LIVING
MY
LIFE

EMMA
GOLDMAN
AN AUTOBIOGRAPHY

Library of Congress Cataloging in Publication Data

Goldman, Emma, 1869-1940.
 Living my life.

 Originally published: New York: Knopf, 1931.
 Includes index.
 1. Goldman, Emma, 1869-1940. 2. Anarchism and anarchists—United
States—Biography. I. Title.
HX843.G6A354 1982   335'.83'0924 [B]   82-19199
ISBN 0-87905-096-9

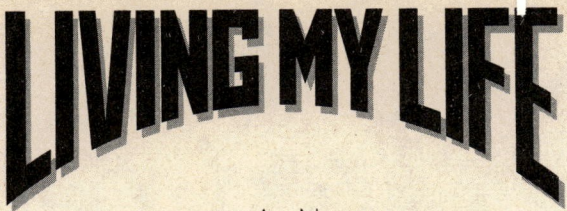

LIVING MY LIFE

A N

A U T O B I O G R A P H Y

O F

EMMA GOLDMAN

 P

A Peregrine Smith Book / Gibbs M. Smith, Inc.
Salt Lake City, Utah 1982

This is a Peregrine Smith Book
Published by Gibbs M. Smith, Inc.

Cover Design by Scott Knudsen

Manufactured in the United States of America

First Peregrine Smith Edition

Introduction

Emma Goldman is a woman of great ability and of personal magnetism, and her persuasive powers are such to make her an exceedingly dangerous woman . . . U. S. Attorney Caffey, 1917

There is nothing wrong with Miss Goldman's gospel that I can see, except this: she is about 8,000 years ahead of her age. Her vision is the vision of every truly great-souled man or woman who has ever lived . . . life is death without the dream. The dream is the reality to which we move . . . universal peace and beauty, Emma Goldman, the daughter of the dream. William Marion Reedy, Editor, *St. Louis Mirror*, 5 November 1908

LIVING MY LIFE IS THE PASSIONATE MEMOIR OF A GREAT WOMAN IN THE history of America's radicalism. It is intimate, accessible, and unflinchingly political. This first publication of a one-volume unabridged paperback edition of *Living My Life* makes available a fascinating literary and political work.

In a fluid and emotional style, Emma Goldman follows her life from her birth in 1869 in Lithuania to her political birth in 1887 in Rochester, New York, when the Haymarket Martyrs were executed in Chicago. She shares her personal triumphs and failures, from her ill-fated marriage in Rochester to the cooperative living arrangements of her New York City activism. She sketches the crucial figures who inspired her and took the time to bring her in to the anarchist movement. And she recalls her own struggle to become confident and independent enough to distinguish her ideas from theirs. Her years of publishing the anarchist magazine, *Mother Earth*, and her tours of the country between 1906 and 1917 on behalf of the publication marked the most active period of her life. She went from town to town, speaking on free love, the drama, birth control, patriotism, militarism, women's emancipation, education, and free speech. The controversies involved in her efforts to exercise her right to speak out against mainstream conventions and ideas helped to spark the formation of free speech clubs throughout the country.

At the center of her autobiography is Emma's struggle to live a life consistent with her anarchist vision. She wrote:

> *I had long realized that I was woven of many skeins, conflicting in shade and texture. To the end of my days I should be torn between the yearning for a personal life and the need of giving all to my ideal. (Living My Life)*

Her book alludes to some of the shadows, the difficulties of maintaining that consistency. It interweaves political essay and confessional.

Yet, the autobiography stops short of serious self-criticism. Emma was torn between wanting to write a very personal memoir—which risked opening herself to criticism—and the desire to write a book which would illustrate unflinching courage. She wanted to be seen as a great example whose bravery and consistency would inspire others.

Goldman minimizes (consciously and unconsciously) her own periodic depression and deep disappointment with the movement and many of the people who were an intimate part of her life, yet she still succeeds in making her book seem open and honest. *Living My Life* offers Emma Goldman's best image of herself in the context of the history of American radicalism and the international anarchist movement.

The book embodies her belief that personal life is integrally related to a larger general political context, and therefore shapes how one participates in public life. So *Living My Life* draws the reader into the inner lives of the leaders of the radical movement in America, Canada, Europe, and Russia—Johann Most, Alexander Berkman, Max Eastman, Mabel Dodge, Jack London, John Reed, Lenin, Havelock Ellis, Margaret Sanger, Voltairine De Cleyre, Peter Kropotkin, and Kate Richards O'Hare. Goldman's acute perceptions of individual personalities make her characterizations particularly valuable and her love stories are intertwined with great historical events.

In wanting her autobiography to convey that her own life was the embodiment of a great ideal, Emma omitted many of the less than heroic parts of her past. She left out much of the detail of her intimacy with Ben Reitman, a doctor and hobo organizer, who was her manager and lover from 1908 until 1918. This, probably the central sexual relationship in her life, tested her selfconfidence and tempted her to abandon her political work. Her love for Ben Reitman made her acutely aware of the conflict between her inner longing for the security of a monogamous relationship and her outer commitment to the ideal of total sexual freedom. She believed that her "dependence on a mere man" weakened her. This obsession made her feel "condemned before the bar of her own reason." Ironically she felt her jealousy intensify at the same time as she was speaking so eloquently on the virtues of free love, and the "causes and possible cures" of jealousy. She wanted the public to know her as a heroine; she could never reconcile such contradictory feelings with her exalted vision. She rationalized her selectiveness in *Living My Life* by insisting that she did not want to give the public "something hot from the flesh to represent the thrillers of the pathologically curious reading public." (Emma Goldman to Hutchins Hapgood, 26 October 1927, Courtesy International Institute of Social History, Amsterdam.) Instead, she wanted her book to mirror her "inner struggle and the social struggle outside." (Emma Goldman to Hutchins Hapgood.) She wrote to her dearest friend and comrade Alexander Berkman about her dilemma:

> *I naturally want to let people see what one can do if imbued with an ideal. What one can endure and how one can overcome all difficulties and suffering in life. Will I be able to do that and yet give also the other side, the woman, the personality in quest for the unattainable in a personal sense? That's going to be the rub. But I mean to do it and try hard to. (Emma Goldman to Alexander Berkman, December 1927. Courtesy International Institute of Social History, Amsterdam.)*

Goldman's portrayal of various episodes in her life makes exciting historical and personal reading. The story of the political repression prior to and during the U. S. entry into World War I is frightening, as it culminates in her deportation in 1919 to the Soviet Union. Her account of her initial enthusiasm and subsequent disillusion with the Soviet regime remains one of the most powerful political critiques of the nascent authoritarian strains of the Bolsheviks. Her book concludes with a discussion of her exile period in Europe in the 1920s, and her decision to write a book about her life in 1928.

When the book appeared, the reviews were on the whole quite positive, several terming the book a classic. But Emma remained preoccupied by the agony of producing such a major work. She likened her struggle to labor pains (The original story of her life was cut down extensively for publication yet it still took over a thousand pages to tell.)—the mammoth length meant that she had given birth to "quintuplets." Almost a year after publication, Emma expressed to an old friend her feelings about both the process of writing her book and what she took as its message.

> *Yes, my dear, it was very painful to relive everything, and much more so than the actual living life. I was much younger, then, and so cocksure that I would continue, till the end of my days, to serve the ideal I had chosen as my goal. It was different while I was writing my book. All my hopes for activity had been buried, really nothing to look forward to, and the past seemed oceans*

*and miles away. To resurrect it all was, indeed, a painful process; but it had
to be done to make the story real and vivid. Well, if the book will bring nothing
else, it is some comfort to know it impresses the reader. In it, I have been able
to let those whose opinion I care about, see me as I was. Perhaps it will also
help the young generation to see that no life is worth anything, which does not
contain a great ideal, and which does not bring forth determination to serve
it to the uttermost. That would be a great reward, indeed. (Emma Goldman
to Gwyneth Roe, January 1932, Paris. Collection of State Historical Society
of Wisconsin)*

It is clear that while writing the autobiography, Emma Goldman felt that
she no longer retained much personal or political power. She felt that "there
was really nothing to look forward to"—as an exile, her freedom of expression, that thing which she held most dear, was restricted. She could barely
survive as a freelance writer and speaker. The autobiography had given her
a large publisher's advance, as well as a chance to rethink and relive the compelling political and personal events of her past. She hoped that if enough
people were inspired by her book, she might be able to create the public
support necessary to persuade the United States government to allow her
back to her beloved America. She felt "nowhere at home" and unsure of her
future.

The autobiography did generate interest in her cause. Its publication in
1931 was followed by a three month speaking tour in the U. S. in 1934.
Although she was officially restricted to speaking only on the drama, Emma
expanded this to include the "drama of world events." Once again she came
alive and spoke with passion, inspiring people to live freely and to dare to
live out their vision. Her political life was not over with the completion of
her autobiography.

Unfortunately, in 1936, when Alexander Berkman killed himself while sick
and in pain, Emma entered a deep depression which made her wish that she
too could die. But once again she was reborn to the cause. The inspiration
of the anarchists in the Spanish Civil War revived her, renewing her belief
in the possibility of realizing her ideals. She warned against the rise of Hitler,
fascism, and even of Stalinism. And her last campaign to save the life of a
young Italian anarchist threatened with deportation from Canada to Mussolini's
Italy allowed her to "die in the saddle" as she wished. Buried near the
Haymarket Martyrs in Chicago's Waldheim Cemetery, Emma was at last allowed to reenter her chosen homeland.

In her long exile from the United States, Emma Goldman remained staunchly American in her character and ideas. America, in spite of its problems,
still represented the New World; the self-made person was an integral part

of her anarchist affirmation of the dominance of the individual. Like many Americans she longed for a world without conflict, a society unblemished by European hierarchies and prejudices. She remained an anarchist with radical notions of how to change society, but to her last breath she longed to return to the youth and promise of America.

Living My Life is an early statement of what it felt like to be a woman in a predominantly male world. Though bitterly disappointed by her brief marriage, she never gave up her search for love and affection. She longed for conventional security, and at the same time insisted on unrestricted sexual freedom for herself and everyone else. As well, her work for birth control, and her need for a broader definition of family than conventional forms could accommodate resonate with the issues raised by the contemporary women's movement.

Emma Goldman was not a Suffragist, and was critical of the massive effort to win women the right to vote, because she was against the State in any form. She believed that woman's freedom would be won "in and through herself," and was often considered a "man's woman" in the context of the suffrage movement.

Emma was a visionary. "Be realistic. Demand the impossible," the slogan of the Paris student uprising in May 1968, might have been Emma's call in the early 20th century. She would settle for nothing short of her dream of a world which realized "everybody's right to beautiful radiant things." Some of Emma Goldman's dreams did come true. Indeed, the world has slowly caught up with the vision of the early radicals. Goldman's work helped to inspire the formation of the American Civil Liberties Union. Free speech is today more firmly established as an indelible right. The discussion and dissemination of birth control literature—which put Goldman in jail in 1916—is now legal and generally accepted. The eight-hour work day is an accepted convention. Modern free schools reflect her concern for encouraging a positive attitude toward freedom early in a child's development. Love and sexuality are not exclusively linked to marriage. Women are finding their independence through their own resources. The anti-conscription work which put Goldman in jail in 1917, and triggered her deportation in 1919, has become part of a legacy of draft resistance in the United States. Her critique of the authoritarianism in the Soviet Union as early as 1921 is now widely accepted within the Left.

Richard Drinnon's first fine biography of Emma Goldman, *Rebel in Paradise*, is a sourcebook for all other Emma Goldman scholarship. Although published works on Goldman are relatively few—a biography for young people, collections of her own essays, a book of letters between Goldman and

Alexander Berkman in exile, a biography published in Spain and another in Bombay, and various scholarly and popular articles—work on Emma Goldman is increasing. Interest in her life had been growing for a number of years even before the prominent role of her character played in *Reds*, the 1981 film about John Reed and Louise Bryant. Scholars have been going back to the letters and papers of Emma Goldman. An Emma Goldman Papers project is collecting, organizing, and indexing all known letters and papers of Emma Goldman for microfilm and a book of selected materials. Two new biographies are due to appear in 1983, both of which draw heavily on letters and other papers which have only recently become available to scholars. There is a book in process on her work on the drama, another on her contribution to the Spanish Civil War, and one on her lover, Ben Reitman. Playwrights and screen writers have been sparking broad audiences with the dramatic inspiration of Emma Goldman's life and her words. Emma Goldman's life does still inspire political activists, as symbolized by the health clinics, community groups, and book stores which have taken her name.

When Emma Goldman died on 14 May 1940 telegrams streamed in from all parts of the world, from people who had been touched by her spirit. An Italian comrade wrote:

> *Emma Goldman, an invincible fighter for the liberation of the human soul has disappeared [yet] she lives now immortally among the great women of the centuries who foresaw a new society and a larger life of peace and happiness for all human kind. (Arturo Giovanitti, telegram sent to Stella Ballantine on 16 May 1940, after the death of Emma Goldman. Courtesy New York Public Library.)*

Living My Life is the living document of Emma Goldman's life, in which she speaks to the unlimited capacity for passion and vision in all of us.

Candace Falk

A Remembrance

Publisher's note: In celebration of this new edition of Living My Life *the publisher asked Meridel LeSueur to share some of her personal memories of Emma Goldman. Ms. LeSeuer is now 82 years old and is the author of many articles and books, including several children's books, as well as* Ripening, *recently published by The Feminist Press.*

EMMA GOLDMAN IS ONE OF THE STRONG AND STRANGE FEMALE figures that have sprung alive in amazing contours in the present woman's movement. I see her now in a new, amazing way, grown alive, a leader of a strange subculture of America, in which images are gestated in one period to emerge in yet another.

I knew her when I was a young radical girl before the First World War when I lived in the anarchist house in New York while attending the American Academy of Dramatic Art. Alexander Berkman had been out of prison for only a few years, *Mother Earth*, the anarchist magazine, was being published, and the anarchists were leading demonstrations of the unemployed, and opposing the draft (for which they were later tried and deported to Russia by J. Edgar Hoover).

I came from the Midwest radical movement with socialist and I.W.W. roots. My mother was a friend of Eleanor Fitzgerald, a Midwesterner who had followed her lover, Ben Reitman when he followed Emma out of Chicago. Alexander Berkman had been in love with my mother. He was often in love. My mother had dreams of me as an actress so I was sent to live in the anarchist house while I attended dramatic school. I am sure the anarchists looked down upon me for attending such a bourgoise school and had just as critical an attitude towards the socialism with which I was brought up. But they took time to teach me things I have never forgotten. Berkman told me about French Impressionism and Cubism. He showed how the realistic, naturalistic bourgoise school of art was reactionary and that revolution was breaking the dead forms of a dying society. He also encouraged me by telling me that being an artist or writer was one of the great energies of humanity—that art should serve the revolutionary movement and the struggle of the people. He taught that one must never betray this bond but become a revolutionary artist for the cause of the revolution. For him there was no higher dedication.

Emma was deeply involved in theatrical activities. She was known for her work in the Yiddish theater. Having the Midwest radicals' suspicion of European culture, I had never even heard of Yiddish culture. She helped bring Alla Nazimova and her Russian theater company to the United States. I heard of Ibsen for the first time at one of her lectures attended by the intellectuals of New York.

And it strikes me now what a strange cultural and ethnic figure Emma Goldman was to me as well as to the feminist movement. I didn't realize until reading modern historical studies the true nature of the feminist radical movement during that time. It was white, Anglo-Saxon, and often racist. In the early days, before meeting Goldman, I had never seen a radical feminist who was Jewish, a peasant, a worker. This illustrates the amazing phenomenon of Emma Goldman, and why her spirit has entered today's feminist movement with such strength and meaning.

My mother was a feminist. She had kidnapped her children out of Texas, because in that state the wife and children were property of the man. She lectured on the Chautauqua circuit on the subect "Love and Bread." She was tried in Kansas City for giving birth control information to a woman with nine children. During that period the sentence for this crime was 99 years! She was saved only because the woman refused to recognize her in court. They gave the poor woman three years in jail. There were wonderful and heroic prairie feminists—Kate Richards O'Hare, Caroline Lowe, Mother Jones, Elizabeth Gurley Flynn—heroic and brave women. I didn't know until I went to New York that there was a difference between the Midwestern and Eastern feminists. The ones I knew back home were all puritan, white, mostly middle-class women. I thought of myself as a puritian/agrarian socialist—not from the factory or city experience nor with an immigrant background. But Emma Goldman represented an entirely different culture.

Also in New York I saw for the first time the Jewish garment workers. I came to love them and they shared with me their experiences and radicalism. Their German and Russian experience was all new to me. This is important even today. The present feminist movement is very middle class and often prejudiced. This perhaps explains why Emma Goldman's autobiography has become so illuminating to the young women of today.

I had never seen a woman like Emma Goldman during my years in the Midwest. She was built differently than prairie women like my mother. She was different in many other ways, too. She was not a Christian. She had no sexual guilt or repression. The other early feminists, like my mother, did not champion the cause of sexual freedom. Many of them felt sex was a humiliating force, symbolic of their repression – of marriage and child bearing – and it represented to them violence, rape, and enslavement. Many of them at that time felt a woman had only two choices: living her own life with a career and a calling as a radical or marriage with sex and children. There was a kind of neurotic fanaticism in the ranks of these feminists. To them sex was a degradation, a trap.

I saw Emma's sexual freedom in her strong stout body. She was direct and forceful and demanded input in her own sexual relationships. The anarchists' philosophy was that there was no possession in sex, that it was a free, rich experience between comrades. I saw that she was immense, varied, fearless – without puritan guilt, melancholy, or oppression. She had her lovers boldly and shamelessly. She chose them and was not chosen by them. What amazed me the most was her enjoyment, her open pride in sex. She defended Ben Reitman, who had followed her from Chicago, when her friends and comrades accused him of not being her equal, of not being an anarchist or even a serious man. She said he was a good lover, that she loved him physically. I had never experienced this before. It shocked me and changed me.

I went with Emma to the weekly solon of Mabel Dodge, whose residence was a gathering place of Village dissidents, radicals, and artists as well as the elite and the wealthy. There I refused the amorous advances of some famous male writers and was rebuked and laughingly dubbed the Corn Virgin from Kansas. I did not want to return and felt culturally rebuked.

I saw Goldman as a source of social nourishment and responsibility. She was a social mother, a nourisher. At the anarchist house there was a can on the newel post, where everyone was supposed to put his contribution to the communal cupboard. I noticed the can was never overladen. Sometimes the comrades would be sitting glumly and nervously around, waiting for Emma to come back. In she swept, like a Yiddish mother, arms full of groceries. She bustled to the kitchen and helped prepare the supper. This was a different part of her radical philosophy – to nourish, to feed, to warm the people.

Sasha (Alexander Berkman), after his years of solitary confinement in prison, at first could not stand to be in a room with more than a couple of people. He was never a charismatic, easy speaker and at first could not even appear on a platform. I was moved by Emma's care and love for him. She always tried to meet his physical needs. In 1936 she was on her way to look after him and his wife when he killed himself. Also, I saw for the first time the effect of intellectual energy on the relationship of a man and a woman. It seemed to me that he taught her. She took his knowledge and made it come alive on the platform and in her writing. It was a communal sharing of talents and knowledge. During the awful years he was in prison she returned his intellectual energy, kept him alive, and brought him back.

During the terrible depression which began in 1912 she led many demonstrations for the garment workers. She fed people, edited the magazine *Mother Earth*, and raised money for the anarchist house. In one tremendous demonstration she led the unemployed into the richest church on Fifth Avenue, where they stayed until they got lodging and food.

I became part of the anarchist house because it seemed to me a beautiful way of living, working together and changing the world. So I began to help mail out *Mother Earth* and to do chores. In the morning, Emma sometimes woke and rang a bell by her bed. Some wag in the kitchen would say, "God's awake" and a lucky person got the privilege of taking her coffee to her.

I was put out of the anarchist house at the beginning of the War because I had dinner with a soldier. He was a young rubber worker from Akron, Ohio who had been drafted. I had known him in Ohio and I had dinner with him the last night before he sailed. Emma said that it was unforgivable to eat with a soldier. I said he was a victim who did not want to go. But she said he had a choice. He never came back from the War.

When war was declared it became very dangerous for radicals. Meetings were broken up. Emma was hunted like a criminal. Then finally there was the famous trial which ended in the deportation of Goldman and Berkman to Russia. I was there. I was at the trial and I went with Eleanor Fitzgerald and the other anarchists to see them leave. I saw her short staunch figure with the hat she nearly always wore, standing by the taller Berkman with his strange cosmopolitan air with his cane and mustache. We waved goodbye to them. They waved back to us and to the America that would never be the same again, and to which they would never be allowed to return. Hoover let her return only in death. I go to her grave at the Haymarket shrine in Chicago where there is a copper relief of her strong woman peasant face, with her little hat on and the glasses, over her great eyes looking to the future.

Now I see clearly what an alive, diverse, powerful woman Emma Goldman was. She had the strength to break the molds of sexual repression and puritanism. She was an immigrant woman who saw and loved the people of America and held a vision of a revolution replete with democratic freedom, art, close relationships amid comrades, sexual love between men and women, great communes of love. Almost alone in America she created this image of the woman of the future. She saw what a woman could be—alive, varied, beautiful, her own power.

Meridel Le Sueur

In Appreciation

SUGGESTIONS THAT I WRITE MY MEMOIRS CAME TO ME WHEN I HAD barely begun to live, and continued all through the years. But I never paid heed to the proposal. I was living my life intensely—what need to write about it? Another reason for my reluctance was the conviction I entertained that one should write about one's life only when one had ceased to stand in the very torrent of it. "When one has reached a good philosophic age," I used to tell my friends, "capable of viewing the tragedies and comedies of life impersonally and detachedly—particularly one's own life—one is likely to create an autobiography worthwhile." Still feeling adolescently young in spite of advancing years, I did not consider myself competent to undertake such a task. Moreover, I always lacked the necessary leisure for concentrated writing.

My enforced European inactivity left me enough time to read a great deal, including biographies and autobiographies. I discovered, much to my discomfiture, that old age, far from ripening wisdom and mellowness, is too often fraught with senility, narrowness, and petty rancour. I would not risk such a calamity, and I began to think seriously about writing my life.

The great difficulty that faced me was lack of historical data for my work. Almost everything in the way of books, correspondence, and similar material that I had accumulated during the thirty-five years of my life in the United States had been confiscated by the Department of Justice raiders and never returned. I lacked even my personal set of the *Mother Earth* magazine, which I had published for twelve years. It was a problem I could see no solution for. Sceptic that I am, I had overlooked the magic power of friendship, which had so often in my life made mountains move. My staunch friends Leonard D. Abbott, Agnes Inglis, W.S. Van Valkenburgh, and others soon put my doubts to shame. Agnes, the founder of the Labadie Library in Detroit, containing the richest collection of radical and revolutionary material in America, came to my aid with her usual readiness. Leonard did his share, and Van spent all his free time in research work for me.

In the matter of European data I knew I could turn to the two best historians in our ranks: Max Nettlau and Rudolf Rocker. No further need to worry with such an array of co-workers.

Still I was not appeased. I needed something that would help me re-create the atmosphere of my own personal life: the events, small or great, that had tossed me about emotionally. An old vice of mine came to my rescue: veritable mountains of letters I had written. Often I had been chided by my pal Sasha, otherwise known as Alexander Berkman, and by my other friends, for my proclivity to spread myself in letters. Far from virtue bringing reward, it was my iniquity that gave me what I needed most—the true atmosphere of past days. Ben Reitman, Ben Capes, Jacob Margolis, Agnes Inglis, Harry Weinberger, Van, my romantic admirer Leon Bass, and scores of other friends readily responded to my request to send me my letters. My niece, Stella Ballantine, had kept everything I had written her during my imprisonment in the Missouri penitentiary. She, as well as my dear friend M. Eleanor Fitzgerald, had also preserved my Russian correspondence. In short, I was soon put into possession of over one thousand specimens of my epistolary effusions. I confess that most of them were painful reading, for at no time does one reveal onself so much as in one's intimate correspondence. But for my purpose they were of utmost value.

Thus supplied, I started for Saint-Tropez, a picturesque fisher nest in the south of France, in company of Emily Holmes Coleman, who was to act as my secretary. Demi, as she is familiarly called, was a wild wood-sprite with a volcanic temper. But she was also the tenderest of beings, without any guile or rancour. She was essentially the poet, highly imaginative and sensitive. My world of ideas was foreign to her, natural rebel and anarchist though she was. We clashed furiously, often to the point of wishing each other in Saint-Tropez Bay. But it was nothing compared to her charm, her profound interest in my work, and her fine understanding for my inner conflicts.

Writing had never come easy to me, and the work at hand did not mean merely writing. It meant reliving my long-forgotten past, the resurrection of memories I did not wish to dig out from the deeps of my consciousness. It meant doubts in my creative ability, depression, and disheartenings. All through that period Demi held out bravely and by her faith and encouragement proved the comfort and inspiration of the first year of my struggle.

Altogether I was very fortunate in the number and devotion of friends who exerted themselves to smooth the way for *Living My Life*. The first to start the fund to secure me from material anxiety was Peggy Guggenheim. Other friends and comrades followed suit, giving without stint from their limited economic means. Miriam Lerner, a young American friend, volunteered to take Demi's place when the latter had to leave for England. Dorothy Marsh, Betty Markow, and Emmy Eckstein typed part of my manuscript as a labor of love. Arthur Leonard Ross, kindest and most lavish of men, gave me his untiring efforts as legal representative and adviser. How could such friend-ship ever be rewarded?

And Sasha? Many misgivings beset me when we began the revision of my manuscript. I feared he might resent seeing himself pictured through my eyes. Would he be detached enough, I wondered, sufficiently objective for the task? I found him remarkably so for one who is so much a part of my story. For eighteen months Sasha worked side by side with me as in our old days. Critical, of course, but always in the finest and broadest spirit. Sasha also it was who suggested the title, *Living My Life*.

My life as I have lived it owes everything to those who had come into it, stayed for long or little, and passed out. Their love, as well as their hate, has gone into making my life worth while.

Living My Life is my tribute and my gratitude to them all.

Emma Goldman
Saint-Tropez, France
January 1931

ILLUSTRATIONS

EMMA GOLDMAN

EMMA GOLDMAN
AT THE AGE OF SEVENTEEN, IN 1886

ABRAHAM GOLDMAN
EMMA GOLDMAN'S FATHER

EDWARD BRADY IN 1893

EMMA GOLDMAN IN 1892

JOHANN MOST IN 1890

EMMA GOLDMAN IN 1912

ALEXANDER BERKMAN
AT THE AGE OF TWENTY-ONE, IN 1892

BEN L. REITMAN

PRISON LABELS

HELENA HOCHSTEIN AND HER SON DAVID

TAUBE GOLDMAN
EMMA GOLDMAN'S MOTHER

EMMA GOLDMAN (MOSCOW, 1921)

LIVING MY LIFE

CHAPTER I

IT WAS THE 15TH OF AUGUST 1889, THE DAY OF MY ARRIVAL IN New York City. I was twenty years old. All that had happened in my life until that time was now left behind me, cast off like a worn-out garment. A new world was before me, strange and terrifying. But I had youth, good health, and a passionate ideal. Whatever the new held in store for me I was determined to meet unflinchingly.

How well I remember that day! It was a Sunday. The West Shore train, the cheapest, which was all I could afford, had brought me from Rochester, New York, reaching Weehawken at eight o'clock in the morning. Thence I came by ferry to New York City. I had no friends there, but I carried three addresses, one of a married aunt, one of a young medical student I had met in New Haven a year before, while working in a corset factory there, and one of the *Freiheit,* a German anarchist paper published by Johann Most.

My entire possessions consisted of five dollars and a small hand-bag. My sewing-machine, which was to help me to independence, I had checked as baggage. Ignorant of the distance from West Forty-second Street to the Bowery, where my aunt lived, and unaware of the enervating heat of a New York day in August, I started out on foot. How confusing and endless a large city seems to the new-comer, how cold and unfriendly!

After receiving many directions and misdirections and making frequent stops at bewildering intersections, I landed in three hours at the photographic gallery of my aunt and uncle. Tired and hot, I did not at first notice the consternation of my relatives at my unexpected arrival. They asked me to make myself at home, gave me breakfast, and then plied me with questions. Why did I come to New York? Had I definitely broken with my husband? Did I have money? What did I intend to do? I was told that I could, of course, stay with them.

"Where else could you go, a young woman alone in New York?" Certainly, but I would have to look for a job immediately. Business was bad, and the cost of living high.

I heard it all as if in a stupor. I was too exhausted from my wakeful night's journey, the long walk, and the heat of the sun, which was already pouring down fiercely. The voices of my relatives sounded distant, like the buzzing of flies, and they made me drowsy. With an effort I pulled myself together. I assured them I did not come to impose myself on them; a friend living on Henry Street was expecting me and would put me up. I had but one desire — to get out, away from the prattling, chilling voices. I left my bag and departed.

The friend I had invented in order to escape the " hospitality " of my relatives was only a slight acquaintance, a young anarchist by the name of A. Solotaroff, whom I had once heard lecture in New Haven. Now I started out to find him. After a long search I discovered the house, but the tenant had left. The janitor, at first very brusque, must have noticed my despair. He said he would look for the address that the family left when they moved. Presently he came back with the name of the street, but there was no number. What was I to do? How to find Solotaroff in the vast city? I decided to stop at every house, first on one side of the street, and then on the other. Up and down, six flights of stairs, I tramped, my head throbbing, my feet weary. The oppressive day was drawing to a close. At last, when I was about to give up the search, I discovered him on Montgomery Street, on the fifth floor of a tenement house seething with humanity.

A year had passed since our first meeting, but Solotaroff had not forgotten me. His greeting was genial and warm, as of an old friend. He told me that he shared his small apartment with his parents and little brother, but that I could have his room; he would stay with a fellow-student for a few nights. He assured me that I would have no difficulty in finding a place; in fact, he knew two sisters who were living with their father in a two-room flat. They were looking for another girl to join them. After my new friend had fed me tea and some delicious Jewish cake his mother had baked, he told me about the different people I might meet, the activities of the Yiddish anarchists, and other interesting matters. I was grateful to my host, much more for his friendly concern and *camaraderie* than for the tea and cake. I forgot the bitterness that had filled my soul over the cruel reception given me by my own kin. New York no longer seemed the monster it had appeared in the endless hours of my painful walk on the Bowery.

Later Solotaroff took me to Sachs's café on Suffolk Street, which, as he informed me, was the headquarters of the East Side radicals, socialists, and anarchists, as well as of the young Yiddish writers and poets. "Everybody forgathers there," he remarked; "the Minkin sisters will no doubt also be there."

For one who had just come away from the monotony of a provincial town like Rochester and whose nerves were on edge from a night's trip in a stuffy car, the noise and turmoil that greeted us at Sachs's were certainly not very soothing. The place consisted of two rooms and was packed. Everybody talked, gesticulated, and argued, in Yiddish and Russian, each competing with the other. I was almost overcome in this strange human medley. My escort discovered two girls at a table. He introduced them as Anna and Helen Minkin.

They were Russian Jewish working girls. Anna, the older, was about my own age; Helen perhaps eighteen. Soon we came to an understanding about my living with them, and my anxiety and uncertainty were over. I had a roof over my head; I had found friends. The bedlam at Sachs's no longer mattered. I began to breathe freer, to feel less of an alien.

While the four of us were having our dinner, and Solotaroff was pointing out to me the different people in the café, I suddenly heard a powerful voice call: "Extra-large steak! Extra cup of coffee!" My own capital was so small and the need for economy so great that I was startled by such apparent extravagance. Besides, Solotaroff had told me that only poor students, writers, and workers were the clients of Sachs. I wondered who that reckless person could be and how he could afford such food. "Who is that glutton?" I asked. Solotaroff laughed aloud. "That is Alexander Berkman. He can eat for three. But he rarely has enough money for much food. When he has, he eats Sachs out of his supplies. I'll introduce him to you."

We had finished our meal, and several people came to our table to talk to Solotaroff. The man of the extra-large steak was still packing it away as if he had gone hungry for weeks. Just as we were about to depart, he approached us, and Solotaroff introduced him. He was no more than a boy, hardly eighteen, but with the neck and chest of a giant. His jaw was strong, made more pronounced by his thick lips. His face was almost severe, but for his high, studious forehead and intelligent eyes. A determined youngster, I thought. Presently Berkman remarked to me: "Johann Most is speaking tonight. Do you want to come to hear him?"

How extraordinary, I thought, that on my very first day in New York I should have the chance to behold with my own eyes and hear the fiery man whom the Rochester press used to portray as the personification of the devil, a criminal, a bloodthirsty demon! I had planned to visit Most in the office of his newspaper some time later, but that the opportunity should present itself in such an unexpected manner gave me the feeling that something wonderful was about to happen, something that would decide the whole course of my life.

On the way to the hall I was too absorbed in my thoughts to hear much of the conversation that was going on between Berkman and the Minkin sisters. Suddenly I stumbled. I should have fallen had not Berkman gripped my arm and held me up. "I have saved your life," he said jestingly. "I hope I may be able to save yours some day," I quickly replied.

The meeting-place was a small hall behind a saloon, through which one had to pass. It was crowded with Germans, drinking, smoking, and talking. Before long, Johann Most entered. My first impression of him was one of revulsion. He was of medium height, with a large head crowned with greyish bushy hair; but his face was twisted out of form by an apparent dislocation of the left jaw. Only his eyes were soothing; they were blue and sympathetic.

His speech was a scorching denunciation of American conditions, a biting satire on the injustice and brutality of the dominant powers, a passionate tirade against those responsible for the Haymarket tragedy and the execution of the Chicago anarchists in November 1887. He spoke eloquently and picturesquely. As if by magic, his disfigurement disappeared, his lack of physical distinction was forgotten. He seemed transformed into some primitive power, radiating hatred and love, strength and inspiration. The rapid current of his speech, the music of his voice, and his sparkling wit, all combined to produce an effect almost overwhelming. He stirred me to my depths.

Caught in the crowd that surged towards the platform, I found myself before Most. Berkman was near me and introduced me. But I was dumb with excitement and nervousness, full of the tumult of emotions Most's speech had aroused in me.

That night I could not sleep. Again I lived through the events of

1887. Twenty-one months had passed since the Black Friday of November 11, when the Chicago men had suffered their martyrdom, yet every detail stood out clear before my vision and affected me as if it had happened but yesterday. My sister Helena and I had become interested in the fate of the men during the period of their trial. The reports in the Rochester newspapers irritated, confused, and upset us by their evident prejudice. The violence of the press, the bitter denunciation of the accused, the attacks on all foreigners, turned our sympathies to the Haymarket victims.

We had learned of the existence in Rochester of a German socialist group that held sessions on Sunday in Germania Hall. We began to attend the meetings, my older sister, Helena, on a few occasions only, and I regularly. The gatherings were generally uninteresting, but they offered an escape from the grey dullness of my Rochester existence. There one heard, at least, something different from the everlasting talk about money and business, and one met people of spirit and ideas.

One Sunday it was announced that a famous socialist speaker from New York, Johanna Greie, would lecture on the case then being tried in Chicago. On the appointed day I was the first in the hall. The huge place was crowded from top to bottom by eager men and women, while the walls were lined with police. I had never before been at such a large meeting. I had seen *gendarmes* in St. Petersburg disperse small student gatherings. But that in the country which guaranteed free speech, officers armed with long clubs should invade an orderly assembly filled me with consternation and protest.

Soon the chairman announced the speaker. She was a woman in her thirties, pale and ascetic-looking, with large luminous eyes. She spoke with great earnestness, in a voice vibrating with intensity. Her manner engrossed me. I forgot the police, the audience, and everything else about me. I was aware only of the frail woman in black crying out her passionate indictment against the forces that were about to destroy eight human lives.

The entire speech concerned the stirring events in Chicago. She began by relating the historical background of the case. She told of the labour strikes that broke out throughout the country in 1886, for the demand of an eight-hour workday. The centre of the movement was Chicago, and there the struggle between the toilers and their bosses became intense and bitter. A meeting of the striking employees of the McCormick Harvester Company in that city was attacked by police; men and women were beaten and several persons killed. To protest against the outrage a mass meeting was called in Haymarket Square on May 4. It was addressed by Albert Parsons, August Spies, Adolph Fischer, and others, and was quiet and orderly. This was attested to by Carter Harrison, Mayor of Chicago, who had attended the meeting to see what was going on. The Mayor left, satisfied that everything was all right, and he informed the captain of the district to that effect. It was getting cloudy, a light rain began to fall, and the people started to disperse, only a few remaining while one of the last speakers was addressing the audience. Then Captain Ward, accompanied by a strong force of police, suddenly appeared on the square. He ordered the meeting to disperse forthwith. "This is an orderly assembly," the chairman replied, whereupon the police fell upon the people, clubbing them unmercifully. Then something flashed through the air and exploded, killing a number of police officers and wounding a score of others. It was never ascertained who the actual culprit was, and the authorities apparently made little effort to discover him. Instead orders were immediately issued for the arrest of all the speakers at the Haymarket meeting and other prominent anarchists. The entire press and *bourgeoisie* of Chicago and of the whole country began shouting for the blood of the prisoners. A veritable campaign of terror was carried on by the police, who were given moral and financial encouragement by the Citizens' Association to further their murderous plan to get the anarchists out of the way. The public mind was so inflamed by the atrocious stories circulated by the press against the leaders of the strike that a fair trial for them became an impossibility. In fact, the trial proved the worst frame-up in the history of the United States. The jury was picked for conviction; the District Attorney announced in open court that it was not only the arrested men who were the accused, but that " anarchy was on trial " and that it was to be exterminated. The judge repeatedly denounced the prisoners from the bench, influencing the jury against them. The witnesses were terrorized or bribed, with the result that eight men, innocent of the crime and in no way connected with it, were convicted. The incited state of the public mind, and the general prejudice against anarchists, coupled with the employers' bitter opposition to the eight-hour movement, constituted the atmosphere that favoured the judicial murder of the Chicago anarchists. Five of them — Albert Parsons, August Spies, Louis Lingg, Adolph Fischer, and George Engel — were sentenced to die by hanging; Michael Schwab and Samuel Fielden were doomed to life imprisonment; Neebe received fifteen years' sentence. The innocent blood of the Haymarket martyrs was calling for revenge.

At the end of Greie's speech I knew what I had surmised all along: the Chicago men were innocent. They were to be put to death for their ideal. But what was their ideal? Johanna Greie spoke of Parsons, Spies, Lingg, and the others as socialists, but I was ignorant of the real meaning of socialism. What I had heard from the local speakers had impressed me as colourless and mechanistic. On the other hand, the papers called these men anarchists, bomb-throwers. What was anarchism? It was all very puzzling. But I had no time for further contemplation. The people were filing out, and I got up to leave. Greie, the chairman, and a group of friends were still on the platform. As I turned towards them, I saw Greie motioning to me. I was startled, my heart beat violently, and my feet felt leaden. When I approached her, she took me by the hand and said: " I never saw a face that reflected such a tumult of emotions as yours. You must be feeling the impending tragedy intensely. Do you know the men?" In a trembling voice I replied: " Unfortunately not, but I do feel the case with every fibre, and when I heard you speak, it seemed to me as if I knew them." She put her hand on my shoulder. " I have a feeling that you will know them better as you learn their ideal, and that you will make their cause your own."

I walked home in a dream. Sister Helena was already asleep, but I had to share my experience with her. I woke her up and recited to her the whole story, giving almost a verbatim account of the speech. I must have been very dramatic, because Helena exclaimed: " The next thing I'll hear about my little sister is that she, too, is a dangerous anarchist."

Some weeks later I had occasion to visit a German family I knew. I found them very much excited. Somebody from New York had sent them a German paper, *Die Freiheit,* edited by Johann Most. It was filled with news about the events in Chicago. The language fairly took my breath away, it was so different from what I had heard at the socialist meetings and even from Johanna Greie's talk. It seemed lava shooting forth flames of ridicule, scorn, and defiance; it breathed deep hatred of the powers that were preparing the crime in Chicago. I began to read *Die Freiheit* regularly. I sent for the literature advertised in the paper and I devoured every line on anarchism I could

get, every word about the men, their lives, their work. I read about
their heroic stand while on trial and their marvellous defence. I saw
a new world opening before me.

The terrible thing everyone feared, yet hoped would not happen,
actually occurred. Extra editions of the Rochester papers carried the
news: the Chicago anarchists had been hanged!

We were crushed, Helena and I. The shock completely unnerved
my sister; she could only wring her hands and weep silently. I was in
a stupor; a feeling of numbness came over me, something too horrible
even for tears. In the evening we went to our father's house. Everybody talked about the Chicago events. I was entirely absorbed in what
I felt as my own loss. Then I heard the coarse laugh of a woman. In
a shrill voice she sneered: "What's all this lament about? The men
were murderers. It is well they were hanged." With one leap I was at
the woman's throat. Then I felt myself torn back. Someone said:
"The child has gone crazy." I wrenched myself free, grabbed a pitcher
of water from a table, and threw it with all my force into the woman's
face. "Out, out," I cried, "or I will kill you!" The terrified woman
made for the door and I dropped to the ground in a fit of crying. I was
put to bed, and soon I fell into a deep sleep. The next morning I woke
as from a long illness, but free from the numbness and the depression
of those harrowing weeks of waiting, ending with the final shock. I had
a distinct sensation that something new and wonderful had been born
in my soul. A great ideal, a burning faith, a determination to dedicate
myself to the memory of my martyred comrades, to make their cause
my own, to make known to the world their beautiful lives and heroic
deaths. Johanna Greie was more prophetic than she had probably
realized.

My mind was made up. I would go to New York, to Johann Most.
He would help me prepare myself for my new task. But my husband,
my parents — how would they meet my decision?

I had been married only ten months. The union had not been happy.
I had realized almost from the beginning that my husband and I were
at opposite poles, with nothing in common, not even sexual blending.
The venture, like everything else that had happened to me since I had
come to America, had proved most disappointing. America, "the
land of the free and the home of the brave" — what a farce it now
seemed to me! Yet how I had fought with my father to get him to let
me go to America with Helena! In the end I had won, and late in

December 1885, Helena and I had left St. Petersburg for Hamburg, there embarking on the steamer *Elbe* for the Promised Land.

Another sister had preceded us by a few years, had married, and was living in Rochester. Repeatedly she had written Helena to come to her, that she was lonely. At last Helena had decided to go. But I could not support the thought of separation from the one who meant more to me than even my mother. Helena also hated to leave me behind. She knew of the bitter friction that existed between Father and me. She offered to pay my fare, but Father would not consent to my going. I pleaded, begged, wept. Finally I threatened to jump into the Neva, whereupon he yielded. Equipped with twenty-five roubles —all that the old man would give me—I left without regrets. Since my earliest recollection, home had been stifling, my father's presence terrifying. My mother, while less violent with the children, never showed much warmth. It was always Helena who gave me affection, who filled my childhood with whatever joy it had. She would continually shoulder the blame for the rest of the children. Many blows intended for my brother and me were given Helena. Now we were completely together—nobody would separate us.

We travelled steerage, where the passengers were herded together like cattle. My first contact with the sea was terrifying and fascinating. The freedom from home, the beauty and wonder of the endless expanse in its varying moods, and the exciting anticipation of what the new land would offer stimulated my imagination and sent my blood tingling.

The last day of our journey comes vividly to my mind. Everybody was on deck. Helena and I stood pressed to each other, enraptured by the sight of the harbour and the Statue of Liberty suddenly emerging from the mist. Ah, there she was, the symbol of hope, of freedom, of opportunity! She held her torch high to light the way to the free country, the asylum for the oppressed of all lands. We, too, Helena and I, would find a place in the generous heart of America. Our spirits were high, our eyes filled with tears.

Gruff voices broke in upon our reverie. We were surrounded by gesticulating people—angry men, hysterical women, screaming children. Guards roughly pushed us hither and thither, shouted orders to get ready, to be transferred to Castle Garden, the clearing-house for immigrants.

The scenes in Castle Garden were appalling, the atmosphere

charged with antagonism and harshness. Nowhere could one see a sympathetic official face; there was no provision for the comfort of the new arrivals, the pregnant women and young children. The first day on American soil proved a violent shock. We were possessed by one desire, to escape from the ghastly place. We had heard that Rochester was the "Flower City" of New York, but we arrived there on a bleak and cold January morning. My sister Lena, heavy with her first child, and Aunt Rachel met us. Lena's rooms were small, but they were bright and spotless. The room prepared for Helena and myself was filled with flowers. Throughout the day people came in and out — relatives I had never known, friends of my sister and of her husband, neighbours. All wanted to see us, to hear about the old country. They were Jews who had suffered much in Russia; some of them had even been in pogroms. Life in the new country, they said, was hard; they were all still possessed by nostalgia for their home that had never been a home.

Among the visitors there were some who had prospered. One man boasted that his six children were all working, selling newspapers, shining shoes. Everybody was concerned about what we were going to do. One coarse-looking fellow concentrated his attention on me. He kept staring at me all the evening, scanning me up and down. He even came over and tried to feel my arms. It gave me the sensation of standing naked on the market-place. I was outraged, but I did not want to insult my sister's friends. I felt utterly alone and I rushed out of the room. A longing possessed me for what I had left behind — St. Petersburg, my beloved Neva, my friends, my books and music. I became aware of loud voices in the next room. I heard the man who had enraged me say: "I can get her a job at Garson and Mayer's. The wages will be small, but she will soon find a feller to marry her. Such a buxom girl, with her red cheeks and blue eyes, will not have to work long. Any man will snatch her up and keep her in silks and diamonds." I thought of Father. He had tried desperately to marry me off at the age of fifteen. I had protested, begging to be permitted to continue my studies. In his frenzy he threw my French grammar into the fire, shouting: "Girls do not have to learn much! All a Jewish daughter needs to know is how to prepare *gefüllte* fish, cut noodles fine, and give the man plenty of children." I would not listen to his schemes; I wanted to study, to know life, to travel. Besides, I never would marry for anything but love, I stoutly maintained. It was really to escape my father's plans for me that I had insisted on going to America. Now attempts to marry me off pursued me even in the new land. I was determined not to be bartered: I would go to work.

Sister Lena had left for America when I was about eleven. I used to spend much time with my grandmother in Kovno, while my people lived in Popelan, a small town in the Baltic Province of Kurland. Lena had always been hostile to me, and unexpectedly I had discovered the reason. I could not have been more than six at the time, while Lena was two years older. We were playing a game of marbles. Somehow sister Lena thought I was winning too often. She flew into a rage, gave me a violent kick, and shouted: "Just like your father! He too cheated us! He robbed us of the money *our* father had left. I hate you! You are not my sister."

The effect of her outburst on me was petrifying. For a few moments I sat riveted to the ground, staring at Lena in silence; then the tension gave way to a fit of crying. I ran to sister Helena, to whom I carried all my childish woes. I demanded to know what Lena had meant when she said my father had robbed her, and why I was not her sister.

As usual Helena took me in her arms, tried to comfort me, and made light of Lena's words. I went to Mother, and from her I learned that there had been another father, Helena's and Lena's. He had died young and Mother had then chosen my father, mine and my baby brother's. She said that my father was also Helena's and Lena's, even if they were his stepchildren. It was true, she explained, that Father had used the money left to the two girls. He had invested it in business and failed. He had meant it for the good of all of us. But what Mother told me did not lessen my great hurt. "Father had no right to use that money!" I cried. "They are orphans. It is a sin to rob orphans. I wish I were grown up; then I could pay back the money. Yes, I must pay back, I must atone for Father's sin."

I had been told by my German nurse that whoever was guilty of robbing orphans would never get to heaven. I had no clear conception of that place. My people, while keeping Jewish rites and going to the synagogue on Saturdays and holidays, rarely spoke to us about religion. I got my idea of God and devil, sin and punishment, from my nurse and our Russian peasant servants. I was sure Father would be punished if I did not pay back his debt.

Eleven years had passed since that incident. I had long forgotten the hurt Lena had caused, but I by no means felt the great affection for her that I bore my dear Helena. All the way to America I had been anxious about what Lena's feelings might be towards me, but when I saw her, heavy with her first child, her small face pale and shrunken, my heart went out to her as if there had never been a shadow between us.

The day after our arrival we three sisters remained alone. Lena told us how lonely she had been, how she had longed for us and for our people. We learned of the hard life that had been hers, first as a domestic servant in Aunt Rachel's house, later as buttonhole-maker in Stein's clothing-factory. How happy she was now, with her own home at last and the joy of her expected child! "Life is still difficult," Lena said; "my husband is earning twelve dollars a week as a tin-smith, working on roofs in the beating sun and in the cold wind, always in danger. He had begun working as a child of eight in Berdichev, Russia," she added, "and he has been working ever since."

When Helena and I retired to our room, we agreed that we must both go to work at once. We could not add to the burden of our brother-in-law. Twelve dollars a week and a child on the way! Some days later Helena got a job retouching negatives, which had been her work in Russia. I found employment at Garson and Mayer's, sewing ulsters ten and a half hours a day, for two dollars and fifty cents a week.

CHAPTER II

I HAD WORKED IN FACTORIES BEFORE, IN ST. PETERSBURG. IN THE winter of 1882, when Mother, my two little brothers, and I came from Königsberg to join Father in the Russian capital, we found that he had lost his position. He had been manager of his cousin's dry-goods store; but, shortly before our arrival, the business failed. The loss of his job was a tragedy to our family, as Father had not managed to save anything. The only bread-winner then was Helena. Mother was forced to turn to her brothers for a loan. The three hundred roubles they advanced were invested in a grocery store. The business yielded little at first, and it became necessary for me to find employment.

Knitted shawls were then much in vogue, and a neighbour told my mother where I might find work to do at home. By keeping at the task many hours a day, sometimes late into the night, I contrived to earn twelve roubles a month.

The shawls I knitted for a livelihood were by no means masterpieces, but somehow they passed. I hated the work, and my eyes gave way under the strain of constant application. Father's cousin who had failed in the dry-goods business now owned a glove factory. He offered to teach me the trade and give me work.

The factory was far from our place. One had to get up at five in the morning to be at work at seven. The rooms were stuffy, unventilated, and dark. Oil lamps gave the light; the sun never penetrated the work-room.

There were six hundred of us, of all ages, working on costly and beautiful gloves day in, day out, for very small pay. But we were allowed sufficient time for our noon meal and twice a day for tea. We could talk and sing while at work; we were not driven or harassed. That was in St. Petersburg, in 1882.

Now I was in America, in the Flower City of the State of New York, in a model factory, as I was told. Certainly, Garson's clothing-works were a vast improvement on the glove factory on the Vassilev-sky Ostrov. The rooms were large, bright, and airy. One had elbow space. There were none of those ill-smelling odours that used to nau-seate me in our cousin's shop. Yet the work here was harder, and the day, with only half an hour for lunch, seemed endless. The iron disci-pline forbade free movement (one could not even go to the toilet without permission), and the constant surveillance of the foreman weighed like stone on my heart. The end of each day found me sapped, with just enough energy to drag myself to my sister's home and crawl into bed. This continued with deadly monotony week after week.

The amazing thing to me was that no one else in the factory seemed to be so affected as I, no one but my neighbour, frail little Tanya. She was delicate and pale, frequently complained of headaches, and often broke into tears when the task of handling heavy ulsters proved too much for her. One morning, as I looked up from my work, I dis-covered her all huddled in a heap. She had fallen in a faint. I called to the foreman to help me carry her to the dressing-room, but the deafening noise of the machines drowned my voice. Several girls near by heard me and began to shout. They ceased working and rushed over to Tanya. The sudden stopping of the machines attracted the foreman's attention and he came over to us. Without even asking the reason for the commotion, he shouted: " Back to your machines! What do you mean stopping work now? Do you want to be fired? Get back at once! " When he spied the crumpled body of Tanya, he yelled: " What the hell is the matter with her? " " She has fainted," I replied, trying hard to control my voice. " Fainted, nothing," he sneered, " she's only shamming."

"You are a liar and a brute! " I cried, no longer able to keep back my indignation.

I bent over Tanya, loosened her waist, and squeezed the juice of an orange I had in my lunch basket into her half-opened mouth. Her face was white, a cold sweat on her forehead. She looked so ill that even the foreman realized she had not been shamming. He excused her for the day. " I will go with Tanya," I said; " you can deduct from my pay for the time." "You can go to hell, you wildcat! " he flung after me.

We went to a coffee place. I myself felt empty and faint, but all we had between us was seventy-five cents. We decided to spend forty on food, and use the rest for a street-car ride to the park. There, in the fresh air, amid the flowers and trees, we forgot our dreaded tasks. The day that had begun in trouble ended restfully and in peace.

The next morning the enervating routine started all over again, continuing for weeks and months, broken only by the new arrival in our family, a baby girl. The child became the one interest in my dull existence. Often, when the atmosphere in Garson's factory threatened to overcome me, the thought of the lovely mite at home revived my spirit. The evenings were no longer dreary and meaningless. But, while little Stella brought joy into our household, she added to the material anxiety of my sister and my brother-in-law.

Lena never by word or deed made me feel that the dollar and fifty cents I was giving her for my board (the car fare amounted to sixty cents a week, the remaining forty cents being my pin-money) did not cover my keep. But I had overheard my brother-in-law grumbling over the growing expenses of the house. I felt he was right. I did not want my sister worried, she was nursing her child. I decided to apply for a rise. I knew it was no use talking to the foreman and therefore I asked to see Mr. Garson.

I was ushered into a luxurious office. American Beauties were on the table. Often I had admired them in the flower shops, and once, unable to withstand the temptation, I had gone in to ask the price. They were one dollar and a half apiece — more than half of my week's earnings. The lovely vase in Mr. Garson's office held a great many of them.

I was not asked to sit down. For a moment I forgot my mission. The beautiful room, the roses, the aroma of the bluish smoke from Mr. Garson's cigar, fascinated me. I was recalled to reality by my employer's question: "Well, what can I do for you?"

I had come to ask for a rise, I told him. The two dollars and a half I was getting did not pay my board, let alone anything else, such as an occasional book or a theatre ticket for twenty-five cents. Mr. Garson replied that for a factory girl I had rather extravagant tastes, that all his "hands" were well satisfied, that they seemed to be getting along all right — that I, too, would have to manage or find work elsewhere. "If I raise your wages, I'll have to raise the others' as well and I can't afford that," he said. I decided to leave Garson's employ.

A few days later I secured a job at Rubinstein's factory at four dollars a week. It was a small shop, not far from where I lived. The house stood in a garden, and only a dozen men and women were employed in the place. The Garson discipline and drive were missing.

Next to my machine worked an attractive young man whose name was Jacob Kershner. He lived near Lena's home, and we would often walk from work together. Before long he began calling for me in the morning. We used to converse in Russian, my English still being very halting. His Russian was like music to me; it was the first real Russian, outside of Helena's, that I had had an opportunity to hear in Rochester since my arrival.

Kershner had come to America in 1881 from Odessa, where he had finished the *Gymnasium*. Having no trade, he became an " operator " on cloaks. He used to spend most of his leisure, he told me, reading or going to dances. He had no friends, because he found his co-workers in Rochester interested only in money-making, their ideal being to start a shop of their own. He had heard of our arrival, Helena's and mine — had even seen me on the street several times — but he did not know how to get acquainted. Now he would no longer feel lonely, he said brightly; we could visit places together and he would lend me his books to read. My own loneliness no longer was so poignant.

I told my sisters of my new acquaintance, and Lena asked me to invite him the next Sunday. When Kershner came, she was favourably impressed; but Helena took a violent dislike to him from the first. She said nothing about it for a long time, but I could sense it.

One day Kershner invited me to a dance. It was my first since I came to America. The very anticipation was exciting, bringing back memories of my first ball in St. Petersburg.

I was fifteen then. Helena had been invited to the fashionable German Club by her employer, who gave her two tickets, so she could bring me with her. Some time previously my sister had presented me with a piece of lovely blue velvet for my first long dress; but before it could be made up, our peasant servant walked off with the material. My grief over its loss made me quite ill for several days. If only I had a dress, I thought, Father might consent to my attending the ball. " I'll get you material for a dress," Helena consoled me, " but I'm afraid Father will refuse." " Then I will defy him ! " I declared.

She bought another piece of blue stuff, not so beautiful as my velvet, but I no longer minded. I was too happy over the prospect of my first ball, of the bliss of dancing in public. Somehow Helena succeeded in getting Father's consent, but at the last moment he changed his mind. I had been guilty of some infraction during the day, and he categorically declared that I would have to stay home. Thereupon Helena said she also would not go. But I was determined to defy my father, no matter what the consequences.

With bated breath I waited for my parents to retire for the night. Then I dressed and woke Helena. I told her she must come with me or I would run away from home. "We can be back before Father wakes up," I urged. Dear Helena — she was always so timid! She had infinite capacity for suffering, for endurance, but she could not fight. On this occasion she was carried away by my desperate decision. She dressed and we quietly slipped out of the house.

At the German Club everything was bright and gay. We found Helena's employer, whose name was Kadison, and some of his young friends. I was asked for every dance, and I danced in frantic excitement and abandon. It was getting late and many people were already leaving when Kadison invited me for another dance. Helena insisted that I was too exhausted, but I would not have it so. "I will dance!" I declared; "I will dance myself to death!" My flesh felt hot, my heart beat violently as my cavalier swung me round the ball-room, holding me tightly. To dance to death — what more glorious end!

It was towards five in the morning when we arrived home. Our people were still asleep. I awoke late in the day, pretending a sick headache, and secretly I gloried in my triumph of having outwitted our old man.

The memory of that experience still vivid in my mind, I accompanied Jacob Kershner to the party, full of anticipation. My disappointment was bitter: there were no beautiful ball-room, no lovely women, no dashing young men, no gaiety. The music was shrill, the dancers clumsy. Jacob danced not badly, but he lacked spirit and fire. "Four years at the machine have taken the strength out of me," he said; "I get tired so easily."

I had known Jacob Kershner about four months when he asked me to marry him. I admitted I liked him, but I did not want to marry so young. We still knew so little of each other. He said he'd wait as long as I pleased, but there was already a great deal of talk about our being out together so much. "Why should we not get engaged?" he pleaded. Finally I consented. Helena's antagonism to Jacob had become almost an obsession; she fairly hated him. But I was lonely —

I needed companionship. Ultimately I won over my sister. Her great love for me could never refuse me anything or stand out against my wishes.

The late fall of 1886 brought the rest of our family to Rochester — Father, Mother, my brothers, Herman and Yegor. Conditions in St. Petersburg had become intolerable for the Jews, and the grocery business did not yield enough for the ever-growing bribery Father had to practise in order to be allowed to exist. America became the only solution.

Together with Helena I had prepared a home for our parents, and on their arrival we went to live with them. Our earnings soon proved inadequate to meet the household expenses. Jacob Kershner offered to board with us, which would be of some help, and before long he moved in.

The house was small, consisting of a living-room, a kitchen, and two bedrooms. One of them was used by my parents, the other by Helena, myself, and our little brother. Kershner and Herman slept in the living-room. The close proximity of Jacob and the lack of privacy kept me in constant irritation. I suffered from sleepless nights, waking dreams and great fatigue at work. Life was becoming unbearable, and Jacob stressed the need of a home of our own.

On nearer acquaintance I had grown to understand that we were too different. His interest in books, which had first attracted me to him, had waned. He had fallen into the ways of his shopmates, playing cards and attending dull dances. I, on the contrary, was filled with striving and aspirations. In spirit I was still in Russia, in my beloved St. Petersburg, living in the world of the books I had read, the operas I had heard, the circle of the students I had known. I hated Rochester even more than before. But Kershner was the only human being I had met since my arrival. He filled a void in my life, and I was strongly attracted to him. In February 1887 we were married in Rochester by a rabbi, according to Jewish rites, which were then considered sufficient by the law of the country.

My feverish excitement of that day, my suspense and ardent anticipation gave way at night to a feeling of utter bewilderment. Jacob lay trembling near me; he was impotent.

The first erotic sensations I remember had come to me when I was about six. My parents lived in Popelan then, where we children had no home in any real sense. Father kept an inn, which was constantly filled with peasants, drunk and quarrelling, and government officials. Mother was busy superintending the servants in our large, chaotic house. My sisters, Lena and Helena, fourteen and twelve, were burdened with work. I was left to myself most of the day. Among the stable help there was a young peasant, Petrushka, who served as shepherd, looking after our cows and sheep. Often he would take me with him to the meadows, and I would listen to the sweet tones of his flute. In the evening he would carry me back home on his shoulders, I sitting astride. He would play horse — run as fast as his legs could carry him, then suddenly throw me up in the air, catch me in his arms, and press me to him. It used to give me a peculiar sensation, fill me with exultation, followed by blissful release.

I became inseparable from Petrushka. I grew so fond of him that I began stealing cake and fruit from Mother's pantry for him. To be with Petrushka out in the fields, to listen to his music, to ride on his shoulders, became the obsession of my waking and sleeping hours. One day Father had an altercation with Petrushka, and the boy was sent away. The loss of him was one of the greatest tragedies of my child-life. For weeks afterwards I kept on dreaming of Petrushka, the meadows, the music, and reliving the joy and ecstasy of our play. One morning I felt myself torn out of sleep. Mother was bending over me, tightly holding my right hand. In an angry voice she cried: " If ever I find your hand again like that, I'll whip you, you naughty child! "

The approach of puberty gave me my first consciousness of the effect of men on me. I was eleven then. Early one summer day I woke up in great agony. My head, spine, and legs ached as if they were being pulled asunder. I called for Mother. She drew back my bedcovers, and suddenly I felt a stinging pain in my face. She had struck me. I let out a shriek, fastening on Mother terrified eyes. "This is necessary for a girl," she said, " when she becomes a woman, as a protection against disgrace." She tried to take me in her arms, but I pushed her back. I was writhing in pain and I was too outraged for her to touch me. " I am going to die," I howled, " I want the *Feldscher* (assistant doctor). The *Feldscher* was sent for. He was a young man, a new-comer in our village. He examined me and gave me something to put me to sleep. Thenceforth my dreams were of the *Feldscher*.

When I was fifteen, I was employed in a corset factory in the

Hermitage Arcade in St. Petersburg. After working hours, on leaving the shop together with the other girls, we would be waylaid by young Russian officers and civilians. Most of the girls had their sweethearts; only a Jewish girl chum of mine and I refused to be taken to the *konditorskaya* (pastry shop) or to the park.

Next to the Hermitage was a hotel we had to pass. One of the clerks, a handsome fellow of about twenty, singled me out for his attentions. At first I scorned him, but gradually he began to exert a fascination on me. His perseverance slowly undermined my pride and I accepted his courtship. We used to meet in some quiet spot or in an out-of-the-way pastry shop. I had to invent all sorts of stories to explain to my father why I returned late from work or stayed out after nine o'clock. One day he spied me in the Summer Garden in the company of other girls and some boy students. When I returned home, he threw me violently against the shelves in our grocery store, which sent the jars of Mother's wonderful *varenya* flying to the floor. He pounded me with his fists, shouting that he would not tolerate a loose daughter. The experience made my home more unbearable, the need of escape more compelling.

For several months my admirer and I met clandestinely. One day he asked me whether I should not like to go through the hotel to see the luxurious rooms. I had never been in a hotel before — the joy and gaiety I fancied behind the gorgeous windows used to fascinate me as I would pass the place on my way from work.

The boy led me through a side entrance, along a thickly carpeted corridor, into a large room. It was brightly illumined and beautifully furnished. A table near the sofa held flowers and a tea-tray. We sat down. The young man poured out a golden-coloured liquid and asked me to clink glasses to our friendship. I put the wine to my lips. Suddenly I found myself in his arms, my waist torn open — his passionate kisses covered my face, neck, and breasts. Not until after the violent contact of our bodies and the excruciating pain he caused me did I come to my senses. I screamed, savagely beating against the man's chest with my fists. Suddenly I heard Helena's voice in the hall. " She must be here — she must be here! " I became speechless. The man, too, was terrorized. His grip relaxed, and we listened in breathless silence. After what seemed to me hours, Helena's voice receded. The man got up. I rose mechanically, mechanically buttoned my waist and brushed back my hair.

Strange, I felt no shame — only a great shock at the discovery that the contact between man and woman could be so brutal and so painful. I walked out in a daze, bruised in every nerve.

When I reached home I found Helena fearfully wrought up. She had been uneasy about me, aware of my meeting with the boy. She had made it her business to find out where he worked, and when I failed to return, she had gone to the hotel in search of me. The shame I did not feel in the arms of the man now overwhelmed me. I could not muster up courage to tell Helena of my experience.

After that I always felt between two fires in the presence of men. Their lure remained strong, but it was always mingled with violent revulsion. I could not bear to have them touch me.

These pictures passed through my mind vividly as I lay alongside my husband on our wedding night. He had fallen fast asleep.

The weeks went on. There was no change. I urged Jacob to consult a doctor. At first he refused, pleading diffidence, but finally he went. He was told it would take considerable time to "build up his manhood." My own passion had subsided. The material anxiety of making ends meet excluded everything else. I had stopped work: it was considered disgraceful for a married woman to go to the shop. Jacob was earning fifteen dollars a week. He had developed a passion for cards, which swallowed up a considerable part of our income. He grew jealous, suspecting everyone. Life became insupportable. I was saved from utter despair by my interest in the Haymarket events.

After the death of the Chicago anarchists I insisted on a separation from Kershner. He fought long against it, but finally consented to a divorce. It was given to us by the same rabbi who had performed our marriage ceremony. Then I left for New Haven, Connecticut, to work in a corset-factory.

During my efforts to free myself from Kershner the only one who stood by me was my sister Helena. She had been strenuously opposed to the marriage in the first place, but now she offered not a single reproach. On the contrary, she gave me help and comfort. She pleaded with my parents and with Lena in behalf of my decision to get a divorce. As always, her devotion knew no bounds.

In New Haven I met a group of young Russians, students mainly, now working at various trades. Most of them were socialists and anarchists. They often organized meetings, generally inviting speakers from New York, one of whom was A. Solotaroff. Life was interesting and colourful, but gradually the strain of the work became too much for my depleted vitality. Finally I had to return to Rochester.

I went to Helena. She lived with her husband and child over their little printing shop, which also served as an office for their steamship agency. But both occupations did not bring in enough to keep them from dire poverty. Helena had married Jacob Hochstein, a man ten years her senior. He was a great Hebrew scholar, an authority on the English and Russian classics, and a very rare personality. His integrity and independent character made him a poor competitor in the sordid business life. When anyone brought him a printing order worth two dollars, Jacob Hochstein devoted as much time to it as if he were getting fifty. If a customer showed a tendency to bargain over prices, he would send him away. He could not bear the implication that he might overcharge. His income was insufficient for the needs of the family, and the one to worry and fret most about it was my poor Helena. She was pregnant with her second child and yet had to drudge from morning till night to make ends meet, with never a word of complaint. But, then, she had been that way all her life, suffering silently, always resigned.

Helena's marriage had not sprung from a passionate love. It was the union of two mature people who longed for comradeship, for a quiet life. Whatever there had been of passion in my sister had burned out when she was twenty-four. At the age of sixteen, while we were living in Popelan, she had fallen in love with a young Lithuanian, a beautiful soul. But he was a *goi* (gentile) and Helena knew that marriage between them was impossible. After a great struggle and many tears Helena broke off the affair with young Susha. Years later, while on our way to America, we stopped in Kovno, our native town. Helena had arranged for Susha to meet her there. She could not bear to go away so far without saying good-bye to him. They met and parted as good friends — the fire of their youth was in ashes.

On my return from New Haven Helena received me, as always, with tenderness and with the assurance that her home was also mine. It was good to be near my darling again, with little Stella and my young brother Yegor. But it did not take me long to discover the pinched condition in Helena's home. I went back to the shop.

Living in the Jewish district, it was impossible to avoid those one did not wish to see. I ran into Kershner almost immediately after my arrival. Day after day he would seek me out. He began to plead with me to go back to him — all would be different. One day he threatened suicide — actually pulled out a bottle of poison. Insistently he pressed me for a final answer.

I was not naïve enough to think that a renewed life with Kershner would prove more satisfactory or lasting than at first. Besides, I had definitely decided to go to New York, to equip myself for the work I had vowed to take up after the death of my Chicago comrades. But Kershner's threat frightened me: I could not be responsible for his death. I remarried him. My parents rejoiced and so did Lena and her husband, but Helena was sick with grief.

Without Kershner's knowledge I took up a course in dressmaking, in order to have a trade that would free me from the shop. During three long months I wrestled with my husband to let me go my way. I tried to make him see the futility of living a patched life, but he remained obdurate. Late one night, after bitter recriminations, I left Jacob Kershner and my home, this time definitely.

I was immediately ostracized by the whole Jewish population of Rochester. I could not pass on the street without being held up to scorn. My parents forbade me their house, and again it was only Helena who stood by me. Out of her meagre income she even paid my fare to New York.

So I left Rochester, where I had known so much pain, hard work, and loneliness, but the joy of my departure was marred by separation from Helena, from Stella, and the little brother I loved so well.

The break of the new day in the Minkin flat still found me awake. The door upon the old had now closed for ever. The new was calling, and I eagerly stretched out my hands towards it. I fell into a deep, peaceful sleep.

I was awakened by Anna Minkin's voice announcing the arrival of Alexander Berkman. It was late afternoon.

CHAPTER III

HELEN MINKIN WAS AWAY AT WORK. ANNA WAS OUT OF A JOB just then. She prepared tea, and we sat down to talk. Berkman inquired about my plans for work, for activity in the movement. Would I like to visit the *Freiheit* office? Could he be of help in any way? He was free to take me about, he said; he had left his job after a fight with the foreman. "A slave-driver," he commented; "he never dared drive me, but it was my duty to stand up for the others in the shop." It was rather slack now in the cigar-making trade, he informed us, but as an anarchist he could not stop to consider his own job. Nothing personal mattered. Only the Cause mattered. Fighting injustice and exploitation mattered.

How strong he was, I thought; how wonderful in his revolutionary zeal! Just like our martyred comrades in Chicago.

I had to go to West Forty-second Street to get my sewing-machine out of the baggage-room. Berkman offered to accompany me. He suggested that on our way back we might ride down to Brooklyn Bridge on the Elevated and then walk over to William Street, where the *Freiheit* office was located.

I asked him whether I could hope to establish myself in New York as a dressmaker. I wanted so much to free myself from the dreadful grind and slavery of the shop. I wanted to have time for reading, and later I hoped to realize my dream of a co-operative shop. "Something like Vera's venture in *What's to be Done?*" I explained. "You have read Chernishevsky?" Berkman inquired, in surprise; "surely not in Rochester?" "Surely not," I replied, laughing; "besides my sister Helena, I found no one there who would read such books. No, not in that dull town. In St. Petersburg." He looked at me doubtfully. "Chernishevsky was a Nihilist," he remarked, "and his works are prohibited in Russia. Were you connected with the Nihilists? They

are the only ones who could have given you the book." I felt indignant. How dared he doubt my word! I repeated angrily that I had
read the forbidden book and other similar works, such as Turgeniev's
Fathers and Sons, and *Obriv (The Precipice)* by Gontcharov. My
sister had got them from students and she let me read them. " I am
sorry if I hurt you," Berkman said in a soft tone. " I did not really
doubt your word. I was only surprised to find a girl so young who had
read such books."

How far I had wandered away from my adolescent days, I reflected. I recalled the morning in Königsberg when I had come upon
a huge poster announcing the death of the Tsar, " assassinated by
murderous Nihilists." The thought of the poster brought back to
my memory an incident of my early childhood which for a time had
turned our home into a house of mourning. Mother had received a
letter from her brother Martin giving the appalling news of the
arrest of their brother Yegor. He had been mixed up with Nihilists,
the letter read, and he was thrown into the Petro-Pavlovsky Fortress
and would soon be sent away to Siberia. The news struck terror in us.
Mother decided to go to St. Petersburg. For weeks we were kept in
anxious suspense. At last she returned, her face beaming with happiness. She had found that Yegor was already on the way to Siberia.
After much difficulty and with the help of a large sum of money she
had succeeded in getting an audience with Trepov, the Governor-
General of St. Petersburg. She had learned that his son was a college
chum of Yegor and she urged it as proof that her brother could not
have been mixed up with the terrible Nihilists. One so close to the
Governor's own son would surely have nothing to do with the enemies
of Russia. She pleaded Yegor's extreme youth, went on her knees,
begged and wept. Finally Trepov promised that he would have the
boy brought back from the *étape.* Of course, he would put him under
strict surveillance; Yegor would have to promise solemnly never to go
near the murderous gang.

Our mother was always very vivid when she related stories of books
she had read. We children used to hang on her very lips. This time,
too, her story was absorbing. It made me see Mother before the stern
Governor-General, her beautiful face, framed by her massive hair,
bathed in tears. The Nihilists, too, I saw — black, sinister creatures
who had ensnared my uncle in their plotting to kill the Tsar. The
good, gracious Tsar — Mother had said — the first to give more

freedom to the Jews; he had stopped the pogroms and he was planning to set the peasants free. And him the Nihilists meant to kill! "Cold-blooded murderers," Mother cried, "they ought to be exterminated, every one of them!"

Mother's violence terrorized me. Her suggestion of extermination froze my blood. I felt that the Nihilists must be beasts, but I could not bear such cruelty in my mother. Often after that I caught myself thinking of the Nihilists, wondering who they were and what made them so ferocious. When the news reached Königsberg about the hanging of the Nihilists who had killed the Tsar, I no longer felt any bitterness against them. Something mysterious had awakened compassion for them in me. I wept bitterly over their fate.

Years later I came upon the term "Nihilist" in *Fathers and Sons.* And when I read *What's to be Done?* I understood my instinctive sympathy with the executed men. I felt that they could not witness without protest the suffering of the people and that they had sacrificed their lives for them. I became the more convinced of it when I learned the story of Vera Zassulich, who had shot Trepov in 1879. My young teacher of Russian related it to me. Mother had said that Trepov was kind and humane, but my teacher told me how tyrannical he had been, a veritable monster who used to order out his Cossacks against the students, have them lashed with *nagaikas,* their gatherings dispersed, and the prisoners sent to Siberia. "Officials like Trepov are wild beasts," my teacher would say passionately; "they rob the peasants and then flog them. They torture idealists in prison."

I knew that my teacher spoke the truth. In Popelan everyone used to talk about the flogging of peasants. One day I came upon a half-naked human body being lashed with the knout. It threw me into hysterics, and for days I was haunted by the horrible picture. Listening to my teacher revived the ghastly sight: the bleeding body, the piercing shrieks, the distorted faces of the *gendarmes,* the knouts whistling in the air and coming down with a sharp hissing upon the half-naked man. Whatever doubts about the Nihilists I had left from my childhood impressions now disappeared. They became to me heroes and martyrs, henceforth my guiding stars.

I was aroused from my reverie by Berkman's asking why I had become so silent. I told him of my recollections. He then related to me some of his own early influences, dwelling particularly on his beloved Nihilist uncle Maxim and on the shock he had experienced on learning that he had been sentenced to die. "We have much in common, haven't we?" he remarked. "We even come from the same city. Do you know that Kovno has given many brave sons to the revolutionary movement? And now perhaps also a brave daughter," he added. I felt myself turn red. My soul was proud. "I hope I shall not fail when the time comes," I replied.

The train was passing narrow streets, the dreary tenements so close by that I could see into the rooms. The fire-escapes were littered with dirty pillows and blankets and hung with laundry streaked with dirt. Berkman touched my arm and announced that the next station was Brooklyn Bridge. We got off and walked to William Street.

In an old building, up two dark and creaking flights, was the office of the *Freiheit*. Several men were in the first room setting type. In the next we found Johann Most standing at a high desk, writing. With a side-glance he invited us to sit down. "My damned torturers there are squeezing the blood out of me," he declared querulously. "Copy, copy, copy! That's all they know! Ask them to write a line — not they. They are too stupid and too lazy." A burst of good-natured laughter from the composing-room greeted Most's outburst. His gruff voice, his twisted jaw, which had so repelled me on my first meeting him, recalled to me the caricatures of Most in the Rochester papers. I could not reconcile the angry man before me with the inspired speaker of the previous evening whose oratory had so carried me away.

Berkman noticed my confused and frightened look. He whispered in Russian not to mind Most, that he was always in such a mood when at work. I got up to inspect the books which covered the shelves from floor to ceiling, row upon row. How few of them I had read, I mused. My years in school had given me so little. Should I ever be able to make up? Where should I get the time to read? And the money to buy books? I wondered whether Most would lend me some of his, whether I dared ask him to suggest a course of reading and study. Presently another outburst grated on my ears. "Here's my pound of flesh, you Shylocks!" Most thundered; "more than enough to fill the paper. Here, Berkman, take it to the black devils in there!"

Most approached me. His deep blue eyes looked searchingly into mine. "Well, young lady," he said, "have you found anything you want to read? Or don't you read German and English?" The harshness of his voice had changed to a warm, kindly texture. "Not English," I said, soothed and emboldened by his tone, "German." He told me I could have any book I wanted. Then he plied me with questions —where I hailed from and what I intended to do. I said I had come from Rochester. "Yes, I know the city. It has good beer. But the Germans there are a bunch of *Kaffern*. Why New York exactly?" he inquired; "it is a hard city. Work poorly paid, not easily found. Have you enough money to hold out?" I was deeply touched by the interest of this man in me, a perfect stranger. I explained that New York had lured me because it was the centre of the anarchist movement, and because I had read of him as its leading spirit. I had really come to him for suggestions and help. I wanted very much to talk to him. "But not now, some other time," I said, "somewhere away from your black devils."

"You have a sense of humour,"—his face lit up—"you'll need it if you enter our movement." He suggested that I come next Wednesday, to help with expediting the *Freiheit,* to write addresses and fold the papers—"and afterwards we may be able to talk."

With several books under my arm and a warm handshake, Most sent me off. Berkman left with me.

We went to Sachs's. I had had nothing to eat since the tea Anna had given us. My escort, too, was hungry, but evidently not so much as the night before: he did not call for extra steak or extra cups of coffee. Or was he broke? I suggested that I was still rich and begged him to order more. He refused brusquely, telling me that he couldn't accept it from anyone out of a job who had just arrived in a strange city. I felt both angry and amused. I explained that I did not wish to hurt him; I believed that one always shared with a comrade. He repented his abruptness, but assured me that he was not hungry. We left the restaurant.

The August heat was suffocating. Berkman suggested a trip to the Battery to cool off. I had not seen the harbour since my arrival in America. Its beauty gripped me again as on the memorable day. But the Statue of Liberty had ceased to be an alluring symbol. How childishly naïve I had been, how far I had advanced since that day!

We returned to our talk of the afternoon. My companion expressed doubt about my finding work as a dressmaker, having no connexion in the city. I replied that I would try a factory, one for corsets, gloves, or men's suits. He promised to inquire among the Jewish comrades who were in the needle trade. They would surely help find a job for me.

It was late in the evening when we parted. Berkman had told me little about himself, except that he had been expelled from the *Gymnasium* for an anti-religious essay he had composed, and that he had left home for good. He had come to the United States in the belief that it was free and that here everyone had an equal chance in life. He knew better now. He had found exploitation more severe, and since the hanging of the Chicago anarchists he had become convinced that America was as despotic as Russia.

"Lingg was right when he said : 'If you attack us with cannon, we will reply with dynamite.' Some day I will avenge our dead," he added with great earnestness. "I too! I too!" I cried; "their death gave me life. It now belongs to their memory — to their work." He gripped my arm until it hurt. "We are comrades. Let us be friends, too — let us work together." His intensity vibrated through me as I walked up the stairs to the Minkin flat.

The following Friday, Berkman invited me to come to a Jewish lecture by Solotaroff at 54 Orchard Street, on the East Side. In New Haven Solotaroff had impressed me as an exceptionally fine speaker, but now, after having heard Most, his talk appeared flat to me, and his badly modulated voice affected me unpleasantly. His ardour, however, made up for much. I was too grateful for the warm reception he had given me on my first arrival in the city to allow myself any criticism of his lecture. Besides, everybody could not be an orator like Johann Most, I reflected. To me he was a man apart, the most remarkable in all the world.

After the meeting Berkman introduced me to a number of people, "all good active comrades," as he put it. "And here is my chum Fedya," he said, indicating a young man beside him; "he is also an anarchist, of course, but not so good as he should be."

The young chap was probably of the same age as Berkman, but not so strongly built, nor with the same aggressive manner about him. His features were rather delicate, with a sensitive mouth, while his eyes, though somewhat bulging, had a dreamy expression. He did not seem to mind in the least the banter of his friend. He smiled good-naturedly and suggested that we retire to Sachs's, "to give Sasha a chance to tell you what a good anarchist is."

Berkman did not wait till we reached the café. "A good anarchist," he began with deep conviction, "is one who lives only for the Cause and gives everything to it. My friend here " — he indicated Fedya —

" is still too much of a *bourgeois* to realize that. He is a *mamenkin sin* (mother's spoilt darling), who even accepts money from home." He continued to explain why it was inconsistent for a revolutionary to have anything to do with his *bourgeois* parents or relatives. His only reason for tolerating his friend Fedya's inconsistency, he added, was that he gave most of what he received from home to the movement. " If I'd let him, he'd spend all his money on useless things — ' beautiful,' he calls them. Wouldn't you, Fedya ? " He turned to his friend, patting him on the back affectionately.

The café was crowded, as usual, and filled with smoke and talk. For a little while my two escorts were much in demand, while I was greeted by several people I had met during the week. Finally we succeeded in capturing a table and ordered some coffee and cake. I became aware of Fedya watching me and studying my face. To hide my embarrassment I turned to Berkman. " Why should one not love beauty ? " I asked; " flowers, for instance, music, the theatre — beautiful things ? "

" I did not say one should not," Berkman replied; " I said it was wrong to spend money on such things when the movement is so much in need of it. It is inconsistent for an anarchist to enjoy luxuries when the people live in poverty."

" But beautiful things are not luxuries," I insisted; " they are necessaries. Life would be unbearable without them." Yet, at heart, I felt that Berkman was right. Revolutionists gave up even their lives — why not also beauty ? Still the young artist struck a responsive chord in me. I, too, loved beauty. Our poverty-stricken life in Königsberg had been made bearable to me only by the occasional outings with our teachers in the open. The forest, the moon casting its silvery shimmer on the fields, the green wreaths in our hair, the flowers we would pick — these made me forget for a time the sordid home surroundings. When Mother scolded me or when I had difficulties at school, a bunch of lilacs from our neighbour's garden or the sight of the colourful silks and velvets displayed in the shops would cause me to forget my sorrows and make the world seem beautiful and bright. Or the music I would on rare occasions be able to hear in Königsberg and, later, in St. Petersburg. Should I have to forgo all that to be a good revolutionist, I wondered. Should I have the strength ?

Before we parted that evening Fedya remarked that his friend had mentioned that I would like to see something of the city. He was free the next day and would be glad to show me some of the sights. " Are you also out of work, that you can afford the time?" I asked. "As you know from my friend, I am an artist," he replied, laughing. "Have you ever heard of artists working?" I flushed, having to admit that I had never met an artist before. "Artists are inspired people," I said, "everything comes easy to them." "Of course," Berkman retorted, "because the people work for them." His tone seemed too severe to me, and my sympathy went out to the artist boy. I turned to him and asked him to come for me the next day. But alone in my room, it was the uncompromising fervour of the "arrogant youngster," as I mentally called Berkman, that filled me with admiration.

The next day Fedya took me to Central Park. Along Fifth Avenue he pointed out the various mansions, naming their owners. I had read about those wealthy men, their affluence and extravagance, while the masses lived in poverty. I expressed my indignation at the contrast between those splendid palaces and the miserable tenements of the East Side. "Yes, it is a crime that the few should have all, the many nothing," the artist said. "My main objection," he continued, "is that they have such bad taste — those buildings are ugly." Berkman's attitude to beauty came to my mind. "You don't agree with your chum on the need and importance of beauty in one's life, do you?" I asked. "Indeed I do not. But, then, my friend is a revolutionist above everything else. I wish I could also be, but I am not." I liked his frankness and simplicity. He did not stir me as Berkman did when speaking of revolutionary ethics; Fedya awakened in me the mysterious yearning I used to feel in my childhood at sight of the sunset turning the Popelan meadows golden in its dying glow, as the sweet music of Petrushka's flute did also.

The following week I went to the *Freiheit* office. Several people were already there, busy addressing envelopes and folding the papers. Everybody talked. Johann Most was at his desk. I was assigned a place and given work. I marvelled at Most's capacity to go on writing in that hubbub. Several times I wanted to suggest that he was being disturbed, but I checked myself. After all, they must know whether he minded their chatter.

In the evening Most stopped writing and gruffly assailed the talkers as "toothless old women," "cackling geese," and other appellations I had hardly ever before heard in German. He snatched his large felt hat from the rack, called to me to come along, and walked out. I followed him and we went up on the Elevated. "I'll take you to Terrace

Garden," he said; " we can go into the theatre there if you like. They are giving *Der Zigeunerbaron* tonight. Or we can sit in some corner, get food and drink, and talk." I replied that I did not care for light opera, that what I really wanted was to talk to him, or rather have him talk to me. " But not so violently as in the office," I added.

He selected the food and the wine. Their names were strange to me. The label on the bottle read: *Liebfrauenmilch*. " Milk of woman's love — what a lovely name ! " I remarked. " For wine, yes," he retorted, " but not for woman's love. The one is always poetic — the other will never be anything but sordidly prosaic. It leaves a bad taste."

I had a feeling of guilt, as if I had made some bad break or had touched a sore spot. I told him I had never tasted any wine before, except the kind Mother made for Easter. Most shook with laughter, and I was near tears. He noticed my embarrassment and restrained himself. He poured out two glassfuls, saying: " *Prosit,* my young, naïve lady," and drank his down at a gulp. Before I could drink half of mine, he had nearly finished the bottle and ordered another.

He became animated, witty, sparkling. There was no trace of the bitterness, of the hatred and defiance his oratory had breathed on the platform. Instead there sat next to me a transformed human being, no longer the repulsive caricature of the Rochester press or the gruff creature of the office. He was a gracious host, an attentive and sympathetic friend. He made me tell him about myself and he grew thoughtful when he learned the motive that had decided me to break with my old life. He warned me to reflect carefully before taking the plunge. " The path of anarchism is steep and painful," he said; " so many have attempted to climb it and have fallen back. The price is exacting. Few men are ready to pay it, most women not at all. Louise Michel, Sophia Perovskaya — they were the great exceptions." Had I read about the Paris Commune and about that marvellous Russian woman revolutionist? I had to admit ignorance. I had never heard the name of Louise Michel before, though I did know about the great Russian. " You shall read about their lives — they will inspire you," Most said.

I inquired whether the anarchist movement in America had no outstanding woman. " None at all, only stupids," he replied; " most of the girls come to the meetings to snatch up a man; then both vanish, like the silly fishermen at the lure of the Lorelei." There was a roguish twinkle in his eye. He didn't believe much in woman's revolutionary zeal. But I, coming from Russia, might be different and he would help me. If I were really in earnest, I could find much work to do. "There is great need in our ranks of young, willing people — ardent ones, as you seem to be — and I have need of ardent friendship," he added with much feeling.

"You?" I questioned; "you have thousands in New York — all over the world. You are loved, you are idolized." "Yes, little girl, idolized by many, but loved by none. One can be very lonely among thousands — did you know that?" Something gripped my heart. I wanted to take his hand, to tell him that I would be his friend. But I dared not speak out. What could I give this man — I, a factory girl, uneducated; and he, the famous Johann Most, the leader of the masses, the man of magic tongue and powerful pen?

He promised to supply me with a list of books to read — the revolutionary poets, Freiligrath, Herwegh, Schiller, Heine, and Börne, and our own literature, of course. It was almost daybreak when we left Terrace Garden. Most called a cab and we drove to the Minkin flat. At the door he lightly touched my hand. "Where did you get your silky blond hair?" he remarked; "and your blue eyes? You said you were Jewish." "At the pigs' market," I replied; "my father told me so." "You have a ready tongue, *mein Kind.*" He waited for me to unlock the door, then took my hand, looked deeply into my eyes, and said: "This was my first happy evening in a long while." A great gladness filled my being at his words. Slowly I climbed the stairs as the cab rolled away.

The next day, when Berkman called, I related to him my wonderful evening with Most. His face darkened. "Most has no right to squander money, to go to expensive restaurants, drink expensive wines," he said gravely; "he is spending the money contributed for the movement. He should be held to account. I myself will tell him."

"No, no, you musn't," I cried. "I couldn't bear to be the cause of any affront to Most, who is giving so much. Is he not entitled to a little joy?"

Berkman persisted that I was too young in the movement, that I didn't know anything about revolutionary ethics or the meaning of revolutionary right and wrong. I admitted my ignorance, assured him I was willing to learn, to do anything, only not to have Most hurt. He walked out without bidding me good-bye.

I was greatly disturbed. The charm of Most was upon me. His remarkable gifts, his eagerness for life, for friendship, moved me deeply. And Berkman, too, appealed to me profoundly. His earnestness, his self-confidence, his youth — everything about him drew me with irresistible force. But I had the feeling that, of the two, Most was more of this earth.

When Fedya came to see me, he told me that he had already heard the story from Berkman. He was not surprised, he said; he knew how uncompromising our friend was and how hard he could be, but hardest towards himself. " It springs from his absorbing love of the people," Fedya added, " a love that will yet move him to great deeds."

For a whole week Berkman did not show up. When he came back again, it was to invite me for an outing in Prospect Park. He liked it better than Central Park, he said, because it was less cultivated, more natural. We walked about a great deal, admiring its rough beauty, and finally selected a lovely spot in which to eat the lunch I had brought with me.

We talked about my life in St. Petersburg and in Rochester. I told him of my marriage to Jacob Kershner and its failure. He wanted to know what books I had read on marriage and if it was their influence that had decided me to leave my husband. I had never read such works, but I had seen enough of the horrors of married life in my own home. Father's harsh treatment of Mother, the constant wrangles and bitter scenes that ended in Mother's fainting spells. I had also seen the debasing sordidness of the life of my married aunts and uncles, as well as in the homes of acquaintances in Rochester. Together with my own marital experiences they had convinced me that binding people for life was wrong. The constant proximity in the same house, the same room, the same bed, revolted me.

" If ever I love a man again, I will give myself to him without being bound by the rabbi or the law," I declared, " and when that love dies, I will leave without permission."

My companion said he was glad to know that I felt that way. All true revolutionists had discarded marriage and were living in freedom. That served to strengthen their love and helped them in their common task. He told me the story of Sophia Perovskaya and Zhelyabov. They had been lovers, had worked in the same group, and together they elaborated the plan for the execution of Alexander II. After the explosion of the bomb Perovskaya vanished. She was in hiding. She had every chance to escape, and her comrades begged her to do so. But she refused. She insisted that she must take the consequences, that she would share the fate of her comrades and die together with Zhelyabov. " Of course, it was wrong of her to be moved by personal sentiment," Berkman commented; " her love for the Cause should have urged her to live for other activities." Again I found myself disagreeing with him. I thought that it could not be wrong to die with one's beloved in a common act — it was beautiful, it was sublime. He retorted that I was too romantic and sentimental for a revolutionist, that the task before us was hard and we must become hard.

I wondered if the boy was really so hard, or was he merely trying to mask his tenderness, which I intuitively sensed in him. I felt myself drawn to him and I longed to throw my arms around him, but I was too shy.

The day ended in a glowing sunset. Joy was in my heart. All the way home I sang German and Russian songs, *Veeyut, vitri, veeyut booyniy,* being one of them. " That is my favourite song, Emma, *dorogaya* (dear)," he said. " I may call you that, may I not? And will you call me Sasha? " Our lips met in a spontaneous embrace.

I had begun to work in the corset factory where Helen Minkin was employed. But after a few weeks the strain became unbearable. I could hardly pull through the day; I suffered most from violent headaches. One evening I met a girl who told me of a silk waist factory that gave out work to be done at home. She would try to get me some, she promised. I knew it would be impossible to sew on a machine in the Minkin flat, it would be too disturbing for everybody. Furthermore, the girls' father had got on my nerves. He was a disagreeable person, never working, and living on his daughters. He seemed erotically fond of Anna, fairly devouring her with his eyes. The more surprising was his strong dislike of Helen, which led to constant quarrelling. At last I decided to move out.

I found a room on Suffolk Street, not far from Sachs's café. It was small and half-dark, but the price was only three dollars a month, and I engaged it. There I began to work on silk waists. Occasionally I would also get some dresses to make for the girls I knew and their friends. The work was exhausting, but it freed me from the factory and its galling discipline. My earnings from the waists, once I acquired speed, were not less than in the shop.

Most had gone on a lecture tour. From time to time he would send me a few lines, witty and caustic comments on the people he was meeting, vitriolic denunciation of reporters who interviewed him and then wrote vilifying articles about him. Occasionally he would include in his letters the caricatures made of him, with his own marginal comments: " Behold the wife-killer! " or " Here's the man who eats little children."

The caricatures were more brutal and cruel than anything I had seen before. The loathing I had felt for the Rochester papers during the Chicago events now turned into positive hatred for the entire American press. A wild thought took hold of me and I confided it to Sasha. " Don't you think one of the rotten newspaper offices should be blown up — editors, reporters, and all? That would teach the press a lesson." But Sasha shook his head and said that it would be useless. The press was only the hireling of capitalism. " We must strike at the root."

When Most returned from his tour, we all went to hear his report. He was more masterly, more witty and defiant against the system than on any previous occasion. He almost hypnotized me. I could not help going up after the lecture to tell him how splendid his talk was. " Will you go with me to hear *Carmen* Monday at the Metropolitan Opera House? " he whispered. He added that Monday was an awfully busy day because he had to keep his devils supplied with copy, but that he would work ahead on Sunday if I would promise to come. " To the end of the world! " I replied impulsively.

We found the house sold out — no seats to be had at any price. We should have to stand. I knew that I was in for torture. Since childhood I had had trouble with the small toe of my left foot; new shoes used to cause me suffering for weeks, and I was wearing new shoes. But I was too ashamed to tell Most, afraid he would think me vain. I stood close to him, jammed in by a large crowd. My foot burned as if it were being held over a fire. But the first bar of the music, and the glorious singing, made me forget my agony. After the first act, when the lights went on, I found myself holding on to Most for dear life, my face distorted with pain. " What's the matter? " he asked. " I must get off my shoe," I panted, " or I shall scream out." Leaning against him, I bent down to loosen the buttons. The rest of the opera I heard supported by Most's arm, my shoe in my hand. I could not tell whether my rapture was due to the music of *Carmen* or the release from my shoe!

We left the Opera House arm in arm, I limping. We went to a café, and Most teased me about my vanity. But he was rather glad, he said, to find me so feminine, even if it was stupid to wear tight shoes. He was in a golden mood. He wanted to know if I had ever before heard an opera and asked me to tell him about it.

Till I was ten years of age I had never heard any music, except the plaintive flute of Petrushka, Father's stable-boy. The screeching of the violins at the Jewish weddings and the poundings of the piano at our singing lessons had always been hateful to me. When I heard the opera *Trovatore* in Königsberg, I first realized the ecstasy music could create in me. My teacher may have been largely responsible for the electrifying effect of that experience: she had imbued me with the romance of her favourite German authors and had helped to rouse my imagination about the sad love of the Troubadour and Leonore. The tortuous suspense of the days before Mother gave her consent to my accompanying my teacher to the performance aggravated my tense expectancy. We reached the Opera a full hour before the beginning, myself in a cold sweat for fear we were late. Teacher, always in delicate health, could not keep up with my young legs and my frenzied haste to reach our places. I flew up to the top gallery, three steps at a time. The house was still empty and half-lit, and somewhat disappointing at first. As if by magic, it soon became transformed. Quickly the place filled with a vast audience — women in silks and velvets of gorgeous hue, with glistening jewels on their bare necks and arms, the flood of light from the crystal chandeliers reflecting the colours of green, yellow, and amethyst. It was a fairyland more magnificent than any ever pictured in the stories I had read. I forgot the presence of my teacher, the mean surroundings of my home; half-hanging over the rail, I was lost in the enchanted world below. The orchestra broke into stirring tones, mysteriously rising from the darkened house. They sent tremors down my back and held me breathless by their swelling sounds. Leonore and the Troubadour made real my own romantic fancy of love. I lived with them, thrilled and intoxicated by their passionate song. Their tragedy was mine as well, and I felt their joy and sorrow as my own. The scene between the Troubadour and his mother, her plaintive song " *Ach, ich vergehe und sterbe hier,*" Troubadour's response in " *O, teuere Mutter,*" filled me with deep woe and made my heart palpitate with compassionate sighs. The spell was broken by the loud clapping of hands and the new flood of light. I, too, clapped wildly, climbed on my bench, and shouted frantically for Leonore and the Troubadour, the hero and heroine of my fairy world. " Come along, come along," I heard my teacher say, tugging at my skirts. I followed in a daze, my body shaken with convulsive sobs, the music ringing in my ears. I had heard other operas in Königsberg and later in St. Petersburg, but the impression of *Trovatore* stood out for a long time as the most marvellous musical experience of my young life.

When I had finished relating this to Most, I noticed that his gaze was far away in the distance. He looked up as if from a dream. He had never heard, he remarked slowly, the stirrings of a child more dramatically told. I had great talent, he said, and I must begin soon to recite and speak in public. He would make me a great speaker — " to take my place when I am gone," he added.

I thought he was only making fun, or flattering me. He could not really believe that I could ever take his place or express his fire, his magic power. I did not want him to treat me that way — I wanted him to be a true comrade, frank and honest, without silly German compliments. Most grinned and emptied his glass to my " first public speech."

After that we went out together often. He opened up a new world to me, introduced me to music, books, the theatre. But his own rich personality meant far more to me — the alternating heights and depths of his spirit, his hatred of the capitalist system, his vision of a new society of beauty and joy for all.

Most became my idol. I worshipped him.

CHAPTER IV

THE 11TH OF NOVEMBER WAS APPROACHING, THE ANNIVERSARY of the Chicago martyrdoms. Sasha and I were busy with preparations for the great event of so much significance to us. Cooper Union had been secured for the commemoration. The meeting was to be held jointly by anarchists and socialists, with the co-operation of advanced labour organizations.

Every evening for several weeks we visited various trade unions to invite them to participate. This involved short talks from the floor, which I made. I always went in trepidation. On previous occasions, at German and Jewish lectures, I had mustered up courage to ask questions, but every time I would experience a kind of sinking sensation. While I was listening to the speakers, the questions would formulate themselves easily enough, but the moment I got up on my feet, I would feel faint. Desperately I would grip the chair in front of me, my heart throbbing, my knees trembling — everything in the hall would turn hazy. Then I would become aware of my voice, far, far away, and finally I would sink back in my seat in a cold sweat.

When I was first asked to make short speeches, I declined; I was sure I could never manage it. But Most would accept no refusal, and the other comrades sustained him. For the Cause, I was told, one must be able to do everything, and I so eagerly wanted to serve the Cause.

My talks used to sound incoherent to me, full of repetitions, lacking in conviction; and always the dismal feeling of sinking would be upon me. I thought everyone must see my turmoil, but apparently no one did. Even Sasha often commented on my calm and self-control. I do not know whether it was due to my being a beginner, to my youth, or to my intense feeling for the martyred men, but I never once failed to interest the workers I had been sent to invite.

Our own little group, consisting of Anna, Helen, Fedya, Sasha, and I, decided on a contribution — a large laurel-wreath with broad black and red satin ribbons. At first we wanted to buy eight wreaths, but we were too poor, since only Sasha and I were working. At last we decided in favour of Lingg: in our eyes he stood out as the sublime hero among the eight. His unbending spirit, his utter contempt for his accusers and judges, his will-power, which made him rob his enemies of their prey and die by his own hand — everything about that boy of twenty-two lent romance and beauty to his personality. He became the beacon of our lives.

At last the long-awaited evening arrived — my first public meeting in memory of the martyred men. Since I had read the accounts in the Rochester papers of the impressive march to Waldheim — the five-mile line of workers who followed the great dead to their last resting-place — and the large meetings that had since been held all over the world, I had ardently looked forward to being present at such an event. Now the moment had at last come. I went with Sasha to Cooper Union.

We found the historic hall densely packed, but with our wreath held high over our heads we finally managed to get through. Even the platform was crowded. I was bewildered until I saw Most standing next to a man and a woman; his presence made me feel at ease. His two companions were distinguished-looking people; the man radiated friendliness, but the woman, clad in a tight-fitting black velvet dress with a long train, her pale face framed in a mass of copper hair, seemed cold and aloof. She evidently belonged to another world.

Presently Sasha said: " The man near Most is Sergey Shevitch, the famous Russian revolutionist, now editor-in-chief of the socialist daily *Die Volkszeitung;* the woman is his wife, the former Helene von Dönniges." " Not the one Ferdinand Lassalle loved — the one he lost his life for?" I asked. " Yes, the same; she has remained an aristocrat. She really doesn't belong among us. But Shevitch is splendid."

Most had given me Lassalle's works to read. They had impressed me by their profound thought, force, and clarity. I had also studied his manifold activities in behalf of the incipient workers' movement in Germany in the fifties. His romantic life and untimely death at the hands of an officer in a duel fought over Helene von Dönniges had affected me deeply.

I was repelled by the woman's haughty austerity. Her long train, the lorgnette through which she scrutinized everybody, filled me with resentment. I turned to Shevitch. I liked him for his frank, kindly face and the simplicity of his manner. I told him I wanted to put our wreath over Lingg's portrait, but it was hung so high that I would have to get a ladder to reach it. " I'll lift you up, little comrade, and hold you until you have hung your wreath," he said pleasantly. He picked me up as if I were a baby.

I felt greatly embarrassed, but I hung the wreath. Shevitch set me down and asked why I had chosen Lingg rather than some one of the other martyrs. I replied that his appeal was strongest to me. Raising my chin gently with his strong hands, Shevitch said: " Yes, he was more like our Russian heroes." He spoke with much feeling.

Soon the meeting began. Shevitch and Alexander Jonas, his co-editor on the *Volkszeitung,* and a number of other speakers in various languages told the story I had first heard from Johanna Greie. I had since read and reread it until I knew every detail by heart.

Shevitch and Jonas were impressive speakers. The rest left me cold. Then Most ascended the platform, and everything else seemed blotted out. I was caught in the storm of his eloquence, tossed about, my very soul contracting and expanding in the rise and fall of his voice. It was no longer a speech, it was thunder interspersed with flashes of lightning. It was a wild, passionate cry against the terrible thing that had happened in Chicago — a fierce call to battle against the enemy, a call to individual acts, to vengeance.

The meeting was at an end. Sasha and I filed out with the rest. I could not speak; we walked on in silence. When we reached the house where I lived, my whole body began to shake as in a fever. An over-powering yearning possessed me, an unutterable desire to give myself to Sasha, to find relief in his arms from the fearful tension of the evening.

My narrow bed now held two human bodies, closely pressed to-gether. My room was no longer dark; a soft, soothing light seemed to come from somewhere. As in a dream I heard sweet, endearing words breathed into my ear, like the soft, beautiful Russian lullabies of my childhood. I became drowsy, my thoughts in confusion.

The meeting . . . Shevitch holding me up . . . the cold face of Helene von Dönniges . . . Johann Most . . . the force and wonder of his speech, his call to extermination — where had I heard that word before ? Ah, yes, Mother — the Nihilists ! The horror I had felt at her cruelty again came over me. But, then, she was not an idealist ! Most was an idealist, yet he, too, urged extermination. Could idealists be cruel? The enemies of life and joy and beauty are cruel. They are relentless, they have killed our great comrades. But must we, too, exterminate?

I was roused from my drowsiness as if by an electric current. I felt a trembling, shy hand tenderly glide over me. Hungrily I reached for it, for my lover. We were engulfed in a wild embrace. Again I felt terrific pain, like the cut of a sharp knife. But it was numbed by my passion, breaking through all that had been suppressed, unconscious, and dormant.

The morning still found me eagerly reaching out, hungrily seeking. My beloved lay at my side, asleep in blissful exhaustion. I sat up, my head resting on my hand. Long I watched the face of the boy who had so attracted and repelled me at the same time, who could be so hard and whose touch was yet so tender. Deep love for him welled up in my heart — a feeling of certainty that our lives were linked for all time. I pressed my lips to his thick hair and then I, too, fell asleep.

The people from whom I rented my room slept on the other side of the wall. Their nearness always disturbed me, and now in Sasha's presence it gave me a feeling of being seen. He also had no privacy where he lived. I suggested that we find a small apartment, and he consented joyfully. When we told Fedya of our plan, he asked to be taken in. The fourth of our little commune was Helen Minkin. The friction with her father had become more violent since I had moved out, and she could not endure it. She begged to come with us. We rented a four-room flat on Forty-second Street and we all felt it a luxury to have our own place.

From the very first we agreed to share everything, to live like real comrades. Helen continued to work in the corset factory, and I divided my time between sewing silk waists and keeping house. Fedya devoted himself to painting. The expense of his oils, canvases, and brushes often consumed more than we could afford, but it never occurred to any one of us to complain. From time to time he would sell a picture to some dealer for fifteen or twenty-five dollars, whereupon he would bring an armful of flowers or some present for me. Sasha would upbraid him for it: the idea of spending money for such things, when the movement needed it so badly, was intolerable to him. His anger had no effect on Fedya. He would laugh it off, call him a fanatic, and say he had no sense of beauty.

One day Fedya arrived with a beautiful blue and white striped silk jersey, considered very stylish then. When Sasha came home and saw the jersey, he flew into a rage, called Fedya a spendthrift and an incurable *bourgeois,* who would never amount to anything in the movement. The two nearly came to blows, and finally both left the flat. I felt sick with the pain of Sasha's severity. I began to doubt his love. It could not be very deep or he would not spoil the little joys that Fedya brought into my life. True, the jersey cost two dollars and a half. Perhaps it was extravagant of Fedya to spend so much money. But how could he help loving beautiful things? They were a necessity to his artist's spirit. I grew bitter, and was glad when Sasha did not return that night.

He stayed away for some days. During that time I was a great deal with Fedya. He had so much that Sasha lacked and that I craved. His susceptibility to every mood, his love of life and of colour, made him more human, more akin to me. He never expected me to live up to the Cause. I felt release with him.

One morning Fedya asked me to pose for him. I experienced no sense of shame at standing naked before him. He worked away for a time, and neither of us talked. Then he began to fidget about and finally said he would have to stop: he could not concentrate, the mood was gone. I went back behind the screen to dress. I had not quite finished when I heard violent weeping. I rushed forward and found Fedya stretched on the sofa, his head buried in the pillow, sobbing. As I bent over him, he sat up and broke loose in a torrent — said he loved me, that he had from the very beginning, though he had tried to keep in the background for Sasha's sake; he had struggled fiercely against his feeling for me, but he knew now that it was of no use. He would have to move out.

I sat by him, holding his hand in mine and stroking his soft wavy hair. Fedya had always drawn me to him by his thoughtful attention, his sensitive response, and his love of beauty. Now I felt something stronger stirring within me. Could it be love for Fedya, I wondered. Could one love two persons at the same time? I loved Sasha. At that very moment my resentment at his harshness gave way to yearning for my strong, arduous lover. Yet I felt Sasha had left something untouched in me, something Fedya could perhaps waken to life. Yes, it must be possible to love more than one! All I had felt for the boy artist must have really been love without my being aware of it till now, I decided.

I asked Fedya what he thought of love for two or even for more persons at once. He looked up in surprise and said he did not know, he had never loved anyone before. His love for me had absorbed him to the exclusion of anyone else. He knew he could not care for another woman while he loved me. And he was certain that Sasha would never want to share me; his sense of possession was too strong.

I resented the suggestion of sharing. I insisted that one can only respond to what the other is able to call out. I did not believe that Sasha was possessive. One who so fervently wanted freedom and preached it so whole-heartedly could never object to my giving myself to someone else. We agreed that, whatever happened, there must be no deception. We must go to Sasha and tell him frankly how we felt. He would understand.

That evening Sasha returned straight from work. The four of us sat down, as usual, to our supper. We talked about various things. No reference was made to Sasha's long absence and there was no chance to speak to him alone about the new light that had come into my life. We all went to Orchard Street to a lecture.

After the meeting Sasha went home with me, Fedya and Helen remaining behind. In our flat he asked permission to come to my room. Then he began to talk, pouring out his whole soul. He said he loved me dearly, that he wanted me to have beautiful things; that he, too, loved beauty. But he loved the Cause more than anything else in the world. For that he would forgo even our love. Yes, and his very life.

He told me about the famous Russian revolutionary catechism that demanded of the true revolutionist that he give up home, parents, sweetheart, children, everything dear to one's being. He agreed with it absolutely and he was determined to allow nothing to stand in the way. " But I do love you," he repeated. His intensity, his uncompromising fervour, irritated and yet drew me like a magnet. Whatever longing I had experienced when near Fedya was silent now. Sasha, my own wonderful, dedicated, obsessed Sasha, was calling. I felt entirely his.

Later in the day I had to meet Most. He had spoken to me about a short lecture tour he was planning for me, but though I did not take it seriously, he had asked me to come to see him about it.

The *Freiheit* office was crowded. Most suggested a near-by saloon, which he knew to be quiet in the early afternoon. We went there. He began to explain his plans for my tour; I was to visit Rochester, Buffalo, and Cleveland. It threw me into a panic. " It is impossible! " I protested; " I don't know a thing about lecturing." He waved my ob-

jections aside, declaring that everybody felt that way in the beginning.
He was determined to make a public speaker of me, and I would simply
have to begin. He had already chosen the subject for me and he would
help me prepare it. I was to speak on the futility of the struggle for
the eight-hour workday, now again much discussed in labour ranks.
He pointed out that the eight-hour campaigns in '84, '85, and '86 had
already taken a toll far beyond the value of the " damned thing."
" Our comrades in Chicago lost their lives for it, and the workers still
work long hours." But even if the eight-hour day were established,
there would be no actual gain, he insisted. On the contrary, it would
serve only to distract the masses from the real issue — the struggle
against capitalism, against the wage system, for a new society. At any
rate, all I would have to do would be to memorize the notes he would
give me. He was sure that my dramatic feeling and my enthusiasm
would do the rest. As usual, he held me by his eloquence. I had no
power to resist.

When I got home, away from Most's presence, I again experienced
the sinking feeling that had come upon me when I had first tried to
speak in public. I still had three weeks in which to read up, but I was
sure I never could go through with it.

Stronger than my lack of faith in myself was my loathing for Rochester. I had completely broken with my parents and my sister Lena,
but I yearned for Helena, for little Stella, now in her fourth year,
and for my youngest brother. Oh, if I were really an accomplished
speaker, I would rush to Rochester and fling my accumulated bitterness
into the smug faces of the people who had treated me so brutally. Now
they would only add ridicule to the hurt they had given me. Anxiously
I waited for the return of my friends.

How great was my astonishment when Sasha and Helen Minkin
grew enthusiastic about Most's plan! It was a marvellous opportunity,
they said. What if I would have to work hard to prepare my talk? It
would be the making of me as a public lecturer, the first woman speaker
in the German anarchist movement in America! Sasha was especially
insistent: I must set aside every consideration, I must think only of how
useful I would become to the Cause. Fedya was dubious.

My three good friends insisted that I stop work to have more time
for study. They would also relieve me of every domestic responsibility. I devoted myself to reading. Now and then Fedya would come
with flowers. He knew that I had not yet spoken to Sasha. He never

pressed me, but his flowers spoke more appealingly than anything he could have said. Sasha no longer scolded him for wasting money. " I know you love flowers," he would say; " they may inspire you in your new work."

I read up a great deal on the eight-hour movement, went to every meeting where the matter was to be discussed; but the more I studied the subject, the more confused I became. " The iron law of wages," " supply and demand," " poverty as the only leaven of revolt " — I could not follow it all. It left me as cold as the mechanistic theories I used to hear expounded in the Rochester Socialist local. But when I read Most's notes, everything seemed clear. The imagery of his language, his unanswerable criticism of existing conditions, and his glorious vision of the new society awakened enthusiasm in me. I continued to doubt myself, but everything Most said seemed irrefutable.

One thought took definite shape in my mind. I would never memorize Most's notes. His phrases, the flower and spice of his invective, were too well known for me to repeat them parrot-like. I would use his ideas and present them in my own way. But the ideas — were they not also Most's? Ah, well, they had become such a part of me that I could not distinguish how far I was repeating him or to what extent they had been reborn as my own.

The day of my departure for Rochester arrived. I met Most for a last talk; I came in a depressed mood, but a glass of wine and Most's spirit soon lifted the weight. He talked long and ardently, made numerous suggestions, and said I must not take the audiences too seriously; most of them were dullards, anyway. He impressed upon me the need of humour. " If you can make people laugh, sailing will be easy." He told me that the construction of my lecture did not matter much. I must talk in the way I related to him my impressions of my first opera. That would move the audience. " For the rest, be bold, be arrogant, I am sure you will be brave."

He took me to the Grand Central in a cab. On the way he moved close to me. He yearned to take me in his arms and asked if he might. I nodded, and he held me pressed to him. Conflicting thoughts and emotions possessed me; the speeches I was going to make, Sasha, Fedya, my passion for the one, my budding love for the other. But I yielded to Most's trembling embrace, his kisses covering my mouth as of one famished with thirst. I let him drink; I could have denied him nothing. He loved me, he said; he had never known such longing for any woman before. Of late years he had not even been attracted to anyone. A feeling of growing age was overcoming him, and he felt worn from the long struggle and the persecution he had endured. More depressing even was the consciousness that his best comrades misunderstood him. But my youth had made him young, my ardour had raised his spirit. My whole being had awakened him to a new meaning in life. I was his *Blondkopf,* his " blue eyes "; he wanted me to be his own, his helpmate, his voice.

I lay back with my eyes closed. I was too overpowered to speak, too limp to move. Something mysterious stirred me, something entirely unlike the urge towards Sasha or the sensitive response to Fedya. It was different from these. It was infinite tenderness for the great man-child at my side. As he sat there, he suggested a rugged tree bent by winds and storm, making one supreme last effort to stretch itself towards the sun. " All for the Cause," Sasha had so often said. The fighter next to me had already given all for the Cause. But who had given all for him? He was hungry for affection, for understanding. I would give him both.

At the station my three friends were already waiting for me. Sasha held out an American Beauty rose to me. " As a token of my love, *Dushenka,* and as a harbinger of luck on your first public quest."

Precious Sasha; only a few days before, when we went shopping on Hester Street, he had protested strenuously because I wanted him to spend more than six dollars for a suit and twenty-five cents for a hat. He would not have it. " We must get the cheapest we can," he reiterated. And now — what tenderness there was under his stern exterior! Like Hannes. Strange, I had never before realized how much alike they were. The boy and the man. Both hard; one because he had never yet tasted life, and the other because it had struck him so many blows. Both equally unyielding in their zeal, both so childlike in their need for love.

The train sped on towards Rochester. Only six months had passed since I had cut loose from my meaningless past. I had lived years in that time.

CHAPTER V

I HAD BEGGED MOST NOT TO GIVE THE TIME OF MY ARRIVAL TO THE German Union in Rochester, before which I was to speak. I wanted to see my beloved sister Helena first. I had written her about my coming, but not the purpose of my visit. She met me at the station and we clung to each other as if we had been separated for decades.

I explained to Helena my mission in Rochester. She stared at me open-mouthed. How could I undertake such a thing, face an audience? I had been away only six months; what could I have learned in such a brief time? Where did I get the courage? And in Rochester, of all cities! Our parents would never get over the shock.

I had never before been angry with Helena; there never had been occasion for it. In fact, it was always I who tried her patience to the breaking-point. But the reference to our parents made me wroth. It brought back Popelan, Helena's crushed young love for Susha, and all the other ghastly pictures. I broke out in a bitter arraignment of our people, especially picking out my father, whose harshness had been the nightmare of my childhood, and whose tyranny had held me even after my marriage. I reproached Helena for having allowed our parents to rob her of her youth. "They came near doing it to me, too!" I cried. I had finished with them when they joined the Rochester bigots and cast me out. My life was now my own, the work I had chosen more precious to me than my life! Nothing could take me from it, least of all consideration for my parents.

The pain in my darling's face checked me. I took her in my arms and assured her that there was nothing to worry about, that our family need not know about my plans. The meeting was to be only before a German union; no publicity would be connected with it. Besides, the Jews on St. Joseph's Street knew nothing about the advanced Germans, or about anything else, for that matter, outside of their own colourless, petty lives. Helena brightened up. She said that if my public speech was as eloquent as my arguments to her, I would make a hit.

When I faced the audience the next evening, my mind was a blank. I could not remember a single word of my notes. I shut my eyes for an instant; then something strange happened. In a flash I saw it — every incident of my three years in Rochester: the Garson factory, its drudgery and humiliation, the failure of my marriage, the Chicago crime. The last words of August Spies rang in my ears: " Our silence will speak louder than the voices you strangle today."

I began to speak. Words I had never heard myself utter before came pouring forth, faster and faster. They came with passionate intensity; they painted images of the heroic men on the gallows, their glowing vision of an ideal life, rich with comfort and beauty: men and women radiant in freedom, children transformed by joy and affection. The audience had vanished, the hall itself had disappeared; I was conscious only of my own words, of my ecstatic song.

I stopped. Tumultuous applause rolled over me, the buzzing of voices, people telling me something I could not understand. Then I heard someone quite close to me: " It was an inspired speech; but what about the eight-hour struggle? You've said nothing about that." I felt hurled down from my exalted heights, crushed. I told the chairman I was too tired to answer questions, and I went home feeling ill in body and mind. I let myself quietly into Helena's apartment and threw myself on the bed in my clothes.

Exasperation with Most for forcing the tour on me, anger with myself for having so easily succumbed to his influence, the conviction that I had cheated the audience — all seethed in my mind together with a new revelation. I could sway people with words! Strange and magic words that welled up from within me, from some unfamiliar depth. I wept with the joy of knowing.

I went to Buffalo, determined to make another effort. The preliminaries of the meeting threw me into the same nervous tension, but when I faced the audience, there were no visions to inflame my mind. In an endless, repetitious manner I made my speech about the waste of energy and time the eight-hour struggle involved, scoffing at the stupidity of the workers who fought for such trifles. At the end of what seemed to me several hours I was complimented on my clear and logical presentation. Some questions were asked, and I answered them with a sureness that brooked no gainsaying. But on the way home from the meeting my heart was heavy. No words of exaltation had come to me, and how could one hope to reach other hearts when one's own remained cold? I decided to wire Most the next morning, begging him to relieve me of the necessity of going to Cleveland. I could not bear to repeat once more the meaningless prattle.

After a night's sleep my decision seemed childish and weak. How could I give up so soon? Would Most have given up like that? Would Sasha? Well, I, too, would go on. I took the train for Cleveland.

The meeting was large and animated. It was a Saturday night, and the workers attended with their wives and children. Everybody drank. I was surrounded by a group, offered refreshments, and asked questions. How did I happen to come into the movement? Was I German? What was I doing for a living? The petty curiosity of people supposed to be interested in the most advanced ideas reminded me of the Rochester grilling on the day of my arrival in America. It made me thoroughly angry.

The gist of my talk was the same as in Buffalo, but the form was different. It was a sarcastic arraignment, not of the system or of the capitalists, but of the workers themselves — their readiness to give up a great future for some small temporary gains. The audience seemed to enjoy being handled in such an outspoken manner. They roared in some places, and in others vigorously applauded. It was not a meeting; it was a circus, and I was the clown!

A man in the front row who had attracted my attention by his white hair and lean, haggard face rose to speak. He said that he understood my impatience with such small demands as a few hours less a day, or a few dollars more a week. It was legitimate for young people to take time lightly. But what were men of his age to do? They were not likely to live to see the ultimate overthrow of the capitalist system. Were they also to forgo the release of perhaps two hours a day from the hated work? That was all they could hope to see realized in their lifetime. Should they deny themselves even that small achievement? Should they never have a little more time for reading or being out in the open? Why not be fair to people chained to the block?

The man's earnestness, his clear analysis of the principle involved in the eight-hour struggle, brought home to me the falsity of Most's position. I realized I was committing a crime against myself and the workers by serving as a parrot repeating Most's views. I understood why I had failed to reach my audience. I had taken refuge in cheap jokes and bitter thrusts against the toilers to cover up my own inner lack of conviction. My first public experience did not bring the result Most had hoped for, but it taught me a valuable lesson. It cured me somewhat of my childlike faith in the infallibility of my teacher and impressed on me the need of independent thinking.

In New York my friends had prepared a grand reception for me; our flat was spotlessly clean and filled with flowers. They were eager for an account of my tour and they felt apprehensive of the effect upon Most of my changed attitude.

The next evening I went out with Most, again to Terrace Garden. He had grown younger during my two weeks' absence: his rough beard was trimmed neatly and he wore a natty new grey suit, a red carnation in his buttonhole. He joined me in a gay mood, presenting me with a large bouquet of violets. The two weeks of my absence had been unbearably long, he said, and he had reproached himself for having let me go just when we had grown so close. But now he would never again let me go — not alone, anyhow.

I tried several times to tell him about my trip, hurt to the quick that he had not asked about it. He had sent me forth against my will, he had been so eager to make a great speaker of me; was he not interested to know whether I had proved an apt pupil?

Yes, of course, he replied. But he had already received the reports from Rochester that I had been eloquent, from Buffalo that my presentation had silenced all opponents, and from Cleveland that I had flayed the dullards with biting sarcasm. "What about my own reactions?" I asked. "Don't you want me to tell you about that?" "Yes, another time." Now he wanted only to feel me near — his *Blondkopf*, his little girl-woman.

I flared up, declaring I would not be treated as a mere female. I blurted out that I would never again follow blindly, that I had made a fool of myself, that the five-minute speech of the old worker had convinced me more than all his persuasive phrases. I talked on, my listener keeping very silent. When I had finished, he called the waiter and paid the bill. I followed him out.

On the street he burst out in a storm of abuse. He had reared a viper, a snake, a heartless coquette, who had played with him like a cat with a mouse. He had sent me out to plead his cause and I had betrayed him. I was like the rest, but he would not stand for it. He would rather cut me out of his heart right now than have me as a lukewarm friend. " Who is not with me is against me," he shouted; " I will not have it otherwise ! " A great sadness overwhelmed me, as if I had just experienced an irreparable loss.

Returning to our flat, I collapsed. My friends were disturbed and did everything to soothe me. I related the story from beginning to end, even to the violets I had mechanically carried home. Sasha grew indignant. " Violets at the height of winter, with thousands out of work and hungry ! " he exclaimed. He had always said that Most was a spendthrift, living at the expense of the movement. And what kind of a revolutionist was I, anyway, to accept Most's favours ? Didn't I know that he only cared for women physically ? Most of the Germans were that way. They considered women only as females. I would have to choose once for all between Most and him. Most was no longer a revolutionist; he had gone back on the Cause.

Angrily he left the house, and I remained bewildered, bruised, with my new-found world in debris at my feet. A gentle hand took mine, led me quietly into my room, and left me. It was Fedya.

Soon a new call came to me, of workers on strike, and I followed it eagerly. It came from Joseph Barondess, whom I had previously met; he was of the group of young Jewish socialists and anarchists who had organized the cloakmakers and other Yiddish unions. The aggregation numbered more informed men and abler speakers than Barondess, but he stood out by reason of his greater simplicity. There was no bombast about this attractive, lanky chap. His mind was not of a scholarly type; it was of a practical turn. He was just the man the workers needed to help them in their daily struggle. Barondess was now at the head of the union, directing the cloakmakers' strike.

Everybody on the East Side who was able to say a few words in public was drawn into the struggle. They were nearly all men, except Annie Netter, a young girl who had already made a name for herself by her untiring activity in the anarchist and labour ranks. She had been one of the most intelligent and indefatigable women workers in various strikes, including those of the Knights of Labor, an organization which had been for a number of years the storm-centre of the intense campaigns of the eighties. It had reached its zenith in the eight-hour fight led by Parsons, Spies, Fielden and the other men who had died in Chicago. It began its downward course when Terence V. Powderly, Grand Master of the Knights of Labor, had allied himself with the enemies of his comrades who were being rushed to their doom. It was well known that Powderly, in return for thirty pieces of silver, had helped to pull the strings that strangled the men in Chicago. Militant workers withdrew from the Knights of Labor, and it became a dumping-ground for unscrupulous job-hunters.

Annie Netter had been among the first to turn from the Judas organization. She was now a member of the Pioneers of Liberty, to which most of the active Jewish anarchists in New York belonged. An ardent worker, she gave unstintingly of her time and meagre earnings. In her efforts she was sustained by her father who had developed himself out of religious orthodoxy to atheism and socialism. He was a man of exceptional quality, a great scholar, of warm humanity, a lover of life and youth. The Netter home, behind their little grocery store, became the oasis for the radical element, an intellectual centre. Mrs. Netter kept open house: the *samovar* and a generous spread of *zakusky* were never off the table. We young rebels were appreciative, if not profitable, customers of the Netter grocery.

I had never known a real home. At the Netters' I basked in the sunny atmosphere of the beautiful understanding that existed between the parents and their children. The gatherings there were intensely interesting, the evenings spent in discussions, enlivened by the entertaining banter of our kindly host. Among the frequenters were some very able young men whose names were well known in the New York ghetto; among others, David Edelstadt, a fine idealistic nature, a spiritual petrel whose songs of revolt were beloved by every Yiddish-speaking radical. Then there was Bovshover, who wrote under the name of Basil Dahl, a high-strung and impulsive man of exceptional poetic gifts. Young Michael Cohn, M. Katz, Girzhdansky, Louis, and other young men of ability and promise used to meet at the Netters', all helping to make the evenings real intellectual feasts. Joseph Barondess often participated, and it was he who sent for me to help in the strike.

I threw myself into the work with all the ardour of my being and I became absorbed in it to the exclusion of everything else. My task was to get the girls in the trade to join the strike. For that purpose meetings, concerts, socials, and dances were organized. At these affairs it was not difficult to press upon the girls the need of making common cause with their striking brothers. I had to speak often and I became less and less disturbed when on the platform. My faith in the justice of the strike helped me to dramatize my talks and to carry conviction. Within a few weeks my work brought scores of girls into the ranks of the strikers.

I became alive once more. At the dances I was one of the most untiring and gayest. One evening a cousin of Sasha, a young boy, took me aside. With a grave face, as if he were about to announce the death of a dear comrade, he whispered to me that it did not behoove an agitator to dance. Certainly not with such reckless abandon, anyway. It was undignified for one who was on the way to become a force in the anarchist movement. My frivolity would only hurt the Cause.

I grew furious at the impudent interference of the boy. I told him to mind his own business, I was tired of having the Cause constantly thrown into my face. I did not believe that a Cause which stood for a beautiful ideal, for anarchism, for release and freedom from conventions and prejudice, should demand the denial of life and joy. I insisted that our Cause could not expect me to became a nun and that the movement should not be turned into a cloister. If it meant that, I did not want it. " I want freedom, the right to self-expression, everybody's right to beautiful, radiant things." Anarchism meant that to me, and I would live it in spite of the whole world — prisons, persecution, everything. Yes, even in spite of the condemnation of my own closest comrades I would live my beautiful ideal.

I had worked myself into a passion, my voice ringing out. I found myself surrounded by many people. There was applause, mingled with protests that I was wrong, that one must consider the Cause above everything. All the Russian revolutionists had done that, they had never been conscious of self. It was nothing but narrow egotism to want to enjoy anything that would take one away from the movement. In the hubbub Sasha's voice was the loudest.

I turned in his direction. He was standing near Anna Minkin. I had noticed their growing interest in each other long before our last altercation. Sasha had then moved out of our flat, where Anna used to be almost a daily visitor. It was now the first time in weeks that I had seen either of them. My heart contracted with yearning for my impetuous, headstrong lover. I longed to call him by the name he loved best, *Dushenka* — to stretch out my arms to him — but his face was set, his eyes full of reproach, and I checked myself. I danced no more that evening.

Presently I was called into the committee room, where I found Joseph Barondess and other strike leaders already at work. Next to Barondess I noticed Professor T. H. Garside, a Scotchman, formerly lecturer for the Knights of Labor, and now at the head of the strike. Garside was about thirty-five, tall, pale, and languid-looking. His manner was gentle and ingratiating, and he resembled somewhat the pictures of Christ. He was always trying to pacify conflicting elements, to smooth things over.

Garside informed us that the strike would be lost if we did not consent to a compromise. I disagreed with him and objected to his proposal. Several members of the committee upheld me, but Garside's influence prevailed. The strike was settled according to his suggestions.

The strenuous weeks of the strike now gave way to less arduous activities: lectures, evenings at the Netters' or at our flat, and efforts to secure employment again. Fedya had begun to work with crayons, enlarging photographs; he declared that he could not keep on wasting our money, Helen's and mine, on paints. He felt he would never become a great painter, anyway. I suspected it was something else: no doubt his desire to earn money so that he could relieve me of hard work.

I had not been feeling very well, especially during periods, on which occasions I always had to take to bed, in excruciating pain for days. It had been so since my great shock when Mother slapped my face. It grew worse when I caught a cold on our way from Königsberg to St. Petersburg. We had to be smuggled across the border, Mother, my two brothers, and I. It was in the latter part of 1881 and the winter was particularly severe. The smugglers had told Mother that we would have to wade through deep snow, even across a half-frozen brook. Mother worried about me because I was taken sick a few days earlier than my time, owing to the excitement of our departure from Königsberg. At five in the morning, shivering with cold and fear, we started out. Soon we reached the brook that separated the German and Russian frontiers. The very anticipation of the icy water was paralysing, but there was no escape; we had to plunge in or be overtaken and perhaps shot by soldiers patrolling the border. A few roubles finally induced them to turn their backs, but they had cautioned us to be quick.

We plunged in, Mother loaded with bundles and I carrying my little brother. The sudden chill froze my blood; then I felt a stinging sensation in my spine, abdomen, and legs, as if I were being pierced with hot irons. I wanted to scream, but terror of the soldiers checked me. Soon we were over, and the stinging ceased; but my teeth kept chattering and I was in a hot sweat. We ran as fast as we could to the inn on the Russian side. I was given hot tea with *maliny,* packed in hot bricks, and covered with a large feather bed. I felt feverish all the way to St. Petersburg, and the pain in my spine and legs was racking. I was laid up for weeks, and my spine remained weak for years afterwards.

In America I had consulted Solotaroff about my trouble, and he took me to a specialist, who urged an operation. He seemed surprised that I could have stood my condition so long and that I had been at all able to have physical contact. My friends informed me that the physician had said I would never be free from pain, or experience full sexual release, unless I submitted to the operation.

Solotaroff asked me whether I had ever wanted a baby. " Because if you have the operation," he explained, " you will be able to have a child. So far your condition has made that impossible."

A child! I had loved children madly, ever since I could remember. As a little girl I used to look with envious eyes on the strange little babies our neighbour's daughter played with, dressing them up and putting them to sleep. I was told they were not real babies, they were only dolls, although to me they were living things because they were so beautiful. I longed for dolls, but I never had any.

When my brother Herman was born, I was only four years old. He replaced the need of dolls in my life. The arrival of little Leibale two years later filled me with ecstatic joy. I was always near him, rocking and singing him to sleep. Once when he was about a year old, Mother put him in my bed. After she left, the child began to cry. He must be hungry, I thought. I remembered how Mother gave him the breast. I, too, would give him my breast. I picked him up in my arms and pressed his little mouth close to me, rocking and cooing and urging him to drink. Instead he began to choke, turned blue in the face, and gasped for breath. Mother came running in and demanded to know what I had done to Baby. I explained. She broke out into laughter, then slapped and scolded me. I wept, not from pain, but because my breast had no milk for Leibale.

My compassion for our servant Amalia had surely been due to the circumstance that she was going to have *ein Kindchen.* I loved babies passionately, and now — now I might have a child of my own and

experience for the first time the mystery and wonder of motherhood!
I closed my eyes in blissful day-dreaming.

A cruel hand clutched at my heart. My ghastly childhood stood
before me, my hunger for affection, which Mother was unable to
satisfy. Father's harshness towards the children, his violent outbreaks, his beating my sisters and me. Two frightful experiences were
particularly fresh in my mind: Once Father lashed me with a strap so
that my little brother Herman, awakened by my cries, came running
up and bit Father on the calf. The lashing stopped. Helena took me
to her room, bathed my bruised back, brought me milk, held me to
her heart, her tears mingling with mine, while Father outside was
raging: " I'll kill her! I will kill that brat! I will teach her to obey! "

Another time, in Königsberg, my people, having lost everything in
Popelan, were too poor to afford decent schooling for Herman and
myself. The city's rabbi, a distant relative, had promised to arrange
the matter, but he insisted on monthly reports of our behaviour and
progress at school. I hated it as a humiliation that outraged me, but
I had to carry the report. One day I was given a low mark for bad behaviour. I went home in trembling fear. I could not face Father — I
showed my paper to Mother. She began to cry, said that I would be
their ruin, that I was an ungrateful and wilful child, and that she
would have to let Father see the paper. But she would plead with
him for me, although I did not deserve it. I walked away from her
with a heavy heart. At our bay window I looked out over the fields
in the distance. Children were playing there; they seemed to belong
to another world — there never had been much play in my life. A
strange thought came to me: how wonderful it would be if I were
stricken with some consuming disease! It would surely soften Father's
heart. I had never known him soft save on *Sukkess,* the autumnal
holiday of rejoicing. Father did not drink, except a little on certain
Jewish fêtes, on this day especially. Then he would grow jolly, gather
the children about him, promise us new dresses and toys. It was the
one bright spot in our lives and we always eagerly looked forward to
it. It happened only once a year. As long as I could think back, I remembered his saying that he had not wanted me. He had wanted a
boy, the pig woman had cheated him. Perhaps if I should become very
ill, near death, he would become kind and never beat me again or let
me stand in the corner for hours, or make me walk back and forth
with a glass of water in my hand. "If you spill a drop, you will get

whipped! " he would threaten. The whip and the little stool were always at hand. They symbolized my shame and my tragedy. After many attempts and considerable punishment I had learned to carry the glass without spilling the water. The process used to unnerve me and make me ill for hours after.

My father was handsome, dashing, and full of vitality. I loved him even while I was afraid of him. I wanted him to love me, but I never knew how to reach his heart. His hardness served only to make me more contrary. Why was he so hard, I was wondering, as I looked out of the bay window, lost in recollections.

Suddenly I felt a terrific pain in my head, as if I had been struck with an iron bar. It was Father's fist that had smashed the round comb I wore to hold my unruly hair. He pounded me and pulled me about, raging: " You are my disgrace! You will always be so! You can't be *my* child; you don't look like me or like your mother; you don't act like us! "

Sister Helena wrestled with him for my life. She tried to tear me away from his grip, and the blows intended for me fell upon her. At last Father became tired, grew dizzy, and fell headlong to the floor. Helena shouted to Mother that Father had fainted. She hurried me along to her room and locked the door.

All my love and longing for my father were turned to hatred. After that I avoided him and never talked to him, unless in answer. I did what I was told mechanically; the gulf between us widened with the years. My home had become a prison. Every time I tried to escape, I was caught and put back in the chains forged for me by Father. From St. Petersburg to America, from Rochester to my marriage, there were repeated attempts to escape. The last and final one was before I left Rochester for New York.

Mother had not been feeling well and I went over to put her house in order. I was on the floor scrubbing while Father was nagging me for having married Kershner, for having left him, and again for returning to him. " You are a loose character," he kept on saying; " you have always disgraced yourself in the family." He talked, while I continued scrubbing.

Then something snapped within me; my lone and woeful childhood, my tormented adolescence, my joyless youth — I flung them all into Father's face. He stood aghast as I denounced him, emphasizing every charge by beating my scrubbing-brush on the floor. Every

cruel incident of my life stood out in my arraignment. Our large barn
of a home, Father's angry voice resounding through it, his ill-treat-
ment of the servants, his iron grip on my mother — everything that
had haunted my days and terrorized my nights I now recalled in my
bitterness. I told him that if I had not become the harlot he repeatedly
called me, it was not his fault. I had been on the verge even of going
on the street more than once. It was Helena's love and devotion that
had saved me.

My words rushed on like a torrent, the brush pounding the floor
with all the hatred and scorn I felt for my father. The terrible scene
ended with my hysterical screams. My brothers carried me up and
put me to bed. The next morning I left the house. I did not see Father
again before I went to New York.

I had learned since then that my tragic childhood had been no exception, that there were thousands of children born unwanted, marred
and maimed by poverty and still more by ignorant misunderstanding.
No child of mine should ever be added to those unfortunate victims.

There was also another reason: my growing absorption in my new-
found ideal. I had determined to serve it completely. To fulfil that
mission I must remain unhampered and untied. Years of pain and of
suppressed longing for a child — what were they compared with the
price many martyrs had already paid? I, too, would pay the price, I
would endure the suffering, I would find an outlet for my mother-need
in the love of *all* children. The operation did not take place.

Several weeks' rest and the loving care of my friends — of Sasha,
who had returned to the house, the Minkin sisters, Most, who called
often and sent flowers, and, above all, the artist boy — gave me back
to health. I rose from my sick-bed renewed in faith in my own strength.
Like Sasha I now felt that I, too, could overcome every difficulty and
face every test for my ideal. Had I not overcome the strongest and
most primitive craving of a woman — the desire for a child?

During those weeks Fedya and I became lovers. It had grown clear
to me that my feelings for Fedya had no bearing on my love for
Sasha. Each called out different emotions in my being, took me into
different worlds. They created no conflict, they only brought fulfilment.

I told Sasha about my love for Fedya. His response was bigger and
more beautiful than I had expected. " I believe in your freedom to

love," he said. He was aware of his possessive tendencies and hated them like everything else he had got from his *bourgeois* background. Perhaps if Fedya were not his friend, he might be jealous; he knew he had a large streak of jealousy in his make-up. But not only was Fedya his friend, he was his comrade in battle; and I was more to him than merely a woman. His love for me was intense, but the revolutionist and the fighter meant more to him.

When our artist friend came home that day, the boys embraced. Late into the night we talked of our plans for further activities. When we separated, we had made a pact — to dedicate ourselves to the Cause in some supreme deed, to die together if necessary, or to continue to live and work for the ideal for which one of us might have to give his life.

The days and weeks that followed were illumined by the glorious new light in us. We became more patient with each other, more understanding.

CHAPTER VI

M OST HAD TOLD ME THAT HE WAS PLANNING A SHORT LECTURE tour through the New England States. Now he informed me that he was about to leave, and he invited me to accompany him. He said that I looked worn and thin and that a change of scene would do me good. I promised to consider his invitation.

The boys urged me to go; Fedya stressed the need of getting away from household duties, while Sasha said it would help me to get acquainted with the comrades and open up a way for further activities.

Two weeks later I went with Most by the Fall River Line to Boston. I had never before seen such a spacious, luxurious boat, such cosy state-rooms; mine, not far from Most's, looked bright with a bunch of lilacs he had sent. We stood on the deck as the boat steamed out, and presently a beautiful green island came into view, with large stately trees shading grey stone buildings. The sight was pleasing after the endless tenement-houses. I turned to Most. His face was ashy, his fist clenched. "What is it?" I cried in alarm. "That is Blackwell's Island Penitentiary, the Spanish Inquisition transferred to the United States," he replied; "soon it will again hold me within its walls."

Soothingly I placed my hand on his convulsed fingers. Gradually they relaxed, and his hand stretched out in mine. We stood for a long time, each absorbed in his thoughts. The night was warm, pungent with the May air. Most's arm was around me as he related his experiences on Blackwell's Island, and of his early life and development.

He was, it seems, the offspring of a clandestine affair. His father had at first led an adventurous life, later becoming a copyist in a lawyer's office. His mother had been a governess in a wealthy family. He was born without legal, moral, or religious sanction; subsequently the union was legalized.

It was his mother who had the most potent influence on him as a child. She taught him his first lessons and, most important of all, kept his young mind free from prevalent religious dogmas. His first seven years were care-free and happy. Then his great tragedy happened — the poisoning of his cheek and the consequent disfigurement of his face as the result of an operation. Perhaps if his beloved mother had remained alive, her affection would have helped him over the taunts his distorted appearance brought upon him, but she had died when he was only nine. Some time later his father married again. His stepmother turned the erstwhile joyous home into a purgatory for the child. His life became unbearable. At fifteen he was taken out of school and apprenticed to a bookbinder. That only changed one hell for another. His deformity pursued him like a curse and caused him untold misery.

He loved the theatre madly, and every pfennig he could save he used to invest in tickets. He became obsessed by a yearning to go on the stage. Schiller's plays, especially *Wilhelm Tell, Die Räuber,* and *Fiesco,* were his inspirations and he longed to play in them. Once he had applied to a manager of a theatre, but he was curtly told that his face was more fit for a clown than for an actor. The disappointment was crushing and made him still more sensitive about his affliction. It became the horror of his existence. It made him pathologically self-conscious, particularly in the presence of women. He wanted them passionately, but the harrowing thought of his deformity always drove him from them. For many years, until he was able to grow a beard, he could not overcome his morbid shyness. It came near driving him to end his life, when he was saved by his spiritual awakening. The new social ideas he had become acquainted with inspired him with a great purpose and made him hold on to life. Blackwell's Island revived his old horror of his appearance. They had there shaved his beard, and the sight of the hideous image looking back at him from a piece of mirror he had smuggled into his cell was more terrifying than the prison. He was sure that a great deal of his fierce hatred of our social system, of the cruelty and injustice of life, was due to his own maimed condition, to the indignities and maltreatment it had caused him.

He spoke with intense feeling. He had been married twice, he continued; both marriages were failures. Since then, he went on, he had given up hope for a great love — until he met me, when the old yearning came upon him again. But with it returned the monster of tormenting shyness. For months a great conflict had been raging within him. Fear that he was repellent to me haunted him. He became obsessed by one thought — to win me, to bind me to himself, to make himself indispensable to me. When he realized that I had talent and the making of a forceful speaker, he clutched at it as a means of reaching my heart. In the cab on the way to Forty-second Street his love had overcome his fears. He hoped that I also loved him, in spite of his affliction. But when I returned from my trip, he saw the change at once: I had awakened to independent thinking, I had slipped out of his reach. It made him frantic, roused bitter recollections, and drove him to attack the one he loved and wanted so much. Now, he concluded, he asked for nothing more than friendship.

I was stirred to my depths by the simple, frank confession of a tormented being. It was too overwhelming for speech. In silence I took Most's hand. Years of suppressed intensity crushed my body, cried out ecstatically, dissolving in me. His kisses mingled with my tears covering the poor mutilated face. It was beautiful now.

During the two weeks of our tour I saw Most alone only occasionally: for an hour or two during the day or while journeying from one city to another. The rest of the time he was busy with comrades. I marvelled how he could talk and drink until the last moment before going on the platform and then speak with such fire and abandon. He seemed oblivious of the audience, yet I was sure that he was aware of everything that went on around him. Most could, in the midst of an oratorical pitch, take out his watch to see if he had not spoken too long. Was his speech studied, I wondered; not at all spontaneous? It troubled me considerably. I hated to think that he did not intensely feel what he said, that his eloquence and his expressive gestures were conscious theatricality rather than inspiration. I was impatient with myself for such thoughts and I could not tell Most about them. Besides, the little time we could spend together was too precious: I was eager to hear about the social struggle in the various countries in which he had played an important part. Germany, Austria, Switzerland, and, later, England had all been Most's arena. His enemies had not been slow to understand the danger of the young, fiery rebel. They strove to crush him. Repeated arrests, years of imprisonment and exile, followed; even the customary immunity accorded to members of the German parliament was denied him.

Most had been elected to the Reichstag by a large Socialist vote,

but unlike his colleagues he soon discovered what was going on behind
the scenes of the " House of Marionettes," as he had nicknamed that
legislative assembly. He realized that the masses had nothing to gain
from that source. He lost faith in the political machinery. By August
Reinsdorf, a very remarkable young German who was later executed
for conspiracy against the life of the Kaiser, Most was introduced to
anarchist ideas. Subsequently, in England, he definitely broke with his
Social Democratic adherents and became the spokesman of anarchism.

Our two weeks together, or what we had of them alone, gave me
more information about the political and economic struggle in European countries than years of reading could have done. Most had
revolutionary history at his fingers' tips: the rise of socialism as
sponsored by Lassalle, Marx, and Engels; the formation of the Social Democratic Party, originally imbued with revolutionary fire, but
gradually absorbing political ambitions; the difference between the
various social schools; the bitter struggle between social democracy
and anarchism, as personified by Marx and Engels on one side and
Michael Bakunin and the Latin sections on the other — a feud that
finally broke the First International.

Most spoke interestingly of his past and he also wanted to know
about my childhood and youthful life. All that had preceded my coming to New York seemed to me insignificant, but Most disagreed
with me about it. He insisted that early environment and conditions
are powerful factors in moulding one's life. He wondered whether
my awakening to social problems was due entirely to the shock the
Chicago tragedy had given me, or whether it was the flowering of
what had its roots in myself, in the past and in the conditions of my
childhood.

I related to him incidents of my recollections — some experiences of
my schooldays, which seemed particularly to interest him.

When I was eight years of age, Father sent me to Königsberg to
live with my grandmother and go to school there. Grandmother was
the owner of a hairdressing parlour managed by her three daughters,
while she herself continued to ply the trade of smuggler. Father took
me as far as Kovno, where we were met by Grandmother. On the way
he sternly impressed upon my mind what a sacrifice it was going to be
for him to pay forty roubles a month for my board and schooling. I
was going to be in a private school, as he would not permit his child
in the *Volkschule*. He was willing to do anything for me if I would

be a good girl, study hard, obey my teachers, grandmother, aunts, and uncles. He would never take me back if there should be any complaint against me and he would come to Königsberg to thrash me. My heart was heavy with fear of my father. I was even too miserable to care for Grandmother's loving reception. I had only one desire, to get away from Father.

Grandmother's quarters in Königsberg were cramped, consisting of only three rooms and a kitchen. The best room had been assigned to my aunt and uncle, while I had to sleep with my youngest aunt. I had always hated sharing my bed with anyone else. In fact, that was a constant bone of contention between my sister Helena and myself. Every night we would repeat the same argument: who should sleep next to the wall and who on the outside? I insisted always on the outside; it gave me the feeling of greater freedom. Now, too, the prospect of having to sleep with my aunt was oppressing me. But there was no other place.

From the very first I took a violent dislike to my uncle. I missed our large yard, the fields, and the hills. I felt stifled and alone in the world. Before long I was sent to school. I made friends there with the other children and began to feel a little less lonely. All went well for a month; then Grandmother had to go away indefinitely. Almost immediately my purgatory began. Uncle insisted that it was no use wasting money on my schooling, and that forty roubles were barely enough for my keep. My aunts protested, but to no purpose. They were afraid of the man who bullied them all. I was taken out of school and put to work in the house.

From early morning, when I had to fetch the rolls, milk, and chocolate for our breakfast, until late at night I was kept busy, making beds, cleaning boots, scrubbing floors, and washing clothes. After a while I was even put to cooking, but my uncle was never satisfied. His gruff voice shouting orders all day long would send cold shivers down my spine. I drudged on. At night I would weep myself to sleep.

I became thin and pale; my shoes were run down at the heels, my clothes were threadbare, and I had no one to go to for comfort. My only friends were the two old maids who owned our flat and lived below, and one of my mother's sisters, a noble soul. She was ill most of the time, and I could rarely get away to see her, but I was often taken in by the two dear ladies, fed on coffee, and treated to burnt almonds, my favourite delicacy. I used to see such sweets in the

Konditorei and look yearningly at them, but I never had ten pfennige to buy any. My two friends gave me all I wanted, as well as flowers from their lovely garden.

I never dared slip into their place until my uncle was away, but their friendly greeting was balm to my aching heart. It was always the same: "*Na, Emmchen, noch immer im Gummi?*" That was because I wore large rubbers, my shoes having become too worn out.

On the rare occasions when I could get away to see my aunt Yetta she insisted that my people must be written to and told to come and take me away. I would not listen to it. I had not forgotten Father's last words; besides, Grandmother was expected every day and I knew she would save me from my dreaded uncle.

One afternoon, after an especially hard day's work and endless errands, Uncle came into the kitchen to say that I would have to deliver one more parcel. I knew by the address that it was far away. Whether from fatigue or because I disliked the man so violently, I took the courage to say that I could not make the journey; my feet hurt me too much. He slapped me full in the face, shouting: "You are not earning your keep! You are lazy!" When he left the room, I went out into the corridor, sat down on the stairs, and began to cry bitterly. All of a sudden I felt a kick in the back. I tried to grab the banister as I rolled to the bottom, landing below in a heap. The clatter roused the sisters, who came running to see what had happened. "*Das Kind is tot!*" they screamed. "The scoundrel has killed her!" They took me to their room and I clung to them, beseeching them not to let me go back to my uncle. A doctor was called, who found no bones broken, but my ankle was sprained. I was put to bed, nursed and petted as I had never been before, except by my own Helena.

The elder of the two sisters, Wilhelmina, went upstairs, stick in hand. I don't know what she said to my uncle, but after that he never came near me again. I remained with my benefactors, basking in their garden and their love, and eating burnt almonds to my heart's content.

Soon my father and grandmother arrived. Aunt Yetta had telegraphed them to come. Father was shocked by my appearance; he actually took me in his arms and kissed me. Such a thing had not happened since I was four. There was a terrible scene between Grandmother and her son-in-law, which ended in his moving out of the house with his wife. Before long, Father took me back to Popelan.

I then discovered that he had been sending forty roubles regularly every month, and that my uncle had just as regularly been reporting to him that I was doing splendidly at school.

Most was deeply moved by my story. He patted my head and kissed my hands. "*Armes Aschenprödelchen,*" he kept on saying; "your childhood was like mine after that beast of a stepmother came to our house." He was now more convinced than ever, he told me, that it was the influence of my childhood that had made me what I was.

I returned to New York much strengthened in my faith, proud of having the confidence and love of Johann Most. I wanted my young friends to see him as he appeared to me. In glowing colours I told them everything that had occurred during the two weeks on tour — everything except the episode on the boat. To do otherwise, I felt, would have meant to tear open Most's heart. I could not bear even the least reflection on anything he said or did.

We had moved to Thirteenth Street. Helen Minkin had gone back to live with her sister, as their father was no longer with them. Sasha, Fedya, and I shared our new flat. It became an oasis for Most from the bedlam of the *Freiheit* office. Often there would be verbal clashes between him and Sasha: nothing personal, it seemed, but about revolutionary consistency, methods of propaganda, the difference in zeal between the German and Russian comrades, and such matters. But I could not free myself from the feeling that underneath there might be something else, something concerning me. Their disputes used to make me uneasy, but as I always succeeded in diverting their particular arguments into general issues, the discussions ended in a friendly manner.

In the winter of that year (1890) the radical ranks were aroused over the report brought from Siberia by George Kennan, an American journalist. His account of the harrowing conditions of the Russian political prisoners and exiles moved even the American press to lengthy comments. We on the East Side had all along known of the horrors through underground messages. A year before, fearful things had taken place in Yakutsk. Politicals who had protested against the maltreatment of their comrades were lured into the prison yard and fired upon by guards; a number of prisoners were killed, among them women, while several others were subsequently hanged in the prison for " inciting an outbreak." We knew of other cases equally terrible, but the American press had kept silent on the inhumanities committed by the Tsar.

Now, however, an American had brought back authentic data and photographs, and he could not be ignored. His story aroused many public-spirited men and women, among them Julia Ward Howe, William Lloyd Garrison, Edmund Noble, Lucy Stone Blackwell, James Russell Lowell, Lyman Abbott, and others, who organized the first society of the Friends of Russian Freedom. Their monthly journal, *Free Russia,* initiated the movement against the proposed extradition treaty with Russia, and their activity and agitation brought splendid results. Among other things they succeeded in preventing the delivery of the famous revolutionist Hartmann into the clutches of the Tsarist henchmen.

When we first learned of the Yakutsk outrage, Sasha and I began discussing our return to Russia. What could we hope to achieve in barren America? It would require years to acquire the language thoroughly, and Sasha had no aspirations to become a public speaker. In Russia we could engage in conspiratorial work. We belonged to Russia. For months we went about nursing the idea, but the lack of necessary funds compelled us to give it up. But now, with George Kennan's *exposé* of the Russian horrors, our plans were revived. We decided to speak to Most about them. He became enthusiastic over the idea. " Emma is fast developing into a good speaker," he said; " when she will have mastered the language, she will become a force here. But you can do more in Russia," he agreed with Sasha. He would issue a confidential appeal for funds to some trustworthy comrades in order to equip Sasha for his trip and for his work afterwards. In fact, Sasha himself could help draw up the document. Most also suggested that it would be advisable for Sasha to learn the printing trade so as to enable him to start a secret press for anarchist literature in Russia.

I was happy to see Most become rejuvenated by his ardour over our plans. I loved him for his confidence in my boy, but my heart contracted with the thought that he did not want me to go also. He surely did not realize what it would mean to me to let Sasha go alone to Russia. No, that could never be, I decided inwardly.

It was agreed that Sasha should go to New Haven; in the printing shop of a comrade there he would familiarize himself with every aspect of the work. I, too, would go to New Haven to be near Sasha.

I would invite Helen and Anna Minkin to join us, and also Fedya. We could rent a house and there we would at last carry out my original purpose: start a co-operative dressmaking establishment. We could work for the Cause, too; organize lectures and invite Most and other speakers, arrange concerts and plays, and raise funds for the propaganda. Our friends welcomed the idea, and Most said he would be glad to have a home and friends to go to, a real place of rest. Sasha immediately left for New Haven. With Fedya I disposed of the household things we could not take with us, and the rest, together with my faithful sewing-machine, we carried to New Haven. Once there, we hung out a shingle: " Goldman and Minkin, Dressmakers," but we were soon compelled to realize that customers were not exactly standing in line on the corner and that it would be necessary at first to earn money by other means. I went back to the corset-factory where I had worked after my first separation from Kershner. Three years only had passed since then, but it seemed ages, my world had changed so completely, and I with it.

Helen joined me in the factory, while Anna remained at home. She was a good seamstress, but she was not able to cut or fit dresses. I prepared the work for her in the evening, so she could finish it in the day-time.

It was a great physical strain to run the machine all day in the factory, come home to prepare supper (no one else in our little commune could cook), then cut and fit dresses for the next day. But I had been in good health for some time and we had a great purpose. Then, too, there were our social interests. We organized an educational group, arranged lectures, socials, and dances. We hardly had time to think of ourselves; our lives were busy and full.

Most came for a series of lectures and visited with us. Solotaroff also, and we celebrated the event in memory of my first hearing him in New Haven. Our group became a centre for the progressive Russian, Jewish, and German elements. Our work, being carried on in foreign languages, did not arouse the attention of the press or police.

Gradually we built up a good clientele, which gave promise of my leaving the factory soon. Sasha was making great headway at the printer's. Fedya had gone back to New York because he could secure no work in New Haven. Our propaganda activities were bringing results. The lectures drew large crowds, much literature was sold, and many subscribers to the *Freiheit* gained. Our life was active and interesting, but presently it was disturbed. Anna, who had been ailing in New York, now grew worse, showing signs of consumption; and one Sunday afternoon, at the close of Most's lecture, Helen became hysterical. There seemed to be no particular cause for her attack, but the next morning she confided to me her love for Most, declaring that she would have to leave for New York, as she could not bear being away from where he was.

I myself had of late not been much with Most alone. He would come to us after his lecture, but there were always other visitors about, and in the evening he would take the train for New York. Occasionally I went to New York at Most's request, but our meetings there generally ended in a scene. He would urge closer contact, which I could not grant. Once he grew angry, declaring he didn't have to beg from me; he could " get Helen any time." I thought he was joking, until Helen's confession. Now I wondered if Most really loved the child.

The following Sunday he lunched at our place and we went out for a walk. I asked him to tell me about his feelings for Helen. " Ridiculous," he replied; " the girl simply needs a man. She thinks she loves me. I am sure any other man would do as well." I resented the insinuation, for I knew Helen; I knew she was not one who could give herself in the way he hinted. " She yearns for love," I replied. Most laughed cynically. " Love, love — it's all sentimental nonsense," he cried; " there is only sex! " So Sasha was right, after all, I thought. Most cared for women only as females. Probably he had also never wanted me for any other reason.

I had realized long before that Most's appeal to me was not physical. It was his intellect, his brilliant abilities, his peculiar, contradictory personality that fascinated me; the suffering and persecution he had endured melted my heart, even though I resented many of his traits. He would charge me with being cold, with not loving him. Once, while we were walking in New Haven, he became especially insistent. My refusal made him angry and he launched into a tirade against Sasha. He had known long ago, he said, that I preferred " that arrogant Russian Jew " who had dared to hold him, Most, to account; to tell him what was in keeping with revolutionary ethics. He had ignored the criticism of " the young fool who knew nothing of life." But he was tired of the whole thing, and that was why he was helping him go to Russia, far away from me. I would have to choose between him and Sasha.

I had been aware of the silent antagonism between the two, but Most had never spoken of Sasha before in such a manner. It stung me to the quick. I forgot Most's greatness; I was conscious only that he had dared to attack what was the most precious thing to me, my Sasha, my wild, inspired boy. I wanted Most and the very hills to know my love for this " arrogant Russian Jew." I cried it out, impulsively, passionately. I, too, was a Russian Jew. Was he, Most, the anarchist, an anti-Semite? And how dare he say that he wanted me all to himself? Was I an object, to be taken and owned? What kind of anarchism was that? Sasha had been right in claiming that Most was no longer an anarchist.

Most kept silent. Presently I heard a moan as of a wounded animal. My outburst came to an abrupt stop. He lay stretched on the ground, face downward, his hands clenched. Various emotions struggled within me — love for Sasha, mortification that I had spoken so harshly, anger with Most, intense compassion for him, as he lay like a child before me, crying. I lifted his head gently. I longed to tell him how sorry I felt, but words seemed banal. He looked up into my face and whispered: " *Mein Kind, mein Kind,* Sasha is a lucky dog to have such love. I wonder if he appreciates it." He buried his head in my lap and we sat in silence.

Suddenly voices broke upon our ears. " Get up, you two, get up! What do you mean making love in public? You are arrested for disorderly conduct." Most was about to raise himself. Cold terror clutched me, not for myself, but for him. I knew that if they recognized him they would take him to the station-house, and the next day the papers would again carry scurrilous stories about him. Quick as lightning the thought came to me to make up some yarn, anything that would prevent a scandal. " I am so glad you have come," I said; " my father had a sudden attack of dizziness. I was hoping someone would pass along so we could get a doctor. Won't one of you gentlemen do something? " The two broke out into loud laughter. " Father, huh, you shrew! Well, if your father will give us five bucks, we'll let you off this time." I fumbled in my purse nervously and got out the only five-dollar bill I owned. The men left, their suggestive laugh grating on my ears.

Most sat bolt upright, trying hard to suppress a chuckle. " You are clever," he said; " but I can see now that I shall never be anything else to you but a father." That evening, after the lecture, I did not go to the station to see Most off.

Early next morning I was torn out of sleep by Sasha. Anna had had a hæmorrhage of the lungs. The physician, hurriedly summoned, said the case was serious and ordered Anna to a sanatorium. Some days later Sasha took her to New York. I remained in New Haven to wind up our affairs. My great plan of a co-operative venture had gone to smash.

·In New York we rented a flat on Forsythe Street. Fedya continued to make crayon enlargements whenever he was lucky enough to get orders. I again took up piece-work. Sasha worked as compositor on the *Freiheit,* still clinging to the hope that Most would enable him to go to Russia. The appeal for funds, composed by Most and Sasha, had been sent out, and we anxiously awaited the results.

I spent much time in the *Freiheit* office, where the tables were piled high with European exchanges. One of them particularly attracted my attention. It was *Die Autonomie,* a German anarchist weekly published in London. While not comparable with the *Freiheit* in force and picturesqueness of language, it nevertheless seemed to me to express anarchism in a clearer and more convincing manner. One time, when I had mentioned the publication to Most, he became enraged. He told me curtly that the people behind the venture were shady characters, that they had been mixed up with " the spy Peukert, who betrayed John Neve, one of our best German comrades, into the hands of the police." It had never occurred to me then to doubt Most and I ceased reading the *Autonomie.*

But nearer acquaintance with the movement and my other experiences showed me Most's partiality. I began to read the *Autonomie* again. Soon I came to the conclusion that, however correct Most might be about the personnel of the paper, its tenets were much closer to what anarchism had come to mean to me than those of the *Freiheit.* The *Autonomie* stressed more the freedom of the individual and the independence of groups. Its entire tone held a powerful appeal for me. My two friends felt the same way. Sasha suggested that we get in touch with the comrades in London.

Before long we learned of the existence of the Group *Autonomie* in New York. Its weekly gatherings were on Saturdays, and we decided to visit the place on Fifth Street. It bore the peculiar name *Zum Groben Michel,* which well corresponded with the rough exterior and gruff manner of its giant owner. The leading spirit of the group was Joseph Peukert.

Having been influenced by Most against Peukert, we long fought the latter's version of the story that held him responsible for the arrest and imprisonment of Neve. But after months of association with Peukert we became convinced that, whatever might have been his share in that terrible affair, he could not have been a deliberate party to treachery.

Joseph Peukert had at one time played a very important rôle in the socialist movement of Austria. But he could in no sense compare with Johann Most. He lacked the vivid personality of the latter, his genius and fascinating spontaneity. Peukert was grave, pedantic, utterly devoid of humour. At first I believed that his sombreness was due to the persecution he had suffered, the accusation of traitor cast against him, which had made him a pariah. But soon I came to understand that his inferiority was conditioned in himself, and that, in fact, it was the dominant force in his hatred of Most. Still our sympathies went out to Peukert. We felt that the feud between the two anarchistic camps — between the followers of Most and those of Peukert — was to a large extent the result of personal vanities. We thought it fair that Peukert be given a hearing before a group of impartial comrades. In this view we were supported by some members of the Pioneers of Liberty, to which both Sasha and Fedya belonged.

At the national conference of the Yiddish anarchist organizations in December 1890 Sasha proposed that the Most-Peukert charges be taken up for a thorough investigation, and that both men be asked to bring their evidence. When Most learned of it, all his personal antagonism and bitterness against Sasha broke out into uncontrolled fury. " That arrogant young Jew," he cried; " that *Grünschnabel* — how dare he doubt Most and the comrades who long ago proved that Peukert was a spy? " Again I felt that Sasha was right in his estimate of Most. Had he not maintained for a long time that Most was a tyrant who wanted to rule with an iron hand under the guise of anarchism? Had he not repeatedly told me that Most was no longer a revolutionist? " You can do what you please," Sasha now said to me, " but I am through with Most and the *Freiheit.*" He would give up his job on the paper at once.

I had been too close to Most, had looked too deeply into his soul, had felt too strongly his charm and fascination, his heights and depths, to give him up so easily. I would go to him and try to smooth his troubled spirit, as I had done so often. I was sure Most loved our beautiful ideal. Had he not given up everything for it? Had he not suffered pain and indignities for its sake? Surely he could be made to see the great harm to the movement which his feud with Peukert had already caused. I would go to him.

Sasha called me a blind worshipper; he had known all along, he said, that Most the man meant more to me than Most the revolutionist. Yet I could not agree with Sasha's rigid distinctions. When I had first heard him emphasize the greater importance of the Cause over life and beauty, something in me had rebelled. But I was never convinced that he was wrong. No one with such singleness of purpose, such selfless devotion, could be wrong. It must be something in myself, I felt, that bound me to the earth, to the human side of those who came into my life. I often thought that I must be weak, that I would never reach Sasha's revolutionary, idealistic heights. But — well, at least I could love him for his zeal. Some day I would show him how great my devotion could be.

I went to the *Freiheit* office to see Most. How changed was his manner to me, what a contrast to my first memorable visit! I felt it even before he said one word. " What do you want with me, now that you are with that dreadful group? " he greeted me. " You have chosen my enemies as your friends." I stepped close to him, remarking that I could not argue in the office. Would he not go out with me that evening — just for old friendship's sake? " Old friendship's sake! " he cried derisively; " it was beautiful while it lasted. Where is it now? You have seen fit to go with my enemies and you have preferred a mere youngster to me! Whoever is not with me is against me! " But while he kept on talking angrily, I thought I detected a change in his tone. It was no longer so harsh. It had been his voice that had originally struck deep into my being; I had learned to love it, to understand its tremulous changeability from the hardness of steel to mellow tenderness. I was always able to distinguish the heights and depths of his emotion by the timbre of his voice. By this I now knew that he was no longer angry.

I took him by the hand. " Please, Hannes, come, won't you? " He pressed me to his heart. " You are a *Hexe;* you are a terrible woman. You will be the undoing of every man. But I love you, I will come."

We went to a café on Sixth Avenue and Forty-second Street. It was a famous gathering-place for theatrical people, gamblers, and prostitutes. He chose the place because comrades never frequented it.

It was a long time since we had been out together, since I had watched the wonderful transformation that Most always underwent after a few glasses of wine. His changed mood would transport me to a different world, a world without discord and strife, without a Cause to bind one, or opinions of comrades to consider. All differences were forgotten. When we separated, I had not spoken to him about the Peukert case.

The next day I received a letter from Most, enclosing data on the Peukert affair. I read the letter first. Again he poured out his heart as on our trip to Boston. His plaint was love, and why it must end; it was not only that he could not continue to share me with another, but that he could no longer support the increasing differences between us. He was sure that I would go on growing, becoming an ever-increasing force in the movement. But this very assurance convinced him that our relations were bound to lack permanence. A home, children, the care and attention ordinary women can give, who have no other interest in life but the man they love and the children they bear him — that was what he needed and felt he had found in Helen. Her attraction for him was not the tempestuous passion I had awakened. Our last embrace was only one more proof of the hold I had on him. It was ecstatic, but it left him in a turmoil, in a conflict, unhappy. The squabbles in the ranks, the precarious condition of the *Freiheit,* and his own impending return to Blackwell's Island, all combined to rob him of peace, to unfit him for work which was, after all, his great task in life. He hoped that I would understand, that I would even help him to find the peace he sought.

I read and reread the letter, locked in my room. I wanted to be alone with all that Most had meant to me, all he had given me. What had I given him? Not so much as even the ordinary woman gives the man she loves. I hated to admit, even to myself, that I lacked what he wanted so much. I knew I could bring him children if I would have the operation. How wonderful it would be to have a child by this unique personality! I sat lost in the thought. But soon something more insistent awakened in my brain — Sasha, the life and work we had together. Would I give it all up? No, no, that was impossible, that should never be! But why Sasha rather than Most? To be sure, Sasha had youth and indomitable zeal. Ah, yes, his zeal — was not that the cement that had bound me to him? But suppose Sasha, too, should want a wife, home, children. What then? Should I be able to give him that? But Sasha would never expect such a thing — he lived only for the Cause and he wanted me also to live only for it.

An agonized night followed that day. I could find no answer and no peace.

CHAPTER VII

AT THE INTERNATIONAL SOCIALIST CONGRESS HELD IN PARIS IN 1889 the decision had been made to turn the first of May into a world-wide holiday of labour. The idea caught the imagination of the progressive workers in every land. The birth of spring was to mark the reawakening of the masses to new efforts for emancipation. In this year, 1891, the decision of the Congress was to find wide application. On the first of May the toilers were to lay down their tools, stop their machines, leave the factories and mines. In festive attire they were to demonstrate with their banners, marching to the inspiring strains of revolutionary music and song. Everywhere meetings were to take place to articulate the aspirations of labour.

The Latin countries had already begun their preparations. The socialist and anarchist publications carried detailed reports of the intense activities scheduled for the great day. In America, too, the call went out to make the first of May an impressive demonstration of the strength and power of the workers. Nightly sessions took place to organize for the event. I was again assigned to canvass the trade unions. The press of the country began a campaign of vituperation, charging the radical elements with plotting revolution. The unions were urged to purge their ranks of the " foreign riff-raff and criminals who came to our country to destroy its democratic institutions." The campaign had its effect. The conservative labour bodies refused to lay down their tools and to participate in the first-of-May demonstration. The others were too small, numerically, and still too terrorized by the attacks on the German unions during the Chicago Haymarket days. Only the most radical among German, Jewish, and Russian organizations held to their original decision. They would demonstrate.

The celebration in New York was arranged by the socialists. They secured Union Square and promised to permit the anarchists to speak from their own platform. But at the last moment the socialist organizers refused to let us erect our platform on the square. Most did not arrive on time, but I was there with a group of young people, including Sasha, Fedya, and several Italian comrades. We were determined to have our say on this great occasion. When it became evident that we could not have our platform, the boys lifted me up on one of the socialist trucks. I began to speak. The chairman left, but in a few minutes he returned with the owner of the wagon. I continued to speak. The man hitched his horse to the truck and started off at a trot. I still continued to speak. The crowd, failing to take in the situation, followed us out of the square for a couple of blocks while I was speaking.

Presently the police appeared and began beating back the crowd. The driver stopped. Our boys quickly lifted me off and hurried me away. The morning papers were filled with a story about a mysterious young woman on a truck who had waved a red flag and urged revolution, "her high-pitched voice putting the horse to flight."

A few weeks later the news arrived that the Supreme Court had decided against John Most's appeal. We knew it meant Blackwell's Island again. Sasha forgot his differences with Most, and I no longer cared that he had cast me out of his heart and life. Nothing mattered now except the cruel fact that Most would be returned to prison, that he would be shaved again, that his deformity, from which he had suffered so much, would again become the butt of ridicule and humiliation.

We were the first in court. Most was brought in, accompanied by his attorneys and his bondsman, our old comrade Julius Hoffmann. Many friends streamed in, Helen Minkin among them. Most seemed indifferent to his doom, holding himself erect and proud. He was again the old warrior, the unflinching rebel.

The proceedings lasted only a few minutes. In the corridor I rushed over to Most, took his hand, and whispered: "Hannes, dear Hannes, I'd give anything to take your place!" "I know you would, my *Blondkopf*. Write to me at the island." Then he was led away.

Sasha accompanied Most to Blackwell's Island. He returned enthusiastic about his splendid bearing: he had never seen him more rebellious, more dignified, more brilliant. Even the newspaper men had been impressed. "We must bury our differences, we must work with Most," Sasha declared.

A mass meeting was decided upon to voice our protest against the decision of the Supreme Court and to raise funds to continue the fight for Most and help make his life in prison as endurable as possible. Sympathy with our imprisoned comrade was general in the radical ranks. Within forty-eight hours we succeeded in filling a large hall, where I was one of the speakers. My speech was not merely about Johann Most, the symbol of universal revolt, the spokesman of anarchism, but also of the man who had been my great inspiration, my teacher and comrade.

During the winter Fedya left for Springfield, Massachusetts, to work for a photographer. After a while he wrote that I could have a job at the same place, taking care of the orders. I was glad of the chance; it would take me away from New York, from the everlasting grind of the sewing-machine. Sasha and I had been supporting ourselves with piece-work on boys' jumpers. Often we worked eighteen hours a day in the one light room of our flat, and I had to do the cooking and the housework besides. Springfield would be a change and a relief.

The work was not hard, and it was soothing to be with Fedya, who was so different from both Most and Sasha. We had many tastes in common outside of the movement: our love for beauty, for flowers, for the theatre. There was very little of the last in Springfield; in fact, the American play and theatre had become abhorrent to me. After Königsberg, St. Petersburg, and the German Irving Place Theatre in New York the ordinary American play seemed flat and tawdry.

Fedya was so successful with his work that it seemed folly to keep on enriching our employer. It occurred to us that we might start out for ourselves and have Sasha with us. Though Sasha had never complained, I could sense in his letters that he was not happy in New York. Fedya suggested that we open our own studio. We decided to go to Worcester, Massachusetts, and to invite Sasha to join us.

We fixed up an office, put out a sign, and waited for customers. But none came, and our little savings were dwindling. We hired a horse and buggy to enable us to visit near-by country places and secure orders from the farmers for crayon enlargements of family photographs. Sasha would drive, and whenever we bumped into trees and sidewalks, he would dilate on the natural cussedness of our horse. Often we travelled for hours before securing any work.

We were struck by the great difference between the New Englanders and the Russian peasant. The latter seldom had enough for himself to eat, yet he would never fail to offer the stranger bread and kvass (cider). The German peasants also, as I remembered from my schooldays, would invite us to their " best room," put milk and butter on the table, and urge us to partake. But here, in free America, where the farmers owned acres of land and much cattle, we were lucky to be admitted at all or be given a glass of water. Sasha used to say that the American farmer lacked sympathy and kindness because he himself had never known want. " He is really a small capitalist," he argued. " It is different with the Russians, or even with the German peasants; they are proletarians. That is why they are warm-hearted and hospitable." I was not convinced. I had worked with proletarians in factories and I did not always find them helpful and generous. But Sasha's faith in the people was infectious and dispelled my doubts.

Frequently we were on the point of giving up. The family we lived with used to advise us to open a lunch-room or ice-cream parlour. The suggestion at first seemed to us absurd; we had neither funds nor aspirations for such a venture. Besides, it was against our principles to engage in business.

Just at that time the radical press was again aroused by new atrocities in Russia. The old yearning took hold of us to return to our native country. But where get enough money for the purpose? The private call sent out by Most had found no adequate response. Then it occurred to us that an ice-cream parlour might prove the means to our end. The more we thought of it, the more convinced we became that it offered the only solution.

Our savings consisted of fifty dollars. Our landlord, who had suggested the idea, said he would lend us a hundred and fifty dollars. We secured a store, and within a couple of weeks Sasha's skill with hammer and saw, Fedya's with his paint and brush, and my own good German housekeeping training succeeded in turning the neglected ramshackle place into an attractive lunch-room. It was spring and not yet warm enough for an ice-cream rush, but the coffee I brewed, our sandwiches and dainty dishes, were beginning to be appreciated, and soon we were kept busy till early morning hours. Within a short time we had paid back our landlord's loan and were able to invest in a soda-water fountain and some lovely coloured dishes. We felt we were on the way to the realization of our long-cherished dream.

CHAPTER VIII

It was May 1892. News from Pittsburgh announced that trouble had broken out between the Carnegie Steel Company and its employees organized in the Amalgamated Association of Iron and Steel Workers. It was one of the biggest and most efficient labour bodies of the country, consisting mostly of Americans, men of decision and grit, who would assert their rights. The Carnegie Company, on the other hand, was a powerful corporation, known as a hard master. It was particularly significant that Andrew Carnegie, its president, had temporarily turned over the entire management to the company's chairman, Henry Clay Frick, a man known for his enmity to labour. Frick was also the owner of extensive coke-fields, where unions were prohibited and the workers were ruled with an iron hand.

The high tariff on imported steel had greatly boomed the American steel industry. The Carnegie Company had practically a monopoly of it and enjoyed unprecedented prosperity. Its largest mills were in Homestead, near Pittsburgh, where thousands of workers were employed, their tasks requiring long training and high skill. Wages were arranged between the company and the union, according to a sliding scale based on the prevailing market price of steel products. The current agreement was about to expire, and the workers presented a new wage schedule, calling for an increase because of the higher market prices and enlarged output of the mills.

The philanthropic Andrew Carnegie conveniently retired to his castle in Scotland, and Frick took full charge of the situation. He declared that henceforth the sliding scale would be abolished. The company would make no more agreements with the Amalgamated Association; it would itself determine the wages to be paid. In fact, he would not recognize the union at all. He would not treat with the employees collectively, as before. He would close the mills, and the men might consider themselves discharged. Thereafter they would have to apply for work individually, and the pay would be arranged with every worker separately. Frick curtly refused the peace advances of the workers' organization, declaring that there was " nothing to arbitrate." Presently the mills were closed. " Not a strike, but a lock-out," Frick announced. It was an open declaration of war.

Feeling ran high in Homestead and vicinity. The sympathy of the entire country was with the men. Even the most conservative part of the press condemned Frick for his arbitrary and drastic methods. They charged him with deliberately provoking a crisis that might assume national proportions, in view of the great numbers of men locked out by Frick's action, and the probable effect upon affiliated unions and on related industries.

Labour throughout the country was aroused. The steel-workers declared that they were ready to take up the challenge of Frick: they would insist on their right to organize and to deal collectively with their employers. Their tone was manly, ringing with the spirit of their rebellious forebears of the Revolutionary War.

Far away from the scene of the impending struggle, in our little ice-cream parlour in the city of Worcester, we eagerly followed developments. To us it sounded the awakening of the American worker, the long-awaited day of his resurrection. The native toiler had risen, he was beginning to feel his mighty strength, he was determined to break the chains that had held him in bondage so long, we thought. Our hearts were fired with admiration for the men of Homestead.

We continued our daily work, waiting on customers, frying pancakes, serving tea and ice-cream; but our thoughts were in Homestead, with the brave steel-workers. We became so absorbed in the news that we would not permit ourselves enough time even for sleep. At daybreak one of the boys would be off to get the first editions of the papers. We saturated ourselves with the events in Homestead to the exclusion of everything else. Entire nights we would sit up discussing the various phases of the situation, almost engulfed by the possibilities of the gigantic struggle.

One afternoon a customer came in for an ice-cream, while I was alone in the store. As I set the dish down before him, I caught the large headlines of his paper: " LATEST DEVELOPMENTS IN HOMESTEAD — FAMILIES OF STRIKERS EVICTED FROM THE COMPANY HOUSES — WOMAN IN CONFINEMENT CARRIED OUT INTO STREET BY

SHERIFFS." I read over the man's shoulder Frick's dictum to the workers: he would rather see them dead than concede to their demands, and he threatened to import Pinkerton detectives. The brutal bluntness of the account, the inhumanity of Frick towards the evicted mother, inflamed my mind. Indignation swept my whole being. I heard the man at the table ask: "Are you sick, young lady? Can I do anything for you?" "Yes, you can let me have your paper," I blurted out. "You won't have to pay me for the ice-cream. But I must ask you to leave. I must close the store." The man looked at me as if I had gone crazy.

I locked up the store and ran full speed the three blocks to our little flat. It was Homestead, not Russia; I knew it now. We belonged in Homestead. The boys, resting for the evening shift, sat up as I rushed into the room, newspaper clutched in my hand. "What has happened, Emma? You look terrible!" I could not speak. I handed them the paper.

Sasha was the first on his feet. "Homestead!" he exclaimed. "I must go to Homestead!" I flung my arms around him, crying out his name. I, too, would go. "We must go tonight," he said; "the great moment has come at last!" Being internationalists, he added, it mattered not to us where the blow was struck by the workers; we must be with them. We must bring them our great message and help them see that it was not only for the moment that they must strike, but for all time, for a free life, for anarchism. Russia had many heroic men and women, but who was there in America? Yes, we must go to Homestead, tonight!

I had never heard Sasha so eloquent. He seemed to have grown in stature. He looked strong and defiant, an inner light on his face making him beautiful, as he had never appeared to me before.

We immediately went to our landlord and informed him of our decision to leave. He replied that we were mad; we were doing so well, we were on the way to fortune. If we would hold out to the end of the summer, we would be able to clear at least a thousand dollars. But he argued in vain — we were not to be moved. We invented the story that a very dear relative was in a dying condition, and that therefore we must depart. We would turn the store over to him; all we wanted was the evening's receipts. We would remain until closing-hours, leave everything in order, and give him the keys.

That evening we were especially busy. We had never before had so many customers. By one o'clock we had sold out everything. Our receipts were seventy-five dollars. We left on an early morning train.

On the way we discussed our immediate plans. First of all, we would print a manifesto to the steel-workers. We would have to find somebody to translate it into English, as we were still unable to express our thoughts correctly in that tongue. We would have the German and English texts printed in New York and take them with us to Pittsburgh. With the help of the German comrades there, meetings could be organized for me to address. Fedya was to remain in New York till further developments.

From the station we went straight to the flat of Mollock, an Austrian comrade we had met in the *Autonomie* group. He was a baker who worked at night; but Peppie, his wife, with her two children was at home. We were sure she could put us up.

She was surprised to see the three of us march in, bag and baggage, but she made us welcome, fed us, and suggested that we go to bed. But we had other things to do.

Sasha and I went in search of Claus Timmermann, an ardent German anarchist we knew. He had considerable poetic talent and wrote forceful propaganda. In fact, he had been the editor of an anarchist paper in St. Louis before coming to New York. He was a likable fellow and entirely trustworthy, though a considerable drinker. We felt that Claus was the only person we could safely draw into our plan. He caught our spirit at once. The manifesto was written that afternoon. It was a flaming call to the men of Homestead to throw off the yoke of capitalism, to use their present struggle as a stepping-stone to the destruction of the wage system, and to continue towards social revolution and anarchism.

A few days after our return to New York the news was flashed across the country of the slaughter of steel-workers by Pinkertons. Frick had fortified the Homestead mills, built a high fence around them. Then, in the dead of night, a barge packed with strike-breakers, under protection of heavily armed Pinkerton thugs, quietly stole up the Monongahela River. The steel-men had learned of Frick's move. They stationed themselves along the shore, determined to drive back Frick's hirelings. When the barge got within range, the Pinkertons had opened fire, without warning, killing a number of Homestead men on the shore, among them a little boy, and wounding scores of others.

The wanton murders aroused even the daily papers. Several came out in strong editorials, severely criticizing Frick. He had gone too far; he had added fuel to the fire in the labour ranks and would have himself to blame for any desperate acts that might come.

We were stunned. We saw at once that the time for our manifesto had passed. Words had lost their meaning in the face of the innocent blood spilled on the banks of the Monongahela. Intuitively each felt what was surging in the heart of the others. Sasha broke the silence. " Frick is the responsible factor in this crime," he said; " he must be made to stand the consequences." It was the psychological moment for an *Attentat;* the whole country was aroused, everybody was considering Frick the perpetrator of a coldblooded murder. A blow aimed at Frick would re-echo in the poorest hovel, would call the attention of the whole world to the real cause behind the Homestead struggle. It would also strike terror in the enemy's ranks and make them realize that the proletariat of America had its avengers.

Sasha had never made bombs before, but Most's *Science of Revolutionary Warfare* was a good text-book. He would procure dynamite from a comrade he knew on Staten Island. He had waited for this sublime moment to serve the Cause, to give his life for the people. He would go to Pittsburgh.

"We will go with you!" Fedya and I cried together. But Sasha would not listen to it. He insisted that it was unnecessary and criminal to waste three lives on one man.

We sat down, Sasha between us, holding our hands. In a quiet and even tone he began to unfold to us his plan. He would perfect a time regulator for the bomb that would enable him to kill Frick, yet save himself. Not because he wanted to escape. No; he wanted to live long enough to justify his act in court, so that the American people might know that he was not a criminal, but an idealist.

"I will kill Frick," Sasha said, "and of course I shall be condemned to death. I will die proudly in the assurance that I gave my life for the people. But I will die by my own hand, like Lingg. Never will I permit our enemies to kill me."

I hung on his lips. His clarity, his calmness and force, the sacred fire of his ideal, enthralled me, held me spellbound. Turning to me, he continued in his deep voice. I was the born speaker, the propagandist, he said. I could do a great deal for his act. I could articulate its meaning to the workers. I could explain that he had had no personal grievance against Frick, that as a human being Frick was no less to him than anyone else. Frick was the symbol of wealth and power, of the injustice and wrong of the capitalistic class, as well as personally responsible for the shedding of the workers' blood. Sasha's act would be directed against Frick, not as a man, but as the enemy of labour. Surely I must see how important it was that I remain behind to plead the meaning of his deed and its message throughout the country.

Every word he said beat upon my brain like a sledge-hammer. The longer he talked, the more conscious I became of the terrible fact that he had no need of me in his last great hour. The realization swept away everything else — message, Cause, duty, propaganda. What meaning could these things have compared with the force that had made Sasha flesh of my flesh and blood of my blood from the moment that I had heard his voice and felt the grip of his hand at our first meeting? Had our three years together shown him so little of my soul that he could tell me calmly to go on living after he had been blown to pieces or strangled to death? Is not true love — not ordinary love, but the love that longs to share to the uttermost with the beloved — is it not more compelling than aught else? Those Russians had known it, Jessie Helfmann and Sophia Perovskaya; they had gone with their men in life and in death. I could do no less.

" I will go with you, Sasha," I cried; " I must go with you! I know that as a woman I can be of help. I could gain access to Frick easier than you. I could pave the way for your act. Besides, I simply must go with you. Do you understand, Sasha? "

We had a feverish week. Sasha's experiments took place at night when everybody was asleep. While Sasha worked, I kept watch. I lived in dread every moment for Sasha, for our friends in the flat, the children, and the rest of the tenants. What if anything should go wrong — but, then, did not the end justify the means? Our end was the sacred cause of the oppressed and exploited people. It was for them that we were going to give our lives. What if a few should have to perish? — the many would be made free and could live in beauty and in comfort. Yes, the end in this case justified the means.

After we had paid our fare from Worcester to New York, we had about sixty dollars left. Twenty had already been used up since our arrival. The material Sasha bought for the bomb had cost a good deal and we still had another week in New York. Besides, I needed a dress and shoes, which, together with the fare to Pittsburgh, would amount to fifty dollars. I realized with a start that we required a large sum of money. I knew no one who could give us so much; besides, I could never tell him the purpose. After days of canvassing in the scorching July heat I succeeded in collecting twenty-five dollars. Sasha finished his preparatory work and went to Staten Island to test the bomb. When he returned, I could tell by his expression that something terrible had happened. I learned soon enough; the bomb had not gone off.

Sasha said it was due either to the wrong chemical directions or to the dampness of the dynamite. The second bomb, having been made from the same material, would most likely also fail. A week's work and anxiety and forty precious dollars wasted! What now? We had no time for lamentations or regrets; we had to act quickly.

Johann Most, of course. He was the logical person to go to. He had constantly propagated the doctrine of individual acts; every one of his articles and speeches was a direct call to the *Tat*. He would be glad to learn that someone in America had come forward at last to commit a heroic act. Most was certainly aware of the heinous crime of Frick: the *Freiheit* had pointed him out as the responsible person. Most would help.

Sasha resented the suggestion. He said it had been evident from Most's behaviour since his release from Blackwell's Island that he wanted nothing more to do with us. He was too bitter over our affiliation with the Group *Autonomie*. I knew Sasha was right. While Most was in the penitentiary, I had written repeatedly to him, but he never replied. Since he had come out, he had not asked to see me. I knew he was living with Helen, that she was with child; and I had no right to break in on their life. Yes, Sasha was right, the gulf had grown too wide.

I recalled that Peukert and one of his friends had been given charge of a small legacy recently left by a comrade. Among the latter's effects a paper was found authorizing Peukert to use the money and a gun for propaganda purposes. I had known the man and I was sure he would have approved of our plan. And Peukert? He was not, like Most, an outspoken champion of individual revolutionary deeds, but he could not fail to see the significance of an act against Frick. He would surely want to help. It would be a wonderful opportunity for him to silence for ever the current suspicions and doubts about him.

I sought him out the following evening. He refused his aid point-blank. He could not give me the money, much less the gun, he declared, unless he knew for whom and for what. I struggled against the disclosure, but, fearing that all might be lost if I failed to get the money, I finally told him it was for an act on the life of Frick, though I did not mention who was to commit the act. He agreed that such a deed would prove of propagandistic value; but he said that he would have to consult the other members of his group before he could give me what I asked. I could not consent to having so many people know about the plan. They would be sure to spread the news, and it would get to the ears of the press. More than these considerations was the distinct feeling that Peukert did not want to have anything to do with the matter. It bore out my first impression of the man: he was not made of the stuff of heroes or martyrs.

I did not have to tell the boys of my failure. It was written on my face. Sasha said that the act must be carried out, no matter how we got the money. It was now clear that the two of us would not be able to go. I would have to listen to his plea and let him go alone. He reiterated his faith in me and in my strength and assured me of the great joy I had given him when I insisted upon going with him to Pittsburgh. "But," he said, "we are too poor. Poverty is always a deciding factor in our actions. Besides, we are merely dividing our labours, each doing what he is best fitted for." He was not an agitator; that was my field, and it would be my task to interpret his act to the people. I cried out against his arguments, though I felt their force. We had no money. I knew that he would go in any event; nothing would stop him, of that I was certain.

Our whole fortune consisted of fifteen dollars. That would take Sasha to Pittsburgh, buy some necessaries, and still leave him a dollar for the first day's food and lodging. Our Allegheny comrades Nold and Bauer, whom Sasha meant to look up, would give him hospitality for a few days until I could raise more money. Sasha had decided not to confide his mission to them; there was no need for it, he felt, and it was never advisable for too many people to be taken into conspiratorial plans. He would require at least another twenty dollars for a gun and a suit of clothes. He might be able to buy the weapon cheap at some pawnshop. I had no idea where I could get the money, but I knew that I would find it somehow.

Those with whom we were staying were told that Sasha would

leave that evening, but the motive for his departure was not revealed. There was a simple farewell supper, everyone joked and laughed, and I joined in the gaiety. I strove to be jolly to cheer Sasha, but it was laughter that masked suppressed sobs. Later we accompanied Sasha to the Baltimore and Ohio Station. Our friends kept in the distance, while Sasha and I paced the platform, our hearts too full for speech.

The conductor drawled out: "All aboard!" I clung to Sasha. He was on the train, while I stood on the lower step. His face bent low to mine, his hand holding me, he whispered: "My sailor girl," (his pet name for me), "comrade, you will be with me to the last. You will proclaim that I gave what was dearest to me for an ideal, for the great suffering people."

The train moved. Sasha loosened my hold, gently helping me to jump off the step. I ran after the vanishing train, waving and calling to him: "Sasha, Sashenka!" The steaming monster disappeared round the bend and I stood glued, straining after it, my arms outstretched for the precious life that was being snatched away from me.

I woke up with a very clear idea of how I could raise the money for Sasha. I would go on the street. I lay wondering how such a notion could have come to me. I recollected Dostoyevsky's *Crime and Punishment,* which had made a profound impression on me, especially the character of Sonya, Marmeladov's daughter. She had become a prostitute in order to support her little brothers and sisters and to relieve her consumptive stepmother of worry. I visioned Sonya as she lay on her cot, face to the wall, her shoulders twitching. I could almost feel the same way. Sensitive Sonya could sell her body; why not I? My cause was greater than hers. It was Sasha — his great deed — the people. But should I be able to do it, to go with strange men — for money? The thought revolted me. I buried my face in the pillow to shut out the light. "Weakling, coward," an inner voice said. "Sasha is giving his life, and you shrink from giving your body, miserable coward!" It took me several hours to gain control of myself. When I got out of bed my mind was made up.

My main concern now was whether I could make myself attractive enough to men who seek out girls on the street. I stepped over to the mirror to inspect my body. I looked tired, but my complexion was good. I should need no make-up. My curly blond hair showed off well with my blue eyes. Too large in the hips for my age, I thought; I was just twenty-three. Well, I came from Jewish stock. Besides, I would wear a corset and I should look taller in high heels (I had never worn either before).

Corsets, slippers with high heels, dainty underwear — where should I get money for it all? I had a white linen dress, trimmed with Caucasian embroidery. I could get some soft flesh-coloured material and sew the underwear myself. I knew the stores on Grand Street carried cheap goods.

I dressed hurriedly and went in search of the servant in the apartment who had shown a liking for me, and she lent me five dollars without any question. I started off to make my purchases. When I returned, I locked myself in my room. I would see no one. I was busy preparing my outfit and thinking of Sasha. What would he say? Would he approve? Yes, I was sure he would. He had always insisted that the end justified the means, that the true revolutionist will not shrink from anything to serve the Cause.

Saturday evening, July 16, 1892, I walked up and down Fourteenth Street, one of the long procession of girls I had so often seen plying their trade. I felt no nervousness at first, but when I looked at the passing men and saw their vulgar glances and their manner of approaching the women, my heart sank. I wanted to take flight, run back to my room, tear off my cheap finery, and scrub myself clean. But a voice kept on ringing in my ears: "You must hold out; Sasha — his act — everything will be lost if you fail."

I continued my tramp, but something stronger than my reason would compel me to increase my pace the moment a man came near me. One of them was rather insistent, and I fled. By eleven o'clock I was utterly exhausted. My feet hurt from the high heels, my head throbbed. I was close to tears from fatigue and disgust with my inability to carry out what I had come to do.

I made another effort. I stood on the corner of Fourteenth Street and Fourth Avenue, near the bank building. The first man that invited me — I would go with him, I had decided. A tall, distinguished-looking person, well dressed, came close. "Let's have a drink, little girl," he said. His hair was white, he appeared to be about sixty, but his face was ruddy. "All right," I replied. He took my arm and led me to a wine house on Union Square which Most had often frequented with me. "Not here!" I almost screamed; "please, not here." I led him to the back entrance of a saloon on Thirteenth Street

and Third Avenue. I had once been there in the afternoon for a glass
of beer. It had been clean and quiet then.

That night it was crowded, and with difficulty we secured a table.
The man ordered drinks. My throat felt parched and I asked for a
large glass of beer. Neither of us spoke. I was conscious of the man's
scrutiny of my face and body. I felt myself growing resentful. Presently he asked: " You're a novice in the business, aren't you? " " Yes,
this is my first time — but how did you know? " " I watched you as
you passed me," he replied. He told me that he had noticed my
haunted expression and my increased pace the moment a man came
near me. He understood then that I was inexperienced; whatever
might have been the reason that brought me to the street, he knew
it was not mere looseness or love of excitement. " But thousands of
girls are driven by economic necessity," I blurted out. He looked at
me in surprise. " Where did you get that stuff? " I wanted to tell him
all about the social question, about my ideas, who and what I was,
but I checked myself. I must not disclose my identity: it would be too
dreadful if he should learn that Emma Goldman, the anarchist, had
been found soliciting on Fourteenth Street. What a juicy story it
would make for the press!

He said he was not interested in economic problems and did not
care what the reason was for my actions. He only wanted to tell me
that there was nothing in prostitution unless one had the knack for
it. " You haven't got it, that's all there is to it," he assured me. He
took out a ten-dollar bill and put it down before me. " Take this and
go home," he said. " But why should you give me money if you don't
want me to go with you? " I asked. " Well, just to cover the expenses
you must have had to rig yourself out like that," he replied; " your
dress is awfully nice, even if it does not go with those cheap shoes
and stockings." I was too astounded for speech.

I had met two categories of men: vulgarians and idealists. The
former would never have let an opportunity pass to possess a woman
and they would give her no other thought save sexual desire. The
idealists stoutly defended the equality of the sexes, at least in theory,
but the only men among them who practised what they preached were
the Russian and Jewish radicals. This man, who had picked me up on
the street and who was now with me in the back of a saloon, seemed
an entirely new type. He interested me. He must be rich. But would a
rich man give something for nothing? The manufacturer Garson

came to my mind; he would not even give me a small raise in wages.

Perhaps this man was one of those soul-savers I had read about, people who were always cleansing New York City of vice. I asked him. He laughed and said he was not a professional busybody. If he had thought that I really wanted to be on the street, he would not have cared. "Of course, I may be entirely mistaken," he added, " but I don't mind. Just now I am convinced that you are not intended to be a streetwalker, and that even if you do succeed, you will hate it afterwards." If he were not convinced of it, he would take me for his mistress. "For always?" I cried. "There you are!" he replied; " you are scared by the mere suggestion and yet you hope to succeed on the street. You're an awfully nice kid, but you're silly, inexperienced, childish." " I was twenty-three last month," I protested, resentful of being treated like a child. " You are an old lady," he said with a grin, " but even old folks can be babes in the woods. Look at me; I'm sixty-one and I often do foolish things." " Like believing in my innocence, for instance," I retorted. The simplicity of his manner pleased me. I asked for his name and address so as to be able to return his ten dollars some day. But he refused to give them to me. He loved mysteries, he said. On the street he held my hand for a moment, and then we turned in opposite directions.

That night I tossed about for hours. My sleep was restless; my dreams were of Sasha, Frick, Homestead, Fourteenth Street, and the affable stranger. Long after waking the next morning the dream pictures persisted. Then my eye caught my little purse on the table. I jumped up, opened it with trembling hands — it did contain the ten dollars! It had actually happened, then!

On Monday a short note arrived from Sasha. He had met Carl Nold and Henry Bauer, he wrote. He had set the following Saturday for his act, provided I could send some money he needed at once. He was sure I would not fail him. I was a little disappointed by the letter. Its tone was cold and perfunctory, and I wondered how the stranger would write to the woman he loved. With a start I shook myself free. It was crazy to have such thoughts when Sasha was preparing to take a life and lose his own in the attempt. How could I think of that stranger and Sasha in the same breath? I must get more money for my boy.

I would wire Helena for fifteen dollars. I had not written my dear sister for many weeks, and I hated to ask her for money, knowing how poor she was. It seemed criminal. Finally I wired her that I had been taken ill and needed fifteen dollars. I knew that nothing would prevent her from getting the money if she thought that I was ill. But a sense of shame oppressed me, as once before, in St. Petersburg, when I had deceived her.

I received the money from Helena by wire. I sent twenty dollars to Sasha and returned the five I had borrowed for my finery.

CHAPTER IX

SINCE OUR RETURN TO NEW YORK I HAD NOT BEEN ABLE TO LOOK for work. The tension of the weeks since Sasha's departure, my desperate struggle against letting him go alone, my street adventure, together with the misery I felt for having deceived Helena, completely upset me. My condition was aggravated now by the agonizing wait for Saturday, July 23, the date set by Sasha for his act. I grew restless and aimlessly walked about in the July heat, spending the evenings in *Zum Groben Michel,* the nights at Sachs's café.

In the early afternoon of Saturday, July 23, Fedya rushed into my room with a newspaper. There it was, in large black letters: " YOUNG MAN BY THE NAME OF ALEXANDER BERGMAN SHOOTS FRICK — ASSASSIN OVERPOWERED BY WORKING-MEN AFTER DESPERATE STRUGGLE."

Working-men, working-men overpowering Sasha? The paper was lying! He did the act for the working-men; they would never attack him.

Hurriedly we secured all the afternoon editions. Every one had a different description, but the main fact stood out — our brave Sasha had committed the act! Frick was still alive, but his wounds were considered fatal. He would probably not survive the night. And Sasha — they would kill him. They were going to kill him, I was sure of it. Was I going to let him die alone? Should I go on talking while he was being butchered? I must pay the same price as he — I must stand the consequences — I must share the responsibility!

I had read in the *Freiheit* that Most was to lecture that evening before the German Anarchist Local No. 1. "He will surely speak of Sasha's act," I said to Fedya. "We must go to the meeting."

I had not seen Most for a year. He now looked aged; Blackwell's Island had left its mark. He spoke in his usual manner, but Sasha's act he mentioned only at the end, in a casual way. " The papers report the attempt on the life of Frick by a young man by the name of Bergman," he said. " It is probably the usual newspaper fake. It must be some crank or perhaps Frick's own man, to create sympathy for him. Frick knows that public opinion is against him. He needs something to turn the tide in his favour."

I did not believe my own ears. I sat dumbfounded, fixedly staring at Most. He was drunk, of course, I thought. I looked about me and saw surprise on many faces. Some in the audience seemed impressed by what he had said. I noticed several suspicious-looking men near the exits; detectives, evidently.

When Most finished, I demanded the floor. I spoke scathingly of a lecturer who dared come before the public in a drunken condition. Or was Most sober, I demanded, and merely afraid of the detectives? Why did he invent the ridiculous story about Frick's " own man "? Did he not know who " Bergman " was?

Objections and protests began to be heard and soon the uproar became so great that I had to stop. Most descended from the platform; he would not answer me. Sick at heart, I left with Fedya. We noticed two men following us. For several hours we zigzagged through the streets, finally succeeding in losing them. We walked to Park Row, there to wait for the Sunday morning papers.

In feverish excitement we read the detailed story about the " assassin Alexander Berkman." He had forced his way into Frick's private office on the heels of the Negro porter who had taken in his card. He had immediately opened fire, and Frick had fallen to the ground with three bullets in his body. The first to come to his aid, the paper said, was his assistant Leishman, who was in the office at the time. Working-men, engaged on a carpenter job in the building, rushed in, and one of them felled Berkman to the ground with a hammer. At first they thought Frick dead. Then a cry was heard from him. Berkman had crawled over and got near enough to strike Frick with a dagger in the thigh. After that he was pounded into unconsciousness. He came to in the station-house, but he would answer no questions. One of the detectives grew suspicious about the appearance of Berkman's face and he nearly broke the young man's jaw trying to open his mouth. A peculiar capsule was found hidden there. When asked what it was, Berkman replied with defiant contempt: " Candy." On examination it proved to be a dynamite cartridge. The police were sure of conspiracy. They were now looking for the accomplices, especially for " a certain Bakhmetov, who had registered at one of the Pittsburgh hotels."

I felt that, on the whole, the newspaper accounts were correct. Sasha had taken a poisoned dagger with him. " In case the revolver, like the bomb, fails to work," he had said. Yes, the dagger was poisoned — nothing could save Frick. I was certain that the papers lied when they said that Sasha had fired at Leishman. I remembered how determined he was that no one except Frick should suffer, and I could not believe that working-men would come to the assistance of Frick, their enemy.

In the Group *Autonomie* I found everybody elated over Sasha's act. Peukert reproached me for not having told him for whom I wanted the money and the gun. I waved him aside. He was a weak-kneed revolutionist, I told him; I was convinced that he had been too concerned about himself to respond to my plea. The group decided that the next issue of the *Anarchist,* its weekly paper, should be entirely devoted to our brave comrade, Alexander Berkman, and his heroic deed. I was asked to write an article about Sasha. Except for a small contribution to the *Freiheit* upon one occasion, I had never written for publication before. I was much worried, fearing I should not be able to do justice to the subject. But after a night's struggle and the waste of several pads of paper, I succeeded in writing an impassioned tribute to " Alexander Berkman, the avenger of the murdered Homestead men."

The eulogistic tone of the *Anarchist* seemed to act on Most like a red rag on a bull. He had stored up so much antagonism against Sasha, and his bitterness was so great against us for our participation in the hated Peukert group, that he now began pouring it out in the *Freiheit,* not openly, but in an indirect and insidious way. The following week the *Freiheit* carried a sharp attack on Frick. But the *Attentat* against him was belittled and Sasha made to appear ludicrous. In his article Most hinted that Sasha had " shot off a toy pistol." The arrest of Nold and Bauer in Pittsburgh Most condemned in unmeasured terms, pointing out that they could have had nothing to do with the attempt on Frick, because they had " mistrusted Berkman from the first."

It was true, of course, that the two comrades knew nothing about the planned act. Sasha had decided before he left not to tell them, but I knew that Most had lied when he said that they mistrusted him. Certainly not Carl Nold; Sasha had written me how friendly Carl had been to him. It was only Most's vindictiveness, his desire to discredit Sasha, that had induced him to write as he did.

It was cruelly disillusioning to find the man I had worshipped, loved, and believed in prove himself so unspeakably small. Whatever his personal feelings against Sasha, whom he had always considered his rival, how could Johann Most, the stormy petrel of my fancy, attack Sasha? Great bitterness welled up in my heart against him. I was consumed by the desire to beat back his thrusts, to proclaim aloud the purity and idealism of Sasha, to shout it so passionately that the whole world should hear and know it. Most had declared war — so be it! I would meet his attacks in the *Anarchist*.

Meanwhile the daily press carried on a ferocious campaign against the anarchists. They called for the police to act, to round up " the instigators, Johann Most, Emma Goldman, and their ilk." My name had rarely before been mentioned in the papers, but now it appeared every day in the most sensational stories. The police got busy; a hunt for Emma Goldman began.

My friend Peppie, with whom I was living, had a flat on Fifth Street and First Avenue, round the corner from the police station. I used to pass the latter frequently, going about openly and spending considerable time at the headquarters of the *Autonomie*. Yet the police seemed unable to find me. One evening, while we were away at a meeting, the police, having discovered my whereabouts at last, broke into the flat through the fire-escape and stole everything they could lay their hands on. My fine collection of revolutionary pamphlets and photographs, my entire correspondence, vanished with them. But they did not find what they came to look for. At the first mention of my name in the papers I had disposed of the material left over from Sasha's experiments. Since the police found nothing incriminating, they went after Peppie's servant, but she was too terrorized by the very sight of an officer to give them information. She stoutly denied that she had ever seen any man in the flat who looked like the photograph of Sasha which the detectives had shown her.

Two days after the raid the landlord ordered us out of the flat. This was followed by a more serious blow — Mollock, Peppie's husband, who was working on Long Island, was kidnapped and spirited away to Pittsburgh, charged with complicity in Sasha's act.

Several days after the *Attentat* militia regiments were marched into Homestead. The more conscious of the steel-workers opposed the move, but they were overruled by the conservative labour element, who foolishly saw in the soldiers protection against new attacks by Pinkertons. The troops soon proved whom they came to protect. It was the Carnegie mills, not the Homestead workers.

However, there was one militiaman who was wide awake enough to see in Sasha the avenger of labour's wrongs. This brave boy gave vent to his feelings by calling in the ranks for " three cheers for the man who shot Frick." He was court-martialled and strung up by his thumbs, but he stuck to his cheers. This incident was the one bright moment in the black and harassing days that followed Sasha's departure.

After a long, anxious wait a letter came from Sasha. He had been greatly cheered by the stand of the militiaman, W. L. Iams, he wrote. It showed that even American soldiers were waking up. Could I not get in touch with the boy, send him anarchist literature? He would be a valuable asset to the movement. I was not to worry about himself; he was in fine spirits and already preparing his court speech — not as a defence, he emphasized, but in explanation of his act. Of course, he would have no lawyer; he would represent his own case as true Russian and other European revolutionists did. Prominent Pittsburgh attorneys had offered their services free of charge, but he had declined. It was inconsistent for an anarchist to employ lawyers; I should make his attitude on the matter clear to the comrades. What was that about Hans Wurst (our nickname for Most in order to shield him) ? Someone had written him that Most had not approved of his act. Could it possibly be? How stupid of the authorities to arrest Nold and Bauer! They had known nothing whatever about his act. In fact, he had told them he was leaving for St. Louis and bidden them good-bye, thereupon taking a hotel room and registering under the name of Bakhmetov.

I pressed the letter to my heart, covering it with kisses. I knew how intensely my Sasha felt, although he had said not one word about his love and his thoughts of me.

I was considerably alarmed about his decision to represent his own case. I loved his beautiful consistency, but I knew that his English, like my own, was too poor to be effective in court. I feared he would have no chance. But Sasha's wish, now more than ever, was sacred to me, and I consoled myself with the hope that he would have a public trial, that I could have his speech translated, and that we might give the whole proceedings countrywide publicity. I wrote him that I agreed with his decision, and that we were preparing a large meeting where his act would be fully explained and his motives properly presented. I told him of the enthusiasm in the *Autonomie* group and in the ranks of the Jewish comrades; of the fine stand the socialist *Volkszeitung* had taken, and of the encouraging attitude of the Italian revolutionists. I added that we all rejoiced over the courage of the young militiaman, but that he was not the only one who admired Sasha and gloried in his act. I tried to put the derogatory items that had appeared in the *Freiheit* as mildly as possible; I did not wish him disturbed. Still, it was bitterly hard to have to admit that Most had justified Sasha's opinion of him.

We began to prepare for the large meeting on behalf of Sasha. Joseph Barondess was one of the first to offer his help. Since I had seen him a year previously, he had been condemned to prison in connexion with a new cloakmaker strike, but had been pardoned by the Governor of New York State at the request of union labour and in response to his own letter asking for a pardon. Dyer D. Lum, who had been a close friend of Albert Parsons, volunteered to speak; Saverio Merlino, the brilliant Italian anarchist, then in New York, would also address the meeting. My spirits rose: Sasha still had true and devoted comrades.

Our large red posters announcing the mass meeting roused the ire of the press. Were the authorities not going to interfere? The police came out with the threat that our gathering would be stopped, but on the appointed evening the audience was so large and looked so determined that the police did nothing.

I acted as chairman, a new experience for me; but we could get no one else. The meeting was very spirited, every one of the speakers paying the highest tribute to Sasha and his deed. My hatred of conditions which compelled idealists to acts of violence made me cry out in passionate strains the nobility of Sasha, his selflessness, his consecration to the people.

" Possessed by a fury," the papers said of my speech the next morning. " How long will this dangerous woman be permitted to go on? " Ah, if they only knew how I yearned to give up my freedom, to proclaim loudly my share in the deed — if only they knew!

The new landlord notified Peppie that she would have either to ask me to move out or vacate. Poor Peppie! She was being made to suffer for me. When I returned home that night, after a late meeting, I missed the night key in my bag. I was sure I had put it there in the morning. Not wishing to wake the janitor, I sat on the stoop waiting for some tenant to arrive. At last someone came and let me into the house. When I tried to open the door of Peppie's apartment, it refused to yield. I knocked repeatedly, but there was no answer. I grew alarmed, thinking something might have happened. I knocked violently, and finally the servant came out and informed me that her mistress had sent her to say that I must keep away from the flat, because she could no longer endure being pestered by the landlord and the police. Dashing past the woman, I seized hold of Peppie in the kitchen and shook her roughly, berating her as a coward. In the bedroom I gathered up my things, while Peppie broke down in tears. She had locked me out, she whimpered, because of the children, who had been frightened by detectives. I walked out in silence.

I went to the home of my grandmother. She had not seen me for a long time, and she was startled by my looks. She insisted that I was ill and that I must remain with her. Grandmother kept a grocery store on Tenth Street and Avenue B. Her two rooms she shared with the family of her married daughter. The only place for me was the kitchen, where I could go in and out without disturbing the others. Grandmother offered to get me a cot, and both she and her daughter busied themselves to prepare breakfast for me and make me at home.

The papers began reporting that Frick was recovering from his wounds. Comrades visiting me expressed the opinion that Sasha, " had failed." Some even had the effrontery to suggest that Most might have been right in saying that " it was a toy pistol." I was stung to the quick. I knew that Sasha had never had much practice in shooting. Occasionally, at German picnics, he would take part in target-shooting, but was that sufficient? I was sure Sasha's failure to kill Frick was due to the cheap quality of his revolver — he had lacked enough money to buy a good one.

Perhaps Frick was recovering because of the attention he was getting? The greatest surgeons of America had been called to his bedside. Yes, it must be that; after all, three bullets from Sasha's revolver had lodged in his body. It was Frick's wealth that was enabling him to recover. I tried to explain this to the comrades, but most of them remained unconvinced. Some even hinted that Sasha was at liberty. I was frantic — how dared they doubt Sasha? I would write him! I would ask him to send me word that would stop the horrible rumours about him.

Soon a letter arrived from Sasha, written in a curt tone. He was provoked that I could even ask for an explanation. Did I not know that the vital thing was the motive of his act and not its physical success or failure? My poor, tortured boy! I could read between the lines how crushed he was at the realization that Frick remained alive. But he was right: the important thing was his motives, and these no one could doubt.

Weeks passed without any indication of when Sasha's trial would begin. He was still kept on " Murderers' Row " in the Pittsburgh jail, but the fact that Frick was improving had considerably changed Sasha's legal status. He could not be condemned to death. Through comrades in Pennsylvania I learned that the law called for seven years in prison for his attempt. Hope entered my heart. Seven years are a long time, but Sasha was strong, he had iron perseverance, he could hold out. I clung to the new possibility with every fibre of my being.

My own life was full of misery. Grandmother's place was too crowded and I could not prolong my visit with her. I went in search of a room, but my name seemed to frighten the landlords. My friends suggested that I give an assumed name, but I would not deny my identity.

Often I would sit in a café on Second Avenue until three in the morning, or I would ride back and forth to the Bronx in a street-car. The poor old horses seemed as tired as I, their pace was so slow. I wore a blue and white striped dress and a long, grey coat that resembled a nurse's uniform. Soon I found that it gave me considerable protection. Conductors and policemen would often ask me whether I had just come off duty and was taking a breath of air. One young policeman on Tompkins Square was particularly solicitous about me. He frequently entertained me with stories in his luscious Irish brogue, or he would tell me just to snooze off, that he would be near enough to protect me. " You look all in, kid," he would say; " you're working too hard, ain't you? " I had told him that I was on day and night duty, with only a few hours' respite. I could not help laughing inwardly over the humour of my being protected by a policeman! I wondered how my cop would act if he knew who the demure-looking nurse was.

On Fourth Street near Third Avenue I had often passed a house which always had a sign out: "Furnished Room to Rent." One day I went in. No questions were asked about my identity. The room was small, but the rent was high, four dollars a week. The surroundings looked rather peculiar, but I hired the room.

In the evening I discovered that the whole house was tenanted by girls. I paid no attention at first, being busy putting my belongings in order. Weeks had passed since I had unpacked my clothes and books. It was such a comforting sensation to be able to take a scrub, to lie down on a clean bed. I retired early, but was awakened at night by someone knocking on my door. "Who is it?" I called, still heavy with sleep. "Say, Viola, ain't you goin' to let me in? I've been knockin' for twenty minutes. What the hell is up? You said I could come to-night." "You're in the wrong place, mister," I replied; "I'm not Viola."

Similar episodes happened every night for some time. Men called for Annette, for Mildred, or Clothilde. It finally dawned on me that I was living in a brothel.

The girl in the room next to mine was a sympathetic-looking youngster, and one day I invited her for coffee. I learned from her that the place was not a "regular dump, with a Madam," but that it was a rooming-house where girls were allowed to bring their men. She asked if I was doing good business, as I was so young. When I told her that I was not in the business, that I was only a dressmaker, the girl jeered. It took me some time to convince her that I was not looking for men customers. What better place could I have found than this house full of girls who must need dresses? I began to consider whether to remain in the house or move out. The thought of living within sight and sound of the life around me made me feel ill. My gracious stranger had been right — I had no knack for such things. There was also the fear that the papers might find out about the nature of the place I was in. Anarchists were already outrageously misrepresented; it would be grist to the capitalistic mill if they could proclaim that Emma Goldman had been found in a house of prostitution. I saw the necessity of moving out. But I remained. The hardships of the weeks since Sasha had gone, the prospect of again having to join the host of the shelterless, outweighed all other considerations.

Before the week was over, I had become the confidante of most of the girls. They competed with one another in being kind to me, in giving me their sewing to do and helping in little ways. For the first time since my return from Worcester I was able to earn my living. I had my own corner and I had made new friends. But my life was not destined to run smoothly for long.

The feud between Most and our group continued. Hardly a week passed without some slur in the *Freiheit* against Sasha or myself. It was painful enough to be called vile names by the man who had once loved me, but it was beyond endurance to have Sasha slandered and maligned. Then came Most's article "*Attentats-Reflexionen* (Reflections on Propaganda by Deed)" in the *Freiheit* of August 27, which was a complete reversal of everything that Most had till then persistently advocated. Most, whom I had heard scores of times call for acts of violence, who had gone to prison in England for his glorification of tyrannicide — Most, the incarnation of defiance and revolt, now deliberately repudiated the *Tat!* I wondered if he really believed what he wrote. Was his article prompted by his hatred of Sasha, or written to protect himself against the newspaper charge of complicity? He dared even make insinuations against Sasha's motives. The world Most had enriched for me, the life so full of colour and beauty, all lay shattered at my feet. Only the naked fact remained that Most had betrayed his ideal, had betrayed us.

I resolved to challenge him publicly to prove his insinuations, to compel him to explain his sudden reversal of attitude in the face of danger. I replied to his article, in the *Anarchist*, demanding an explanation and branding Most as a traitor and a coward. I waited for two weeks for a reply in the *Freiheit*, but none appeared. There were no proofs, and I knew that he could not justify his base accusations. I bought a horsewhip.

At Most's next lecture I sat in the first row, close to the low platform. My hand was on the whip under my long, grey cloak. When he got up and faced the audience, I rose and declared in a loud voice: "I came to demand proof of your insinuations against Alexander Berkman."

There was instant silence. Most mumbled something about "hysterical woman," but he said nothing else. I then pulled out my whip and leaped towards him. Repeatedly I lashed him across the face and neck, then broke the whip over my knee and threw the pieces at him. It was all done so quickly that no one had time to interfere.

Then I felt myself roughly pulled back. "Throw her out! Beat her up!" people yelled. I was surrounded by an enraged and threatening crowd and might have fared badly had not Fedya, Claus, and other friends come to my rescue. They lifted me up bodily and forced their way out of the hall.

Most's change of position regarding propaganda by deed, his inimical attitude towards Sasha's act, his insinuations against the latter's motive, and his attacks upon me caused widespread dissension in the anarchist ranks. It was no more a feud between Most and Peukert and their adherents. It raised a storm within the entire anarchist movement, splitting it into two inimical camps. Some stood by Most, others defended Sasha and eulogized his act. The strife grew so bitter that I was even refused admission to a Jewish meeting on the East Side, the stronghold of Most's faithful. My public punishment of their adored teacher roused furious antagonism against me and made me a pariah.

Meanwhile we were anxiously waiting for the date of Sasha's trial to be set, but no information was forthcoming. In the second week of September I was invited to speak in Baltimore, my lecture being scheduled for Monday, the 19th. As I was about to ascend the platform, a telegram was handed to me. The trial had taken place that very day and Sasha had been condemned to twenty-two years in prison! Railroaded to a living death! The hall and the audience began to swim before my eyes. Someone took the telegram out of my hands and pushed me into a chair. A glass of water was held to my lips. The meeting must be called off, the comrades said.

I looked wildly about me, gulped down some water, snatched up the telegram, and leaped to the platform. The yellow piece of paper in my hand was a glowing coal, its fire searing my heart and flaming it into passionate expression. It caught the audience and raised it to ferment. Men and women jumped to their feet, calling for vengeance against the ferocious sentence. Their burning fervour in the cause of Sasha and his act resounded like thunder through the great hall.

The police burst in with drawn clubs and drove the audience out of the building. I remained on the platform, the telegram still in my hand. Officers came up and put the chairman and me under arrest. On the street we were pushed into a waiting patrol wagon and driven to the station-house, followed by the incensed crowd.

I had been surrounded by people from the moment the crushing news had come, compelled to suppress the turmoil in my soul and force back

the hot tears that kept swelling in my throat. Now, free from intrusion, the monstrous sentence loomed up before me in all its horror.
Twenty-two years! Sasha was twenty-one, at the most impressionable
and vivid age. The life he had not yet lived was before him, holding
out the charm and beauty his intense nature could extract. And now
he was cut down like a strong young tree, robbed of sun and of light.
And Frick was alive, almost recovered from his wounds and now
recuperating in his palatial summer house. He would go on spilling the
blood of labour. Frick was alive, and Sasha doomed to twenty-two
years in a living tomb. The irony, the bitter irony of the thing, struck
me full in the face.

If only I could shut out the ghastly picture and give vent to tears,
find forgetfulness in everlasting sleep! But there were no tears, there
was no sleep. There was only Sasha — Sasha in convict's clothes, captive behind stone walls — Sasha with his pale set face pressed to the
iron bars, his steady eyes gazing intently upon me, bidding me go on.

No, no, no, there must be no despair. I would live, I would fight for
Sasha. I would rend the black clouds closing on him, I would rescue
my boy, I would bring him back to life!

CHAPTER X

WHEN I RETURNED TO NEW YORK TWO DAYS LATER, HAVING been discharged by the Baltimore police magistrate with a strong admonition never again to come back to the city, a letter from Sasha was awaiting me. It was written in very small but distinct script and gave the details of the Monday in court. He had repeatedly tried to learn the date of his trial, the letter read, but he could not procure any information about it. On the morning of the 19th he was suddenly ordered to get ready. He had barely time to gather up the sheets of his speech. Strange and antagonistic faces met him in the court-room. In vain he strained his eye for the sight of his friends. He realized that they, too, must have been kept in ignorance of the day of the trial. Yet he hoped against hope for the miracle. But there was not a friendly face anywhere. He was confronted with six indictments, all manufactured from the one act, and among them one charging him with an attempt on the life of John G. A. Leishman, Frick's assistant. Sasha declared that he knew nothing of Leishman; it was Frick whom he had come to kill. He demanded that he be tried on that charge alone, and that the other indictments be quashed, because they were all involved in the major charge. But his objection was overruled.

The jurors were selected in a few minutes, Sasha making no use of his right of challenge. What difference did it make? They were all alike, and he would be convicted anyhow. He declared to the Court that he scorned to defend himself; he wanted only to explain his act. The interpreter assigned to him translated haltingly and wrongly, and after several attempts to correct him Sasha discovered to his horror that the man was blind, as blind as justice in the American courts. He then tried to address the jury in English, but he was impatiently stopped by Judge McClung, who declared that " the prisoner has said enough already." Sasha protested, but in vain. The

District Attorney stepped into the jury-box and held a low conversation with the talesmen, whereupon they brought in a verdict of guilty without even leaving their seats. The Judge was curt and denunciatory. He passed sentence on each count separately, including three indictments for "entering a building with felonious intent," giving the prisoner the maximum on each charge. The total amounted to twenty-one years in the Western Penitentiary of Pennsylvania, at the expiration of which time an additional year was to be served in the Allegheny County Workhouse for "carrying concealed weapons."

Twenty-two years of slow torture and death! He had done his duty, Sasha's letter concluded, and now the end had come. He would depart as he had determined, by his own will and hand. He wanted no effort made in his behalf. It would be of no use and he could not give his consent to an appeal to the enemy. No need of further help for him; whatever campaign could be made must be for his act, and I was to see to that. He was sure that no one else felt and understood his motives so well, no one else could clarify the meaning of his deed with the same conviction. His one deep longing now was for me. If he could only look into my eyes once more and press me to his heart— but as that was denied him, he would keep on thinking of me, his friend and comrade. No power on earth could take that away from him.

I felt Sasha's spirit lifted above everything earthly. Like a brilliant star it illumined my own dark thoughts and brought home to me the realization that there was something greater than personal ties or even love: an all-embracing devotion that understands all and gives all to the last breath.

Sasha's terrible sentence aroused Most to a virulent attack on the courts of Pennsylvania and the judicial criminal who could give a man twenty-two years for an act that legally called for only seven. His article in the *Freiheit* increased my bitterness against him, for had he not helped to weaken the effect of Sasha's deed? I was certain that the enemy would not have dared to railroad Sasha if there had been a concerted radical protest in his behalf. I held Most much more responsible for the inhuman sentence than the Court of the State of Pennsylvania.

Sasha was by no means without friends. They proved their loyalty from the very first. Now two groups came forward to organize the campaign for the commutation of his sentence. The East Side group comprised various social elements, labour men, and leading Jewish socialists. Among them were M. Zametkin, an old Russian revolutionary; Louis Miller, an energetic and influential man in the ghetto; and Isaac Hourwitch, a comparatively recent arrival in America after his exile in Siberia. The last was especially ardent as a spokesman for Sasha. There was also Shevitch, who had from the beginning defended Sasha in the German daily *Volkszeitung,* of which he was editor-in-chief. Our friend Solotaroff, Annie Netter, young Michael Cohn, and others were the most active in the East Side group.

The moving spirit of the American group was Dyer D. Lum, a man of exceptional abilities, a poet and writer on economic and philosophical subjects. With him were John Edelman, the gifted architect and publicist; William C. Owen, an Englishman of literary talents, and Justus Schwab, the well-known German anarchist.

It was most encouraging to see the splendid solidarity in the cause of Sasha. I kept him informed of the efforts in his behalf, painting them in exaggerated colours to cheer him. But nothing seemed to avail; he was in the grip of the twenty-two-year sentence. " It is no earthly use to try to do anything for me," he wrote. " It will take years to accomplish a commutation, and I know that Frick and Carnegie will never consent to it. Without their approval the Pennsylvania Board of Pardons will not act. Besides, I cannot continue for long in this living tomb." His letters were dispiriting, but I held on grimly. I knew his indomitable will and his iron strength of character. I clung tenaciously to the hope that he would arouse himself and not allow himself to be crushed. That hope alone gave me the courage to go on. I joined the newly organized efforts for him. Night after night I was at some meeting voicing the meaning and message of Sasha's act.

Early in November came the first sign of Sasha's reawakened interest in life. His letter informed me that he might have the privilege of a visitor. Prisoners were entitled to one visit a month, but only from a near relative. Could I get his sister from Russia to come to see him? I understood what he meant and wrote him immediately to get the pass.

I had been invited by anarchist groups in Chicago and St. Louis to speak at the approaching anniversary of the 11th of November and I decided to combine the trip with a visit to Sasha. I would go as his married sister, under the name of Niedermann. I was certain that the prison authorities knew nothing about Sasha's sister in Russia. I would impersonate her and they would never suspect my identity. I was hardly known then. The pictures of me in the papers in connexion with

Sasha's act were so unlike me that no one could have recognized me from them. To see my boy again, to press him to my heart, to bring him hope and courage — I lived for nothing else during the weeks and days before the visit.

In a fever I made my preparations. My first stop was to be St. Louis; then Chicago; finally Pittsburgh. A letter from Sasha arrived a few days before my departure. It contained a pass from the Chief Prison Inspector of the Western Penitentiary for Mrs. E. Niedermann, sister of Prisoner A-7, for a visit on the 26th of November. Sasha had asked me to instruct his sister to remain in Pittsburgh two days. In view of the fact that she was coming all the way from Russia to see him, the Inspector had promised him a second visit. I was wild with joy, impatient of every hour that kept me from him. The pass for my visit became my amulet. I would not part with it for a moment.

I arrived in Pittsburgh early on the morning of Thanksgiving Day. I was met by Carl Nold and Max Metzkow, the latter a German comrade who had faithfully stood by Sasha. Nold and Bauer were out on bail awaiting trial " for complicity in the attempt on Frick's life." I had been in correspondence with Carl for some time and I was glad of the opportunity to meet the young comrade who had been kind to Sasha. He was of small stature, frail, with intelligent eyes and a shock of black hair. We greeted each other like old friends.

In the afternoon I went out to Allegheny, accompanied by Metzkow. It was decided that Nold should stay away; he was often followed by detectives and we were afraid that my identity might be discovered before I had a chance to get inside the prison. Not far from the penitentiary Metzkow remained to await my return.

The grey stone building, the high forbidding walls, the armed guards, the oppressive silence in the hall where I was told to wait, and the minutes creeping into endless time settled on my heart with the weight of a nightmare. In vain I tried to shake myself free. At last a harsh voice called: "This way, Mrs. Niedermann." I was taken through several iron doors, along twisting corridors, into a small room. Sasha was there, a tall guard beside him.

My first impulse was to rush up to him and cover him with kisses, but the presence of the guard checked me. Sasha approached me and put his arms around me. As he bent over to kiss me, I felt a small object pass into my mouth.

For weeks I had been looking forward eagerly, anxiously to this visit. A thousand times I had gone over in my mind all I would say to him of my love and undying devotion, of the struggle I was making for his release, but all I could do was to press his hand and look into his eyes.

We began to speak in our beloved Russian, but we were stopped immediately by the cold command of the guard: "Talk English. No foreign languages here." His lynx-like eyes followed our every movement, watched our lips, crept into our very minds. I became tongue-tied, numb in every nerve. Sasha, too, was mute; his fingers kept on playing with my watch-chain and he seemed to hold on to it as a drowning man to a straw. Neither of us could utter a word, but our eyes spoke to each other — of our fears, our hopes, our yearnings.

The visit lasted twenty minutes. Another embrace, another touch of our lips, and our " time was up." I whispered to him to hold on, to hold out, and then I found myself on the prison steps. The iron gate clattered shut behind me.

I wanted to scream, to throw my weight against the door, to pound it with my fists. But the gate stared back at me and mocked. I walked along the front of the prison and into the street. I walked, silently weeping, towards the spot where I had left Metzkow. His presence brought me back to reality and made me conscious of the object Sasha had given me with his kiss. I took it out of my mouth — a small roll tightly wrapped. We went into the back room of a saloon and I unwound the several layers of paper. At last appeared a note with Sasha's diminutive handwriting, each word standing out like a pearl before me. "You must go to Inspector Reed," it read; " he promised me a second pass. Go to his jewellery shop tomorrow. I am counting on you. I'll give you another message of importance — the same way."

I went to Reed's store the next day. I looked shabby in my thread-bare coat amid the sparkling jewellery, silver, and gold. I asked to see Mr. Reed. He was a tall, emaciated, thin-lipped creature, with hard and piercing eyes. No sooner had I given my name than he exclaimed: " So this is Berkman's sister! " Yes, he had promised him a second visit, though he did not deserve any kindness. Berkman was a murderer, he had tried to kill a good Christian man. I held on to myself by sheer force; my chance to see Sasha again was at stake. He would call up the prison, Reed continued, to find out at what time I could be admitted. I was to return in an hour.

My heart sank. I had a distinct premonition that there would be no more visits for Sasha. But I came back as directed. As soon as Mr. Reed saw me, his face turned purple and he fairly leaped at me. " You deceiver ! " he yelled. " You have already been at the penitentiary ! You sneaked in under a false name as his sister. You don't get away with such lies here — you have been recognized by a guard ! You are Emma Goldman, that criminal's mistress ! There will be no more visits. You might as well make up your mind about it — Berkman will never get out alive ! "

He had gone behind the glass counter, which was covered with silverware. In my indignation and rage I swept everything to the floor — plates, coffee-pots and pitchers, jewellery and watches. I seized a heavy tray and was about to throw it at him when I was pulled back by one of the clerks, who shouted to someone to run for the police. Reed, white with fear and frothing at the mouth, signalled to the clerk. " No police," I heard him say; " no scandal. Just kick her out." The clerk advanced towards me, then stopped. " Murderer, coward ! " I cried; " if you harm Berkman, I will kill you with my own hands ! "

No one moved. I walked out and boarded a street-car. I made sure of not being followed before returning to Metzkow's home. In the evening, when he came back with Nold from work, I told them what had happened. They were alarmed. They regretted that I had lost control of myself, because it would react on Sasha. They agreed that I would have to get out of Pittsburgh at once. The Inspector might put detectives on my trail and have me arrested. The Pennsylvania authorities had been trying to get me ever since Sasha's act.

I was shocked by the thought that Sasha might indeed have to suffer as a result of my outbreak. But the threat of the Inspector that Sasha would never come out of prison alive had been too much for me. I was sure Sasha would understand.

The night was black as I walked with Nold to the station to take the train for New York. The steel-foundries belched huge flames that reflected the Allegheny hills blood-red and filled the air with soot and smoke. We made our way past the sheds where human beings, half man, half beast, were working like the galley-slaves of an era long past. Their naked bodies, covered only with small trunks, shone like copper in the glare of the red-hot chunks of iron they were snatching from the mouths of the flaming monsters. From time to time the steam rising from the water thrown on the hot metal would completely envelop the men; then they would emerge again like shadows. " The children of hell," I said, " damned to the everlasting inferno of heat and noise." Sasha had given his life to bring joy to these slaves, but they had remained blind and continued in the hell of their own forging. "Their souls are dead, dead to the horror and degradation of their lives."

Carl related to me what he knew about Sasha in his Pittsburgh days. It was true that Henry Bauer had suspected Sasha. Henry was a fanatical follower of Most, who had warned him against us as renegades, telling him that we had allied ourselves with "that spy Peukert." When Sasha arrived at the height of the Homestead trouble, Bauer was already prejudiced against him. Henry had confided to Nold that he would examine Sasha's bag while he was asleep and that if he found anything incriminating, he would kill Sasha. With loaded gun Bauer had slept in the same room with Sasha, alert for any suspicious movement and ready to shoot. Nold had been so impressed with Sasha by his open countenance and directness that he could not possibly suspect him. He had agreed with Bauer, trying to convince him that Most was unfair and prejudiced against everyone who disagreed with him. Carl no longer believed so implicitly in Hannes.

Carl's story filled me with horror. What if Sasha had happened to have something in his bag that Bauer might have taken as justifying his suspicions! Enough for the blind Most-worshipper to shoot him! And Most, to what depths his hatred of Sasha had driven him, to what despicable methods! What was there in human passion that forced men to such lengths? My own, for instance, that compelled me to horsewhip Most, to hate him now as he had always hated Sasha, to hate the man I had once loved, the man who had been my ideal. It was all so painfully disturbing, so frightful. I could not grasp it.

Of his own trial Carl spoke lightly. He would even welcome a few years in prison to be near Sasha, to help him bear his heavy ordeal. Faithful Carl! His trust in Sasha and his faith brought me close to him, made him very dear.

Far in the distance, as the train sped on, I could still see the belching flames shoot against the black sky, lighting up the hills of Allegheny. Allegheny, which held what was most precious to me immured perhaps for ever! I had planned the *Attentat* together with him; I had let him go alone; I had approved of his decision to have no lawyer. I strove to shake off the consciousness of guilt, but it would give me no rest until I found forgetfulness in sleep.

CHAPTER XI

OUR WORK FOR THE COMMUTATION OF SASHA'S SENTENCE CONtinued. At one of our weekly meetings, in the latter part of December, I became conscious of the steady gaze of a man in the audience. He was tall and broad, well built, with soft blond hair and blue eyes. I particularly noticed the peculiar motion of his right leg, swinging back and forth regularly, while his hand kept steadily playing with matches. His monotonous movements were making me drowsy and I repeatedly had to rouse myself with an effort. Finally I walked over to the man and playfully took the matches away from him, remarking: " Children are not allowed to play with fire." " All right, grandmother," he replied in the same spirit, " but you should know that I am a revolutionist. I love fire. Don't you? " He smiled at me, exposing beautiful white teeth. " Yes, in its right place," I retorted, " not here, with so many people about. It makes me nervous. And please stop moving your leg." The man apologized; a bad habit he had acquired in prison, he remarked. A feeling of shame overcame me; I thought of Sasha. I begged the man to go on and not to mind me. Perhaps some day he would tell me about his prison experience. " I have a dear friend there now," I said. Evidently he understood whom I meant. " Berkman is a brave man," he replied. " We know about him in Austria and we admire him tremendously for what he did."

I learned that his name was Edward Brady and that he had just arrived from Austria after completing a term of ten years in prison for the publication of illegal anarchist literature. I found him the most scholarly person I had ever met. His field was not limited, like Most's, to social and political subjects; in fact, he rarely talked about them to me. He introduced me to the great classics of English and French literature. He loved to read Goethe and Shakespeare to me,

or translate passages from the French, Jean Jacques Rousseau and
Voltaire being his favourites. His English, although with a German
accent, was perfect. On one occasion I asked him where he had received his schooling. " In prison," he replied unhesitatingly. He modi-
fied it by adding that he had passed through the *Gymnasium* first;
but it was in prison that he had done his real studying. His sister used
to send him English and French dictionaries, and he made it his practice to memorize so many words every day. In solitary confinement he
had always read aloud to himself. It was the only way to survive.
Many went crazy, particularly those who had nothing with which to
occupy their minds. But for people with ideals prison is the best school,
he said. " Then I ought to get to prison as quickly as possible," I remarked, " because I am awfully ignorant." " Don't be in such a hurry,"
he replied; " we have only just met and you are too young for prison."
" Berkman was only twenty-one," I told him. " Yes, that is the pity of
it." His voice trembled. " I was thirty when I was imprisoned. I had
already lived intensely."

He asked about my childhood and schooldays, evidently trying to
change the subject. I had only had three and a half years of *Realschule*
in Königsberg, I told him. The régime was harsh, the instructors brutal; I learned scarcely anything. Only my teacher of German had been
kind to me. She was a sick woman, slowly dying of consumption, but
patient and tender. She would often invite me to her home and give
me extra lessons. She was particularly anxious for me to know her favourite writers: Marlitt, Auerbach, Heise, Lindau, and Spielhagen.
She loved Marlitt more than the others; so I, too, loved Marlitt. We
used to read her novels together and we would both grow tearful over
the unhappy heroines. My teacher worshipped the royal house; Fred-
erick the Great and Queen Louise were her idols. " The poor Queen
so cruelly treated by that butcher, Napoleon — the gracious, beautiful Queen," she would say with much feeling. She often recited to me
the poem, the daily prayer of the good Queen:

> *Wer nie sein Brot in Tränen ass —*
> *Wer nie die kummervollen Nächte auf seinem Bette weinend sass —*
> *Der kennt euch nicht, Ihr himmlischen Mächte.*

The moving stanza completely captured me. I, too, became a devotee
of Queen Louise.

Two of my teachers had been altogether terrible. One, a German

Jew, was our instructor in religion; the other taught geography. I hated them both. Occasionally I would avenge myself on the former for his constant beatings, but I was too terrorized by the other even to complain at home.

The great joy of our religious instructor used to be to beat the palms of our hands with a ruler. I used to organize schemes to annoy him: stick pins in his upholstered chair, stealthily tie his long coat-tails to the table, put snails in his pockets — anything I could think of to pay him back for the pain of his ruler. He knew I was the ring-leader and he beat me the more for it. But it was a frank feud that could be met in the open.

Not so with the other man. His methods were less painful, but more dreadful. Every afternoon he would keep one or two of the girls after school-hours. When everybody had left the building, he would send one girl to the next class-room, then force the other on his knee and grasp her breasts or put his hands between her legs. He would promise her good marks if she kept quiet and threaten instant dismissal if she talked. The girls were terrorized into silence. I did not know for a long time about these things, until one day I found myself on his knee. I screamed, reached for his beard, and pulled it violently in my attempt to wriggle out of his hold. He jumped up, and I fell to the floor. He ran to the door to see if anyone was coming in response to my cry; then he hissed into my ear: " If you breathe one word, I'll kick you out of school."

For several days I was too sick with fright to return to school, but I would not say anything. The dread of being dismissed brought back the remembrance of Father's fury whenever I returned with bad marks. I went back to school at last, and for some days the geography lessons passed without incident. Because of my poor eyesight I had to stand close to the map. One day the teacher whispered to me: " You will remain behind." " I will not! " I whispered back. The next moment I felt a stinging pain in my arm. He had stuck his nails into my flesh. My cries broke up the class and brought other instructors to the room. I heard our teacher telling them that I was a dullard, that I never knew my lessons and therefore he had to punish me. I was sent home.

At night my arm hurt a great deal. Mother noticed that it was all swollen and she sent for the doctor, who questioned me. His kindly manner led me to tell him the whole story. " Terrible! " he exclaimed; " the fellow belongs to the madhouse." A week later when I returned to school our geography-teacher was no longer there. He had gone on a journey, we were told.

When the time came for me to join Father in St. Petersburg, I hated to go. I could not part from my sick teacher of German, who had taught me to love everything Teutonic. She had induced one of her friends to give me French and music lessons and had promised to help me through the *Gymnasium*. She wanted me to continue my education in Germany, and I dreamed of studying medicine so that I could be helpful in the world. After much pleading and many tears Mother consented to let me remain with my grandmother in Königsberg, provided I would pass the entrance examination for the *Gymnasium*. I worked day and night and I passed. But to become enrolled I needed a certificate of good character from my religious teacher. I loathed the idea of asking the man for anything; but I felt that my whole future depended on it, and I went to him. In front of the whole class he announced that he would never give me " a good character." I had none, he declared; I was a terrible child and would grow into a worse woman. I had no respect for my elders or for authority, and I would surely end on the gallows as a public menace. I went home heart-broken, but Mother promised to permit me to continue my studies in St. Petersburg. Unfortunately her plans did not materialize. I got only six months of study in Russia. However, the spiritual influences from my association with Russian students were most valuable.

" Those teachers must have been regular beasts," Brady declared; " but you will admit that your religious fellow had a prophetic eye. You are already considered a public menace, and if you go on, you may be given a distinguished death. But console yourself; better people die on the gallows than in palaces."

Gradually a beautiful comradery matured between Brady and me. I now called him Ed. " The other sounds conventional," he had said. At his suggestion we started reading French together, beginning with *Candide*. I read slowly, haltingly, my pronunciation atrocious. But he was a born teacher, and his patience was boundless. On Sundays Ed would play host in the two-room apartment to which I had moved. Fedya and I would be ordered out of the flat until the meal was ready. Ed was a marvellous cook. On rare occasions I would be given the privilege of watching him prepare the meal. He would explain minutely, with evident gusto, every dish and I soon proved a much better pupil in cooking than in French. I learned to prepare many dishes before we were through reading *Candide.*

On Saturdays when I did not have to lecture, we used to visit the saloon of Justus Schwab, the most famous radical centre in New York. Schwab was the traditional Teuton in appearance, over six feet tall, broad-chested, and straight as a tree. On his wide shoulders and strong neck rested a magnificent head, framed in curly red hair and beard. His eyes were full of fire and intensity. But it was his voice, deep and tender, that was his peculiar characteristic. It would have made him famous if he had chosen an operatic career. Justus was too much the rebel and the dreamer, however, to care about such things. The rear room of his little place on First Street was a Mecca for French Communards, Spanish and Italian refugees, Russian politicals, and German socialists and anarchists who had escaped the iron heel of Bismarck. Everyone gathered at Justus's. Justus, as we affectionately called him, was the comrade, adviser, and friend of all. The circle was interspersed with many Americans, among them writers and artists. John Swinton, Ambrose Bierce, James Huneker, Sadakichi Hartmann, and other literati loved to listen to Justus's golden voice, drink his delicious beer and wine, and argue world-problems far into the night. Together with Ed I became a regular frequenter. Ed would dilate on the subtleties of some English, French, or German word, a group of philologists his forum. I would clash swords with Huneker and his friends about anarchism. Justus loved those battles and would urge me on. Then he would pat me on the back and say: " Emmachen, your head is not made for a hat; it is made for the rope. Just look at those soft curves — the rope would easily snuggle into them." At which Ed would wince.

The sweet companionship with Ed did not eliminate Sasha from my mind. Ed was also deeply interested in him and he joined the groups that were carrying on a systematic campaign in Sasha's behalf. Meanwhile Sasha had established an underground mail route. His official notes contained little about himself, but they spoke kindly of the prison chaplain, who had given him books and was showing human interest. His underground letters evidenced how outraged he felt over the sentence of Bauer and Nold. But they also breathed a little hope; he no longer felt so alone, with his two comrades under the same roof. He was trying to establish communication with them, his friends having been placed in a different wing of the prison. For the present, letters from the outside were his only link with life. I must urge our friends to write him often.

The consciousness that my correspondence would be read by the prison censor haunted me. The written words seemed cold and matter-of-fact, yet I wanted Sasha to feel that whatever happened in my life, whoever entered it, he would remain in it always. My letters left me dissatisfied and unhappy. But life went on. I had to work ten, sometimes twelve hours a day at the sewing-machine to earn my living. Almost nightly meetings and the need of improving my neglected education kept me engaged all the time. Somehow Ed made me feel that need more than anyone else had done.

Our friendship gradually ripened into love. Ed became indispensable to me. I had known for a long time that he also cared for me. Of unusual reserve, he had never spoken of his love, but his eyes and his touch were eloquent of it. He had had women in his life before. One of them had given him a daughter, who was living with her mother's parents. He felt grateful to those women, he would often say. They had taught him the mysteries and subtleties of sex. I could not follow Ed when he spoke of these matters, and I was too shy to ask for an explanation. But I used to wonder what he meant. Sex had seemed a simple process to me. My own sex life had always left me dissatisfied, longing for something I did not know. I considered love more important than all else, love which finds supreme joy in selfless giving.

In the arms of Ed I learned for the first time the meaning of the great life-giving force. I understood its full beauty, and I eagerly drank its intoxicating joy and bliss. It was an ecstatic song, profoundly soothing by its music and perfume. My little flat in the building known as the " Bohemian Republic," to which I had moved lately, became a temple of love. Often the thought would come to me that so much peace and beauty could not last; it was too wonderful, too perfect. Then I would cling to Ed with a trembling heart. He would hold me close and his unfailing cheer and humour would dispel my dark thoughts. " You are overworked," he would say. " The machine and your constant anxiety about Sasha are killing you."

In the spring I fell ill, began to lose weight, and grew too weak to walk across the room. Physicians ordered immediate rest and a change of climate. My friends persuaded me to leave New York and I went to Rochester, accompanied by a girl who volunteered as nurse.

My sister Helena thought her place too cramped for a patient and she secured for me a room in a house with a large garden. She spent every spare moment with me, unfailing in her love and care. She took me to a lung-specialist who discovered an early stage of tuberculosis and put me on a special diet. Presently I began to improve, and within two months I had recovered sufficiently to take walks. My doctor was planning to send me for the winter to a sanatorium, when developments in New York gave a different turn to the situation.

The industrial crisis of that year had thrown thousands out of employment, and their condition now reached an appalling state. Worst of all was the situation in New York. Jobless workers were being evicted; suffering was growing and suicides multiplying. Nothing was being done to alleviate their misery.

I could no longer remain in Rochester. My reason told me it was reckless to go back in the middle of my cure. I had grown much stronger and had gained weight. I coughed less and the hæmorrhages had stopped. I knew, however, that I was far from well. But something stronger than reason was drawing me back to New York. I longed for Ed; but more compelling was the call of the unemployed, of the workers of the East Side who had given me my labour baptism. I had been with them in their previous struggles; I could not stay away from them now. I left notes behind for the physician and Helena; I did not have the heart to face them.

I had wired Ed and he met me joyously. But when I told him that I had returned to devote myself to the unemployed, his mood changed. It was insanity, he urged; it would mean the loss of everything I had gained in health through my rest. It might even prove fatal. He would not permit it — I was his now — his, to love and protect and watch over.

It was bliss to know that someone cared so much for me, but I felt it at the same time a handicap. His " to hold and protect "? Did he consider me his property, a dependent or a cripple who had to be taken care of by a man? I had thought he believed in freedom, in my right to do as I wished. It was anxiety about me, fear for my health, he assured me, that prompted his words. But if I was determined to resume my efforts, he would help. He was no speaker, but he could be useful in other ways.

Committee sessions, public meetings, collection of food-stuffs, supervising the feeding of the homeless and their numerous children, and, finally, the organization of a mass meeting on Union Square entirely filled my time.

The meeting at Union Square was preceded by a demonstration, the marching columns counting many thousands. The girls and women were in front, I at their head carrying a red banner. Its crimson waved proudly in the air and could be seen for blocks. My soul, too, vibrated with the intensity of the moment.

I had prepared my speech in writing and it seemed to me inspiring, but when I reached Union Square and saw the huge mass of humanity, my notes appeared cold and meaningless.

The atmosphere in the ranks had become very tense, owing to the events of that week. Labour politicians had appealed to the New York legislature for relief of the great distress, but their pleas met with evasions. Meanwhile the unemployed went on starving. The people were outraged by this callous indifference to the suffering of men, women, and children. As a result the air at Union Square was charged with bitterness and indignation, its spirit quickly communicating itself to me. I was scheduled as the last speaker and I could barely endure the long wait. Finally the apologetic oratory was over and my turn came. I heard my name shouted from a thousand throats as I stepped forward. I saw a dense mass before me, their pale, pinched faces upturned to me. My heart beat, my temples throbbed, and my knees shook.

" Men and women," I began amidst sudden silence, " do you not realize that the State is the worst enemy you have? It is a machine that crushes you in order to sustain the ruling class, your masters. Like naïve children you put your trust in your political leaders. You make it possible for them to creep into your confidence, only to have them betray you to the first bidder. But even where there is no direct betrayal, the labour politicians make common cause with your enemies to keep you in leash, to prevent your direct action. The State is the pillar of capitalism, and it is ridiculous to expect any redress from it. Do you not see the stupidity of asking relief from Albany with immense wealth within a stone's throw from here? Fifth Avenue is laid in gold, every mansion is a citadel of money and power. Yet there you stand, a giant, starved and fettered, shorn of his strength. Cardinal Manning long ago proclaimed that ' necessity knows no law ' and that ' the starving man has a right to a share of his neighbour's bread.' Cardinal Manning was an ecclesiastic steeped in the traditions of the Church, which has always been on the side of the rich against the poor. But he had some humanity, and he knew that hunger is a compelling force. You, too, will have to learn that you have a right to share your neighbour's bread. Your neighbours — they have not only stolen your bread, but they are sapping your blood. They will go on robbing you, your children, and your children's children, unless you wake up, unless you become daring enough to demand your rights. Well, then, demonstrate before the palaces of the rich; demand work. If they do not give you work, demand bread. If they deny you both, take bread. It is your sacred right!"

Uproarious applause, wild and deafening, broke from the stillness like a sudden storm. The sea of hands eagerly stretching out towards me seemed like the wings of white birds fluttering.

The following morning I went to Philadelphia to secure relief and help organize the unemployed there. The afternoon papers carried a garbled account of my speech. I had urged the crowd to revolution, they claimed. "Red Emma has great swaying power; her vitriolic tongue was just what the ignorant mob needed to tear down New York." They also stated that I had been spirited away by some husky friends, but that the police were on my track.

In the evening I attended a group meeting, where I met a number of anarchists I had not known before. Natasha Notkin was the active spirit among them. She was the true type of Russian woman revolutionist, with no other interests in life but the movement. A mass meeting was decided upon for Monday, August 21. On that morning the papers brought the news that my whereabouts had been discovered, that detectives were on their way to Philadelphia with a warrant for my arrest. I felt that the important thing for me was to manage to get into the hall and address the meeting before my arrest could take place. It was my first visit to Philadelphia, where I was unknown to the authorities. The New York detectives would hardly be able to identify me by the pictures that had so far appeared in the press. I decided to go to the hall unaccompanied and slip in unnoticed.

The streets near by were blocked with people. No one recognized me as I walked up the flight of steps leading to the meeting-place. Then one of the anarchists greeted me: "Here's Emma!" I waved him aside, but a heavy hand was immediately on my shoulder, and a voice said: "You're under arrest, Miss Goldman." There was a commotion, people ran towards me, but the officers drew their guns and held back the crowd. A detective gripped my arm and pulled me down the stairs into the street. I was given the choice of riding in the patrol wagon or walking to the police station. I chose to walk. The officers attempted to handcuff me, but I assured them there was no need of it, as I did not intend to escape. On our way a man broke through the crowd and ran up to me. He held out his wallet, in case I needed money. The detectives promptly nabbed him and he was put under arrest. I was taken to police headquarters, in the tower of the City Hall, and locked up for the night.

In the morning I was asked whether I was willing to go back with the detectives to New York. "Not of my own free will," I declared. "Very well, we'll keep you until your extradition has been arranged." I was taken into a room where I was weighed, measured, and photographed. I fought desperately against the photographing, but my head was held pinioned. I closed my eyes, and the photograph must have resembled a sleeping beauty that looked like an escaped felon.

My New York friends were alarmed. They deluged me with telegrams and letters. Ed wrote guardedly, but I sensed his love between the lines. He wanted to come to Philadelphia, bring money, and get a lawyer, but I wired him to await developments. Many comrades visited me in the jail, and from them I learned that the meeting had been allowed to proceed after my arrest. Voltairine de Cleyre had taken my place and had protested vigorously against my suppression.

I had heard about this brilliant American girl and I knew that she had been influenced, like myself, by the judicial murder in Chicago, and that she had since become active in anarchist ranks. I had long wanted to meet her and I had visited her upon my arrival in Philadelphia, but I found her ill in bed. She always suffered a sick spell after a meeting, and she had lectured the previous evening. I thought it splendid of her to have gone to the meeting from a sick-bed and to have spoken in my behalf. I was proud of her comradeship.

The second morning after my arrest I was transferred to Moyamensing Prison to await extradition. I was put into a fairly large cell, its door of solid sheet iron, with a small square in the centre opening from the outside. The window was high and heavily barred. The cell contained a sanitary toilet, running water, a tin cup, a wooden table, a bench, and an iron cot. A small electric lamp hung from the ceiling. From time to time the square in the door would open and a pair of eyes would look in, or a voice would call for the cup and it would be passed back to me filled with tepid water or soup and a slice of bread. Except for such interruptions silence prevailed.

After the second day the stillness became oppressive and the hours crept on endlessly. I grew weary from constant pacing between the window and the door. My nerves were tense with the strain for some human sound. I called for the matron, but no one answered. I banged my tin cup against the door. Finally it brought response. My door was unlocked and a large woman with a hard face came into the cell. It was against the rules to make so much noise, she warned me. If I did it again, she would have to punish me. What did I want? I wanted my mail, I told her. I was sure there was some from my friends, and I also wanted books to read. She would bring a book, but there was no mail, the matron said. I knew she was lying, for I was certain Ed had written, even if no one else. She went out, locking the door after her. Presently she returned with a book. It was the Bible and it recalled to my mind the cruel face of my religious instructor in school. Indignantly I flung the volume at the matron's feet. I had no need of religious lies; I wanted some human book, I told her. For a moment she stood horror-stricken; then she began raging at me. I had desecrated God's word; I would be put in the dungeon; later on I would burn in hell. I replied heatedly that she did not dare punish me, because I was a prisoner of the State of New York, that I had not yet been tried and therefore still had some civil rights. She flung out, slamming the door after her.

In the evening I had a violent headache, caused by the electric light scorching my eyes. I again knocked on the door and demanded to see the doctor. Another woman came, the prison physician. She gave me some medicine and I asked her for some reading-matter, or at least some sewing. Next day I was given towels to hem. Eagerly I stitched by the hour, my thoughts with Sasha and Ed. With crushing clarity I saw what Sasha's life in prison meant. Twenty-two years! I should go mad in a year.

One day the matron came to announce that extradition had been granted and that I was to be taken to New York. I followed her into the office, where I was handed a large package of letters, telegrams, and papers. I was informed that several boxes of fruit and flowers had come for me, but that it was against the rules for prisoners to have such things. Then I was handed over to a heavy-set man. A cab waited outside the prison and we were driven to the station.

We travelled in a Pullman car, and the man introduced himself

as Detective-Sergeant —. He excused himself, saying he was only doing his duty; he had six children to support. I asked him why he had
not chosen a more honourable occupation and why he had to bring
more spies into the world. If *he* did not do it, someone else would, he
replied. The police force was necessary; it protected society. Would
I have dinner? He would have it brought to the car to save my going
to the diner. I consented. I had not eaten anything decent for a week;
besides, the City of New York was paying for the unsolicited luxury
of my journey.

Over the dinner the detective referred to my youth and the life
" such a brilliant girl, with such abilities " had before her. He went
on to say that I never would earn anything by the work I was doing,
not even my salt. Why shouldn't I be sensible and " look out for number one " first? He felt for me because he was a *Yehude* himself.
He was sorry to see me go to prison. He could tell me how to get
free, even to receive a large sum of money, if I would only be sensible.

" Out with it," I said; " what's on your mind? "

His chief had instructed him to tell me that my case would be
quashed and a substantial sum of money presented to me if I would
give way a little. Nothing much, just a short periodic report of what
was going on in radical circles and among the workers on the East
Side.

A horrible feeling came over me. The food nauseated me. I gulped
down some ice-water from my glass and threw what was left into the
detective's face. " You miserable cur! " I shouted; " not enough that
you act as a Judas, you try even to turn me into one — you and your
rotten chief! I'll take prison for life, but no one will ever buy me! "

" All right, all right," he said soothingly; " have it your own way."

From the Pennsylvania Station I was driven to the Mulberry Street
Police Station, where I was locked up for the night. The cell was
small and ill-smelling, with only a wooden plank to sit or lie down
upon. I heard the clank of cells being locked and unlocked, crying and
hysterical weeping. But it was a relief not to see the bloated face and
not to have to breathe the same air with the loathsome detective.

The next morning I was taken before the Chief. The detective had
told him everything and he was furious. I was a fool, a stupid goose
who did not know what was good for her. He would put me away
for years where I could do no more harm. I let him rave, but before
I left, I told him that the whole country should learn how corrupt the

Chief of Police of New York can be. He raised a chair as if to strike me with it. Then, changing his mind, he called for a detective to take me back to the station-house.

I was overjoyed to find Ed, Justus Schwab, and Dr. Julius Hoffmann waiting for me there. In the afternoon I was brought before a judge and charged with inciting to riot on three counts. My trial was set for the 28th of September; my bail, to the amount of five thousand dollars, was given by Dr. Julius Hoffmann. In triumph my friends took me to Justus's den.

In my accumulated mail I found an underground letter from Sasha. He had read about my arrest. " Now you are indeed my sailor girl," he wrote. He had at last established communication with Nold and Bauer and they were arranging a *sub rosa* prison publication. They had already chosen a name; it was to be called " *Gefängniss-Blüthen* (Prison Blossoms)." I felt a weight lifted off my heart. Sasha had come back, he was beginning to take an interest in life, he would hold out! At most he would have to serve seven years on the first charge. We must work energetically to get his sentence commuted. I was light-hearted and happy in the thought that we might yet succeed in wrenching Sasha from his living grave.

Justus's place was crowded. People I had never before seen now came to express their sympathy. I had suddenly become an important personage, though I could not understand why, since I had done or said nothing that merited distinction. But I was glad to see so much interest in my ideas. I never doubted for a moment that it was the social theories I represented, and not I personally, that was attracting attention. My trial would give me a wonderful chance for propaganda. I must prepare for it. My defence in open court should carry the message of anarchism to the whole country.

I missed Claus Timmermann in the crowd and wondered what could be keeping him away. I turned to Ed and asked what had happened to cause Claus to neglect such an opportunity for free drinks. Ed was at first evasive, but on my insisting he informed me that the police had raided my grandmother's grocery store, expecting to find me there. Later on they arrested Claus. Knowing that he was often under the influence of liquor, the police hoped to learn from him my whereabouts. But Claus refused to talk, whereupon they beat him into unconsciousness and then railroaded him to six months in Blackwell's Island on the charge of resisting arrest.

As my own trial was approaching, Fedya, Ed, Justus, and other friends urged the need of counsel. I knew they were right. Sasha's mock trial had proved that, and now also the fate of Claus. I, too, would have no chance if I went into court without an attorney. But it seemed like a betrayal of Sasha to consent to legal defence. He had refused to compromise, although he knew that a long sentence was awaiting him. How could I do it? I would defend myself.

A week before the trial I received a *sub rosa* letter from Sasha. He had come to realize that as revolutionists we had small chance in an American court in any event, but we were altogether lost without legal defence. He did not regret his own stand; he still held that it was inconsistent for an anarchist to have a legal representative or to spend the workers' money on lawyers; but he felt that my situation was different. As a good speaker I could do much propaganda for our ideals in court, and a lawyer would protect my right to talk. He suggested that some prominent attorney of liberal views, such as Hugh O. Pentecost, might offer his services gratis. I knew it was Sasha's concern for my welfare that induced him to urge me to something he had so bravely denied himself. Or was it that his own experience had taught him our mistake? Sasha's letter and an offer of free counsel from an unexpected quarter changed my mind. The offer came from A. Oakey Hall.

My friends were delighted. A. Oakey Hall was a great jurist, besides being a man of liberal ideas. He had once been mayor of New York, but had proved to be too humane and democratic for the politicians. His affair with a young actress presented the opportunity to make Hall politically impossible. Hall, tall, distinguished-looking, vivacious, gave one the impression of a much younger man than his white hair indicated. I was curious to know why he was willing to take my case free of charge. He explained that it was partly out of sympathy with me and partly because of his antagonism to the police. He knew their corruption, he knew how easily they swear away a man's freedom, and he was anxious to expose their methods. My case would give him the opportunity. The issue of free speech being of national importance, my defence would bring his name before the public again. I liked the man's frankness and agreed to let him plead my case.

My trial began on the 28th of September before Judge Martin, lasting ten days, during which time the court-room was filled with reporters and my friends. The prosecuting attorney presented three indictments against me, but Oakey Hall spoiled his scheme. He pointed out that one could not justly be tried on three separate charges for one offence, and he was sustained by the Judge. Two of the three counts were set aside and I was tried only on the charge of inciting to riot.

At noon on the first day of the trial I went out to lunch with Ed, Justus, and John Henry Mackay, the anarchist poet. But when the court adjourned and my attorney was about to accompany me home, we were stopped. For the remainder of the trial, we were informed, I would be in the custody of the court. I would have to be sent to the Tombs. My counsel protested that I was out on bail, and that only in cases of murder was such procedure permissible. But to no purpose. I had to remain in custody. My friends gave me an ovation, cheering and singing revolutionary songs, the voice of Justus thundering above the rest. I called to them to keep our banner flying and to drink my portion, in addition to their own, to the day when courts and jailers would be no more.

The star witness for the State was Detective Jacobs. He produced notes, taken by him on the Union Square platform, as he claimed, and purporting to represent a verbatim account of my speech. He quoted me as urging " revolution, violence, and bloodshed." Twelve persons who had been at the meeting and had heard me speak came forward to testify in my behalf. Every one of them stated that it would have been a physical impossibility to take notes at my meeting because of the overcrowding on the platform. Jacobs's notes were submitted to a handwriting expert, who declared that the writing was too regular and even to have been written in a standing position in a crowded place. But neither his testimony nor that of the witnesses for the defence availed against the statements of the detective. When I took the stand in my own behalf, District Attorney MacIntyre persisted in questioning me on everything under the sun except my Union Square speech. Religion, free love, morality — what were my opinions on those subjects? I attempted to unmask the hypocrisy of morality, the Church as an instrument for enslavement, the impossibility of love that is forced and not free. Constant interruptions by MacIntyre and orders from the Judge to reply only with yes or no finally compelled me to give up the task.

In his closing speech MacIntyre waxed eloquent over what would happen if " this dangerous woman " were allowed to go free. Property would be destroyed, the children of the rich would be exterminated, the streets of New York would stream with blood. He talked himself into such frenzy that his starched collar and cuffs became flabby and began dripping sweat. It made me more uncomfortable than his oratory.

Oakey Hall delivered a brilliant address ridiculing Jacobs's testimony and castigating the police methods and the stand of the Court. His client was an idealist, he declared; all the great things in our world have been promulgated by idealists. More violent speeches than Emma Goldman had ever made were never prosecuted in court. The moneyed classes of America were seeing red since Governor Altgeld had pardoned the three surviving anarchists of the group hanged in Chicago in 1887. The New York Police sought in the Union Square meeting an opportunity to make Emma Goldman an anarchist target. It was clear that his client was the victim of police persecution. He closed his speech with an eloquent plea for the right of free expression and the acquittal of the prisoner.

The Judge enlarged on law and order, the sanctity of property, and the need of protecting " free American institutions." The jury deliberated for a long time; it was evidently loath to convict. Once the foreman came back for instructions: the jury seemed especially impressed by the testimony of one of my witnesses, a young reporter on the New York *World*. He had been at the meeting and had written a detailed account of it. When he saw his story in the paper the following morning, it was so garbled that he had at once offered to testify to the actual facts. While he was on the witness-stand, Jacobs bent over to MacIntyre, whispered something, and a court attendant was sent out. He soon returned with a copy of the *World* of the morning after the meeting. The reporter could not charge some desk editor in open court with having tampered with his account. He became embarrassed, confused, and obviously very miserable. His report as printed in the *World,* and not as testified to by him on the witness-stand, decided my fate. I was found guilty.

My attorney insisted on an appeal to the higher court, but I refused. The farce of my trial had strengthened my opposition to the State and I would ask no favours from it. I was ordered back to the Tombs until the 18th of October, the day set for sentence.

Before being taken to jail I was allowed a short visit with my friends. I repeated to them what I had already told Oakey Hall: I would not consent to an appeal. They agreed that nothing could be gained except some respite while the case would be pending. A moment's weakness overcame me, the thought of Ed and of our love, so young, so full of happy possibilities. The temptation was great. But — I must go the way many had gone before me. I would get a year or two; what was that compared with Sasha's fate? I would go the way.

In the interval before my sentence the papers carried sensational stories about " anarchists planning to storm the court-room " and " preparations for a forcible rescue of Emma Goldman." The police were getting ready to " cope with the situation," radical quarters were being watched, and the court-house was well guarded. No one except the prisoner, counsel, and press representatives would be allowed in the court building on the day of sentence.

My attorney sent word to my friends of his decision not to be present in court on that date because of my " stubbornness in refusing an appeal to a higher tribunal." But Hugh O. Pentecost would be on hand, not as counsel, but as friend, to protect my legal rights and demand that I be permitted opportunity to speak. Ed informed me that the New York *World* had offered to publish the statement I had prepared for the Court. It would reach a great many more people in that way than my talk in the court-room. I wondered that the *World,* which had carried a falsified report of my Union Square speech, should now offer to publish my statement. Ed said that there was no accounting for the inconsistencies of the capitalist press. At any rate, the *World* had promised to permit him to see the proofs, and thus we should be assured against misrepresentation. My statement would appear in a special edition immediately after sentence had been passed. My friends urged me to let the *World* have the manuscript, and I consented.

On the way from the Tombs to the court New York looked as if it were under martial law. The streets were lined with police, the buildings surrounded by heavily armed cordons, the corridors of the court-house filled with officers. I was called to the bar and asked if I had " anything to say why sentence should not be passed." I had considerable to say; should I be given the chance? No, that was impossible; I could only make a very brief statement. Then I would say only that I had expected no justice from a capitalist court. The Court might do its worst, but it was powerless to change my views, I said.

Judge Martin sentenced me to one year in Blackwell's Island

Penitentiary. On my way to the Tombs I heard the news-boys shout: "Extra! Extra! Emma Goldman's speech in court!" and I felt glad that the *World* had kept its promise. I was at once placed in the Black Maria and taken to the boat that delivers prisoners to Blackwell's Island.

It was a bright October day, the sun playing on the water as the barge sped on. Several newspaper men accompanied me, all pressing me for an interview. "I travel in queenly state," I remarked in light mood; "just look at my satraps." "You can't squelch that kid," a young reporter kept on saying, admiringly. When we reached the island, I bade my escorts good-bye, admonishing them not to write any more lies than they could help. I called out to them gaily that I would see them again within a year and then followed the Deputy Sheriff along the broad, tree-lined gravel walk to the prison entrance. There I turned towards the river, took a last deep breath of the free air, and stepped across the threshold of my new home.

CHAPTER XII

I WAS CALLED BEFORE THE HEAD MATRON, A TALL WOMAN WITH A stolid face. She began taking my pedigree. "What religion?" was her first question. "None, I am an atheist." "Atheism is prohibited here. You will have to go to church." I replied that I would do nothing of the kind. I did not believe in anything the Church stood for and, not being a hypocrite, I would not attend. Besides, I came from Jewish people. Was there a synagogue?

She said curtly that there were services for the Jewish convicts on Saturday afternoon, but as I was the only Jewish female prisoner, she could not permit me to go among so many men.

After a bath and a change into the prison uniform I was sent to my cell and locked in.

I knew from what Most had related to me about Blackwell's Island that the prison was old and damp, the cells small, without light or water. I was therefore prepared for what was awaiting me. But the moment the door was locked on me, I began to experience a feeling of suffocation. In the dark I groped for something to sit on and found a narrow iron cot. Sudden exhaustion overpowered me and I fell asleep.

I became aware of a sharp burning in my eyes, and I jumped up in fright. A lamp was being held close to the bars. "What is it?" I cried, forgetting where I was. The lamp was lowered and I saw a thin, ascetic face gazing at me. A soft voice congratulated me on my sound sleep. It was the evening matron on her regular rounds. She told me to undress and left me.

But there was no more sleep for me that night. The irritating feel of the coarse blanket, the shadows creeping past the bars, kept me awake until the sound of a gong again brought me to my feet. The cells were being unlocked, the doors heavily thrown open. Blue and white striped figures slouched by, automatically forming into a line, myself a part of it. " March! " and the line began to move along the corridor down the steps towards a corner containing wash-stands and towels. Again the command: " Wash! " and everybody began clamouring for a towel, already soiled and wet. Before I had time to splash some water on my hands and face and wipe myself half-dry, the order was given to march back.

Then breakfast: a slice of bread and a tin cup of warm brownish water. Again the line formed, and the striped humanity was broken up in sections and sent to its daily tasks. With a group of other women I was taken to the sewing-room.

The procedure of forming lines — " Forward, march! " — was repeated three times a day, seven days a week. After each meal ten minutes were allowed for talk. A torrent of words would then break forth from the pent-up beings. Each precious second increased the roar of sounds; and then sudden silence.

The sewing-room was large and light, the sun often streaming through the high windows, its rays intensifying the whiteness of the walls and the monotony of the regulation dress. In the sharp light the figures in baggy and ungainly attire appeared more hideous. Still, the shop was a welcome relief from the cell. Mine, on the ground floor, was grey and damp even in the day-time; the cells on the upper floors were somewhat brighter. Close to the barred door one could even read by the help of the light coming from the corridor windows.

The locking of the cells for the night was the worst experience of the day. The convicts were marched along the tiers in the usual line. On reaching her cell each left the line, stepped inside, hands on the iron door, and awaited the command. " Close! " and with a crash the seventy doors shut, each prisoner automatically locking herself in. More harrowing still was the daily degradation of being forced to march in lock-step to the river, carrying the bucket of excrement accumulated during twenty-four hours.

I was put in charge of the sewing-shop. My task consisted in cutting the cloth and preparing work for the two dozen women employed. In addition I had to keep account of the incoming material and the outgoing bundles. I welcomed the work. It helped me to forget the dreary existence within the prison. But the evenings were torturous. The first few weeks I would fall asleep as soon as I touched the pillow. Soon, however, the nights found me restlessly tossing about, seeking sleep in vain. The appalling nights — even if I should get the customary two months' commutation time, I still had nearly two hundred and ninety of them. Two hundred and ninety — and Sasha? I used to lie awake and mentally figure in the dark the number of days and nights before him. Even if he could come out after his first sentence of seven years, he would still have more than twenty-five hundred nights! Dread overcame me that Sasha could not survive them. Nothing was so likely to drive people to madness, I felt, as sleepless nights in prison. Better dead, I thought. Dead? Frick was not dead, and Sasha's glorious youth, his life, the things he might have accomplished — all were being sacrificed — perhaps for nothing. But — was Sasha's *Attentat* in vain? Was my revolutionary faith a mere echo of what others had said or taught me? " No, not in vain! " something within me insisted. " No sacrifice is lost for a great ideal."

One day I was told by the head matron that I would have to get better results from the women. They were not doing so much work, she said, as under the prisoner who had had charge of the sewing-shop before me. I resented the suggestion that I become a slave-driver. It was because I hated slaves as well as their drivers, I informed the matron, that I had been sent to prison. I considered myself one of the inmates, not above them. I was determined not to do anything that would involve a denial of my ideals. I preferred punishment. One of the methods of treating offenders consisted in placing them in a corner facing a blackboard and compelling them to stay for hours in that position, constantly before the matron's vigilant eyes. This seemed to me petty and insulting. I decided that if I was offered such an indignity, I would increase my offence and take the dungeon. But the days passed and I was not punished.

News in prison travels with amazing rapidity. Within twenty-four hours all the women knew that I had refused to act as a slave-driver. They had not been unkind to me, but they had kept aloof. They had been told that I was a terrible " anarchist " and that I didn't believe in God. They had never seen me in church and I did not participate in their ten-minute gush of talk. I was a freak in their eyes. But when they learned that I had refused to play the boss over them, their reserve broke down. Sundays after church the cells would be opened to permit the women an hour's visit with one another. The next Sunday I received visits from every inmate on my tier. They felt I was their friend, they assured me, and they would do anything for me. Girls working in the laundry offered to wash my clothes, others to darn my stockings. Everyone was anxious to do some service. I was deeply moved. These poor creatures so hungered for kindness that the least sign of it loomed high on their limited horizons. After that they would often come to me with their troubles, their hatred of the head matron, their confidences about their infatuations with the male convicts. Their ingenuity in carrying on flirtations under the very eyes of the officials was amazing.

My three weeks in the Tombs had given me ample proof that the revolutionary contention that crime is the result of poverty is based on fact. Most of the defendants who were awaiting trial came from the lowest strata of society, men and women without friends, often even without a home. Unfortunate, ignorant creatures they were, but still with hope in their hearts, because they had not yet been convicted. In the penitentiary despair possessed almost all of the prisoners. It served to unveil the mental darkness, fear, and superstition which held them in bondage. Among the seventy inmates, there were no more than half a dozen who showed any intelligence whatever. The rest were outcasts without the least social consciousness. Their personal misfortunes filled their thoughts; they could not understand that they were victims, links in an endless chain of injustice and inequality. From early childhood they had known nothing but poverty, squalor, and want, and the same conditions were awaiting them on their release. Yet they were capable of sympathy and devotion, of generous impulses. I soon had occasion to convince myself of it when I was taken ill.

The dampness of my cell and the chill of the late December days had brought on an attack of my old complaint, rheumatism. For some days the head matron opposed my being taken to the hospital, but she was finally compelled to submit to the order of the visiting physician.

Blackwell's Island Penitentiary was fortunate in the absence of a "steady" physician. The inmates were receiving medical attendance from the Charity Hospital, which was situated near by. That institution had six weeks' post-graduate courses, which meant frequent changes in the staff. They were under the direct supervision of a visiting physician from New York City, Dr. White, a humane and kindly man. The treatment given the prisoners was as good as patients received in any New York hospital.

The sick-ward was the largest and brightest room in the building. Its spacious windows looked out upon a wide lawn in front of the prison and, farther on, the East River. In fine weather the sun streamed in generously. A month's rest, the kindliness of the physician, and the thoughtful attention of my fellow prisoners relieved me of my pain and enabled me to get about again.

During one of his rounds Dr. White picked up the card hanging at the foot of my bed giving my crime and pedigree. " Inciting to riot," he read. " Piffle! I don't believe you could hurt a fly. A fine inciter you would make! " he chuckled, then asked me if I should not like to remain in the hospital to take care of the sick. "I should, indeed," I replied, " but I know nothing about nursing." He assured me that neither did anyone else in the prison. He had tried for some time to induce the city to put a trained nurse in charge of the ward, but he had not succeeded. For operations and grave cases he had to bring a nurse from the Charity Hospital. I could easily pick up the elementary things about tending the sick. He would teach me to take the pulse and temperature and to perform similar services. He would speak to the Warden and the head matron if I wanted to remain.

Soon I took up my new work. The ward contained sixteen beds, most of them always filled. The various diseases were treated in the same room, from grave operations to tuberculosis, pneumonia, and childbirth. My hours were long and strenuous, the groans of the patients nerve-racking; but I loved my job. It gave me opportunity to come close to the sick women and bring a little cheer into their lives. I was so much richer than they: I had love and friends, received many letters and daily messages from Ed. Some Austrian anarchists, owners of a restaurant, sent me dinners every day, which Ed himself brought to the boat. Fedya supplied fruit and delicacies weekly. I had so much to give; it was a joy to share with my sisters who had neither friends nor attention. There were a few exceptions, of course; but the majority had nothing. They never had had anything before and they would have nothing on their release. They were derelicts on the social dung-heap.

I was gradually given entire charge of the hospital ward, part of my duties being to divide the special rations allowed the sick prisoners. They consisted of a quart of milk, a cup of beef tea, two eggs, two crackers, and two lumps of sugar for each invalid. On several occasions milk and eggs were missing and I reported the matter to a day matron. Later she informed me that a head matron had said that it did not matter and that certain patients were strong enough to do without their extra rations. I had had considerable opportunity to study this head matron, who felt a violent dislike of everyone not Anglo-Saxon. Her special targets were the Irish and the Jews, against whom she discriminated habitually. I was therefore not surprised to get such a message from her.

A few days later I was told by the prisoner who brought the hospital rations that the missing portions had been given by this head matron to two husky Negro prisoners. That also did not surprise me. I knew she had a special fondness for the coloured inmates. She rarely punished them and often gave them unusual privileges. In return her favourites would spy on the other prisoners, even on those of their own colour who were too decent to be bribed. I myself never had any prejudice against coloured people; in fact, I felt deeply for them because they were being treated like slaves in America. But I hated discrimination. The idea that sick people, white or coloured, should be robbed of their rations to feed healthy persons outraged my sense of justice, but I was powerless to do anything in the matter.

After my first clashes with this woman she left me severely alone. Once she became enraged because I refused to translate a Russian letter that had arrived for one of the prisoners. She had called me into her office to read the letter and tell her its contents. When I saw that the letter was not for me, I informed her that I was not employed by the prison as a translator. It was bad enough for the officials to pry into the personal mail of helpless human beings, but I would not do it. She said that it was stupid of me not to take advantage of her goodwill. She could put me back in my cell, deprive me of my commutation time for good behaviour, and make the rest of my stay very hard. She could do as she pleased, I told her, but I would not read the private letters of my unfortunate sisters, much less translate them to her.

Then came the matter of the missing rations. The sick women began to suspect that they were not getting their full share and complained to the doctor. Confronted with a direct question from him, I had to tell the truth. I did not know what he said to the offending matron, but the full rations began to arrive again. Two days later I was called downstairs and locked up in the dungeon.

I had repeatedly seen the effect of a dungeon experience on other women prisoners. One inmate had been kept there for twenty-eight days on bread and water, although the regulations prohibited a longer stay than forty-eight hours. She had to be carried out on a stretcher; her hands and legs were swollen, her body covered with a rash. The

descriptions the poor creature and others had given me used to make
me ill. But nothing I had heard compared with the reality. The cell
was barren; one had to sit or lie down on the cold stone floor. The
dampness of the walls made the dungeon a ghastly place. Worse yet
was the complete shutting out of light and air, the impenetrable blackness, so thick that one could not see the hand before one's face. It gave
me the sensation of sinking into a devouring pit. " The Spanish Inquisition come to life in America " — I thought of Most's description.
He had not exaggerated.

After the door shut behind me, I stood still, afraid to sit down or to
lean against the wall. Then I groped for the door. Gradually the blackness paled. I caught a faint sound slowly approaching; I heard a key
turn in the lock. A matron appeared. I recognized Miss Johnson, the
one who had frightened me out of my sleep on my first night in the
penitentiary. I had come to know and appreciate her as a beautiful personality. Her kindness to the prisoners was the one ray of light in their
dreary existence. She had taken me to her bosom almost from the first,
and in many indirect ways she had shown me her affection. Often at
night, when all were asleep, and quiet had fallen on the prison, Miss
Johnson would enter the hospital ward, put my head in her lap, and
tenderly stroke my hair. She would tell me the news in the papers to
distract me and try to cheer my depressed mood. I knew I had found
a friend in the woman, who herself was a lonely soul, never having
known the love of man or child.

She came into the dungeon carrying a camp-chair and a blanket.
" You can sit on that," she said, " and wrap yourself up. I'll leave the
door open a bit to let in some air. I'll bring you hot coffee later. It will
help to pass the night." She told me how painful it was for her to see
the prisoners locked up in the dreadful hole, but she could do nothing
for them because most of them could not be trusted. It was different
with me, she was sure.

At five in the morning my friend had to take back the chair and
blanket and lock me in. I no longer was oppressed by the dungeon.
The humanity of Miss Johnson had dissolved the blackness.

When I was taken out of the dungeon and sent back to the hospital,
I saw that it was almost noon. I resumed my duties. Later I learned
that Dr. White had asked for me, and upon being informed that I
was in punishment he had categorically demanded my release.

No visitors were allowed in the penitentiary until after one month had been served. Ever since my entry I had been longing for Ed, yet at the same time I dreaded his coming. I remembered my terrible visit with Sasha. But it was not quite so appalling in Blackwell's Island. I met Ed in a room where other prisoners were having their relatives and friends to see them. There was no guard between us. Everyone was so absorbed in his own visitor that no one paid any attention to us. Still we felt constrained. With clasped hands we talked of general things.

My second visit took place in the hospital, Miss Johnson being on duty. She thoughtfully put a screen to shut us out from the view of the other patients, she herself keeping at a distance. Ed took me in his arms. It was bliss to feel again the warmth of his body, to hear his beating heart, to cling hungrily to his lips. But his departure left me in an emotional turmoil, consumed by a passionate need for my lover. During the day I strove to subdue the hot desire surging through my veins, but at night the craving held me in its power. Sleep would come finally, sleep disturbed by dreams and images of intoxicating nights with Ed. The ordeal was too torturing and too exhausting. I was glad when he brought Fedya and other friends along.

Once Ed came accompanied by Voltairine de Cleyre. She had been invited by New York friends to address a meeting arranged in my behalf. When I had visited her in Philadelphia, she had been too ill to speak. I was glad of the opportunity to come closer to her now. We talked about things nearest to our hearts — Sasha, the movement. Voltairine promised to join me, on my release, in a new effort for Sasha. Meanwhile she would write to him, she said. Ed, too, was in touch with him.

My visitors were always sent up to the hospital. I was therefore surprised one day to be called to the Warden's office to see someone. It proved to be John Swinton and his wife. Swinton was a nationally known figure; he had worked with the abolitionists and had fought in the Civil War. As editor-in-chief of the New York *Sun* he had pleaded for the European refugees who came to find asylum in the United States. He was the friend and adviser of young literary aspirants, and he had been one of the first to defend Walt Whitman against the misrepresentations of the purists. Tall, erect, with beautiful features, John Swinton was an impressive figure.

He greeted me warmly, remarking that he had just been saying to Warden Pillsbury that he himself had made more violent speeches during the abolition days than anything I said at Union Square. Yet he had not been arrested. He had told the Warden that he ought to be ashamed of himself to keep " a little girl like that " locked up. " And what do you suppose he said? He said he had no choice — he was only doing his duty. All weaklings say that, cowards who always put the blame on others." Just then the Warden approached us. He assured Swinton that I was a model prisoner and that I had become an efficient nurse in the short time. In fact, I was doing such good work that he wished I had been given five years. " Generous cuss, aren't you? " Swinton laughed. " Perhaps you'll give her a paid job when her time is up? " " I would, indeed," Pillsbury replied. " Well, you'd be a damn fool. Don't you know she doesn't believe in prisons? Sure as you live, she'd let them all escape, and what would become of you then? " The poor man was embarrassed, but he joined in the banter. Before my visitor took leave, he turned once more to the Warden, cautioning him to " take good care of his little friend," else he would " take it out of his hide."

The visit of the Swintons completely changed the attitude of the head matron towards me. The Warden had always been quite decent, and she now began showering privileges on me: food from her own table, fruit, coffee, and walks on the island. I refused her favours except the walks; it was my first opportunity in six months to go out in the open and inhale the spring air without iron bars to check me.

In March 1894 we received a large influx of women prisoners. They were nearly all prostitutes rounded up during recent raids. The city had been blessed by a new vice crusade. The Lexow Committee, with the Reverend Dr. Parkhurst at its head, wielded the broom which was to sweep New York clean of the fearful scourge. The men found in the public houses were allowed to go free, but the women were arrested and sentenced to Blackwell's Island.

Most of the unfortunates came in a deplorable condition. They were suddenly cut off from the narcotics which almost all of them had been habitually using. The sight of their suffering was heart-breaking. With the strength of giants the frail creatures would shake the iron bars, curse, and scream for dope and cigarettes. Then they would fall exhausted to the ground, pitifully moaning through the night.

The misery of the poor creatures brought back my own hard struggle to do without the soothing effect of cigarettes. Except for the ten weeks of my illness in Rochester, I had smoked for years, sometimes as many as forty cigarettes a day. When we were very hard pressed for money, and it was a toss-up between bread and cigarettes, we would generally decide to buy the latter. We simply could not go for very long without smoking. Being cut off from the satisfaction of the habit when I came to the penitentiary, I found the torture almost beyond endurance. The nights in the cell became doubly hideous. The only way to get tobacco in prison was by means of bribery. I knew that if any of the inmates were caught bringing me cigarettes, they would be punished. I could not expose them to the risk. Snuff tobacco was allowed, but I could never take to it. There was nothing to be done but to get used to the deprivation. I had resisting power and I could forget my craving in reading.

Not so the new arrivals. When they learned that I was in charge of the medicine chest, they pursued me with offers of money; worse still, with pitiful appeals to my humanity. " Just a whiff of dope, for the love of Christ ! " I rebelled against the Christian hypocrisy which allowed the men to go free and sent the poor women to prison for having ministered to the sexual demands of those men. Suddenly cutting off the victims from the narcotics they had used for years seemed ruthless. I would have gladly given the addicts what they craved so terribly. It was not fear of punishment which kept me from bringing them relief; it was Dr. White's faith in me. He had trusted me with the medicines, he had been kind and generous — I could not fail him. The screams of the women would unnerve me for days, but I stuck to my responsibility.

One day a young Irish girl was brought to the hospital for an operation. In view of the seriousness of the case Dr. White called in two trained nurses. The operation lasted until late in the evening, and then the patient was left in my charge. She was very ill from the effect of the ether, vomited violently, and burst the stitches of her wound, which resulted in a severe hæmorrhage. I sent a hurry call to the Charity Hospital. It seemed hours before the doctor and his staff arrived. There were no nurses this time and I had to take their place.

The day had been an unusually hard one and I had had very little sleep. I felt exhausted and had to hold on to the operating-table with my left hand while passing with my right instruments and sponges. Suddenly the operating-table gave way, and my arm was caught. I screamed with pain. Dr. White was so absorbed in his manipulations that for a moment he did not realize what had happened. When he at last had the table raised and my arm was lifted out, it looked as if every bone had been broken. The pain was excruciating and he ordered a shot of morphine. " We'll set her arm later. This has got to come first." " No morphine," I begged. I still remembered the effect of morphine on me when Dr. Julius Hoffmann had given me a dose against insomnia. It had put me to sleep, but during the night I had tried to throw myself out of the window, and it had required all of Sasha's strength to pull me back. The morphine had crazed me, and now I would have none of it.

One of the physicians gave me something that had a soothing effect. After the patient on the operating-table had been returned to her bed, Dr. White examined my arm. "You're nice and chubby," he said; " that has saved your bones. Nothing has been broken — just flattened a bit." My arm was put in a splint. The doctor wanted me to go to bed, but there was no one else to sit up with the patient. It might be her last night: her tissues were so badly infected that they would not hold the stitches, and another hæmorrhage would prove fatal. I decided to remain at her bedside. I knew I could not sleep with the case as serious as it was.

All night I watched her struggle for life. In the morning I sent for the priest. Everyone was surprised at my action, particularly the head matron. How could I, an atheist, do such a thing, she wondered, and choose a priest, at that! I had declined to see the missionaries as well as the rabbi. She had noticed how friendly I had become with the two Catholic sisters who often visited us on Sunday. I had even made coffee for them. Didn't I think that the Catholic Church had always been the enemy of progress and that it had persecuted and tortured the Jews? How could I be so inconsistent? Of course, I thought so, I assured her. I was just as opposed to the Catholic as to the other Churches. I considered them all alike, enemies of the people. They preached submission, and their God was the God of the rich and the mighty. I hated their God and would never make peace with him. But if I could believe in any religion at all, I should prefer the Catholic Church. " It is less hypocritical," I said to her; " it makes allowance for human frailties and it has a sense of beauty." The Catholic sisters and the priest had not tried to preach to me like the missionaries, the minister, and the vulgar rabbi. They left my soul to its own fate; they talked to me about human things, especially the priest, who was a cultured man. My poor patient had reached the end of a life that had been too hard for her. The priest might give her a few moments of peace and kindness; why should I not have sent for him? But the matron was too dull to follow my argument or understand my motives. I remained a " queer one," in her estimation.

Before my patient died, she begged me to lay her out. I had been kinder to her, she said, than her own mother. She wanted to know that it would be my hand that would get her ready for the last journey. I would make her beautiful; she wanted to look beautiful to meet Mother Mary and the Lord Jesus. It required little effort to make her as lovely in death as she had been in life. Her black curls made her alabaster face more delicate than the artificial methods she had used to enhance her looks. Her luminous eyes were closed now; I had closed them with my own hands. But her chiselled eyebrows and long, black lashes were remindful of the radiance that had been hers. How she must have fascinated men! And they destroyed her. Now she was beyond their reach. Death had smoothed her suffering. She looked serene in her marble whiteness now.

During the Jewish Easter holidays I was again called to the Warden's office. I found my grandmother there. She had repeatedly begged Ed to take her to see me, but he had declined in order to spare her the painful experience. The devoted soul could not be stopped. With her broken English she had made her way to the Commissioner of Corrections, procured a pass, and come to the penitentiary. She handed me a large white handkerchief containing matzoth, *gefüllte* fish, and some Easter cake of her own baking. She tried to explain to the Warden what a good Jewish daughter her *Chavele* was; in fact, better than any rabbi's wife, because she gave everything to the poor. She was fearfully wrought up when the moment of departure came, and I tried to soothe her, begging her not to break down before the Warden. She bravely dried her tears and walked out straight and proud, but I knew she would weep bitterly as soon as she got out of sight. No doubt she also prayed to her God for her *Chavele*.

June saw many prisoners discharged from the sick-ward, only a few beds remaining occupied. For the first time since coming to the hospital I had some leisure, enabling me to read more systematically. I had accumulated a large library; John Swinton had sent me many books, as did also other friends; but most of them were from Justus Schwab. He had never come to see me; he had asked Ed to tell me that it was impossible for him to visit me. He hated prison so much that he would not be able to leave me behind. If he should come, he would be tempted to use force to take me back with him, and it would only cause trouble. Instead he sent me stacks of books. Walt Whitman, Emerson, Thoreau, Hawthorne, Spencer, John Stuart Mill, and many other English and American authors I learned to know and love through the friendship of Justus. At the same time other elements also became interested in my salvation — spiritualists and metaphysical redeemers of various kinds. I tried honestly to get at their meaning, but I was no doubt too much of the earth to follow their shadows in the clouds.

Among the books I received was the *Life of Albert Brisbane,* written by his widow. The fly-leaf had an appreciative dedication to me. The book came with a cordial letter from her son, Arthur Brisbane, who expressed his admiration and the hope that on my release I would allow him to arrange an evening for me. The biography of Brisbane brought me in touch with Fourier and other pioneers of socialist thought.

The prison library had some good literature, including the works of George Sand, George Eliot, and Ouida. The librarian in charge was an educated Englishman serving a five-year sentence for forgery. The books he handed out to me soon began to contain love notes framed in most affectionate terms, and presently they flamed with passion. He had already put in four years in prison, one of his notes read, and he was starved for the love of woman and companionship. He begged me at least to give him the companionship. Would I write him occasionally about the books I was reading? I disliked becoming involved in a silly prison flirtation, yet the need for free, uncensored expression was too compelling to resist. We exchanged many notes, often of a very ardent nature.

My admirer was a splendid musician and played the organ in the chapel. I should have loved to attend, to be able to hear him and feel him near, but the sight of the male prisoners in stripes, some of them handcuffed, and still further degraded and insulted by the lip-service of the minister, was too appalling to me. I had seen it once on the fourth of July, when some politician had come over to speak to the inmates about the glories of American liberty. I had to pass through the male wing on an errand to the Warden, and I heard the pompous patriot spouting of freedom and independence to the mental and physical wrecks. One convict had been put in irons because of an attempted escape. I could hear the clanking of his chains with his every movement. I could not bear to go to church.

The chapel was underneath the hospital ward. Twice on Sundays

I could listen on the stairway to my prison flame playing the organ. Sunday was quite a holiday: the head matron was off duty, and we were free from the irritation of her harsh voice. Sometimes the two Catholic sisters would come on that day. I was charmed with the younger one, still in her teens, very lovely and full of life. Once I asked her what had induced her to take the veil. Turning her large eyes upwards, she said: " The priest was young and so beautiful ! " The " baby nun," as I called her, would prattle for hours in her cheery young voice, telling me the news and gossip. It was a relief from the prison greyness.

Of the friends I made on Blackwell's Island the priest was the most interesting. At first I felt antagonistic to him. I thought he was like the rest of the religious busybodies, but I soon found that he wanted to talk only about books. He had studied in Cologne and had read much. He knew I had many books and he asked me to exchange some of them with him. I was amazed and wondered what kind of books he would bring me, expecting the New Testament or the Catechism. But he came with works of poetry and music. He had free access to the prison at any time, and often he would come to the ward at nine in the evening and remain till after midnight. We would discuss his favourite composers — Bach, Beethoven, and Brahms — and compare our views on poetry and social ideas. He presented me with an English-Latin dictionary as a gift, inscribed: " With the highest respect, to Emma Goldman."

On one occasion I asked him why he never gave me the Bible. " Because no one can understand or love it if he is forced to read it," he replied. That appealed to me and I asked him for it. Its simplicity of language and legendry fascinated me. There was no make-believe about my young friend. He was devout, entirely consecrated. He observed every fast and he would lose himself in prayer for hours. Once he asked me to help him decorate the chapel. When I came down, I found the frail, emaciated figure in silent prayer, oblivious of his surroundings. My own ideal, my faith, was at the opposite pole from his, but I knew he was as ardently sincere as I. Our fervour was our meeting-ground.

Warden Pillsbury often came to the hospital. He was an unusual man for his surroundings. His grandfather had been a jailer, and both his father and himself had been born in the prison. He understood his wards and the social forces that had created them. Once he remarked to me that he could not bear " stool-pigeons "; he preferred the prisoner who had pride and who would not stoop to mean acts against his fellow convicts in order to gain privileges for himself. If an inmate asseverated that he would reform and never again commit a crime, the Warden felt sure he was lying. He knew that no one could start a new life after years of prison and with the whole world against him unless he had outside friends to help him. He used to say that the State did not even supply a released man with enough money for his first week's meals. How, then, could he be expected to " make good? " He would relate the story of the man who on the morning of his release told him: " Pillsbury, the next watch and chain I steal I'll send to you as a present." " That's my man," the Warden would laugh.

Pillsbury was in a position to do much good for the unfortunates in his charge, but he was constantly hampered. He had to allow prisoners to do cooking, washing, and cleaning for others than themselves. If the table damask was not properly rolled before ironing, the laundress stood in danger of confinement to the dungeon. The whole prison was demoralized by favouritism. Convicts were deprived of food for the slightest infraction, but Pillsbury, who was an old man, was powerless to do much about it. Besides, he was eager to avoid a scandal.

The nearer the day of my liberation approached, the more unbearable life in prison became. The days dragged and I grew restless and irritable with impatience. Even reading became impossible. I would sit for hours lost in reminiscences. I thought of the comrades in the Illinois penitentiary brought back to life by the pardon of Governor Altgeld. Since I had come to prison, I realized how much the release of the three men, Neebe, Fielden, and Schwab, had done for the cause for which their comrades in Chicago had been hanged. The venom of the press against Altgeld for his gesture of justice proved how deeply he had struck the vested interests, particularly by his analysis of the trial and his clear demonstration that the executed anarchists had been judicially killed in spite of their proved innocence of the crime charged against them. Every detail of the momentous days of 1887 stood out in strong relief before me. Then Sasha, our life together, his act, his martyrdom — every moment of the five years since I had first met him I now relived with poignant reality. Why was it, I mused, that Sasha was still so deeply rooted in my being? Was not my love for Ed more ecstatic, more enriching? Perhaps it was his act that had bound me to him with such powerful cords. How insignificant was my own prison experience compared with what Sasha was suffering in the Allegheny purgatory! I now felt ashamed that, even for a moment, I could have found my incarceration hard. Not one friendly face in the court-room to be near Sasha and comfort him — solitary confinement and complete isolation, for no more visits had been allowed him. The Inspector had kept his promise; since my visit in November 1892, Sasha had not again been permitted to see anyone. How he must have craved the sight and touch of a kindred spirit, how he must be yearning for it!

My thoughts rushed on. Fedya, the lover of beauty, so fine and sensitive! And Ed. Ed — he had kissed to life so many mysterious longings, had opened such spiritual sources of wealth to me! I owed my development to Ed, and to the others, too, who had been in my life. And yet, more than all else, it was the prison that had proved the best school. A more painful, but a more vital, school. Here I had been brought close to the depths and complexities of the human soul; here I had found ugliness and beauty, meanness and generosity. Here, too, I had learned to see life through my own eyes and not through those of Sasha, Most, or Ed. The prison had been the crucible that tested my faith. It had helped me to discover strength in my own being, the strength to stand alone, the strength to live my life and fight for my ideals, against the whole world if need be. The State of New York could have rendered me no greater service than by sending me to Blackwell's Island Penitentiary!

CHAPTER XIII

THE DAYS AND WEEKS THAT FOLLOWED MY RELEASE WERE LIKE A nightmare. I needed quiet, peace, and privacy after my prison experience, but I was surrounded by people, and there were meetings nearly every evening. I lived in a daze: everything around me seemed incongruous and unreal. My thoughts continued in captivity; my fellow convicts haunted my waking and sleeping hours, and the prison noises kept ringing in my ears. The command " Close ! " followed by the crash of iron doors and the clank-clank of the chains, pursued me when I faced an audience.

The strangest experience I had was at the meeting arranged to welcome me on my release. It took place in the Thalia Theatre and the house was crowded. Many well-known men and women of various social groups in New York had come to celebrate my liberation. I sat listless, in a stupor. I strove to keep contact with reality, to listen to what was going on, to concentrate on what I intended to say, but it was in vain. I kept drifting back to Blackwell's Island. The vast audience imperceptibly changed to the pale, frightened faces of the women prisoners, the voices of the speakers took on the harshness of the head matron. Presently I became conscious of the pressure of a hand on my shoulder. It was Maria Louise, who was presiding at the meeting. She had called me several times and had announced that I was the next to address the gathering. " You seem as if asleep," she said.

I got to my feet, walked to the footlights, saw the audience rise to greet me. Then I tried to speak. My lips moved, but there was no sound. Hideous figures in fantastic stripes emerged from every aisle, slowly moving towards me. I grew faint and helplessly turned to Maria Louise. In a whisper, as if fearing to be overheard, I begged her to explain to the audience that I felt dizzy and that I would speak later. Ed was near and he led me behind the stage into a dressing-

room. I had never before lost control of myself or of my voice, and
the occurrence frightened me. Ed talked reassuringly, telling me that
every sensitive person carried the prison in his heart for a long time.
He urged me to leave the city with him, find a quiet place and greater
peace. Dear Ed, his soft voice and tender way always soothed me.
Now, too, they had the same effect.

Presently the sound of a beautiful voice reached the dressing-room.
Its speech was unfamiliar to me. " Who is speaking now ? " I asked.
" That is Maria Rodda, an Italian girl anarchist," Ed replied; " she is
only sixteen years old and has just come to America." The voice electri-
fied me and I was eager to see its owner. I stepped to the door leading
to the platform. Maria Rodda was the most exquisite creature I had
ever seen. She was of medium height, and her well-shaped head, covered with black curls, rested like a lily of the valley on her slender neck.
Her face was pale, her lips coral-red. Particularly striking were her
eyes: large, black coals fired by an inner light. Like myself, very few
in the audience understood Italian, but Maria's strange beauty and
the music of her speech roused the whole assembly to tensest enthusiasm. Maria proved a veritable ray of sunlight to me. My spooks vanished, the prison weights dropped off; I felt free and happy, among
friends.

I spoke after Maria. The audience again rose, to a man, applauding. I sensed that the people were spontaneously responsive to my
prison story, but I was not deceived; I knew intuitively that it was
Maria Rodda's youth and charm that fascinated them and not my
speech. Yet I, too, was still young — only twenty-five. I still had attraction, but compared with that lovely flower, I felt old. The sorrows
of the world had matured me beyond my years; I felt old and sad. I
wondered whether a high ideal, made more fervent by the test of fire,
could stand out against youth and dazzling beauty.

After the meeting the closer comrades gathered at Justus's place.
Maria Rodda was with us and I was anxious to know all about her.
Pedro Esteve, a Spanish anarchist, acted as interpreter. I learned that
Maria had been a schoolmate of Santa Caserio, their teacher having
been Ada Negri, the ardent poetess of revolt. Through Caserio,
Maria, then barely fourteen, had joined an anarchist group. When
Caserio killed Carnot, President of France, their group had been
raided and Maria, with all the other members, was sent to prison. On
her release she came to America, together with her younger sister.
What they learned about Sasha and me convinced them that America,

like Italy, was persecuting idealists. Maria felt that she had work to do among her countrymen in the United States. Would I help her, would I be her teacher, she now begged me. I pressed her close to me as if to ward off the cruel thrusts I knew life would give her. I would be Maria's teacher, friend, comrade. The gnawing voice of envy of an hour ago was silent.

On the way to my room I spoke to Ed about Maria. To my surprise he did not share my enthusiasm. He admitted that she was ravishing, but he thought her beauty would not endure, much less her enthusiasm for our ideals. "Latin women mature young," he said; "they grow old with their first child, old in body and in spirit." "Well, then, Maria should guard against having children if she wants to devote herself to our movement," I remarked. "No woman should do that," Ed replied, emphatically. "Nature has made her for motherhood. All else is nonsense, artificial and unreal."

I had never before heard such sentiments expressed by Ed. His conservatism roused my anger. I demanded to know if he thought me also nonsensical because I preferred to work for an ideal instead of producing children. I expressed contempt for the reactionary attitude of our German comrades on these matters. I had believed that he was different, but I could see that he was like the rest. Perhaps he, too, loved only the woman in me, wanted me only as his wife and the bearer of his children. He was not the first to expect that of me, but he might as well know that I would never be that — never! I had chosen my path; no man should ever take me from it.

I had stopped walking. Ed also stood still. I saw the pained expression on his face, but all he said was: "Please, dearest, come along or we shall soon have a large audience." He took me gently by the arm, but I freed myself and hastened off alone.

My life with Ed had been glorious and complete, without any rift. But now it came; my dream of love and true comradeship suffered a rude awakening. Ed had never stressed his longing, except when he had protested against my joining the movement of the unemployed. I thought then that it was only his concern for my health. How was I to know that it was something else, the interest of the male? Yes, that is what it was, the man's instinct of possession, which brooks no deity except himself. Well, it should not be, even if I had to give him up. All my senses cried out for him. Could I live without Ed, without the joy he gave me?

Weary and miserable, my thoughts dwelt on Ed, on Maria Rodda, and on recollections of Santa Caserio. The latter's image brought to my mind the revolutionary events in France of recent occurrence. A number of *Attentats* had taken place there. There had been also the protests of Émile Henri and Auguste Vaillant against the political corruption, the frenzied speculation with the Panama Canal funds, and the resultant failure of the banks, in which the masses lost their last savings, causing widespread misery and want. Both had been executed. Vaillant's act had had no fatal result; no one had lost his life or even been wounded. Yet he was also condemned to death. Many leading men, among them François Coppée, Émile Zola, and others had pleaded with President Carnot to commute his sentence. He refused, ignoring even the pathetic letter of Vaillant's little child, a girl of nine, who had petitioned for the life of her father. Vaillant was guillotined. Some time later President Carnot, while driving in his carriage, was stabbed to death by a young Italian. On his dagger was found the inscription: "Revenge for Vaillant." The Italian's name was Santa Caserio, and he had tramped on foot from Italy to avenge his comrade, Vaillant.

I had read about his act and other similar occurrences in the anarchist papers Ed used to smuggle into prison. In the light of them my personal grief over my first serious quarrel with Ed now appeared like a mere speck on the social horizon of pain and blood. One by one the heroic names of those who had sacrificed their lives for their ideal or were still being martyred in prison came before me: my own Sasha and the others — all so finely attuned to the injustice of the world, so high-minded, driven by social forces to do the very thing they abhorred most, to destroy human life. Something deep in my consciousness rebelled against such tragic waste, yet I knew there was no escape. I had learned the fearful effects of organized violence: inevitably it begets more violence.

Sasha's spirit, fortunately, however, always hovered over me, helping me to forget everything personal. His letter of welcome on my release was the most beautiful I had so far received from him. It testified not only to his love and his faith in me, but also to his own valour and strength of character. Ed had kept the copies of the *Gefängniss-Blüthen,* the little underground magazine that Sasha, Nold, and Bauer were editing in prison. Sasha's will to life was apparent in every word, in his determination to fight on and not to permit the enemy to crush him. The spirit of the boy of twenty-three was extraordinary. It shamed me for my own faint heart. Yet I knew that the personal would always play a dominant part in my life. I was not hewn of one piece, like Sasha or other heroic figures. I had long realized that I was woven of many skeins, conflicting in shade and texture. To the end of my days I should be torn between the yearning for a personal life and the need of giving all to my ideal.

Ed came early the next day. He was his usual well-poised, outwardly calm self again. But I had looked into the turbulent waters of his soul too often to be misled by his reserve. He suggested that we take a trip. I had been out of prison about a fortnight and we had not yet had one complete day alone. We went to Manhattan Beach. The November air was sharp, the sea stormy; but the sun shone brightly. Ed was never much of a talker, but on this day he spoke a great deal about himself, his interest in the movement, his love for me. His ten years' incarceration had given him much time for reflection. He had come out believing as deeply in the truth and beauty of anarchism as when he had first entered prison. He continued to believe in the ultimate triumph of our ideas, but was now convinced that that time was far off. He no longer looked for great changes in his own lifetime. All he could do was to arrange his own life as nearly true to his vision as possible. In that life he wanted me; he wanted me with all the strength of his being. He admitted that he would be happier if I would give up the platform and devote my time to study, to writing or a profession. That would not keep him in constant anxiety about my life and freedom. "You are so intense, so impetuous," he said, "I fear for your safety." He begged me not to be angry because he believed that woman was primarily a mother. He was sure that the strongest motive in my devotion to the movement was unsatisfied motherhood seeking an outlet. "You are a typical mother, my little Emma, by build, by feeling. Your tenderness is the greatest proof of it."

I was profoundly stirred. When I could find words, poor inadequate words, to convey what I felt, I could only tell him again of my love, of my need of him, of my longing to give him much of what he craved. My starved motherhood — was that the main reason for my idealism? He had roused the old yearning for a child. But I had silenced the voice of the child for the sake of the universal, the all-absorbing passion of my life. Men were consecrated to ideals and yet were fathers of children. But man's physical share in the child is only a moment's; woman's part is for years — years of absorption in one human being to the exclusion of the rest of humanity. I would never give up the one for the other. But I would give him my love and devotion. Surely it must be possible for a man and a woman to have a beautiful love-life and yet be devoted to a great cause. We must try. I proposed that we find a place where we could live together, no longer separated by silly conventions — a home of our own, even if poor. Our love would beautify it, our work would give it meaning. Ed became enthusiastic over the idea and took me in his arms. My strong, big lover, he had always hated the least demonstration of affection in public. Now in his joy he forgot that we were in a restaurant. I teased him on his having renounced his good manners, but he was like a child, gay and frolicsome as I had never seen him before.

Nearly four weeks passed before we could carry out our plans. The papers had turned me into a celebrity, and I soon learned the German truism: "*Man kann nicht ungestraft unter Palmen wandeln.*" I knew of the American craze for celebrities, especially the American women's hunt for anyone in the limelight, be it prize-fighter, baseball-player, matinée idol, wife-killer, or decrepit European aristocrat. Thanks to my imprisonment and the space given to my name in the newspapers, I also became a celebrity. Every day brought stacks of invitations to luncheons and dinners. Everyone seemed eager to " take me up."

Of the many invitations showered on me I welcomed most one from the Swintons. They wrote asking me to come to dinner and to bring Ed and Justus. Their apartment was simply and beautifully furnished and full of curios and gifts. I saw a lovely *samovar* sent them by Russian exiles in recognition of Swinton's tireless work in behalf of Russian freedom, an exquisite set of Sèvres given him by French Communards who had escaped the fury of Thiers and Galliffet after the short-lived Paris Commune of 1871, beautiful peasant embroidery from Hungary, and other gifts of appreciation of the splendid spirit and personality of the great American libertarian.

On our arrival John Swinton, tall and erect, with a silk cap on his white hair, proceeded to scold me for what I had said about the Negroes in prison. He had read in the New York *World* my disclosures of conditions in the penitentiary. He liked the article, but he was grieved to see that Emma Goldman had " the white man's prejudice against the coloured race." I was dumbfounded. I could not understand how anyone, least of all a man like John Swinton, could read race prejudice into my story. I had pointed out the discrimination

practised between sick and starved white women and Negro favourites. I should have protested as much had coloured women been robbed
of their rations. "To be sure, to be sure," Swinton replied; "still,
you should not have emphasized the partiality. We white people have
committed so many crimes against the Negro that no amount of extra
kindness can atone for them. The matron is no doubt a beast, but I
forgive her much for her sympathy with the poor Negro prisoners."
"But she was not moved by such considerations!" I protested; "she
was kind because she could use them in every despicable way." Swinton
was not convinced. He had been closely allied with the most active
abolitionists, he had fought and been wounded in the Civil War; it
was apparent that his feeling for the coloured race had made him
partial. There was no use arguing the matter further; moreover, Mrs.
Swinton was calling us to the table.

They were charming hosts. John was especially gracious and full
of warmth. He was a man of wide experience in people and affairs and
he proved a veritable mint of information to me. I learned for the
first time of his share in the campaign to save the Chicago anarchists
from the gallows and of other public-spirited Americans who had
valiantly defended my comrades. I became acquainted with Swinton's
activities against the Russian-American Extradition Treaty, and the
part he and his friends had played in the labour movement. The evening with the Swintons showed me a new angle of my adopted country. Until my imprisonment I had believed that except for Albert
Parsons, Dyer D. Lum, Voltairine de Cleyre, and a few others America
was barren of idealists. Her men and women cared only for material
acquisitions, I had thought. Swinton's account of the liberty-loving
people who had been and still were in every struggle against oppression changed my superficial judgment. John Swinton made me see
that Americans, once aroused, were as capable of idealism and sacrifice as my Russian heroes and heroines. I left the Swintons with a
new faith in the possibilities of America. On our way down town I
talked with Ed and Justus, telling them that from now on I meant to
devote myself to propaganda in English, among the American people.
Propaganda in foreign circles was, of course, very necessary, but real
social changes could be accomplished only by the natives. Their enlightenment was therefore much more vital, we all agreed.

At last Ed and I had a place of our own. With one hundred and fifty
dollars I received from the New York *World* for my article on prisons

we furnished a four-room flat on Eleventh Street. Most of our furniture was second-hand, but we had a new bed and couch. The latter, together with a desk and a few chairs, made up my sanctum. Ed was surprised when I stressed the need of a room for myself. It was hard enough to be separated during work hours, he said; in our free hours he wanted me near him. But I held out for my own corner. My childhood and youth had been poisoned by being compelled to share my room with someone else. Ever since I had become a free being, I had insisted on privacy for at least a part of the day and the night.

But for this little cloud our life in our own home started gloriously. Ed was earning only seven dollars a week as an insurance agent, but he seldom returned from work without a flower or some other gift, a lovely china cup or a vase. He knew my love for colour and he never forgot to bring something that would help make our place cheerful and bright. We had many visitors, far too many for Ed's peace of mind. He wanted quiet and to be alone with me. But Fedya and Claus had shared my life in the past, had been part of my struggle. I needed their companionship.

Claus had got along satisfactorily on Blackwell's Island. He had missed his precious beer, of course, but otherwise he had done well. After his release from the island Claus started an anarchist paper, *Der Sturmvogel,* of which he was the main contributor, besides setting up, printing, and even delivering the paper. But, busy as he was, he could not keep out of mischief. Ed had little patience with my friend, whom he nicknamed *Pechvogel.*

Fedya had secured a position on a New York publication soon after my imprisonment. He was doing pen-and-ink sketches and was already being recognized as one of the best in his field. He had begun at fifteen dollars a week, regularly contributing to my needs during my ten months in the penitentiary. Now that he was earning twenty-five, he insisted on my taking at least ten, so as to make any appeal to our comrades unnecessary, which he knew I could not bear. He had remained the same loyal soul, more matured, with growing confidence in himself and his art.

He felt that in order to keep his position he could no longer appear openly in our ranks. But his interest in the movement continued and his anxiety for Sasha did not abate. During my imprisonment he had helped to buy things for Sasha. It was little enough one was permitted in the Western Penitentiary: condensed milk, soap, underwear, and socks. Ed had looked after the matter. Now I was eager to attend to these things myself and I also decided to begin a new campaign for the commutation of Sasha's sentence.

I had been out two months, but I did not forget the unfortunates in prison. I wanted to do something for them. I needed money for this purpose and I also wanted to earn my own living.

Much against Ed's wishes, I began to work as a practical nurse. Dr. Julius Hoffmann sent me his private patients after treating them in St. Mark's Hospital. Dr. White had told me before I left the prison that he would give me work in his office. He could not recommend his patients to me, he had said. " They are mostly stupid, they would be afraid you'd poison them." The dear man kept his word: he employed me for several hours a day, and I also got work in the newly organized Beth-Israel Hospital on East Broadway. I loved my profession and I was able to earn more money than at any time previously. The joy of no longer having to grind at the machine, in or out of a shop, was great; greater still the satisfaction of having more time for reading and for public activity.

Ever since I had come into the anarchist movement I had longed for a friend of my own sex, a kindred spirit with whom I could share the inmost thoughts and feelings I could not express to men, not even to Ed. Instead of friendship from women I had met with much antagonism, petty envy and jealousy because men liked me. Of course, there were exceptions: Annie Netter, always big and generous, Natasha Notkin, Maria Louise, and one or two others. But my bond with these was the movement; there was no close personal, intimate point of contact. The coming into my life of Voltairine de Cleyre held out the hope of a fine friendship.

After her visit to me in prison she had kept on writing wonderful letters of comradeship and affection. In one of them she had suggested that on my release I come straight to her. She would make me rest before her fire-place, she would wait on me, read to me, and try to make me forget my ghastly experience. Shortly after that she wrote another letter saying that she and her friend A. Gordon were coming to New York and were anxious to visit me. I did not want to refuse her — she meant so much to me — but I could not bear to see Gordon. On my first visit to Philadelphia I had met the man at a group circle and he impressed me badly. He was a follower of Most and as such would hate me. At the gathering of the comrades he had denounced

me as a disrupter of the movement, charging me with being in it only
for sensational ends. He would not participate in any meeting where
I was to speak. Not being naïve enough to believe that my imprisonment had added to my importance, I could see no cause for Gordon's
change towards me. I wrote this frankly to Voltairine, explaining that
I preferred not to see Gordon. I was permitted only two visits a
month; I would not give up Ed's visit, the other being taken up by
near friends. Since then I had not heard any more from Voltairine,
but I ascribed her silence to illness.

On my release I had received many letters of congratulation from
friends who shared my ideas as well as from persons unknown to me.
But not one word did I get from Voltairine. When I expressed my
surprise to Ed, he informed me that Voltairine had felt much hurt
because I had refused to permit Gordon to visit me on the island.
I was sorry to learn that such a splendid revolutionist could turn from
me because I did not care to see a friend of hers. Noticing my disappointment, Ed remarked: " Gordon is not only her friend, he is more
than that." But it made no difference; I did not see why a free woman
should expect her friends to accept her lover. I felt that Voltairine
had shown herself too narrow ever again to enable me to be free and
at ease with her. My hope of a close friendship with her was destroyed.

I was somewhat consoled by another woman, young and beautiful,
coming into my life. Her name was Emma Lee. During my imprisonment she had written Ed expressing interest in my case. Her letters
were signed only with her initials; her handwriting being very masculine, Ed had thought her to be a man. " Imagine my surprise," Ed
told me on one of his visits, " when a young and charming woman
walked into my bachelor quarters." But not only was Emma Lee
charming; she also had brains and a fine sense of humour. I was
drawn to her from the first moment when Ed brought her to see me in
prison. After my release Emma Lee and I were much together. At
first she was very reticent about herself, but in the course of time
I learned her story. She had become interested in me because she had
been in prison herself and knew its horrors. She had become a free-
thinker and had emancipated herself from the belief that love is
justified only when sanctioned by law. She had met a man who assured
her that he shared her ideas. He was married and very unhappy. In
her, he said, he had found more than a comrade; he had fallen in love

with her. She loved him in return, but their relationship in the bigoted atmosphere of a small Southern town was soon made impossible. They went to Washington, but there, too, persecution followed. They planned to remove to New York, and Emma Lee returned to her native town to dispose of a piece of property she owned. She had not been there more than a week when her place was set on fire. The house was insured, and presently Emma was arrested on the charge of incendiarism. She was convicted and given five years in prison. During the entire time the man gave no sign of life; he left her to her doom and was keeping under cover in some Eastern city.

Her bitter disillusionment was harder to bear than the imprisonment. The descriptions Emma Lee gave of life in the Southern penitentiary made existence on Blackwell's Island seem like paradise. In that hell-hole Negro convicts, male and female, were flogged for the least infraction of the rules. White women had either to submit to the keepers or starve. The atmosphere was lurid with vile talk and viler acts by keepers and prisoners alike. Emma was forced to be on constant guard against the demands of the Warden and the prison doctor. On one occasion they nearly drove her to murder in self-defence. She would not have come out alive if she had not succeeded in getting a note to a friend in the town, a woman. This friend interested some people who began quietly petitioning the Governor, finally obtaining a pardon for Emma Lee after she had served two years.

Since then she had devoted herself entirely to bringing about fundamental changes in prison conditions. She had already succeeded in getting her former tormentors removed from office, and now she was co-operating with the Society for Prison Reform.

Emma Lee was a rare soul, educated, refined, and free-minded, although she had not read much libertarian literature. Through her own affairs she had also emancipated herself from the anti-Negro prejudice of the Southerner. Most admirable to me was her lack of bitterness towards men. Her own love tragedy had not narrowed her outlook on life. Men were egotistical and thoughtless towards women's needs, she would say; even the freest of them wanted only to possess women. But they were interesting and entertaining. I did not agree with her about the egotism of men, and when I would cite Ed as an exception, she would reply: " There is no doubt he loves you, but — but! " However, they got on famously. They fought about everything, but it was all done in a friendly spirit. I was their common tie. No woman except my own sister Helena loved me as much as Emma did. As for Ed, he showed his affection in so many ways that I could not doubt him. Yet I knew that of the two it was Emma Lee who had looked deeper into my soul.

Emma Lee was employed in the Nurses' Settlement on Henry Street and I often visited her there, sometimes as the guest of the women at the head of the institution. Miss Lillian D. Wald, Lavinia Dock, and Miss MacDowell were among the first American women I met who felt an interest in the economic condition of the masses. They were genuinely concerned with the people of the East Side. My contact with them, as with John Swinton, brought me close to new American types, men and women of ideals, capable of fine, generous deeds. Like some of the Russian revolutionists they, too, had come from wealthy homes and had completely consecrated themselves to what they considered a great cause. Yet their work seemed palliative to me. " Teaching the poor to eat with a fork is all very well," I once said to Emma Lee; " but what good does it do if they have not the food? Let them first become the masters of life; they will then know how to eat and how to live." She agreed with my view that, sincere as the settlement workers were, they were doing more harm than good. They were creating snobbery among the very people they were trying to help. A young girl who had been active in a shirtwaist-makers' strike, for instance, was taken up by them and exhibited as the pet of the settlement. The girl put on airs and constantly talked of the " ignorance of the poor," who lacked understanding for culture and refinement. " The poor are so coarse and vulgar ! " she once told Emma. Her wedding was soon to take place at the settlement, and Emma invited me to attend the affair.

It was gaudy, almost vulgar. The bride, dressed in cheap finery, looked utterly out of place in that background. Not that the settlement women were living in luxury; on the contrary, everything was of the simplest, though of the best quality. The very simplicity of the environment exaggerated the shamed poverty of the married couple and the embarrassment of their orthodox parents. It was very painful to behold, most of all the self-importance of the bride. When I congratulated her on choosing such a fine-looking fellow for her husband, she said: " Yes, he's quite nice, but of course he's not of my sphere. You see, I am really marrying below my station."

All winter Ed had been suffering from fallen arches; much walking and climbing of stairs was causing him unbearable pain. In the early spring his condition became so bad that he had to give up his job with the insurance agency. I was earning enough for both of us, but Ed would not accept "support from a woman." My proud sweetheart was compelled to join the ranks of the unemployed looking for work. There was nothing in the great city of New York for a man of his culture and knowledge of languages. "If I were a hod-carrier or a tailor," he would say, "I could get a job. But I'm only a useless intellectual." He worried, lost sleep, grew thin, and became very de-pressed. His worst misery was that he had to remain at home while I went to work. His male self-respect could not endure such a situation.

It occurred to me that we might try something like our ice-cream parlour in Worcester. It had been successful there; why not in New York? Ed approved of the project and suggested that we proceed at once.

I had saved a little money, and Fedya offered us more. Friends advised Brownsville: it was a growing centre, and a store could be got not far from the race-tracks, where thousands of people were passing daily. So to Brownsville we went, and fixed up a beautiful place. Thousands did pass by there, but they kept on passing. They were in a hurry to get to the race-track, and on their way home they had already visited some ice-cream store nearer the track. Our daily receipts were not enough to cover our expenses. We could not even keep up the weekly payments on the furniture we had bought for the two rooms we had rented in Brownsville. One afternoon a wagon drove up and proceeded to collect beds, tables, chairs, and everything else we had. Ed tried to laugh away our plight, but he was evidently unhappy. We gave up the business and returned to New York. In three months we had lost five hundred dollars, besides the work Ed, Claus, and I had put into the wretched venture.

I had realized at the very beginning of my nursing work that I should have to take up a regular course in a training-school. Practical nurses were paid and treated like servants, and without a diploma I could not hope to get employment as a trained nurse. Dr. Hoffmann urged me to enter St. Mark's Hospital, where he could get me credits for one year because of my experience. It was a great opportunity, but there was also another and a more alluring one. It was Europe.

Ed had always talked with glee of Vienna, of its beauty, charm, and possibilities. He wanted me to go there to study in the Allgemeines

Krankenhaus. I could take up midwifery and other branches of nursing, he advised me. It would give me greater material independence later on and also enable us to be more together. It would be hard to endure another year's separation when I had barely been given back to him; but he was willing to let me go, knowing it was for my good. It seemed a fantastic idea for people as poor as we, but gradually Ed's enthusiasm infected me. I agreed to go to Vienna, but I would combine my trip abroad with a lecture tour in England and Scotland. Our British comrades had often asked me to come over.

Ed had found a job in the wood work shop of a Hungarian acquaintance. The man offered to lend him money, but Fedya insisted on his priority as my old friend. He would pay my passage and send me twenty-five dollars a month during my entire stay in Vienna.

There was a dark shadow, however: the thought of Sasha in prison. Europe was so far away! Ed and Emma Lee promised to keep in correspondence with him and look after his needs. Sasha himself urged me to go. Nothing could be done for him now, he wrote, and Europe would give me the opportunity to meet our great people — Kropotkin, Malatesta, Louise Michel. I should be able to learn much from them and be better equipped for my activities in the American movement. It was just like my consecrated Sasha to think of me always in terms of the Cause.

On the 15th of August 1895, exactly six years since my new life in New York had begun, I sailed for England. My departure was quite different from my arrival in New York in 1889. I was very poor then, poor in more than merely material things. I was a child, inexperienced and alone in the whirlpool of the American metropolis. Now I had experience, a name; I had been through the crucible; I had friends. Above all, I had the love of a beautiful personality. I was rich, yet I was sad. The Western Penitentiary lay heavily on my heart, with the thought of Sasha there.

I again travelled steerage, my means not permitting more than sixteen dollars for the passage. But there were only a few passengers, some of whom had been no longer in the States than I. They considered themselves Americans and they were treated accordingly, with more decency than the poor emigrants who had pilgrimed over as I did to the Promised Land in 1886.

CHAPTER XIV

OUTDOOR MEETINGS IN AMERICA ARE RARE, THEIR ATMOSPHERE always surcharged with impending clashes between the audience and the police. Not so in England. Here the right to assemble constantly in the open is an institution. It has become a British habit, like bacon for breakfast. The most opposing ideas and creeds find expression in the parks and squares of English cities. There is nothing to cause undue excitement and there is no display of armed force. The lone bobby on the outskirts of the crowd is there as a matter of form; it is not his duty to disperse meetings or club the people.

The social centre of the masses is the out-of-door meeting in the park. On Sundays they flock there as they do to music-halls on weekdays. They cost nothing and they are much more entertaining. Crowds, often numbering thousands, drift from platform to platform as they would at a country fair, not so much to listen or learn as to be amused. The main performers at these gatherings are the hecklers, who hugely enjoy bombarding the speakers with questions. Pity him who fails to get the cue from these tormentors or who is not quick enough at repartee. He soon finds himself confused and the helpless butt for boisterous ridicule. All this I learned after I nearly came to grief at my first meeting in Hyde Park.

It was a novel experience to talk out of doors, with only a lone policeman placidly looking on. Alas, the crowd, too, was placid. It felt like climbing a steep mountain to speak against such inertia. I soon grew tired and my throat began to hurt, but I kept on. All at once the audience began to show signs of life. A volley of questions, like bullets, came flying at me from all directions. The unexpected attack, finding me quite unprepared, bewildered and irritated me. I felt my trend of thought slip from me, and my anger rise. Then a man in front called out: " Don't mind it, old girl, go right on. Heckling is a good old British custom." "Good, you call it?" I retorted; "I think it is rotten to interrupt a speaker like that. But all right, fire away, and don't blame me if you get the worst of the bargain." "That's right, old dear," the audience shouted; "go ahead, let's see what you can do."

I had been speaking on the futility of politics and its corrupting influence when the first shot was fired. "How about honest politicians — don't you believe there are such?" "If there are, I never heard of one," I hurled back. "Politicians promise you heaven before election and give you hell after." "'Ear! 'Ear!" they screamed in approval. I had barely got back to my speech when the next bolt struck me. "I say, old girl, why do you speak of heaven? — Do you believe in such a place?" "Of course not," I replied; "I was only referring to the heaven you stupidly believe in." "Well, if there is no heaven, where else would the poor get their reward?" another heckler demanded. "Nowhere, unless they insist on their right here — take their reward by gaining possession of the earth." I continued that even if there were a heaven, the common people would not be tolerated there. "You see," I explained, "the masses have lived in hell so long they would not know how to behave in heaven. The angel at the gate would kick them out for disorderly conduct." This was followed by another half-hour of fencing, which kept the crowd in spasms. Finally they called for the hecklers to stop, admit defeat, and let me go on.

My fame travelled quickly; the crowds grew in size at every meeting. Our literature sold in large quantities, which delighted my comrades. They wanted me to remain in London because I could do so much good there. But I knew that out-of-door speaking was not for me. My throat would not hold out under the strain and I could not bear the disturbing noises of the street traffic so close at hand. Besides, I realized that people standing up for hours grew too restless and weary to be able to concentrate or to follow a serious talk. My work meant too much to me to turn it into a circus for the amusement of the British public.

More than my exploits in the park I enjoyed meeting people and witnessing the vital spirit which prevailed in the anarchist movement. In the United States activities were being carried on almost exclusively among the foreign element. There were few native anarchists in America, while the movement in England supported several weekly and monthly publications. One of them was *Freedom,* among whose contributors and co-workers were some very brilliant and talented people, including Peter Kropotkin, John Turner, Alfred Marsh, William Wess, and others. *Liberty* was another anarchist publication, issued in London by James Tochatti, a follower of the poet William Morris. The *Torch* was a little paper published by two sisters, Olivia and Helen Rossetti. They were only fourteen and seventeen years old, respectively, but developed in mind and body far beyond their age. They did all the writing for the paper, even setting the type and attending to the press work themselves. The *Torch* office, formerly the nursery of the girls, became a gathering-place for foreign anarchists, particularly those from Italy, where severe persecution was taking place. The refugees naturally flocked to the Rossettis, who were themselves of Italian origin. Their grandfather, the Italian poet and patriot Gabriele Rossetti, had been condemned to death in 1824 by Austria, under whose yoke Italy then was. Gabriele fled to England, settling in London, where he became Professor of Italian at King's College. Olivia and Helen were the daughters of Gabriele Rossetti's second son, William Michael, the famous critic. Evidently the girls had inherited their revolutionary tendencies as well as their literary talents. While in London, I spent much time with them, greatly enjoying their prodigious hospitality and the inspiring atmosphere of their circle.

One of the members of the *Torch* group was William Benham, familiarly known as the " boy anarchist." He attached himself to me, constituting himself my companion at the meetings as well as on trips through the city.

Anarchist activities in London were not limited to the natives. England was the haven for refugees from all lands, who carried on their work without hindrance. By comparison with the United States the political freedom in Great Britain seemed like the millennium come. But economically the country was far behind America.

I had myself experienced want and I knew of the poverty in the large industrial centres of the United States. But never had I seen such abject misery and squalor as I did in London, Leeds, and Glasgow. Its effects impressed me as not being the results of yesterday or even of years. They were century-old, passed on from generation to generation, apparently rooted in the very marrow of the British masses. One of the most appalling sights was that of able-bodied men running ahead of a cab for blocks to be on the spot in time to open the door for a "gentleman." For such services they would receive a penny, or tuppence at most. After a month's stay in England I understood the reason for so much political freedom. It was a safety-valve against the fearful destitution. The British Government no doubt felt that as long as it permitted its subjects to let off steam in unhampered talk, there was no danger of rebellion. I could find no other explanation for the inertia and the indifference of the people to their slavish conditions.

One of my aims in visiting England was to meet the outstanding personalities in the anarchist movement. Unfortunately Kropotkin was out of town, but would be back before I left. Enrico Malatesta was in the city. I found him living behind his little shop, but there was no one to interpret for me, and I could not speak Italian. His kindly smile, however, mirrored a congenial personality and made me feel as if I had known him all my life. Louise Michel I met almost immediately upon my arrival. The French comrades I stayed with had arranged a reception for my first Sunday in London. Ever since I had read about the Paris Commune, its glorious beginning and its terrible end, Louise Michel had stood out sublime in her love for humanity, grand in her zeal and courage. She was angular, gaunt, aged before her years (she was only sixty-two); but there was spirit and youth in her eyes, and a smile so tender that it immediately won my heart. This, then, was the woman who had survived the savagery of the respectable Paris mob. Its fury had drowned the Commune in the blood of the workers and had strewn the streets of Paris with thousands of dead and wounded. Not being appeased, it had also reached out for Louise. Again and again she had courted death; on the barricades of Père Lachaise, the last stand of the Communards, Louise had chosen the most dangerous position for herself. In court she had demanded the same penalty as was meted out to her comrades, scorning clemency on the grounds of sex. She would die for the Cause. Whether out of fear or awe of this heroic figure, the murderous Paris *bourgeoisie* had not dared to kill her. They preferred to doom her to slow death in New Caledonia. But they had reckoned without the fortitude of Louise Michel, her devotion and capacity for consecration to her fellow sufferers. In New Caledonia she became the hope and inspiration of the exiles. In sickness she nursed their bodies; in depression she cheered their spirits. The amnesty for the Communards brought Louise back with the others to France. She found herself the acclaimed idol of the French masses. They adored her as their *Mère Louise, bien aimée.*

Shortly after her return from exile Louise headed a demonstration of unemployed to the Esplanade des Invalides. Thousands were out of work for a long time and hungry. Louise led the procession into the bakery shops, for which she was arrested and condemned to five years' imprisonment. In court she defended the right of the hungry man to bread, even if he has to " steal " it. Not the sentence, but the loss of her dear mother proved the greatest blow to Louise at her trial. She loved her with an absorbing affection and now she declared that she had nothing else to live for except the revolution. In 1886 Louise was pardoned, but she refused to accept any favours from the State. She had to be taken forcibly from prison in order to be set at liberty.

During a large meeting in Havre someone fired two shots at Louise while she was on the platform talking. One went through her hat; the other struck her behind the ear. The operation, although very painful, called forth no complaint from Louise. Instead she lamented her poor animals left alone in her rooms and the inconvenience the delay would cause her woman friend who was waiting for her in the next town. The man who nearly killed her had been influenced by a priest to commit the act, but Louise tried her utmost to have him released. She induced a famous lawyer to defend her assailant and she herself appeared in court to plead with the judge in his behalf. Her sympathies were particularly stirred by the man's young daughter, whom she could not bear to have become fatherless by the man's being sent to prison. Louise's stand did not fail to influence even her fanatical assailant.

Later Louise was to participate in a great strike in Vienne, but she was arrested in the Gare du Lyon as she was about to board the train. The Cabinet member responsible for the massacre of the working-men in Fourmies saw in Louise a formidable force that he had repeatedly tried to crush. Now he demanded her removal from jail to an insane asylum on the ground that she was deranged and dangerous. It was this fiendish plan to dispose of Louise that induced her comrades to persuade her to move to England.

The vulgar French papers continued to paint her as a wild beast, as *" Là Vierge Rouge,"* without any feminine qualities or charm.

The more decent wrote of her with bated breath. They feared her, but they also looked up to her as something far above their empty souls and hearts. As I sat near her at our first meeting, I wondered how anyone could fail to find charm in her. It was true that she cared little about her appearance. Indeed, I had never seen a woman so utterly oblivious of anything that concerned herself. Her dress was shabby, her bonnet ancient. Everything she wore was ill-fitting. But her whole being was illumined by an inner light. One quickly succumbed to the spell of her radiant personality, so compelling in its strength, so moving in its childlike simplicity. The afternoon with Louise was an experience unlike anything that had happened till then in my life. Her hand in mine, its tender pressure on my head, her words of endearment and close comradeship, made my soul expand, reach out towards the spheres of beauty where she dwelt.

After my return from Leeds and Glasgow, where I spoke at large meetings and became acquainted with many active and devoted workers, I found a letter from Kropotkin asking me to visit him. At last I was to realize my long-cherished dream, to meet my great teacher.

Peter Kropotkin was a lineal descendant of the Ruriks and in the direct succession to the Russian throne. But he gave up his title and wealth for the cause of humanity. He did more: since becoming an anarchist he had forgone a brilliant scientific career to be better able to devote himself to the development and interpretation of anarchist philosophy. He became the most outstanding exponent of anarchist communism, its clearest thinker and theoretician. He was recognized by friend and foe as one of the greatest minds and most unique personalities of the nineteenth century. On my way to Bromley, where the Kropotkins lived, I felt nervous. I feared I should find Peter difficult of approach, too absorbed in his work for ordinary social intercourse.

But five minutes in his presence put me at my ease. The family was away and Peter himself received me in such a gracious and kindly manner that I felt at home with him at once. He would have tea ready directly, he said. Meanwhile should I like to see his carpenter shop and the articles he had made with his own hands? He took me into his study and pointed with great pride to a table, a bench, and some shelves he had fashioned. They were very simple things, but he gloried in them; they represented labour and he had always stressed the need of combining mental activity with manual effort. Now he could demonstrate how well the two can be blended. No artisan ever looked more lovingly and with greater reverence upon the things created by his hands than did Peter Kropotkin, the scientist and philosopher. His wholesome joy in the products of his toil were symbolic of the burning faith he had in the masses, in their capacity to create and fashion life.

Over the tea which he himself prepared, Kropotkin asked me about conditions in America, about the movement, and about Sasha. He had followed the latter's case and he knew every phase of it, expressing great regard and concern for Sasha. I related to him my impressions of England, the contrasts between its poverty and extreme wealth alongside of political freedom. Was it not a bone thrown to the masses to pacify them, I asked. Peter agreed with my view. He said that England was a nation of shopkeepers engaged in buying and selling instead of producing the necessaries required to keep her people from starvation. " The British *bourgeoisie* has good reason to fear the spread of discontent, and political liberties are the best security against it. English statesmen are shrewd," he continued; " they have always seen to it that the political reins should not be pulled too tightly. The average Britisher loves to think he is free; it helps him to forget his misery. That is the irony and pathos of the English working classes. Yet England could feed every man, woman, and child of her population if she would but release the vast lands now held in monopoly by an old, decaying aristocracy." My visit with Peter Kropotkin convinced me that true greatness is always coupled with simplicity. He was the personification of both. The lucidity and brilliance of his mind combined with his warm-heartedness into the harmonious whole of a fascinating and gracious personality.

I was sorry to leave England; during my short visit I had met many people and made friends and I was enriched by personal contact with my great teachers. The days were indeed glorious. Never had I seen such a luscious green of trees and grass, such a profusion of gardens, parks, and flowers. At the same time I had never seen such dreary and dismal poverty. Nature herself seemed to be discriminating between rich and poor. The clear blue sky in Hampstead looked a dirty grey in the East End, the sunshine a blot of dull yellow. The crass distinctions between the different social layers in England were appalling. They increased my hatred of injustice and my determination to work for my ideal. I begrudged the loss of time which my proposed training as a nurse would involve. But I consoled myself with the hope that I should be better equipped on my return to America. I could not remain in London: my course was to begin on the first of October. I had to leave for Vienna.

Vienna proved even more fascinating than Ed had described it. Ringstrasse, the principal street, with its array of splendid old mansions and gorgeous cafés, the spacious promenades lined with stately trees, and particularly the Prater, more forest than park, made the city one of the most beautiful I had ever seen. The whole was enhanced by the gaiety and light-heartedness of the Viennese people. London seemed a tomb by comparison. There was colour here, life and joy. I longed to become part of it, to throw myself into its generous arms, to sit in the cafés or in the Prater and watch the crowds. But I had come for another purpose; I could not afford to be distracted.

My studies included, besides the subject of midwifery, a course in children's diseases. In my short experience as nurse I had seen how ill-fitted most graduate nurses were to take care of children. They were harsh and domineering and lacked understanding. My own childhood had been made hideous by these things, but it had also filled me with sympathy for children. I had much more patience with them than with grown-ups. Their dependence, aggravated by illness, always moved me deeply. I wanted not merely to give them affection, but to equip myself for their care.

The Allgemeines Krankenhaus, which gave courses on and treated every ill of the human body, offered splendid opportunities to the eager and willing student. I found the place a remarkable institution, a veritable city in itself, with its thousands of patients, nurses, doctors, and care-takers. The men in charge of the departments were world-renowned in their particular spheres. The obstetric courses were fortunate in having at their head a famous gynecologist, Professor Braun. He was not only a splendid teacher, but also a lovable man. His lectures were never dry or tedious. In the very midst of an explanation or even during an operation the Herr Professor would enliven things by a humorous anecdote or by remarks embarrassing to the German lady students. In explaining, for example, the comparatively large birth-rate during the months of November and December, he would say: "It's the carnival, ladies. During that gayest Vienna festival even the most virtuous girls get caught. I do not mean to say that they give way easily to their natural urge. It is only that Nature has made them so fertile. A man has only to look at them, so to speak, and they become pregnant. So we must put it all on Nature and not blame the young things." Again, Professor Braun would outrage some of the more moral students by relating the story of a certain female patient. Several of the male students had been asked to examine her and diagnose the case. One by one they carried out the order, but no one ventured to speak out. They were waiting for the Professor to give his opinion. After his examination the great man said: " Gentlemen, it is a case most of you have already had, or you have it now, or you will have it in the future. Very few can resist the charm of its origin, the pain of its development, or the price of its cure. It happens to be syphilis."

Among those attending the obstetric courses were a number of Jewish girls from Kiev and Odessa. One had even come all the way from Palestine. None of them knew enough German to understand the lectures. The Russians were very poor, compelled to exist on ten roubles a month. It was an inspiration to find such courage and perseverance for the sake of a profession. But when I expressed my admiration, the girls replied that it was quite an ordinary thing: thousands of Russians, both Jewish and Gentile, were doing it. All the students abroad lived on very little; why could not they? " But your lack of German," I asked; " how will you get the lectures or read the text-books? How do you expect to pass your examinations? " They did not know, but they would manage somehow. After all, every Jew understands a little German, they said. Two of the girls were especially sympathetic to me. They were living in a wretched little hole, while I had a large and beautiful room. I asked them to share it with me. I knew that we should have to do night duty in the hospital, but most likely not at the same time. Our living together would reduce their expenses, and I should also be able to help them with their German. Soon our place became a centre for the Russian students of both sexes.

I was known in Vienna as Mrs. E. G. Brady. I had to come abroad under that name, for I should not have been admitted under my own. I had emancipated myself from the notion that one must not assume a fictitious name. I could, of course, have procured a passport on Kershner's citizenship papers, but I had not used his name since I left him. In fact, after that I saw him only once, in 1893, when I was ill in Rochester. I had nothing but painful recollections of that name. Brady was Irish, and I knew it would arouse no suspicion as to my identity. Passports could then be had for the asking.

In Vienna I had to be extremely careful. The Habsburgs were

despotic, the persecution of socialists and anarchists severe. I could therefore not associate openly with my comrades, as I did not wish to be expelled. But it did not prevent me from meeting interesting people active in various social movements.

My studies and frequent night duty in the hospital did not lessen my interest in the cultural events of Vienna, its music and theatres. I met a young anarchist, Stefan Grossmann, who was remarkably well informed about the life of the city. He had many traits I disliked: his efforts to hide his origin in chameleon-like acceptance of every silly Gentile habit irritated me. The very first time I met Grossmann he told me that his fencing-master had admired his *germanische Beine* (Germanic legs). " I don't think that's much of a compliment," I replied; " now, if he had admired your Yiddish nose, that would be something to boast about." However, he came often, and gradually I learned to like him. He was an omnivorous reader and a great admirer of the new literature — Friedrich Nietzsche, Ibsen, Hauptmann, von Hoffmansthal and its other exponents who were hurling their anathemas against old values. I had read some of their works in snatches in the *Arme Teufel,* the weekly published in Detroit by Robert Reitzel, a brilliant writer. It was the one German paper in the States that kept its readers in contact with the new literary spirit in Europe. What I had read in its columns from the works of the great minds that were stirring Europe only whetted my appetite.

In Vienna one could hear interesting lectures on modern German prose and poetry. One could read the works of the young iconoclasts in art and letters, the most daring among them being Nietzsche. The magic of his language, the beauty of his vision, carried me to undreamed-of heights. I longed to devour every line of his writings, but I was too poor to buy them. Fortunately Grossmann had a supply of Nietzsche and other moderns.

I had to do my reading at the expense of much-needed sleep; but what was physical strain in view of my raptures over Nietzsche? The fire of his soul, the rhythm of his song, made life richer, fuller, and more wonderful for me. I wanted to share these treasures with my beloved, and I wrote him long letters depicting the new world I had discovered. His replies were evasive; Ed evidently did not share my fervour for the new art. He was more interested in my studies and in my health, and he urged me not to tax my energies with idle reading. I was disappointed, but I consoled myself that he would appreciate the revolutionary spirit of the new literature when he had a chance to read it for himself. I must get money, I decided, to bring back a supply of books to Ed.

Through one of the students I learned of a lecture course given by an eminent young professor, Sigmund Freud. I found, however, that it would be difficult to attend his series, only physicians and holders of special cards being admitted. My friend suggested that I enroll for the course of Professor Bruhl, who also was discussing sex problems. As one of his students I should have a better chance to secure admission to Freud.

Professor Bruhl was an old man with a feeble voice. The subjects he treated were mystifying to me. He talked of "Urnings," "Lesbians," and other strange topics. His hearers, too, were strange: feminine-looking men with coquettish manners and women distinctly masculine, with deep voices. They were certainly a peculiar assembly. Greater clarity in these matters came to me later on when I heard Sigmund Freud. His simplicity and earnestness and the brilliance of his mind combined to give one the feeling of being led out of a dark cellar into broad daylight. For the first time I grasped the full significance of sex repression and its effect on human thought and action. He helped me to understand myself, my own needs; and I also realized that only people of depraved minds could impugn the motives or find " impure " so great and fine a personality as Freud.

My various interests in Vienna kept me occupied the greater part of the day. Still I managed to attend plays and hear a good deal of music. I heard for the first time the entire *Ring des Nibelungen* and other works of Wagner. His music had always stirred me; the Vienna performances — magnificent voices, splendid orchestra, and masterly leadership — were enthralling. After such an experience it was painful to sit through a Wagner concert conducted by his son. One night Siegfried Wagner conducted his own composition *Der Bärenhäuter*. It was pale enough; but when it came to a work of his illustrious father, he was completely ineffectual. I left the concert in disgust.

Vienna brought me many new experiences. One of the greatest was Eleonora Duse as Magda in Sudermann's *Heimat*. The play itself was a new dramatic event, but what Duse put into it of herself transcended Sudermann's talents and gave to his work its real dramatic depth. Years before, in New Haven, I had seen Sarah Bernhardt in *Fedora*. Her voice, her gestures, her intensity were a revelation. I thought then that no one could rise to greater heights, but Eleonora Duse attained a higher zenith. Hers was a genius too rich and too complete for artifice, her interpretation too real for stage tricks. There were no violent gestures, no unnecessary movements, no studied volume of sound. Her voice, rich and vibrant, held rhythm in every tone, her expressive features reflecting her own wealth of emotion. Eleonora Duse interpreted every nuance of the turbulent nature of Magda blended with her own spirit. It was art reaching towards the heavens, itself a star on the firmament of life.

When examinations drew near, I could no longer indulge in the temptations of the fascinating city on the Danube. Soon I was the proud holder of two diplomas, one for midwifery and one for nursing: I could return home. But I was loath to leave Vienna; it had given me so much. I lingered on for two more weeks. During that time I was a great deal with my comrades and learned much from them about the anarchist movement in Austria. At several small gatherings I lectured on America and our struggle in that country.

Fedya had sent me my return fare, second class, and a hundred dollars to buy myself some clothes. I preferred to invest the money in my beloved books, purchasing a supply of the works of the writers that were making literary history, especially the dramatists. No amount of wardrobe could have given me so much joy as my precious little library. I did not even dare to risk shipping it in my trunk. I took the books with me in a suit-case.

Standing on the deck as the French liner steamed towards the New York dock, I spied Ed long before he saw me. He stood near the gangplank holding a bunch of roses, but when I came down, he failed to recognize me. It was late afternoon of a rainy day, and I wondered whether it was because of the dusk, my large hat, or the fact that I had grown thin. For a moment I stood watching him scanning the passengers, but when I saw his anxiety growing, I tiptoed up from behind and put my hands over his eyes. He spun round quickly, pressed me tempestuously to his heart, and exclaimed in a trembling voice: " What is the matter with my *Schatz?* Are you ill? " " Nonsense! " I replied, " I have only grown more spiritual. Let's get home and I'll tell you all about it."

Ed had written me that he had changed our quarters for a more comfortable flat, which Fedya had helped to decorate. What I found far excelled my expectations. Our new home was an old-fashioned apartment in the German-inhabited part of Eleventh Street. The windows of the large kitchen overlooked a beautiful garden. The front room was spacious and high-ceilinged, simply but cosily furnished with lovely old mahogany. There were rare prints on the walls, and my books were arranged on shelves. The place had atmosphere and taste.

Ed played the host to me at an elaborate dinner he had prepared, with wine sent by Justus Schwab. He was rich now, he informed me; he was earning fifteen dollars a week! Then he related news of our friends: Fedya, Justus, Claus, and, most of all, Sasha. While I was abroad, I had not been able to keep in direct touch with Sasha, and Ed had acted as our go-between, which meant anxious delays. I was overjoyed to learn that there was mail for me from my brave boy. I thought it wonderful that he should have been able to send out a missive to reach me on the very day of my arrival. Sasha's letter was, as always, permeated with his fine spirit. It contained no complaint about his own life, but showed great interest in activities outside, in my work and impressions of Vienna. Europe was so far away, he wrote; my return to America brought me closer, although he knew that he would never see me again. Perhaps I would come to Pittsburgh on a lecture tour. It would mean something to feel me in the same city.

Before my departure for Europe our friend Isaac Hourwich had proposed that we aid Sasha by an appeal to the Supreme Court on the ground of the illegal proceedings at his trial. After considerable effort and expense we had succeeded in procuring the trial records. It was then discovered that there were no legal reasons on which any procedure for a revision was to be based. Representing his own case, Sasha had omitted to take exceptions to the Judge's rulings, as a result of which no appeal could be made.

During my stay in Vienna several of our American friends had suggested an application to the Board of Pardons. Inwardly I rebelled against such a step on the part of an anarchist. I was certain that Sasha would not approve of it, and therefore I did not even write to him about the proposal. During my absence abroad he had been repeatedly put into the dungeon and kept in solitary confinement until his health gave way. I began to think that consistency, while admirable in oneself, was criminal if allowed to stand in the way of another. It led me to set aside all considerations and to implore Sasha to let us appeal to the Board of Pardons. His reply indicated that he felt indignant and hurt that I should want him to beg for pardon. His act bore its own justification, he wrote; it was a gesture of protest against the injustice of the capitalist system. The courts and the pardon boards were the bulwarks of that system. I must have grown less revolutionary, or perhaps it was only my concern for him that had decided me in favour of such a step. In any case he did not wish me to act against my principles in his behalf.

Ed had sent me that letter to Vienna. It had made me unhappy. It disappointed me, but it did not abate my efforts. Friends in Pennsylvania had informed me that the personal signature of the applicant for a pardon was not necessary in that State. I again wrote to Sasha, emphasizing that I considered his life and freedom too valuable to the movement to refuse to make an appeal. Some of the greatest revolutionists had, when serving long terms, appealed in order to gain their freedom. But if he still felt it inconsistent to take the step for his own sake, would he not permit our friends to do so for mine? I could no longer bear, I explained, the consciousness of his being in prison for an act in which I had been almost as much involved as he. My plea seemed to make some impression on Sasha. In his reply he reiterated that he had no faith whatever in the Board of Pardons; but his friends on the outside were in a better position to judge the step they intended to take and therefore he would offer no further objections. He added that there were certain other matters he would like to talk over; could not Emma Lee try to get a permit?

Emma had moved to Pittsburgh, where she secured a position in a hotel as supervisor of its linen department. She had begun a correspondence with the prison chaplain, whom she gradually interested in an attempt to have Sasha's right to visits restored. After months of waiting the chaplain succeeded in having a permit sent to Emma Lee. But when she called at the penitentiary, the Warden refused to let her see Sasha. " I, and not the chaplain, am the sole authority here," he told Emma; " as long as I am in charge, no one will be allowed to see Prisoner A-7."

Emma Lee felt that a violent protest on her part would only hurt Sasha's chances with the Board of Pardons. She showed greater control than I had on that fatal day at Inspector Reed's store. We continued to cling to the hope that our efforts would tear Sasha from the clutches of the enemy.

I communicated with Voltairine de Cleyre, reminding her of her promise to help in our efforts for Sasha. She replied promptly by composing a public call in his behalf, but she sent it to Ed instead of to me. For a moment I felt angry at what I considered a slight, but when I read the document, my wrath melted away. It was a prose poem full of moving power and beauty. I wrote her my thanks without reference to our misunderstanding. She did not reply.

The campaign for the appeal was launched, the entire radical element supporting our efforts. A prominent Pittsburgh lawyer had become interested and consented to take the case to the Pennsylvania Board of Pardons.

We worked energetically, driven on by great expectations. Sasha's hopes, too, were reviving; life, pulsating life, now seemed to open before him. But our joy was short-lived. The Board refused to act on the appeal. Berkman would have to complete his first seven years' sentence before the " actual wrong " of his other sentences could be considered, the Board held. It was evident that nothing displeasing to Carnegie and Frick would be done.

The shock to me was crushing, and I dreaded its effect on Sasha. How should I write to him, what should I say to help him over the cruel blow? Ed's reassuring words that Sasha was brave enough to hold out until 1897 did not help me. I lost hope that a commutation would ever be granted him. The threat of Inspector Reed that Sasha would not be allowed out alive was ringing in my ears. Before I could bring myself to write him, a letter arrived from Sasha. He had not banked much on a favourable outcome, his letter read, and he was not much disappointed. The action of the Board merely proved once more the close alignment of the American Government and the plutocracy. It was what we anarchists had always claimed. The promise of the Board to reconsider the appeal in 1897 was merely a trick to hoodwink public opinion and to tire out the friends who had been working for him. He was sure the flunkeys of the steel interests would never act in his behalf. But it did not matter. He had survived the first four years and he meant to keep on fighting. " Our enemies shall never have the chance to say that they have broken me," he wrote. He knew he could always count on my support and on that of the new friends he had gained. I must not despair or relax in my zeal for our Cause. My Sasha, my wonderful Sasha — he was not only brave, as Ed had said; he was a tower of strength. As so often since that day when the steam monster at the Baltimore and Ohio Station had snatched him away from me, he stood out like a shining meteor on the dark horizon of petty interests, personal worries, and the enervating routine of everyday existence. He was like a white light that purged one's soul, inspiring even awe at his detachment from human frailties.

CHAPTER XV

A RENAISSANCE WAS NOW TAKING PLACE IN ANARCHIST RANKS; greater activity was being manifested than at any time since 1887, especially among American adherents. *Solidarity,* an English publication started in 1892 by S. Merlino and suspended later on, reappeared in '94, gathering about itself a number of very able Americans. Among them were John Edelman, William C. Owen, Charles B. Cooper, Miss Van Etton, an energetic trade-unionist, and a number of others. A social science club was organized, with weekly lectures. The work attracted considerable attention among the intelligent native element, not failing, of course, also to call forth virulent attacks in the press. New York was not the only city where anarchism was being expounded. In Portland, Oregon, the *Firebrand,* another English weekly, was being published by a group of gifted men and women, including Henry Addis and the Isaak family. In Boston Harry M. Kelly, a young and ardent comrade, had organized a co-operative printing shop which was publishing the *Rebel.* In Philadelphia activities were carried on by Voltairine de Cleyre, H. Brown, Perle McLeod, and other courageous advocates of our ideas. In fact, all over the United States the spirit of the Chicago martyrs had been resurrected. The voice of Spies and his comrades was finding expression in the native tongue as well as in every foreign language of the peoples in America.

Our work had received considerable incentive through the arrival of two British anarchists, Charles W. Mowbray and John Turner. The former had come in 1894, shortly after my release from prison, and was now active in Boston. John Turner, who was the more cultivated and better informed of the two, had been invited to the States by Harry Kelly. For some reason his lectures were at first poorly attended and it became necessary for us in New York to look after the arrangements. I had met John and his sister Lizzie during my stay in London. Both of them had strongly appealed to me by reason of their warmth, geniality, and friendliness. I loved especially to talk to John; he was familiar with the social movements in England and was himself closely allied with the trade-union and co-operative elements, as well as with the *Commonweal,* founded by William Morris. But his best efforts were devoted to the propaganda of anarchism. John Turner's coming to America gave me an opportunity to test my ability to speak in English, as I often had to preside at his meetings.

The free-silver campaign was at its height. The proposition for the free coinage of silver at the ratio with gold of sixteen to one had become a national issue almost overnight. It gained in strength by the sudden ascendancy of William Jennings Bryan who had stampeded the Democratic Convention by an eloquent speech and the catch phrase: "You shall not press down upon the brow of labour the crown of thorns, you shall not crucify mankind upon the cross of gold." Bryan was running for the presidency: the "silver-tongued" orator had caught the fancy of the man in the street. The American liberals, who so easily fall for every new political scheme, went over to Bryan on free silver almost to a man. Even some anarchists were carried away by his slogans. One day a well-known Chicago comrade, George Schilling, arrived in New York to enlist the co-operation of the Eastern radicals. George was an ardent follower of Benjamin Tucker, the leader of the individualist school of anarchism, and a contributor to his paper, *Liberty.* But, unlike Tucker, he was closer to the labour movement and also more revolutionary than his teacher. The wish for a popular awakening in the United States was father to George's belief that the free-silver issue would become a force to undermine both monopoly and the State. The vicious attacks on Bryan in the press helped his cause by leading George and many others to regard him as a martyr. The papers spoke of Bryan as a "tool in the blood-stained hands of Altgeld, the anarchist, and Eugene Debs, the revolutionist."

I could not share the enthusiasm for Bryan, partly because I did not believe in the political machine as a means of bringing about fundamental changes, and also because there was something weak and superficial about Bryan. I had a feeling that his main aim was to get into the White House rather than "strike off the chains" from the people. I resolved to steer clear of him. I sensed his lack of sincerity and I did not trust him. For this attitude I was assailed from two different sides on the same day. First it was Schilling who urged me to join the free-silver campaign. "What are you Easterners going to do," he asked when I met him, "when the West marches in revolutionary ranks towards the East? Are you going to continue talking, or will you join forces with us?" He assured me that my name had travelled to the West and that I could be a valuable factor in the popular movement to free the masses from their despoilers. George was very optimistic in his ardour, but he failed to convince me. We parted as friends, George shaking his head over my lack of judgment about the impending revolution.

In the evening we had a visitor, the former Burgess of Homestead, a man named John McLuckie. I remembered his determined stand during the steel strike against the importation of blacklegs and I appreciated his solidarity with the workers. I was glad to meet the large, jovial fellow, a true type of the old Jeffersonian democrat. He told me that he had been asked by Voltairine to see me about Sasha. He had gone to her to inform her that Berkman was no longer in the Western Penitentiary. He, as well as many other people in Homestead, believed that Berkman had never intended to kill Frick; he had committed the act only to arouse sympathy for the latter. The excessive sentence he had been given was merely a ruse on the part of the Pennsylvania courts to deceive the public. The Homestead workers felt sure that Alexander Berkman had been let out of prison long ago. Voltairine had given McLuckie material which proved how ridiculous his story was and had sent him to me for more proofs.

I listened to the man, unable to conceive that anyone in his senses could believe such a thing about Sasha. He had sacrificed his youth, he had already spent five years in the penitentiary, had suffered the dungeon, solitary confinement, and brutal physical attacks. Persecution by the prison authorities had even driven him to attempt suicide. Yet he was being suspected by the very people for whom he was willing to lay down his life. It was preposterous, cruel. I stepped into my room, took Sasha's letters, and handed them to McLuckie. "Read," I said, "and then tell me if you still believe the impossible stories you have just told me."

He took up one of the letters from the pile, read it carefully, then scanned several others. Presently he held out his hand. "My dear, brave girl," he said, "I am sorry, I am awfully sorry, to have doubted your friend." He assured me that he now realized how wrong he and his people had been. "You can count on me to help," he added, feel-

ingly, "in any effort you may make to get Berkman out of prison."
Then he referred to Bryan, dwelling on the exceptional opportunity to
assist Sasha if I would join the free-silver campaign. My activities
would bring me in close contact with the prominent politicians of the
Democratic Party, and they could afterwards be approached to secure a pardon. He himself would undertake to see the leaders and he
was certain of success if he could assure them of my services. He
pointed out that I would have no responsibilities about the business
end. He would travel with me and arrange everything. Of course, I
would be paid a generous salary.

McLuckie was frank and decent, though evidently childishly ignorant of my ideas. Perhaps it was also his suggestion that I might help
Sasha that made him sympathetic to me. Still, I could have nothing
to do with Bryan, feeling he would use the workers merely as a
stepping-stone to power.

My visitor took no offence. He left with regrets that I was so lacking in practical sense, but he promised faithfully to enlighten his people in Homestead in regard to Berkman.

Together with Ed and several other close friends I discussed the
possible origin of the dreadful rumours about Sasha. I was sure that
they had been created by the attitude of Most. I remembered that
the press had widely commented on Most's statement that Sasha had
used a "toy pistol to shoot Frick up a bit." Johann Most — my life
was so full I had nearly forgotten him. The bitterness his betrayal of
Sasha had aroused had given way to a dull feeling of disappointment
in the man who had once meant so much to me. The wound he had
struck had partly healed, yet leaving behind a sensitive scar. Mc-
Luckie's visit had torn the wound open again.

My encounters with Schilling and McLuckie made me aware of a
large new field for activity. What I had done so far was only the first
step of usefulness in our movement. I would go on a tour now, study
the country and its people, come close to the pulse of American life.
I would bring to the masses the message of a new social ideal. I was
eager to start at once, but I determined first to become more pro-
ficient in English and to earn some money. I did not want to be dependent on the comrades or take pay for my lectures. Meanwhile I
could continue my work in New York.

I was full of enthusiasm for the future, but in proportion as my
spirits rose, Ed's interest in my aims waned. I had known for a long

time that he begrudged every moment which took me away from him. I was also aware of our decided differences as far as the woman question was concerned. But outside of that, Ed had moved along with me, had always been helpful and ready to aid in my efforts. Now he became disgruntled, critical of everything I was doing. As the days passed, he grew more morose. Often on my return from a late meeting I would find him with a set face, frigidly silent, nervously swinging his leg. I yearned to come close to him, to share my thoughts and plans with him; but his reproachful look would numb me. In my room I would wait expectantly, but he would remain away and then I would hear him wearily drag himself to bed. It hurt me to the quick, for I loved him deeply. Outside of my interest in the movement and Sasha, my great passion for Ed had displaced everything else.

I still had a very tender feeling for my erstwhile artist lover, the more so because I thought he needed me. On my return from Europe I had found him very much changed. He had risen in his profession and was earning considerable money. He remained as generous to me as in our days of poverty, having aided me financially all through my stay in Vienna and later furnishing my new apartment. Indeed, there was no change in his attitude towards me. But it did not take me long to discover that the movement had lost its former meaning for Fedya. He now lived in a different circle, and his interests were different. Art auctions absorbed him, and all his leisure he spent at sales. He had craved beauty so long that, now that he had some means, he wanted to gorge himself with it. Studios became his great passion. Every few months he would furnish one with the most exquisite things, only to discard it shortly for another, which he would decorate with new hangings, vases, canvases, carpets, and what not. All the beautiful things in our flat had come from his *ateliers*. I could not bear the thought of Fedya's wandering so far away from our past interests that he would not offer any more financial help to the movement. But as he had never had much sense of material values, I was not surprised to find him so extravagant. I was even concerned more about his choice of new friends, nearly all of them men who worked on newspapers. A dissipated, cynical lot they were, their main objects in life being drink and women. Unhappily they had succeeded in imbuing Fedya with the same spirit; I was grieved to see my idealistic friend going the way of so many empty in head and heart. Sasha had always felt that the social struggle would prove a mere passing phase in Fedya's life, but I had hoped that when Fedya should be drawn into other channels, they would be those of art. His drift towards meaningless and trivial pleasures, for which he was entirely too fine, was most painful. Fortunately he still felt close to us. He had great regard for Ed, and his affection for me, while no longer the same as in the past, was yet warm enough to counteract, at least partly, the disintegrating influence of his new surroundings.

He came often to our house. On one occasion he asked me to pose, this time for a pen-and-ink sketch he had promised Ed. During the sittings I thought of our common past, of our affection that had been so tender, perhaps too tender to survive the sway Ed's personality exercised over me; probably also because Fedya's love was too yielding for my turbulent nature, which could find expression only in the clashing of wills, in resistance and the surmounting of obstacles. Fedya still attracted me, but it was Ed who consumed me with intense longing, Ed who turned my blood to fire, Ed whose touch intoxicated and exalted me. The sudden change from his usual self to a discontented and hypercritical attitude was too galling to endure. But my pride would not let me make the first step to break his silence. Fedya told me that Ed had greatly admired his sketch of me and had praised it as a splendid piece of work, expressive of much of my being. In my presence, however, Ed would not say a word about it.

But one evening Ed's reserve broke down. "You are drifting away from me!" he cried excitedly. "I can see that my hopes of a beautiful life with you must be given up. You have wasted a year in Vienna, you have acquired a profession only to throw it over for those stupid meetings. You have no concern about anything else; your love has no thought of me or my needs. Your interest in the movement, for which you are willing to break up our life, is nothing but vanity, nothing but your craving for applause and glory and the limelight. You are simply incapable of a deep feeling. You have never understood or appreciated the love I have given you. I have waited and waited for a change, but I see it is useless. I will not share you with anybody or anything. You will have to choose!" He paced the room like a caged lion, turning from time to time to fasten his eyes on me. All that had been accumulating in him for weeks now streamed out in accusation and reproaches.

I sat in consternation. The familiar old demand that I "choose" kept droning in my ears. Ed, who had been my ideal, was like the others. He would have me forswear my interests and the movement, sacrifice everything for love of him. Most had repeatedly given me the same ultimatum. I stared at him unable to speak or move, while he continued stalking about the room in uncontrolled anger. Finally he picked up his coat and hat and left.

For hours I sat as if paralysed; then a violent ring brought me to my feet. It was a call to a confinement case. I took the bag which I had been keeping ready for weeks and walked out with the man who had come for me.

In a two-room flat on Houston Street, on the sixth floor of a tenement-house, I found three children asleep and the woman writhing in labour pains. There was no gas-jet, only a kerosene lamp, over which I had to heat the water. The man looked blank when I asked him for a sheet. It was Friday. His wife had washed Monday, he told me, and all the bed-linen had got dirty since. But I might use the table-cloth; it had been put on that very evening for the Sabbath. " Diapers or anything else ready for the baby?" I asked. The man did not know. The woman pointed to a bundle which consisted of a few torn shirts, a bandage, and some rags. Incredible poverty oozed from every corner.

With the use of the table-cloth and an extra apron I had brought I prepared to receive the expected comer. It was my first private case, and the shock over Ed's outburst helped to increase my nervousness. But I steeled myself and worked on desperately. Late in the morning I helped to bring the new life into the world. A part of my own life had died the evening before.

For a week my grief over Ed's absence was dulled by work. The care of several patients and Dr. White's operations, at which I assisted, left me little time for repining. The evenings were occupied with meetings in Newark, Paterson, and other near-by towns. But at night, alone in the flat, the scene with Ed haunted and tortured me. I knew he cared for me, but that he could leave as he did, stay away so long, and give no sign of his whereabouts made me resentful. It was impossible to reconcile myself to a love that denied the beloved the right to herself, a love that throve only at the expense of the loved one. I felt I could not submit to such a sapping emotion, but the next moment I would find myself in Ed's room, my burning face on his pillow, my heart contracting with yearning for him. At the end of two weeks my longing mastered all my resolutions; I wrote him at his place of work and begged him to return.

He came at once. Folding me to his heart, between tears and laughter, he cried: " You are stronger than I; I have wanted you every moment, ever since I closed that door. Every day I meant to come back, but I was too cowardly. Nights I have been walking round the house like a shadow. I wanted to come in and beg you to forgive and forget. I even went to the station when I knew you had to go to Newark and Paterson. I could not bear to think of your going home alone late at night. But I was afraid of your scorn, afraid you would send me away. Yes, you are braver and stronger than I. You are more natural. Women always are. Man is such a silly, civilized creature! Woman has retained her primitive impulses and she is more real."

We took up our common life again, but I spent less time on my public interests. Partly it was due to the numerous calls on my professional services, but more to my determination to devote myself to Ed. As the weeks passed, however, the still small voice kept on whispering that the final rupture would only temporarily be deferred. I clung desperately to Ed and his love to ward off the impending end.

My profession of midwife was not very lucrative, only the poorest of the foreign element resorting to such services. Those who had risen in the scale of material Americanism lost their native diffidence together with many other original traits. Like the American women they, too, would be confined only by doctors. Midwifery offered a very limited scope; in emergencies one was compelled to call for the aid of a physician. Ten dollars was the highest fee; the majority of the women could not pay even that. But while my work held out no hope of worldly riches, it furnished an excellent field for experience. It put me into intimate contact with the very people my ideal strove to help and emancipate. It brought me face to face with the living conditions of the workers, about which, until then, I had talked and written mostly from theory. Their squalid surroundings, the dull and inert submission to their lot, made me realize the colossal work yet to be done to bring about the change our movement was struggling to achieve.

Still more impressed was I by the fierce, blind struggle of the women of the poor against frequent pregnancies. Most of them lived in continual dread of conception; the great mass of the married women submitted helplessly, and when they found themselves pregnant, their alarm and worry would result in the determination to get rid of their expected offspring. It was incredible what fantastic methods despair could invent: jumping off tables, rolling on the floor, massaging the stomach, drinking nauseating concoctions, and using blunt instruments. These and similar methods were being tried, generally with great injury. It was harrowing, but it was understandable. Having a large brood of children, often many more than the weekly wage of the father could provide for, each additional child was a curse, " a curse of God," as orthodox Jewish women and Irish Catholics repeatedly told me. The men were generally more resigned, but the women cried out against Heaven for inflicting such cruelty upon them. During their labour pains some women would hurl anathema on God and man, especially on their husbands. " Take him away," one of my patients cried, " don't let the brute come near me — I'll kill him ! " The tortured creature already had had eight children, four of whom had died in infancy. The remaining were sickly and undernourished, like most of the ill-born, ill-kept, and unwanted children who trailed at my feet when I was helping another poor creature into the world.

After such confinements I would return home sick and distressed, hating the men responsible for the frightful condition of their wives and children, hating myself most of all because I did not know how to help them. I could, of course, induce an abortion. Many women called me for that purpose, even going down on their knees and begging me to help them, " for the sake of the poor little ones already here." They knew that some doctors and midwives did such things, but the price was beyond their means. I was so sympathetic; wouldn't I do something for them ? They would pay in weekly instalments. I tried to explain to them that it was not monetary considerations that held me back; it was concern for their life and health. I would relate the case of a woman killed by such an operation, and her children left motherless. But they preferred to die, they avowed; the city was then sure to take care of their orphans, and they would be better off.

I could not prevail upon myself to perform the much-coveted operation. I lacked faith in my skill and I remembered my Vienna professor who had often demonstrated to us the terrible results of abortion. He held that even when such practices prove successful, they undermine the health of the patient. I would not undertake the task. It was not any moral consideration for the sanctity of life; a life unwanted and forced into abject poverty did not seem sacred to me. But my interests embraced the entire social problem, not merely a single aspect of it, and I would not jeopardize my freedom for that one part of the human struggle. I refused to perform abortions and I knew no methods to prevent conception.

I spoke to some physicians about the matter. Dr. White, a conservative, said: " The poor have only themselves to blame; they indulge their appetites too much." Dr. Julius Hoffmann thought that children were the only joy the poor had. Dr. Solotaroff held out the hope of great changes in the near future when woman would become more intelligent and independent. " When she uses her brains more," he would tell me, " her procreative organs will function less." It seemed more convincing than the arguments of the other medicos, though no more comforting; nor was it of any practical help. Now that I had learned that women and children carried the heaviest burden of our ruthless economic system, I saw that it was mockery to expect them to wait until the social revolution arrives in order to right injustice. I sought some immediate solution for their purgatory, but I could find nothing of any use.

My home life was anything but harmonious, though externally all seemed smooth. Ed was apparently calm and contented again, but I felt cramped and nervous. If I attended a meeting and was detained later than expected, it would make me uneasy and I would hasten home in perturbation. Often I refused invitations to lecture because I sensed Ed's disapproval. Where I could not decline, I worked for weeks over my subject, my thoughts dwelling on Ed rather than on the matter in hand. I would wonder how this point or that argument might appeal to him and whether he would approve. Yet I never could get myself to read him my notes, and if he attended my meetings, his presence made me self-conscious, for I knew that he had no faith in my work. It served to weaken my faith in myself. I developed strange nervous attacks. Without preliminary warning I would fall to the ground as if knocked down by a heavy blow. I did not lose consciousness, being able to see and understand what was going on around me, but I was not able to utter a word. My chest felt convulsed, my throat compressed; I had an agonizing pain in my legs as if the muscles were being pulled asunder. This condition would last from ten minutes to an hour and leave me utterly exhausted. Solotaroff, failing to diagnose the trouble, took me to a specialist, who proved no wiser. Dr. White's examination also gave no results. Some physicians said it was hysteria, others an inverted womb. I knew the latter was the real cause, but I would not consent to an operation. More and more I had become convinced that my life would never know harmony in love for very long, that strife and not peace would be my lot. In such a life there was no room for a child.

From various parts of the country came requests for a series of lectures. I was very eager to go, but I lacked the courage to broach the matter to Ed. I knew he would not consent, and his refusal would most likely bring us nearer to a violent separation. My physicians had strongly advised a rest and change of scene, and now Ed surprised me by insisting that I ought to go away. " Your health is more important than any other consideration," he said, " but first you must drop the silly notion that you have to earn your own living." He was making enough for both now, and it would make him happy if I would give up my nursing and stop making myself ill by helping hapless brats into the world. He welcomed the opportunity to take care of me, to afford me leisure and recuperation. Later on, he said, I should be in condition to go on a tour. He realized how much I wanted it and he knew what an effort it was to me to play the devoted wife. He enjoyed the home I had made so beautiful for him, he went on, but he could see that I was not contented. He was sure a change would do me good, give me back my old spirit, and bring me back to him.

The weeks that followed were happy and peaceful. We were much together, making frequent trips to the country, attending concerts and operas. We took up reading together again, and Ed helped me to understand Racine, Corneille, Molière. He cared only for the classics; Zola and his contemporaries were repellent to him. But when alone during the day I indulged in the more modern literature, besides planning a number of lectures for my forthcoming tour.

In the midst of my preparations came the news of tortures in the Spanish prison of Montjuich. Three hundred men and women, mostly trade-unionists, with a sprinkling of anarchists, had been arrested in 1896 as a result of a bomb explosion in Barcelona during a religious procession. The entire world was appalled by the resurrection of the Inquisition, by prisoners being kept for days without food or water, flogged, and burned with hot irons. One even had had his tongue cut out. The fiendish methods were used to extort confessions from the unfortunates. Several went mad and in their delirium implicated their innocent comrades, who were immediately condemned to death. The person responsible for these horrors was the Prime Minister of Spain, Canovas del Castillo. Liberal-minded papers in Europe, like the *Frankfurter Zeitung* and the Paris *Intransigeant,* were arousing public sentiment against the nineteenth-century Inquisition. Advanced members of the House of Commons, the Reichstag, and the Chamber of Deputies

were calling for action to stay the hand of Canovas. Only America
remained dumb. Excepting the radical publications, the press maintained a conspiracy of silence. Together with my friends I strongly felt
the necessity of breaking through that wall. In conference with Ed,
Justus, John Edelman, and Harry Kelly, who had come from Boston,
and with the co-operation of Italian and Spanish anarchists, we decided
to start our campaign with a large mass meeting. A demonstration in
front of the Spanish Consulate in New York was to follow. As soon
as our efforts became public, the reactionary papers began to urge the
authorities to stop " Red Emma," that term having stuck to me since
the Union Square meeting. On the night of our gathering the police
appeared in full force, crowding even the platform so that the speakers could hardly make a gesture without touching an officer. When my
turn came to speak, I gave a detailed account of the methods that
were being used in Montjuich, and called for a protest against the
Spanish horrors.

The pent-up emotions of the audience, aroused to a high pitch,
broke into thunderous applause. Before it fully subsided, a voice from
the gallery called out: " Miss Goldman, don't you think someone of
the Spanish Embassy in Washington or the Legation in New York
ought to be killed in revenge for the conditions you have just described? " I felt intuitively that my questioner must be a detective,
attempting to trap me. There was a movement among the police near
me as if preparing to lay hands on me. The audience was hushed in
tense expectation. For a moment I paused; then I replied calmly and
deliberately: " No, I do not think any one of the Spanish representatives in America is important enough to be killed, but if I were in
Spain now, I should kill Canovas del Castillo."

Several weeks later came the news that Canovas del Castillo had
been shot dead by an anarchist whose name was Angiolillo. At once the
New York papers started a veritable hunt for the leading anarchists
to secure their opinions of the man and his deed. Reporters pestered
me day and night for interviews. Did I know the man? Had I been in
correspondence with him? Had I suggested to him that Canovas be
killed? I had to disappoint them. I did not know Angiolillo and had
never corresponded with him. All I knew was that he had acted while
the rest of us had only talked about the fearful outrages.

We learned that Angiolillo had lived in London and that he was
known among our friends as a sensitive young man, an ardent student,

a lover of music and books, poetry being his passion. The Montjuich tortures had haunted him and he decided to kill Canovas. He went to Spain, expecting to find the Prime Minister in Parliament, but he learned that Canovas was recuperating from his " labours of State " at Santa Agueda, a fashionable summer resort. Angiolillo journeyed there. He met Canovas almost immediately, but the man was accompanied by his wife and two children. " I could have killed him then," Angiolillo said in court, " but I would not risk the lives of the innocent woman and children. It was Canovas I wanted; he alone was responsible for the crimes of Montjuich." He then visited the Castillo villa, introducing himself as the representative of a conservative Italian paper. When he was face to face with the Prime Minister, he shot him dead. Mme Canovas ran in at that moment and hit Angiolillo full in the face. " I did not mean to kill your husband," Angiolillo apologized to her, " I aimed only at the official responsible for the Montjuich tortures."

The *Attentat* of Angiolillo and his frightful death vividly recalled to me the period of July 1892. Sasha's Calvary had now lasted five years. How close I had come to sharing a similar fate! — the lack of a paltry fifty dollars had prevented my accompanying Sasha to Pittsburgh — but can one estimate the spiritual travail and suffering the experience involved? Yet the price was worth the lesson I had gained from Sasha's deed. Since then I had ceased to regard political acts, as some other revolutionists did, from a merely utilitarian standpoint or from the view of their propagandistic value. The inner forces that compel an idealist to acts of violence, often involving the destruction of his own life, had come to mean much more to me. I felt certain now that behind every political deed of that nature was an impressionable, highly sensitized personality and a gentle spirit. Such beings cannot go on living complacently in the sight of great human misery and wrong. Their reactions to the cruelty and injustice of the world must inevitably express themselves in some violent act, in supreme rending of their tortured soul.

I had spoken in Providence a number of times without the least trouble. Rhode Island was still one of the few States to maintain the old tradition of unabridged freedom of speech. Two of our open-air gatherings, attended by thousands, went off well. But the police had evidently decided to suppress our last meeting. Arriving with several friends at the square where the assembly was to take place, we found a member of the Socialist Labor Party talking, and, not wishing to in-

terfere with him, we set up our box farther away. My good comrade
John H. Cook, a very active worker, opened the meeting, and I began
to speak. Just then a policeman came running towards us, shouting:
" Stop your jabbering! Stop it this minute or I'll pull you off the box! "
I went on talking. Someone called out: " Don't mind the bully — go
right on! " The policeman came up, puffing heavily. When he got his
breath he snarled, " Say, you, are you deaf? Didn't I tell you to stop?
What d'you mean not obeying the law? " " Are you the law? " I retorted; " I thought it is your duty to maintain the law, not to break it.
Don't you know the law in this State gives me the right of free
speech? " " The hell it does," he replied, " I'm the law." The audience
began hooting and jeering. The officer started to pull me off the improvised platform. The crowd looked threatening and began closing
in on him. He blew his whistle. A patrol wagon dashed up to the
square, and several policemen broke through the crowd with their
clubs swinging. The officer, still holding on to me, shouted: " Drive
those damn anarchists back so I can get this woman. She's under arrest." I was led to the patrol wagon and literally thrown into it.

At the police station I demanded to know by what right I had been
interfered with. " Because you're Emma Goldman," the sergeant at the
desk replied. " Anarchists have no rights in this community, see? " He
ordered me locked up for the night.

It was the first time since 1893 that I had been arrested, but, constantly expecting to fall into the clutches of the law, I had made it a
practice to carry a book with me when going to meetings. I wrapped my
skirts around me, climbed up on the board placed for a bed in my
cell, pressed close to the barred door, through which shimmered a
light, and started to read. Presently I became aware of someone moaning in the adjoining cell. " What is it? " I called in a whisper; " are
you ill? " A woman's voice replied between sobs: " My children, my
motherless children! Who is going to take care of them now? My
sick husband, what'll become of him? " Her weeping became louder.
" Say, you drunken lout, stop that squealing! " a matron shouted from
somewhere. The crying was checked, and I heard the woman walking
up and down her cell like a caged animal. When she quieted down a
little I asked her to tell me her troubles; perhaps I could be of help. I
learned that she was the mother of six children, the eldest fourteen,
the baby only a year old. Her husband had been ill for ten months, unable to work, and in her despair she had helped herself to a loaf of
bread and a can of milk from the grocery store in which she had once

worked. She was caught in the act and turned over to the police. She begged to be let off for the night in order not to frighten her family, but the officer insisted on her going with him, not even giving her a chance to send a message to her home. She was brought to the station-house after the evening meal. The matron told her she could order some food if she had the price. The woman had not eaten all day; she was faint with hunger and ill with anxiety; but she had no money.

I rapped for the matron and asked her to send out for supper for me. In less than fifteen minutes she returned with a tray of ham and eggs, hot potatoes, bread, butter, and a large pot of coffee. I had given her a two-dollar bill, and she handed back fifteen cents. " You have fancy prices here," I said. " Sure thing, kid, did you think this was a charity joint? " Seeing that she was in a good humour, I requested her to pass part of the meal to my neighbour. She did, but not without commenting: " You're a regular fool to waste such a feed on a common sneak-thief."

The next morning I was taken, together with my neighbour and other unfortunates, before a magistrate. I was held over under bond, and as the amount could not be raised immediately I was returned to the station-house. At one o'clock in the afternoon I was again called for, this time to see the Mayor. That individual, no less bulky and bloated than the policeman, informed me that if I would promise under oath never to return to Providence he would let me go. " That's nice of you, Mayor," I replied; " but inasmuch as you have no case against me, your offer isn't quite so generous as it appears, is it? " I told him that I would make no promises whatever, but that if it would relieve his mind, I could tell him that I was about to start on a lecture tour to California. " It may take three months or more, I don't know. But I do know that you and your city cannot do without me much longer than that, so I am determined to come back." The Mayor and his flunkies roared, and I was released.

On my arrival in Boston I was shocked by a report in the local papers of the shooting at Hazleton, Pennsylvania, of twenty-one strikers. The men were miners on their way to Latimer, in the same State, to induce the workers there to join the strike. The Sheriff had met them on the public road and would not allow them to go on. He commanded them to return to Hazleton, and when they refused, he and his posse opened fire.

The papers stated that the Sheriff had acted in self-defence; the mob had been threatening. Yet there was not one casualty among the posse, while twenty-one working-men had been mowed down and a number of others wounded. It was evident from the report that the men had gone out with empty hands, without any intention of offering resistance. Everywhere workers were slain, everywhere the same butchery! Montjuich, Chicago, Pittsburgh, Hazleton — the few for ever outraging and crushing the many. The masses were the millions, yet how weak! To awaken them from their stupor, to make them conscious of their power — that is the great need. Soon, I told myself, I should be able to reach them throughout America. With a tongue of fire I would rouse them to a realization of their dependence and indignity! Glowingly I visioned my first great tour and the opportunities it would offer me to plead our Cause. But presently my reverie was disturbed by the thought of Ed. Our common life — what would become of it? Why could it not go hand in hand with my work? My giving to humanity would only increase my own need, would make me love and want Ed more. He would, he must, understand; he had himself suggested my going away for a time. The image of Ed filled me with warmth, but my heart fluttered with apprehension.

I had been away from Ed only two weeks, but my longing for him was more intense than it had been on my return from Europe. I could hardly contain myself until the train came to a stop in the Grand Central Station, where he met me. At home everything seemed new, more beautiful and enticing. Ed's endearing words sounded like music in my ears. Sheltered and protected from the strife and conflict outside, I clung to him and basked in the sunshine of our home. My eagerness to go on a long tour paled under the fascination of my lover. A month of joy and abandon followed, but my dream was soon to suffer a painful awakening.

It was caused by Nietzsche. Ever since my return from Vienna I had been hoping that Ed would read my books. I had asked him to do so and he promised he would when he had more time. It made me very sad to find Ed so indifferent to the new literary forces in the world. One evening we were gathered at Justus's place at a farewell party. James Huneker was present and a young friend of ours, P. Yelineck, a talented painter. They began discussing Nietzsche. I took part, expressing my enthusiasm over the great poet-philosopher and dwelling on the impression of his works on me. Huneker was surprised. " I did not know you were interested in anything outside of propaganda," he remarked. " That is because you don't know anything about anarchism," I replied, " else you would understand that it embraces every phase of life and effort and that it undermines the old, outlived values." Yelineck asserted that he was an anarchist because he was an artist; all creative people must be anarchists, he held, because they need scope and freedom for their expression. Huneker insisted that art has nothing to do with any ism. " Nietzsche himself is the proof of it," he argued; " he is an aristocrat, his ideal is the superman because he has no sympathy with or faith in the common herd." I pointed out that Nietzsche was not a social theorist but a poet, a rebel and innovator. His aristocracy was neither of birth nor of purse; it was of the spirit. In that respect Nietzsche was an anarchist, and all true anarchists were aristocrats, I said.

Then Ed spoke. His voice sounded cold and constrained, and I sensed the tempest behind it. " Nietzsche is a fool," he said, " a man with a diseased mind. He was doomed from birth to the idiocy which finally overtook him. He will be forgotten in less than a decade, and so will all those other pseudo-moderns. They are contortionists in comparison with the truly great of the past."

" But you haven't read Nietzsche! " I objected heatedly; " how can you talk about him? " " Oh, yes, I have," he retorted, " I read long ago all the silly books you brought from abroad." I was dumbfounded. Huneker and Yelineck turned on Ed, but my hurt was too great to continue the discussion.

He had known how I had wanted him to share my books, how I had hoped and waited for him to recognize their value and significance. How could he have kept me in suspense, how could he have remained silent after he had read them? Of course, he had a right to his opinion: that I believed implicitly. It was not his differing from me that had stabbed me to the quick; it was his scorn and ridicule of what had come to mean so much to me. Huneker, Yelineck, strangers in a measure, welcomed my appreciation of the new spirit, while my own lover made me appear silly, childish, incapable of judgment. I wanted to run away from Justus's place, to be alone; but I checked myself. I could not bear an open conflict with Ed.

Late at night, when we returned home, he said to me: " Let's not spoil our beautiful three months; Nietzsche is not worth it." I felt wounded to the heart. " It isn't Nietzsche, it is you — you," I cried excitedly. " Under the pretext of a great love you have done your utmost to chain me to you, to rob me of all that is more precious to me than life. You are not content with binding my body, you want also to bind my spirit! First the movement and my friends — now it's the books I love. You want to tear me away from them. You're rooted in the old. Very well, remain there! But don't imagine you will hold me to it. You are not going to clip my wings, you shan't stop my flight. I'll free myself even if it means tearing you out of my heart."

He stood leaning against the door of his room, his eyes closed, giving no sign of having heard a word I said. But I no longer cared. I stepped into my own room, my heart cold and empty.

The last few days were outwardly calm, even friendly, Ed helping me to prepare for my departure. At the station he embraced me. I knew he wanted to say something, but he remained silent. I, too, could not speak.

When the train pulled out and Ed's form receded, I realized that our life would never be the same any more. My love had received too violent a shock. It was now like a cracked bell; never again would it ring the same clear, joyous song.

CHAPTER XVI

MY FIRST STOP WAS PHILADELPHIA. I HAD VISITED THE CITY MANY times since my arrest in 1893, always addressing Jewish audiences. On this occasion I was invited to lecture in English before several American organizations. While in the City of Brotherly Love I stayed at the house of Miss Perle McLeod, the president of the Ladies' Liberal League. I should have preferred the warmer hospitality of my old friend Natasha Notkin, with whom I felt at home, in the congenial atmosphere of my Russian comrades, but it had been suggested that the apartment of Miss McLeod was more accessible to the Americans who would want to meet me.

The meetings were not badly attended, but, still aching from the distressing scene with Ed, I did not feel fully equal to the situation, and my lectures lacked inspiration. Yet my visit was not altogether useless. I gained a footing and made a number of friends, among them a most interesting woman, Susan Patten. I knew through Sasha that she was one of his constant American correspondents. I liked her on account of that and for her fine spirit.

In Washington I spoke before a German free-thought society. After the lecture I met a group of *Reitzel Freunde,* as the readers of the *Armer Teufel* called themselves. Most of them looked more like butchers than idealists. One man, who boasted of being an employee of the United States Government, talked much of beauty in art and letters — not for the ignorant mob, of course, but for the choice few. He had no patience with anarchism, because "it wanted to make all alike." "How could a hod-carrier, for instance, claim the same rights as I, an educated man?" he asked me. He didn't think that I seriously believed in such equality, or that any other leading anarchist did. He was sure we were merely using it as a bait. He did not blame us at all; "the rabble should be made to pay."

"How long have you been reading the *Armer Teufel*?" I inquired. "Since its first issue," he proudly replied. "And that is all you got from it? Well, all I can say is that my friend Robert has been casting his pearls before a swine." The man jumped to his feet and angrily left the room amidst the boisterous laughter of the rest of the company.

Another Reitzel "friend" introduced himself as a brewer from Cincinnati. He moved closer to me and began to talk of sex. He had heard that I was the "great champion of free love" in the United States. He was delighted to see that I was not only clever, as I had just proved, but also young and charming, not at all like the rigid blue-stocking he had imagined me to be. He, too, believed in free love, though he didn't think most men and women were ripe for it, especially women who always try to hold on to the man. But "Emma Goldman, that's another matter." His lewd and smirking manner nauseated me. I turned my back upon him and went to my room. Very tired, I fell asleep almost immediately. I was awakened by a persistent tap-tap on my door. "Who is it?" I called. "A friend," came in reply; "won't you open?" It was the voice of the brewer from Cincinnati. Jumping out of bed, I shouted as loud as I could: "If you don't leave instantly, I shall wake the whole house!" "Please, please!" he pleaded through the door, "don't make any scene. I'm a married man, with grown children. I thought you believed in free love." Then I heard him hurrying off.

Of what avail are lofty ideals, I wondered. The government clerk who dares put himself above the hod-carrier; the respectable pillar of society, to whom free love is only a means for clandestine affairs — both readers of Reitzel, the brilliant rebel and idealist! Their heads and hearts have remained as sterile as the Sahara. The world must be full of such people, the world I have set out to awaken. A sense of futility came over me and of dismal isolation.

On the way from Washington to Pittsburgh it poured incessantly. I was chilled to the bone and oppressed by the memory of Homestead and of Sasha. Always on my visits to the Steel City a heavy weight would settle on my heart. The sight of the belching fires from the huge furnaces scorched my soul.

The presence at the station of Carl Nold and Henry Bauer somewhat cheered my dejection. My two comrades had been liberated from the Western Penitentiary in May of that year (1897). I had never met Bauer before, but Carl brought back the days of our first meeting, in November 1892. The friendship begun then had become strengthened through our correspondence while Carl was in prison. Our meeting now was to cement further the bond between us. It was good to see the dear, vivacious face again. Prison had made him more thoughtful, yet it had not dampened his joy in life. Bauer, large and jovial, towered over us like a giant. " The elephant and his family," he remarked, walking between us, while Carl and I vainly tried to keep pace with his huge steps.

On my former visits in Pittsburgh I had always stopped with my good friend Harry Gordon and his family. Harry was one of our best workers, a faithful and enthusiastic friend. Mrs. Gordon, a simple and tender-hearted woman, was very much attached to me. She always went out of her way to make my stay in her home as pleasant and comfortable as her husband's small wages would permit. I loved being with the Gordons, and I asked my companions to take me to them. They, however, were bent on celebrating my arrival first.

There were to be no lectures in Pittsburgh. Carl and Henry had begun a new move for Sasha's release, an appeal to the Board of Pardons to be backed exclusively by labour elements. I had no faith left in such steps, but I did not want to communicate my pessimism to my friends. Both of them were in a jovial mood. They had arranged a little dinner in a near-by restaurant, in a room all by ourselves where we would be undisturbed. We drank our first glass standing, in silence. It was to Sasha. His spirit hovered over us and brought us closer to each other in our common aims and work. Then Carl and Henry recounted to me their prison experience and the years they had spent under the same roof with Sasha. They had brought out a message for me which they feared to trust to the mails: Sasha was planning an escape.

His scheme was a masterly one; it fairly took my breath away. But even if he should succeed in getting out of prison, I reflected, where would he go? In America he would have to keep under cover for the rest of his life. He would be a haunted man, to be captured in the end. It would be different in Russia. Similar escapes had been repeatedly carried out there. But Russia had a revolutionary spirit and the political was a persecuted unfortunate in the eyes of the workers and the peasant; he could count on their sympathy and assistance. In the United States, on the other hand, nine-tenths of the workers themselves would immediately join in the hunt for Sasha. Nold and Bauer agreed with me, but they asked me not to communicate my fears to Sasha. He had reached the limit of endurance; his eyes were failing, his health was breaking down, and he had again been brooding on suicide. The hope of escape and the elaboration of his plan energized his fighting spirit. We must not discourage him, but perhaps we would induce him to wait until every legal means for his release had been tried.

So deeply engrossed had we become in our talk that we had lost all sense of time. In surprise we discovered that it was long after midnight. My companions thought it too late to go to the Gordons' and suggested taking me to a little hotel kept by a reader of the *Armer Teufel*. On the way I related to them my experience with the Washington *Reitzel Freunde,* but Bauer assured me that the Pittsburgh hotel man was of a different type. He really turned out to be very friendly. " Indeed, there is surely room for Emma Goldman in my place," he said genially. We were about to mount the stairs when the hysterical voice of a woman burst upon our ears. " A room for Emma Goldman! " she screamed. " This is a respectable family hotel, no place for that shameless creature, the free lover of a convict! " " Let's get out of this," I urged my friends. Before we had a chance to move, the hen-pecked husband banged his fist on the counter, demanding to know who was boss. " Tell me that, you Xantippe! " he yelled. " Am I, or am I not, master in this house? " With a devastating look in my direction the woman slunk out of the room. The master became calm and kindly again. He couldn't let me go out in the awful weather, he protested; I must stay at least for the night. But I had had enough, and we left.

" Why not come to my den? " Carl suggested. Together with his wife and little boy he occupied one room and a kitchen, and they would be glad to share them with me. Dear, generous Carl did not know the dread I had of going into people's houses uninvited. But I was very tired and weary and I did not wish to hurt Carl. " I will go anywhere you take me, Carolus, even to hell," I said; " only let's get there quickly."

At last we reached Nold's place, in Allegheny, Bauer having gone home. The door opened on a dimly lit room. A buxom young woman, somewhat dishevelled, met us, and Carl introduced her to me. I had the impression that she resented my intrusion. The place was small, containing only one bed, in which the child lay sleeping. I looked questioningly at Carl. " It's all right, Emma," he said; " Nellie and I will sleep on the floor, and you will share the bed with the kid." I hesitated, inclined to leave, but the rain was coming down in torrents. I turned to the woman to apologize for the discomfort I was causing, but she would not listen; in silence she walked into the kitchen, closing the door. Half dressed, I lay down on the bed alongside of the little boy and immediately fell asleep. I was awakened by someone shouting: " He's killing me! Help! Police! " The room was pitch-dark. I jumped up in terror, not realizing at first what was happening. Groping, I found a table and matches. When I had struck a light, I saw two bodies rolling on the floor, fighting. The woman held Carl pressed down with her knees and was trying to get at his throat, at the same time yelling for the police. Carl was beating back her hands and making frantic efforts to extricate himself. I had never seen a more disgusting sight. I pulled the woman off Carl, snatched up my things, and was out on the street before either of them had come to his senses. My mind in a turmoil, I ran in the beating rain to Henry's place, rousing him out of bed and telling him what had happened. He accompanied me immediately on my search for a hotel. Carl had dashed out after me, and the three of us walked in the downpour to Pittsburgh, the hotels in Allegheny being closed at that late hour. We canvassed a number of hostelries, but were refused everywhere, no doubt because I looked so wet and disreputable, without any suitcase, for that had been left at Carl's. It was nearly morning when at last we found a little hotel that would receive me.

With shaking knees and chattering teeth I crawled into bed, drawing the blankets over my face to shut out the hideousness of life. But in vain I sought forgetfulness in sleep. Dark shadows seemed to envelop me on every side. The sinister walls of the penitentiary that held Sasha, his years of suffering, my own prison days, the ghastly experience of an hour ago, all blended into a grinning, fantastic mockery of darkness and despair. Yet somewhere in the distance there quivered a faint shimmer of light. I knew it; I recognized it; it emanated from Ed. The thought of our love, our home, pierced the gloom for an instant. I stretched out trembling hands, but they encountered only empty space, empty and cold as my own heart.

Three days later I arrived in Detroit. The lure of that city had always been to me Robert Reitzel. His wit and peerless pen had fascinated me from the time I began to read his paper. His courageous

defence of the Chicago martyrs and his bold effort to save their lives
had impressed him on my mind as an unflinching rebel and fighter.
The vision I had of him had become strengthened by his stand in behalf of Sasha. While Most, knowing Sasha and his revolutionary
ardour, had calumniated him and disparaged his act, Reitzel had
gloried in the man and his *Attentat.* His article *" Im Hochsummer
fiel ein Schuss "* was an exalted and moving tribute to our brave boy.
It brought Reitzel very close to me and made me long to know him
personally.

Almost five years had passed since I had first met the editor of
the *Armer Teufel,* while he was visiting New York. The recollection
of that experience now stood out vividly before me. It was late one
evening, while still at my sewing-machine, that I heard violent knocking on the shutters of my window. " Let in the errant knights ! "
boomed the bass of Justus. Beside him I saw a man almost as tall and
broad-shouldered as himself, whom I at once recognized as Robert
Reitzel. Before I could greet him, he began to upbraid me playfully.
" A fine anarchist you are ! " he thundered. " You preach the need of
leisure, and work longer than a galley-slave. We have come to break
your chains, and we are going to take you with us if we have to use
force. March ! Little girl, get ready ! Come on out here, since you
don't seem too anxious to invite us into your virgin chamber." My
unexpected visitors were standing in full view of the street-lamp.
Reitzel wore no hat. A shock of blond hair, already considerably
greyed, fell in confusion over his high forehead. He looked big and
strong, more youthful and vital than Justus. He was holding on to the
windowsill with both hands, his eyes inquisitively scrutinizing my face.
" What's the verdict ? " he exclaimed; " am I acceptable ? " " Am
I ? " I questioned in return. " You have passed long ago," he replied,
" and I have come to give you the prize, to offer myself as your
knight."

Soon I was walking between the two men in the direction of Justus's
place. There we were met by hilarious hurrahs and *" Hoch soll er
leben,"* and calls for more wine. Justus, with his usual graciousness,
rolled up his sleeves, got behind the counter, and insisted on playing
host. Robert gallantly offered his arm to lead me to the head of the
table. As we walked up the aisle Justus intoned the wedding-march
from *Lohengrin.* The strains were taken up by the whole group of
men, who had splendid voices.

Robert was the spirit of the gathering. His humour was more sparkling than the wine freely partaken of by all present. The amount he consumed transcended even Most's ability in that regard; and the more he imbibed, the more eloquent he grew. His stories, very colourful and amusing, came gushing like water from a brook. He was inexhaustible. Long after most of the others had caved in, my knight kept on singing and talking of life and love.

It was almost daybreak when, accompanied by Robert, I stepped into the street, clinging to his arm. A great longing possessed me to embrace the fascinating man at my side, so fine and beautiful in body and mind. I felt sure he was also strongly attracted to me; he had shown it all through the evening in his every glance and touch. As we walked along I could feel his agitation of passionate desire. Where could we go? The thought flitted through my mind, as in increasing excitement I walked close to him, waiting and madly hoping that he would make some suggestion.

"And Sasha?" he suddenly asked. "Do you hear often from our wonderful boy?" The spell was broken. I felt thrust back into the world of misery and strife. During the rest of the walk we talked of Sasha and his act, of Most's attitude and its dire effects. It was another Robert now; it was the rebel and fighter against injustice.

At my door he took me in his arms, with hot breath whispering: "I want you! Let's forget the ugliness of life." Gently I freed myself from his embrace. "Too late, my dear," I replied; "the mysterious voices of the night are silent, the dissonances of the day have begun." He understood. Gazing affectionately into my eyes, he said: "This is only the beginning of our friendship, my brave Emma. We will meet again soon in Detroit." I threw my window wide open and watched the rhythmic swing of his well-knit body until he disappeared round the corner. Then I went back to my life and to my machine.

A year later came the news of Reitzel's illness. He was suffering from spinal tuberculosis, which resulted in the paralysis of his lower extremities. He was bedridden, like Heine, whom he so greatly admired and whom in a certain measure he resembled in spirit and feeling. But even in his mattress-grave Robert could not be daunted. Every line he wrote was a clarion call to freedom and battle. From his sick-bed he had prevailed on the Central Labor Union of his city to invite me as speaker to that year's eleventh of November commemora-

tion. " Come a few days earlier," he had written me, " so that we can
resume our friendship of the days when I was still young."

I arrived in Detroit late in the afternoon on the day of the scheduled meeting and was met by Martin Drescher, whose stirring poems
had often appeared in the *Armer Teufel*. To my amusement and the
astonishment of the crowd at the station, Drescher, tall and awkward,
kneeled before me, holding out a bunch of red roses, and delivering
himself of the following: " From your knight, my Queen, with his
undying love." " And who may be the knight?" I queried. " Robert,
of course! Who else would dare send his love to the Queen of the
Anarchists?" The crowd laughed, but the man on his knees before
me was not disturbed. To save him from catching a bad cold (there
was snow on the ground) I held out my hand, saying: " Now, vassal,
take me to my castle." Drescher got up, bowed low, gave me his arm,
and solemnly led me to a cab. " To the Randolph Hotel," he commanded. On our arrival there, we found half a score of Robert's
friends awaiting us. The owner himself was one of the *Armer Teufel*
admirers. " My best room and wines are at your disposal," he announced. I knew it was Robert's thoughtfulness and friendship that
had paved the way and secured for me the affection and hospitality
of his circle.

Turner Hall was filled to the limit, the audience in tune with the
spirit of the evening. The event was made more festive by the singing
of a chorus of children and the masterly reading of a fine revolutionary
poem by Martin Drescher. I was scheduled to speak in German. The
impression on me of the Chicago tragedy had not paled with the passing years. That night it seemed more poignant, perhaps because of the
nearness of Robert Reitzel, who had known, loved, and fought for our
Chicago martyrs and who was himself now slowly dying. The memory
of 1887 took living form, personifying their Calvary and inspiring
me to heights of exaltation, of hope and life springing from heroic
death.

At the conclusion of the meeting I was called back to the platform
to receive from the hands of a golden-haired maiden of five a huge
bouquet of red carnations, too large for her wee body. I pressed the
child to my heart and carried her off, bouquet and all.

Later in the evening I met Joe Labadie, a prominent individualist anarchist of picturesque appearance, who introduced to me the

Reverend Dr. H. S. McCowan. Both expressed regret that I had not spoken in English. "I came especially to hear you," Dr. McCowan informed me, whereupon Joe, as everyone affectionately called Labadie, remarked: "Well, why don't you offer Miss Goldman your pulpit? Then you could hear our ' Red Emma ' in English." "That's an idea!" the minister replied; "but Miss Goldman is opposed to churches; would you speak in one?" "In hell if need be," I said, "provided the Devil won't pull at my skirts." "All right," he exclaimed, "you shall speak in my church, and no one shall pull at your skirts or curtail a word of what you want to say." We agreed that my lecture should be on anarchism, it being a subject most people knew almost nothing about.

With the flowers my " knight " had sent me came also a note asking me to visit him any time after the meeting, since he would be awake. It seemed strange for a sick person to keep such late hours, but Drescher assured me that Robert felt best after sundown. His house was the last on the street, overlooking a large open space. "Luginsland," Robert had named it; it was all his eye had looked upon for the past three and a half years. His inner vision, though, keen and penetrating, wandered to distant lands and climes, bringing to him all the cultural wealth they contained. The bright light streaming through his bay window could be seen from afar; it reminded me of a lighthouse, with Robert Reitzel its keeper. Song and laughter sounded from the house. On entering Reitzel's room I found it filled with people; the smoke was so thick that it obscured Robert from view and blurred the faces of those present. His voice called out jovially: "Welcome to our sanctum! Welcome to the den of your adoring knight!" Robert, in a white shirt open wide at the neck, sat in bed propped up against a mountain of pillows. Except for the ashy colour of his face, the increased greyness of his hair, and his thin, transparent hands, there was no indication of his illness. His eyes alone spoke of the martyrdom he was suffering. Their care-free light was gone. With aching heart I put my arms around him, pressing his beautiful head to me. "So motherly?" he objected. "Aren't you going to kiss your knight?" "Of course," I stammered.

I had almost forgotten the others in the room, to whom Robert now began introducing me as the " Vestal of the Social Revolution." "Look at her!" he cried, "look at her; does she resemble the monster pictured by the press, the fury of a hetæra? Behold her black dress and white collar, prim and proper, almost like a nun." He was making me embarrassed and self-conscious. " You are praising me as if I were a horse you wanted to sell," I finally objected. It did not dismay him in the least. " Didn't I say you are prim and proper ? " he declared triumphantly; " you don't live up to your reputation. *Wein her*," he called; " let's drink to our Vestal ! " The men surrounded Robert's bed, glasses in hand. He emptied his to the dregs and then flung it against the wall. " Emma is now one of us. Our pact is sealed; we will be true to her to our last breath ! "

An account of the meeting and of my speech had preceded me to Reitzel, the manager of his paper having brought back a glowing report. When I mentioned McCowan's invitation, Robert was delighted. He knew the Reverend Doctor, whom he considered a rare exception in the " outfit of soul-savers." I told Robert about my friend in Blackwell's Island, the young priest, relating how fine and understanding he was. " A pity you met him in prison," Robert teased me, " else you might have found in him an ardent lover." I was sure I could not love a priest. " That's nonsense, my dear — love has no concern with ideas," he replied; " I have loved girls in every town and village and they were not remotely so interesting as your priest seems to be. Love has nothing to do with any ism, and you'll find it out when you grow older." In vain I insisted that I knew all about it. I was no child, being nearly twenty-nine. I was confident I should never fall in love with anyone who did not share my ideas.

The next morning I was awakened in my hotel by the announcement that a dozen reporters were waiting to interview me. They were eager for a story on my proposed speech in Dr. McCowan's church. They showed me the morning papers with the glaring headlines: " EMMA SHOWS MOTHER INSTINCT — FREE LOVER IN A DETROIT PULPIT — RED EMMA CAPTURES HEART OF MCCOWAN — CONGREGATIONAL CHURCH TO BE TURNED INTO HOTBED OF ANARCHY AND FREE LOVE."

For several succeeding days the front page of every paper in Detroit was filled with the impending desecration of the church and the portending ruin of the congregation by " Red Emma." Reports about members' threatening to leave and committees' besieging poor Dr. McCowan followed one another. " It will mean his neck," I said to Reitzel when I saw him the day before the meeting, " and I'd hate to be the cause of it." But Robert held that the man knew what he was doing; it was only right for him to stick to his guns, if only to test his independence in the church. "At any rate, I must offer to with-draw," I suggested, "to give McCowan a chance to recall his invitation if he feels like it." A friend was dispatched to the minister, but he sent word that he would go through with his plan no matter what happened. "A church that refuses the right of expression to the most unpopular person or creed is no place for me," he said. "You must not mind the consequences to me."

In the Tabernacle the Reverend Dr. McCowan presided. In a short speech, which he read from a prepared text, he set forth his own position. He was not an anarchist, he declared; he had never given much thought to it and he really knew very little about it. It was for that reason that he had visited Turner Hall on the night of November 11. Unfortunately Emma Goldman had spoken in German, and when it was suggested that he might hear her in English in his own pulpit, he had accepted the idea at once. He felt that the members of his church would be glad to hear the woman who had for years been persecuted as a "social menace"; as good Christians, he thought, they would be charitable to her. He then turned over the pulpit to me.

I had decided to stick strictly to the economic side of anarchism and to avoid as far as possible matters of religion and sexual problems. I felt I owed it to the man who was making such a courageous stand. At least his congregation should have no cause to say that I had used the Tabernacle to attack their God or to undermine the sacred institution of marriage. I succeeded better than I had expected. My lecture, lasting an hour, was listened to without any interruption and was much applauded at the end. "We won!" Dr. McCowan whispered to me when I sat down.

He rejoiced too soon. The applause had barely died away when an elderly woman rose belligerently. "Mr. Chairman," she demanded, "does Miss Goldman believe in God or does she not?" She was followed by another. "Does the speaker favour killing off all rulers?" Then a small, emaciated man jumped to his feet and in a thin voice cried: "Miss Goldman! You're a believer in free love, aren't you? Now, wouldn't your system result in houses of prostitution at every lamp-post?"

"I shall have to answer these people straight from the shoulder," I remarked to the minister. "So be it," he replied.

"Ladies and gentlemen," I began, "I came here to avoid as much as possible treading on your corns. I had intended to deal only with the basic issue of economics that dictates our lives from the cradle to the grave, regardless of our religion or moral beliefs. I see now that it was a mistake. If one enters a battle, he cannot be squeamish about a few corns. Here, then, are my answers: I do not believe in God, because I believe in man. Whatever his mistakes, man has for thousands of years past been working to undo the botched job your God has made." The house went frantic. " Blasphemy! Heretic! Sinner! " the women screamed. " Stop her! Throw her out! "

When order was restored, I continued: " As to killing rulers, it depends entirely on the position of the ruler. If it is the Russian Tsar, I most certainly believe in dispatching him to where he belongs. If the ruler is as ineffectual as an American president, it is hardly worth the effort. There are, however, some potentates I would kill by any and all means at my disposal. They are Ignorance, Superstition, and Bigotry — the most sinister and tyrannical rulers on earth. As for the gentleman who asked if free love would not build more houses of prostitution, my answer is: they will all be empty if the men of the future look like him."

There was instant pandemonium. In vain the chairman pounded for order. People jumped up on benches, waved their hats, shouted, and would not leave the church until the lights were turned out.

The next morning most of the papers reported the Tabernacle meeting as a disgraceful spectacle. There was general condemnation of the action of Dr. McCowan in permitting me to speak in the Tabernacle. Even the famous agnostic Robert Ingersoll joined the chorus. " I think that all the anarchists are insane, Emma Goldman among the rest," he stated; " I also think that the Reverend Dr. McCowan is a generous man — not afraid. However, it is not commendable for a crazy man or woman to be invited to talk before any public assemblage." Dr. McCowan resigned from the church. " I'm going to a mining town," he told me; " I am sure the miners will appreciate my work much better." I was sure they would.

My correspondence with Ed after I left New York was of a friendly nature, though constrained. When I reached Detroit, I found a long letter from him in the old loving spirit. He made no reference to our last scene. He was anxiously waiting for me to return, he wrote, and he hoped to have me back for the holidays. " When one's sweetheart is married to public life, one must learn to be *genügsam* [content with little]," his letter read. I could not imagine Ed being *genügsam*, but I understood that he was trying to meet my needs. I loved Ed and I wanted him, but I was determined to go on with my work. I greatly missed him, however, and his charm, which had not ceased to attract me. I wired him that I was on my way to visit sister Helena and that I should be home within a week.

Outside of a brief visit after my release from prison, I had not been in Rochester since 1894. It seemed ages, so much had happened in my life. Changes had also taken place in the fortunes of my beloved sister Helena. The Hochsteins now occupied more comfortable quarters in a little house with a touch of green in the back. Their steamship agency, though yielding small returns, had nevertheless improved their condition. Helena continued to shoulder the main burden; her children needed her even more than before, and so did the business. Most of their customers were Lithuanian and Lettish peasants, who performed the hardest labour in the United States. Their wages were small, yet they managed to send money to their families and bring them over to America. Poverty and drudgery had made them dull and suspicious, and this required tact and patience in dealing with them. My brother-in-law, Jacob, usually extremely reserved and quiet, would often lose his temper when confronted with such stupidity. But for Helena most of the customers would have turned to some better business man than Jacob Hochstein, the scholar. She knew how to smooth the troubled waters. Her sympathies were with these wage-slaves and she understood their psychology. She did more than merely sell them tickets and forward their money; she entered into their barren lives. She wrote their letters home for them and helped them over many difficulties. Nor were they the only ones to come to Helena to be comforted and aided. Almost the entire neighbourhood brought their troubles to her. While my precious sister would lend an attentive ear to everybody's tale of woe, she herself never complained, never lamented her own unfulfilled hopes, the dreams and aspirations of her youth. I realized keenly what a force was lost in the rare creature; hers was a large nature compressed in too limited a space.

The day of my arrival offered no chance for communion with Helena. In the evening, when the children were asleep and the office closed, we could talk. She would not pry into my life; what I told her she accepted with understanding and affection. She herself spoke mostly about the children, hers and Lena's, and of the hard life of our parents. I knew well enough her reasons for constantly dwelling on the difficulties of our father. She strove to bring me closer to him and to help to a better understanding. She had suffered greatly because of our mutual antagonism, which in me had developed into hatred. She had been horrified at the message I had sent her three years previously when she had notified me that Father was near Death's door. He had undergone a dangerous operation on his throat, and Helena had called me to his bedside. " He should have died long ago," I had wired back. Since then she had tried repeatedly to change my attitude towards the man whose harshness had marred the childhood of all of us.

The memory of our sad past had made Helena more kind and generous. It was her beautiful spirit and my own development that gradually healed me of the bitterness I bore my father. I came to understand that it is ignorance rather than cruelty that makes parents do so many dreadful things to their helpless children. During my short stay in Rochester in 1894, I had seen my father for the first time in five years. I still felt estranged, but no longer so hostile. On that visit I found Father physically broken, a mere shadow of his former strong and energetic self. His condition was constantly growing worse. Ten hours' work in the shop on dry food were destructive to his weakened and nervous state of health, aggravated by the taunts and indignities he had to endure. He was the only Jew, a man of nearly fifty, a foreigner not familiar with the language of the country. Most of the youngsters who worked with him were of foreign parents, but they had acquired the worst American traits without any of the fine qualities. They were crude, coarse, and heartless. They throve on the pranks and tricks they played on the " sheeny." Repeatedly they had so molested and harassed him as to cause him to faint. He would be brought home, only to compel himself to go back the next day. He could not afford to lose the job that paid him ten dollars a week.

The sight of Father so ill and worn softened the last vestige of my animosity towards him. I began to regard him as one of the mass of the exploited and enslaved for whom I was living and working.

In our talks Helena had always argued that Father's violence in his youth had been due to his exceptional energy, which found no adequate outlet in such a small place as Popelan. He had been ambitious for himself and his family, dreaming of the large city and the big things he could do there. The peasants eked out a poor existence on their land; but most of the Jews, with practically every profession closed to them, lived upon the peasants. Father was too honest for such methods, and his pride smarted under daily indignities from the officials he had to deal with. The failure of his life, the lack of opportunity to put his abilities to good use, had embittered him and made him ill-natured and hard towards his own.

My years of contact with the lives of the masses, the social victims in and out of prison, and my wide reading had shown me the dehumanizing effect of misplaced energy. In numerous instances I had watched people who had started life with ambition and hope being thwarted by a hostile environment. Only too often they had grown vindictive and ruthless. The understanding I gained through my own struggle had come to my sister through her highly sensitive nature and her unusual intuitiveness. She was wise without having known much of life.

I saw a great deal of my sister Lena and her family on this visit. She already had four children, and a fifth was on the way. She was worn by too frequent child-bearing and the struggle to make ends meet. The only joy Lena had was her children. The most radiant of the four was little Stella, who had always been my sunbeam in grey Rochester. She was ten now, very intelligent, high-strung, and full of exaggerated fancies about her *Tante Emma,* as she called me. Since my previous visit Stella had begun to correspond with me, in quaint and extravagant outpourings of the yearnings of her young soul. The severity of her father and his preference for her younger sister were great and real tragedies to the sensitive child. Having to share the same bed with her caused Stella great misery. Her people had no patience with " such whims "; besides, they were too poor to afford extra space. But I understood Stella only too well: her tragedy was a repetition of what I myself had suffered at her age. I was happy in the thought that the little one had Helena near, to whom she could take her troubles, and that she felt the need of confiding in me. " I hate the people who are mean to my *Tante Emma,*" Stella wrote when she was barely seven. " When I grow up, I will fight for her."

There was also my brother Yegor. Until the age of fourteen he was, like most American boys, crude and wild. He loved Helena because she had been so devoted to him. I had evidently not so impressed myself on his mind. I was just a sister, like Lena — nothing to be excited about. But on my visit in 1894 I seemed to awaken a deeper feeling in him. Since then he had become, like Stella, closely attached

to me, perhaps because I had prevailed upon Father not to compel
the boy to continue at school. Yegor had shown himself clever at his
studies, and this led the old man to hope that his youngest son would
realize his own bankrupt ambitions to be a man of learning. His
eldest boy, Herman, had proved a disappointment in this regard. He
could do wonders with his hands, but he hated school, and Father
finally lost hope of ever seeing his Herman become a " man of the professions." He sent him to a machine shop, where the boy soon proved
that he was much more at home with the most intricate machine than
with the simplest book lesson. He became a new being, serious and concentrated. Father could not get over the disappointment; yet hope
springs eternal. With Yegor doing well at school, Father again began
to vision college diplomas. But again his plans were frustrated. My
visit saved the situation. My arguments in behalf of " our baby " had
a better effect than the pleas I had once urged in my own behalf.
Yegor went to work in the same shop with Herman. Subsequently
the boy underwent a radical change : he became enamoured of study.
The life of a working-man and the lunch-basket he had so greatly admired lost their glamour. The shop, with its noises and coarseness,
revolted him. To read and learn was now his ambition. Contact with
the misery of the workers' lot brought Yegor closer to me. " You
have become my heroine," he wrote me ; " you have been in prison,
you are with the people and in touch with the aims of youth." I would
understand his awakening, he added; his hopes were centred on me,
for only I could induce our father to permit him to go to New York.
He wanted to study. But, strange to say, instead of being glad, Father
objected. He had lost faith in the fickle boy, he declared. Besides, the
wages Yegor was earning were needed in the house now that his own
health was failing and he could not continue much longer at work. It
required days of pleading and my offer to take Yegor to my home in
New York before Father yielded. Yegor had his wish and now saw
his dream about to be fulfilled, and thus I won his lasting devotion.

My stay in Rochester this time proved to be my first unclouded
visit with my family. It was a novel experience to be accepted with
warmth and affection by those who had always been strangers to me.
My dear sister Helena and the two young lives that needed me helped
me to closer communion with my parents.

On my way to New York I thought much about my frequent talks
with Ed in regard to my taking up a course of medicine. It had been

my aspiration when I was still in Königsberg, and my studies in Vienna had again awakened that desire. Ed had seized upon the idea with enthusiasm, assuring me he would soon be able to pay my way through college. My arrangements to have Yegor in New York with us and to assist him would, however, postpone the realization of my hope of becoming a doctor. I also feared Ed might resent the new obstacle and dislike having my brother in the house. I would certainly not force him on Ed.

I found Ed in splendid condition and fine spirits. Our little apartment looked festive, as my sweetheart always made it on my homecomings. Far from objecting to my plans about Yegor, Ed immediately consented to have him: with my brother in the house, he said, he would not feel so lonely during my absences. Did Yegor talk much, he inquired anxiously. He himself could sit for hours without uttering a word, and he was greatly relieved when I told him that Yegor was a studious and reticent boy. As to my proposed study of medicine, Ed was confident that we should be able to carry out the idea before long. He was " on the way to riches," he assured me with a serious face; his partner had perfected an invention, a novelty in albums, which would certainly prove a great success. "We want you as our third partner," he announced jubilantly; " you might take the contraption on the road with you on your next tour." Again, as in the early stages of our life, he began to indulge in fancies of the things he would do for me when we became rich.

Yegor arrived after New Year's Day. Ed liked him from the first, and before long my brother was completely charmed by my beloved. I was soon to go on a new tour, and it was a great comfort to know that my two " children " would keep each other company in my absence.

CHAPTER XVII

EQUIPPED WITH A DOZEN CAREFULLY PREPARED LECTURES AND supplied with a sample of the invention, I started out full of hope to win converts to our Cause and orders for the new album. My percentage on the sales would help to pay my travelling expenses, relieving me of the unpleasant necessity of the comrades supporting my tours.

Charles Shilling, a Philadelphia anarchist, whom I had met on my previous visits in that city, had undertaken all arrangements for my lectures and had also invited me to stay with his family. Both he and Mrs. Shilling were charming hosts, and Charles a most effective organizer. In six large meetings I spoke on the New Woman, the Absurdity of Non-Resistance to Evil, the Basis of Morality, Freedom, Charity, and Patriotism. Lecturing in English was still rather difficult, but I felt at home when the questions began. The more opposition I encountered, the more I was in my element and the more caustic I became with my opponents. After ten days of intensive activities and warm *camaraderie* with the Shillings and other new friends, I left for Pittsburgh.

Carl, Henry, Harry Gordon, and Emma Lee had arranged fourteen lectures in the Steel City and adjoining towns, except in the place I wanted most to go to, Homestead. No hall could be had there. My first pilgrimage was, as always, to the Western Penitentiary. I went out with Emma Lee. We walked close to the wall, and she noticed that now and then I ran my hand along the rough surface. If only thoughts and feelings could be transferred, the intensity of mine would penetrate the grey pile and reach through to Sasha. Almost five years had passed since his imprisonment. The Warden and the keepers had tried their utmost to break his spirit, but they had reckoned without Sasha's power of resistance. He remained undaunted, clinging with every fibre to the determination to come back to life and freedom. In that he was sustained by many friends, none more devoted than Harry Kelly, the Gordons, Nold, and Bauer. They had been working for months on the new appeal for pardon. Their efforts, begun in November 1897, found support among various elements. Through the help of Harry Kelly, who was canvassing the workers' organizations in Sasha's behalf, strong resolutions favouring his release had been passed by the United Labor League of Western Pennsylvania. The American Federation of Labor, at its convention in Cincinnati, the Bakers' International Union, the Boston Central Union, and many other labour bodies throughout the United States had taken favourable action. Two of the best Pittsburgh lawyers had been engaged, and the necessary funds raised. There was tremendous interest in Sasha and his case, and our friends were certain of results. I felt rather sceptical, but as I walked along the prison wall that separated me from our brave boy, I hoped against hope that I might be proved wrong.

Continuous lecturing and meeting many people were a strenuous job. It brought on several nervous attacks, which left me weak and spent. Yet I could not rest. I begrudged every minute that took me away from my work, especially because popular interest in our ideas seemed so great. Some of the newspapers, contrary to their usual custom, gave fair reports of my meetings; the Pittsburgh *Leader* even published a whole-page story, actually saying kind things about me. " Miss Goldman does not look at all the vicious being she is pictured," it wrote among other things. " You would not judge from her personal appearance that she carried bombs about in her clothes or that she was capable of the incendiary utterances which have marked her platform career. On the contrary, she is rather prepossessing than otherwise. As she converses, her face lights up with intelligent ardour. Indeed, the chances are ninety-nine in a hundred that a stranger asked to guess what and who she was would tell you she was a school-teacher or a woman whose mind runs in progressive channels."

The writer surely believed he was bestowing a compliment when he said I looked like a school-teacher. He meant it for the best, no doubt, but my vanity was hurt, nevertheless. Did I really look so inane, I wondered.

In Cleveland I delivered three lectures. The reports in the papers were very amusing. One simply stated that " Emma Goldman is crazy" and "her doctrines demoniacal ravings." Another enlarged upon my "fine manners, more like a lady than a bomb-thrower."

To Detroit I returned as to a dear old friend, and I went to Robert Reitzel straight from the train. His condition had been steadily growing worse, but his will to live would not be extinguished. I found my knight paler and more emaciated than before. The suffering he had been through since my last visit lined his face, but he had not lost his characteristic wit and humour. It was both joy and agony to see him. Yet he would not have me sad. He launched into stories that were convulsing by virtue of his great gift for comical recital. Particularly funny were his experiences as pastor of a German Reformed congregation, a position he held when he first came to America. Once he was requested to preach in Baltimore. The evening before he had spent in the circle of gay friends, with whom he worshipped at the shrine of wine and song till early dawn. Spring was in the air; the trees were alive with birds singing lustily to their mates. All of nature was vibrant with naked voluptuousness. The spirit of adventure was upon Robert when he walked out into the breaking day. Hours later he was found riding astride a beer-barrel, stripped to the skin, and stentoriously serenading the lady of his heart. Alas, she happened to be the fair daughter of a prominent member of the congregation that had invited the young pastor. There was no German sermon in Baltimore that day.

Unforgettable were the hours I spent with my knight. The sunshine of his spirit drew me into its orbit and made me reluctant to tear myself away. I wished I could pour sustenance into the sick body from the youth and strength that were mine.

Cincinnati was dull and disappointing after Detroit. A complaining letter from Ed made it doubly so. He could not bear my long absence, he wrote; better a thousand times to make a radical break, to live without me, than to have me only in snatches. I replied, assuring Ed of my love and of my desire for a home with him; but I reiterated that I would not be bound and kept in a cage. In such a case I should have to give up our common life altogether. What I prized most was freedom, freedom to do my work, to give myself spontaneously and not out of duty or by command. I could not submit to such demands; rather would I choose the path of a homeless wanderer; yes, even go without love.

St. Louis was not less dreary, but on the last day the police came to the rescue. They broke up the meeting in the middle of my speech and hustled everybody out. There was some consolation in the thought that the extensive quotations from my speech in the papers would reach a greater audience than the hall could hold. Moreover, the action of the authorities gained me many friends among Americans who still believed in freedom of expression.

Chicago, city of our Black Friday, cause of my rebirth! Next to Pittsburgh it was the most ominous and depressing to me. But I no longer felt as friendless there as on previous occasions when the fury of 1887 was still active and the opposition from the followers of Most was blind and bitter against me. My imprisonment and succeeding activities had won me friends and turned the tide in my favour. I now had the support of various labour unions which the efforts of Peukert had secured for me. Since 1893 he had been living in Chicago and spreading propaganda there. I found sweet hospitality with Comrade Appel, a prominent local anarchist, who, together with his vivacious wife and children, made their home a pleasant place to visit. The *Free Society* group was doing splendid work in Chicago, and a series of fifteen lectures had been arranged by them for me.

The gatherings themselves were of the usual character, with no special incidents occurring. But several events lent significance to my stay in the city, proving a lasting factor in my life. Among them were my meeting Moses Harman and Eugene V. Debs, and my rediscovery of Max Baginski, a young comrade from Germany.

In the exciting August days of 1893, in Philadelphia, when the police were hunting for me, two young men had called to see me. One was my old friend John Kassel; the other was Max Baginski. I was particularly glad to meet Max, who was one of the young rebels who had played such an important part in the revolutionary movement in Germany. He was of medium height, spiritual-looking, and frail, as if he had just been through a long illness. His blond hair stood up in defiance of the persuasions of a comb, his intelligent eyes appearing small through the thick glasses he wore. His pronounced features were an unusually high forehead and a face contour that looked as Slavic as his name sounded. I tried to engage him in conversation, but he seemed depressed and indisposed to talk. I wondered whether the large scar on his neck was the cause of his self-consciousness. In the years following I did not see Max again until my release from prison, and then only casually. Subsequently I heard that he had gone to Chicago to take charge of the *Arbeiter Zeitung,* the publication formerly edited by August Spies.

On my previous visits to Chicago I had refrained from going to the office of the paper to seek out Baginski. I had heard that he was a staunch adherent of Most, and I had suffered too much persecution from the latter's followers to care to meet any more of them. The appearance of a friendly notice in the *Arbeiter Zeitung* about my lectures, and an unaccountable urge to see Max again, induced me to look him up on my arrival in the city.

The office of the *Arbeiter Zeitung,* made famous by the Chicago events, was on Clark Street. The medium-sized room was divided by a grating, behind which I saw a man writing. By the scar on his neck I recognized Max Baginski. At the sound of my voice he rose quickly, opened the wire door, and with a buoyant: " Well, dear Emma, are you here at last ? " he embraced me. The greeting was so unexpectedly warm that it immediately quieted my apprehensions of him as a blind follower of Most. He asked me to wait a moment to enable him to finish the last paragraph of the article he was writing. " Done! " he exclaimed cheerily after a short time; "let's get out of this prison. We'll go to lunch at the Blue Ribbon Restaurant."

It was past noon when we reached the place; five o'clock found us still there. The silent, depressed young man of my brief encounter in Philadelphia was very much alive and an interesting conversationalist, now intensely serious, again light-hearted as a boy. We discussed the movement, Most and Sasha. Far from being fanatical and narrow, Max showed greater breadth, sympathy, and understanding than I had found among even the best of the German anarchists. He greatly admired Most, he said, for the heroic struggle he had made and the persecutions he had endured. Yet Most's attitude towards Sasha had produced a very painful impression on Max and his co-workers in the *"Jungen"* group in Germany. They had all sided with Sasha, and still did, Max assured me; but since his coming to America he had begun better to appreciate Most's tragedy in the alien land in which he could never take root. In the United States Most was out of his sphere, without the inspiration and impetus that come from the life and struggle of the masses. Most, of course, had considerable German support in the country, but it is only the native element in a country that can bring about fundamental changes. It must have been the helplessness of his position in America and the absence of a native anarchist movement that had caused Most to turn against propaganda by deed and, with it, against Sasha.

I could not accept Max's explanation of Most's betrayal of what he had propagated for years. But his generous attempt objectively to analyse the causes that had brought about the change in Most gave me an insight into the character of Max. There was nothing petty about him, no trace of rancour or desire to censor, no vestige of a partisan spirit. He impressed me as a big personality; to be with him was like breathing the pure air of green fields.

My joy in Max was heightened by the discovery that he shared my admiration for Nietzsche, Ibsen, and Hauptmann, and that he knew many more whose names I had not even heard. He had known Gerhart Hauptmann personally and had accompanied him on his rounds through the districts where the weavers live in Silesia. Max was then editor of a labour paper, *Der Proletarier aus dem Eulengebirge*, published in the locality which had furnished the dramatist with the material for his two powerful social canvases, *Die Weber* and *Hannele*. The ghastly poverty and wretchedness had embittered the weavers and had made them suspicious. They were loath to talk to the young man with the ascetic face resembling a priest who had come to question them about their lives. But they knew Max. He was of the people and with them, and they trusted him.

Max related to me some of his experiences on his tramps with Gerhart Hauptmann. Everywhere they found appalling misery. Once they came upon an old weaver in a barren hut. On a bench lay a woman with a little baby, covered with rags. The child's emaciated body was a mass of sores. There was no food and no wood in the house. Utter destitution grinned from every corner. In another place there lived a widow with her grand-daughter of thirteen, a girl of extraordinary beauty. They shared the room with a weaver and his wife. All during his talk with them Hauptmann had kept stroking the child's head. "It was no doubt she who gave him the inspiration for his Hannele," Max commented; "I know how he was impressed by that tender flower in its dreadful environment." For a long time afterwards Hauptmann continued sending gifts to the little girl. He could sympathize with those disinherited because he knew from personal experience what poverty was; he had often gone hungry while a student in Zürich.

I felt I had found a kindred spirit in Max, one with understanding and appreciation of what had come to mean so much to me. The wealth of his mind and his sensitive personality held irresistible appeal. Our intellectual kinship was spontaneous and complete, finding also its emotonal expression. We became inseparable, each day revealing to me new beauty and depth in his being. He was matured mentally far beyond his years, while psychically he was of the world of romance, of rare gentleness and refinement.

Another great event during my stay in Chicago was meeting Moses Harman, the courageous champion of free motherhood and woman's economic and sexual emancipation. His name had first become familiar to me through reading *Lucifer,* the weekly paper he was publishing. I knew of the persecution he had endured and of his imprisonment by the moral eunuchs of America, with Anthony Comstock at their head. Accompanied by Max, I visited Harman at the office of *Lucifer,* which was also the home that he shared with his daughter Lillian.

One's mental picture of great personalities usually proves false upon nearer contact. With Harman it was the contrary; I had not sufficiently visualized the charm of the man. His erect carriage (in spite of a lame leg, the result of a Civil War bullet), his striking head, with its flowing white hair and beard, together with his youthful eyes, combined to make the man a most impressive figure. There was nothing austere or forbidding about him; in fact, he was all kindliness. That characteristic explained his supreme faith in the country that had struck him so many blows. I was no stranger to him, he assured me. He had been outraged by the treatment I had received at the hands of the police, and he had protested against it. " We are comrades in more than one respect," he commented, with a pleasant smile. We spent the evening discussing problems affecting woman and her emancipation. During the talk I expressed doubt as to whether the approach to sex, so coarse and vulgar in America, was likely to change in the near future and Puritanism be banished from the land. Harman was sure it would. " I have seen such great changes since I began my work," he said, " that I am convinced we are not far now from a real revolution in the economic and sexual status of woman in the United States. A pure and ennobling feeling about sex and its vital rôle in human life is bound to develop." I called his attention to the growing power of Comstockism. "Where are the great men and women who can check that stifling force? " I asked; " outside of yourself and a handful of others the Americans are the most puritanical people in the world." " Not quite," he replied; " don't forget England, which has only recently suppressed Havelock Ellis's great work on sex." He had faith in America and in the men and women that had been fighting for years, even suffering calumny and imprisonment for the idea of free mother-hood.

During my stay in Chicago I attended a Labour convention in session in the city. I met a number of people there prominent in trade-union and revolutionary ranks, among them Mrs. Lucy Parsons, widow of our martyred Albert Parsons, who took an active part in the proceedings. The most striking figure at the convention was Eugene V. Debs. Very tall and lean, he stood out above his comrades in more than a physical sense; but what struck me most about him was his naïve unawareness of the intrigues going on around him. Some of the delegates, non-political socialists, had asked me to speak and had the chairman put me on the list. By obvious trickery the Social Democratic politicians succeeded in preventing my getting the floor. At the conclusion of the session Debs came over to me to explain that there had been an unfortunate misunderstanding, but that he and his comrades would have me address the delegates in the evening.

In the evening neither Debs nor the committee was present. The audience consisted of the delegates that had extended the invitation to me and of our own comrades. Debs arrived, all out of breath, almost at the close. He had tried to get away from the various sessions in order to hear me, he said, but he had been detained. Would I forgive him and take lunch with him the next day? I had the feeling that possibly he had been a party to the petty conspiracy to suppress me. At the same time I could not reconcile his frank and open demeanour with mean actions. I consented. After spending some time with him I was convinced that Debs was in no way to blame. Whatever the politicians in his party might be doing, I was sure that he was decent and high-minded. His belief in the people was very genuine, and his vision of socialism quite unlike the State machine pictured in Marx's communist manifesto. Hearing his views, I could not help exclaiming: "Why, Mr. Debs, you're an anarchist!" "Not Mister, but Comrade," he corrected me; "won't you call me that?" Clasping my hand warmly, he assured me that he felt very close to the anarchists, that anarchism was the goal to strive for, and that all socialists should also be anarchists. Socialism to him was only a stepping-stone to the ultimate ideal, which was anarchism. "I know and love Kropotkin and his work," he said; "I admire him and I revere our murdered comrades who lie in Waldheim, as I do also all the other splendid fighters in your movement. You see, then, I am your comrade. I am with you in your struggle." I pointed out that we could not hope to achieve freedom by increasing the power of the State, which the socialists were aiming at. I stressed the fact that political action is the death-knell of the economic struggle. Debs did not dispute me, agreeing that the revolutionary spirit must be kept alive notwithstanding any political objects, but he thought the latter a necessary and practical means of reaching the masses.

We parted good friends. Debs was so genial and charming as a human being that one did not mind the lack of political clarity which made him reach out at one and the same time for opposite poles.

The following day I visited Michael Schwab, one of the Chicago martyrs whom Governor Altgeld had pardoned. Six years in the Joliet Penitentiary had undermined his health, and I found him in the hospital with tuberculosis. It was amazing to witness with what endurance and fortitude an ideal can imbue one. Schwab's wasted body, the hectic flush on his cheeks, his eyes shining with the fatal fever in his blood, convincingly spoke of the tortures he had endured during the harrowing trial, through the months of waiting for reprieve, followed by the execution of his comrades, and his own long years in prison. Yet Michael said hardly a word about himself, nor did he permit a complaint to escape him. His ideal was uppermost in his mind, and everything bearing upon it was still his sole interest. I felt with a feeling of awe for the man whose staunch and proud spirit the cruel powers had failed to break.

My presence in Chicago gave me the opportunity to fulfil a wish of long standing: to do honour to our precious dead by placing a wreath upon their grave in Waldheim Cemetery. Before the monument erected to their memory we stood in silence, Max and I, our hands clasped. The inspired vision of the artist had transformed stone into a living presence. The figure of the woman on a high pedestal, and the fallen hero reclining at her feet, were expressive of defiance and revolt, mingled with pity and love. Her face, beautiful in its great humanity, was turned upon a world of pain and woe, one hand pointing to the dying rebel, the other held protectingly over his brow. There was intense feeling in her gesture, and infinite tenderness. The tablet on the back of the base was engraved with a significant passage from Governor Altgeld's reasons for pardoning the three surviving anarchists.

It was nearly dark when we made our way out of the cemetery. My thoughts wandered back to the time when I had opposed the erection of the monument. I had argued that our dead comrades needed no stone to immortalize them. I realized now how narrow and bigoted I had been, and how little I had understood the power of art. The monument served as the embodiment of the ideals for which the men had died, a visible symbol of their words and their deeds.

Before I left Chicago, the news reached me of Robert Reitzel's death. While his friends knew that the end was only a question of weeks, yet we were stunned. My own loss was the more poignant because of my closeness to my dear "knight." His rebellious ardour and artistic soul stood so vividly before me that I could not think of him as dead. It was particularly on my last visit to him that I came fully to appreciate his true greatness, the heights to which he could rise. A thinker and poet, he was not content merely to fashion beautiful words; he wanted them to be living realities, to help in awakening the masses to the possibilities of an earth freed from the shackles the privileged few had forged. His dream was of things radiant, of love and freedom, of life and joy. He had lived and fought for that dream with all the passion of his soul.

Now Robert was dead, his ashes strewn over the lake. His great heart beat no more; his turbulent spirit was at rest. Life continued on its course, made more desolate without my knight, robbed of the force and beauty of his pen, the poetic splendour of his song. Life continued, and with it grew stronger the determination for greater effort.

Denver was a centre of our work, with a number of men and women of the individualist as well as of the communist school of anarchism active there. They were nearly all native born; some of them could trace their ancestry to the pioneers of colonial days. Lizzie and William Holmes, co-workers of Albert Parsons and his close friends, and their circle were persons of keen and clear minds, grounded in the economic aspects of the social struggle and well-informed otherwise also. Lizzie and William had been in the thick of the eight-hour struggle in Chicago and were contributors as well to the *Alarm* and other radical publications. The death of Albert Parsons had been an even greater blow to them than to most comrades because of their year-long friendship. Now living in Denver in poor quarters and barely earning enough to sustain life, they were still as devoted to the Cause as in the days when their faith was young and their hopes high. We spent much time discussing the movement and particularly the period of 1887. Their picture of Albert Parsons, the rebel and the man, was most vivid: To Parsons, anarchism had not been a mere theory of the future. He had made it a living force in his everyday existence, in his home life and relations with his fellows. Descended from an old Southern family that prided itself on caste, Albert Parsons felt kinship with the most degraded of humanity. He had grown up in an atmosphere that tenaciously clung to the idea of slavery as a divine right, and State honours as the only thing worth while in the world. He not only repudiated both, but married a young mulatto. There was no room for colour distinctions in Albert's ideal of human brotherhood, and love was more powerful than man-made barriers. The same generous quality had impelled him to leave his place of safety and deliberately walk into the clutches of the Illinois authorities. The urge of sharing the fate of his comrades was more important than anything else. And yet Albert passionately loved life. His fine spirit manifested itself even in his last moments. Far from giving way to rancour or lamentations, Parsons intoned his favourite song, *Annie Laurie,* its strains ringing in his prison cell on the very day of execution.

My journey from Denver to San Francisco through the Rocky Mountains was replete with new experience and sensations. I had looked at the Swiss mountains when I had stopped for a few days in Switzerland on my way from Vienna. But the sight of the Rockies, austere and forbidding, was overwhelming. I could not free myself from the thought of the puerility of all man's efforts. The whole human race, myself included, appeared like a mere blade of grass, so insignificant, so pathetically helpless, in the face of those crushing mountains. They terrified me, yet held me by their beauty and grandeur. But when we reached the Royal Gorge, and our train slowly picked its way along the winding arteries hewn by the hand of Labour, relief came and renewed faith in my own strength. The forces that had penetrated those colossi of stone were everywhere at work bearing witness to the creative genius and inexhaustible resources of man.

To see California for the first time in early spring, after twenty-four hours through drab Nevada, was like beholding a fairyland after a nightmare. Never before had I seen nature so lavish and resplendent. I was still under its spell when the scene changed to one of less exuberance, and the train pulled into Oakland.

My stay in San Francisco was most interesting and delightful. It enabled me to do the best work I had accomplished till then, and it brought me in contact with many free and rare spirits. The headquarters of anarchist activity on the Coast was *Free Society,* edited and published by the Isaak family. They were unusual people, Abe Isaak, Mary, his wife, and their three children. They had been Mennonites, a liberal religious sect in Russia, of German origin. In America the Isaaks had first settled in Portland, Oregon, where they came under the influence of anarchist ideas. Together with some native comrades, among whom were Henry Addis and H. J. Pope, the Isaaks founded an anarchist weekly called the *Firebrand.* Because of the appearance in the latter of Walt Whitman's poem, " A Woman Waits for Me," their paper was suppressed, its publishers arrested, and H. J. Pope imprisoned for obscenity. The Isaak family then started *Free Society,* later moving to San Francisco. Even the children co-operated in the undertaking, often working eighteen hours a day, writing, setting up type, and addressing wrappers. At the same time they did not neglect other propagandist activities.

The particular attraction of the Isaaks for me was the consistency of their lives, the harmony between the ideas they professed and their application. The comradeship between the parents and the complete freedom of every member of the household were novel things to me. In no other anarchist family had I seen children enjoy such liberty or so independently express themselves without the slightest hindrance from their elders. It was amusing to hear Abe and Pete, boys of sixteen and eighteen respectively, hold their father to account for some alleged infraction of principle, or criticize the propaganda value of his articles. Isaak would listen with patience and respect, even if the manner of the criticism were adolescently harsh and arrogant. Never once did I see the parents resort to the authority of superior age or wisdom. Their children were their equals; their right to disagree, to live their own lives and learn, was unquestioned.

" If you can't establish freedom in your own home," Isaak often said, " how can you expect to help the world to it? " To him and to Mary that was just what freedom meant: equality of the sexes in all their needs, physical, intellectual, and emotional.

The Isaaks maintained this attitude in the *Firebrand,* and now again in *Free Society.* For their insistence on sex equality they were severely censored by many anarchists in the East and abroad. I had welcomed the discussion of these problems in their paper, for I knew from my own experience that sex expression is as vital a factor in human life as food and air. Therefore it was not mere theory that had led me at an early stage of my development to discuss sex as frankly as I did other topics and to live my life without fear of the opinion of others. Among American radicals in the East I had met many men and women who shared my view on this subject and had the courage to practise their ideas in their sex life. But in my own immediate ranks I was very much alone. It was therefore a revelation to find that the Isaaks felt and lived as I did. It helped to establish a strong personal bond between us besides our common anarchist ideal.

Notwithstanding nightly lectures in San Francisco and adjoining towns, a mass meeting to celebrate the first of May, and a debate with a socialist, we still found time for frequent social gatherings jovial enough to be disapproved by the purists. But we did not mind it. Youth and freedom laughed at rules and strictures, and our circle consisted of people young in years and in spirit. In the company of the Isaak boys and the other young chaps I felt like a grandmother — I was twenty-nine — but in spirit I was the gayest, as my young admirers often assured me. We had the joy of life in us, and the California wines were cheap and stimulating. The propagandist of an unpopular cause needs, even more than other people, occasional light-hearted irresponsibility. How else could he survive the hardships and travail of existence? My San Francisco comrades could work strenuously; they took their tasks very seriously; but they could also love, drink, and play.

CHAPTER XVIII

AMERICA HAD DECLARED WAR WITH SPAIN. THE NEWS WAS NOT unexpected. For several months preceding, press and pulpit were filled with the call to arms in defence of the victims of Spanish atrocities in Cuba. I was profoundly in sympathy with the Cuban and Philippine rebels who were striving to throw off the Spanish yoke. In fact, I had worked with some of the members of the Junta engaged in underground activities to secure freedom for the Philippine Islands. But I had no faith whatever in the patriotic protestations of America as a disinterested and noble agency to help the Cubans. It did not require much political wisdom to see that America's concern was a matter of sugar and had nothing to do with humanitarian feelings. Of course there were plenty of credulous people, not only in the country at large, but even in liberal ranks, who believed in America's claim. I could not join them. I was sure that no one, be it individual or government, engaged in enslaving and exploiting at home, could have the integrity or the desire to free people in other lands. Thenceforth my most important lecture, and the best-attended, was on Patriotism and War.

In San Francisco it went over without interference, but in the smaller California towns we had to fight our way inch by inch. The police, never loath to break up anarchist meetings, stood complacently by and thus encouraged the patriotic disturbers who sometimes made speaking impossible. The determination of our San Francisco group and my own presence of mind saved more than one critical situation. In San Jose the audience looked so threatening that I thought it best to dispense with a chairman and carry the meeting myself. As soon as I began to speak, bedlam broke loose. I turned to the trouble-makers with the request that they choose someone of their own crowd to conduct the meeting. " Go on! " they shouted; " you're only bluffing. You know you wouldn't let us run your show!" "Why not?" I called back. "What we want is to hear both sides, isn't that so?" "Betcher life!" someone yelled. "We must secure order for that, mustn't we?" I continued; "I seem unable to do so. Supposing one of you boys comes up here and shows me how to keep the rest quiet until I have stated my side of the story. After that you can state yours. Now be good American sports."

Boisterous cries, shouts of "Hurrah," calls of "Smart kid, let's give her a chance!" kept the house in confusion for a few minutes. Finally an elderly man stepped up on the platform, banged his cane on the table, and in a voice that would have crumbled the walls of Jericho, bellowed: "Silence! Let's hear what the lady has to say!" There was no further disturbance during my speech of an hour, and when I finished, there was almost an ovation.

Among the most interesting people I met in San Francisco were two girls, the Strunsky sisters. Anna, the elder, had attended my lecture on Political Action. She had been indignant, I afterwards learned, because of my "unfairness to the socialists." The next day she came to visit me "for a little while," as she said. She remained all afternoon, and then invited me to her home. There I met a group of students, among them Jack London, and the younger Strunsky girl, Rose, who was ill. Anna and I became great friends. She had been suspended from Leland Stanford University because she had received a male visitor in her room instead of in the parlour. I told Anna of my life in Vienna and of the men students with whom we used to drink tea, smoke, and discuss all through the night. Anna thought that the American woman would establish her right to liberty and privacy, once she secured the vote. I did not agree with her. I argued that the Russian woman had long ago established, even without the vote, her social and moral independence. Out of it had developed a beautiful *camaraderie,* which makes the relations of the sexes so fine and wholesome among advanced Russians.

I wanted to go to Los Angeles, but I knew no one there capable of organizing my meetings. The few German anarchists I had corresponded with in that city advised me not to come. Certain of my lectures, especially the one on the sex question, they wrote, would militate against their work. I had almost abandoned the idea of Los Angeles when encouragement came from an unexpected quarter. A young man whom I knew as Mr. V., from New Mexico, offered to act as my manager. He was to be in Los Angeles on business, he informed me, and he would be glad to help me arrange one meeting. Mr. V., who was a fine Jewish type, at first attracted my attention at my lectures; he attended every evening and always asked intelligent questions. He was also a frequent visitor at the house of the Isaaks and was evidently interested in our ideas. He was a likable person and I agreed to have him organize one lecture.

In due time my " manager " wired me that all was ready. When I arrived, he met me at the station with a bunch of roses and took me to a hotel. It was one of the best in Los Angeles and I felt it inconsistent for me to put up at such a fashionable place; but Mr. V. argued that it was mere prejudice, a thing he had not expected from Emma Goldman. " Don't you want the meeting to be a success? " he asked. " Of course," I replied, " but what has it to do with staying in expensive hotels? " " Very much," he assured me; " it will help advertise the lecture." " Such matters are not considered from that viewpoint in anarchist ranks," I protested. " The worse for your ranks," he retorted; " that's why you reach so few people. Wait till the meeting; then we will talk." I consented to remain.

The luxurious room he had reserved for me, filled with flowers, was another surprise. Then I discovered a black velvet dress prepared for me. " Is this going to be a lecture or a wedding? " I demanded of Mr. V. " Both," he replied promptly, " though the lecture is to come first."

He had rented one of the best theatres in the town, and surely, my manager expostulated, I must understand that I could not appear in the shabby dress I had worn in San Francisco. Moreover, if I did not like the gown he had chosen, I could change it. It was necessary that I make the best possible showing on my first visit to Los Angeles. " But what interest have you in doing all this? " I persisted. " You told me you are not an anarchist." " I'm on the road to being one," he replied. " Now be sensible. You agreed to have me as your manager, so let me manage this affair in my own way." " Are all managers so solicitous? " I inquired. " Yes, if they know their business and like their artists a little," he said.

The following days the papers were full of Emma Goldman, " under the management of a wealthy man from New Mexico." To avoid the reporters Mr. V. took me out for long walks and rides in the Mexican quarter of the town, to restaurants and cafés. One day he induced me to accompany him to a Russian friend of his, who turned out to be the most fashionable tailor in town and who talked me into letting him take my measurements for a suit. On the afternoon of the lecture I found a simple but beautiful black chiffon dress in my room. Things appeared mysteriously, as in the fairy-tales my German nurse used to tell me. Almost every day brought new surprises, happening in a strange but unostentatious manner.

The meeting was large and rather tumultuous, with patriots present in great numbers. They repeatedly attempted to create confusion, but the clever chairmanship of the " rich man from New Mexico " steered the evening to a peaceful conclusion. Then many people came up to introduce themselves as radicals and to urge me to remain in Los Angeles, offering to arrange more lectures for me. From the obscurity of a complete stranger I had become almost a celebrity, thanks to the efforts of my manager.

Late that evening, in a little Spanish restaurant, away from the crowds, Mr. V. asked me to marry him. Under ordinary circumstances I should have considered such an offer an insult, but everything the man had done was in such good taste that I could not be angry with him. " I and marriage ! " I exclaimed. " You didn't ask whether I love you. Besides, have you so little faith in love that you must put a lock and key on it ? " " Well," he replied, " I don't believe in your free-love stuff. I should want you to continue your lectures ; I'd be happy to help you and secure you so that you will be able to do more and better work. But I couldn't share you with anyone else."

The old refrain ! How often had I heard it since I had become a free human being. Radical or conservative, every male wants to bind the woman to himself. I told him flatly : " No ! "

He refused to take my answer as final. I might change my mind, he said. I assured him there was no chance of my marrying him : I did not propose to forge chains for myself. I had done it once before ; it should not happen again. I wanted only " that free-love stuff " ; no other " stuff " had any meaning to me. But Mr. V. was not in the least perturbed. His love was not of the moment only, he felt confident. He would wait.

I bade him good-bye, left the fashionable hotel, and went to stay with some Jewish comrades I had met. For another week I lectured at well-attended meetings, later organizing a group of sympathizers to continue the work. Then I returned to San Francisco.

As a sequel to my activities in Los Angeles an article appeared in the *Freiheit* denouncing me for having stayed in an expensive hotel and having allowed a rich man to arrange my meeting. My behaviour had "queered anarchism with the workers," the writer claimed. Considering that anarchism had never before had a hearing in Los Angeles in English, and that as a result of my meeting systematic propaganda was now about to be carried on among Americans, the charges seemed to me ridiculous. It was another of the many silly accusations that often appeared against me in Most's weekly. I ignored it, but *Free Society* published a reply by a German comrade who called attention to the good results accomplished by my visit to Los Angeles.

In New York Ed and my brother Yegor met me at the station. Yegor was overjoyed to have me back; Ed, always reserved in public, now appeared unusually so. I thought it was due to my brother's presence, but when he continued to keep aloof even when we were alone, I realized that some change had taken place in him. He was as attentive and considerate as usual, and our home as sweet as ever; but he had become different.

For my part, I was not conscious of any emotional change towards Ed — I knew it even before my return. Now, in his presence, I felt sure that, whatever our intellectual differences, I still loved and wanted him. But his frigid behaviour held me in check.

Although very busy during my tour, I had not neglected the commission Ed had given me for his firm. I had solicited orders for the "invention" and had succeeded in closing several substantial contracts with large stationery stores in Western cities. Ed was delighted and praised my efforts. But about my tour and my work, he asked no questions and showed not the slightest interest. This served to add resentment to my dissatisfaction with the condition of things at home. The haven that had given me so much joy and peace now became stifling.

Fortunately there was no time for brooding. The textile strike in Summit, New Jersey, was demanding my services. It presented the usual situation; meetings were either prohibited or broken up by police clubs. It required skilful manœuvring to meet in the woods outside of Summit. I was kept very much engaged, with hardly any time to see Ed. On the rare occasions when we were together, he would remain silent. Only his eyes spoke and they were full of reproach.

When the strike was over I decided to have it out with Ed. I could

bear the situation no longer. I did not get to it for several weeks, however, owing to the international hunt for anarchists that resulted from
the shooting of the Empress of Austria by Luccheni. Though I had
never before heard the name of the man, I was nevertheless shadowed
by the police and pilloried by the press as if I were the one who had
killed the unfortunate woman. I refused to raise the cry of " Crucify! "
against Luccheni, especially because I had learned through the Italian
anarchist press that he had been a child of the street, forced into
military service in his youth. He had witnessed the savagery of war
on the African front, had been brutally treated in the Army, and had
led a life of wretchedness ever since. It was sheer desperation that had
driven the man to his deed of misplaced protest. Everywhere in our
social scheme life was cheap, wasted, and degraded. Why should this
boy, then, be expected to have any reverence for it? I declared my
sympathy with the woman who had long been *persona non grata* at
the Austrian court and who therefore could not have been responsible
for the crimes committed by the Crown. I saw no propagandistic value
in Luccheni's act. He was a victim no less than the Empress; I refused
to join in the savage condemnation of the one or in the sickening sentimentality expressed for the other.

My attitude again called forth the anathema of the press and the
police. Naturally I was not alone; nearly every leading anarchist
throughout the world had to endure similar attacks. But in the States,
and particularly in New York City, I was the black sheep.

Luccheni's act had evidently struck terror into the hearts of the
crowned and even the elected rulers, between whom the bonds of
sympathy were evident. The secret conclaves of the powers resulted
in the decision to hold an international anti-anarchist congress in Rome.
The revolutionary and liberty-loving elements in the United States
and Europe realized the impending danger to freedom of thought and
expression and immediately set to work to stem the tide. Everywhere
meetings were held to protest against the international conspiracy of
authority. In New York no hall could be found where my appearance
would be tolerated.

In the midst of this work came an urgent request from the Alexander Berkman Defense Association in Pittsburgh for greater activity
in behalf of his pardon. The case, which was to be heard in September,
was now set for December 21. The attorneys advised that the decision of the Board of Pardons would largely depend on the stand of

Andrew Carnegie in the matter and therefore they urged seeing the steel-magnate. It was an inane suggestion, which would certainly not be approved by Sasha; such a step was sure to put us all in a ridiculous position. I knew no one likely to consent to approach Carnegie, and I was positive he would not act in the case, anyway. Some of our well-wishers insisted, nevertheless, that he was humane and interested in advanced ideas. As proof of it they adduced the fact that, some time previously, Carnegie had invited Peter Kropotkin to be his guest. I knew that Peter had refused the doubtful honour, replying in effect that he could not accept the hospitality of a man whose interests had imposed an inhumanly excessive sentence on his comrade Alexander Berkman and continued to keep him buried in the Western Penitentiary. Carnegie's eagerness to have Kropotkin visit him was an indication that he would listen favourably to a plea for the liberation of Sasha, some of our friends held. I opposed the idea, but finally succumbed to the arguments of Justus and Ed, who pointed out that we should not allow our own feelings to stand in the way of Sasha's freedom. Justus suggested that we write to Benjamin R. Tucker, requesting him to see Carnegie in the matter.

I knew Tucker only through his writings in *Liberty,* the individualist-anarchist publication, of which he was founder and editor. He wielded a forceful pen and he had done much to introduce his readers to some of the best works in German and French literature. But his attitude towards communist-anarchists was very narrow and charged with insulting rancour. "Tucker doesn't impress me as a large nature," I said to Justus, who insisted that I was wrong and that we must at least give the man a chance. A short letter, signed by Justus Schwab, Ed Brady and me, was sent to Benjamin R. Tucker, stating our case and asking whether he would consent to see Carnegie, who was expected shortly from Scotland.

Tucker's reply was a lengthy epistle setting forth the conditions on which he would approach Carnegie. He would, he wrote, say to him: " In determining your attitude you surely will take it for granted, as I take it for granted, that they approach you as penitent sinners asking forgiveness and seeking remission of penalty. Their very appearance before you in person or by proxy on such an errand must be taken to indicate that what they once regarded as a wise act of heroism they now regard as a foolish act of barbarism . . . that the six years of Mr. Berkman's imprisonment have convinced them of the error of their ways. . . . Any other explanation of the prayer of these petitioners is inconsistent with their lofty character; certainly it is not to be supposed for a moment that men and women of their courage and dignity after shooting a man down deliberately and in cold blood would then descend to the basely humiliating course of begging their victims to grant them the freedom to assault them again. . . . I myself do not appear here today before you as a penitent sinner. In my record in this matter there is nothing for which I have occasion to apologize. I reserve all my rights. . . . I have refused to commit, counsel, or sanction violence, but since circumstances may arise when a policy of violence might seem advisable, I decline to surrender my liberty of choice. . . ."

The letter contained not a word about Sasha's sentence, which, even from a legal view-point, was barbarous; not a word about the torture he had already endured; not a single expression of ordinary humanity from Mr. Tucker, the exponent of a great social ideal. Nothing but cold calculation how to belittle Sasha and his friends while at the same time advancing his own lofty position. He was incapable of seeing that one might feel a wrong done to others more intensely than one done to oneself. He could not grasp the psychology of a man whom the brutality of Frick during the Homestead lock-out had caused to express his protest by an act of violence. Nor was he apparently willing to comprehend that Sasha's friends could endeavour to secure his liberation without necessarily having become convinced of " the error of their ways."

We now turned to Ernest Crosby, a leading single-taxer and Tolstoyan, who was also a gifted poet and writer. He was a man of a very different calibre, understanding and sympathetic even where he did not entirely agree. He visited us in the company of a younger man, whom I knew to be Leonard D. Abbott. When we placed our case before Mr. Crosby, he agreed at once to see Carnegie. There was only one thing that troubled him, he explained. If Carnegie should demand a guarantee that Alexander Berkman, when free, would not again commit an act of violence, what answer was he to give? He himself would never ask such a thing, aware that no one could say what he might do under pressure. But as the intermediary he felt it necessary to be informed by us on the matter. Of course, it was impossible for us to give such a guarantee, and I knew that Sasha would never make any pledges of " reform " or allow them to be made for him.

The matter finally ended with our decision not to apply to Carnegie at all. Sasha's case was not even brought before the Board of Pardons at the time intended. Its members were found to be too prejudiced against him, and it was hoped that the new Board, which was to take office in the following year, might prove more impartial.

After long efforts to procure a hall for our protest meeting against the anti-anarchist congress we succeeded in obtaining Cooper Union. It still adhered to the principle established by its founder to give every political opinion a hearing. My friends feared that I should be arrested, but I was determined to see the thing through. I felt desperate at the attempt to crush the last vestiges of free speech, and sick at heart over my personal life at home. In fact, I was really hoping for an arrest as an escape from everybody and everything.

On the eve of the meeting Ed unexpectedly broke his silence. " I can't bear to have you face this danger," he said, " without trying once more to reach you. While you were on tour, I had definitely decided to stifle my love and try to meet you on terms of comradeship. But I realized the absurdity of such a decision the moment I saw you at the station. Since then I have gone through a severe struggle, deciding even to leave you altogether. But I cannot do it. I would let things drift till you go on tour again, but now that you are in danger of arrest, I have to speak out, to try to bridge the gap between us."

" But there is no gap," I exclaimed excitely, " unless you persist in making one! Of course, I have outgrown many of the conceptions still so dear to you. I can't help it; but I love you, don't you understand? I love you, no matter what or who comes into my life. I need you, and I need our home. Why will you not be free and big and take what I can give? "

Ed promised to try again, to do anything not to lose me. Our reunion brought back memories of our young love in my little flat in the Bohemian Republic.

The meeting at Cooper Union passed without trouble. Johann Most, who had promised to address the audience, failed to appear. He would not speak on the same platform with me; he still preserved all his bitterness.

Three weeks later Ed fell ill with pneumonia. All my care and love were pitted against the great dread I felt at the possibility of losing the precious life. The big strong man, who used to make light of illness and who had often hinted " that such things were inherent only in the female species," now clung to me like an infant and would not have me out of sight even for a moment. His impatience and irascibility transcended those of ten sick women. But he was so ill that I did not mind his constant demands upon my care and attention.

Fedya and Claus came to offer their help as soon as they learned of Ed's condition. One of them would relieve me at night to permit me a few hours' rest. During the crisis my anxiety was too intense for sleep. Ed was in a high fever, tossing about and even trying to jump out of bed. His vacant look gave no indication of recognition, yet he would grow more restless at the touch of either of the boys. At one moment when he had got quite frenzied, Fedya and Claus were about to try to hold him down by force. " Let me manage him myself," I said, bending over my darling, trying to pour my very soul into his wild eyes and pressing him to my anxious heart. Ed struggled for a while, then his rigid body relaxed, and with a sigh he fell back on his pillow, all covered with sweat.

At last the crisis was over. In the morning Ed opened his eyes. His hand groped for mine, and in a faint voice he asked: " Dear nurse, must I kick the bucket? " " Not this time," I comforted him, " but you must be very quiet." His face lit up with his old beautiful smile, and he dozed off again.

When Ed was already on his feet, though still very weak, I had to leave for a meeting I had promised to address long before his illness. Fedya remained with him. When I returned, late at night, Fedya was gone and Ed fast asleep. There was a note from Fedya saying that Ed was feeling fine and had urged him to go home.

In the morning Ed was still asleep. I took his pulse and noticed that he was breathing heavily. I became alarmed and sent for Doctor Hoffmann. The latter expressed concern over Ed's unusually protracted sleep. He asked to see the box of morphine he had left for Ed to take. Four powders were missing! I had given Ed one before going away, and I had impressed upon Fedya that he was not to get any more. Ed had taken four times the ordinary dose — no doubt in an attempt to end his life! He wanted to die — now — after I had barely rescued him from the grave! Why? Why?

" We must get him on his feet and walk the floor with him," the doctor ordered; " he is alive, he is breathing; we must keep him alive." We supported his drooping body up and down the room, from time to time applying ice to his hands and face. Gradually his face began to lose its deathly pallor, and his lids responded to pressure.

" Who would ever have thought that a reserved and quiet person like Ed would be capable of such a thing? " the doctor remarked. " He'll sleep on for many more hours, but no need to worry. He'll live."

I was shocked by Ed's attempted suicide and tried to fathom what particular cause had induced his action. On several occasions I was on the point of asking him for an explanation, but he was in such cheerful humour and recuperating so well that I was afraid to dig up the ghastly affair. He himself never referred to it.

Then one day he surprised me by mentioning that he had not intended to take his life at all. My leaving him to go to the meeting when he was still so ill had enraged him. He knew from past experience that he could stand a large dose of morphine, and he swallowed several powders, " just to scare you a little and cure you of your mania for meetings, which stops at nothing, not even at the illness of the man you pretend to love."

His words staggered me. I felt that the seven years of our life together had failed to make Ed grasp the pain and travail of my inner growth. A " mania for meetings " — that was all that it meant to him.

There followed days of conflict between my love for Ed and the realization that life had lost its content and meaning. At the end of my bitter struggle I knew that I must leave him. I told Ed that I should have to go, for good.

" Your desperate act to tear me from my work," I said, " has convinced me that you have no faith in me or my aims. Whatever little of it you had in former years is no more. Without your faith and your co-operation our relationship has no value to me." " I love you more now than I did in the early days! " he interrupted me excitedly. " It is no use, dear Ed, to deceive ourselves or each other," I continued. " You want me only as your wife. Well, that is not enough for me. I need understanding, harmony, the exaltation that results from unity of ideas and purpose. Why go on until our love is poisoned by bitterness and made ugly with recrimination? Now we can still part as friends. I'm going on tour anyway; it will be less painful that way."

His frenzied pacing of the room came to a stop. He looked at me in silence, as if trying to penetrate my innermost being. " You're all wrong, you're terribly wrong," he cried desperately; then he turned and left the room.

I began preparations for my tour. The day of departure was approaching, and Ed pleaded with me to permit him to see me off. I declined; I was afraid I might give way at the last moment. That day Ed came home at noon to have lunch with me. Both of us pretended to be cheerful. But at parting his face darkened for a moment. Before leaving he embraced me, saying: "This isn't the end, dearest — it cannot be! This is your home, now and for ever!" I could not speak; my heart was too full of grief. When the door had closed on Ed, I was unable to restrain my sobs. Every object about me assumed a strange fascination, speaking to me in many tongues. I realized that to linger meant to weaken my determination to leave Ed. With palpitating heart I walked out of the house I had loved and cherished as my home.

CHAPTER XIX

THE FIRST STOP ON MY TOUR WAS IN BARRE, VERMONT. THE ACTIVE group there consisted of Italians employed mostly in the stone-quarries, which furnished the principal industry of the city. Very little time was left me for introspection into my personal life; there were numerous meetings, debates, private gatherings, and discussions. I found generous hospitality with my host, Palavicini, a comrade who had worked together with me in the textile strike in Summit. He was a cultivated man, well-informed not only on the international labour movement, but also on the new tendencies in Italian art and letters. At the same time I met also Luigi Galleani, the intellectual leader of the Italian activities in the New England States.

Vermont was under the blessings of Prohibition, and I was interested in learning its effects. In company with my host I made the rounds of some private homes. To my astonishment I found that almost all of them had been turned into saloons. In one such place we came upon a dozen men visibly under the influence of liquor. Most of them were city officials, my companion informed me. The stuffy kitchen, with the children of the family inhaling the foul air of whisky and tobacco, constituted the drinking-den. Many such places were thriving under the protection of the police, to whom part of the income was regularly paid. "That is not the worst evil of Prohibition," my comrade remarked; "its most damnable side is the destruction of hospitality and good-fellowship. Formerly you could offer a drink to callers or have one offered to you. Now, with most people turned into saloon-keepers, your friends expect you to buy booze or to buy it from you."

Another result of Prohibition was the increase of prostitution. We visited several houses on the outskirts of the town, all doing a flourishing business. Most of the "guests" were travelling salesmen, with a sprinkling of farmers. By the closing of the saloons the brothel became the only place where the men coming into town could find some distraction.

After two weeks' activity in Barre the police suddenly decided to prevent my last meeting. The official reason for it was supposed to be my lecture on war. According to the authorities, I had said: " God bless the hand that blew up the Maine." It was of course obviously ridiculous to credit me with such an utterance. The unofficial version was more plausible. " You caught the Mayor and the Chief of Police in Mrs. Colletti's kitchen, dead drunk," my Italian friend explained, " and you have looked into their stakes in the brothels. No wonder they consider you dangerous now and want to get you out."

It was not until I reached Chicago that I began to make my efforts count. As on my preceding tour, I was invited to speak by many labour organizations, including the conservative Woodworkers' Union, which had never before allowed an anarchist within its sacred portals. A number of lectures were also arranged for me by American anarchists. It was strenuous work and I should probably not have been able to carry it through but for the exhilarating companionship of Max Baginski.

As on previous occasions, my headquarters were again with the Appels. At the same time Max and I rented a little place near Lincoln Park, our *Zauberschloss* (fairy-castle), as he christened it, to which we might escape in our free hours. There we would often feast on the basketfuls of delicacies, fruit, and wine the extravagantly big-natured Max would bring. Then we would read *Romeo und Juliet auf dem Lande,* the beautiful story by Gottfried Keller, and the works of our favourites: Strindberg, Wedekind, Gabriele Reuter, Knut Hamsun, and, best of all, Nietzsche. Max knew and understood Nietzsche and deeply loved him. It was only by the aid of his remarkable appreciation that I became aware of the full significance of the great poet-philosopher. After readings came long walks in the park and talks about interesting people in the German movement, about art and literature. The month in Chicago was filled with interesting work, the fine comradeship of new friends, and exquisite hours of joy and harmony with Max.

The Paris Exposition, which was being planned for 1900, suggested the idea to our European comrades of holding an anarchist congress at about the same time. There would be reduced fares, and many of our friends would be able to come from different countries.

I had received an invitation; I spoke to Max about it and asked him to come with me. A trip to Europe together — the very thought of it transported us with ecstasy. My tour would last till August; then we could carry out our new plan. We might journey to England first; I was sure the comrades would want me to lecture there. Then to Paris. "Think of it, dearest — Paris!" "Wonderful, glorious!" he cried. "But the fare — have you thought of that, my romantic Emma?" "That's nothing. I will rob a church or a synagogue — I'll get the money somehow! We must go anyhow. We must go in quest of the moon!" "Two babes in the woods," Max commented; "two sane romantics in a crazy world!"

On my way to Denver I made a side trip to Caplinger Mills, an agricultural district in south-western Missouri. My only previous contact with farm life in the United States had been years before when I had canvassed Massachusetts farmers for orders to enlarge the pictures of their worthy ancestors. I had found them so dull, so rooted in old social traditions, that I did not even care to tell them what I stood for. I was sure they would think me possessed of the devil. It very much surprised me, therefore, to receive an invitation from Caplinger Mills to lecture there. The comrade who wrote that she had arranged my meetings was Kate Austen, whose articles I had read in *Free Society* and other radical publications. Her writings showed her to be a logical thinker, well-informed, and of revolutionary fibre, while her letters to me indicated an affectionate, sensitive being.

At the station I was met by Sam Austen, Kate's husband, who announced that Caplinger Mills was twenty-two miles distant from the railroad. "The roads are very bad," he said; "I'm afraid I'll have to tie you to the seat of my wagon, else you may be shaken out." I soon found he had not been exaggerating. We had hardly covered half the way when there came a violent jolt and the cracking of wheels. Sam landed in a ditch, and when I attempted to get up, I felt sore all over. He lifted me out of the wagon and set me down by the wayside. Waiting and rubbing my aching joints, I tried to smile to encourage Sam.

While he was tinkering the broken wheel, my thoughts went back to Popelan and our long rides in the big sleigh drawn by a fiery *troika*. My blood tingled with the mystery of the night, the starry heavens above me, the white-clad expanse, the music of the merry bells, and the peasant songs of Petrushka at my side. The danger from the

wolves, whose howling could be heard in the distance, made the outings more adventurous and romantic. On our return home there would
be a feast of hot potato pancakes baked in delicious goose grease,
steaming tea with *varenya* (jam) Mother had made, and vodka for
the servants. Petrushka always let me taste a little from his glass.
" You're a regular drunkard," he would tease me. That was indeed
my reputation since the day when they had found me in a stupor in
our cellar underneath a beer-barrel. Father would never permit us
to taste liquor, but one day — I was about three years old then —
I had trotted down to the cellar, put my mouth to a faucet, and drank
the queer-tasting stuff. I woke up in my bed, deathly sick, and would
no doubt have been given a sound thrashing had not our dear old
nurse kept me hidden away from Father. . . .

At last we arrived in Caplinger Mills at the Austen farm. " Put
her to bed right away and give her a hot drink," Sam directed, " else
she'll hate us for the rest of her life for having taken her over that
road." After a hot bath and a good massage I felt much refreshed,
though still aching in every joint.

My week with the Austens showed me new angles of the small
American farmer's life. It made me see that we had been wrong to
regard the farmer in the States as belonging to the *bourgeoisie.* Kate
said it was true only of the very rich landowner who raised everything on a large scale; the vast mass of farmers in America were even
more dependent than the city workers. They were at the mercy of the
bankers and the railroads, not to speak of their natural enemies,
storm and drought. To combat the latter and nourish the leeches who
sap the farmer he must slave endless hours in every kind of weather
and live almost on the edge of penury. It is his toilsome lot that makes
him hard and close-fisted, Kate thought. She lamented especially the
drab existence of the farmer's wife. " The womenfolk have nothing
but cares, drudgery, and frequent child-bearing."

Kate had come to Caplinger only after her marriage. Before that
she had lived in small towns and villages. Left in charge of eight
brothers and sisters at her mother's death, when she herself was
only eleven years old, she had had no time for much study. Two years
in a district school was all the learning her father had been able to
afford for her. I wondered how she had managed to gain so much
knowledge as her numerous articles implied. " From reading," she
informed me. Her father had been a constant reader, at first of

Ingersoll's works, later of *Lucifer* and other radical publications. The events in Chicago in 1887 had exerted upon her, as also upon me, the greatest influence. Since then she had closely followed the social struggle and had studied everything she could get hold of. The range of her reading, judging by the books I found in the Austen household, was very wide. Works on philosophy, on social and economic questions, and on sex were side by side with the best in poetry and fiction. They had been her school. She was thoroughly informed, besides possessing an enthusiasm extraordinary in a woman who had hardly come in contact with life.

" How can a woman of your brains and abilities go on living in such a dull and limited sphere ? " I inquired.

"Well, there is Sam," she replied, "who shares everything with me and whom I love, and the children. And there are my neighbours who need me. One can do much even here."

The attendance at my three meetings testified to Kate's influence. From a radius of many miles the farmers came, on foot, in wagons, and on horseback. Two lectures I gave in the little country schoolhouse, the third in a large grove. It was a most picturesque gathering, with the faces of my listeners lit up by lanterns they had brought with them. From the questions some of the men asked, which centred mainly on the right to the land under anarchism, I could see that at least some of them had not come out of mere curiosity, and that Kate had awakened them to the realization that their own difficulties were part of the larger problems of society.

The whole Austen family dedicated itself to me during my stay. Sam took me over the fields on horseback, having given me a sober old mare to ride. The children fulfilled my wishes almost before I had a chance to express them, and Kate was all affectionate devotion. We were much alone together, which gave her a chance to tell me about herself and her surroundings. The greatest objection some of her neighbours had to her was her stand on the sex question. " What would you do if your husband fell in love with another woman ? " a farmer's wife had once asked her. " Wouldn't you leave him ? " " Not if he still loved me," Kate had promptly replied. " And shouldn't you hate the woman ? " " Not if she were a fine person and really loved Sam." Her neighbour had said that if she didn't know Kate so well, she would consider her immoral or crazy ; even as it was, she was sure Kate could not possibly love her husband or she would never consent to share him with anybody else. " The joke of it is," Kate added, " that the husband of this neighbour is known to be after every skirt, and she is not aware of it. You have no idea what the sexual practices of these farmers are. But it is the result mostly of their dreary existence," she hastened to add; " no other outlet, no distraction, no colour of any sort in their lives. It is different in the city; even the poorest working-man there can sometimes go to a show or a lecture, or find some interest in his union. The farmer has nothing but long and arduous toil in the summer, and empty days in the winter. Sex is all they have. How should these people understand sex in its finer expressions, or love that cannot be sold or bound? It's an uphill fight, but we must strive on," my dear comrade concluded.

Time passed only too quickly. Presently I had to leave in order to keep my engagements in the West. Sam offered to take me to the station by a shorter route, which was " only fourteen miles." Kate and the rest of the family accompanied us.

CHAPTER XX

AT THE HEIGHT OF MY CALIFORNIA ACTIVITIES A LETTER CAME that shattered my visions of harmonious love: Max wrote me that he and his comrade " Puck " were about to go abroad together, financed by a friend. I laughed aloud at the folly of my hopes. After the failure with Ed how could I have dreamed of love and understanding with anyone else? Love and happiness — empty, meaningless words, vain reaching out for the unattainable. I felt robbed by life, defeated in my yearning for a beautiful relationship. I still had my ideal to live for, as I consoled myself, and the work I had set myself to do. Why expect more from life? But where get strength and inspiration to keep up the struggle? Men had been able to do the world's work without the sustaining power of love; why should not also women? Or is it that woman needs love more than man? A stupid, romantic notion, conceived to keep her for ever dependent on the male. Well, I would not have it; I would live and work without love. There is no permanency anywhere in nature or in life. I must drain the moment and then let the goblet fall to the ground. It is the sole protection against taking root, only to be painfully pulled up again. My young friends in San Francisco had been calling. The vision of life with Max had stood in the way. Now I could respond; I must respond in order to forget.

After visiting Portland and Seattle I went to Tacoma, Washington. Everything had been prepared for a meeting there, but when I arrived, I found that the owner of the hall had backed out, and no other place could be secured. At the last moment, when all hopes had been given up, the spiritualists came to the rescue. I delivered several lectures before them, but at the subject of Free Love even they balked. Evidently the spirits continued in heaven the moral standards they had set during their embodiment.

Spring Valley, Illinois, a large mining section, had a strong anarchist group, consisting mostly of Belgians and Italians. They had
invited me for a series of lectures, culminating in a demonstration on
Labour Day. Their efforts were crowned with great success. Although
it was broiling hot, the miners turned out with their wives and children, dressed in their finest. I headed the procession, carrying a large
red flag. In the garden hired for the speeches the platform had no
awning. I spoke with the hot sun beating down on my head, which
had already begun to ache during the long march. In the afternoon, at
our picnic, the comrades brought nineteen babies to be baptized by
me in " true anarchist fashion," as they said. I got on an empty beer-
barrel, no other stand being available, and addressed the audience.
I felt that the ones who needed baptism were really the parents,
baptism in the new ideas of the rights of the child.

The local papers the following day carried two leading stories:
one that Emma Goldman " drank like a trooper "; the other that
she " had baptized anarchist children in a barrel of beer."

During my previous visit in Detroit with Max I had met one of
Robert Reitzel's staunchest friends, Herman Miller, and another
devotee of the *Armer Teufel,* Carl Stone. Miller was president of the
Cleveland Brewing Company and a man of considerable means. How
he ever came to his position was a puzzle to all who knew him. He
was a dreamer and visionary, a lover of freedom and beauty, and a
very generous spirit. For years he had been the main support of the
Armer Teufel. His finest trait was his art of giving. Even when he
tipped a waiter, it was done in a delicate and almost apologetic way.
As for his friends, Herman fairly showered gifts on them, in a manner
as though they were bestowing a favour on him. On this occasion my
host outdid himself in thoughtfulness and generosity. The days spent
with him and Stone, in the company of the Ruedebusches, Emma
Clausen, and other friends, were a round of good fellowship and
comradeship.

Both Miller and Stone showed great interest in my struggle and
plans for the future. Asked about the latter, I informed them that
I had none, except to work for my ideal. Didn't I wish to secure myself
materially, by having some profession, for instance, Herman suggested. I had always wanted to study medicine, I told him, but had
never had the means for it. I was completely taken off my feet by Herman's unexpectedly offering to finance my studies. Stone also wanted to

share the expense, but the two friends thought it impracticable to turn the entire amount over to me. " I understand you always have a string of people needing help; you will be sure to give the money away," Herman said. They agreed to secure me for five years with an income of forty dollars a month. The same day Herman, accompanied by Julia Ruedebusch, took me to the best store in Detroit, " to help rig Emma out for her trip." A beautiful blue Scotch cloth cape was among the numerous things I cherished from my shopping tour. Carl Stone presented me with a gold watch; it was clam-shaped, and I wondered why he had chosen such a peculiar form. " In token of a gift you have, so rare in your sex: the ability to keep mum," he said. " That is indeed a compliment from a male!" I retorted, to the amusement of the rest.

Before I took leave of my dear friends in Detroit, Herman shyly and unobtrusively put an envelope in my hand. " A love-letter," he said, " to be read on the train." The "love-letter" contained five hundred dollars, with a note: " For your passage, dear Emma, and to keep you from care until we meet in Paris."

The last hope of legal redress for Sasha was gone when the new Board of Pardons refused to hear our appeal. There was nothing left except the desperate venture Sasha had been planning for a considerable time — an escape. His friends used every means to dissuade him from the idea during the campaign made in his behalf by Carl, Henry, Gordon, and Harry Kelly. With the possibility of release gone, I could do nothing but submit to Sasha's wishes, though with an anxious heart.

His letters, after I informed him that we would go ahead with his scheme, showed him to have undergone a wonderful transformation. He was buoyant again, full of hope and vigour. Soon he would send a friend to us, he wrote, a most trustworthy person, a fellow prisoner whom he called " Tony." The man would be released within a few weeks, and he would then bring us the necessary details of the plan. " It will not fail if my instructions are faithfully carried out," he wrote. He explained that two things would be required: dependable comrades of grit and endurance, and some money. He was sure I would find both.

Before long " Tony " was released, but certain preparatory work in Sasha's behalf kept him in Pittsburgh, and we could not get in personal touch with him. I learned, however, that Sasha's plan involved the digging of a tunnel from the outside into the prison, and that Sasha had entrusted "Tony" with all the necessary diagrams and measurements to enable us to do the work. The scheme seemed fantastic, the desperate design of one driven to stake everything, even his life, upon the throw of a card. Yet I was carried away by the project, so cleverly conceived, and worked out with utmost care. I reflected a long time upon whom to approach in regard to the undertaking. There were plenty of comrades who would be willing to risk their lives to rescue Sasha, but few who had the requisites for such a difficult and hazardous task. I finally decided upon our Norwegian friend Eric B. Morton, whom we had nicknamed "Ibsen." He was a veritable viking, in spirit and physique, a man of intelligence, daring, and will-power.

The plan appealed to him at once. Without hesitation he promised to do anything that would be required, and he was ready to start there and then. I explained that there would be an unavoidable delay; we had to wait for "Tony." Something was apparently detaining him much longer than he had expected. I was loath to leave for Europe without being sure that Sasha's plan was being carried out and I confessed to Eric that I felt uneasy about going at all. "It will be maddening to be three thousand miles away while Sasha's fate is hanging in the balance," I said. Eric understood my feelings in the matter, but he thought that as far as the proposed tunnel was concerned, I could do nothing. "In fact, your absence may prove of greater value," he argued, "than your presence in America. It will serve to ward off suspicion that something is being done for Sasha." He agreed with me that the question of Sasha's safety after the escape was of paramount importance. He feared, as I did, that Sasha could not remain very long in the country without being apprehended. "We'll have to get him away as quickly as possible to Canada or Mexico, and thence to Europe," he suggested. "The tunnel will require months of work, and that will give you time to prepare a place for him abroad. There he will be recognized as a political refugee, and as such he will not be extradited."

I knew Eric was a very level-headed man, entirely reliable. Still I hated to go away without seeing "Tony," learning the details of the plan, and finding out all he could tell us about Sasha. Eric quieted my apprehensions by promising to take charge of the entire matter and to begin operations as soon as "Tony" arrived. He was a man of convincing manner and strong personality, and I had the fullest faith in his courage and ability to carry out successfully Sasha's directions. He was, moreover, splendid company, full of cheer, and with a fine sense of humour. At parting he jubilantly assured me that together with Sasha we should soon all meet in Paris to celebrate his escape.

Still "Tony" failed to appear and his absence filled me with misgivings. Involuntarily I thought of the unreliability of prisoners' promises. I remembered the great things several of the women in Blackwell's Island were going to do for me upon their release. They were all soon drawn into the whirlpool of life and personal interests, their best prison intentions slipping away from them. It is rare indeed that a released prisoner is willing and able to carry out the promises made to his fellow sufferers remaining behind the bars. "Tony" was probably like the majority, I thought. Still, I had several weeks yet before sailing — perhaps "Tony" would turn up in the meantime.

Since leaving New York on my last tour I had not corresponded with Ed, but on my return I had received a letter from him begging me to come to the apartment and occupy it until I left for Europe. He could not endure the idea that I should be with strangers when I had a home of my own. "There is no reason for your not staying here," he wrote; "we are still friends, and the flat, with everything in it, is yours." At first I was inclined to refuse; I dreaded a revival of our former relationship and the old struggle. But Ed was so persistent in his letters that I finally returned to the place that had been my home for so many years. Ed was charming, full of tact, considerately non-invasive. Our flat had separate entrances; we came and went our different ways. It was the busy season for Ed's firm, and my time was fully occupied by raising money for Sasha's project and getting ready for my trip abroad. On my occasional free evenings or Saturday afternoons Ed would invite me to dinner or to the theatre, afterwards going to Justus's place. He never once referred to our old life. Instead we discussed my plans for Europe and he seemed greatly interested in them. He was pleased to hear that Herman Miller and Carl Stone were to finance my study of medicine, and he promised to pay me a visit in Europe, as he was planning to go abroad the following year. His mother had been ailing of late; she was growing old and he was anxious to see her as soon as possible.

Justus's place continued to be the most interesting in New York, but its former gaiety was dampened by the alarming condition of its host. I had not been informed, while touring the country, of his illness, and on my return I was appalled to find him wasted and weak. His friends had urged him to go for a rest; Mrs. Schwab and their son could manage the place in his absence. But Justus would not consent. He laughed and joked as usual, but his glorious voice had lost its old ring. It was heart-rending to see our " giant oak " beginning to break.

Funds to carry out Sasha's undertaking had to be raised under cover of a supposed new legal move. Only very few comrades could be told about the real object for which the money was needed. The man who could help most was S. Yanofsky, editor of the *Freie Arbeiter Stimme,* the Yiddish anarchist weekly. He had only recently come from England, where he had edited the *Arbeiter Freund;* he was clever and wielded an incisive pen. I knew him as a worshipper of Most, which was no doubt the reason for his antagonistic attitude towards me at our first meeting. His sarcastic manner had made a disagreeable impression on me, and I disliked having to approach him. But it was for Sasha's sake, and I went to see him.

To my surprise I found Yanofsky very much interested and willing to help. He expressed doubts about the chances of the plan's success, but when I informed him that Sasha was desperate at the thought of continuing eleven more years in his grave, Yanofsky promised to do his utmost to raise the necessary money. With " Ibsen " and several other reliable friends in Pittsburgh to look after the undertaking, and with Yanofsky to assist with the financial end, my anxiety was considerably allayed.

Harry Kelly was then in England. I had written him about my coming to Europe and he immediately invited me to stay in the house where he was living with his wife and child. The London comrades, Harry wrote, were planning a large eleventh-of-November meeting and would be glad to have me as one of the speakers. At the same time a letter arrived from the anarchists in Glasgow, inviting me for lectures. Besides, there was much to be done for our congress. I had received credentials as a delegate from several groups. Some of the American comrades, among them Lizzie and William Holmes, Abe Isaak, and Susan Patten, asked me to present their papers on various topics. I had a great deal of work before me and it was time to start on my journey. But to my distress there was still no word from " Tony."

One evening I went to Justus's place, where I had promised to meet

Ed. I found him in the circle of his philologic cronies, discussing, as usual, the etymology of words. An old literary friend, whom I had not seen for a long time, was there, and while I waited for Ed, I conversed with him. It grew late, but Ed showed no disposition to leave. I told him I was going home, and I left, accompanied by the writer, who lived in the same neighbourhood. At my door I bade him good-bye and immediately went to bed.

I awoke from a ghastly dream that terrified me by lightning and rumbling. But the thunder and crashing of things seemed to continue, and presently I became aware that it was real, happening next door, in Ed's room. He must be crazed by drink, I thought. Yet I had never seen Ed intoxicated to the extent of losing control of himself. What had happened to make Ed so violent as to come home and smash up things in the middle of the night? I wanted to call, to cry out to him, but I was somehow restrained by the continued clatter of objects falling and breaking. After a while it subsided and I heard Ed throw himself heavily on the couch. Then all was quiet.

I kept awake, my eyes burning, my heart beating tumultuously. At daybreak I dressed hastily and opened the door separating my room from Ed's. The sight was appalling: the floor was littered with broken furniture and china; the sketch Fedya had made of me, which Ed had cherished as his greatest treasure, lay torn and trampled upon, its frame smashed. Table and chairs were overturned and broken. In the midst of the confusion lay Ed, half-dressed and fast asleep. In anger and disgust I ran back to my room, slamming the door behind me.

I saw Ed once more, the next day, before I sailed. His haggard look of misery sealed my lips. What was there to say or explain? The debris of our things were the symbol of our wrecked love, of the life that had been so full of colour and promise.

Many friends came to the steamer to say adieu to me and to Mary Isaak, who was sailing with me. Ed was not among them, and I was grateful for it. It would have been even more difficult to control my tears in his presence. It was most painful to say good-bye to Justus, whom we all knew to be dying of tuberculosis. He looked very ill, and I felt saddened by the thought that I might never see him alive again. It was hard also to part from my brother. I was glad to be able to leave him some money, and I would contribute to his needs from the monthly allowance my Detroit friends were to send me. I could manage on less; I had done it in Vienna. The boy had taken deep hold on my heart; he was so tender and considerate that his affection had become something very precious in my life. As the big liner steamed out, I remained on deck to watch the receding silhouettes of New York.

Our crossing was uneventful, except for a raging storm. We arrived in London two days too late for the eleventh-of-November meeting and at the height of the Boer War. In the house where Harry Kelly and his family were living there was only one room vacant, and that was in the basement. Even in clear weather it had but little daylight, while on foggy days the gas-jet had to be kept going all the time. The fire-place warmed only one's side or back, never the entire body, and I constantly had to keep changing my position to balance, to some extent, the atmospheric difference between the fire and the cold room.

Having been in London during its best season, in late August and September, I used to think that people exaggerated when they spoke of the horrors of the London fogs, the dampness and greyness of its winter. But I realized this time that they had hardly done justice to the reality. The fog was like a monster, stealthily creeping up and enveloping the victim in its chilly embrace. Mornings I would awaken with a leaden feeling, my mouth parched. In vain the hope of enjoying a ray of light by opening the blinds; the blackness from the outside would soon creep into the room. Poor Mary Isaak, coming from sunny California, was depressed by the London weather even worse than I. She had planned to stay a month, but after one week she was anxious to leave.

CHAPTER XXI

THE WAR MADNESS IN ENGLAND WAS SO GREAT, SOME OF THE comrades informed me, that it would be almost impossible to deliver my lectures as had been planned. Harry Kelly was of the same opinion. "Why not hold anti-war mass meetings?" I suggested. I referred to the splendid gatherings we had in America during the Spanish War. Now and then there had been attempts at interference, and several lectures had to be given up, but on the whole we had been able to carry through our campaign. Harry thought, however, that it would be impossible in England. His description of violent attacks on speakers (the jingo spirit being at its height) and of meetings being broken up by patriotic mobs sounded discouraging. He was sure it would be even more dangerous for me, a foreigner, to speak on the war. I was in favour of trying it, anyhow. I simply could not be in England and keep silent on the matter. Did not Great Britain believe in free speech? "Mind you," he warned me, "it is not the authorities who interfere with meetings, as in America; it is the mob itself, both rich and poor." I insisted, nevertheless, on making an attempt. Harry promised to consult the other comrades about it.

At the invitation of the Kropotkins I went out with Mary Isaak to Bromley. This time Mrs. Kropotkin and her little daughter, Sasha, were at home. Both Peter and Sophia Grigorevna received us with affectionate cordiality. We discussed America, our movement there, and conditions in England. Peter had visited the States in 1898, but I was at the time on the Coast and unable to attend his lectures. I knew, however, that his tour had been very successful and that he had left a most gratifying impression. The proceeds of his meetings had helped to revive *Solidarity* and inject new life into our movement. Peter was particularly interested in my tours through the Middle West and California. "It must be a splendid field," he remarked, "if you can cover the same ground three times in succession." I assured him that it was, and that much of the credit for my success in California had been due to *Free Society.* "The paper is doing splendid work," he warmly agreed, "but it would do more if it would not waste so much space discussing sex." I disagreed, and we became involved in a heated argument about the place of the sex problem in anarchist propaganda. Peter's view was that woman's equality with man had nothing to do with sex; it was a matter of brains. "When she is his equal intellectually and shares in his social ideals," he said, " she will be as free as he." We both got somewhat excited, and our voices must have sounded as if we were quarrelling. Sophia, quietly sewing a dress for her daughter, tried several times to direct our talk into less vociferous channels, but in vain. Peter and I paced the room in growing agitation, each strenuously upholding his side of the question. At last I paused with the remark: " All right, dear comrade, when I have reached your age, the sex question may no longer be of importance to me. But it is *now,* and it is a tremendous factor for thousands, millions even, of young people." Peter stopped short, an amused smile lighting up his kindly face. " Fancy, I didn't think of that," he replied. " Perhaps you are right, after all." He beamed affectionately upon me, with a humorous twinkle in his eye.

During dinner I broached the plan for the anti-war meetings. Peter was even more emphatic than Harry had been. It was out of the question, he thought; it would endanger my life; moreover, because I was a Russian, my stand on the war would unfavourably affect the status of the Russian refugees. " I'm not here as a Russian, but as an American," I protested. " Moreover, what do these considerations matter when such a vital issue as war is involved? " Peter pointed out that it mattered very much to people who had death or Siberia staring them in the face. He insisted, nevertheless, that England was still the only asylum in Europe for political refugees and that its hospitality should not be forfeited by meetings.

My first public appearance in London, in the Athenæum Hall, was a dismal failure. I had caught a severe cold that affected my throat so that my speaking was painful not only to myself but to the audience as well. I could hardly be heard. No less distressing was my nervousness when I learned that the most distinguished Russian refugees and some noted Englishmen had come to hear me. The names of those Russians had always symbolized to me all that was heroic in the struggle against the tsars. The thought of their presence filled me with awe. What could I say to such men, and how say it?

Harry Kelly acted as chairman, straightway proceeding to tell the audience that his comrade Emma Goldman, who had faced squadrons of police in America, had just confided to him that she was panicky before this assembly. The latter thought it a good joke and laughed heartily. Inwardly I raged at Harry, but the good humour of the audience and its evident desire to put me at my ease somewhat relieved my nervous tension. I plodded through my lecture, aware all the time that I was delivering a rotten speech. The questions that followed, however, gave me back my self-possession. I felt more in my element, and I did not care any more who was present. I regained my ordinary determined and aggressive manner.

My meetings in the East End offered no difficulties. There I was among my people; I knew their lives, hard and barren everywhere, but more so in London. I was able to find the right words to reach them; I was my own self in their midst. My nearer comrades were a warm and genial lot. The moving spirit of the work in the East End was Rudolph Rocker, a young German, who presented the peculiar phenomenon of a Gentile editor of a Yiddish paper. He had not associated much with Jews until he came to England. In order to fit himself the better for his activities in the ghetto, he had lived among the Jews and mastered their language. As editor of the *Arbeiter Freund* and by his brilliant lectures Rudolph Rocker was doing more for the education and revolutionizing of the Jews in England than the ablest members of their own race.

The same good-fellowship which prevailed among my Jewish comrades was evident also in the English anarchist circles, especially in the group that published *Freedom*. That monthly had gathered about it a coterie of able contributors and workers who co-operated most harmoniously. It was a joy to find things going so well, to meet the dear old friends and make so many new ones.

At a social evening at the Kropotkins', I met a number of illustrious people, among them Nikolai Tchaikovsky. He had been the genius of the revolutionary movement of the Russian youth in the seventies that crystallized in the famous circles bearing his name. It was a great event to meet the man who was to me the personification of everything that was inspiring in the emancipation movement of Russia. He was of magnificent physique and idealistic appearance, a personality that

could easily appeal to young and eager souls. Tchaikovsky was surrounded by friends, but after a while he came over to the corner where
I was sitting and engaged me in conversation. Peter had told him that
I intended to study medicine. How did I propose to do it and go on
with my activities at the same time, he wondered. I explained that
I planned to come to England for lectures, during the summer, perhaps even go to America; in any case I did not think of giving up the
movement altogether. " Unless you do that," he said, " you'll be a
bad doctor; and if you are in earnest about your profession, you'll
become a bad propagandist. You can't do both." He advised me to
think it over before undertaking something that was sure to destroy
my usefulness in the movement. His words disturbed me. I was confident that I could do both things if I was determined enough and
continued with my social interests. But somehow he had succeeded in
putting doubt into my mind. I began to question myself; did I really
want to take five years out of my life to gain a doctor's degree?

Before long, Harry Kelly came to inform me that some of the comrades had agreed to arrange an anti-war meeting and that steps would
be taken to ensure security. Their plan was to bring a score of men
from Canning Town, a suburb known for the fighting spirit and
strength of its men. They would protect the platform and prevent a
possible rush of the jingoes. Tom Mann, the labour man who had
played a leading part in the recent dockers' strike, would be asked to
preside. I should have to be smuggled into the hall before the patriots
could have a chance to do anything, Harry explained. Tchaikovsky
was to attend to that.

On the appointed day, accompanied by my escort, I reached South
Place Institute a few hours before the crowd began to gather. Very
soon the hall was filled. When Tom Mann stepped on to the platform,
there was loud booing, which drowned the applause of our friends.
For a time the situation looked hopeless, but Tom was an experienced
speaker, skilled in the handling of crowds. The audience soon subsided. When I made my appearance, however, the patriots got out of
leash again. Several tried to get on the platform, but the Canning
Town men held them back. I stood silent for some moments, not
knowing just how to approach the infuriated Britishers. I was certain
I could achieve nothing by the direct and blunt manner that had invariably succeeded with my American audiences. Something different
was needed, something that would touch their pride. My visit in 1895

and my experiences this time had taught me to know the pride of Englishmen in their traditions. " Men and women of England! " I shouted above the din, " I have come here in the firm belief that a people whose history is surcharged with the spirit of rebellion and whose genius in every field is a shining star upon the firmament of the world can be naught but liberty- and justive-loving. Nay, more, the immortal works of Shakespeare, Milton, Byron, Shelley, and Keats, to mention only the greatest in the galaxy of poets and dreamers of your country, must needs have enlarged your vision and quickened your appreciation of what is the most precious heritage of a truly cultivated people; I mean the grace of hospitality and a generous attitude towards the stranger in your midst."

Complete silence in the hall.

" Your behaviour tonight hardly sustains my belief in the superior culture and breeding of your country," I went on; " or is it that the fury of war has so easily destroyed what it has taken centuries to build up? If that is so, it should be enough to repudiate war. Who is there who would supinely sit by when what is best and highest in a people is being throttled before his very eyes? Certainly not your Shelley, whose song was of liberty and revolt. Certainly not your Byron, whose soul could find no peace when the greatness of Greece was endangered. Not they, not they! And you, are you so forgetful of your past, is there no echo in your soul of your poets' songs, your dreamers' dreams, your rebels' calls? "

Silence continued, my hearers apparently bewildered by the unexpected turn of my speech, dumbfounded by the high-sounding words and compelling gestures. The audience became absorbed in my talk, carried to a pitch of enthusiasm which finally broke forth in loud applause. After that it was easy sailing. I delivered my lecture on War and Patriotism as I had given it all through the United States, merely changing the parts that had dealt with the causes of the Spanish-American hostilities to those behind the Anglo-Boer War. I concluded with the gist of Carlyle's idea of war as a quarrel between two thieves, themselves too cowardly to fight, compelling boys of one village and another into uniforms with guns in their hands and then letting them loose like ferocious beasts against each other.

The house went wild. Men and women waved their hats and shouted themselves hoarse in approval. Our resolution, a powerful protest against the war, was read by the Chair and adopted with only one dissenting voice. I bowed in the direction of the objector and said:

" There is what I call a brave man who deserves our admiration. It requires great courage to stand alone, even if one is mistaken. Let us all join in hearty applause for our daring opponent."

Even our guard from Canning Town could no longer hold back the surging crowd. But there was no danger any more. The audience had turned from fierce antagonism to equally burning devotion, ready to protect me to the last drop of its blood. In the committee room Tchaikovsky, who had joined in enthusiastic demonstration, waving his hat like an excited youngster, embraced me, praising my mastery of the situation. " I am afraid I was somewhat of a hypocrite," I remarked. " All diplomats are," he replied, " but diplomacy is necessary at times."

My first mail from America contained letters from Yegor, Ed, and Eric Morton. My brother wrote that Ed had sought him out the day after my departure and had begged him to come back to the house, as he could not bear the loneliness. " You know, my dear *Chavele,* I always liked Ed," his letter read; " I simply couldn't refuse, and so I went back. Two weeks later Ed brought some woman into the apartment and she has been there ever since. It made me sick to see her among your things, in the atmosphere you had created. That's why I moved out again." Ed had asked Yegor to take the furniture, books, and other things that belonged to me, but he could not do it: he felt too unhappy over the whole matter. Ed had consoled himself quickly, I reflected. Well, why not? I wondered who the woman was.

Ed's letter contained no mention of the new relationship in his life. He merely inquired what he should do with my things. He was planning to move up-town, he wrote, and he did not want to take what he had always considered mine. I cabled him that I wanted nothing but my books and asked him to pack them in a box and store it with Justus.

Eric wrote in his usual jovial way. All was well with our plans. A house had been rented, and he was going to move into it with his friend K. They were expecting a strenuous ordeal, because K " was preparing for her forthcoming concert." They had already hired a piano so she could practise, and he would be busy with his invention. The money I had left him would cover the trip of himself and K to Pittsburgh and keep them going for a time. " As to our engineer, T, he seems to suffer from self-importance, but he will do. Everything else when we meet in Paris to celebrate my invention."

I was amused at the manner in which Eric had worded his letter, with a view to safety, of course. But even I was puzzled by some of its contents. K was no doubt Kinsella, his friend, whom I had met in Chicago. But what on earth did he mean by a concert and a piano? I knew the woman had a good voice and was also a trained pianist, but what would she do with these talents in the house from which the tunnel was to be dug? The " engineer " was apparently " Tony." Evidently he had shown up at last, but it was obvious that Eric did not like him. I hoped that they could get along until the project was completed. I must write dear Eric, I decided, to be very, very patient.

During my London stay I also spoke at a German meeting arranged by comrades of the *Autonomie* Club. In the discussion I was attacked by a young German. " What does Emma Goldman know about the life of the workers, anyway? " my opponent demanded; " she never worked in a factory and she's just like the other agitators, having a good time, travelling round and enjoying herself. We, the proletarians, we of the blue blouse, are the only ones who have a right to talk about the suffering of the masses." It was obvious that the boy knew nothing about me, nor did I find it necessary to enlighten him on my work in factories and my knowledge of the lives of the people. But I was intrigued by his reference to the blue blouse. What could that signify, I wondered.

After the meeting two men of about my own age came up to see me. They begged me not to hold all the comrades responsible for the stupid attack of the youth. They knew him well; he was doing nothing in the movement except boast of his proletarian trade mark, the blue blouse. In the early period of the movement, the men explained, the German intelligentsia began to wear the blue blouse of the workers, partly in protest against conventional and formal attire, but more especially to be able to approach the masses more easily. Since then some charlatans in the social movement had used that mode of dressing as a sign of their adherence to strict revolutionary principles. " And also because they haven't a white shirt," the dark-looking man put in, " or because they don't have to wash their necks so often." I laughed heartily and asked him why he was so vindictive. " Because I can't bear sham! " the man replied almost gruffly. The two introduced themselves as Hippolyte Havel and X, the former a Czech, the latter a German. X soon excused himself, and Havel asked me to take dinner with him.

My escort was of small stature, very dark, with large eyes gleaming in his pale face. He was dressed fastidiously, even to the point of gloves, which no men in our ranks wore. It struck me as dandyish, especially in a revolutionist. In the restaurant I noticed that Havel took off only one glove, keeping the other on all through the meal. I was on the point of asking him the reason, but he seemed so self-conscious that I did not wish to embarrass him. After a few glasses of wine he became more animated, talking in nervous staccato sentences. He had come to London from Zürich, he told me, and though not long in the city, he knew it well and would be happy to take me about. It would have to be Sunday afternoon, or late in the evening, his only free time.

Hippolyte Havel proved to be a veritable encyclopædia. He knew everybody and everything in the movement of the various European countries. I detected bitterness in his tone when he spoke of certain comrades in the *Autonomie* Club. It affected me unpleasantly, but on the whole he was exceedingly entertaining. It was already too late to catch a bus, and Havel hailed a cab to take me home. When I offered to pay the driver, he became incensed. " Just like an American, flaunting your money! I'm working, and I can afford to pay! " he protested. I ventured to suggest that for an anarchist he was strangely conventional to object to a woman's right to pay. Havel smiled for the first time during the whole evening, and I could not help noticing that he had beautiful white teeth. When I shook his hand, still encased in the glove, he gave a suppressed groan. " What is it? " I asked. " Oh, nothing," he replied, " but for a little lady you do have a strong grip."

There was something strange and exotic about the man. He was evidently very nervous and ungenerous in his estimate of people. Still, he was fascinating, even disturbing.

My Czech comrade came frequently, sometimes with his friend, but usually alone. He was far from gay company; in fact, he rather depressed me. Unless he had drunk a little, it was difficult to get him to converse; at other times he seemed tongue-tied. Gradually I learned that he had come into the movement when only eighteen and that he had been in prison several times, once for a term of eighteen months. On the last occasion he had been sent to the psychopathic ward, where he might have remained had he not aroused the interest of Professor Krafft-Ebing, who declared him sane and helped him back to freedom. He had been active in Vienna and expelled from there, after which he had tramped through Germany, lecturing and writing for anarchist publications. He had visited Paris, but was not allowed to remain there long, being expelled. Finally he had gone to Zürich and thence to London. As he had no trade, he was compelled to accept any kind of job. At the time, he was working in an English boarding-house as an all-round man. His duties began at five in the morning and consisted in lighting the fires, cleaning the boots of the guests, washing dishes, and doing other kinds of " degrading and humiliating work." " But why degrading? Labour is never degrading," I protested. "Labour, as it is now, is always degrading!" he insisted vehemently; " in an English boarding-house it is even worse; it is an outrage on all human sensibilities, besides the drudgery it involves. Look at my hands!" With a nervous jerk he tore off his glove and the bandage underneath. His hand, red and swollen, was a mass of blisters. " How did it happen, and how can you keep on working?" I asked. " I got it from cleaning filthy boots in the early morning chill and carrying coals and wood to keep the fires going. What else can I do without a trade in a foreign country? I might starve, sink into the gutter, or end in the Thames," he added. " But I'm not just ready for it. Besides, I'm only one of the many thousands; why fuss about it? Let's talk about more cheerful things." He continued conversing, but I hardly heard what he said. I took his poor blistered hand, conscious of an irresistible desire to put it to my lips, in infinite sympathy and tenderness.

We went about together a good deal, visiting the poor quarters, Whitechapel and similar districts. On week-days the streets were littered with foul rubbish, and the smell of fried fish was nauseating. On Saturday nights the spectacle was even more harrowing. I had seen drunken women on the Bowery, old social dregs, their scraggy hair loose. their incongruous hats tilted to one side and skirts sweeping the sidewalk. " Bummerkes," the Jewish children called them. It used to make me furious to see the thoughtless youngsters taunt and chase those poor derelicts. But nothing compared in brutality and degradation with the sights I witnessed in the East End of London: drunken women lurching out of the public houses, using the vilest language and fighting until they would literally tear the clothes off one another. Small boys and girls hanging round the drinking-places in sleet and cold, infants in dilapidated carriages in a stupor from the whisky-soaked " suckers," the elder children keeping watch and greedily drinking the ale their parents would bring out to them from time to time. Too often I saw such pictures, more terrible than any conceived by Dante. Every time, filled with rage, disgust, and shame, I would promise myself never to go back to the East End, yet I would invariably return. When I broached the situation to some of my comrades, they thought me overwrought. Such conditions existed in every large city, they claimed; it was capitalism with its resultant sordidness. Why should I feel more disturbed in London than anywhere else?

Gradually I began to realize that the pleasure I found in Havel's company was due to more than ordinary comradeship. Love was making its claims again, daily more insistent. I was afraid of it, afraid of the new pain, the new disappointments in store. Yet my need of it in the dismal surroundings was stronger than my apprehensions. Havel, too, cared for me. He had grown more timid, more restless and fidgety. He had been in the habit of coming to see me alone, but one evening he visited me with his friend, who remained for hours and showed no intention of leaving. I suspected that Havel had brought him because he did not trust himself to be alone with me, and that only increased my yearning. Finally, long after midnight, his friend left. No sooner was he gone than we found ourselves, hardly conscious how, in each other's embrace. London receded, the cry of the East End was far away. Only the call of love sounded in our hearts, and we listened and yielded to it.

I felt reborn with the new joy in my life. We would go together to Paris and later to Switzerland, we decided. Hippolyte also wanted to study and we planned to live very frugally on thirty dollars a month, ten out of my forty going to my brother. Hippolyte thought he could earn a little with articles, but we would not mind if we should have to forgo some comforts. We had each other and our love. But it was first necessary to induce my sweetheart to give up his dreadful job. I wanted him to have a month's rest from his boarding-house grind. It took considerable argument to persuade him, but two weeks away from cleaning filthy boots raised his spirits so much that he seemed a different being.

One afternoon we called on the Kropotkins. Hippolyte was a great admirer of the *Genossenschafts-Bewegung,* a co-operative movement more advanced, as he believed, than the British. He soon got into heated discussion with Peter, who did not see any particular merit in the German experiment. I had noticed on previous occasions that

Hippolyte could not hold his own in an argument. He would grow irritable and frequently become personal. He tried to avoid it with Peter, but, the discussion presently getting beyond his control, he broke off suddenly and became oppressively silent. Kropotkin was unpleasantly impressed, and, on the pretext of having work to do, I made haste to leave. On the street he began to abuse Peter, denouncing him as the " pope of the anarchist movement," who could not tolerate a dissenting opinion. I felt outraged and we exchanged hot words. By the time we reached my room we realized how childish it was to allow our tempers to becloud our young love.

Accompanied by Hippolyte, I attended the Russian New Year *vetcherinka,* which proved a great event for me. There I met some of the outstanding personalities of the Russian colony, among them I. Goldenberg, with whom I had worked in New York in the campaign against the Russian-American Extradition Treaty; E. Serebriakov, well known for his revolutionary activities; V. Tcherkesoff, a prominent theoretician of anarchism, as well as Tchaikovsky and Kropotkin. Almost everyone present had a record of heroic effort, of years of prison and exile. Among those present was also Michael Hambourg, with his sons Mark, Boris, and Jan, already promising musicians.

The affair was more sedate than similar gatherings in New York. Serious problems were discussed, only the younger people caring to dance. Later in the evening Peter entertained us at the piano, while Tcherkesoff swung twelve-year-old Sasha Kropotkin round the floor, their example followed by some of the others. Tchaikovsky, towering high above me, bowed comically when he asked me to dance. It was a memorable evening.

In Glasgow, the first stop on my Scottish tour, the meetings had been arranged by our good comrade Blair. Smith, who was also my host. Everybody was very kind and friendly to me, but the city itself proved a nightmare, in some respects even worse than London. On a Saturday night, returning home on the tramway, I counted seven children on the street, dirty and undernourished, staggering along with their mothers, all under the influence of drink.

Edinburgh was a treat after·Glasgow, spacious, clean, and attractive, with poverty not so obvious. It was there I first met Tom Bell, of whose propagandistic zeal and daring we had heard much in America. Among his exploits was a free-speech experiment he had made while in Paris. He had urged the French anarchists to make a stand for open-air meetings, on the English plan, but the Paris comrades considered such an attempt impossible. Tom decided to demonstrate that it was feasible to speak in the open regardless of the police.

He distributed handbills announcing that on the following Sunday afternoon he would, on his own responsibility, hold an open-air meeting at the Place de la République, one of the busy centres of Paris. When he reached the square at the appointed time, there was a great crowd waiting. As he made his way to the centre of the Place, several police agents approached him. Not sure whether he was the announced speaker, they hesitated a moment. Tom had picked out his lamp-post, one with a big ornamental base half-way up and a cross-piece at the top. Just as the police stepped up to him, he sprang up the post. His feet were firm on the base, and in a second his wrist was chained to the cross-piece. He had secured by a padlock a strong steel chain round his wrist, and now he quickly whipped the two ends round the cross-piece and fastened them by another padlock that locked automatically. The police got after him at once, but they could do nothing; the man was securely chained. They sent for a file. Meanwhile the crowd kept increasing and Tom went on nonchalantly talking to them. The officers raged, but he continued his speech till his voice gave out. Then he produced the key, opened the padlock and coolly came down. The police threatened him with terrible things " for insults to the Army and the law," but all Paris laughed at them and held them up to ridicule. The authorities thought it best to hush up the matter, and Tom was not prosecuted. After a fortnight in jail he was expelled as " too dangerous a man to be allowed loose in France."

Another of Tom Bell's exploits took place on the occasion of the visit of Tsar Nicholas II to England. The Queen was at Balmoral at the time. The royal schedule was to have the Tsar land at Leith, where he would be met by the Prince of Wales (later King Edward VII); subsequently he was to come to Windsor and London.

Tom Bell agreed with his friend McCabe to help in the reception of the Tsar. McCabe had a shrivelled hand and arm, but he was as game as Tom. Together they laid their plans. They were in Edinburgh at the time, and when they reached Leith, they found an enormous number of police at the dock, including British, Russian, and French secret-service men. The streets were barricaded and lined all the way by soldiers and bobbies, with detectives swarming everywhere. Behind the barricade was a row of Highlanders; behind them territorials, these again supported by infantry. The situation looked hopeless — no chance for any action. Tom Bell and McCabe decided to separate; "each knew that the other would do his damnedest," as Tom afterwards said. He heard a faint cheer from the school-children as the pretty uniforms went by. Then came the carriages. The Tsar's was easily distinguished. Tom made out the Russian autocrat sitting in the back seat, the Prince of Wales facing him. It seemed impossible to do anything, up to the last moment, and it was possible only at that moment and at no other. The guards had been alert and vigilant till — just as the Tsar's carriage came level with them. In an instant Tom dived right through them, under the barricade and to the side of the carriage, shouting into the Tsar's face: "Down with the Russian tyrant! To hell with all the empires!" Just at that moment he became conscious of his friend Mac, who had also got through, also shouting close by.

The British authorities did not dare bring Bell and McCabe before a Scottish jury. Most probably they feared that prosecution would mean more publicity. Not one word appeared in the papers about the incident. "The Tsar appeared pale," they wrote. No doubt. He cut his visit short, going home again, not through Leith or any other Scottish seaport, but from an obscure fishing-village, whence he was taken to his yacht by boat.

I was naturally eager to meet the adventurous comrade. I found him living with John Turner's sister Lizzie, the lovely girl I had met in London in 1895. Tom was a very sick man, suffering from asthma, but he was picturesque — tall, with red hair and beard, just the type capable of unusual performances.

I departed from England for Paris, together with Hippolyte, arriving in that city on a drizzling January morning and stopping in a hotel on Boulevard Saint-Michel. Four years previously, in 1896, I had visited the city on my way from Vienna. That experience had been a great disappointment. The people I then stopped with, German anarchists, lived in a suburb, worked hard during the day, and were too tired to go out at night, and my French was not sufficient to enable me to go about alone. On the only free Sunday, friends had taken me to the Bois de Boulogne. Outside of that I had seen practically nothing of Paris, which I had longed so much to know, but I had promised myself that some day I would return to enjoy the delights of the wonderful city.

Now the opportunity was at hand at last, made more wonderful by the rebirth of love in my life. Hippolyte had been in Paris before and knew its charms; he made a perfect companion. For a month we were completely engrossed in the wonders of the city and in each other. Every street, every stone almost, had its revolutionary story, every district its heroic legend. The beauty of Paris, her reckless youth, her thirst for joy and ever-changing moods, held us in their sway. The Mur des Fédérés at Père Lachaise revived the memory of the high hopes and the black despair of the last days of the Commune. It was there that the rebels had made their last heroic stand, finally to be slain by order of Thiers and Galliffet. Place de la Bastille, once the dreaded tomb of the living dead, razed to the ground by the accumulated wrath of the people of Paris, brought back to us the unspeakable pain and suffering that glowed into regenerating hope in the days of the great revolution, whose history had so much influenced our own lives.

Our cares and worries were forgotten in the world of beauty, in the treasures of architecture and art, created by the genius of man. The days were passing like a dream from which one feared to awaken. But I had come to Paris also for another purpose. It was time to begin the preparatory work for our congress.

France had been the cradle of anarchism, fathered for a long time by some of her most brilliant sons, of whom Proudhon was the greatest. The battle for their ideal had been strenuous, involving persecution, imprisonment, and often even the sacrifice of life. But it had not been in vain. Thanks to them anarchism and its exponents had come to be regarded in France as a social factor to be reckoned with. No doubt the French *bourgeoisie* continued to dread anarchism and to persecute it through the machinery of the State. I had occasion to witness the brutal manner in which the French police handled radical crowds, as well as proceedings in the French courts when dealing with social offenders. Still, there was a vast difference in the approach and methods used by the French in dealing with anarchists from the American way. It was the difference between a people seasoned in revolutionary traditions and one which had merely skimmed the surface of a struggle for independence. That difference was everywhere apparent, strikingly so in the anarchist movement itself. In the various groups I did not meet a single comrade who used the high-sounding term " philosophic " to mask his anarchism, as many did in America, because they thought it more respectable.

We were soon carried into the tide of the varied activities that went on in the anarchist ranks. The revolutionary-syndicalist movement, given new impetus by the fertile mind of Pelloutier, was permeated with anarchist tendencies. Nearly all the leading men of the organization were outspoken anarchists. The new educational efforts, known as the *Université Populaire,* were backed almost exclusively by anarchists. They had succeeded in enlisting the support and co-operation of university men in every field of learning, giving popular lectures on various branches of science before large classes of workers. Neither were the arts neglected. The volumes of Zola, Richepin, Mirbeau, and Brieux and the splendid plays produced in the Théâtre Antoine were a part of anarchist literature similar to the writings of Kropotkin, while the works of Meunier, Rodin, Steinlen, and Grandjouan were discussed and appreciated in revolutionary ranks to a greater extent than by the *bourgeois* elements that lay claim to being the sponsors of art. It was inspiring to visit the anarchist groups, watch their efforts, and observe the growth of our ideas on French soil.

My studies of the movement, however, did not allay my personal interest in people, always stronger with me than theories. Hippolyte was quite the reverse; he disliked meeting people and he was diffident in their presence. After a short while I knew nearly every one of the leading personalities in our movement in France, as well as those connected with other social work in Paris. Among the latter was the circle of *L'Humanité Nouvelle,* which published a magazine of the same name. Its able editor, Auguste Hamon, author of *La Psychologie du Militaire,* as also its contributors, belonged to a group of young artists and writers keenly alive to their time and its needs.

Of the people I met I was most impressed by Victor Dave. He was an old comrade who during forty years had participated in anarchist activities in various European countries. He had been a member of the first International, a co-worker of Michael Bakunin, and the teacher of Johann Most. He had begun a brilliant career as a student of history and philosophy, but later he chose to dedicate himself to his social ideal. I had learned much of Dave's history from Johann Most, who greatly admired him. I also knew the part he had played in the events that led to the accusations against Peukert in connexion with the arrest and conviction of John Neve. Dave was still certain of Peukert's guilt, yet there was no trace of personal animosity in him. He was kindly and jovial. Though sixty, he was as alert in mind and spirit as in his student days. Eking out a meagre existence as contributor to anarchist and other publications, he yet retained the buoyancy and humour of youth. I spent much time with him and his lifelong companion, Marie, an invalid for many years, but still interested in public affairs. Victor was a great linguist and as such invaluable in helping me to arrange the material I had brought for the congress and in making translations into different languages.

The most fascinating thing about Victor Dave was his innate feeling for life and ready enjoyment of fun. He was the freest and gayest among the many comrades I met in Paris, a companion after my own heart. But our good humour was often marred by Hippolyte's fits of extreme depression. From the very first he had taken a strong dislike to Victor. He would refuse to join us on our outings, yet peevishly resent having been left behind. Ordinarily his feeling would express itself in mute reproach, but the least quantity of liquor would incite him to abuse Victor. At first I took his outbreaks lightly, but gradually they began to affect me, making me uneasy when I was away from him. I loved the boy; I knew his unhappy past had left wounds in his soul that made him morbidly self-conscious and suspicious. I wanted to help him to a better understanding of himself and a broader approach to others. I hoped that my affection would soften his virulence. When sober, he regretted his attacks on Victor, and at such moments he would be all tenderness, clinging to our love. It led me to hope that he might outgrow his acrimonious moods. But the scenes kept recurring, and my apprehension increased.

In the course of time I realized that Hippolyte's resentment was directed not only against Victor, but against every man of my acquaintance. Two Italians I had worked with in behalf of Cuban freedom, as well as during the Summit strike, arrived in Paris to attend the Exposition. They came to see me and invited me out to dinner. On my return I found Hippolyte in a ferment of wrathful indignation. Some time later my good friend Palavicini came over with his wife and child. Hippolyte immediately began to concoct impossible stories about the man. Life with Hippolyte was growing more distressing, yet I could not think of parting.

CHAPTER XXII

A LETTER FROM CARL STONE UNEXPECTEDLY CHANGED MY PLANS regarding the study of medicine. " I thought it was understood when you left for Europe," he wrote, " that you were to go to Switzerland to study medicine. It was solely for that purpose that Herman and I offered to give you an allowance. I now learn that you are at your old propaganda and with a new lover. Surely you do not expect us to support you with either. I am interested only in E. G. the woman — her ideas have no meaning whatever to me. Please choose." I wrote back at once: " E. G. the woman and her ideas are inseparable. She does not exist for the amusement of upstarts, nor will she permit anybody to dictate to her. Keep your money."

I could not believe that Herman Miller had had anything to do with the miserable letter. I was sure that I should hear from him in due time. Of the amount he had given me I still had enough money left for several months. The two hundred dollars from Stone I had turned over to Eric to be used in connexion with the tunnel. I experienced a sense of relief that the matter was closed. When the allowance stopped and no word reached me from Herman, I concluded that he also had changed his mind. It was rather disappointing, but I was happy that I should no longer be dependent on moneyed people. Tchaikovsky was right, after all; one could not devote himself to an ideal and to a profession at the same time. I would return to America to take up my work.

One evening as I was about to go with Hippolyte to an important committee session, the hotel maid handed me a visiting-card. I was overjoyed to see on it the name of Oscar Panizza, whose brilliant writings in the *Armer Teufel* had delighted me for years. Presently a tall, dark man entered, introducing himself as Panizza. He had learned through Dr. Eugene Schmidt of my presence in Paris and was anxious

to " meet Cassandra, our dear Robert's friend." He asked me to spend
the evening with him and Dr. Schmidt. " We are going up to see Oscar
Wilde first," he said, " and we want you to come with us. Afterwards
we will have dinner."

What a marvellous event to meet Panizza and Wilde the same
evening! In a flurry of anticipation I knocked at Hippolyte's door to
tell him about it. I found him pacing his room, waiting for me in great
irritation. " You don't mean you are not going to the session! " he
cried angrily. " You have promised, you are expected, you have undertaken work to do! You can meet Oscar Wilde some other time, and
Panizza too. Why must it be tonight? " In my excitement I had forgotten all about the session. Of course, I could not go back on it. With
heavy heart I went downstairs to tell Panizza that I was not able to
come that evening. Could we not meet tomorrow or the next day? We
agreed on the following Saturday, at luncheon. He would invite Dr.
Schmidt again, but he could not promise as to Oscar Wilde. The latter
was in poor health and not always able to be about; but he would try
his best to arrange a meeting.

On Friday Dr. Schmidt called to say that Panizza had left unexpectedly, but he was to return to Paris before long, and he would see
me then. The doctor must have read disappointment on my face. " It is
lovely outside," he remarked, " come for a walk." I was grateful, sick
with regret for having given up the rare opportunity of meeting Oscar
Wilde and of spending an evening with Panizza.

During our walk in the Luxembourg I told the doctor of the indignation I had felt at the conviction of Oscar Wilde. I had pleaded his case
against the miserable hypocrites who had sent him to his doom.
" You! " the doctor exclaimed in astonishment, " why, you must have
been a mere youngster then. How did you dare come out in public for
Oscar Wilde in puritan America? " " Nonsense! " I replied; " no daring is required to protest against a great injustice." The doctor smiled
dubiously. " Injustice? " he repeated; " it wasn't exactly that from the
legal point of view, though it may have been from the psychological."
The rest of the afternoon we were engaged in a battle royal about in-
version, perversion, and the question of sex variation. He had given
much thought to the matter, but he was not free in his approach, and
I suspected that he was somewhat scandalized that I, a young woman,
should speak without reservations on such tabooed subjects.

On my return to the hotel I found Hippolyte in a state of sulky depression. Somehow it irritated me more than on any previous occasion. Without a word I left for my room. On my table lay a pile of letters, among them one that sent my pulse beating faster. It was from Max. He and Puck were in Paris, he wrote. They had arrived the previous night and were anxious to see me. I ran to Hippolyte, waving the letter and crying: " Max is in town! Think of it — Max! " He stared at me as if I had lost my wits. " Max — what Max? " he asked darkly. " Why, Max Baginski! What other Max could mean so much to me? " No sooner had I spoken than I realized my tactlessness. But to my surprise Hippolyte exclaimed: " Max Baginski! Why, I know all about him and I wanted to meet him long ago. I am glad he is here." Never before had I heard my " bitter Putzi," as I called him, express such a warm interest in a member of his own sex. Throwing my arms around his neck, I cried: " Let's go to Max right away! " He pressed me to him and looked intently into my eyes. " What is it? " I asked. " Oh, just to reassure myself of your love," he replied. " If only I could be certain of it, I should want nothing else in the world." " Silly boy," I said, " of course you can be sure of it." He declined to accompany me to see Max and Puck; he wanted me to see them first. Later he would meet us.

On my way the precious moments I had lived through with Max sprang vividly to life. It did not seem possible that a year had passed since. Even the shock of his going to Europe without me became resurrected in its old poignancy. Much had happened during the year to help me over the blow, but now it came back with renewed force. Why see Max — why start it all over again, I asked myself bitterly. He could not have cared if he was able to give me up so easily. I would not go through the same agony again. I would write him a note to tell him that it would be best for us not to meet any more. I stepped into a café, got paper and pen, and began to write. I started several times, but could not formulate my thought. I was in the throes of ever-increasing agitation. At last I paid the waiter and almost ran in the direction of the hotel where Max was stopping.

At the sight of his dear face, at the sound of his gay greeting, " Well, my little one, do we actually meet in Paris! " a change instantly came over me. The sweet tenderness of his voice dissolved my resentment and soothed the storm within me. Puck also welcomed me with the greatest warmth. She looked better and more vivacious than in Chicago. Soon the three of us were on our way to my hotel to get

Hippolyte. Our evening together, which lasted until three o'clock in the morning, was a merry celebration, worthy of the spirit of Paris. I was particularly happy to see the effect Max exerted on Hippolyte. The latter ceased to be moody; he became more sociable and less resentful towards other men.

Some of the documents I had received to be read at the congress treated of the importance of the discussion of sex problems in the anarchist press and lectures. Kate Austen's paper was particularly strong, giving the history of the American movement for freedom in love. Kate was no mincer of words; frankly and directly she set forth her views of sex as a vital factor in life. Victor assured me that certain French comrades would not consent to have Kate's paper read at the congress; surely not to discuss it. I could hardly believe it. The French, of all people! Victor explained that not being puritanical does not always mean being free. "The French have not the same serious attitude towards sex as the idealists in America," he said. "They are cynical about it and cannot see more than the mere physical side. Our older French comrades have always loathed such an attitude, and in protest against it they have outdone the Puritans. They now fear that any discussion of sex would serve only to increase the misconceptions of anarchism." I was not convinced, but a week later Victor informed me that one group had definitely decided not to have the American reports dealing with sex read at the congress. They might be taken up at private gatherings, but not at public meetings with the press representatives present.

I protested, and declared that I would immediately get in touch with the comrades in the United States and ask them to relieve me of the credentials and the instructions they had given me. While realizing that the matter in question was only one of the numerous issues involved in anarchism, yet I could not co-operate with a congress that attempted to silence opinion or suppress views that failed to meet the approval of certain elements.

One day, while in a café with Max and Victor, I read in the afternoon papers about the killing of King Humbert by an anarchist. The name of the *Attentäter* was Gaetano Bresci.

I remembered the name as that of an active comrade of the anarchist group in Paterson, New Jersey. Strange that he should have committed such an act, I thought; he had impressed me so differently from most of the other Italians I knew. He was not at all of an excitable temperament and not easily aroused. What could have induced him to take the life of the King of Italy, I wondered. Victor ascribed the protracted hunger riots in Milan, in 1898, as the probable cause of Bresci's deed. Many workers' lives had been lost on that occasion through the attack of the soldiery upon the starving and unarmed people. They had marched towards the palace to demonstrate their misery, the women carrying their children in their arms. They had found the palace surrounded by a strong military force under command of General Bava Beccaris. The people ignored the order to disperse, whereupon the General gave the signal that resulted in a massacre of the demonstrants. King Humbert complimented Beccaris upon his "brave defence of the royal house," decorating him for his murderous work.

Max and Victor agreed with me that those tragic events must have induced Bresci to come all the way from America to carry out his act. Max thought I was lucky not to be in the States, else I would surely be held responsible in some way for the death of Humbert, as had invariably been the case in the past whenever any political act of violence took place anywhere in the world. I was less concerned about such an eventuality than over the fate that awaited Bresci. I knew what tortures would be his lot in prison and I recalled the fearful treatment of Luccheni, a similar victim of the ruthless social struggle.

We remained for some time in the café, discussing the incredible waste of human life involved in the terrible war of the classes in every country. I confided to my friends the doubts that had been assailing me since Sasha's act, though I fully realized the inevitability of such deeds resulting from existing conditions.

Shortly afterwards I learned through Victor that the Neo-Malthusian Congress was soon to meet in Paris. Its sessions would have to be secret because the French Government proscribed any organized attempt to limit offspring. Dr. Drysdale, the pioneer of birth limitation, and his sister were already in Paris, and other delegates were arriving from various countries. In France it was largely Paul Robin and Madeleine Verné, who were backing the Neo-Malthusian movement, Victor explained.

I knew Madeleine Verné, but who was Paul Robin? My friend informed me that he was one of the great libertarians in the field of education. Out of his own means he had bought a large tract of land on which he established a school for destitute children. Sempuis, the place was called. Robin had taken homeless waifs from the street or from orphan asylums, the poorest and the so-called bad children. " You should see them now! " Victor said; " Robin's school is a living example of what can be done in education by an attitude of understanding and love for the child." He promised to afford me an opportunity to attend the Neo-Malthusian Congress and to visit Sempuis.

The Neo-Malthusian conference, having to meet under cover, every session in a different place, had a very small attendance, of not more than a dozen delegates. But what it lacked in numbers it made up in vital interest. Dr. Drysdale, the venerable advocate of family limitation, was full of enthusiasm for the cause. Miss Drysdale, his sister, Paul Robin, and their co-workers were admirable in the simplicity and earnestness with which they presented the subject, and very brave in the demonstration of preventive methods. I marvelled at their ability to discuss such a delicate matter so frankly and in such an inoffensive manner. I thought of my former patients on the East Side and the blessing it would have meant to them if they could have procured the contraceptives described at these sessions. The delegates were amused when I told them of my vain efforts, as midwife, to find some way of helping the poor women in the States. They thought that, with Anthony Comstock supervising American morals, it would take many years before methods to prevent conception could be discussed openly in that country. I pointed out to them, however, that even in France they had to meet in secret and I assured them that I knew many people in America brave enough to do good, even if prohibited, work. At any rate, I decided to take the matter up on my return to New York. I was complimented on my attitude by the delegates and supplied with literature and contraceptives for my future work.

My money was dwindling fast, but still we could not forgo the pleasure of visiting theatres and museums and hearing music. The concerts at the Trocadero were particularly interesting, among them those by the Finnish orchestra, including folk-songs by magnificent artists, with Mme Aïno Ackté, the prima donna of the Paris Opéra, as the soloist. The Russian Balalaika Orchestra, Wagner performances, and a recital by Ysaye, the magician of the violin, were rare treats. A favourite place was the Théâtre Libre, managed by Antoine; it was the only dramatic venture in Paris worth seeing. With the exception of

Sarah Bernhardt, the Coquelins, and Mme. Réjane, the Paris stage impressed me as declamatory. Compared with Eleonora Duse even " Divine Sarah " appeared theatrical. The one play in which she was her great self was *Cyrano de Bergerac,* with Coquelin playing Cyrano to her Roxane. The group under Antoine had abolished the star system; their ensemble acting was of the highest order.

During my stay in Europe I could not correspond with Sasha directly. Our letters passed through a friend, entailing long delays. Sasha was permitted to write only one letter a month; on rare occasions, thanks to the friendship of the prison chaplain, he was allowed an extra letter. In order to keep in touch with as many correspondents as possible, Sasha had devised a scheme of dividing his writing-paper into four, five, or even six separate parts, each filled on both sides with diminutive writing, clear as an etching. The recipient of his letter on the outside would cut the sheet according to the indicated divisions and then mail the various parts as directed. His last note to me had been cheerful, even jocular. He had asked for souvenirs of the Exposition and detailed accounts of things happening in Paris. But that was over two months ago, nothing having reached me since. Eric also wrote seldom, only a line or two about the " invention," which was apparently progressing slowly. I was beginning to grow anxious. Max and Hippolyte tried to explain away my fears and forebodings, but it was evident that they were also very uneasy.

One morning I was awakened at an early hour by Hippolyte violently knocking on my door. He entered excitedly, a French newspaper in his hand. He started to say something; his lips moved, but he could not utter a word. " What is it? " I cried in instinctive apprehension. " Why don't you speak? " " The tunnel, the tunnel! " he whispered hoarsely; " it has been discovered. It is in the paper."

With fainting heart I thought of Sasha, his terrible disappointment at the failure of the project, the disastrous consequences, his desperate position. Sasha again thrust back into the black hopelessness of eleven more years in his inferno. What now? What now? I must go back to America at once. I should have never gone away! I had failed Sasha, I felt; I had left him when he needed me most. Yes, I must go back to America as quickly as possible.

But that very afternoon a cable from Eric B. Morton prevented my putting the plan into immediate action. " Sudden illness. Work suspended. Sailing for France," the message read. I should have to await his arrival.

The nervous tension of the days that followed would have been beyond my endurance were it not for the intensive work I had to do. Within a fortnight Eric appeared. I hardly recognized him; the change he had undergone since I saw him in Pittsburgh was appalling. The big, strong viking had grown very thin, his face ashen and covered with blisters full of pus.

As soon as Tony finally got in touch with him, Eric related, he went to Pittsburgh to attend to the preliminary arrangements. His first impression of Tony was not very favourable. Tony seemed obsessed by his self-importance over his part in Sasha's projects. Sasha had devised a special cipher for underground communications, and Tony, being the only person able to read it, exploited the situation by arbitrary behaviour and directions. Not a mechanic, Tony had little idea of the difficulties involved in the construction of the tunnel, and the danger attending the digging of it. The house they had rented on Sterling Street was almost directly opposite the main gate of the prison and about two hundred feet distant from it. From the cellar of the house the tunnel had to be dug in a slightly circular line in the direction of the southern gate, then underneath it and into the prison yard towards an outhouse indicated by Sasha on his diagram. Sasha was to manage somehow to leave the cell-block, reach the outhouse unobserved, tear up its wooden flooring, and, opening the tunnel, crawl through into the cellar of the house. There he would find citizen's clothes, money, and cipher directions where to meet his friends. But work on the tunnel was taking more time and money than had been expected. Eric and the other comrades working on the tunnel came upon unexpected difficulties in the rocky formation of the soil in the neighbourhood of the prison wall. It was found necessary to dig underneath its foundations, and there Eric and his co-workers were nearly asphyxiated by poisonous fumes leaking into the tunnel from some unknown source. This unforeseen trouble resulted in much delay and involved the installation of machinery to supply fresh air to the men toiling prostrate in the narrow passage deep in the bowels of the earth. The sounds of digging might attract the attention of the alert look-outs on the prison wall, and Eric hit upon the idea of hiring a piano and inviting a woman friend of his, Kinsella, a splendid musician, to come to his aid. Her singing and playing masked the noises from below, and the guards on the wall greatly enjoyed the fine performances of Kinsella.

The "invention" was a most ingenious undertaking, but also very dangerous, requiring great engineering skill and the utmost care in avoiding the least suspicion on the part of the prison guards and the passers-by on the street. At the first sign of danger the pianist would press an electric button near at hand to warn the diggers underground to cease operations immediately. Then all would remain quiet till she would again burst out into song. The staccato piano chords would be the signal that all was well. " Digging under such conditions was no snap," Eric continued. " To save time and expense we had decided to make the tunnel very narrow, just wide enough for a person to crawl through. Our work therefore could not be carried on even by kneeling. We had to lie flat on the stomach and do the drilling with one hand. It was so exhausting it was impossible to keep at it more than half an hour at a time. Naturally progress was slow. But what was more exasperating was that Tony constantly shifted from one idea to another. We wanted to keep strictly to Sasha's plans. The latter insisted on it all the time and we felt that he, being on the inside, knew best. But Tony was bent on carrying out his own notions. Sasha evidently considered it too dangerous to give us directions even in his underground letters; he did so only in his cipher, which no one except Tony could read. Therefore we were compelled to take our instructions from Tony. Well, at last the tunnel was finished."

" And then — and then? " I cried unable to contain myself any longer.

" Why, didn't anyone write you? " Eric asked in surprise. " When Sasha tried to make his escape through the hole in the prison yard where the tunnel terminated, according to Tony's directions, he found it covered with a pile of bricks and stone. They were putting up a new building in the penitentiary and they had emptied a wagon-load of rock just over the spot that Tony had selected as the terminal of the tunnel. You can imagine how Sasha must have felt about it, and the danger to which he had exposed himself by escaping from the cell-house only to have to return again. The most dreadful thing about it was that, as we learned later, Sasha had repeatedly warned Tony against ending the tunnel in the middle of the prison yard, as Tony had proposed to him. Sasha was absolutely against it, knowing that it was bound to prove a failure. His original plan called for the tunnel to terminate in a deserted outhouse, about twenty feet from that hole. Believing that we had dug the tunnel to the point desired by Sasha, and that our work was completed, we departed for New York, only Tony remaining in Pittsburgh. Sasha was desperate at Tony's arbitrary change from his instructions. He insisted that the digging be continued farther and up to the outhouse, according to his diagram. Tony finally realized the fatal results of his mad obstinacy. He notified Sasha that his wishes would be carried out and he immediately left for New York to see us with a view to raising more money to complete the tunnel. Our house opposite the prison was left vacant. During Tony's absence children playing in the street somehow got into the cellar, discovered the secret passage, and notified their parents, among whom was the agent of the house. Strange to say, he proved also to be a guard in the Western Penitentiary."

I sat silent, crushed by the thought of what Sasha must have gone through during the weeks and months of suspense and anxious waiting for the completion of the tunnel, only to have all his hopes blighted almost in sight of liberty.

"The most amazing thing is," Eric continued, "that to this day the prison officials have been unable to find out for whom the tunnel was intended. The police departments of Pittsburgh and Allegheny, as well as the State authorities, agreed that the tunnel was one of the cleverest pieces of engineering they had ever seen. The Warden and the Board of Prison Inspectors suspect Sasha, but they can find no proof to support their charges, while the police claim the tunnel was intended for a certain Boyd, a prominent forger serving a long term. No clues have been discovered; but at any rate they put Sasha in solitary."

"In solitary!" I screamed. "No wonder I haven't heard from him for so long!" "Yes, he's under very severe punishment," Eric admitted. The purgatory Sasha had already endured, the ghastly years still ahead of him, flitted through my mind. "They will kill him!" I groaned. I knew they were killing him inch by inch, and here I was away in Paris and unable to help him, to do anything, anything! "Better a thousand times for me to have been in prison than to sit by and helplessly see them murdering Sasha!" I cried. "That wouldn't do Sasha any good," Eric retorted; "in fact, it would make it harder for him, harder to bear his lot. You must realize that, so why eat your heart out?"

Why, why? Could I explain what those years had been to me, ever since that black day in July 1892. Life is inexorable; it does not let you pause at any point. My own life had been crowded with events, following each in quick succession. There had been little time to indulge in retrospection of the past, but it had eaten into my consciousness, and nothing could ever still its gnawing. Yet life kept on its course. There was no cessation.

Eric was hardly able to keep on his feet. He was completely exhausted by what he had endured working in the tunnel; its poisonous fumes had infected his blood and produced a serious skin-disease. His condition became so bad that he had to be put to bed and I nursed him for weeks. But the dear man, true viking that he was, kept laughing and joking, with never a word of complaint or regret over the perilous hardships he had endured in the luckless venture to aid Sasha's escape.

Our scheduled congress did not take place. At the last moment the authorities prohibited the public gathering of foreign anarchists. We held some sessions, nevertheless, in private homes, in the environs of Paris. Under the circumstances and in view of the necessary secrecy of our proceedings, we had time to discuss only the most urgent problems.

The presence of Eric involved additional expenditure, and I found it imperative to earn some money. He had worked his way across and he did not have a cent left. A number of friends were living in the same hotel with me and I conceived the idea of preparing breakfast and luncheon for them. It was a big job to cook for twelve and even more persons on a single alcohol burner. Hippolyte was very helpful, being much better at marketing than I, as well as a first-class chef. Our "boarders" were nearly all foreign comrades, easily satisfied with the meals we served. It enabled us to earn a little money, though far from enough. Hippolyte and I contrived to take small parties to the Exposition. I did pretty well, though it was boring to guide dull Americans about. One chap, on seeing Voltaire's statue, demanded to know who "that guy" was and what had been his business. Several school-teachers, who had been recommended to me by a friend, almost fell into a faint when they saw the nude statues in the Luxembourg. I would return home thoroughly disgusted with the rôle of cicerone.

One afternoon I came back to my hotel determined never again to serve as guide to sightseers unless it be to a certain very hot place. In my room I found a huge bouquet of flowers and a note beside it. The handwriting was unfamiliar, the contents puzzling: "An admirer of long standing would like you to join him for a pleasant evening. Will you meet him tonight at the Café du Chatelet? You may bring a friend along." I wondered who the man could be.

The " admirer of long standing " turned out to be none other than Eric. With him were three other comrades from America. " What's up? " both Hippolyte and I asked simultaneously. " Have you discovered a gold-mine? " " Not exactly," Eric replied; " my grandmother, who died a few months ago, left me a legacy of seven hundred francs, which I received today. We're going to blow it all in tonight." " Don't you want to get back to the United States? " I inquired. " Of course I do." " Then let me have half of your legacy for your return fare," I suggested; " the rest I am perfectly willing to help you blow in." Laughingly he turned three hundred and fifty francs over to me for safe-keeping.

We dined, wined, and made merry. Everyone was gay and still firm on his feet when at two o'clock in the morning we landed at the Rat Mort, a famous Montmartre cabaret, where Eric ordered champagne. Across from us sat a very attractive French girl, and Eric asked if he might invite her to our table. " Sure," I said, " the only woman in the company of five men, I can afford to be generous." The girl joined us, drank, and danced with the boys. Our viking, remarkably lithe despite his two hundred pounds, danced like a nymph. After an exciting waltz the boys lifted their glasses in a toast to E. G., and I drank mine down without a stop. Suddenly all went black before me.

I woke up in my room with a splitting headache, deathly ill. The French girl of the cabaret was sitting near my bed. " What has happened? " I demanded. *" Rien du tout, chérie;* you felt a bit sick last night," she replied. I asked her to call my friends, and in a short time Eric and Hippolyte entered. " I feel as if I had been poisoned," I told them. " Not quite," Eric retorted; " but one of the boys poured a glass of cognac into your champagne." " And then? " " Then we had to carry you downstairs. We hailed a cab, but we could not make you get into it. You sat down on the sidewalk and shouted that you were Emma Goldman, the anarchist, protesting that you would not be forced. It took the five of us to get you into the cab." I was dumbfounded; I could not remember a thing about it.

" We were none of us any too steady on our feet," Eric went on. " But we sobered up quick enough when we saw in what condition you were." " And the girl — how does she happen to be here? " I asked. " She simply would not let us take you without her accompanying you. She must have thought we were bandits intending to rob you. She insisted on coming with us." " But the poor girl lost her earnings for the night," I protested.

Hippolyte put twenty francs in an envelope and sent the girl home in a cab. In the late afternoon she returned to me. " What do you mean by insulting me ? " she cried, almost weeping; " do you think a girl who makes her living on the street has no feelings ? That she would take money for helping a friend in distress ? No, indeed, nursing isn't my profession, and I won't be paid for it." I held out my hand to her and drew her down to me. I was affected almost to tears by the beauty of that child-woman and her fine, tender spirit.

The inspiring atmosphere of our movement in Paris and my other delightful experiences in the city made me wish to prolong my stay. But it was time to leave. Our money was almost entirely exhausted. Besides, detectives had already been at the hotel looking for information about Mme Brady. It was a wonder the police had not yet ordered me out of the country. Victor Dave suggested that it was because of the Exposition; the authorities wanted to avoid unpleasant publicity about foreigners. On an early morning, dark and drizzling, Eric, Hippolyte, and I drove to the railroad station. We were followed by several secret-service men in a cab and one on a bicycle. They waved good-bye to us as the train pulled out, but one of them we found in the compartment next to our coupé. He followed us to Boulogne, leaving only when we boarded the boat.

Only thanks to the gift sent me by my dear friend Anna Stirling were we able to pay our hotel bills and fares, and still have about fifteen dollars left. It would be enough for tips and other expenses during our journey. I knew I could borrow some money in New York, and Eric said he would wire to Chicago for funds, when necessary.

When the steamer was a few hours out, Hippolyte became seasick, getting worse with the increasing motion. On the third day he was so ill that the doctor ordered iced champagne. He looked so yellow and thin that I was afraid he would not last to the end of the trip. Meanwhile Eric had developed a ravenous appetite. Three times each day he would begin at the top of the menu and end at the bottom. " Don't make the waiter work so hard! " I pleaded with him; " we haven't enough money for tips." But he kept on feeding. He was a born sailor, he loved the sea, and he grew jollier and more hungry every day. At the end of the crossing I had just two dollars and fifteen cents left, which

I divided among the stewards and stewardesses that had served Hippolyte and me. Our viking was left to face the music. The brave fellow, who had for months lived in constant danger of a cave-in in the tunnel, now quailed before the employees of the ship. He actually kept in hiding. The dining-room steward was inexorable and he pursued Eric. But when the latter stood before him shamefaced, like a schoolboy, with his pockets turned inside out, the cruel steward took pity and let him go.

My precious " baby " brother, tall and handsome, was at the dock to greet me. He was considerably surprised to see me return with a bodyguard of two. We went immediately to a pawnshop to hock my clamshell watch, for which I received ten whole dollars, enough to pay for a week's rent in a Clinton Street room and treat the company to dinner.

CHAPTER XXIII

DIRECTLY I WAS SETTLED IN MY NEW ROOM, I WENT TO SEE JUSTUS Schwab. I found him in bed, a mere shadow of his former self. A lump rose in my throat at the sight of our giant so wasted. I knew that Mrs. Schwab worked very hard taking care of the saloon and I begged her to let me nurse Justus. She promised, though she was sure that the sick man would have no one attend him but herself. We were all aware of the tender relationship that existed between Justus and his family. His wife had been his companion all through the years. She had always been the picture of health, but Justus's illness, worry, and overwork were visibly telling on her; she had lost her bloom and looked wan.

While I was talking to Mrs. Schwab, Ed came in. He became embarrassed on seeing me; I also was confused. He quickly regained control of himself and approached us. Mrs. Schwab excused herself by saying she had to look after her patient, and we were left alone. It was a painful moment, to which neither of us could for some time find the right approach.

I had not been in touch with Ed during my stay abroad, but I knew of his life through our common friends, who had written me about the birth of Ed's child. I asked him how it felt to be a father. He became animated at once, launching into a pæan over his little daughter and enlarging upon her charm and remarkable intelligence. I was amused to see that baby-hater waxing so enthusiastic. I remembered that he had always refused to move into a house where there were children. " I see you don't believe me," he remarked presently; " you are astonished that I am so excited about it. Well, it isn't because *I* happen to be the father, but because my little girl is really an exceptional child." It was amazing to hear it from the man who used to say that " most human beings are foolish, but parents are both foolish and blind: they imagine their children to be prodigies and expect the whole world to be of the same opinion."

I assured him that I did not doubt him, but in order that I might make quite certain he had better let me see the wonder-child. "You really want to see her? You really want me to bring her to you?" he cried. "Why, yes, of course," I replied; "you know I have always been fond of children — why should I not be of yours?" He was silent for a while. Then he said: "Our love has not been much of a success, has it?" "Is love ever?" I responded; "ours lasted seven years, which most people would consider a long time." "You have grown wise during the past year, dear Emma," he answered. "No, only older, dear Ed." We parted with the promise of meeting again soon.

At the Russian New Year's *vetcherinka* Ed was present in the company of a woman — his wife, I was sure. She was large, and she talked in a rather loud voice. Ed had always abhorred this trait in women; how did he stand it now? Friends besieged me, and comrades from the East Side came to question me about the movement in England and in France. I did not see Ed again that evening.

The most urgent necessity on my arrival in America was to secure employment. I had left my visiting-card with several of my medical friends, but weeks passed and not a single call came. Hippolyte tried to get something to do on the Czech anarchist weekly. There was plenty of work there, but no payment; it was considered unethical to accept money for writing for an anarchist paper. All the foreign-language publications, with the exception of the *Freiheit* and the *Freie Arbeiter Stimme*, were got out by the voluntary labour of men who earned their living at some trade, giving their evenings and Sundays gratis to the needs of the movement. Hippolyte, not having a profession, was even more helpless in New York than he had been in London. Boarding-houses in America rarely employed men.

At last on Christmas Eve Dr. Hoffmann sent for me. "The patient is a morphine addict," he informed me, "a very difficult and trying case. The night nurse had to be given a week off; she could not stand the strain. You have been called to substitute for a week." The prospect was not enticing, but I needed work.

It was almost midnight when I arrived with the doctor at the patient's house. In a large room on the second floor a woman was lying half dressed on the bed, in a stupor. Her face, framed in a mass of black hair, was white and she was breathing heavily. Looking about,

I noticed on the wall the portrait of a heavy man peering at me out of small, hard eyes. I recognized the likeness as that of a person I had seen before, but I could not recollect where or under what circumstances. Dr. Hoffmann began giving me directions. The patient's name was Mrs. Spenser, he said. He had been treating her for some time, trying to cure her of the drug habit. She had been making good progress, but recently she had suffered a relapse and taken to morphine again. Nothing could be done for her until she came out of her stupor. I should watch her pulse and keep her warm. Mrs. Spenser hardly stirred during the night. I tried to while away the time by reading, but I could not concentrate. The picture of the man on the wall haunted me. When the day nurse arrived, the patient was still asleep, though breathing more normally.

Soon my week was nearly over. During the entire time Mrs. Spenser had shown no interest in her surroundings. She would open her eyes, stare vacantly, and doze off to sleep again. When I came on duty on the sixth night, I found her fully conscious. Her hair looked neglected and I asked her whether she would like me to comb and braid it. She consented gladly. While I was doing it, she inquired what my name was. " Goldman," I said. " Are you related to Emma Goldman, the anarchist ? " " Very much so," I replied, " I am the guilty party." To my surprise she appeared much pleased to have such a " famous person " for her nurse. She asked me to take full charge of her case, saying that she liked me better than her other nurses. It was flattering to my professional vanity, but I did not feel it right to have the other nurses discharged on my account. Besides, the strain of twenty-four hours' straight duty would make it impossible for me to give her the care she needed. She begged me to stay, promising that I should have every afternoon off and a rest during the night.

Some time later Mrs. Spenser inquired whether I knew the original of the portrait. I told her he looked familiar, but that I could not place him. She did not discuss the matter further.

The house, the furniture, the large library of good books, all bespoke the intelligence and good taste of their owner. There was a curious, mystifying air about the apartment, heightened by the daily visits of a woman, coarse-looking and gaudily attired. The moment she arrived my patient would send me on an errand. I welcomed the opportunity for a walk in the fresh air, wondering at the same time who the person might be with whom Mrs. Spenser had always to be alone. At first I suspected that the strange visitor might be supplying her with drugs, but as there were no evil consequences to my patient, I dismissed the matter as not being my concern.

At the end of the third week Mrs. Spenser was able to go downstairs to her parlour. In the process of putting the sick-room in order I came across peculiar slips of paper marked: "Jeannette, 20 times; Marion, 16; Henriette, 12." There were about forty names of women, each checked off by a number. What a strange record! I thought. When about to join my patient in the sitting-room, I was arrested by a voice that I recognized as that of Mrs. Spenser's visitor. "MacIntyre was at the house again last night," I heard her say, "but none of the girls wanted him. Jeannette said she preferred twenty others to that filthy creature." Mrs. Spenser must have heard my step, for the conversation suddenly broke off, and she called through the door, "Is that you, Miss Goldman? Please come in." As I entered, the tea-tray I carried crashed to the ground, and I stood staring at a man sitting next to my patient on the sofa. It was the original of the portrait and I immediately recognized him as the detective-sergeant who had been instrumental in sending me to the penitentiary in 1893.

The slips of paper, the report I had just overheard — I understood it all in a flash. Spenser was the keeper of a "house," and the detective her paramour. I fled to the second storey, filled with the one idea of getting out and away from the house. Hastening downstairs with my suit-case, I saw Mrs. Spenser at the bottom of the stairs, hardly able to stand, her hands nervously gripping the banister. I realized that I could not leave her in that state; I was responsible to Dr. Hoffmann, for whom I must wait. I led Mrs. Spenser to her room and put her to bed.

She burst into hysterical sobbing, begging me not to go away and assuring me that I should never have to see the man again; she would even have his portrait removed. She admitted being the keeper of a house. "I dreaded to have you find it out," she said, "but I did think that Emma Goldman, the anarchist, would not condemn me for being a cog in a machine I did not create." Prostitution was not of her making, she argued; and since it existed, it did not matter who was "in charge." If not she, it would be someone else. She did not think keeping girls was any worse than underpaying them in factories; at least she had always been kind to them. I could inquire of them myself if I wished. She talked incessantly, weeping herself into exhaustion. I remained.

Mrs. Spenser's "reasons" did not influence me. I knew that

everyone offered the same excuse for vile deeds, the policeman as well as the judge, the soldier as well as the highest war-lord; everybody who lives off the labour and degradation of others. I felt, however, that in my capacity as nurse I could not concern myself with the particular trade or occupation of my patients. I had to minister to their physical needs. Besides, I was not only a nurse, I was also an anarchist who knew the social factors behind human action. As such, even more than as a nurse I could not refuse her my services.

My four months with Mrs. Spenser gave me considerable experience in psychology. She was an unusual person, intelligent, observant, and understanding. She knew life and men, all sorts of men, in every social stratum. The house she kept was " high-class "; among its patrons were some of the strongest pillars of society: doctors, lawyers, judges, and preachers. The man whom the girls " hated like the pest " was none other, I found out, than a New York lawyer prominent in the nineties — the very same who had assured the jury that Emma Goldman, if free, would endanger the lives of the children of the rich and cover the streets of New York with blood.

Indeed, Mrs. Spenser knew men, and, knowing them, she felt nothing but contempt and hatred for them. Over and again she would say that not one of her girls was so depraved as the men who bought them, or so barren of common humanity. Her sympathies were always on the side of the girls when a " guest " complained. That she had intense feeling for suffering she often demonstrated, and not only in her dealings with the girls, many of whom I met and talked with; she was kind to every beggar on the street. She loved children passionately. When she would come upon some urchin, no matter how ragged or filthy, she would pet him and give him money. Repeatedly I heard her lament: " If I only had a child! A child of my own! "

Her story was a veritable novel. As a girl of sixteen, very beautiful, she fell in love with a dashing army officer in Ruthenia, her native country. By promises of marriage he made her his mistress. When she became pregnant, he took her to Vienna, where an operation almost killed her. After she had recuperated, the man went with her to Cracow, where he left her in a house of prostitution. She had no money, did not know a soul in the city, and found herself a slave in the house. Later one of the patrons bought her free and took her on a long voyage. For five years she travelled over Europe with her keeper, and then she again was stranded, without friends, the street her only refuge. Several years passed. She had grown wise; she had saved some money and she decided to go to America. Here she drifted into acquaintance with a wealthy politician. When he left her, she had enough money to open up a house.

The remarkable trait about Mrs. Spenser was that she had not become affected by the life through which she had passed. There was not a coarse grain in her and she remained touchingly sensitive, a lover of music and of good literature.

Dr. Hoffmann's treatment gradually weaned her from the use of drugs, but it left her physically weak and subject to attacks of dizziness. She could not go out alone and I became her companion as well as nurse. I read to her, accompanied her to concerts, the opera, and the theatre, occasionally even to lectures in which she was interested.

While nursing Mrs. Spenser I became engaged in work preparatory to the projected visit of Peter Kropotkin. He had notified us that he was coming to America to deliver a series of lectures at the Lowell Institute on Ideals in Russian Literature, and that he would also be able to talk on anarchism if we wished it. We were enthusiastic over the prospect. I had missed the lectures of our dear comrade on his previous tour. In England I had had no opportunity to hear him. We all felt that Peter's lectures and gracious personality would be of inestimable value to our movement in the United States. When Mrs. Spenser heard of my activity, she immediately offered to relieve me evenings, so that I might have more leisure to devote to the work.

From all parts of the city people came streaming in to Grand Central Palace to hear Peter Kropotkin on the first Sunday afternoon in May. For once even the papers were decent: they could not gainsay the man's charm, the power of his intellect, the simplicity and logic of his delivery and argumentation. In the audience was also Mrs. Spenser, completely carried away by the speaker.

A social evening was being prepared for Kropotkin, an unofficial affair, to enable him to meet the comrades and others in sympathy with our ideas. Mrs. Spenser inquired whether she would be admitted. "What if your friends find out who I am?" she asked anxiously. I assured her that my friends were in no way akin to Anthony Comstock and that no one would by word or deed make her feel out of place. She looked wonderingly at me out of her luminous eyes.

The evening before the social gathering several of the more intimate comrades dined with our beloved teacher. I related the story of

Mrs. Spenser. Peter was much interested; she was a real human document, he thought. Indeed, he would meet my patient, and autograph a copy of his *Memoirs* for her, as she had requested. Before I left, Peter embraced me. " You are giving a convincing example of the beauty and humanity of our ideals," he remarked. I knew that he, so rich in compassion, understood why I had remained to care for the social pariah.

At last my patient was far enough advanced in her cure to dispense with me. I was eager to go on tour. The comrades in a number of cities had been urging me to come for lectures. There were also other reasons. One of them was Pittsburgh. I had no hopes of being able to see Sasha; he had been deprived of visits entirely after my dreadful encounter with Prison Inspector Reed. Since the failure of the tunnel my tortured boy had been in solitary, with all his privileges taken away. The rare *sub rosa* notes he was able to send out gave no indication of what he was enduring. They only helped to increase my feeling of the hopelessness of his situation. I kept on writing to him, but it was like sending letters into the void. I had no way of knowing whether they reached him. The prison authorities would never let me see Sasha again, but they could not prevent me from going to Pittsburgh, where I could feel nearer to him.

Hippolyte had left for Chicago to work on the *Arbeiter Zeitung*. The offer of employment had come at a period when life had become insupportable to him, and he in turn had added much to my unhappiness. The thought that he would now have the soothing companionship of Max, as well as work he was fitted to do, gave me much consolation. I was planning to meet him in Chicago.

Ed came often to visit me or to invite me to dinner. He was charming and there was no sign of the storm that had tossed us about for seven years. It had given way to a calm friendship. He did not bring his little daughter and I suspected that the mother must have objected to my seeing the child. Whether she also resented our companionship I had no way of knowing. Ed never mentioned her. When he learned that I was about to begin a lecture tour, he asked me again to act as the representative of his firm.

Before leaving for the West I kept a previous engagement in Paterson, New Jersey, where the local Italian group had arranged a meeting for me. Our Italian comrades were always most hospitable, and on this occasion they prepared an informal social to follow my lecture. I was glad of the opportunity to find out more about Bresci and his life. What I learned from his closest comrades convinced me once more how difficult it is to gain a real insight into the human heart and how likely we all are to judge men by superficial indications.

Gaetano Bresci was one of the founders of *La Questione Sociale,* the Italian anarchist paper published in Paterson. He was a skilful weaver, considered by his employers a sober, hard-working man, but his pay averaged only fifteen dollars a week. He had a wife and child to support; yet he managed to donate weekly contributions to the paper. He had even saved a hundred and fifty dollars, which he lent to the group at a critical period of *La Questione Sociale.* His free evenings and Sundays he used to spend in helping with the office work and in propaganda. He was beloved and respected for his devotion by all the members of his group.

Then one day Bresci had unexpectedly asked that his loan to the paper be returned. He was informed that it was impossible; the paper had no funds and had, in fact, a deficit. But Bresci insisted and even refused to offer any explanation for his demand. Finally the group succeeded in securing enough money to pay back the debt to Bresci. But the Italian comrades bitterly resented Bresci's behaviour, branding him as a miser, who loved money above his ideal. Most of his friends even ostracized him.

A few weeks later came the news that Gaetano Bresci had killed King Humbert. His act brought home to the Paterson group the realization of how cruelly they had wronged the man. He had insisted on the return of his money in order to secure the fare to Italy! No doubt the consciousness of the injustice done Bresci rested heavier on the Italian comrades than his resentment against them. To make amends, in a sense, the Paterson group charged itself with the support of their martyred comrade's child, a beautiful little girl. His widow, on the other hand, gave no indication that she either understood the spirit of her child's father or was in sympathy with his great sacrifice.

The subject of my lecture in Cleveland, early in May of that year, was Anarchism, delivered before the Franklin Liberal Club, a radical organization. During the intermission before the discussion I noticed a man looking over the titles of the pamphlets and books on sale near the platform. Presently he came over to me with the question: " Will you suggest something for me to read? " He was working in Akron, he explained, and he would have to leave before the close of the meeting.

He was very young, a mere youth, of medium height, well built, and carrying himself very erect. But it was his face that held me, a most sensitive face, with a delicate pink complexion; a handsome face, made doubly so by his curly golden hair. Strength showed in his large blue eyes. I made a selection of some books for him, remarking that I hoped he would find in them what he was seeking. I returned to the platform to open the discussion and I did not see the young man again that evening, but his striking face remained in my memory.

The Isaaks had moved *Free Society* to Chicago, where they occupied a large house, which was the centre of the anarchist activities in that city. On my arrival there, I went to their home and immediately plunged into intense work that lasted eleven weeks. The summer heat became so oppressive that the rest of my tour had to be postponed until September. I was completely exhausted and badly in need of rest. Sister Helena had repeatedly asked me to come to her for a month, but I had not been able to spare the time before. Now was my opportunity. I would have a few weeks with Helena, the children of my two sisters, and Yegor, who was spending his vacation in Rochester. He had two college chums with him, he had written me; to make the circle of young people complete I invited Mary, the fourteen-year-old daughter of the Isaaks, to come with me for a holiday. I had earned some money on orders for Ed's firm and I could afford to play Lady Bountiful to the young people and grow younger with them.

On the day of our departure the Isaaks gave me a farewell luncheon. Afterwards, while I was busy packing my things, someone rang the bell. Mary Isaak came in to tell me that a young man, who gave his name as Nieman, was urgently asking to see me. I knew nobody by that name and I was in a hurry, about to leave for the station. Rather impatiently I requested Mary to inform the caller that I had no time at the moment, but that he could talk to me on my way to the station. As I left the house, I saw the visitor, recognizing him as the handsome chap of the golden hair who had asked me to recommend him reading-matter at the Cleveland meeting.

Hanging on to the straps on the elevated train, Nieman told me that he had belonged to a Socialist local in Cleveland, that he had found its members dull, lacking in vision and enthusiasm. He could not bear to be with them and he had left Cleveland and was now working in Chicago and eager to get in touch with anarchists.

At the station I found my friends awaiting me, among them Max.

I wanted to spend a few minutes with him and I begged Hippolyte to take care of Nieman and introduce him to the comrades.

The Rochester youngsters took me to their hearts. My two sisters' children, my brother Yegor and his chums, and young Mary, all combined to fill the days with the loveliness only young ardent souls can give. It was a new and exhilarating experience, to which I completely abandoned myself. The roof of Helena's house became our garden and the gathering-place where my youthful friends confided to me their dreams and aspirations.

Our picnics with the young folks were especially delightful. Harry, sister Lena's eldest child, was a Republican at ten, a regular campaign spellbinder. It was fun to hear him defend McKinley, his hero, and argue against *Tante* Emma. He shared the family admiration for me, regretting, however, that I did not belong to his camp. Saxe, Harry's brother, was of an entirely different type. In character he resembled Helena much more than his own mother, having a good deal of the former's shyness and timidity, and giving the same impression of sadness. He also shared Helena's boundless capacity for love. His ideal was David, Helena's youngest son, whose word was sacred to Saxe. This was not surprising, because David was a splendid specimen of a boy. Of fine physique and pleasing appearance, his unusual musical talents and his love of fun won him the heart of everyone. I loved all these children, but next to Stella it was Saxe who came nearest my heart, perhaps mainly because I was aware that he lacked the coarser equipment necessary for the struggle of life.

My holiday in Rochester was somewhat marred by a notice in *Free Society* containing a warning against Nieman. It was written by A. Isaak, editor of the paper, and it stated that news had been received from Cleveland that the man had been asking questions that aroused suspicion, and that he was trying to get into the anarchist circles. The comrades in Cleveland had concluded that he must be a spy.

I was very angry. To make such a charge, on such flimsy grounds! I wrote Isaak at once, demanding more convincing proofs. He replied that, while he had no other evidence, he still felt that Nieman was untrustworthy because he constantly talked about acts of violence. I wrote another protest. The next issue of *Free Society* contained a retraction.

The Pan-American Exposition, held at Buffalo, interested me and I had long wanted also to see the Niagara Falls. But I could not leave my precious youngsters behind and I did not have enough money to take them with me. Dr. Kaplan, a Buffalo friend, who knew that I was holidaying with my family, solved our difficulties. He had asked me before to pay him a visit and bring my friends along. When I wrote him that my means would not allow such a luxury, he called me up on the long-distance telephone and offered to contribute forty dollars towards expenses and be our host for a week. In merry anticipation of the adventure, I took the older children to Buffalo. We were treated to a round of festivities, "did" the Falls, saw the Exposition, and enjoyed music and parties, as well as gatherings with comrades, at which the young generation participated in the discussions on a footing of equality.

On our return to Rochester I found two letters from Sasha. The first, *sub rosa*, dated July 10, had evidently been delayed in transmission. Its contents threw me into despair. It read:

> From the hospital. Just out of the strait jacket, after eight days.
>
> For over a year I was in the strictest solitary; for a long time mail and reading-matter were denied me. . . . I have passed through a great crisis. Two of my best friends died in a frightful manner. The death of Russell, especially, affected me. He was very young, and my dearest and most devoted friend, and he died a terrible death. The doctor charged the boy with shamming, but now he says it was spinal meningitis. I cannot tell you the awful truth—it was nothing short of murder, and my poor friend rotted away by inches. When he died, they found his back one mass of bedsores. If you could read the pitiful letters he wrote, begging to see me and to be nursed by me! But the Warden wouldn't permit it. In some manner his agony seemed to communicate itself to me, and I began to experience the pains and symptoms that Russell described in his notes. I knew it was my sick fancy; I strove against it, but presently my legs showed signs of paralysis, and I suffered excruciating pain in the spinal column, just like Russell. I was afraid that I would be done to death like my poor friend. . . . I was on the verge of suicide. I demanded to be relieved from the cell, and the Warden ordered me punished. I was put in the strait jacket. They bound my body in canvas, strapped my arms to the bed, and chained my feet to the posts. I was kept that way eight days, unable to move, rotting in my own excrement. Released prisoners called the attention of our new Inspector to my case. He refused to believe that such things were being done in the penitentiary. Reports spread that I was going blind and insane. Then the Inspector visited the hospital and had me released from the jacket.

I am in pretty bad shape, but they have put me in the general ward now, and I am glad of the chance to send you this note.

The fiends! It would have been a convenient way to send Sasha into the madhouse or to make him take his own life. I was sick with the thought that I had been living in a world of dreams, youthful fancies and gaiety, while Sasha was undergoing hellish tortures. My heart cried out: "It isn't fair that he alone should go on paying the price — it isn't fair!" My young friends clustered around me in compassion. Stella's large eyes were filled with tears. Yegor held out the other letter, saying: "This is of a later date. It may have better news." I was almost afraid to open it. I had barely read the first paragraph when I cried in joy: "Children — Stella — Yegor! Sasha's term has been commuted! Only five years more and he will be free! Think of it, only five more years!" Breathlessly I went on reading. "I can visit him again!" I exclaimed. "The new Warden has restored his privileges — he can see his friends!" I ran about the room laughing and crying.

Helena rushed up the stairs, followed by Jacob. "What is it? What has happened?" I could only cry: "Sasha! My Sasha!" Gently my sister drew me down on the sofa, took the letter from my hand, and read it aloud in a trembling voice:

> *Direct to Box A 7.*
> *Allegheny City, Pa.*
> *July 25, 1901.*

DEAR FRIEND,—

I cannot tell you how happy I am to be allowed to write to you again. My privileges have been restored by our new Inspector, a very kindly man. He has relieved me from the cell, and now I am again on the range. The Inspector requested me to deny to my friends the reports which have recently appeared in the papers concerning my condition. I have not been well of late, but now I hope to improve. My eyes are very poor. The Inspector has given me permission to have a specialist examine them. Please arrange for it through our local comrades.

There is another piece of very good news, dear friend. A new commutation law has been passed, which reduces my sentence by $2\frac{1}{2}$ years. It still leaves me a long time, of course; almost four years here, and another year in the workhouse. However, it is a considerable gain, and if I should not get into solitary again, I may—I am almost afraid to utter the thought—I may live to come out. I feel as if I am being resurrected.

The new law benefits the short-timers proportionately much more than the men with longer sentences. Only the poor lifers do not share in it. We were very anxious for a while, as there were many rumours that the law would be declared unconstitutional. Fortunately, the attempt to nullify its benefits proved ineffectual. Think of men who will see something unconstitutional in allowing the prisoners a little more good time than the commutation statute of 40 years ago. As if a little kindness to the unfortunates—really justice—is incompatible with the spirit of Jefferson! We were greatly worried over the fate of this statute, but at last the first batch has been released, and there is much rejoicing over it.

There is a peculiar history about this new law, which may interest you; it sheds a significant side-light. It was especially designed for the benefit of a high Federal officer who was recently convicted of aiding two wealthy Philadelphia tobacco-manufacturers to defraud the Government of a few millions, by using counterfeit tax stamps. Their influence secured the introduction of the commutation bill and its hasty passage. The law would have cut their sentences almost in two, but certain newspapers seem to have taken offence at having been kept in ignorance of the "deal," and protests began to be voiced. The matter finally came up before the Attorney General of the United States, who decided that the men in whose special interest the law was engineered could not benefit by it, because a State law does not affect U.S. prisoners, the latter being subject to the Federal Commutation Act. Imagine the discomfiture of the politicians! An attempt was even made to suspend the operation of the statute. Fortunately it failed, and now the "common" State prisoners, who were not at all meant to profit, are being released. The legislature has unwittingly given some unfortunates here much happiness.

I was interrupted in this writing by being called out for a visit. I could hardly credit it: the first comrade I have been allowed to see in nine years! It was Harry Gordon, and I was so overcome by the sight of the dear friend, I could barely speak. He must have prevailed upon the new Inspector to issue a permit. The latter is now Acting Warden, owing to the serious illness of Captain Wright. Perhaps he will allow me to see my sister. Will you kindly communicate with her at once? Meantime I shall try to secure a pass. With renewed hope, and always with green memory of you,

ALEX

" At last, at last the miracle ! " Helena exclaimed amid tears. She had always admired Sasha. Since his imprisonment she had taken a keen interest in his condition and in every bit of news that had come out of his living grave. She had shared my grief, and now she rejoiced with me over the wonderful news.

Once more I stood within the prison walls of the Western Penitentiary, with fast-beating heart straining to catch the sound of Sasha's step. Nine years had passed since that November day in 1892 when for a fleeting moment I had been brought face to face with him, only again to be wrenched away — nine years replete with the torment of endless time.

" Sasha ! " I rushed forward with outstretched arms. I saw the guard, beside him a man in a grey suit, the same greyness in his face. Could it really be Sasha, so changed, so thin and wan ? He sat mute at my side, fumbling with the fob of my watch-chain. I waited tensely, listening for a word. Sasha made no sound. Only his eyes stared at me, sinking into my very soul. They were Sasha's eyes, startled, tortured eyes. They made me want to weep. I, too, was mute.

" Time's up ! " The sound almost froze my blood. With heavy steps I turned to the corridor, out of the enclosure, through the iron gate into the street.

The same day I left Allegheny City for St. Louis, where I was met by Carl Nold, whom I had not seen for three years. He was the same kind Carl, eager for news of Sasha. He had already learned of the unexpected change in his status and he was highly elated over it. " So you have seen him ! " he cried. " Tell me quickly all about him."

I told him what I could of the ghastly visit. When I had finished he said : " I am afraid your visit to the prison came too soon after his year in solitary. A whole year of enforced isolation, never a chance to exchange a word with another human being, or to hear a kindly voice. You grow numb and incapable of giving expression to your longing for human contact." I understood Sasha's fearful silence.

The following day, September 6, I canvassed every important stationery and novelty store in St. Louis for orders for Ed's firm, but I failed to interest anyone in my samples. Only in one store was I told to call the next day to see the boss. As I stood at a street-corner wearily waiting for a car, I heard a newsboy cry : " Extra ! Extra ! President McKinley shot ! " I bought a paper, but the car was so jammed that it was impossible to read. Around me people were talking about the shooting of the President.

Carl had arrived at the house before me. He had already read the account. The President had been shot at the Exposition grounds in Buffalo by a young man by the name of Leon Czolgosz. " I never heard the name," Carl said; " have you ? " " No, never," I replied. " It is fortunate that you are here and not in Buffalo," he continued. " As usual, the papers will connect you with this act." " Nonsense ! " I said, " the American press is fantastic enough, but it would hardly concoct such a crazy story."

The next morning I went to the stationery store to see the owner. After considerable persuasion I succeeded in getting an order amounting to a thousand dollars, the largest I had ever secured. Naturally I was very happy over it. While I was waiting for the man to fill out his order, I caught the headline of the newspaper lying on his desk: " ASSASSIN OF PRESIDENT MCKINLEY AN ANARCHIST. CONFESSES TO HAVING BEEN INCITED BY EMMA GOLDMAN. WOMAN ANARCHIST WANTED."

By great effort I strove to preserve my composure, completed the business, and walked out of the store. At the next corner I bought several papers and went to a restaurant to read them. They were filled with the details of the tragedy, reporting also the police raid of the Isaak house in Chicago and the arrest of everyone found there. The authorities were going to hold the prisoners until Emma Goldman was found, the papers stated. Already two hundred detectives had been sent out throughout the country to track down Emma Goldman.

On the inside page of one of the papers was a picture of McKinley's slayer. " Why, that's Nieman ! " I gasped.

When I was through with the papers, it became clear to me that I must immediately go to Chicago. The Isaak family, Hippolyte, our old comrade Jay Fox, a most active man in the labour movement, and a number of others were being held without bail until I should be found. It was plainly my duty to surrender myself. I knew there was neither reason nor the least proof to connect me with the shooting. I would go to Chicago.

Stepping into the street, I bumped into " V.," the " rich man from New Mexico " who had managed my lecture in Los Angeles some years before. The moment he saw me he turned white with fear. " For God's sake, Emma, what are you doing here ? " he cried in a quavering voice; " don't you know the police of the whole country are looking for you? " While he was speaking, his eyes roved uneasily over the street. It was evident he was panicky. I had to make sure that he would not disclose my presence in the city. Familiarly I took his arm and whispered: " Let's go to some quiet place."

Sitting in a corner, away from the other guests, I said to him: " Once you assured me of your undying love. You even made me an offer of marriage. It was only four years ago. Is anything left of that affection? If so, will you give me your word of honour that you will not breathe to anybody that you have seen me here? I do not want to be arrested in St. Louis — I intend to give Chicago that honour. Tell me quickly if I can depend on you to keep silent." He promised solemnly.

When we reached the street, he walked away in great haste. I was sure he would keep his word, but I knew that my former devotee was no hero.

When I told Carl I was going to Chicago, he said that I must be out of my senses. He pleaded with me to give up the idea, but I remained adamant. He left me to gather up a few trusted friends, whose opinion he knew I valued, hoping they would be able to persuade me not to surrender myself. They argued with me for hours, but they failed to change my decision. I told them jokingly that they had better give me a good send-off, as we probably should never again have an opportunity for a jolly evening together. They engaged a private dining-room at a restaurant, where we were treated to a Lucullan meal, and then they accompanied me to the Wabash Station, Carl having secured a sleeper for me.

In the morning the car was agog with the Buffalo tragedy, Czolgosz and Emma Goldman. " A beast, a bloodthirsty monster! " I heard someone say; " she should have been locked up long ago." " Locked up nothing! " another retorted; " she should be strung up to the first lamp-post."

I listened to the good Christians while resting in my berth. I chuckled to myself at the thought of how they would look if I were to step out and announce: " Here, ladies and gentlemen, true followers of the gentle Jesus, here is Emma Goldman! " But I did not have the heart to cause them such a shock and I remained behind my curtain.

Half an hour before the train pulled into the station I got dressed. I wore a small sailor hat with a bright blue veil, much in style then. I left my glasses off and pulled the veil over my face. The platform was jammed with people, among them several men who looked like detectives. I asked a fellow-passenger to be kind enough to keep an eye on my two suit-cases while I went in search of a porter. I finally got one, walking the whole length of the platform to my luggage, then back again with the porter to the check-room. Securing my receipt, I left the station.

The only person who knew of my coming was Max, to whom I had sent a cautious wire. I caught sight of him before he saw me. Passing him slowly, I whispered: "Walk towards the next street. I'll do the same." No one seemed to follow me. After some zigzagging with Max and changing half a dozen street-cars we reached the apartment where he and Millie ("Puck") lived. Both of them expressed the greatest anxiety about my safety, Max insisting that it was insanity to have come to Chicago. The situation, he said, was a repetition of 1887; the press and the police were thirsty for blood. "It's *your* blood they want," he repeated, while he and Millie implored me to leave the country.

I was determined to remain in Chicago. I realized that I could not stay at their home, nor with any other foreign comrades. I had, however, American friends who were not known as anarchists. Max notified Mr. and Mrs. N., who I knew were very fond of me, of my presence and they came at once. They also were worried about me, but they thought I would be safe with them. It was to be only for two days, as I was planning to give myself up to the police as quickly as possible.

Mr. N., the son of a wealthy preacher, lived in a fashionable neighbourhood. "Imagine anybody believing I would shelter Emma Goldman," he said when we had arrived in his house. Late in the afternoon, on Monday, when Mr. N. returned from his office, he informed me that there was a chance to get five thousand dollars from the Chicago *Tribune* for a scoop on an interview. "Fine!" I replied; "we shall need money to fight my case." We agreed that Mr. N. should bring the newspaper representative to his apartment the next morning, and then the three of us would ride down to police headquarters together. In the evening Max and Millie arrived. I had never before seen my friends in such a state of nervous excitement. Max reiterated that I must get away, else I was putting my head in the noose. "If you go to the police, you will never come out alive," he warned me. "It will be the same as with Albert Parsons. You must let us get you over to Canada."

Millie took me aside. " Since Friday," she said, " Max has not slept or taken food. He walks the floor all night and keeps on saying: ' Emma is lost; they will kill her.' " She begged me to soothe Max by promising him that I would escape to Canada, even if I did not intend doing so. I consented and asked Max to make the necessary arrangements to get me away. Overjoyed, he clasped me in his arms. We arranged for Max and Millie to come the next morning with an outfit of clothes to disguise me.

I spent the greater part of the night tearing up letters and papers and destroying what was likely to involve my friends. All preparations completed, I went to sleep. In the morning Mrs. N. left for her office, while her husband went to the Chicago *Tribune*. We agreed that if anyone called, I was to pretend to be the maid.

About nine o'clock, while taking a bath, I heard a sound as if someone was scratching on the window-sill. I paid no attention to it at first. I finished my bath leisurely and began to dress. Then came a crash of glass. I threw my kimono over me and went into the dining-room to investigate. A man was clutching the window-sill with one hand while holding a gun in the other. We were on the third floor and there was no fire-escape. I called out: " Look out, you'll break your neck! " " Why the hell don't you open the door? Are you deaf? " He swung through the window and was in the room. I walked over to the entrance and unlocked it. Twelve men, led by a giant, crowded into the apartment. The leader grabbed me by the arm, bellowing: " Who are you? " " I not speak English — Swedish servant-girl." He released his hold and ordered his men to search the place. Turning to me, he yelled: " Stand back! We're looking for Emma Goldman." Then he held up a photo to me. " See this? We want this woman. Where is she? " I pointed my finger at the picture and said: " This woman I not see here. This woman big — you look in those small boxes will not find her — she too big." " Oh, shut up! " he bawled; " you can't tell what them anarchists will do."

After they had searched the house, turning everything upside down, the giant walked over to the book-shelves. " Hell, this is a reg'lar preacher's house," he remarked: " look at them books. I don't think Emma Goldman would be here." They were about to leave when one of the detectives suddenly called: " Here, Captain Schuettler, what about this? " It was my fountain-pen, a gift from a friend, with my name on it. I had overlooked it. " By golly, that's a find! " cried the

Captain. " She must have been here and she may come back." He ordered two of his men to remain behind.

I saw that the game was up. There was no sign of Mr. N. or the *Tribune* man, and it could serve no purpose to keep the farce up longer. " I am Emma Goldman," I announced.

For a moment Schuettler and his men stood there as if petrified. Then the Captain roared: " Well, I'll be damned! You're the shrewdest crook I ever met! Take her, quick! "

When I stepped into the cab waiting at the curb, I saw N. approaching in the company of the *Tribune* man. It was too late for the scoop, and I did not want my host recognized. I pretended not to see them.

I had often heard of the third degree used by the police in various American cities to extort confessions, but I myself had never been subjected to it. I had been arrested a number of times since 1893; no violence, however, had ever been practised on me. On the day of my arrest, which was September 10, I was kept at police headquarters in a stifling room and grilled to exhaustion from 10.30 a.m. till 7 p.m. At least fifty detectives passed me, each shaking his fist in my face and threatening me with the direst things. One yelled: " You was with Czolgosz in Buffalo! I saw you myself, right in front of Convention Hall. Better confess, d'you hear? " Another: " Look here, Goldman, I seen you with that son of a bitch at the fair! Don't you lie now — I seen you, I tell you! " Again: " You've faked enough — you keep this up and sure's you're born you'll get the chair. Your lover has confessed. He said it was your speech made him shoot the President." I knew they were lying; I knew I had not been with Czolgosz except for a few minutes in Cleveland on May 5, and for half an hour in Chicago on July 12. Schuettler was most ferocious. His massive bulk towered above me, bellowing: " If you don't confess, you'll go the way of those bastard Haymarket anarchists."

I reiterated the story I had told them when first brought to police headquarters, explaining where I had been and with whom. But they would not believe me and kept on bullying and abusing me. My head throbbed, my throat and lips felt parched. A large pitcher of water stood on the table before me, but every time I stretched out my hand for it, a detective would say: " You can drink all you want, but first answer me. Where were you with Czolgosz the day he shot the President? " The torture continued for hours. Finally I was taken to the

Harrison Street Police Station and locked in a barred enclosure, exposed to view from every side.

Presently the matron came to inquire if I wanted supper. "No, but water," I said, "and something for my head." She returned with a tin pitcher of tepid water, which I gulped down. She could give me nothing for my head except a cold compress. It proved very soothing, and I soon fell asleep.

I woke up with a burning sensation. A plain-clothes man held a reflector in front of me, close to my eyes. I leaped up and pushed him away with all my strength, crying: "You're burning my eyes!" "We'll burn more before we get through with you!" he retorted. With short intermissions this was repeated during three nights. On the third night several detectives entered my cell. "We've got the right dope on you now," they announced; "it was you who financed Czolgosz and you got the money from Dr. Kaplan in Buffalo. We have him all right, and he's confessed everything. Now what you got to say?" "Nothing more than I have already said," I repeated; "I know nothing about the act."

Since my arrest I had had no word from my friends, nor had anyone come to see me. I realized that I was being kept *incommunicado*. I did get letters, however, most of them unsigned. "You damn bitch of an anarchist," one of them read, "I wish I could get at you. I would tear your heart out and feed it to my dog." "Murderous Emma Goldman," another wrote, "you will burn in hell-fire for your treachery to our country." A third cheerfully promised: "We will cut your tongue out, soak your carcass in oil, and burn you alive." The description by some of the anonymous writers of what they would do to me sexually offered studies in perversion that would have astounded authorities on the subject. The authors of the letters nevertheless seemed to me less contemptible than the police officials. Daily I was handed stacks of letters that had been opened and read by the guardians of American decency and morality. At the same time messages from my friends were withheld from me. It was evident that my spirit was to be broken by such methods. I decided to put a stop to it. The next time I was given one of the opened envelopes, I tore it up and threw the pieces into the detective's face.

On the fifth day after my arrest I received a wire. It was from Ed, promising the backing of his firm. "Do not hesitate to use our name. We stand by you to the last." I was glad of the assurance,

because it relieved me of the need of keeping silent about my movements on business for Ed's house.

The same evening Chief of Police O'Neill of Chicago came to my
cell. He informed me that he would like to have a quiet talk with me.
" I have no wish to bully or coerce you," he said; " perhaps I can
help you." " It would indeed be a strange experience to have help
from a chief of police," I replied; " but I am quite willing to answer
your questions." He asked me to give him a detailed account of my
movements from May 5, when I had first met Czolgosz, until the day
of my arrest in Chicago. I gave him the requested information, but
without mentioning my visit to Sasha or the names of the comrades
who had been my hosts. As there was no longer any need of shielding
Dr. Kaplan, the Isaaks, or Hippolyte, I was in a position to give
practically a complete account. When I concluded — what I said being taken down in shorthand — Chief O'Neill remarked: " Unless
you're a very clever actress, you are certainly innocent. I think you
are innocent, and I am going to do my part to help you out." I was
too amazed to thank him; I had never before heard such a tone from
a police officer. At the same time I was sceptical of the success of his
efforts, even if he should try to do something for me.

Immediately following my conference with the Chief I became
aware of a decided change in my treatment. My cell door was left
unlocked day and night, and I was told by the matron that I could
stay in the large room, use the rocking-chair and the table there, order
my own food and papers, receive and send out mail. I began at once
to lead the life of a society lady, receiving callers all day long, mostly
newspaper people who came not so much for interviews as to talk,
smoke, and relate funny stories. Others, again, came out of curiosity.
Some women reporters brought gifts of books and toilet articles.
Most attentive was Katherine Leckie, of the Hearst papers. She
possessed a better intellect than Nelly Bly, who used to visit me in
the Tombs in 1893, and had a much finer social feeling. A strong
and ardent feminist, she was at the same time devoted to the cause of
labour. Katherine Leckie was the first to take my story of the third degree. She became so outraged at hearing it that she undertook to
canvass the various women's organizations in order to induce them
to take the matter up.

One day a representative of the *Arbeiter Zeitung* was announced.
With joy I saw Max, who whispered to me that he could secure ad-

mission only in that capacity. He informed me that he had received a letter from Ed with the news that Hearst had sent his representative to Justus Schwab with an offer of twenty thousand dollars if I would come to New York and give him an exclusive interview. The money would be deposited in a bank acceptable to Justus and Ed. Both of them were convinced, Max said, that Hearst would spend any amount to railroad me. "He needs it to whitewash himself of the charge of having incited Czolgosz to shoot McKinley," he explained. The Republican papers of the country had been carrying front-page stories connecting Hearst with Czolgosz, because all through the McKinley administration the Hearst press had violently attacked the President. One of the newspapers had cartooned the publisher standing behind Czolgosz, handing him a match to light the fuse of a bomb. Now Hearst was among the loudest of those demanding the extermination of the anarchists.

Justus and Ed, as well as Max, were unconditionally opposed to my return to New York, but they had felt it their duty to inform me of Hearst's offer. "Twenty thousand dollars!" I exclaimed; "what a pity Ed's letter arrived too late! I certainly would have accepted the proposal. Think of the fight we could have made and the propaganda!" "It is well you still keep your sense of humour," Max remarked, "but I am happy the letter came too late. Your situation is serious enough without Mr. Hearst to make it worse."

Another visitor was a lawyer from Clarence Darrow's office. He had come to warn me that I was hurting my case by my persistent defence of Czolgosz; the man was crazy and I should admit it. "No prominent attorney will accept your defence if you ally yourself with the assassin of the President," he assured me; "in fact, you stand in imminent danger of being held as an accessory to the crime." I demanded to know why Mr. Darrow himself did not come if he was so concerned, but his representative was evasive. He continued to paint my case in sinister colours. My chances of escape were few at best, it seemed, too few for me to allow any sentimentality to aggravate it. Czolgosz was insane, the man insisted; everybody could see it, and, besides, he was a bad sort to have involved me, a coward hiding behind a woman's skirts.

His talk was repugnant to me. I informed him that I was not willing to swear away the reason, character, or life of a defenceless human being and that I wanted no assistance from his chief. I had never met

Darrow, but I had long known of him as a brilliant lawyer, a man of broad social views, an able writer and lecturer. According to the papers he had interested himself in the anarchists arrested in the raid, especially the Isaaks. It seemed strange that he should send me such reprehensible advice, that he should expect me to join the mad chorus howling for the life of Czolgosz.

The country was in a panic. Judging by the press, I was sure that it was the people of the United States and not Czolgosz that had gone mad. Not since 1887 had there been evidenced such lust for blood, such savagery of vengeance. " Anarchists must be exterminated! " the papers raved; " they should be dumped into the sea; there is no place for the vultures under our flag. Emma Goldman has been allowed to ply her trade of murder too long. She should be forced to share the fate of her dupes."

It was a repetition of the dark Chicago days. Fourteen years, years of painful growth, yet fascinating and fruitful years. And now the end! The end? I was only thirty-two and there was yet so much, so very much, undone. And the boy in Buffalo — his life had scarce begun. What was his life, I wondered; what the forces that drove him to this doom? " I did it for the working people," he was reported to have said. The people! Sasha also had done something for the people; and our brave Chicago martyrs, and the others in every land and time. But the people are asleep; they remain indifferent. They forge their own chains and do the bidding of their masters to crucify their Christs.

CHAPTER XXIV

BUFFALO WAS PRESSING FOR MY EXTRADITION, BUT CHICAGO asked for authentic data on the case. I had already been given several hearings in court, and on each occasion the District Attorney from Buffalo had presented much circumstantial evidence to induce the State of Illinois to surrender me. But Illinois demanded direct proofs. There was a hitch somewhere that helped to cause more delays. I thought it likely that Chief of Police O'Neill was behind the matter.

The Chief's attitude towards me had changed the behaviour of every officer in the Harrison Street Police Station. The matron and the two policemen assigned to watch my cell began to lavish attentions on me. The officer on night duty now often appeared with his arms full of parcels, containing fruit, candy, and drinks stronger than grape-juice. " From a friend who keeps a saloon round the corner," he would say, " an admirer of yours." The matron presented me with flowers from the same unknown. One day she brought me the message that he was going to send a grand supper for the coming Sunday. " Who is the man and why should he admire me? " I inquired. " Well, we're all Democrats, and McKinley is a Republican," she replied. " You don't mean you're glad McKinley was shot? " I exclaimed. " Not glad exactly, but not sorry, neither," she said; " we have to pretend, you know, but we're none of us excited about it." " I didn't want McKinley killed," I told her. " We know that," she smiled, " but you're standing up for the boy." I wondered how many more people in America were pretending the same kind of sympathy with the stricken President as my guardians in the station-house.

Even some of the reporters did not seem to be losing sleep over the case. One of them was quite amazed when I assured him that in my professional capacity I would take care of McKinley if I were called upon to nurse him, though my sympathies were with Czolgosz. "You're a puzzle, Emma Goldman," he said, "I can't understand you. You sympathize with Czolgosz, yet you would nurse the man he tried to kill." "As a reporter you aren't expected to understand human complexities," I informed him. "Now listen and see if you can get it. The boy in Buffalo is a creature at bay. Millions of people are ready to spring on him and tear him limb from limb. He committed the act for no personal reasons or gain. He did it for what is his ideal: the good of the people. That is why my sympathies are with him. On the other hand," I continued, "William McKinley, suffering and probably near death, is merely a human being to me now. That is why I would nurse him."

"I don't get you, you're beyond me," he reiterated. The next day there appeared these headlines in one of the papers: "EMMA GOLD-MAN WANTS TO NURSE PRESIDENT; SYMPATHIES ARE WITH SLAYER."

Buffalo failed to produce evidence to justify my extradition. Chicago was getting weary of the game of hide-and-seek. The authorities would not turn me over to Buffalo, yet at the same time they did not feel like letting me go entirely free. By way of compromise I was put under twenty-thousand-dollar bail. The Isaak group had been put under fifteen-thousand-dollar bail. I knew that it would be almost impossible for our people to raise a total of thirty-five thousand dollars within a few days. I insisted on the others being bailed out first. Thereupon I was transferred to the Cook County Jail.

The night before my transfer was Sunday. My saloon-keeper admirer kept his word; he sent over a huge tray filled with numerous goodies: a big turkey, with all the trimmings, including wine and flowers. A note came with it informing me that he was willing to put up five thousand dollars towards my bail. "A strange saloon-keeper!" I remarked to the matron. "Not at all," she replied; "he's the ward heeler and he hates the Republicans worse than the devil." I invited her, my two policemen, and several other officers present to join me in the celebration. They assured me that nothing like it had ever before happened to them — a prisoner playing host to her keepers. "You mean a dangerous anarchist having as guests the guardians of law and order," I corrected. When everybody had left, I noticed that my day watchman lingered behind. I inquired whether he had been changed to night duty. "No," he replied, "I just wanted to tell you that you are not the first anarchist I've been assigned to watch. I was on duty when Parsons and his comrades were in here."

Peculiar and inexplicable the ways of life, intricate the chain of events! Here I was, the spiritual child of those men, imprisoned in the city that had taken their lives, in the same jail, even under the guardianship of the very man who had kept watch in their silent hours. Tomorrow I should be taken to Cook County Jail, within whose walls Parsons, Spies, Engel, and Fischer had been hanged. Strange, indeed, the complex forces that had bound me to those martyrs through all my socially conscious years! And now events were bringing me nearer and nearer — perhaps to a similar end?

The newspapers had published rumours about mobs ready to attack the Harrison Street Station and planning violence to Emma Goldman before she could be taken to the Cook County Jail. Monday morning, flanked by a heavily armed guard, I was led out of the station-house. There were not a dozen people in sight, mostly curiosity-seekers. As usual, the press had deliberately tried to incite a riot.

Ahead of me were two handcuffed prisoners roughly hustled about by the officers. When we reached the patrol wagon, surrounded by more police, their guns ready for action, I found myself close to the two men. Their features could not be distinguished: their heads were bound up in bandages, leaving only their eyes free. As they stepped to the patrol wagon, a policeman hit one of them on the head with his club, at the same time pushing the other prisoner violently into the wagon. They fell over each other, one of them shrieking with pain. I got in next, then turned to the officer. "You brute," I said, "how dare you beat that helpless fellow?" The next thing I knew, I was sent reeling to the floor. He had landed his fist on my jaw, knocking out a tooth and covering my face with blood. Then he pulled me up, shoved me into the seat, and yelled: "Another word from you, you damned anarchist, and I'll break every bone in your body!"

I arrived at the office of the county jail with my waist and skirt covered with blood, my face aching fearfully. No one showed the slightest interest or bothered to ask how I came to be in such a battered condition. They did not even give me water to wash up. For two hours I was kept in a room in the middle of which stood a long table. Finally a woman arrived who informed me that I would have to be searched. "All right, go ahead," I said. "Strip and get on the table," she ordered. I had been repeatedly searched, but I had never before been offered such an insult. "You'll have to kill me first, or get your keepers to put me on the table by force," I declared; "you'll never get me to do it otherwise." She hurried out, and I remained alone. After a long wait another woman came in and led me upstairs, where the matron of the tier took charge of me. She was the first to inquire what was the matter with me. After assigning me to a cell she brought a hot-water bottle and suggested that I lie down and get some rest.

The following afternoon Katherine Leckie visited me. I was taken into a room provided with a double wire screen. It was semi-dark, but as soon as Katherine saw me, she cried: " What on God's earth has happened to you? Your face is all twisted! " No mirror, not even of the smallest size, being allowed in the jail, I was not aware how I looked, though my eyes and lips felt queer to the touch. I told Katherine of my encounter with the policeman's fist. She left swearing vengeance and promising to return after seeing Chief O'Neill. Towards evening she came back to let me know that the Chief had assured her the officer would be punished if I would identify him among the guards of the transport. I refused. I had hardly looked at the man's face and I was not sure I could recognize him. Moreover, I told Katherine, much to her disappointment, that the dismissal of the officer would not restore my tooth; neither would it do away with police brutality. " It is the system I am fighting, my dear Katherine, not the particular offender," I said. But she was not convinced; she wanted something done to arouse popular indignation against such savagery. " Dismissing wouldn't be enough," she persisted; " he should be tried for assault."

Poor Katherine was not aware that I knew she could do nothing. She was not even in a position to speak through her own paper: her story about the third degree had been suppressed. She promptly replied by resigning; she would no longer be connected with such a cowardly journal, she had told the editor. Yet not a word had she breathed to me of her trouble. I learned the story from a reporter of another Chicago daily.

One evening, while engrossed in a book, I was surprised by several detectives and reporters. " The President has just died," they announced. " How do you feel about it? Aren't you sorry? " " Is it possible," I asked, " that in the entire United States only the President passed away on this day? Surely many others have also died at the same time, perhaps in poverty and destitution, leaving helpless dependents behind. Why do you expect me to feel more regret over the death of McKinley than of the rest? "

The pencils went flying. " My compassion has always been with

the living," I continued; "the dead no longer need it. No doubt that
is the reason why you all feel so sympathetic to the dead. You know
that you'll never be called upon to make good your protestations."
" Damned good copy," a young reporter exclaimed, " but I think
you're crazy."

I was glad when they left. My thoughts were with the boy in Buffalo, whose fate was now sealed. What tortures of mind and body were
still to be his before he would be allowed to breathe his last! How
would he meet the supreme moment? There was something strong
and determined about his eyes, emphasized by his very sensitive face.
I had been struck by his eyes on first seeing him at my lecture in Cleveland. Was the idea of his act already with him then or had some particular thing happened since that compelled his deed? What could
it have been? " I did it for the people," he had said. I paced my cell
trying to analyse the probable motives that had decided the youth in
his purpose.

Suddenly a thought flitted through my mind — that notice by Isaak
in *Free Society*! — the charge of " spy " against Nieman because he
had " asked suspicious questions and tried to get into the anarchist
ranks." I had written Isaak at the time, demanding proofs for the
outrageous accusation. As a result of my protest *Free Society* had
contained a retraction to the effect that a mistake had been made. It
had relieved me and I had given the matter no further thought. Now
the whole situation appeared in a new light, clear and terrible. Czolgosz must have read the charge; it must have hurt him to the quick to
be so cruelly misjudged by the very people to whom he had come for
inspiration. I recalled his eagerness to secure the right kind of books.
It was apparent that he had sought in anarchism a solution of the
wrongs he saw everywhere about him. No doubt it was that which had
induced him to call on me and later on the Isaaks. Instead of finding
help the poor youth saw himself attacked. Was it that experience,
fearfully wounding his spirit, that had led to his act? There must also
have been other causes, but perhaps his great urge had been to prove
that he was sincere, that he felt with the oppressed, that he was no spy.

But why had he chosen the President rather than some more direct
representative of the system of economic oppression and misery?
Was it because he saw in McKinley the willing tool of Wall Street and
of the new American imperialism that flowered under his administration? One of its first steps had been the annexation of the Philippines,

an act of treachery to the people whom America had pledged to set free during the Spanish War. McKinley also typified a hostile and reactionary attitude to labour: he had repeatedly sided with the masters by sending troops into strike regions. All these circumstances, I felt, must have exerted a decisive influence upon the impressionable Leon, finally crystallizing in his act of violence.

Throughout the night thoughts of the unfortunate boy kept crowding in my mind. In vain I sought to divest myself of the harassing reflections by reading. The dawning day still found me pacing my cell, Leon's beautiful face, pale and haunted, before me.

Again I was taken to court for a hearing and again the Buffalo authorities failed to produce evidence to connect me with Czolgosz's act. The Buffalo representative and the Chicago judge sitting on the case kept up a verbal fight for two hours, at the end of which Buffalo was robbed of its prey. I was set free.

Ever since my arrest the press of the country had been continually denouncing me as the instigator of Czolgosz's act, but after my discharge the newspapers published only a few lines in an inconspicuous corner to the effect that " after a month's detention Emma Goldman was found not to have been in complicity with the assassin of President McKinley."

Upon my release I was met by Max, Hippolyte, and other friends, with whom I went to the Isaak home. The charges against the comrades arrested in the Chicago raids had also been dismissed. Everyone was in high spirits over my escape from what they had all believed to be a fatal situation. " We can be grateful to whatever gods watch over you, Emma," said Isaak, " that you were arrested here and not in New York." " The gods in this case must have been Chief of Police O'Neill," I said laughingly. " Chief O'Neill! " my friends exclaimed; " what did he have to do with it? " I told them about my interview with him and his promise of help. Jonathan Crane, a journalist friend of ours present, broke out into uproarious laughter. " You are more naïve than I should have expected, Emma Goldman," he said; " it wasn't you O'Neill cared a damn about! it was his own schemes. Being on the *Tribune,* I happen to know the inside story of the feud in the police department." Crane then related the efforts of Chief O'Neill to put several captains in the penitentiary for perjury and bribery. " Nothing could have come more opportunely for those blackguards than the cry of anarchy," he explained; "they seized upon it as the police did in 1887; it was their chance to pose as saviours of the country and incidentally to whitewash themselves. But it wasn't to O'Neill's interest to let those birds pose as heroes and get back into the department. That's why he worked for you. He's a shrewd Irishman. Just the same, we may be glad that the quarrel brought us back our Emma."

I asked my friends their opinion as to how the idea of connecting my name with Czolgosz had originated. "I refuse to believe that the boy made any kind of a confession or involved me in any way," I stated; "I cannot think that he was capable of inventing something which he must have known might mean my death. I'm convinced that no one with such a frank face could be so craven. It must have come from some other source."

"It did!" Hippolyte declared emphatically. "The whole dastardly story was started by a *Daily News* reporter who used to hang round here pretending to sympathize with our ideas. Late in the afternoon of September 6 he came to the house. He wanted to know all about a certain Czolgosz or Nieman. Had we associated with him? Was he an anarchist? And so forth. Well, you know what I think of reporters — I wouldn't give him any information. But unfortunately Isaak did."

"What was there to hide?" Isaak interrupted. "Everybody about here knew that we had met the man through Emma, and that he used to visit us. Besides, how was I to know that the reporter was going to fabricate such a lying story?"

I urged the Chicago comrades to consider what could be done for the boy in the Buffalo jail. We could not save his life, but we could at least try to explain his act to the world and we should attempt to communicate with him, so that he might feel that he was not forsaken by us. Max doubted the possibility of reaching Czolgosz. He had received a note from a comrade in Buffalo informing him that no one was permitted to see Leon. I suggested that we secure an attorney. Without legal aid Czolgosz would be gagged and railroaded, as Sasha had been. Isaak advised that a lawyer be engaged in the State of New York, and I decided to leave immediately for the East. My friends argued that it would be folly to do so; I should surely be arrested the moment I reached the city, and turned over to Buffalo, my fate sealed. But it was unthinkable to me to leave Czolgosz to his doom without making an effort in his behalf. No considerations of personal safety should influence us in the matter, I told my friends, adding that I would remain in Chicago for the public meeting that must be organized to explain our attitude to Czolgosz and his *Attentat*.

On the evening of the meeting one could not get within a block of Brand's Hall, where it was to be held. Strong detachments of police were dispersing the people by force. We tried to hire another hall, but the police had terrorized the hall-keepers. Our efforts to hold a meeting being frustrated, I resolved to state my position in *Free Society*.

"Leon Czolgosz and other men of his type," I wrote in my article, entitled: "The Tragedy of Buffalo," "far from being depraved creatures of low instincts are in reality supersensitive beings unable to bear up under too great social stress. They are driven to some violent expression, even at the sacrifice of their own lives, because they cannot supinely witness the misery and suffering of their fellows. The blame for such acts must be laid at the door of those who are responsible for the injustice and inhumanity which dominate the world." After pointing out the social causes for such acts as that of Czolgosz, I concluded: "As I write, my thoughts wander to the young man with the girlish face about to be put to death, pacing his cell, followed by cruel eyes:

> Who watch him when he tries to weep
> And when he tries to pray,
> Who watch him lest himself should rob
> The prison of its prey.

My heart goes out to him in deep sympathy, as it goes out to all the victims of oppression and misery, to the martyrs past and future that die, the forerunners of a better and nobler life." I turned the article over to Isaak, who promised to have it set up at once.

The police and the press were continuing their hunt for anarchists throughout the country. Meetings were broken up and innocent people arrested. In various places persons suspected of being anarchists were subjected to violence. In Pittsburgh our good friend Harry Gordon was dragged out into the street and nearly lynched. A rope already around his neck, he was saved at the last moment by some bystanders who were touched by the pleading of Mrs. Gordon and her two children. In New York the office of the *Freie Arbeiter Stimme* was attacked by a mob, the furniture demolished, and the type destroyed. In no case did the police interfere with the doings of the patriotic ruffians. Johann Most was arrested for an article in the *Freiheit* reproducing an essay on political violence by Karl Heinzen, the famous '48 revolutionist, then dead many years. Most was out on bail awaiting his trial. The German comrades in Chicago arranged an affair to raise funds for his defence and invited me to speak. Our feud of 1892 was a matter of the past to me. Most was again in the clutches of the police, in danger of being sent to Blackwell's Island, and I gladly consented to do all I could for him.

Returning to the Isaak home after the meeting, I found the proofs of my article. Looking them over, I was surprised by a paragraph that changed the entire meaning of my statement. It was, I was sure, no other than Isaak, the editor, who was responsible for the change. I confronted him, demanding an explanation. He readily admitted that he had written the little paragraph, " to tone down the article," he explained, " in order to save *Free Society*." " And incidentally your skin! " I retorted hotly. " For years you've been denouncing people as cowards who could not meet a dangerous situation. Now that you yourself are face to face with one, you draw in your horns. At least you should have asked my permission to make the change."

It required a long discussion to alter Isaak's attitude. He saw that my view was sustained by the rest of the group — his son Abe, Hippolyte, and several others — whereupon he declared that he renounced all responsibility in the matter. My article finally appeared in its original form. Nothing happened to *Free Society*. But my faith in Isaak was shaken.

On my way back to New York I stopped off in Rochester. Arriving in the evening, I walked to Helena's place in order to avoid recognition. A policeman was stationed at the house, but he did not know me. Everyone gasped when I made my appearance. " How did you get by? " Helena cried; " didn't you see the officer at the door? " " Indeed I saw him, but he evidently didn't see me," I laughed. " Don't you folks worry about any policeman; better give me a bath," I cried lightly. My nonchalance dispelled the family's nervous tension. Everybody laughed and Helena clung to me in unchanged love.

All through my incarceration my family had been very devoted to me. They had sent me telegrams and letters, offering money for my defence and any other help I might need. Not a word had they written about the persecution they had been subjected to on my account. They had been pestered to distraction by reporters and kept under surveillance by the authorities. My father had been ostracized by his neighbours and had lost many customers at his little furniture store. At the same time he had also been excommunicated from the synagogue. My sister Lena, though in poor health, had also been given no peace. She had been terrorized by the police ordering Stella to appear at headquarters, where they had kept the child the whole day, plying her with questions about her aunt Emma Goldman. Stella had bravely refused to answer, defiantly proclaiming her pride and faith in her *Tante* Emma. Her courage, combined with her youth and beauty, had won general admiration, Helena said.

Even more cruel had been the teachers and pupils of the public school. " Your aunt Emma Goldman is a murderess," they had taunted our children. School was turned into a hideous nightmare for them. My nephews Saxe and Harry had suffered most. Harry's grief over the violent death of his hero was more real than with most of the adults in the country. He deeply felt the disgrace that his own mother's sister should be charged with responsibility for it. Worse yet, his schoolmates denounced him as an anarchist and criminal. The persecution aggravated his misery and completely alienated him from me. Saxe's unhappiness, on the other hand, resulted from his strong feeling of loyalty to me. His mother and Aunt Helena loved Emma and they had told him she was innocent. They must know better than his schoolmates. Their boisterous aggressiveness had always repelled him; now more than ever he avoided them. My unexpected appearance and outwitting the officer on guard must have quickened Saxe's imagination and increased his admiration for me. His flushed face and shining eyes were eloquent of his emotion. His hovering near me all evening said more than his quivering lips could tell.

It was balm to my bruised spirit to find such a haven of love and peace in the circle of my family. Even my sister Lena, who had often in the past disapproved of my life, now showed warmest affection. Brother Herman and his gentle wife lavished attentions upon me. The imminent danger I had faced, which still threatened me, had served to establish a bond between my family and me stronger than we had ever felt before. I wanted to prolong my happy stay in Rochester to recuperate from the ordeal of Chicago. But the thought of Czolgosz tormented me. I knew that in New York I could make some effort in his behalf.

At the Grand Central Station I was met by Yegor and the two chums who had spent that wonderful month with us in Rochester. Yegor looked distressed; he had tried hard to find a place for me, but had failed. No one would rent even a furnished room to Emma Goldman. Our friends who happened to have a vacant room would not run the risk of my staying with them for fear of being evicted. One of the boys offered to let me have his room for a few nights. " No need to worry," I comforted Yegor; " I am taken care of for the present, and in the meantime I will find an apartment."

After a long search for a flat I realized that my brother had not been exaggerating. No one would have me. I went to see a young prostitute I had once nursed. " Sure, kid, stay right here! " she welcomed me. " I'm tickled to death to have you. I'll bunk with a girl friend for a while."

The encouraging telegram I had received in Chicago from Ed had been followed by a number of letters assuring me that I could count on him for whatever I might need: money, help and advice, and, above all, his friendship. It was good to know that Ed remained so staunch. When we met upon my return to New York, he offered me the use of his apartment while he and his family would be staying with friends. " You won't find much changed in my place," he remarked; " all your things are intact in the room that is my sanctum, where I often dream of our life together." I thanked him, but I could not accept his generous proposal. He was too tactful to press the matter, except to inform me that his firm owed me several hundred dollars in commissions.

" I need the money badly," I confided to Ed, " to send somebody to Buffalo to see Czolgosz. Possibly something can be done for him. We also ought to organize a mass meeting at once." He stared at me in bewilderment. " My dear," he said, shaking his head, " you are evidently not aware of the panic in the city. No hall in New York can be had and no one except yourself would be willing to speak for Czolgosz." " But no one is expected to eulogize his act! " I argued; " surely there must be a few people in the radical ranks who are capable of sympathy for a doomed human being." " Capable perhaps," he said doubtfully, " but not brave enough to voice it at this time." " You may be right," I admitted, " but I intend to make sure of it."

A trusted person was dispatched to Buffalo, but he soon returned without having been able to visit Czolgosz. He reported that no one was permitted to see him. A sympathetic guard had disclosed to our messenger that Leon had repeatedly been beaten into unconsciousness. His physical appearance was such that no outsider was admitted, and for the same reason he could not be taken to court. My friend further reported that, notwithstanding all the torture, Czolgosz had made no confession whatever and had involved no one in his act. A note had been sent in to Leon through the friendly guard.

I learned that an effort had been made in Buffalo to secure an attorney for Czolgosz, but no one would accept his defence. That made me even more determined to raise my voice in behalf of the poor unfortunate, denied and forsaken by everyone. Before long, however, I became convinced that Ed had been right. No one among the English-speaking radical groups could be induced to participate in a meeting to discuss the act of Leon Czolgosz. Many were willing to protest against my arrest, to condemn the third degree and the treatment I had received. But they would have nothing to do with the Buffalo case. Czolgosz was not an anarchist, his deed had done the movement an irreparable injury, our American comrades insisted. Most of the Jewish anarchists, even, expressed similar views. Yanofsky, editor of the *Freie Arbeiter Stimme,* went still further. He kept up a campaign against Czolgosz, also denouncing me as an irresponsible person and declaring that he would never again speak from the same platform with me. The only ones who had not lost their heads were of the Latin groups, the Italian, Spanish, and French anarchists. Their publications had reprinted my article on Czolgosz that had appeared in *Free Society*. They wrote sympathetically of Leon, interpreting his act as a direct result of the increasing imperialism and reaction in this country. The Latin comrades were anxious to help with anything I might suggest, and it was a great comfort to know that at least some anarchists had preserved their judgment and courage in the madhouse of fury and cowardice. Unfortunately the foreign groups could not reach the American public.

In desperation I clung to the hope that by perseverance and appeals I should be able to rally some public-spirited Americans to express ordinary human sympathy for Leon Czolgosz, even if they felt that they must repudiate his act. Every day brought more disappointment and heart-ache. I was compelled to face the fact that I had been fighting against an epidemic of abject fear that could not be overcome.

The tragedy in Buffalo was nearing its end. Leon Czolgosz, still ill from the maltreatment he had endured, his face disfigured and head bandaged, was supported in court by two policemen. In its all-embracing justice and mercy the Buffalo court had assigned two lawyers to his defence. What if they did declare publicly that they were sorry to have to plead the case of such a depraved criminal as the assassin of " our beloved " President! They would do their duty just the same! They would see to it that the rights of the defendant were protected in court.

The last act was staged in Auburn Prison. It was early dawn, October 29, 1901. The condemned man sat strapped to the electric chair. The executioner stood with his hand on the switch, awaiting the signal. A warden, impelled by Christian mercy, makes a last effort to save the sinner's soul, to induce him to confess. Tenderly he says: " Leon, my boy, why do you shield that bad woman, Emma Goldman? She is not your friend. She has denounced you as a loafer, too lazy to work. She said you had always begged money from her. Emma Goldman has betrayed you, Leon. Why should you shield her? "

Breathless silence, seconds of endless time. It fills the death chamber, creeps into the hearts of the spectators. At last a muffled sound, an almost inaudible voice from under the black mask.

" It doesn't matter what Emma Goldman has said about me. She had nothing to do with my act. I did it alone. I did it for the American people."

A silence more terrible than the first. A sizzling sound — the smell of burnt flesh — a final agonized twitch of life.

CHAPTER XXV

IT WAS BITTER HARD TO FACE LIFE ANEW. IN THE STRESS OF THE past weeks I had forgotten that I should again have to take up the struggle for existence. It was doubly imperative; I needed forgetfulness. Our movement had lost its appeal for me; many of its adherents filled me with loathing. They had been flaunting anarchism like a red cloth before a bull, but they ran to cover at his first charge. I could no longer work with them. Still more harrowing was the gnawing doubt of the values I had so fervently believed in. No, I could not continue in the movement. I must first take stock of my own self. Intensive work in my profession, I felt, was the only refuge. It would fill the void and make me forget.

I had lost my identity; I had assumed a fictitious name, for no landlord was willing to lodge me, and most of my erstwhile comrades and friends proved equally brave. The situation revived memories of 1892, of the nights spent in Tompkins Square, or riding in horsecars to Harlem and back to the Battery, and later among the girls in the house on Fourth Street. I had endured that life rather than make the concession of changing my name. It was weak and inconsistent, I had then thought, to give in to popular prejudices. Some of those who now denied Czolgosz had praised me for joining the homeless brigade rather than compromise. All this had no meaning for me any longer. The struggle and disappointment of the past twelve years had taught me that consistency is only skin-deep in most people. As if it mattered what name you took, as long as you kept your integrity. Indeed, I would take another name, the most common and inoffensive I could think of. I became Miss E. G. Smith.

I met with no further objections from landlords. I rented a flat on First Street; Yegor and his chum Dan moved in with me, our furniture purchased on the instalment plan. Thereupon I went out to call on my physicians, to apprise them of the fact that henceforth they could recommend me as E. G. Smith.

By the end of the day's tramp I gained one more proof that I had become a pariah. Several doctors I visited, men who had known me for years and who had always been entirely satisfied with my work as a nurse, were indignant that I had dared to call on them. Did I want to get their names in the papers or cause them trouble with the police? I was being shadowed by the authorities; how could I expect them to recommend me? Dr. White was more humane. He had never credited the stories connecting me with Czolgosz, he assured me; he was certain that I was incapable of murder. Still he could not employ me in his office. "Smith is an ordinary enough name," he said, "but how long do you suppose it will be before you are discovered? I cannot take the chance; it would mean my ruin." He was anxious, however, to help me in some other manner, perhaps with money. I thanked him and went my way.

I visited Dr. Julius Hoffmann and Dr. Solotaroff. They at least had not changed towards me and they were eager to recommend cases. Unfortunately my good friend Solotaroff had fallen ill with an affection of the heart and was compelled to give up his outside practice. His office patients rarely needed nurses, but he promised to speak to other East Side doctors. Dear, faithful comrade, since I had climbed those six flights of stairs to his flat on my first arrival in New York twelve years previously, he had never failed me once.

It was evident my prospects were not very bright. I knew it involved a desperate struggle to win new ground, but I was determined to start all over again. I would not submit passively to the forces that were trying to crush me. "I must, I will, go on, for the sake of Sasha and of my brother, who need me," I told myself.

Sasha! I had not heard from him for nearly two months, and I also had been unable to write him. While under arrest, I could not express myself freely, and the last month had been too dreary and depressing. I was sure that of all people my dear Sasha would understand the social meaning of the Buffalo shot, and that he would appreciate the boy's integrity. Dear Sasha! Since the unexpected commutation of his prison term his spirit had grown buoyant. "Only five years more," he had written in his last letter; "just think, dear friend, only five years more!" To see him free at last, resurrected; what were all my hardships compared with that moment? In that hope I plodded on.

Occasionally I was called to a case; at other times I had orders for dresses.

I seldom went out. We could not afford music or theatres, and I dreaded to appear at public meetings. The last one, shortly after my return from Chicago, had nearly ended in a riot. I had gone to hear my old friend Ernest Crosby speak at the Manhattan Liberal Club. I had attended its weekly meetings since 1894, often participated in the discussions, and was known by everybody. The moment I entered the hall this time, I sensed an atmosphere of antagonism. Except for Crosby and several others, the audience seemed to resent my presence. At the close of the lecture, as the people were filing out of the hall, a man called out: " Emma Goldman, you are a murderess, and fifty million people know it!" In a moment I found myself surrounded by an excited crowd, crying: " You're a murderess! " Some voices were raised in my defence, but they were drowned in the general clamour. A clash was imminent. I got up on a chair and shouted: " You say fifty million people know that Emma Goldman is a murderess. The population of the United States being considerably more than that, there must be a great number willing to inform themselves before making irresponsible accusations. It is a tragedy to have a fool in the family, but to have fifty million maniacs in a nation is a calamity indeed. As good Americans you should refuse to swell their number."

Someone laughed, others followed, and soon the audience was in good humour again. But I left sick with disgust, determined to stay away from meetings, even from people. I saw only the few friends that came to our house, and occasionally I visited Justus.

Justus had been opposed to my coming to New York. Even now he feared for my safety; I was in danger of being kidnapped and taken to Buffalo, he thought, and he strongly urged a body-guard for me. It was good to see him so concerned, and I sought to humour him. His old friends, among them Ed and Claus, often gathered in his place to cheer him. We all knew that Death was daily creeping nearer and that before long he would claim his toll.

Early one morning Ed called to tell me that the end had come. I was asked to be one of the speakers at the funeral of Justus, but I felt compelled to refuse. I knew I could not express in words what he had meant in my life. Champion of freedom, sponsor of labour's cause, pleader for joy in life, Justus had a surpassing capacity for friendship, a veritable genius for responding generously and beautifully. He had always been reticent about his own great life and work. For me to sing his praises in the market-place would have been a breach of faith. The vast throng of people from every rank that followed the remains to the crematorium testified to the deep affection and high regard Justus had inspired in those who knew him.

The loss of Justus increased the dullness of my life. The small circle of friends who used to meet at his place was now scattered; more and more I withdrew into my own four walls. The struggle for the necessities of existence became more severe. Solotaroff, ill again, could not help me with employment; Dr. Hoffmann was out of the city. I was again compelled to take piece-work from the factory. I had advanced in the trade; I was sewing gaudy silk morning gowns now. The many ruffles, ribbons, and laces required painstaking effort, affecting my lacerated nerves until I felt like screaming. The one bright spot in the drabness that was now my life was my dear brother and his chum Dan.

Yegor had brought him to me when I was still living in my little room on Clinton Street. He had attracted me from the first, and I knew that he was also strongly drawn to me. I was thirty-two, while he only nineteen, naïve and unspoiled. He had laughed at my misgivings over the difference in our ages; he did not care for young girls, he said; they were generally stupid and could give him nothing. I was younger than they, he thought, and much wiser. He wanted me more than anyone else.

His pleading voice had been like music to me; yet I had struggled against it. One of my reasons for going on tour in May had been the hope of escaping my growing affection for the boy. In July, when we all met in Rochester, the storm I had repressed so long swept over me and engulfed us both. Then came the Buffalo tragedy and the horrors in its wake. They stifled the mainsprings of my being. Love seemed a farce in a world of hate. Since we had moved into our little flat, we were thrown together a great deal, and love again raised its insistent voice. I responded. It made me forget the other calls — of my ideal, my faith, my work. The thought of a lecture or meeting had become repugnant to me. Even concerts and theatres had lost their attraction because of my fear, grown almost to an obsession, of meeting people or being recognized. Dejection was upon me, the feeling that my existence had lost its meaning and was bereft of content.

Life dragged on with its daily cares and worries. By far the greatest of them was Sasha's reported condition. Friends in Pittsburgh had written that he was again being persecuted by the prison authorities, and that his health was breaking down. At last, on December 31, a letter arrived from him. No greater New Year's gift could have come to me. Yegor knew that I liked to be alone on such occasions, and he thoughtfully tiptoed out of the room.

I pressed my lips to the precious envelope, opening it with trembling fingers. It was a long *sub rosa* letter, dated December 20 and written on several slips of paper in the very small script Sasha had acquired, each word standing out clear and distinct.

" I know how your visit and my strange behaviour must have affected you," he wrote. " The sight of your face after all these years completely unnerved me. I could not think, I could not speak. It was as if all my dreams of freedom, the whole world of the living, were concentrated in the shiny little trinket that was dangling from your watch-chain. I couldn't take my eyes off it, I couldn't keep my hand from playing with it. It absorbed my whole being. And all the time I felt how nervous you were at my silence, and I couldn't utter a word."

The frightful months since my visit to Sasha had obscured the poignancy of my disappointment at that time. His lines again revived it. But his letter showed how closely he had followed the events. " If the press mirrored the sentiments of the people," he continued, " the nation must have suddenly relapsed into cannibalism. There were moments when I was in mortal dread for your very life, and for the safety of the other arrested comrades. . . . Your attitude of proud self-respect and your admirable self-control contributed much to the fortunate outcome. I was especially moved by your remark that you would faithfully nurse the wounded man, if he required your services, but that the poor boy, condemned and deserted by all, needed and deserved your sympathy and aid more than the President. More strikingly than your letters, that remark discovered to me the great change wrought in us by the ripening years. Yes, in us, in both, for my heart echoed your beautiful sentiment. How impossible such a thought would have been to us in the days of a decade ago! We should have considered it treason to the spirit of revolution; it would have outraged all our traditions even to admit the humanity of an official representative of capitalism. Is it not significant that we two — you living in the very heart of anarchist thought and activity, and I in the atmosphere of absolute suppression and isolation — should have arrived at the same evolutionary point after ten years of divergent paths? "

The dear, faithful pal — how big and brave it was of him so frankly to admit the change! As I read on I grew even more astounded at the amount of knowledge Sasha had acquired since his imprisonment. Works of science, philosophy, economics, even metaphysics — he had evidently read a great many of them, critically studied and digested them. His letter stirred a hundred memories of the past, of our common life, our love, our work. I was lost in recollections; time and space disappeared; the intervening years became blotted out, and I relived the past. My hands caressed the letter, my eyes dreamily wandering over the lines. Then the word "Leon" fastened my gaze, and I continued to read:

"I have read of the beautiful personality of the youth, of his inability to adapt himself to brutal conditions, and of the rebellion of his soul. It throws a significant light upon the causes of the *Attentat*. Indeed, it is at once the greatest tragedy of martyrdom and the most terrible indictment of society that it forces the noblest men and women to shed human blood, though their souls shrink from it. The more imperative it is that drastic methods of this character be resorted to only as a last extremity. To prove of value they must be motived by social rather than individual necessity and be aimed against a direct and immediate enemy of the people. The significance of such a deed is understood by the popular mind, and in that alone lies the propagandistic, educational import of an *Attentat,* except if it is exclusively an act of terrorism."

The letter dropped from my hand. What could Sasha mean? Did he imply that McKinley was not "an immediate enemy of the people"? Not a subject for an *Attentat* of "propagandistic, educational import"? I was bewildered. Had I read right? There was still another passage: "I do not believe that Leon's deed was terroristic, and I doubt whether it was educational, because the social necessity for its performance was not manifest. That you may not misunderstand, I repeat: as an expression of personal revolt it was inevitable, and in itself an indictment of existing conditions. But the background of social necessity was lacking, and therefore the value of the act was to a great extent nullified."

The letter fell to the floor, leaving me in a daze. A strange, dry voice screamed out: "Yegor! Yegor!"

My brother ran in. "What has happened, dear? You're all trembling. What's the matter?" he cried in alarm. "The letter!" I whispered hoarsely. "Read it; tell me if I've gone mad."

"A beautiful letter," I heard him say, "a human document, though Sasha does not see social necessity in Czolgosz's act."

"But how can Sasha," I cried in desperation, "he of all people in the world — himself misunderstood and repudiated by the very workers he had wanted to help — how can *he* misunderstand so?"

Yegor tried to soothe me, to explain what Sasha had meant by "the necessary social background." Picking up another slip of the letter, he began reading to me:

"The scheme of political subjection is subtle in America. Though McKinley was the chief representative of our modern slavery, he could not be considered in the light of a direct and immediate enemy of the people. In an absolutism the autocrat is visible and tangible. The real despotism of republican institutions is far deeper, more insidious, because it rests on the popular delusion of self-government and independence. That is the source of democratic tyranny, and as such it cannot be reached with a bullet. In modern capitalism economic exploitation rather than political oppression is the real enemy of the people. Politics is but its handmaid. Hence the battle is to be waged in the economic rather than the political field. It is therefore that I regard my own act as far more significant and educational than Leon's. It was directed against a tangible, real oppressor, visualized as such by the people."

Suddenly a thought struck me. Why, Sasha is using the same arguments against Leon that Johann Most had urged against Sasha. Most had proclaimed the futility of individual acts of violence in a country devoid of proletarian consciousness and he had pointed out that the American worker did not understand the motives of such deeds. No less than I had Sasha then considered Most a traitor to our cause as well as towards himself. I had fought Most bitterly for it — Most, who had been my teacher, my great inspiration. And now Sasha, still believing in acts of violence, was denying "social necessity" to Leon's deed.

The farce of it — the cruel, senseless farce! I felt as if I had lost Sasha — I broke down in uncontrollable sobbing.

In the evening Ed came for me. We had agreed several days previously to celebrate the New Year together, but I felt too crushed to go. Yegor pleaded with me, saying it would help to distract me. But I was shaken to the roots. When the New Year came, I lay ill in bed.

Dr. Hoffmann was again treating Mrs. Spenser and I was called to nurse her. The work compelled me to take life up once more. I followed my daily routine almost unconsciously, out of habit, my mind brooding on Sasha. It was peculiar self-deception on his part, I kept on saying to myself, to believe that his act had been more valuable than Leon's. Had the years of solitary confinement and suffering led him to think his act had been better understood by the people than Czolgosz's was? Perhaps it had served him as a prop to lean on during his terrible prison years. It was that, no doubt, that had kept him alive. Yet it seemed incredible that a man of his clarity and judgment should be so blind to the value of Leon's political act.

I wrote Sasha several times pointing out that anarchism does not direct its forces against economic injustices only, but that it includes the political as well. His replies only emphasized the wide difference in our view-points. They increased my misery and made me realize the futility of continuing the discussion. In despair I stopped writing.

After the death of McKinley the campaign against anarchism and its adherents continued with increased venom. The press, the pulpit, and other public mouthpieces were frantically vying with each other in their fury against the common enemy. Most ferocious was Theodore Roosevelt, the new-fledged President of the United States. As Vice-President he succeeded McKinley to the presidential throne. The irony of fate had, by the hand of Czolgosz, paved the way to power for the hero of San Juan. In gratitude for that involuntary service Roosevelt turned savage. His message to Congress, intended largely to strike at anarchism, was in reality a death-blow to social and political freedom in the United States.

Anti-anarchist bills followed each other in quick succession, their congressional sponsors busy inventing new methods for the extermination of anarchists. Senator Hawley evidently did not consider his professional wisdom sufficient to slay the anarchist dragon. He declared publicly that he would give a thousand dollars to get a shot at an anarchist. It was a cheap offer considering the price Czolgosz had paid for his shot.

In my bitterness I felt that the American radicals who had shown the white feather when courage and daring were so needed were mainly responsible for the developments. No wonder the reactionaries so brazenly clamoured for despotic measures. They saw themselves complete masters of the situation in the country, with hardly any organized opposition. The Criminal Anarchy law, rushed through the New York legislature, and a similar statute in New Jersey, helped to strengthen my conviction that our movement in the United States was paying dearly for its inconsistencies.

Signs of an awakening in our ranks gradually began to manifest themselves; voices were being raised against the impending danger to American liberties. But I had the feeling that the psychological moment had been neglected; nothing could be done to stem the tide of reaction. At the same time I could not reconcile myself to the fearful situation. My indignation was roused by the mad pack howling for our lives. Yet I remained benumbed and inert, unable to do anything except torment myself with everlasting whys and wherefors.

In the midst of the harassing situation we were ordered out of our flat, the landlord having somehow learned my identity. With great difficulty we found quarters in the very heart of the ghetto, on Market Street, on the fifth floor of a congested tenement. East Side landlords were used to having every kind of radical as their tenants. Moreover, the new place was cheaper and had the advantage of light rooms. It was fatiguing to climb so many flights of stairs a score of times a day, but it was preferable to having heavy-footed tenants over our heads. Orthodox Jews take Jehovah literally, especially his command to multiply. There was not a family in the house with fewer than five children, and some had eight or ten. Notwithstanding my love for children, I could not have remained long in the flat with the constant tramp of little feet over my head.

My good friend Solotaroff succeeded in inducing several East Side doctors to give me employment. Their patients, Jews and Italians, were mostly from the poorest families, their living-quarters consisting generally of two or three rooms for six or more people. Their incomes averaged about fifteen dollars a week, and the trained nurse was paid four dollars a day. For them nurses were luxuries indulged in only in very serious illness. Nursing under such conditions was not only difficult, but extremely painful. I was pledged to keep up the standard of pay in my profession. I could not give my services for a lower price, and therefore had to find other ways of helping those poor people than by merely taking care of their sick.

I was mostly on night duty because few nurses were willing to take night cases, while I preferred them. The presence of relatives and their constant interference, much talking and weeping, and, above all, their horror of fresh air made day work most trying for me. " You wicked one ! " an old lady once berated me for opening a window in the sick-room; " do you want to kill my child? " At night I had a free hand to give my patients the attention they needed. With the help of a book and a large pot of coffee, brewed by myself, the night hours passed quickly.

While I never refused any case, whatever the nature of the disease, I preferred to nurse children; they are so pathetically helpless when ill; they respond so gratefully to patience and kindness.

Working under an assumed name brought me many amusing experiences. Once a young socialist I knew called me to nurse his mother. She had double pneumonia, he informed me; she was a large woman and very hard to handle. About to accompany the man, I noticed that he was fidgety, as if he wanted to say something, but did not know how. " What is it? " I asked. His mother had been violently antagonistic to me during the McKinley panic, he confided to me; she had repeatedly said: " If I had that woman, I would soak her in kerosene and burn her alive." He wanted me to know it before taking the case. " It was generous of your mother," I said, " but in her present condition she will hardly be able to carry out her threat." My young socialist was very much impressed.

After three weeks of struggle our patient succeeded in cheating the black-hooded gentleman. She had sufficiently recovered to do without a night nurse, and I was preparing to leave. To my surprise the young socialist announced that his mother wanted the day nurse discharged and me in her place. " Miss Smith is a wonderful nurse," she had told her son. " Do you know who she really is? " he asked: " it's the terrible Emma Goldman! " " My God," his mother cried, " I hope you have not told her what I said about her." The boy admitted that he had. " And she nursed me so fine? Oi, a wonderful nurse! "

With the advent of warm weather the number of my patients decreased. I did not regret it; I was very tired and needed a rest. I wanted more time for reading and leisure to be with Dan, Yegor, and Ed. A sweet and harmonious *camaraderie* with the latter had replaced our turbulent emotions of the past. Our separation had had a profound effect on Ed, made him more tolerant and mellow, more understanding. In his little girl and in much reading he found solace. Our intellectual companionship had never before been so stimulating and enjoyable.

I had everything a human being could wish, yet there was chaos in my mind, an ever-growing craving in my heart. I longed to take up the old struggle, to make my life count for more than a mere round of personal interests. But how get back — where begin again? It seemed to me that I had burned the bridges behind me, that I could never again span the gap that had grown so wide since the dreadful Buffalo days.

One morning the young English anarchist William McQueen called on me. I had met him on my first tour through England in 1895; he had arranged my meetings in Leeds and had been my host. I had also met him several times since his arrival in America. He now came to invite me to speak in Paterson in behalf of the striking silk-weavers. McQueen and the Austrian anarchist Rudolph Grossmann were going to address a mass meeting, and the strikers had asked me to come.

It was the first time since the Czolgosz tragedy that I had been approached by workers, or even by my own comrades. I seized upon the chance as a desert wanderer falls upon a well.

The night before the meeting I had a nightmare, waking up with screams that brought Yegor to my bed. In a cold sweat and shaking in every nerve I related to my brother all I could remember of my oppressive dream.

I dreamed I was in Paterson. The large hall was crowded, myself on the platform. I stepped to the edge and began to speak. I seemed to be carried along on the human sea at my feet. The waves rose and fell in tune with the inflections of my voice. Then they rushed away from me, faster and faster, carrying the people with them. I remained on the platform, all alone, my voice hushed in the silence around me. Alone, yet not quite. Something was stirring, taking form, growing before my eyes. I stood tense, breathlessly waiting. The form was advancing, coming to the very edge of the platform, carrying itself erect, head thrown back, its large eyes gleaming into mine. My voice struggled in my throat, and with a great effort I cried out: " Czolgosz! Leon Czolgosz! "

Fear possessed me that I should not be able to speak at the Paterson meeting. In vain I sought to rid myself of the feeling that when I stepped upon the platform, the face of Czolgosz would emerge from the crowd. I wired McQueen that I could not come.

The next day the papers carried the news of the arrest of McQueen and Grossmann. It horrified me to think that I had allowed a dream to keep me from responding to the call of the strikers. I had permitted myself to be influenced by a spook and had stayed safe at home

while my young comrades were in danger. " Will the Czolgosz tragedy haunt me to the end of my days? " I kept asking myself. The answer came sooner than I anticipated.

" BLOODY RIOTS — WORKERS AND PEASANTS KILLED — STUDENTS
WHIPPED BY COSSACKS. . . ." The press was filled with the events
that were happening in Russia. Once more the struggle against tsarist
autocracy was being brought to the attention of the world. The appalling brutality on one side, the glorious courage and heroism on the
other, tore me out of the lethargy that had paralysed my will since
the Buffalo days. With accusing clarity I realized that I had left the
movement at its most critical moment, had turned my back on our
work when I was most needed, that I had even begun to doubt my
life's faith and ideal. And all because of a handful that had proved to
be base and cowardly.

I tried to excuse my faint-heartedness by the deep concern I felt in
the forsaken boy. My indignation against the weaklings had sprung, I
argued with myself, from my sympathy with Czolgosz. No doubt that
had been the impelling motive for my stand — so impelling, indeed,
that it had even turned me against Sasha because he had failed to see
in Czolgosz's act what had been so clear to me. My bitterness had extended to that dear friend and had made me forget that he was in
prison and still needed me.

Now, however, another thought hammered in my brain, the thought
that there might have been other motives, motives not quite so selfless
as I had made myself and others believe. My own inability to face the
first great issue in my life now made me see that the self-assurance with
which I had always proclaimed that I could stand alone had deserted
me the moment I was called upon to make good. I had not been able
to bear being repudiated and shunned; I could not brave defeat. But,
instead of admitting it to myself at least, I had kept on beating my
wings in blind fury. I had become embittered and had drawn back
within myself.

The qualities I had most admired in the heroes of the past, and also
in Czolgosz, the strength to stand and die alone, had been lacking in
me. Perhaps one needs more courage to live than to die. Dying is of a
moment, but the claims of life are endless — a thousand small and
petty things which tax one's strength and leave one too spent to meet
the testing hour.

I emerged from my tortuous introspection as from a long illness, not yet in possession of my former vigour, but with a determination to try once more to steel my will to meet the exigencies of life, whatever they might be.

My first faltering step after the months of spiritual death was a letter to Sasha.

The news from Russia stirred the East Side radicals into intense activity. Trade-unionists, socialists, and anarchists set aside their political differences, the better to be able to help the victims of the Russian régime. Large meetings were held and funds raised for the sufferers in prison and exile. I took up the work with new-born strength. I stopped nursing in order to devote myself entirely to the needs of Russia. At the same time there was also enough happening in America to tax our utmost energies.

The coal-miners were on strike. Conditions in the coal districts were appalling and aid was urgently needed. The politicians in the labour movement were busy talking for the press and doing little for the strikers. Whatever backbone they had shown in the beginning of the strike caved in when the man with the Big Stick appeared on the scene. President Roosevelt suddenly evinced an interest in the miners. He would help the strikers, he announced, if their representatives would be reasonable and give him a chance to go after the mine-owners. That was manna for the politicians in the unions. They immediately transferred the burden of responsibility to the presidential shoulders of Teddy. No need to worry any more; his official wisdom would find the right solution of vexing problems. Meanwhile the miners and their families were starving and the police browbeating those who came to the coal region to encourage the strikers.

The radical elements refused to be duped by the President's interest, nor did they have greater faith in the sudden change of heart of the employers. They worked steadily to raise funds and keep up the spirit of the men. The heat had grown too oppressive for public meetings, which meant a lull in our efforts. Still we were able to canvass unions, hold picnics, and arrange other affairs to raise money. My return to public activity rejuvenated me and gave me a new interest in life.

I was asked to undertake a lecture tour for the purpose of raising funds for the miners and the victims in Russia. We had reckoned, however, without the authorities in the strike districts. Our people there could secure no halls; on the rare occasions when a landlord was brave enough to rent us his place, the police broke up our gatherings. In several towns, among them Wilkesbarre and McKeesport, I was met by the guardians of the law at the station and turned back. It was finally decided that I should concentrate my efforts in the larger cities of the strike regions. In these I met with no difficulties until I reached Chicago.

My first lecture there dealt with Russia and took place in a crowded West Side hall. As usual the police were present, but they did not interfere. "We believe in freedom of speech," one of the officials told our committee, "so long as Emma Goldman talks on Russia." Fortunately my work for the miners was almost exclusively in the unions, and the police could do nothing there.

My last lecture was to be given at the Chicago Philosophical Society, an organization with a free platform. Their weekly gatherings had always been held in Handel Hall, on which the society had a long lease. The owners of the place had never before objected to either the speakers or their subjects, but on the Sunday scheduled for my talk Handel Hall was barred to the people. The janitor, pale and trembling, declared that detectives had been "to see" him. They had informed him about the Criminal Anarchy Law, which would make him liable to arrest, imprisonment, and a fine if he allowed Emma Goldman to speak. It happened that no such law had been passed in Illinois, but what did that matter? I delivered the proscribed lecture, nevertheless. Another hall-keeper, better versed in his legal rights and not so easily frightened, consented to let me speak on the dangerous subject of the Philosophic Aspects of Anarchism.

My tour was trying and strenuous, made more so by the necessity of speaking surrounded by watch-dogs ready to spring on me at any moment, as well as by being compelled to change halls at a moment's notice. But I welcomed the difficulties. They helped to rekindle my fighting spirit and to convince me that those in power never learn to what extent persecution is the leaven of revolutionary zeal.

I had barely returned home when news came of Kate Austen's death. Kate, the most daring, courageous voice among the women of America! Risen from the depths, she had reached intellectual heights many educated people could not touch. She loved life, and her soul was aflame for the oppressed, the suffering, and the poor. How splendid she had been all through the Buffalo tragedy! Only a month ago she had written, within the shadow of her own death, a glowing tribute to Czolgosz. And now she was gone, and with her one of the truly great personalities in our ranks. Her death was the loss not merely of a comrade, but also of a precious friend. Excepting Emma Lee she was the only woman who had come close to me and who understood the complexities of my being better than I did myself. Her sensitive response had helped me through many hard moments. Now she was dead, and my heart was heavy.

In a hectic life like mine sorrows and joys follow each other so rapidly that they leave no time to dwell too long on either. My grief over Kate's loss was still acute when another shock came. Voltairine de Cleyre was shot and severely wounded by a former pupil of hers. A telegram from Philadelphia informed me that she was in the hospital in a critical condition and suggested that I raise money for her care.

I had seen little of Voltairine since our unfortunate misunderstanding in 1894. I had heard that she was not well and that she had gone to Europe to regain her health. On my last visit in Philadelphia I had been told that she was having a severe struggle to make a living by teaching English to Jewish immigrants and giving music lessons, while at the same time keeping up her activities in the movement. I admired her energy and industry, but I was hurt and repelled by what seemed to me her unreasonable and small attitude toward me. I could not seek her out, nor had she communicated with me in all these years. Her fearless stand during the McKinley hysteria had helped much to increase my respect for her, and her letter in *Free Society* to Senator Hawley, who had said he would give a thousand dollars to have a shot at an anarchist, had made a lasting impression on me. She had sent her address to the senatorial patriot and had written him that she was ready to give him the pleasure to shoot an anarchist free of charge, on the sole condition that he permit her to explain to him the principles of anarchism before he fired.

"We must begin to raise money for Voltairine at once," I said to Ed. I knew she would resent a public appeal in her behalf, and Ed agreed that it was necessary to approach our friends privately on the matter. Solotaroff, first to be advised by us, responded beautifully, even though he was in poor health and his office practice was yielding very little. He suggested that Gordon, Voltairine's former lover, should be seen; he had become a successful physician and he was financially well able to help Voltairine, who had done so much for him. Solotaroff volunteered to speak to Gordon.

The result of our canvass was very encouraging, though we also met with some disagreeable experiences. An East Side friend of Voltairine's declared that he did not believe in " private charity," and there were also others whose sympathies had become blunted by material success. But generous souls made up for the rest, and soon we collected five hundred dollars. Ed went to Philadelphia with the money. Upon his return he reported that two of the bullets had been extracted. The third could not be touched because it was embedded too close to the heart. Voltairine's main concern, Ed told us, was about the boy who had attempted her life and she had already declared that she would not prosecute him.

Max and Millie were visiting New York for Christmas, and the occasion proved an unexpected and joyful treat. Ed had been urging me for some time to permit him to realize his long-cherished dream of dressing me up in " decent clothes." The time had come to carry out his promise, he insisted; I must go with him to the best shops and give my fancy free rein.

I realized as soon as we were in the fashionable emporium that an untrammelled fancy is an expensive thing, and I did not want to bankrupt Ed. "Let's run away quickly," I whispered; "this is no place for us." "Run away? Emma Goldman run away?" Ed teased; "you'll stay long enough to have your measurements taken and leave the rest to me."

On Christmas Eve boxes began to arrive at my apartment: a wonderful coat with a real astrakhan collar, muff, and turban to match. There were also a dress, silk underwear, stockings, and gloves. I felt like Cinderella. Ed beamed when he called and found me all rigged out. "That's the way I have always wanted you to look," he exclaimed; " some day everybody may be able to have beautiful things like these."

At the Hofbrau Haus we found Max and Millie already waiting for us. Millie was also dressed for the occasion, and Max was in fine mettle. He asked whether I had married a Rockefeller or struck a gold-mine. I was entirely too swell for a proletarian like himself, he laughed. " Such duds deserve at least three bottles of *Trabacher*," he cried, forthwith ordering them. We were the merriest party in the place.

Millie preceded Max to Chicago. He lingered on for a few days and we spent the time in long walks, visiting galleries and concerts. On the evening of his departure I accompanied Max to the station. While we stood on the platform, chatting, we were approached by two men who turned out to be detectives. They put us under arrest and took us to the police station, where we were cross-examined and then discharged. "On what grounds were we arrested?" I demanded. "Just on general principles," the desk sergeant answered pleasantly. "Your principles are rotten!" I retorted heatedly. "Go on, now," he roared, "you're Red Emma, ain't you? That's enough."

A letter from Solotaroff informed me that Gordon had refused to aid Voltairine. The latter had drudged for years to help him through college, and now that she was ill, he had not even a kind word for her. My intuition about him had been correct. We agreed that she should not be told of the cruel indifference of the man who had meant so much to her.

Voltairine not only refused to prosecute the youth who had shot her, but even appealed to our press to aid his defence. "He is sick, poor, and friendless," she wrote; "he is in need of kindness, not prison." In a letter to the authorities she pointed out that the boy had been jobless for a long time and that as a result of worry he suffered from delusions. But the law had to have its pound of flesh: the youth was found guilty and given a sentence of six years and nine months.

The effect of the verdict on Voltairine caused a very serious relapse that kept us in anxious suspense for weeks. Finally she was declared out of danger and able to leave the hospital.

The Philadelphia papers furnished an amusing side to the tragic incident. Like the rest of the American press they had for years been filled with invectives against anarchism and anarchists. "Fiends incarnate — champions of murder and destruction — cowards" were among the most delicate epithets applied to us. But when Voltairine refused to prosecute her assailant and pleaded in his behalf, the same editors wrote that "anarchism is really the doctrine of the Nazarene, the gospel of forgiveness."

CHAPTER XXVI

THE ANTI-ANARCHIST IMMIGRATION LAW WAS AT LAST SMUGGLED through Congress, and thereafter no person disbelieving in organized government was to be permitted to enter the United States. Under its provisions men like Tolstoy, Kropotkin, Spencer, or Edward Carpenter could be excluded from the hospitable shores of America. Too late did the lukewarm liberals realize the peril of this law to advanced thought. Had they opposed in a concerted manner the activities of the reactionary element, the statute might not have been passed. The immediate result of this new assault on American liberties, however, was a very decided change of attitude towards anarchists. I myself now ceased to be considered anathema; on the contrary, the very people who had been hostile to me began to seek me out. Various lecture forums, like the Manhattan Liberal Club, the Brooklyn Philosophical Society, and other American organizations invited me to speak. I accepted gladly because of the opportunity I had been wanting for years to reach the native intelligentsia, to enlighten it as to what anarchism really means. At these gatherings I made new friends and met old ones, among them Ernest Crosby, Leonard D. Abbott, and Theodore Schroeder.

At the Sunrise Club I came to know many persons of advanced ideas. Among the most interesting were Elizabeth and Alexis Ferm, John and Abby Coryell. The Ferms were the first Americans I met whose ideas on education were akin to mine; but while I merely advocated the need of a new approach to the child, the Ferms translated their ideas into practice. In the Playhouse, as their school was called, the children of the neighbourhood were bound by neither rules nor text-books. They were free to go or come and to learn from observation and experience. I knew no one else who so well understood child psychology as Elizabeth and who was so capable of bringing out the best in the young. She and Alexis considered themselves single-taxers, but in reality they were anarchists in their views and lives. It was a great treat to visit their home, which was also the school, and to witness the beautiful relationship that existed between them and the children.

The Coryells had much of the same quality, John possessing exceptional depth of mind. He impressed me as being more European than American, and indeed he had seen much of the world. As a young man he had been United States consul at Canton, China. Later he had lived in Japan, had travelled extensively, and had associated with people of various countries and races. It had served to give him a wider outlook on life and a deeper understanding of human beings. John had considerable talent as a writer; he was the author of the original Nick Carter stories, and he had earned a name and money under the pseudonym of Bertha M. Clay. He was also a frequent contributor to the *Physical Culture* magazine, because of his interest in health matters and because it gave him his first chance to express himself freely on the subjects he had at heart. He was one of the most generous persons I had ever met. His writings had brought him a fortune, of which he had kept almost nothing, having given lavishly to those in need. His greatest charm lay in his rich sense of humour, no less incisive because of his polished manner. The Coryells and the Ferms became my dearest American friends.

I also saw a great deal of Hugh O. Pentecost. He had undergone many changes since I had first met him during my trial in 1893. He did not impress me as a strong character, but he was among the most brilliant speakers in New York. He lectured Sunday mornings on social topics, his eloquence attracting large audiences. Pentecost was a frequent visitor at my apartment, where he used to " feel natural," as he often said. His wife, a handsome, middle-class woman, keenly disliked her husband's poor friends, and her eyes were upon the influential subscribers to his lectures.

Once I had arranged a little party in my flat, with Pentecost as one of my guests. Shortly before the party I met Mrs. Pentecost and asked her if she would like to come. " Thank you so much," she said, " I shall be delighted; I love slumming." " Isn't it fortunate? " I remarked. " Otherwise you would never meet interesting people." She did not attend the party.

My public life grew colourful. Nursing became less strenuous when several of my " charges " moved out of my apartment and thus reduced my expenses. I could afford to take longer rests between cases. It gave me the opportunity to do much reading that had been neglected for some time. I enjoyed my new experience of living alone. I could go and come without considering others and I did not always find a crowd at home upon my return from a lecture. I knew myself well enough to realize that I was not easy to live with. The dreadful months following the Buffalo tragedy had driven me desperate with the struggle to find my way back to life and work. The timid radicalism of the people on the East Side had made me impatient and intolerant with the striplings who talked about the future, yet did nothing in the present. I enjoyed the boon of retirement and the companionship of a few chosen friends, the dearest among them Ed — no longer jealously watching, possessively demanding every thought and every breath, but giving and receiving free and spontaneous joy.

Often he would visit me weary and depressed. I knew it was the growing friction in his home; not that he had ever spoken about it, but now and then a chance remark disclosed to me that he was not happy. Once, in the course of a conversation, he remarked: " In prison I used to take solitary confinement rather than share my cell with anybody. The constant jabber of a cell-mate used to drive me frantic. Now I have to listen to incessant talk, and there is no solitary for me to get away to." On another occasion he gave vent to irony regarding the girls and women that pretend to hold advanced ideas until they have safely captured their man and then fiercely turn against those ideas for fear of losing their provider. To cheer him I would turn the talk into other channels, or ask about his daughter. At once his face would light up and his depression lift. One day he brought me a picture of the little one. I had never seen such a striking resemblance. I was so moved by the beautiful face of the child that unthinkingly I cried out: " Why don't you ever bring her to see me? " " Why? " he replied, vehemently; " the mother! The mother! If you only knew the mother! " " Please, please! " I remonstrated; " don't say anything more; I don't want to know about her! " He began excitedly to pace the floor, breaking out into a torrent of words. " You must; you must let me speak! " he cried. " You must let me tell you all I have suppressed so long." I tried to stop him, but he paid no attention.

" Rage and bitterness against you drove me to that woman," he continued, tempestuously; " yes, and to drink. For weeks after our last break-up I kept drinking. Then I met the woman. I had seen her at radical affairs before, but she had never meant anything to me. Now she excited me; I was maddened by the loss of you and by drink. So I took her home. I quit working and gave myself up to a wild debauch, hoping to blot out the resentment I felt against you for going away." With a sharp pain in my heart I seized his hand, crying: " Oh, Ed, not resentment?" " Yes, yes! Resentment!" he repeated; " even hate! I felt it then because you had so easily given up our love and our life. But don't interrupt me; I must get it out of my system."

We sat down. Putting his hand over mine, he continued somewhat more calmly: " The drunken debauch went on for weeks. I wasn't aware of time, I didn't go anywhere or see anybody. I stayed at home in a stupor of drink and sex. One day I woke up with my mind terribly clear. I was sick of myself and of the woman. I told her brutally that she would have to go; that I had never intended our affair to be a permanent thing. She did what women usually do; she said I was a cruel and unscrupulous seducer. When she saw that it did not impress me, she began weeping and begging and finally she declared that she was pregnant. I was staggered; I felt it was impossible, yet I didn't believe she would deliberately invent such a thing. I had no money and I could not let her shift for herself. I was trapped and I had to go through with it. A few months under the same roof made me realize that we didn't have a single thought in common. Everything about her repelled me; her shrill voice all over the house, her constant chatter and gossip. They grated on my nerves and often drove me out of the house, but the thought that she was carrying my child always brought me back. Two months before it was born, she taunted me, during one of our bickering wrangles, with having tricked me. She had not been pregnant at all when she had first told me. I decided then and there to leave her as soon as the child was born. You'll laugh, but the birth of the little one woke strange chords in my soul. It made me forget all that was lacking in my life. I stayed."

" Why torture yourself, dear Ed?" I tried to soothe him; " why rake up the past?" He brushed me gently aside. " You must listen," he insisted; " you had everything to do with the beginning; it's only fair you should listen to the very end."

" When you returned from Europe," he went on, " the contrast between our past life and my present existence appeared more glaring. I wanted to take my child and come to you to plead once more for our love. But you were wrapped up in other people and in your public activities. You seemed to be completely cured of what you had once felt for me."

"You were wrong!" I cried, "I still loved you even when we had drifted apart." "I see it now, my dear, but at the time you appeared indifferent and aloof," he replied. "I could not turn to you. I sought what relief I could in my child. I read, and I found — yes, I found — some forgetfulness in the works we used to argue about; I could understand them better. But my nerves had become blunted; I no longer winced at the sound of the shrill voice. Her recriminations had made me hard and cynical. Besides, I had discovered a way to stop the stream," he added with a chuckle. "What was it?" I asked, glad of his lighter tone; "perhaps I could also use it on some people." "Well, you see," he explained, "I take out my watch, hold it up to the lady's face, and tell her I'll give her five minutes to get through. If by that time she still keeps it up, I leave the house." "And it works?" I inquired. "Like magic. She dashes into the kitchen, and I go into my room and lock the door." I laughed, though I really wanted to cry at the thought of Ed, who had always loved refinement and peace, forced into degrading, vulgar scenes.

"The break has come, though, at last," he went on. "It had to, anyway, even if you and I had not become good friends again. It was bound to come as soon as I began to realize the effect those quarrels were having on the child." He added that for a long time he had wanted to go to Europe to see his mother again, but he had lacked the means. Now he was in a position to do so. He would take his child to Vienna with him, and he asked me to accompany him.

"How do you mean, take the child?" I cried. "The mother, what about her? It's her child, too, isn't it? It must mean everything to her. How can you rob her of it?" Ed got on his feet and raised me up also. His face close to mine, he said: "Love! Love! Haven't you always insisted that the love of the average mother either smothers the child with kisses or kills it with blows? Why this sudden sentimentality for the poor mother?" "I know, I know, my dear," I answered; "I haven't changed my views. Just the same, the woman endures the agony of birth and she nourishes the infant with her own substance. The man does almost nothing, and yet he claims the child. Can't you

see how unjust it is, Ed? Go to Europe with you? I'd do it at once.
But I cannot have a mother robbed of her child on my account." He
charged me with not being free; I was like all feminists who rail
against man for the wrongs he supposedly does to woman, without
seeing the injustices that the man suffers, and also the child. He would
go anyway and take his little girl along. Never would he allow his
child to grow up in an atmosphere of strife.

Ed left me in a turmoil of conflicting emotions. I had to admit to
myself that it had indeed been I who had driven him into that woman's
arms. I knew, as I had known when I had gone away from him, that
I could not have acted otherwise. All the same, I had been the cause.
I recalled vividly Ed's violent outburst on that terrible night; it was
evidence enough of his agony of spirit. There was no blinking my part
in his misery; why, then, did I refuse him now when he needed me
even more? Why did I deny him the help he asked for his child?
The woman certainly meant nothing to me; why should I have scruples
about her loss? I had always held that the mere physical process of
motherhood does not make a woman a real mother; yet I had talked
to Ed against robbing her!

After much thought I concluded that my feeling in regard to the
mother of Ed's child was deeply embedded in my sentiments for
motherhood in general, that blind, dumb force that brings forth life
in travail, wasting woman's youth and strength, and leaving her in
old age a burden to herself and to those to whom she has given birth.
It was this helplessness of motherhood that had made me recoil from
adding to its pain.

The next time Ed came I tried to explain this to him, but he could
not follow me. He said he had always credited me with being able to
reason like a man, objectively; now he felt I was arguing subjectively,
like all women. I replied that the reasoning faculties of most men had
not impressed me to the point of wishing to imitate them, and that I
preferred to do my own thinking as a woman. I repeated what I had
already told him: that I should be supremely happy to go with him
if he went alone, or to visit him in Europe some time later, but that
I could not run off with another woman's child.

I was afraid that my stand would throw a shadow on my new friendship with Ed, but he proved to be big and fine about it. His visits became beautiful events. He was planning to leave for Europe in June,
together with his child.

Early in April he told me he would be very busy for a week. His firm had to buy a large stock of lumber, and the transaction was to keep him out of town for a few days. But he would remain in touch with me and wire the moment he got back. During his absence I was called on a night case in Brooklyn, to nurse a consumptive boy. It was a long and tedious journey to and fro; I would return home very tired, barely able to take my bath, and fall asleep as soon as I struck the pillow. One morning, very early, I was roused out of bed by persistent and violent ringing. It was Timmermann, whom I had not seen for more than a year. "Claus!" I cried; "what brings you at such an hour?"

His manner was unusually quiet and he looked strangely at me. "Sit down," he said at last in a solemn voice; "I have something to tell you." I wondered what had happened to him. "It's about Ed," he began. "Ed!" I cried, suddenly alarmed; "is anything the matter with him? Is he ill? Have you a message for me?"

"Ed — Ed — " he stammered — "Ed has no more messages." I held out my hand as if to ward off a blow. "Ed died last night," I heard Claus say in a shaken voice. I stood staring at him. "You're drunk!" I cried; "it can't be!" Claus took my hand and gently pulled me down beside him. "I'm a messenger of evil; of all your friends I had to be the one to bring you this news. Poor, poor girl!" He stroked my hair furtively. We sat in silence.

Finally Claus spoke. He had gone to Ed's house to meet him for supper; he had waited until nine o'clock, but Ed did not return, so he decided to leave. At that moment a cab drove up to the house. The driver inquired for Brady's apartment, saying that Mr. Brady was in the cab, sick. Would someone help to carry him up? Neighbours came out and surrounded the cab. Ed was inside, sunk back in the seat, unconscious and breathing heavily. People carried him upstairs, while Claus ran for a doctor. When he came back the cabman was gone. All he had been able to tell was that he had been called to a saloon near the Long Island station, where he had found the gentleman hunched up in a chair, bleeding from a cut on his face. He was conscious, but able only to give his address. The saloon-keeper explained that the gentleman had asked for a drink and had taken it standing at the bar. Then he had paid and started towards the toilet. On the way he had suddenly fallen down in a heap, striking his forehead against the bar. That was all any of them knew.

The doctor had worked frantically to revive Ed; but it was in vain. He died without regaining consciousness.

Claus's voice was droning in my ears, but I barely heard what he was saying. Nothing mattered but that Ed had been stricken among strangers, stuffed into a cab, alone at the moment of his greatest need. Oh, Ed, my splendid friend, robbed of life when so close to the fullness of it! The cruelty of it, the senseless cruelty! My heart cried out in protest, my throat choked with tears that would not come to my eyes to relieve my poignant grief.

Claus got to his feet remarking that he must notify other friends and help with the funeral arrangements. "I will go with you!" I declared. "I will see Ed again." "Impossible!" Claus objected. "Mrs. Brady has already stated that she will not let you in. She said you had robbed her of Ed when he was alive and she will keep you away now that he is dead. You would only have to go through with an ugly scene."

I remained alone with memories of my life with Ed. In the late afternoon Yegor came, shaken by the news. He had loved Ed and was profoundly overcome now. His sweet concern melted my frozen heart. With his arms about me I found the tears that would not come before. We sat close together, talking of Ed, his life, his dreams, and premature end. It grew late and I remembered the sick boy in Brooklyn waiting for me. I might not be near my precious dead, but I could at least go to the aid of my young patient struggling for life.

Funerals had always been abhorrent to me; I felt that they expressed grief turned inside out. My loss was too deep for it. I went to the crematory and found the ceremony over, the coffin already closed. The friends who knew of my bond with Ed lifted the cover again for me. I approached to look at the dear face, so beautifully serene in sleep. The silence about me made death less gruesome.

Suddenly a shriek echoed through the place, followed by another and another. A female voice, hysterically crying: "My husband! My husband! He is mine!" The shrieking woman, her black widow's veil resembling a crow's wings, threw herself between me and the coffin, pushing me back and falling over the dead. A little blonde girl with frightened eyes, suffocating with sobs, was clutching at the woman's dress.

For a moment I stood petrified with horror. Then I slowly moved towards the exit, out into the open, away from the revolting scene. My mind was full of the child, the replica of its father, its life now to be so different from what he had intended.

CHAPTER XXVII

MEMORIES OF MY FORMER LIFE WITH ED FILLED ME WITH LONG-ing for what had again been just within my reach, only to be snatched away. Recollections of the past compelled me to look into the most hidden crevices of my being; their strange contradictions tore me between my hunger for love and my inability to have it for long. It was not only the finality of death, as in the case of Ed, nor the circumstances that had robbed me of Sasha in the springtime of our lives, that always came between. There were other forces at work to deny me permanency in love. Were they part of some passionate yearning in me that no man could completely fulfil or were they in-herent in those who for ever reach out for the heights, for some ideal or exalted aim that excludes aught else? Was not the price they exacted conditioned in the very nature of the thing I wished to achieve? The stars could not be climbed by one rooted in a clod of earth. If one soared high, could he hope to dwell for long in the absorbing depths of passion and love? Like all who had paid for their faith, I too would have to face the inevitable. Occasional snatches of love; nothing permanent in my life except my ideal.

Yegor remained in my flat, while I accompanied my patient and his mother to Liberty, New York. I had never nursed consumptives before and had not witnessed their indomitable will to live and the consuming fires of their withering flesh. At the moment when every-thing seemed at an end, my patient would take a new leap, followed by days of rekindled hope for a future of work that would tax the vitality of the strongest. Here was the boy of eighteen, a mere bundle of bone and skin, with burning eyes and hectic cheeks, talking of the life he might never have.

With his reawakened will invariably came the urge of the body, the craving for sex. It was not until I had spent four months with him that I realized what the youth had been desperately trying to suppress. I was far from the thought that it was my presence that was adding fuel to the smouldering fires within him. A few things had aroused my suspicion, but I had put them aside as signs of my patient's feverish state. Once, as I was taking his pulse, he suddenly seized my hand and pressed it excitedly in his own. At another time, when I bent over to straighten his covers, I felt his hot breath very close to the back of my neck. Often I noticed his large burning eyes following me about.

The boy slept in the open, on the screened veranda. To be within reach, at night I stayed in the room adjoining the porch. His mother was always with him part of the day to give me some time to rest. Her bedroom was behind the dining-room, farthest away from the veranda. The care of my tubercular case was more exacting than any I had nursed before, but years of experience had made me alert to the least stirring of a patient. It was hardly ever necessary for the boy to use the little bell on his table; I could hear him the moment he began to move.

One night I had gone in to my patient several times to find him peacefully slumbering; very tired, I also fell asleep. I was awakened by a feeling of something pressing on my chest. I discovered my patient sitting on my bed, his hot lips pressed to my breast, his burning hands caressing my body. Anger made me forget his precarious condition. I pushed him away and leaped to the floor. "You madman!" I cried; "get to your bed at once or I will call your mother!" He held cut his hands in silent entreaty and started to walk towards the porch. Half-way over, he fell down, shaken by a paroxysm of coughing. Frightened out of my resentment, I was for a moment at a loss what to do. I dared not call his mother; his presence in my room would make her think I had failed her son when he had called me. Nor could I leave him where he was. He weighed little, and desperation increases one's strength. I raised him up and carried him to his bed. His excitement brought on a new hæmorrhage, and my anger gave way to pity for the poor boy, so near death, yet so tenaciously reaching out for life.

All through his attack he clung to my hand, between fits of coughing begging me to spare his mother and forgive him for what he had done. I kept on turning over in my mind how I could resign. It was clear I should have to leave. What excuse could I give? I could not tell his mother the truth; she would not believe it of her son, and even if she did, she would be too shocked and hurt to understand the urge that had impelled the boy. I should have to say that I was tired out by constant nursing and needed rest; and of course I would give her time to find another nurse. But weeks passed before I could carry out my resolve. My patient was very ill and his mother herself almost a physical wreck from anxiety. When at last the patient had once more escaped his doom and was better again, I begged to be allowed to go.

On my return to New York I found that I should have to look for a new abode again: once more my neighbours had objected to having Emma Goldman in the house. I moved into a larger place, my brother Yegor and our young comrade Albert Zibelin sharing the apartment with me. Various elements were combined in Albert's make-up; his father, an active anarchist, was French; his mother an American Quaker of sweet and gentle disposition. He was born in Mexico, where as a child he had roamed freely in the hills. Later he lived with Elisée Reclus, the celebrated French scientist and exponent of anarchism. His fine heritage and the beneficial influences in his early life had produced splendid results in Albert; he was beautiful in body and spirit. He grew into an ardent lover of freedom and became a tender and thoughtful friend, altogether a rare character among the young American boys of my acquaintance.

This time our co-operative venture began more promisingly. Each member talked less of equal responsibility and did more to relieve the burden of the others. It was doubly fortunate for me because of the many calls of the movement upon my energies. With Albert as chef, and the help of Yegor and Dan, when the latter visited us, I was able to devote myself more to my public interests, which were shared also by the boys.

Since I had begun writing to Sasha again, we had been drawing closer together. He had not quite three years more to endure, and he was full of new hope, planning what he would do after his release. For several years past he had been much interested in one of his prison mates, a consumptive boy by the name of Harry. In every letter Sasha referred to his friend, especially while I was nursing my tubercular patient. I had to keep him informed of the methods and treatment I applied. His interest in Harry had even suggested to him the study of medicine when he should leave prison. Meanwhile he was eager for what I could send him: medical books, journals, and everything else bearing on the white plague.

Sasha's letters breathed a zest in life that carried me along and filled me with increased admiration for him. I, too, began to dream and plan for the great moment when my heroic boy would be free again and united with me in life and work. Only thirty-three months more and his martyrdom would be at an end!

Meanwhile John Turner had announced his coming to the States. He had been in America in 1896 and had lectured extensively during seven months. He was planning a new tour and wished especially to study the conditions of the men and women employed as clerks and sales-people in the United States. He had been very successful in England with the Shop Assistants' Union, which he had developed into a powerful organization. Under his leadership the status of those employees had been improved to a very considerable degree. While the conditions of that class of workers in America were not quite so bad as in England prior to the efforts of Turner and his union colleagues, we were sure that the men needed awakening. There was no one so capable of accomplishing it as John Turner.

For that reason, as well as because of the contribution Turner would make to the more general spread of our ideas, we hailed his proposed visit and immediately began to arrange a series of lectures for our brilliant English comrade. His first meeting we organized for October 22 at Murray Hill Lyceum.

Like so many others, John Turner had become an anarchist as a result of the Haymarket tragedy of 1887. His attitude to the State and to political action had induced him to refuse the candidacy for Parliament offered him by his union. "My place is among the rank and file," Turner had stated at the time; "my work is not in so-called 'public affairs,' which are part of the organized exploitation of labour. Even the small palliatives possible through Parliament would be gained by organized Labour much quicker by pressure from outside than by the representatives inside the House of Commons." His stand showed his grasp of social forces and his devotion to his ideal. While he had never ceased to work for anarchism, he considered activity in the unions his most vital purpose. He maintained that anarchism without the masses is bound to remain a mere dream, lacking living force. He felt that to reach the toilers one must take part in their daily economic struggle.

His opening address was on "Trade Unionism and the General Strike." Murray Hill Lyceum was filled to the doors with people from every walk of life. The police were present in large numbers. I in-

troduced our British comrade to the audience and then went to the
rear of the hall to look after our literature. When John had finished
speaking, I noticed several plain-clothes men approach the platform.
Sensing trouble, I hastened over to John. The strangers proved immigration officials who declared Turner was under arrest. Before the
audience had time to realize what was happening, he was rushed out
of the hall.

Turner was given the honour of being the first to fall under the
ban of the Federal Anti-Anarchist Law passed by Congress on March
3, 1903. Its main section reads: "No person who disbelieves in or
who is opposed to all organized governments, or who is a member
of or affiliated with any organization entertaining or teaching such
disbelief in or opposition to all governments . . . shall be permitted
to enter the United States." John Turner, well known in his own
country, respected by thinking people and having access to every
European land, was now to be victimized by a statute conceived in
panic and sponsored by the darkest elements in the United States.
When I announced to the audience that John Turner had been arrested and would be deported, the meeting unanimously resolved that
if our friend had to go, it should not be without a fight.

The Ellis Island authorities thought they were going to have it all
their own way. For several days no one, not even his lawyer, was
allowed to see Turner. Hugh O. Pentecost, whom we engaged to
represent the prisoner, immediately started habeas corpus proceedings.
That stayed the deportation and checked the arbitrary methods of
the Ellis Island Commissioner. At the first hearing the judge sustained,
of course, the immigration authorities by ordering Turner deported.
But we still had an appeal to the Federal Supreme Court in reserve.
Most of our comrades opposed such a step as inconsistent with our
ideas, a waste of money that could achieve no results. While I had no
illusions about what the Supreme Court was likely to do, I felt that
the fight for Turner would be splendid propaganda by bringing the
absurd law to the attention of the intelligent public. Last but not
least it would serve to awaken many Americans to the fact that the
liberties guaranteed in the United States, among which the right of
asylum was the most important, had become nothing but empty
phrases to be used as fire-crackers on the Fourth of July. The main
point, however, was whether Turner would be willing to continue
a prisoner on Ellis Island, perhaps for many months, until the Supreme

Court should decide his case. I wrote to ask him about it, receiving an immediate reply to the effect that he was "enjoying the hospitality of Ellis Island," and that he was entirely at our disposal to help make the fight.

While there had been a decided change in public opinion towards me since 1901, I was still very much taboo to the majority. I realized that if I wished to help Turner and participate in the activities against the deportation law, I had better remain in the background. My assumed name of Smith secured for me a willing ear with people who were sure to see red on meeting Emma Goldman. Still, a goodly number of American radicals knew me and were advanced enough not to be frightened by my ideas. With their help I succeeded in organizing a permanent Free Speech League, its members coming from various liberal elements. Among them were Peter E. Burroughs, Benjamin R. Tucker, H. Gaylord Wilshire, Dr. E. B. Foote, Jr., Theodore Schroeder, Charles B. Spahr, and many others well known in progressive circles. At its first meeting the league decided to have Clarence Darrow represent Turner before the Supreme Court.

The next step taken by the league was to arrange a meeting in Cooper Union. The Free Speech Leaguers were mostly professional men and very busy. It was left to me to do the suggesting and directing and to pester people until they promised their support. I had to visit numerous unions, as a result of which I collected sixteen hundred dollars. What was more difficult, I succeeded in persuading Yanofsky, editor of the *Freie Arbeiter Stimme,* who was at first opposed to the appeal, to open his columns to our publicity. Gradually I got other persons interested, the most active being Bolton Hall and his secretary, A. C. Pleydell, both untiring in their work on the case.

Bolton Hall, whom I had met several years before, was one of the most charming and gracious personalities it has been my good fortune to know. An unconditional libertarian and single-taxer, he had entirely emancipated himself from his highly respectable background except for his conventional dress. His frock-coat, high silk hat, gloves, and cane made him a conspicuous figure in our ranks, particularly so when he visited trade unions in behalf of Turner, or when he appeared before the American Longshoremen's Union, whose organizer and treasurer he was. But Bolton knew what he was about. He claimed that nothing impressed working-men so much as his fashionable attire. To my remonstrances he would reply: "Don't you see it is my silk hat that gives my speech importance?"

The Cooper Union meeting met with tremendous success, the speakers representing all shades of political opinion. Some were apologetic for having come to plead in behalf of an anarchist; as congressmen and college professors they could not afford to be as outspoken as they felt. Others, more daring, however, set the real tone of the meeting. Among them were Bolton Hall, Ernest Crosby, and Alexander Jonas. Letters and telegrams were read from William Lloyd Garrison, Edward M. Shepard, Horace White, Carl Schurz, and the Rev. Dr. Thomas Hall. They were unconditional in their condemnation of the outrageous law and of the attempts of Washington to destroy the fundamental principles guaranteed by the Declaration of Independence and the Constitution of the United States.

I sat in the audience, very much gratified with the results of our efforts, amused to think that most of those good people on the platform were unaware that it was Emma Goldman and her anarchist comrades who had arranged and managed the meeting. No doubt some of the respectable liberals, those who always offered profuse apologies for every bold step they contemplated making, would have been shocked out of their wits had they known that "wild-eyed anarchists" had had anything to do with the affair. But I was a hardened sinner; I did not feel the least scruple for having gone into a conspiracy to induce the timid gentlemen to express themselves on such a vital issue.

Amidst the excitement of the campaign I was called by Dr. E. B. Foote to a case. I had tried several times previously to get work with him, but although he was a prominent free-thinker, he had yet fought shy of employing the dangerous Emma Goldman. Since the Turner appeal we had come in contact a good deal, and that was probably what had changed his mind. At any rate he sent for me to take charge of one of his patients, and New Year's Eve 1904 found me at the bedside of the man entrusted to my care. The midnight merry-making on the street awakened memories of the great day, a year past, spent with Max, Millie, and Ed.

Being compelled to move to new quarters every now and then had become a habit with me, and I no longer minded it. I now rented part of a flat at 210 East Thirteenth Street, the rest of the apartment being occupied by Mr. and Mrs. Alexander Horr, friends of mine. I was preparing to go on tour. Yegor had work outside the city, and Albert was leaving for France, so I was glad when the Horrs offered to share their flat. Little did I dream that I was going to remain ten years in the place.

The Free Speech League had asked me to visit a number of cities in behalf of the John Turner fight, and I had also received two other invitations: one from the garment-workers in Rochester, and the other from miners in Pennsylvania. The Rochester tailors had had trouble with some clothing firms, among them that of Garson and Meyer. It was strangely significant that I should be called to speak to the wage-slaves of the man who had once exploited my labour for two dollars and fifty cents a week. I welcomed the opportunity, which would also enable me to see my family.

Within the last few years I had felt more drawn to my people, Helena remaining nearest to me. I always stayed with her on my visits to Rochester, and my folks had learned to take it as a matter of course. My arrival this time was the occasion for a general family reunion. It gave me a chance to get in closer touch with my brother Herman and his charming young wife, Rachel. I learned that the boy who could not memorize his lessons at school had become a great mechanical expert, his specific line the construction of intricate machinery. When it grew late and the other members of the family retired, I remained with my dear Helena. We always had much to say to each other, and it was nearly morning when we separated. Sister consoled me by saying I could sleep late.

I had hardly dozed off when I was awakened by a messenger bringing a letter. Glancing at the signature first, in a half-drowsy state, I saw with surprise that it was signed "Garson." I read it several times to make sure that I was not dreaming. He felt proud that a daughter of his race and city had achieved nation-wide fame, he wrote; he was glad of her presence in Rochester and he would consider it an honour to welcome me at his office soon.

I handed the letter to Helena. "Read it," I said, "and see how important your little sister has become." When she got through, she asked: "Well, what are you going to do?" I wrote on the back of the letter: "Mr. Garson, when I needed you, I came to you. Now that you seem to need me, you will have to come to me." My anxious sister was worried about the outcome. What could he want and what would

I say or do? I assured her that it was not difficult to guess what Mr.
Garson wanted, but I intended, nevertheless, to have him tell it
to me in person and in her presence. I would receive him in her store
and treat him "as a lady should."

In the afternoon Mr. Garson drove up in his carriage. I had
not seen my former employer for eighteen years, and during that
time I had hardly given him a thought. Yet the moment he entered,
every detail of the dreadful months in his shop stood out as clearly
as if it had happened but yesterday. I saw the shop again and his
luxurious office, American Beauties on the table, the blue smoke of
his cigar swelling in fantastic curves, and myself standing trembling,
waiting until Mr. Garson would deign to notice me. I visioned it all
again and I heard him saying harshly: "What can I do for you?"
Everything to the minutest detail I recalled as I looked at the old
man standing before me, silk hat in hand. The thought of the injustice and humiliation his workers were suffering, their driven and
drained existence, agitated me. I could barely suppress the impulse
to show him the door. If my life depended on it, I could not
have asked Mr. Garson to sit down. It was Helena who offered
him a chair — more than he had done for me eighteen years
before.

He sat down and looked at me, evidently expecting me to speak
first. "Well, Mr. Garson, what can I do for you?" I finally asked.
The expression must have recalled something to his mind; it seemed
to confuse him. "Why, nothing at all, dear Miss Goldman," he presently replied; "I just wanted to have a pleasant talk with you." "Very
well," I said, and waited. He had worked hard all his life, he related,
"just like your father, Miss Goldman." He had saved penny by
penny and in that way had accumulated a little money. "You may not
know how difficult it is to save," he went on, "but ask your father.
He works hard, he is an honest man, and he is known in the whole
city as such. There isn't another man in Rochester more respected
and who has so much credit as your father."

"Just a moment, Mr. Garson," I interrupted; "you forgot something. You forgot to mention that you had saved by the assistance of
others. You were able to put aside penny by penny because you had
men and women working for you."

"Yes, of course," he said apologetically, "we had 'hands' in our
factory, but they all made good livings."

"And were they all able to open factories from their savings of penny by penny?"

He admitted that they were not, but it was because they were ignorant and spendthrift. "You mean they were honest working-men like my father, don't you?" I continued. "You've spoken in such high terms of my father, you certainly will not accuse him of being a spendthrift. But though he has worked like a galley-slave all his life, he has accumulated nothing and he has not been able to start a factory. Why do you suppose my father and others remained poor, while you succeeded? It is because they lacked the forethought to add to their shears the shears of ten others, or of a hundred or several hundred, as you have done. It isn't the saving of pennies that makes people rich; it is the labour of your 'hands' and their ruthless exploitation that has created your wealth. Eighteen years ago there was an excuse for my ignorance of it, when I stood like a beggar before you, asking for a rise of a dollar and a half in pay. There is no excuse for you, Mr. Garson—not now, when the truth of the relation between labour and capital is being cried from the house-tops."

He sat looking at me. "Who would have thought that the little girl in my shop would become such a grand speaker?" he said at last. "Certainly not you!" I replied, "nor could she have if you had had your way. But let's come down to your request that I visit your office. What is it you want?"

He began talking about labour's having its rights; he had acknowledged the union and its demands (whenever reasonable) and had introduced many improvements in his shop for the benefit of his workers. But times were hard and he had sustained heavy losses. If only the grumblers among his employees would listen to reason, be patient awhile, and meet him half-way, everything could be amicably adjusted. "Couldn't you put this before the men in your speech," he suggested, "and make them see my side a little? Your father and I are great friends, Miss Goldman; I would do anything for him if he should be in trouble—lend him money or help in any way. As to his brilliant daughter, I have already written you how proud I am that you come from my race. I should like to prove it by some little gift. Now, Miss Goldman, you are a woman, you must love beautiful things. Tell me what you'd like best."

His words did not rouse my anger. Perhaps it was because I had expected some such offer from his letter. My poor sister was regarding me with her sad, anxious eyes. I rose quietly from my chair; Garson did the same and we stood facing each other, a senile smile on his withered face.

"You've come to the wrong person, Mr. Garson," I said; "you cannot buy Emma Goldman."

"Who speaks of buying?" he exclaimed. "You're wrong; let me explain."

"No need of it," I interrupted him. "Whatever explanation is necessary I will make tonight before your workers who have invited me to speak. I have nothing more to say to you. Please go."

He edged out of the room, silk hat in hand, followed by Helena, who saw him to the door.

After careful consideration I decided to say nothing at the meeting about his offer. I felt it might obscure the main issue, the wage dispute, and possibly affect the chances of a settlement in favour of the employees. Moreover, I did not want the Rochester papers to get hold of the story; it would have been too much grist for their scandal-mongering mills. But I did relate to the workers that evening the venture of Garson into political economy, repeating the explanation he had given as to how he had acquired his wealth. My audience was greatly amused, which was the only result of Garson's visit.

During my brief stay in Rochester I had another caller, much more interesting than Mr. Garson: a newspaper woman who introduced herself as Miss T. She came to interview me, but she stayed to tell a remarkable story. It was about Leon Czolgosz.

She had been on the staff of one of the Buffalo dailies in 1901, she related, assigned to the Exposition grounds during the President's visit. She had stood very near McKinley and had watched the people filing by to shake his hand. In the procession she noticed a young man pass along with the rest, a white handkerchief wrapped around his hand. Reaching the President, he raised a revolver and fired. A panic followed, the crowd scattering in all directions. Bystanders picked up the wounded McKinley and carried him into Convention Hall; others pounced upon the assailant and beat him as he lay prostrate. Suddenly there was a fearful scream. It came from the boy on the ground. A burly Negro was over him, digging his nails into the youth's eyes. The ghastly scene made her sick with horror. She hastened to her paper's office to write her account.

When the editor had read her story, he informed her that the stuff about the Negro gouging Czolgosz's eyes would have to come out. "Not that the anarchist dog didn't deserve it," he remarked; "I'd have done it myself. But we need the sympathy of our readers for the President, not for his murderer."

Miss T. was not an anarchist; in fact, she knew nothing of our ideas, and she was against the man who had attacked McKinley. But the scene she had witnessed and the brutality of the editor softened her towards Czolgosz. She tried repeatedly to get an assignment to interview him in jail, but without success. She learned from other reporters that Czolgosz had been so badly beaten and tortured that he could not be seen. He was ill and it was feared he might not live to be taken to court. Some time later she was ordered to cover the trial.

The court-room was guarded by a heavily armed force and filled with curiosity-seekers, mostly well-dressed women. The atmosphere was tense with excitement, all eyes on the door from which the prisoner was to enter. Suddenly there was a stirring in the crowd. The door was flung open, and a young man, supported by policemen, was half-carried into the room. He looked pale and emaciated; his head was bandaged, his face swollen. It was a repulsive sight until one caught his eyes — large, wistful eyes, that kept roving over the court-room, searching with terrible intensity, apparently for some familiar face. Then they lost their intentness, turning brilliant as if illumined by some inner vision. "Dreamers and prophets have such eyes," Miss T. continued; "I was filled with shame to think that I did not have the courage to cry out to him that he was not alone, that I was his friend. For days afterwards those eyes haunted me. During two years I couldn't go near a newspaper office; even now I am only doing free-lance work. The moment I think of a steady job that might bring me another such experience, I see those eyes. I have always wanted to meet you," she added, "to tell you about it."

I pressed her hand in silence, too overcome to speak. When I had mastered my emotion, I told her I wished I could believe that Leon Czolgosz had been conscious that there was at least one friendly spirit near him in that court-room full of hungry wolves. What Miss T. told me bore out all that I had guessed and what I had learned about Leon in 1902 when I visited Cleveland. I had hunted up his parents; they were dark people, the father hardened by toil, the stepmother with a dull, vacant look. His own mother had died when he was a baby;

at the age of six he had been forced into the street to shine shoes and sell papers; if he did not bring enough money home, he was punished and deprived of meals. His wretched childhood had made him timid and shy. At the age of twelve he began his factory life. He grew into a silent youth, absorbed in books and aloof. At home he was called "daft"; in the shop he was looked upon as queer and "stuck-up." The only one to be kind to him was his sister, a timid, hard-working drudge. When I saw her, she told me that she had been once to Buffalo to see Leon in jail, but he had asked her not to come again. "He knew I was poor," she said; "our family was pestered by the neighbours, and father was fired from his job. So I didn't go again," she repeated, weeping.

Perhaps it was just as well, for what could the poor creature give to the boy who had read queer books, had dreamed queer dreams, had committed a queer act, and had even been queer in the face of death. People out of the ordinary, those with a vision, have ever been considered queer; yet they have often been the sanest in a crazy world.

In Pennsylvania I found the condition of the miners since the "settlement" of the strike worse than in 1897 when I had gone through the region. The men were more subdued and helpless. Only our own comrades were alert, and even more determined since the shameful defeat of the strike, brought about by the treachery of the union leaders. They were working part time, barely earning enough to live on, yet somehow they managed to contribute to the propaganda. It was inspiring to see such consecration to our cause.

Two experiences stood out on my trip. One happened down in a mine, the other in the home of a worker. As on my previous visits, I was taken to the pit to talk to the men in one of the shafts during lunch-hour. The foreman was away, and the miners eager to hear me. I sat surrounded by a group of black faces. During my talk I caught sight of two figures huddled together — a man withered with age and a child. I inquired who they were. "That's Grandpa Jones," I was told; "he's ninety and he has worked in the mines for seventy years. The kid is his great-grandchild. He says he's fourteen, but we know he's only eight." My comrade spoke in a matter-of-fact manner. A man of ninety and a child of eight working ten hours a day in a black pit!

After the first meeting I was invited by a miner to his home for the night. The small room assigned me had already three occupants: two children on a narrow cot, and a young girl in a folding bed. I was to share the bed with her. The parents and their infant girl slept in the next room. My throat felt parched; the stifling air in the room made me cough. The woman offered me a glass of hot milk. I was tired and sleepy; the night was heavy with the breathing of the man, the pitiful wailing of the infant, and the monotonous tramp of the mother trying to quiet her baby.

In the morning I asked about the child. Was it ill or hungry that it cried so much? Her milk was too poor and not enough, the mother said; the baby was bottle-fed. A horrible suspicion assailed me. "You gave me the baby's milk!" I cried. The woman attempted to deny it, but I could see in her eyes that I had guessed correctly. "How could you do such a thing?" I upbraided her. "Baby had one bottle in the evening, and you looked tired and you coughed; what else could I do?" she said. I was hot with shame and overcome with wonder at the great heart beneath that poverty and those rags.

Back in New York from my short tour, I found a message from Dr. Hoffmann calling me again to nurse Mrs. Spenser, I could undertake only day duty, my evenings being taken up with the Turner campaign. The patient consented to the arrangement, but after a few weeks she urged me to take care of her during the night. She had become more to me than merely a professional case, but her present surroundings were repugnant. It was one thing to know that she lived from the proceeds of a brothel, quite different to have to work in such a house. To be sure, my patient's business now went by the respectable name of a Raines hotel. Like all legislation for the elimination of vice, the Raines Law only multiplied the very thing it claimed to abolish. It relieved the keepers of responsibility towards the inmates and increased their revenue from prostitution. The customers no longer had to come to Mrs. Spenser. The girls were now compelled to solicit on the street. In rain or cold, well or ill, the unfortunates had to hustle for business, glad to take anyone who consented to come, no matter how decrepit or hideous he might be. They had, furthermore, to endure persecution from the police and pay graft to the department for the right to "work" in certain localities. Each district had its price, according to the amount the girls were able to get from the men. Broadway, for instance, paid more in graft than the Bowery. The policeman on the beat took care that there should be no unauthorized competition. Any girl who dared trespass on another's beat was arrested and often sent to the workhouse. Naturally the girls clung to their territory and fought the intrusion of any colleague who did not "belong" there.

The new law also resulted in certain arrangements between the Raines-hotel-keepers and the street girl: the latter received a percentage from the liquor she could induce her guests to consume. That became her main source of income since brothels had been abolished and she was thrown out on the street. She was forced to accept what she could from the man, especially because he had also to pay for the hotel room. To meet the many claims on her she had to imbibe heavily in order to induce her customers to drink more. To see those poor slaves and their males going in and out of Mrs. Spenser's hotel all through the night, tired, harassed, and generally drunk, to be compelled to overhear what went on, was more than I could bear. Moreover, Dr. Hoffmann had told me that there was no hope of permanent cure for our patient. Her persistent use of drugs had broken her will and weakened her power of resistance. No matter how well we should succeed in weaning her, she would always go back to them. I informed my patient that I must resign. She flew into a rage, berating me bitterly and concluding by saying that if she could not have me when she wanted me, she preferred that I leave altogether.

I needed all my strength for public work, of which the John Turner campaign was the most important. While his appeal was pending, the attorneys succeeded in getting our comrade out on five-thousand-dollar bail. He immediately started on tour, visiting a number of cities and delivering lectures to crowded houses. Had he not been arrested and threatened with deportation, he would have reached only very limited audiences, whereas now the press dealt at length with the Anti-Anarchist Law and with John Turner, and large crowds had the opportunity of hearing anarchism expounded in a logical and convincing manner.

John had come to America on a leave of absence from his union. It was nearing expiration and he resolved to return to England without waiting for the verdict of the Supreme Court. When the decision was finally handed down, it proved to be just what we had expected. It upheld the constitutionality of the Anti-Anarchist Law and sustained the order for Turner's deportation. However, the ridiculous statute would hereafter defeat its own ends: European comrades wishing to come to the United States would no longer feel bound to confide their ideas to the busybodies of the Immigration Department.

Henceforth I gave more time to English propaganda, not only because I wanted to bring anarchist thought to the American public, but also to call attention to certain great issues in Europe. Of these the struggle for freedom in Russia was among the least understood.

CHAPTER XXVIII

For a number of years the Friends of Russian Freedom, an American group, had been doing admirable work in enlightening the country about the nature of Russian absolutism. Now that society was inactive and the splendid efforts of the radical Yiddish press were confined entirely to the East Side. The sinister propaganda carried on in America by the representatives of the Tsar through the Russian Church, the Consulate, and the New York *Herald,* under the ownership of James Gordon Bennett, was widespread. These forces combined to picture the autocrat as a kind-hearted dreamer not responsible for the evils in his land, while the Russian revolutionists were denounced as the worst of criminals. Now that I had greater access to the American mind, I determined to use whatever ability I possessed to plead the heroic cause of revolutionary Russia.

My efforts, together with the other activities in behalf of Russia, received very considerable support by the arrival in New York of two Russians, members of the Socialist-Revolutionary Party, Rosenbaum and Nikolaev. They came unannounced and unheralded, but the work they accomplished was of far-reaching consequences and paved the way for the visits of a number of distinguished leaders of the Russian libertarian struggle. Within a few weeks after his arrival Rosenbaum succeeded in welding together the militant elements of the East Side into a section of the S. R. Although aware that this party did not agree with our ideas of a non-governmental society, I became a member of the group. It was their work in Russia that attracted me and compelled me to help in the labours of the newly formed society. Our spirits were greatly raised by the news of the approaching visit of Catherine Breshkovskaya, affectionately called Babushka, the Grandmother of the Russian Revolution.

Those familiar with Russia knew of Breshkovskaya as one of the most heroic figures in that country. Her visit would therefore be an event of exceptional interest. We had no anxiety about her success with the Yiddish population — her fame guaranteed it. But the American audiences knew nothing about her, and it might be difficult to get them interested. Nikolaev, who was very close to Babushka, informed us that she was coming to the States not only to raise funds, but also to arouse public sentiment. He visited me frequently to discuss methods of co-operating with the Friends of Russian Freedom. George Kennan was perhaps the only American who knew Babushka and who had written about her; Lyman Abbott, of the *Outlook,* was also interested. Nikolaev suggested that I see them. I laughed at his naïveté in believing that Emma Goldman could approach those ultra-respectable people. "If I go under my own name," I told him, "I should queer Breshkovskaya's chances, while under the obscure name of Smith I'd get no recognition at all." Alice Stone Blackwell came to my mind.

In 1902 I had come across some translations of Russian poetry by Miss Blackwell, and later I had read her sympathetic articles about the Russian struggle. I had written her expressing my appreciation, and in her reply she had asked me to recommend someone who could translate Jewish poetry into English prose. I did so, and thereafter we continued in correspondence. I now wrote to Miss Blackwell about our efforts to get in touch with Americans in behalf of Russia, mentioning Nikolaev, who could give her detailed information about present conditions in his country. Miss Blackwell responded at once. She was soon to be in New York, she wrote; she would visit me and also bring with her the Honourable William Dudley Foulke, president of the recently reorganized Society of the Friends of Russian Freedom.

Foulke was an ardent devotee of Roosevelt. "The poor man is sure to have a stroke when he finds out who Miss Smith is," I remarked to Nikolaev. I had no worry about Miss Blackwell; she was of old New England stock and an energetic champion of liberty. She knew my identity. But Roosevelt's man — what would happen when he came? Nikolaev lightly dismissed my apprehensions, saying that in Russia the greatest revolutionists had worked under fictitious names.

Before long, Alice Stone Blackwell arrived, and while we were having tea, there came a knock at the door. I opened it to a short, stout man all out of breath after his climb of the five flights. "Are you Miss Smith?" he panted. "Yes," I replied brazenly; "you are Mr. Foulke, aren't you? Please come in." The good Rooseveltian Republican in Emma Goldman's flat at 210 East Thirteenth Street, sipping tea and discussing ways and means to undermine the Russian autocracy, would certainly have made a delicious story for the press. I took great care to keep the newspapers out of it, however, and the conspiratory session went off without a hitch. Both Miss Blackwell and the Honourable William D. Foulke were much impressed by Nikolaev's account of the horrors in Russia.

Several weeks later Miss Blackwell informed me that a New York branch of the Friends of Russian Freedom had been organized, with the Reverend Minot J. Savage as president, and Professor Robert Erskine Ely as secretary, the body planning to do everything in its power to bring Mme Breshkovskaya before the American public. It was a quick and gratifying result of our little gathering. But Ely! I had met him during Peter Kropotkin's visit in 1901; an extremely timid man, he seemed, for ever in fear that his connexion with anarchists might ruin his standing with the backers of the League for Political Economy, of which he was head. To be sure, Kropotkin was an anarchist, but he was also a prince and a scientist, and he had lectured before the Lowell Institute. I felt that to Ely the *prince* was the important feature about Kropotkin. The British have royalty and love it, but some Americans love it because they would like to have it. It did not matter to them that Kropotkin had discarded his title in joining the revolutionary ranks. Dear Peter had been not a little shocked to discover it. I remembered the anecdote he had told us about his stay in Chicago, when his comrades had arranged for him to go to Waldheim to visit the graves of Parsons, Spies, and the other Haymarket martyrs. The same morning a group of society women, led by Mrs. Potter Palmer, invited him to a luncheon. "You will come, Prince, will you not?" they pleaded. "I am sorry, ladies, but I have a previous engagement with my comrades," he excused himself. "Oh, no, Prince; you *must* come with us!" Mrs. Palmer insisted. "Madam," Peter replied, "you may have the Prince, and I will go to my comrades."

My impression of Professor Ely made me feel that it would be better for his peace of mind, as well as for the work for Babushka, if he were not enlightened about E. G. Smith's identity. I was again obliged to act through an intermediary, as in the Turner case, remaining in the background. If timorous souls were deceived, it was not of my choosing; it was their narrow-mindedness that made it necessary.

When Catherine Breshkovskaya arrived, she was immediately surrounded by scores of people, many of them moved more by curiosity than by genuine interest in Russia. I did not wish to swell the number, and so I waited. Nikolaev had told her about me and she asked to see me.

The women in the Russian revolutionary struggle, Vera Zassulitch, Sophia Perovskaya, Jessie Helfman, Vera Figner, and Catherine Breshkovskaya, had been my inspiration ever since I had first read of their lives, but I had never met one of them face to face. I was greatly excited and awed when I reached the house where Breshkovskaya was staying. I found her in a barren flat, badly lighted and inadequately heated. Dressed in black, she was wrapped in a thick shawl, a black kerchief over her head, leaving the ends of her waving grey hair exposed. She gave the impression of a Russian peasant woman, except for her large grey eyes, expressive of wisdom and understanding, eyes remarkably youthful for a woman of sixty-two. Ten minutes in her presence made me feel as if I had known her all my life; her simplicity, the tenderness of her voice, and her gestures, all affected me like the balm of a spring day.

Her first appearance in New York was at Cooper Union and proved the most inspiring manifestation I had seen for years. Babushka, who had never before had a chance to face such a vast gathering, was somewhat nervous at first. But when she got her bearings, she delivered a speech that swept her audience off its feet. The next day the papers were practically unanimous in their tributes to the grand old lady. They could afford to be generous to one whose attack was levelled against far-off Russia instead of their own country. But we welcomed the attitude of the press because we knew that publicity would arouse interest in the cause Babushka had come to plead. Subsequently she spoke in French at the Sunrise Club before the largest assembly in the history of that body. I acted as interpreter, as I did also at most of the private gatherings arranged for her. One of these took place at 210 East Thirteenth Street and was attended by a crowd far too big for my small apartment. Ernest Crosby, Bolton Hall, the Coryells, Gilbert E. Roe, and many members of the University Settlement were present, among them Phelps Stokes, Kellogg Durland, Arthur Bullard, and William English Walling, as well as women prominent in radical ranks. Lillian D. Wald, of the Nurses' Settlement, responded warmly; she arranged receptions for Babushka and succeeded in interesting scores of people in the Russian cause.

Often after the late gatherings Babushka would come with me to my flat to spend the night. It was amazing to see her run up the five flights with an energy and vivacity that put me to shame. "Dear Babushka," I once said to her, "how have you been able to keep your youth after so many years of prison and exile?" "And how did you manage to retain yours, living in this soul-destroying, materialistic country?" she returned. Her long exile had never been stagnant; it was always rejuvenated by the stream of politicals passing through. "I had much to inspire and sustain me," she said; "but what have you in a country where idealism is considered a crime, a rebel an outcast, and money the only god?" I had no answer except that it was the example of those who had gone before, herself included, and the ideal we had chosen that gave us courage to persevere. The hours with Babushka were among the richest and most precious experiences of my propaganda life.

Our strenuous work for Russia at this time received additional significance by the news of the appalling tragedy of January 22 in St. Petersburg. Thousands of people, led by Father Gapon, assembled before the Winter Palace to appeal to the Tsar for relief, had been brutally mowed down, massacred in cold blood by the autocrat's henchmen. Many advanced Americans had held aloof from Babushka's work. They were willing enough to pay homage to her personality, her courage and fortitude; they were sceptical, however, about her description of conditions in Russia. Things could not be quite so harrowing, they claimed. The butchery on "Bloody Sunday" gave tragic significance and incontestable proof to the picture Babushka had painted. Even the lukewarm liberals could no longer close their eyes to the situation in Russia.

At the Russian New Year's ball we greeted the advent of 1905 standing in a circle, Babushka dancing the *kazatchok* with one of the boys. It was a feast for the eyes to see the woman of sixty-two, her spirit young, cheeks ruddy, and eyes flashing, whirling about in the popular Russian dance.

In January Babushka went on a lecture tour, and I could turn to other interests and activities. My dear Stella had come from Rochester in the late fall to live with me. It had been her great dream to do so since early childhood. My narrow escape during the McKinley hysteria had changed the attitude of my sister Lena, Stella's mother, making her more kindly and affectionate towards me. She no longer begrudged me Stella's love, having learned to understand how deep was my concern for her child. Stella's parents realized that their daughter would have better opportunity for development in New York, and that she would be safe with me. I was happy in the anticipation of having with me my little niece, whose birth had brightened my dark youth. Yet when the long-awaited moment arrived, I was too busy with Babushka to give much time to Stella. The old revolutionist was captivated by my niece, and she in turn completely fell under Babushka's charm. Still we both longed to have more of each other, and now, with the departure of the revolutionary "Grandmother," we could at last come closer together.

Stella soon found a position as secretary to a judge, who would no doubt have died of horror had he known that she was the niece of Emma Goldman. I took up nursing again, but before long, Babushka returned from her Western tour and once more I had to devote my time to her and her mission. She had confided to me that she required a dependable person to be entrusted with the task of smuggling ammunition into Russia. I thought at once of Eric and I told her of the courage and endurance he had shown while digging the tunnel for Sasha. She was particularly impressed by the fact that Eric was an excellent sailor and capable of running a launch. " That would facilitate the transport through Finland and it would arouse less suspicion than if attempted by land," she had said. I put Babushka in touch with Eric. He made a most favourable impression on her. "Just the person needed for the job," she said, " cool-headed, brave, and a man of action." When she returned to New York, Eric accompanied her, arrangements for his sailing having already been made. It was good to see our jolly viking again before he left on his perilous journey.

Before the grand old lady's departure I gave her a farewell party at 210 East Thirteenth Street, attended by her old friends and the many new ones the dear woman had made. She lent atmosphere to the evening, infecting everybody with her big and free spirit. There was no cloud on "Grandmother's" brow, although she knew, as we all did, what dangers she would face in returning to the lair of Russian autocracy.

Not until Babushka left the country did I realize how strenuous the month had been. I was utterly exhausted and unable to face the ordeal of nursing. I had realized for some time past that I could not keep up much longer the hard work, responsibility, and anxiety my profession involved while continuing my platform activities. I had tried taking cases of body massage, but I found them even more of a strain than nursing. I had spoken of my predicament to one of my American friends, a woman manicurist who was making a comfortable living by working only five hours a day in her own office. She suggested that I could do the same with facial and scalp massage. Many professional women needed it for the restfulness it gave them, and she would recommend her clients to me. It seemed absurd for me to engage in such a thing, but when I spoke to Solotaroff about it, he urged that it was the best thing I could do to earn my living and still have time left for the movement. My good friend Bolton Hall was of the same opinion; he at once offered to lend me money to fix up a place and also promised to be my first patient. "Even if your skill won't bring back hair on my head," he remarked, "I will have you pinned down for an hour to listen to my arguments on single tax." Some of my Russian friends saw the undertaking in a different light; a massage parlour would well serve, they thought, as a cover for the Russian work we were to go on with. Stella greatly favoured the idea because it would relieve me of the long hours of nursing. The result of it all was that I went in search of an office, which I found without much difficulty on the top floor of a building on Broadway at Seventeenth Street. It was a small place, but it had a view over the East River and plenty of air and sunlight. With the borrowed capital of three hundred dollars and a few lovely draperies lent me by women friends, I established myself in a very attractive parlour.

Before long, patients began to arrive. By the end of June I had earned enough to cover expenses and pay back part of my debt. It was hard work, but most of those who came for treatment were interesting people; they knew me and there was no need of hiding my identity. Still more important, I did not have to work in noisy, congested quarters, and I was relieved from the anxiety I used to feel over the probable outcome of my nursing cases. Every rise in the temperature of my charges used to alarm me, and a death would upset me for weeks. In all my years of nursing I had never learned detachment or indifference to suffering.

During the hot summer months many of my patients left for the country. Stella and I decided that we also needed a vacation. In our search for a suitable place we came upon Hunter Island, in Pelham Bay, near New York, as ideal a spot as we could wish for. But it belonged to the city and we had not the least notion how to secure the necessary permission to pitch a tent. Stella had an inspiration; she would ask her judge. A few days later she came triumphantly waving a piece of paper. "Now, darling," she cried, "will you still insist that judges are useless? Here is the permit to pitch a tent on Hunter Island!"

A friend of mine, Clara Felberg, together with her sister and brother, joined us. We were just beginning to settle down on our island and enjoy its peace and beauty when Clara brought back from New York the announcement that the Paul Orleneff troupe was stranded in the city. Its members had been thrown out of their apartment for failure to pay the rent, and they were without means of livelihood.

Pavel Nikolayevitch Orleneff and Mme Nazimova had come to America in the early part of 1905, taking the East Side by storm with their wonderful production of Tchirikov's *The Chosen People*. It was said that Orleneff had been prevailed upon by a group of writers and dramatists in Russia to take the play abroad as a protest against the wave of pogroms then sweeping Russia. The Orleneff troupe arrived at the very height of our activities for Babushka, which had prevented my getting in touch with the Russian players. But I had attended every performance. With the exception of Joseph Kainz, I knew no one to compare with Paul Orleneff, and even Kainz had created nothing so overwhelming as Orleneff's Raskolnikov in *Crime and Punishment,* or his Mitka Karamazov. His art was, like that of Eleonora Duse, the very living of every nuance of human emotion. Alla Nazimova was very fine as Leah in *The Chosen People,* as she was in all her rôles. As to the rest of the cast, nothing like its ensemble acting had ever been seen on the American stage before. It was therefore a shock to learn that Orleneff's troupe, who had given us so much, should find themselves stranded, without friends or funds. We might pitch a tent for Orleneff on our island, I thought, but how help his ten men? Clara promised to borrow some money, and within a week the entire troupe was on the island with us. It was a motley crowd and a motley life, and our hopes for a restful summer soon went by the board. During the day, when Stella and I had to return to the heat of the city, we regretted that Hunter Island had ceased to be a secluded spot. But at night, sitting around our huge bonfire, with Orleneff in the centre, guitar in hand, softly strumming an accompaniment to his own singing, the whole troupe joining in on the chorus, the strains echoing far over the bay as the large *samovar* buzzed, our regrets of the day were forgotten. Russia filled our souls with the plaint of her woe.

The spiritual proximity of Russia brought Sasha poignantly near. I knew how profoundly he would enjoy our inspiring nights; how he would be stirred and soothed by the songs of the native land he had always passionately loved. It was the month of July 1905. Just thirteen years before, he had left me to stake his life for our cause. His Calvary was soon to end, but only to continue in another place; he still had to serve another year in the workhouse. The judge who had added the extra year to the inhuman sentence of twenty-one now appeared more barbarous than on that trial day in September 1892. But for that, Sasha would be free now, out of the power of his jailers.

It somewhat lessened my misery to think that Sasha would have to spend only seven months in the workhouse, the Pennsylvania law granting five months' commutation on his final year. But even that consolation was soon destroyed. A letter from Sasha informed me that, though he was legally entitled to a five months' reduction, he had learned that the workhouse authorities had decided to regard him as a "new" prisoner and to allow him only two months' time off, provided his behaviour was "good." Sasha was to be forced to drain the bitter cup to the last drop.

Several months previously Sasha had sent to me a friend whom he called "Chum." His name was John Martin, I learned, and he was socialistically inclined. He was a civilian instructor in the prison weaving-shops; he had accepted the job less out of necessity than because he was planning to aid the prisoners. He had learned about Sasha shortly after he had come to work in the Western Penitentiary. Since then he had got in close touch with him and had been able to help him a little. I knew from Sasha's letters that the man used to take great risks in order to do kind things for him and others.

John Martin broached a new appeal to the Pardon Board, to get the year in the workhouse set aside. He could not bear to think that Alex, as he called Sasha, after so many years in one hell should have to go to another. I was deeply touched by Martin's beautiful spirit, but we had failed in our previous attempts to rescue Sasha and I was sure that we could expect no better success now. Moreover, I knew that he himself would not want it tried. He had endured thirteen years and I was certain he would prefer to stand the additional ten months rather than have to go begging again. My attitude was justified by a letter from Sasha. He wanted nothing from the enemy, he wrote.

The sickening anxiety of the days preceding his transfer was finally over. Two days later I received his last note from the penitentiary. It read:

> DEAREST GIRL:
> It's Wednesday morning, the 19th, at last!
>
> > *Geh stiller, meines Herzens Schlag*
> > *Und schliesst euch alle meine alten Wunden,*
> > *Denn dieses ist mein letzter Tag,*
> > *Und dies sind seine letzten Stunden!*[1]
>
> My last thoughts within these walls are of you, dear friend, the Immutable.
>
> > SASHA

Only ten months more to the 18th of May, the glorious day of liberation — the day of your triumph, Sasha, and mine!

When I returned to our camp that afternoon, Orleneff was the first to notice my feverish excitement. "You look inspired, Miss Emma," he cried: "what wonderful thing has happened to you?" I told him about Sasha, of his youth in Russia, his life in America, his *Attentat* and long years in prison. "A character for a great tragedy!" Orleneff exclaimed enthusiastically; "to interpret him, to visualize him to the people — I'd love to play the part!" It was balm to see the great artist so carried away by the force and beauty of Sasha's spirit.

Orleneff urged me to help him get in touch with my American friends, to be his interpreter and manager. Like the genius he was, he lived only in his art; he knew and cared for nothing else. It was enough to watch Orleneff saturate himself with the part he was to play, to realize how truly great an artist he was. Every nuance and shade of the character he was to interpret was created by him beforehand inch by inch, agonized over for weeks, until it assumed a complete and living form. In his efforts for perfection he was re-

---

[1] "Go slower, beating heart of mine — and close, ye bleeding wounds — this is my final day — and these its waning hours."

lentless with himself and equally so with his troupe. More than once in the middle of the night the obsessed creature would tear me out of my sleep by shouting and yelling outside my tent: "I have it! I have it!" Drowsy with sleep, I would inquire what the great find was, and it would prove to be a new inflection in Raskolnikov's monologue or some significant gesture in Mitka Karamazov's drunkenness. Orleneff was literally afire with inspiration. It gradually communicated itself to me, causing me to scheme how to make the world see his art as it was unfolded to me in the unforgettable weeks on Hunter Island.

For some time I could do little except take care of Pavel Nikolayevitch and his numerous guests. Several dependable newspapermen whom I knew interviewed Orleneff about his plans, and meanwhile work began on the Third Street hall that was being remodelled into a theatre. Orleneff insisted on going to town every day to direct this work, which necessitated disputes with the owner over every detail. Paul could not speak anything except Russian, and there was no one but myself to interpret for him. I had to divide my time between my office and the future theatre. In the late afternoon we would return to our island, half-dead with heat and fatigue, Orleneff a nervous wreck from the thousand petty irritations with which he was entirely unfitted to cope.

The superabundance of poison ivy on Hunter Island and the legions of mosquitoes finally drove us into the city. Only the troupe of sturdy peasant actors remained, compelled to defy both pests because they had no other place to go. After Labour Day the number of my patients increased and the preliminary work for the Russian performances began, involving a large correspondence and a personal canvass of my American friends. James Huneker, whom I had not seen for several years, promised to write about Orleneff, and other critics also pledged support. Our efforts were aided by a number of wealthy Jews, among them the banker Seligman.

The members of the East Side Committee on their return from the country set to work in earnest to fulfil their promise to Orleneff. There were readings of plays in some of their homes, especially at Solotaroff's and at Dr. Braslau's, the latter now the host of Pavel Nikolayevitch. Themselves the parents of an artist daughter, Sophie, who had already begun to train for an operatic career, Doctor and Mrs. Braslau could well understand the psychology and moods of their guest.

They had much feeling for him and patience, while some of the East Siders talked about him in terms of dollars and cents. The Braslaus were charming people, genuine, hospitable Russian souls; the evenings in their home always gave me a feeling of freedom and release.

The radical Jewish press actively aided the work of publicity. Abe Cahan, of the socialist daily *Forward,* often attended the readings of plays and wrote a great deal of the significance of Orleneff's art. Considerable publicity was also given him by the *Freie Arbeiter Stimme* and other East Side Yiddish papers.

The various activities, including my office work and lectures, filled my time. Nor did I neglect the friends who were wont to gather at my apartment. Among my many visitors were M. Katz and Chaim Zhitlovsky. Katz held a special place in my affections: he and Solotaroff had been my most faithful friends during my ostracism following the feud with Most and later again at the time of the McKinley hysteria. In fact, I had been thrown together with dear Katz much more than with Solotaroff, both in our work and in more intimate social gatherings.

Zhitlovsky had come to America with Babushka. A Socialist Revolutionist, he was also an ardent Judaist. He never tired urging upon me that as a Jewish daughter I should devote myself to the cause of the Jews. I would say to him that I had been told the same thing before. A young scientist I had met in Chicago, a friend of Max Baginski, had pleaded with me to take up the Jewish cause. I repeated to Zhitlovsky what I had related to the other: that at the age of eight I used to dream of becoming a Judith and visioned myself in the act of cutting off Holofernes' head to avenge the wrongs of my people. But since I had become aware that social injustice is not confined to my own race, I had decided that there were too many heads for one Judith to cut off.

Our circle at 210 East Thirteenth Street was increased by the arrival from Chicago of Max, Millie, and their six-months-old baby girl. The State and Church champions of the sanctity of motherhood had shown their true colours as soon as they discovered that Millie had dared to become a mother without the permission of established authority. She was forced to give up her position as a teacher in the Chicago schools, which she had held for a number of years. It happened at a very unfortunate time, after Max had left the editorial staff of the *Arbeiter Zeitung.* The paper, founded by August Spies, had been gradually deserting its non-political policy. Max had for years fought the Socialist politicians who were trying to turn the *Arbeiter Zeitung* into a vote-catching medium. No longer able to endure the atmosphere of strife and intrigue, he had resigned.

Max hated the dehumanizing spirit of the city and its crushing grind. He longed for nature and the soil. Thanks to the generosity of my friend Bolton Hall, I found myself in a position to offer Max and his little family a small place in the country, three and a half miles out of Ossining, which Bolton had given me when I was being pestered by the landlords. "No one will be able to drive you out of it," he had said; "you can have it to use for the rest of your life, or you can pay for it when you strike a gold-mine." The house was old and shaky, and there was no water on the premises. But its rugged beauty and seclusion, and the gorgeous view from the hill, made up for what was lacking in comfort. With Hall's permission, Max, Millie, and their baby settled on the farm.

The number of my patients had increased considerably, among them being women representing fourteen different professions, besides men from every walk of life. Most of the women claimed to be emancipated and independent, as indeed they were in the sense that they were earning their own living. But they paid for it by the suppression of the mainsprings of their natures; fear of public opinion robbed them of love and intimate comradeship. It was pathetic to see how lonely they were, how starved for male affection, and how they craved children. Lacking the courage to tell the world to mind its own business, the emancipation of the women was frequently more of a tragedy than traditional marriage would have been. They had attained a certain amount of independence in order to gain their livelihood, but they had not become independent in spirit or free in their personal lives.

CHAPTER XXIX

THE NEWS OF THE RUSSIAN REVOLUTION OF OCTOBER 1905 WAS electrifying and carried us to ecstatic heights. The many tremendous events that had happened since the massacre in front of the Winter Palace had kept us in far-away America in constant tension. Kalayev and Balmashov, members of the Fighting Organization of the Social Revolutionary Party, had taken the lives of Grand Duke Sergius and Shipiaghin in retaliation for the butchery of January 22. Those acts had been followed by a general strike throughout the length and breadth of Russia, participated in by large sections from every stratum in society. Even the most insulted and degraded human beings, the prostitutes, had made common cause with the masses and had joined the general strike. The ferment in the Tsar-ridden land had finally come to a head; the subdued social forces and the pent-up suffering of the people had broken and had at last found expression in the revolutionary tide that swept our beloved *Matushka Rossiya*. The radical East Side lived in a delirium, spending almost all of its time at monster meetings and discussing these matters in cafés, forgetting political differences and brought into close comradeship by the glorious events happening in the fatherland.

It was at the very height of those events that Orleneff and his troupe made their first appearance in the little theatre on Third Street. Who cared if the place was ugly, the acoustics unspeakably bad, the stage too small to move about on, the scenery atrociously painted, the incongruous properties borrowed from a dozen different friends? We were too full of new-born Russia, too inspired by the thought of the great artists that were to depict for us the dreams of life. When the curtain rose for the first time, triumphant joy rolled like thunder from the audience to the people on the stage. It raised them to heights of artistic expression that surpassed anything they had done before.

The little theatre became an oasis in New York dramatic art. Hundreds of Americans attended the performances, and even though they did not understand the language, they were carried away by the magic of the Orleneff troupe. Sunday evenings were professional nights, the theatre filled to overflowing with theatre-managers and men and women of the stage. Ethel Barrymore and her brother John, Grace George, Minnie Maddern Fiske and Harrison Grey Fiske, her husband, Ben Greet, Margaret Anglin, Henry Miller, and scores of others, besides every writer and critic in town, were frequent guests. " Miss Smith," as Orleneff's manager, received them, took them back-stage to see the idol, and interpreted their compliments to him, taking care, however, not always to render his replies.

On one occasion, at an after-theatre party given for Orleneff and Mme Nazimova by a certain very prominent theatre-manager, the host began asking Orleneff some rather peculiar questions: " Why do you hold your head in such a queer way in the part of Oswald, when you first appear on the stage? . . . Don't you think it would be more effective if you could cut the talk of that guy in *Crime and Punishment?* . . . Couldn't you make more money if you gave plays with happy endings?" I transmitted the questions all at once. " Tell the man he's a fool!" Orleneff cried, his brows drawn angrily together; " tell him he should be a chimney-sweep and not a theatre-manager. Tell him to go to hell!" He let loose a deluge of Russian oaths too spicy for the respectable Anglo-Saxon ear. Nazimova sat tense, talking French and pretending not to hear, yet watching me stealthily out of large and anxious eyes. My interpretation of Orleneff's outburst was somewhat " diplomatic."

The Russian Revolution had barely begun to flower when it was thrust back into the depths and stifled in the blood of the heroic people. Cossack terror stalked through the land, torture, prison, and the gallows doing their deadly work. Our bright hopes turned to blackest despair. The whole East Side profoundly felt the tragedy of the crushed masses.

The renewed massacres of Jews in Russia brought tears and sorrow to numerous Jewish homes in America. In their disappointment and bitterness, even advanced Russians and Jews turned against everything Russian, and as a result the audience at the little theatre began to dwindle. And then, out of the darkness of some slimy corner, came hideous whispers that Orleneff had members of the Black Hundred, the organized Russian Jew-baiters, in his troupe. A veritable boycott followed. No Jewish store, restaurant, or café would accept posters or advertisements of the Russian plays. The radical press protested vehemently against these utterly unfounded rumours, but without effect. Orleneff was heart-broken over the malicious charges. He had put his very soul into Nachman, the hero of *The Chosen People,* and had pleaded for the Russian cause. Ruin was staring him in the face, with creditors pressing on every side, and the performances barely paying for rent.

Orleneff had once told me of a testimonial performance that had been arranged for him and Mme Nazimova in London by Beerbohm Tree. It had been a brilliant affair, attended by the most distinguished men and women of the British stage. It occurred to me that we might try a similar plan in New York. It would help raise the desperately needed money and perhaps also calm the troubled waters of the East Side, for I knew from years of experience the effect of American opinion upon the immigrant members of my race. I accompanied Orleneff to Arthur Hornblow, editor of the *Theatre Magazine,* who had repeatedly expressed his admiration for the Russian troupe. Mr. Hornblow also knew the person behind Miss Smith and had always been very charming to that dangerous individual.

Mr. Hornblow gave us a royal welcome. He liked the idea of the testimonial and he suggested that the three of us call on Harrison Grey Fiske, lessee of the Manhattan Theatre and successful manager of Mrs. Fiske. Mr. Fiske was interested immediately; he would give us all the help we needed and he also would induce his wife to participate. But he could not offer us the theatre; it had been condemned by the building-department and was soon to be torn down. The interview over, Mr. Hornblow asked us to wait in the hall, as he had something private to say to Mr. Fiske. Soon the latter came out of his office and, placing both hands on my shoulders, cried: "Emma Goldman, aren't you ashamed of yourself to come to me under an assumed name? Don't you know that Mrs. Fiske and I have always been denounced as rebels and trouble-makers because we introduce modern plays and refuse to bow to the theatre trust? Miss Smith, indeed! Who the hell is Miss Smith? Emma Goldman — that's the girl! Now shake, and don't ever doubt me again."

More help and encouragement came from other quarters. Four matinées in the Criterion Theatre and two out-of-town engagements — Boston for a week, and Chicago for a fortnight — put new life into the Russian troupe. The matinées were made possible by a group of American women, admirers of Orleneff, the most active among them being Ethel Barrymore and two society women, cousins of President Roosevelt.

The Boston and Chicago engagements took considerable correspondence to materialize. When everything was ready, Orleneff insisted that I accompany the troupe. In Boston it was the Twentieth Century Club that did the most to aid Orleneff and Nazimova. At the various receptions given in their honour by the club I met Professor Leo Wiener and other Harvard men, Mrs. Ole Bull, who was very active for the success of the troupe, Mr. Nathan Haskell Dole, the translator of Russian works, Dr. Konikov, and scores of other leading Bostonians.

Chicago proved to be much more satisfactory. The social groups of the city backing the venture, including the Jewish and Russian radicals, combined to fill the Studebaker Theatre night after night. Notwithstanding the numerous social affairs, I repeatedly managed to steal away to deliver lectures arranged by my comrades. My "double" life would have shocked many a Puritan, but I led it quite bravely. I had got used to shedding the skin of Miss Smith and wearing my own, but on several occasions the process failed to work.

The first time was when Orleneff and his leading lady were invited to the home of Baron von Schlippenbach, the Russian consul. I told Orleneff that not even for his sake could Emma Goldman be comfortable, in any guise, under the roof of a person that represented the Russian imperial butcher. Another occasion was in connexion with the Hull House. I had met Jane Addams as E. G. Smith at the office of the Studebaker Theatre when she had come to order seats. It had been a business transaction, on neutral ground, calling for no enlightenment as to my identity. But to come to her sanctum under an assumed name, when she herself was supposed to stand for advanced social ideas, seemed an unfair advantage and was distasteful to me. I therefore called up Miss Addams to tell her that Miss Smith could not attend her Orleneff party, but that Emma Goldman would, if welcome. I could hear by the catch in her breath that the disclosure had been made somewhat too suddenly.

When I related the incident to Orleneff, he got very angry. He knew that Jane Addams had made a great fuss over Kropotkin during his visit in Chicago, that she had hung her place with Russian peasant work, and that she and her helpers had worn Russian peasant costumes. How could she, then, object to me, he wondered. I explained that Peter, who hated display of any kind, certainly had had nothing to do with the Russianization of Hull House; furthermore, I did not happen to be known to Miss Addams as a princess.

There were other receptions for my Russians, one at the University, the other at the home of Mrs. L. C. Counley-Ward. I attended both of them under my safe passport. Mrs. Ward lived on the lake front in a palatial home. There was a large crowd at the party, more curious than interested. The hostess herself was very unpretentious and most charming. It was, however, her mother, a woman of eighty, a sweet and distinguished-looking lady, who won my heart. In simple manner she entertained us with an account of her exploits in the abolition movement and in the pioneer work for woman's emancipation. Her flushed face and bright eyes evidenced that she still preserved the rebellious spirit of her youth, and I felt uncomfortable to have stolen into her gracious presence under a false name. The next day I wrote her and her daughter asking forgiveness for my deception and explaining the reason that compelled me to live and work under a pseudonym. I received beautiful letters from both of them, saying that they had understood it was Emma Goldman who had honoured their home. For a number of years thereafter we kept in touch with each other.

Upon our return to New York, Orleneff informed me that he would like to remain in America for several seasons if a guarantee fund could be raised. I submitted the idea to some of the people interested in the Russian troupe. At the end of several conferences sixteen thousand dollars was raised and more pledged. Someone suggested that Orleneff go under the management of Charles Frohman. Orleneff felt outraged; he had never submitted to such a yoke in Russia, he declared; much less would he do it in America. There was only one manager he would recognize, and that was "Miss Emma." He knew that I would never attempt to interfere, as the ordinary manager usually does, with what he was to play or how.

The disappointment over the committee's determination to change his management, and the decision of Mme Nazimova to remain in America and prepare herself for the English stage, had a very depressing effect on Orleneff. He was so set on leaving the country that he would no longer continue with the testimonial we had planned.

During my connexion with his work Orleneff had often urged me to accept a salary. At no time had there been enough money in his treasury for such an extra expense, and he always insisted that the company be paid first, even when he and Nazimova had to go short. The little they did get was due entirely to her resourcefulness. Out of almost nothing at all and with the help of only her Russian maid Alla Nazimova managed to create all the costumes, not alone for herself, but for the whole troupe; thus also were all the court dresses for *Tsar Feodor,* rich and colourful as they were, made by her. But small as the returns were, Orleneff wanted me to have a share in them. I had refused because I had been earning my living, and I could not bear to be an additional burden. Orleneff had once asked me what I would like to do most if I had money, and I had replied that I should want to publish a magazine that would combine my social ideas with the young strivings in the various art forms in America. Max and I had often discussed such a venture, greatly needed. It had been our cherished dream for a long time, though apparently hopeless. Now Orleneff broached the matter again, and I submitted my plan to him. He offered to give a special performance for the purpose and promised to see Nazimova about playing Strindberg's *Countess Julia,* a drama she had always wanted to present with him. He did not care particularly for the part of Jean, he said, but "You have done so much for me," he added, "I will stage the piece."

Before long, Orleneff had set a definite date for the performance. We rented the Berkeley Theatre, printed announcements and tickets, and, with the help of Stella and a few young comrades, set to work to fill the house. At the same time we arranged a gathering at 210 East Thirteenth Street, to which we invited a number of people we knew would be interested in the magazine venture we had in mind: Edwin Björkman, the translator of Strindberg, Ami Mali Hicks, Sadakichi Hartmann, John R. Coryell, and some of our comrades. When our friends left that night, the expected child had a name, *The Open Road,* as well as foster-parents and a host of others anxious to help in its care.

I walked on air. At last my preparatory work of years was about to take complete form! The spoken word, fleeting at best, was no longer to be my only medium of expression, the platform not the only place where I could feel at home. There would be the printed thought, more lasting in its effect, and a place of expression for the young idealists in art and letters. In *The Open Road* they should speak without fear of the censor. Everybody who longed to escape rigid moulds, political and social prejudices, and petty moral demands should have a chance to travel with us in *The Open Road*.

Amidst the rehearsals of *Countess Julia* a swarm of creditors descended upon Orleneff. They had him arrested and the theatre closed, and I had to drop my work to find bondsmen and someone to pay his rent. When things were arranged and Orleneff released, he was too distressed by his experience to continue the rehearsals. There were only two weeks left before the opening night, and I knew he would not go on the stage unless he was sure of his part. To relieve his misery I suggested that he give some other play in which he had already appeared. We agreed on *Ghosts,* the character of Oswald being among Orleneff's greatest creations. Unfortunately, theatre audiences do not care to see the same play many times; when the change of program was announced, a number of people demanded their money back. They wanted to see *Countess Julia* and nothing else. We should have had a substantial turn-out, anyhow, had the gods not chosen the night of the performance for sending down a torrent of rain. The thousand dollars or more we had hoped to realize dwindled down to two hundred and fifty, a sorry capital with which to launch a magazine. Our disappointment was great, but we refused to let it affect our zeal.

We had enough for the first number, which we decided to issue in the historic revolutionary month of March. What other free-lance publication had ever started with more? Meanwhile we sent out a general appeal to our friends. Among the responses we received one from Colorado bearing the heading: *The Open Road*. It threatened to set the law on us for infringement of copyright! Poor Walt Whitman would have surely turned in his grave if he knew that someone had dared to legalize the title of his great poem. But there was nothing for us to do except to christen the child differently. Friends sent in new names, but we did not find one expressing our meaning.

While visiting the little farm one Sunday, Max and I went for a buggy ride. It was early in February, but already the air was perfumed by the balm of spring. The soil was beginning to break free from the grip of winter, a few specks of green already showing and indicating life germinating in the womb of Mother Earth. "Mother Earth," I thought; "why, that's the name of our child! The nourisher of man, man freed and unhindered in his access to the free earth!" The title

rang in my ears like an old forgotten strain. The next day we returned to New York and prepared the copy for the initial number of
the magazine. It appeared on the first of March 1906, in sixty-four
pages. It's name was *Mother Earth.*

Paul Orleneff sailed back to Russia soon afterwards, leaving a
large part of himself in the hearts of all of us who had exulted in his
genius. The American theatre and what passed as drama in the country seemed, thereafter, commonplace and vulgar to me. But I had new
work to do, fascinating and absorbing.

With *Mother Earth* off the press and mailed to our subscribers, I
left a substitute in my office and, together with Max, started on tour.
We had large audiences in Toronto, Cleveland, and Buffalo. It was
my first visit to the last-named city since 1901. The police were still
haunted by the shades of Czolgosz; they were in force and commanded that no language but English be spoken. That prevented Max
from delivering his address, but I did not permit the opportunity to
pass without paying my respects to the police. The second meeting, the
next evening, was stopped before we could get into the hall.

While still in Buffalo, we received the news of the death of Johann
Most. He had been on a lecture tour and had died in Cincinnati, fighting for his ideal to the very last. Max had loved Most devotedly
and he was quite unnerved by the blow. And I — all my early feeling
for Hannes now perturbed me as if there had never been the bitter
clash that separated us. Everything he had given me in the years when
he had inspired and taught me stood before me now and made me
realize the senselessness of that feud. My own long struggle to find
my bearings, the disillusionments and disappointments I had experienced, had made me less dogmatic in my demands on people than I
had been. They had helped me to understand the hard and lonely
life of the rebel who had fought for an unpopular cause. Whatever
bitterness I had felt against my old teacher had given way to deep
sympathy long before his death.

I had tried on several occasions to let him feel the change in me,
but his unyielding attitude convinced me that there had been no corresponding change in him. The first time I had approached him, after
many years, had been in 1903, at a reception given upon his release
after his third term at Blackwell's Island. His hair had grown white,
yet his face was still ruddy and his blue eyes shone with the old fire.
We collided near the steps of the platform, he coming down as I was

going up to speak. Without the least sign of recognition, without a word, he stepped coldly aside to let me pass. Later in the day I saw him surrounded by a lot of hangers-on. I longed to go over and take him by the hand, as in the old days, but his cold stare was still upon me and made me turn away.

In 1904 Most gave a performance of Hauptmann's *Weavers* at the Thalia Theatre. His interpretation of Baumert was a superb piece of acting that brought back to memory all he had told me of his passionate yearning for the theatre. How different his life might have been had he been able to satisfy that craving! Recognition and glory instead of hatred, persecution, and prison.

Again the old feeling for Most welled up in my heart, and I went behind the stage to tell him how splendidly he had played. He accepted my praise in the same manner as he did that of the scores of others who flocked about him. It apparently meant nothing more to him.

The last time I saw Most was at the great memorial meeting for Louise Michel. She had died while lecturing in Marseilles, in February 1905. Her death had united all the revolutionary sections of New York in a demonstration in honour of the wonderful woman. Together with Catherine Breshkovskaya and Alexander Jonas, Most represented the old guard that came to pay homage to the dead rebel and fighter. I was listed to speak after Most. We stood on the platform side by side for a moment. It was the first time in years that we had been seen together in public, and the audience evidenced great enthusiasm. Most turned away from me, without even a greeting, and left without another look in my direction.

And now the old warrior was dead! Sadness overcame me at the thought of the suffering that had made him so inexorable and harsh.

When Max and I returned to New York, we learned that a memorial meeting was being arranged for Most, to take place in the Grand Central Palace. We were both asked to speak. I was informed that the invitation to me had been protested against by some of Most's supporters, especially his wife, who considered it " sacrilegious " for Emma Goldman to pay tribute to Johann Most. I had no desire to intrude, but the younger comrades in the German ranks, as well as many of the Yiddish anarchists, insisted on my speaking.

On the appointed afternoon the place was crowded, every German and Yiddish labour organization being represented at the gathering.

There were also great numbers from our own ranks, from every foreign-language anarchist group. It was an impressive affair and proved the great appreciation of the genius and spirit of Johann Most. I spoke only a short time, but I was told afterwards that my tribute to my old teacher had affected even my enemies in the *Freiheit* group.

CHAPTER XXX

MY OFFICE LEASE WAS ABOUT TO EXPIRE, AND FROM SOME RE-marks of the janitor I gathered that it would not be renewed. I was not disturbed, as I had decided to discontinue massaging. I could not attend to all the work myself and I did not care to exploit help. Moreover, *Mother Earth* was requiring all my time. The friends who had enabled me to open the beauty parlour were indignant at my giving it up when it was beginning to show success. I had paid my debts and I even had a little surplus on hand. The experience I had gained and the people I had met were worth much more than material returns. Now I would be free, free from disguise and subterfuge. There was also something else from which I had to free myself. It was my life with Dan.

Too great differences in age, in conception and attitude, had gradu-ally loosened our ties. Dan was a college boy of the average American level. Neither in our ideas nor in our views of social values had we much in common. Our life lacked the inspiration of mutuality in aim and purpose. As time passed, the certainty kept growing that our re-lationship could not continue. The end came abruptly one night, when I was bruised with endless misunderstanding. When I returned to my apartment in the afternoon of the following day, Dan had departed, and thus one more fond hope had been buried with the past.

I was free to devote myself entirely to *Mother Earth*. But even more important was the approaching event I had longed for and dreamed about during fourteen years — Sasha's release.

May 1906 came at last. Only two more weeks remained till Sasha's resurrection. I had become restless, assailed by perturbing thoughts. What would it be like to stand face to face with Sasha again, his hand in mine, with no guard between us? Fourteen years are a long time, and our lives had flowed in different channels. What if they had

moved too far apart to enable them to converge again into the life
and comradeship that had been ours when we had parted? The
thought of such a possibility sickened me with fear. I busied myself
to still my fluttering heart: *Mother Earth,* arrangements for a short
tour, preparations for lectures. I had planned to be the first at the
prison gate when Sasha would step out into freedom, but a letter from
him requested that we meet in Detroit. He could not bear to see me
in the presence of detectives, reporters, and a curious mob, he wrote.
It was a bitter disappointment to have to wait longer than I had
planned, but I knew his objection was justified.

Carl Nold now lived with a woman friend in Detroit. They occupied a small house, surrounded by a garden, away from the noise and
confusion of the city. Sasha could rest quietly there. Carl had shared
Sasha's lot under the same prison roof and had remained one of his
staunchest friends. It was only fair that he should participate in the
great moment with me.

Buffalo, Toronto, Montreal, meetings, crowds — I went through
them in a daze, conscious only of one thought — *the 18th of May,*
the date of Sasha's release. I reached Detroit on the early morning of
that day, with the vision of Sasha impatiently pacing his cell before
his final liberation. Carl met me at the station. He had arranged a
public reception for Sasha and a meeting, he informed me. I listened
confused, constantly watching the clock striking off the last prison
minutes of my boy. At noon a telegram arrived from friends in
Pittsburgh: "Free and on the way to Detroit." Carl snatched up
the wire, waved it frantically, and shouted: "He is free! Free!"
I could not share his joy; I was oppressed by doubts. If only the
evening would come and I could see Sasha with my own eyes!

Tense I stood at the railroad station, leaning against a post. Carl
and his friend were near, talking. Their voices sounded afar, their
bodies were blurred and faint. Out of my depths suddenly rose the
past. It was July 10, 1892, and I saw myself at the Baltimore and
Ohio Station in New York, standing on the steps of a moving train,
clinging to Sasha. The train began moving faster; I jumped off and
ran after it, with outstretched hands, crying frantically: "Sasha!
Sasha!"

Someone was tugging at my sleeve, voices were calling: "Emma!
Emma! The train is in. Quick — to the gate!" Carl and his girl ran
ahead, and I too wanted to run, but my legs felt numb. I remained

riveted to the ground, clutching at the post, my heart throbbing violently.

My friends returned, a stranger walking between them, with swaying step. "Here is Sasha!" Carl cried. That strange-looking man — was that Sasha, I wondered. His face deathly white, eyes covered with large, ungainly glasses; his hat too big for him, too deep over his head — he looked pathetic, forlorn. I felt his gaze upon me and saw his outstretched hand. I was seized by terror and pity, an irresistible desire upon me to strain him to my heart. I put the roses I had brought into his hand, threw my arms around him, and pressed my lips to his. Words of love and longing burned in my brain and remained unsaid. I clung to his arm as we walked in silence.

On reaching the restaurant Carl ordered food and wine. We drank to Sasha. He sat with his hat on, silent, a haunted look in his eyes. Once or twice he smiled, a painful, joyless grin. I took off his hat. He shrank back embarrassed, looked about furtively, and silently put his hat on again. His head was shaved! Tears welled up into my eyes; they had added a last insult to the years of cruelty; they had shaved his head and dressed him in hideous clothes to make him smart at the gaping of the outside world. I choked back my tears and forced a merry tone, pressing his pale, transparent hand.

At last Sasha and I were alone in the one spare room of Carl's home. We looked at each other like children left in the dark. We sat close, our hands clasped, and I talked of unessential things, unable to pour out what was overflowing in my heart. Utterly exhausted, I wearily dragged myself to bed. Sasha, shrinking into himself, lay down on the couch. The room was dark, only the gleam of Sasha's cigarette now and then piercing the blackness. I felt stifled and chilled at the same time. Then I heard Sasha groping about, come closer, touch me with trembling hands.

We lay pressed together, yet separated by our thoughts, our hearts beating in the silence of the night. He tried to say something, checked himself, breathed heavily, and finally broke out in fierce sobs that he vainly tried to suppress. I left him alone, hoping that his tortured spirit might find relief in the storm that was shaking him to the roots. Gradually he grew calm and said he wanted to go out for a walk, the walls were crushing him. I heard him close the door, and I was alone in my grief. I knew with a terrible certainty that the struggle for Sasha's liberation had only begun.

I woke up with the feeling that Sasha needed to go away somewhere, alone, to a quiet place. But meetings and receptions had been
arranged in Detroit, Chicago, Milwaukee, and New York; the comrades wanted to meet him, to see him again. The young people
especially were clamouring to behold the man who had been kept
buried alive for fourteen years for his *Attentat*. I was beset with
anxiety about him, but there would be no escape for him, I felt, until
all the scheduled affairs were over. He would then be able to go to
the little farm and perhaps find his way slowly back to life.

The Detroit papers were full of our visit with Carl, and before we
left the city, they even had me married to Alexander Berkman and
on our honeymoon. In Chicago the reporters were constantly on our
trail, the meetings under heavy police guard. The reception in Grand
Central Palace, New York, because of its size and the intense enthusiasm of the audience, depressed Sasha even more than the others.
But now the misery was at an end and we went out to the little
Ossining farm. Sasha was pleased with it; he loved its wildness,
seclusion, and quiet. And I was filled with new hope for him and for
his release from the grip of the prison shadows.

Having been starved for so many years, he now ate ravenously.
It was extraordinary what an amount of food he could absorb,
especially of his favourite Jewish dishes, of which he had been deprived so long. It was nothing at all for him to follow up a substantial
meal with a dozen *blintzes* (a kind of Yiddish pancake containing
cheese or meat) or a huge apple pie. I cooked and baked, happy in
his enjoyment of the food. Most of my friends were in the habit of
paying court to my culinary art, but no one ever did so much justice
to it as my poor, famished Sasha.

Our country idyll was short-lived. The black phantoms of the past
were again pursuing their victim, driving him out of the house and
robbing him of peace. Sasha roamed the woods or lay for hours
stretched on the ground, silent and listless.

The quiet of the country increased his inner turmoil, he told me.
He could not endure it; he must go back to town. He must find work
to occupy his mind or he would go mad. And he must make a living;
he would not be supported by public collections. He had already declined to accept the five hundred dollars the comrades had raised
for him, and had distributed the money among several anarchist publications. There was another thing that tormented him: the thought

of his unfortunate comrades of so many years. How could he enjoy peace and comfort, knowing that they were deprived of both? He had pledged himself to voice their cause and to cry out against the horrors within prison walls. Yet he was doing nothing but eating, sleeping, and drifting. He could not go on that way, he said.

I understood his suffering, and my heart bled for my dear one, so bound by the past. We returned to 210 East Thirteenth Street, and there the struggle grew more intense, the struggle for adjustment to living. In his depleted physical condition Sasha could find no work to do, and the atmosphere surrounding me appeared strange and alien to him. With the passing weeks and months his misery increased. When we were alone in the flat, or in the company of Max, he breathed a little freer, and he was not unhappy with Becky Edelson, a young comrade who often came to visit us. All my other friends irritated and disturbed him; he could not bear their presence and he always looked for some excuse to leave. Generally it was dawn before he returned. I would hear his weary steps as he went to his room, hear him fling himself dressed upon his bed and fall into restless sleep, always disturbed by frightful nightmares of his prison life. Repeatedly he would awaken with fearful shrieks that chilled my blood with terror. Entire nights I would pace the floor in anguish of heart, racking my brain for some means to help Sasha find his way back to life.

It occurred to me that a lecture tour might prove a wedge to it. It would enable him to unburden himself of what lay so heavily on his mind—prison and its brutality—and it would help him perhaps to readjust himself to life away from the work he considered mine. It might bring back his old faith in himself. I prevailed upon Sasha to get in touch with our people in a few cities. Soon he had numerous applications for lectures. Almost immediately it brought about a change; he became less restless and depressed, somewhat more communicative with the friends who came to see me, and he even showed an interest in the preparations for the October issue of *Mother Earth*.

That number was to contain articles on Leon Czolgosz, in memory of the fifth anniversary of his death. Sasha and Max strongly favoured the idea of a memorial issue, but other comrades fought against it on the ground that anything about Czolgosz would hurt the cause as well as the magazine. They even threatened to withdraw their material support. I had promised myself when I started *Mother Earth* never to permit anyone, whether group or individual, to dictate its policy; opposition now made me the more determined to go through with my plan of dedicating the October number to Czolgosz.

As soon as the magazine was off the press, Sasha began his tour. His first stops were Albany, Syracuse, and Pittsburgh. I hated the idea of his going back to the dreadful city so soon, particularly because I knew that according to the provisions of the Pennsylvania commutation law Sasha remained at the mercy of the authorities of that State for eight years, during which period they had the legal right to arrest him at any time for the slightest offence and send him back to the penitentiary to complete his full term of twenty-two years. Sasha was set, however, on lecturing in Pittsburgh, and I clung to the faint hope that speaking in that city might free him from his prison nightmare. I felt relieved when a telegram came from him saying that the Pittsburgh gathering had been a success, and that all was well.

His next stop was Cleveland. On the day after his first meeting in that city I received a wire informing me that Sasha had left the house of the comrade with whom he had spent the night and had not yet returned. It did not disturb me very much, knowing how the poor boy dreaded contact with people. He had probably decided to go to a hotel, I thought, to be by himself, and he would undoubtedly appear for the lecture in the evening. But at midnight another wire notified me that he had not attended the meeting, and that the comrades were worried. I, too, became alarmed and telegraphed Carl in Detroit, the next city Sasha was expected in. There could be no answer the same day, and the night, full of black forebodings, seemed to stand still. The morning newspapers carried large headlines about the "disappearance of Alexander Berkman, the recently freed anarchist."

The shock completely unnerved me. I was too paralysed at first to form any idea of what might have happened to him. Finally two possibilities presented themselves: that he had been kidnapped by the authorities in Pittsburgh, or — more likely and terrible — that he might have ended his life. I was frantic that I had failed to plead with him not to go to Pittsburgh. Yet, though fearful of his danger, the more dreadful thought persisted in my brain, the thought of suicide. Sasha had been in the throes of such depression that he had said repeatedly he did not care to live, that prison had unfitted him for life. My heart rebelled in passionate protest against the cruel forces that could drive him to leave me just when he had come back. I was tormented by bitter regrets that I had suggested the idea of the lecture tour.

For three days and three nights we in New York and our people in every city searched police stations, hospitals, and morgues for Sasha, but without result. Cables came from Kropotkin and other European anarchists inquiring about him, and streams of people besieged my flat. I was nearly mad with uncertainty, yet dreaded to make up my mind that Sasha had taken the fatal step.

I had to go to Elizabeth, New Jersey, to address a meeting. Long public life had taught me not to expose joy or sorrow to the idle gaze of the market-place. But how hide what now was obsessing my every thought? I had promised weeks previously, and I was compelled to go. Max accompanied me. He had already bought our tickets and we were almost at the railroad gate. Suddenly I was seized by a feeling of some impending calamity. I stopped short. "Max! Max!" I cried, "I can't go! Something is pulling me back to the flat!" He understood and urged me to return. It would be all right, he assured me; he would explain my absence and speak in my stead. Hastily pressing his hand, I dashed off to catch the first ferry-boat back to New York.

On Thirteenth Street near Third Avenue I saw Becky running towards me, excitedly waving a yellow slip of paper. "I've been looking for you everywhere!" she cried. "Sasha is alive! He is waiting for you at the telegraph office on Fourteenth Street!" My heart leaped to my throat. I snatched the paper from her. It read: "Come. I am waiting for you here." I ran full speed towards Fourteenth Street. When I got to the office, I came face to face with Sasha. He was leaning against the wall, a small hand-bag at his side.

"Sasha!" I cried; "oh, my dear — at last!" At the sound of my voice he pulled himself together, as if out of a harrowing dream. His lips moved, but he remained silent. His eyes alone told of his suffering and despair. I took his arm and steadied him, his body shaking as in a chill. We had almost reached 210 East Thirteenth Street when he suddenly cried: "Not here! Not here! I can't see anybody in your flat!" For a moment I did not know what to do; then I hailed a cab and told the driver to go to the Park Avenue Hotel.

It was dinner-hour, and the lobby filled with guests. Everybody was in evening dress; conversation and laughter blended with the strains of music from the dining-hall. When we were alone in a room,

Sasha grew dizzy and had to be helped to the couch, where he fell down in a heap. I ran to the telephone and ordered whisky and hot broth. He drank eagerly, indicating that it refreshed him. He had not eaten in three days, nor taken off his clothes. I prepared a bath for him, and while helping him to undress, my hand suddenly came in contact with a steel object. It was a revolver he was trying to hide in his hip pocket.

After the bath and another hot drink Sasha spoke to me. He had hated the idea of the tour the moment he got out of New York, he said. The approach of each lecture would throw him into a panic and fill him with an irresistible desire to escape. The meetings had been badly attended and lacked spirit. The homes of the comrades he had stopped with were congested, with no separate corner for him. More terrible even had been the constant stream of people, the incessant questions. Still he had kept on. Pittsburgh had somewhat relieved his depression; the presence of a horde of police, detectives, and prison officials had roused his fighting spirit and had lifted him out of himself. But Cleveland was a ghastly experience from the moment he arrived. There was no one to meet him at the station, and he spent the day in an exhausting search to locate comrades. The audience in the evening was small and inert; after the lecture came an endless ride to the farm of the comrade whose guest he was to be. Worn and sick unto death, he fell into a heavy sleep. He awoke in the middle of the night and was horrified to find a strange man snoring at his side. His years of solitude in prison had made close human proximity a torture to him. He rushed out of the house, into the country road, to look for some hiding-place where he could be alone. But peace would not come, nor relief from the feeling that he was unfit for life. He determined to end it.

In the morning he walked to the city and bought a revolver. He decided to go to Buffalo. No one knew him there, no one would discover him in life or claim him in death. He roamed through the city all day and night, but New York drew him with irresistible force. Finally he went there and spent two days and nights circling around 210 East Thirteenth Street. He was in constant terror of meeting anyone, yet he could not keep away. Each time on returning to his squalid little room on the Bowery he would take up the revolver for the final gesture. He went to the park nearby, determined to make an end. The sight of little children playing turned his mind to the past and the "sailor girl." "And then I knew that I could not die without seeing you again," he concluded.

His story held me breathless, unable and afraid to break its thread. Sasha's inner conflict was so overwhelming that my own excruciating uncertainty during those three days seemed nothing in comparison. Infinite tenderness filled me for the man who had already died a thousand deaths and who was again attempting to escape life. I became possessed of a burning craving to defeat the ominous forces that were pursuing my unfortunate friend.

I held out my hand to him and begged him to come home with me. "Only Stella is there, my dearest," I pleaded, "and I will see that no one intrudes upon you." At the flat I found Stella, Max, and Becky waiting anxiously for our return. I took Sasha through the corridor into my room and put him to bed. He went off to sleep like a weary child.

Sasha remained in bed for several days, asleep most of the time and only half-aware of his surroundings during his waking hours. Max, Stella, and Becky relieved me in taking care of him; no one else was allowed to disturb the quiet in my apartment.

A group of young anarchists had arranged a gathering to discuss Leon Czolgosz and his act. At the meeting three of the boys were arrested. I knew nothing about the matter until I was awakened early one morning by violent ringing of the bell and informed of the arrest. We immediately called a meeting to protest against the suppression of free speech, the announced speakers being Bolton Hall, Harry Kelly, John Coryell, Max Baginski, and I. On the appointed evening Sasha, who was beginning to feel a little better, wanted to go. Fearing he might be upset again, I persuaded him to attend the theatre with Stella instead.

When I arrived with Max and the Coryells in the hall, we found a small audience, but the walls were lined with policemen. Young Julius Edelson, brother of Becky, who had been arrested at the previous meeting, but had been bailed out by Bolton Hall, had just ascended the rostrum. He had spoken about ten minutes when there came a commotion; several officers dashed forward and pulled Julius off the platform, while other policemen charged the crowd, drawing the chairs from under the people, dragging the girls out by the hair, and clubbing the men. Crying and cursing, the audience rushed for the exits. When I got to the stairs with Max, a policeman gave him a violent kick that nearly sent him down to the bottom, while another struck me in the back and told me I was under arrest. "You're just the one we want!" he roared; "we'll teach you how to protest!" In the patrol wagon I found myself in the company of eleven "dangerous criminals," all of them young boys and girls, members of the offending group. Bolton Hall and Harry Kelly and the Coryells had somehow escaped the brutality of the police. Pending our indictment we were admitted to bail.

Our arrest produced one beneficial result; it immediately roused Sasha's fighting spirit. "My resurrection has come!" he cried, when he heard of what had happened at the meeting; "there is work for me to do now!" My joy over Sasha's awakening, and the realization of the danger the arrested youngsters were facing, increased my strength and energy. Soon we organized for the fight, with Hugh O. Pentecost and Meyer London as our legal advisers and with considerable material support from our American and foreign friends. Already at the police-court hearing it became evident that there was no case against us, but the District Attorney was out for glory. What better way of getting it than by saving the city from anarchy? It was an easy job now, with the Criminal Anarchy Law on the statute-book. The judge seemed willing enough to oblige the District Attorney, but most of the criminal anarchists before him looked so young and inoffensive that His Honour was dubious about any jury's convicting them. To save his face he held us over for "further examination."

While I always preferred certainty in such matters, I should have welcomed the delay had I been able to continue my lecture work. But the police kept up a systematic raid upon all English anarchist activities; not in the open manner in which they had suppressed the meeting, but in a more insidious way. They terrorized the hall-keepers, thereby making it practically impossible for me to get a hearing in any public place in New York. Even so harmless an affair as a *Mother Earth* masked ball, arranged to raise funds for our publication, was broken up. Fifty officers had come down to the hall and ordered the people to get out, tearing off their masks. When that failed to provoke trouble, they forced the owner to close the hall. It meant a great financial loss.

We organized a *Mother Earth* Club, giving weekly lectures on various topics and occasionally also musicales. The police were furious; they had been hounding us for nine weeks, and still we would not be put down. Something more drastic and intimidating had to be done to save the sacred institutions of law and order. The next move of the authorities took place at a meeting that was to be addressed by Alexander Berkman, John R. Coryell, and Emma Goldman. They arrested all the speakers. A criminal anarchist, fifteen years of age, who happened to be at the door was also taken along to complete the quartet. I had intended to speak on the " Misconceptions of Anarchism," a lecture I had delivered only two weeks previously before the Brooklyn Philosophical Society. Detectives from the newly created Anarchist Squad had been present, yet no arrest had taken place. It was obvious that they had not dared to interfere with a non-anarchist society, even though the speaker was Emma Goldman. It might have taught the Brooklyn philosophers that it was not anarchism but the Police Department that was destroying the little liberty that still existed in the United States. On the way to the police station the inspector in charge of the Anarchist Squad asked me whether I did not intend to cease my agitation. When I assured him that I was more determined than ever to go on, he informed me that thereafter I would be arrested every time I attempted to speak in public.

For a while it seemed as if Sasha had really found himself again and would be able to continue with me in our common life and work. He had been eager for activity since the day of our arrest, but after two months his interest gave way again to the gloom which had pursued him since he got out of prison. He thought that the main reason for his depression was his material dependence on me, which was galling to him. To free him from it I induced a good comrade to lend Sasha some money to set up a small printing shop. It helped to revive Sasha's spirits and he began to work assiduously to advance the venture. Presently he was installed in a complete printing outfit of his own that enabled him to do small jobs. But the happiness was not to last; new difficulties besieged him. He could not get a union label because as a compositor he was not permitted to do pressman's work, while to employ a pressman would be exploitation. He found himself in the same position I had been in with my massage establishment, and, rather than live off the labour of others or do non-union jobs, he gave up his shop. The old misery was upon him again.

Gradually I came to see that it was not so much the question of earning a living that harassed Sasha as something deeper and more bitter to face: the contrast between his dream-world of 1892 and my reality of 1906. The world of ideals he had taken with him to prison at twenty-one had defied the passage of time. Perhaps it was fortunate that it was so; it had been his spiritual support through all the terrible fourteen years, a star to illumine the blackness of his prison existence. It had even coloured his mind's-eye view of the outside world — of the movement, his friends, and especially myself. During that time life had kicked me about, forced me into the current of events, to sink or to swim — I had ceased to be the little "sailor girl" whose image had remained with Sasha from former days. I was a woman of thirty-seven who had undergone profound changes. I no longer fitted into the old mould, as he had expected me to. Sasha saw and felt it almost immediately upon his release. He had tried to understand the mature personality which had burst forth from the shell of the inexperienced girl, and, failing, he became resentful, critical, and often condemnatory of my life, my views, and my friends. He charged me with intellectual aloofness and revolutionary inconsistency. Every thrust from him cut me to the quick and made me cry out my grief. Often I wanted to run away, never to see him again, but I was held by something greater than the pain: the memory of his act, for which he alone had paid the price. More and more I realized that to my last breath it would remain the strongest link in the chain that bound me to him. The memory of our youth and of our love might fade, but his fourteen years' Calvary would never be eradicated from my heart.

A way out of the distressing situation suggested itself in the imperative need of my going on tour for *Mother Earth*. Sasha could remain in charge as editor of the magazine; it would help to release him from his cramped feeling and enable him to find freer expression. He liked Max, and there were able contributors to assist him: Voltairine de Cleyre, Theodore Schroeder, Bolton Hall, Hippolyte Havel, and others. Sasha readily accepted the plan, and I was relieved that he did not suspect how hard it was for me to go away so soon after he had come back to me. His release — I had waited for it with such intensity, and now I should not even be with him on the first anniversary of the day so long and anxiously looked forward to.

The death of Hugh O. Pentecost came as a shock to all of us who knew and appreciated the man and his work. The news reached us through the press, as we were not informed by his widow. Pentecost had been a firm believer in cremation as the more beautiful way of disposing of a person's remains. Naturally everybody expected him to be cremated and many of his friends planned to attend and send floral tributes. Great was our astonishment when we learned that Hugh O. Pentecost had been buried instead, and that he had been given a funeral in accordance with religious rites. It was sheerest irony, considering that the one thing which Hugh O. had held high throughout his entire life was free-thought. His political changes had been many: single-taxer, socialist, and anarchist — he had been all of them at one time or another. It was different with his attitude to religion and the Church. Irrevocably he had turned from them to convinced atheism. The presence of a minister at his grave was therefore the worst outrage to his memory, and an insult to his free-thought friends. It seemed like the fulfilment of a subconscious fear Pentecost had often voiced to me: "It is very hard to live decently, but still harder to die decently." Another of his frequent expressions was that love is more difficult to escape than hate. He meant the kind of love that binds one with soft arms and tender words stronger than chains. His inability to tear himself away from those "soft arms" had been behind the repeated changes of his social ideas. It had even led him to play false to the memory of the Chicago anarchists, among whose staunchest defenders he had been until ambition made him seek the post of Assistant District Attorney of New York. "I may have been mistaken," he had declared, "in saying that the Haymarket trial was a miscarriage of justice." Neither in life nor in death had Hugh O. Pentecost been permitted to remain true to himself.

Our work for Russia received considerable zest by the arrival of Grigory Gershuni. He had escaped from Siberia in a cabbage-barrel and had come to the States via California. Gershuni had been a schoolteacher, believing that only by the education of the masses could Russia be redeemed from the yoke of the Romanoffs. For many years he had been an ardent Tolstoyan, opposed to every form of active resistance. But incessant opposition and violence by the despotism had gradually taught Gershuni the inevitability of the methods pursued by the militant revolutionists in his country. He had joined the Fighting Organization of the Socialist-Revolutionist Party and had become one of its dominant figures. He had been condemned to death, but ultimately his sentence was commuted to lifelong imprisonment in Siberia.

Grigory Gershuni, like all the great Russians I had met, was of touching simplicity, extremely reticent about his own heroic life and fired to the exclusion of any personal interest by the vision of the liberation of the Russian masses. Moreover, he possessed what many Russian rebels lacked: a keen, practical sense, exactitude, and responsibility for tasks undertaken.

I saw much of this exceptional man during his stay in New York. I learned that his extraordinary escape had been aided by two young anarchists. Working in the carpenter shop of the prison, they had skilfully drilled undetectable air-holes in the barrel to be used by Gershuni, later nailing him up within. Gershuni never tired of praising the devotion and daring of those two boys, mere children in years, yet so courageous and dependable in their revolutionary zeal.

About this time we began to prepare for the celebration of *Mother Earth's* first birthday. It seemed incredible that the magazine should have survived the hardships and difficulties of the past twelve months. The failure of some of the New York literati to live up to their promises to write for it had been only one of the ill winds which had pursued my child. They were enthusiastic at first, until they realized that *Mother Earth* pleaded for freedom and abundance in life as the basis of art. To most of them art meant an escape from reality; how, then, could they be expected to support anything that boldly courted life? They left the new-born one to shift for itself. Their places were soon filled, however, by braver and freer spirits, among them Leonard Abbott, Sadakichi Hartmann, Alvin Sanborn, all of whom regarded life and art as the twin flames of revolt.

This difficulty overcome, another arose: condemnation from my own ranks. *Mother Earth* was not revolutionary enough, they claimed, the reason no doubt being that it treated anarchism less as a dogma than as a liberating ideal. Fortunately many of my comrades stood by me, giving generously to the support of the magazine. And my own personal friends, even those who were not anarchists, were faithfully devoted to the publication and to every fight I made against continued police persecution. Altogether it was a rich and fruitful year, full of promise for the future of *Mother Earth*.

CHAPTER XXXI

OUR HEARINGS ON THE CHARGE OF CRIMINAL ANARCHY WERE repeatedly postponed and finally dropped altogether. That set me free to start on my projected tour to the Coast, the first since 1897. Before I had gone very far, my meetings were stopped by the police in three cities — Columbus, Toledo, and Detroit.

The action of the authorities in Toledo was especially reprehensible because the Mayor, Brand Whitlock, was supposed to be a man of advanced ideas, known as a Tolstoyan and "philosophical" anarchist. I had met a number of American individualists who called themselves philosophical anarchists. On closer acquaintance they invariably proved neither philosophers nor anarchists, and their belief in free speech always had a "but" to it.

Mayor Whitlock, however, was also a single-taxer, a member of a group of Americans who stood out as the most valiant champions of free speech and press. In fact, the single-taxers had always been the first to support me in my fights against police interference. I was therefore greatly surprised to find a single-tax mayor guilty of the same arbitrary attitude as any ordinary city official. I asked some of his admirers how they could explain such behaviour on the part of a man like Whitlock. Much to my astonishment, they informed me that he was under the impression that I had come to Toledo for the express purpose of fomenting trouble among the automobile-workers then on strike. He was trying to bring about a settlement between the bosses and their employees, and he thought it best not to permit me to speak.

"Evidently your Mayor knows that his settlement is likely to benefit the owners and not the strikers," I remarked, "else he would not fear what I might say."

I informed them that until I arrived in Toledo, I had not even known about the strike. I had come to lecture on the "Misconceptions of Anarchism." I cheerfully admitted, however, that if the strikers asked me to speak, I should tell them to steer clear of politicians, who are the worst meddlers and who help to break the backbone of every economic struggle. This was reported to a group of American liberals, who at once set to work to arrange a special meeting for me.

The most spirited among them was a venerable old woman, Mrs. Kate B. Sherwood. In abolition times she had helped many a fugitive slave to safety, and she did not change with the years. She was a fervent feminist, a great libertarian in economic and educational fields, as well as a lovable personality. The dear lady must have read the Riot Act to the Mayor, because there was no further interference in Toledo with my lectures.

In Minneapolis I had an amusing experience. I was invited to address an organization of professional men known as the Spook Club. I was told that no woman had ever before been admitted into the holy presence of the Spookers, but that I had been made an exception. Not believing in special privileges, I wrote to the club that in my capacity as nurse I had never known nervousness when I had to lay out the dead. But to face living corpses alone would prove disconcerting to me. I would brave the task of preparing the Spookers for burial if I could have a few husky members of my own sex to assist me. The poor Spook Club was flabbergasted. To consent to my request involved the danger of a female invasion. To refuse was to expose themselves to public ridicule. Male conceit conquered its lily-white purity. "Bring your regiment along, Emma Goldman," the Spookers replied, "and take the consequences." My women friends and I created almost a revolution in the club. Alas, not in the heads, but only in the hearts of the Spookers. We made them conscious that there is nothing duller in all the world than exclusive gatherings of men or of women, who are yet never able to eliminate each other from their minds. On this occasion everybody felt relief from sex obsession, natural and at ease. The evening was very interesting. Indeed, I was assured that it was considered the most stimulating intellectual treat in the club's history, and the most hilarious besides.

The liberal attitude of the Spookers towards me was only part of the general change which had taken place in the past six years in regard to anarchism. The tone of the press was no longer so vindictive. The papers in Toledo, Cincinnati, Toronto, Minneapolis, and

Winnipeg were extraordinarily decent in their reports of my meetings. In a long editorial one Winnipeg paper said:

> Emma Goldman has been accused of abusing freedom of speech in Winnipeg, and Anarchism has been denounced as a system that advocates murder. As a matter of fact, Emma Goldman indulged, while in Winnipeg, in no dangerous rant and made no statement that deserved more than moderate criticism of its wisdom or logic. Also, as a matter of fact, the man who claims that Anarchism teaches bomb-throwing and violence doesn't know what he is talking about. Anarchism is an ideal doctrine that is now, and always will be, utterly impracticable. Some of the gentlest and most gifted men of the world believe in it. The fact alone that Tolstoi is an Anarchist is conclusive proof that it teaches no violence.
>
> We all have a right to laugh at Anarchy as a wild dream. We all have a right to agree or disagree with the teachings of Emma Goldman. But we should not make ourselves ridiculous by criticizing a lecturer for the things that she did not say, nor by denouncing as violent and bloody a doctrine that preaches the opposite of violence.

After my coast-to-coast lecture tour I returned to New York at the end of June with a net result of a considerable number of subscribers to *Mother Earth* and a substantial surplus from the sale of literature to sustain the magazine during the inactive summer months.

In the early spring our European comrades had issued a call for an anarchist congress to be held in Amsterdam, Holland, in August. Some of the groups in the cities I had visited had requested me to attend the gathering as their delegate. It was gratifying to have the confidence of my comrades, and Europe always had its lure for me. But there was Sasha, only one year out of prison, and I had already been away from him for months. I longed to see him again and to try to bridge the gap which his imprisonment had created between us.

Sasha had done splendidly on *Mother Earth* while I was away. He had surprised everybody by the vigour of his style and the clarity of his thoughts. It was an amazing achievement for a man who had gone into prison ignorant of the English language and who had never written for publication before. His letters to me during my four months on tour were free from depression, and he showed much interest in the magazine and my work. I was proud of Sasha and his efforts, and I was full of hope that we might yet dispel the clouds that had been hanging in our sky since he had re-entered the outside world. These considerations made me hesitate to go to Amsterdam. I would decide when I reached New York, I told my comrades.

On my return I found Sasha as I had left him — in the same mental turmoil, in torturing conflict between the vision that had inspired his deed and the reality that confronted him now. He continued to dwell in the past, in the mirage he had created for himself during his living death. Everything in the present was alien to him, made him wince and avoid it. It was bitter irony that I, of all Sasha's friends, should cause him the deepest disappointment and pain — I who had never had him out of my mind in all the cruel years, or out of my heart, no matter who else had been there, not even Ed, whom I had loved more deeply and intensely than anyone else. Yet it was I who most roused Sasha's impatience and resentment; not in a personal sense, but because of the changes I had undergone in my attitude to life, to people, and to our movement. We did not seem to have a single thought in common. Yet I felt bound to Sasha, bound for ever by the tears and blood of fourteen years.

Often, when I could no longer bear up under his censure and condemnation, I would fight back with harsh and bitter words, then run to my room and cry out in pain against the differences that were tearing us apart. Yet I would always come back to Sasha, feeling that whatever he had said or done was nothing in the light of what he had endured. I knew *that* would ever weigh heaviest in the balance with me and bring me to his side at every moment of his need. Just now it seemed that I was of little help. Sasha appeared to feel more at ease when I was away.

I decided to comply with the request of my Western comrades to represent them at the anarchist congress. Sasha said he would continue on the magazine until my return, but that his heart was not in *Mother Earth*. He wanted a weekly propaganda paper that would reach the workers. He had already discussed the project with Voltairine de Cleyre, Harry Kelly, and other friends. They had agreed with him that such a paper was needed and had promised to sign an appeal for the necessary funds. They had been worried, however, that I might misunderstand, that I might consider the new publication a competitor of *Mother Earth*. "What a ridiculous notion," I protested; "I claim no monopoly of the movement. By all means try to get out a weekly paper. I will add my name to the call." Sasha was quite moved, embraced me tenderly, and sat down to write the appeal. My poor boy! If only I could have had the assurance that his project would bring him peace, help him back to life and to the work his mastery of language and his pen should enable him to do!

More and more I was beginning to see that there was an inner resentment in Sasha, perhaps not even conscious, against being part of the activities I had created for myself. He longed for something of his own making, something that would express his own self. I hoped fervently that the weekly paper would prove the means of his release and that it might succeed.

I was getting ready for my trip abroad; Max was going, too, representing some German groups at the Amsterdam congress. We both needed to get away from our environment for a while. The farm had not turned out the roseate reality he had hoped for. A farm never does for city people who come to the land with romantic notions about nature and with no ability to cope with her hardships. Our place in Ossining had proved too primitive and the winter too harsh for Max's little daughter. Another reason was the isolation of Millie, which she was unable to bear. My friends had moved to the city and were trying desperately to make ends meet, Max by occasional articles for German papers and contributions to *Mother Earth,* Millie by sewing. The stress she had endured since the birth of her child had made her nervous and irritable, and Max shrank into his shell at the least disharmony. Like myself he longed to get away from conditions that were agonizing, yet of no one's making.

Sasha was much more alive now, thanks to his plan for a weekly paper. There was also another factor that helped to raise his spirits. He had gained many friends among our young comrades, and he was especially attracted by young Becky Edelson. I felt considerably relieved about him. *Mother Earth* also did not worry me; I left it secure until my return and I was certain of its quality, with Sasha as its editor, and John Coryell, Hippolyte Havel, and others as collaborators.

Hippolyte and I had long ago drifted apart in our old relation, but our friendship had remained as strong as before, as had also our common interest in the social struggle. His great historical knowledge and his feeling for events made him most valuable to our magazine.

In the middle of August 1907 Max and I waved our friends goodbye from the Holland-America pier. Besides our mission at the congress, we both looked upon our trip as a quest for something to fill our inner void. The calm sea and the ever-soothing companionship of Max helped me to relax from the tension of the months preceding and following Sasha's liberation. By the time we reached Amsterdam, I was again in full control of myself, eager with anticipation of the people I should meet, our congress, and the work to be done.

I had heard a great deal about the extreme cleanliness of the Dutch, but until I went for a walk in Amsterdam on the morning after our arrival, I did not know how uncomfortable Hollanders could make it for the passers-by. I had gone out with Max to take a look at the quaint old town. We found every balcony adorned with buxom servants in colourful dress, arms and legs bare, furiously beating carpets and rugs. A pleasant picture indeed, but the whirlwind of dust and dirt they were lustily shaking on to our defenceless heads filled our throats and covered our clothes. Still we could have stood it if we had not been at the same time treated to a shower of cold water meant for the plants. The unexpected bath was more than the Dutch cleanliness we had bargained for.

The congress was my third attempt to attend an international anarchist gathering. In 1893 such a conclave had been planned, and it was to take place during that year's exposition in Chicago. I had been chosen to represent several New York groups, but my trial and imprisonment had prevented my attendance. At the eleventh hour the Chicago police had prohibited the congress, but it was held just the same — in the most unlikely place imaginable. A comrade, employed as clerk in one of the city departments, had smuggled a dozen delegates into a room in the City Hall.

The second time had been in Paris, in 1900, where I was closely connected with the preparatory work of our congress. The French police, too, had made open conferences impossible. The sessions held under cover, while exciting enough, had made constructive work impossible.

It was certainly a commentary on democratic America and republican France that an international anarchist congress, prohibited in both countries, should have the right to meet quite openly in monarchical Holland. Eighty men and women, most of them hounded and persecuted in their own countries, were here able to address large meetings, gather in daily session, and discuss openly such vital problems as revolution, syndicalism, mass insurrection, and individual acts of violence, without any interference from the authorities. We went about the city singly or in groups, had social gatherings in restaurants or cafés, talked, and sang revolutionary songs until early morning hours, yet we were not shadowed, spied upon, or in any way molested.

More remarkable still was the attitude of the Amsterdam press. Even the most conservative newspapers treated us, not as criminals or lunatics, but as a group of serious people who had come together for a serious purpose. Those papers were opposed to anarchism, yet they did not misrepresent us or distort anything said at our sessions.

One of the vital subjects discussed at length by the congress was the problem of organization. Some delegates deprecated Ibsen's idea, as presented by Dr. Stockmann in *An Enemy of the People,* to the effect that the strongest is he who stands alone. They preferred Peter Kropotkin's view, so brilliantly elucidated in all his books, that it is mutual aid and co-operation that secure the best results. Max and I, however, stressed the need of both. We held that anarchism does not involve a choice between Kropotkin and Ibsen; it embraces both. While Kropotkin had thoroughly analysed the social conditions that lead to revolution, Ibsen had portrayed the psychologic struggle that culminates in the revolution of the human soul, the revolt of individuality. Nothing would prove more disastrous to our ideas, we contended, than to neglect the effect of the internal upon the external, of the psychologic motives and needs upon existing institutions.

There is a mistaken notion in some quarters, we argued, that organization does not foster individual freedom; that, on the contrary, it means the decay of individuality. In reality, however, the true function of organization is to aid the development and growth of personality. Just as the animal cells, by mutual co-operation, express their latent powers in the formation of the complete organism, so does the individuality, by co-operative effort with other individualities, attain its highest form of development. An organization, in the true sense, cannot result from the combination of mere nonentities. It must be composed of self-conscious, intelligent individualities. Indeed, the total of the possibilities and activities of an organization is represented in the expression of individual energies. Anarchism asserts the possibility of an organization without discipline, fear, or punishment and without the pressure of poverty: a new social organism, which will make an end to the struggle for the means of existence — the savage struggle which undermines the finest qualities in man and ever widens the social abyss. In short, anarchism strives towards a social organization which will establish well-being for all.

There were many interesting and vital personalities in the group of delegates, among them Dr. Friedberg, once member of the Social Democratic Party and Alderman of Berlin, who had become a brilliant exponent of the general strike and anti-militarism. Notwithstanding an indictment for high treason hanging over him, he took a most active part in the proceedings of the congress, oblivious of the danger awaiting him on his return home. There were also Luigi Fabbri, one of the ablest contributors to the educational Italian magazine *Università Populare;* Rudolph Rocker, who was doing splendid work among the Jewish population of London as lecturer and editor of the Yiddish *Arbeiter Freind;* Christian Cornelissen, one of the keenest intellects in our movement in Holland; Rudolph Grossmann, publisher of an anarchist paper in Austria; Alexander Schapiro, active among revolutionary trade unions in England; Thomas H. Keell, one of our most devoted workers on the London *Freedom;* and other capable and energetic comrades.

The French, Swiss, Belgian, Austrian, Bohemian, Russian, Serbian, Bulgarian, and Dutch delegates were all men of spirit and ability, but the most outstanding personality among them was Enrico Malatesta. Of fine and sensitive nature, Malatesta had already in his youth embraced revolutionary ideals. Later he met Bakunin, in whose circle he was the youngest, affectionately called "Benjamin." He wrote a number of popular pamphlets that found wide distribution, particularly in Italy and Spain, and he was editor of various anarchist publications. But his literary activities did not prevent him from participating also in the actual daily struggles of the workers. He had played an important rôle, together with the celebrated Carlo Cafiero and the famous Russian revolutionist Sergius "Stepniak" (Kravtchinsky), in the uprising in Benevento, Italy, in 1877. His interest in popular rebellion runs like a red thread throughout his life. Whether he happened to be in Switzerland, France, England, or the Argentine, an uprising in his native country always brought him to the aid of the people. In 1897 he had again taken an active part in the rebellion in southern Italy. His entire life was one of storm and stress, his energies and exceptional abilities devoted to the service of the anarchist cause. But whatever his work in the movement, he always insisted on remaining materially independent of it, earning his living by manual labour, which was a principle of his life. The considerable inheritance from his father, consisting of land and houses in Italy, he had deeded without any remuneration to the workers who occupied them, himself continuing to exist most frugally on the earnings of his own hands. His name was one of the best-known and best-beloved in Latin countries.

I had met this grand old anarchist fighter in London in 1895, for a few brief moments. On my second visit, in 1899, I discovered that Enrico Malatesta had gone to the States to lecture and edit the Italian anarchist paper *La Questione Sociale*. While there, he was shot by a deluded Italian patriot, but Enrico, true anarchist that he was, refused to prosecute his assailant. In Amsterdam I had the first real chance to come into daily contact with him. Max and I quickly fell under the spell of Malatesta. We loved his capacity to throw off the weight of the world and give himself to play in his leisure. Every moment spent with him was a joy, whether he exulted over the sight of the sea or frolicked in a public garden.

The most important constructive result of our congress was the formation of an International Bureau. Its secretariate consisted of Malatesta, Rocker, and Schapiro. The purpose of the bureau, the headquarters of which were in London, was to bring into closer contact the anarchist groups and organizations of the various countries, to make a thorough and painstaking study of the labour struggle in every land, and to supply data and material concerning it to the anarchist press. The bureau was also to begin immediate preparations for another congress, to be held in the near future in London.

Upon the closing of our sessions we attended the anti-militarist congress, arranged by the Dutch pacifist anarchists, among whom Domela Nieuwenhuis was the most prominent. Domela's origin had certainly not forecast his becoming an enemy of authority. His ancestors were nearly all ministers of the Church. He himself had been a preacher of the Lutheran faith, but his progressive spirit lifted him out of the narrow path of theology. Domela joined the Social Democratic Party, became its foremost representative in Holland, and was elected the first Socialist member of Parliament. But he did not remain there very long. Like Johann Most and the great French anarchist Pierre Proudhon, Nieuwenhuis soon realized that nothing vital could come for liberty from parliamentary activities. He resigned his post, declaring himself an anarchist.

Since then he had devoted all his time and large private fortune to our movement, especially to the propaganda of anti-militarism. Domela was of striking and winning appearance — tall and straight, with expressive features, large blue eyes, flowing white hair and beard. He radiated kindness and sympathy and was the embodiment of the ideal he fought for. One of his characteristic traits was a broad tolerance. He was for years a vegetarian and teetotaller, yet meat and wine never left his table. "Why should my family or guests be deprived of anything that I do not care for?" he once said as he poured out the wine for us at dinner.

Before we left for France, I had occasion to address a gathering of Dutch transport workers. Once more I saw the difference between the independence of the Dutch workers, in spite of their monarchy, and democratic United States, where most of the people know precious little of independence. Several detectives had sneaked into the meeting. They were discovered by the committee, however, and were unceremoniously put out. I could not help comparing this show of spirit to the lack of it in American trade unions, so infested with the Pinkerton detective pest.

At last we were back in Paris, her lure again upon me, her reckless youth in my veins. I grew younger and more eager for all that my beloved city on the Seine could give. There was much more to learn and to absorb than in previous years.

There was also my own Stella, whom I had not seen for many months. She and dear old Victor Dave awaited us at the station and carried us off to a café. Stella was already quite Parisienne, proud of her French and her familiarity with restaurants where the cuisine was good and prices reasonable. Victor, his hair whiter, still preserved his youthful gait and his former capacity for fun. We joked and laughed more during our first dinner in Paris than I had laughed in months. The particular cause for our merriment was Stella's unsuspecting boss, no less a personage than the American Consul, whose secretary she was. Emma Goldman's devoted niece, and still the Consulate had not been blown up!

While we were yet in Holland, news had come that Peter Kropotkin had at last been readmitted to France. Peter loved the country and its people. To him France signified the cradle of liberty, the French Revolution the symbol of all that the world had of social idealism. To be sure, France was very short of the glory my great teacher had invested her with; his own eighteen months' incarceration in a French prison and subsequent expulsion had demonstrated it. Yet by some peculiar partiality Peter hailed France as the banner-bearer of freedom and the most cultured country in the world. We knew that nothing he had personally suffered had changed his feeling about the French people, and we rejoiced that he was now able to satisfy his longing to return.

Peter was already in Paris when we arrived, living but a few doors from my hotel, on Boulevard Saint-Michel. I found him in higher spirits than I had ever seen him before; he looked more vigorous and vivacious. Pretending not to know the reason, I inquired what had brought about the happy change. "Paris, Paris, my dear!" he cried. "Is there any other city in the world that gets into one's blood like Paris?" We discussed the movement in France and the work of the local groups. His favourite child was *Temps Nouveaux,* the paper he had helped to establish, yet his sense of the rights of other groups, even if they disagreed with him, was too great and his love of justice too strong to discourage the opposing elements. There was something large and beautiful about him. No one could be in his presence very long without feeling inspired by him.

Though he was busy with many things, especially the revision of his manuscript of *The Great French Revolution,* Peter would not let me go until I had told him everything about our congress. He was particularly pleased with our stand on organization and our insistence on the right of individual as well as collective revolt.

With the help of Monatte I was able to make a study of syndicalism in action at the Confédération du Travail. The leaders were nearly all anarchists, men of a much sturdier and more interesting type than one usually meets in Paris. Not only were Pouget, Pataud, Delasalle, Grueffulhieus, and Monatte brilliant exponents of new labour theories; they also had practical knowledge and experience in the daily struggle of the workers. Together with their colleagues they had converted the Bourse du Travail into a beehive of activity. Every union had its office there; many published their papers in the common printing shop, *La Voix du Peuple,* the weekly organ of the C. G. T., being perhaps the most instructive and ably edited labour paper in the world. There were night classes where the workers were taught every aspect of the intricate industrial system. Lectures were given on scientific and economic subjects, and a well-equipped dispensary and *crèche* were maintained by the workers themselves. The institution represented a practical effort to teach the masses how to make the coming revolution and how to help the new social life to birth.

Observation and study at the very source of syndicalism convinced me that it represented the economic arena where Labour could match its strength against the organized forces of its capitalist foe.

To these experiences were added others, no less enlightening, with the group of modern artists who by pen and brush were voicing the social protest, with Steinlen and Grandjuan doing the most forceful work. I did not find Steinlen, but Grandjuan proved to be a simple, kindly soul, a born rebel, the artist and idealist in the truest sense. He was at work on a set of drawings depicting phases of proletarian life. His idea was to portray Labour, pathetic in dumb helplessness, slowly awakening to the consciousness of germinating strength. He expressed his belief that the mission of art is to inspire the vision of a new dawn. "In this respect all our artists are revolutionaries," Grandjuan assured me. "Steinlen and the others are doing for art what Zola, Mirbeau, Richepin, and Rictus have done for letters. They are bringing art in rapport with the currents of life, the great human struggle for the right to know and live life."

I spoke to Grandjuan about *Mother Earth* and what it had been trying to do in America. He at once offered to make a cover-design for it, and before I left Paris, he sent it to me. It was significant in conception and expressive in its design.

The trial of nine anti-militarists and a splendid educational experiment at Rambouillet, near Paris, by Sébastien Faure, were among my other important experiences during this visit to France. The group involved in the trial consisted of one girl and eight boys, the oldest not more than twenty-three years of age. They had distributed a manifesto among soldiers urging them to use their arms against their superiors instead of against their brother working-men — certainly a very grave offence from the standpoint of military interests. In an American court those youths would have been browbeaten, terrorized, and railroaded to prison for a long term. In Paris they became the accusers, thundering anathema against the State, patriotism, militarism, and war. Far from being interfered with, the defiant denunciation of the young prisoners was listened to with attention and respect. The bold *plaidoirie* of the counsel for the defence, the distinguished persons who came to testify to the idealism of the accused, and the entire atmosphere of the court combined to make the anti-militarist trial one of the most dramatic events I had witnessed.

True, the prisoners were found guilty and sentenced to small terms, the longest being three years. Since it was France, the girl was set free altogether. In my adopted country their punishment would have been incomparably more severe and they would have undoubtedly been held also for contempt of court because of their frank avowal of their opinions and acts and the ridicule they heaped on the judge and the prosecuting attorney.

It struck me that behind the difference between American and French legal procedure was a fundamental difference in attitude to social revolt. Frenchmen had gained from their Revolution the understanding that institutions are neither sacred nor unalterable, and that social conditions are subject to change. Rebels are therefore considered in France the precursors of coming upheavals.

In America the ideals of the Revolution are dead — mummies that must not be touched. Hence the hatred and condemnation which meet the social and political rebel in the United States.

Long before I came to Paris, I had read in our French press of a unique educational experiment by the anarchist Sébastien Faure. I had heard him speak in 1900 and was carried away by his truly great eloquence. Moreover, Sébastien Faure's unusual personal history made me feel that the modern school organized by him must be of more than ordinary interest.

Beginning life as a priest, Faure had broken the shackles of Catholicism and become its formidable foe. In 1897, during the Dreyfus affair, he had joined the campaign led by Emile Zola, Anatole France, Bernard Lazare, and Octave Mirbeau against the reactionary forces in France. Faure became a fervent spokesman of Dreyfus, lecturing throughout the country, exposing the military clique that had railroaded an innocent man to Devil's Island to cover its own corruption. After that, Faure completely emancipated himself from belief in authority, whether in heaven or upon earth. Anarchism became his goal, the work for its achievement his passionate endeavour.

"La Ruche" (the Beehive), as Faure's school was called, was situated on the outskirts of Rambouillet, an ancient French village. With only a few people to help him, Faure had turned a wild, uncultivated stretch of land into a flourishing farm growing fruit and vegetables. He had taken twenty-four orphan children and those of parents too poor to pay and was housing, feeding, and clothing them at his own expense. He had created an atmosphere at La Ruche that released the life of the child from discipline and coercion of any sort. He had discarded the old methods of education and in their place he established understanding for the needs of the child, confidence and trust in its possibilities, and respect for its personality.

Not even at Cempuis, the school of the venerable libertarian Paul Robin, which I had visited in 1900, was the spirit of comradeship and co-operation between pupils and teachers so complete as at La Ruche. Robin, too, felt the need of a new approach to the child, but he still remained somewhat tied to the old text-books on education. La Ruche had freed itself also from them. The hand-painted wall-paper in the dormitory and class-rooms, picturing the life of plants, flowers, birds, and animals, had a more quickening effect on the imagination of the children than any "regular" lessons. The free grouping of the children around their teachers, listening to some story or seeking explanation for puzzling thoughts, amply made up for lack of old-fashioned instruction. In discussing problems of the education of the young, Faure showed an exceptional grasp of child psychology. The results accomplished by his school within two years were highly gratifying. "It is surprising how frank, kind, and affectionate the children are to each other," he said. "The harmony between themselves and the adults at La Ruche is highly encouraging. We should feel at fault were the children to fear or honour us merely because we are their elders. We leave nothing undone to gain their confidence and love; that accomplished, understanding will replace duty; confidence, fear; and affection, sternness." No one has yet fully realized the wealth of sympathy, kindness, and generosity hidden in the soul of the child. The effort of every true educator should be to unlock that treasure — to stimulate the child's impulses and call forth the best and noblest tendencies. What greater reward can there be for one whose life-work is to watch over the growth of the human plant than to see it unfold its petals and to observe it develop into a true individuality?

My visit to La Ruche was a valuable experience that made me realize how much could be done, even under the present system, in the way of libertarian education. To build the man and woman of the future, to unshackle the soul of the child — what grander task for those who, like Sébastien Faure, are pedagogues, not by the mere grace of a college degree, but innately, born with the gift to create, as the poet or the artist is?

Paris, always enriching one with new impressions, made it difficult for me to leave. Many friends had also endeared themselves to me, among them Max Nettlau, whom I had first met in London in 1900 and who had introduced me there to the museums and other British art treasures. In Paris I saw much of Nettlau. He was one of the most intellectual men of our movement, a scientist and historian. At the time he was collecting additional material for his monumental work on Michael Bakunin.

A few days before we left Paris, there arrived Jo Davidson, the young American sculptor. I had known him in New York and was interested in his work. He had found a studio, he told us, but there was not much in it. I had quite an outfit in my *ménage* — dishes, pots, kettles, a coffee-percolator, and an alcohol lamp on which I had often prepared feasts for a dozen visitors. In triumphal procession we carried the swag through the streets, Jo with a large bundle on his back, Max on one side of him, frying-pan and kettle slung over his shoulders, I on the other with the coffee-pot. When everything had been safely deposited in Jo's studio, we retired to a café to celebrate the inauguration of a budding artist in real Bohemian life.

Amid brilliant sunshine Max and I left Paris. It was bleak and penetrating when we reached London, with no change in the weather during our stay of two weeks. The first thing to greet us on our arrival were press dispatches from America reporting that the Federal authorities were planning to keep me out of the country under the provisions of the Anti-Anarchist Law. I paid no attention to the matter at first, believing it to be a newspaper fabrication. I was a citizen by my marriage to Kershner. Before long, letters from several attorney friends in the United States confirmed the rumours. They informed me that Washington was determined to refuse me readmission, and they urged me to sail back as quickly and quietly as possible.

Meetings for me had already been arranged in Scotland and I felt I ought not to disappoint my comrades. I decided to go on with my work, but soon I was made to realize that I should not be able to leave England without the United States Government's being apprised of my movements.

It was after a lecture in Holborn Town Hall in London that I became aware that I was being watched by Scotland Yard. A score of detectives dogged my heels from the moment I left the meeting-place. Rudolph Rocker, Milly, his wife, Max, and several other friends were with me at the time. We zigzagged London for hours, now and then stopping at restaurants and saloons, but our "shadows" kept close by and would not relinquish their prey. Finally the Rockers suggested that we go to their flat in the East End; we must lead the detectives to believe that we were going to spend the night at their home, which would be our only chance to get away unobserved early in the morning. The lights in the house were turned out and we sat in the dark, conspiring how to delude Scotland Yard. At dawn Milly went down to reconnoitre. No one was in sight. Friends in another part of the city were awaiting us. We were taken to a suburb, to the house of our horticulturist comrade Bernard Kampfmayer. He and his wife were not active in the movement at the time and therefore not under surveillance by the authorities. I hated to disappoint our Scottish comrades, but I could not afford to risk being held up on my arrival in America and forced into a legal fight. I therefore resolved to return home. After three days with our hosts, Max and I left for Liverpool, sailing from there to New York via Montreal.

The Canadian immigration authorities proved less inquisitive than the American and we experienced no trouble whatever getting into Canada. On the way from Montreal to New York the Pullman porter took our tickets, together with a generous tip, and he did not show up again until we were safely in New York. It was two weeks later, at my first public appearance, that the newspapers learned of my being back in the States. They tried frantically to find out how I had managed to get in and I suggested that they inquire of the immigration authorities.

On my return I found *Mother Earth* in a deplorable condition financially. Very little had come in during my absence, and the monthly expenses had far exceeded the amount I had left for the maintenance of the magazine. Something had to be done at once, and, being the only one who could raise funds, I lost no time in arranging various affairs to secure aid for the publication and also decided upon an immediate tour.

Sasha's critical attitude to me had not changed; if anything, it had become more pronounced. At the same time his interest in young Becky had grown. I became aware that they were very close to each other, and it hurt me that Sasha did not feel the need of confiding in me. I knew that he was not communicative by nature, yet something within me felt both offended and injured at his apparent lack of trust. I had realized even before I left for Europe that my physical

attraction for Sasha had died with his prison years. I had clung to
the hope that when he learned to understand my life, to know that
my having loved others had not changed my love for him, his old
passion would flame up again. It was painful to see that the new love
that had come to Sasha completely excluded me. My heart rebelled
against the cruel thing, but I knew that I had no right to complain.
While I had experienced life in all its heights and depths, Sasha had
been denied it. For fourteen years he had been starved for what youth
and love could give. Now it had come to him from Becky, ardent and
worshipful as only an eager girl of fifteen can be. Sasha was two
years younger than I, thirty-six, but he had not lived for fourteen
years, and in regard to women he had remained as young and naïve
as he had been at twenty-one. It was natural that he should be attracted to Becky rather than to a woman of thirty-eight who had
lived more intensely and variedly than other women double her age.
I saw it all clearly enough, yet at the same time I felt sad that he should
seek in a child what maturity and experience could give a hundredfold.

Barely five weeks after my return from Europe I was again on a
tramp through Massachusetts, Connecticut, and the State of New
York. Then came Philadelphia, Baltimore, Washington, D. C., and
Pittsburgh. The Chief of Police in Washington at first announced that
he would not let me speak. When some prominent liberals called his
attention to the fact that he had no business to interfere with the right
of free speech, he told my committee that they could go ahead with
my meetings. At the same time he revoked the licence of the hall-
keeper. When the owner threatened a legal fight, the Chief issued
a temporary licence permitting entertainments and meetings "not
objectionable to the district authorities." My meetings did not take
place.

Pittsburgh brought back many memories — Sasha's martyrdom and
the pilgrimages I used to make to the prison, the hopes I had cherished
and that had not been fulfilled. Yet gladness was in my soul: Sasha
had escaped his prison grave and I had had a large share in bringing
it about. No one could take that consolation away from me.

CHAPTER XXXII

ALL THROUGH THE WINTER OF 1907 AND 1908 THE COUNTRY WAS in the grip of financial depression. Thousands of workers in every large city were idle, in poverty and misery. The authorities, instead of devising ways and means to feed the starving, aggravated the appalling conditions by interfering with every attempt to discuss the causes of the crisis.

The Italian and Jewish anarchists in Philadelphia had called a meeting for the purpose. Voltairine de Cleyre and Harry Weinberg, an eloquent Yiddish agitator, addressed the gathering. Someone in the audience urged a demonstration in front of the City Hall to demand work. The speakers advised against it, but the crowd surged out into the street. Half-way to the City Hall the workers were attacked by the police and beaten. The next day Voltairine and Weinberg were arrested and held under fifteen-hundred-dollar bail each, charged with inciting to riot.

In Chicago the police had dispersed a large demonstration of the unemployed, using the same methods upon the defenceless men and women. Similar outrages had happened throughout the country. Touring under such conditions was a great strain and yielded barely enough to pay expenses; my situation was aggravated by a very severe cold I had caught, which racked me with a fearful cough. But I kept on in the hope of a favourable change by the time I should reach Chicago. I planned to stay with my dear friends Annie and Jake Livshis. The fourteen meetings organized for me would be successful, I thought, for I had become well known in Chicago and had many friends willing to help.

Two days before my arrival a Russian youth who had been clubbed by the police during the unemployment demonstration called at the house of the Chief of Police, with the intention of taking his life, as the papers reported. I did not know the boy, yet my meetings were immediately suppressed and my name was connected with the matter. Upon my arrival in Chicago I was not met by the friends who had invited me to be their guest, but by two other comrades, one of them a stranger to me. Hurriedly they led me away from the crowd and informed me that the Livshis' house was surrounded by detectives, and that I would be taken instead to the home of the comrade I had now met for the first time. Both men advised me to leave the city at once, since the police were determined not to permit me to speak. I refused to be stampeded. "I will stay in Chicago and do what I have done in similar situations: fight for our right to be heard," I declared.

At the home of my host I became aware that his wife was terrorized lest the police find out that I was with them. All through the night she kept going to the window to see whether they had not already arrived. In the morning she began quarrelling with her husband over my having been brought into the house. I was sure to get them into trouble, she said, and they would be ostracized by their neighbours.

I should have gone to a hotel, but it was certain that I would not be admitted. Fortunately, two Russian-American girls came to invite me. One of them, Dr. Becky Yampolsky, I knew through correspondence. Her apartment consisted of an office and a living-room, she informed me, but she would be glad to share the latter with me. I accepted eagerly. At Yampolsky's I met William Nathanson, a young student active in the Yiddish anarchist movement. He offered to help in anything I might decide to undertake. His comradely spirit and Becky's hospitable concern soon made me forget the madhouse I had escaped.

My first question was about the unfortunate boy, whose name was Lazarus Overbuch. Who was he and why had he gone to the Chief of Police? I was informed that very little was known about him. He had not been in our ranks, nor had he belonged to any anarchist group. It had been learned through his sister that he had not been long in America. In Russia he and his family had been among the victims of the terrible Kishinev massacre. During the march of the unemployed in Chicago he had witnessed similar brutalities practised upon workers for daring to demonstrate their poverty and need. In a free country, as he believed America to be, he saw the same inhumanity and cruelty. No one knew the exact reason for his visit to the Chief of Police. The boy had been killed by the Chief's son almost directly after he had been admitted into the house.

At the inquest Chief Shippey stated that Overbuch, after handing him a letter, had tried to shoot his son, one bullet having lodged in his body. On examination it was found that young Shippey had not been wounded at all. Overbuch was killed by a thirty-eight-calibre gun, while according to the Chief's statement, the revolver found on the boy was of thirty-two calibre. That did not prevent the police, however, from starting raids on everyone known to be an anarchist, as well as closing up the headquarters of our comrades and confiscating their library.

The old trick of the police of terrorizing landlords made it impossible to get any hall for me. Every step I made was watched. Detectives were on my trail from the moment it became known that I was staying at the house of my young medical friend. Meanwhile the papers continued to print fantastic stories about anarchism and Emma Goldman, and how we were conspiring to defeat the police. Washington got busy. Commissioner of Immigration Sargent declared he did not know how Emma Goldman had managed to return to America after her trip to Amsterdam. He admitted that he had directed an inquiry to discover the official who had neglected his instructions not to permit me to re-enter. It was tragicomic to see a powerful country moving heaven and hell to gag one little woman. It was fortunate that my bump of vanity was only mildly developed.

When I had almost given up hope of being able to speak in Chicago, Becky Yampolsky brought word that Dr. Ben L. Reitman had offered us a vacant store he was using for gatherings of unemployed and hobos. We could hold our meetings there, he had said, and he had also asked to see me to discuss the matter. In the press accounts of the unemployed parade in Chicago, Reitman had been mentioned as the man who had led the march and who had been among those beaten by the police. I was curious to meet him.

He arrived in the afternoon, an exotic, picturesque figure with a large black cowboy hat, flowing silk tie, and huge cane. "So this is the little lady, Emma Goldman," he greeted me; "I have always wanted to know you." His voice was deep, soft, and ingratiating. I replied that I also wanted to meet the curiosity who believed enough in free speech to help Emma Goldman.

My visitor was a tall man with a finely shaped head, covered with a mass of black curly hair, which evidently had not been washed for some time. His eyes were brown, large, and dreamy. His lips, disclosing beautiful teeth when he smiled, were full and passionate. He looked a handsome brute. His hands, narrow and white, exerted a peculiar fascination. His finger-nails, like his hair, seemed to be on strike against soap and brush. I could not take my eyes off his hands. A strange charm seemed to emanate from them, caressing and stirring.

We discussed the meeting. Dr. Reitman said that the authorities had assured him that they did not object to my speaking in Chicago. "It is up to her to find a place," they had told him. He was glad to help me put them to a test. His place could seat over two hundred people; it was filthy, but his hobos would help him clean it up. Once I had carried through the venture in his hall, it would be easy to get any place I wanted. With much enthusiasm and energy my visitor elaborated on the plan to defeat the police by our gathering at the headquarters of the Brotherhood Welfare Association, as he called his place. He stayed several hours, and when he went away, I remained restless and disturbed, under the spell of the man's hands.

With the help of his hobos Reitman cleaned his store, built a platform, and arranged benches to seat two hundred and fifty people. Our girls prepared little curtains to make the place attractive and to shut out the curious gaze. All was ready for the event, the press carrying sensational stories about Reitman and Emma Goldman, who were conspiring against police orders. On the afternoon of the scheduled gathering the store was visited by officials from the building and fire departments. They questioned the doctor as to how many he expected to seat. Sensing trouble, he said fifty. "Nine," decided the building-department. "The place is not safe for more," echoed the fire department. With one stroke our meeting was condemned, and the police scored another victory.

This new outrage aroused even some of the newspapers. The *Inter-Ocean* opened its columns to me, and for several days my articles appeared on its pages, reaching many thousands of readers with each issue. I was thus enabled to place before a large public the tragic Overbuch case, the part played by the Chief and his son, and the conspiracy to suppress free speech, and finally also to present my ideas, in complete freedom from censorship. The editor, of course, reserved the right to put glaring headlines over my article and to denounce anarchism in his editorials; but as I wrote over my own signature, what I had to say was not in the least affected by anything else that appeared in the paper.

The *Inter-Ocean* was anxious to stage a *coup* over the police. They offered me an automobile from which to address crowds in the city; they would supply reporters, photographers, flash-lights, and other paraphernalia "to make the venture hum." I would not consent to such a circus performance; it could not establish my right of free speech and it would give only a vulgar atmosphere to what was sacred to me.

Meeting-places being closed, I suggested to the comrades that we arrange a social and concert at the Workmen's Hall, my name not to appear in the public announcements. I would try to elude the watch-dogs and get into the hall at the appointed time. Only a few members of our group were apprised of the plan, the others being left under the impression that the sole purpose of the social was to raise funds for our fight.

One outsider was drawn into our secret, and that was Ben Reitman. Some comrades objected on the ground that the doctor was a new-comer and as such not to be trusted. I argued that the man had shown a large spirit in offering his place, and that he had been of great help in securing publicity for our efforts. There could be no doubt about his interest. I did not convince the objectors, but the other comrades agreed that Reitman should be told.

That night I could not sleep. I tossed about in a disturbed state of mind, questioning myself why I had pleaded so warmly for a person I really knew almost nothing about. I had always opposed ready confidence in strangers. What was there in this man that had made me trust him? I had to admit to myself that it was his intense attraction to me. From the moment he had first entered Yampolsky's office, I had been profoundly stirred by him. Our being much together since had strengthened his physical appeal for me. I was aware that he also had been aroused; he had shown it in every look, and one day he had suddenly seized me in an effort to embrace me. I had resented his presumption, though his touch had thrilled me. In the quiet of the night, alone with my thoughts, I became aware of a growing passion for the wild-looking handsome creature, whose hands exerted such fascination.

On the evening of our social gathering, March 17, I succeeded in slipping away through the back entrance of Yampolsky's house while the detectives were waiting for me out in front. I got safely through the police lines near the hall. The audience was large and many officers were inside, stationed against the walls. The concert had begun and someone was playing a violin solo. In the half-light I walked to the front of the platform. When the music was over, Ben Reitman ascended the platform to announce that a friend they all knew would address the gathering. I quickly got up and began to speak. The first tones of my voice and the ovation by the crowd brought the police to the platform. The Captain in charge pulled me off by force, almost ripping open my dress. At once confusion broke out. Fearing that some of our young people might be moved to a rash act, I called out: "The police are here to cause another Haymarket riot. Don't give them a chance. Walk out quietly and you will help our cause a thousand times more." The audience applauded and intoned a revolutionary song, filing out in perfect order. The Captain, infuriated because he had failed to gag me altogether, pushed me towards the exit, cursing and swearing. When we got to the stairs, I refused to budge until my coat and hat, which remained in the hall, were brought to me. I was standing with my back against the wall, waiting for my wraps, when I saw Ben Reitman dragged out by two officers, pushed down the stairs and into the street. He passed me without a look or a word. It affected me disagreeably, but I thought that he had pretended not to know me in order to dupe the officers. He would surely come to Yampolsky's when he had shaken off the police, I reassured myself. I was led out, followed by policemen, detectives, newspaper men, and a large crowd to the door of Becky Yampolsky's home.

I found our comrades already in her office, discussing in what manner the authorities and reporters had learned that I would be present at the gathering. I sensed that they were suspecting Reitman. I felt indignant, but said nothing; I expected he would soon come and speak for himself. But the night wore on and the doctor failed to appear. The suspicion of my comrades grew stronger and communicated itself to me. "He must have been detained by the police," I tried to explain. Faithful Becky and Nathanson agreed that that must be the reason, but the others doubted it. I spent a wretched night, clinging to my faith in the man, yet fearing that he might be at fault.

Reitman called early next morning. He had not been arrested, he said, but for certain important reasons he could not come to Becky's after the meeting. He had no idea who had notified the press and the authorities. I looked searchingly at him, trying to fathom his soul. Whatever doubts I had had the night before melted like ice at the first rays of the sun. It seemed impossible that anyone with such a frank face could be capable of treachery or deliberate lies.

The action of the police resulted in most of the newspapers, which had formerly incited the authorities to "stamp out anarchy," in editorial protests against my having been brutally treated. Some stated that it had not been the police but Emma Goldman's coolness and courage that had prevented bloodshed. One paper wrote: "Captain Mahoney acted contrary to orders in ejecting Emma Goldman from Workmen's Hall, where she was to have lectured. By preventing her from speaking, they played into her hands and gave point to the passionate assertions of her followers that there is no such thing as a constitutional right of free speech."

For days following, the Chicago press published articles and letters of protest by well-known men and women. One was from William Dudley Foulke, voicing his indignation against the suppression of Emma Goldman and free speech. Another was signed by Dr. Kuh, a prominent Chicago physician. The most gratifying result was the stand of Rabbi Hirsch in regard to the action of the police at our social. The next Sunday his sermon was devoted to an objective exposition of anarchism. Among other things he pointed out the stupidity of the authorities in attempting by violent methods to stamp out an ideal that had as its spokesmen some of the noblest spirits of the world. An additional contribution to the change of attitude was made by Dr. Kuh when he invited me to his house to meet his brother and other friends interested in the fight for free speech. The formation of a Free Speech League resulted, with some of the most prominent radicals in Chicago as members.

The league urged me to remain in the city until it could establish my right to speak. Unfortunately compliance with their wishes was excluded on account of the lecture dates already arranged in Milwaukee and other Western towns. It was agreed that I should return later.

The suppression of my meetings in Chicago advertised me through the length and breadth of the country as I had not been since the Buffalo tragedy. I had repeatedly visited Milwaukee before, but I had not been able to attract much attention. Now the attendance was far beyond the capacity of our halls, and great numbers had to be turned away. Even the socialists came in force, among them Victor Berger, their leader. I had met him once before and had found him as intolerant of the ideas I represented as only a Marxian socialist can be. Now he even praised me for the fight I had been making. The demand for anarchist literature increased to a most gratifying degree.

I had every reason to be satisfied with the Milwaukee response and to be happy in the circle of my good comrades, yet I was restless and discontented. A great longing possessed me, an irresistible craving for the touch of the man who had so attracted me in Chicago. I wired for him to come, but once he was there, I fought desperately against an inner barrier I could neither explain nor overcome. After my scheduled meetings I returned with Reitman to Chicago. The police were no longer on my trail, and for the first time in weeks I was able to enjoy some privacy, to move about freely, and to talk with friends without fear of being under surveillance. To celebrate my release from the everlasting presence of detectives the doctor took me out to dinner. He spoke of himself and his youth, telling me of his wealthy father, who had divorced his mother and left her in poverty to shift for herself and her two children. The boy's *Wanderlust* had asserted itself at the age of five, always luring him to the railroad tracks. He ran away at the age of eleven, tramped over the United States and Europe, always close to the depths of human existence, to vice and crime. He had worked as janitor in the Chicago Polytechnic, where the professors took an interest in him. He had married at the age of twenty-three and was divorced soon after a child had come from the short union. He spoke of his passion for his mother, the influence of a Baptist preacher on him, and of many adventures, some colourful and some bleak, all of which had gone into the making of his life.

I was enthralled by this living embodiment of the types I had only known through books, the types portrayed by Dostoyevsky and Gorki. The misery of my personal life, the hardships I had endured through the weeks in Chicago, seemed to vanish. I was care-free and young again. I craved life and love, I yearned to be in the arms of the man who came from a world so unlike mine.

That night at Yampolsky's I was caught in the torrent of an elemental passion I had never dreamed any man could rouse in me. I responded shamelessly to its primitive call, its naked beauty, its ecstatic joy.

The day brought me back to earth and to the work for my ideal, which brooked no other god. On the eve of my departure from Minneapolis for Winnipeg some friends invited me to a restaurant for dinner. Ben was to meet us there later. We were a gay party, making merry in the last hours of my strenuous Chicago stay. Soon Ben arrived, and with him came a heightened mood.

Not far from us sat a group of men, one of whom I recognized as Captain Schuettler, whose presence seemed to me to pollute the very air. Suddenly I saw him motion towards our table. To my amazement, Ben rose and walked over to Schuettler. The latter greeted him with a jovial: "Hello, Ben," familiarly pulling him down to his side. The others, evidently police officials, all seemed to know Ben and be on friendly terms with him. Anger, disgust, and horror all mingled together, beat against my temples, and made me feel ill. My friends sat staring at each other and at me, which increased my misery.

Ben Reitman, whose embrace had filled me with mad delight, chumming with detectives! The hands that had burned my flesh were now close to the brute who had almost strangled Louis Lingg, near the man who had threatened and bullied me in 1901. Ben Reitman, the champion of freedom, hob-nobbing with the very sort of people who had suppressed free speech, who had clubbed the unemployed, who had killed poor Overbuch. How could he have anything to do with them? The terrible thought struck me that he might be a detective himself. For some moments I was utterly dazed. I tried to eliminate the dreadful idea, but it kept growing more insistent. I recalled our social on March 17 and the treachery that had brought the police and the reporters to that gathering. Was it Reitman who had informed them? Was it possible? And I had given myself to that man! I, who had been fighting the enemies of freedom and justice for nineteen years, had exulted in the arms of a man who was one of them.

I strove to control myself and suggested to my friends that we leave. The comrades who accompanied me to the train were kind and understanding. They talked of the good work I had done and their plans for my return. I was grateful for their tact, but I longed for the train to take me away. At last it pulled out and I was alone, alone with my thoughts and the storm in my heart.

The night was endless. I tossed about between nerve-racking doubts and shame that I could still reach out for Ben. In Milwaukee I found a wire from him asking why I had rushed away. I did not reply. Another telegram in the afternoon said: "I love you, I want you.

Please let me come." I replied: "Do not want love from Schuettler's friends." In Winnipeg a letter awaited me, a mad outpouring of passion, and a piteous pleading to let him explain.

My days were busy with work for the meetings, which made it less difficult to be brave and resist my desire for Ben. But the nights were a raging conflict. My reason repudiated the man, but my heart cried out for him. I fought frantically against his lure, trying to stifle my craving by throwing myself completely into my lectures.

On the way back from Canada I was held up at the American border, taken off the train by the immigration inspector, and plied with questions as to my right to enter the United States. The satrap of Washington had evidently studied the anti-anarchist statutes. He puffed and sweated for his promotion rather than for the glory of Uncle Sam. I informed him I had lived in the country twenty-three years, while the Anti-Anarchist Law applied only to persons who had been in the country less than three years. Moreover, I was an American citizen by marriage. The immigration officer almost collapsed. He had seen medals dangling in the air and he hated to let them escape.

Returning to Minneapolis, I again found letters from Ben beseeching me to let him come. I struggled against it for a time, but in the end a strange dream decided the issue. I dreamed that Ben was bending over me, his face close to mine, his hands on my chest. Flames were shooting from his finger-tips and slowly enveloping my body. I made no attempt to escape them. I strained towards them, craving to be consumed by their fire. When I awoke, my heart kept whispering to my rebellious brain that a great passion often inspired high thoughts and fine deeds. Why should I not be able to inspire Ben, to carry him with me to the world of my social ideals?

I wired: "Come," and spent twelve hours between sickening doubt and mad desire to believe in the man. It could not be that my instinct should be so misleading, I reiterated to myself — that anyone worthless could so irresistibly appeal to me.

Ben's explanation of the Schuettler scene swept my doubts away. It was not friendship for the man or connexion with the police department that had made him known to them, he said. It was his work among tramps, hobos, and prostitutes, which often brought him in contact with the authorities. The outcasts always came to him when in trouble. They knew and trusted him and he understood them much better than the so-called respectable people. He had been part of the underworld himself, and his sympathies were with the derelicts of society. They had made him their spokesman, and as such he frequently called on the police to plead in their behalf. "It never was anything else," Ben pleaded; "please believe me and let me prove it to you." Whatever might have been at stake, I had to believe in him with an all-embracing faith.

CHAPTER XXXIII

WHILE MY MEETINGS WERE BEING SUPPRESSED IN CHICAGO, Sasha was subjected to similar persecution in the East. His lectures were stopped in a number of cities in Massachusetts, and the Union Square demonstrations of the unemployed at which he presided were forcibly dispersed by the police. I was worried about Sasha and wired him to let me know whether it was necessary for me to return to New York. The next morning I read in the newspapers that a bomb had exploded at Union Square, and that Alexander Berkman was arrested in connexion with it. I forgot our disagreements. Sasha was in trouble, and I not at his side to help and comfort him! I resolved to leave for New York immediately, but before I could carry out my decision, a telegram came from Sasha, telling me that the authorities had tried to implicate him in the Union Square affair; failing in that, they had charged him with "inciting to riot." That charge also had to be dropped for lack of proof. A letter explained that there was no need for me to worry and that the only victim of the tragic affair at Union Square was a young comrade, Selig Silverstein, a gentle fellow who had been badly clubbed. He had been mangled by the explosion and had later been tortured at police headquarters. Physical suffering and mental anguish had brought about his end. Sasha's description of the police brutality, and of the comrade so brave and stoical to the last, increased my hatred of the machinery of government and its organized violence. It made me more determined to go on with my work until the last breath.

Before I started out for California, Ben asked to let him come with me on the tour. He had enough money to pay his own way, he assured me. He would help with the work, arrange meetings, sell literature, or do anything else to be near me. The suggestion made me happy with anticipation. It would be wonderful to have someone with me on the long and weary tramps through the country, someone who was lover, companion, and manager. Yet I hesitated. My lectures, deducting my own expenses, left only small margins for *Mother Earth*. They could hardly bring enough to cover an additional burden, and I was not willing to accept Ben's co-operation without his sharing in the results. There was also another consideration — my comrades. They had helped faithfully, if not always efficiently; they were sure to see in Ben an interloper. He was from another world; moreover, he was impetuous and not always tactful. Clashes would surely follow, and I already had had to face far too many. I found it difficult to decide, but my need of Ben, of what his primitive nature could yield, was compelling. I resolved to have him; let the rest take care of itself.

Sitting beside Ben in the rushing train, his hot breath almost touching my cheek, I listened to him reciting one of his favourite Kipling stanzas:

> I sits and looks across the sea
> Until it seems that no one's left but you and me.

"You and me, my blue-eyed Mommy," he whispered.

Was this to be the beginning of a new chapter in my life, I wondered. What was it going to bring? My whole being was suffused with a feeling of comfort and security. Blissfully I closed my eyes and nestled closer to my lover. This was a new and great force, which I knew had come to stay.

The meetings in San Francisco were being looked after by my friend Alexander Horr; not expecting any trouble where I had never been interfered with before, I felt at ease.

I had reckoned, however, without the ambitious Chief of Police of San Francisco. Envious, perhaps, of the laurels carried off by his colleagues in the East, Chief Biggey seemed anxious to gain similar glory. He was at the station himself, accompanied by a retinue of officers and equipped with a large automobile. They all piled in and dashed after the taxi that was taking Ben, Horr, and me to the St. Francis Hotel. There he stationed four detectives to watch over my welfare.

The pomp of my entry into the hotel aroused the misgivings of the management and the curiosity of the guests. Unable to account for the unexpected homage, I turned to Horr for an explanation.

"Don't you know," he said with a perfectly sober face, "rumours have gone abroad that you are coming to San Francisco to blow up

the American fleet now in the harbor." "Stop your ridiculous invention," I replied; "you do not expect me really to believe that." He
insisted that he was in earnest, that Biggey had boasted that he
would protect the fleet against "the whole bunch of Emma Goldman
and her gang." My friend had purposely reserved a room for me at the
highly respectable St. Francis; one living in such a place would not
be suspected of association with bombs. "Never mind what people will
think," I retorted; "this place is loud and gaudy, and I can't endure
having to run the gauntlet of the rich and vulgar people here." Poor
Horr looked crest-fallen and went to find other quarters.

Meanwhile I was not left in peace. I was besieged by reporters
with cameras, photographed against my will, and asked endless questions, the main one being whether I had really come to blow up the
fleet.

"Why waste a bomb?" I replied. "What I should like to do with
the fleet, with the entire Navy, and the Army too, would be to dump
them in the bay. But as I have not the power to do it, I have come
to San Francisco to point out to the people the uselessness and waste
of military institutions, whether they operate on land or on sea."

At midnight my friend returned. He had found a place, although
it was very far from town. It was the cottage of Joe Edelsohn, in
which there was room enough for Ben and me. I knew Joe as a splendid
comrade, and I was glad to be able to get out of the St. Francis Hotel,
however far I'd have to walk. The three of us, together with all our
baggage, loaded into a taxi and, followed by four detectives in another
car, arrived at Joe's house. The plain-clothes men remained on watch,
in the morning replaced by mounted police. This was kept up all
through my stay in the city.

One day Ben took me to the Presidio, the military encampment at
San Francisco. He knew the chief physician of its hospital; he had
worked with him during the earthquake and had assisted in taking
care of patients. We were followed to the very door of the hospital,
but we had the satisfaction of seeing the detectives kept out, while
Emma Goldman, the foe of militarism, was entertained by the physician in charge and shown through the wards.

My meetings were veritable battle encampments. For blocks the
streets were lined with police in autos, on horseback, and on foot.
Inside the hall were heavy police guards, the platform surrounded
by officers. Naturally this array of uniformed men advertised our

meetings far beyond our expectations. Our hall had a seating capacity of five thousand, and it proved too small for the crowds that clamoured for admittance. Lines formed hours before the time set for the opening of my lectures. Never in all the years since I had first gone on tour, with the exception of the Union Square demonstration in 1893, had I seen masses so eager and enthusiastic. It was all due to the stupendous farce staged by the authorities at huge expense to San Francisco taxpayers.

The most interesting meeting took place one Sunday afternoon when I spoke on "Patriotism." The crowds struggling to get in were so large that the doors of the hall had to be closed very early to prevent a panic. The atmosphere was charged with indignation against the police, who were flaunting themselves importantly before the assembled people. My own endurance had almost reached breaking-point because of the annoyances caused by the authorities, and I went to the meeting determined to vent in no uncertain terms my protest. When I looked into the faces of the excited audience, I sensed at once that very little encouragement from me would be needed to arouse them to violent action. Even the dull mind of Biggey responded to the temper of the situation. He came over to beg that I try to pacify the people. I promised on condition that he would reduce the number of his men in the hall. He consented and gave orders to the officers to file out. Out they marched, like guilty schoolboys, accompanied by the jeering and hooting of the crowd.

The subject I had selected for the meeting was particularly timely because of the patriotic stuff which had been filling the San Francisco papers for days past. The presence of so vast an audience testified that I had chosen well. The people were certainly eager to hear some other version of the nationalist myth. "Men and women," I began, "what is patriotism? Is it love of one's birthplace, the place of childhood's recollections and hopes, dreams and aspirations? It is the place where, in childlike naïveté, we used to watch the passing clouds and wonder why we, too, could not float so swiftly? The place where we used to count the milliard glittering stars, terror-stricken lest each one an eye should be, piercing the very depths of our little souls? Is it the place where we would listen to the music of the birds and long to have wings to fly, even as they, to distant lands? Or the place where we would sit at Mother's knee, enraptured by tales of great deeds and conquests? In short, is it love for the spot, every inch representing dear and precious recollections of a happy, joyous, and playful child-hood?

"If that were patriotism, few American men of today could be called upon to be patriotic, since the place of play has been turned into factory, mill, or mine, while deafening sounds of machinery have replaced the music of the birds. Nor can we hear any longer the tales of great deeds, for the stories our mothers tell today are but those of sorrow, tears, and grief.

"What, then, is patriotism? 'Patriotism, sir, is the last resort of scoundrels,' said Dr. Johnson. Leo Tolstoy, the greatest anti-patriot of our times, defined patriotism as the principle that justifies the training of wholesale murderers; a trade that requires better equipment for the exercise of man-killing than the making of such necessities as shoes, clothing, and houses; a trade that guarantees better returns and greater glory than that of the honest workingman."

The uproarious applause that interrupted me showed that the five thousand people were in sympathy with my ideas. I proceeded with an analysis of the origin, nature, and meaning of patriotism, and its terrific cost to every country. At the close of my speech of an hour, delivered amid tense silence, a storm rolled over me and I felt myself surrounded by men and women clamouring to shake my hand. I was dizzy from the excitement and oblivious of what was being said to me. Suddenly I became aware of a tall figure in the uniform of a soldier holding out his hand to me. Before I had time to think, I took it. When the audience saw that, pandemonium broke loose. People threw their hats in the air, stamped their feet, and yelled in uncontrolled joy over the sight of Emma Goldman clasping hands with a soldier. It all happened so quickly that I had no time to ask the man's name. All he said was: "Thank you, Miss Goldman," and then he slipped away as unobserved as he appeared. It was a dramatic ending to a highly dramatic situation.

The next morning I read in the papers that a soldier leaving Emma Goldman's meeting had been followed by plain-clothes men to the Presidio, and that they had reported him to the military authorities. Later the press stated that the soldier's name was William Buwalda, that he had been placed under military arrest and would be "court-martialled for attending Emma Goldman's meeting and for shaking hands with her." It seemed preposterous; nevertheless we set to work immediately to organize a committee for his defence and to raise money for his fight. After that Ben and I left for Los Angeles.

The most interesting events in that city, outside of large and lively meetings, were a debate with Mr. Claude Riddle, a socialist, and a visit with George A. Pettibone. I had debated with a number of socialists before, but my opponent this time proved the most fair-minded of them all. That was a crime in the eyes of his party and he was at once suspended from membership. It was a coincidence no less interesting than significant that a United States soldier and a socialist should fall under the ban at the same time for daring to have anything to do with Emma Goldman.

George A. Pettibone, with Charles H. Moyer and William D. Haywood, had been the victim of a conspiracy to crush the Western Miners' Federation. For years the mine-owners of Colorado had waged relentless war against the workers' organization without success. When they discovered that the spirit of the union could not be broken and the leaders neither bullied nor bought, they sought other means to destroy them. In February 1906 the three had been arrested in Denver on the charge of having killed Ex-Governor Steunenberg. So complete was the autocracy of money and power that the prisoners were rushed to Boise City without a semblance of legality, the train and extradition papers having been prepared even before the arrest. The only evidence against the labour defendants had been furnished by a Pinkerton spy, Harry Orchard.

For a year their lives had hung in the balance. The press in general had been inciting the Idaho authorities to send them to the gallows. The tone in this man-hunt had been set by President Roosevelt, who had branded Moyer, Haywood, and Pettibone as "undesirable citizens."

The immediate and concerted campaign of labour and radical bodies throughout the country had succeeded in frustrating the mine-owners. In this agitation the anarchists had played a large part, devoting their energy and means to save the indicted men. I had lectured about the case all through the country, while *Mother Earth* had proclaimed their innocence and urged the workers to declare a general strike, if need be, to rescue their comrades from the noose. On the day of their acquittal the *Mother Earth* group had wired Roosevelt: "Undesirable citizens victorious. Rejoice." It was an expression of our contempt for the man who, though President of the United States, had joined the pack of hounds.

I had had no opportunity of meeting any of the three men before or since the trial. In Los Angeles I learned that Pettibone was living in the city in the strictest retirement, his health shattered by his jail experience. When he heard of my arrival, he sent a friend to tell me that he had wanted for many years to meet me.

I found him with the stamp of death on his face, but with enthusiasm for labour's cause still shining in his eyes. He talked of many things, among them of the judicial murder in Chicago, in 1887, which had proved a great factor in awakening his rebellious spirit, as it had mine. He dwelt on the events that had been meant to furnish a second eleventh of November, but instead had turned into a red-letter day for the labour forces. He related many incidents of his conflicts with the Pinkertons and told how he used to make game of their cowardice and stupidity. He spoke of the authorities having attempted to induce him to turn against his comrades. "Just think of it!" he said; "they appealed to my interests as a business man and the chances I'd have to get free and become prosperous. How were those soul-and-mind-impoverished creatures to know that I would have preferred death a thousand times rather than hurt one hair of the other boys."

In Portland, Oregon, we learned the cheerful news that the two halls rented for my lectures, the Arion, belonging to a German society, and the Y.M.C.A., had been refused at the last moment. Fortunately the city had a number of people to whom the right of free speech was not merely a theory. Foremost among them was ex-Senator Charles Erskine Scott Wood, distinguished lawyer, writer, and painter and a man of considerable cultural influence in the town. He was a fine-looking man of gracious personality, and a libertarian in the truest sense. He had been instrumental in securing the two halls, and he was very much distressed that the owners should have backed out. He tried to console me with the assurance that the Arion Society could be held legally responsible, because they had signed a contract for the rental of their hall. When I told him that I never invoked the law against anyone, although the law had often been invoked against me, Mr. Wood exclaimed: "So that's the kind of dangerous anarchist you are! Now that I have found you out, I shall have to take others into my confidence. I shall have to ask them to meet the real Emma Goldman." Within a few days he not only introduced various persons to me, but he also inspired Mr. Chapman, one of the editors of the *Oregonian,* to write about my lectures, and the Reverend Doctor Elliot, a Unitarian minister, to offer me his church. He induced a considerable number of prominent men and women of the city to declare themselves publicly in favour of my right to be heard.

After this it was easy sailing. A hall was secured, and the meetings were attended by large and representative audiences. Mr. Wood presided at my first lecture and delivered a brilliant introductory speech. With such a backing I should have captured my hearers even if I had been less aroused on this occasion. I was at a high emotional pitch over the news in the morning papers of the treatment accorded William Buwalda. He had been court-martialled, dismissed from the Army, degraded, and sentenced to the military prison on Alcatraz Island for five years. This, notwithstanding the admission of his superior officers that he had been an exemplary soldier in the United States Army for fifteen years. That was the punishment meted out to the man whose crime, as General Funston had stated, had consisted in "attending Emma Goldman's meeting in uniform, applauding her speech, and shaking hands with that dangerous anarchist woman."

My subject was "Anarchism." What better argument did I need than the outrage by the State on William Buwalda, by the State and its military machine, from which there is no redress or escape? My speech was fiery, igniting everyone present, even those who had come out of curiosity. At the close of my lecture I made an appeal for an immediate campaign to arouse public opinion against the sentence of Buwalda. The assembly generously responded with money and pledges to organize the work for his speedy release. Mr. Wood was chosen treasurer, and a considerable sum was contributed on the spot.

The audiences at my meetings kept increasing, the crowds representing every social stratum; lawyers, judges, doctors, men of letters, society women, and factory girls came to learn the truth about the ideas they had been taught to fear and to hate.

We had started for Butte, Montana, after successful meetings in Seattle and Spokane. The trip gave me opportunity to observe the Western farmer and the Indians on the reservations. The Montana farmer differed very little from his New England brother. I found him just as inhospitable and close-fisted as the farmers Sasha and I had canvassed for crayon portraits in 1891. Montana is among the most beautiful States, its soil rich and fertile far beyond the unyielding

New England sod. Yet those farmers were unkind, greedy, and suspicious of the stranger. The Indian reservation revealed to me the blessings of the white man's rule. The true natives of America, once masters of the length and breadth of the land, a simple and sturdy race possessing its own art and conception of life, had dwindled to mere shadows of what they had once been. They were infected with venereal disease; their lungs were eaten by the white plague. In return for their lost vigour they had received the gift of the Bible. The kindly and helpful spirit of the Indians was very cheering after the forbidding attitude of their white neighbours.

My tour, more eventful than any previous one, was at an end, and I was on my way to New York. Ben remained in Chicago for a visit with his mother and would join me in the autumn. It was a painful wrench to separate after the intimacy of four months. Only four months since that strange being had come so unexpectedly into my life, and already I felt him in every pore, consumed by longing for his presence!

I had tried all through the months to explain to myself the appeal Ben had for me. With all my absorption in him, I was not deceived about the difference that existed between us. I knew from the first that we had intellectually very little in common, that our outlook on life, our habits, our tastes, were far apart. In spite of his degree of M.D. and his work for the outcast, I had felt Ben to be intellectually crude and socially naïve. He had profound sympathy for society's derelicts, he understood them, and he was their generous friend, but he had no real social consciousness or grasp of the great human struggle. Like many liberal Americans, he was a reformer of surface evils, without any idea of the sources from which they spring. That alone should have been enough to keep us apart, and there were still other and graver differentiations.

Ben was typically American in his love of publicity and of show. The very things I most disliked were inherent in the man I now loved with a fierce passion. Our first serious disagreement had been over a newspaper photographer Ben had "wished" on me without my knowledge or consent. It was during our trip from Chicago to Salt Lake City. The man was on the train and Ben must needs tell him that Emma Goldman was among the passengers. At the next stop, as I was walking along the platform, I suddenly found myself confronting a camera ready to "shoot." I had been often annoyed by invasive American methods and I always ran from them. But there was no place to run to this time. Instinctively I held up a paper before my face. To Ben it was merely a caprice. He could not understand my deep-seated repulsion to the habitual imposition of the newspaper men. He could not comprehend that one who had been so long before the public could still shrink from the vulgarity of being made a public show.

Through all my travels I had managed to keep to myself while *en route* from one city to another. On this tour our fellow-passengers, the train crew, and even the station-masters knew the glad tidings that Emma Goldman was in their midst. Our car became a magnet that drew all the curiosity-mongers who were about. It was manna to Ben, but torture to me.

Moreover, Ben had the American swagger, which he would display with particular gusto at our meetings and in the homes of comrades. The antagonism his manner aroused caused me great distress and I lived in constant fear of what he might do next. Indeed, there were many elements in my lover to jar my nerves, outrage my taste, and sometimes even make me suspicious of him. Yet it all did not weigh in the scale against the magic that bound me to him and filled my soul with new warmth and colour.

I could find but two explanations of the riddle: First, Ben's child-like nature, unspoiled, untrained, and utterly lacking in artifice. Whatever he said or did came spontaneously, dictated by his intensely emotional nature. It was a rare and refreshing trait, though not always pleasant in its effects. The second was my great hunger for someone who would love the woman in me and yet who would also be able to share my work. I had never had anyone who could do both.

Sasha had been but a short time in my life, and he had been too obsessed by the Cause to see much of the woman who craved expression. Hannes and Ed, who had loved me profoundly, had wanted merely the woman in me; all the others had been attracted by the public personality only. Fedya belonged to the past. He had married, had a child, and disappeared from my ken. My friendship with Max, still as fragrant as it had always been, was less of the senses than of the understanding. Ben had come when I had greatest need of him; our four months together had proved that in him were combined the emotions I had yearned for so long.

Already he had greatly enriched my life. As helpmate in my work he had shown his interest and his worth. With complete absorption and abundance of energy Ben had achieved wonders in the size of our meetings and the increased sales of literature. As travelling companion he had made my trip a new, delightful experience. He was touchingly tender and solicitous, most comforting in releasing me from the petty annoyances and details involved in travelling. As lover he had unleashed elements in me that made all differences between us disappear as so much chaff in a storm. Nothing mattered now except the realization that Ben had become an essential part of myself. I would have him in my life and in my work, whatever the cost.

That the cost would not be small I already knew by the opposition to him which was growing in our ranks. Some of my comrades sensed Ben's possibilities and his value to the movement. Others, however, were antagonistic to him. Of course, Ben did not feel at ease under those circumstances. He could not understand why people standing for freedom should object to anyone's behaving naturally. He was particularly nervous about my New York friends. How would they act towards him and our love? Sasha — what would he say? My account of Sasha's act, his imprisonment and suffering, had stirred Ben profoundly. "I can see Berkman is your greatest obsession," he had once said to me; "no one will ever have a chance alongside of him." "Not an obsession, but a fact," I had told him; "Sasha has been in my life so long that I feel we have grown together like the Siamese twins. But you need fear no rivalry from him. Sasha loves me with his head, not with his heart."

He was not convinced and I could see he was worried. I myself was apprehensive because of the difference in their personalities. Yet I hoped that Sasha, who had touched the depths of life, would understand Ben better than the rest. As for Max, I knew that, whatever his reaction to Ben, he was too considerate to cast any shadow on my love.

More and more the upkeep of *Mother Earth* was draining my energies. The support from our comrades and from my American friends, considerable as it was, proved insufficient. My tours had become the main source of revenue for the magazine, for the publication of our literature and the other expenses involved. The last tour had left us an unusually large margin, yet by August we were again without funds. My new lecture course could not begin until October. Fortunately help came from an unexpected quarter.

My friend Grace Potter, one of the contributors to *Mother Earth,* was working on the New York *World*. She induced her editor to accept an article from me on "What I Believe." I would be paid two hundred and fifty dollars for it, Grace informed me, and I could write with full freedom. I accepted, glad of the opportunity to reach a large audience and at the same time also to earn some money. After the article appeared, exactly as I had written it, I was given the right to publish it in brochure form. "What I Believe" became the bestseller of years. Now we could pay the printer for the current issue and have enough money left for Ben's trip to New York.

I waited for his arrival like a schoolgirl in love for the first time. He came with his old eagerness, ready to throw himself into the work of our magazine. He was his own self when we were alone, but he became a changed creature in the presence of my friends. With them he would grow nervous, inarticulate, and dull, or he would ask silly questions that made them suspicious of him. I was sick with disappointment. I knew that it was only panic that made Ben so awkward and I believed that he would feel more at home on the farm. There life was simpler — Ben would find himself; and Sasha, who was with Becky and other friends on the farm, would be patient and help him along.

My hopes proved vain. Not that Sasha or the other friends were unkind to Ben, but the atmosphere was strained, and no one seemed to find the right word. The situation acted on Ben as on a child expected to be on its good behaviour. He began to show off and brag, boast of his exploits, and talk nonsense, which made matters worse. I felt ashamed of Ben, bitterly resentful of my friends, and angry with myself for having brought him into their midst.

My deepest grief was Sasha. He said nothing to Ben, but he said plenty of cutting things to me. He scoffed at the idea that I could love such a man. It was nothing but a temporary infatuation, he felt sure. Ben lacked social feeling, he had no rebel spirit, and he did not belong in our movement, he insisted. Moreover, he was too ignorant to have passed through college or to have earned a degree. He would write to the university to find out. This, coming from Sasha, completely unnerved me. "You are a zealot," I cried; "you judge human quality by your criterion of one's value to the Cause, as the Christians do from the standpoint of the Church. That has been your attitude towards me since your release. The years of struggle and travail I suffered for my growth mean nothing to you, because you are

bound in the confines of your creed. With all your talk of the movement, you thrust back the outstretched hand of a man who comes to
learn about your ideals. You and the other intellectuals prate about
human nature, yet when someone out of the ordinary appears, you
don't even try to understand him. But all that can have no bearing on
my feeling for Ben. I love him, and I will fight for him to the death!"

I left the farm with Ben. I was sick from the scene with Sasha, the
harsh words I had hurled in his face; and I was tortured by my own
doubts. I had to admit to myself that much that Sasha had said about
Ben was true. I could see his defects much better than anyone else and
I knew how lacking he was. But I could not help loving him.

It had been my plan to devote the winter to New York. I was tired
out from trains, strange places, and other people's "atmosphere."
Here I had my home, limited and crowded though it was. *Mother
Earth* also needed my presence. I was certain that if I lectured through
the winter, I should attract large Yiddish and English audiences. I
had talked it over with Ben and he had decided to move to New York
and devote himself to my task.

But now Ben hated the city and hated 210 East Thirteenth Street.
He could never do any good there, he felt. With me on the road he
would be able to put his energies into the work and he would grow,
develop, and become a force. I, too, wanted to get away from the
disharmony and the censure of the people nearest to me. I was anxious
to give Ben a better chance, to help him to an understanding of himself, to bring out what was finest in him.

The previous year I had received an invitation from Australia.
J. W. Fleming, our most active comrade there, had even raised enough
money for my fare. At that time I could not decide to go away so far
and make the long journey alone. With Ben at my side the voyage
would be turned into a joy and give me a much needed rest, free from
strife. Ben was wild with the idea of Australia; he could talk of nothing
else and was eager to start at once. But there were many arrangements
to make before I could go on a two years' tour. We decided to leave in
October for California, lecturing on the way. By February we would
cover the ground, raise enough money to secure the New York end
for a time, then sail to the new land, where there were new friends to
win, fresh minds and hearts to awaken.

My one anxiety was *Mother Earth*. Would Sasha consent to continue in charge? On my return from the last tour I had found him

better adjusted to life, much surer of himself and more devoted to our magazine than he had been. He had, besides, created many activities of his own while I was away. He had organized the Anarchist Federation, with groups all over the country, and had gained many admirers and friends. When I submitted my Australian plan to Sasha, he expressed surprise that I should have made such a sudden decision, but he assured me that I could be at ease about our work in New York. He would look after everything, and with Max and Hippolyte to help him the magazine and the office would be secure. I was sad that Sasha should show no regret whatever about my going away for so long, but I was too absorbed in my new venture to allow his lack of interest to affect me.

We shipped fifteen hundred pounds of literature to Victoria, Australia. We got in touch with our friends all along the route to California, and within a few weeks our arrangements were made. Ben was all eagerness to discover new ground. "All the world shall know what my Mommy can do," he proclaimed.

On Labour Day a meeting of the unemployed was to take place in Cooper Union. Ben was helping to arrange it and he was also asked to speak. I wanted him to make a good impression and urged him to prepare his notes. He tried industriously, but nothing came of his efforts. It was not of any particular importance what he might say, he told me; he wanted the audience to hear Emma Goldman, and as I had not been invited, I must write out what I would want to say at such a gathering. The suggestion was as fantastic as most of Ben's ideas, but rather than have him make a rambling talk, I prepared a short paper on the meaning of Labour Day.

Cooper Union was crowded. The "anarchist police squad" was present in force, as were also Sasha, Becky, Hippolyte, and I. All went well, Ben holding the audience better than I had expected while he was reading his paper. At the end he announced that what he had just read had been prepared by that "much maligned woman the anarchist Emma Goldman." The house applauded thunderously, but the committee in charge of the meeting became panicky. The chairman offered a profuse apology for the "unfortunate occurrence" and sailed into a violent attack on Ben. The latter had already left the platform and could therefore not reply. Sasha rose to protest. Before he had a chance to be properly heard by the crowd, the police pulled him out of the hall and placed him under arrest. Becky, who had followed Sasha, was also arrested and both were rushed to the station-house. They were confronted by a burly desk sergeant, who received them with the remark: "You should have been brought here on a stretcher." When Hippolyte called at the police station to find out about our friends, he was refused information. "We have that son of a b— anarchist Berkman at last," he was told; "we'll fix him this time."

The New York police department had tried repeatedly to get Sasha into their clutches. The previous year, after the Union Square bomb explosion, they had almost succeeded in involving him. I was naturally worried and at once got in touch with Meyer London, the socialist attorney, and other friends, to help us rescue Sasha.

For hours London and Hippolyte waited at the police station to see Sasha and Becky before they would be taken to the night court. Finally they were informed that the case would not come up until morning. No sooner had they left than the two prisoners were hustled into court, tried, and convicted without a chance to say a word in their defence. Sasha was sentenced to the workhouse for five days on the charge of disorderly conduct, while Becky was fined ten dollars for "vagrancy."

Not wanting to involve me, Becky had refused to say where her home was. As a matter of fact, she had been living with us for more than two years. She had been arrested at one of our meetings, which caused her expulsion from high school. Her home conditions were desperately poor and cramped and I had invited her to our flat. Her fine was paid by our dear friend Bolton Hall.

The papers the next day were filled with lurid stories of a "riot prevented by the prompt action of the police," and as usual I was pestered by reporters for days. I did not mind the annoyance, too happy in the thought that Sasha had been given a short sentence. What were five days to a man who had served fourteen years? I went to Blackwell's Island to see him. Memories of my own sojourn on the island and of my two visits to the Western Penitentiary came to my mind. How different the situation had been then — how hopeless and bleak Sasha's chances to come out alive! Now we both joked over the five days. "I can do them on one toe," Sasha laughed. I left him with the old certainty that whatever our disagreements, our friendship was of an eternal quality. I still felt the hurt caused by his attitude towards Ben, yet I knew that nothing could ever come beween us.

Everything was ready for my departure. Ben was to precede me to do advance work. A few days before leaving he sent me a letter thirty pages long, a rambling, incoherent account of things he had done since we first met. He had been reading *The Power of a Lie,* by the Norwegian author Boyer, he wrote; it had struck deep into him, and he felt impelled to confess to me the falsehoods he had told and the mean things he had done while on tour with me. It was giving him no rest. He could keep silent no longer.

He had lied when he had told me that it was not he who had disclosed the plan of my speaking at the social in Chicago last March. He had not informed the police, but he had confided it to a reporter, who had promised to keep it to himself. He had lied when he had given "important matters" as the reason for not calling on me that evening to explain about the presence of the police. He had gone straight from the hall to a girl he cared about. He had lied when he had assured me that he had money to pay his way on the trip with me. He had borrowed the money, gradually paying it back from the sales of our literature. He had also taken money from the receipts to send to his mother. He loved her passionately, and he had always looked after her. He had not dared to tell me that his mother depended on him, because he feared I would send him away. Every time I had expressed surprise that money was apparently missing from our accounts, he had lied. The excuses he had given for so often vanishing after my meetings or for staying away during the day were all false. He had gone with other women, women he had met at the lectures or somewhere else. In nearly every city he had gone with women. He did not love them, but they attracted him physically to the point of obsession. He had always had such obsessions and probably always would have. These women had never meant anything more than a moment's distraction. He always forgot them afterwards; often he did not even know their names. Yes, he had gone with other women during the four months; yet he loved only me. He had loved me from the first, and each day his passion for me had increased. I was the greatest force in his life, my work his deepest concern. He would prove it if I only would not send him away, if I would forgive him his lies and his betrayal, if only I would again have confidence in him. But even if I should send him away after I had read the letter, he would still feel relieved that he had confessed to me. He realized now how disintegrating and crushing is the power of a lie.

I had the feeling of sinking into a swamp. In desperation I clutched the table in front of me and tried to cry out, but no sound came from my throat. I sat numb, the terrible letter seeming to creep over me, word by word, and drawing me into its slime.

I was brought back to myself by Sasha's arrival. Sasha — at this moment — of all people! How he would feel justified by this letter in all he had said about Ben! I broke out in uncontrollable laughter.

"Emma, your laugh is terrible. It cuts like a knife. What is it?"

"Nothing, nothing, only I must get out on the street or I shall choke."

I snatched up my coat and hat and ran down the five flights. I walked for hours, the letter burning in my head.

This was the man whom I had taken into my heart, my life, my work! Fool, lovesick fool that I was, blinded by passion not to see what everyone else saw. I, Emma Goldman, to be carried away like any ordinary woman of forty by a mad attraction for a young man, a stranger picked up at a chance meeting, an alien to my every thought and feeling, the reverse of the ideal of man I had always cherished. No, no! It was impossible! The letter could not be true; it was all an invention, imaginary; it could not be real. Ben was impressionable, susceptible to every influence, always seeing his own reflection in the books he read. He loved to dramatize himself and his life. The tragedy of the peasant in Boyer's novel who thoughtlessly, even needlessly, tells a lie and is forced to lie for the rest of his life to sustain his first falsehood is vividly depicted. Ben must have read himself into that character. That was all. That *must* be all. All this I thought as I walked for hours, torn between my intense desire to believe in him, and my feeling that I had given myself to a man lacking all integrity, a creature I could never trust again.

Days of anguish followed, tortured by attempts to explain and excuse Ben's acts, attempts irritating and vain. Over and again I repeated to myself: "Ben comes from a world where lies prevail in all human relations. He does not know that free spirits in their love and tasks honestly and frankly share everything life brings; that among people with ideals no one need cheat, steal, or lie. He is of another world. What right have I to condemn, I who claim to teach new values of life?" "But his obsessions? His going with every woman?" My heart cried out in protest. "Women he does not love, does not even respect. Can you justify that, too? No, no!" came from the depths of my woman's soul. "Yes," replied my brain, "if it is his nature, his dominant need, how can I object? I have propagated freedom in sex. I have had many men myself. But I loved them; I have never been able to go indiscriminately with men. It will be painful, lacerating, to feel myself one of many in Ben's life. It will be a fearful price to pay for my love. But nothing worth while is gained except at heavy cost. I've paid dearly for the right to myself, for my social ideal, for everything I have achieved. Is my love for Ben so weak that I shall not be able to pay the price his freedom of action demands?" There was no answer. In vain did I strive to harmonize the conflicting elements that were warring in my soul.

Dazed and hardly aware of my surroundings, I jumped out of bed. It was still dark. Like a sleep-walker I got into my clothes, felt my way to Sasha's room, and shook him out of sleep.

"I must go to Ben," I said. "Will you take me to him?"

Sasha was startled. He switched on the light and searchingly looked at me. But he asked no questions and said nothing. He hurriedly dressed and accompanied me.

We walked in silence. My head swam, my feet were unsteady. Sasha put my arm in his. In my purse was a key to the house where Ben was rooming. I let myself in, then turned to Sasha for a moment. Without a word I closed the door and ran up the two flights, bursting into Ben's room.

He jumped up with a cry. "Mommy, you've come at last! You have forgiven, you have understood." We clung to each other, everything else wiped out.

CHAPTER XXXIV

IN PLANNING OUR TOUR TO TAKE PLACE DURING THE PRESIDEN-
tial campaign we had overlooked the interest of the American
masses in the political circus. The result was failure of the initial part
of our trip. In Indianapolis, the first city to bring out a large attendance, my lecture was suppressed in the usual manner. The Mayor
expressed regret that the police had overstepped their powers, but of
course he could not act against the department. The Chief said that
stopping the meeting might have been bad law, but that it was good
common sense.

We were more fortunate in St. Louis, where we experienced no
interference. There I met William Marion Reedy, the editor of the
St. Louis *Mirror*. He and his paper were an oasis in the desert of
American intellectuality. Reedy, a man of ability, broad culture, and
rich humour, also possessed a courageous spirit. His fellowship made
our stay in St. Louis a pleasant event and brought me large and varied
audiences. After my departure he published in his weekly an article
that he called "The Daughter of the Dream." No finer appreciation
of my ideas and no greater tribute to me had ever been written by a
non-anarchist before.

In Seattle Ben and I were arrested. His offence consisted in putting
his weight too heavily against the door of the hall, which he had
found barred; mine was in protesting against his arrest. At the
station-house it developed that the price of my manager's offence was
a dollar and a half, representing the amount the landlord demanded
for his broken lock. After we paid for this injury to the sanctity of
property, we were both released. Of course, there were no further
meetings in Seattle and no redress for the loss we had sustained.

In Everett no hall was open to us. In Bellingham our train was met
by detectives. They followed us to the hotel, and when we went out to

find a restaurant, they put us under arrest. "Would you please wait
until we have dined?" Ben asked with an engaging smile. "Sure,"
said our protectors, "we will wait." It was bright and warm in the
restaurant, drizzling and chilly outside, but we took no pity on our
watch-dogs. We lingered long over our meal, well aware that we
should have the whole night before us in a place neither warm nor
bright. In the station-house we were presented with the warrant. It
was a document worthy of immortality. "Emma Goldman and Dr.
Ben L. Reitman," it read, "anarchists and outlaws, having conspired
to hold an unlawful assembly," and so forth in the same spirit. We
were given the choice between leaving Bellingham at once or going
to the city jail. It being the first hospitality offered us in the State
of Washington, we decided in favour of the jail. At midnight the
offer to get out of town was repeated, but having already made myself at home in the cell, I refused to leave. Ben did likewise.

In the morning we were taken before a magistrate, who placed us
under five-thousand-dollar bail. It was only too apparent that the
judge knew that the police had undertaken more than they would be
able to carry through. We could not be tried for merely "attempting"
to hold a meeting, but we were at their mercy, just the same. We
knew no one in town likely to bail us out, and we had no means of
getting in touch with a lawyer. I was interested, however, to find out
how far legalized stupidity could go.

In the afternoon two strangers arrived. They introduced themselves as Mr. Schamel, attorney, and Mr. Lynch. The former volunteered his services gratis; the latter offered to be our bondsman.

"But you don't know us," I said in astonishment. "How can you
risk so much money?"

"Oh, yes," said Mr. Schamel, "we do know you. We are not
anarchists, but we feel that anyone who will stand up for an ideal
as you have done is worthy of trust."

If I had not been afraid of shocking them, I should have embraced
them in open court. The old fossil on the bench, who had blustered
when we appeared friendless before him in the morning, was personified politeness now. We were quickly bailed out, entertained at a
restaurant by our new friends, and accompanied to the train.

When we reached Blaine, on the Canadian border, a man came
into our car, walked straight up to me, and inquired: "You are
Emma Goldman, are you not?" — "And who are you?" — "I am

a Canadian immigration inspector. I have orders to invite you to leave the train." What could one do but comply with such a gentlemanly request? At the office the inspector in charge seemed very much surprised that I looked like a lady and had no bombs about me. He assured us that he had gathered from the stories in the American press that I was a very dangerous person. He had therefore decided to hold up my entry into Canada until he could receive instructions from Ottawa. Meanwhile he asked me, as his guest, to make myself at home in his hut. I could have anything I wanted in the way of food and drink. In case of delay we would be given the best rooms in the local hotel. He spoke in a polite manner, his tone more friendly than I had ever heard from an American official. While the result was the same, I did not feel quite so indignant over the new interference.

The next morning our jovial inspector informed us that Ottawa had wired to let Emma Goldman proceed. There was no law in monarchical Canada to forbid my entry into the country. American democracy, with its anti-anarchist laws, was made to appear rather ludicrous.

San Francisco held a special attraction. The ex-soldier William Buwalda, as a result of our agitation in his behalf, had been pardoned by President Roosevelt. He was released after ten months' imprisonment, two weeks before our arrival in the city.

Owing to a terrific rain-storm my first meeting, in the Victory Theatre, was poorly attended. We were not discouraged, however, because of the wide publicity given my series of eight lectures and two debates. The following afternoon William Buwalda called on me, a very different man in his civilian clothes from the soldier whose hand I had clasped for a fleeting moment that memorable afternoon on the platform of Walton's Pavilion. His fine, open face, intelligent eyes, and firm mouth were indicative of an independent character. I wondered how he had stood fifteen years of military service without becoming warped. Buwalda related that he had joined the Army mainly because of tradition. American-born, he was of Dutch stock and nearly all the men of his family had done military service in Holland. He had believed in American freedom and he had considered its army forces a necessary protection. On several occasions he had come across my name in the papers. He had thought Emma Goldman a crank and had paid little attention to articles about me. "That is not very flattering," I interrupted: "how could you be so rude to a lady?"

"It is true, though," he replied with a smile. Military people live in a world of their own, he explained, and he had been particularly occupied for several years past. He had taken up a course of veterinary surgery because he was passionately fond of horses, and he had also studied shorthand. Added to his duties in the barracks, it had kept him too busy for other interests.

He had come upon my meeting accidentally, while out for a walk. He had seen the large crowd and the police before the Walton Pavilion. It had made him curious and he thought it a good opportunity to practise his stenography by taking down the speech. "Then you appeared," he continued, "a little, unassuming figure in black, and you started to talk. I began to feel disturbed. I thought at first it was the heat in the hall and the tense atmosphere. I did not forget the purpose that had brought me. For a while I was able to follow you; then I became distracted by your voice. I felt myself carried along by your sledge-hammer arraignment of all I held high. I was filled with resentment. I wanted to raise my voice in protest, to challenge your statements before the whole assembly. But the more I resisted your influence, the more I fell under its sway. Your eloquence held me breathless to the end of your speech. I felt confused and eager to escape. Instead I was caught by the crowd and found myself standing on the platform holding out my hand to you."

"And then?" I asked. "Did you see the detectives following you? Did you realize that they would cause you trouble?"

"I don't remember how I got out of the hall, and I did not feel that I had done anything wrong. I was upset by what I had heard and in the grip of the turmoil you had caused in me. All the way to the Presidio I kept thinking: 'She's wrong, she's entirely wrong! Patriotism is not the last resort of scoundrels. Militarism isn't only murder and destruction!' After the plain-clothes men had reported me to my superior officer, I was put under arrest. I thought it was all a mistake, that I had been taken for someone else and that I should be freed in the morning. To think otherwise would have meant that you were right, and my whole being rebelled against that. For several days I clung to the belief that you had misrepresented the Government which I had served for fifteen years; that my country was too fair and too just to be guilty of your unreasonable charges. But when I was brought before the military tribunal, I began to see that you had spoken the truth. I was asked what you had done for me that I should mix with such a dangerous person, and I replied: 'She has made me think.' Yes, you had made me think, Emma Goldman, for the first time in all my forty years."

I held out my hand to him and said: "Now that you are free from your military shackles, we can shake hands without fear. Let us be friends."

He took my hand eagerly. "Friends for life and comrades as well, dear, big, little Emma."

I was so carried away by his story that I had forgotten it was time to prepare for my meeting. Never being able to eat before a lecture, I did not mind going without dinner. But for my guest I had proved a poor hostess. My new comrade gallantly assured me that he did not care for food.

When we came within a block of the hall, we saw the streets filled with people. I thought it was our announcements that had brought out the vast crowd, but when we reached the Victory Theatre, I was received with open arms by detectives and put under arrest. Buwalda protested and was also arrested. We were hustled into the patrol wagon to find that Ben, too, had met with the same fate. As the wagon rattled through the streets, he hurriedly related that the police had ordered everyone out of the theatre, freely using their clubs. He had objected to their methods, of course, and was put under arrest. He had sent someone with a warning to me, but evidently the comrade had found me gone.

At police headquarters William Buwalda was discharged with a severe reprimand for associating with "dangerous criminals." Ben and I were charged with "conspiracy, making unlawful threats, using force and violence, and disturbing the public peace." In the morning we were taken before a judge, who held us for trial under sixteen-thousand-dollar bail each. The same day Alexander Horr was arrested for distributing a handbill protesting against the action of the authorities. The task of raising our bond and arranging for counsel and publicity fell to Cassius V. Cook, a man I had met only casually a few years before. But he proved to be a tower of strength.

Within a few days Sasha and other New York friends telegraphed that five thousand dollars would be sent towards our bail and that money was being raised for our defence. From all over the country protests and contributions began pouring in. Charles T. Sprading, of Los Angeles, whom I had first met in Denver on my maiden tour to the Coast in 1897, our buoyant Charlie, of ready wit and merry pranks, wired two thousand dollars as bail. The Forresters, and other friends, helped in a similar way. What did our trouble matter with such good comradeship to aid us?

Our lawyers, Messrs. Kirk and King, intelligent and brave men, exerted themselves in our behalf, and within a few days Mr. Kirk succeeded in having our bail released. We were to be liberated and placed in his custody. But unexpectedly another indictment came, charging us with "unlawful assemblage, denouncing as unnecessary all organized government," and — horror of horrors — with "preaching anarchist doctrines." Bail was set at two thousand dollars each. I was to be tried first, Ben to follow.

Among the sensational reports in the San Francisco press regarding the raid of our meeting and our arrest was one enlarging upon " Emma Goldman's lack of sentiment and feeling." While in jail, she had been given a telegram announcing her father's death, the paper stated, which she received without the least sign of emotion. As a matter of fact, my father's end, though not unexpected, had affected me deeply and had recalled to me the details of his wasted life. An invalid for over thirty years, he had of late been more frequently ill than usually. When I had seen him on my last visit to Rochester, in October, I had been shocked to find him so near death. The giant he had once been was now shattered by the storms of life.

With the passing years had come to me better understanding of Father, and mutual sympathy had drawn us gradually closer. My beloved Helena had had much to do with my change towards him. It was helped also by my awakening to the complexities of sex as a force dominating our feelings. I had learned to understand better my own turbulent nature, and my experiences had made me see what had been obscure to me so long in the character of my father. His violence and hardness had only been symptoms of an intensely sexual nature that had failed to find adequate expression.

My parents had been brought together in the traditional Jewish orthodox fashion, without love. They were mismated from the first. Mother had been left a widow at twenty-three, with two children, a little store her only earthly possession. Whatever love she had had died with the young man to whom she had been married at the age of fifteen. Father had brought into the match a fire of passionate youth. His wife was only one year his senior and radiantly beautiful. The impelling need of his nature drove him to her and made him more insistent in proportion as Mother fought back his insatiable hunger. My coming had marked her fourth childbirth, each one nearly bringing her to the grave. I recalled some remarks I had heard her make when I was too young to understand their meaning. They illuminated much that had been dark to me and caused me to realize what a purgatory my parents' intimacy must have been for them both. No doubt they would have been shocked had anyone called to their attention the true source of the struggle between them and of Father's uncontrollable temper. With the decline of health came also a lessening of his erotic vitality and a resultant psychic change. Father grew more mellow, patient, and kindly. The affection he had rarely shown his own children he now lavished on those of my two sisters. When I once referred to the harsh methods he had used towards us, he assured me that it could not be true. The tenderness that had come into his nature blotted out even the remembrance of past severity. The best in him, formerly hidden by emotional stress, by the struggle for existence and years of physical suffering, came into its own at last. He now felt and gave us a newly born affection, which in its turn awakened our love for him.

The court farce in San Francisco, ending in our acquittal, did more for anarchism than months of our propaganda might have accomplished. But the most significant event was William Buwalda's letter to the military authorities and his entry into our ranks. The historic document, published in the May 1909 issue of *Mother Earth,* read as follows:

Hudsonville, Michigan
April 6, 1909

Hon. Joseph M. Dickinson,
Secretary of War,
Washington, D. C.

Sir: —

After thinking the matter over for some time I have decided to send back this trinket[1] to your Department, having no further use for such baubles, and enable you to give it to some one who will appreciate it more than I do.

It speaks to me of faithful service, of duty well done, of friendships inseparable, friendships cemented by dangers and hardships

---

[1] The medal awarded William Buwalda for faithful service in the Philippines.

and sufferings shared in common in camp and in the field. But, sir, it also speaks to me of bloodshed—possibly some of it unavoidably innocent—in defence of loved ones, of homes; homes in many cases but huts of grass, yet cherished none the less.

It speaks of raids and burnings, of many prisoners taken and, like vile beasts, thrown in the foulest of prisons. And for what? For fighting for their homes and loved ones.

It speaks to me of G. O. 100, with all its attendant horrors and cruelties and sufferings; of a country laid waste with fire and sword; of animals useful to man wantonly killed; of men, women, and children hunted like wild beasts, and all this in the name of Liberty, Humanity, and Civilization.

In short, it speaks to me of War—legalized murder, if you will— upon a weak and defenceless people. We have not even the excuse of self-defence.

                              Yours sincerely,
                              Wm. Buwalda
                              R. R. No. 3
                              Hudsonville, Michigan

Our departure for Australia had been set for January. The arrest and subsequent free-speech fight in San Francisco forced us to postpone it until April. At last we were ready, our trunks packed, a grand farewell party arranged for us. We were about to secure passage when a telegram from Rochester demolished our plans. "Washington revoked Kershner's citizenship papers," it read; "dangerous to leave country."

My sister had written me months before that two suspicious-looking individuals had been snooping about to secure data on Kershner. He had left the city years previously and nothing had been heard from him since then. Not finding Kershner, the men had pestered his parents and tried to get information from them. I had dismissed the matter from my mind at the time as of no consequence. But now the blow came. I was deprived of my citizenship without even an opportunity to contest the action of the Federal authorities. I knew that if I should leave the country, I should not be permitted to re-enter it. My Australian tour had to be abandoned at a great financial loss, not to mention the expenditures invested by our Australian friends in preparing for my activities there. It was a bitter disappointment, much mitigated, fortunately, by the undaunted optimism of my hobo manager. His zeal merely increased with the obstacles we encountered. His energy was dynamic and tireless.

Australia eliminated from our itinerary, we went to Texas instead. El Paso, San Antonio, and Houston were new ground. I was cautioned to avoid the Negro question, but though I made no concessions to the prejudices of the South, I was in no way molested, nor was there any police interference. I even walked with Ben from El Paso to Mexico and back again before the United States immigration inspector had time to realize the chance he had missed to save his Government from the Emma Goldman menace.

CHAPTER XXXV

I NEEDED A REST BADLY, BUT, OUR TOUR THIS TIME HAVING brought us more glory than cash, I could not afford to take it. In fact, we were so short of funds that we were compelled to reduce the size of *Mother Earth* from sixty-four to thirty-two pages. Our financial condition made it necessary for me to start lecturing again. Ben joined me in New York in the latter part of March, and by the 15th of April he had succeeded in organizing for me a series of lectures on the drama. All went well at first, but May proved to be a record-breaker. During that month I was stopped by the police in eleven different places.

I had had similar experiences before, but the Chief of Police of New Haven outdid his colleagues by a novel way of interference. He allowed Ben and me to enter the hall we had hired, and then placed a detachment of officers at the doors to keep everybody else out. Great numbers, among them many students who had come to hear me, found themselves barred. The Chief soon learned, however, that "originality" is a costly thing. The local papers, which had never before protested against the infringement of Emma Goldman's rights, now pilloried the police for "interfering with a peaceable assembly."

The authorities of New York had always been stupid in their methods of persecuting anarchists; but never had their folly been quite so great as when they swept down on Lexington Hall on the third Sunday of my lecture course. The seditious subject on that occasion was "Henrik Ibsen as the Pioneer of Modern Drama." Before the opening of the meeting several detectives had called on the hall-keeper and threatened him and his family with arrest if he allowed me to speak. The poor man was frightened, but the rent had already been paid and Ben held the receipt. The landlord could do nothing and the plain-clothes men left, taking him along to the station-house.

Just as I started to speak, the Anarchist Squad arrived, spreading themselves out in the hall. The moment I uttered the name "Henrik Ibsen," the sergeant in charge jumped to the platform and bellowed: "You're not sticking to your subject. If you do it again, we'll stop the meeting."

"That is exactly what I am doing," I replied quietly, and continued with my lecture.

The officer kept interfering, repeatedly ordering me to "stick to my subject." Somewhat impatiently I said: "I am sticking to my subject. Ibsen is my subject."

"Nothing of the kind!" he yelled. "Your subject is the drama and you're talking about Ibsen."

The merriment of the audience added to the indignation of my scholarly interruptor. Before I could proceed, he commanded his men to clear the hall, which they did by pulling the chairs from under the people and using their sticks freely.

It happened that these Sunday morning lectures were attended almost exclusively by Americans, some of whom traced their ancestry to the Pilgrim Fathers. Among them was Mr. Alden Freeman of East Orange, the son of a prominent Standard Oil Company shareholder. It was his first experience with the police and he was naturally indignant at their behaviour, as were also the other blue-blooded Americans.

To us, for years targets of persecution, the breaking up of my lecture was no unusual happening. Not only my meetings, but gatherings of workers had been frequently suppressed without the least cause. In the twenty years of my public activity I had always been in uncertainty to the very last minute as to whether I should be permitted to speak or not, and whether I should sleep in my own bed or on a board in a police station.

When the *Mayflower* descendants had read about such police tactics, they had undoubtedly thought I had given cause; that I had perhaps urged the use of violence or bombs. They had never objected, nor had the press. This time, however, the affront was offered to "real" Americans, among them even the son of a millionaire, the partner and bosom-friend of Rockefeller. Such a thing could not be tolerated. Even the New York *Times* waxed indignant, and the other dailies followed suit. Letters of protest began to fill the papers. My good friend William Marion Reedy, of the St. Louis *Mirror,* and Mr. Louis F. Post, of the *Public,* branded the persecution of Emma Goldman as a deliberate conspiracy of the police of the country to Russianize the American Constitution. As a result of the situation there was formed a Free Speech Society, and a manifesto was issued signed by American men and women in every walk of life. Writers, painters, sculptors, lawyers, doctors, and people of every shade of opinion came forward to fight the New York police methods.

Mr. Alden Freeman had throughout his life believed that free speech was a fact and not a mere pretence. He was genuinely shocked to come face to face with reality and he at once identified himself with the campaign of the newly created committee to establish free speech. Mr. Freeman was confident that I would be permitted to speak in East Orange, his home town, and generously offered to arrange a meeting for me there. He also invited me to be his guest at the luncheon of the Mayflower Society, of which he was a member. "Once people see that you are not as you have been described in the papers, they will be glad to come and hear you," he said.

The Mayflowerites proved to be uninteresting, the speeches dull. Towards the end of the luncheon my presence became known. A bomb hurled into the unsuspecting gathering could have produced no more disastrous effect. There was dead silence for a moment. Then some of the guests scrambled to their feet and haughtily marched out. The women present seemed too paralysed to move and fumbled for their smelling-bottles. Some of them looked daggers at Mr. Freeman. Only a few reckless ones ventured to face the dragon. It was amusing to me, but painfully disappointing to my host, the second blow within a short time to his cherished ideas of American freedom and traditions.

The third came soon after the luncheon. The Mayflower Society discussed his expulsion or forced resignation because he had dared to bring Emma Goldman into their presence. But it did not dismay Mr. Freeman. Bravely he proceeded to arrange a meeting for me in his home town.

On the appointed evening we found the hall barred by the police, who announced that there would be no lecture. Mr. Freeman then invited the assembled audience to his home; the meeting would take place on his lawn, he declared. Triumphantly we marched through the streets of aristocratic East Orange, past palatial dwellings, followed by a vast crowd, including police and reporters. It was a demonstration such as the quiet town had never seen before.

Mr. Freeman's house was a fine mansion, surrounded by a beautiful garden. It was private ground, and the police knew that their authority stopped where property rights began. They did not dare to trespass and remained outside the gate. The garage where our gathering took place was more comfortable than some workmen's homes. The coloured lights trembled like shadows in the night, throwing fantastic silhouettes. It was a picture suggesting the legendary birthplace of the Christ-child, the hallelujahs changed into a song of freedom and revolt.

As a result of the East Orange episode people I had never heard of before came to offer their help, subscribe to *Mother Earth,* and secure our literature. By the grace of the police club they had been made to realize that Emma Goldman was neither assassin, witch, nor crank, but a woman with a social ideal the authorities were trying to suppress.

The Free Speech Society began its campaign with a large meeting in Cooper Union. Although it was the end of June and scorchingly hot, the old historic hall was crowded with people of the most diversified social and political tendencies. The speakers also differed on almost every issue, but all were held together by a common bond: the imperative need to put a stop to the growing despotism of the police department. Mr. Alden Freeman presided and gave a humorous account of how he, the son of a Standard Oil man, had been "driven into the arms of anarchism," He continued in a serious tone to describe the purpose of the gathering. " If Emma Goldman sat on this platform with a gag between her teeth, and a policeman on each side of her," he declared, "the picture would simply and plainly express the reason for our being here tonight and would also explain why it is that letters and telegrams of protest and sympathy are pouring in upon the Free Speech Committee from the Atlantic to the Pacific, and from the Gulf to the Great Lakes."

The speakers that followed expressed themselves in a similar vein, the most brilliant talk being made by Voltairine de Cleyre, who contended that " free speech means nothing if it does not mean the freedom to say what others don't like to hear."

Almost an immediate effect of the meeting and of the energetic campaign of the committee was the dismissal by Mayor McClellan of Police Commissioner General Bingham, whose military régime had been responsible for the suppressive methods,

While busy with these activities, I received a letter from a man on the editorial staff of the Boston *Globe,* informing me that a contest for a new Declaration of Independence was being planned by the paper. Several radicals had already promised to participate; would not I also like to send in a contribution? The writer further stated that the best essay would be published in the *Globe* and would be paid for. I replied that though in these days few Americans cared for independence, I would participate for the fun of it. My article, which I kept almost entirely in the form of the Declaration of Independence, giving it new phrasing and meaning, was forwarded to the *Globe,* and in the course of time I received an envelope containing a check and the galley proofs of my Declaration. The accompanying letter from my newspaper friend explained that the owner had chanced upon the proofs on the editor's desk. "Send that woman a check and return her damned anarchist declaration," he had ordered; "I don't want her in the *Globe*."

The current issue of *Mother Earth* was about to go to press, and we just had time to insert my article by leaving out a less important one. On the 4th of July the new Declaration of Independence was read by thousands, as we sold many copies and distributed a great number free of charge.

In September I went with Ben on a short tour through Massachusetts and Vermont. We were stopped, stopped, and stopped, either by direct police interference or by the intimidation of the hall-owners. In Worcester, Massachusetts, I spoke out of doors, thanks to the aid of the Reverend Dr. Eliot White and his wife, Mrs. Mabel A. White. They followed the example of our friend Alden Freeman and extended to us the hospitality of their spacious lawn. Anarchism was heard there not under the Stars and Stripes, but under a more appropriate canopy — the limitless sky and the myriads of glittering stars, while the large trees shaded us from the curious who had come to stare.

The most important event of our Worcester visit was an address given by Sigmund Freud on the twentieth anniversary of Clark University. I was deeply impressed by the lucidity of his mind and the simplicity of his delivery. Among the array of professors, looking stiff and important in their university caps and gowns, Sigmund Freud, in ordinary attire, unassuming, almost shrinking, stood out like a giant among pygmies. He had aged somewhat since I had heard him in

Vienna in 1896. He had been reviled then as a Jew and irresponsible innovator; now he was a world figure; but neither obloquy nor fame had influenced the great man.

On my return to New York new struggles absorbed me. There was the shirtwaist-makers' strike, involving fifteen thousand employees, and that of the steel-workers at McKeesport, Pennsylvania. Money had to be raised for both fights. The anarchists always being among the first to respond to every need, I had to address numerous meetings and visit labour bodies to plead the cause of their fellow unionists.

Then came the uprising in Spain. In protest against the slaughter in Morocco the Spanish workers had declared a general strike. As usual the American press misrepresented the situation. It necessitated an immediate campaign on our part to present the events in their true light and significance. Our Spanish comrades in America called for my help and I gave it gladly.

Before long we received the news of the arrest in Barcelona of Francisco Ferrer, anarchist and libertarian educationist, who was charged with responsibility for the general strike. We realized the imminent danger facing our comrade and the necessity of arousing intelligent American public opinion in his behalf.

In Europe many noted men and women of advanced thought had already begun an intensive campaign in favour of Francisco Ferrer. In America there were too few to make a similar effort, and the situation therefore required the greater activity on our part. Meetings, conferences, *Mother Earth,* and a constant stream of people kept us busy from early morning until late hours of night.

I had an engagement in Philadelphia, where Ben had preceded me by several days. On his arrival he was informed by comrades that all radical gatherings had of late been suppressed in the City of Brotherly Love. Ben, still imbued with American trust in police officials, went to see the Director of Public Safety, who was the tsar of Philadelphia. That potentate not only received him gruffly, but declared that he would never permit Emma Goldman to speak in "his" city. The local single-taxers passed resolutions denouncing the despotic decision and sent a committee to the City Hall to demand that I be given the right to speak. Seeing that I had friends among Americans, the dictator in the police department drew in his horns. "Emma Goldman can speak," he declared, "if she will submit to a small formality: to let me read her lecture notes."

I would, of course, do nothing of the kind, since I did not believe in censorship. Thereupon the director decided that I could not speak. " The meeting can proceed," he announced, " but Emma Goldman will not be allowed in the Odd Fellows' Temple, if I have to call out the whole police department to prevent her."

He kept his promise. He placed six plain-clothes men at my unsolicited disposal, who were stationed at the entrance of the little hotel where I was stopping. In the evening, when I started for Odd Fellows' Hall, accompanied by the attorney of the Philadelphia Free Speech League, the detectives followed at our heels. For blocks the hall was lined with police on foot, on horseback, and in automobiles. Not only was I barred from entering, but I was forced to return to the hotel along the route dictated by the officers, who would not let me out of sight until I was back in my room. The meeting took place and was addressed by anarchists, socialists, and single-taxers, but not by Emma Goldman, and thus Philadelphia was saved.

The single-taxers and the members of the Free Speech League insisted that the case should be tested in the courts. I had no faith in legal procedure, but my friends argued that if I refused, the police would undoubtedly continue their tactics, whereas a legal fight would focus public attention on their Russian methods of trying to gag me. Voltairine de Cleyre also was in favour of having a test made, and I consented.

Meanwhile the papers carried sensational stories about the situation, and the detectives remained at the hotel. The owner, somewhat of a liberal, was exceedingly decent to me, but the undesirable publicity was injuring his business. We therefore moved to one of the larger hostelries. I was just beginning to unpack my things in the new place when I was informed by telephone that there had been a mistake: the rooms assigned to us had been reserved before and there were no others vacant in the house. The same thing happened in several other hotels. There were no objections to Ben, but they would not have me.

I finally found shelter with some American friends. During three weeks their place was under constant watch and I was shadowed from the moment I left the house until I returned. Moreover, the police tried to bribe my host's servant to watch my room and report what was happening. But the dear soul refused. She helped me instead to escape for one whole day from the vigilance of the detectives.

My presence was urgently needed in New York. On Sunday morning, October 13, this servant took Ben and me through the back entrance, across several yards, and out into an alley. Without having been observed we reached the railroad station and were soon speeding east.

Our mission in New York was a mass meeting to commemorate Francisco Ferrer, the victim of popery and militarism in Spain.

The Romish Church had for eight years waged a relentless war against Francisco Ferrer. He had dared to strike her in her most vulnerable spot. Between 1901 and 1909 he had founded 109 modern schools and his example and influence had led the liberal elements to organize three hundred non-sectarian educational institutions. Catholic Spain had never before witnessed such daring, but it was mainly Ferrer's Modern School that gave the Church fathers no peace. They were wroth at the attempt to free the child from superstition and bigotry, from the darkness of dogma and authority. Church and State saw the danger to their dominion of centuries and they tried to crush Ferrer. They had almost succeeded in 1906. At that time they had caused his arrest in connexion with Morral's attempt on the life of the Spanish King.

Mateo Morral, a young anarchist, had devoted his private fortune to the library of the Modern Schools and had worked with Ferrer in the capacity of librarian. After the failure of his act he had ended his own life. It was then that the Spanish authorities discovered the connexion of Mateo Morral with the Modern School. Francisco Ferrer was arrested. It was known throughout Spain that Ferrer was opposed to acts of political violence, that he firmly believed in and preached modern education as against force. It did not save him, however, from the powers that be. World-wide protests had rescued him in 1906, but now Church and State insisted on their pound of flesh.

While Francisco Ferrer was being sought by the authorities he was living with a comrade ten miles from Barcelona. He was in perfect safety there and he could have escaped the fury of the Church and military cliques which demanded his death. Then he read the official proclamation that anyone harbouring him would be shot. He decided to give himself up. The anarchist friends at whose house he was staying were a poor family with five children; they knew their danger, yet they pleaded with Ferrer to remain with them. To quiet their fears for his safety, he promised. But at night, while everyone was asleep,

Ferrer left through the window of his room and walked to Barcelona. He was recognized a short distance from the city and arrested.

After a mock trial Francisco Ferrer was condemned to death and shot within the walls of Montjuich prison. He died as he had lived, proclaiming with his last breath: " Long live the Modern School!"

After the Francisco Ferrer commemoration meeting in New York I returned to Philadelphia to continue our free-speech fight. While awaiting the court's decision in the test case, a social gathering was arranged in my room for the committee backing our campaign. We were quietly discussing things over our coffee when there came violent knocking. Several officers rushed into the room.

" You're holding a secret meeting," their leader declared, and ordered the people out.

" How dare you intrude upon my birthday party?" I replied. " These are my guests who have come to celebrate my birthday. Is that a crime in Philadelphia?"

" Birthday, eh?" the officer sneered; "I didn't know anarchists celebrated birthdays. We'll wait outside to see how late you'll celebrate."

Some of the single-taxers who were present were very indignant; not, however, because the police had forcibly disturbed our friendly circle, but on account of their violation of the sacredness of private property. My visitors soon dispersed and I was left wondering whether the greater difficulty confronting us anarchists was the hold upon man of the sanctity of property or his belief in the State.

Our campaign closed with a large meeting under the auspices of the Free Speech League. Leonard D. Abbott presided, while among the speakers were ex-Congressman Robert Baker, Frank Stephens, Theodore Schroeder, George Brown (the "shoemaker philosopher"), Voltairine de Cleyre, and Ben Reitman. Letters protesting against my gagging were read from Horace Traubel, Charles Edward Russell, Rose Pastor Stokes, Alden Freeman, William Marion Reedy, and others.

Some time later the Director of Public Safety in Philadelphia was dismissed from office on charges of graft and bribery.

CHAPTER XXXVI

IN THE LATTER PART OF 1909 NEW YORK AGAIN EXPERIENCED A vice crusade. The reformers had discovered the white-slave traffic! They got busy, though they were without the slightest notion regarding the sources of the evil they were trying to eradicate.

I had had considerable opportunity to come in contact with prostitution; first in the house in which I was once compelled to live, then during the two years when I nursed Mrs. Spenser, and finally at Blackwell's Island. I had also read and gathered much material on the subject. I therefore felt much better equipped to discuss the problem than the moral busybodies who were now attracting so much attention. I prepared a lecture on the white-slave traffic, dealing with its causes, effects, and possible elimination. It became the strongest drawing card in my new course and also aroused the most heated criticism and discussion. The lecture was published in the January issue of *Mother Earth* and subsequently in pamphlet form.

Shortly afterwards Ben and I went on our annual tour. Everywhere we met with complaints from our subscribers that they had not received the January number of the magazine. I wired Sasha about it and he went after the postal authorities. He was informed that some copies had been held up on the complaint of Anthony Comstock. While we felt flattered that we were at last given a place among other victims of Comstockery, we nevertheless demanded to know the reason for the unexpected honour.

After several calls Sasha succeeded in getting into the august presence of the keeper of American morals. Comstock admitted that *Mother Earth* had been held up, but denied that it had been done on his complaint.

"The matter is now in my hands," he told Sasha; "the reason for it is Miss Goldman's article on the white-slave traffic." At Comstock's request Sasha accompanied him to the office of the District Attorney, where St. Anthony held a secret conference lasting two hours. After that came a prolonged consultation with the Chief Post Office Inspector. Finally the censor declared that nothing objectionable had been found in the article.

The next day the New York *Times* contained an interview with Comstock in which he entirely denied the whole matter. It was "a scheme of Emma Goldman to attract attention to her publication," he stated. He had made no complaint against the magazine, he said, nor had it been held up by the Post Office. It required another week of energetic work by Sasha, canvassing various postal departments and repeatedly wiring to Washington, before the January issue was finally released.

If Comstock had been decent enough at least to inform us of his intention in advance, we should have printed fifty thousand copies of the proscribed number. Even as it was, his interference helped to advertise our publication. The demand for *Mother Earth* greatly increased, but unfortunately we had only our usual edition on hand.

For the first time since the free-speech fight in Chicago in 1908 I could go back to that city. The police, perhaps mindful of the publicity they had given anarchism at that time by their treatment of me, actually assured Ben that I should not be molested any more. The promise made my manager enthusiastic with anticipation of the work awaiting us in his native town. He wired for dates and subjects and then threw himself with all his elemental strength into the arrangements for a series of lectures.

Chicago had been significant in my life. I owed my spiritual birth to the martyrs of 1887. Ten years later I found Max there, whose understanding and tender companionship had not ceased to inspire and sustain me through the years. It was also in Chicago, in 1901, that I had been brought close to death because of my attitude towards Leon Czolgosz, and was it not Chicago that had given me Ben? Ben, with all his faults, irresponsibility, and obsessions — the man who had already caused me greater agony of spirit than anyone else in my life, and who had brought me deeper devotion and a complete consecration to my work. Only two years we had been together, and during that period he had tested my soul a hundred times, my brain always in rebellion against the strange boy whose nearness was yet a vital need to me.

I had been lecturing in the city on Lake Michigan since 1892, but it was only on this visit that I realized its possibilities. Within ten days I addressed six English and three Yiddish meetings, attended by large crowds that were sufficiently interested to pay admission and to purchase large quantities of our literature. It was certainly a notable achievement, and it was brought about almost entirely through the efforts of Ben. My satisfaction in having gained ground in Chicago was mingled with pride in him, pride because his most antagonistic opponents in our ranks had come to see and admire his sincerity and his talent for organizing. In this city at least Ben had conquered the hearts of many comrades and had won their co-operation and support.

In my travels through the United States I had always found university towns the most indifferent to the social struggle. American student bodies were ignorant of the great issues in their native land and lacked sympathy with the masses. I was therefore not enthusiastic when Ben suggested our invading Madison, Wisconsin.

Great was my surprise when I discovered an entirely new note in the University of Wisconsin. I found the professors and pupils vitally interested in social ideas, and a library containing the best selection of books, papers, and magazines. Professors Ross, Commons, and Jastrow and several others proved to be exceptions to the average American educator. They were progressive, alive to the problems of the world, and modern in the interpretation of their subjects.

A group of students invited us to lecture in the Y.M.C.A. hall on the campus. Ben spoke on the relation between education and agitation, and I discussed the difference between Russian and American college men. It was news to our hearers to learn that the Russian intelligentsia saw in education, not a mere means to a career, but something to enable them to understand life and the people, so that they could teach and help them. American students, on the other hand, were interested mostly in their diplomas. As to the social struggle, American university men knew little about it and cared still less. Our talks on this occasion were followed by spirited discussions and proved to us that our audiences had become very much aware of their relation to the masses and of their debt to the workers who produced all wealth.

The trustees of the Y.M.C.A. building could think of nothing wiser than to refuse the hall for our further gatherings. It was, of course, the best advertising for our meetings. It brought scores of students to the hall we had secured in town and made them more eager than ever to hear us speak. Subsequently I learned from the librarian that there had been a greater demand for books on anarchism since I had come to the city than during the entire previous existence of the library.

The excitement my presence in Madison created and the large attendance at our meetings were too much for the conservative townsfolk. Their spokesman, the *Democrat,* sounded the alarm against "the spirit of anarchy and the revolution rampant in college." The editor chose as his special target Professor Ross, who had been my host and who had also advised the students to go to my lectures and had even attended them himself. The newspaper almost caused the dismissal of the professor. Fortunately he had left on a long-planned trip to China shortly after my visit. The ravings of the *Democrat* soon died out, and when Dr. Ross returned from the Orient, he was able to take up his work without further molestation.

As manager of the Orleneff troupe I had often attended social functions, but as propagandist I had always managed to keep away from idle entertainments. The man who now steered me through the shoals of society luncheons and would-be Bohemian dinners was William Marion Reedy, the brilliant editor of the St. Louis *Mirror.* His suave manner could smuggle the most dangerous contraband into the enemy's camp. There were many questions hurled at me at my first luncheon with the "nice" people of St. Louis, where plenty of water was served and little spirit. The one enlivening element at the affair was Bill Reedy, who was like sparkling wine at a prayer-meeting.

My second appearance was at the Artists' Guild, a society composed of "respectable" Bohemians. Their bohemianism made me think of Jack London's exploits in the East End of London as portrayed in his *Children of the Abyss,* when he had stood in the bread-line, waited hours to be given a chance to shovel coal, and had himself locked up in the workhouse, in the comforting consciousness that at any time he could go back to his lodgings, take a bath, change his linen, and eat a hearty dinner.

The majority of the Guilders impressed me as people to whom "bohemianism" was a sort of narcotic to help them endure the boredom of their lives. Of course there were others, those who knew the struggle that is the lot of every sincere and free person, whether he

aspires to an ideal in life or in art. To them I addressed my talk on
"Art in Life," pointing out, among other things, that life in all its
variety and fullness is art, the highest art. The man who is not part
of the stream of life is not an artist, no matter how well he paints
sunsets or composes nocturnes. It certainly does not mean that the
artist must hold a definite creed, join an anarchist group or a socialist
local. It does signify, however, that he must be able to feel the
tragedy of the millions condemned to a lack of joy and beauty. The
inspiration of the true artist has never been the drawing-room. Great
art has always gone to the masses, to their hopes and dreams, for
the spark that kindled their souls. The rest, "the many, all too many,"
as Nietzsche called mediocrity, have been mere commodities that
can be bought with money, cheap glory, or social position.

My lecture on the drama was particularly apropos because of the
efforts which were being made at the time by ministers and virtuous
ladies to purify the stage. It was, however, my talk on Francisco
Ferrer that brought the largest audience and aroused the deepest
interest.

More satisfactory than "breaking into society" were the hours
spent at Faust's with Billy Reedy and the sweet companionship of
Ben and Ida Capes. In theory Bill and I were five thousand years
apart. He had said as much in his pen portrait of me, "The Daughter of the Dream." But in reality the editor of the St. Louis *Mirror*
was very much of an anarchist. His breadth of vision, tolerance, and
generous support of every social rebel brought him very near to me.
We had many literary tastes in common, and his rich Irish humour
and ready wit enlivened the hours we passed together.

I told him about another evening I had spent at Faust's, in 1901,
with Carl Nold and the other friends, before I had gone to Chicago
to give myself up to the police. "You sat here enjoying food and
drink while two hundred detectives were searching for you up and
down the land!" he exclaimed. "Oh, my God, my God, what a
woman!" He broke into spasms, his eyes bulging in wonder, his fat
belly shaking with laughter. After receiving several slaps on the back
and a few gulps of water, Billy regained his breath, but he continued
to cry all through the evening: "Oh, my God, what a woman!"

The Capeses were near to me in a deeper sense than Bill because of
the bond of our ideal and our struggle for it. Long before I had met
them, I had heard of their zeal in our cause and their ever-ready response to its needs. Much later I learned how Ben had become

awakened to social consciousness. " It was at one of your meetings in St. Louis," he told me; " I had come with a bunch of kids to rotten-egg you because you were an enemy of God and man. Your talk that evening moved me profoundly and changed the entire course of my life. I had come to scoff, and I remained to pray to the new vision you had created for me." Since then he had never faltered in his devotion to this vision, nor to our friendship, which became stronger and more beautiful through the years.

Michigan State University is only ten hours removed from the University of Wisconsin, but in spirit it was fifty years behind. Instead of broad-minded professors and keen students, I was confronted with five hundred university rowdies in our hall, whistling, howling, and acting like lunatics. I had addressed difficult crowds in my day — long-shoremen, sailors, steel-workers, miners, men aroused by war hysteria. They resembled boarding-school girls compared with the tough gang that had come this time, evidently intent upon breaking up the meeting. Before I reached the hall, these believers in the sanctity of private property had torn up all our literature. This done, they were amusing themselves by throwing pieces of coal at the cut-glass vase on the platform. The place was packed with men, only one other woman besides myself being present, Dr. Maud Thompson. She, poor soul, was jammed in at the door and could not reach the platform. In any event she would have done no good, as I had no intention of appealing to the "chivalry" of these adolescents.

Several students who had entertained us at a fraternity dinner grew anxious about my safety and offered to call the police. I felt that such a step would only aggravate the situation and perhaps cause a riot. I informed them that I would face the music myself and take the consequences.

My appearance on the platform was greeted with shouts, bells, stamping of feet, and cries of "Here she is, the anarchist bomb-thrower; here's the free lover! You can't speak in our town, Emma! Get out — you'd better get out!"

I saw clearly that if the situation was to be met, I must not show nervousness or lose patience. I folded my arms and stood there facing the young savages while the deafening noises continued. During a slight lull I said: "Gentlemen, I can see you are in a sporting mood, you want a contest. Very well, you shall have it. Just go on with the noise. I will wait until you are through."

There was an amazed silence for a moment, and then they again broke loose. I continued to stand, my arms folded, all my will-power concentrated in my stare. Gradually the yelling subsided and then someone cried: "All right, Emma, let's hear about your anarchism!" The cry was taken up by others, and after a while comparative quiet prevailed. Then I began to speak.

I talked for an hour amid repeated interruptions, but before long, silence settled over the assembly. Their behaviour, I told them, was the best proof of the effects of authority and of its system of education. "You are the result of it," I said; "how can you know the meaning of freedom of thought and speech? How can you feel respect for others or be kind and hospitable to a stranger in your midst? Authority at home, in the school, and in the body politic destroys those qualities. It turns the individual into a parrot repeating time-worn slogans, until he becomes incapable of thinking for himself or of feeling social wrongs. But I believe in the possibilities of youth," I continued, "and you are young, gentlemen, very, very young. That is fortunate, because you are still uncorrupted and impressionable. The energy you have so ably demonstrated this afternoon could be put to better use. It could be applied for the benefit of your fellows. But you have wasted your efforts in smashing a beautiful vase and in destroying the literary labours of men and women who live, work, and often die for their vision of a better future."

As soon as I had finished, they broke out with the college yell. It was the highest tribute, I was told later, that I could receive. Towards the evening a committee of students came to my hotel to offer apologies for the behaviour of their comrades and to pay the damage for the literature and vase. "You won, Emma Goldman," they said, "you have made us ashamed. Next time you visit our city, we will give you a different welcome."

This was not the only interesting event that happened to us in Ann Arbor. There was also the meeting with Dr. William Boehm, instructor at the university, and with his wife, Dr. Maud Thompson, a very fine woman of tender nature. On the day of my lecture Ben and I had been their guests at luncheon. We spent the hour in a heated argument with Boehm, an adherent of "scientific socialism." At the meeting afterwards he forgot our theoretic differences; comradely sympathy and concern spoke louder than his cold science, and he was ready to fight for me.

In Buffalo we found an unusual personality in the secretary of the

Mayor. Only America could produce such a contradiction: he was a radical and a non-believer, yet he was at the same time bound by his New England conscience. He was a dreamer of great dreams, wasting his energies in small deeds; a politician and an opportunist, afraid of public opinion, yet recklessly ignoring it. He had nothing to gain and considerable to lose in urging the Mayor to let me speak. But he championed my rights with a Puritan doggedness.

The Chief of Police attempted to stop my meeting. The Mayor, urged on by his secretary, refused to acquiesce. It was a contest in which superior intelligence scored over official narrow-mindedness.

The ways of the gods are strange; for some reason there was no further interference on this tour. We went on our way quietly, ploughing old fields, breaking new ground, and meeting interesting people who added zest and colour to our work.

Fair newspaper treatment of an anarchist was by no means an everyday occurrence. In Denver, much to my surprise, three papers devoted their columns to verbatim accounts of my lectures. The dramatic critic of the local *Times* even made a discovery. "Emma Goldman," he wrote, "is being treated as an enemy of society because, like Dr. Stockmann in Ibsen's *Enemy of the People,* she is pointing out our ills and defects."

As the divorce-mill of the country, Reno attracts a certain class of women. They flock there to buy their freedom from one owner in order to sell themselves more profitably, as often is the case, to another. Respectability has it easy. No heart-aches, no soul-struggle of the free woman, who suffers a thousand torments in the readjustment from an old to a new emotional experience. Just a piece of paper, easily obtainable when one has money to appease public opinion and one's own conscience. Yet the divorcees in the hotel where we had registered were scandalized.

"What, Emma Goldman under the same roof with us! Emma Goldman, the champion of free love! Such a person cannot be tolerated," they declared. What could the poor owner do? The divorcees, like the poor, are always there and are profitable guests. I had to leave the hotel. The humour of the situation was that the very women who had objected to my staying in the same place with them helped to crowd my lectures on "The Failure of Marriage" and "The Meaning of Love."

It was in Reno that I was inaugurated into the art of gambling.

I had never before seen gambling-houses wide open, with people besieging the roulette tables. It was interesting to watch the expression and behaviour of the men and women obsessed by the passion. I, too, tried my "luck," but after losing fifty cents I gave up the attempt to coax fortune.

In San Francisco I learned that Jack London lived in the neighbourhood. I had met him with other young socialist students at the Strunskys' on my first visit to California, in 1897. I had since read most of his works and I was naturally eager to renew our acquaintance. There was also another reason: the Modern School the Ferrer Association was planning to establish in New York. We had been fortunate in securing the active help of some very vital persons in its educational work, among them Lola Ridge, Manuel Komroff, Rose and Mary Yuster. I wanted to interest Jack London in our project. I wrote requesting him to attend my lecture on Francisco Ferrer.

His reply was characteristic. "Dear Emma Goldman," it read, "I have your note. I would not go to a meeting even if God Almighty were to speak there. The only time I attend lectures is when I am to do the talking. But we want you *here*. Will you not come to Glen Ellen and bring whomever you have with you?"

Who could resist such an amiable invitation? I had only two friends with me, Ben and my erstwhile attorney, E. E. Kirk, but even if I had brought a whole caravan, Jack and Charmian London would have welcomed them, so warm and genuine was the hospitality of those two dear people.

How different was the real Jack London from the mechanical, bell-button socialist of the *Kempton-Wace Letters!* Here was youth, exuberance, throbbing life. Here was the good comrade, all concern and affection. He exerted himself to make our visit a glorious holiday. We argued about our political differences, of course, but there was in Jack nothing of the rancour I had so often found in the socialists I had debated with. But, then, Jack London was the artist first, the creative spirit to whom freedom is the breath of life. As the artist he did not fail to see the beauties of anarchism, even if he did insist that society would have to pass through socialism before reaching the higher stage of anarchism. In any case it was not Jack London's politics that mattered to me. It was his humanity, his understanding of and his feeling with the complexities of the human heart. How else could he have created his splendid *Martin Eden*, if he did not have in himself the elements that had contributed to the soul-struggle and undoing of his hero? It was this Jack London, and not the devotee of a mechanistic creed, who lent meaning and joy to my visit to Glen Ellen.

Charmian, Jack's wife, was a gracious hostess, gentle and loving in her expectant motherhood. She was as active and spirited as if she were not so near to the birth of her child — too strenuous, I feared, in her daily occupations. During our three days' stay Charmian hardly rested, except after dinner, when she would sew on the outfit for the baby while we argued, joked, and drank into the wee hours of the morning.

For fifteen years before this my lectures had been made possible by my comrades, who had always given me their best assistance. But they had never been able to reach a large American public. Some of them had been too centred in their own language-group activities to trouble about interesting the native element. The results during those years were scant and unsatisfactory. Now with Ben as my manager my work was lifted out of its former narrow confines. On this tour I visited thirty-seven cities in twenty-five States, among them many places where anarchism had never been discussed before. I lectured one hundred and twenty times to vast audiences, of which twenty-five thousand paid admission, besides the great number of poor students or unemployed admitted without charge. The most gratifying part of the enlarged scope of my work was that ten thousand pieces of literature were sold and five thousand distributed free. Not least important were the various free-speech fights, with the entire expense for them raised at our own gatherings. Nor had other activities been neglected. Our appeals for the newly organized Francisco Ferrer Association and for many strikes had brought considerable material response.

Nevertheless I was roundly condemned by some of the comrades. They considered it really treason that I, an anarchist, should travel with a manager, and an ex-tramp at that, a man of unsettled habits, who was not even a comrade. I was not disturbed, however, though it was painful to find such sectarianism in our ranks. I took heart in the certainty that during the past two years I had done better work and that I had made anarchism more widely known than in the previous years. And it had been the skill and devotion of Ben that had brought it about.

CHAPTER XXXVII

MAY 18, THE DAY OF SASHA'S RESURRECTION, REMAINED GRAVEN on my heart, although my yearly tours had always prevented my being with him on the anniversary of his release. In a spiritual sense, however, neither space nor time could separate me from Sasha or make me forget the day I had longed and worked for throughout the years of his imprisonment. On May 18 this year a telegram from him found me in Los Angeles. It filled me with great joy, for it brought the news that he had determined to begin his prison memoirs. I had often urged him to write them, believing that if he could re-create his prison life on paper, it might help him to get rid of the phantoms that were making his readjustment to life so difficult. Now he had decided it at last, on Our Day, the day that represented the most significant moment in both our lives. I immediately notified him that I would soon return to relieve him in the *Mother Earth* office, and that I would devote myself for the rest of the summer to his needs.

I was also to do some writing, to revise my lectures for publication. Ben had put that bee in my bonnet and had talked of it all through our tour. I thought that I could not find time for it; moreover, no publisher would accept a book by me. But Ben already visioned my essays as a best-seller at our meetings; his optimism and persistence were too infectious to withstand for long.

Formerly upon the completion of our tours Ben had always remained in Chicago with his mother, to whom he was fondly attached. This time I wanted to have him in New York to give me more leisure to be with Sasha and also for my own writing. But the *Wanderlust* was in Ben's blood, as compelling as in his old tramp days. Not to burden *Mother Earth,* he would work his way across to Europe, he said. Since we had always been separated during a part of the summer, it would make no difference, he argued, whether he was in Chicago or in London.

Shortly after Ben's departure, Sasha and I went out to the little farm. We loved the beauty and restfulness of the place. He pitched a tent on one of the highest hills, which gave him a gorgeous view over the Hudson. I was occupied in setting the house in order. Meanwhile Sasha began to write.

Notwithstanding the many police raids I had suffered since Sasha had gone to Pittsburgh in 1892, I had managed to rescue some copies of "The Prison Blossoms," which he had published *sub rosa* in the penitentiary. Carl Nold, Henry Bauer and several other friends also had kept copies. They were helpful to Sasha, but they were insignificant in comparison with the memory of what he had lived through in that house of the living dead. All the horrors he had known, the agony of body and soul, the suffering of his fellow-prisoners, all this he had now to dig out from the depths of his being and re-create. The black spectre of fourteen years again began to haunt his waking and sleeping hours.

Day after day he would sit at his desk staring into vacancy, or he would write as if driven by furies. What he had written he often wanted to destroy, and I would wrestle with him to save it, as I had fought through all the years to save him from his grave. Then would come days when Sasha would vanish into the woods to escape human contact, to escape me, and above all to escape himself and the ghosts that had come to life since he had begun to write. I would torment myself to find the right way and the right word with which to soothe his harassed spirit. It was not only because of my affection for him that I took up this struggle each day; it was also because I perceived in the very first chapter of his writing that Sasha was in the birth-throes of a great work. No price on my part seemed too high to help it to life.

While on the farm, one evening I fell and hurt myself. A friend, a young medical man who was visiting us, diagnosed my injury as a broken knee-cap, but I would not give up the writing I had planned to do that night. With a cold compress over my knee, my leg suspended, I worked until six in the morning. After a few hours' sleep I felt no pain, and, having to be in New York that day, I busied myself with preparing supplies. I baked, made my special brand of "Boston" beans and compote, and then walked three and a half miles to the railroad station. When I tried to get on the train, I knew there was something very wrong with my knee. That night was excruciating, and in the morning I had to send for a physician. He supported the previous diagnosis of a broken knee-cap and advised an operation. Two other medical friends agreed with him and suggested the St. Francis Hospital.

"Dr. Stewart, the famous surgeon, is there," one of my friends said; "he would do a fine job."

"Dr. Stewart!" I exclaimed; "not the man who was called to treat McKinley?"

"The very one," he replied.

"What a strange coincidence!" I remarked. "Do you think he will consent when he learns who I am?"

"Of course," my friend assured me; "besides, you can register as Kershner."

After an X-ray had been taken, Dr. Stewart came to tell me that my knee-bone was broken on the side. "But how did you manage to tear your ligaments?" he asked. When I told him I had been on my feet all day, he threw up his hands. But he did not intend to operate, he informed me. "Knees never work the same after an operation," he said; "I will give you the slow treatment, the conservative method. It takes more time and patience, but it is better in the end," he remarked with a twinkle in his eye.

"Found out," I thought; "this about the conservative method is for my special benefit."

It was an unpleasant pill for an anarchist to swallow, but female vanity decided against a stiff knee, and I consented to the "conservative method." I was taken back to my flat and laid up for weeks in a plaster cast and splints. Meanwhile Sasha's writing had been interrupted and my own book postponed, which was harder to bear than the pain in my knee. Learning of my accident, Ben cut short his stay abroad and returned to New York. It was soothing and comforting to have him, and I was almost glad I had been laid up.

In another week I was back on the farm, hopping about on crutches, acting as light domestic for five persons, spending the evenings with Sasha, and the nights on my book, which I completed in two months. As I had foreseen, no publisher would accept my manuscript. Ben urged that we get the book out ourselves. Our printer was willing to give us credit, but where get the other necessary funds? "Borrow," my optimistic manager advised; "we'll sell enough on our next tour to pay back the entire cost."

Ben was attending to the office of *Mother Earth* and to the publication of my book, and I returned again to our Ossining farm, where Sasha was still working on his memoirs. Our intention was to remain there as long as the weather would permit, but unexpected events soon changed our plans. News came of the explosion in the Los Angeles *Times* building and of the impending danger to a group of anarchists in Japan. Both matters necessitated immediate and concentrated effort on our part, and we hastened back to New York early in October.

The Merchants' and Manufacturers' Association of Los Angeles, with Harrison Grey Otis, the owner of the Los Angeles *Times,* at their head, had for years carried on a relentless war on the Pacific Coast against organized labour. Their determined opposition had frustrated every attempt to organize the workers in Los Angeles and thus enable them to improve their condition. In consequence Otis and his paper were bitterly hated by the labour elements in California.

On the night of October 1 an explosion blew up the *Times* building, involving the sacrifice of twenty-two employees. Otis raised the cry of "Anarchy!" The press, the State, and the Church combined in an attack on everybody known to sympathize with labour, many preachers being the most rabid in their thirst for vengeance. Even before the cause of the *Times* explosion had been ascertained, the anarchists were being held responsible. We took up the challenge of the enemy and warned the toilers that it was not only anarchism that was in danger but also organized labour. We felt this work to be of paramount importance at the moment, to which all other efforts had to be subordinated. Sasha had no more chance to continue his memoirs.

At the same time news reached us from Japan about the arrest of a number of anarchists for an alleged plot on the life of the Mikado. The outstanding figure of the group was Denjiro Kotoku. He knew his country better than European writers like Lafcadio Hearn, Pierre Loti, or Mme Gauthier, who had painted Japan in roseate colours. Kotoku had personally experienced the miserable conditions under which the workers slaved, and the barbarism of the political régime. For years he had devoted himself to awaking the intelligentsia and the masses of Japan to the needs of the situation. He was a man of brilliant mind, an able writer, and the translator of some of the works of Karl Marx, Leo Tolstoy, and Peter Kropotkin. In co-operation with Lien Sun Soh and Mme Ho Chin he had propagated anarchism in the University of Tokio among Japanese and Chinese students. The Government had repeatedly imprisoned him for his activities, without dampening our comrade's ardour. The authorities finally decided to "eliminate" him by involving him in the plot against the Emperor.

On November 10 the Associated Press announced that "the special tribunal appointed to try the plotters against the life of the Mikado found twenty-six persons guilty, including the ringleaders, Kotoku and his wife, Sugano Kano. The Court recommended the severest penalty under clause 73, which provides capital punishment for conspirators against the Imperial family."

There was no time to lose if anything was to be done to stay the hand of the executioner in Japan. With the help of our friend Leonard D. Abbott, president of the Free Speech League, we initiated a protest that soon assumed national proportions. Letters and telegrams were forwarded to the Japanese Ambassador in Washington, the Consul-General in New York, and the American newspapers. A committee of persons prominent in public life interviewed the Japanese representatives in the United States. The great American protest was evidently not to the liking of the satraps of the Mikado. They strove their utmost to blacken the character of the condemned men and exerted their persuasive powers to prevail upon our committee to give up their efforts. In response we intensified our work, holding private and public meetings, bombarding the press, and otherwise working strenuously to arouse public opinion over the judicial crime about to be committed in Japan.

Among the many friends who participated in this campaign was Sadakichi Hartmann, poet, writer, painter, and a marvellous reader of the poems and stories of Whitman and Poe. I had first met him in 1894; subsequently he had become a steady contributor to our magazine. Partly Japanese himself, Sadakichi was familiar with conditions in Japan and the case of Kotoku. At our request he wrote a powerful manifesto that was widely distributed in behalf of the condemned comrades.

In January 1911 Ben and I again started on our annual tour. Before we left, my selected lectures, *Anarchism and Other Essays,* came off the press. The book also contained a biographic sketch of the author by Hippolyte Havel, comprising the most significant events of my public career. Some of the lectures in the volume had been repeatedly suppressed by the police. Even when I had been able to deliver them, it had never been without anxiety and travail. They represented a mental and spiritual struggle of twenty years, the conclusions arrived at after much reflection and growth. I owed the inspiration to write the book to Ben, but the main assistance, including the revision and the reading of proofs, was due to Sasha. It was hard to say which of us was the happier at seeing my first literary effort in print.

Before going on tour I was able to participate in the inauguration of the Francisco Ferrer Centre at St. Mark's Place, New York, which was organized by the efforts of Leonard D. Abbott, Harry Kelly, Sasha, and other friends. There the Ferrer Association began Sunday and evening classes, preparatory to the Modern School, which we hoped would emerge from our humble beginnings. My great satisfaction at the event was due not only to the funds I had helped to raise, but also to having secured Bayard Boyesen as instructor and secretary of our school.

Mr. Boyesen had been a member of the Department of English and Comparative Literature at Columbia University. Profoundly stirred by the martyrdom of Francisco Ferrer, he had presided at our second memorial meeting. Being censured for it by the president of Columbia, Boyesen resigned his post at the university. He was induced to join the Ferrer Association and to assume the secretaryship of the Modern School. In this capacity he could expect neither salary nor glory, but his interest in the proposed educational venture outweighed all other considerations.

Nothing of particular moment happened on our tour till we reached Columbus, Ohio. There we were gagged and had to begin a fight for free speech. It happened that the United Mine Workers were having their convention in the city at the time. The militant elements were incensed over the action of the police. They staged a demonstration in our hall in protest against the interference and also against their own leaders because the latter had voted down a motion to have me address the convention. The result was an " invitation " to me from the latter. The curious document read:

DEAR MADAM:
   Pursuant to the action of our Convention you are hereby cordially invited to address the delegates of the United Mine Workers

of America at one P.M. tomorrow, January 19th, in session at Memorial Hall.

Subsequent to this action of our Convention, notice was served on us by the custodian that before addressing the delegation it will be necessary to get permission from the County Commissioners; otherwise you would not be allowed. I would suggest that you have Mr. Reitman take this matter up with the Commissioners and avoid any complications or unpleasantness which might ensue if you undertook to deliver an address without permission of the Commissioners.

However, I assure you that as far as our Convention is concerned there would be no objection.

Very truly yours,
EDWIN PERRY
Secretary-Treasurer, U. M. W. of A.

P. S. Have just been advised by the Custodian that the Commissioners refuse to allow you to speak under any circumstances tomorrow morning at the Memorial Hall.

When our miner friends of the rank and file were informed of the ruse to prevent my speaking, they decided unanimously to march to the meeting-place that we had secured; but first they would go to Memorial Hall, where the convention was holding its sessions. And then the unexpected happened. The custodians of Memorial Hall shut their doors, not only to me, but to all the delegates. Even those who had opposed my speaking now felt outraged, and joined the procession to our hall.

I was introduced by Delegate E. S. McCullough, an eloquent man, and received by the audience with enthusiasm. The most gratifying aspect of the situation was the genuine response of the delegates to the necessity of the general strike as the most effective weapon at labour's command.

In Detroit we received the appalling news of the execution of our comrades in Japan. Denjiro Kotoku and his wife, Sugano Kano, Dr. S. Oishi, a physician educated in the United States, A. Morichiki, agricultural engineer, and their co-workers had been judicially assassinated. Their crime had been, as with our Chicago martyrs, love of their fellows and consecration to an ideal.

"Long live anarchy!" Denjiro Kotoku had cried with his last breath.

"Banjoi! (For ever)," had replied his companions in death. "I have lived for liberty and I die for liberty, for liberty is my life," had exclaimed Sugano Kano. The East had met the West, united by the same tie of blood.

William Marion Reedy's efforts in my behalf this year brought even greater results than on the previous occasions in St. Louis. Thanks to him and his friend Alice Martin, who was at the head of a dancing-school, I was enabled to speak in the Odeon Recital Hall. My subjects "Kotoku" and "Victims of Morality" attracted great numbers of people who had never before ventured near an anarchist meeting. The lectures at the Women's Wednesday Club on "Tolstoy" and "Galsworthy's *Justice*" proved rather strong food for the delicate palates of the St. Louis society ladies.

On this visit I made the acquaintance of Roger Baldwin, Robert Minor, and Zoe Akins. Baldwin was helpful in arranging a luncheon at one of the large hotels, where I met a group of social workers and reformers. He had also been instrumental in securing the Women's Wednesday Club for the two drama lectures. He was a very pleasant person, though not very vital, rather a social lion surrounded by society girls, whose interest in the attractive young man was apparently greater than in his uplift work.

Robert Minor, a talented cartoonist, impressed me as more effective and interesting, both as an artist and as a socialist.

Zoe Akins, exotic and vivacious, proved to be a strange American product. Of an ultra-conservative family, her early influences reactionary to the last degree, she yet was trying to break her bonds and find untrammelled expression for her life. A frequent visitor at my hotel, she entertained me with the amusing recital of her exploits in dodging her respectable relatives in order to spend time with her Bohemian friends.

On my return to Madison, Wisconsin, I found Professor Ross and the other instructors less "reckless" than on my previous visit. The cause of it was no doubt the university appropriation bill, pending before the legislature. However they may dislike the idea, professors are also proletarians; intellectual proletarians, to be sure, but even more dependent upon their employer than ordinary mechanics. State universities cannot function without appropriations; hence the need of caution on the part of the faculty. But the students were not deterred. They came in much larger numbers than in the previous year.

The State of Kansas, like Massachusetts, lives on past glory. Had

it not given John Brown to the cause of the slaves? Had not the
rebel voice of Moses Harman sounded there? Had it not been the
stronghold of free thought? Whatever its historic claim to progress,
Kansas now gave no sign of it. The Church and Prohibition had evidently performed the last rites at the interment of liberalism. Lack
of interest in ideas, smugness, and self-complacency characterized
most cities of the State of Kansas.

The exception was Lawrence, the university seat. Here it was
largely a group of advanced students who put life into an otherwise
sleepy town. The most active among them was Harry Kemp. He
prevailed upon the Good Government Club, a body of law-students,
to invite the dangerous anarchist to address them on "Why Laws
Fail." My interpretation proved a novel experience to them. Some
argued and fought against my view-point with youthful arrogance.
Others admitted that I had helped them to see the flaws in the scheme
which they had heretofore considered perfect.

Our own meetings were attended by members of the faculty and
students. My talk on "Victims of Morality" ended in a hilarious
manner. In the course of the lecture I pointed out that men, no matter
how loose in their own sexual habits, always insist that the women
they marry must be "pure" and virtuous. During the discussion a
man in the audience arose to protest. "I am forty," he announced,
"and I have remained pure." He was sickly looking, quite evidently
emotionally starved. "I would advise a medical examination," I replied. In an instant, the house was in an uproar. The cause of the
hilarity I learned only after the meeting. Harry Kemp informed me
that my virtuous opponent was a professor of botany, who was
always very frank in his lectures on plant life, but extremely rigid
on the subject of sex among human beings. I wished I had known
that the poor man was on the faculty. I might not have been so
drastic in my reply. I hated smugness, yet I was sorry to have made
the Puritan professor a target for adolescent mischief.

I found California seething with discontent. The Mexican revolution and the arrest of the two McNamara brothers had aroused
labour on the Pacific Coast to a high pitch. The despotic régime of
Diaz and the ruthless exploitation of the Mexican people by native
and American interests had been unmasked by Ricardo Flores Magón
and his brother Enrique, the representatives of the Junta of the
Mexican Liberal Party. Their contentions were fully supported by

Carlo de Fornaro in his book *Diaz, Tsar of Mexico*. For his disclosures Mr. Fornaro, a well-known New York artist, was arrested
for criminal libel and sentenced to prison for a year, the United States
Government thus acting as lackey for the American oil interests in
Mexico. Another volume, *Barbarous Mexico*, by John Kenneth Turner, had also severely arraigned the legalized robbery of the helpless
peons and castigated the despicable rôle America was playing in their
enslavement.

The revolution in Mexico was the expression of a people awakened
to the great economic and political wrongs in their land. The struggle
inspired large numbers of militant workers in America, among them
many anarchists and I.W.W.'s (Industrial Workers of the World),
to help their Mexican brothers across the border. Thoughtful persons on the Coast, intellectuals as well as proletarians, were imbued
with the spirit behind the Mexican revolution.

Another factor to intensify the atmosphere was the new attempt
to crush labour. Since the explosion of the *Times* building in the previous year (October 1910) a veritable man-hunt had been carried on
by the private detective agency of William J. Burns in the interests of
California employers. John J. McNamara, secretary-treasurer of
the International Association of Bridge and Structural Iron Workers,
was kidnapped and taken back to California. He was charged with
having caused the Los Angeles *Times* explosion and other acts of
dynamiting. At the same time his brother J. B. McNamara and a man
known as Ortie McManigal were also arrested.

Though denounced by the press as anarchists, the McNamara
brothers were, as a matter of fact, good Roman Catholics and members of the conservative American Federation of Labor. Perhaps they
would have been the first to resent the charge of anarchy, since they
knew nothing of our ideas and were unaware of their relation to the
struggle of the workers. Simple trade-unionists, the McNamaras did
not realize that the conflict between capital and labour is a social issue
embracing all life, and that its solution is not a mere matter of higher
wages or shorter hours; they did not know that the problem involved
the abolition of the wage system, of all monopoly and special privileges. But while the McNamaras were not anarchists, they were of the
exploited class, and therefore we were with them. We saw in their
persecution another attempt of the plutocracy to crush organized
labour. To us their case was a repetition of the conspiracy in Chicago

in 1887 and in Idaho in 1906. It was the identical policy of wealth and power everywhere — in Spain, Italy, Russia, Japan, and the United States. The McNamaras were our brothers, their cause ours. From this view-point the anarchists of the entire United States rallied to the support of the men awaiting their doom in the Los Angeles County Jail.

The intense feeling created by these events partially found an outlet on the Coast at my meetings, which were attended by great numbers. I delivered eleven lectures in Los Angeles, two in San Diego, two in Fresno, and eight in San Francisco, as well as participating in a debate. Puget Sound was equally responsive. Portland, Seattle, and Spokane gave us large audiences.

Since the Haywood, Moyer, and Pettibone trial in Boise City I had wanted to go there, but we had had no opportunity to make the trip. On this tour we were within four hundred miles, by no means a small jump. But what were four hundred miles to an old tramp like Ben and a wandering Jew like me? Nor were we deterred by the fact that we knew no one in the city who could help with meetings. My efficient manager had broken virgin soil before; he would attempt it again. When I reached Boise, twenty-four hours after Ben, I found all arrangements made for two Sunday lectures. There was a police ordinance against paid admission on the Sabbath, but the Boise people knew how to evade the law. "You simply give everyone a piece of literature equivalent to your admission charge, see?" the hall landlady had instructed Ben.

The following day we drove out to the Idaho penitentiary where Haywood, Moyer, and Pettibone had been incarcerated. Since then another star was there, the spy Harry Orchard. It seemed just retribution that he, the detectives' tool who had helped to prepare the trap for his comrades, should have been caught in it himself. He was a self-confessed desperado of eighteen murders. The State had used his testimony in its effort to hang the labour leaders and in gratitude had spared his life. It would no doubt have let him go free altogether if it had dared to face the widespread indignation. I could not help thinking of the significant similarity in the new crime the State of California was preparing by using the spy Ortie McManigal to destroy the brothers McNamara.

Harry Orchard, a stocky individual with a bull's neck, sallow complexion, and shifting eyes, was a "model" prisoner, we were told,

"religious and devout." He knew what was good for him, the Judas
of his class. I felt as if something loathsome were crawling near me;
I could not remain in the prison to breathe the same air with him. To
me the worst of human monstrosities had always been the informer
and the spy.

The most interesting aspect of our tour was the absence of police
interference. It was the first time in my public career that I had been
left free to carry my message. I enjoyed the novel experience and
made good use of it, knowing that I should not be left in peace for
long.

When I returned to New York, I found myself viciously attacked,
this time not by the authorities, but by a socialist publication. I was
charged with being in the employ of the Russian Tsar! This astound-
ing revelation appeared in the London *Justice*, May 13, 1911, the
official organ of the Social Democratic Party of England.

> The notorious Emma Goldman has been attacking the socialists
> of Milwaukee lately. She says they are cheap politicians without
> any revolutionary purposes—pretty much what our "impossibil-
> ists" say of us! Emma Goldman has had a remarkably free run in
> the United States for a good many years, and some people have
> wondered how it is that this female fire-brand should carry on her
> propaganda of violence so long and with such impunity. But it is
> not generally known that Emma Goldman is in the pay of the
> police, though the fact has leaked out recently. At one time she was
> employed by Mr. A. E. Olarovsky, of the Russian Secret Police in
> San Francisco, as an agent and a spy. It is the same, we may be
> sure, in nine cases out of ten, with those "prominent" anarchists
> who only kill people with their mouths, who are never on hand
> when an outrage occurs, and who manage to escape so mysteri-
> ously when their associates are arrested.

I was at first sick about this crazy charge. But then I remembered
that denunciation equally scurrilous had been cast against a greater
person than I, Michael Bakunin, the father of anarchism. The men
who had hounded Bakunin were Friedrich Engels and Karl Marx.
Since that time, when the founders of socialism had split the First
International by their demagogic methods, socialists everywhere had
used similar tactics. I felt flattered that I should meet with the same
fate as my illustrious comrade and I considered it beneath my self-

respect to reply to such calumny. Just the same, I would have given much to trace the origin of the damnable story.

It seemed preposterous for any sane person to believe me capable of such treachery. My friends in England and the United States protested vigorously. Members of labour organizations did so through their unions in the form of resolutions. In England proofs were demanded of the editor of *Justice,* but no proofs were forthcoming. At the anniversary dinner of the Francisco Ferrer Center in New York, Moses Openheimer, an old socialist, and my friends Harry Kelly and Leonard D. Abbott paid their respects to the man responsible for the base invention. This was followed by a letter signed by a large number of men and women prominent in the world of labour, art, and letters.

> Editor of *Justice*
>   London, England
>
>   We note in your issue of May 13th, in an article entitled "Anarchist Agents," the statement:
>   "It is not generally known that Emma Goldman is in the pay of the police, though the fact has leaked out recently. At one time she was employed by Mr. A. E. Olarovsky, of the Russian Secret Police in San Francisco, as an agent and a spy."
>   We write to protest in the most emphatic manner against this outrageous slander. It passes our comprehension why you should soil your columns by printing such an absolutely unsupported charge against one of the most devoted and beloved representatives of the radical movement in America. Emma Goldman has given the best years of her life to the anarchist cause. Her integrity is above suspicion. There is not an iota of truth in the charge.

The protest was widely circulated in socialist and liberal papers, but there was no retraction from the editor of *Justice.*

My friend Rose Strunsky, who was then in England, undertook to see the man, but somehow he could nowhere be found. She submitted the matter to Mr. H. M. Hyndman, the head of the British Social Democratic Party. He was requested to compel the editor, Mr. Harry Quelch, to give proof of his accusation. Mr. Hyndman promised, but he never did so.

As a law-abiding British subject Mr. Quelch knew the libel laws of his country. It would have been an easy thing for me to sue him for malicious slander. He would have been forced to produce proof or pay damages and perhaps also go to prison. But I adhere to my anarchist views and to my refusal to invoke the law against anybody, no matter how great his villainy. Evidently Quelch had speculated on that, and I had no other way to compel him to retract. However, the protest in my behalf had one effect. It silenced him. Neither in his paper nor on the platform did he ever again mention my name.

Shortly afterwards another charge was made against me, this time by detective William J. Burns. In a newspaper interview he declared that "Emma Goldman was urging working-men to contribute to the defence of the murderers McNamara." I stated in the press that I not only urged the workers to contribute, but that I also called on them to deliver a mortal blow to "justice" that was supported by spies and a government maintained by and for detectives. It was a commentary on the London followers of Marx that an American detective should be better informed about Emma Goldman than they.

During the summer Sasha and I again went out to our retreat on the Hudson and he resumed work on his book. Fortunately, I had no writing to do and I was not handicapped by crutches any more. I could devote my time to Sasha and look after his comfort. I sought to encourage him in his work: with him I had lived through the agony of his prison years, and now the turmoil of his spirit re-echoed in my heart.

The end of the summer saw his *Prison Memoirs* completed. It was a document profoundly moving, a brilliant study of criminal psychology. I was filled with wonder to see Sasha emerge from his Calvary an artist with a rare gift of music in his words.

"Now for New York and the publishers!" I cried; "surely there will be many who will appreciate the dramatic appeal of your work, the understanding and sympathy for those you have left behind."

We hastened back to the city and I began to canvass the publishers. The more conservative houses refused even to read the manuscript the moment they learned the author's name. "Alexander Berkman, the man who shot Frick!" the representative of a large firm exclaimed; "no, we can't have him on our shelves." "It is a vital literary work," I urged; "aren't you interested in that and in his interpretation of prisons and crime?" They were looking for such a book, he said, but they could not afford to risk the name of the author.

Some publishers asked whether Alexander Berkman would be

willing to use a pseudonym. I resented the suggestion and pointed out that *Prison Memoirs* was a personal story, the product of years of suffering and pain. Could the writer be expected to hide his identity concerning something that was flesh of his flesh and blood of his blood?

I turned to some of the " advanced " publishers and they promised to read the manuscript. I waited anxiously for weeks, and when they at last requested me to come, I found them enthusiastic. "It is a remarkable work," one said, "but would Mr. Berkman leave out the anarchist part?" Another insisted on eliminating the chapters relating to homosexuality in prison. A third suggested other changes. Thus it went on for months. I clung to the hope that someone of literary and human judgment would accept the manuscript. I still believed that we could discover in America what Dostoyevsky had found in tsarist Russia — a publisher courageous enough to issue the first great American study of a "House of the Dead." In vain.

Finally we decided to publish the book ourselves. In our predicament I turned to my friend Gilbert E. Roe, a lawyer by profession, an anarchist by feeling, and one of the kindest of men it has been my good fortune to know.

Through all the years since we had first met, Gilbert and Mrs. Roe remained among my staunchest friends and most generous contributors to our work. From the initial issue of *Mother Earth* the Roes had been among the first to respond to every appeal for help. When I informed Gilbert that Sasha's manuscript had been turned down by many publishers, and that we wanted the *Mother Earth* Publishing Association to have the honour of giving the book to the American public, my good friend said simply: "All right. We will arrange an evening in our apartment and invite some people to hear you read parts of the manuscript. Then we will make an appeal for subscriptions." "Read Sasha's work?" I cried in alarm; "I'll never be able to do it. It is too vital a part of my own life. I shall be sure to break down." Gilbert scoffed at the idea of my being nervous at a small private gathering, considering that I had so often faced thousands in my public work.

When I arrived with the manuscript, the guests were already at Roe's. I felt myself growing faint and covered with a cold sweat. Gilbert took me to the dining-room and handed me a stiff drink. "To give strength to your weak knees," he teased. We returned to a darkened room, with only one light for me at the desk. I began to read. Soon the assembled people seemed to vanish, and Sasha emerged. Sasha at the Baltimore and Ohio Station, Sasha as I saw him in convict clothes in prison, and then Sasha resurrected at the railroad station in Detroit. All the agony, all the hope and despair I had shared with him, leaped up in my throat as I read.

"Whether it is the manuscript or your reading," Gilbert presently remarked, "it is a tremendous piece of work."

Five hundred dollars was pledged that evening towards the expense of publication. A few days later Gilbert took me to see Lincoln Steffens, who contributed two hundred dollars. We now had enough on hand to start setting up the book, but we were advised against putting out such a work in the spring. Besides, Sasha wanted to go over the manuscript once more. Our flat was a beehive, with people coming and going all day long. The *Mother Earth* office was not much quieter. Matters relating to the movement kept us engaged all the time. Not before the summer was Sasha able to get away to our little shack on the Hudson for the final revision of his *Prison Memoirs*.

CHAPTER XXXVIII

THE MCNAMARA DRAMA, STAGED IN THE COURTS OF LOS ANGELES, held the entire country in tense anticipation and then came to a sudden farcical end. The McNamaras confessed! Unexpectedly, to everyone's amazement, they pleaded guilty to the charges on which they were being tried. The reactionary press was jubilant; the Merchants' and Manufacturers' Association, Harrison Grey Otis, William J. Burns, and their crew of spies, whose mission it was to send these men to their death, now offered fervent thanks for the lucky turn affairs had taken. Had they not from the first proclaimed the McNamara brothers anarchists and dynamiters?

The prosecution and the informers had reason to be grateful to the circumstances that had induced the plea of guilty. It was a blow to Labour that even Detective Burns had never dreamed of being able to deliver. Alas, those responsible for the confession came not from the enemy's ranks, but from the camp of Labour itself, from the circle of "well-intentioned" friends.

It would be unfair to lay upon any one person the entire responsibility for the ludicrous end of what had begun as an epoch-making event in the history of the industrial war in the United States. The ignorance of John J. and James B. McNamara about the social significance of their case must share the blame for the irreparable blunder they had made. Had the McNamaras had revolutionary spirit and the intellectual powers of Sasha and other social rebels, there would have been a proud avowal of their acts and an intelligent analysis of the causes that had compelled them to resort to violence. In such a case there could have been neither the feeling nor the admission of guilt. But the McNamara brothers were only trade-unionists who saw in their struggle no more than a feud between their organization and the steel interests.

Yet, however unfortunate the limitations of these two victims, the timidity of their counsel and the credulity of the reformers among their friends were far more blame-worthy. Such people never seem to learn from experience. No matter how often they had seen the lion devour the lamb, they continued to cling to the hope that the nature of the beast might change. If only the lion could get to know the lamb better, they argued, or talk matters over, he would surely learn to appreciate his gentle brother and thereby grow gentle himself. It was therefore not difficult for the prosecutors of the McNamaras to say to them: " Now, gentlemen, induce the prisoners to plead guilty. Get them to confess and we give you our word of honour that their lives will be saved and there will be no further man-hunt, no more arrests, no prosecution of anybody in the labour ranks connected with their acts. Believe us, gentlemen. We may roar like lions, but we have soft hearts. We feel with the poor lambs in the Los Angeles County Jail. Get them to confess and they shall not be doomed. This is a gentlemen's agreement. Now shake, and let's all be lambs."

And those infants believed. They accepted the promise of the sly and cunning beasts. They went forth inspired by the great mission fate had placed before them to bring the lion and the lamb together. But it was not long before the taste of the tender mutton helped to whet the lion's appetite for more of it. A renewed man-hunt followed, arrests upon arrests, indictments by the score, and savage persecution of the victims caught in the dragnet.

Now J. J. and J. B. McNamara were hurled from their pedestal into the dust. They were dragged through the mire, reviled, and branded by the very supporters who had recently strewn roses in their path. The wretched apostates now beat their chests and cried: " We have been deceived, we did not know that the McNamaras were guilty, and that they had used violence. They are criminals."

The collapse of the trial disclosed the appalling hollowness of radicalism in and out of the ranks of labour, and the craven spirit of so many of those who presume to plead its cause.

A few clear minds and staunch souls remained, all too few when compared with the pack that were calling down anathema upon the two victims. These refused to be swayed by the panic which followed on the heels of the McNamara confession. Among the small minority in the United States most anarchists stood by the deserted labour leaders because they were victims of a system supported by violence and unyielding to any other method in the industrial struggle.

The *Mother Earth* group registered its protest in our magazine and on the platform against the cheap apology of those who claimed to have been "deceived in thinking the McNamaras innocent." We held that if such excuses were sincere, then the trade-unionists and the reformers, as well as the political socialists, were fools and not competent to be teachers of the people. We pointed out that he who remains ignorant of the causes of the class conflict makes himself responsible for its existence.

Every time I lectured on the McNamara case, police and detectives were on my trail, but I did not care. In fact, I should have welcomed arrest. Prison seemed preferable to the world of cowardice and impotence. Nothing happened, however, and I went on with our work. The next job was already at hand, the Lawrence strike.

Twenty-five thousand textile workers, men, women, and children, were involved in the struggle for a fifteen-per-cent increase in their wage. For years they had toiled fifty-six hours a week for an average weekly pay of eight dollars. Out of the strength of these people the mill-owners had grown immensely rich. Poverty and misery had at last driven the Lawrence textile workers to strike. The struggle was hardly under way when the mill lords began to show their teeth. In this they had the support of the State, and even of the college authorities. The Governor of Massachusetts, himself a mill-owner, sent the militia to protect his interests and those of his mill-owning colleagues. The president of Harvard was, as one of the stockholders, equally interested in dividends from the Lawrence mills. The result of this unity between State, capitalism, and seats of learning in Massachusetts was a horde of police, detectives, soldiers, and collegiate ruffians let loose on the helpless strikers. The first victims of the reign of military terror were Anna Lapezo and John Ramo. During a skirmish the girl was shot and the young man bayoneted to death by a soldier. Instead of apprehending the perpetrators of the crime, the State and local authorities arrested among others, Joseph Ettor and Arturo Giovannitti, the two foremost strike leaders. These men were conscious rebels, backed by the Industrial Workers of the World and by the other revolutionary elements in the country. Labour in the East rallied with particular generosity to the support of the Lawrence strikers and to the defence of the two men. The gap left by the arrest of Ettor and Giovannitti was immediately filled by Bill Haywood and Elizabeth Gurley Flynn. Haywood's years of experience in the labour struggle, his determination and tact, made him a distinctive power in the Lawrence situation. On the other hand, Elizabeth's youth, charm, and eloquence easily won everybody's heart. The names of the two and their reputation gained for the strike country-wide publicity and support.

I had known and admired Elizabeth since I had first heard her, years before, at an open-air gathering. She could not have been more than fourteen years of age at the time, with a beautiful face and figure and a voice vibrant with earnestness. She made a strong impression on me. Later I used to see her in the company of her father at my lectures. She was a fascinating picture with her black hair, large blue eyes, and lovely complexion. I often found it hard to take my eyes off her, sitting in the front row at my meetings.

The splendid free-speech fight she had made in Spokane with other members of the I.W.W., and the persecution she had endured, brought Elizabeth Gurley Flynn very near to me. And when I heard she was ill, after the birth of her child, I felt great sympathy for this young rebel, one of the first American women revolutionists of proletarian background. My interest in her had served to increase my efforts in raising funds, not only for the Spokane fight, but for Elizabeth's own use during her first months of young motherhood.

Since she had returned to New York we were often thrown together, in meetings and in more intimate ways. Elizabeth was not an anarchist, but neither was she fanatical or antagonistic, as were some of her comrades who had emerged from the Socialist Labor Party. She was accepted in our circles as one of our own, and I loved her as a friend.

Bill Haywood had but recently come to live in New York. We had met almost immediately and became very friendly. Bill also was not an anarchist, but, like Elizabeth, he was free from narrow sectarianism. He frankly admitted that he felt much more at home with the anarchists, and especially with the *Mother Earth* group, than with the zealots in his own ranks.

The most notable characteristic of Bill was his extraordinary sensitiveness. This giant, outwardly so hard, would wince at a coarse word and tremble at the sight of pain. On one occasion, when he addressed our eleventh-of-November commemoration, he related to me the effect the crime of 1887 had had on him. He was but a youngster at the time, already working in the mines. "Since then," he told me, "our Chicago martyrs have been my greatest inspiration, their courage my guiding star." The apartment at 210 East Thirteenth Street became

Bill's retreat. Frequently he spent his free evenings at our place. There he could read and rest to his heart's content, or drink coffee " black as the night, strong as the revolutionary ideal, sweet as love."

At the height of the Lawrence strike I was approached by Mr. Sol Fieldman, a New York socialist, in regard to two debates on the difference in theory and tactics between socialism and anarchism. I had debated with socialists all through the United States, but never in my own city. I was glad of the opportunity, and the proposal caught Ben's fancy. Nothing but Carnegie Hall would do, he declared; he was sure we could jam it, and off he went to rent the place. But he returned with a sad face; the hall was free for one evening only. For the second date he had to be content with the Republic Theatre.

It occurred to me that the debates presented a splendid occasion to raise a substantial sum for the Lawrence strike, and Mr. Fieldman agreed. Nothing was said as to who should make the appeal, but I set my heart upon having Big Bill do it. He, in the very thick of the battle, was the most appropriate person for the purpose.

Mr. Fieldman wanted to supply the chairman from his own ranks. I made no objections, because it was of no moment to me who presided. On the day of the debate my opponent informed me that he was still without a chairman and that he had been severely censured by his socialist comrades for having proposed the debate. "Very well, we'll wire for Bill Haywood," I said; " he'll be glad to preside and he is the man to make the appeal." But Mr. Fieldman refused. He would prefer even an anarchist, he said, to Haywood. I insisted that it must be Bill for the appeal, no matter who presided. In the evening, when I came to Carnegie Hall, Fieldman was still without a chairman, nor would he consent to Bill. "All right, there will be no debate," I announced; "but I myself will tell the audience the reason for it." The categorical imperative frightened him into submission.

The audience knew that Bill came straight from the Lawrence scene. The feeling the strike had aroused now broke out in an ovation for Bill. His simple appeal for the heroic men and women of Lawrence moved everybody to response. Within a few minutes the platform was strewn with money, and Mr. Fieldman was on all fours gathering in the harvest of Bill's appeal. The amount contributed was five hundred and forty-two dollars, a very large sum from an audience of working people who had already paid admission to the debate.

Then the bull-fight began, but, alas, the bull turned out to be a very tame animal. Mr. Fieldman knew his catechism. He recited his Marxist rosary with the fluency and precision which comes from practice, but not one original or independent thought did he advance. In roseate colours he painted the marvellous achievements of social democracy in Germany, dwelling on its party strength of four million votes and its even greater number of adherents in trade-union ranks, consisting of eight millions. "Think of what those twelve million socialists can do," he cried triumphantly; "stop wars, take possession of the means of production and distribution. Not by violence, but by their political power! As to the State, did not Engels say that it will die of itself?" It was a grand socialist speech, ably delivered. But it was no debate.

The historic data and the current facts I advanced to prove the deterioration of socialism in Germany, the betrayal on the part of most socialists who had achieved power, the tendency in their ranks everywhere towards petty reforms — all that Mr. Fieldman conveniently ignored. Each time he rose to reply, he repeated verbatim what he had said in his opening round.

Our debate on political versus direct action, at the Republic Theatre, was more spirited. Many I.W.W. boys were present and gave the proceedings heightened colour. The Lawrence strike served me as an illuminating example of direct action. My opponent did not feel quite so sure of himself as when he had presented the socialist theory with such finality. He was especially nonplussed by the questions hurled at him from the gallery by an I.W.W. boy: "How would political action serve the mass of migratory workers, who are never long enough in one place to be able to register for voting, or the millions of boys and girls under age and without right to the ballot? Is not direct mass action their only medium, and the most effective to gain economic redress? The textile workers in Lawrence, for instance; should they have waited until they had voted their socialist comrades into the Massachusetts legislature?"

My opponent sweated trying to wriggle out of a definite answer. When he did finally meet the issue, it was to say that the socialists do believe in strikes, but that when they should gain the majority and come into political power, there would be no further need of such methods. This was too much for the overall brigade. They howled with laughter, stamped their feet, and intoned I.W.W. songs.

Our activities did not leave us much leisure for sociability or intellectual enjoyment. The return to America of Paul Orleneff with a new company came as a great surprise and brought joy to all of us who had known the man from his first visit. Paul looked older; his face was more lined, and his eyes had more *Weltschmerz* in them. But he remained the same naïve, unworldly creature, living only in the realm of his art.

The people who could help him to some success were the men of the Yiddish press, particularly Abe Cahan and the other Jewish writers. Orleneff would not listen to my suggestion that he seek them out. It was not resentment, he said, at the unkind treatment during the latter part of his visit in 1905. "You see, Miss Emma," he explained, "for almost a year I have been living Ibsen's Brand. You know what his motto is: 'No compromise; all or nothing.' Can you imagine Brand going about knocking at the door of the editors? If I should do what Brand would scorn to do, I'd ruin my conception of the character."

Before long, Orleneff left America. He could not acclimatize himself in this country or accept its attitude to art. The realization also that the tie which had bound him to Alla Nazimova was definitely broken excluded his continued stay. They were separated now by the gap which must always exist between a truly creative artist and one interested mainly in material success.

In Chicago I had the opportunity of meeting the famous Russian revolutionary Vladimir Bourtzeff. I was greatly interested in his recital of the arduous mission that had come to him of unmasking Azeff as a police spy. Azeff was undoubtedly a most exceptional phenomenon in revolutionary annals. Not that there had not been before, or since, traitors in revolutionary ranks. But Azeff was no ordinary spy, and even today the psychology of the man remains an unsolved enigma. For years he had not only been a member of the Fighting Organization of the Socialist-Revolutionary Party of Russia, but also the all-powerful head of that terrorist body. He had planned and had successfully executed numerous acts against the highest dignitaries of the Tsarist Government, and he enjoyed the absolute confidence of all his co-workers. When Bourtzeff charged Azeff, the ultra-terrorist, with being an agent of the Russian Secret Service, even the nearest friends of the accuser thought him demented. The mere suggestion of such a possibility was considered treason to the revolution, for Azeff personified the very spirit of the Russian revolutionary movement. Bourtzeff, however, was a man of dogged tenacity who possessed an unerring intuition in such matters. He had exposed a number of spies previously, and his sources of information had always proved to be entirely reliable. Yet even he underwent a long inner struggle before he could bring himself to believe in the guilt of the trusted head of the Fighting Organization. The data Bourtzeff secured were incontrovertible and damned Azeff as a man who had during a period of twenty years managed to dupe the Russian Secret Service and the revolutionists at the same time. Bourtzeff succeeded in proving Azeff a traitor to both sides, and both resolved to punish Azeff by death for his monumental deceit. Yet even at the eleventh hour Azeff tricked them, by escaping without leaving a trace.

Except for the good-fellowship of my comrades in Denver, the city had always been a disappointment to me. There even Ben's energy had failed to arouse interest in our work. This time the number of my friends was augmented by Lillian Olf, Lena and Frank Monroe, John Spiss, May Courtney, and other American anarchists, as well as by new comrades among the Yiddish element. But the public at large remained away from our meetings. Then it happened that the Denver *Post* asked me to write a series of articles on the growing social unrest. At the same time several newspaper women I knew offered to arrange a special lecture at the Brown Palace Hotel. The subject they chose was Rostand's *Chantecler*.

I had long since become convinced that the modern drama is a fruitful disseminator of new ideas. My first experience in that regard was in 1897, when I had talked to a group of miners on George Bernard Shaw's plays. It was during their lunch-hour, and we were four hundred feet below the ground. My audience clustered around me, their black faces lit up now and then by the gleam of their lamps. Their eyes, deep-sunken, looked dull at first, but as I continued speaking, they began glowing with understanding of the social significance of Shaw's works. My well-dressed audience in the luxurious ballroom of the Brown Palace Hotel reacted in the same manner as the miners had. They, too, saw themselves reflected in the dramatic mirror. Several teachers of the university and of the high school urged me to deliver a drama course. Among them one woman particularly attracted my attention, Miss Ellen A. Kennan, who had a very scholarly mind. She offered to maintain the class until I returned. Thus my visit to Denver for five lectures lengthened into fourteen and resulted also in five articles for the *Post*.

Among the interesting features of my stay in the city was the opening performance of *Chantecler,* with Maude Adams in the title rôle, which I attended by request to review the play in the press. I had liked Miss Adams in her demure parts, but in stature and voice she impressed me as miscast in the rôle of Chanticler.

San Diego, California, had always enjoyed considerable freedom of speech. Anarchists, socialists, I.W.W. men, as well as religious sects, had been in the habit of speaking out of doors to large crowds. Then the city fathers of San Diego passed an ordinance doing away with the old custom. The anarchists and I.W.W.'s initiated a free-speech fight, with the result that eighty-four men and women were thrown into jail. Among them was E. E. Kirk, who had defended me in San Francisco in 1909; Mrs. Laura Emerson, a well-known woman rebel; and Jack Whyte, one of the most intelligent I.W.W. boys in California.

When I arrived with Ben in Los Angeles in April, San Diego was in the grip of a veritable civil war. The patriots, know as Vigilantes, had converted the city into a battle-field. They beat, clubbed, and killed men and women who still believed in their constitutional rights. Hundreds of them had come to San Diego from every part of the United States to participate in the campaign. They travelled in box cars, on the bumpers, on the roofs of trains, every moment in danger of their lives, yet sustained by the holy quest for freedom of speech, for which their comrades were already filling the jails.

The Vigilantes raided the I.W.W. headquarters, broke up the furniture, and arrested a large number of men found there. They were taken out to Sorrento to a spot where a flag-pole had been erected. There the I.W.W.'s were forced to kneel, kiss the flag, and sing the national anthem. As an incentive to quicker action one of the Vigilantes would slap them on the back, which was the signal for a general beating. After these proceedings the men were loaded into automobiles and sent to San Onofre, near the county line, placed in a cattle-pen with armed guards over them, and kept without food or drink for eighteen hours. The following morning they were taken out in groups of five and compelled to run the gauntlet. As they passed between the double line of Vigilantes, they were belaboured with clubs and blackjacks. Then the flag-kissing episode was repeated, after which they were told to "hike" up the track and never come back. They reached Los Angeles after a tramp of several days, sore, hungry, penniless, and in deplorable physical condition.

In this struggle, in which the local police were on the side of the Vigilantes, several I.W.W. men lost their lives. The most brutal murder was that of Joseph Mikolasek, who died on May 7. He was one of the many rebels who had attempted to fill the gap caused by the arrest of their speakers. When he ascended the platform, he was assaulted by the police. With difficulty he dragged himself to the socialist headquarters and thence home. He was followed by detectives, who attacked him in his house. One officer fired and severely wounded him. In self-defence Mikolasek had picked up an ax, but his body was riddled with bullets before he had a chance to lift it against his assailants.

On every tour to the Coast I had lectured in San Diego. This time we were also planning meetings there after the close of our Los Angeles engagements. Reports from San Diego and the arrival of scores of wounded Vigilante victims decided us to go at once. Especially after the killing of Mikolasek we felt it imperative to take up the free-speech fight waged there. First, however, it was necessary to organize relief for the destitute boys who had escaped their tormentors and had reached us alive. With the help of a group of women we organized a feeding-station at the I.W.W. headquarters. We raised funds at my meetings and collected clothing and food-stuffs from sympathetic store-keepers.

San Diego was not content with the murder of Mikolasek; it would not permit him even to be buried in the city. We therefore had his body shipped to Los Angeles, and prepared a public demonstration in his honour. Joseph Mikolasek had been obscure and unknown in life, but he grew to country-wide stature in his death. Even the police of the city were impressed by the size, dignity, and grief of the masses that followed his remains to the crematorium.

Some comrades in San Diego had undertaken to arrange a meeting, and I chose a subject which seemed to express the situation best — Henrik Ibsen's *An Enemy of the People.*

On our arrival we found a dense crowd at the station. It did not occur to me that the reception was intended for us; I thought that some State official was being expected. We were to be met by our friends Mr. and Mrs. E. E. Kirk, but they were nowhere to be seen, and Ben suggested that we go to the U. S. Grant Hotel. We passed unobserved and got into the hotel autobus. It was hot and stuffy inside and we climbed up on top. We had barely taken our seats when someone shouted: "Here she is, here's the Goldman woman!" At once the cry was taken up by the crowd. Fashionably dressed women stood up in their cars screaming: "We want that anarchist murderess!" In an instant there was a rush for the autobus, hands reaching up to pull me down. With unusual presence of mind, the chauffeur started the car at full speed, scattering the crowd in all directions.

At the hotel we met with no objections. We registered and were shown to our rooms. Everything seemed normal. Mr. and Mrs. Kirk called to see us, and we quietly discussed final arrangements for our meeting. In the afternoon the head clerk came to announce that the Vigilantes had insisted on looking over the hotel register to secure the number of our rooms; he would therefore have to transfer us to another part of the house. We were taken to the top floor and assigned to a large suite. Later on, Mr. Holmes, the hotel manager, paid us a visit. We were perfectly safe under his roof, he assured us, but he could not permit us to go down for our meals or leave our rooms. He would have to keep us locked in. I protested that the U. S. Grant Hotel was not a prison. He replied that he could not keep us incarcerated against our will, but that, as long as we remained the guests of the house, we should have to submit to his arrangement for our safety. "The Vigilantes are in an ugly mood," he warned us; "they are determined not to let you speak and to drive you both out of town." He urged us to leave of our own account and volunteered to escort us. He was a kindly man and we appreciated his offer, but we had to refuse it.

Mr. Holmes had barely left when I was called on the telephone. The speaker said that his name was Edwards, that he was at the head of the local Conservatory of Music, and that he had just read in the papers that our hall-keeper had backed out. He offered us the recital hall of the conservatory. "San Diego still seems to have some brave men," I said to the mysterious person at the other end of the telephone, and I invited him to come to see me to talk over his plan. Before long a fine-looking man of about twenty-seven called. In the course of our conversation I pointed out to him that I might cause him trouble by speaking in his place. He replied that he did not mind; he was an anarchist in art and he believed in free speech. If I were willing to take a chance, so was he. We decided to await developments.

Towards evening a bedlam of auto horns and whistles filled the street. "The Vigilantes!" Ben cried. There was a knock at the door, and Mr. Holmes came in, accompanied by two other men. I was wanted downstairs by the city authorities, they informed me. Ben sensed danger and insisted that I ask them to send the visitors up. It seemed timid to me. It was early evening and we were in the principal hotel of the city. What could happen to us? I went with Mr. Holmes, Ben accompanying us. Downstairs we were ushered into a room where we found seven men standing in a semicircle. We were asked to sit down and wait for the Chief of Police, who arrived before long. "Please come with me," he addressed me; "the Mayor and other officials are awaiting you next door." We got up to follow, but, turning to Ben, the Chief said: "You are not wanted, doctor. Better wait here."

I entered a room filled with men. The window-blinds were partly drawn, but the large electric street light in front disclosed an agitated mass below. The Mayor approached me. "You hear that mob," he said, indicating the street; "they mean business. They want to get you and Reitman out of the hotel, even if they have to take you by force. We cannot guarantee anything. If you consent to leave, we will give you protection and get you safely out of town."

"That's very nice of you," I replied, "but why don't you disperse the crowd? Why don't you use the same measures against these people that you have against the free-speech fighters? Your ordinance makes it a crime to gather in the business districts. Hundreds of I.W.W.'s, anarchists, socialists, and trade-union men have been clubbed and arrested, and some even killed, for this offence. Yet you allow the Vigilante mob to congregate in the busiest part of the town and obstruct traffic. All you have to do is to disperse these law-breakers."

"We can't do it," he said abruptly; "these people are in a dangerous mood, and your presence makes things worse."

"Very well, then, let me speak to the crowd," I suggested. "I could do it from a window here. I have faced infuriated men before and I have always been able to pacify them."

The Mayor refused.

"I have never accepted protection from the police," I then said, "and I do not intend to do so now. I charge all of you men here with being in league with the Vigilantes."

Thereupon the officials declared that matters would have to take their course, and that I should have only myself to blame if anything happened.

The interview at an end, I went to call Ben. The room I had left

him in was locked. I became alarmed and pounded on the door. There
was no answer. The noise I made brought a hotel clerk. He unlocked
the door, but no one was there. I ran back to the other room and met
the Chief, who was just coming out.

"Where is Reitman?" I demanded. "What have you done with
him? If any harm comes to him, you will pay for it if I have to do
it with my own hands."

"How should I know?" he replied gruffly.

Mr. Holmes was not in his office, and no one would tell me what
had become of Ben Reitman. In consternation I returned to my room.
Ben did not appear. In dismay I paced the floor, unable to decide what
steps to take or whom to approach to help me find Ben. I could not
call any person I knew in the city without endangering his safety, least
of all Mr. Kirk; he was already under indictment in connexion with
the free-speech fight. It had been brave of him and his wife to meet
us; it was sure to aggravate his situation. The circumstance that the
Kirks did not return as they had promised proved that they were
being kept away.

I felt helpless. Time dragged on, and at midnight I dozed off from
sheer fatigue. I dreamed of Ben, bound and gagged, his hands groping
for me. I struggled to reach him and woke up with a scream, bathed
in sweat. There were voices and loud knocking at my door. When I
opened, the house detective and another man stepped in. Reitman was
safe, they told me. I looked at them in a daze, hardly grasping their
meaning. Ben had been taken out by the Vigilantes, they explained,
but no harm had come to him. They had only put him on a train for
Los Angeles. I did not believe the detective, but the other man looked
honest. He reiterated that he had been given absolute assurance that
Reitman was safe.

Mr. Holmes came in. He corroborated the man and begged me to
consent to leave. There was no object in my remaining any longer in
town, he urged. I would not be allowed to lecture and I was only endangering his own position. He hoped I would not take undue advantage because I was a woman. If I remained, the Vigilantes would drive
me out of town anyhow.

Mr. Holmes seemed genuinely concerned. I knew there was no
chance of holding a meeting. Now that Ben was safe, there was no
sense in harassing Mr. Holmes any further. I consented to leave,
planning to take the Owl, the 2:45 A.M. train, for Los Angeles. I

called for a taxi and drove to the station. The town was asleep, the streets deserted.

I had just purchased my ticket and was walking towards the Pullman car when I caught the sound of approaching autos — the fearful sound I had first heard at the station and later at the hotel. The Vigilantes, of course.

"Hurry, hurry!" someone cried; "get in quick!"

Before I had time to make another step, I was picked up, carried to the train, and literally thrown into the compartment. The blinds were pulled down and I was locked in. The Vigilantes had arrived and were rushing up and down the platform, shouting and trying to board the train. The crew was on guard, refusing to let them on. There was mad yelling and cursing — hideous and terrifying moments till at last the train pulled out.

We stopped at innumerable stations. Each time I peered out eagerly in the hope that Ben might be waiting to join me. But there was no sign of him. When I reached my apartment in Los Angeles, he was not there. The U. S. Grant Hotel men had lied in order to get me out of town!

"He's dead! He's dead!" I cried in anguish. "They've killed my boy!"

In vain I strove to drive the terrible thought away. I called up the Los Angeles *Herald* and the San Francisco *Bulletin* to inform them about Ben's disappearance. Both papers were unequivocal in their condemnation of the Vigilante reign of terror. The guiding spirit of the *Bulletin* was Mr. Fremont Older, perhaps the only man on a capitalist paper brave enough to plead labour's cause. He had made a valiant fight for the McNamaras. Mr. Older's enlightened humanity had created on the Coast a new attitude towards the social offender. Since the San Diego fight he had kept up a fearless attack on the Vigilantes. Mr. Older and the editor of the *Herald* promised to do their utmost to unearth Ben.

At ten o'clock I was called on the long-distance phone. A strange voice informed me that Dr. Reitman was boarding the train for Los Angeles and that he would arrive in the late afternoon. "His friends should bring a stretcher to the station." "Is he alive?" I shouted into the receiver. "Are you telling the truth? Is he alive?" I listened breathlessly, but there was no response.

The hours dragged on as if the day would never pass. The wait at the station was more excruciating still. At last the train pulled in. Ben lay in a rear car, all huddled up. He was in blue overalls, his face deathly pale, a terrified look in his eyes. His hat was gone, and his hair was sticky with tar. At the sight of me he cried: "Oh, Mommy, I'm with you at last! Take me away, take me home!"

The newspaper men besieged him with questions, but he was too exhausted to speak. I begged them to leave him alone and to call later at my apartment.

While helping him to undress, I was horrified to see that his body was a mass of bruises covered with blotches of tar. The letters I.W.W. were burned into his flesh. Ben could not speak; only his eyes tried to convey what he had passed through. After partaking of some nourishment and sleeping several hours, he regained a little strength. In the presence of a number of friends and reporters he told us what had happened to him.

"When Emma and the hotel manager left the office to go into another room," Ben related, "I remained alone with seven men. As soon as the door was closed, they drew out revolvers. 'If you utter a sound or make a move, we'll kill you,' they threatened. Then they gathered around me. One man grabbed my right arm, another the left; a third took hold of the front of my coat, another of the back, and I was led out into the corridor, down the elevator to the ground floor of the hotel, and out into the street past a uniformed policeman, and then thrown into an automobile. When the mob saw me, they set up a howl. The auto went slowly down the main street and was joined by another one containing several persons who looked like business men. This was about half past ten in the evening. The twenty-mile ride was frightful. As soon as we got out of town, they began kicking and beating me. They took turns at pulling my long hair and they stuck their fingers into my eyes and nose. 'We could tear your guts out,' they said, 'but we promised the Chief of Police not to kill you. We are responsible men, property-owners, and the police are on our side.' When we reached the county line, the auto stopped at a deserted spot. The men formed a ring and told me to undress. They tore my clothes off. They knocked me down, and when I lay naked on the ground, they kicked and beat me until I was almost insensible. With a lighted cigar they burned the letters I.W.W. on my buttocks; then they poured a can of tar over my head and, in the absence of feathers, rubbed sage-brush on my body. One of them attempted to push a cane into my rectum. Another twisted my testicles. They forced me to kiss the flag and sing *The Star Spangled Banner*. When they tired of the fun, they gave me my underwear for fear we should meet any women. They also gave me back my vest, in order that I might carry my money, railroad ticket, and watch. The rest of my clothes they kept. I was ordered to make a speech, and then they commanded me to run the gauntlet. The Vigilantes lined up, and as I ran past them, each one gave me a blow or a kick. Then they let me go."

Ben's case was but one out of many since the struggle in San Diego had begun, but it helped to focus greater attention on the scene of savagery. A number of labour and radical journalists went to that city to gather material at first hand. The Governor of California appointed Colonel H. Weinstock as special commissioner to investigate the situation. Guarded and cautious as his subsequent report was, it yet substantiated every charge made by the victims of Vigilante rule. It aroused indignation even among the conservative elements of the country.

In Los Angeles the tide of sympathy rose very high and we drew unusually large crowds. On the evening of our protest meeting we had to address our audience in two halls. We could have filled several more if we had had them and enough speakers to go round.

San Francisco, fruitful for years, turned out an enormous crowd this time. Our comrades were spared the labour and expense of advertising; the Vigilantes had done that for us. Their action inspired the San Francisco city officials to give us a glad welcome. The Mayor, the Chief of Police, and hordes of detectives came to meet us at the station, though not to interfere. Our halls, larger than in Los Angeles, yet proved not big enough to hold the masses who came to the lectures, while the rush on our literature floored even Ben, who was seldom content with sales.

The climax was reached with our meeting in the Trade Council Hall. Our friend Anton Johannsen, a well-known labour man, presided. He urged a boycott against the approaching fair in San Diego, "until its citizens are cured of their rabies." Ben recounted the details of the Vigilante attack upon him. I gave a brief report of my experience and then delivered the treasonable lecture, "The Enemy of the People."

Before we left for Portland, we were able to turn over a substantial fund to the San Diego free-speech fight, send money for the Ettor-

Giovannitti defence, and also free *Mother Earth* for a while from a considerable debt.

Mainly responsible for the madness of San Diego were two newspapers. They started the cry of "Anarchist and I.W.W. peril!" The inhabitants were kept in constant fear of dynamite and bombs, which were said to have been smuggled in on barges to blow up the town. The evil spirit of the Vigilante activities was a certain reporter on one of these newspapers. Such fame and glory as his must needs arouse envy in the hearts of other capitalist sheets. A Seattle newspaper set to work to emulate its San Diego colleagues. Long before our arrival it began a campaign calling on the good American patriots to protect the flag and save Seattle from anarchy. Some senile Spanish War veterans suddenly discovered their lost manhood and offered to do their duty. "Five hundred brave soldiers will meet Emma Goldman at the station," the newspaper announced, "and drive her back."

The story, whether true or invented, put everybody in a panic. Our friends in Portland begged us not to proceed to Seattle. Our comrades in Seattle, anxious for our safety, offered to call off the meetings. But I insisted on going through with our program.

Arriving in Seattle, we learned that Mayor Cotteril was a staunch single-taxer. He announced that he would not interfere with free speech, and that he would send the police to protect our meetings. The courage of the tottering veterans evidently caved in at the last moment; they did not appear to give us the promised reception, but the police were on hand. They crowded the hall and stationed themselves on the roofs. They even searched the people who came to my lectures for weapons. The lurid articles in the *Times* and the array of blue-coats naturally did much to intimidate a great many people. I had to request the Mayor to be less solicitous about our safety and call off our protectors. He did, whereupon the audiences took heart to attend my meetings.

On the Sunday of my first lecture a sealed note was left at my hotel for me. The anonymous writer warned me of a plot against my life: I was going to be shot when about to enter the hall, he assured me. Somehow I could give no credence to the story. Not wishing to cause my comrades any anxiety, however, I did not mention the matter to my friend C. V. Cook, who came to escort me to the hall. I told him that I preferred to go alone.

I was never more calm than as I walked leisurely from the hotel to the meeting-place. When within half a block of it I instinctively raised to my face the large bag I always carried. I got safely into the hall and walked towards the platform still holding the bag in front of my face. All through the lecture the thought persisted in my brain: "If I could only protect my face!" In the evening I repeated the same performance, holding my bag to my face all the way to the hall. The meetings went off well, without any sign of the plotters.

For days after, I tried to find some plausible explanation for my silly action with the bag. Why had I been more concerned about my face than about my chest or any other part of my body? Surely no man would think of his face under such circumstances. Yet I, in the presence of probable death, had been afraid to have my face disfigured! It was a shock to discover in myself such ordinary female vanity.

CHAPTER XXXIX

ON MY RETURN EAST I LEARNED OF THE DEATH OF VOLTAIRINE DE Cleyre. Her end affected me very deeply; her whole life had been a continuous chain of suffering. Death had come after an operation for an abcess on the brain which had impaired her memory. A second operation, her friends had been informed, would have deprived her of the power of speech. Voltairine, always stoical in pain, preferred death. Her end, on June 19, was a great loss to our movement and to those who valued her strong personality and unusual talents.

In compliance with her last request Voltairine was buried in Waldheim Cemetery, near the graves of our Chicago comrades. Their martyrdom had awakened Voltairine's soul as it had so many other fine spirits. But few had so completely consecrated themselves to their cause as she, and fewer still had her genius to serve the ideal with singleness of purpose.

Arrived in Chicago, I went out to Waldheim with Annie Livshis, a dear common friend. Voltairine had made her home with Annie and Jake Livshis, and she had been tenderly nursed by our devoted comrades to the very last. I went to the cemetery with red carnations in my arms, while Annie carried red geraniums to be added to those she had already planted on the fresh grave. These were the only monument Voltairine had ever wanted.

Voltairine de Cleyre was born of a Quaker mother and a French father. The latter, in his youth an admirer of Voltaire, had named his daughter after the great philosopher. Later her father, having turned conservative, had placed her in a Catholic convent school, from which Voltairine subsequently escaped, rebelling against the authority of both. She was exceptionally gifted as poet, writer, and lecturer. She would have gained high position and renown had she been one to market her talents, but she would not accept even the simplest com-

forts for her activities in the various social movements. She shared the
fate of the lowly whom she sought to teach and inspire. Revolutionary
vestal, she lived as the poorest of the poor in dreary and wretched
surroundings, taxing her body to the utmost, sustained only by her
ideal.

Voltairine began her public career as a pacifist, and for many years
she sternly set her face against revolutionary methods. But greater
familiarity with European developments, the Russian Revolution of
1905, the rapid growth of capitalism in her own country, with all its
resultant violence and injustice, and particularly the Mexican Revolution, subsequently changed her attitude. After an inner struggle, Voltairine's intellectual integrity compelled her to admit her error frankly
and to stand up bravely for the new vision. She did so in a number
of essays and especially when she took up work for the Mexican Revolution, which she considered of most vital consequence. She devoted
herself entirely to it, writing, lecturing, and collecting funds. In her
the movement for liberty and humanism, especially the anarchist cause,
lost one of its most gifted and tireless workers.

As I stood beside Voltairine's grave, in the shadow of the monument dedicated to the memory of our comrades, I felt that another
martyr had been added to them. She was the prototype of the sculp-
tured Waldheim figure, beautiful in her spiritual defiance and filled
with the revolt of a flaming ideal.

The year 1912, rich with varied experiences, closed with three important events: the appearance of Sasha's book, the twenty-fifth anniversary of the eleventh of November, and the seventieth birthday of
Peter Kropotkin.

Sasha was reading the final proofs of his *Prison Memoirs*. In renewed agony he was living through again every detail of the fourteen
years, and experiencing harrowing doubt as to whether he had succeeded in making them real in his work. He kept revising until our
bill for author's corrections mounted to four hundred and fifty dollars.
He was worried and exhausted, yet he hung on, going over his proofs
again and again. The final chapters had to be taken from him almost
by force to save him from the curse of his tormenting anxiety.

And now the book was ready at last. Verily, not a book, but a life
suffered in the solitude of interminable prison days and nights, with
all their pain and grief, their disillusionments, despair, and hope.
Tears of joy sprang to my eyes as I held the precious volume in my

hands. I felt it my triumph as well as Sasha's — *our* fulfilment of twenty years, giving the promise of Sasha's real resurrection from his prison nightmare, and my own release from the gnawing regret of not having shared his fate.

Prison Memoirs of an Anarchist was widely reviewed and acclaimed a work of art and a deeply moving human document. "A story of prison life by an author who spent fourteen years behind the bars gathering his material ought to have value as a human document," commented the New York *Tribune*. "When the writer, furthermore, wields his pen in the manner of the Slavic realists and is compared by critics with such men as Dostoyevsky and Andreieff, his work must possess a tremendous fascination as well as a social value."

The literary critic of the New York *Globe* stated that "nothing could exceed the uncanny spell exercised by this story. Berkman has succeeded in making you live his prison experiences with him, and his book is probably as complete a self-revelation as is humanly possible."

Such praise from the capitalist press helped to accentuate my disappointment over Jack London's attitude towards Sasha's book. Having been requested to write a preface for it, Jack had asked to see the manuscript. After he had read it, he wrote us in his impetuous way how tremendously he was impressed by it. But his preface turned out to be a lame apology for the fact that he, a socialist, was writing an introduction to the work of an anarchist. At the same time it was a condemnation of Sasha's ideas. Jack London had not failed to see the human and the literary qualities of the book. What he wrote was even more laudatory than most of the reviews. But London insisted on using his preface for a long discussion of his own social theories versus anarchism. Inasmuch as Sasha's book did not deal with theories, but with life, Jack's attitude was absurd. His argument was summarized in his dictum: "The man who can't shoot straight can't think straight." Evidently Jack assumed that the world's best thinkers were also the best shots.

Sasha, who had gone to see Jack, pointed out that the great Danish critic Georg Brandes, though not an anarchist, had written a sympathetic preface to Peter Kropotkin's *Memoirs of a Revolutionist* without attempting to air his own theories. As artist and humanist Brandes had appreciated the big personality of Kropotkin.

"Brandes was not writing in America," London replied. "If he had been, he would most likely have displayed a different attitude."

Sasha understood; Jack London feared offending his publishers and incurring the censure of his party. The artist in Jack longed to soar, but the man in him kept his feet on the ground. His own best literary efforts, as he himself said, were buried in his trunk because his publishers wanted only works sure to bring financial results. And there were Glen Ellen and also other responsibilities to meet. Jack left no doubt on the matter, by remarking: "I have a family to support." Perhaps he did not realize how self-condemnatory his justification was.

Sasha refused Jack's preface. Instead we asked our friend Hutchins Hapgood to write an introduction to *Prison Memoirs*. He had never proclaimed himself an adherent of any ism, nor did he sign his letters: "Yours for the revolution," as Jack London used to do. He was, however, enough of a literary rebel and social iconoclast to appreciate the spirit of Sasha's book.

Jack London was not the only one who condemned while praising. There were others, even in our own ranks, among them S. Yanofsky, the editor of the *Freie Arbeiter Stimme*. He was one of the speakers at the banquet given to celebrate the appearance of Sasha's book. He was the only one of the five hundred guests who interjected a discordant note into the otherwise beautifully harmonious evening. Yanofsky paid high tribute to Sasha's *Memoirs* as the "mature product of a mature mind," but he "regretted the useless and futile act of a silly boy." I felt outraged by the man's denouncing the *Attentat* on the occasion of the birth of Sasha's book, a work conceived in that heroic moment of July 1892 and nourished by tears and blood throughout the dark and terrible years that followed. When I was called upon to speak, I turned upon the man who presumed to represent a great ideal and yet who was lacking in the least understanding of one so truly the idealist.

"To you the impressionable youth of Alexander Berkman appears silly," I said, "and his *Attentat* futile. You are by no means the first to take such a stand towards the idealist whose humanity can tolerate no injustice and endure no wrong. From time immemorial the wise and practical have denounced every heroic spirit. Yet it has not been they who have influenced our lives. The idealists and visionaries, foolish enough to throw caution to the winds and express their ardour and faith in some supreme deed, have advanced mankind and have enriched the world. The one whose work we are here to celebrate happens to be such a futile visionary. His act was the protest of a sensitive spirit that would rather perish for his ideal than continue for a lifetime as a smug inhabitant of a complaisant and callous world. If our comrade did not perish, it was certainly not due to the mercy of those who had openly declared he should not survive his living grave. It was due entirely to the same traits that inspired Alexander Berkman's act: his unwavering purpose, his indomitable will, and his faith in the ultimate triumph of his ideal. These elements have gone into the making of the ' silly ' youth, into his act and into his martyrdom of fourteen years. It is these same elements that have inspired the creation of *Prison Memoirs*. Whatever greatness and humanity the book possesses, they are woven of these elements. There is no gap between the silly youth and the mature man. There is a continuous flow, a red thread that winds like a leitmotif throughout the entire life of Alexander Berkman."

November 11, 1887 — November 11, 1912! Twenty-five years, an infinitesimal fraction of time in the upward march of the race, but an eternity for him who dies many deaths in the course of his life. The twenty-fifth anniversary of the Chicago martyrdom intensified my feeling for the men I had never personally known, but who by their death had become the most decisive influence in my existence. The spirit of Parsons, Spies, Lingg, and their co-workers seemed to hover over me and give deeper meaning to the events that had inspired my spiritual birth and growth.

November 11, 1912 came at last. Numerous labour organizations and anarchist groups worked feverishly to make the anniversary an impressive memorial. They arrived in large numbers in the hall, their flaming red banners covering the balconies and walls. The platform was decorated in red and black. The life-size portraits of our comrades were hung with wreaths. The presence of the hateful Anarchist Squad only helped to increase the bitter resentment of the crowd against the forces that had crushed the Haymarket victims.

I was one of the many speakers eager to pay tribute to our precious dead and to recall once more the valour and heroism of their lives. I awaited my turn, stirred to the roots by the historic occasion, its great social significance and personal meaning to me. Memories of the distant past flitted through my mind — Rochester and a woman's voice ringing like music in my ears: " You will love our men when you learn

to know them, and you will make their cause your own!" In times of
ascent to heights, in days of faint-heartedness and doubt, in hours
of prison isolation, of antagonism and censure from one's own kind,
in failure of love, in friendships broken and betrayed — always their
cause was mine, their sacrifice my support.

I stood erect before the dense mass of people. Its tense feeling
mingled with mine, and all our hate and all our love were concentrated
in my voice. "They are not dead," I cried; "they are not dead, the
men we have come to honour tonight! Out of their quivering bodies
dangling from the noose, new lives have emerged to take up the
strains throttled on the scaffold. With a thousand voices they proclaim that our martyrs are not dead!"

Preparatory work was beginning for the celebration of the seventieth birthday of Peter Kropotkin. He was a prominent figure in the
realm of learning, recognized as such by the foremost men of
the world. But to us he meant much more than that. We saw in him
the father of modern anarchism, its revolutionary spokesman and brilliant exponent of its relation to science, philosophy, and progressive
thought. As a personality he towered high above most of his contemporaries by virtue of his humanity and faith in the masses. Anarchism to him was not an ideal for the select few. It was a constructive
social theory, destined to usher in a new world for all of mankind.
For this he had lived and laboured all his life. The seventieth anniversary of such a person was therefore of great moment to all who knew
and loved him.

Months before, we had written to his admirers in European coun-
tries, and to our own leading comrades, for contributions to the Kro-
potkin-birthday edition of *Mother Earth*. Everybody responded generously. Now the December issue was ready, containing tributes to
Peter Kropotkin by Georg Brandes, Edward Carpenter, Professor
George D. Herron, Tom Mann, J. Morrison-Davidson, Bayard
Boyesen, Anna Strunsky Walling and her husband, Rose Strunsky,
Leonard D. Abbott, and leading anarchists throughout the world.
In conjunction with the special Kropotkin issue of our magazine a
big meeting took place in Carnegie Hall, arranged by us in co-opera-
tion with the *Freie Arbeiter Stimme* Association. As on the pages of
Mother Earth, every speaker paid tribute to Kropotkin, our common
teacher and inspiration.

Peter was deeply moved by these expressions of love and affection. In token of appreciation he sent us the following letter:

DEAR COMRADES AND FRIENDS:

First of all, let me express to you my warmest, heartiest thanks for all the kind words and thoughts you have addressed to me, and then to voice through your pages the same heartiest thanks to all the comrades and friends who have sent me such warm and friendly letters and telegrams on the occasion of my seventieth birthday.

I need not tell you, nor could I word it on paper, how deeply I was touched by all these expressions of sympathy, and how I felt that "something brotherly" which keeps us anarchists united by a feeling far deeper than the mere sense of solidarity in a party; and I am sure that that feeling of brotherhood will have some day its effect, when history will call upon us to show what we are worth, and how far we can act in harmony for the reconstruction of society upon a new basis of equality and freedom.

And then let me add that if all of us have contributed to some extent to the work of liberation of exploited mankind, it is because our ideas have been more or less the expression of the ideas that are germinating in the very depths of the masses of the people. The more I live, the more am I convinced that no truthful and useful social science, and no useful and truthful social action is possible but the science which bases its conclusions, and the action which bases its acts, upon the thoughts and the inspirations of the masses. All sociological science and all social actions which do not do that must remain sterile.

With full heart with you,

PETER KROPOTKIN

The effect on Ben of his San Diego experience proved to be stronger and more lasting than any of us had expected. He remained in the throes of those harrowing days and he became a victim of the *idée fixe* that he must return there. He followed his activities with even more than his wonted energy, working as if driven by furies and driving everybody else in turn. I became to him a means rather than an end, the end being meetings, meetings, meetings, and plans for more meetings. But I saw that he did not really live in his work, or in our love. His whole being was centred on San Diego, and it became almost a hallucination with him. He taxed my powers of endurance, and often my affection, by his constant insistence on starting for the Coast. His restlessness kept increasing and he was not content until we were finally on our way.

Our Los Angeles friends were strongly opposed to our returning to San Diego. They said that Ben's obsession was nothing but bravado, and that I was weak in giving in to his irrational scheme. They even brought the matter to the attention of the audience at our last meeting, urging a unanimous vote against our going.

I knew that our friends were concerned only for our safety, but I could not agree with them. I did not feel about San Diego as Ben did; to me it was but one of the many towns in the United States where free speech had been gagged and its defenders maltreated. To such places I always kept returning until the right of free speech was again established there. That was one of the motives for my wanting to go back to San Diego, but it was by no means the strongest motive. I was certain that Ben would not be freed from the hold of that city unless he returned to the scene of the May outrage. My love for him had grown more intense with the years. I could not permit him to go to San Diego alone. I therefore informed my comrades that I would go with Ben, no matter what might be awaiting us there. It seemed incredible that any group of people, however savage in time of excitement, would repeat such brutalities after the lapse of a year, particularly since the Vigilantes and San Diego had been placed in the pillory by country-wide condemnation.

An active worker in our ranks volunteered to precede us to San Diego, secure a hall, and advertise my lecture, which was again to be on "An Enemy of the People." Before long he notified us that all was well and promising.

After our last meeting in Los Angeles we were taken by our friends Dr. and Mrs. Percival T. Gerson to the railroad station. On the way Ben's excitement reached such a pitch that the doctor suggested a sanatorium instead of San Diego. But Ben insisted that nothing would cure him except to go back. In the train he became deathly pale, and large drops of perspiration poured over his face. His body shook with nervousness and fear. All night he tossed about sleeplessly in his berth.

Except for my concern about him I was singularly calm. I was wide awake and sat up reading *Comrade Yetta* by "Albert Edwards." An interesting book always made me forget a difficult situation. This volume was by Arthur Bullard, one of our friends who had co-operated with us during Babushka's visit to New York. His power-ful story and its Russian theme brought back to me the days gone by. The last two hours of our trip Ben was fast asleep, and I was so lost in the past that I was unaware we were nearing San Diego. The bustle of our fellow-passengers recalled me to reality. I dressed hurriedly and then woke Ben.

It was early dawn, and only a few passengers got off the train. The platform was deserted as we made our way towards the exit. But before we had proceeded far, five men suddenly confronted us. Four of them exposed detective badges and informed us that we were under arrest. I demanded the reason for our detention, but they gruffly ordered us to come with them.

San Diego was asleep as we walked to the police station. Something in the appearance of the man accompanying the officers seemed famil-iar to me. I strove to remember where I had seen him before. Then it dawned on me that it was he who had come to my room in the U. S. Grant Hotel to tell me that I was wanted by the authorities. I recog-nized him as the reporter who had caused our former difficulties there. He was a leader of the Vigilantes!

Ben and I were locked up. There was nothing to be done but await developments. I again took up my book. Weary, I put my head on the little cell table and dozed off.

"You must have been very tired to sleep like that," the matron said as she woke me. "Didn't you hear the racket?" She looked fixedly at me. "Better have some coffee," she added, not unkindly. "You may need your strength before the day is over."

Noises and yelling came from the street. "The Vigilantes," the matron said in a low voice. There were loud cries outside and I could hear voices calling: "Reitman! We want Reitman!" Then came the tooting of automobile horns and the shriek of the riot signal. And again cries of "Reitman!" My heart sank.

The riot call boomed and howled. The noises beat like tomtoms on my brain. Why had I ever let Ben come, I thought; it was madness, madness! They could not forgive him for returning. They wanted his life!

In a frenzy I rapped on my cell door. The matron arrived and with her the Chief of Police and several detectives.

"I want to see Dr. Reitman!" I demanded.

"That's what we've come for," the Chief replied. "He wants you to consent to being taken out of town, and your other comrade too."

"What other comrade?"

"The chap who arranged your meeting. He's in the jail, and lucky for him he is."

"You're playing the benefactor again," I retorted; "but you won't dupe me this time. Take those two out of town. *I* will not go under your protection."

"All right," he growled. "Come and talk to Reitman yourself."

The pale horror staring at me out of Ben's eyes made me realize the meaning of fear as I had never seen it before. "Let's get out of town," he whispered, trembling. "We can't hold the meeting anyway. Chief Wilson promises to get us away safe. Please say yes."

I had completely forgotten our meeting. It was my objection to leaving under police protection that made me urge Ben to go himself.

"It is your life that is in danger," I said; "they don't want me. No harm will come to me. But in any case I can't run away."

"All right, I'll stay too," he replied determinedly.

I struggled with myself for a moment. I knew that if I let him stay, I should jeopardize his life and possibly also the safety of the other comrade. There was no other way out; I should have to consent.

No play was ever staged with greater melodrama than our rescue from the San Diego jail and our ride to the railroad station. At the head of the procession marched a dozen policemen, each carrying a shot-gun, with revolvers sticking in their belts. Then came the Chief of Police and the Chief of Detectives, heavily armed, Ben between them. I followed with two officers on each side. Behind me was our young comrade. And behind him more police.

Our appearance was greeted with savage howls. As far as the eye could reach, there was a swaying, jostling human pack. The shrill cries of women mingled with the voices of the men, drunk with the lust of blood. The more venturesome of them tried to make a rush for Ben.

"Back, back!" shouted the Chief. "The prisoners are under the protection of the law. I demand respect for the law. Get back!"

Some applauded him, others jeered. He proudly led the procession through the phalanxes of police, accompanied by the yelling of the frenzied crowd.

Automobiles were waiting us, gaily bedecked with American flags. One of them had rifles posted at every corner. Police and plain-clothes men stood on the running-board. I recognized the reporter among them. We were piled into this armed citadel, Chief Wilson standing over us like a stage hero, with a shot-gun pointed at the mob. Cameras from houses and tree-tops began to click, the sirens screamed, the riot call boomed again, and off we dashed, followed by the other cars and the angry bellowing of the mob.

At the railroad station we were pushed into a Pullman, six policemen crowding around Ben. Just as the train was about to start, a man ran in, shoved the officers aside, and spat full in Ben's face. Then he rushed out again.

"That's Porter," Ben cried, "the leader of last year's attack on me!"

I thought of the savagery of the mob, terrifying yet fascinating at the same time. I realized why Ben's previous experience had so obsessed him until it had driven him back to San Diego. I felt the overwhelming power of the crowd's concentrated passion. I knew I should find no peace until I had returned to it, to subdue it or to be destroyed.

I would go back, I promised myself, but not with Ben. There was no relying on him in a critical moment. I knew he had imaginative flights, but strength of will he had not. He was impulsive, but he lacked stamina and a sense of responsibility. These traits of his character had repeatedly clouded our lives and made me tremble for our love. I grieved to realize that Ben was not of heroic stuff. He was not of the texture of Sasha, who had courage enough for a dozen men and extraordinary coolness and presence of mind in moments of danger.

Perhaps courage, I thought, is nothing remarkable in those who know no fear. I was sure Sasha had never known fear. And I, during the McKinley panic, had I feared for my life? No, I had had no fear for myself, though I had often felt it for others. It was always this, and my exaggerated sense of responsibility, that compelled me to do things I hated to do. Are we really courageous, we who do not know fear, if we remain firm in the face of danger? Ben was consumed with terror, yet he went back to San Diego. Was that not real courage? Inwardly I strove to exonerate Ben, to find some justification for his readiness to run away.

The train sped on. Ben's face was close to mine, his voice whispering endearments, his eyes gazing pleadingly into mine. As so often before, all my doubts and all my pain dissolved in my love for my impossible boy.

In Los Angeles and San Francisco we were fêted as heroes, though we had both shamefully run away. I did not feel very comfortable about it, but I was gratified by the exceptional interest in my lectures. The two that drew the largest audiences were those on "Victims of Morality" and on *Prison Memoirs of an Anarchist*.

Upon our return to New York Ben urged a larger house to give us better living-quarters and also enough room for a combination office and book-shop. He was sure he could build up a good trade to help make *Mother Earth* independent of tours. Ben was anxious to have his mother under the same roof with him, especially now that she was not well.

We found a place at 74 East One Hundred and Nineteenth Street, a ten-room house in good condition. The parlour, conveniently seating a hundred people, was the very thing we needed for small sessions and social gatherings; the basement was light and spacious enough for an office and book-shop; the upper floors would afford privacy for each of us. I had never dreamed of such comfort, yet the cost of the rent and heating was lower than our previous expenditures for these items. The large house would need someone to look after it, because I should be busy revising my drama lectures for publication.

I decided to invite my friend Rhoda Smith as housekeeper. She was a few years younger than I and full of the light-heartedness of the French race. But beneath her lightness were the sterling qualities of kindness and dependability. She was a splendid housekeeper and cook, and, like most French women, very skilful with her hands. No less deft was she with her tongue, especially when she had looked a little too deeply into her glass. Her language, always very spicy, would then become hot. Not everyone could stand its flavour or its sting.

We needed a secretary for our office work, and Ben suggested a friend of his, Miss M. Eleanor Fitzgerald. I had first met her in Chicago, during our free-speech campaign. She was a striking girl with red hair, delicate skin, and blue-green eyes. Very fond of Ben, she had no inkling of his ways with women. She did not know of my relationship with Ben and she was considerably shocked when I told her that we were very much more to each other than merely manager and lecturer. Miss Fitzgerald (or "Lioness," as Ben called her, because of her red mane of hair) was a most likable person, with something very fine and large about her. In fact, she was the only real personality among all the obsessions Ben had imposed on me through the years. Ben kept stressing the need of a secretary. "Lioness" was very competent, he assured me; she had held several responsible positions, and had recently become manager of a sanatorium in South Dakota. She was interested in our work and she would be glad to give up her job and join us in New York.

Our new quarters were ready and we began breaking up our old home. When I had first moved into 210 East Thirteenth Street, in 1903, to share the flat with the Horrs, we were the first tenants in the recently built house. Since then the police had repeatedly tried to have me put out, but my landlord remained steadfast, arguing that I had never given cause for complaint, and that I was the oldest tenant. The others, indeed, had changed so often in nationality, character, and station that I had lost count. From business men to day-labourers, from preachers to gamblers, from Jewish women with wigs on their heads to street girls flaunting their charms on the stoop, they were a constant human tide coming in, staying awhile, and ebbing again.

There were no facilities for heating at 210, except the kitchen stove, and my room was farthest from it. It faced the yard and looked right into the windows of a large printing house. The nerve-racking buzz of its linotypes and presses never let up. My room was the living-room, dining-room, and *Mother Earth* office, all in one. I slept in a little alcove behind my bookcase. There was always someone sleeping in front, someone who had stayed too late and lived too far away or who was too shaky on his feet and needing cold compresses or who had no home to go to.

All the other tenants of the house were in the habit of applying to us when ill or in trouble. Our most frequent callers, usually in the wee hours of the morning, were the gamblers. Expecting a raid, they would run up the fire-escape to ask us to hide their paraphernalia. " In your place," they once told me, " the police may look for bombs, but never for chips." Everyone in distress came to us in 210 as to an oasis in the desert of their lives. It was flattering, but at the same time wearying, never to have any privacy by day or at night.

Our little flat had grown very dear to me; a good deal of my life had been spent in it. It had witnessed a decade of the most varied activities, and men and women famous in the annals of life had laughed and cried there. The Russian campaigns of Catherine Bresh-kovskaya and of Tchaikovsky, the Orleneff work, free-speech fights and revolutionary propaganda, not to speak of the many personal dramas, with all their griefs and joys, had flowed through the historic place. The entire kaleidoscope of human tragedy and comedy had been reflected in colourful variegation within the walls of 210. No wonder my good friend Hutch Hapgood often urged that together we write the story of that "home of lost dogs." He was especially insistent on emphasizing its romance and pathos whenever we both felt young and gay and desperately flirted our way into each other's hearts. Alas, I was fond of his wife, and he of Ben, and so we remained shamelessly faithful, and the story unwritten.

Ten years had streamed by in a rushing current, with little leisure to reflect on how dear the place had grown to me. Only when the time came to leave it did I realize how rooted I had become at 210. Taking a last look at the empty rooms, I walked out with a feeling of deep loss. Ten most interesting years of my life left behind!

CHAPTER XL

AT LAST WE WERE INSTALLED IN OUR NEW QUARTERS. BEN AND Miss Fitzgerald were in charge of the office, Rhoda of the house, while Sasha and I took care of the magazine. With each one busy in his own sphere, the differences in character and attitude had more scope for expression without mutual invasiveness. We all found "Fitzi," as we called our new co-worker, a most charming woman, and Rhoda also liked her, though she often took delight in shocking our romantic friend by her peppery jokes and stories.

Ben was happy to have his mother with him. She had two sons, but her entire world was centred in Ben. Her mental horizon was very narrow; she was unable even to read or write and felt no interest in anything except the little home Ben had made for her. In Chicago she had lived among her pots and kettles, untouched by the stream outside. She loved her son and she was always most patient with his moods, no matter how irrational they were. He was her idol who could do no wrong. As to his numerous affairs with women, she was sure it was they who led her child astray. She had hoped her son would become a successful doctor, honoured, respected, and rich. Instead he had dropped his practice when he had barely begun it, "took up" with a woman nine years his senior, and got himself involved with a dangerous lot of anarchists. Ben's mother was always respectful when she met me, but I could sense her keen dislike.

I understood her very well: she was one of the millions whose minds have been stunted by the limitations of their lives. Her approval or disapproval would have mattered little to me if it had not been that Ben was as madly obsessed by his mother as she by him. He realized how little there was in common between them. Her attitude and manner jarred on him and would drive him away whenever he came to Chicago to visit her. Yet her hold was beyond his control. She was constantly on his mind, his passion for her a menace to his love for any other woman. His mother-complex had caused me much suffering and even despair. Yet I loved Ben in spite of all our differences. I longed for peace and harmony with him. I wanted to see him happy and contented, and I consented to his plan to bring his mother to New York.

She was given the best room in the house, supplied with her own furniture, so as to make her feel more at home. Ben always took his breakfast alone with her, with no one near to disturb their idyll. At our common meals she was given the seat of honour and treated by everybody with utmost consideration. But she felt ill at ease, out of her environment. She longed for her old Chicago place and she became dissatisfied and unhappy. Then, one unfortunate day, Ben began to read *Sons and Lovers* by D. H. Lawrence. From the very first page he lived in the book with his mother. He saw in it the story of himself and of her. The office, our work, and our life were blotted out. He could think of nothing but the story and his mother, and he began to imagine that I — and everyone else — was treating her badly. He would have to take her away, he decided; he must give up everything and live only for his mother.

I was in the midst of my drama manuscript. There were lectures on hand, a large undertaking for *Mother Earth,* and the campaign in behalf of J. M. Rangel, Charles Cline, and their I.W.W. comrades arrested in Texas while on their way to Mexico to participate in the revolution in that country. All of the men were Mexicans except Cline, who was an American. They had been attacked by an armed posse, and in the skirmish three of the Mexicans and a deputy sheriff had lost their lives. Now fourteen men, including Rangel and Cline, were awaiting trial on charges of murder. Publicity was needed to arouse the workers of the East to the peril of the situation. I reasoned, I argued, I pleaded with Ben not to permit Lawrence's book to rob him of his senses. But to no avail. Scenes with Ben became more frequent and violent. Our life was daily growing more impossible. A way out had to be found. I could not share my misery with anyone, least of all with Sasha, who had from the beginning been opposed to the scheme of the house and a life with Ben and his mother under the same roof.

The break came. Ben had started again the old plaint about his mother. I listened in silence for a while, and then something snapped in me. The desire seized me to make an end of Ben as far as I was concerned, to do something that would shut out for ever every thought and every memory of this creature who had possessed me all these years. In blind fury I picked up a chair and hurled it at him. It whirled through space and came crashing down at his feet.

He made a step towards me, then stopped and stared at me in wonder and fright.

"Enough!" I cried, beside myself with pain and anger. "I've had enough of you and your mother. Go, take her away — today, this very hour!"

He walked out without a word.

Ben rented a small flat for his mother and went to live with her. He began again attending to the office. We still had that much in common, but the rest seemed dead. I found forgetfulness in more intensive work. I lectured several times a week, participated in the campaign for the I. W. W. boys arrested in connexion with the miners' strike in Canada, and at the same time continued working on my drama book, dictating the manuscript to Fitzi.

I had come to know her better since she had joined the *Mother Earth* group. She was a rare personality, cast in a generous spiritual mould. Her father was Irish, but on her mother's side she came from American pioneer stock, the earliest settlers in Wisconsin. Fron them Fitzi had inherited her independence and self-reliance. At the age of fifteen she had joined the Seventh Day Adventists, defying the ire of her father. But her search for truth did not terminate there. Her idea of God, as she often said, was much more beautiful and more tolerant than the Adventist conception. So one day she stood up in the midst of the religious service, announced to the assembly that she had not found the truth among them, and walked out of the little country church and out of the ranks of the believers. She became interested in free-thought and radical activities. Socialism disappointed her as being essentially another Church with new dogmas. Her large nature found greater attraction in the freedom and scope of anarchist ideas. I grew to love Fitzi for her inherent idealism and understanding spirit, and we gradually came very close to each other.

The close of the year was at hand, and we had not yet held a house-warming in our new place. New Year's was decided upon as the right moment for our party of friends and active supporters of *Mother Earth* to help kick out the Old with all its trouble and pain and gaily meet the New no matter what it might bring. Rhoda was all excitement and she worked hard and late to make ready for the festive occasion. New Year's Eve brought the procession of friends, among them poets, writers, rebels, and Bohemians of various attitude, behaviour, and habit. They argued about philosophy, social theories, art, and sex. They ate the delicious things Rhoda had prepared and drank the wines our generous Italian comrades had supplied. Everybody danced and grew gay. But my thoughts were with Ben, whose birthday it was. He was thirty-five and I nearing forty-four. That was a tragic difference in age. I felt lonely and unutterably sad.

Still young was the new year when the country began to echo with new outrages against labour. The horrors in West Virginia were followed by cruelties in the hop-fields of Wheatfield, California, in the mines of Trinidad, Colorado, and in Calumet, Michigan. The police, the militia, and gangs of armed citizens were carrying on a reign of despotism.

In Wheatfield twenty-three thousand hop-pickers, who had come in answer to a newspaper advertisement, found themselves confronted by conditions not decent even for cattle. They were kept at work all day without rest or proper food, even without drinking-water. To quench their thirst in the scorching heat they were compelled to buy lemonade at five cents a glass from members of the Durst family, the owners of the hop-field. Unable to endure such a state of affairs, the pickers sent a delegate to Durst. The delegate was assaulted and beaten up, whereupon the men struck. The local authorities, aided by the Burns Detective Agency, the Citizens' Alliance, and subsequently the National Guard, terrorized the strikers. They broke up a gathering of the workers and opened fire without provocation. Two men were killed and a number wounded; the District Attorney and a deputy sheriff also lost their lives. Many of the strikers were put through the " third degree," one of them, grilled without sleep for fourteen days to extract a confession, attempted suicide. Another, who had lost his arm in the police attack, hanged himself.

The latest victim of these American Black Hundreds was Mother Jones, a famous native agitator. In truly tsarist manner she was deported from Trinidad at the order of General Chase, who threatened to imprison her *incommunicado* if she dared to return. In Calumet, Moyer, the president of the Western Federation of Miners, was shot

in the back and driven out of town. Similar happenings in various
parts of the country decided me to give a lecture dealing with the
right of labour to self-defence. The Radical Library of Philadelphia
invited me to speak on that subject in the Labor Temple. Before I
reached the hall, the police drove everybody out and locked the place.
I delivered my talk none the less, in the quarters of the Radical Library, as well as in New York and in a number of other cities.

My relation with Ben, which had grown more strained, finally
became unbearable. Ben was no less unhappy than I. He decided to
return with his mother to Chicago and take up the practice of medicine again. I did not try to detain him.

For the first time I was to give a full course of lectures on " The
Social Significance of the Modern Drama " in New York, both in
English and in Yiddish. The Berkeley Theatre on Forty-fourth Street
was rented for the purpose. It was disheartening to start out on an
important venture without Ben, for the first time in six years. His
departure, which had given me a feeling of release, now resistlessly
drew me to him. He was ever present in my thoughts, and my hunger
for him kept growing. Nights I would determine to cut myself loose
once and for all and not even accept his letters. The morning would
find me eagerly scanning my mail for the handwriting so electrifying
in its effect on me. No man I had loved had ever so paralysed my
will before. I fought against it with all my strength, but my heart
wildly called for Ben.

I could see from his letters that he was going through the same
purgatory as I, and that he also could not free himself. He yearned to
return to me. His attempt to take up the practice of medicine had
failed; I had made him see his profession in a new light, he wrote, and
he felt how inadequate it was to give relief. He knew that the poor
needed better working- and living-conditions; they needed sunshine,
fresh air, and rest. What could powders and pills do for them? A
great many physicians realize that the health of their patients does
not depend on their prescriptions. They know the true remedy, but
they prefer to grow rich on the credulity of the poor. He could never
again become one of those, Ben wrote. I had spoiled him for that. I
and my work had become too vital a part of his life. He loved me.
He knew it now better than at any time since we had first met. He
knew he had been impossible in his behaviour in New York. He had
never felt free or at ease with my friends. They had not shown faith

in him, and that had made him more antagonistic towards them. And I, too, had seemed changed when in New York; I made him feel inferior to Sasha, and I was more critical of him than when we were alone on tour. We must try again, he pleaded; we must go away, just by ourselves, on tour. He wanted nothing else.

His letters were like a narcotic. They put my brain to sleep, but they made my heart beat faster. I clung to the assurance of his love.

Again, in the winter, the country was in the throes of unemployment. Over a quarter of a million persons were out of work in New York, and other cities were stricken in no lesser degree. The suffering was augmented by the extraordinarily severe weather. The papers minimized the appalling state of affairs; the politicians and reformers remained lukewarm. A few palliatives and the threadbare suggestion of an investigation were all they could offer to meet the widespread misery.

The militant elements resolved upon action. The anarchists and the I.W.W.'s organized the unemployed and secured considerable relief for them. At my Berkeley Theatre lectures and other meetings appeals for the jobless met with generous response. But it was a mere drop in the ocean of need.

Then an unexpected thing happened, which gave the situation compelling publicity. Out of the ranks of starved and frozen humanity the slogan came to visit religious institutions. The unemployed, led by a vivid youth named Frank Tannenbaum, began a march on the churches of New York.

We all had loved Frank for his wide-awakeness and his unassuming ways. He had spent much of his free time in our office, reading and helping in the work connected with *Mother Earth*. His fine qualities held out the hope that Frank would some day play an important part in the labour struggle. None of us had expected however that our studious, quiet friend would so quickly respond to the call of the hour.

Whether out of fear or because of the realization of the significance of the march on the churches, several of them gave shelter, food, and money to the bands of unemployed. Emboldened by their success, one hundred and eighty-nine jobless men, with Frank at their head, went to one of the Catholic churches in the city. Instead of receiving them with loving-kindness a priest at St. Alphonsus Church, turned traitor to his God, who had commanded that one give all to the poor. In connivance with two detectives the priest trapped Frank Tannenbaum and had him and several of the unemployed arrested.

Frank was condemned to serve a year in the penitentiary and to pay a five-hundred-dollar fine, which meant an additional five hundred days' imprisonment. He made a splendid stand, his speech in his own defence being intelligent and defiant.

The most outrageous aspect of the Tannenbaum arrest and conviction was the silence maintained by the so-called sponsors of the oppressed. Not a finger did the socialists raise to awaken the public to the obvious conspiracy on the part of the authorities and the St. Alphonsus Church to " make an example " of Frank Tannenbaum. The New York *Call,* a socialist daily, sneered at the convicted boys and even said that Frank Tannenbaum had deserved a spanking.

The Socialist Party and some prominent I.W.W. leaders tried to paralyse the activities of the jobless. This only helped to increase the zeal of the Conference of the Unemployed, which consisted of various labour and radical organizations. A mass meeting at Union Square was decided upon and the date fixed for March 21. Neither the Socialists nor the I.W.W.'s would participate. It was Sasha who was the active spirit of the movement. He had a double share to perform, as I was hard at work finishing my manuscript, lecturing frequently, and supervising our office.

The mass meeting was large and spirited; it reminded me of a similar event in the same place and for the same purpose, the demonstration of August 1893. Apparently nothing had changed since then. Now as then capitalism was relentless, the State crushing every individual and social right, and the Church in league with them. Now as then those daring to give voice to the suffering of the dumb multitude were persecuted and jailed, and the masses too seemed to have remained as ever in their submissive helplessness. The thought was depressing and made me want to run away from the square. But I stayed. I stayed because deep down in me there was the certainty that there is no sameness in nature. Eternal change, I knew, is for ever at work, life always is in flux, new currents flowing from the dried-up springs of the old. I stayed, and I spoke to the huge crowd as I could speak only when really lifted out of myself.

I left the square after my speech, while Sasha remained at the meeting. When he came home, I learned that the demonstration had ended in a parade up Fifth Avenue, the vast assembly marching and carrying a large black flag as a symbol of their revolt. It must have been a menacing sight to the dwellers on Fifth Avenue no less than to the police, for the latter did not interfere. The unemployed marched all the way to the Ferrer Center, from Fourteenth to One Hundred and Seventh Street, where they were treated to a substantial meal, given tobacco and cigarettes, and provided with temporary lodgings.

This demonstration was the beginning of a city-wide campaign for the unemployed. Sasha, whose valour had endeared him to everyone who knew about his life, was its organizing and directing influence. In his tireless efforts he had the support of a large number of our young rebels, who vigorously worked with him.

My Berkeley Theatre series brought some interesting and amusing experiences. One was the help I was able to give a stranded group of Welsh players; the other an offer to go on the vaudeville stage. My drama lectures afforded me free access to the theatres, and thus I happened to attend the initial performance of a play called *Change,* by J. O. Francis, a Welsh dramatist. It proved to be the most powerful social drama I had seen in the English language. The appalling conditions of the Welsh miners and their desperate struggle to wrench a few pitiful pennies from their masters was as moving as Zola's *Germinal.* Besides this theme the play also treated the age-long struggle between the stubborn acquiescence of the old generation in things as they are and the bold aspirations of the young. *Change* was a stirring work of social significance and it was magnificently interpreted by the Welsh group. No wonder that most reviewers damned the play. A friend informed me that the Welsh troupe was stranded, and asked me to interest the radical element in its behalf.

At a special matinée performance, which I had helped to arrange, I met a number of New York dramatists and literati. One very popular playwright expressed surprise that such an arch-destructionist as I should care for creative drama. I tried to explain to him that anarchism represented the urge of expression in every phase of life and art. Seeing his uncomprehending look, I remarked: "Even those who only *think* they are dramatists will have opportunity in a free society. If they lack real talent, they will still have other honourable professions to choose from, like shoemaking, for instance."

After the performance many of those present expressed their willingness to come to the rescue of the stranded players. I arranged to bring the matter also to the attention of my Sunday audiences and made an appeal in *Mother Earth*. The following Sunday I delivered a lecture on *Change*. The entire Welsh company were present as my guests, and I succeeded in arousing enough interest to keep their theatre going for several weeks. Not the least help to them were the advance notices which our friends in every city gave them when they were touring the country.

At the close of my drama course I was approached by a representative of the Victoria Theatre, a vaudeville house owned by Oscar Hammerstein. He offered me an engagement to appear twice a day, naming a thousand dollars as my approximate weekly salary. I laughed it off at first. The suggestion of going on the vaudeville stage did not appeal to me. But the man kept on urging the advantages of reaching large audiences not to mention the money I would earn. I dismissed the proposal as ridiculous, but gradually the idea of the opportunities the venture would give prevailed upon me. The poverty of the unemployed affected the receipts of our meetings; most people could not afford such luxuries as books or lectures now. The hope that our new quarters might diminish our expenses had also failed to materialize. Several weeks on the vaudeville stage would free me from the everlasting economic grind. They might give me a year to myself, to cut loose from everybody and everything, a year to drift, to read books for their inherent value and not merely for the use they might be to my lectures. This hope silenced all my objections, and I went to Hammerstein's.

The manager informed me that he would have to try me out first, to see what was the drawing power of my name. We went back-stage, where he introduced me to some of the performers. It was a motley crowd of dancers, acrobats, and men with trained dogs. "I'll have to sandwich you in," the manager said. He was not sure whether I was to come on before the high kicker or after the trained dogs. At any rate I could not have more than ten minutes. From behind the curtain I watched the pitiful efforts to amuse the public, the horrible contortions of the dancer, whose flabby body was laced into youthful appearance, the cracked voice of the singer, the cheap jokes of the funny man, and the coarse hilarity of the crowd. Then I fled. I knew I could not stand up in such an atmosphere to plead my ideas, not for all the money in the world.

The last Sunday at the Berkeley Theatre was turned into a gala night. Leonard D. Abbott presided, and among the speakers were the noted actress Mary Shaw, the first to defy American purists with her performances of *Ghosts* and of *Mrs. Warren's Profession;* Fola La Follette, gifted and frankly outspoken; and George Middleton, who had a volume of one-act plays to his credit. They dwelt on what the drama meant to them, and what a powerful factor it was in awakening social consciousness in people who might not be reached in any other way. They were very appreciative of my work, and I was grateful to them for making me feel that my efforts had brought some of the American intelligentsia into closer rapport with the struggle of the masses. The evening strengthened my conviction that whatever contribution I had made in that direction had been due in part to my never having permitted anyone to "sandwich" me in.

My Berkeley lectures brought me a valuable gift in the form of my drama notes in typewriting. Stenographers had often tried to take down my speeches, but in vain. My delivery was too rapid, they said, especially when I was carried away by my theme. A young man named Paul Munter was the first in his profession to beat my flow of words with his stenographic speed. He attended my entire series, for six weeks, and at the end presented me with my course in perfectly type-written sheets.

Paul's gift proved to be of great value in the preparation of my manuscript of *The Social Significance of the Modern Drama.* Thanks to it the work was less difficult than the writing of my essays, though I had been in a more tranquil state of mind then; I still had hopes of a harmonious life with Ben. Little was left of that hope now. Perhaps therefore I clung more tenaciously to its remaining shreds. Ben's pleading letters from Chicago added fuel to the smouldering fires of my longing. After two months I began to realize the wisdom of the Russian peasant saying: "If you drink, you'll die, and if you don't drink, you'll die. Better drink and die."

To be away from Ben meant sleepless nights, restless days, sickening yearning. To be near him involved conflict and strife, daily denial of my pride. But it also meant ecstasy and renewed vigour for my work. I would have Ben and go with him on tour again, I decided. If the price was high, I would pay it; but I would drink, I would drink!

Sasha had never been more thoughtful and considerate than during the months of my struggle to free myself from Ben. He was stimulatingly helpful with the revision of my drama book; in fact, I let him do most of it himself. I felt the work safe in his hands: he was scrupulously conscientious about not changing the spirit or tendency of my writing. We also collaborated on *Mother Earth*. There were wonderful nights when we would prepare copy for the printer and drink strong coffee to keep us going till the break of day. They brought us closer to each other than we had been for a long time past — not that anything could ever loosen our common bonds or affect our friendship, which had stood the test of so many fires.

Depending upon Sasha to read the proofs of my book, and with Fitzi in charge of the office, I could now start on tour. Fitzi had proved herself not only very efficient, but a real friend as well, a beautiful soul, whose interest in our labours made me ashamed of my early doubts of her. Sasha had also realized that his former objections to the "stranger" were groundless. They had become friends and worked harmoniously together. Everything was ready for my departure.

My drama book was off the press, looking quite attractive in its simple attire. It was the first English volume of its kind to point out the social meaning of thirty-two plays by eighteen authors of different countries. My only regret was that my own adopted land had to be left out. I had tried diligently to find some American dramatist who could be placed alongside the great Europeans, but I could discover no one. Commendable beginnings there were by Eugene Walter, Rachel Crothers, Charles Klein, George Middleton, and Butler Davenport. The dramatic master, however, was not yet in sight. He would no doubt appear some day, but meanwhile I had to be content with calling the attention of America to the works of the foremost playwrights of Europe and the social significance of modern dramatic art.

At a lecture in Toledo a visiting-card had been left on my table. It was from Robert Henri, who had requested that I let him know what lectures I was planning to deliver in New York. I had heard of Henri, had seen his exhibitions, and had been told that he was a man of advanced social views. Subsequently, at a Sunday lecture in New York, a tall, well-built man came up and introduced himself as Robert Henri. "I enjoy your magazine," he said, "especially the articles on Walt Whitman. I love Walt, and I follow everything that is written about him."

I learned to know Henri as an exceptional personality, a free and generous nature. He was in fact an anarchist in his conception of art and its relation to life. When we started the Ferrer evening classes, he quickly responded to the invitation to instruct our art students. He also interested George Bellows and John Sloan, and together they helped to create a spirit of freedom in the art class which probably did not exist anywhere else in New York at that time.

Later Robert Henri asked me to sit for my portrait. I was very busy at the time; besides, several people had already tried to paint me, with little success. Henri said he wanted to depict the "real Emma Goldman." "But which is the real one?" I asked; "I have never been able to unearth her." His beautiful studio in Gramercy Park, far removed from the dirt and noise of the city, and the sweet hospitality of Mrs. Henri were balm to me. There were talks on art, literature, and libertarian education. Henri was well versed in these subjects; he possessed, moreover, unusual intuition for every sincere striving. During those illuminating hours I learned of the art-school he had started some years before. "The students are left entirely to themselves," he said, "to develop whatever is in them. I merely answer questions or give suggestions on the solution of their more difficult problems." He never sought to impose his ideas on his pupils.

I was naturally anxious to see the portrait, but, knowing Henri's sensitiveness about showing unfinished work, I did not ask for it. I was not in New York when the painting was done, but some time later my sister Helena wrote me that she had seen it at an exhibition in Rochester. "I should not have known it was you if your name had not been under it," she told me. Several other friends agreed with her. I was certain, however, that Henri had tried to portray what he conceived to be the "real Emma Goldman." I never saw the painting, but I prized the memory of the sittings, which had given me so much of value.

CHAPTER XLI

THE TRAIN WAS SPEEDING TOWARDS CHICAGO. MY HEART WAS outwinging it, all aflutter with the yearning to join Ben at last. I was scheduled to deliver twelve lectures and give a drama course in the city. During my stay I came upon the new literary publication called the *Little Review,* and shortly afterwards I met its editor, Margaret C. Anderson. I felt like a desert wanderer who unexpectedly discovers a stream of fresh water. At last a magazine to sound a note of rebellion in creative endeavour! The *Little Review* lacked clarity on social questions, but it was alive to new art forms and was free from the mawkish sentimentality of most American publications. Its main appeal to me lay in its strong and fearless critique of conventional standards, something I had been looking for in the United States for twenty-five years. "Who is this Margaret Anderson?" I inquired of the friend who had shown me a copy of the magazine. "A charming American girl," he replied, " and she is anxious to interview you." I told him I did not care to be interviewed, but that I did want to meet the editor of the *Little Review.*

When Miss Anderson came to my hotel, I went to the elevator to meet her. I was surprised to see a *chic* society girl, and, thinking that I must have misunderstood the name, I turned back to my room. "Oh, Miss Goldman," the girl called, "I am Margaret Anderson!" Her butterfly appearance was disappointing, so radically different from my mental picture of the *Little Review* editor. My tone was cold as I asked her into my room, but it did not seem to affect my visitor in the least. "I came to invite you to my place," she said impetuously, "just to rest and relax a little; you look so tired and you are always surrounded by so many people." At her home I would need to see no one, she ran on, I should be entirely undisturbed and could do as I pleased. "You can bathe in the lake, take walks, or just lie perfectly still," she coaxed; "I will wait on you and play for you." She had a taxi waiting for us to go at once. I was overwhelmed by the wordy avalanche and I felt remorseful at the frigid reception I had given the generous girl.

In a large apartment facing Lake Michigan I found, besides Miss Anderson, the latter's sister with her two children, and a girl named Harriet Dean. The entire furniture consisted of a piano, piano-stool, several broken cots, a table, and some kitchen chairs. However this strange *ménage* managed to pay the undoubtedly large rent, there was evidently no money for anything else. In some mysterious way, though, Margaret Anderson and her friend procured flowers, fruit, and dainties for me.

Harriet Dean was as much a novel type to me as Margaret, yet the two were entirely unlike. Harriet was athletic, masculine-looking, reserved, and self-conscious. Margaret, on the contrary, was feminine in the extreme, constantly bubbling over with enthusiasm. A few hours with her entirely changed my first impression and made me realize that underneath her apparent lightness was depth and strength of character to pursue whatever aim in life she might choose. Before long I saw that the girls were not actuated by any sense of social injustice, like the young Russian intelligentsia, for instance. Strongly individualized, they had broken the shackles of their middle-class homes to find release from family bondage and bourgeois tradition. I regretted their lack of social consciousness, but as rebels for their own liberation Margaret Anderson and Harriet Dean strengthened my faith in the possibilities of my adopted country.

My visit with them was entertaining and restful. I was happy to find two young American women who were seriously interested in modern ideas. We spent our time talking and discussing. In the evening Margaret would play the piano and I would sing Russian folksongs or relate to the girls some episodes of my life.

Margaret's playing was not that of a trained artist. There was a certain original and vibrant quality in it, particularly when no strangers were present. At such moments she was able to give full expression to all her emotion and intensity. Music stirred me profoundly, but Margaret's playing exerted a peculiar effect, like the sight of the sea, which always made me uneasy and restless. I had never learned to swim and I feared deep water, yet on the beach I would be filled with a desire to reach out towards the waves and become submerged in their embrace. Whenever I heard Margaret play, I was overcome by the same sensation and an uneasy craving. The days spent at her home on Lake Michigan passed all too quickly, but during the rest of my stay in Chicago Margaret and " Deansie " were never away from my side for very long.

Through Margaret I met most of the contributors to the *Little Review,* among them Ben Hecht, Maxwell Bodenheim, Caesar, Alexander Kaun, Allen Tanner, and others. Able writers they were, yet none of them possessed the all-absorbing ardour and daring of Margaret Anderson.

Harriet Monroe, of the *Poetry Magazine,* and Maurice Browne, of the Little Theatre, belonged to the same circle. I was particularly interested in the new dramatic experiment of Mr. Browne. He had talent and sincerity, but he was too dominated by the past to make the Little Theatre an effective influence. The Greek drama and the classics were certainly of great value, I often told him, but thoughtful people were nowadays seeking dramatic expression of the human problems of our own day. As a matter of fact, no one in Chicago outside of Mr. Browne's troupe and their small circle of adherents was aware of the existence of the Little Theatre. Life simply passed it by. The greater the pity, because Maurice Browne was very much in earnest about his efforts.

On this visit in Chicago I was fortunate to hear some very fine music. Percy Grainger, Alma Gluck, Mary Garden, and Casals concerted in the city during my stay. Such an array of artists was a rare treat.

Alma Gluck gripped me with her first tones. Her Hebrew chants especially gave full sway to the range of her rich voice. The sorrows of six thousand years were made poignantly real by her exquisite singing.

Mary Garden I had seen on previous occasions. Once in St. Louis she had been denied a theatre for her performance of *Salome,* which the moral busybodies had declared indecent. Some reporter had called Mary Garden's attention to the similarity of her fight for free expression to that of Emma Goldman, and Mary had spoken in high praise of me. She knew nothing about anarchism, she had said, or anything about my ideas, but she admired my stand for freedom. I wrote her my appreciation. In reply she asked me to let her know next time we happened to be in the same city. Later, in Portland,

Mary had recognized me in the front row just as some admirers had presented her with a huge basket of roses. Stepping to the edge of the stage, she picked out the largest and reddest ones and threw them into my lap with an airy kiss. Years before, in 1900, when in Paris, she had delighted me by her rendering of Charpentier's *Louise* and Massenet's *Thaïs*. But never had I seen her so lovely and fascinating as in the opera *Pelléas et Mélisande,* which I attended in the Chicago Auditorium with Margaret Anderson. She was youth, naïvité, and the earth-spirit exquisitely blended into one.

The greatest musical event during my stay in Chicago was the playing of the Spanish 'cellist Casals. I had always loved the 'cello best, but until I heard this conjuror, I had guessed little of its possibilities. Casal's touch unlocked its treasures, made it vibrate like the human soul and sing in velvet tones.

Unexpectedly came the shocking news of the massacre of workers in Ludlow, Colorado, of the shooting of strikers and the burning of women and children in their tents. Drama lectures appeared trifling, with the flames of Ludlow rising to the sky.

The coal-miners in southern Colorado had been on strike for months. The Colorado Fuel and Iron Company, a Rockefeller combine, appealed to the State for "protection" while at the same time they were shipping thugs and gunmen to the coal region. The miners were evicted from their huts, which were on company property. With their wives and children they pitched tents and prepared for the long winter. The Rockefeller interests prevailed upon Governor Ammon to call out the militia to "keep order."

Arriving in Denver with Ben, I learned that the labour leaders would be glad to accept funds I might raise at my lectures, but that they did not care to have it known that they were in any way connected with my efforts. No more encouragement did I receive from our own comrades in Ludlow. The authorities would not permit me to come to the city, they wrote, and if I did get there, the papers would proclaim that I was behind the strike. It was painful to know that I was not wanted by the very people for whom I had worked all my life.

Fortunately I had an independent forum, *Mother Earth* and my lectures. On my own platform I should be free to denounce the Ludlow crime and point out its lesson to labour. We started our meetings, and within two weeks I was able to demonstrate that a few militants imbued with idealism could focus greater attention on a pressing social issue than large organizations that lacked the courage to speak out. My lectures helped to turn the full light of publicity on Ludlow. Ludlow, Wheatland, the invasion of Mexico by Federal troops — they were all streams from the same source. I discussed them before audiences reaching into the thousands, and we succeeded in raising large sums for the various struggles.

On our arrival in Denver we had found twenty-seven I.W.W. boys in jail. They had been arrested as a result of a free-speech campaign and had been tortured in the sweat-box for refusing to work on the rock-pile. Our efforts in their behalf were successful. On their release they marched through the streets with banners and songs to our hall, where they were received in the spirit of comradeship and solidarity.

One of the interesting experiences of my Denver stay was meeting Julia Marlowe Sothern and Gustave Frohman. We discussed modern plays. Frohman was sure they did not interest the theatre-going public, and I argued that New York had also another public, more intelligent and appreciative than the one in the habit of flocking to Broadway. That public, I insisted, would support a theatre giving the dramas of Ibsen, Strindberg, Hauptmann, Shaw, and the Russians. I offered to prove that a repertory theatre, with prices running from fifty cents to a dollar and a half, could be made self-sustaining. Mr. Frohman thought I was an impractical optimist. He was interested, however, and he promised to talk the matter over further with me when we were both back in New York.

I had seen Miss Marlowe and Sothern in *The Sunken Bell,* by Gerhart Hauptmann. I did not care for his Heinrich, but Julia Marlowe as Rautendelein was sublime, and she was equally great as Katharina in *The Taming of the Shrew* and also as Juliet. Miss Marlowe must have been nearing forty at the time. She was rather heavy for youthful parts, yet her superb acting at no time broke the illusion of Rautendelein, the lithe, wild mountain-spirit, or the unsophisticated naïveté of Juliet, the child-woman.

Sothern was stiff and uninteresting, but Julia made up for both by her charm, grace, and unaffectedness. She sent flowers to my lectures and a kindly greeting to " ease the task of always having to be before the public." Well she knew how painful it often was.

While Ben and I were busy with our meetings in the West, Sasha was engaged in strenuous activities in New York. With Fitzi, Leonard

D. Abbott, the comrades of anarchist groups, and the young members of the Ferrer School he was conducting the unemployed movement and the anti-militarist campaign. Their persistency in fighting for free speech in New York had resulted in the repeated breaking up of their gatherings by mounted police, involving incredible brutality and violence. But their perseverance and defiance of arbitrary official regulations in the end impressed public opinion and they won the right of assembly in Union Square without police permission. From Sasha's brief notes I could only guess what was happening in New York, but soon the newspapers were filled with accounts of the work of the Anti-Militarist League, which Sasha had founded, and the demonstrations in behalf of the Ludlow miners held in New York and in Tarrytown, Rockefeller's citadel. It was wonderful to me to see Sasha's old spirit rising to the battle, and to observe his extraordinary skill in organizing and handling the work.

The New York activities resulted in a number of arrests, among them that of Becky Edelsohn and several boys from the Ferrer School. Sasha wrote that Becky had been splendid at her trial, where she had conducted her own defence. On being convicted she had declared a forty-eight-hour hunger strike in protest. It was the first time that a political prisoner had done this in America. I had always known Becky to be brave, though her lack of responsibility and perseverance in her personal life had for years been a source of irritation to me. I was therefore very glad to see her show such strength of character. It is often the exceptional moment that discovers unsuspected qualities.

Liberal and radical elements in New York were co-operating in protest against the Ludlow butchery. The "Silent Parade" in front of Rockefeller's office, organized by Upton Sinclair and his wife, and the various other demonstrations were arousing the East to the appalling conditions in Colorado.

I eagerly scanned the papers from New York. I had no anxiety about Sasha, for I knew how dependable and cool he was in times of danger. But I longed to be at his side, in my beloved city, to take part with him in those stirring activities. My engagements, however, kept me in the West. Then came the news of an explosion in a tenement-house on Lexington Avenue which cost the lives of three men — Arthur Caron, Charles Berg, and Karl Hanson — and of an unknown woman. The names were unfamiliar to me. The press was filled with the wildest rumours. The bomb, it was reported, had been intended for Rockefeller, whom the speakers at the New York meetings had charged with direct responsibility for the Ludlow massacres. The premature explosion had probably saved his life, the papers declared. Sasha's name was dragged into the case, and the police were looking for him and the owner of the Lexington apartment, our comrade Louise Berger. Word came from Sasha that the three men who had lost their lives in the explosion were comrades who had worked with him in the Tarrytown campaign. They had been badly beaten up by the police at one of the Union Square demonstrations. The bomb might have been intended for Rockefeller, Sasha wrote, but in any case the men had kept their intentions to themselves, for neither he nor anyone else knew how the explosion had occurred.

Comrades, idealists, manufacturing a bomb in a congested tenement-house! I was aghast at such irresponsibility. But the next moment I remembered a similiar event in my own life. It came back with paralysing horror. In my mind I saw my little room in Peppi's flat, on Fifth Street, its window-blinds drawn, Sasha experimenting with a bomb, and me watching. I had silenced my fear for the tenants, in case of an accident, by repeating to myself that the end justified the means. With accusing clarity I now relived that nerve-racking week in July 1892. In the zeal of fanaticism I had believed that the end justifies the means! It took years of experience and suffering to emancipate myself from the mad idea. Acts of violence committed as a protest against unbearable social wrongs — I still believed them inevitable. I understood the spiritual forces culminating in such *Attentats* as Sasha's, Bresci's, Angiolillo's, Czolgosz's, and those of others whose lives I had studied. They had been urged on by their great love for humanity and their acute sensitiveness to injustice. I had always taken my place with them as against every form of organized oppression. But though my sympathies were with the man who protested against social crimes by a resort to extreme measures, I nevertheless felt now that I could never again participate in or approve of methods that jeopardized innocent lives.

I was worried about Sasha. He was the spirit of the tremendous campaign in the East, and I feared the police would involve him in their dragnet. I wanted to return to New York, but his letters held me back. He was perfectly safe, he wrote, and there were plenty of people to help him in the work. He had succeeded in obtaining the bodies of the dead comrades for cremation, and he was planning a monster demonstration at Union Square. The authorities definitely declared in the press that no public funeral would be permitted. All the radical groups, including the I.W.W., repudiated Sasha's intention. Even Bill Haywood warned him to desist from his plan because he was "sure to cause another eleventh of November." But Sasha's group refused to be terrorized. He publicly announced that he would stand responsible for anything that might happen at the meeting, on condition that no police officers be permitted within the lines of the demonstration.

The public funeral took place in spite of official prohibition. Union Square seethed with a crowd of twenty thousand people. At the last moment the police had decided not to permit Sasha, who was to preside at the demonstration, to reach the square. Detectives and reporters besieged our house. Sasha appeared on the front stoop to talk to them and they asked to see the urn containing the cremated remains of the Lexington Avenue victims. He stepped back into the house and then slipped out through the back and some neighbouring yards. He had taken the precaution to order a red automobile to wait for him in a nearby street. At a furious pace it was driven to Union Square. For blocks all approaches to the square were crowded. It seemed impossible to reach the platform. But before Sasha could open the door of the machine, police officers — in their excitement undoubtedly taking the automobile to be that of the Fire Chief — obsequiously cleared a lane for the auto right through the crowd to the very front of the platform. When Sasha stepped out, the officers were amazed to see who it was. He quickly ascended the platform. It was too late for the police to do anything without causing a blood bath.

Now the remains of the dead comrades, Sasha wrote me, were deposited in a specially designed urn in the form of a clenched fist rising from the depths. The urn was exposed in the office of *Mother Earth*, which had been decorated with wreaths and red and black banners. Thousands passed through our quarters to pay the last tribute to Carron, Berg, and Hanson.

I was happy to learn that the perilous situation in New York had ended so favourably. But when I received copies of the July issue of *Mother Earth*, I was dismayed at its contents. The Union Square speeches were published there in full; with the exception of Sasha's own address and those of Leonard D. Abbott and Elizabeth Gurley

Flynn, the harangues were of a most violent character. I had tried always to keep our magazine free from such language, and now the whole number was filled with prattle about force and dynamite. I was so furious that I wanted the entire issue thrown into the fire. But it was too late; the magazine had gone out to the subscribers.

The persistent efforts of one man in Portland, Oregon, exerted an influence in that town that for its potency could hardly be equalled in any other American city. I refer to my friend Charles Erskine Scott Wood. By position he belonged to the ultra-conservative set, yet he was among the most unflinching opponents of the social layer from which he sprang. It was owing to his efforts that the Public Library was granted to so dangerous a person as I was considered to be. Mr. Wood presided at my first lecture, which was on " Intellectual Proletarians," and his presence brought an enormous audience.

Portland was in the throes of a prohibition campaign. My talk on " Victims of Morality," which touched on this subject, resulted in an uproar. It was one of the most exciting evenings in my public career. The prohibitionists and the pro-liquorists almost came to blows on the occasion.

The following day a man called on Mr. Wood and offered to buy my lecture notes, not the part dealing with the suppression of sex, but the one where I had enlarged on the right of grown-ups to choose their drinks. The caller represented the Saloon-Keepers' League, and his organization wanted my notes as propaganda in their anti-prohibition campaign. Mr. Wood informed him that he would submit the offer to me, but that I was a " queer creature " and would probably not consent to having only half of my lecture published. " But she will be paid," the man cried, " and any price she wants! " Needless to say, I declined to appear as an agent of the Saloon-Keepers' League.

The power of the Montana copper-kings, faithfully supported by the Catholic Church, made Butte and other smelting-towns in the State barren ground except for the sweet hospitality of my friends Annie and Abe Edelstadt, the latter a brother of our dead poet. The system of espionage had been perfected by the bosses. Their employees were surrounded by spies not only when at work, but also in their free hours. The " spotters " dogged every step of the men and made detailed reports on their behaviour. In consequence those modern slaves lived in fear of displeasing their masters and losing their jobs. The situation was aggravated by reaction in the union ranks. The Western Federation of Miners, long in the control of corrupt and unscrupulous officials, helped to silence the voice of labour protest. But pressure from above begets rebellion. The break had to come. The aroused workers dynamited the Union Hall, drove their leaders out of town, and organized a new union along revolutionary lines.

It was a changed atmosphere that greeted us on our arrival in Butte. No particular efforts were necessary to arouse interest in my lectures. The people came in a body and openly demonstrated their independence. They fearlessly asked questions and participated in the discussion. If any " spotters " were in the audience, they were unknown to the men, who would have certainly given them short shrift.

Very significant also was the presence of many women, especially at my lecture on " Birth-control." Formerly they would not have dared to inquire about such matters even privately; now they stood up in a public assembly and frankly avowed their hatred of their position as domestic drudges and child-bearers. It was an extraordinary manifestation, most encouraging to me.

All through the years no decent hall had been accessible to us in Chicago. I had often been compelled to speak in dreadful places, generally in the rear of a saloon. That did not, however, prevent the so-called better class from attending my lectures. Not rarely the street in front of the hall would be lined with automobiles, thus providing a chance for the Wobblies, and even for some of my own comrades, to protest against my " educating the bourgeoisie." My last lecture in Chicago in April had been nearly broken up by a drunken man who had drifted in from the saloon and who insisted on taking charge of the proceedings. At the close of the meeting two strangers left their visiting-cards with Ben. They asked him to let them know when I would return to Chicago and promised to secure an appropriate place for my future lectures.

Having received many promises, few of which had ever been fulfilled, I had little faith in this one. Nevertheless I wrote the strangers that I would meet them on my way back from the Coast. After leaving Butte I proceeded to Chicago, where I also intended to visit Margaret Anderson and Deansie. The men proved to be a rich advertising-agent and a stock-broker! We discussed the best means of organizing a series of drama lectures and it was decided to secure the Fine Arts recital hall. The men offered to finance the venture and I wondered why they should do it, unless it be that wealthy Jews love to engage in " uplift " work. I made it clear to them that I must remain as free to speak in the fashionable place as in the back room of a saloon. It was agreed that I should wire my lecture dates later on.

When I arrived in New York I was confronted with a serious financial situation. Sasha's activities among the unemployed, together with the anti-militarist and Ludlow campaigns, had swallowed up most of the funds I had sent to our office from my tour. We could not meet the obligations of *Mother Earth,* much less the expense of the house, which in my absence had been turned into a free-for-all lodging- and feeding-place. We were in debt to our printer and to the mailing-house, and money was owed to every store-keeper in the neighbourhood. The strain of the agitation he had carried on, the danger and the responsibility he had faced, had left Sasha in a high-strung and irritable state. He was sensitive to my criticism, and hurt that I should even mention money matters. I had hoped for rest, harmony, and peace after six months of constant lecturing and the struggle involved in my tour. Instead I was swamped with new cares.

I was dazed by the situation and I felt very indignant with Sasha. Entirely absorbed in his own propaganda, he had given me no thought. He was the revolutionist of old, with the same fanatical belief in the Cause. His sole concern was the movement, and I was to him but a means for it. He was nothing more to himself than that; how could I expect to be any more to him?

Sasha did not understand my resentment. He grew impatient at my mentioning money matters. He had spent our funds for the movement; the latter was more important than my drama lectures, he said. I spoke bitterly to him, telling him that without my drama lectures he would have had no means to finance his activities. The clash made us both unhappy. Sasha withdrew into himself.

The only ones I could turn to in my misery were my dear nephew Saxe and my old friend Max. Both were very understanding, but neither of them was worldly enough to be of much assistance to me. I should have to face the situation alone.

I decided to give up our house and to declare myself bankrupt. My friend Gilbert E. Roe, to whom I confided my troubles, laughed at my strange notion. " Bankruptcy is resorted to by those who want to get out of paying debts," he said; " it will involve you in year-long litigation, and your creditors will attach every penny you make to the end of your days." He offered to lend me money, but I could not accept his generosity.

Then a new idea struck me. I would tell the printer exactly how I stood. The frank and open way is always the best, I decided. My creditors proved to be very accommodating. They lost no sleep over the money I owed them, they said; I could be depended on to make good. It was finally arranged that I pay my indebtedness in monthly instalments. Our mailing-house even declined my promissory notes. " Pay what you can and when you can," the manager said; " your word is good enough for us."

I resolved to start from the bottom up again; to rent a small place — one room for an office, the other for my living-quarters — and to accept every lecture engagement I could secure, and practise the strictest economy in order to keep up *Mother Earth* and my work. I wired Ben dates for my dramatic course in Chicago, and then I went out to look for a new home. It was a discouraging task; the Lexington Avenue explosion and the publicity given to Sasha's activities were fresh in the public mind, and the landlords were timid. But at last I found a two-room loft on One Hundred and Twenty-fifth Street, and I set to work to make it fit for my use.

Sasha and Fitzi came to help me get my new place in order, but our relations were strained. Yet Sasha was too deeply rooted in my being to permit me to remain angry with him very long. There was also something else to change my resentful attitude. The realization had come to me that it was not Sasha, but I who was at fault. Not only since my return from the last tour, but all through the eight years since his release from prison, it was I who had been responsible for the breaks that came between us. I had committed a great wrong against him. Instead of giving him a chance to find his way back to life, after his resurrection, I had brought him into my atmosphere, into an environment that could only be galling to him. I had done this in the mistaken belief, usual with mothers, that they know best what is good for their children; fearing the latter will be crushed in the world outside, they desperately try to shield them from the experiences so essential to their growth. I had committed the same mistake in regard to Sasha. Not only had I not urged him to launch out for

himself, but I had trembled at every step he made, because I could not
see him exposed to new suffering and hardships. Yet I had saved him
from nothing; I had only awakened his resentment. Perhaps he was
not even aware of it, yet it was always there, breaking out in one form
or another. Sasha had always wanted his own work and his own place.
I had offered him everything one human being can give to another, but
I had not helped him to what he wanted and needed most. There was
no blinking the hard fact. But now that Sasha had found a woman
who could give him both love and understanding, it was my opportunity to repair the wrong I had done him.

I would enable them to go on a cross-country tour, I decided. Once
Sasha reached California, he could carry out his dream of a paper of
his own.

Fitzi and Sasha eagerly responded to my suggestion for a tour.
I arranged with my young friend Anna Baron, who used to do part-
time typing for us, to take care of the business side of the *Mother
Earth* office. Max and Saxe were to look after the editorial work of
the magazine. There were also Hippolyte and other friends to help.
Sasha felt rejuvenated, and there was no further friction between us.

One day my friend Bolton Hall called on me. I had worked hard
and he no doubt noticed my exhausted condition. " Why not go out to
the little farm in Ossining? " he suggested. " Not for worlds," I replied, " as long as my pest is there." " What pest? " he queried in
wonder. " Why, Micky, whom for years I have tried vainly to
escape." " You mean Herman Mikhailovitch, the timid-looking fellow
who used to help in the *Mother Earth* office and the Ferrer Center? "
" The very one," I told him; " his apparent timidity has been my
curse for a long time." Dear Bolton looked his blank surprise. " Tell
me about it," he urged.

I related the story to Bolton. Herman had been a reader of *Mother
Earth* for a long time, had faithfully paid his subscription, and often
ordered literature. He lived in Brooklyn, but none of us had ever
met him. Then one day I received a letter from Omaha asking permission to arrange my meetings there. It was from Herman. Glad
that someone in that city had offered to assist, I wired him to go
ahead. On my arrival there I found our unknown comrade in rags
and looking starved. Ben helped him and we also procured his release when he was locked up for distributing our handbills announcing
my meetings. Before I left the city I enabled him to join the painters'

union and secure a job. In Minneapolis three days later we were unexpectedly faced by Herman. He wanted to organize my meetings
along the route, he declared. I assured him that I appreciated his
offer, but that I already had one manager; two would be too much to
endure. Herman said nothing more, but when we reached the next
town, he was there, and again in the next and in the next. There was
no shaking him off; he was either ahead of us or at our rear. The proceeds from my lectures were not sufficient to pay his railroad fare, and
I feared lest Herman meet some accident while stealing rides. He became an additional worry and burden. In Seattle I could not stand it
any more. He would find a job, he said, if I would secure him for a
few weeks. I did, and he solemnly promised to remain in Seattle. When
we came to Spokane, who should meet us but Herman Mikhailovitch?
He did not like the West, he declared, and had decided to return to
New York. For the rest of our tour Herman stuck like glue. He was
a good worker, ready to do anything to help my meetings; and he
was shrewd enough to make himself indispensable to Ben. I gave a
sigh of relief when we finally arrived in New York.

Nothing was heard from Herman for some time. Then he showed
up again, all in rags. He was working in a laundry, he told me, eighteen
hours a day for five dollars a week. In the midst of his story he fell to
the floor in a faint. A hurried agreement with Sasha and Hippolyte, to
the effect that Herman could earn his keep by assisting in the office,
saved him from returning to the laundry, and incidentally also from
further fainting spells. He was an intelligent chap, but fame affects
some people worse than liquor. Touring with us, getting arrested,
and seeing his name in the papers had turned Herman's head. His
condition became worse after Ben put him up as one of his stars at
a hobo meeting. Herman shared honours with Chuck Connor, the
Chinatown celebrity, Sadakichi Hartmann, of weird dance fame,
Hutchins Hapgood, widely known for his books on the underworld,
Arthur Bullard, intellectual Bohemian and globe-trotter, Ben Reitman, pseudo-king of Hoboland, and others of the over- and underworld *milieu*.

Herman, now christened Micky, delivered himself of an oration
on that occasion, speaking with unchallenged authority on tramping
as a superior art. "Everywhere you are forced to sell your labour,"
he declared, " but on the open road you are free from work. I have
pledged myself to be the master of my soul. Rather than work for a

boss, I will let others work for me unless I can choose my occupation."
He was hailed as a hero and accepted by the fraternity as one of
their own.

The next day the papers had write-ups about Micky, " the Irish
Jew who had taken a pledge never to work." Micky walked on air,
his head held high, his chest expanded, and looking the world contemptuously in the face. In our office he wisely refrained from flaunting
his fame — until Ben and I went on tour. Then he declared that he
had his own life to live and great things to perform. The boys
promptly told him they could not survive such importance in the same
house.

In Omaha I was faced by Micky again. He would not be an expense, he assured me; he only wanted to be connected with my work.
I could not deny him that. Micky continued as my shadow, ever on my
heels, from town to town. I admired his perseverance, though he got
on my nerves fearfully. His presence became all-pervading. Then he
began to gossip about my New York friends and particularly about
Ben, who had been especially patient with him. That broke the camel's
back, and Micky fled from my sight.

When we were back in New York, Ben brought the cheerful news
that Micky had landed in the city that very day, half-starved and
frozen from a long tramp. " Rig him out, give him money, shelter,
and food," I said, " only don't bring him here; his attentions are entirely too much for me." Ben did as I asked, but he never stopped
talking of poor Micky's plight, and on Christmas Eve he brought
him to me as a gift. A snow-storm was raging, and we had a spare
room. How could I send the poor creature away?

No sooner did Micky feel secure than he again began to demonstrate his superiority, criticizing, reprimanding, and straining everybody's patience to the breaking-point. In rage one day he raised a
cane against Saxe, who had grown tired of listening to his bragging.
My presence saved Micky from the sound thrashing he deserved. I
told him categorically that he would have to find another place. When
we returned from a meeting that night, we found our furnace sabo-
taged and Micky locked in his room. He was on a hunger strike, his
note on my desk informed me, and he would keep it up until I would
consent to his remaining in the house. The boys offered to throw him
bodily into the street, but I refused to let them do so, hoping Micky
would change his mind.

Four days passed, and he was still locked in. I took a pail of water and resolutely climbed up to his room. He opened as soon as he heard my voice. I told him that if he would not get up within five minutes, I would give him a cold shower-bath. He began to weep and to charge me with being cruel. He loved me more than anyone else, he declared; he was my true friend, but now he must die, since I would not requite his affection. He would die right there, and I must help him do so. The boys had suggested that Micky's pranks were due to jealousy, and I had laughed at the silly notion. At last poor Micky's secret was out! But I remained stern. "A nice kind of love is yours, to want to burden me with your death," I said; "don't you think there are worthier causes to go to the electric chair for?" I told him to get up, take a bath, put on clean clothes, and have some food; later on we would decide on the best way for him to commit suicide. He asked permission to go out on the farm and I gladly consented. But, once there, he began pestering me with letters, two and three of them every day, complaining of cold and hunger and threatening suicide again.

"No doubt Micky knows you have a sick conscience," Bolton teased me; "and, besides, consider his unrequited love," he added with a merry twinkle in his eye. "But I'll get him off the farm all right, and I promise not to leave him destitute." Bolton wrote Micky that he had been informed of his illness and poverty, and that thereupon he had notified the authorities of the poorhouse: an officer would call for him in a few days. By return mail Bolton received a reply from Micky to the effect that he was no pauper, and that he had saved enough money to take him to the Coast. Micky left. "Clever man, this Micky," Bolton commented, "but I didn't know you could be so easily imposed on."

The little place at Ossining was at last free from the pest, and I longed for a much-needed rest. But in the confusion I had quite forgotten that young Donald, the son of my dear friend Gertie Vose, was living in the house that I was giving up. Sasha had written me when I was in the West that the boy had come to him with a letter from his mother, and that he had taken him in. Gertie Vose was an old rebel whom I had met in 1897, but I had not seen her son in eighteen years. When I met him again in our house he produced on me a very disagreeable effect, which was probably due to his high-pitched voice or to his shifting look, which seemed to avoid my eyes. But he was Gertie's son, alone and out of work. He seemed undernourished and he was wretchedly dressed. I proposed that he go out for a rest to our little place in Ossining. He told me that he had intended to return home after the Tarrytown campaign, but he was waiting for his mother to send him the fare. He seemed appreciative of my offer, and the next day he left for the farm.

In my new quarters I took up my activities again. Readjustment to the altered conditions involved many hardships, but they were made more bearable by the presence of my good friend Stewart Kerr, who had a room above my little office. He had formerly shared with us our apartment at 210 East Thirteenth Street; of a considerate and non-invasive nature, Stewart was touchingly thoughtful of my welfare and very helpful in numerous ways. It was comforting to have him as my neighbour, the two of us being the only tenants living in the little house.

I was busy preparing the new drama course I had promised to deliver in Chicago and a series of lectures on the war. Three months had passed since its outbreak in Europe. Outside of *Mother Earth* and our anti-militarist campaign in New York I had not been able to raise my voice in the West against the slaughter, except on one occasion, in Butte, when I had spoken from an automobile to a large crowd and denounced the criminal stupidity of war. I felt that but for the socialist betrayal of their ideals, the great catastrophe would have been impossible. In Germany the party counted twelve million adherents. What a power to prevent the declaration of hostilities! But for a quarter of a century the Marxists had trained the workers in obedience and patriotism, trained them to rely on parliamentary activity and, particularly, to trust their socialist leaders blindly. And now most of those leaders had joined hands with the Kaiser! Instead of making common cause with the international proletariat, they had called upon the German workers to rise to the defence of " their " fatherland, the fatherland of the disinherited and degraded. Instead of declaring the general strike and thus paralysing war preparations, they had voted the Government money for slaughter. The socialists of the other countries, with certain notable exceptions, had followed their example. No wonder, for the German social democracy had for decades been the pride and inspiration of the socialists throughout the world.

My drama course under the auspices of my two wealthy patrons proved to be a most disagreeable experience. Mr. L., the advertising genius, had taken it upon himself to "edit" the announcements I had sent. Indeed, he had changed their entire character, handling the subjects of my lectures as if they had been chewing-gum ads.

Then happened something to shock the tender sensibilities of my patrons. My first drama talk fell on November 10, a day of momentous importance to me. It had been the last day on earth of my comrades martyred in Chicago twenty-seven years before. I introduced my lecture by contrasting the changes in the public attitude towards anarchism between 1887 and 1914. The vision of our precious dead was before me, bearing witness to the last prophecy of August Spies: "Our silence will be more powerful than the voices you strangle today." In 1887 Chicago's sole answer to anarchism was the gallows; in 1914 it was eagerly listening to the ideas for which Parsons and his comrades had died. During my brief introduction I saw one of my backers and his family, in the first row, uncomfortably fidgeting in their seats; some people in the rear ostentatiously left the hall. Unconcernedly I went on with the subject of the evening, "The American Drama."

Subsequently my backers informed Ben that I had "missed the opportunity of a lifetime." They had induced the "wealth and influence of Chicago" to attend my lectures, "the rich Rosenwalds among them." They would have helped to secure my drama work for the rest of my life, and then "Emma Goldman had to spoil in ten minutes all that we had worked weeks to achieve."

I felt as if I had been put up on the block for sale. The incident had a most depressing effect on me. Try as I would, I could not get my usual intensity into my further drama talks. It was different when I discussed the war. In my own hall, under no obligations to anyone, I could freely express my abhorrence of slaughter and frankly discuss whatever phase of the social question I took up. At the close of my drama course we reimbursed my "patrons" for their outlay. I did not regret the experience; it taught me that patronage is paralysing to one's integrity and independence.

My stay in Chicago was lent charm by my two young friends Margaret and Deansie. Both consecrated themselves to me and turned the office of the *Little Review* over to my needs. The girls were as poor as church mice, never sure of their next meal, much less able to pay the printer or the landlord. Yet there were always fresh flowers on the desk to cheer me. Since the unforgettable days I had spent with Margaret in the spring when we had both enjoyed the hospitality of Mr. and Mrs. Roe at their home in Pelham Manor, something very new and precious had grown up between us. Three weeks of almost daily association with her, her fine understanding and intuition, had increased our mutual affection.

Chicago had charm, but I could not linger. Other voices were calling, calling me to take up the struggle again. I still had a number of cities to cover. Sasha and Fitzi had left on their lecture tour, and I was urgently needed at home.

CHAPTER XLII

ELENA AND OUR YOUNG FOLKS IN ROCHESTER ALWAYS BROUGHT me back to that city even when I did not have to lecture there. This year there were additional reasons for visiting my home town: an opportunity to speak on the war, and the great family event of David Hochstein's first concert with the local symphony orchestra.

The Victoria Theatre had been secured for my lecture by an anarchist workman known as Dashuta. An idealist of the best type, he had paid out of his meagre savings the entire expense of the meeting and he had used all his leisure to make the lecture widely known. His help meant infinitely more to me than the " security for life " offered by the Chicago rich.

On my arrival in Rochester I found my people in anxious suspense over David's forthcoming concert. Well I knew how my sister Helena yearned for the dreams and aspirations of her own frustrated life to be realized in her youngest son. At the first signs of his talent my timid sister had developed determination and strength to defy every difficulty that beset the beloved child's artistic career. She drudged and saved to enable her children, particularly David, to have the opportunities she herself had been deprived of in life, and she was consumed by a great longing to give herself to the uttermost. On my visits she would sometimes pour out her heart to me, never complaining, but only regretting that she was able to do " so little " for her dear ones.

Now the crowning moment of her struggle had arrived. David had returned from Europe the finished artist she had slaved to help him become. Her heart trembled for his triumph. The cold critics, the unappreciative audience — what would her darling's playing mean to them? Would they understand his genius? She refused seats in a box.

"It might disturb him to see me," she said. She would feel more comfortable with Jacob in the gallery.

I had heard David in New York and I knew how his playing had impressed everyone. He was truly an artist. Handsome and of good appearance, he made a striking figure on the platform. I felt no anxiety about his Rochester engagement. My sister's excitement, however, had communicated itself to me, and all during the concert my thoughts were with her whose fierce love and hope were now being fulfilled. David's violin charmed the audience and he was acclaimed with an enthusiasm seldom accorded a young artist in his native town.

Arriving in New York, I was approached by the Newspaper Enterprise Association, controlled by the Scripps-Howard newspapers, for an essay on how the American people could help establish peace on earth and good will towards men. The subject, if treated adequately, would have required a volume, but I was asked to "keep it down" to a thousand words. The opportunity to reach a large audience, however, was too valuable to miss. In my article I pointed out that the first step to good will demands a reversal of Christ's command to "render unto Cæsar the things which are Cæsar's and unto God the things that are God's." Ceasing to pay tribute to despots in heaven and on earth, I wrote, would tend towards peace among men.

On my return from a short tour I was surprised to find Donald Vose still in New York. He looked more shabby than I had seen him last, and though it was cold December, he was without an overcoat. Every day he came to our office and remained for hours "to warm up," as he said. "What about the money you expected?" I asked him; "did it ever come?" He had received it, he told me, but he had been promised a good job in New York and he had decided to stay on. Nothing had come of it, however, and now his fare was used up and he had to write home for more. It sounded plausible, yet somehow I was not impressed. His constant presence was getting on my nerves.

Soon reports began to drift in that Donald was spending money on drink and that he was nightly treating his companions. I thought at first that it was mere gossip; the boy apparently could not afford an overcoat; where would he get money for drink? But the reports became more frequent, and I got suspicious. I knew his mother Gertie to be too poor to support her son, as were also most of her friends. Writing her would only make her uneasy, and I therefore communicated with some of our friends in the West. They investigated the matter in Seattle, Tacoma, and the Home Colony, where Gertie lived. No money was being supplied to Donald from any of those places. My apprehensions increased. Shortly afterwards Donald came to tell me that his fare had arrived at last and that he was returning West. I was relieved and I felt also a little ashamed of my distrust.

A week after Donald's departure we read about the arrest of Matthew A. Schmidt in New York and of David Caplan on Puget Sound. We knew that the two men were " wanted " in connexion with the Los Angeles *Times* explosion. The " gentlemen's agreement " made by the State of California to refrain from further prosecution of labour men after the McNamara confession was broken again. Donald Vose came to my mind, and my old suspicions were revived. Various circumstances pointed to his connexion with the arrest of the men. It seemed preposterous to think a child of Gertie Vose capable of treachery, yet I could not free myself from the thought that Donald was somehow responsible for the arrests.

Soon no room was left for doubt. Proofs sent to us by dependable friends on the Coast disclosed that Donald Vose was in the pay of Detective William J. Burns and that he had betrayed Matthew A. Schmidt and David Caplan. The son of our old comrade Gertie, raised in anarchist circles and a guest in our house, turned Judas! It was a staggering blow, one of the worst I had received in my twenty-five years of public life.

The first step I decided upon was a frank avowal in *Mother Earth* of the facts in the case and an explanation of how Donald Vose had happened to live in our house. But it would crush my dear friend Gertie to learn that her own child was a spy! Gertie had been so happy that her son was now " in the right atmosphere," and that he would take up the work for which she had spent her life. I wondered how the clear-thinking and observant woman could have remained so blind to the true nature of her son. She never would have sent him to our house if she had had the slightest inkling of his true nature. I hesitated to disclose the truth about Donald. Yet sooner or later Gertie would have to face the fact; moreover, there was so much involved in Donald's relation to us and to our work that I could not keep the matter under cover. Our people must be warned against him, I finally decided.

I wrote an article for our magazine giving the whole history of the case. But before it was set up, I received the request from those connected with the defence of Schmidt and Caplan to delay publishing anything about Donald because he was expected to testify at the trial. I had always hated subterfuge, but I could not ignore the wishes of the people in charge of the defence of Caplan and Schmidt.

The tenth anniversary of *Mother Earth* was approaching. It seemed nothing short of a miracle for our magazine to have survived a whole decade. It had faced the condemnation of enemies and the unfriendly criticism of well-wishers and had had a hard struggle to keep alive. Even most of those who had helped at its birth had expressed misgivings about its continued existence. Their fears were not groundless, in view of the reckless founding of the magazine. Blissful ignorance of the publishing business, combined with the ridiculous nest-egg of two hundred and fifty dollars — how could anyone hope to succeed with such a start? But my friends had overlooked the most important factors in the heritage of *Mother Earth,* a Yiddish perseverance and a boundless enthusiasm. These had proved to be stronger than gilt-edged securities, large income, or even popular support. From the very beginning I had outlined for it a twofold purpose: to voice without fear every unpopular progressive cause, and to aim for unity between revolutionary effort and artistic expression. To achieve these ends I had to keep *Mother Earth* untrammelled by party policies, even by anarchist policies, free from sectarian favouritism and from every outside influence, however well-intentioned. For this I was charged even by some of my comrades with using the magazine for my personal ends, and by socialists with being in the employ of capitalism and of the Catholic Church.

Its survival was due in no little measure to the devotion of a small band of comrades and friends who helped to realize my dream of an independent radical spokesman in the United States. The tributes paid at the tenth anniversary by readers in America and abroad testified to the niche in people's hearts my child had made for itself. Some of the praise was especially touching because it came from persons with whom I had been compelled to clash swords over the war.

After my return from the Neo-Malthusian Conference, held in Paris in 1900, I had added to my lecture series the subject of birth-control. I did not discuss methods, because the question of limiting offspring represented in my estimation only one aspect of the social struggle and I did not care to risk arrest for it. Moreover, I was so continually on the brink of prison because of my general activities that it seemed unjustifiable to court extra trouble. Information on methods I gave only when privately requested for it. Margaret Sanger's difficulties with the postal authorities over her publication of *The Woman Rebel,* and the arrest of William Sanger for giving his wife's pamphlet on methods of birth-control to a Comstock agent, made me aware that the time had come when I must either stop lecturing on the subject or do it practical justice. I felt that I must share with them the consequences of the birth-control issue.

Neither my birth-control discussion nor Margaret Sanger's efforts were pioneer work. The trail was blazed in the United States by the grand old fighter Moses Harman, his daughter Lillian, Ezra Heywood, Dr. Foote and his son, E. C. Walker, and their collaborators of a previous generation. Ida Craddock, one of the bravest champions of women's emancipation, had paid the supreme price. Hounded by Comstock and faced with a five-year sentence, she had taken her own life. She and the Moses Harman group were the pioneers and heroes of the battle for free motherhood, for the right of the child to be born well. The matter of priority, however, in no way lessened the value of Margaret Sanger's work. She was the only woman in America in recent years to give information to women on birth-control and she had revived the subject in her publication after many years of silence.

E. C. Walker, president of the Sunrise Club, had invited me to speak at one of its fortnightly dinners. His organization was among the few libertarian forums in New York open to free expression. I had often lectured there on various social topics. On this occasion I chose birth-control as my theme, intending openly to discuss methods of contraception. I faced one of the largest audiences in the history of the club, numbering about six hundred persons, among them physicians, lawyers, artists, and men and women of liberal views. Most of them were earnest people who had come together to lend moral support to the test case that this first public discussion represented. Everyone felt certain that my arrest would follow, and some friends had come prepared to go bail for me. I carried a book with me in case I should have to spend the night in the station-house. That possibility did not disturb me, but I did feel uneasy because I knew that some of the diners had come out of curiosity, for the sex thrills they expected to experience on this evening.

I introduced my subject by reviewing the historical and social aspects of birth-control and then continued with a discussion of a number of contraceptives, their application and effects. I spoke in the direct and frank manner that I should use in dealing with ordinary disinfection and prophylaxis. The questions and the discussion that followed showed that I had taken the right approach. Several physicians complimented me on having presented so difficult and delicate a subject in a " clean and natural manner."

No arrest followed. Some friends feared I might be picked up on my way home, and insisted on seeing me to my door. Days passed and the authorities had taken no steps in the matter. It was the more surprising in view of the arrest of William Sanger for something he had not said nor written himself. People wondered why I, who had been so frequently arrested when I had not broken the law, should be allowed to go unpunished when I had done so deliberately. Perhaps Comstock's failure to act was due to the fact that he knew that those who were in the habit of attending the Sunrise Club gatherings were probably already in possession of contraceptives. I must therefore deliver the lecture at my own Sunday meetings, I decided.

Our hall was packed, mostly with young people, among them students from Columbia University. The interest evinced by my audience was even greater than at the Sunrise dinner, the questions put by the young folks of a more direct and personal nature. I did not mince matters, yet there was no arrest. Evidently I should have to make another test — on the East Side.

I had to postpone the matter for a while because of previous engagements. Students from the Union Theological Seminary, frequent attendants at my Sunday lectures, had invited me to address them. I had consented after having warned the boys that they were likely to meet with opposition from the faculty. As soon as it became known that the heathen was to invade the theological sanctum, a tempest broke out which lasted beyond the day set for my lecture. The students insisted on their right of hearing whom they pleased until the faculty gave in, and another date was agreed upon.

In the mean time I had to deliver another lecture, on the " Failure of Christianity," with particular reference to Billy Sunday, whom I considered the modern clown of religion and whose circus was in Paterson at the time. In view of the tsarist methods employed by the authorities in dealing with strike meetings and radical gatherings, the

police protection given Billy and his performances was doubly outrageous. Our comrades in Paterson were planning some protest, and
they invited me to speak. I felt that it would not be fair to discuss
Billy Sunday without first learning the calibre of the man and seeing
what he was passing out as religion. I went with Ben to Paterson to
hear the self-appointed voice of Christ.

Never did Christianity appear to me so divested of meaning and
decency. Billy Sunday's vulgar manner, his coarse suggestiveness,
erotic flagellation, and disgusting lasciviousness, clad in theological
phraseology, stripped religion of the least spiritual significance. I was
too nauseated to hear him to the end. Fresh air brought relief from
the atmosphere of the lewd mouthings and sexual contortions with
which he goaded his audience to salacious hysteria.

Some days later I lectured in Paterson on the " Failure of Christianity " and cited Billy Sunday as the symbol of its inner collapse.
The next morning's newspapers stated that I had provoked the wrath
of God by my blasphemy. I learned that the hall in which I had spoken
had caught fire after I had left and burned to the ground.

My tour this year met with no police interference until we reached
Portland, Oregon, although the subjects I treated were anything but
tame: anti-war topics, the fight for Caplan and Schmidt, freedom in
love, birth-control, and the problem most tabooed in polite society,
homosexuality. Nor did Comstock and his purists try to suppress me,
although I openly discussed methods of contraception before various
audiences.

Censorship came from some of my own comrades because I was
treating such " unnatural " themes as homosexuality. Anarchism was
already enough misunderstood, and anarchists considered depraved;
it was inadvisable to add to the misconceptions by taking up per-
verted sex-forms, they argued. Believing in freedom of opinion, even
if it went against me, I minded the censors in my own ranks as little
as I did those in the enemy's camp. In fact, censorship from comrades had the same effect on me as police persecution; it made me
surer of myself, more determined to plead for every victim, be it one
of social wrong or of moral prejudice.

The men and women who used to come to see me after my lectures
on homosexuality, and who confided to me their anguish and their
isolation, were often of finer grain than those who had cast them

out. Most of them had reached an adequate understanding of their differentiation only after years of struggle to stifle what they had considered a disease and a shameful affliction. One young woman confessed to me that in the twenty-five years of her life she had never known a day when the nearness of a man, her own father and brothers even, did not make her ill. The more she had tried to respond to sexual approach, the more repugnant men became to her. She had hated herself, she said, because she could not love her father and her brothers as she loved her mother. She suffered excruciating remorse, but her revulsion only increased. At the age of eighteen she had accepted an offer of marriage in the hope that a long engagement might help her grow accustomed to a man and cure her of her " disease." It turned out a ghastly failure and nearly drove her insane. She could not face marriage and she dared not confide in her fiancé or friends. She had never met anyone, she told me, who suffered from a similar affliction, nor had she ever read books dealing with the subject. My lecture had set her free; I had given her back her self-respect.

This woman was only one of the many who sought me out. Their pitiful stories made the social ostracism of the invert seem more dreadful than I had ever realized before. To me anarchism was not a mere theory for a distant future; it was a living influence to free us from inhibitions, internal no less than external, and from the destructive barriers that separate man from man.

Los Angeles, San Diego, and San Francisco were record-breaking in the size of our meetings and the interest shown. In Los Angeles I was invited by the Women's City Club. Five hundred members of my sex, from the deepest red to the dullest grey, came to hear me speak on " Feminism." They could not excuse my critical attitude towards the bombastic and impossible claims of the suffragists as to the wonderful things they would do when they got political power. They branded me as an enemy of woman's freedom, and club-members stood up and denounced me.

The incident reminded me of a similar occasion when I had lectured on woman's inhumanity to man. Always on the side of the under dog, I resented my sex's placing every evil at the door of the male. I pointed out that if he were really as great a sinner as he was being painted by the ladies, woman shared the responsibility with him. The mother is the first influence in his life, the first to cultivate his conceit and self-importance. Sisters and wives follow in the mother's footsteps, not to mention mistresses, who complete the work begun by the mother. Woman is naturally perverse, I argued; from the very birth of her male child until he reaches a ripe age, the mother leaves nothing undone to keep him tied to her. Yet she hates to see him weak and she craves the manly man. She idolizes in him the very traits that help to enslave her — his strength, his egotism, and his exaggerated vanity. The inconsistencies of my sex keep the poor male dangling between the idol and the brute, the darling and the beast, the helpless child and the conqueror of worlds. It is really woman's inhumanity to man that makes him what he is. When she has learned to be as self-centred and as determined as he, when she gains the courage to delve into life as he does and pay the price for it, she will achieve her liberation, and incidentally also help him become free. Whereupon my women hearers would rise up against me and cry: " You're a man's woman and not one of us."

Our experience in San Diego two years previously, in 1913, had exerted the same effect on me as the night ride in 1912 had on Ben. I was set on returning to deliver my suppressed lecture. In 1914 one of our friends had gone to San Diego to try to secure a hall. The socialists, who had their own place, refused to have anything to do with me. Other radical groups were equally brave, so that my plan had to be abandoned. Only temporarily, I had promised myself, however.

This year, 1915, I was fortunate in having to deal with real men instead of with mere apologies in male attire. One of them was George Edwards, the musician who had offered us the Conservatory of Music on the occasion of our first trouble with the Vigilantes. The other was Dr. A. Lyle de Jarnette, a Baptist minister who had resigned from the Church and had founded the Open Forum. Edwards had become a thorough anarchist who devoted his time and abilities to the movement. He had set to music Voltairine de Cleyre's *The Hurricane,* Olive Schreiner's *Dream of Wild Bees,* and " The Grand Inquisitor " from Dostoyevsky's *Brothers Karamazov.* Now he was determined to help me come back to San Diego and establish the right of free speech there. Dr. Jarnette had organized the Open Forum as a protest against Vigilante suppression. The association had since grown into a large and vital body. Arrangements were made for me to deliver three lectures there, in an attempt to break the San Diego conspiracy.

The recently electer mayor of the city, reputed to be a liberal, had assured the Open Forum that I would be allowed to speak, and that no Vigilante interference would be permitted. It was a new tone for San Diego, probably due to the circumstance that its exposition had greatly suffered as a result of the three-year boycott. But our former experiences in the city did not justify too much trust in official declarations. We·preferred to prepare ourselves for possible emergencies.

I had long before decided that I would return to San Diego without Ben. I had planned to go alone, but fortunately Sasha was in Los Angeles at the time. I knew I could count on his poise in a difficult situation and on his utter fearlessness in the face of the gravest danger. Sasha and my romantic admirer Leon Bass left for San Diego two days ahead of me to look over the field. Accompanied by Fitzi and Ben Capes, I departed quietly from Los Angeles in an auto. Nearing the Vigilante city, the picture of Ben surrounded by fourteen thugs rose before me. They had covered the same route, with Ben at the mercy of savages who were beating and humiliating him. I thought of him writhing in pain, with no one to succour him or alleviate his terror. Barely three years had passed. I was free, with dear friends at my side, securely riding through the balmy night. I could enjoy the beauty around me, the golden Pacific on one side, majestic mountains on the other, their fantastic formations towering above us. The very glory of this magnificent country-side must have been mockery to Ben, a mockery in league with his torturers. May 14, 1912 — June 20, 1915 — what an incredible change! Yet what might be awaiting us in San Diego?

We arrived at four-thirty in the morning and drove straight to the small hotel where Sasha had engaged rooms for us. He reported that the hall-keeper had declared that I could not speak in his place, but that Dr. Jarnette and the other members of the Open Forum were determined to see our plans through. The hall was theirs by yearly lease, the key was in their hands, and it had been decided to take possession of the hall and guard every entrance.

When our meeting opened, at eleven in the morning, we became aware that a number of Vigilantes were present. The situation was tense, the atmosphere charged with suppressed excitement. It furnished a fitting background for my subject, which was Ibsen's *Enemy of the People*. Our men were on the alert, and no untoward incident took place, the Vigilantes evidently not daring to start any hostile demonstration.

The afternoon lecture was on Nietzsche, and again the hall was crowded, but this time the Vigilantes remained away. In the evening I spoke on the struggle of Margaret and William Sanger, dealing with the importance of birth-control. The day ended without any disturbance. I felt that our triumph was due mostly to the comrades martyred for free speech three years previously — to Joseph Mikolasek, who had been murdered in the fight, and the hundreds of I.W.W.'s and other victims, including Ben, who had been beaten, thrown into prison and driven out of town. The thought of them steeled me and urged me on.

Ben insisted on visiting San Diego again, and he returned there later on, not in any public capacity, but just to convince himself that he was not afraid. He went to the exposition in the company of his mother and several friends. No one paid any attention to them. The Vigilante conspiracy had been broken.

Among my numerous friends in Los Angeles none was more helpful in my work and welfare than Dr. Percival T. Gerson, together with his wife. They interested scores of people in my lectures, gave me the opportunity to address gatherings in their home, and entertained me lavishly. It was also Dr. Gerson who procured for me an invitation to speak before the Severance Club, named in honour of Caroline M. Severance, co-worker of Susan B. Anthony, Julia Howe, and the group of militants of the preceding generation.

Before I began my lecture, I was introduced to a man who, in the absence of the president, had been asked to preside. There was nothing striking about him as he sat buried in my volume of *Anarchism and Other Essays*. In his opening remarks this chairman, whose name was Tracy Becker, astonished the audience by the announcement that he had been connected with the District Attorney's office in Buffalo when President McKinley was killed. Until very recently he had considered Emma Goldman a criminal, he said — not one who had courage to do murder herself, but one who unscrupulously played on weak minds and induced them to commit crimes. During the trial of Leon Czolgosz he felt certain, he continued, that it was I who had instigated the assassination of the President and he had thought that I ought to be made to pay the extreme penalty. Since he had read my books and had talked to some of my friends, he realized his mistake and he now hoped that I would forgive him the injustice he had done me.

Dead silence followed his remarks, and everybody's eyes were turned on me. I felt frozen by the sudden resurrection of the Buffalo tragedy, and in an unsteady voice, at first, I declared that since we are all links in the social chain, no one can avoid responsibility for such deeds as that of Leon Czolgosz; not even the chairman. He who remains indifferent to the conditions that result in violent acts of protest cannot escape his share of blame for them. Even those of us who see clearly and work for fundamental changes are not entirely exempt from guilt. Too absorbed in efforts for the future, we often turn a deaf ear to those who reach out for sympathetic understanding and who hunger for the fellowship of kindred spirits. Leon Czolgosz had been one of such.

I talked with growing feeling as I proceeded to describe the bleak background of the boy, his early environment and life. I related the impressions of the Buffalo newspaper woman who had sought me out to tell me what she had experienced during Czolgosz's trial, and I pointed out the motives of Leon's act and martyrdom. I felt no resentment against the man who had confessed his eagerness to send me to the electric chair. Indeed, I rather admired him for frankly admitting his error. But he had revived in my memory the fury of that period, and I was in no mood to meet him or to listen to his idle pleasantries.

The San Francisco Exposition was at its height, and the population of the city had almost doubled. Our meetings, totalling forty within one month, successfully competed with the gate receipts of the big show. The great event was my appearance at the Congress of Religious Philosophies. The astonishing thing was made possible by Mr. Power, who was in charge of the sessions of the congress. He had known me in the East, and when he learned of my presence in San Francisco, he invited me to speak.

The public conclave of the religious philosophers took place in the Civic Auditorium, one of the largest halls in the West. The place of the chairman, a reverend gentleman who suddenly fell ill when he heard that I was to speak, was taken by a member of the newspaper fraternity. I was thus between the devil and the deep sea, and I began my talk on atheism by saying so. My introduction put the audience in a light mood. Surrounded on the platform by gentlemen of the cloth of every known denomination, I needed all my humour to rise to the solemnity of the occasion.

Atheism is rather a delicate subject to handle under such circumstances, but somehow I managed to pull through. I saw consternation on the faces of the theologians, who protested that my treatment of religion was scandalous. But the vast audience evidently enjoyed it, for its hilarious approval came perilously near breaking up the congress when I got through. I was followed by a rabbi, who began by saying that " in spite of all Miss Goldman has said against religion, she is the most religious person I know."

CHAPTER XLIII

On my arrival in New York after my protracted Western lecture tour I hoped to get a long-needed rest. But the fates and Sasha willed it otherwise. He had just returned from Los Angeles to work in the East in behalf of Matthew A. Schmidt and David Caplan, and he immediately drew me into his intensive campaign.

Sasha's presence on the Coast during my last San Diego experience was due to a rather unexpectedly happy turn of affairs. When he had started out on his Western lecture tour, in the fall of 1914, he had not intended to go farther than Colorado. That was owing to his arrest on the very eve of his leaving New York. Fitzi had preceded him to Pittsburgh to make the preliminary arrangements for the meetings. Sasha's New York friends had meanwhile arranged a farewell party in his honour. At midnight the company, returning home, sang revolutionary songs. A policeman ordered them to cease singing, and in the altercation that followed he lifted his night-stick to strike Bill Shatoff, our old friend and co-worker. Sasha's presence of mind undoubtedly saved Bill from serious injury. He gripped the policeman's upraised arm so that the latter let the club fall out of his hand. More officers arrived and the whole company were arrested. In the morning they were condemned to short terms in the workhouse for "disturbing the peace," except Sasha, who was charged with assaulting an officer and inciting to riot. The magistrate insisted on his standing trial there and then, saying that his sentence would not exceed two years. The policeman had come to court with his entire arm painted with iodine and bandaged, and his statement to the judge was to the effect that Sasha had attacked him without the least provocation and that only the arrival of more police had saved his life. It was clearly the intention to "railroad" Sasha. The police, having failed to stop his unemployment activities and Ludlow strike protests, were evidently determined to wreak vengeance on him this time.

Sasha refused to have the case proceed before the police magistrate. The charges against him, classed as felonies, gave him the legal right of trial by jury. Moreover, he was scheduled to speak the same evening in Pittsburgh, and he decided to take his chances in criminal court.

Our friend Gilbert E. Roe bailed him out and promised to look after the case during his absence. Sasha departed for Pittsburgh, but when he reached Denver, he was warned by Roe to go no farther west, so as to be able to return to New York within forty-eight hours if he was called for trial. The situation looked serious, Sasha being in danger of a five-year prison term.

For weeks he remained lecturing in Colorado, anxious to go to California to aid in the defence of Matthew A. Schmidt and David Caplan, who were awaiting trial in Los Angeles in connexion with the *Times* building explosion. Then one day he received a telegram from New York, reading: " Case against you dismissed. You are free to go where you please. Congratulations."

It was Gilbert E. Roe who had managed to have the indictments against Sasha quashed by convincing the new District Attorney of New York that the charges were the result of police enmity.

Now Sasha was in New York, working strenuously in behalf of the Caplan-Schmidt defence. On the Coast he had organized a wide publicity campaign in their behalf, and as a result of his efforts the International Workers' Defence League had requested him to tour the country and form defence branches along the route. It was just the kind of activity Sasha was particularly fitted for, and he devoted himself passionately to saving the two indicted men from the fate that had been his in Pennsylvania.

Equipped with credentials from various labour organizations, he had left Los Angeles, stopping at all the larger industrial cities on his way east, so that by the time he reached New York he had already rallied a goodly part of organized labour to the support of the prisoners in the Los Angeles jail.

Sasha immediately enlisted me for the Caplan-Schmidt campaign, as he did everyone else he could get into the work. It was good to have him near again and to co-operate with him. The Caplan-Schmidt mass meeting he organized, at which we were both to speak, and the numerous other efforts for the defence he was making were too important to let me consider my need of rest. The reactionary forces on the Coast arrayed against labour were feverishly active. They were poisoning the public mind against the men about to be tried; to prejudice the case they were spreading the rumour that David Caplan had turned State's evidence. The preposterous story had just made its appearance in the New York newspapers. Aware of the effect of such statements even upon the radicals, it became necessary to take a stand against the outrageous slander. I had known David fifteen years and had been closely connected with him in the movement during that time; I was absolutely convinced of his integrity.

When the date of the Caplan-Schmidt trial became known, Sasha returned to the Coast to start a bulletin, as part of the publicity he was making for the case.

The conflagration in Europe was spreading; already six countries had been swept by it. America was also beginning to catch fire. The jingo and military cliques were growing restive. "Sixteen months of war," they cried, "and our country is still keeping aloof!" The clamour for "preparedness" began, people joining in who but yesterday waxed hot against the atrocities of organized slaughter. The situation called for more energetic anti-war agitation. It became doubly necessary when we learned of the attitude of Peter Kropotkin.

Rumours had been filtering through from England that Peter had declared himself in favour of the war. We ridiculed the idea, certain that it was a newspaper fabrication to charge our Grand Old Man with pro-war sentiments. Kropotkin, the anarchist, humanitarian, and gentlest of beings — it was preposterous to believe that he could favour the European holocaust. But presently we were informed that Kropotkin had taken sides with the Allies, defending them with the same vehemence that the Haeckels and the Hauptmanns were championing "their" fatherland. He was justifying all measures to crush the "Prussian menace," as those in the opposite camp were urging the destruction of the Allies. It was a staggering blow to our movement, and especially to those of us who knew and loved Peter. But our devotion to our teacher and our affection for him could not alter our convictions nor change our attitude to the war as a struggle of financial and economic interests foreign to the worker and as the most destructive factor of what is vital and worth while in the world.

We determined to repudiate Peter's stand, and fortunately we were not alone in this. Many others felt as we did, distressing as it was to turn against the man who had so long been our inspiration. Enrico Malatesta showed far greater understanding and consistency than Peter, and with him were Rudolph Rocker, Alexander Schapiro, Thomas H. Keell, and other native and Jewish-speaking anarchists in Great Britain. In France Sébastien Faure, A. Armand, and members of the anarchist and syndicalist movements, in Holland Domela Nieuwenhuis and his co-workers maintained a firm attitude against the wholesale murder. In Germany Gustav Landauer, Erich Mühsam, Fritz Oerter, Fritz Kater, and scores of other comrades retained their senses. To be sure, we were but a handful in comparison with the war-drunk millions, but we succeeded in circulating throughout the world the manifesto issued by our International Bureau, and we increased our energies at home to expose the true nature of militarism.

Our first step was the publication in *Mother Earth* of Peter Kropotkin's pamphlet on " Capitalism and War," embodying a logical and convincing refutation of his new position. In numerous meetings and protests we pointed out the character, significance, and effects of war, my lecture on " Preparedness " showing that " readiness," far far from assuring peace, has at all times and in all countries been instrumental in precipitating armed conflicts. The lecture was repeatedly delivered before large and representative audiences, and it was among the first warnings in America against the military conspiracy behind the protestations of peace.

Our people in the States were awakening to the growing danger, and demands for speakers and for literature began pouring into our office from every part of the country. We were not rich in good English agitators, but the situation was urgent, and I was continually busy filling the gap.

I went about the country, speaking almost every evening, my days occupied with numerous calls on my time and energy. At last even my unusual powers of endurance gave way. Returning to New York after a lecture in Cleveland, I was taken ill with the grippe. I was too ill to be transferred to a hospital. After I had spent two weeks in bed, the physician in charge ordered me taken to a decent hotel room, my own quarters lacking all comforts. On my arrival at the hotel I was too weak to register, and Stella, my niece, wrote my name in the guest book. The clerk looked at it and then retired to an inner office. He returned to say that a mistake had been made; there was no vacant room for me in the place. It was a cold and grey day, the rain coming down in torrents, but I was compelled to return to my old quarters.

The incident resulted in strong protests in the press. One communication in particular attracted my attention; it was a long and caustic letter upbraiding the hotel people for their inhumanity to a patient. The statement, signed "Harry Weinberger, Attorney-at-Law, New York," was by a man I did not know personally, but whose name I had heard mentioned as that of an active single-taxer and member of the Brooklyn Philosophical Society.

In the mean time Matthew Schmidt had been sacrificed to the vengeance of the Merchants' and Manufacturers' Association, the Los Angeles *Times,* and the State of California. One of the main witnesses against him was Donald Vose. In open court, face to face with his victim, he admitted being in the employ of Detective William J. Burns. As his agent Vose had ferreted out the whereabouts of David Caplan. He enjoyed the hospitality of the latter for two weeks, gained his confidence, and learned that Schmidt was somewhere in New York. Then he was ordered east by Burns, instructed to frequent anarchist circles and be on the alert for the first chance to reach Matthew Schmidt. On the witness-stand Vose boasted that the prisoner at the bar had confessed his guilt to him. Schmidt was convicted, the jury recommending imprisonment for life.

There was no more reason for withholding the publication of what I considered Donald Vose's perfidy. The January 1916 issue of *Mother Earth* contained the too-long-delayed article about him.

Gertie Vose stood by her son. I understood her maternal feeling, but in my estimation it did not excuse a rebel of thirty years' standing. I never wanted to see her again.

Conviction did not break the strong spirit of Matthew A. Schmidt or influence his faith in the ideals for which he was to be buried for the rest of his life. His statement in court, setting forth the causes behind the social war, was illuminating in its clarity, simplicity, and courage. Though facing a life sentence, he did not lose his rich humour. In the midst of his recital of the real facts in the case he turned to the jury with the remark: " Let me ask you, gentlemen, do you believe a man like Donald Vose? You wouldn't whip your dog on the testimony of such a creature; no honest man would. Any man who would believe Vose would not deserve to have a dog."

Interest in our ideas was growing throughout the country. New anarchist publications began to appear: *Revolt* in New York, with Hippolyte Havel as its editor; the *Alarm* in Chicago, issued by a local group of comrades, and the *Blast* in San Francisco, with Sasha and Fitzi at its head. Directly or indirectly I was connected with all of them. It was, however, the *Blast* that was closest to my heart. Sasha had always wanted a forum from which to speak to the masses, an anarchist weekly labour paper to arouse the workers to conscious revolutionary activity. His fighting spirit and able pen were enough to assure the *Blast* vitality and courage. The co-operation of Robert Minor, the powerful cartoonist, added much to the value of the publication.

Robert Minor had wandered far since the days when I first met him in St. Louis. He had definitely broken with the milk-and-water brand of socialism and had given up a lucrative position on the New York *World* for a twenty-five-dollar-a-week job on the socialist daily *Call*. "This will free me," he once told me, "from making cartoons that show the blessings of the capitalistic régime and injure the cause of labour." In the course of time Bob had developed into a revolutionist and subsequently into an anarchist. He devoted his energy and abilities to our movement. *Mother Earth, Revolt,* and the *Blast* were considerably strengthened by his trenchant brush and pen.

From Philadelphia, Washington, and Pittsburgh came calls for a series of lectures to extend over several months. The initiative of our comrades was a satisfying and stimulating sign; such a venture had never before been tried with one speaker, but our friends were eager to attempt it. I realized the strain it would involve to travel continually from town to town, lecture every evening, then rush back to speak at my Friday and Sunday meetings in New York. But I welcomed the opportunity to awaken interest in the Los Angeles case, agitate against the war, and help circulate our various publications.

My English lectures in Philadelphia were hardly worth the weekly effort. They were poorly attended; the few who did come were sluggish and inert, like the social atmosphere in the City of Brotherly Love. There were only two persons whose friendship recompensed me for the otherwise dreary experience, Harry Boland and Horace Traubel.

Harry was an old devotee and always generously helpful in every struggle I made. Horace Traubel I had first met at a Walt Whitman dinner in 1903. He had impressed me as the outstanding personality among the Whitmanites. I enjoyed the hours spent in his sanctum, filled with Whitman material and books, as well as with the files of his own unique paper, the *Conservator*. Most interesting were his reminiscences of the Good Gray Poet, whose latter years of life Horace had shared. I got more from him of Walt than from any biographer I had read, and I also got much of Horace Traubel, who revealed himself and his own humanity in his talks about his beloved poet.

Another man brought close to me by Horace was Eugene V. Debs. I had met him previously on several occasions and had clashed swords with him in a friendly way over our political differences, but I knew little of his real personality. Horace, an intimate friend of Debs's, made him vibrant to me in the heights and depths of his character. The comradeship I felt for Horace ripened into a beautiful friendship during my visits to Philadelphia. The city's empty boast of brotherly love was redeemed by none so much as by Horace Traubel, whose love embraced mankind.

Results in Washington, D. C., surprised everybody and, most of all, our active workers Lillian Kisliuk and her father. Lillian had for years lived in the capital, but had always been sceptical about the success of lectures in her city, and particularly about having two a week. It was her enthusiasm for our ideas, however, that had induced her to undertake the task.

The Pittsburgh arrangements were in charge of our very able friend Jacob Margolis, who was assisted by a group of young American comrades, among them Grace Loan, very vivid and intense, her husband, Tom, and his brother, Walter. The Loans were most refreshing by their genuineness and zeal, and they gave promise of great usefulness to our cause. They had all worked like beavers to make my meetings a success, but unfortunately the result was not commensurate with their efforts. On the whole, however, my series of meetings in the stronghold of the steel-trust were well worth while, especially because Jacob Margolis had succeeded in inducing a club of lawyers to invite me to address them.

I had heretofore faced the representatives of the law only as a prisoner. On this occasion it was my turn — not to pay back in kind, but to tell the judges and prosecutors among my hearers what I thought of their profession. I confess I did it with glee, without remorse or pity for the predicament of the gentlemen who had to listen without being able to punish me even for contempt of court.

My lectures in New York that winter included the subject of birth-control. I had definitely decided some time previously to make public the knowledge of contraceptives, particularly at my Yiddish meetings, because the women on the East Side needed that information most. Even if I were not vitally interested in the matter, the conviction of William Sanger and his condemnation to prison would have impelled me to take up the question. Sanger had not been actively engaged in the birth-control movement. He was an artist, and he had been tricked by a Comstock agent into giving him a pamphlet which his wife, Margaret Sanger, was circulating. He could have pleaded ignorance and thus avoided punishment. His bold defence in court earned him the deserved appreciation of all right-thinking people.

My lectures and attempts at lecturing on birth-control finally resulted in my arrest, whereupon a public protest was arranged in Carnegie Hall. It was an impressive gathering, with our friend and ardent co-worker Leonard D. Abbott presiding. He presented the historical aspects of the subject, while Doctors William J. Robinson and J. S. Goldwater spoke from the medical point of view. Dr. Robinson was an old champion of the cause; together with the venerable Abraham Jacobi, he was the pioneer of birth-control in the New York Academy of Medicine. Theodore Schroeder and Bolton Hall illuminated the legal side of family limitation, and Anna Strunsky Walling, John Reed, and a number of other speakers dwelt on its social and human value as a liberating factor, particularly in the lives of proletarians.

My trial, after several preliminary hearings, was set for April 20. On the eve of that day a banquet took place at the Brevoort Hotel, arranged by Anna Sloan and other friends. Members of the professions and of various social tendencies were present. Our good old comrade H. M. Kelly spoke for anarchism, Rose Pastor Stokes for socialism, and Whidden Graham for the single-taxers. The world of art was represented by Robert Henri, George Bellows, Robert Minor, John Sloan, Randall Davey, and Boardman Robinson. Dr. Goldwater and other physicians participated. John Francis Tucker, of the Twilight Club, was toast-master and he lived up to his reputation as one of the wittiest men in New York. An entertaining discussion was provided by John Cowper Powys, the British writer, and Alexander

Harvey, an editor of *Current Literature*. Powys expressed himself as appalled by his ignorance of birth-control methods, but he insisted that though he personally was not interested in the matter, yet he belonged to the occasion because of his constitutional objection to any suppression of free expression.

When at the close I was given the floor to reply to the various points raised, I called the attention of the guests to the fact that the presence of Mr. Powys at a banquet given to an anarchist was by no means his first libertarian gesture. He had given striking proof of his intellectual integrity some years previously in Chicago when he had refused to speak at the Hebrew Institute because that institution had denied its premises to Alexander Berkman. The latter had been announced to speak on the Caplan-Schmidt case. At the last moment the directors of the Institute closed its doors. Thereupon the Chicago workers had boycotted the reactionary organization and founded their own Workmen's Institute. Shortly afterwards Mr. Powys had arrived to deliver a series of lectures at the Hebrew Institute. When informed of the attitude of its directors to Berkman, Mr. Powys had cancelled his engagements. His action was especially commendable because all he knew of Berkman was the misrepresentations he had read in the press.

Rose Pastor Stokes demonstrated direct action at the banquet. She announced that she had with her typewritten sheets containing information on contraceptives and that she was ready to hand them out to anyone who wanted them. The majority did.

In court the next day, April 20, I pleaded my own case. The District Attorney interrupted me continually by taking exceptions, in which he was sustained by two of my three judges. Presiding Judge O'Keefe proved to be unexpectedly fair. After some tilts with the young prosecutor I took the stand in my own behalf. It gave me the opportunity to expose the ignorance of the detectives who testified against me and to deliver in open court a defence of birth-control.

I spoke for an hour, closing with the declaration that if it was a crime to work for healthy motherhood and happy child-life, I was proud to be considered a criminal. Judge O'Keefe, reluctantly I thought, pronounced me guilty and sentenced me to pay a fine of one hundred dollars or serve fifteen days in the workhouse. On principle I refused to pay the fine, stating that I preferred to go to jail. It called forth an approving demonstration, and the court attendants cleared the room. I was hurried off to the Tombs, whence I was taken to the Queens County Jail.

Our following Sunday meeting, which I could not attend, since my forum was now a cell, was turned into a protest against my conviction. Among the speakers was Ben, who announced that pamphlets containing information about contraceptives were on the literature table and could be taken free of charge. Before he had got off the platform, the last of the pamphlets had been snatched up. Ben was arrested on the spot and held for trial.

In Queens County Jail, as on Blackwell's Island years previously, I saw it demonstrated that the average social offender is made, not born. One must have the consolation of an ideal to survive the forces designed to crush the prisoner. Having such an ideal, the fifteen days were a lark to me. I read more than I had for months outside, prepared material for six lectures on American literature, and still had time for my fellow prisoners.

Little did the New York authorities foresee the results of the arrests of Ben and me. The Carnegie Hall meeting had awakened interest throughout the country in the idea of birth-control. Protests and public demands for the right to contraceptive information were reported from numerous cities. In San Francisco forty leading women signed a declaration to the effect that they would get out pamphlets and be ready to go to prison. Some proceeded to carry out the plan and they were arrested, but their cases were discharged by the judge, who stated that there was no ordinance in the city to prohibit the propagation of birth-control information.

The next Carnegie Hall meeting was held as a greeting upon my release. The occasion was under the auspices of prominent persons in New York, but the actual organization work was done by Ben and his " staff," as he called our active boys and girls. Birth-control had ceased to be a mere theoretic issue; it became an important phase of the social struggle, which could be advanced more by deeds than by words. Every speaker stressed this point. It was again Rose Pastor Stokes who carried wishes into action. She distributed leaflets on contraceptives from the platform of the famous hall.

The sole disturbing element was Max Eastman, who declared a few minutes before the opening of the meeting that he would not preside if Ben Reitman should be allowed to speak. In view of Eastman's socialistic ideas and his past insistence on the right of free speech this ultimatum shocked everyone on the committee. The fact that Ben was under indictment for the very thing for which the meeting had been called made Mr. Eastman's attitude all the more incomprehensible.

I suggested to him to withdraw, but his friends persuaded him to preside. The incident once more proved how poorly some alleged radicals in America have grasped the true meaning of freedom and how little they care about its actual application in life. The " cultural " leader of socialism in the United States and editor of the *Liberator* permitted personal dislikes to stand in the way of what he claimed to be his " high ideal."

Ben's trial took place on May 8 in Special Sessions, before Judges Russell, Moss, and McInerney. The last-named was the man who had sent William Sanger to prison for a month. Ben pleaded his own case, making a splendid defence for birth-control. He was found guilty, of course, and sentenced to the workhouse for sixty days, because, as Judge Moss put it, he had " acted with deliberation, premeditation, and forethought, in defiance of the law." Ben cheerfully admitted the imputation.

His conviction was followed by a large protest meeting in Union Square. A touring-car was our platform, and we spoke to the working masses that were streaming out from the factories and shops. Bolton Hall presided; Ida Rauh and Jessie Ashley handed out the forbidden pamphlets. At the close of the meeting they were all arrested, including the chairman.

In the excitement of the birth-control campaign I did not forget other important issues. The European slaughter was continuing, and the American militarists were growing bloodthirsty at the smell of the red stream. Our numbers were few, our means limited, but we concentrated our best energies to stem the tide of war.

The Easter uprising in Ireland was culminating tragically. I had entertained no illusions about the rebellion, heroic as it was; it lacked the conscious aim of complete emancipation from economic and political rule. My sympathies were naturally on the side of the revolting masses and against British imperialism, which had oppressed Ireland for so many centuries.

Extensive reading of Irish literature had endeared the Gaelic people to me. I loved them as painted by Yeats and Lady Gregory, Murray and Robinson, and above all by Synge. They had shown me the remarkable similarity between the Irish peasant and the Russian moujik I knew so well. In their naïve simplicity and lack of sophistication, in the motif of their folk-melodies, and in their primitive attitude towards law-breaking, which sees in the offender an unfortunate rather than a criminal, they were brothers. The Irish poets seemed to me more expressive even than the Russian writers, their language being their people's own tongue. The debt I owed to Celtic literature and to my Irish friends in America, and my feeling for the oppressed everywhere, combined in my attitude to the uprising. In *Mother Earth* and on the platform I voiced my solidarity with the people risen in rebellion.

The quality of some of the victims of British imperialism was made vivid to me by Padraic Colum. He had been in close touch with the martyred leaders and spoke with knowledge and understanding of the events of Easter week. Lovingly he remembered Padraic H. Pearse, the poet and teacher, James Connolly, the proletarian rebel, and Francis Sheehy-Skeffington, a most gentle and genuine soul. Colum's description made the men live again and moved me profoundly. At my request he wrote an account of the events for *Mother Earth,* which was published in our magazine together with Padraic H. Pearse's stirring poem " The Pæan of Freedom."

No less than Great Britain our own country writhed in the throes of reaction. After Matthew A. Schmidt had been condemned to life imprisonment there came the conviction of David Caplan, who was sentenced to ten years in the California State prison at San Quentin. The quarters of the Magón brothers, champions of Mexican liberty, were raided in Los Angeles, and Ricardo and Enrico Magón arrested. In northern Minnesota thirty thousand iron-ore miners were waging a desperate struggle for more bearable conditions of existence. The mine-owners, aided by the Government, sought to break the strike by arresting its leaders, including Carlo Tresca, Frank H. Little, George Andreychin, and others active in behalf of the toilers. Arrests followed arrests throughout the country, accompanied by the utmost police brutality and encouraged by the subservience of the courts to the demands of capital.

Ben was meanwhile serving his sentence in the Queens County Jail. His letters breathed a serenity I had never known him to feel before. I was due to leave on my tour. There were many friends to look after Ben in my absence, and we planned to have him join me in California upon his release. There was no reason for anxiety about him, and he himself urged me to go, yet I was loath to leave him in prison. For eight years he had shared the pain and joy of my struggle. How would it be, I wondered, to tour again without Ben, without his elemental activity, which had helped so much to make my meetings a success? And how should I bear the strain of the struggle without Ben's affection and the comfort of his presence? The thought chilled me, yet the larger purpose, which was my life, was too vital to be affected by personal needs. I left alone.

CHAPTER XLIV

IN DENVER I HAD THE RATHER UNUSUAL EXPERIENCE OF SEEING A judge preside at my lecture on birth-control. It was Ben B. Lindsey. He spoke with conviction on the importance of family limitation and he paid high tribute to my efforts. I had first met the Judge and his very attractive wife several years previously and I had spent time with them whenever I visited Denver. Through friends I had learned of the shameful treatment he had received at the hands of his political enemies. They had not only circulated the most scurrilous reports about his public and private integrity, but they had even directed their attacks against Mrs. Lindsey, anonymously threatening and terrorizing her. Yet I found Judge Lindsey free from bitterness, generous towards his enemies, and determined to pursue his own course.

While in the city, I had the opportunity of attending a lecture by Dr. Stanley Hall on " Moral Prophylaxis." I was familiar with his work and I believed him to be a pioneer in the field of sex psychology. In his writings I had found the subject illumined sympathetically and with understanding. Dr. Hall was introduced by a minister, which circumstance may have handicapped his freedom of expression. He talked badly and endlessly on the need of the churches' taking up sex instruction as " a safeguard for chastity, morality, and religion," and he voiced antiquated notions that had no bearing either on sex or on psychology. It made me sad to see him grown so feeble, particularly mentally, since we had met at the celebration of the twentieth anniversary of Clark University and at my own lectures. I felt sorry for the American people who were accepting such infantile stuff as authoritative information.

My lectures in Los Angeles were organized by Sasha, who had specially come for the purpose from San Francisco, where he was publishing the *Blast*. He had worked energetically, and my meetings proved to be successful in every way. Yet I missed Ben, Ben with all his weaknesses, his irresponsibility and ways that were so often harsh. But my longings were stilled by the urgent needs of the Los Angeles situation.

My lecture on "Preparedness" happened to fall on the day of the Preparedness Parade. We could have chosen no more opportune date had we known in advance of the planned militarist demonstration. In the afternoon the people of Los Angeles were treated to a patriotic spectacle, at which they were assured that "the lover of peace must go armed to the teeth," while in the evening they heard it emphasized that "he who goes armed is the greatest menace to peace." Some patriots had come to our meeting with the intention of breaking it up. They changed their minds, however, when they saw that our audience was not in a mood to listen to jingo appeals.

The brothers Ricardo and Enrico Flores Magón were being held in the Los Angeles jail, and the local comrades had so far not succeeded in bailing them out. Twice before had these men been railroaded to prison for their bold advocacy of liberty for the Mexican people. During their ten years' residence in the United States they had been imprisoned five years. Now Mexican influence in America sought to send them up for the third time. The people who knew and loved the Magóns were too poor to bail them out, while those who had means believed them to be the dangerous criminals they were pictured by the press. Even some of my American friends, I found, had been influenced by the newspaper ravings. Sasha and I set to work to secure the needed ten-thousand-dollar bond. Because of the official denunciation of everything Mexican our task proved to be extremely difficult. We even had to compile material to show that the only offence of the Magóns consisted in their selfless devotion to the cause of Mexican liberty. After much effort we succeeded in procuring their release on bond. The happy surprise on the faces of Ricardo and Enrico, who doubted the possibility of bailing them out, was the highest appreciation of our work in their behalf.

An impressive scene took place in court when the Magón brothers appeared for their hearing. The court-room was filled with Mexicans. When the judge entered, not one of them stood up, but when the Magóns were led in, they rose to a man and bowed low before them. It was a magnificent gesture that demonstrated the place these two brothers held in the hearts of those simple people.

In San Francisco Sasha and Fitzi had prepared everything to make my month's stay in the city pleasant and useful. My first lectures were most satisfactory, and they held out much promise for the rest of my series. I had my own apartment, as I was expecting Ben to join me in July. But I spent a great deal of my free time with Sasha and Fitzi in their place.

On Saturday, July 22, 1916, I was lunching with them. It was a golden California day, and the three of us were in a bright mood. We were a long time over our luncheon, Sasha regaling us with a humorous account of Fitzi's culinary exploits. The telephone rang, and he stepped into his office to answer it. When he returned, I noticed the extremely serious expression on his face, and I intuitively felt that something had happened.

"A bomb exploded in the Preparedness Parade this afternoon," he said; "there are killed and wounded." "I hope they aren't going to hold the anarchists responsible for it," I cried out. "How could they?" Fitzi retorted. "How could they not?" Sasha answered; "they always have."

My lecture on "Preparedness" had originally been scheduled for the 20th. But we learned that the liberal and progressive labour elements had arranged an anti-preparedness mass meeting for the same evening, and, not wishing to conflict with the occasion, postponed my talk for the 22nd. It struck me now that we had barely escaped being involved in the explosion; had my meeting taken place as scheduled, prior to the tragedy, everyone connected with my work would have undoubtedly been held responsible for the bomb. The telephone call had come from a newspaper man who wanted to know what we had to say about the explosion — the usual question of reporters and detectives on such occasions.

On the way to my apartment I heard newsboys calling out extra editions. I bought the papers and found what I had expected — glaring headlines about an "Anarchist Bomb" all over the front pages. The papers demanded the immediate arrest of the speakers at the anti-preparedness meeting of July 20. Hearst's *Examiner* was especially bloodthirsty. The panic that followed on the heels of the explosion exposed strikingly the lack of courage, not only of the average person, but of the radicals and liberals as well. Before the 22nd of July they had filled our hall every evening for two weeks, waxing enthusiastic over my lectures. Now at the first sign of danger they ran to cover like a pack of sheep at the approach of a storm.

On the evening following the explosion there were just fifty people at my meeting, the rest of the audience consisting of detectives. The atmosphere was very tense, everybody fidgeting about, apparently in terror of another bomb. In my lecture I dealt with the tragedy of the afternoon as proving more convincingly than theoretic dissertations that violence begets violence. Labour on the Coast had been opposed to the preparedness parade, and union members had been asked not to participate. It was an open secret in San Francisco that the police and the newspapers had been warned that something violent might happen if the Chamber of Commerce kept insisting on the public demonstration of its mailed fist. Yet the " patriots " had permitted the parade to take place, deliberately exposing the participants to danger. The indifference to human life on the part of those who had staged the spectacle gave a foretaste of how cheaply life would be considered should America enter the war.

A reign of official terror followed the explosion. Revolutionary workers and anarchists were, as always, the first victims. Four labour men and one woman were immediately arrested. They were Thomas J. Mooney and his wife, Rena, Warren K. Billings, Edward D. Nolan, and Israel Weinberg.

Thomas Mooney, long a member of Moulders' Union, Local 164, was known throughout California as an energetic fighter in the cause of the workers. For many years he had been an effective factor in various strikes. Because of his incorruptibility he was cordially hated by every employer and labour politician on the Coast. The United Railways had tried, a few years previously, to put Mooney behind the bars, but even the farmer jury had refused to credit the frame-up against him. Recently he had sought to organize again the motormen and conductors of the street-car combine. He had attempted, unsuccessfully, to call a strike of the platform-men a few weeks before the parade, and the United Railways marked him for their victim. They posted bulletins on the car barns, warning their men to have nothing to do with the " dynamiter Mooney," on pain of immediate discharge.

On the night following the posting of the bulletins, some power-towers of the company were blown up, and those who knew smiled at the obvious attempt of the railway bosses to " get " Mooney by the peculiarly " timely " branding of him as a dynamiter.

Warren K. Billings, formerly president of the Boot and Shoe Workers' Union, had for years been active in labour struggles, and the employers had once before succeeded in railroading him to prison on a trumped-up charge in connexion with strike troubles in San Francisco.

Edward D. Nolan was a man greatly admired and respected by labour elements on the Coast for his clear social vision, intelligence, and energy. He had, a few days previous to the preparedness parade, returned from Baltimore, where he had been sent as a delegate to the Machinists' convention. Nolan was also chief of the pickets in the local machinists' strike, and he had long since been put on the employers' black-list.

Israel Weinberg was a member of the executive board of the Jitney Bus Operators' Union, which had incurred the enmity of the United Railways by seriously embarrassing its receipts. The street-car company was trying to drive the jitneys off the principal streets, and the opportunity to discredit the Jitney Bus Union by charging a prominent member with murder was not to be lost by District Attorney Fickert of San Francisco, whom the railways had helped to office that he might quash the indictments against their corrupt officials — which he promptly did as soon as elected.

Mrs. Rena Mooney, the wife of Tom Mooney, was a well-known music-teacher. An energetic and devoted woman, her arrest was a police *coup* to prevent her efforts in behalf of Tom.

To charge these men with responsibility for the preparedness-parade explosion was a deliberate attempt to strike Labour a deadly blow through its most energetic and uncompromising representatives. We expected a concerted response in behalf of the accused from the liberal and radical elements, regardless of political differences. Instead we were confronted by complete silence on the part of the very people who had for years known and collaborated with Mooney, Nolan, and their fellow-prisoners.

The McNamara confession was still haunting, ghostlike, the waking and sleeping hours of their erstwhile friends among the labour politicians. There was not a single prominent man in the unions on the Coast who now dared speak up for his arrested brothers. There was no one to offer a penny for their defence. Not one word appeared even in *Organized Labor,* the organ of the powerful building trades, of which Olaf Tweetmore was editor. Not a word in the *Labor Clarion,* the official weekly of the San Francisco Labor Council and of the State Federation of Labor. Even Fremont Older, who had so staunchly defended the McNamaras and who had always bravely championed every unpopular cause, was silent now, in the face of the evident Chamber of Commerce conspiracy to hang innocent men.

It was a desperate situation. Only Sasha and I dared speak up for the prisoners. But we were known as anarchists and it was a question whether the accused, of whom only Israel was an anarchist, would wish to have us affiliated with their defence; they might feel that our names would hurt their case rather than do them good. I myself knew them but slightly, and Warren K. Billings I had never met. But we could not sit by idly and be a party to the conspiracy of silence. We should have come to their assistance even if we had thought them guilty of the charges, but Sasha knew all of the accused well and he was absolutely certain of their innocence. He considered none of them capable of throwing a bomb into a crowd of people. His assurance was sufficient guarantee for me that they had had no connexion whatever with the preparedness-parade explosion.

During the two weeks following the tragedy of July 22 the *Blast* and my meetings were the only expression of protest against the terrorist campaign carried on by the local authorities, at the behest of the Chamber of Commerce. Robert Minor, summoned by Sasha from Los Angeles, came to help in our preparations for the defence of the accused innocent men.

Ben, who had arrived from New York upon the completion of his prison term, was violently opposed to my remaining in San Francisco to finish my lecture series. My meetings were under police surveillance, the hall filled with hordes of detectives, whose presence kept my audiences away. He could not stand defeat; the mere handful of faithful friends in our hall, holding a thousand, was too much for him. Something else also seemed to be on his mind. He was more than usually restless and he besought me to discontinue my lectures and leave the city. But I could not go back on my engagements and I stayed on. I succeeded in raising at my meetings a hundred dollars and in borrowing a considerable sum for the defence of the arrested labour men. But so terrified was San Francisco that no attorney of standing would accept the case of the prisoners, who had already been condemned by every paper in the city.

It required several weeks of the most strenuous effort on our part to awaken some semblance of interest even among the radicals. With Sasha, Bob Minor, and Fitzi in charge of the activities, I now felt free to continue my tour, though I was very uneasy about their own fate.

The *Blast's* unconditional support of Mooney and his comrades had already subjected Sasha and his associates, Fitzi and our good " Swede " Carl, to the scrutiny of the police authorities. Some days after the explosion, detectives had forcibly entered the *Blast* office and had for hours ransacked it, taking away everything they could lay their hands on, including the California subscription list of *Mother Earth*. They had taken Sasha and Fitzi to headquarters, severely grilled them on their activities, and threatened to arrest them.

The sublime and the ridiculous often overlap each other. At the height of all the worry and anxiety about the San Francisco situation, while on my way to Portland with Ben, he was seized with one of his periodic fits to " nurse his soul, tabulate his ideas, and get acquainted with himself." His plaint was again that he could not continue for ever a " mere office boy," carrying bundles and selling literature; he had other ambitions; he wanted to write. He had wanted to write all along, he said, but I had never given him the chance. Sasha, he declared, was my god, Sasha's life and work my religion. In every difficulty that had arisen between him and Sasha I had always sided with the latter, he said. Ben had never been permitted his way in anything; I had even denied him his longing for a child. He insisted he had not forgotten that I had told him I had made my choice and that I could not allow a child to handicap my work in the movement. My attitude had hung over him like a pall, he declared, and it had made him afraid to confess that he had been living with another girl. His yearning for a child, always very strong, had become more compelling since he had met that girl. During his imprisonment in the Queens County Jail he had determined to allow nothing to stand in the way of the fulfilment of his great wish.

" But you have a child," I said, " your little Helen! Have you ever shown paternal love for her, or even the least interest, except on Valentine's Day, when I would pick out your cards for her? "

He was only a mere youth when the child was born, he replied; and the whole thing had been an accident. Now he was thirty-eight, with a " conscious feeling for fatherhood."

I knew there was no use in arguing. Unlike his confession in the first year of our love, which had struck me like a bolt of lightning out of a clear sky, this new disclosure hardly shocked or wounded me. The other had left scars too deep to heal or ever to allow me freedom from doubt. I had always guessed his deceptions; so accurately, indeed, that he called me a Sherlock Holmes " from whose eyes nothing is hidden."

Peculiar irony of circumstances! In New York Ben had started a " Sunday-school class," which exposed me to the ridicule of my comrades. " A Sunday-school in an anarchist office! " they laughed; " Jesus in the sanctum of the atheist." I sided with Ben. Free speech included his right to Jesus, I said. I knew that Ben was no more a Christian than the millions of others who proclaim themselves followers of the Nazarene. It was rather the personality of the " Son of Man " that appealed to Ben, as it had ever since his early youth. His religious sentimentalism would do no thinking person any harm, I thought. Most of his Sunday-school pupils were girls who were much more attracted to their teacher than to his Lord. I felt that Ben's religious emotionalism was stronger than his anarchistic convictions, and I could not deny him his right of expression.

To maintain consistency in a world of crass contradictions is not easy, and I had frequently been anything but consistent in regard to Ben. His love-affairs with all sorts of women had caused me too many emotional upheavals to allow me to act always in consonance with my ideas. Time, however, is a great leveller of feeling. I no longer cared about Ben's erotic adventures, and his newest confession did not affect me deeply. But it was indeed the height of tragicomedy that my stand in favour of Ben's Sunday-school in the *Mother Earth* office should result in an affair with one of his girl pupils. And then my anxiety about leaving Ben in the jail and going on tour without him at the very time he was absorbed in his new obsession! It was all so absurd and grotesque — I felt unutterably weary and possessed only of a desire to get away somewhere and forget the failure of my personal life, to forget even the cruel urge to struggle for an ideal.

I decided to go to Provincetown for a month, to visit with Stella and her baby. With them I would rest and perhaps find peace, peace.

Stella a mother! It seemed such a short while since she herself had been a little baby, the one ray of sunshine in my bleak Rochester days. When she was about to give birth to her child, I longed to be with her in that supreme moment. Instead I had been obliged to lecture in Philadelphia, while my heart palpitated with anxiety for my dear Stella in the throes of bringing forth new life. Time had passed with giant strides, and now I beheld Stella radiant in her young motherhood, and her little one, six months old, a striking replica of what my niece had looked at that age.

The charm of Provincetown, Stella's care, and the baby's loveliness filled my visit with a delight I had not known in years. There was also Teddy Ballantine, Stella's husband, a man of fine texture, vital and interesting, and the frequent calls of persons of outstanding individuality, such as Susan Glaspell, George Cram Cook, and my old friends Hutch Hapgood and Neith Boyce, the latter a most intriguing personality. There were also John Reed and adventurous Louise Bryant, more sophisticated than she had been in Portland two years before. There was beautiful Mary Pine, already doomed by consumption, her transparent skin and the lustre of her eyes heightened by a mass of copper hair. There was crude Harry Kemp, comically clumsy and awkward alongside of ethereal Mary. Variegated in mind and heart was that Provincetown group, and its company stimulating, but no one exerted such a restful effect on me as did Max, who had come at my invitation to spend a few weeks with me. He had remained unchanged, his fine spirit and intuitive understanding even more mellowed with the years. Kind and wise, he always found the right word to soothe distress. An hour with him was like a spring day, and I found solace and peace at his side. A month spent with him, in the circle of Stella's little family, would make me strong to conquer the world.

Alas, there was no month and no conquest! The eternal struggle for liberty was calling. Letters and telegrams from Sasha cried for help to save the five lives endangered in San Francisco. Could I think of rest, he indignantly demanded, while Tom Mooney and his comrades were facing death? Had I forgotten San Francisco, the terrorized prejudice against the victims in jail there, the cowardice of the labour leaders, the lack of funds for the defence of the prisoners, and the impossibility of securing a good lawyer for them? A note of desperation, unusual with Sasha, sounded in his letters, and he besought me to return to New York to secure for the defence a man prominent in the legal profession. That failing, I should go to Kansas City and try to prevail upon Frank P. Walsh to take the case.

My peace was gone; the forces of reaction had broken in on my golden freedom and had robbed me of the rest I needed so much. I even resented Sasha's strange impatience, but somehow I felt guilty. I was tormented by the feeling that I had broken faith with the victims of a social system which I had fought for twenty-seven years. Days of inner conflict and of galling indecision followed. Then came Sasha's telegram informing me that Billings had been convicted and sentenced to prison for life. There was no more hesitancy on my part. I prepared to leave for New York.

On the last day of my Provincetown stay I went for a walk with Max across the dunes. The tide was out. The sun hung like a golden disk, no ripple on the transparent blue of the ocean in the distance. The sand seemed a sheet of white stretched far out and disappearing into the coloured crystal of the waters. Nature breathed repose and wondrous peace. My mind, too, was at rest; peace had come with my resolve. Max was frolicsome, and I felt in tune with his mood. We slowly made our way across the vast expanse towards the sea. Oblivious of the world of strife outside, we were held rapt by the spell of the enchantment around us. Fishermen returning laden with their spoils recalled us to the lateness of the day. With light step we started on our way back, our gay song ringing in the air.

We were barely half-way across to the beach when we caught the sound of gurgling water rising from somewhere. Sudden apprehension silenced our song. We turned to look back, and then Max gripped my hand and we ran for the shore. The tide was welling in with a fast sweep. It rose from a cove that emptied into the sea at that point. It was already close behind us, the waves rushing over the sand with increasing speed and volume. The terror of being caught drove us on. Now and then our feet would sink in the soft sand, but the foaming peril at our back kept steeling the instinctive will to live.

Terrified, we reached the bottom of a hill. With a last effort we scrambled up and fell exhausted on the green soil. We were safe at last!

On our way to New York we stopped off in Concord. I had always wanted to visit the home of America's past cultural epoch. The museum, the historic houses, and the cemetery were the only remaining witnesses of its days of glory. The inhabitants gave little indication that the quaint old town had once been a centre of poetry, letters, and philosophy. There was no sign that men and women had existed in Concord to whom liberty was a living ideal. The present reality was more ghostlike than the dead.

We visited Frank B. Sanborn, the biographer of Henry David Thoreau, the last of the great Concord circle. It was Sanborn who, half a century before, had introduced John Brown to Thoreau, Emerson, and Alcott. He looked the typical aristocrat of intellect, his manner simple and gracious. With evident pride he spoke of the days when together with his sister he had, at the point of a gun, driven the tax-collectors from his homestead. He talked with reverence of Thoreau, the great lover of man and of beast, the rebel against the encroachments of the State on the rights of the individual, the supporter of John Brown when even his own friends had denied him. In detail Sanborn described to us the meeting Thoreau had carried through in memory of the black man's champion, in spite of almost unanimous opposition from the Concord coterie.

Sanborn's estimate of Thoreau bore out my conception of the latter as the precursor of anarchism in the United States. To my surprise, Thoreau's biographer was scandalized at my remark. " No, indeed! " he cried; " anarchism means violence and revolution. It means Czolgosz. Thoreau was an extreme non-resistant." We spent several hours trying to enlighten this contemporary of the most anarchistic period of American thought about the meaning of anarchism.

From Provincetown I had written Frank P. Walsh about the San Francisco situation, telling him that I would go to Kansas City to talk the matter over further if there was any chance of his taking charge of the Mooney defence. His reply awaited me in New York. He could not accept my suggestion, Walsh wrote; he was involved in an important criminal case in his own city, and he had also undertaken to line up the liberal elements in the East for the Woodrow Wilson campaign. He was of course interested in the San Francisco labour cases, his letter continued; he would soon be in New York and take the question up with me; perhaps he would be able to make some useful suggestions.

Frank P. Walsh was the most vital person I had met in Kansas City. He did not flaunt his radicalism in public, but he could always be depended upon to aid an unpopular cause. By nature he was a fighter; his sympathies were with the persecuted. I was aware of his interest in the labour struggle, and his letter therefore greatly disappointed me. Moreover, it was puzzling. If he could come to New York to take charge of the Wilson campaign, he could not be so tied up at home. Or did he consider electioneering more important than the five lives in peril on the Coast, I wondered. I was sure he was not familiar with the real state of affairs in San Francisco, and I decided to put the situation clearly before him. Perhaps it would induce him to change his mind.

At the Wilson campaign headquarters in New York, presided over by Frank P. Walsh, George West, and other intellectuals, I had a long talk with Walsh about the Mooney case. He seemed much impressed and he assured me that he would like to step in and do something for the prisoners. It was a serious situation, he said, but a far graver issue was facing the country — the war. The militarist elements were anxious for Wilson to get out of office so they could have their own man as President. It was up to all liberal-minded and peace-loving persons to re-elect Woodrow Wilson, Walsh emphasized. Even the anarchists, he thought, ought to set aside at this crucial moment their objections to participation in politics and help keep Wilson in the White House because " he has kept us out of war so far." It was my duty in particular, Walsh insisted, not to neglect the chance to demonstrate that my efforts against war were not mere talk. I could effectively silence the charge that I preached violence and destruction by proving that I was indeed the true champion of peace.

I was not a little surprised to find Frank P. Walsh such a defender of politics, after the very decided stand he had taken in behalf of the Mexican Revolution. I had once gone to Kansas City to solicit his contribution to that struggle, and he had eagerly responded, at the same time expressing his belief that action speaks louder than words. It was a far cry indeed from that attitude to his present notion that investing Woodrow Wilson with more political power would " save the world."

I left Walsh with a feeling of impatience at the credulity of this radically minded man and his co-workers in the Wilson campaign. It was an additional proof to me of the political blindness and social muddle-headedness of American liberals.

I knew no one in the New York legal profession whom I could approach in connexion with the Mooney case. I therefore had to inform Sasha of my failure. He replied that he himself was coming to New York to see what could be done. The International Workers' Defence League of San Francisco had requested him to go east to secure an able attorney and to rouse the labour elements to the peril of the arrested men.

In the latter part of October Bolton Hall's trial in connexion with our birth-control meeting at Union Square the previous May took place. A number of witnesses, including myself, testified that the defendant had given no contraceptive information on that occasion, and Bolton Hall was found not guilty. On leaving the court-room I was arrested on the same charge of which Hall had just been acquitted.

Persecution of birth-control advocates went merrily on. Margaret Sanger, her sister Ethel Byrne, a trained nurse, and their assistant, Fanya Mandell, were rounded up in a raid on Mrs. Sanger's clinic in Brooklyn. They had been tricked by a woman detective, who posed as the mother of four children, to give her contraceptives. Among the other cases were those of Jessie Ashley and of several I.W.W. boys. The guardians of law and morality throughout the country were determined to suppress the spread of information on birth-control.

The various hearings and trials in connexion with this matter proved that at least the judges were being educated. One of them declared that he distinguished between persons who gave out birth-control information free because of personal conviction and those who sold it. Certainly no such differentiation had been made previously, in William Sanger's case, in Ben's, or in mine. Even more striking proof that the agitation for family limitation was beginning to have an effect was given by Judge Wadhams during the trial of a woman charged with theft. Her husband, tubercular and out of work for a long time, was unable to support his large family. In summing up the causes that had led the prisoner to crime Judge Wadhams remarked that many nations in Europe had adopted birth-regulation with seemingly excellent results. " I believe we are living in an age of ignorance," he continued, " which at some future time will be looked upon aghast as we now look back on the dark ages. We have before us the case of a family increasing in numbers, with a tubercular husband, the woman with a child at her breast and with other small children at her skirts, in poverty and want."

We had reason to feel that it was worth going to jail if the urgency of limiting offspring was getting to be admitted even by the bench. Direct action, and not parlour discussion, was responsible for these results.

Early in November Sasha arrived in New York, and in less than two weeks he was able to rally to the support of the San Francisco fight nearly all of the organized Jewish labour, as well as a number of American trade unions. He was equally successful in his efforts to secure an attorney. By aid of some friends he prevailed upon W. Bourke Cockran, the famous lawyer and orator, to examine the transcript of the Billings case. Cockran was so impressed by Sasha's presentation of it and so aroused by the obvious frame-up that he offered to go to the Coast without a fee and take charge of the defence of Mooney, Nolan, and the other San Francisco prisoners. Sasha also prevailed upon the United Hebrew Trades, the largest and most influential central Jewish labour organization in the country, to call a mass meeting in Carnegie Hall to protest against the conspiracy of big business in California. The delegates of that body being fully occupied with their own duties, the entire brunt of organizing the mass meeting and securing speakers fell to Sasha and the active and efficient young comrades who were helping him in the campaign. Unfortunately, I could give him no assistance, owing to my lecture engagements in various points between New York and the Middle West. I promised, however, to speak at Carnegie Hall, even if it necessitated my return from Chicago to do so.

After seventeen lectures in that city and four in Milwaukee I hastened back to New York, arriving on the morning of December 2, the day of the big gathering. In the afternoon a demonstration took place on Union Square, a protest in favour of Mooney and his comrades and also in behalf of Carlo Tresca and his fellow victims of the Minnesota steel interests at the Mesaba Range strike. The evening meeting in Carnegie Hall was attended by a very large audience, which was addressed by Frank P. Walsh, Max Eastman, Max Pine, secretary of the Hebrew Trades, Arturo Giovannitti, poet and labour leader, Sasha, and myself. It fell to me to make the appeal for funds, and the assembly generously responded with aid for the Californians' defence. The same night I left for the West to continue my interrupted tour.

At my lecture in Cleveland on " Family Limitation " Ben conceived the idea of calling for volunteers to distribute birth-control pamphlets. A number of people responded. At the end of the meeting Ben was arrested. A hundred persons, each carrying the forbidden pamphlet, followed him to the jail, but only Ben was held for trial. We immediately organized a Free Speech League, which combined with the local birth-control organization to fight the case.

Cleveland had for years been a free-speech stronghold, owing to the libertarian conditions established there by the single-tax mayor, the late Tom Johnson. Brave citizens of different political views had since zealously guarded those liberties. Among them I had many friends, but none more helpful than Mr. and Mrs. Carr, Fred Shoulder, Adeleine Champney, and our old philosopher Jacobs. They had always exerted themselves to make my public work successful and to enhance my leisure hours by charming fellowship. It was therefore a severe shock to see this exceptional city go back on its traditions. But the ready response to our call to organize a fight against the suppression held out the hope that the right of free expression would again prevail in Tom Johnson's home town.

Similar experiences attended my lectures in various cities, as well as those of other advocates of family limitation. Sometimes it was Ben who was arrested, at other times I and the friends who were actively co-operating with us, or other lecturers who were trying to enlighten the people on the proscribed issue. In San Francisco the *Blast* was held up by the post-office on account of an article on birth-control and because of *lèse-majesté* against Woodrow Wilson. Birth-control had become a burning issue, and the authorities exerted every effort to silence its advocates. Nor did they shrink from foul means to accomplish their ends. In Rochester Ben was arrested for having sold at one of our meetings a copy of Dr. William J. Robinson's *Family Limitation* and Margaret Sanger's pamphlet *What Every Woman Should Know*. The arresting officers were seemingly ignorant that those publications were being openly sold in book-shops. But it soon appeared that there was method in their madness. At the police station a pamphlet on contraceptives was "found" between the pages of Dr. Robinson's book. We knew some detective had placed it there to "get" Ben. And, indeed, he was held for trial.

While still on tour, I received a telegram from Harry Weinberger, my New York attorney, informing me that I had been denied a jury trial. On January 8 my case came up before three judges. Presiding Judge Cullen warned me severely that he would not permit any theories of the defendant to be aired in court. But he might have saved himself the trouble, because my case collapsed before either my lawyer or I had a chance to say anything. The evidence given by the detectives to the effect that I had distributed birth-control pamphlets on Union Square in May was so obviously contradictory that even the Court refused to take it seriously. I was acquitted.

Ben was not so fortunate, however, in regard to the Cleveland charge against him. He had been subpœnaed for my trial, and as his own was to take place the following day, he had wired his Cleveland attorney and bondsman to secure a postponement. They replied that he need have no anxiety, and that they would get him an extension of time. To make doubly sure, Ben telegraphed and also sent a copy of the subpœna to the Cleveland court. But on the afternoon of January 9 he received word from his lawyer, informing him that, far from consenting to a postponement, Judge Dan Cull had issued a warrant for Ben's arrest for contempt of court. Ben took the first train to Cleveland. The next morning his case was called. Judge Cull "graciously" consented to dismiss the charge of contempt of court and to try Ben only on the birth-control case. The Judge was a Roman Catholic and rigidly opposed to any form of sex hygiene. He talked at length about the carnal sins of the flesh and denounced birth-control and anarchism. Of the twelve jurymen five were Catholics. The others were apparently loath to convict, for they held out for thirteen hours without coming to an agreement. The Court sent them back, however, with instructions to remain out until they could bring in a verdict. Long hours in a stuffy room will cause most juries to grow unanimous. Ben was found guilty and sentenced to six months in the workhouse and to pay a thousand dollars' fine. It was the heaviest penalty imposed for a birth-control offence. Ben made a frank avowal of his belief in family limitation, and on the advice of counsel he appealed the case.

The result of the trial was due mainly to the absence of proper publicity. Margaret Sanger had lectured in the city a short time previously, and it had been expected that she would take note of the situation and urge her hearers to rally to Ben's support. Her refusal to do so had incensed our friends at the inexcusable breach of solidarity, but unfortunately no time had been left to arouse public sentiment in regard to Ben's case.

It was not the first occasion on which Mrs. Sanger had failed to aid birth-control advocates caught in the meshes of the law. While my trial in New York was pending, she was touring the country and lecturing at meetings arranged by our comrades, largely at my suggestion. Strange to say, Mrs. Sanger, who had begun her birth-control work in our quarters on One Hundred and Nineteenth Street, would not even mention my approaching trial. Once, at a meeting in the Bandbox Theatre, she was called to account for her silence by Robert Minor. She upbraided him for daring to interfere with her affairs.

In Chicago Ben Capes had to resort to questions from the floor during a meeting to compel Mrs. Sanger to refer to my work for birth-control. Similar occurrences happened in Detroit, Denver, and San Francisco. From numerous places friends wrote me that Mrs Sanger had given the impression that she considered the issue as her own private concern. Subsequently Mr. and Mrs. Sanger publicly repudiated birth-control leagues organized by us, as well as our entire campaign for family limitation.

The lack of backing for Ben in Cleveland taught us the need of an organized protest in connexion with his coming trial in Rochester. On the eve of it a large meeting took place, the local speaker, Dr. Mary E. Dickinson, sharing the platform with Dolly Sloan, Ida Rauh, and Harry Weinberger, all of whom had come from New York for the occasion. The next day an effective demonstration was staged in court. Willis K. Gillette proved to be a very exceptional judge. I almost envied Ben the opportunity of being tried before a man who believed that the court is a place where the defendant should feel unafraid to speak out. With such a judge and with the fighting persistency of an attorney like Harry Weinberger, Ben was sure of fair treatment. He declared that he did not believe in the law that forbids giving birth-control information. He had broken it before and he would do it again, he said. But in the case on trial he was innocent, he maintained, because he did not know how the contraceptive pamphlet had happened to be in Dr. Robinson's book. He was acquitted.

We felt that we had reason for some satisfaction with our share in the campaign. We had presented the ideas of family limitation throughout the length and breadth of the country, bringing the knowledge of methods into the lives of the people who needed them most. We were ready now to leave the field to those who were proclaiming birth-control as the only panacea for all social ills. I myself had never considered it in that light; it was unquestionably an important issue, but by no means the most vital one.

In San Francisco the *Blast* had been suppressed and its office raided twice because of the paper's anti-war work and its efforts in behalf of Mooney. During the last raid Fitzi was brutally handled and her arm almost broken by an official ruffian. It became impossible to continue the publication on the Coast, and Fitzi brought it to New York, where she joined Sasha in his activities for the California defence.

Tom Mooney had been convicted and sentenced to death. Neither the eloquence of W. Bourke Cockran, nor the absolute demonstration that the leading witnesses of the prosecution had perjured themselves availed anything. The grip of the Chamber of Commerce upon official justice in California proved to be stronger than the most unshakable evidence in favour of the labour defendant. There was hardly a citizen in San Francisco who did not know that the State's witnesses, the McDonalds and the Oxmans, were of the very dregs of debased humanity, their testimony bought and paid for by District Attorney Charles Fickert, the willing tool of the employers. But innocence did not count. The bosses who had declared themselves for the " open shop " had determined to hang Tom Mooney, as a warning to other labour organizers, and Mooney's doom was sealed.

Nor was the State of California the only section of the country where law and order had centred all their might to crush the workers and effectively stifle further protest on the part of the disinherited and humiliated. In Everett, Washington, seventy-four I.W.W. boys were fighting for their lives, and in every other State of the Union the jails and prisons were filled with men convicted for their ideals.

The political sky in the United States was darkening with heavy clouds, and the portents were daily growing more disquieting, yet the masses at large remained inert. Then, unexpectedly, the light of hope broke in the east. It came from Russia, the land tsar-ridden for centuries. The day so long yearned for had arrived at last — the Revolution had come!

CHAPTER XLV

THE HATED ROMANOVS WERE AT LAST HURLED FROM THEIR throne, the Tsar and his cohorts shorn of power. It was not the result of a political *coup d'état;* the great achievement was accomplished by the rebellion of the entire people. Only yesterday inarticulate, crushed, as they had been for centuries, under the heel of a ruthless absolutism, insulted and degraded, the Russian masses had risen to demand their heritage and to proclaim to the whole world that autocracy and tyranny were for ever at an end in their country. The glorious tidings were the first sign of life in the vast European cemetery of war and destruction. They inspired all liberty-loving people with new hope and enthusiasm, yet no one felt the spirit of the Revolution as did the natives of Russia scattered all over the globe. They saw their beloved *Matushka Rossiya* now extend to them the promise of manhood and aspiration.

Russia was free; yet not truly so. Political independence was but the first step on the road to the new life. Of what use are " rights," I thought, if the economic conditions remain unchanged. I had known the blessings of democracy too long to have faith in political scene-shifting. Far more abiding was my faith in the people themselves, in the Russian masses now awakened to the consciousness of their power and to the realization of their opportunities. The imprisoned and exiled martyrs who had struggled to free Russia were now being resurrected, and some of their dreams realized. They were returning from the icy wastes of Siberia, from dungeons and banishment. They were coming back to unite with the people and to help them build a new Russia, economically and socially.

America also was contributing its quota. At the first news of the Tsar's overthrow thousands of exiles hastened back to their native country, now the Land of Promise. Many had lived in the United

States for decades and acquired families and homes. But their hearts dwelt more in Russia than in the country they were enriching by their labour, which nevertheless scorned them as " foreigners." Russia was welcoming them, her doors wide open to receive her sons and daughters. Like swallows at the first sign of spring they began to fly back, orthodox and revolutionists for once on common ground — their love and longing for their native soil.

Our own old yearning, Sasha's and mine, began to stir again in our hearts. All through the years we had been close to the pulse of Russia, close to her spirit and her superhuman struggle for liberation. But our lives were rooted in our adopted land. We had learned to love her physical grandeur and her beauty and to admire the men and women who were fighting for freedom, the Americans of the best calibre. I felt myself one of them, an American in the truest sense, spiritually rather than by the grace of a mere scrap of paper. For twenty-eight years I had lived, dreamed, and worked for that America. Sasha, too, was torn between the urge to return to Russia and the necessity of continuing his campaign to save the life of Mooney, whose fatal hour was fast approaching. Could he forsake the doomed man and the others whose fate hung in the balance?

Then came Wilson's decision that the United States must join the European slaughter to make the world safe for democracy. Russia had great need of her revolutionary exiles, but Sasha and I now felt that America needed us more. We decided to remain.

The declaration of war by the United States dismayed and over-awed most of the middle-class pacifists. Some even suggested that we terminate our anti-militarist activities. A certain woman, a member of the Colony Club of New York, who had repeatedly offered to supply money for anti-war work in the European countries now demanded that we discontinue our agitation. Having declined her previous offers, I felt free to tell her that true charity begins at home. I could see no reason for giving up the stand on war that I had maintained for a quarter of a century, just because Woodrow Wilson had tired of his watchful waiting. I could not alter my convictions merely because he had ceased to be " too proud " to let American boys do the fighting, while he and other statesmen remained at home.

With the collapse of the pseudo-radicals the entire burden of anti-war activity fell upon the more courageous militant elements. Our group in particular redoubled its efforts, and I was kept feverishly busy travelling between New York and nearby cities, speaking and organizing the campaign.

A contingent of Russian exiles and refugees was preparing to leave for their native land, and we helped to equip its members with provisions, clothing, and money. Most of them were anarchists, and all of them were eager to participate in the upbuilding of their country on a foundation of human brotherhood and equality. The work of organizing the return to Russia was in charge of our comrade William Shatoff, familiarly known as Bill.

This revolutionary anarchist, compelled to take refuge in America from the tyranny of the Russian autocracy, had during his ten years' sojourn in the United States shared the life of the true proletarian and was always in the thick of the struggle for the betterment of the workers' condition. Having worked as a labourer, longshoreman, machinist, and printer, Bill was familiar with the hardships, insecurity, and humiliation that characterize the existence of the immigrant toiler. Many a weaker man would have perished spiritually, but Bill had the vision of an ideal, an inexhaustible energy, and a keen intellect. He devoted his life to the enlightenment of the Russian refugees. He was a splendid organizer, an eloquent speaker, and a man of courage. These qualities enabled him to gather into one great body the various small groups of Russians in America. He was eminently successful in helping to weld them into a powerful and solidaric organization, known as the Union of Russian Workers, which embraced the United States and Canada. Its aim was the education and revolutionary development of the vast numbers of Russian workers whom the Greek Catholic Church in America sought to ensnare, as it had done at home. Bill Shatoff and the comrades active with him had for years worked to awaken their dark Russian brothers to their economic situation and to enlighten them on the importance of organized co-operation. Most of them were unskilled men, labouring long hours and ruthlessly exploited at most arduous toil in mines and mills and on the railroads. Thanks to Bill's energy and devotion, these masses were gradually united into a strong body of rebels.

Shatoff was also for a time manager of the Ferrer Center, and in that capacity his intelligence and enthusiasm proved as efficient as in everything else he undertook.

No less fine was our Bill in the personal relationships of life. Charming and jovial, he was a splendid companion, dependable in every emergency and especially in difficult situations. A staunch and brave friend, Bill insisted on accompanying Sasha when the latter was in danger of attack by San Francisco detectives because of his work in behalf of Mooney. On Sasha's journey to various cities Bill acted as his self-constituted body-guard, and it afforded me great relief to know that any person attempting to do violence to Sasha would meet with the additional resistance of our stout-hearted Bill.

With the first news of the miracle that had taken place in Russia, Shatoff began organizing the thousands of his radical compatriots eager to return home. Like a true captain of a ship he had determined to see everyone safely on his way, without thought of himself. He would go last, he told us, when we urged that his experience and abilities would be more valuable in Russia than in America. He remained until his own departure had grown almost perilous.

I had known for some time of the presence in New York of Mme Alexandra Kolontay and Leon Trotsky. From the former I had received several letters and a copy of her book on woman's share in the world's work. She had asked me to meet her, but I had been unable to spare the time. Later on I had invited her to dinner, but she was prevented by illness from coming. Leon Trotsky I had also never met before, but I happened to be in the city when an announcement was made of a farewell meeting which he was to address before leaving for Russia. I attended the gathering. After several rather dull speakers Trotsky was introduced. A man of medium height, with haggard cheeks, reddish hair, and straggling red beard stepped briskly forward. His speech, first in Russian and then in German, was powerful and electrifying. I did not agree with his political attitude; he was a Menshevik (Social Democrat), and as such far removed from us. But his analysis of the causes of the war was brilliant, his denunciation of the ineffective Provisional Government in Russia scathing, and his presentation of the conditions that led up to the Revolution illuminating. He closed his two hours' talk with an eloquent tribute to the working masses of his native land. The audience was roused to a high pitch of enthusiasm, and Sasha and I heartily joined in the ovation given the speaker. We fully shared his profound faith in the future of Russia.

After the meeting we met Trotsky to bid him good-bye. He knew about us and he inquired when we meant to come to Russia to help in the work of reconstruction. "We will surely meet there," he remarked.

I discussed with Sasha the unexpected turn of events that made us feel closer to Trotsky, the Menshevik, than to Peter Kropotkin, our comrade, teacher, and friend. The war was producing strange bedfellows, and we wondered whether we should still feel near to Trotsky when in the course of time we should reach Russia, for we had only postponed, not given up, our return there.

Shortly after Trotsky's departure the first group of our comrades sailed. We gave them a joyous send-off at a large party attended by many of our American friends, who also generously contributed to the needs of the men. Sasha had conceived the idea of a manifesto to the Russian workers, peasants, and soldiers, and we wrote it just in time to send it with the group. Among them were a number of men and women who had worked with us in our various campaigns in the *Blast* and *Mother Earth*. The manifesto was entrusted to Louise Berger and S.F., our closest and most dependable friends. It was an appeal to the masses of Russia to voice their protest to Washington against the condemnation of Tom Mooney and Warren K. Billings. We thought it the only method left to save the innocently convicted men.

In the spirit of her military preparations America was rivalling the most despotic countries of the Old World. Conscription, resorted to by Great Britain only after eighteen months of war, was decided upon by Wilson within one month after the United States had decided to enter the European conflict. Washington was not so squeamish about the rights of its citizens as the British Parliament had been. The academic author of *The New Freedom* did not hesitate to destroy every democratic principle at one blow. He had assured the world that America was moved by the highest humanitarian motives, her aim being to democratize Germany. What if he had to Prussianize the United States in order to achieve it? Free-born Americans had to be forcibly pressed into the military mould, herded like cattle, and shipped across the waters to fertilize the fields of France. Their sacrifice would earn them the glory of having demonstrated the superiority of *My Country, 'Tis of Thee* over *Die Wacht am Rhein*. No American president had ever before succeeded in so humbugging the people as Woodrow Wilson, who wrote and talked democracy, acted despotically, privately and officially, and yet managed to keep up the myth that he was championing humanity and freedom.

We had no illusions about the outcome of the conscription bill pending before Congress. We regarded the measure as a complete denial of every human right, the death-knell to liberty of conscience, and we determined to fight it unconditionally. We did not expect to be able to stem the tidal wave of hatred and violence which compulsory service was bound to bring, but we felt that we had at least to make known at large that there were some in the United States who owned their souls and who meant to preserve their integrity, no matter what the cost.

We decided to call a conference in the *Mother Earth* office to broach the organization of a No-Conscription League and draw up a manifesto to clarify to the people of America the menace of conscription. We also planned a large mass meeting as a protest against compelling American men to sign their own death-warrants in the form of forced military registration.

Because of previously arranged lecture dates in Springfield, Massachusetts, I was unfortunately not able to be present at the conference, set for May 9. But as Sasha, Fitzi, Leonard D. Abbott, and other clear-headed friends would attend, I felt no anxiety about the outcome. It was suggested that the conference should take up the question of whether the No-Conscription League should urge men not to register. *En route* to Springfield I wrote a short statement giving my attitude on the matter. I sent it with a note to Fitzi asking her to read it at the gathering. I took the position that, as a woman and therefore myself not subject to military service, I could not advise people on the matter. Whether or not one is to lend oneself as a tool for the business of killing should properly be left to the individual conscience. As an anarchist I could not presume to decide the fate of others, I wrote. But I could say to those who refused to be coerced into military service that I would plead their cause and stand by their act against all odds.

By the time I returned from Springfield the No-Conscription League had been organized and the Harlem River Casino rented for a mass meeting to take place on May 18. Those who had participated at the conference had agreed with my attitude regarding registration.

In the midst of our activities Sasha met with a serious accident. I was living again in the little room behind the *Mother Earth* office in One Hundred and Twenty-fifth Street, while Sasha and Fitzi had moved the *Blast* to the room on the upper floor, formerly occupied by our friend Stewart Kerr. There was no telephone connexion in the house except in my office, and one day Sasha, hurrying to answer a call, slipped and fell down the whole length of the steep stairway. Upon examination the ligaments of his left foot were found torn, and a physician ordered him to bed. Sasha would not listen to it; with the amount of work on hand and with only a few comrades to look after it, he could not rest, he said. Though in great pain and able only to hop about on crutches, he was bent on attending the meeting at the Harlem River Casino.

On May 18 Fitzi and I resorted to every feminine trick we could think of to persuade our cripple to remain at home, but he insisted on coming with us. He was helped by two husky comrades down the stairs and lifted into a taxi, and the same performance was repeated later at the hall.

Almost ten thousand people filled the place, among them many newly rigged-out soldiers and their woman friends, a very boisterous lot indeed. Several hundred policemen and detectives were scattered through the hall. When the session opened, a few young " patriots " tried to rush the stage entrance. Their attempt was foiled, because we had prepared for such a contingency.

Leonard D. Abbott presided, and on the platform were Harry Weinberger, Louis Fraina, Sasha, myself, and a number of other opponents of forced military service. Men and women of varying political views supported our stand on this occasion. Every speaker vigorously denounced the conscription bill which was awaiting the President's signature. Sasha was particularly splendid. Resting his injured leg on a chair and supporting himself with one hand on the table, he breathed strength and defiance. Always a man of great self-control, his poise on this occasion was remarkable. No one in the vast audience could have guessed that he was in pain, or that he gave a single thought to his helpless condition if we should fail to carry the meeting to a peaceful end. With great clarity and sustained power Sasha spoke as I had never heard him before.

The future heroes were noisy all through the speeches, but when I stepped on the platform, pandemonium broke loose. They jeered and hooted, intoned *The Star-Spangled Banner,* and frantically waved small American flags. Above the din the voice of a recruit shouted: "I want the floor!" The patience of the audience had been sorely tried all evening by the interrupters. Now men rose from every part of the house and called to the disturber to shut up or be kicked out. I knew what such a thing would lead to, with the police waiting for a chance to aid the patriotic ruffians. Moreover, I did not want to deny free speech even to the soldier. Raising my voice, I appealed to the assembly to permit the man to speak. "We who have come here to protest against coercion and to demand the right to think and act in accordance with our consciences," I urged, "should recognize the right of an opponent to speak and we should listen quietly and grant him the respect we demand for ourselves. The young man no doubt believes in the justice of his cause as we do in ours, and he has pledged his life for it. I suggest therefore that we all rise in appreciation of his evident sincerity and that we hear him out in silence." The audience rose to a man.

The soldier had probably never before faced such a large assembly. He looked frightened and he began in a quavering voice that barely carried to the platform, although he was sitting near it. He stammered something about "German money" and "traitors," got confused, and came to a sudden stop. Then, turning to his comrades, he cried: "Oh, hell! Let's get out of here!" Out the whole gang slunk, waving their little flags and followed by laughter and applause.

Returning from the meeting home we heard newsboys shouting extra night editions — the conscription bill had become a law! Registration day was set for June 4. The thought struck me that on that day American democracy would be carried to its grave.

We felt that May 18 was the beginning of a period of historic importance. To Sasha and myself the day had also a profound personal meaning. It was the twelfth anniversary of his resurrection from the Western Penitentiary of Pennsylvania, the first time in years that he and I were together in the same city and on the same platform.

Streams of callers besieged our office from morning till late at night; young men, mostly, seeking advice on whether they should register. We knew, of course, that among them were also decoys sent to trick us into saying that they should not. The majority, however, were frightened youths, fearfully wrought up and at sea as to what to do.

They were helpless creatures about to be sacrificed to Moloch. Our sympathies were with them, but we felt that we had no right to decide the vital issue for them. There were also distracted mothers, imploring us to save their boys. By the hundreds they came, wrote, or telephoned. All day long our telephone rang; our offices were filled with people, and stacks of mail arrived from every part of the country asking for information about the No-Conscription League, pledging support and urging us to go on with the work. In this bedlam we had to prepare copy for the current issues of *Mother Earth* and the *Blast,* write our manifesto, and send out circulars announcing our forthcoming meeting. At night, when trying to get some sleep, we would be rung out of bed by reporters wanting to know our next step.

Anti-conscription meetings were also taking place outside of New York and I was busy organizing branches of the No-Conscription League. At such a gathering in Philadelphia the police came down with drawn clubs and threatened to beat up the audience if I dared mention conscription. I proceeded to talk about the freedom the masses in Russia had gained. At the close of the meeting fifty persons retired to a private place, where we organized a No-Conscription League. Similar experiences were repeated in many cities.

A week after the Harlem River Casino meeting I received a telegram from Tom Mooney indicating the hoplessness of further legal proceedings in his case and urging an appeal to the people of the country. His telegram read:

San Francisco
May 25, 1917

Superior Court today held Oxman for trial. Chief Justice Angellotti said evidence of Oxman's guilt overwhelming. Special committee appointed by San Francisco Labor Council and Building Trades Council appeared in person before Attorney General Webb requesting answer on his disposition of Judge Griffin's request confessing error in my case. Attorney General said that records did not show error and it would be impossible confess same.

Powerful publicity, monster demonstrations, absolutely necessary for successful outcome. California lynch-law crowd fighting desperately to save themselves.

This precludes new trial unless the unforeseen happens. Give these facts wide publicity.

Tom Mooney

The conviction of Warren K. Billings, in spite of absolute proof of his innocence, had caused the defence to investigate the witnesses for the prosecution. Virtually every one of them was proved to be a tool of District Attorney Charles Fickert, and several confessed that their testimony for the State was purchased by threats and bribery. The jury also was found to have been tampered with by agents of the Chamber of Commerce. It was too late to save Billings, but it warned the defence of what it had to expect in the trial of Tom Mooney.

Fickert realized that some of his old witnesses, exposed as perjurers and professional prostitutes, could not be used against Mooney. He therefore prepared others of a similar calibre, the star among them being a certain Frank C. Oxman, an alleged Western cattleman. It was mainly on the evidence of Oxman that Mooney was convicted. He testified that he was in San Francisco on Preparedness Day, and he identified Mooney as the man whom he saw placing a suit-case (supposedly of explosives) on a street-corner along the route of the march. An investigation proved that Oxman had not been in San Francisco on the date of the parade. Moreover, a letter by Oxman to his friend F. E. Rigall was produced, in which Oxman urged him to earn " a piece of money " by coming to testify against Mooney. Rigall was at the time in Niagara Falls and had never been in San Francisco. The proof of Oxman's perjury was so overwhelming that District Attorney Fickert was compelled to bring him to trial.

Notwithstanding all these developments, in spite even of the admission of the trial judge, Franklin A. Griffin, that Mooney had been convicted on false testimony, the Supreme Court of California refused to intervene. Mooney was doomed to die!

The country-wide campaign that Sasha had started for Mooney almost a year previously had meanwhile borne fruit. The case had been taken up by radical and progressive labour organizations throughout the land, and many liberal organizations as well as influential individuals had become interested. Work to save the convicted man from the gallows continued without abatement.

At the peace meeting in Madison Square Garden, arranged jointly by the more radical anti-war organizations on June 1, several of our young comrades were arrested for distributing announcements for our Hunt's Point Palace meeting on June 4. Learning of it, we dispatched a letter to the District Attorney, taking entire responsibility for what the arrested boys had done. We pointed out that if it was a crime to give out the handbill, we, its authors, were the guilty persons. The letter was signed by Sasha and me, and we enclosed a special-delivery stamp for an immediate reply. But no answer came and no action was taken against us.

The arrested boys included Morris Becker, Louis Kramer, Joseph Walker, and Louis Sternberg. They were charged with conspiracy to advise people not to submit to the Conscription Law. Their trial took place before Federal Judge Julius M. Mayer. Kramer and Becker were convicted, the jury recommending clemency for the latter. The Judge's idea of clemency was a scurrilous denunciation of the defendants. He called Kramer a coward and gave him the limit of the law, two years in the Federal penitentiary at Atlanta and ten thousand dollars' fine. Becker received one year and eight months and was also condemned to pay a similar fine. The other two boys, Sternberg and Walker, were acquitted. Harry Weinberger had conducted their defence in his usual able way and he appealed their case. Louis Kramer, while in the Tombs awaiting transfer to Atlanta, refused to register for the draft and was sentenced to serve an additional year.

The June issue of *Mother Earth* appeared draped in black, its cover representing a tomb bearing the inscription: "IN MEMORIAM — AMERICAN DEMOCRACY." The sombre attire of the magazine was striking and effective. No words could express more eloquently the tragedy that turned America, the erstwhile torch-bearer of freedom, into a grave-digger of her former ideals.

We strained our capital to the last penny to issue an extra large edition. We wanted to mail copies to every Federal officer, to every editor, in the country and to distribute the magazine among young workers and college students. Our twenty thousand copies barely sufficed to supply our own needs. It made us feel our poverty more than ever before. Fortunately an unexpected ally came to our assistance: the New York newspapers! They had reprinted whole passages from our anti-conscription manifesto, some even reproducing the entire text and thus bringing it to the attention of millions of readers. Now they copiously quoted from our June issue and editorially commented at length on its contents.

The press throughout the country raved at our defiance of law and presidential orders. We duly appreciated their help in making our voices resound through the land, our voices that but yesterday had called in vain. Incidentally the papers also gave wide publicity to our meeting scheduled for June 4.

Our busy and exciting life was not conducive to Sasha's speedy recovery. He continued to suffer much pain and discomfort. Most of his writing had to be done in bed or with his leg perched up on a chair. He could barely hop about on crutches, but he was again adamant in his decision to attend the mass meeting. We knew he was suffering, but he cracked jokes and scolded Fitzi and me because we were making "too much fuss."

When we got within half a dozen blocks of Hunt's Point Palace, our taxi had to come to a stop. Before us was a human dam, as far as the eye could see, a densely packed, swaying mass, counting tens of thousands. On the outskirts were police on horse and on foot, and great numbers of soldiers in khaki. They were shouting orders, swearing, and pushing the crowd from the sidewalks to the street and back again. The taxi could not proceed, and it was hopeless to try to get Sasha to the hall on his crutches. We had to make a detour around vacant lots until we reached the back entrance of the Palace. There we came upon a score of patrol wagons armed with search-lights and machine-guns. The officers stationed at the stage door, failing to recognize us, refused to let us pass. A reporter who knew us whispered to the police sergeant in charge. "Oh, all right," he shouted, "but nobody else will be admitted. The place is overcrowded."

The sergeant had lied; the house was only half filled. The police were keeping the people from getting in, and at seven o'clock they had ordered the doors locked. While they were denying the right of entry to workers, they permitted scores of half-drunken sailors and soldiers to enter the hall. The balcony and the front seats were filled with them. They talked loudly, made vulgar remarks, jeered, hooted, and otherwise behaved as befits men who are preparing to make the world safe for democracy.

In the room behind the stage were officials from the Department of Justice, members of the Federal attorney's office, United States marshals, detectives from the "Anarchist Squad," and reporters. The scene looked as if set for bloodshed. The representatives of law and order were obviously keyed up for trouble.

Among the "alien enemies" in the hall and on the platform were men and women prominent in the field of education, art, and letters. One of them was the distinguished Irish rebel Mrs. Sheehy-Skeffington, the widow of the pacifist author murdered in the Dublin uprising the previous year. A lover of peace and an eloquent pleader for freedom and justice, she was a sweet and gentle soul. In her was personified the spirit of our gathering, the respect for human life and liberty that was seeking public expression that evening.

When the meeting was opened and Leonard D. Abbott took the chair, he was greeted by the soldiers and sailors with catcalls, whistles, and stamping of feet. This failing of the desired effect, the uniformed men in the gallery began throwing on the platform electric lamps which they had unscrewed from the fixtures. Several bulbs struck a vase holding a bunch of red carnations, sending vase and flowers crashing to the floor. Confusion followed, the audience rising in indignant protest and demanding that the police put the ruffians out. John Reed, who was with us, called on the police captain to order the disturbers removed, but that official declined to intervene.

After repeated appeals from the chairman, supported by some women in the audience, comparative quiet was restored. But not for long. Every speaker had to go through the same ordeal. Even the mothers of prospective soldiers, who poured out their anguish and wrath, were jeered by the savages in Uncle Sam's uniform.

Stella was one of the mothers to address the audience. It was the first time she had to face such an assembly and endure insults. Her own son was still too young to be subject to conscription, but she shared the woe and grief of other, less fortunate, parents, and she could articulate the protest of those who had no opportunity to speak. She held her own against the interruptions and carried the audience with her by the earnestness and fervour of her talk.

Sasha was the next speaker; others were to follow him, and I was to speak last. Sasha refused to be helped to the platform. Slowly and with great effort he managed to climb up the several steps and then walked across the stage to the chair placed for him near the footlights. Again, as on May 18, he had to stand on one leg, resting the other on the chair and supporting himself with one hand on the table. He stood erect, his head held high, his jaw set, his eyes clear and unflinchingly turned on the disturbers. The audience rose and greeted Sasha with prolonged applause, a token of their appreciation of his appearance in spite of his injury. The enthusiastic demonstration seemed to enrage the patriots, most of whom were obviously under the influence of drink. Renewed shouts, whistles, stamping, and hysterical cries of the women accompanying the soldiers greeted Sasha. Above the clamour a hoarse voice cried: "No more! We've had enough!" But Sasha would not be daunted. He began to speak, louder and louder, berating the hoodlums, now reasoning with them, now holding them up to scorn. His words seemed to impress them. They became quiet. Then, suddenly, a husky brute in front shouted: "Let's charge the platform! Let's get the slacker!" In an instant the audience were on their feet. Some ran up to grab the soldier. I rushed to Sasha's side. In my highest pitch I cried: "Friends, friends — wait, wait!" The suddenness of my appearance attracted everyone's attention. "The soldiers and sailors have been sent here to cause trouble," I admonished the people, "and the police are in league with them. If we lose our heads there will be bloodshed, and it will be our blood they will shed!" There were cries of "She's right!" "It's true!" I took advantage of the momentous pause. "Your presence here," I continued, "and the presence of the multitude outside shouting their approval of every word they can catch, are convincing proof that you do not believe in violence, and it equally proves that you understand that war is the most fiendish violence. War kills deliberately, ruthlessly, and destroys innocent lives. No, it is not we who have come to create a riot here. We must refuse to be provoked to it. Intelligence and a passionate faith are more convincing than armed police, machine-guns, and rowdies in soldiers' coats. We have demonstrated it tonight. We still have many speakers, some of them with illustrious American names. But nothing they or I could say will add to the splendid example you have given. Therefore I declare the meeting closed. File out orderly, intone our inspiring revolutionary songs, and leave the soldiers to their tragic fate, which at present they are too ignorant to realize."

The strains of the *Internationale* rose above the approval shouted by the audience, and the song was taken up by the many-throated mass outside. Patiently they had waited for five hours and every word that had reached them through the open windows had found a strong echo in their hearts. All through the meeting their applause had thundered back to us, and now their jubilant song.

In the committee room a reporter of the New York *World* rushed up to me. "Your presence of mind saved the situation," he congratulated me. "But what will you report in your paper?" I asked. "Will you tell of the rough-house the soldiers tried to make, and the refusal of the police to stop them?" He would, he said, but I was certain that no truthful report would be published, even if he should have the courage to write it.

The next morning the *World* proclaimed that "Rioting accompanied the meeting of the No-Conscription League at Hunt's Point Palace. Many were injured and twelve arrests made. Soldiers in uniform sneered at the speakers. After adjournment the real riot began in the adjacent streets."

The alleged riot was of editorial making and seemed a deliberate attempt to stop further protests against conscription. The police took the hint. They issued orders to the hall-keepers not to rent their premises for any meeting to be addressed by Alexander Berkman or Emma Goldman. Not even the owners of places we had been using for years dared disobey. They were sorry, they said; they did not fear arrest, but the soldiers had threatened their lives and property. We secured Forward Hall, on East Broadway, which belonged to the Jewish Socialist Party. It was small for our purpose, barely big enough to seat a thousand people, but no other place was to be had in entire New York. The awed silence of the pacifist and anti-military organizations which followed the passing of the registration bill made it doubly imperative for us to continue the work. We scheduled a mass meeting for June 14.

It was not necessary for us to print announcements. We merely called up the newspapers, and they did the rest. They denounced our impudence in continuing anti-war activities, and they sharply criticized the authorities for failing to stop us. As a matter of fact, the police were working overtime waylaying draft-evaders. They arrested thousands, but many more had refused to register. The press did not report the actual state of affairs; it did not care to make it known that large numbers of Americans had the manhood to defy the government. We knew through our own channels that thousands had determined not to shoulder a gun against people who were as innocent as themselves in causing the world-slaughter.

One day, while I was dictating letters to my secretary, an old man came into the *Mother Earth* office and asked for Berkman. Sasha was engaged in the rear room. Engrossed in work, I did not take the time even to invite the caller to sit down. I pointed to the back, indicating that he might enter. In a few minutes Sasha called me in. He introduced the visitor as James Hallbeck, for years a subscriber of *Mother Earth* and the *Blast*, whom he had met in San Francisco. The name was familiar to me and I remembered the man's ready response to our appeals. Sasha told me that the comrade wanted to make a

contribution to our work. We needed money for our campaign desperately and I was glad that someone had come forward with an offer.
The indifferent reception I had given Hallbeck made me somewhat
embarrassed when he handed me his cheque. I apologized by explaining how busy we were, but he assured me that he understood and that
it was perfectly all right. He had very little time, he said, and, hastily
bidding us good-bye, he edged his way out. When I looked at the
cheque, I discovered to my amazement that it was for three thousand
dollars. I was sure the old comrade had made a mistake and I quickly
went to call him back. But he shook his head and assured me that
there was no error about it. I begged him to return to the office and
tell us something about himself. I could not take the money without
knowing whether he had enough left to secure his old age.

He told us that he had emigrated from Sweden to America sixty
years previously. A rebel since his youth, the judicial murder of our
Chicago comrades had made him an anarchist. For a quarter of a
century he had lived in California as a wine-grower and he had saved
a little money. His own needs were small, and he had no kin in the
United States, never having married. His three sisters in the old
country were in comfortable circumstances, and they would also get
a modest legacy after his death. He was very much interested in the
No-Conscription campaign, and, being too old to participate actively,
he had decided to put a little money at our disposal for the work. We
need have no scruples about accepting the cheque, he assured us. "I
am eighty," he added, "and I have not much longer to live. I want
to feel that whatever I can spare will benefit the cause I have believed
in during the largest part of my life. I don't want the State or the
Church to profit by my death." Our venerable comrade's simple manner, his devotion to our work and generous gesture, affected us too profoundly for banal expressions of thanks. Our hand-clasp showed our
appreciation, and he left us as unostentatiously as he had come. His
cheque was deposited in the bank as a fund for anti-war activities.

June 14, the day of our Forward Hall meeting, arrived. In the late
afternoon I was called on the telephone, and a strange voice warned
me against attending the gathering. The man had overheard a plot
to kill me, he informed me. I asked for his name, but he declined to
give it; nor would he consent to see me. I thanked him for his interest
in my welfare and hung up the receiver.

Jocularly I told Sasha and Fitzi that I must prepare my will. "But

I shall probably reach a disgusting old age," I remarked. To be prepared for any eventuality, however, I decided to leave a note directing that "the $3000 contributed by James Hallbeck should remain in charge of Alexander Berkman, my lifelong friend and comrade in battle, to be applied to anti-war work and the support of imprisoned conscientious objectors." The *Mother Earth* fund, consisting of $329, was to pay our office debts; our stock of books was to be sold and the proceeds used for the needs of the movement. My personal library I bequeathed to my youngest brother and Stella. My only property, the little farm in Ossining, which my friend Bolton Hall had recently deeded to me, I left to Ian Keith Ballantine, Stella's little boy. Sasha and Fitzi witnessed the document with their signatures.

Reaching East Broadway, where Forward Hall is located, we were met, not by ordinary plotters, but by the entire police department. At least it seemed so to us, judging by the number of New York's "finest" that lined the street and the whole of Rutgers Square adjacent to our meeting-place. The crowd had been pushed back to the farthest end of the square. Those who had succeeded in getting into the building found themselves locked in and held as prisoners, as it were. No conspirators having designs upon my life had the ghost of a chance to get near me or Sasha, so closely were we encircled by husky officers, who hurried us into the building.

The hall was filled to suffocation. There were police galore and an array of Federal officials, but no soldiers. Forward Hall had probably never before held such a large American attendance. People seemed to realize that free expression on the war and conscription had become a rarity, and they were eager to lend their support.

The meeting was very spirited and our program was carried out without a hitch. But at the close every man in the hall who appeared subject to the draft was detained by the officers, and those who could not show a registration card were placed under arrest. It was apparently the intention of the Federal authorities to use our meeting as a trap. We therefore resolved to hold no more public gatherings unless we could make sure that those who had not complied with the registration law would keep away. We decided to concentrate more on the printed word.

On the following afternoon we were all busy in our offices. Sasha and Fitzi were on the upper floor, preparing the next issue of the *Blast*. I worked with my new secretary, Pauline, while our friend

Carl, the "Swede," was mailing our circulars. He was a staunch and dependable comrade who had been with us for a long time, first in Chicago, where he had helped with my lectures, then in San Francisco, where he was associated with the *Blast,* and now in New York. Carl was among the most trustworthy and level-headed men in our ranks. Nothing could ruffle his even temper or make him give up a task once undertaken. He was being assisted in the office by two other active comrades, Walter Merchant and W. P. Bales, who were true American rebels.

Above the hum of conversation and the clicking of the typewriter we suddenly heard the heavy stamping of feet on the stairway, and before any one of us had a chance to see what was the matter, a dozen men burst into my office. The leader of the party excitedly cried: "Emma Goldman, you're under arrest! And so is Berkman; where is he?" It was United States Marshal Thomas D. McCarthy. I knew him by sight; of late he had always stationed himself near the platform at our No-Conscription meetings, his whole attitude one of impatient readiness to spring upon the speakers. The newspapers had reported him as saying that he had repeatedly wired Washington for orders to arrest us.

"I hope you will get the medal you crave," I said to him. "Just the same, you might let me see your warrant." Instead he held out a copy of the June *Mother Earth* and demanded whether I was the author of the No-Conscription article it contained. "Obviously," I answered. "since my name is signed to it. Furthermore, I take the responsibility for everything else in the magazine. But where is your warrant?"

McCarthy declared that no warrant was necessary for us; *Mother Earth* contained enough treasonable matter to land us in jail for years. He had come to get us and we had better hurry up.

Leisurely I walked towards the stairs and called: "Sasha, Fitzi — some visitors are here to arrest us." McCarthy and several of his men roughly pushed me aside and dashed up to the *Blast* office. The deputy marshals took possession of my desk and began examining the books and pamphlets on our shelves, throwing them in a pile on the floor. A detective grabbed W. P. Bales, the youngest of our group, and announced that he was also under arrest. Walter Merchant and Carl were commanded to stand back until the search was over.

I started for my room to change my dress, aware that a night's free lodging was in store for me. One of the men rushed up to detain me, taking hold of my arm. I wrenched myself loose. "If your chief didn't have the guts to come up here without a body-guard of thugs," I said to him, "he should at least have instructed you not to act like one. I'm not going to run away. I only want to dress for the reception awaiting us, and I don't propose to let you act as my maid." The men ransacking my desk laughed coarsely. "She's a caution," one remarked, "but it's all right, officer, let her go to her room." When I emerged with my book and small toilet outfit, I found that Fitzi and Sasha, who was still on crutches, were already down. McCarthy was with them.

"I want the membership list of the No-Conscription League," he demanded.

"We ourselves are always ready to receive our friends the police," I retorted; "but we are careful not to take chances with the names and addresses of those who cannot afford the honour of an arrest. We don't keep the No-Conscription list in our office, and you can't find out where it is."

The procession started down the stairs to the waiting automobiles, McCarthy and his assistants in front, Sasha and I behind them. In the rear two deputy marshals leading Bales, followed by officers of the "bomb squad." With Sasha I was given the place of honour in the Chief Marshal's car. We fairly flew through the congested streets, frightening people by the screeching of the horn and sending them scampering in all directions. It was after six o'clock and masses of workers were streaming from the factories, but McCarthy would not permit the chauffeur to slacken up, nor did he heed the frantic signals of the traffic policemen along the route. When I called his attention to the fact that he was breaking the speed regulations and endangering the lives of the pedestrians, he replied importantly: " I represent the United States Government."

In the Federal Building we were joined by Harry Weinberger, our pugnacious lawyer and unfailing friend. He asked for immediate arraignment and release on bail, but our arrest had purposely been staged for the late afternoon after the official closing hour. We were ordered to the Tombs prison.

The following morning we were taken before United States Commissioner Hitchcock. The prosecutor, Federal Attorney for the District of New York, Harold A. Content, charged us with " conspiracy against the draft " and demanded that our bail be set high. The commissioner fixed the bonds at twenty-five thousand dollars each. Mr. Weinberger protested, but in vain.

In the Tombs we were held *incommunicado* for several days. Subsequently we learned that the raiders had seized everything they could lay their hands on in the offices of *Mother Earth* and the *Blast,* including subscription lists, cheque-books, and copies of our publications. They had also confiscated our correspondence files, manuscripts intended for publication in book form, as well as my typewritten lectures on American literature and other valuable material that we had spent years in accumulating. The treasonable matter consisted of works by Peter Kropotkin, Enrico Malatesta, Max Stirner, William Morris, Frank Harris, C. E. S. Wood, George Bernard Shaw, Ibsen, Strindberg, Edward Carpenter, the great Russian writers, and other such dangerous explosives.

Our friends hastened to our aid in a spirit of most splendid solidarity. Our dear comrades Michael and Annie Cohn were in the lead with large sums of money. Agnes Inglis of Detroit sent financial help, as did scores of others from various parts of the country. Equally inspiring was the attitude of many poor working-men. They not only contributed their meagre savings, but even offered their trinkets to help raise the fifty-thousand-dollar bond demanded by the United States Government.

I wanted Sasha bailed out first because of his injured leg, which still needed treatment; I did not mind remaining in the Tombs, for I was resting and enjoying an absorbing book Margaret Anderson had sent me. It was *A Portrait of the Artist As a Young Man,* by James Joyce. I had not read that author before and I was fascinated by his power and originality.

The Federal authorities were not anxious to let us out of prison. The three hundred thousand dollars' worth of real estate offered as our bond was refused on a flimsy technicality by Assistant Federal Attorney Content, who declared that nothing but cash would be accepted. There was enough on hand to bail out one of us. Sasha, always gallant, refused to come out first, and therefore the bond was given for me and I was released.

Although the newspapers could easily verify who had contributed towards my bail, the New York *World* had the temerity to print a story in its issue of June 22 to the effect that " a report is current that the Kaiser furnished the $25,000 for Emma's release." It was an indication of the extent to which the press would go to help dispose of undesirable elements.

The Federal grand jury brought in an indictment charging us with conspiracy to defeat the "selective" draft. The maximum penalty for this offence was two years' imprisonment and ten thousand dollars' fine. Our trial was set for June 27. I had only five days to prepare for my defence, while Sasha was still in the Tombs. It was imperative to concentrate all our energies on raising his bail.

But there was Ben, once more unable to face a vital issue and emotionally torn betwixt and between. No court decision had yet been handed down on his appeal from the Cleveland conviction. He had returned to New York when we began our No-Conscription campaign, and with his usual energy he had thrown himself into the work. All went well for some weeks, and then Ben again became, as he had so often before, a prey to his emotional upheavals. This time it was the young woman of his Sunday class. She was neither in danger nor in want, and her child was not expected for months to come. But Ben succumbed. At the very height of our anti-war campaign he left for Chicago to join the prospective mother. His failure to remain at his post at such a critical moment both exasperated and pained me. In vain I sought to explain away his apparent lack of stamina and courage by remembering that he could not have foreseen our arrest. Yet he had not returned when he knew that we were already in custody. Did it not prove breach of faith? The thought that Ben would deny me in my hour of need was tormenting. I felt deeply grieved and humiliated at the same time.

At last we succeeded in procuring the twenty-five-thousand-dollar cash bond demanded for Sasha, and on June 25 he was released from the Tombs. We were entirely at one regarding our trial. We did not believe in the law and its machinery, and we knew that we could expect no justice. We would therefore completely ignore what was to us a mere farce; we would refuse to participate in the court proceedings. Should this method prove impractical, we would plead our own case, not in order to defend ourselves, but to give public utterance to our ideas. We decided to go into court without an attorney. Our resolve was not due to any dissatisfaction with our counsel, Harry Weinberger. On the contrary, we could have wished for no abler attorney and more devoted friend. He had already rendered us services far beyond any monetary recompense, and he had done so although fully aware that we could not pay adequately. We fully appreciated Harry and we felt safe in his hands. But our trial would have meaning only, if we could turn the court-room into a forum for the presentation of the ideas we had been fighting for throughout all our conscious years. No lawyer could help us in this, and we were not interested in anything else.

Harry Weinberger understood our attitude, but he strongly advised us against meeting the prosecution with folded arms. It would make no impression whatever in an American court, he said; we should be given the maximum penalty, and nothing would be gained for our principles. But if we would plead our own case, he would give us every legal assistance and suggestion possible.

The day before our trial I met by appointment a number of people at the Brevoort Hotel, before whom I placed our intention of ignoring the prosecution. Among those present were Frank Harris, John Reed, Max Eastman, Gilbert E. Roe, and several others. After I had explained why I had called the conference, Frank Harris, with whom I had been friendly for years, became enthusiastic with the idea. "Emma Goldman and Alexander Berkman, the arch-champions of active resistance, meeting their enemies with folded arms — fine! Splendid!" he cried. In any European court such a stand would prove to be a magnificent gesture, he declared; but an American judge would only consider us flagrantly contemptuous, and the newspapermen would as little know what to make of us as the scribes of two thousand years ago had made of the Carpenter of Nazareth. Frank did not think we would be given a chance to carry out our plan, but in any event he was with us and we could fully count on his support.

John Reed did not believe in deliberately stepping into the lion's den. If one must go, one should fight all the way through, he thought. Whatever our decision, however, he would help in every way he could.

Max Eastman was not impressed by our suggestion. His opinion was that we could achieve more by a legal fight, with the aid of a competent lawyer to conduct our defence. It was more important, he held, that we should be free to continue our anti-war work than to go to prison without having tried every legal recourse.

It was Tuesday, June 27, at 10 a.m., when, together with Sasha, still on crutches, I walked through the crowded court-room in the Federal Building to face the prosecution. Judge Julius M. Mayer and

Assistant United States District Attorney Harold A. Content, their Prussianism carefully hidden, like wrinkles on a woman's face, under the thick paint of Americanism, were in their appointed places. Surrounding them were the lesser stars in the play about to be staged. In the background was a mob of soldiers, State and Federal officials, court attendants looking like hold-up men, and a contingent of reporters. American flags and bunting added to the high spots of the scene. Only a few of our friends had been admitted.

I moved for postponement on the grounds that my co-defendant, Alexander Berkman, suffering from an injury to his leg, was unable to stand the strain of a prolonged trial. As we had been released on bail only a few days, we had had no time to familiarize ourselves with the indictment, I also declared. Attorney Content protested, and Judge Mayer denied my motion.

Thereupon I said that, in view of the evident intention of the Government to turn the prosecution into persecution, we preferred to take no part whatever in the proceedings. His Honour had apparently never heard of such a thing before. He looked puzzled. Then he announced that he would appoint counsel to defend us. "In our free United States even the poorest are accorded the benefit of legal defence," he said. Upon our refusal the Court ruled that our trial should proceed after the noon recess. During luncheon we conferred with Harry Weinberger and other friends and returned to court in fighting trim.

June 27 happened to be my forty-eighth birthday. It marked twenty-eight years of my life spent in an active struggle against compulsion and injustice. The United States now symbolizing concentrated coercion, I could not have wished for a more appropriate celebration than to meet its challenge. It gave me much joy to feel that my friends had, in the excitement of the moment, not forgotten the event. On my return to court they presented me with flowers and gifts. The demonstration of their love and esteem on this special occasion moved me profoundly.

Active participation in our trial having been thrust upon us, Sasha and I determined to use it to best advantage. We decided to wring from our enemies every chance to propagate our ideas. Should we succeed, it would be the first time since 1887 that anarchism had raised its voice in an American court. Nothing else was worth considering in comparison with such an achievement.

I had known Sasha twenty-eight years. As far as one human being can foretell how another will act under stress or when confronted with the unexpected, I had always believed that I could in reference to him. But Sasha as a brilliant lawyer was a revelation even to me, his oldest friend. At the end of the first day I almost pitied the unfortunate talesmen whom he had been catechizing for hours. Like bullets Sasha fired his questions at the prospective jurymen, examining them on social, political, and religious matters, making them writhe at the exposure of their ignorance and prejudice, and almost convincing the victims themselves that they were not fit to try intelligent men. His flashes of humour and charming manners captivated the spectators.

When Sasha had finished quizzing the jurymen, they could hardly restrain their expression of relief. I followed to question them on marriage, divorce, sex enlightenment of the young, and birth-control. Would my radical views on these matters prevent their rendering an unbiased verdict? It was with the greatest difficulty that I was able to get my questions across. I was often interrupted by the Federal Attorney, became involved in verbal clashes with him, and was repeatedly admonished by the Judge to confine myself to " relevant " matters.

We knew very well that the twelve men we had finally selected could not and would not render an unbiased verdict. But by our examination of the talesmen we had succeeded in uncovering the social issues involved in the trial, had created a libertarian atmosphere, and had broached problems never before mentioned in a New York court.

Attorney Content opened his case by stating that he would prove that in our writings and speeches we had urged men not to register. As evidence he produced copies of *Mother Earth,* the *Blast,* and our No-Conscription manifesto. Cheerfully we admitted our authorship of every word, insisting, however, that the prosecution quote page and line where advice not to register was given. Unable to do so, Content called Fitzi to the witness-stand and tried to make her say that we had worked for profit. Though utterly irrelevant to the crime charged against us, the Court permitted the procedure. In her quiet, unruffled manner Fitzi very soon punctured this bubble.

The next " proof," played up as a trump card, was the insinuation of German money. " Emma Goldman deposited three thousand dollars in the bank a few days prior to her arrest. Where did that money come from? " the prosecutor demanded triumphantly. Everybody present pricked up his ears, and the reporters got busy with their pencils. We laughed inwardly. We could picture to ourselves their faces, now bursting with vindictiveness, when our venerable comrade James Hallbeck should testify. Our one regret was that we should have to call the poor soul into the stuffy court-room on such a scorching July day.

He came, a simple and unassuming little man, with a large heart and brave spirit. He recited his story on the witness-stand exactly as he had told it to us when he had brought his generous gift. " But why did you give Emma Goldman three thousand dollars?" Content demanded in a rage. "Nobody just throws away so much money."

"No, I did not throw it away," he answered with dignity. Emma Goldman and Alexander Berkman were his comrades, he explained. They were doing the work he believed in, but was too old to do. That was why he gave them the money. The German-money fuse fizzled out.

The next card was not original. It had been played in my first round with the State of New York in 1893. A detective, who in this case claimed also to be a stenographer, produced notes purporting to be a verbatim report of my speech at the Harlem River Casino. He quoted me as having said on that occasion: " We believe in violence, and we will use violence."

On cross-examination we brought out the fact that the detective had made his notes while standing on a shaky table, and that the highest number he could take was one hundred a minute. We confronted him with the champion stenographer, Paul Munter. The latter testified that it was difficult even for him to take Emma Goldman, especially in any intense speech, and yet his record was one hundred and eighty words a minute. Munter was followed by the proprietor of the Harlem River Casino. Though called by the prosecution, he told the Court that he had not heard me use the expression imputed to me, and he had listened very attentively to my talk. The meeting had been perfectly orderly in spite of a group of soldiers who had tried to cause trouble, he stated, "and it was Emma Goldman who saved the situation on that occasion." A sergeant of the Coast Guard corroborated his testimony.

The uninitiated wondered why the prosecution should stress what I had said on the 18th of May, *before* conscription had become a law, while no reference was made to my speeches *after* the bill had been passed. We knew the reason. At our last meetings we had had stenographers who sat on the platform in everybody's view. But we had been unable to secure a competent man for May 18. The State had evidently been apprised of that fact; therefore the stenographic detective was very convenient for the prosecution.

We produced a number of witnesses to show that the phrase " we believe in violence and we will use violence " had never been uttered by me or any other speaker at our gatherings. Our first witness was Leonard D. Abbott, admired by everybody for his charm and respected even by the most conservative for his sincerity. He had presided at the meetings of May 18 and June 4. He denied emphatically that I had used the words attributed to me at the Harlem River Casino or anywhere else. In fact, he told the Court, he had been somewhat disappointed with my speech, because he had expected a more extreme attitude. As to my having advised young men not to register, that could easily be disproved by a letter I had sent to the gathering at the *Mother Earth* office on May 9, Leonard stated.

His testimony was supported by a conscientious objector who related that he had gone to our office for advice about registration and had been told by us that we preferred to leave registration or military service to the conscience of those eligible for the draft. After him came Helen Boardman, Martha Gruening, Rebecca Shelley, Anna Sloan, and Nina Liederman. These women had all worked with us from the very beginning of the No-Conscription campaign, and they reiterated that they had never heard us urge anyone not to register.

The Federal Attorney demanded that we produce the original text of my letter, insinuating that the contents had been changed in the transcription. He knew that the original copy, like most of our other papers and documents, had been confiscated in the raid and was now in his possession. Yet he had the effrontery to make the demand. He did not produce the letter; it would have belied the charge against me.

However, the prosecution was resourceful; other devices were tried out. Now it was an attempt to play on the prejudices of the jury by creating the impression that our witnesses were mostly foreigners. Much to the chagrin of Federal Attorney Content, it soon developed that most of them had a background older than his own. Helen Boardman, for instance, was the sort of foreigner whose ancestors had come over in the Mayflower, and Anna Sloan was of old Irish-American stock. He had the same poor luck with our men witnesses, among whom were John Reed, Lincoln Steffens, Bolton Hall, and other " real " Americans.

Sasha followed the prosecution with a brief outline of our case. He declared that the charge of conspiracy was the height of absurdity, considering that he and his co-defendant had openly propagated anti-militarism for twenty-eight years. It was therefore a conspiracy known to a hundred millions of our population. As Sasha continued talking, presenting our case with keen logic and incisive manner, some of the jurymen seemed impressed and showed lively interest. Content did not fail to take note of it. At the first opportunity he picked up a copy of *Mother Earth* of July 1914. I had quite forgotten that several copies of that issue had been left in our office. Some of the boys and girls who had participated in the unemployment campaign that Sasha had organized and in the demonstration after the Lexington tenement explosion had long drifted out of our ranks. Most of them had proved worthless, carried away by momentary excitement, but their violent effusions had unfortunately remained in cold print and they were now taken advantage of by the prosecution. Content proceeded to read the choicest bits, straining to impress the jury that all of us sponsored physical force and the use of dynamite. "It is true, Miss Goldman was at that time absent on a tour," he remarked, "and she could therefore not be held responsible for the articles in this particular number." It was an attempt to throw the entire burden on Sasha. I was on my feet before he got through. "The prosecutor knows perfectly well," I declared, "that I am the owner and publisher of *Mother Earth,* and that I am responsible for everything that appears in the magazine, whether I happen to be present at its publication or not." I demanded whether we were being tried for ancient history; otherwise it was difficult to understand why an issue that had appeared three years before the United States went into the war, which had neither been held up by the postal authorities nor objected to by the State of New York, should now be used in the case. It was irrelevant, I declared. But my objections were ruled out by His Honour.

Every day increased the tension in court. The atmosphere grew more antagonistic, the official attendants more insulting. Our friends were either kept out or treated roughly when they succeeded in gaining admittance. On the street below, a recruiting station had been erected, and patriotic harangues mingled with the music of a military band. Each time the national anthem was struck up, everybody in court was commanded to rise, the soldiers present standing at attention. One of our girls refused to get up and she was dragged out of the room by force. A boy was literally kicked out. Sasha and I remained seated throughout the display of patriotism by the mailed fist. What could the officials do? They could not very well order us removed from this Punch and Judy show; we at least had that advantage.

After endlessly repetitious "evidence" of our crime, which in reality proved nothing, the prosecution closed its case. The last round in the contest between ideas and organized stupidity was set for July 9. This left us about forty-eight hours to prepare our arraignment of the forces that had plunged the world into a vale of tears and blood. Since the beginning of our trial we had been compelled to keep up a terrific pace, and we felt exhausted. For the past week we had enjoyed the hospitality of Leonard D. Abbott and his wife, Rose Yuster, and now we pilgrimed to Stella's little place at Darien for a short rest.

I woke the next morning with the bright sunshine streaming into my room and wide stretches of blue hanging over the luscious green of trees and lawn. The air was pungent with the aroma of the earth, the lake was vibrant with soft music, and all of nature breathed enchantment. I, too, was under her magic spell.

On our return to court Monday, July 9, we found the stage set for the last act of the tragicomedy that had already lasted a week. Judge Mayer, Federal Attorney Content, and a large company of performers in the badly constructed plot were already on the stage. The house was filled with invited official guests and *claqueurs* to lead the applause. Scores of pressmen were present to review the show. Not many of our friends had been able to gain admittance, but there were more than on previous days.

Prosecutor Content could in no way compare in ability and forcefulness with his colleague who had prosecuted me in 1893; he had been drab and colourless all through the trial and stereotyped in his address to the jury. At one moment he had attempted to climb to oratorical heights. "You think this woman before you is the real Emma Goldman," he declared, "this well-bred lady, courteous, and with a pleasant smile on her face? No! The real Emma Goldman can be seen only on the platform. There she is in her true element, sweeping all caution to the winds! There she inflames the young and drives them to violent deeds. If you could see Emma Goldman at her meetings, you would realize that she is a menace to our well-ordered institutions." It was therefore the jury's duty to save the country from *that* Emma Goldman by bringing in a verdict of guilty.

Sasha followed the prosecutor. He held the close attention of the men in the box, as well as of the entire court-room, for two hours. That was no small feat in an atmosphere oozing with prejudice and hate. His playful and witty handling of the so-called evidence to prove our "crime" caused much merriment and often loud laughter. This was promptly stopped by stern rebukes from the bench. The testimony of the government thoroughly demolished, Sasha proceeded with an *exposé* of anarchism, masterly in its simple directness and clarity.

I spoke after Sasha, for an hour. I discussed the farce of a government undertaking to carry democracy abroad by suppressing the last vestiges of it at home. I took up the contention of Judge Mayer that only such ideas are permissible as are "within the law." Thus he had instructed the jurymen when he had asked them if they were prejudiced against those who propagate unpopular ideas. I pointed out that there had never been an ideal, however humane and peaceful, which in its time had been considered "within the law." I named Jesus, Socrates, Galileo, Giordano Bruno. "Were they ' within the law ' ? " I asked. "And the men who set America free from British rule, the Jeffersons and the Patrick Henrys? The William Lloyd Garrisons, the John Browns, the David Thoreaus and Wendell Phillipses — were they within the law ? "

At that moment the strains of the *Marseillaise* floated through the window, and the Russian Mission marched past on its way to the City Hall. I seized upon the occasion. "Gentlemen of the jury," I said, " do you hear the stirring melody? It was born in the greatest of all revolutions, and it was most emphatically not within the law! And that delegation your government is now honouring as the representatives of new Russia. Only five months ago every one of them was considered what you have been told we are: criminals — not within the law! "

During the proceedings His Honour was assiduously reading. His desk was littered with the literature confiscated in our offices, and he seemed absorbed — now in Sasha's *Memoirs*, now in my *Essays*, now in *Mother Earth*. His application had led some friends to believe that the Judge was interested in our ideas and inclined to be fair.

Judge Mayer fully rose to our expectations. In his charge to the jury he declared with much solemnity: " In the conduct of this case, the defendants have shown remarkable ability. An ability which might have been utilized for the great benefit of this country, had they seen fit to employ themselves in behalf of it rather than against it. In this country of ours we regard as enemies those who advocate the abolition of our government and those who counsel disobedience to our laws by those of minds less strong. American liberty was won by the fore-fathers, it was maintained by the Civil War, and today there are the thousands who have already gone, or are getting ready to go, to foreign lands to represent their country in the battle for liberty." He then instructed the jury that " whether the defendants are right or wrong can have no bearing on the verdict. The duty of the jury is merely to weigh the evidence presented as to the innocence or guilt of the defendants of the crime as charged."

The jury filed out. The sun had set. The electric lights looked yellow in the dusk. Flies buzzed, their swirl mingling with the whisperings in the room. The minutes crept on, clammy with the day's heat. The jury returned; its deliberation had lasted just thirty-nine minutes.

" What is your verdict ? " the foreman was asked.

" Guilty," he answered.

I was on my feet. " I move that the verdict be set aside as absolutely contrary to the evidence."

" Motion denied," Judge Mayer said.

" I further move," I went on, " that sentence be deferred for a few days, and that our bail be continued at the sum already fixed in our case."

" Denied," ruled the Judge.

His Honour asked the usual meaningless question as to whether the defendants had anything to say why sentence should not be imposed.

Sasha replied: " I think it only fair to suspend sentence and give us a chance to clear up our affairs. We have been convicted because we are anarchists, and the proceeding has been very unjust." I also added my protest.

" In the United States, law is an imperishable thing," the Court declared in imposing sentence, " and for such people as would nullify our laws we have no place in our country. In a case such as this I can but inflict the maximum sentence which is permitted by our laws."

Two years in prison with a fine of ten thousand dollars each. The Judge also instructed the Federal Attorney to send the records of the trial to the immigration authorities in Washington with his recommendation to deport us at the expiration of our prison terms.

His Honour had done his duty. He had served his country well and merited a rest. He declared court adjourned and turned to leave the bench.

But I was not through. "One moment, please," I called out. Judge Mayer turned to face me. "Are we to be spirited away at such neck-breaking speed? If so, we want to know it now. We want everybody here to know it."

"You have ninety days in which to file an appeal."

"Never mind the ninety days," I retorted. "How about the next hour or two? Can we have that to gather up a few necessary things?"

"The prisoners are in the custody of the United States Marshal," was the curt answer.

The Judge again turned to leave. Again I brought him to a stop. "One more word!" He stared at me, his heavy-set face flushed. I stared back. I bowed and said: "I want to thank you for your leniency and kindness in refusing us a stay of two days, a stay you would have accorded the most heinous criminal. I thank you once more."

His Honour grew white, anger spreading over his face. Nervously he fumbled with the papers on his desk. He moved his lips as if to speak, then abruptly turned and left the bench.

CHAPTER XLVI

THE AUTOMOBILE SPED ON. IT WAS FILLED WITH DEPUTY MAR-
shals, with me in their midst. Twenty minutes later we reached
the Baltimore and Ohio Station. The hand of time seemed set back
twenty-five years. I visioned myself at the same station a quarter of a
century ago, straining towards the disappearing train which was bearing Sasha away, leaving me desolate and alone. A gruff voice startled
me. " Are you seeing ghosts? " it demanded.

I was in a compartment, a big man and a woman at my side, the
deputy marshal and his wife. Then I was left with the woman.

The day's heat, the excitement, and three hours' wait in the Federal
Building had exhausted me. I felt worn and sticky in my sweaty
clothes. I started for the wash-room, and the woman followed me. I
objected. She regretted she could not let me go unattended; her instructions were not to permit me out of sight. She had a rather kindly
face. I assured her that I would not try to escape, and she consented
to close the door half-way. Having cleaned up, I crawled into my berth
and immediately fell asleep.

I was awakened by the loud voices of my keepers. The man's coat
was already off and he was proceeding to undress. " You don't mean
you're going to sleep here? " I demanded.

"Sure," he answered, "what's wrong? My wife is here. You've got
nothing to fear."

What more could morality wish for than the presence of the
deputy's wife? It wasn't fear, I told him; it was disgust.

The watchful eyes of the law were closed in sleep, but its mouth was
wide open, emitting a rattle of snores. The air was putrid. Anxious
thoughts about Sasha beset me. A quarter of a century had passed,
crammed with events and rich in the interplay of light and shade.
The painful frustration with Ben — friendships shattered — others

that had never lost their bloom. The earth-spirit often in conflict with the impelling aspirations of the ideal, and Sasha ever dependable all through the long span of time and always my comrade in the struggle. The thought was soothing, and the strain of weeks found relief in blessed sleep.

My male escort stayed away from the compartment most of the day, his presence gracing only our meals, which were brought to us from the diner. At the luncheon I asked the deputy marshal why I was being taken to the Missouri State Prison, at Jefferson City. There was no Federal prison for women, he explained; there used to be one, but it was discontinued because it " did not pay."

" And male federals, do they pay?" I inquired.

" Sure," he said; " there are so many of them that the U. S. Government is planning another prison. One of them is in Atlanta, Georgia," he added, " and that is where your friend Berkman has been taken."

I led him to talk about Atlanta. He assured me that it was a very strict place, and that " Berk" would have a bad time of it if he did not behave himself. Then he remarked with a sneer: " He's an old hand at prisons, ain't he?"

" Yes, but he has survived, and he will prove a match for Atlanta, too, with all its strictness," I retorted hotly.

The lady deputy kept to herself. It gave me a chance to write, read, and think. We changed trains at St. Louis, which afforded me an opportunity for a little exercise while waiting for the local to Jefferson City. I peered eagerly about to discover a familiar face, but I realized that our comrades in St. Louis could not have known when I would reach their town.

Arriving in Jefferson City, my escorts offered to take me to the penitentiary in a taxi. I requested that we walk. It might be my last chance for a long while, I thought. They readily consented, no doubt because they could pocket the price and charge it to their expense accounts.

When my guardians had delivered me to the head matron of the prison, they assured me that they had enjoyed my company. They had not believed that an anarchist would give so little trouble, they remarked. The wife added that she had grown to like me and was sorry to leave me behind. Rather a doubtful compliment, I felt.

With the exception of my two weeks in Queens County Jail, I had somehow managed to steer clear of prisons since my " rest-cure " on Blackwell's Island. There had been numerous arrests and several trials, but no other convictions. A disgusting record for one who could boast of the never-failing attention of every police department in the country.

"Any disease?" the head matron demanded abruptly.

I was somewhat taken aback at the unexpected concern over my health. I answered her that I had nothing to complain of except that I needed a bath and a cold drink.

"Don't be impudent and pretend you don't know what I mean," she sternly reproved me. " I mean the disease immoral women have. Most of those delivered here have it."

"Venereal disease is not particular whom it strikes," I told her; "the most respectable people have been known to be victims of it. I don't happen to have it, which is due perhaps much more to luck than to virtue."

She looked scandalized. She was so self-righteous and prim, she needed to be shocked, and I was catty enough to enjoy watching the effect.

After having been subjected to the routine search for dope and cigarettes, I was given a bath and informed that I could keep my own underwear, shoes and stockings.

My cell contained a cot with stiff but clean sheets and blankets, a table and a chair, a stationary wash-stand with running water, and, blessing of blessings, a toilet built in a little alcove, hidden from view by a curtain. So far my new home was a decided improvement over Blackwell's Island. Two things marred my pleasant discovery. My cell faced a wall that shut off the air and light, and all through the night the clock in the prison yard struck every fifteen minutes, whereupon stentorian voices would call out: " All's well." I tossed about, wondering how long it would take to get used to this new torture.

Twenty-four hours in the prison gave me an approximate idea of its routine. The institution had a number of progressive features: more frequent visits, the opportunity to order foodstuffs, the privilege of writing letters three times a week, according to the grade one had reached, recreation in the yard daily and twice on Sunday, a bucketful of hot water every evening, and permission to receive packages and printed matter. These were great advantages over

conditions in Blackwell's Island. The recreation was especially gratifying. The yard was small and had but little protection from the sun,
but the prisoners were free to walk about, talk, play, and sing, without
interference from the matron who presided in the yard. On the other
hand, the prevailing labour system required definite tasks. The latter
were so difficult to accomplish that they kept the inmates in constant
trepidation. I was informed that I would be excused from making
the complete task, but that was small comfort. With a woman serving
a life sentence on one side of me, and another doomed to fifteen years,
both forced to do the full amount of work, I did not care to take
advantage of my exemption. At the same time I feared that I might
never be able to accomplish the task. The subject was the main topic
of discussion and the greatest worry of the inmates.

After a week spent in the shop I began suffering excruciating pain
in the back of my neck. My condition was aggravated by the first news
from New York. Fitzi's letter conveyed what I already knew, that
Sasha had been taken to Atlanta. It was far away, she wrote, and it
would prevent our friends from visiting him. She had many worries
and hardships to face. The Federal authorities, in co-operation with
the New York police, had terrorized the proprietor of our office. He
had ordered Fitzi to remove *Mother Earth* and the *Blast,* without
even giving her a week's notice. After much effort she had succeeded
in finding quarters on Lafayette Street, but it was questionable whether
she would be permitted to remain there. The patriotic hysteria was increasing, the press and the police vying with each other to exterminate
every radical activity. Dear, brave Fitzi, and our valiant "Swede"!
They had had to carry the whole burden since our arrest. But faithfully they had kept at their post, concerned only about us, with never
any complaint about their own difficulties. Even now Fitzi wrote
nothing about herself. Dear, sweet soul.

Other letters and several telegrams were more cheering. Harry
Weinberger wrote that Judge Mayer had refused to sign the application for our appeal, nor would any other Federal judge give his
signature. But Harry was sure that he could induce one of the Supreme
Court justices to accept the papers, and that would enable us to be
released on bail.

A letter came from Frank Harris, offering to send me reading-
matter and anything else permitted in the prison. Another was from
my jovial old friend William Marion Reedy. Now that I was living

in his State, he wrote, and was his neighbour, as it were, he was anxious to secure for me the right kind of hospitality. He and Mr. Painter, the warden of the penitentiary, had been college chums, and he had written him that he ought to be proud to have Emma Goldman as his guest. He had cautioned him to treat her right, or he would go after him. I should consider myself lucky, his letter read, to have two years' freedom from my hectic activities. It would mean a good rest and it should also mean the autobiography he had long ago advised me to write. "Now is your chance: you have a home, three meals a day and leisure — all free of charge. Write your life. You have lived it as no other woman. Tell us about it." He had already shipped a box containing paper and pencils, he informed me, and he would persuade Mr. Painter to let me have a typewriter. I must "buckle down and write the book," he concluded.

Like many another, my dear old friend Bill had caught the war fever. Yet he was big enough to continue his interest and friendship, regardless of my stand. But his idea of writing in prison caused me to smile. It showed how little even such a clear-headed man realized the effect of imprisonment; to believe that one could adequately express one's thoughts in captivity, after nine hours' daily drudgery. Just the same, his letter made me very happy.

There were loving messages from Stella, my sisters, and even my dear old mother, who wrote in Yiddish. Very touching were the letters of our St. Louis comrades. They would look after my needs, they wrote; they were so near Jefferson City, they would send me fresh food every day. They would be happy if they could do the same for Sasha, but he was too far away. They hoped friends living in the South would look after his needs.

Two weeks after I had been delivered to the prison, the same deputy marshal and his wife arrived to take me back to New York. Irrepressible Harry Weinberger had succeeded in getting Supreme Court Justice Louis D. Brandeis to sign the application for our appeal, which admitted Sasha and me to bail and temporary freedom. The appeal included also the cases of Morris Becker and Louis Kramer. Harry had scored a victory over Judge Mayer. I was sure that our liberty would be of short duration; still, it was good to return to our friends and resume the work where it had been interrupted by our arrest.

It was with emotions quite different from those I had felt on my way to prison that I boarded the train for New York. My escorts, too, seemed changed. The deputy informed me that there would be no need this time to watch me so closely. Only his wife would share my compartment. He wanted me to feel as free as if I were travelling alone, and he hoped that I would have no complaints to make to the reporters. I understood. At the station in St. Louis I was given an ovation by a group of comrades, and of course there were also representatives of the press. The deputy became demonstratively magnanimous. I could invite my people to the station restaurant, he suggested, while he would remain at a neighbouring table. I enjoyed the dear companionship of my friends.

The return journey had many pleasant features, the main one being the absence of the deputy. His wife also did not intrude, both remaining outside my compartment. The door was left ajar, more to afford me air than to keep me in view. It was an unusually close day, and I had a foretaste of what was to be meted out to such a godless creature when I should have joined the departed.

In the Tombs the keepers received the prodigal daughter with glad acclaim. It was late and the prison had closed for the day, but I was permitted a bath. The head matron was an old friend of mine, of the birth-control fight days. She believed in family limitation, she had confided to me, and she had been kind and solicitous, once even attending our Carnegie Hall meeting as my guest. When the other matrons left, she engaged me in conversation and remarked that she saw no reason to be excited about what the Germans had done to the Belgians. England had treated Ireland no better during hundreds of years and recently again during the Easter uprising. She was Irish, and she had no use for the Allies. I explained that my sympathies were not with any of the warring countries, but with the people of every land, because they alone have to pay the terrible price. She looked rather disappointed, but she gave me clean sheets for my bunk, and I liked her as a good Irish soul.

In the morning friends came to see me, among them Harry Weinberger, Stella, and Fitzi. I inquired about Sasha. Had he been brought back, and how was his leg? Fitzi averted her face.

"What is it?" I asked anxiously.

"Sasha is in the Tombs," she replied in a dead voice; "he will be safer there for a while."

Her tone and manner filled me with apprehension. Urged to tell me the worst, she informed me that Sasha was wanted in San Francisco. He had been indicted for murder in connexion with the Mooney case.

The Chamber of Commerce and the District Attorney had carried out their threat to "get" Sasha. They were going to have revenge for the splendid work he had done to expose the frame-up against five lives. Billings had already been put out of the way, immured for life, and Tom Mooney was facing death. Their next prey was Sasha. I knew they meant to murder him. Instinctively I raised my hand as if to ward off a blow.

I fully realized only when I was bailed out what Fitzi had meant by saying that Sasha would be safer in the Tombs. Released on bail, he would be in danger of being kidnapped and spirited away to California. Such things had happened before. After Sasha's arrest in 1892, our comrade Mollock had been secretly taken from New Jersey by Pennsylvania detectives who hoped to connect him with the attack on Frick. In 1906 Haywood, Moyer, and Pettibone had been abducted from Colorado to Idaho, and in 1910 the McNamara brothers had met with a like fate in Indiana. If the Government dared resort to such methods with members of powerful labour organizations, native-born at that, why not with a "foreign" anarchist? It was clear we could not risk bailing Sasha out. No time was to be lost if his extradition was to be prevented. Governor Whitman was a reactionary and would probably oblige the unscrupulous crew on the Coast; nothing but a mighty protest on the part of organized labour could stop him.

We immediately set to work, Fitzi, the "Swede," and I. We called a group of people together to organize a publicity committee. Then we invited the labour leaders at the head of the Jewish trade unions. A large gathering was held, attended by men and women influential in the world of labour and letters, which resulted in the formation of an active committee, with Dolly Sloan as secretary-treasurer.

The response of the United Hebrew Trades was immediate and whole-hearted, and the joint board of the Amalgamated Clothing Workers of America followed suit. The former offered to head the appeal for Sasha and to get us a hearing by every union.

Sasha's life was at stake. Conferences with labour men, canvassing unions, arranging meetings and theatre benefits, circularizing organizations, press interviews, and a vast correspondence crowded every minute of those nerve-racking days.

Sasha himself was in gay spirits. To see his visitors he had to be taken from the Tombs to the Federal Building and back again, which afforded him a walk in the fresh air. He had not yet been able to discard his crutches, and hobbling along was rather uncomfortable. But when one faces the possible loss of one's life, promenading even on crutches is a great boon. Marshal McCarthy supervised our visits and he acted rather decently. He made no objections when we brought many friends to see Sasha and he did not have us watched too obviously. In fact, he tried his best to gain our good will. On one occasion he remarked to me: " I know you hate me, Emma Goldman, but just you wait until the espionage bill is passed; then you'll thank me for having arrested you and Berkman in the early stages of the game. Now you get only two years, but later you would get twenty. Own up, wasn't I your friend? "

" None better," I admitted; " I'll see that you get a vote of thanks."

Our visits with Sasha were turned into merry family reunion. His genial humour and equanimity in the face of imminent danger gained him the respect even of the members of the Marshal's office. They asked for copies of his *Memoirs* and later they told us how greatly the book had impressed them. After that they became very cordial, and we were delighted for Sasha's sake.

Gradually our work was bringing results. The United Hebrew Trades issued a strong appeal to organized labour to rally to the support of Sasha. The joint board of the cloakmakers' union voted five hundred dollars for our campaign and promised to contribute more. The Joint Board of Furriers, the International Brotherhood of Bookbinders, Typographical Union Local 83, and other organizations co-operated with us in the most solidaric manner. They proposed that a representative delegation of at least a hundred labour men be sent to Governor Whitman to protest against Sasha's extradition to California, and steps were immediately taken to put before Whitman the facts of the judicial crime already perpetrated in San Francisco.

Uncertain how long I should remain at liberty, I had not taken an apartment. I shared with Fitzi her flat and spent an occasional weekend with Stella in Darien. One day Dolly Sloan asked me to stay with her while her husband was absent from the city. Their studio was large, very quaint and charming; and I enjoyed Dolly's hospitality. She was an energetic little lady and most eager to help in our campaign for Sasha, but she was not physically strong enough to endure the continual strain, and she often had to take to bed. Unfortunately, I had so much to do and was feeling so bad myself that I could give her little time. She was not bedridden, however, and was able to get about a great deal.

One morning I left her apparently in improved condition. She had had a good night's sleep and she intended remaining home to rest. I worked all day in the office, and in the evening I canvassed several organizations meeting in different parts of the city. The last was the union of the stage mechanics and electrical workers. They were supposed to meet at midnight, but I had to wait three hours in a narrow, stuffy passage piled up with boxes, one of which served me as a seat. When I was finally given the floor, I could see hostility written on every face. It was like swimming against a heavy tide to speak in the atmosphere thick with prejudice and the smell of bad tobacco and stale beer. When I had concluded my address, quite a number of those present expressed themselves as willing to support the campaign for Sasha, but the politicians in official positions were opposed. Berkman was an enemy of the country, they argued, and they would have nothing to do with him. I left them to fight the matter out among themselves.

Returning to Sloan's studio, I could not unlock the door. I rang in vain for a long time, then knocked loudly. At last I heard someone turn the key on the inside, and a woman was facing me. I recognized Pearl, the former wife of Robert Minor. She demanded whether I could not see the new lock on the door and did not guess that it was to keep me out. She was taking care of Mrs. Sloan and I was not wanted in the house. In astonishment I stared at her, then pushed her aside and walked in. The door to Dolly's room was ajar and I saw her lying on her bed evidently in a stupor. I was alarmed by her condition and turned to the woman for an explanation. She merely reiterated that Mrs. Sloan had ordered her to change the lock. But I knew she was lying.

I went out into the street. The day was breaking; I did not want to go to wake Fitzi, who needed sleep so badly. I walked over to Union Square. Once more I had been shut out, a homeless creature, as in the days I had believed gone for ever.

I rented a furnished room. Fitzi agreed with me that Dolly could have had nothing to do with the changing of the lock. It was known to everybody that Pearl Minor was bitterly opposed to all Bob's friends.

For some unaccountable reason she had a special grudge against me. It was stupid of her, but I was aware that she was the product of an orphanage, her mind and heart warped by her miserable childhood.

In the midst of those trying days there came another and far greater shock. I learned that my nephew David Hochstein had waived exemption and volunteered for the army. His mother, all unconscious of the blow awaiting her, was on her way to New York to meet him. My sister had only recently lost her husband after a short illness. I could not bear to think how the news about David would affect her. David, her beloved son, in whom she had concentrated all her hopes — a soldier! His young life to be given for something Helena had always hated as the crime of crimes!

Life's a fiendish contradiction! To think that David, Helena's child, should of his own free will offer himself for the army. He had never been politically or socially conscious, and I was therefore not surprised when told that he had registered. I was sure he would not be drafted. His break-down from tuberculosis a few years previously, though arrested, had yet left his lungs in such a condition that he was certain to be exempted. The news that he had submitted himself to the examination board in New York instead of in Rochester, and that he had said nothing about the state of his health, came as a shock. I could not believe that the boy had deliberately done so, that he believed in the war or in his country's ethical claims. Helena's children were too much like their parents to think that wars are worth fighting or that they solve anything. What, then, could have been the reason, I wondered, to induce David voluntarily to join the army? Perhaps something personal, or the popular maelstrom had caught him too unawares to resist. Whatever the cause, it was appalling that this richly endowed youth, with a brilliant artistic career just begun, should be among the first to offer himself.

I visited Helena at Darien. Her appearance told me more than words. The frightened expression in her eyes made me fear that she would not survive the blow of the vain sacrifice of her boy. I found David also there, and I longed to talk to him. But I remained dumb. Notwithstanding his family affection for me and my love for him, we had remained distant. How could I now hope to reach his mind? I had proclaimed that the choice of military service must be left to the conscience of every man. How could I attempt to impose my views on David, even if I could hope to persuade him, which I did not? I remained tongue-tied. But I argued hotly with Helena that her son was only one of the many, and her tears but a drop in the ocean already shed by the mothers of the world. Yet abstract theories are not for those whose tragedies are open wounds. I saw the agony in my sister's face and I knew there was nothing I could say or do to bring her relief. I returned to New York to continue our campaign for Sasha.

Every day brought new evidence of the love and esteem he enjoyed on the East Side. The radical Yiddish press outdid itself in championing his cause. Particularly did S. Yanofsky, the editor of the *Freie Arbeiter Stimme,* exert himself. That was especially gratifying because he had never been very comradely with either Sasha or me, and in our stand on the war we had completely drifted apart. Abe Cahan, the editor of the socialist *Forward,* was also very sympathetic and stressed the urgency of coming to Sasha's support. In fact, everyone in the radical Jewish circles heartily co-operated with us. A special group to aid our efforts was composed of the Yiddish writers and poets, among them Abraham Raisin, Nadir, and Sholom Asch.

With these strong drawing cards we organized a series of affairs, a theatre performance to raise funds, on which occasion Asch and Raisin spoke between the acts; a mass meeting in Cooper Union at which Sidney Hillman, president of the Amalgamated Clothing Workers, Alex Cohen, Morris Sigman, and other prominent labor men publicly protested in behalf of Sasha. Large meetings took place in Forward Hall and in the Brooklyn Labor Lyceum. For the same purpose were organized also a number of English meetings. The New York *Call,* the socialist daily, wrote forcibly against Sasha's extradition. It was peculiar to see the paper wax so enthusiastic in the campaign, considering that it had remained silent during our arrest and trial.

Fortunately there was no police interference, and our gatherings were attended by thousands of people. Much encouraged, we arranged a special affair at the Kessler Theatre. But Marshal McCarthy had apparently decided that I had already enjoyed too much freedom of speech and should therefore be stopped " for her own good." He announced that he would prohibit the meeting if I should attempt to address the audience. The purpose of the gathering being too important to risk having it disrupted, I promised to comply.

S. Yanofsky, a very clever man with a vitriolic tongue, was the last speaker. He talked eloquently of the Billings-Mooney case and the attempt of the San Francisco bosses to drag Sasha into their net. Then he proceeded to pay his respects to Marshal McCarthy. "He has gagged Emma," he declared, "too stupid to realize that her voice will now carry far beyond the walls of this theatre." At that moment I stepped upon the stage with a handkerchief stuck in my mouth. The audience shrieked with laughter, stamped their feet, and screamed. "You can't stop *that* speech," they shouted.

McCarthy looked sheepish, but I had kept my promise.

The agitation in behalf of Sasha was spreading. More labour bodies were constantly added to our list, among them the important New Jersey State Federation. This feat was accomplished by our Fitzi, and it had been no easy task to reach that by no means radical organization. She charmed people into sympathy and action — not merely by her Irish name and beautiful auburn hair, but by her fine and suave personality. Little did anyone outside of her immediate friends sense the Celtic temperament behind her tranquil manner.

Our activities in New York multiplied to such an extent that I could not accept the numerous invitations which came from other cities to address meetings arranged in behalf of Sasha. I had to select the most important calls, among them that for three lectures in Chicago.

Max Pine, general secretary, and M. Finestone, assistant secretary, of the United Hebrew Trades, were desirous of having Morris Hillquit, the socialist attorney, go to Albany with our delegation, to address Governor Whitman against Sasha's extradition. I had known Morris Hillquit for many years. When I first came to New York, I used to attend the joint gatherings of anarchists and socialists, among whom there were also the two brothers Hilkowitch. One occasion of those days had been particularly memorable. It was a Yom Kippur celebration held as a protest against Jewish orthodoxy. Speeches on free thought, dances, and plenty of eats took the place of the traditional fast and prayers. The religious Jews resented our desecration of their holiest Day of Atonement, and their sons came down in strong force to meet our boys in pitched battle. Sasha, who always loved a fight, was, of course, the leader and easily the most effective in repulsing the attack. While the affray was going on in the street, anarchist and socialist orators were holding forth inside the hall, young Morris Hilkowitch having the floor at the time. Over two decades had passed since then — Hilkowitch had changed his name to the more euphonious Hillquit and had become a successful lawyer, a leading Marxian theoretician, and an important personage in the Socialist Party. Socialism had never appealed to me, though there were many socialists among my friends. I liked them because they were freer and bigger than their creed. Mr. Hillquit I knew very slightly, but I considered his writings as lacking in vision. We had no common ground; he had risen high in the estimation of respectable society, while I remained a pariah.

The war, and particularly America's entry into the dance of death, had shifted many positions and contacts. People formerly closely allied in ideas and effort were now far apart, while others widely separated in the past found now a strong bond. Morris Hillquit had dared to stand out against the war. No wonder he now discovered himself in the same boat with Alexander Berkman, Emma Goldman, and their associates. The frenzied attacks on him by our common enemies and his erstwhile comrades bridged the chasm of the past as well as our theoretic differences. Indeed, I felt much closer to Hillquit than to many of my own comrades whose social vision had been gassed. Nevertheless, I experienced a sense of strangeness to come face to face with the man for the first time in twenty-seven years.

Hillquit was probably no more than three or four years older than Sasha, but he looked at least fifteen years his senior. His hair was thickly streaked with grey, his face lined, and his eyes weary. He had won success, renown, and wealth. Sasha's life had been a Golgotha, yet how different the two men appeared! However, Hillquit had remained simple in his ways, his manner was gracious, and I soon felt at home with him.

He was not very reassuring about Sasha's chances. At any other time, he said, it would not have been difficult to defeat extradition. In the present war hysteria, with Sasha convicted on a Federal conspiracy charge, the outlook was not very promising.

His candidacy for the mayoralty of New York on the Socialist ticket kept Mr. Hillquit exceedingly busy, but he unhesitatingly responded to the invitation to appear before Governor Whitman with the labour delegation. His campaign meetings were the first gatherings of the kind I had ever attended without being sickened by their inanity. I had no more faith in what Hillquit might achieve if elected mayor than anyone else in his place, though I did not doubt the sincerity of his intentions. His electoral campaign had great anti-war propaganda value. It presented the only chance in the hysteria-crazed country for some freedom of speech, and as an experienced orator and clever lawyer Morris Hillquit knew how to steer safely between dangerous patriotic cliffs.

I was glad that he made such good use of his election opportunities, yet I had to decline the invitation of his brother to participate in the work. I had told him how much I had enjoyed hearing the brilliant Morris and his speeches against war. " Why not join us, then ? " he suggested; " you could be of great help in our campaign." He sought to persuade me to set aside my opposition to political action on that exceptional occasion. " Think of the good you could do by helping stem the tide of the war madness," he urged.

But I had grown to like Morris too much to assist him to a political job. One might wish such a thing on one's enemies, not on one's friends.

Our activities for Sasha and the San Francisco cases received unexpected and far-reaching impetus through news from Russia : demonstrations in their behalf had taken place in Petrograd and Kronstadt. It was the answer to the message we had sent to the councils of workers, soldiers, and sailors by the refugees that had departed in May and June. We had followed it up with cables that our good friend Isaac A. Hourwich and our efficient secretary Pauline had succeeded in getting through to Russia after we had learned of Sasha's indictment in San Francisco. With joyful heart I visited Sasha, knowing what the demonstration of solidarity in Russia would mean to him. I tried to appear calm, but he soon sensed that something must have happened. At hearing the glorious tidings his face lit up and his eyes filled with wonder. But, as usual when profoundly stirred, he was silent. We sat quietly, our hearts beating in unison with gratitude to our *Matushka Rossiya*.

The problem was now how to use the demonstrations in Russia to best advantage. We had wide connexions and channels to bring the matter to the attention of the labour bodies, by meetings and circulars, but other means were needed to interest those who were in a position to intercede for our friends in San Francisco. Sasha suggested that I confer with his friend Ed Morgan, a former socialist, now an Industrial Worker of the World. He had been very active in behalf of Mooney and he might prove of great help in his case, Sasha thought.

I had known Morgan for some time. He was a good-hearted fellow, genuine and tireless when given a task. But I was not sure of his

abilities and he was fearfully long-winded. I had no doubts about his
willingness to do what we should request, but I was dubious about his
chances of accomplishing anything vital in Washington. I was wrong.
Ed Morgan proved a wizard. In a short time he succeeded in getting
more publicity for our purpose than we had got in months. His first
step in the capital had been to find out President Wilson's favourite
morning papers, his second to bombard them with news items about
the agitation in Russia over the San Francisco frame-up. Then Morgan buttonholed influential officials in Washington, made them familiar with the happenings on the Coast, and enlisted their sympathies.
The net results of this one man's efforts were a Federal investigation
ordered by President Wilson into the labour situation in San Francisco.

I had seen too many official investigations to expect much from
this one; still, it held out the hope that the skeleton in the family
closet of Big Business and Fickert and Co. would at last be dragged
into the light of day. Morgan and many of our trade-union associates
were more optimistic. They looked for the complete exoneration and
release of Billings, Mooney, and their co-defendants, as well as of
Sasha. I could not share their faith, but it did not lessen my admiration
for Ed Morgan's splendid achievement.

Shortly afterwards came further news from Russia of still greater
moment. A resolution proposed by the sailors of Kronstadt and
adopted at a monster meeting called for the arrest of Mr. Francis,
the American Ambassador in Russia, who was to be held as hostage
until the San Francisco victims and Sasha should be free. A delegation
of armed sailors had marched to the American Embassy in Petrograd
to carry out the decision. Our old comrade Louise Berger, who with
other Russian refugees had returned to her native land after the
outbreak of the Revolution, served as their interpreter. Mr. Francis
had solemnly assured the delegation that it was all a mistake, and that
the lives of Mooney, Billings, and Berkman were in no danger. But
the sailors were insistent, and Mr. Francis in their presence cabled to
Washington and promised to exert himself further with the American
Government to secure the release of the San Francisco prisoners.

The threat of the sailors evidently had an effect on the Ambassador,
with the result that President Wilson was moved to prompt action.
Whatever the message of the President to Governor Whitman, our
delegation found the latter in a very receptive mood. Moreover, quantity is always appreciated by aspiring politicians, and the labour dele-

gation consisted of a hundred men, representing nearly a million organized workers of New York. With them were Morris Hillquit and
Harry Weinberger, who impressed upon the Governor that Alexander
Berkman did not stand alone, and that his extradition would be resented by labour all through the United States. Mr. Whitman thereupon decided to telegraph District Attorney Fickert for the records
of the case and promised to postpone final action until he had thoroughly acquainted himself with the indictment against Sasha.

It was a victory indeed, though it did only temporarily delay proceedings. But instead of sending the requested documents, the San
Francisco prosecutor wired Albany that " the Berkman extradition
would not be pressed for the present." We had known all along that
Fickert could not afford to produce the records, since they did not
contain a scintilla of evidence to connect Sasha with the explosion.

The demand for extradition not having been granted within the
legally allowed thirty days, Sasha could not be detained in prison
longer. The Warden of the Tombs was anxious to get rid of him;
he had already upset the prison routine too much, the administration
said. His numerous visitors and the stacks of letters and messages he
was receiving added to the burdens of the prison officials, not to speak
of the excitement among the other prisoners who had become interested in the Berkman case. " Take him away, for the love of Mike,"
the Warden urged; " you are out on bail, so why don't you raise
his? " I assured him that the bond was on hand, and I should love
nothing better than to relieve him of the worry Sasha's presence was
causing him. But my friend had decided to sign himself back to the
Tombs for another thirty days to keep the promise made by his
attorney. San Francisco had informed Governor Whitman that they
needed more time to prepare the record requested by him. Though
Sasha could not lawfully be compelled to wait for them, Weinberger
had consented to prove that we had nothing to be afraid of in Fickert's
records. The Warden stared incredulously. An anarchist feeling bound
to live up to a pledge which he had not even given himself! " You
people are a crazy lot! " he said. " Who ever heard of a man's insisting on remaining in prison when he has a chance to get out? " But he
would treat Sasha right, he added, and maybe I would speak a good
word for him to Mr. Hillquit, who was sure to be the next mayor
of New York. I tried to tell him that I had no influence with the future socialist mayor, but it was to no purpose. It was sheer anarchist

cussedness, the Warden reiterated, not to help a fellow who had been such a friend to us.

America, only seven months in the war, had already outstripped in brutality every European land with three years' experience in the business of slaughter. Non-combatants and conscientious objectors from every social stratum were filling the jails and prisons. The new Espionage Law turned the country into a lunatic asylum, with every State and Federal official, as well as a large part of the civilian population, running amuck. They spread terror and destruction. Disruption of public meetings and wholesale arrests, sentences of incredible severity, suppression of radical publications and indictments of their staffs, beating of workers — even murder — became the chief patriotic pastime.

In Bisbee, Arizona, twelve hundred I.W.W.'s were manhandled and driven across the border. In Tulsa, Oklahoma, seventeen of their comrades were tarred and feathered and in a half-dead condition left in the sage-brush. In Kentucky Dr. Bigelow, a single-taxer and pacifist, was kidnapped and whipped for a speech he was *about* to deliver. In Milwaukee a group of anarchists and socialists met an even more terrible fate. Their activities had aroused the ire and envy of an unfrocked Catholic priest. He was especially enraged over the audacity of the young Italians who heckled him at his open-air meetings. He set the police on them and they charged the crowd with drawn clubs and guns. Antonio Fornasier, an anarchist, was instantly killed. Augusta Marinelli, another comrade, was mortally wounded, dying in the hospital five days later. In the general shooting several officers were slightly injured. Arrests followed. The Italian club-rooms were raided, literature and pictures destroyed. Eleven persons, including a woman, were held responsible for the riot caused by the uniformed ruffians. While the Italians were under arrest, an explosion took place in the police station. The perpetrators were unknown, but the prisoners were tried for that bomb. The jury was out just seventeen minutes, returning a verdict of guilty. The ten men and Mary Baldini were given twenty-five years each, and the State appropriated Mary's five-year-old child, although her people were willing and able to take care of it.

Through the length and breadth of the country stalked the madness of jingoism. One hundred and sixty I.W.W.'s were arrested in Chicago and held for trial on charges of treason. Among them were Bill Haywood, Elizabeth Gurley Flynn, Arturo Giovannitti, Carlo Tresca, and our old comrade Cassius V. Cook. Dr. William J. Robinson, editor of the New York *Critic and Guide,* was imprisoned for expressing his opinion on war. Harry D. Wallace, president of the League of Humanity and author of *Shanghaied in the European War,* was sentenced to twenty years' imprisonment for a lecture delivered in Davenport, Iowa. Another victim of this frightfulness was Louise Olivereau, an idealist of the finest type of American womanhood, who was condemned in Colorado to forty-five years' imprisonment for a circular in which she voiced her abhorrence of human slaughter. There was hardly a city or town in the wide United States where the jails did not contain some men and women who would not be terrorized into patriotic slaughter.

The most appalling crime was the murder of Frank Little, a member of the executive board of the I.W.W., and of another poor fellow who happened to bear a German name. Frank Little was a cripple, but that did not deter the masked bandits. In the dead of night they dragged the helpless man from his bed in Butte, Montana, carried him to an isolated spot, and strung him to a railroad trestle. The other " alien enemy " was similarly lynched, whereupon it was found that the man's room was decorated with a large American flag and his money was invested in Liberty Bonds.

The assaults on life and on free speech were supplemented by the suppression of the printed word. Under the Espionage Law and similar statutes passed in the war fever the Postmaster General had been constituted absolute dictator over the press. Even private distribution had become impossible for any paper opposed to the war. *Mother Earth* became the first victim, soon followed by the *Blast,* the *Masses,* and other publications, and by indictments against their editorial staffs.

The reactionaries were not the only element responsible for the patriotic orgy. Sam Gompers handed over the American Federation of Labor to the war baiters. The liberal intelligentsia, with Walter Lippmann, Louis F. Post, and George Creel in the lead, socialists like Charles Edward Russell, Arthur Bullard, English Walling, Phelps Stokes, John Spargo, Simons, and Ghent, all shared in the glory. The Socialist war phobia, the resolutions of their Minneapolis Conference, their patriotic special train, draped in red, white, and blue, their urging of every worker to support the war, all helped to destroy reason and justice in the United States.

On the other hand, the Industrial Workers of the World and those socialists who had not gone back on their ideals had by their blind self-sufficiency in the past also helped to sow the seeds of the crop they were now reaping. As long as persecution had been directed only against anarchists, they had refused to take notice or even to comment on the matter in their press. Not one of the I.W.W. papers had protested against our arrest and conviction. At the Socialist meetings not a single speaker would denounce the suppression of the *Blast* and *Mother Earth*. The New York *Call* thought the issue of free speech, when it was not itself directly concerned, deserving only of a few perfunctory lines. When Daniel Kiefer, the staunch fighter for freedom, had sent in a protest, it appeared in the *Call* thoroughly expurgated, with every reference to our magazines, to Sasha, and to me left out. The silly people were unable to foresee that the reactionary measures, always aimed first at the most unpopular ideas and their exponents, must in the course of time inevitably also be applied to them. Now the American Huns no longer discriminated between one radical group and another: liberals, I.W.W.'s, socialists, preachers, and college professors were being made to pay for their former short-sightedness.

In comparison with the patriotic crime wave the suppression of *Mother Earth* was a matter of insignificance. But to me it proved a greater blow than the prospect of spending two years in prison. No offspring of flesh and blood could absorb its mother as this child of mine had drained me. A struggle of over a decade, exhausting tours for its support, much worry and grief, had gone into the maintenance of *Mother Earth,* and now with one blow its life had been snuffed out! We decided to continue it in another form. The circular letter I had sent out to our subscribers and friends, informing them of the suppression of the magazine and of the new publication I was contemplating, brought many promises of help. Some, however, declined to have anything to do with the matter. It was reckless to defy the war sentiment of the country, they wrote. They could not give their support to such a purpose — they could not afford to get into trouble. Too well I knew that consistency and courage, like genius, are the rarest of gifts. Ben, of my own intimate circle, was sadly lacking in both. Having endured him for a decade, how could I condemn others for running to cover in danger?

A new project was sure to make Ben enthusiastic. The idea of a *Mother Earth Bulletin* caught his fancy, and his usual energy was put into motion at once to bring the publication about. But we had drifted apart too far. He wanted the *Bulletin* kept free from the war; there were so many other matters to discuss, he argued, and continued opposition to the Government was sure to ruin what we had built up during so many years. We must be more cautious, more practical, he insisted. Such an attitude seemed incredible in one who had been quite reckless in his anti-war talks. It was strange and ludicrous to see Ben in that rôle. His change, like everything else about him, was without reason or consistency.

Our strained relations could not last. One day the storm burst, and Ben left. For good. Listless and dry-eyed, I sank into a chair. Fitzi was near me, soothingly stroking my head.

CHAPTER XLVII

THE *MOTHER EARTH BULLETIN* LOOKED SMALL COMPARED WITH our previous publication, but it was the best we could do in those harassing days. The political sky was daily growing darker, the atmosphere charged with hate and violence, and no sign of relief anywhere in the wide United States. And again it was Russia to shed the first ray of hope upon an otherwise hopeless world.

The October Revolution suddenly rent the clouds, its flames spreading to the remotest corners of the earth, carrying the message of fulfilment of the supreme promise the February Revolution had held out.

The Lvovs and the Miliukovs had pitted their feeble strength against the great giant, a people risen in rebellion, and had been crushed in their turn, like the Tsar before them. Even Kerensky and his party had also failed to learn the great lesson; they forgot their pledges to the peasants and workers as soon as they had ascended to power. For decades the Social Revolutionists — next to the anarchists, although far more numerous and better organized — had been the most potent leaven in Russia. Their lofty ideal and aims, their heroism and martyrdom, had been the luminous beacon to draw thousands to their banner. For a brief period their party and its leaders, Kerensky, Tchernov, and others, had remained attuned to the spirit of the February days. They had abolished the death-penalty, thrown open the prisons of the living dead, and brought hope to every peasant's hut and worker's hovel, to every man and woman in bondage. They had proclaimed freedom of speech, press, and assembly for the first time in the history of Russia, grand gestures that met with the acclaim of all liberty-loving people in the world.

To the masses, however, the political changes had represented only the outward symbol of the real liberty to come — cessation of war, access to the land, and reorganization of the economic life. These were to them the fundamental and essential values of the Revolution. But Kerensky and his party had failed to rise to the situation. They had ignored the popular need, and the onrushing tide swept them away. The October Revolution was the culmination of passionate dreams and longings, the bursting of the people's wrath against the party that it had trusted and that had failed.

The American press, never able to see beneath the surface, denounced the October upheaval as German propaganda, and its protagonists, Lenin, Trotsky, and their co-workers, as the Kaiser's hirelings. For months the scribes fabricated fantastic inventions about Bolshevik Russia. Their ignorance of the forces that had led up to the October Revolution was as appalling as their puerile attempts to interpret the movement headed by Lenin. Hardly a single newspaper evidenced the least understanding of bolshevism as a social conception entertained by men of brilliant minds, with the zeal and courage of martyrs.

Unfortunately the American press did not stand alone in the misrepresentation of the Bolsheviki. Most of the liberals and socialists were with them. It was the more urgent for the anarchists and other real revolutionists to take up cudgels for the vilified men and their part in hastening events in Russia. In the columns of the *Mother Earth Bulletin,* from the platform, and by every other means we defended the Bolsheviki against calumny and slander. Though they were Marxists and therefore governmentalists, I sided with them because they had repudiated war and had the wisdom to stress the fact that political freedom without corresponding economic equality is an empty boast. I quoted from Lenin's pamphlet *Political Parties and the Problems of the Proletariat* to prove that his demands were essentially what the Social Revolutionists had wanted, but had been too timid to carry out. Lenin strove for a democratic republic managed by soviets of workers, soldiers, and peasant deputies. He demanded the immediate convocation of the Constituent Assembly, speedy general peace, no indemnities and no annexations, and the abolition of secret treaties. His program included the return of the land to the peasant population according to need and actual working ability, control of industries by the proletariat, the formation of an International in every land for the complete abolition of the existing governments and capitalism, and the establishment of human solidarity and brotherhood.

Most of these demands were entirely in keeping with anarchist ideas and were therefore entitled to our support. But while I hailed and honoured the Bolsheviki as comrades in a common fight, I refused to credit them with what had been accomplished by the efforts of the entire Russian people. The October Revolution, like the February overthrow, was the achievement of the masses, their own glorious work.

Again I longed to return to Russia and to participate in the task of re-creating her new life. Yet once more I was detained by my adopted country, firmly held by two years' prison sentence. However, I still had two months at my disposal before the decision of the United States Supreme Court should be handed down, and I could accomplish something in the meantime.

The United States Supreme Court, always slow in its grinding, had often required years to bring forth its Solomonic wisdom. But it was war time, and press and pulpit were howling for the pound of flesh to be cut from the anarchists and other rebels. The august body in Washington responded quickly. December 10 was to be the decisive day — Lawyers' Day, really, for no fewer than seven members of the profession would argue the unconstitutionality of conscription and the question of conspiracy involved in the cases of Kramer and Becker, Berkman and Goldman.

Our attorney, Harry Weinberger, had gone to Washington. His brief contained a thorough analysis of the various phases of the situation, but what appealed most to us was the progressive view taken by him of the human values and the social vision that were the key-note of his argument. To us it was a foregone conclusion that most of the gentlemen of the Supreme Court were too old and feeble to stand out against the patriotic clamour. But the few remaining days till December 10 were mine, and I decided to employ them for a hurried tour; I would carry the message of the Russian Revolution to the people and tell them the truth about the Bolsheviki.

The Mooney prosecution was in trouble; the Federal investigators were looking too searchingly into its crooked game. Added to this was the movement in San Francisco for Fickert's recall. The District Attorney had also cause for chagrin because of the refusal of Governor Whitman to deliver Sasha until the records in his case should be forthcoming. It was a rotten deal to give a man who had already served his masters so well in the Billings-Mooney trials. But Fickert did not despair. He would prove that his loyalty to big business could not be dampened. He still had three other criminals in his clutches — Rena Mooney, Israel Weinberg, and Edward D. Nolan. He would first get rid of them; then, when the Supreme Court should have decided Berkman's fate, he would secure him also. For the sake of one's duty one must learn to practise patience, and the San Francisco District Attorney could afford to bide his time. He notified Albany that he would temporarily withdraw his demand for the extradition of Alexander Berkman.

Sasha had to put up a twenty-five-thousand-dollar bond in the Federal conspiracy case. The esteem and popularity which he enjoyed among the workers immediately brought the Yiddish labour organizations and individual friends to his rescue. But it took much more time and a great deal of effort to overcome the red tape of the law. At last that was also mastered, and Sasha was once more a free man. It was no small satisfaction to everyone connected with our work to have him in our midst again. As to Sasha, he resembled a boy playing hooky from school. He was light-hearted and gay, though he knew, as we all did, that he would soon have to go to another prison for a longer stay. His leg had not yet healed and he needed a rest. I proposed that he take advantage of his short respite and go to the country, but he could not think of it, he said, so long as San Francisco was holding its victims. Our agitation had considerably shaken Fickert's self-assurance. His failure to secure Sasha's extradition had been followed by other misfortunes. Weinberg had been acquitted after the jury had deliberated for three minutes only, and the exposure of the prosecution's evidence as perjury had compelled the District Attorney to drop proceedings against Rena Mooney and Ed Nolan. But, the overwhelming proofs of frame-up notwithstanding, the two labour men had not escaped his clever manipulations. Two innocent men, one immured for life, the other facing death! How, then, could Sasha permit himself a vacation? It was impossible, he decided. A few days after his release he was again immersed in the San Francisco campaign.

A new worker in the Mooney field now appeared, Lucy Robbins. I had met her on my tours, but somehow we had not been close. I knew, however, that Lucy was an efficient organizer, and that she had been active in the labour and radical movements. While I was lecturing in Los Angeles in 1915, Lucy and Bob Robbins had looked me up. I had found them delightful company, and a friendship sprang up between us. Lucy disproved the male contention regarding woman's lack of mechanical ability. She was a born engineer and among the first in the country to devise and build an auto-house, which for comfort and charm excelled many a worker's apartment. It was unique, with its diminutive cupboards and dressers, and contained even a bath. In addition Lucy and Bob carried with them a complete printing outfit. In this ingenious house on wheels they made their way from coast to coast, with Lucy as the chauffeur. At points along the route they solicited printing orders, filled them on the spot, and thus earned their living-expenses. Their travelling companions were a phonograph and two little dogs, one of which was an uncompromising anti-Semite. As soon as any Jewish melody would be played, the four-footed Jew-hater would start up an unearthly howl and he would not desist until the offensive music stopped. That was the only disturbing element in the otherwise happy life of my new friends on their perambulations.

They arrived in New York for a brief stay, but when they learned that they could be of help in our campaign for Mooney, they at once volunteered to remain. They put their wheeled castle in storage and went to live in a little room in the Lafayette Street house where our office was located. Lucy soon proved herself as capable in interesting unions and organizing big affairs as she had been as an architect, constructor, mechanic, and Jack of all trades. She understood *Realpolitik* long before the term had become a vogue. She would grow impatient with our idea that neither love nor war justifies all means. We, on the other hand, were anything but sympathetic with her tendency to get results even if the goal were lost in the process. We scrapped a great deal, but it did not lessen our regard for Lucy as a good worker and friend. She was a vital creature with unlimited energy, whom no one could escape. I was happy that Sasha and Fitzi now had Lucy as their aide-de-camp. I felt sure that the three of them would make things hum.

Harry Weinberger brought the news that the Supreme Court was not likely to reach our cases until the middle of January, and he also informed us that we should be given a month's time after the decision before being called upon to surrender. That was encouraging in view of the difficulty of holding out-of-town meetings near Christmas.

Our stand against conscription and our condemnation to prison had gained us many new friends, among them Helen Keller. I had long wanted to meet this remarkable woman who had overcome the most appalling physical disabilities. I had attended one of her lectures, which was to me an affecting experience. Helen Keller's phenomenal conquest had strengthened my faith in the almost illimitable power of the human will.

When we had begun our campaign, I wrote to her asking her support. Not receiving a reply for a long time, I concluded that her own life was too difficult to permit interest in the tragedies of the world. Weeks later came a message from her that filled me with shame for having doubted her. Far from being self-absorbed, Helen Keller proved herself capable of an all-embracing love for humanity and profound feeling for its woe and despair. She had been absent with her teacher-companion in the country, she wrote, where she had heard of our arrest.

" My heart was troubled," the letter continued, " and I wanted to do something and I was trying to make up my mind what to do when your letter came. Believe me, my very heart-pulse is in the revolution that is to inaugurate a freer, happier society. Can you imagine what it is to sit idling these days of fierce action, of revolution and daring possibilities? I am so full of longing to serve, to love and be loved, to help things along, and to give happiness. It seems as if the very intensity of my desire must bring fulfilment, but, alas, nothing happens. Why have I this passionate desire to be a part of a noble struggle when fate has sentenced me to days of ineffectual waiting? There is no answer. It is tantalizing almost to the point of frenzy. But one thing is sure — you can always count upon my love and support. Those who are blinded in eye because they refuse to see tell us that in times like these wise men hold their tongues. But you are not holding your tongue, nor are the I.W.W. comrades holding their tongues — blessings upon you and them. No, Comrade, you must not hold your tongue, your work must go on, although all the earthly powers combine against it. Never were courage and fortitude so terribly needed as now. . . ."

This letter was soon followed by our meeting, which took place at a ball given by the *Masses*. The affair was to serve as a demonstration of solidarity with the indicted group of the publication — Max Eastman, John Reed, Floyd Dell, and Art Young. I was glad to learn that Helen Keller was present. The marvellous woman, bereft of the most vital human senses, could nevertheless, by her psychic strength, see and hear and articulate. The electric current of her vibrant fingers on my lips and her sensitized hand over mine spoke more than mere tongue. It eliminated physical barriers and held one in the spell of the beauty of her inner world.

1917 had been a year of most intense activity, and it deserved to receive a fitting farewell. Our New Year's party in Stella's and Teddy's quarters appropriately performed the pagan rites. For once we forgot the present and ignored what tomorrow might bring. The bottles popped, the glasses clinked, and hearts grew young in play and dance. The beautiful clog-dancing of our Julia, Ian's coloured mammy, and her friends enhanced the general hilarity. Faithful and loving was our Julia, full of frolic and fun. She was the soul of our circle and my right hand in making the mountains of sandwiches our friends devoured. Gaily we welcomed the new year. Life was alluring and every hour of freedom precious. Atlanta and Jefferson were far away.

My short lecture tour that followed was hectic and exciting, with no halls large enough to hold the crowds, enthusiasm for Russia running high everywhere.

In Chicago I had nine meetings arranged by the Non-Partisan Radical League, with William Nathanson, Bilov, and Slater as its active members. And of course there was Ben, making a success of his medical practice, but, like Raskolnikov, always stealing back to the scene of his old crimes.

Never before had Chicago shown such spontaneous fervour and response as at my lectures on Russia. Additional interest was lent to the occasion by the decision of the United States Supreme Court, handed down January 15, declaring the Draft Law constitutional. Forcible conscription, compelling the youth of the country to die across the seas, received the approving seal of the highest court in the land. Protest against human slaughter was declared outlawed. God and the ancient gentlemen had spoken, and their infinite wisdom and mercy were the supreme law.

So sure had we been that the decision would reflect the general war psychosis and sustain the lower courts that we had two weeks previously bidden our friends farewell in the *Bulletin*. We wrote:

> Be of good cheer, good friends and comrades. We are going to prison with light hearts. To us it is more satisfactory to stay behind bars than to remain MUZZLED in freedom. Our spirit will not be daunted, nor our will broken. We will return to our work in due time.

This is our farewell to you. The light of Liberty burns low just now. But do not despair, friends. Keep the spark alive. The night cannot last forever. Soon there will come a rift in the darkness, and the New Day break even in this country. May each of us feel that we have contributed our mite toward the great Awakening.

EMMA GOLDMAN
ALEXANDER BERKMAN

After Chicago came Detroit, where the success of my four meetings was assured by the organizing skill of my friends Jake Fishman and his handsome and capable wife, Minnie. People came *en masse*, reflecting the new-born hope, whose name was Russia, awakened in the breasts of these American wage-slaves. My announcement of the Political Prisoners' Amnesty League which I was planning to organize in New York before entering the Jefferson prison was received with frenzied acclaim, and a large sum was added to the fund started in Chicago.

In Ann Arbor it was Agnes Inglis, an old friend and a splendid worker, who had made the necessary arrangements for my two lectures. But the noble Daughters of the American Revolution willed it otherwise. Some of those ancient females protested to the mayor, and he, poor soul, happened to be of German parentage. What could he do but carry out the spirit of true American independence? My meetings were suppressed.

The end of January terminated the hopes many of our friends had naïvely entertained. The Supreme Court declined to grant us a rehearing or to delay the course of legal justice further. February 5 was set for our recommitment to prison. Seven more days of freedom, the nearness of loved ones, the association of faithful friends — we poured ourselves into every second. Our last evening in New York was devoted to our final public appearance and to the organization of the Political Prisoners' Amnesty League.

Delegates of the Union of Russian Workers from every part of the United States and Canada were holding a conference in New York. Sasha and I had been invited as the guests of honour. An ovation greeted us on our appearance, the entire assembly rising to welcome us. Sasha was the first speaker. In honour of the October Revolution and as a token of special appreciation of the conference he meant to say a few words in Russian. He indeed began in that language, but he got no further than " *Dorogiye tovaristchi* (Dear comrades)," continuing in English. I thought I could do better, but I was mistaken. So completely had we become identified with the life and speech of America that we had lost the fluent use of our native tongue. Yet we had always kept in touch with Russian affairs and literature and had co-operated with radical Russian efforts in the United States. We promised our audience, however, to address them the next time in their own beautiful language — perchance in the land of liberty.

The frosty day had played havoc with Stella's gas, but greater conspiracies had been concocted by candlelight. Ours was the formation of the Political Prisoners' Amnesty League. Leonard D. Abbott, Dr. C. Andrews, Prince Hopkins, Lillian Brown, Lucy and Bob Robbins, and others of our co-workers were present at the birth of the new organization. Prince Hopkins was chosen permanent chairman, with Leonard as treasurer, and Fitzi as secretary. The funds I had collected for the purpose in Chicago and Detroit were turned over as the starting capital of the new body. It was late, or rather early February 4, when our friends bade us hail and farewell. There were still the proofs to be read of my brochure *The Truth about the Bolsheviki,* but Fitzi considerately undertook to see the pamphlet safely through.

A few hours later we proceeded to the Federal Building to surrender. I offered to make the trip to the prison by myself and pay my own fare, but my suggestion met with the incredulous smiles of the officials. The deputy marshal and his lady again shared my compartment on our way to the Jefferson City penitentiary.

My fellow-prisoners greeted me as a long-lost sister. They were very sorry that the Supreme Court had decided against me, but since I had to serve my sentence, they had hoped that I would be returned to Jefferson City. I might help to bring about some improvements, they thought, if I could manage to get at Mr. Painter, the Warden. He was considered "a good man," but they rarely saw him, and they were sure he did not know what was going on in the female wing.

Already during my first stay of two weeks I had realized that the inmates in the Missouri penitentiary, like those at Blackwell's Island, were recruited from the lowest social strata. With the exception of my cell neighbour, who was a woman above the average, the ninety-odd prisoners were poor wretches of the world of poverty and drabness. Coloured or white, most of them had been driven to crime by conditions that had greeted them at birth. My first impression was strengthened by daily contact with the inmates during a period of twenty-one months. The contentions of criminal psychologists notwithstanding, I found no criminals among them, but only unfortunates, broken, hapless, and hopeless human beings.

The Jefferson City prison was a model in many respects. The cells were double the size of the pest holes of 1893, though they were not light enough, except on very sunny days, unless one was so fortunate as to have a cell directly facing a window. Most of them had neither light nor ventilation. Perhaps Southern people do not care for much fresh air; the precious element certainly seemed tabooed in my new boarding-house. Only in extremely hot weather were the corridor windows opened. Our life was very democratic in the sense that we all received the same treatment, were made to inhale the same vitiated air and bathe in the same tub. The great advantage, however, was that one was not compelled to share one's cell with anyone else. This blessing could be appreciated by those only who had endured the ordeal of the continuous proximity of another human being.

The contract labour system had been officially abolished in the penitentiary, I was told. The State was now the employer, but the obligatory task the new boss imposed was not much lighter than the toil the private contractor had exacted. Two months were allowed to learn the trade, which consisted in sewing jackets, overalls, auto coats, and suspenders. The tasks varied from forty-five to a hundred and twenty-one jackets a day, or from nine to eighteen dozen suspenders. While the actual machine work on the different tasks was the same, some of them required double physical exertion. The full complement of work was demanded without regard to age or physical condition. Even illness, unless of a very serious nature, was not considered sufficient cause for relieving the worker. Unless one had previous experience in sewing, or a special aptitude for it, the achievement of the task was a source of constant trouble and worry. There was no consideration for human variations, no allowance for physical limitations, except for a few favourites of the officials, who were usually the most worthless.

The shop was dreaded by all the inmates, particularly on account of the foreman. He was a boy of twenty-one who had been in charge of the treadmill since he was sixteen. An ambitious young man, he was very clever in pressing the tasks out of the women. If insults failed, the threat of punishment brought results. The women were so terrorized by him that they rarely dared to speak up. If anyone did, she became his special target for persecution. He was not even averse to robbing them of a part of their work and then reporting them for impudence, thus increasing their punishment for being short of the task. Four unfavourable marks a month meant a drop in the grade, which in return brought a loss of " good time."

The Missouri penitentiary was run on the merit system, of which Grade A was the highest. To attain that goal meant to have one's sentence reduced almost by half, at least so far as the State prisoners were concerned. We Federals might work ourselves to death without benefiting by our efforts. The only reduction of time we were allowed was the usual two months off each year. The dread of failing to reach Class A whipped the non-Federals beyond their strength in an attempt to accomplish the task.

The foreman was of course but a cog in the prison machine, the centre of which was the State of Missouri. It was doing business with private firms, drawing its customers from every part of the United States, as I soon discovered by the labels we had to sew on the things we manufactured. Even poor old Abe had been turned into a sweater of convict labour: the Lincoln Jobbing House of Milwaukee had the picture of the Liberator on its label, bearing the legend: " True to his country, true to our trade." The firms bought our labour for a song and they were therefore in a position to undersell those employing union labour. In other words, the State of Missouri was slave-driving and tormenting us, and in addition also acting as scab on the organized workers. In this commendable enterprise the official bully in our shop was very useful. Captain Gilvan, the acting warden, and Lilah Smith, the head matron, made up the triple alliance in control of the prison régime.

Gilvan used to administer flogging when that method of reformation was in vogue in Missouri. Other forms of punishment had since taken its place: deprivation of recreation, being locked up for forty-eight hours, usually from Saturday to Monday, on a diet of bread and water, and the " blind " cell. The latter measured about four feet by eight and was entirely dark; only one blanket was permitted and the daily food-allowance consisted of two slices of bread and two cups of water. In that cell prisoners were kept from three to twenty-two days. There were also bullrings, which, however, were not used on white women during my stay.

Captain Gilvan loved to punish the inmates in the blind cell and to hang them up by the wrists. "You must make the task," he would bellow; "no such thing as ' can't.' I punish cheerfully, mark you that!" He forbade us to leave our work without permission, even to go to the toilet. Once in the shop, after a more than usually brutal outbreak on his part, I approached him. "I must tell you that the task is sheer torture, especially for the older women," I said; "the insufficient food and constant punishment make things even worse." The Captain turned livid. "Look here, Goldman," he growled; "you're up to mischief. I have suspected it since your arrival. The convicts have never complained before, and they have always made the task. It's you who's putting notions into their heads. You had better look out. We have been kind to you, but if you do not stop your agitation, we will punish you like the rest, do you hear?"

"That's all right, Captain," I replied, "but I repeat that the task is barbarous and no one can make it regularly without breaking down."

He walked away, followed by Miss Smith, and I returned to my machine.

The shop matron, Miss Anna Gunther, was a very decent sort. She would patiently listen to the complaints of the women, often excuse them from work if they were ill, and even overlook a shortage in the task. She had been exceedingly kind to me, and I felt guilty over having left my place without permission. She did not reproach me, but said that I had been rash to talk to the Captain as I had. Miss Anna was a dear soul, the only moral prop the inmates had. Alas, she was only a subordinate.

The reigning queen was Lilah Smith. A woman in the forties, she had been employed in penal institutions since her teens. Of small stature, but compactly built, in appearance she suggested rigidity and coldness. She had an ingratiating manner, but underneath were the hardness and severity of the Puritan, hating implacably every emotion that had dried up in her own being. Neither pity nor compassion dwelt in Lilah's breast, and she was ruthless when she sensed them in anyone else. The fact that my fellow-prisoners liked and trusted me was enough to damn me in her eyes. Aware that I was in the good graces of the Warden, she never showed her antagonism openly. Hers was the insidious way.

The nerve-racking noises in the shop and the furious drive of the work laid me low the first month. My old stomach complaint became aggravated, and I suffered great pain in my neck and spine. The prison physician had anything but a good reputation among the inmates. He knew nothing, they claimed, and was too afraid of Miss Smith to excuse a prisoner from the shop, however ill she might be. I had seen inmates barely able to keep on their feet sent back to work by the doctor. The female department had no dispensary where patients could be examined. Even the seriously ill were kept in their cells. I hated to go to the doctor, but my agony became so unbearable that I had to see him. His gentle manner surprised me. He had been told that I was feeling bad, he said; why hadn't I come sooner? I must have a rest and not resume work until permitted by him, he ordered. His unexpected interest was certainly a far cry from the treatment other prisoners were receiving from him. I wondered whether his kindness to me was not due to the intercession of Warden Painter.

The doctor came to my cell every day, massaged my neck, entertained me with amusing stories, and even ordered a special broth. My improvement was slow, particularly because of the depressing effect of my cell. Its dirty grey walls, the lack of light and ventilation, and my inability to read or do anything else to while away the time made the day oppressively long. Former occupants of the cell had made pitiful attempts to beautify their prison house by family photos and newspaper pictures of their matinée idols. Black-and-yellow patches had been left on the wall, their fantastic outlines adding to my nervous restlessness. Another factor in my misery was the sudden stoppage of my mail; not a word came from anybody for ten days.

Two weeks in the cell made me realize why prisoners preferred the torture of the task. Some sort of occupation is the only escape from despair. None of the inmates enjoyed being idle. The shop, terrible as it was, was better than being locked up in the cells. I returned to work. It was a bitter struggle between physical pain, which drove me to my cot, and mental torment, which forced me back to the shop.

At last I was handed a large package of mail with a note from Mr. Painter saying that he had had to submit my incoming and outgoing correspondence to a Federal inspector in Kansas City, by orders from Washington. It made me feel very important to be considered dangerous even while in prison. Just the same, I wished that Washington were less attentive now, when every line I sent out or received was being read by the head matron and the Warden.

Subsequently I learned the cause of the renewed concern of the Federal authorities in my thoughts and expressions. Mr. Painter had given me permission to write a weekly letter to my attorney, Harry Weinberger. I had commented to the latter on Senator Phelan's speech in Congress against Tom Mooney. Thousands of appeals had been pouring in on the Governor of California to save Mooney's life. For a United States Senator to deliver himself of a vindictive attack at such a moment was both disgraceful and cruel. Naturally my remarks were not very complimentary to Mr. Phelan. I had forgotten that America since entering the war had turned every official into a Gessler, and that homage to his hat had become a national duty.

My mail contained much distressing news along with affection and cheer. Fitzi's apartment had been raided. At night, while she and our young secretary, Pauline, were asleep, Federal agents and detectives had broken into the house and rushed into her room before the girls had a chance to get dressed. The officers were looking for an I.W.W. conscript who had deserted, they claimed. Fitzi knew nothing about the man, but that did not stop the raiders from ransacking her desk, examining letters, and confiscating everything, including the plates of Voltairine de Cleyre's *Selected Works,* which we had published after her death.

Stella's letter evidenced her anxiety about the *Mother Earth* Bookshop, which she and our faithful "Swede" had started in Greenwich Village. Suspicious-looking individuals had been constantly at their heels, and conditions were getting so appalling that people hardly dared to breathe. The March number of the *Bulletin,* which Stella had sent, came as a harbinger of spring. It contained an account of Harry Weinberger's visit in Atlanta with Sasha and our two boys. Sasha had impressed on him the urgent need of continuing the fight for Tom Mooney's life. Cessation of our efforts for him might prove disastrous, he had warned Harry. My brave pal! How deeply he felt for the San Francisco victims and how ardently he had laboured for them! Even now he showed more concern for Mooney than for his own fate. It was bracing to feel his spirit in the *Bulletin,* and that of the other friends who had contributed. It was a wrench to decide to let the paper die, but, knowing Stella was in danger, I wrote her to discontinue its publication and close the book-shop.

In shipping us so far from New York, Washington had no doubt meant to make our lot the harder. There could have been no other reason for burying Sasha in Atlanta, when he could have been sent to Leavenworth, which is more accessible than the State of Georgia.

Jefferson City being only three hours' ride from St. Louis and an important railroad centre. I had more applications for visits than I could fill. I should have laughed over the frustration of Uncle Sam were it not that he had succeeded in striking Sasha. Conditions in Atlanta, I was informed, were nothing short of feudal. After fourteen years in the Pennsylvania purgatory Sasha was again being made to suffer more than I.

My first visitor was Prince Hopkins, chairman of the Political Prisoners' Amnesty League. He was on tour for that body, organizing branches, collecting data on the number of victims in prison, and raising funds. Hopkins inquired whether there was any other work in the prison I might do to save my health, and he offered to see the Warden. I told him that one of the women in the linen-mending room was to be released in the near future, and that there would be a vacancy. Soon after my visitor had left, I received a letter from him saying that Mr. Painter had promised to speak to Miss Smith about changing my employment, but a later note from the Warden was to the effect that the head matron had previously selected someone else for the job.

Ben Capes came to see me, a veritable beam of sunshine, his joyous nature shedding balm. My activities outside had been too absorbing for me fully to appreciate the boy, or perhaps one clings more hungrily in prison to one's kindred. Ben's friendship had never seemed more precious than on this visit. He sent in an enormous box of delicacies from the most expensive Jefferson City grocery, and my fellow-prisoners expressed the hope that my other visitors might prove equally extravagant. Our lean Tuesdays and Fridays, when fish was served that was neither fresh nor plentiful, would cease to be our hungry days. The food was never wholesome or sufficient for hard-working people, but Tuesdays and Fridays meant practically starvation.

Prison life tends to make one wondrously resourceful. Some of the women had devised an original dumb-waiter, consisting of a bag attached by strings to a broomstick. The contraption would be passed through the bars of an upper-tier cell, and I, directly underneath, would fish the bag in, fill it with sandwiches and goodies, then push it out far enough to enable my upper neighbour to pull the bag up again. The same procedure would be repeated with my neighbour below. Then the things would be passed from cell to cell along each gallery. The orderlies shared in the bounty, and by their help I was able also to feed the occupants of the rear tiers.

Various friends kept me supplied with eatables, especially St. Louis comrades. They even ordered a spring mattress for my cot and arranged with a Jefferson City grocer to send me anything I ordered. It was this helpful solidarity that enabled me to share with my prison companions.

The visit of Benny Capes increased my disappointment in " Big Ben." The grief he had caused me, especially in the course of the last two years of our life, undermined my faith in him and filled my cup with bitterness. I had determined after his last departure from New York to break the bond that had chained me so long. Two years in prison would, I hoped, help me do it. But Ben kept on writing as if nothing had happened. His letters, breathing the old assurance of his love, were like coals of fire. I could not believe him any more, yet I wanted to believe. I refused his plea to permit him to visit me. I even intended to ask him to stop writing, but he himself was facing a prison sentence, incurred during the period of our association, and that still linked him to me. His approaching fatherhood added fuel to my emotional stress. His minute description of the feelings engendered in him, and his delight in the little garments prepared for the expected child, afforded me a glimpse into an unsuspected aspect of Ben's character. Whether it was the defeat of my own motherhood or the pain that another should have given Ben what I would not, his rhapsodies increased my resentment against him and everyone connected with him. The announcement of the birth of his son also contained the information that the Appellate Court in Cleveland had sustained the verdict against him. He was leaving for that city, Ben wrote, to serve his sentence of six months in the workhouse. He was to be torn away from what he had looked forward to so eagerly and go to prison. Once more an inner voice spoke for him, submerging everything else in my heart.

At last I was assigned to a cell facing a window, which permitted the sun to look in upon me occasionally. The Warden had also instructed the head matron to allow me to take three baths a week. These privileges soon changed my condition for the better. He had furthermore promised to have my cell whitewashed, but he could not keep his word. The whole prison badly needed a new coat of paint, but Mr. Painter had failed to secure an appropriation for it. He could not make an exception of me, and I agreed with him. I devised something else to cover up the hideous patches on the walls — *crêpe* paper of a lovely green which Stella had sent me. With it I panelled the entire cell, and presently it began to look quite attractive, its cosiness enhanced by beautiful Japanese prints I had received from Teddy and a shelf of books I had accumulated.

There was no library in the female department, nor were we allowed to take out books from the men's wing. Once I asked Miss Smith why we could not get reading-matter from the male library. " Because I can't trust the girls to go there alone," she said, " and I have no time to accompany them. They would be sure to start flirtations." " What harm would that do? " I remarked naïvely, and Lilah was scandalized.

I requested Stella to see some publishers and also to induce our friends to send me books and magazines. Before long, four leading New York houses supplied me with many volumes. Most of them were above the understanding of my fellow inmates, but they soon learned to appreciate good novels.

The beneficial effect of reading was demonstrated to me by a Chinese girl who was serving a long term for killing her husband. She was a lonely creature, always keeping to herself and never communicating with the other prisoners. Up and down she would walk in the yard, muttering to herself. She was showing the first signs of insanity.

One day I received a Chinese magazine from comrades in Peking, with my picture on the front page. More ignorant of Chinese than the girl was of English, I gave her the journal. The sight of the familiar script brought tears to her eyes. The next day she tried to tell me in her broken English how wonderful it was to have something to read and how interesting the publication was. " You gland ladee," she kept repeating; " says muchee you zhis," pointing to the magazine. We became friends and she confided to me how she had come to kill the man she loved. They had become Christians. The minister who had married them told them that Christians in wedlock are bound by God for life, one man to one woman. Then she discovered that her husband had other women, and when she protested, he beat her up. He had often told her that he would always have other women besides her, and she killed him for that. Since then she believed all " Chlistians " false and she would never trust them again. She had thought that I, too, was a " Chlistian," but she read in the magazine that I was a non-believer. She would trust me, she said, but she objected to my friendly relations with the coloured inmates. They were inferior and dishonest, she was convinced. I pointed out that some people made the same objections to her race, and that in California

Chinese had been mobbed. She knew it, but she vehemently insisted that Chinese "no smell, no ignolant, diflent people."

Heathen that I was, I lost the privilege of recreation on Sunday afternoons because I failed to attend chapel services. I had minded the deprivation a great deal when I occupied the dark and damp cell, but now I welcomed it. It was quiet in the block, with the women out in the yard, and I was able to immerse myself in reading and writing. Among the books sent me was one from my friend Alice Stone Blackwell, containing the letters of Catherine Breshkovskaya and a biographic sketch of her. It was symbolic of the eternal recurrence of the struggle for freedom that I should be able to read the account of our Little Grandmother's exile under the tsars while I myself was a prisoner. Great as her persecution had been, she had never been forced to do hard labour, nor had any other women politicals in Russia. How surprised Catherine would be if I were to describe to her our shop, as bad a *katorga* as any in the Romanov autocracy! In one of her letters to Miss Blackwell, Babushka commented: "You, dearest, can write without fearing to be arrested, imprisoned, or exiled." In another she waxed enthusiastic over *The New Freedom,* by the former Princeton professor, now President of the United States. I wondered what the dear old lady would say if she could see with her own eyes what her hero in the White House had done to the country — the abrogation of all liberties, the raids, arrests, and reactionary fury his régime had brought in its wake.

The news of Breshkovskaya's arrival in America filled me with hope that an authentic word would at last be said for Soviet Russia and an effective protest voiced against conditions in America. I knew that Babushka was opposed, no less than I, to the socialism of the Bolsheviki; she would therefore be equally critical of their drift towards dictatorship and centralization. But she would appreciate their services to the October Revolution and she would defend them against the lies and calumnies in the American press. Surely the grand old lady would hold Woodrow Wilson to account for his share in the conspiracy to crush the Revolution. The anticipation of what she would do somewhat eased the poignancy of my own helplessness in prison.

The reports of her first public appearance in Carnegie Hall, under the auspices of Cleveland Dodge and other plutocrats, and her bitter denunciation of the Bolsheviki came as a fearful shock. Catherine Breshkovskaya, one of those whose revolutionary work for the past

fifty years had paved the way for the October upheaval, was now surrounded by the worst enemies of Russia, working hand in glove with
White generals and Jew-baiters, as well as with the reactionary element in the United States. It seemed incredible. I wrote Stella for
accurate information, meanwhile continuing to cling to my faith in
her who had been my inspiration and guiding star. Her simple grandeur, the charm and beauty of her personality, which I had learned
to love during our common work in 1904 and 1905, had too deeply
impressed me for me to give Babushka up so easily. I would write her.
I would tell her of my own stand regarding Soviet Russia; I would
assure her that I believed in her right of criticism, but I would plead
with her not to lend herself as an unwitting tool to those who were
trying to crush the Revolution. Stella was coming to visit me and I
would have her smuggle out my letter to Babushka, type it, and deliver it to her in person.

I had attained to the highest ambition of my fellow sufferers in
the penitentiary: I was placed in Grade A. Not entirely through my
own efforts, though, for I was still unable to make the full task. I was
indebted for it to the kindness of several coloured girls in the shop.
Whether it was due to greater physical strength, or because they had
been longer at the tasks, most of the Negro inmates succeeded better
than the white women. Some of them had acquired such dexterity that
they were often able to finish their tasks by three o'clock in the afternoon. Poor and friendless and desperately in need of a little money,
they would help out those who fell behind. For this service they were
entitled to five cents per jacket. Unfortunately, most of the whites
were too poor to pay. I was considered the millionaire; my exchequer
was often called upon to extend " loans," and I gladly complied. But
the girls helping me with my work would not accept remuneration.
They even felt hurt at the very suggestion of it. I was sharing my
food and books with them, they protested; how could they take
money from me? They agreed with my little Italian friend, Jennie
de Lucia, who had constituted herself my maid. " No take money from
you," she had declared, and the other women all echoed her sentiment.
Thanks to those kind souls, I reached Grade A, which entitled me to
send out three letters a week — really four, including the extra letter
I had been writing regularly to my counsellor.

On the eve of June 27 my coloured friends presented me with a
full task of jackets for the following day. They had remembered my

birthday. " It would be so nice if Miss Emma could keep out of the shop on that day," they had said. The next morning my table was covered with letters, telegrams, and flowers from my own kin and comrades, as well as with innumerable packages from friends in different parts of the country. I was proud to have so much love and attention, but nothing touched me so deeply as the gift of my fellow-sufferers in prison.

The Fourth of July was approaching and the women were all aflutter. They had been promised a cinema, recreation twice on that day, and also a dance. Not with male partners — the good Lord forbid! — but among themselves. They could order soft drinks from the grocery, and it was to be a festive day. Alas, the cinema proved inane and the holiday dinner poor. The women became disgruntled, particularly because of the refusal of Miss Smith to release a coloured girl from the blind cell, put there on the complaint of one of the matron's favourites, also coloured, who was suspected as a stool-pigeon and cordially disliked. It was too much to see her dolled up and running the Fourth of July show, while her victim was on bread and water. Several of the women made for the informer, and the grand day ended in a free-for-all fight. Miss Smith was compelled to punish her favourite as well as her assailants, and they were all locked up in the dungeon.

In my next letter I commented on the events of the patriotic day. My epistle was held up and then returned to me with instructions that no account of anything happening in prison could be sent out. I had often before discussed local matters in letters that Mr. Painter had permitted to pass, and I concluded that my Fourth of July narrative had not gone further than the head matron.

A three days' visit from my dear Stella proved a more real holiday for me than the Fourth of July. I was able to hand her my letter for Babushka, several notes my cell neighbours wanted smuggled out, and samples of the fake shop labels. They were three days of freedom from the shop, spent with my beloved child in our own world, a visit long awaited and quickly passed, to be followed by the reaction of the prison routine.

In my letter to Babushka I had begged her not to think that I denied her the right of criticism of Soviet Russia, or that I wished her to gloss over the faults of the Bolsheviki. I pointed out that I differed with them in ideas and that my stand against every form of dictatorship was irrevocable. But that was not important, I insisted, while every government was at the throat of the Bolsheviki. I pleaded with her to bethink herself, not to go back on her glorious past and the high hopes of Russia's present generation.

Babushka had grown feebler and whiter, Stella told me, but she had remained the old rebel and fighter, her heart aflame for the people as of yore. Still, it was true that she was permitting reactionary elements to make use of her. It was impossible to doubt Babushka's integrity or to think her capable of conscious betrayal, but I could not approve her attitude towards the soviets. Granted that her criticism was justified, I reasoned, why did she not proclaim it from a radical platform to the workers, instead of addressing the wretched gang that was conniving to undo the achievements of the Revolution? I could not forgive her that, and I scorned her suggestion that I would some day be on her side and work with her against the Bolsheviki, who were defying the entire reactionary world. And how could a woman like Breshkovskaya remain unseeing and inarticulate in the face of the dreadful situation in America, I wondered. Not since Peter Kropotkin's attitude on the World War had anything so affected me as her tacit approval of the frightfulness around her.

As for those native liberals and socialists who were serving as war drummers for the Government, I felt only disgust for the Russells, Bensons, Simonses, Ghents, Stokeses, Creels, and Gomperses. They had never been anything but political trimmers; they were merely fulfilling their destiny. It was more difficult to understand the Germanophobia of men like George D. Herron, English Walling, Arthur Bullard, and Louis F. Post. Someone had sent me Herron's book *The Need of Crushing Germany*. Never had I read a more bloodthirsty and vicious misrepresentation of a people. And that from the man who had left the Church because of his revolutionary internationalism!

Similarly Arthur Bullard in his volume *Mobilising America* repeated the falsifications spread by him and his worthy companions George Creel and Company. Bullard, the erstwhile enthusiast of the University Settlement, who had done such valiant work in Russia in 1905, had now thrown his ideals and literary talent on the dung-heap of reaction. I almost felt glad that his friend Kellogg Durland had not lived to join those spokesmen of murder and destruction. His death by his own hand, resulting from a frustrated love-affair, had at least the merit of striking only the two persons concerned, but the betrayal

·of their ideals by the American intelligentsia was a calamity to the whole country. I could not help feeling that this group was even more responsible for the widespread atrocities in the United States than the out-and-out jingoes.

It was the more joy to see that some few had retained their sanity and courage. Randolph Bourne, whose brilliant analysis of war we had reprinted in *Mother Earth,* continued to expose the lack of character and judgment among the liberal intelligentsia. With him were Professors Cattell and Dana, both dismissed from Columbia University for their heresies, as well as other academicians who had refused to silence their disbelief in war. Most gratifying also was the young radical generation and the mettle most of them had shown. Neither prison nor torture could induce them to take up arms. Max Frucht and Elwood B. Moore, of Detroit, and H. Austin Simons, the Chicago poet, had declared themselves willing to undergo any penalty rather than become soldiers. They went to prison, as did Philip Grosser, Roger Baldwin, and scores of others.

Roger Baldwin had proved a great surprise. In former years he had impressed me as rather confused in his social views, a person who tried to be all things to all men. His stand at his trial for evading the draft, his frank avowal of anarchism, and his unreserved repudiation of the right of the State to coerce the individual had made me conscious of guilt towards him. I wrote him confessing my unkind judgment and assuring him that his example had given me a salutary lesson of the need of greater care in the appraisement of people.

The prisons and military barracks were filled with conscientious objectors who were defying the most harrowing treatment. The most conspicuous case among them was that of Philip Grosser.

He had registered as an objector to war on political grounds, and he had declined to sign an enlistment card. Though it constituted a Federal civil offence, the youth was turned over to the military authorities and sentenced to thirty years' imprisonment for refusal to obey military orders. He was subjected to every form of torture, including chaining to the cell door, underground dungeon, and physical violence. Incarcerated in various prisons, he was finally sent to the Federal military penitentiary on Alcatraz Island, California, where he determinedly continued his refusal to participate in anything connected with militarism. Most of his time there he spent in the dark and damp cell of the hell-hole known as Uncle Sam's Devil's Island.

CHAPTER XLVIII

THE ESPIONAGE ACT RESULTED IN FILLING THE CIVIL AND MILI-
tary prisons of the country with men sentenced to incredibly long
terms; Bill Haywood received twenty years, his hundred and ten
I.W.W. co-defendants from one to ten years, Eugene V. Debs ten
years, Kate Richards O'Hare five. These were but a few among the
hundreds railroaded to living deaths.

Then came the arrest of a group of our young comrades in New
York, comprising Mollie Steimer, Jacob Abrams, Samuel Lipman, Hy-
man Lachowsky, and Jacob Schwartz. Their offence consisted in circulating a printed protest against American intervention in Russia.
Every one of those youths was subjected to the severest third degree,
and Schwartz fell dangerously ill as a result of savage beating. They
were kept in the Tombs, where large numbers of other radicals were
also awaiting trial or deportation, among them our faithful " Swede."
Their brave, determined stand for an ideal's sake glaringly contrasted
with Ben's inconsistency. His attempt to offer his medical services to
the army had capped the climax. If his prison term were at last served,
I felt, it would give me the strength to emancipate myself from him,
to become free from my emotional bondage. In this hope I had pestered Stella and Fitzi to raise his fine, so that he should not have to
serve more time in payment. But my fear had been groundless; the
fine was remitted before his release. Ben did not even have the grace
to inform me or the girls in New York about it. I received the news
from Agnes Inglis, one of my dearest and most considerate friends,
who came to visit me in prison. Later Ben wrote me; he told all about
his son, his mother, his wife, and his plans and urged me to see him.
I did not consider that his letter required a reply.

Agnes Inglis was the type to whom friendship was a sacrament.
Never once did she fail me after we first came in close contact in 1914.

She had been attracted to my work, she once told me, by my pamphlet *What I Believe*. She belonged to a wealthy family of orthodox Presbyterians, and it involved a great inner conflict to free herself from the middle-class morality and traditions of her environment, but with rare spiritual courage she overcame her heritage and gradually developed into a woman of independent and original attitude. She gave most generously of her time, energy, and means to every progressive cause and always participated in our campaigns for free speech. Agnes combined her active interest in the social struggle with a broad humanity in personal relations. I had come to appreciate her qualities as comrade and friend, and it was a great treat to have her visit me for two days.

Before she left the city, she called once more at the penitentiary, and the head matron brought her to the shop. I had not expected her and was startled when I saw Agnes standing in the door of our treadmill. Her affrighted eyes roved all over the place, finally settling on me. She started to walk towards my machine, but I stopped her with a gesture and then waved her my good-bye. I could not endure a demonstration of our affection in the presence of my shop-mates, who had so little of it in their own lives.

The war for democracy was celebrating its triumphs at home as abroad. One of its characteristic features was the dooming of Mollie Steimer's group to long prison terms. They were all mere youths. Yet United States District Judge Henry D. Clayton, a veritable Jeffreys, sentenced the boys to twenty years' imprisonment and Mollie to fifteen, with deportation at the expiration of their terms. Jacob Schwartz had been saved His Honour's mercy; he had died on the day of the opening of the trial, from injuries inflicted upon him by police blackjacks. In his Tombs cell was found an unfinished note in Yiddish, written in his dying hour. It read:

> Farewell, comrades. When you appear before the Court I will be with you no longer. Struggle without fear, fight bravely. I am sorry to have to leave you. But this is life itself. After your long martyr—

"The intelligence, courage, and fortitude shown by our comrades at their trial, particularly by Mollie Steimer," a friend wrote to me, "was profoundly impressive." Even the newspaper men could not help referring to the dignity and strength of the girl and her co-defendants.

These comrades had come from the working masses and were hardly known even to us. By their simple act and magnificent bearing they had added their names to the galaxy of heroic figures in the struggle for humanity.

The torrent of war news would have submerged the important case on trial before Judge Clayton but for the acumen of counsel for the defence. Harry Weinberger realized the significance of the underlying issues and he called on the witness-stand men of national reputation, thereby compelling the press to take notice. He subpœnaed Raymond Robins, one of the heads of the American Red Cross in Russia, and Mr. George Creel, of the Federal Information Bureau, who had been responsible for the so-called " Sisson documents." Thus the truth was exposed about the deliberate attempt to prejudice the world against Russia by forgeries which were to serve as ground for military intervention against the Revolution. Weinberger showed that President Woodrow Wilson had, without the knowledge of the people of the United States and without the consent of Congress, illegally sent American troops to Vladivostok and Archangel. Under those circumstances, he declared, the defendants had done a just and laudable act in calling public attention by their protest against waging war with Russia, with which America was officially at peace.

The influenza epidemic raging through the country had reached our prison, and thirty-five inmates were stricken down. In the absence of any hospital facilities, the patients were kept in their cells, exposing the other inmates to infection. At the first sign of the disease I had offered my services to the physician. He knew I was a trained nurse and he welcomed my aid. He promised to see Miss Smith about letting me take care of the sick, but days passed without bringing results. Later I learned that the head matron had refused to take me out of the shop. I was already enjoying too many privileges, she had said, and she would not stand for more.

Not being officially permitted to nurse, I sought means to aid the sick unofficially. Since the influenza invasion our cells were being left unlocked at night. The two girls assigned to nursing were so hardworked that they would sleep all through the night, and the orderlies were my friends. That offered me a chance to make hurried calls from cell to cell and do what little was possible to make the patients more comfortable.

On November 11, at ten in the morning, the electric power in our shop was switched off, the machines stopped, and we were informed that there would be no further work that day. We were sent to our cells, and after lunch we were marched to the yard for recreation. It was an unheard-of event in the prison and everyone wondered what it could mean. My thoughts dwelt in the days of 1887. I had intended to strike against work on the anniversary that marked the birth of my social consciousness. But there were so few women able to go to the shop that I did not want to add to the number of absentees. The unexpected holiday gave me the opportunity to be alone for spiritual communion with my martyred Chicago comrades.

During recreation in the yard I missed Minnie Eddy, one of the inmates. She was the most unfortunate creature in the prison, constantly in trouble about her work. Though she tried very hard to complete the allotted task, she seldom succeeded. If she rushed, her work was bad; if she slowed down, she failed to finish the day's work. She was bullied by the foreman, reprimanded by the head matron, and often punished. In her desperation Minnie spent the few cents she received from her sister to pay for help. She was very appreciative of the least kindness and she became inseparable from me. Of late she had been complaining of dizziness and severe pain in the head. One day she had fainted away at her machine. It was apparent that Minnie was seriously ill. Yet Miss Smith refused to exempt her from work. The woman was shamming, the matron claimed, though we knew better. The doctor, by no means a brave or aggressive man, would not dispute Lilah.

Failing to see Minnie in the yard, I assumed that she had probably received permission to remain in the cell. But when we returned from recreation, I discovered that she was in punishment, locked up on bread and water. We expected her to be released the next day.

Late in the evening the prison silence was torn by deafening noises coming from the male wing. The men were banging on bars, whistling, and shouting. The women grew nervous, and the block matron hastened over to reassure them. The declaration of armistice was being celebrated she said. "What armistice?" I asked. "It's Armistice Day," she replied; "that's why you have been given a holiday." At first I hardly grasped the full significance of the information, and then I, too, became possessed of a desire to scream and shout, to do something to give vent to my agitation. "Miss Anna, Miss Anna!"

I called the matron back. " Come here, please, come here ! " She approached again. "You mean that hostilities have been stopped, that the war has come to an end and the prisons will be opened for those who refused to take part in the slaughter? Tell me, tell me ! " She put her hand soothingly on mine. " I have never seen you so excited before," she said; " a woman of your age, working yourself up to such a pitch over such a thing ! " She was a kindly soul, but she knew nothing outside her prison duties.

Minnie Eddy was not released the next day, as I had hoped she would be. On the contrary, suspecting that someone was secretly feeding her, the head matron ordered her transferred to the blind cell. I pleaded with Miss Smith that Minnie might die if she continued on bread and water and was forced to sleep on the damp floor. Lilah told me gruffly to mind my own business. I waited another few days and then I notified the Warden that I had something urgent to see him about. Miss Smith no doubt suspected the contents of my sealed envelope, but she did not dare hold back letters addressed to Mr. Painter. He came, and I reported Minnie's case to him. The same evening Minnie was sent back to her cell.

On Thanksgiving, she was allowed to come to the dining-room for the special dinner, which consisted of pork of questionable quality. Starved for days, she ate ravenously. A week before, her sister had sent her a basket of fruit, and as a privilege Minnie was permitted to receive it. Most of it had meanwhile become decayed, and I warned her not to touch it, promising to send her eggs and other things from my supply. At midnight the coloured orderly woke me to say that she had heard Minnie cry in pain, and when she had reached her cell, she had found the woman in a faint on the floor. Her door was locked and she did not dare call Miss Smith. I insisted that she must be summoned. After a while we heard groaning in Minnie's cell, followed by sobbing, and then the matron's receding steps. The orderly reported that Miss Smith had poured cold water over Minnie, struck her several times, and ordered her to get up from the floor.

The following day Minnie was placed in an isolated rear cell, with only a mattress on the floor. She became delirious, her cries resounding through the corridor. We learned that she had refused nourishment and that an attempt at forcible feeding had been made. But it was too late. She died on the twenty-second day of her punishment.

The misery and tragedies of prison life were aggravated by sad news from the outside. My brother Herman's wife, our beautiful Ray, had died from heart-trouble. Helena also was in a terrible state of mind. No word from David had reached her for weeks, and she was beside herself with dread that something might have happened to him.

A ray of light came with the commutation of Tom Mooney's death-sentence to life imprisonment. It was a travesty on justice to immure a man for life who had been proved innocent by the State's own witnesses. Nevertheless, the commutation was an achievement, due mostly, I felt, to the effective work our people had done. Without the campaign Sasha, Fitzi, and Bob Minor had inaugurated in San Francisco and New York, there would have been no demonstrations in Russia and other European countries. It was the international scope of the Mooney-Billings case that had impressed President Wilson to the extent of inducing him to cause a Federal investigation. The same moral force had prompted him to intercede with the Governor of California for Mooney's life. The agitation organized by Sasha and his associates had at last snatched Tom Mooney from death. Time was thereby gained for further work to give Mooney and Billings liberty. I was happy at these developments and proud of Sasha and the success of his strenuous efforts. I fervently wished that he might be free to bring to completion the victory which had come near costing his own life.

The prison had been quarantined and all visits stopped, excepting of course the incoming and released prisoners. Several new ones arrived, among them Ella. She was sent up on a Federal charge and she brought to me what I had been missing so much — intellectual companionship with a kindred spirit. My fellow inmates had been kind to me and I had not lacked affection, but we belonged to different worlds. It would have only made them self-conscious of their lack of development had I broached my ideas to them or discussed the books I read. But Ella, though still in her teens, shared my conception of life and values.

She was a proletarian child, familiar with poverty and hardship, strong, and socially conscious. Gentle and sympathetic, she was like a beam of sunshine, bringing cheer to her fellow prisoners and great joy to me. The women reached out for her hungrily, though she was an enigma to them. "What are you here for," one inmate asked Ella — "picking pockets?" "No." "Soliciting men?" "No." "Selling dope?" "No," laughed Ella, "for none of these things." "Well, what else could you have done to have got eighteen months?" "I am an anarchist," Ella replied. The girls thought it funny to go to prison for "just being something."

Christmas was approaching and my companions were in nervous wonderment as to what the day of days would bring them. Nowhere is Christianity so utterly devoid of meaning as in prison, nowhere its precepts so systematically defied, but myths are more potent than facts. Fearfully strong is their hold on the suffering and despairing. Few of the women could expect anything from the outside; some had not even a single human being to give them a thought. Yet they clung to the hope that the day of their Saviour's birth would bring them some kindness. The majority of the convicts, of infantile mentality, talked of Santa Claus and the stocking with naïve faith. It served to help them over their degradation and misery. Forsaken by God, by man forgot, it was their only refuge.

Long before Christmas, gifts began to arrive for me. Members of my family, comrades, and friends fairly deluged me with presents. Soon my cell began to look like a department store, and every day brought additional packages. As usual, our dear Benny Capes, in response to my request for trinkets for the inmates, sent a huge consignment. Bracelets, ear-rings, necklaces, rings, and brooches, enough to make the Woolworth stock feel ashamed, and lace collars, handkerchiefs, stockings, and other things sufficient to compete with any store on Fourteenth Street. Others were equally generous. My old friends Michael and Annie Cohn were particularly lavish. An invalid for years and in constant torment, Annie was yet most thoughtful of others. She was indeed a rare spirit of brave patience and selfless kindness. Our staunch friends for a quarter of a century, Annie and Michael had always been among the first to come to our assistance whenever aid was needed, co-operating in our efforts in the movement, sharing our burdens, helping and giving without stint. Hardly a week had passed since my imprisonment without a cheering letter and gifts from them. For Christmas Annie sent me a special parcel — everything prepared with her own hands, as Michael affectionately wrote. Wonderful Annie, a martyr to physical ailments, steadily growing worse, her suffering increasing, living only in her devotion to others!

It was a problem to divide the gifts so as to give each what she might like best, without arousing envy or suspicion of preference and favouritism. I called to my aid three of my neighbours, and with their expert advice and help I played Santa Claus. On Christmas Eve, while our fellow-prisoners were attending the movies, a matron accompanied us to unlock the doors, our aprons piled high with gifts. With gleeful secrecy we flitted along the tiers, visiting each cell in turn. When the women returned from the cinema, the cell-block resounded with exclamations of happy astonishment. " Santa Claus 's been here! He's brung me something grand! " " Me, too! Me, too! " re-echoed from cell to cell. My Christmas in the Missouri penitentiary brought me greater joy than many previous ones outside. I was thankful to the friends who had enabled me to bring a gleam of sunshine into the dark lives of my fellow-sufferers.

On New Year's again the prison was filled with noisy hilarity. Fortunate indeed are they whom each year brings nearer to the passionately longed-for hour of release. Not so the poor creatures sent up for life. No hope or cheer for them in the new day or new year. Little Aggie kept to her cell, wailing over her fate. A piteous sight the poor woman was, withered at thirty-three, her years spent in the penitentiary since she was eighteen. She had been condemned to death for killing her husband. The murder was the result of a drunken card-row between Aggie's husband and the boarder. It probably was not the young bride who had wielded the fatal poker, but her " own man " had managed to wriggle out of responsibility. He had turned State's evidence and had helped to send the child to her doom. Her extreme youth had saved her from the noose; her sentence was commuted to life imprisonment. I found Aggie one of the sweetest and kindest of beings, capable of strong attachments. After she had been in prison ten years, she was permitted to keep a dog some visitor had given her. His name was Riggles, and an ugly beast he was. But to Aggie he was beauty personified, the most precious thing she possessed and her only tie in life. No mother could have given greater love and attention to her child than Aggie gave her pet. She would never ask anything for herself, but for Riggles she would beg. The brightening of her otherwise dead eyes when she would take Riggles into her arms was a key to the heart-hunger of the unfortunate the law's stupidity had stamped a hardened criminal.

And there was my other neighbour Mrs. Schweiger, a " bad woman," as the head matron called her. A devout Catholic, tragically mismated, she could find no escape in divorce. Ill health, which unfitted her for child-bearing, added to the misery and loneliness of her life. Her husband sought distraction with other women, and she was left to brood and weep, a prisoner in her own home. In a fit of homicidal melancholia she had emptied a pistol into him. She was of German parentage, which did not add to Lilah Smith's liking for her.

With the New Year came the shock of David's death. For months rumours of the boy's end had hung like a pall over his family. Helena's appeals to Washington for news of her son had brought no results. The United States Government had done its duty; it had shipped David with thousands of others to the fields of France. It could not be bothered by the anguish of those left behind. It was from an officer returned from France that Stella had learned of Dave's tragic fate.

The boy had preferred a responsible position, though dangerous, to the safety of the military orchestra to which he had been assigned, his comrade reported to Stella. He lost his life on October 15, 1918, in the Bois de Rappe, in the Argonne forest, killed one month before Armistice Day, in the prime and glory of his youth. My poor sister was still ignorant of the blow awaiting her. She would be informed as soon as official confirmation was received, Stella's letter said. I foresaw the effect of the terrible news on Helena and I felt sickening apprehension for her sake.

For the first time in months I had a caller again, our dear friend and co-worker M. Eleanor Fitzgerald — "Fitzi." Following our imprisonment she had accepted a position with the Provincetown Players, where she worked as arduously as she had with us. At the same time she continued her activities in the Mooney-Billings campaign, the Political Prisoners' Amnesty League, and as well took care of our boys in prison. I realized only when I saw her again how hard she must have been working. She looked worn and fatigued, and I regretted having scolded her in a letter because she had not written me in a long time.

She came to Jefferson on her way back home from the Mooney Conference in Chicago. She had also gone to see Sasha in Atlanta. Her visit with him, she told me, had proved most unsatisfactory, because it had been very brief and under a rigid watch. But she had managed to smuggle out a note from him to me. I had had no direct word from Sasha since the last day of our trial, a year before, and the familiar handwriting brought a lump to my throat. Fitzi's replies to my questions were evasive, and I suspected that all was not well with Sasha. He was having a frightful time of it, she reluctantly admitted. He had been put in the dungeon for circulating a protest to the Warden against the brutal clubbing of defenceless prisoners. He had earned the bitter enmity of the officers by denouncing the unprovoked murder of a young Negro inmate who was shot in the back for "impudence." All his Christmas parcels, except one, had been denied him. The other gifts sent to him had graced the dinner-table of the officials. He looked haggard and sick, Fitzi said. "But you know Sasha," she hastened to add; "nothing can break his spirit or dampen his sense of humour. He joked and laughed while I was with him and I joined in, choking back my tears." Yes, I knew Sasha, and I was certain he would survive. Only eight months more — had he not shown his powers of endurance during his fourteen years in Pennsylvania?

Fitzi could tell me little that was encouraging about the Mooney Conference in Chicago, which she had helped to organize. Most of the labour politicians were busy side-tracking the Mooney activities, she informed me. There was a disheartening lack of unanimity in favour of a general strike in behalf of Mooney and Billings. Moreover, there was evidently a deliberate attempt to hush up publicity. More "diplomatic" methods were to be used to liberate the men. The participation of anarchists was to be discouraged. They had been the first to sound the alarm in the San Francisco cases, and Sasha had consecrated himself to the work, even at the jeopardy of his own life. Now the anarchists and their efforts were to be eliminated from the fight. It was not the first time, nor would it be the last, that anarchists burned their fingers in pulling the chestnuts out of the fire for others, but if Billings and Mooney should regain their freedom, we should feel our work amply repaid. Fitzi, of course, had no intention of relaxing her efforts to bring about a general strike, and I knew that the brave girl would do her best.

The hardest thing to bear in prison is one's utter powerlessness to do aught for one's loved ones in distress. My sister Helena had given me more affection and care than my parents. Without her my childhood would have been even more barren. She had saved me many blows and had soothed my youth's sorrows and pains. Yet in her own greatest need I could do nothing to help her.

If only I could believe that my sister was still able, as in the past, to feel the suffering of humanity at large, then I would point out to her that there were other stricken mothers, their loss no less poignant than hers, and other tragedies more appalling even than David's untimely death. In former days Helena would have understood, and her own grief might have been mellowed by universal suffering. Would she now? From the letters of my sister Lena and of Stella I could see that Helena's springs of social sympathy had dried up with the tears she had shed for her son.

Time is the greatest healer, and it might also heal my sister's wounds, I thought. I held to that ray of hope and I looked forward to my approaching release, when I might take my darling away somewhere and perhaps bring her a little peace by loving communion.

My sorrow was augmented by still another loss, that of my friend Jessie Ashley, valiant rebel. No other American woman of her position had allied herself so completely with the revolutionary movement as Jessie. She had taken a vital part in the I.W.W. activities, the free-speech and birth-control campaigns, giving personal service and much of her means. She had been with us in the No-Conscription League and in every move we had made against the draft and the war. When Sasha and I were held under fifty-thousand-dollar bail, Jessie Ashley was the first to contribute ten thousand dollars in cash towards our bond. The news of her death after a short illness had come unexpectedly. David and Jessie — one of my own blood, the other much closer in spirit — their passing affected me deeply. Yet it was the horrible fate of two other persons, known to me by name only, that proved even a greater blow — that of Rosa Luxemburg and Karl Liebknecht.

Social democracy had been their goal, and anarchists their special *bête noire*. They had fought us and our ideas, not always even by fair means. At last social democracy triumphed in Germany. Popular wrath had frightened the Kaiser out of the country, and the brief revolution had made an end to the house of Hohenzollern. Germany was proclaimed a republic, with the socialists at the political helm. But, oh, the cruel irony of the shades of Marx! Luxemburg and Liebknecht, who had helped to build up the Socialist Party of Germany, were crushed by the régime of their orthodox comrades risen to power.

With Easter came spring's awakening, flooding my cell with warmth and filling it with the perfume of flowers. Life was gaining new meaning — only six more months to liberty!

April added another political, Mrs. Kate Richards O'Hare, to our company. I had met her once before, when she had called at the prison on her visit to Jefferson City to see Governor Gardner. She had been convicted under the Espionage Law, but she was emphatic that the Supreme Court would reverse the verdict, and that in any event she would not serve time in our place. I had been disagreeably impressed by her dogmatic manner and her belief that exceptions would be made in her behalf, but I wished her luck. When I came upon her dressed in the penitentiary uniform of striped gingham, waiting to fall in line with us as we were marching to the dining-room, I felt sorry indeed that her expectations had miscarried. I wanted to take her by the hand and say something that would ease her first and most trying prison hours, but talking or demonstration of feeling was strictly tabooed. Moreover, Mrs. O'Hare looked rather forbidding. Of tall stature, she carried herself with hauteur, her expression appearing more rigid because of her steel-grey hair. I found it difficult to say something warm even when we reached the yard.

Mrs. O'Hare was a socialist. I had read the little publication she had been issuing together with her husband, and I considered her socialism a colourless brand. Had we met on the outside, we should have probably argued furiously and have remained strangers for the rest of our lives. In prison we soon found common ground and human interest in our daily association, which proved more vital than our theoretical differences. I also discovered a very warm heart beneath Kate's outer coldness and found her a woman of simplicity and tender feeling. We quickly became friends, and my fondness for her increased in proportion as her personality unfolded itself to me.

Soon we politicals — Kate, Ella, and I — were nicknamed " the trinity." We spent much time together and became very neighbourly. Kate had the cell on my right, and Ella was next to her. We did not ignore our fellow-prisoners or deny ourselves to them, but intellectually Kate and Ella created a new world for me, and I basked in its interests, its friendship and affection.

Kate O'Hare had been taken away from her four children, the youngest of whom was about eight — an ordeal that would have taxed the strength of many a woman. Kate, however, was splendid. She knew that her children were well cared for by their father, Frank O'Hare. Besides, in point of intelligence and maturity her children were far above their age. They were their mother's real comrades and not merely the offspring of her womb. Their spirit was Kate's greatest moral support.

Frank O'Hare visited Kate every week and occasionally even more often, keeping her in touch with her friends and their work. He mimeographed her letters and circulated them through the land. The bitter edge of incarceration was thus taken away from Kate. An additional factor to help her over the hardest period was her extraordinary adaptability. She was able to fit into any situation and to go about everything in her quiet, methodical manner. Even the dreadful noises in the shop, and its maddening grind, seemed to have little effect on her. Nevertheless, she suffered a break-down before she had been with us two months. She had over-estimated her strength when she attempted to master the task sooner than any one of us had been able to do it.

But Kate kept her courage and she was greatly sustained by Frank, who had already begun to work for her pardon. She had been convicted for an anti-war speech, but the O'Hares had big political connexions. It was therefore reasonably certain that Kate would not have to serve long. I myself had declined the offer of friends to gain clemency for me. But it was different with Kate, who believed in the political machine. I hoped, however, that in her appeal would also be included the other political prisoners.

Meanwhile Kate was bringing about changes in the Missouri penitentiary which I had in vain been trying for fourteen months to accomplish. She had an advantage in the presence of her husband nearby, in St. Louis, and access to the press, and we often banteringly discussed which of the two was of more value. Her letters to O'Hare, criticizing the lack of a library for the women, and her condemnation of our food, standing for two hours before being served, had appeared in the *Post Dispatch* and brought immediate improvement. The head matron announced that books could henceforth be had from the men's department, and the food was served hot, " for the first time in the ten years I've been here," as Aggie commented.

In the interim an unusual feature was introduced by the Warden independently of Kate's influence. It was announced that we were to have picnics every second Saturday in the city park. So extraordinary was the innovation that we felt inclined to consider it a joke, too good to be true. But when we were assured that the first outing would actually take place the following Saturday, that we could spend the whole afternoon in the park, where the male band would play dance music, the women lost their heads and forgot all about the prison rules. They laughed and wept, shouted, and acted generally as if they had gone mad. The week was tense with excitement, everyone working to exhaustion to make the task, so as not to be left behind when the great day should arrive. During recreation the sole talk was of the picnic, and in the evenings the cell block was filled with whispered conversation about the impending event — how to fix up to look nice, how it would feel to walk about in the park. And would the band boys be near enough to talk to? No débutante was ever more wrought up over her first ball than the poor creatures, most of whom had not stepped out of the prison walls for a decade.

The picnic did take place, but to us — to Kate, Ella, and me — it was a ghastly experience. There were heavily armed guards behind and in front of us, and not a step was permitted outside the prescribed area. Guards surrounded the prison orchestra, while the matrons let no woman out of sight the moment dancing began. The supper was most depressing. The whole thing was a farce and an insult to human dignity. But to our unfortunate fellow-convicts it was like manna to the Jews in the desert.

In my next letter to Stella I quoted Tennyson's *Light Brigade*. In the course of the week the Warden sent for me to ask what I had meant by my reference. I told him that I should prefer to remain in my cell Saturday afternoon rather than picnic by the grace of an armed force. There was no danger of any woman's escaping, with the open country-side offering no place to hide. "Don't you see, Mr. Painter," I appealed to him, "it is not the park which will prove an influence for good? It will be your trust in the women, their feeling that at least once in two weeks they are given a chance to eliminate the prison from their consciousness. That sense of freedom and release will create a new morale among the inmates."

The following Saturday there were fewer guards and they did not flaunt their weapons in our faces. Limit restrictions were abolished, and the entire park was ours. The band boys were permitted to meet the girls at the soda-water stand and to treat them to pop and ginger ale. Our suppers in the park were gradually discarded, having proved too hard a task for the two matrons to supervise. But none of us minded it, since we were given another two hours of recreation in the prison yard after supper. The inmates had now something to look forward to and live for. Their state of mind changed; they worked with more zest, and their former distress and irritableness decreased.

One day an unexpected visitor was announced — S. Yanofsky, the editor of our Yiddish anarchist weekly in New York. He was on a lecture tour to California and he could not pass Jefferson City without seeing me, he said. I was pleased to know that my bitter opponent and censor of yester-year had gone out of his way to pay me a visit. His stand on the war, and particularly his worship of Woodrow Wilson, had completely alienated me from him. It was discouraging that a man of his ability and perspicacity should be carried away by the general psychosis. But, after all, his inconsistency was no worse than that of Peter Kropotkin, who had taken the lead which all the other pro-war anarchists had followed. Yanofsky, however, had gone even further in his enthusiasm for the Allies. He had written a veritable panegyric on Woodrow Wilson and had waxed poetic about "the pride of the Atlantic," that it might carry his hero to European shores for the great feast of peace. Such idolatry of one old gentleman for another outraged not only my principles, but also my conception of good taste.

Our conviction and the shameful manner in which we had been spirited out of New York must have touched something very deep in Yanofsky's heart. He wrote and spoke in our defence, helped to raise funds, and evidenced great concern over our fate. But it was mainly our struggle to rescue Sasha from the San Francisco trap that had established closer rapport between Yanofsky and me. His wholehearted co-operation and his genuine interest in Sasha had shown him capable of devoted comradeship I had never suspected in him before.

My mail had again been held up for ten days. The contents of two letters I had written had been found to be of a treasonable nature. I had ridiculed in them the Congressional committee that was investigating bolshevism in America; I had also attacked the high-handed autocracy of Attorney General A. Mitchell Palmer and his régime, as well as Messrs. Lusk and Overman, the New York State Senators delving into radicalism. Those Rip van Winkles had suddenly awakened to find that some of their countrymen had actually been thinking and reading about social conditions, and that other subversive elements had even dared to write books on the subject. It was a crime to be nipped in the bud if American institutions were to be saved. Of the insidious works those of Goldman and Berkman were the worst, and *Prison Memoirs of an Anarchist,* and *Anarchism and Other Essays* deserved to be put on the Index Expurgatorius.

My delayed mail brought news from Harry Weinberger about the treatment of Sasha in the Atlanta Federal prison and of our counsel's protest to Washington in connexion with it. Sasha had been confined in an underground dungeon, deprived of all his privileges, including mail and reading-matter, and kept on a reduced diet. The solitary was breaking down his health, and Weinberger had threatened a campaign of publicity against the palpable persecution of his client by the prison administration. Our comrades Morris Becker and Louis Kramer, as well as several other politicals in Atlanta, were sharing a similar fate.

Among my letters was also one containing details of the harrowing death of the brilliant German anarchist Gustav Landauer. Another prominent victim had been added to the number that included Rosa Luxemburg, Karl Liebknecht, and Kurt Eisner. Landauer had been arrested in connexion with the revolution in Bavaria. Not satisfied with shooting him, the reactionary fury had resorted to the dagger to finish up its ghastly job.

Gustav Landauer was one of the intellectual spirits of the "*Jungen*" (the "Young"), the group that had seceded from the German Social Democratic Party in the early nineties. Together with the other rebels he had founded the anarchist weekly, *Der Sozialist.* Gifted as a poet and writer, the author of a number of books of sociological and literary value, he soon made his publication one of the most vital in Germany.

In 1900 Landauer had drifted from the Kropotkin communist-anarchist attitude to the individualism of Proudhon, which change also involved a new conception of tactics. Instead of direct revolutionary mass action he favoured passive resistance, advocating cultural and co-operative efforts as the only constructive means of fundamental social change. It was sheer irony of fate that Gustav Landauer, turned Tolstoyan, should lose his life in connexion with a revolutionary uprising.

While the Kaiser's socialists were busy annihilating their own political kin, the fate of their country was decided at Versailles. The labour pains of the peace negotiators were long and distressing, the result a still-born child more hideous in a measure than the war. Its fearful effect on the German people and the rest of the world completely vindicated our stand against the slaughter which was to end all slaughter. And Woodrow Wilson, that innocent at the diplomatic gaming-table, how easily he had been duped by the European sharks! The President of the mighty United States had held the world in the palm of his hand. Yet how pathetic was his failure, how complete his collapse! I kept wondering how our worshipful American intelligentsia felt at seeing their idol no longer protected by his Presbyterian mask. The war to end war terminated in a peace that carried a rich promise of more terrible wars.

Among my literary correspondents I greatly enjoyed Frank Harris and Alexander Harvey. Harris had always been very thoughtful, supplying me with his magazine and also frequently writing to me. Owing to his stand on the war, few of his epistles had reached me the previous year, nor any copies of *Pearsons'*, of which Frank was the editor. But in 1919 I was permitted to receive my mail more regularly. I liked Harris's publication more for its brilliant editorials than its social attitude. We were too far apart in our conception of the changes necessary to bring humanity relief. Frank was opposed to the abuse of power; I to the thing itself. His ideal was a benevolent despot ruling with a wise head and generous hand; I argued that " there ain't no such animal " and could not be. We often clashed, yet never in an unkind way. His charm was not in his ideas, but in his literary quality, in his incisive and witty pen and his caustic comments on men and affairs.

Our first clash, however, was not over theories. I had read his *The Bomb* and had been profoundly moved by its dramatic power. The true historic background was wanting, but as fiction the book was of a high order, and I felt it would help to dispel the ignorant prejudices against my Chicago comrades. I had included the volume among the literature we sold at my lectures, and it had been reviewed by Sasha in *Mother Earth* and advertised in our columns.

We had been roundly condemned for it by Mrs. Lucy Parsons, the widow of Albert Parsons. She denounced *The Bomb* because Harris had not kept to the actual facts, and also because Albert emerged from the pages of the book a rather colourless person. Frank Harris claimed to have written, not a history, but a novel of a dramatic event. I had no quarrel with him on that score. But Mrs. Parsons was entirely right in repudiating Harris's erroneous conception of Albert Parsons.

I had expressed my surprise to Frank at his apparent failure to appreciate the personality of Parsons. Far from being colourless or weak, he should have been, together with Louis Lingg, the hero of the drama. Parsons had deliberately walked into the arena to share the fate of his comrades. He had done more; he scorned a chance to save his own life by accepting a pardon because it did not include the lives of the other men.

In reply Frank explained that he had made Lingg the outstanding personality in his novel because he had been impressed by the determination, fearlessness, and stoicism of the boy. He had admired Lingg's contempt for his enemies, and his proud choice of death by his own hand. Since he could not have two heroes in one story, he had given preference to Lingg. In my next letter I called his attention to the fact that the best Russian writers, such as Tolstoy and Dostoyevsky, often had more than one hero in their works. Moreover, the sharp contrast between Parsons and Lingg would have only enhanced the dramatic interest of *The Bomb* had the true grandeur of Albert Parsons been faithfully portrayed. Harris admitted that the values of the Haymarket tragedy had by no means been exhausted in his book; perhaps some day he would write a story from another angle, with Albert Parsons as the dominant figure.

Alexander Harvey's correspondence greatly amused me. He worshipped at the shrine of Greek and Latin culture; nothing that had come to us since counted for much in his estimation. " Believe me," one of his letters read, " the truest conscientious objector was Sophocles. The decay of the ancients goes hand in hand with the loss of liberty. You yourself remind me of Antigone. There is something splendid and Greek in your life and in your gospel." I wanted him to explain the existence of slavery in his beloved old world, and I asked for enlightenment on how it happened that I, who had never looked at a Latin or Greek grammar, should yet prize liberty above everything else. His only explanation was several volumes of Greek plays in English translation.

My library had been greatly enlarged by many books friends had sent me, among them works by Edward Carpenter, Sigmund Freud, Bertrand Russell, Blasco Ibañez, Barbusse, and Latzko, and *Ten Days that Shook the World.* John Reed's story, engrossingly thrilling, helped me to forget my surroundings. I ceased to be a captive in the Missouri penitentiary and I felt myself transferred to Russia, caught by her fierce storm, swept along by its momentum, and identified with the forces that had brought about the miraculous change. Reed's narrative was unlike anything else I had read about the October Revolution — ten glorious days, indeed, a social earthquake whose tremors were shaking the entire world.

While still in the atmosphere of Russia, I received — significant coincidence! — a basketful of deep-red roses, ordered by Bill Shatoff, of Petrograd. Bill, our co-worker in many fights in America, our jovial comrade and friend, in the very midst of the Revolution, surrounded by enemies within and without, facing danger and death, thinking of flowers for me!

CHAPTER XLIX

LIFE IN PRISON, UNLESS ONE HAS VITAL INTERESTS OUTSIDE, IS deadly dull. Until Kate arrived, our existence in Jefferson had been no exception. But the publicity campaign kept up by Frank O'Hare by means of his wife's letters brought many surprises and unexpected results. After the library and the hot food came an influx of convict plumbers, carpenters, and mechanics to install shower-baths. Then the walls of our wing were whitewashed and preparations were being made to whitewash the cells. Presently Kate received an offer to be excused from the shop. "Is it only because of the pull you have outside?" I asked her. "My friends have tried hard to relieve me from machine work, but I am still pegging away at it." "You have never been together with Mr. Painter on a political job," Kate laughed; "we are friends." "You mean you know each other from behind the scenes?" I questioned. "Precisely," giggled Kate, "and now you understand why Mr. Painter is willing to do things for me." Kate refused to be released from the shop; it would spoil her chance of keeping up her criticism of evils that needed to be reformed.

Meanwhile it became known that an investigator was to visit the penitentiary. The usual investigating fraternity inspires prisoners with anything but confidence. This man, however, was from the *Survey,* the liberal research magazine. Winthrop Lane had published a report of the unique strike of the politicals in the Leavenworth disciplinary barracks, and we had been impressed by his sympathetic understanding of the protestants in prison; his coming was therefore looked forward to with interested suspense.

When I was called down to the office, I was surprised to find myself alone with Mr. Lane. It was a pleasant experience to be able to converse with a human being without the surveillance of the head matron, which we always had to endure at visits. Mr. Lane had already investigated the blocks and the punishment cells in the men's wing, and we discussed penal institutions in general. I did not suggest that he visit the shop, assuming that he would do so as a matter of course. But to my amazement Mr. Lane failed to come to see the women at work. Whatever his report about our place, it would be wanting, I feared, without his personal observation of the very thing that caused all the hardships and trouble in the prison.

My fiftieth birthday I spent in the Missouri penitentiary. What more fitting place for the rebel to celebrate such an occasion? Fifty years! I felt as if I had five hundred on my back, so replete with events had been my life. While at liberty I had hardly noticed age creeping up, perhaps because I had counted my real birth from 1889, when, as a girl of twenty, I had first come to New York. Like our Sasha, who would jestingly give his age minus his fourteen years in the Western Penitentiary, I used to say that my first twenty years should not be held against me, for I had merely existed then. The prison, however, and still more the misery abroad in every land, the savage persecution of radicals in America, the tortures social protestants were enduring everywhere, had an ageing effect on me. The mirror lies only to those who want to be deceived.

Fifty years — thirty of them in the firing line — had they borne fruit or had I merely been repeating Don Quixote's idle chase? Had my efforts served only to fill my inner void, to find an outlet for the turbulence of my being? Or was it really the ideal that had dictated my conscious course? Such thoughts and queries swirled through my brain as I pedalled my sewing-machine on June 27, 1919.

The week before, I had again fallen ill and had been told by the physician to stay in my cell. Feeling particularly weak on my birthday, I had remained in bed, hoping that Dr. McNearney would understand that I needed a rest. To my astonishment an orderly came to tell me that the doctor had ordered me back to the shop. I was certain that McNearney knew nothing about it, and that it was the head matron's doing. But I was too weary of the continual struggle with her, and I dragged myself to work. At noon I discovered that the lady had imposed an additional punishment on me. She had not delivered the flowers, packages, and stack of mail received for me. In the evening I found half of the flowers and plants wilted from the excessive heat.

It was provoking — they had committed no offence, and I thought it petty revenge to have denied them drink and air. I proceeded to clean and bathe them in salt water. Some raised their drooping heads and seemed to revive. They nodded tender birthday messages from my darling Stella and from many other known and unknown well-wishers. A beautiful pink rose rambler plant had come from my troubadour of many years, Leon Bass. No adversity in domestic and business life could dim his interest in our ideas or his devotion to me. Leon was a true knight of old, serving without thought of reward. His solicitude for my welfare was most touching and a rare trait among radicals, who seem to think that people in public life have no personal needs or desires.

Many familiar names were among those of the fifty signers of the birthday message I received from New York and the thirty-five signatures of another from Los Angeles. A box of oranges from a friend's own grove in California; luscious apples and preserves from Butler Davenport, my friend for years, whose dramas were performed in the quaint little theatres built by himself on his estates in Connecticut and in New York. From East and West the congratulatory messages came, expressing appreciation of my work and what I had meant to the writers.

My own family's affection for me had grown with the years. Sister Lena had blossomed out like a flower in her love for me. Her life, filled with hardships and pain, might have corroded the heart of many another woman. But Lena had become more gentle and understanding, even humble. "I do not presume to compare my love for you with Helena's," she once wrote me, "but I love you just the same." It made me remorseful to think of the poor affection I had given her in the past. My old mother had also come very close to me of late years. She kept sending me gifts, things made by her own trembling hands. Her birthday letter, written in Yiddish, was filled with affection for her most wayward child.

The thought of Helena was the only cloud on my birthday sky. Her daughter Minnie had come all the way from Manila to help her mother over their great loss. But my sister was wrapped in her precious dead, and the living could do nothing to loosen its hold. Helena alone had failed me on the day she had always filled with her love before. But I understood.

I felt myself very rich indeed. An abundance of affection and loyalty was my share, and it bore witness that my life and work had been worth the suffering and travail.

A few months after Kate had arrived she was granted the privilege of her typewriter, and my correspondents had been blessing her ever since. "Such a relief," they wrote, "not to have to spend hours in puzzling out your hieroglyphics." On a previous occasion, when I had acquired a Blickensdoerfer, they had also rejoiced to be free from the ordeal of trying to decipher my letters. Alas, their glee had been premature, because my typing did not prove more legible than my handwriting. I was trying hard to improve, stoically enduring the pains in my neck from constant practice, but the heartless lot did not begin to appreciate it. They had even suggested I should be psychoanalyzed for the peculiar complex that made me strike the wrong keys. They kept on finding fault with my most perfect copy. But when Kate became my "secretary," all complaints ceased.

She was thorough in everything, particularly in mechanical things, and adept at handling machines, however intricate. Her father had been a mechanic, and Kate had grown up in his shop, dabbling in machinery since she had been a tot. Later she had become her parent's assistant, and her greatest pride was her membership in the Machinists' Union. But what is a union card among friends? Out of her bigness of heart, Kate scabbed for me. Besides the day's task and her own mail after work hours, she also did my letters. Shamelessly I took advantage of her good nature and exploited her for my correspondence. The Federal authorities had robbed me of my forum and of *Mother Earth,* and letters became my platform. Censorships had taught me to express proscribed ideas in guileless disguise.

With my good old comrade Jacob Margolis I argued hotly the merits and demerits of Soviet Russia. I agreed with him on the danger to the Revolution from the dictatorship of the proletariat, but I fought his lack of faith in the men who had helped October to birth and who were defending its gains against a hostile world. I stressed the point that the time would undoubtedly come when the anarchists would have to take issue with the Lenin-Trotsky group, but not while Russia was in danger from enemies within and without. My comrade replied that he certainly had no intention of siding with the interventionists. He was concerned, however, in keeping anarchism free from any affiliations with the political school that had always fought us in the past and would crush us in Russia just as soon as they should feel their State machine strong enough for it. Our controversy continued for a considerable time, proving as stimulating as a personal talk with Jake.

Other letters to New York friends were in defence of Robert Minor, our co-worker in various campaigns. His cabled articles on Russia, which had appeared in one of the New York dailies, caused much indignation in radical ranks. While some of his criticisms of the Bolsheviki were plausible, they contained passages obviously not from Bob's pen. I felt that his reports were being doctored. I urged that it was infantile to suspect everybody as a traitor who did not fully accept the dicta of Lenin, Trotsky, or Zinoviev. They were human, like the rest of us, and likely to make mistakes. To call attention to the latter could not harm the Revolution. As for the apparently garbled accounts, we should have to wait for Robert Minor's return to America, when he could explain things.

On his return to America, Minor proved that his European articles had been deliberately altered in New York editorial rooms to hurt Russia and to injure his standing in radical ranks. He planned to see Sasha and me as soon as we should be released and to give us a full report of the situation in Russia.

An article in the *Liberator* signed "X" contained a violent attack on the anarchists in Russia. Stella had been assured by Max Eastman that a refutation from me would be published, and I devoted several Sundays to an analysis of the charges made against my Russian comrades. I pointed out that the writer had not adduced a single proof for his assertions, that he had shown gross ignorance of his subject, and that he had even lacked the courage to sign his name. I demanded that he come out in the open so that we could argue the matter fairly. A letter from Max Eastman spoke highly of my article and assured me that it would soon appear. But he did not keep his promise, and my refutation was not published.

I was not surprised. On a previous occasion Max Eastman had demonstrated his peculiar conception of free speech and press. His poetic soul had always craved these rights for himself and his group, but not for anarchists. Max Eastman was living up to the good old Marxist tradition.

Lack of fairness to an opponent is essentially a sign of weakness. And, truth to tell, Max Eastman was neither strong nor brave. His spiritual somersault at his trial, and his sudden glorification of the policies of America's "greatest statesman in the White House," testified to it. Well, what of it? He possessed other gifts worthy a king's ransom: he was a poet and handsome. Better a Napoleon in his own domain than a common soldier in the social battle.

It saddened me to learn that Catherine Breshkovskaya had left America without replying to my appeal. Nor had she expressed any protest against the crimes committed by Uncle Sam in the name of lofty ideals. Miss Alice Stone Blackwell had questioned her silence in the face of so much wrong. In reply the veteran fighter had said that she could not jeopardize her chances of helping the destitute children of Russia, for which purpose she had come to the United States.

Kate's repeated complaints about unfairness to the Federal prisoners finally brought an official investigator to question us. We were compelled to make the same task as the State prisoners and we were equally punished in case of failure. But we did not receive the same benefits. Advancement to Grade A gave the Federals only the right of a third letter a week whereas the State prisoners were rewarded by the reduction of five months on each year and were also made eligible to parole. The investigator interviewed us separately. His efforts were apparently exhausted by a significant remark to Kate. "You and Miss Goldman," he said, "must have stiffened the backs of these girls. I always find it difficult to get prisoners to talk frankly. But this time they expressed themselves freely and they all told the same story." The Federals desperately clung to the hope that the investigation would bring results. I did not try to discourage them, though I knew that even Mr. Lane, of the *Survey,* had failed to have his critical article on conditions in our prison accepted by the magazine.

A new batch of letters from Frank Harris served to strengthen the mutual-admiration society that had sprung up between us. I had been greatly impressed by his *Contemporary Portraits,* naming those of Carlyle, Whistler, Davidson, Middleton, and Sir Richard Burton as the most successful. Among the short stories I had chosen *Montes the Matador, The Stigmata,* and *Magic Glasses.* I wrote Frank that I regarded them as his literary masterpieces. I knew that he was inclined to feel hurt if one did not consider all his works great, and I feared that my preferences might impair our friendship. But Frank

Harris heaped coals of fire on my sinful head by calling me "a great and unerring critic." "You will be out soon," one of his letters read, "which delights my soul; but I will still be boiling in the fires of the Philistines. Why do they not deport me? I would thus save passage money." He asked permission to arrange a banquet in my honour when I should be released. He had made no mention of Sasha, and I informed him that, though I appreciated his offer, I could not accept any testimonial of a public character that did not also include my old pal.

A similar reception was being planned by Mrs. Margaret Sanger, as Stella notified me. I felt much surprised at it. Friendship is best tested in time of danger. While Sasha's fate was hanging in the balance in connexion with San Francisco, Mrs. Sanger had offered no help and showed no interest. She had been good enough to permit her name on the list of his publicity committee, but every leading radical had done no less. Outside of that she had kept cautiously in the background, though she had always claimed to be a very particular friend of Sasha. I had no desire to hurt Mrs. Sanger, but I had to decline her proposal.

On August 28, 1919 Sasha and I had completed twenty months of our two-year sentence. Wicked anarchists though we were, we had earned four months each for good behaviour. We had done our bit much longer than many of the boys in the dug-outs. We should have been honourably discharged from service and allowed to return from the prison front. But Judge Julius Mayer had willed it otherwise by placing a high valuation on our heads. Twenty thousand dollars' fine! A United States commissioner was sent to the penitentiary to question me about my financial standing. He looked incredulous when I told him that anarchist propaganda is a pleasure and not a paying business. He grew still more dubious when I explained that the Kaiser, having been unseemly hurried in his departure from Germany, had neglected to make provision for our welfare. The commissioner decided to "look into the matter." Meanwhile Berkman and I would have to serve an extra month in payment of our fine, he declared. Two months for twenty thousand dollars! When did Sasha and I ever expect to earn so much money in so short a time?

Only thirty days. Then release from the hateful shop, the control, the surveillance, the thousand humiliations prison involves. Back to life and work again — with Sasha. Back to my family, comrades, and friends. An alluring fantasy, soon dispelled by the immigration authorities. Ellis Island was waiting for the two distinguished guests. I wondered who would compete for my favours next. Would it be Russia, the long-awaited, or America, my old flame? In our uncertain fortunes only one thing was certain: Sasha and I would meet the future as we had always met it in the past.

The last days were drawing near. I had but one thing to regret: the friends I should have to leave behind. Little Ella, grown into my heart as my own child, still had six months to serve. I was less anxious about Kate, who was sure of a pardon before long. Ella would then have no one with her, and I grieved to part from her. And there were also poor little Aggie, the lifer, the coloured orderly Addie, serving ten years, and the other unfortunates who had become dear to me. I had tried to interest some of my women friends in New York in Addie. Several had responded and offered to give her a job when she was paroled. Did I know what she was "in for," they had inquired, "and would she be all right?" I could never bring myself to ask my fellow-prisoners on what charges they had been sent up. I would wait until they confided to me of their own accord. I told Addie what my correspondents had said. "I don't blame them at all," she commented; "they might think I'm here for stealin' or usin' dope. Tell 'em I'm here for killin' my man, who played me false." Convicts have their own code of ethics, I wrote back, and they can be trusted to live up to them, which is more than could be said of a great many people outside. Alice Stone Blackwell had asked no questions; she had secured employment for Addie and she would even pay her fare. But there the head matron had stepped in. She frightened Addie by telling her that "Emma Goldman's friends are Bolsheviki and bad women." She would only queer her chances for parole if the board should learn that she had such sponsors. Addie implored me to do nothing further in her case.

During my imprisonment death had robbed me of two more friends, Horace Traubel and Edith de Long Jarmuth. I had not known of their illness, and the news was a great shock. The poetic beauty of Horace's life accompanied him even to his grave. The church caught fire just as his friends had gathered to pay their last tribute. Red flames shooting on high greeted his remains. It seemed appropriately symbolic of Horace Traubel, the rebel and man.

Edith de Long Jarmuth, Japanese-looking with her blue-black hair, almond-shaped eyes, and marble-white skin, was like a lotus flower in alien soil. She was a strange and ethereal figure in her wealthy and heavy bourgeois home in Seattle. Later her apartment on Riverside Drive in New York became the rendezvous of radicals and intellectual Bohemians. Edith was their magnet, and she felt alive to their ideas and work. Her own interests, however, had no social roots; they sprang from her yearning for the exotic and the picturesque. In life as in art Edith was a dreamer who lacked creative strength. One loved her more for what she was than for what she did. Her personality and native charm were her greatest gifts.

Saturday, September 28, 1919, I left the Missouri penitentiary, accompanied by my faithful Stella, who had come from New York for the occasion. Only technically free, I was taken to the Federal Building to make an affidavit that I possessed no real estate or cash. The Federal agent looked me up and down. "You're dressed so swell, funny you claim to be poor," he commented. "I am a multimillionaire in friends," I replied.

The fifteen-thousand-dollar bond demanded by the Government pending inquiries by the Immigration Bureau was secured, and I was at last at liberty.

CHAPTER L

IN ST. LOUIS WE WERE ALMOST MOBBED BY FRIENDS, REPORTERS, and camera-men who had come to meet us at the station. I could not bear to see many people and I was eager to be left alone.

Stella grew uneasy on hearing that on our way east I intended to stop off in Chicago, where Ben was living. She implored me to give up the idea. "You will only lose the peace you have gained through months of struggle to free yourself from Ben," she pleaded. There was no need for anxiety, I assured her. In the isolation and loneliness of the cell one finds the courage to face the nakedness of one's soul. If one survives the ordeal, one is less hurt by the nakedness of other souls. I had worked my way through much anguish and travail to a better understanding of my relation with Ben. I had dreamed of having ecstatic love without the pettiness and jarring conditioned in it. But I learned to see that the great and the small, the beautiful and the mean, that had made up our life were inseparable springs from the same source, flowing to a common outlet. In my clarified perception the fine things in Ben now stood out in bolder relief, and the little no longer mattered. One so primitive as he, who was always moved by his emotions, could not do things half-way. He gave without measure or restraint. His best years, his tremendous zest for work, he had devoted to me. It is not unusual for woman to do as much for the man she loves. Thousands of my sex had sacrificed their own talents and ambitions for the sake of the man. But few men have done so for women. Ben was one of the few; he had dedicated himself completely to my interests. Emotionalism had guided his passion as it had his life. But, like nature unleashed, he would destroy with one hand the lavish gifts of the other. I had revelled in the beauty and strength of his giving, and I had recoiled from and struggled against the self-centred egotism which ignored and annihilated obstacles in the soul of the loved one. Erotically Ben and I were of the same earth, but in a cultural sense we were separated by centuries of time. With him social impulses, sympathy with mankind, ideas, and ideals were moods of the moment, and as fleeting. He had no means of sensing basic verities or inner need to convert them into his own.

My life was linked with that of the race. Its spiritual heritage was mine, and its values were transmuted into my being. The eternal struggle of man was rooted within me. That made the abyss between us.

In the solitude of prison I had lived away from the disturbing presence of Ben. Often my heart had called for him, but I had silenced its cry. I had promised myself after our last break never to see him again until I should have made order out of my emotional chaos. I had fulfilled my pledge; nothing was now left of the conflict that had lasted so many years. Neither love nor hate. Only a new friendliness and a clearer appreciation of what the man had given me. I was no longer afraid to meet Ben.

In Chicago he called, bringing a large bouquet of flowers. It was the same old Ben, instinctively reaching out and his eyes opening wide in wonder at meeting no response. No change in him nor understanding for mine. He wanted to give me a party at his home. Would I come, he asked. "Of course," I said, "I will come to meet your wife and your child." I went. The dead had buried their dead, and I felt serene.

In Rochester my people received me with their usual affection. Helena had been in Maine, whence she had written me: "I don't know how I got here. Minnie brought me. How anybody can think to divert me from my great sorrow, I cannot understand. The more I see of nature and people, the greater my loss. My misfortune goes everywhere with me." On our way to Rochester Stella had described Helena's condition and had cautioned me to be prepared. But my worst mental picture was not so horrible as the sight my dear sister presented. Emaciated to the bone, she was a bent old woman, moving with lifeless steps. Her face was shrunken and ashy, unutterable despair in her hollow eyes. I held her close to me, her poor little body convulsed with sobs. She had done nothing but weep since the news of David's death, my people told me; her life was ebbing out in tears. "Take me away, let me live with you in New York," she pleaded. It had been her dream in our youth to be always near me. Now the moment had come to realize it, she reiterated. I was filled with pity and fear. My existence was so precarious, new uncertainties and dangers were already facing me. Could Helena stand such a life? But everything else had failed to save her from herself. She needed something to occupy her mind, physical exertion especially. Perhaps looking after her daughter and me would take her away from her dead. It was a last hope, and I held it out to her. I told her I would rent an apartment in New York at once, and soon Minnie could bring her to me. She sighed deeply and seemed somewhat consoled.

With Helena's collapse the care of two families had fallen upon my sister Lena. She worked for everybody without complaint; she drudged far beyond her strength and asked no reward. Lena was of the stuff of the millions who go through life unpraised by poet, unsung by lyre, heroic in their silent strength. The gloom I had found on my home-coming was broken only by the golden glow of Ian, our adorable baby of four, and by the sprightly energy of my mother, who was eighty-one. She was in poor health, but still busy with her charity interests, and she was the moving spirit in the numerous lodges to which she belonged. She was the *grande dame par excellence,* more careful of her toilet than her daughters. Always strong and self-assertive, Mother had, since Father's death, become a veritable autocrat. No statesman or diplomat excelled her in wit, shrewdness, and force of character. Whenever I visited Rochester, Mother had new conquests to report. For years the orthodox Jews of the city had discussed the need of an orphanage and a home for the indigent aged. Mother did not waste words; she located two sites, purchased them on the spot, and for months canvassed the Jewish neighbourhood for contributions to pay off the mortgage and build the institutions the others had only talked about. There was no prouder queen than Mother on the opening day of the new orphanage. She invited me to " come and speak a piece " on the great occasion. I had once told her that my aim was to enable the workers to reap the fruit of their labours, and every child to enjoy our social wealth. A mischievous twinkle had come into her still sparkling eyes as she replied: " Yes, my daughter, that is all very good for the future; but what is to become of our orphans now, and the old and decrepit who are alone in the world? Tell me that." And I had no answer to give.

One of her exploits had been to put the Rochester manufacturer of shrouds out of business because of exorbitant charges. The owner of the business, a woman, had a monopoly of furnishing the burial garments without which no orthodox Jew may be laid to final rest. An old woman of the poorest class needed a shroud, but her family could not pay the high price asked for it. When my mother learned of it, she at once proceeded in her usual energetic manner. She called on the heartless creature who had enriched herself on the dead, and demanded that the garment be supplied at once without pay, threatening to ruin her in case of refusal. The manufacturer remained unmoved, and my mother set to work forthwith. She bought white material and with her own hands made a shroud for the pauper; then she called on the largest dry-goods store in the city and succeeded in convincing the owner of the riches he would store up in heaven if he would sell the material in quantities at cost price. " Anything for you, Mrs. Goldman," the man had said, Mother reported proudly. Then she organized a group of Jewish women to sew the shrouds, and she made it known in the community that the garments would be furnished for ten cents apiece. The clever scheme brought about the bankruptcy of the monopolist.

Many anecdotes circulated about my mother, characteristic of her vitality and broad sympathies, but none amused me so much as the story of how Mrs. Taube Goldman had put the chairlady of a powerful lodge " in her place." At one of the meetings Mother had talked rather too long. Another member asked for the floor, and the chairlady timidly suggested that Mrs. Goldman had already exceeded her time. Drawing herself up to full stature, my mother defiantly announced: " The whole United States Government could not stop my daughter Emma Goldman from speaking, and a fine chance you have to make her mother shut up! "

Mother had not always known how to express her affection to her children, except to our " baby " brother, whom she had always loved best. But I remembered the occasion on which she gave me the greatest proof in her power that she also loved me. Mysteriously she had taken me aside to tell me that she had made her will and that she had deeded me her most cherished treasure. Would I promise to make use of it after her death? From a bureau drawer Mother took out her jewel-case and solemnly held it out to me. " Here, my daughter, is what I am leaving you," she said as she handed me the medals she had received from various charity organizations. Repressing my laughter with difficulty, I assured her that I had already received too many medals of my own, though less shiny than hers; I could not very well wear any more, but I would keep hers in loving esteem.

Harry Weinberger had gone to Atlanta to meet Sasha on his release. The fates had never been kind to him in prison; this time they robbed him of three days. Instead of September 28, Sasha was released on October 1. A number of detectives faced him on his discharge, among them representatives of Prosecutor Fickert of San Francisco. They attempted to claim Sasha as their prisoner, but Federal officers declared that they had prior claim upon him. Friends supplied his fifteen-thousand-dollar bond for appearance before the immigration authorities, and at last Sasha was again in our midst. He looked haggard and pale, but otherwise apparently his usual stoical and humorous self. But soon we realized that it was only the flush of his release and the joy of being free, for Sasha was very ill. Uncle Sam's prison had succeeded in accomplishing in twenty-one months what the Western Penitentiary of Pennsylvania had failed to do in fourteen years. Atlanta had broken his health and had sent him back a physical wreck, with the horrors of his experience burned into his soul.

Sasha had been kept in an underground dungeon for protesting against the brutalities practised on the other inmates. The cell was too small to move about in and fetid with the bucket of excrement that was emptied only once in twenty-four hours. He was allowed only two small slices of bread and one cup of water a day. Later on, for interceding for a coloured prisoner, he was again punished by the "hole," which measured two and a half feet by four and a half, and where he could not even stand up straight. The "hole" was provided with double doors, one iron-barred, the other "blind," thus entirely excluding all light and air. In that cell, known as "the tomb," one is subjected to gradual suffocation. It is the worst punishment known in the Atlanta penitentiary, and it is designed to break the prisoner's spirit and force him to beg for mercy. Sasha refused to do so. To keep from suffocating he had to lie flat on the floor with his mouth close to the groove where the double doors fit into the stone casing. Only thus could he keep alive. Released from "the tomb," he was for three months deprived of his mail privileges, allowed no books or other reading-matter, and not permitted any exercise whatever. After that he remained continuously in solitary and isolation for seven-and-a-half months, from February 21 to the day of his discharge, October 1.

The memory of Atlanta haunted Sasha upon his release. At night he would wake up in a cold sweat, tortured by the nightmare of his recent experience. His prison phantoms were no new misery to me, but Fitzi had not seen him in such a state, and it unnerved her. She had gone through much suffering and worry since 1916, and she was run down and depressed. Together with the responsibilities of her position in the Provincetown Playhouse, she had carried almost the entire brunt of the preparations for the Mooney general strike, the amnesty campaign, and the National Amnesty Day. The raising of funds for bail and trials and the care of imprisoned politicals had fallen mostly to her. With the help of a handful of comrades, among them Pauline, Hilda and Sam Kovner, Minna Lowensohn, and Rose Nathanson, Fitzi had accomplished a tremendous amount of work.

More wearing than the physical exertion involved in these activities had been her deep disappointment in the new element that had come into the Billings-Mooney fight. The labour politicians had well-nigh emasculated the militant spirit of the campaign for the California men. Owing to their faint-heartedness, the general strike, set for the first week of July, had completely failed. The same conservative elements had voted against and ruined the chances of a successful general strike in October. Some of the radical organizations were not much more encouraging; they had refused to include in the proposed protest the other political and labour prisoners. Fitzi had justly stressed the argument that the demand for a general amnesty would strengthen the movement for Mooney and Billings, but even so militant a man as Ed Nolan had at first voted against her proposal, though later he changed his attitude and supported her stand. The lack of vision and backbone on the part of the majority of the labour organizations had caused a split and had greatly injured all the rebels in prison.

Sasha's condition was growing steadily worse. An examination by our friend Dr. Wovschin showed the need of an operation, but with stubborn indifference Sasha ignored the physician's advice. Fitzi and I had to conspire with the doctor to take our patient by surprise. Late one afternoon Wovschin arrived with an assistant for a second examination. Sasha was away, we knew not where. On his return we learned that he had been invited to a veritable Jewish feast, specially prepared for him by the mother of Anna Baron, our former *Mother Earth* secretary. Dr. Wovschin was disgusted; he had never operated on anyone immediately after a grand repast. But it had to be now or never. The physician succeeded in coaxing Sasha on to the table under the pretext of having to look him over once more. Then he quickly proceeded to give him ether. Sasha, resisting the anæsthetic, put up a fierce fight, shouting that the Deputy Warden was trying to kill him and swearing to finish the s.o.b. I had unfortunately been detained by an important engagement, and when I hastened back home, I met Fitzi on the street running to a drug store. White as a ghost, she told me that enough ether had already been given Sasha to put several men to sleep, but more was still needed. I found the room looking like a battle-field. The eye-glasses of the assistant physician were smashed and his face lacerated. Dr. Wovschin had also not escaped damage. Sasha was on the table, already unconscious, but still gritting his teeth and denouncing the Deputy Warden. I took his hand in mine and spoke soothingly to him. Presently I felt my pressure returned, and then he quieted down.

When he came to after the operation, he opened his eyes and stared in terror at the foot of the bed. "The goddam Deputy!" he cried, about to leap at his throat. We held him down, assuring him that he was among friends. "Fitzi and I are near you, dear," I whispered; "no one will harm you." He looked incredulously at me. "I can see him plainly right there," he insisted. It took much effort to persuade him that he was only imagining himself still in Atlanta. He gazed steadily into my eyes. "If you say so, it must be true, and I believe you," he said at last, "but how strange is the human mind!" He went peacefully off to sleep.

On my return from Jefferson City I found destroyed what we had slowly built up through a long period of years. The literature confiscated in the raid had not been returned to us, and *Mother Earth,* the *Blast,* Sasha's *Prison Memoirs,* and my essays were under the ban. The large sums of money raised while we were in prison, including the three thousand dollars contributed by our old Swedish comrade, had gone for appeals in cases of conscientious objectors, in the political-amnesty activities, and in other work. We had nothing left, neither literature, money, nor even a home. The war tornado had swept the field clean, and we had to begin everything anew.

Among my first callers was Mollie Steimer, who came accompanied by another comrade. I had never met either of them before, but Mollie's remarkable stand at her trial, and all I knew about her, made me feel as if she had always been in my life. I was glad to meet the brave girl face to face and to tell her of my admiration and love. She was diminutive and quaint-looking, altogether Japanese in features and stature. But she had shown exceptional strength and she was typical of the Russian revolutionists in her earnestness and the severity of her dress.

Mollie and her escort informed me that they had come as delegates of their group to ask me to write for their *Bulletin,* which they were publishing underground. Unfortunately I could not comply with their request. Even if I were not already overburdened with too much work, I could not ally myself with secret activities. I told them that I had thought of continuing *Mother Earth sub rosa,* but had discarded the plan because of the hazard it involved for others. I was not afraid of danger if I could meet it in the open, but I did not want to be trapped by spies and informers, who are always found in secret revolutionary bodies. Mollie understood my attitude. She had not yet recovered from the shock she had experienced at the treachery of Rosansky, the boy who had delivered her and her comrades to the police. She felt, however, that, with every breath of freedom suppressed in the country, our ideas must be spread even at the risk of possible betrayal. I held that the results of such methods are not commensurate with the risk, and I refused to have anything to do with such inadequate efforts. My visitors were much disappointed, the young man even indignant. I disliked hurting them, but I could not alter my decision.

An additional disagreement between us was due to my attitude to Soviet Russia. My young comrades thought that the Bolsheviki, representing a government, should be treated by anarchists like other governments. I insisted that Soviet Russia, the object of attack by the combined reactionists of the world, was not at all to be considered as an ordinary government. I did not object to criticism of the Bolsheviki, but I could not approve active opposition to them, anyway not until they should be in a less dangerous situation.

I longed to take little Mollie in my arms, but she looked stern in her youthful fervour. I let her depart with just a friendly handshake.

She was a wonderful girl, with an iron will and a tender heart, but she was fearfully set in her ideas. "A sort of Alexander Berkman in skirts," I jokingly remarked to Stella. Mollie was a true factory child of revolutionary spirit. She had gone to work at the age of thirteen and she had continued in the shop until she fell into the hands of the authorities. She was essentially of the idealistic youth of Russia in times of the Tsar, who sacrificed their lives before they had scarcely begun to live. What a fearful fate — from the factory to the Missouri prison for fifteen years, with no joy in between for my lovely young comrade!

I found a cozy apartment, and soon Minnie arrived with her mother, and the three of us moved in. For a while it seemed as if Helena would get herself in hand. She was busy attending to the *ménage,* sewing and mending. To afford her more work, I used to invite many friends to dinner. Dutifully my sister would prepare the food, serve it attractively, and charm everybody with her personality. But soon the novelty wore off and the old woe was again upon her. It was no use — her life was crushed, she kept on saying; it had lost meaning and purpose. Everything in her was dead, dead as David in the Bois de Rappe. She could not continue, she insisted, she must make an end of it, and I must help her out of her purgatory. Day after day she would repeat her piteous appeal, and call me cruel and inconsistent for my refusal. I had always claimed that everyone had a right to do with his life what he willed, and that persons suffering from incurable disease should not be compelled to live. And yet I was refusing her the relief I would give even a sick animal.

It was madness, and yet I felt that Helena was right. I was inconsistent. I saw her dying by inches with a desperate determination to escape from life. It would be an act of humanity to help her do so. I had no doubt as to the justification of making an end to one's misery or aiding another in it when there is no hope of recovery. Moved by Helena's plea, I would decide to comply with her wishes; and yet I could not bring myself to cut short her life — the life of one who had been mother, sister, friend to me, everything I had had in my childhood. I continued to struggle with her in the silent hours of the night. In the day-time, when I had to leave her, I would go through sickening terror lest on my return home I should find her dashed on the sidewalk. I could not absent myself unless I knew that someone was staying with her when Minnie and I were out.

My deportation hearing, twice postponed, was finally set for October 27. Sasha had already made his statement prior to leaving Atlanta. He had refused to answer the questions of the Federal immigration agent, who had called on him in the prison to give him " a hearing " in the matter of deportation. Instead he had issued a declaration of his position, in which he said:

> The purpose of the present hearing is to determine my "attitude of mind." It does not, admittedly, concern itself with my actions, past or present. It is purely an inquiry into my views and opinions.
>
> I deny the right of anyone—individually or collectively—to set up an inquisition of thought. Thought is, or should be, free. My social views and political opinions are my personal concern. I owe no one responsibility for them. Responsibility begins only with the effect of thought expressed in action. Not before. Free thought, necessarily involving freedom of speech and press, I may tersely define thus: no opinion a law—no opinion a crime. For the government to attempt to control thought, to prescribe certain opinions or proscribe others, is the height of despotism.
>
> This proposed hearing is an invasion of my conscience. I therefore refuse, most emphatically, to participate in it.
>
> ALEXANDER BERKMAN

Sasha, not being a citizen and not caring about that side of the issue, nevertheless joined me in my fight against deportation because he considered such governmental methods as the worst form of autocracy. I also had an additional reason for contesting the Washington scheme to drive me out of the country. The United States Government still owed me an explanation for the shady methods it had employed in 1909 to rob me of my citizenship. And I was determined to have them disclosed.

I had always longed to revisit Russia, and after the February-October Revolution I had definitely decided to return to my native land to help in its reconstruction. But I wanted to go of my own free will, at my own expense, and I denied the right of the government to force me. I was aware of its brutal strength, but I did not propose to submit without a fight. I was no more deceived in its outcome than I had been in regard to our trial. Now, as then, I was concerned primarily in publicly disclosing the utter hollowness of American political claims and the pretence that heralded citizenship is a sacred and inalienable right.

At my hearing before the immigration officials I found the inquisitors sitting at a desk piled high with my dossier. The documents, classified, tabulated, and numbered, were passed on to me for inspection. They consisted of anarchist publications in different languages, most of them long out of print, and of reports of speeches I had delivered a decade previously. No objection had been made to them at the time by the police or the Federal authorities. Now they were being offered as proof of my criminal past and as justification for banishing me from the country. It was a farce I could not participate in, and I consequently refused to answer any questions. I remained silent throughout the " hearing," at the end of which I handed to my examiners a statement, reading in part:

> If the present proceedings are for the purpose of proving some alleged offence committed by me, some evil or antisocial act, then I protest against the secrecy and third-degree methods of this so-called " trial." But if I am not charged with any specific offence or act, if—as I have reason to believe—this is purely an inquiry into my social and political opinions, then I protest still more vigorously against these proceedings, as utterly tyrannical and diametrically opposed to the fundamental guarantees of a true democracy. Every human being is entitled to hold any opinion that appeals to her or him without making herself or himself liable to persecution. . . .
>
> The free expression of the hopes and aspirations of a people is the greatest and only safety in a sane society. In truth, it is such free expression and discussion alone that can point the most beneficial path for human progress and development. But the object of deportations and of the Anti-Anarchist Law, as of all similar repressive measures, is the very opposite. It is to stifle the voice of the people, to muzzle every aspiration of labour. That is the real and terrible menace of the star-chamber proceedings and of the tendency of exiling those who do not fit into the scheme of things our industrial lords are so eager to perpetuate.
>
> With all the power and intensity of my being I protest against the conspiracy of imperialist capitalism against the life and the liberty of the American people.   Emma Goldman

The newspapers reported Mollie Steimer to be on a hunger-strike. We all felt very anxious about her, because the police, State and Federal, had been hounding our comrade ever since she had been released on bail. Within eleven months she had been arrested eight times, kept in station-houses for a night or a week, released and re-arrested without definite charges being preferred against her. In the recent raid of the Russian People's House, where the Workers' Council had their offices, Mollie had been hauled in by the immigration authorities, held for eight days, and then released on a thousand-dollar bond. Later, while walking on the street with a friend, she was accosted by two detectives and told that " the boss wanted " her. She was held in the office of the head of the New York " bomb squad " for three hours without being questioned, then taken to the station-house and locked up. The following morning she read in the press that she was charged with " inciting to riot." She was transferred to the Tombs and after a week's detention released on five thousand dollars' bail. She had barely reached her home when she was visited by three detectives with a Federal warrant for her arrest and taken to Ellis Island. There she had been held ever since. The entire machinery of the United States Government was being employed to crush the slip of a girl, weighing less than eighty pounds.

Fifteen years in prison were facing Mollie, and I wanted to prevail upon her not to waste her strength by a hunger-strike. As her counsellor, Harry Weinberger was permitted to visit her, and the commissioner allowed me to accompany him. We found her in a very weakened condition, but her will indomitable. She showed no trace of any ill feeling as a result of our previous disagreement. On the contrary, she was very glad to see me, sweet and friendly.

She was being kept locked up all the time, Mollie informed us, denied the right to mingle with the other politicals and to associate with those to be deported. She had repeatedly protested in vain, and finally she had decided on a hunger-strike. I agreed that her provocation was certainly extreme, but I urged that her life was too important to our movement to jeopardize her health. Would she terminate her strike if we should persuade the commissioner to change his treatment of her? She was reluctant at first, but finally consented. This time I did not hesitate to take my splendid comrade in my arms. She was like a little child to me whom I longed to shield from the cruelty of the world.

We succeeded in prevailing upon the commissioner to permit Mollie the right of association with her comrades. To save his face he promised " to look into the matter first," and make a change provided Miss Steimer would " meet him half-way." We sent Mollie the message and got her consent to supply her with food.

The same evening a reception dinner for Sasha and me was taking place at the Brevoort Hotel, arranged by our indefatigable Dolly Sloan. We had opposed the plan of an exclusive affair; we preferred Carnegie Hall or some large theatre where a popular admission price would permit large numbers to attend. But no place in Greater New York could be secured except the Brevoort, whose management alone lived up to their hospitable traditions. The evening was somewhat marred by the inevitable exclusion of many friends who had travelled from afar to be with us on the occasion. But the fine spirit of the evening made up for that disappointment. Lola Ridge, our gifted rebel poet, inspired the audience by reciting a graphic poem she had dedicated to Sasha and me, and the other speakers were equally generous in paying tribute to us. Even our old co-worker Harry M. Kelly, who had drifted away from us because of the World War, was again in our midst, the same kindly soul.

I spoke of our heroic young rebels on Ellis Island and of Mollie, whose courage and revolutionary integrity put many a man to shame. The Mollies of the rising generation had sprung from the soil we older anarchists had helped to plough, I said. They were our children of the spirit and they would carry further their heritage. In this proud consciousness we might look with assurance towards the future.

A similar affair in behalf of Kate Richards O'Hare was arranged by the group of radical women that were working for Kate's pardon. Crystal Eastman presided, the speakers of the evening including Elizabeth Gurley Flynn and me. I talked about Kate's life in the Jefferson City prison and of the good she had achieved for the unfortunates there. I dwelt on the fine spirit of her comradeship, and I related some personal details of our sojourn in the penitentiary that illustrated Kate's character. Her complex about her hair particularly amused the audience. Not for anything would she appear in the shop without an elaborate coiffure. The ritual required considerable time and effort, and, as there was no opportunity for it in the morning, Kate used to devote the last evening hours to it. Once I was awakened at night by Kate lustily swearing. "What is it, Kate?" I called to her. "Stuck again by a hairpin, darn it," she replied. "You will be vain," I teased her. "Sure," she retorted; "how else am I to show off my beauty? Nothing in this world can be had without a price, as you well know yourself." "Well, I would not pay for such foolishness as curled hair." "Why, E. G., how you talk. Just ask your male friends, and you'll find out that a fine coiffure is more important than the best speech." The diners roared, and I was sure most of them agreed with Kate.

The gods had never been miserly in providing me with care and work. No sooner had Sasha left his sick-bed than another patient was on hand: Stella was laid up and had to be nursed. My only chance for rest was when some friends managed to kidnap me, as my friend Aline Barnsdall presently did.

I had first met her at my lectures in Chicago. She was keenly interested in the drama and she had staged some modern plays in that city. We spent many pleasant hours together, and I had an opportunity of learning that she was also wide awake to social problems, particularly to free motherhood and birth-control. Her interest in the Mooney-Billings case proved that her attitude was not mere theory. She had been among the first to contribute to the defence and she had also extended a large loan for the purpose. It was not until I was sent to prison, however, that Aline made me feel that she really cared for me. Her coming to Chicago from the Coast to welcome me on my release brought her very near and helped to cement our friendship, begun four years before. On her arrival in New York she carried me off and made me forget for a while the troubles of the world.

One day, as we sat discussing my approaching deportation, I happened to quote Ibsen to the effect that it is the struggle for the ideal that counts, rather than the attainment of it. My life had been rich and colourful, and I had nothing to regret. "What about material results?" Aline suddenly asked. "Nothing except my good looks," I replied jestingly. My friend grew thoughtful and then inquired whether I would be able to cash a cheque. I could, I told her, but it were better for her not to have my name in her cheque-book. Aline declared that she had the right to dispose of her money as she pleased; the government had no business to control such things. Then she handed me a cheque for five thousand dollars, to be applied to the fight against my deportation or for my needs if I should be compelled to leave the country.

I did not trust myself to thank Aline for her gracious gesture; I had to get my emotions in hand first. Later in the evening I told her that the most disturbing feeling in regard to my deportation was the dread of dependence. Never once since I had come to America had I known the fear of not being able to stand on my own feet. I should rather keep my independence in poverty than give it up for wealth. It was the only treasure which I guarded as a miser does his possessions. To be driven out of the land I had called my own, where I had toiled and suffered for years, was not a cheerful prospect. But to come to other shores penniless and without the hope of immediate adjustment was for me a calamity indeed. It was not the dread of poverty or want; it was the fear of having to do the bidding of those who have the power to withhold the means of existence. This spectre had worried me most. " Your cheque is not an ordinary gift," I said to Aline; " it will be the means of keeping me free, and it will enable me to retain my independence and self-respect. Do you understand? " She nodded, and my heart expanded in gratitude no words could express.

A year had passed since the Armistice, and political amnesty had been granted in every European country. America alone failed to open her prison doors. Instead, official raids and arrests increased. There was hardly a city where workers known as Russians or suspected of sympathy with radical ideas were not being picked up, taken at their work-benches or on the street. Behind these raids stood Attorney General Mitchell Palmer, panicky at the thought of radicals. Many of the arrests were accompanied by brutal manhandling of the victims. New York, Chicago, Pittsburgh, Detroit, Seattle, and other industrial centres had their detention houses and jails filled with these " criminals." I was besieged by requests for lectures. The Federal deportation mania was terrorizing the foreign workers of the country, and there were many calls upon me to speak on the matter and enlighten the people on the subject.

Our own fate was hanging in the balance, and Sasha was still an invalid. It seemed preposterous to begin a lecture tour, yet I could not refuse. I had a foreboding that it would be my last opportunity to raise my voice against the shame of my adopted land. I consulted Sasha and he agreed that I ought to go. I suggested that he come with me; it would help him to forget Atlanta and enable him to be with our comrades for perhaps the last time, and he consented.

Our friends and counsel unconditionally opposed our undertaking the campaign. The question of our deportation was still under consideration by the Federal Government, and it was therefore inadvisable to prejudice our case, they argued. But Sasha and I felt that it was the psychological moment to speak out in behalf of Russia. We could not allow personal interests to influence our decision.

From New York to Detroit and thence to Chicago we made a whirl-wind tour, our movements watched by local and Federal agents, every utterance noted down and attempts made to silence us. Unperturbed we continued. It was our last supreme effort and we felt our die had been cast.

Notwithstanding sensational press reports of police interference, warnings to keep away from our gatherings, and similar methods calculated to deter our audiences from attending, our meetings in Detroit, as well as in Chicago, were crowded by thousands. No ordinary assemblies, these; monster demonstrations they were, a tempest of vehement indignation against government absolutism and of homage to ourselves. It was the eloquent voice of the awakened collective soul, thrilled by new hope and aspiration. We merely articulated its yearnings and dreams.

During the farewell dinner given us by our friends in Chicago, on December 2, reporters dashed in with the news of Henry Clay Frick's death. We had not heard of it before, but the newspaper men suspected that the banquet was to celebrate the event. "Mr. Frick has just died," a blustering young reporter addressed Sasha. "What have you got to say?" "Deported by God," Sasha answered dryly. I added that Mr. Frick had collected his debt in full from Alexander Berkman, but he had died without making good his own obligations. "What do you mean?" the reporters demanded. "Just this: Henry Clay Frick was a man of the passing hour. Neither in life nor in death would he have been remembered long. It was Alexander Berkman who made him known, and Frick will live only in connexion with Berkman's name. His entire fortune could not pay for such glory."

The next morning brought a telegram from Harry Weinberger informing us that the Federal Department of Labor had ordered our deportation, and that we must surrender on December 5. We had two more days of freedom and another lecture on hand. There was much to attend to in New York, and Sasha left to arrange our affairs there. I remained for the last meeting. However the storm might rage and the waves mount high, I was determined to face it to the end.

The next day I took the fastest train for New York, Kitty Beck and Ben Capes accompanying me. It was a royal send-off that was given me on leaving Chicago. Our friends and comrades almost monopolized the station platform, the sea of faces expressive of the most precious token of complete solidarity and affection.

I was on the fastest American train, travelling in state with my two companions. "A sleeper or compartment on what may be your last trip in the U. S.?" my friends had declared; "never!" A drawing-room was none too good, and champagne to go with it. Somehow Benny had managed to unearth a couple of bottles in spite of Prohibition. He was an old hand at getting on the good side of porters, and he captured our darky's heart. Our porter had been busying himself about our room and sniffing the air all the time. "Great stuff," he grinned, closing one eye. "Bet your life, George," Benny admitted; "can you get us a bucket of ice?" "Yah, sah, a whole chest." We had not enough bottles to fill a refrigerator, Ben told him, but he might "come in on the swag" if he would bring an extra glass. The sly Negro proved to be a philosopher and artist. His observations on life were keen and his mimicry of the passengers and their foibles masterly.

Kitty and I, left alone, talked into the wee hours of the morning. Her life had been very tragic, perhaps because nature had made her all too lavish. Giving was to her a ritual, to serve to the uttermost her only impulse. Whether it was the man she loved, a friend, or a beggar, a stray cat or a dog, Kitty always emptied the fullness of her heart. She could exact nothing for herself, yet I have seldom known a being so in need of affection. Those in her life accepted from her as a matter of course; few, if any, of them understood the craving of her own heart. Kitty was born to give, not to receive. That was at once her supreme achievement and her defeat.

At the Grand Central terminal in New York friends awaited us, including Sasha, Fitzi, Stella, Harry, and other intimates. There was no time left even to go to my apartment to bid my dear Helena good-bye. We piled into taxis and drove straight to Ellis Island. There Sasha and I surrendered, while Harry Weinberger prepared to demand the return of the thirty thousand dollars deposited as our bond.

"That is the end, Emma Goldman, isn't it?" a reporter remarked. "It may only be the beginning," I flashed back.

CHAPTER LI

THE ROOM I WAS ASSIGNED TO ON THE ISLAND ALREADY CONTAINED two occupants, Ethel Bernstein and Dora Lipkin, who had been rounded up at the raid of the Union of Russian Workers. The documents discovered there consisted of English grammars and text-books on arithmetic. The raiders had beaten up and arrested those found on the premises for possessing such inflammatory literature.

To my amazement I learned that the official who had signed the order for our deportation was Louis F. Post, Assistant Secretary of Labor. It seemed incredible. Louis F. Post, ardent single-taxer, champion of free speech and press, former editor of the *Public,* a fearless liberal weekly, the man who had flayed the authorities for their brutal methods during the McKinley panic, who had defended me, and who had insisted that even Leon Czolgosz should be safeguarded in his constitutional rights — he now a champion of deportation? The radical who had offered to preside at a meeting arranged after my release in connexion with the McKinley tragedy, now favouring such methods? I had been a guest at his home and entertained by him and Mrs. Post. We had discussed anarchism and he had admitted its idealist values, though he had doubted the practicability of their application. He had assisted us in various free-speech fights and he had vigorously protested by pen and voice against John Turner's deportation. And he, Louis F. Post, had now signed the first order for deporting radicals!

Some of my friends suggested that Louis F. Post, being an official of the Federal Government, could not go back on his oath to support the mandates of the law. They failed to consider that in accepting office and taking the oath he had gone back on the ideals he had professed and worked for during all his previous years. If he were a man of integrity, Louis F. Post should have remained true to himself and should have resigned when Wilson forced the country into war.

He should have resigned at least when he found himself compelled to order the deportation of people for the opinions they entertained. I felt that Post had covered himself with ignominy.

The lack of stamina and backbone on the part of such American radicals was tragic. But why expect a braver stand from Louis F. Post than from his teacher Henry George, the father of single-tax, who had failed my Chicago comrades at the eleventh hour? His voice carried great weight at the time and he could have helped to save the men in whose innocence he had believed. But political ambition proved stronger than his sense of justice. Louis F. Post was now following in the footsteps of his admired single-tax apostle.

I sought comfort in the thought that there still were some single-taxers of integrity and moral strength. Bolton Hall, Harry Weinberger, Frank Stephens (my comrades in many free-speech fights), Daniel Kiefer, and scores of others had stood their ground — against war and the new despotism. Frank Stephens, arrested as a conscientious objector, had in protest even declined to accept bail. Daniel Kiefer was another libertarian of true metal. Liberty was a living force in his private life as in his public activities. He was one of the first single-taxers to take an active part against America's entry into the war and against the " selective " draft. He heartily abhorred renegades of the type of Mitchell Palmer, Newton D. Baker, and other weak-kneed Quakers and pacifists. Nor did he spare his friend Louis F. Post for his betrayal.

Judge Julius M. Mayer, of the United States District Court, dismissed Harry Weinberger's writ of habeas corpus and refused to admit us to bail. But the hearing elicited valuable information. The attorney for the United States Government stated that Jacob Kershner had been dead for years; in fact, he was dead at the time his citizenship was revoked, in 1909. The official admission definitely stamped the action of the Federal authorities as a deliberate attempt to deprive me of citizenship by disfranchising the *dead* Jacob Kershner.

Our counsel was not one to accept defeat easily. Beaten at one place, he would train his guns upon another. The United States Supreme Court was his next objective. He would apply for a writ of error, he informed us, and he would insist on our being admitted to bail. Then we could proceed with the fight for my citizenship. Harry was irrepressible, and I was glad to take advantage of every hour left me on American soil.

Sasha and I had long before decided to write a pamphlet on deportation. We knew that the Ellis Island authorities would confiscate such a manuscript, and it therefore became necessary to prepare and send it out secretly. We wrote at night, our room-mates keeping watch. In the morning, during our joint walks, we would discuss what we had written and exchange suggestions. Sasha made the final revision and gave it to friends to smuggle out.

Each day brought scores of new candidates for deportation. From various States they came, most of them without clothes or money. They had been kept in jails for months and were then shipped to New York just as they were at the time of their unexpected arrest. In that condition they were facing a long voyage in the winter. We bombarded our people with requests for clothing, blankets, shoes, and other wearing-apparel. Soon supplies began to arrive, and great was the rejoicing among the prospective deportees.

· The condition of the emigrants on Ellis Island was nothing short of frightful. Their quarters were congested, the food was abominable, and they were treated like felons. These unfortunates had cut their moorings in the homeland and had pilgrimed to the United States as the land of promise, liberty, and opportunity. Instead they found themselves locked up, ill-treated, and kept in uncertainty for months. I marvelled that things had changed so little since my Castle Garden days of 1886. The emigrants were not permitted to mingle with us, but we managed to get from them notes that strained all our linguistic acquirements, almost every European language being represented. It was little enough we were in a position to do for them. We interested our American friends and did the best we could to show the forsaken strangers that not all of the United States was represented by official barbarians. We were loaded with work, and neither Sasha nor I could complain of ennui.

An attack of neuralgia proved very timely. The island dentist failed to alleviate my pain; the commissioner, however, refused to let my own dentist attend me. My agony becoming unbearable, I made a vigorous protest, and finally the island authorities promised to communicate with Washington for instructions. For forty-eight hours my teeth became a Federal issue. Secret diplomacy at last solved the great problem. Washington consented to let me go to my dentist, accompanied by a male guard and a matron.

The dentist's reception room became my rendezvous. Fitzi, Stella, Helena, Yegor, our little Ian, dear old Max, and other friends gathered there. Waiting for treatment became a joy, time passing all too quickly.

Harry Weinberger was meeting with unexpected difficulties in Washington, due to bureaucratic pettiness and red tape. The Clerk of the Court refused to accept his papers because they were not in printed form. Harry successfully appealed to Chief Justice White. On December 11 he was permitted to argue his motion, but the Court denied us the writ of error. A stay of deportation for Sasha was also refused. The documents in my case were ordered printed and returned within one week.

I decided that if Sasha was to be driven out of the country, I would go with him. He had come into my life with my spiritual awakening, he had grown into my very being, and his long Golgotha would for ever remain our common bond. He had been my comrade, friend, and co-worker through a period of thirty years; it was unthinkable that he should join the Revolution and I remain behind.

"You are staying to make the fight, aren't you?" Sasha asked me at recreation that day. I could do much for the deportees, he added, as well as for Russia, if I should establish my right to remain in the United States. The same old Sasha, I thought; always considering propaganda values first. I could hardly restrain the pang I felt over his detachment even at such a moment. Yet I knew the real Sasha; I knew that although he would not admit it even to himself, there was a great deal of the all-too-human underneath his rigid revolutionary exterior. "It's no use, old scout," I said; "you can't get rid of me so easily. I have made my decision, and I am going with you." He gripped hard my hand, but he said not a word.

Few days remained to us on the hospitable United States shores, and our girls were busy as beavers with the final preparations. No effort was too hard for my darling Stella, no task too difficult for Fitzi. They went about their work with aching hearts, yet they were always cheery when with us. Separation from them and from Max, Helena, and other loved ones was poignant indeed. Some day we might all meet again, however — all except Helena. I entertained no such hopes concerning my poor sister. I had a feeling she could not last much longer, and I knew she intuitively echoed my thought. We clung to each other desperately.

Saturday, December 20, was a hectic day, with vague indications that it might be our last. We had been assured by the Ellis Island authorities that we were not likely to be sent away before Christmas, certainly not for several days to come. Meanwhile we were photographed, finger-printed, and tabulated like convicted criminals. The day was filled with visits from numerous friends who came individually and in groups. Self-evidently, reporters also did not fail to honour us. Did we know when we were going, and where? And what were my plans about Russia? " I will organize a Society of Russian Friends of American Freedom," I told them. " The American Friends of Russia have done much to help liberate that country. It is now the turn of free Russia to come to the aid of America."

Harry Weinberger was still very hopeful and full of fight. He would soon get me back to America, he insisted, and I should keep myself ready for it. Bob Minor smiled incredulously. He was greatly moved by our approaching departure; we had fought together in many battles and he was fond of me. Sasha he literally idolized and he felt his deportation as a severe personal loss. The pain of separation from Fitzi was somewhat mitigated by her decision to join us in Soviet Russia at the first opportunity. Our visitors were about to leave when Weinberger was officially notified that we were to remain on the island for several more days. We were glad of it and we arranged with our friends to come again, perhaps for the last time, on Monday, no callers being allowed on the island on the Lord's day.

I returned to the pen I was sharing with my two girl comrades. The State charge of criminal anarchy against Ethel had been withdrawn, but she was to be deported just the same. She had been brought to America as a child; her entire family were in the country, as well as the man she loved, Samuel Lipman, sentenced to twenty years at Leavenworth. She had no affiliations in Russia and was unfamiliar with its language. But she was cheerful, saying that she had good cause to be proud: she was barely eighteen, yet she had already succeeded in making the powerful United States Government afraid of her.

Dora Lipkin's mother and sisters lived in Chicago. They were working people too poor to afford a trip to New York, and the girl knew that she would have to leave without even bidding her loved ones good-bye. Like Ethel, she had been in the country for a long time, slaving in factories and adding to the country's wealth. Now she was being kicked out, but fortunately her lover was also among the men to be deported.

I had not met either of the girls before, but our two weeks on Ellis

Island had established a strong bond between us. This evening my room-mates again kept watch while I was hurriedly answering important mail and penning my last farewell to our people. It was almost midnight when suddenly I caught the sound of approaching footsteps. " Look out, someone's coming! " Ethel whispered. I snatched up my papers and letters and hid them under my pillow. Then we threw ourselves on our beds, covered up, and pretended to be asleep.

The steps halted at our room. There came the rattling of keys; the door was unlocked and noisily thrown open. Two guards and a matron entered. " Get up now," they commanded, "get your things ready! " The girls grew nervous. Ethel was shaking as in fever and helplessly rummaging among her bags. The guards became impatient. " Hurry, there! Hurry! " they ordered roughly. I could not restrain my indignation. " Leave us so we can get dressed! " I demanded. They walked out, the door remaining ajar. I was anxious about my letters. I did not want them to fall into the hands of the authorities, nor did I care to destroy them. Maybe I should find someone to entrust them to, I thought. I stuck them into the bosom of my dress and wrapped myself in a large shawl.

In a long corridor, dimly lit and unheated, we found the men deportees assembled, little Morris Becker among them. He had been delivered to the island only that afternoon with a number of other Russian boys. One of them was on crutches; another, suffering from an ulcerated stomach, had been carried from his bed in the island hospital. Sasha was busy helping the sick men pack their parcels and bundles. They had been hurried out of their cells without being allowed even time to gather up all their things. Routed from sleep at midnight, they were driven bag and baggage into the corridor. Some were still half-asleep, unable to realize what was happening.

I felt tired and cold. No chairs or benches were about, and we stood shivering in the barn-like place. The suddenness of the attack took the men by surprise and they filled the corridor with a hubbub of exclamations and questions and excited expostulations. Some had been promised a review of their cases, others were waiting to be bailed out pending final decision. They had received no notice of the nearness of their deportation and they were overwhelmed by the midnight assault. They stood helplessly about, at a loss what to do. Sasha gathered them in groups and suggested that an attempt be made to reach their relatives in the city. The men grasped desperately at that last hope and appointed him their representative and spokesman. He succeeded in prevailing upon the island commissioner to permit the men to telegraph, at their own expense, to their friends in New York for money and necessaries.

Messenger boys hurried back and forth, collecting special-delivery letters and wires hastily scribbled. The chance of reaching their people cheered the forlorn men. The island officials encouraged them and gathered in their messages, themselves collecting pay for delivery and assuring them that there was plenty of time to receive replies.

Hardly had the last wire been sent when the corridor filled with State and Federal detectives, officers of the Immigration Bureau and Coast Guards. I recognized Caminetti, Commissioner General of Immigration, at their head. The uniformed men stationed themselves along the walls, and then came the command: " Line up! " A sudden hush fell upon the room. " March! " It echoed through the corridor.

Deep snow lay on the ground; the air was cut by a biting wind. A row of armed civilians and soldiers stood along the road to the bank. Dimly the outlines of a barge were visible through the morning mist. One by one the deportees marched, flanked on each side by the uniformed men, curses and threats accompanying the thud of their feet on the frozen ground. When the last man had crossed the gangplank, the girls and I were ordered to follow, officers in front and in back of us.

We were led to a cabin. A large fire roared in the iron stove, filling the air with heat and fumes. We felt suffocating. There was no air nor water. Then came a violent lurch; we were on our way.

I looked at my watch. It was 4:20 A.M. on the day of our Lord, December 21, 1919. On the deck above us I could hear the men tramping up and down in the wintry blast. I felt dizzy, visioning a transport of politicals doomed to Siberia, the *étape* of former Russian days. Russia of the past rose before me and I saw the revolutionary martyrs being driven into exile. But no, it was New York, it was America, the land of liberty! Through the port-hole I could see the great city receding into the distance, its sky-line of buildings traceable by their rearing heads. It was my beloved city, the metropolis of the New World. It was America, indeed, America repeating the terrible scenes of tsarist Russia! I glanced up — the Statue of Liberty!

Dawn was breaking when our barge pulled up alongside of the large ship. We were quickly transferred and assigned to a cabin. It was six o'clock. Exhausted, I crawled into my bunk and immediately fell asleep.

I was awakened by someone pulling at my covers. A white figure stood at my berth, probably the stewardess. Was I ill, she asked, to remain in bed so long. It was already six o'clock in the evening. I had shut out the hideous sights in twelve hours of blessed sleep. Stepping into the corridor, I was startled by someone roughly grabbing me by the shoulder. "Where are you going?" a soldier demanded. "To the toilet, if you must know it. Any objection?" He loosed his hold and followed me; he waited till I emerged again, and accompanied me back to the cabin. My girl companions informed me that guards had been stationed at our door since our arrival, and that they had also been escorted to the place of pressing needs every time they left the cabin.

At noon the next day we were conducted by the sentry to the officers' dining-room. At a large table sat the captain and his retinue, civilian and military. A separate table was assigned to us.

After lunch I requested to see the Federal official in charge of the deportees. He proved to be F. W. Berkshire, an immigration inspector detailed to manage the *Buford* expedition. Did we like our cabin and was the food good, he inquired solicitously. We had no complaints to make, I told him, but how about our men comrades? Could we take our meals with them and meet them on deck? "Impossible," Berkshire said. I then demanded to see Alexander Berkman. Also impossible. Thereupon I informed the inspector that I had no desire to cause trouble, but that I would give him twenty-four hours to change his mind about allowing me to talk to my friend. If my demand should be refused, at the expiration of that time I would go on a hunger-strike.

In the morning Sasha was brought under escort to see me. It seemed weeks since I had beheld his dear face. He told me that the conditions of the men were harrowing. They were cooped up in the hold of the ship, forty-nine in a place barely large enough for half that number. The rest of them were in two other compartments. The bunks, three tiers high, were old and worn out; those in the lower ones bumped their heads against the wire netting of the uppers every time they turned around. The boat, built at the end of the last century, had been used as a transport in the Spanish-American War and later discarded as unsafe. The floor of the steerage was wet all the time, the beds and blankets damp. Only salt water was to be had for washing, and no soap. The food was abominable, especially the bread, half-baked and uneatable. And, worst of all, there were only two toilets for the two hundred and forty-six men.

Sasha advised against pressing our request to eat with the men. It would be better to save what we could from our food for the sick boys who could not stomach the rations given them. Meanwhile he was trying to see what improvements he could secure. He was negotiating with Berkshire a list of demands he had submitted. I was happy to see Sasha full of vital energy again. He had forgotten his own physical troubles the moment he saw that the others were depending on him.

The officers celebrated Christmas in the dining-room in grand style. Ethel and Dora were too ill to leave their berths, and I could not bear to be alone with our jailers. Their Christmas feast was the veriest mockery to me. During the day we were taken out on deck, but not allowed to see the men. Insistence by Sasha and myself finally resulted in permission for him and Dora's friend to visit us.

Friction had developed between the deportees and those in charge of the *Buford*. The men were given no exercise in the fresh air, and Sasha had protested in the name of his comrades. The Federal representative, Immigration Inspector Berkshire, seemed willing to grant the demands, but he evidently stood in awe of those commanding a large force of soldiers. The inspector referred the men to the "chief," but Sasha refused to apply to the latter on the ground that the deportees were political and not military prisoners. Prisoners they were, indeed, continuously locked below deck, with sentries stationed day and night at the doors. Berkshire seemed to realize that our comrades were determined, and no doubt he felt that their resentment of the treatment they were receiving was justified. On Christmas Day he informed Sasha that the "higher authorities" had granted the demanded exercise.

Even then we were not allowed to associate with them. Political prisoners in other countries could freely mingle together during recreation hours regardless of sex, but American puritanism considered such things improper. To save morality we were kept locked in our cabin while the men were out for an airing. They had to remain on the lowest deck, with the waves often sweeping the boat and drenching them.

We were in rough waters, and many of the deportees fell ill. The coarse and badly cooked food was causing general stomach-complaints, and the dampness of the bunks laid many of the men low with rheumatism. The ship's doctor, too busy to attend the increasing number of patients, called upon Sasha to aid him. My offer to serve as nurse had been refused, but my hands were fully occupied with my two girl companions, who had to keep to their beds almost all the time. It was a very strained atmosphere those Christmas days, with forebodings of impending strife.

Our guards were extremely antagonistic, but with the passing of time I seemed to detect a gradual change. At first very forbidding and taciturn, their severity presently began to decrease. They entered into conversation with us, always on the alert, however, for the approach of an officer. Soon they confided to me that they had been tricked. The order for duty had reached them only the day previous to embarkation. They were in ignorance about the purpose and probable length of the voyage, and they had no idea of our destination. They had been told that they were to guard dangerous criminals being shipped somewhere. They were bitter against their officers, and some cursed them openly.

The sentry who had so roughly grabbed me the first day was holding out longest against us. One evening I kept watching him as he paced up and down in front of our cabin. He looked exhausted with the endless walking and I suggested that he sit down for a while. When I placed a camp-chair before him, his reserve broke down. " I daren't," he whispered, " the sergeant may be along." I offered to change rôles with him: I would remain on the look-out. " My God!" he exclaimed, unable to restrain himself any longer, " they told us you were a desperado, that you had killed McKinley and are always plotting against someone." From that moment he became very friendly, ready to do us any service. He had apparently spoken of the incident to his buddies, and they began to hang around our door, eager to show us some kindness. Our cabin had also a special attraction for them: my good-looking young companion Ethel. The soldiers were wild about her, discussed anarchism every free moment at their disposal, and became greatly interested in our fate. They hated their superiors. They would like to drop them into the sea, they said, because they were treated as chattel slaves and punished on every pretext.

One of the lieutenants also was very courteous and humane. He borrowed from me some books, and when he returned them, I found a note containing the news that Kalinin had become President of

Soviet Russia and hinting that we were not to be taken to any parts occupied by the Whites. Uncertainty as to our exact destination had all the time been a source of great anxiety and worry among the deportees. The information of the friendly officer proved a great relief in allaying our worst fears.

Meanwhile our men comrades were busy " agitating " their guards and fraternizing with them. The soldiers offered them their extra shoes and clothing for sale — " Might come handy in Russia," they said. Sasha's tact and his rich stock of humorous stories helped to win the hearts of Uncle Sam's boys. Posting a sentry as their look-out, they would crowd into his compartment and ask for funny yarns. He knew how to arouse their interest, and presently they began to put questions about the Bolsheviki and the soviets. They were eager to know what changes the Revolution had made, and they heard with amazement that in the Red Army the soldiers themselves elected their officers, and that even a commissar or general did not dare insult a private. They thought it wonderful that officers and men were on a footing of equality, and that all shared the same rations.

The steerage quarters were cold and wet. Many of the deportees had been given no opportunity to provide themselves with warm clothing, and there was much suffering as a result. Sasha suggested that those who had supplies should share what they could spare with their less fortunate comrades, and the men responded beautifully. Bags, suit-cases, and trunks were unpacked, everyone donating whatever he did not absolutely require for himself. Coats, underwear, hats, socks, and other apparel were piled up in one of the compartments below deck, and a commission was selected for distribution. The story of the proceedings, as told to me by Sasha, strikingly evidenced the splendid solidarity and fellow-feeling of the deportees. Themselves not too well provided for, they gave of their very last. The distribution had proved so fair and just that there had not been a single complaint.

The strains of Russian melodies, ringing from a hundred throats, were resounding through the *Buford*. The men were on deck, and their lusty voices rose above the rolling of the waves, reaching us in our cabin. The powerful baritone of the leader intoned the first stanzas, and then the entire crowd joined in the chorus. Revolutionary songs they sang, forbidden old Russian folk-tunes surcharged with the grief and yearning of the peasant, or echoing Nekrassov's women who heroically followed their lovers to prison and exile. All aboard grew silent, even the guards ceasing their march and listening with strained ears to the heart-rending melodies.

Sasha had become chummy with the assistant steward, and by means of him we organized a mail service. Copious notes passed every day between us, and we kept each other informed of happenings. Our friend, whom we had christened " Mac," became so devoted that he began to take a personal interest in our fate. He was very clever and ingenious, and he managed to appear at the most unexpected moments, just when he was needed. He seemed suddenly to develop the habit of walking with his hands under his apron, and he never came to us without some little gift hidden about his person. Delicacies from the pantry, sweet morsels from the captain's table, even fried chicken and pastry, we would find stuck away under our beds or in Sasha's bunk. And then one day he brought to Sasha several soldiers who confided to him that they had come as delegates of their comrades in arms. They had a serious mission. It was an offer to supply the deportees with guns and ammunition, to arrest all those in charge, turn the command of the *Buford* over to Sasha, and sail with all aboard to Soviet Russia.

It was January 5, 1920 when we reached the English Channel. The mail-bag carried away by the pilot contained our first letters to the United States. For the sake of safety they were addressed to Frank Harris, Alexander Harvey, and other American friends whose correspondence was subject to less scrutiny than that of our own people. Mr. Berkshire had also consented to let us send a cable to America. The favour was rather costly, amounting to eight dollars, but it was worth the relief our friends would feel at the message that we were alive and still safe.

When we left the English Channel, we were followed by an Allied destroyer. Twofold fear on the part of the *Buford* authorities was responsible for the presence of the warship. Our men had repeatedly complained about the quality of the bread rationed to them. Their protest ignored, they had threatened to strike. Mr. Berkshire brought Sasha " strict orders from the Colonel " for the deportees to submit. The men laughed in his face. " Berkman is the only ' Colonel ' *we* recognize," they shouted. The military chief sent for Sasha. He stormed about the disorganization of the ship's discipline, raved about the deportees fraternizing with the soldiers, and threatened to have the men searched for hidden weapons. Sasha boldly declared that his comrades would resist. The Colonel did not press the matter, and it was evident that he felt he could not rely on the force under his command. Sasha offered to solve the difficulty by putting two of the deportees, who were cooks, in charge of the bakery, without pay. The Colonel was loath to accept what he considered a reflection upon his supreme authority, but Sasha insisted and he won Berkshire to his side. Sasha's plan was finally adopted, and henceforth everyone enjoyed bread of the best quality. What might have proved serious trouble had thus been averted, but the talk of a strike, and the organized stand of our comrades, had had its effect on the commanding officers. Confidence in their exclusive power shaken, an Allied destroyer was a useful thing to have near. With a crowd on the *Buford* that had no respect for epaulets and gold braid, with two hundred and forty-nine radicals on hand who believed in strikes and direct action, the warship was a veritable godsend.

Another reason was the *Buford* itself. The battered old tub had been unseaworthy at the start, and the long journey had not improved her condition. The United States Government had been fully aware that the boat was unsafe, yet it had entrusted five hundred or more lives to it. We were heading for German waters and the Baltic Sea, the latter still thickly dotted with mines. The British destroyer was sadly needed in such a hazardous situation. The captain realized the imminent peril. He ordered the life-boats held in readiness and authorized Sasha to take charge of twelve of them and organize the men for quick action in case of alarm.

Many of the deportees had left considerable sums in American banks and postal savings. They had been denied time to draw their money, nor had they been given an opportunity to transfer it to their families. Sasha proposed to Berkshire that a statement be prepared of their holdings, to be sent to America with authorization for their kin to collect. The inspector seized upon the idea, but he left the work to Sasha. For days and late into the nights he worked tirelessly, collecting data and taking down depositions. When he got through, thirty-three affidavits were completed, disclosing that $45,470.39 had remained in the States. Some of the men had deposited their money in private banks and they preferred not to trust the government that had driven them out like dogs. It was all they had from long years of drudgery and economy.

After nineteen days of dangerous cruising we at last reached the Kiel Canal. Badly battered, the *Buford* had to remain for twenty-four hours for repair. The men were locked below deck, and special guards stationed on watch. German barges came alongside of our ship. They were in front of our cabin, and I threw them a note through the porthole, telling them who we were. They consented to forward a letter, and I covered two sheets in the smallest German script I could write, describing our deportation, the reaction we left behind, and the treatment of the revolutionists imprisoned without benefit of amnesty. I addressed the letter to the *Republik,* organ of the Independent Socialists, and I added an appeal to the German workers to make their revolution as fundamental as that of Russia.

The men locked in the steerage and almost suffocating in the vile air made vigorous protests, demanding the daily exercise they had won after the first days of the journey. Meanwhile they were bombarding the German workers on the dock with missiles in which messages had been secreted. Presently the repair men, their work done and my letter safe in their hands, pulled away, shouting cheers for the political deportees from America and *die soziale Revolution.* It was a stirring demonstration of comradely solidarity which even war could not destroy.

We learned that our destination was Libau, in western Latvia, but two days later a radiogram notified the captain that fighting was continuing on the Baltic front, and the course of the *Buford* was changed. Again we were at sea in more senses than one. Deportees and crew became impatient and irritable with the drawn-out, perilous voyage. Longing filled me for those I had left behind and sickening uncertainty of the things ahead. Roots embedded in the soil of one's entire life are not easily transplanted. I felt uneasy and restless, between hope and doubt. My spirit was still in the United States.

The ghastly trip was over at last. We had reached Hango, a Finnish port. Supplied with three days' rations, we were turned over to the local authorities. America's obligation was at an end and so were her fears.

On our trip through Finland we were kept locked in the train, with sentries with fixed bayonets inside the cars and on the platforms. Ethel and Dora, as well as a number of the men comrades, were ill, but though our train stopped at stations having buffets, no one was allowed to step out for purchases. On the border, at Teryoki, our compartments were unlocked and the sentries withdrawn. We were permitted to look after our supplies, but to our consternation we discovered that the greater part of our provisions had been appropriated by the Finnish soldiers. Presently there appeared a representative of the Finnish Foreign Office and a military officer of the General Staff. They were very anxious to be rid of the American political deportees and they demanded that we cross over at once to Russia. We refused to comply without first notifying Soviet Russia of our arrival. There followed negotiations with the Finnish authorities, and finally we were granted permission to send two radios, one to Moscow, addressed to Chicherin, People's Commissar for Foreign Affairs, the other to our old friend Bill Shatoff in Petrograd. Within a short time the Soviet committee arrived. Chicherin had sent Feinberg as his representative, while the Petrograd Soviet delegated Zorin, Secretary of the Communist Party of that city, to receive us. Mme Andreyeva, Gorki's wife, accompanied them. Arrangements were quickly made to transfer our luggage from the train across the border. Just at that moment the complete rout of Denikin by the valiant Red Army was announced, and the air was rent by the joyous hurrahs of our two hundred and forty-nine deportees.

All was ready. It was the twenty-eighth day of our journey, and at last we were on the threshold of Soviet Russia. My heart trembled with anticipation and fervent hope.

CHAPTER LII

SOVIET RUSSIA! SACRED GROUND, MAGIC PEOPLE! YOU HAVE COME to symbolize humanity's hope, you alone are destined to redeem mankind. I have come to serve you, beloved *matushka*. Take me to your bosom, let me pour myself into you, mingle my blood with yours, find my place in your heroic struggle, and give to the uttermost to your needs!

At the border, on our way to Petrograd, and at the station there, we were received like dear comrades. We who had been driven out of America as felons were welcomed on Soviet soil as brothers by her sons and daughters who had helped to set her free. Workers, soldiers, and peasants surrounded us, took us by the hand, and made us feel akin to them. Pale-faced and hollow-cheeked they were, a light burning in their sunken eyes, and determination breathing from their ragged bodies. Danger and suffering had steeled their wills and made them stern. But underneath beat the old childlike, generous Russian heart, and it went out to us without stint.

Music and song greeted us everywhere and wondrous tales of valour and never-failing fortitude in the face of hunger, cold, and devastating disease. Tears of gratitude burned in my eyes and I felt great humility before those simple folk risen to greatness in the fire of the revolutionary struggle.

In Petrograd, after a third reception, *Tovarishtch* Zorin, in whose company we had made the trip, invited Sasha and me to come with him to a waiting automobile. Darkness covered the big city, fantastic shadows over the glistening snow on the ground. The streets were entirely deserted, the grave-like silence disturbed only by the rattling of our car. We sped on, several times halted by human forms suddenly emerging from the blackness of the night. Soldiers they were, heavily armed, their flashlights searchingly on us. *" Propusk, tovarishtch!*

(Pass-card, comrade!)," was their curt demand. "Military precautions," our escort explained; "Petrograd has only recently escaped the menace of Yudenich. Too many counter-revolutionists are still lurking about for us to take any chances." We continued on our way, and as the automobile turned a corner and passed a brightly lighted building, Zorin remarked: "The Cheka and our jail — generally empty, though." Presently we halted before a large house, lights streaming from its many windows. "The Astoria, a fashionable hotel in tsarist times," Zorin informed us, "now the First House of the Petro-Soviet." We were to room there, he added, while the rest of the deportees would be housed in the Smolny, formerly the most exclusive boarding-school for the daughters of the aristocracy. "And the girls?" I inquired. "Ethel Bernstein and Dora Lipkin — I could not bear to be separated from them." Zorin promised to secure a room for them in the Astoria, although only party members were quartered in that Soviet house, mostly high officials, as well as special guests. He led us to his apartment, while places for us were being prepared.

Liza, Zorin's wife, bade us a hearty welcome, her greeting as kindly as Zorin's attitude had been throughout the day. She felt sure we were hungry. She had not much to offer us, but we should partake of everything she had, which proved to be herring, *kasha,* and tea. The Zorins looked none too well fed themselves, and I promised myself to replenish their scanty larder when our trunks were unpacked. Our American friends had provided us with a huge trunkful of supplies and we had also rescued some of the rations given us on leaving the *Buford.* I chuckled inwardly at the thought of the United States Government unwittingly feeding the Russian Bolsheviks.

The Zorins had lived in America, though we had never met them there. But they knew us, and Liza said that she had attended some of my lectures in New York. Both spoke English with a strong foreign accent, but more fluently than we did Russian. Thirty-five years in the States with almost no practice in our native tongue had paralysed our ability to use it. Besides, the Zorins had much to relate to us and they could do it in English. They told us of the Revolution, its achievements and hopes, and many other things we wanted to learn about. Their story of the events leading up to October and the developments since, though more detailed, was somewhat repetitious of what we had already heard at our receptions. It concerned the blockade and its fearful toll; the iron ring that surrounded Russia and the devastating sabotage of the interventionists; the armed attacks by Denikin, Kolchak, and Yudenich; the havoc wrought by them and the revolutionary spirit that kept at its height against terrible odds, fighting on numerous fronts and routing its enemies. Fighting also on the industrial front, building the new Russia out of the ruins of the old. Already much constructive work had been achieved, they informed us; we should have the opportunity to see it with our own eyes. Schools, workers' colleges, social protection of mother and child, care of the aged and the sick, and much more were made possible by the dictatorship of the proletariat. Of course, Russia was very far yet from perfection, with every hand raised against her. The blockade, the intervention, the counter-revolutionary plotters — foremost amongst them the Russian intelligentsia — they were the greatest menace. It was they who were responsible for the fearful obstacles the Revolution encountered and for the ills the country was suffering.

The herculean tasks facing Russia now made our past struggles in America appear pitifully insignificant; our real test by fire was yet before us! I trembled at the thought of my possible failure, my inability to scale the heights already attained by the obscure and dumb millions. In their earnestness and obvious consecration the Zorins symbolized this greatness and I felt proud to have them as friends. It was past midnight before we could tear ourselves away from them.

In the hotel corridor we ran into a young woman who told us that she was on her way to the Zorins' to call us. A friend from America was waiting, eager to see us. We followed her to an apartment on the fourth floor, and when the door was opened, I found myself in the embrace of our old comrade Bill Shatoff. "Bill, you here!" I cried in surprise; "why, Zorin told me you had left for Siberia!"

"Why were you not at the border to meet us? Didn't you receive our radio?" Sasha chimed in.

"None of your American speed," Bill laughed: "let me hug you first, dear Sasha, and let's have a glass to your safe arrival in revolutionary Russia. Then we'll talk." He led us to a divan, placing himself between us. The others present greeted us warmly: Anna (Bill's wife), her sister Rose, and the latter's husband. I had met the girls in New York, but I had not recognized Rose in the dim light of the corridor.

Bill had put on considerable weight since the farewell send-off we had given him in New York. His military uniform accentuated his bulging lines and made his face look rather hard. But he was the same old Bill, impulsive, affectionate, and jovial. He pelted us with a volley of questions about America, the San Francisco labour cases, our imprisonment and deportation. "Never mind all that for the present," we parried; "better tell us first about yourself. How do you happen still to be in Petrograd? And why were you not on the reception committee for the American deportees?" Bill looked somewhat embarrassed and sought to dodge our questions, but we were insistent. I could not bear the uncertainty about Zorin and I was not willing to suspect him of deliberate deception. "I see you have not changed," Bill teased; "you are the same old persistent pest." He tried to explain that in the strenuous life of Russia people had no time for mere sociability. He and Zorin, having different duties, rarely met. That might explain Zorin's impression that he had departed. His Siberian journey had been settled upon weeks previously, but, owing to the difficulty of procuring the necessary equipment for his trip, had been delayed. Even now much was to be attended to before he would be ready to leave. It might keep him in the city for another fortnight, but he did not mind it now that we were with him — it would give us time to talk things over, about America and Russia. He had received our radio and he had asked to be on the committee, but he was refused. It had been considered unwise to allow him to give us our first impressions of Russia, in order not to prejudice us. "It! It!" both Sasha and I exclaimed. "Who is that dictatorial 'it' that orders your Siberian trip and that refuses you the right to meet your old comrades and friends? And why could you not have come on your own account?" "The dictatorship of the proletariat," Bill replied, patting me on the back indulgently; "but of that some other time. Now I just want to tell you," he continued earnestly, "that the Communist State in action is exactly what we anarchists have always claimed it would be — a tightly centralized power, still more strengthened by the dangers to the Revolution. Under such conditions one cannot do as one wills. One does not just hop on a train and go, or even ride the bumpers, as I used to in the United States. One needs permission. But don't get the idea that I miss my American 'blessings.' Me for Russia, the Revolution, and its glorious future!"

Bill was certain we would come to feel just as he did about things in Russia. No need to worry about trifles like *propusks* during our first hours together. "*Propusks!* I have a whole trunkful of them, and so will you soon," he concluded, a mischievous twinkle in his eye. I caught his mood and dismissed my questions. I was dazed by the impressions that had crowded the day. Was it really only one day, I wondered. I seemed to have lived years since our arrival.

Bill Shatoff did not leave for another fortnight, and we spent together most of our time, often into the wee hours of the morning. The revolutionary canvas he unrolled before us was of far larger scope than had been painted before by anyone else. It was no longer a few individual figures thrown on the picture, their rôle and importance accentuated by the vast background. Great and small, high and low, stood out in bold relief, imbued with a collective will to hasten the complete triumph of the Revolution. Lenin, Trotsky, Zinoviev, with their small band of inspired comrades, had a tremendous part to play, Bill declared with enthusiastic conviction; but the real power behind them was the awakened revolutionary consciousness of the masses. The peasants had expropriated the masters' land all through the summer of 1917 . . . workers had taken possession of the factories and shops . . . the soldiers had flocked back by the hundred thousands from the warring fronts . . . the Kronstadt sailors had translated their anarchist motto of direct action into the everyday life of the Revolution . . . the Left Socialist Revolutionists, as also the anarchists, had encouraged the peasantry in socializing the land. . . . All these forces had helped to energize the storm that broke over Russia, finding full expression and release in the terrific sweep of October.

Such was the epic of dazzling beauty and overwhelming power, infused with palpitating life by the ardour and eloquence of our friend. Presently Bill himself broke the spell. He had shown us the transformation in the soul of Russia, he continued; he would have to let us see her ills of the body as well. "Not to prejudice you," he emphasized, "as has been feared by people whose criterion of revolutionary integrity is a membership card." Before long we would ourselves meet the appalling afflictions that were sapping the country's strength, he said. His object was merely to prepare us — to help us diagnose the source of the disease, to point out the danger of its spreading and enable us to see that only the most drastic measures could effect a cure. The Russian experience had taught him that we anarchists had been the romanticists of revolution, forgetful of the cost it would entail, the frightful price the enemies of the Revolution would exact, the fiendish methods they would resort to in order to destroy its gains.

One cannot fight fire and sword with only the logic and justice of one's ideal. The counter-revolutionists had combined to isolate and starve Russia, and the blockade was taking frightful toll of human life. The intervention and the destruction in its wake, the numerous White attacks, costing oceans of blood, the hordes of Denikin, Kolchak, and Yudenich; their pogroms, bestial revenge, and the general havoc wrought had imposed on the Revolution a warfare that its most far-sighted exponents had never dreamed about. A warfare not always in keeping without romantic ideas of revolutionary ethics, indispensable none the less to drive off the hungry wolves ready to tear the Revolution limb from limb. He had not ceased to be an anarchist, Bill assured us; he had not become indifferent to the menace of a Marxian State machine. That danger was no longer a subject for theoretic discussion, but an actual reality because of the existing bureaucracy, inefficiency, and corruption. He loathed the dictatorship and its handmaiden, the Cheka, with their ruthless suppression of thought, speech, and initiative. But it was an unavoidable evil. The anarchists had been the first to respond to Lenin's essentially anarchistic call to revolution. They had the right to demand an accounting. "And we will! Never doubt that," Bill fairly shouted, "we will! But not now, not now! Not while every nerve must be strained to save Russia from the reactionary elements which are desperately fighting to come back to power." He had not joined the Communist Party, and never would, Bill assured us. But he was with the Bolsheviki and he would continue until every front had been liquidated and the last enemy driven to cover, like Yudenich, Denikin, and the rest of the tsarist gang. "And so will you, dear Emma and Sasha," Bill concluded; "I am certain of it."

Our comrade was the enthusiastic bard of old, his song the saga of the Revolution, the most stupendous event of our time. Its miracles were many, its horrors and woe the martyrdom of a people nailed to the cross.

Bill was entirely right, we thought. Nothing was of moment compared with the supreme need of giving one's all to safeguard the Revolution and its gains. The faith and fervour of our comrade swept me along to ecstatic heights. Yet I could not entirely free myself from an undercurrent of uneasiness one often feels when left alone in the dark. Resolutely I strove to drive it back, moving like a sleep-walker through enchanted space. Sometimes I would stumble back to earth only half-aroused by a harsh voice or an ugly sight. The gagging of free speech at the session of the Petro-Soviet that we had attended, the discovery that better and more plentiful food was served Party members at the Smolny dining-room and many similar injustices and evils had attracted my attention. Model schools where the children were stuffed with sweets and candies, and side by side with them schools dismal, poorly equipped, unheated, and filthy, where the little ones, hungry all the time, were herded together like cattle. A special hospital for Communists, with every modern comfort, while other institutions lacked the barest medical and surgical necessities. Thirty-four different grades of rations — under alleged *Communism!* — while some markets and privileged stores were doing a lively business in butter, eggs, cheese, and meat. The workers and their womenfolk standing long hours in endless queues for their ration of frozen potatoes, wormy cereals, and decayed fish. Groups of women, their faces bloated and blue, accompanied by Red soldiers and bargaining with them for their pitiful wares.

I talked to Zorin about these things, to the young anarchist Kibalchich, living in the Astoria, to Zinoviev and others, pointing out these contradictions. How were they to be justified or explained? All of them repeated the same refrain: "What will you, with the blockade around us, the sabotage of the intelligentsia, the attacks of Denikin, Kolchak, and Yudenich!" They alone were to blame, they reiterated. Old evils could not be eradicated until the fronts were liquidated. "Come and work with us," they said, "you and Berkman. You can have any position you choose and you can help us a great deal."

I was profoundly moved to see these people reaching eagerly out for willing hands. We would join them; we would work with them with our best energy and strength as soon as we found our bearings, knew where we belonged and where we could be of greatest use.

Zinoviev did not look the formidable leader his reputation would have led one to assume. He impressed me as flabby and weak. His voice was adolescent, high-pitched and lacking in appeal. But he had faithfully helped the Revolution to its birth and he was indefatigably working for its further development, we had been told. He certainly deserved confidence and respect. "The blockade," he reiterated, "Kolchak, Denikin, Yudenich, the counter-revolutionist Savinkov, as well as the Menshevik traitors and the Socialist Revolutionists of the Right, are a constant menace. They are eternally plotting vengeance and the death of the Revolution." Zinoviev's plaint added tragic momentum to the general chorus. I joined in with the rest.

Soon, however, other voices rose from the depths, harsh, accusing voices that greatly disturbed me. I had been asked to attend a conference of anarchists in Petrograd, and I was amazed to find that my comrades were compelled to gather in secret in an obscure hiding-place. Bill Shatoff had spoken with great pride of the courage shown by our comrades in the Revolution and on the military fronts, and he had extolled the heroic part they had played. Why should people with such a record, I wondered, be driven under cover.

Presently came the answer — from workers in the Putilov Iron-works, from factories and mills, from the Kronstadt sailors, from Red Army men, and from an old comrade who had escaped while under sentence of death. The very brawn of the revolutionary struggle was crying out in anguish and bitterness against the people they had helped place in power. They spoke of the Bolshevik betrayal of the Revolution, of the slavery forced upon the toilers, the emasculation of the soviets, the suppression of speech and thought, the filling of prisons with recalcitrant peasants, workers, soldiers, sailors, and rebels of every kind. They told of the raid with machine-guns upon the Moscow headquarters of the anarchists by the order of Trotsky; of the Cheka and the wholesale executions without hearing or trial. These charges and denunciations beat upon me like hammers and left me stunned. I listened tense in every nerve, hardly able clearly to understand what I heard, and failing to grasp its full meaning. It couldn't be true — this monster indictment! Had not Zorin pointed the jail out to us and assured us that it was almost empty? Capital punishment, he had said, had been abolished. And had not Bill Shatoff paid glowing tribute to Lenin and his co-workers, glorifying their vision and valour? Bill had not covered up the dark spots on the Soviet horizon; he had explained the reason for them and the methods they had forced upon the Bolsheviki, and indeed upon all rebels serving the Revolution.

The men in that dismal hall must be mad, I thought, to tell such impossible and preposterous stories, wicked to condemn the Communists for the crimes they must know were due to the counter-revolutionary gang, to the blockade and the White generals attacking the Revolution. I proclaimed my conviction to the gathering, but my voice was drowned in the laughter of derision and jeers. I was roundly denounced for my wilful blindness. "That's the gag they have given you!" my comrades shouted at me. "You and Berkman have fallen for it and swallowed it whole. And Zorin, the bigot who hates anarchists and would shoot them all in cold blood! Bill Shatoff, too, the renegade!" they shouted; "you believe them and not us. Wait, wait until you have seen things with your own eyes. You will sing another song then."

When the indignant uproar had subsided, the fugitive from the death-sentence demanded the floor. His pale face was deeply furrowed, suffering spoke from his large, hunted eyes, and he talked in a voice trembling with suppressed excitement. He dwelt at length on the recent events and the difficulties in the way of the Revolution. The anarchists did not close their eyes to the counter-revolutionary menace, he said. They were fighting it tooth and nail, as proved by the numerous comrades on the fronts and the great numbers that had laid down their lives in the battles against the enemy. In fact, it was Nestor Makhno, an anarchist, who with his peasant rebel army of *povstantsy* had helped to rout Denikin and thus saved Moscow and the Revolution at the most critical period. Anarchists in every part of Russia were at the very moment on the firing line, driving back the enemies of the Revolution. But they were also fighting the plague that had brought in the counter-revolutionary pest: the Brest-Litovsk peace, which had disintegrated the revolutionary spirit of the masses and had been the first wedge to break the proletarian forces and their unity. The anarchists and the Left Social Revolutionists had opposed it from the very first as a perilous step and a breach of faith on the part of the Bolsheviki. The policy of the *razverstka,* introduced by the Bolsheviki, the forcible gathering of products by irresponsible military detachments, had added fuel to the fires of popular bitterness. It had aroused hatred among the peasants and workers and had made them fertile soil for counter-revolutionary plots. "Shatoff knows all this," the man cried; "why did he hide these facts from you? But Bill Shatoff has become a 'Sovietsky' anarchist and he is serving the men in the Kremlin. That is why Lenin has saved him from the Cheka and has exiled him to Siberia instead. Workers and peasants, soldiers and sailors had been shot for lesser offences than the shady manipulations with his *bourgeois* cronies that Shatoff engaged in as virtual governor of Petrograd. The Bolsheviki are grateful masters. Shatoff

had ruled Petrograd with an iron hand. He had himself rushed after
the fleeing Kanegiesser, the slayer of the sadist Uritsky, chief of the
Petrograd Cheka. Shatoff, the anarchist, had caught the unfortunate
prey, brought him back in triumph, and turned him over to the Cheka
to be shot!"

"Stop, stop!" I screamed; "I've had enough of your lies! Bill
would never do such a thing. I have known Bill for years as the kindest
and gentlest of beings. I could never believe him capable of such
things." In rage I struck out at these people who called themselves
anarchists and yet were so vindictive and mean-spirited. I fought for
the integrity of Zorin and defended Zinoviev as an able and energetic
leader. I championed Bill, my old comrade and friend, extolling the
nobility of his character, his big spirit and clear vision. I refused to
have my burning faith extinguished by the poisonous fumes I had been
inhaling for three days.

Sasha had been laid up with a severe cold and was too ill to attend
the conference of the anarchist group. But I had kept him informed,
and now I burst into his room in great mental turmoil to tell him of
this last dreadful day. He dismissed the charges as the irresponsible
prattle of ineffective and disgruntled men. The Petrograd anarchists
were like so many in our ranks in America who used to do least and
criticize most, he said. Perhaps they had been naïve enough to expect
anarchism to emerge overnight from the ruins of autocracy, from the
war and blunders of the Provisional Government. It was absurd to
denounce the Bolsheviki for the drastic measures they were using,
Sasha urged. How else were they to free Russia from the strangle-
hold of counter-revolution and sabotage? So far as he was concerned,
he did not think any methods too harsh to deal with this. Revolutionary necessity justified all measures, however we might dislike them.
As long as the Revolution was in jeopardy, those seeking to undermine it must pay the penalty. Single-hearted and clear-eyed as ever was
my old pal. I agreed with him; still, the ugly reports of my comrades
kept disturbing me.

Sasha's illness had driven back the phantoms of my sleepless nights.
Physicians were few, medicine scarce, and disease rampant in Petrograd. Zorin had immediately sent out for a doctor, but the patient's
fever was too alarming for a long wait. My old professional experience never served a better purpose. With the help of my small, well-

equipped medicine chest which the kindly doctor of the *Buford* had given me, I succeeded in breaking Sasha's fever. Two weeks of careful nursing brought him out of bed, looking thin and pale, but on the road to complete recovery. About this time two men were sent up to see us: George Lansbury, editor of the London *Daily Herald,* and Mr. Barry, an American correspondent. They had not been expected and no provision had been made for an English-speaking person to meet them. They did not understand a word of Russian and they wanted to get to Moscow. We communicated their plight to Mme Ravich, head of the Interior Department and chief of the Foreign Office in Petrograd. She requested Sasha to accompany the English visitors to Moscow, and he consented.

His departure left me free to go about again. The Zorins were always willing to take me to places of interest, but I was beginning to pick up my Russian and I preferred to go alone. The anarchist conference having been held under cover, I had not been in a position to talk to the Zorins about it, much less tell them what I had heard. It made me feel somewhat guilty in their presence. Added to it was my impression that Zorin was purposely keeping me away from certain things. I had asked him whether I could visit some factories. He had promised to secure a *propusk* for me, but he had failed to do so. He had also shown impatience with Liza when she had asked me to address the girls of a shop-collective. Not that I had consented; my Russian was still too halting. Moreover, I had come to Russia to learn and not to teach. Zorin seemed greatly relieved at my refusal. I had paid no attention to his peculiar attitude at the time, but when he also broke his promise to take me to the mills, I began to wonder whether there was not something wrong there. I did not believe that conditions were as bad as described at the conference; why, then, should Zorin refuse to let me see them? However, my relations with the Zorins continued very friendly. They were ardent rebels, utterly without thought of themselves and their needs. They were unwilling to accept anything from us, though always ready to share their own meagre supplies. Zorin was particularly adamant. Every time I would bring some of our American provisions, he would warn me that we should soon go hungry ourselves if we continued giving our things away. Liza also was difficult to persuade. She was expecting her baby, and I was urging her to let me help her prepare a few things for the new arrival. "Nonsense," she would reply; "in proletarian Russia no one fusses about baby clothes; we leave that to the pampered *bourgeois* women in capitalist countries. We have more important things to do."

I would argue that the babies of today were going to be the inheritors of that future she was working for. Shouldn't their first needs be considered even before their birth? But Liza would laugh it off and call me sentimental, not at all the fighter she had thought me. I liked and admired their sterling qualities, in spite of their narrow partisan traits. I did not see quite so much of them, however, as in the first weeks. There was no need for it, as I could now go about by myself; moreover, other people had come into my life.

One thing Bill Shatoff had told us about was certainly not overdrawn: the matter of *propusks*. They played a greater rôle in Soviet Russia than passports had under the tsars. One could not even get in or out of our hotel without a permit, not to speak of visiting any Soviet institution or important official. Almost everyone carried portfolios stocked with *propusks* and *oodostoverenyas* (identification papers). Zorin had told me that they constituted a necessary precaution against counter-revolutionary plotters, but the longer I stayed in Russia, the less I saw their value. Paper was at a high premium, yet reams upon reams of it were used for "permits," and much time was wasted in securing them. On the other hand, the very quantity of them defeated any real control. What sane counter-revolutionist, I argued, would expose himself to discovery by standing for hours in line waiting for a *propusk*? He could more easily secure it in other ways. But it was useless; every Communist I met seemed to suffer from counter-revolutionary fixation, no doubt due to the attacks already endured. How could I take issue with them? My stay in Russia had been too short for me to advise them on the most practical method of coping with the enemies of the Revolution. And what did the pesky pieces of paper matter in view of the great things already achieved? Everywhere I witnessed sublime courage, selfless devotion, and simple grandeur on the part of those holding the revolutionary fort against the entire inimical world. Thus I reasoned with myself, determinedly refusing to see the reverse side of Russia's face. But its scarred and twisted countenance would not be ignored. It kept calling me back, urging me to look, forcing me to view its suffering. I wanted to see only its beauty and radiance, longed passionately to believe in its strength and power, yet the very hideousness of the other side compelled with an irresistible appeal. "Look, look!" it grinned, "within reach of Petrograd are vast stretches of forest, enough to heat every home and make every factory wheel turn. Yet the city is perishing from cold, and the machines are frozen. The *razverstka* (forcible collection of food) drains the peasantry to feed Petrograd, they are told; fertile Ukraine is forced to ship carloads of provisions northward, yet the population of the cities is starving. A goodly half of the provisions somehow vanishes along the route, the rest reaching, in the main, the markets rather than the hungry masses; and the constant shootings on the Gorokhovaya (Cheka headquarters), have you been deaf to those? And the planned prison for morally defective children — has your indignation not been aroused by this, you who have for thirty-five years hurled anathema at the traducers of child-life? What about all these ghastly blotches so skilfully hidden by Communist rouge?"

Like a rabbit in a trap I dashed about in my cage, beating against the bars of these fearful contradictions. Blindly I reached out for someone to ward off the mortal blow. Zinoviev and John Reed, who had just returned from Moscow, could explain, I thought. And Maxim Gorki, he would surely tell me which side of the Russian face was the real one and which one false. He would help me, he the great realist, whose clarion voice had thundered against every wrong and who had castigated the crimes against childhood in words of fire.

I dispatched a note to Gorki, requesting him to see me. I felt lost in the labyrinth of Soviet Russia, stumbling constantly over the many obstacles, vainly groping for the revolutionary light. I needed his friendly, guiding hand, I wrote him. Meanwhile I turned to Zinoviev. "Forests within easy reach of Petrograd," I said; "why must the city freeze?" "Any amount of fuel," Zinoviev replied; "but of what avail? Our enemies have destroyed our means of transportation; the blockade has killed off our horses as well as our men. How are we to get at the woodland?" "What about the population of Petrograd?" I persisted. "Could it not be appealed to for co-operation? Could it not be induced to go *en masse* with pick and ax and ropes to haul wood for its own use? Would not such a concerted effort alleviate much suffering and at the same time decrease the antagonism against your party?" It might help to diminish the misery from cold, Zinoviev replied, but it would interfere with the carrying out of the main political policies. What were they? "Concentration of all power in the hands of the proletarian *avant-garde*," Zinoviev explained, "the *avant-garde* of the Revolution, which is the Communist Party." "Rather a dear price to pay," I objected. "Unfortunately," he agreed; "but the dictatorship of the proletariat is the only workable program during a revolutionary period. Anarchist groups, free initiative of communes, as your great teachers have suggested, may be feasible in centuries to come, but not now in Russia, with the Denikins and Kolchaks ready to crush us. They have doomed the whole of Russia, yet your comrades fret about the fate of one city." One city, with a million and a half inhabitants reduced to four hundred thousand! A mere bagatelle in the eyes of the Communist political program! Disheartened, I left the man so cock-sure of his party's wisdom, so ensconced in the heavenly Marxian constellation and self-conscious of being one of its major stars.

John Reed had burst into my room like a sudden ray of light, the old buoyant, adventurous Jack that I used to know in the States. He was about to return to America, by way of Latvia. Rather a hazardous journey, he said, but he would take even greater risks to bring the inspiring message of Soviet Russia to his native land. "Wonderful, marvellous, isn't it, E.G.?" he exclaimed. "Your dream of years now realized in Russia, your dream scorned and persecuted in my country, but made real by the magic wand of Lenin and his band of despised Bolsheviks. Did you ever expect such a thing to happen in the country ruled by the tsars for centuries?"

"Not by Lenin and his comrades, dear Jack," I corrected, "though I do not deny their great part. But by the whole Russian people, preceded by a glorious revolutionary past. No other land of our days has been so literally nurtured by the blood of her martyrs, a long procession of pioneers who went to their death that new life may spring from their graves."

Jack insisted that the young generation cannot for ever be tied to the apron-strings of the old, particularly when those strings are tightly drawn around its throat. "Look at your old pioneers, the Breshkovskayas and Tchaikovskys, the Chernovs and Kerenskys and the rest of them," he cried heatedly; "see where they are now! With the Black Hundreds, the Jew-baiters, and the ducal clique, aiding them to crush the Revolution. I don't give a damn for their past. I am concerned only in what the treacherous gang has been doing during the past three years. To the wall with them! I say. I have learned one mighty expressive Russian word, '*razstrellyat*'!" (execute by shooting).

"Stop, Jack! Stop!" I cried; "this word is terrible enough in the mouth of a Russian. In your hard American accent it freezes my blood. Since when do revolutionists see in wholesale execution the only solution of their difficulties? In time of active counter-revolution it is no doubt inevitable to give shot for shot. But cold-bloodedly and merely for opinion's sake, do you justify standing people against the wall under such circumstances?" I went on to point out to him that the Soviet Government must have realized the futility of such methods, not to speak of their barbarity, because it had abolished capital punishment. Zorin had told me that. Was the decree revoked, that Jack spoke so glibly of standing men against the wall? I mentioned the frequent shooting I heard in the city at night. Zorin had said that it was target practice of *kursanty* (Communist students at the military training-school for officers). "Do you know anything about it, Jack?" I questioned. "Tell me the truth."

He did know, he said, that five hundred prisoners, considered counter-revolutionists, had been shot on the eve the decree was to go into force. It had been a stupid blunder on the part of over-zealous Chekists and they had been severely reprimanded for it. He had not heard of any other shootings since, but he had always thought me a revolutionist of the purest dye, one who would not shirk any measure in defence of the Revolution. He was surprised to see me so worked up over the death of a few plotters. As if that mattered in the scales of the world revolution!

"I must be crazy, Jack," I said, "or else I never understood the meaning of revolution. I certainly never believed that it would signify callous indifference to human life and suffering, or that it would have no other method of solving its problems than by wholesale slaughter. Five hundred lives snuffed out on the eve of a decree abolishing the death-penalty! You call it a stupid blunder. I call it a dastardly crime, the worst counter-revolutionary outrage committed in the name of the Revolution."

"That's all right," said Jack, trying to calm me; "you are a little confused by the Revolution in action because you have dealt with it only in theory. You'll get over that, clear-sighted rebel that you are, and you'll come to see in its true light everything that seems so puzzling now. Cheer up, and make me a cup of the good old American coffee you have brought with you. Not much to give you in return for all my country has taken from you, but greatly appreciated in starving Russia by her native son."

I marvelled at his capacity to change so quickly to a light tone. It was the same old Jack, with his zest for the adventures of life. I longed to join in his gay mood, but my heart was heavy. Jack's appearance had brought back memories of my recent life, my people, Helena and those dear to me. Not a word from anyone had reached me in two months. Uncertainty about them added to my depression and restlessness. Sasha's letter, suggesting that I come to Moscow, put new energy into me. Moscow was much more alive than Petrograd, he wrote, and there were interesting people to meet. A few weeks in the capital might help to clarify the revolutionary situation to me. I wanted to go immediately. I had already learned, however, that in Soviet Russia one does not just buy a ticket and board a train. I had seen people standing in queues for days and nights to obtain a permit for their journey and then again wait in long lines to purchase their tickets. Even with the helpful co-operation of Zorin it required ten days before I could leave. He had arranged for me to be in the party of Soviet officials going to Moscow, he informed me. Demyan Bedny, the official poet, would be there and he would place me in the Hotel National. Zorin was as obliging as ever, though somewhat distant.

Arrived at the station, I found myself in distinguished company. Karl Radek, who had escaped the fate of Liebknecht, Rosa Luxemburg, and Landauer, was there. Chiperovich, head of the Petrograd labour unions, Maxim Gorki, and several lesser lights were also in the same car with me.

Gorki had previously replied to my letter and had asked me to call for a talk. I did, but there was no talk. I found him suffering from a heavy cold and constantly coughing, while four women were fluttering about him, ministering to his needs. When he saw me in the car, he said we could have our postponed talk *en route;* he would come to my compartment later. I waited eagerly the largest part of the day. Gorki did not appear, nor anyone else except the porter with sandwiches and tea for the Soviet party. Radek, in the next compartment, was evidently holding court. In true Russian fashion everybody talked at once. But the little, nervous Radek managed to outstrip the others. For hours he rattled on. My brain grew weary and I dozed off.

I was roused from my sleep by a gaunt and lanky figure towering above me. Maxim Gorki stood before me, his peasant face deeply lined with pain. I asked him to sit down beside me and he crumpled into the seat, a tired and languid man, much older than his fifty years.

I had looked forward with much anticipation to the chance of talking to Gorki, yet now I did not know how to begin. " Gorki knows nothing about me," I was saying to myself. . . . " He may think me merely a reformer, opposed to the Revolution as such. Or he may even get the impression that I am just fault-finding on account of personal grievances or because I could not have ' buttered toast and grape-fruit for breakfast ' or other material American blessings." Such an interpretation had actually been given to the complaint of Morris Becker about the unbearably putrid air in the shop where he was working, the unnecessary filth and dirt. " You are a pampered *bourgeois*," the Commissar had bellowed at him; " you pine for the comforts of capitalist America. The proletarian dictatorship has more important things to consider than ventilation or lockers to keep your bread and tea clean." I had laughed to tears over that story, but now I was upset by the apprehension lest Maxim Gorki consider me also a pampered *bourgeois,* dissatisfied because I had failed to find in Soviet Russia the flesh-pots of capitalist America. But it was ridiculous to think Gorki capable of the silly prattle of a subordinate Bolshevik official, I sought to reassure myself. Surely the seer who could detect beauty in the meanest life and discover nobility in the basest was too penetrating to misunderstand my groping. He more than any other man would grasp its cause and its pain.

At last I began by saying that I should first have to introduce myself before I could talk to him about the things that were distressing me. " Hardly necessary," Gorki interrupted; " I know a good deal about your activities in the United States. But even if I knew nothing about you, the fact that you were deported for your ideas would be proof enough of your revolutionary integrity. I need nothing more." " That is most kind of you," I replied, " yet I must insist on a little preliminary." Gorki nodded, and I proceeded to tell him of my faith in the Bolsheviki from the very beginning of the October Revolution, and my defence of them and of Soviet Russia at a time when even very few radicals dared speak up for Lenin and his comrades. I had even turned from Catherine Breshkovskaya, who had been our torch for a generation. It had been no easy task to cry in the wilderness of fury and hate in defence of people who in point of theory had always been my political opponents. But who could think of such differences when the life of the Revolution was at stake? Lenin and his co-workers personified that life to me and to my nearest comrades and friends. Therefore we had fought for them and we would have cheerfully given our lives for the men who were holding the revolutionary fort. " I hope you will not consider me boastful or think that I have exaggerated the difficulties and dangers of our struggle in America for Soviet Russia," I said. Gorki shook his head and I continued: " I also hope you will believe me when I say that, though an anarchist, I had not been naïve enough to think that anarchism could rise overnight, as it were, from the debris of old Russia."

He stopped me with a gesture of his hand. " If that is so, and I do not doubt you, how can you be so perplexed at the imperfections you find in Soviet Russia? As an old revolutionist you must know that revolution is a grim and relentless task. Our poor Russia, backward and crude, her masses, steeped in centuries of ignorance and darkness, brutal and lazy beyond any other people in the world! " I gasped at his sweeping indictment of the entire Russian people. His charge was terrible, if true, I told him. It was also rather novel. No Russian writer had ever spoken in such terms before. He, Maxim Gorki, was the first to advance such a peculiar view, and the first not to put all the blame upon the blockade, the Denikins and Kolchaks. Somewhat irritated, he replied that the " romantic conception of our great literary genuises " had entirely misrepresented the Russian and had wrought no end of evil. The Revolution had dispèlled the bubble of the goodness and naïveté of the peasantry. It had proved them shrewd, avaricious, and lazy, even savage in their joy of causing pain. The rôle played by the counter-revolutionary Yudeniches, he added, was too obvious to need special emphasis. That is why he had not considered it necessary even to mention them, nor the intelligentsia, which had been talking revolution for over fifty years and then was the first to stab it in the back with sabotage and conspiracies. But all these were contributory factors, not the main cause. The roots were inherent in Russia's brutal and uncivilized masses, he said. They have no cultural traditions, no social values, no respect for human rights and life. They cannot be moved by anything except coercion and force. All through the ages the Russians had known nothing else.

I protested vehemently against these charges. I argued that in spite of his evident faith in the superior qualities of other nations, it was the ignorant and crude Russian people that had risen first in revolt. They had shaken Russia by three successive revolutions within twelve years, and it was they and their will that gave life to " October."

" Very eloquent," Gorki retorted, " but not quite accurate." He admitted the share of the peasantry in the October uprising, though even that, he thought, was not conscious social feeling, but mere wrath accumulated for decades. If not checked by Lenin's guiding hand, it would have surely destroyed rather than advanced the great revolutionary aims. Lenin, Gorki insisted, was the real parent of the October Revolution. It had been conceived by his genius, nurtured by his vision and faith, and brought to maturity by his far-sighted and patient care. Others had helped to deliver the lusty child, particularly the small band of Bolsheviki, aided by the Petrograd workers, together with the sailors and soldiers of Kronstadt. Since the birth of October it was again Lenin who was steering its development and growth.

" Miracle-worker, your Lenin," I cried; " but I seem to remember that you have not always thought him a god or his comrades infallible." I reminded Gorki of his scathing arraignment of the Bolsheviki in the journal *Zhizn,* edited by him in the days of Kerensky. What had caused his change? He had attacked the Bolsheviki, Gorki acknowledged, but the march of events had convinced him that a revolution in a primitive country with a barbarous people could not survive without resort to drastic methods of self-defence. The Bolsheviki had made many mistakes and they continued doing so. They admitted it themselves. But the suppression of the rights of the individual for the sake of the whole, the Cheka, prison, terror, and death were not of their choice. These methods had been forced upon Soviet Russia and they were unavoidable in the revolutionary struggle.

He looked exhausted, and I did not detain him when he rose to leave. He shook my hand and walked out with a weary gait. I, too, was tired and unutterably sad. Which of the two Gorkis, I wondered, had come closer to the Russian soul. Was it the creator of *Makar Tchudra* and *Tchelkash,* the author of *In the Depths,* of *Twenty-six and One,* the " dumb and cruel savages " of the Russian mass? How human Gorki had made them, how childlike and guileless, how moving in their frustration! He had lived with them, in the " nethermost where there is naught but murk and slush "; he had heard their " harsh cry for life," and he had " come up to bear witness to the suffering he had left behind." Was that the true soul of Russia, or was it as pictured by

Gorki the worshipper of Lenin? "A hundred million people, cruel savages needing barbarous methods to keep them in leash." Did he actually believe such monstrous things, or had he invented them to enhance the glory of his god?

Maxim Gorki had been my idol, and I would not see his feet of clay. I became convinced, however, of one thing: neither he nor anyone else could solve my problems. Only time and patient seeking could do it, aided by sympathetic understanding of cause and effect in the revolutionary struggle of Russia.

The occupants of the car had retired, and all was quiet. The train sped on. I tried to gain some sleep, but found myself thinking of Lenin. What was this man and what the power that drew everyone to him, even those who disagreed with his course? Trotsky, Zinoviev, Bukharin, and the other prominent men I had come across, all differed on many problems, yet were unanimous in their appraisal of Lenin. His was the clearest mind in Russia, everyone assured me, of iron will and dogged perseverance in pursuit of his aims, no matter what the cost. It was peculiar, though, that no one ever referred to any generous impulses of the man. I thought of Dora Kaplan, Lenin's assailant. Her story, told me by a friend of Bill Shatoff, who was entirely for the Bolsheviki and Lenin, had been among the first shocks of my Petrograd days. He roundly condemned the attack on Lenin as fraught with most disastrous effects on Russia had Lenin not survived his wounds. But he spoke with the highest regard of Dora and her revolutionary idealism and strength of character, which baffled even her Cheka tormentors. She had been motivated by her conviction that Lenin had betrayed the Revolution by his Brest-Litovsk negotiations. Her attitude was shared by her entire party, the Left Socialist Revolutionists, as well as by the anarchists. Even a goodly number in Communist ranks held the same view. Trotsky, Bukharin, Joffe, and other foremost Bolsheviki had strenuously fought their leader on the issue of making peace with the Kaiser. Lenin's influence, supported by his ingenious slogan of a *peredishka* (getting one's breath), had conquered all opposition. Many claimed that the *peredishka* would, in reality, prove a *zadishka* (death by strangulation). It would mean the end of the Revolution, they insisted, and Lenin would be responsible for it. Dora Kaplan, a mere slip of a girl, had translated the mental turmoil of the moment into action. She had attempted to slay Lenin before he could slay the Revolution!

"Only the Cheka works fast in Russia," my informant had

remarked with a cynical smile. " No time was wasted on a trial, and no chances were taken with a hearing." Torture having failed to induce Dora Kaplan to involve others in her act, she was put out of her agony by a steadier hand than hers. Lenin had gained the love and adulation of millions in every land, but he did nothing to save that unfortunate young woman. The ghastly story had haunted me for weeks. Relief came and renewed faith in Lenin's humanity when I learned that he had saved Bill Shatoff from the " quick action " of the Cheka. He could rise to generous heights, after all, I thought. Perhaps he had been too ill to intercede for Dora in time; possibly, also, the fact of her being tortured had been kept from him. Almost two months had passed since then. Now I was on my way perhaps to meet the man once hounded as a criminal and exile and who was now holding the fate and future of Russia in his hands.

Half asleep I heard the porter call out " Moscow! " When I reached the platform, I found that my fellow-passengers had already departed, including Demyan Bedny. I had had no means of notifying Sasha of my arrival, and no one else in the capital knew of my coming. I felt quite lost in the noise and bustle of the station and helpless with my bags and bundles. I had been warned that things had a way of vanishing in Russia under one's very eyes. I could not go in search of an *izvostchik* and I stood irresolutely wondering what to do. Presently a familiar voice struck my ears. It was Karl Radek talking to some friends. He had not come near me during the entire journey, nor did he show any sign that he knew my identity. I felt awkward about turning to him for help. Suddenly he wheeled round and approached me. Was I waiting for anyone, he inquired, or could he be of aid? I could have hugged the dear little man for his kindly interest, but I was afraid of scandalizing him by such a display of " *bourgeois* sentimentality." I had frequently heard the expression used with great derision. I assured Radek that he was more chivalrous than the chaperon Zorin had given me. He had faithfully promised to see me safely to Moscow and secure a room for me there, and he had basely run away. " Chivalry, nonsense! " laughed Radek; " we are comrades, aren't we, even if you are not a member of my party? " " But how do you know who I am? " " News travels quickly in Russia," he replied. " You're an anarchist, you are Emma Goldman, and you were driven out of plutocratic America. That's three good reasons to entitle you to my comradeship and assistance."

He invited me to accompany him and to give the " comrade chauffeur " directions where to let me off. I explained that I had only the
name and number of the street where my comrade Alexander Berkman
was stopping. He was not expecting me and he would probably not
be in. Moreover, he had no room of his own. Radek demanded to
know " what swine " had left me " in such a predicament." I remarked
that he would not apply such a term to the man if he knew how important he was. " Why, he is substituting official jingles for the daily
bread," I said. " Demyan! " Radek shrieked; " just like that fat
pig to shirk a difficult task." It was certainly not going to be easy to
secure a room for me in Moscow, he remarked; the city was overcrowded and few quarters were available. But I should not worry;
he'd take me to his apartment in the Kremlin and then we should see.

After the desolation of Petrograd, Moscow appeared a veritable
cauldron of activity. Crowds everywhere, almost everyone lugging
bundles or pulling loaded sleighs, rushing about and jostling, pushing
and swearing as only Russians can. Very conspicuous was the number
of soldiers and hard-faced men in leather jackets, with guns in their
belts. Jack Reed had not exaggerated when he told me that Moscow
was like an armed camp. Petrograd also did not lack military display,
but in the ten weeks I had spent there, I did not see so many men in
uniform, much less Chekists, as on my first morning in Moscow.

Radek and his car were evidently well known to the sentries along
our route. We were not halted, not even when the auto dashed through
the portals of the Kremlin. The sight of its stone walls brought back
to me memories of the tsarist régime. Through the centuries its rulers
had dwelt in the magnificence of the huge palaces, their drunken orgies
and black deeds echoing through the vast halls. More miraculous than
legend, I mused, were the changing faces of time. But yesterday en-
trenched in inviolate power, their authority inalienable as the stars,
today hurled from their thrones, bemoaned by a handful, by the many
forgot. The builders of the new Russia in the seats of the mighty of
old seemed incongruous in the extreme. How could they feel comfortable or at ease in the creeping shadows of the gruesome past, I wondered. A few hours in the Kremlin were enough to give me the uncanny
feeling of the dead trying to come to life again. The generous hospitality of Mme Radek, and her chubby baby blissfully unconscious of
the surroundings of the bygone days, helped to dispel my oppressive
thoughts. Karl Radek was a veritable dynamo of energy, all the time

rushing about, hastening to the telephone, dashing back to pick up the baby and dandle it on his knees, talking and giggling like a school-girl. He apparently could not sit still a minute, not even during the meal. He seemed everywhere and nowhere at the same time. Mme Radek, who mothered her husband more than her baby, did not seem to mind his nervous state. Every time he went up like a balloon, her restraining hand would gently detain him and threaten to feed him like the infant if he did not finish the morsel she had set before him. It was an amusing scene, though somewhat wearing through constant repetition.

After luncheon my host invited me to his study. We entered a tall and stately room flooded with sunshine. Beautifully carved old furniture was about, the walls lined with books from floor to ceiling. Here Radek became a changed man. His nervousness disappeared and a strange poise was upon him. He began speaking of the German Revolution and the failure of the Socialists to make it as thorough as the Russian October. No fundamental changes had taken place, he declared. The few radical achievements were insignificant, and the cowardly Socialist Government had not even disarmed the counter-revolutionary Junkers. No wonder the Spartacus uprising had been stifled in the blood of the workers. He spoke with deep feeling about the dreadful end of Karl Liebknecht, Rosa Luxemburg, and the anarchist Gustav Landauer. I had reason to be proud of my comrade, he said, for he was a great mind and a rare spirit. Though scholar and humanist, Landauer had joined the masses in the Revolution and died as he lived, heroic to the end. " If only we had such anarchists as Gustav Landauer to work with us!" Radek exclaimed enthusiastically. " But you do have many anarchists working with you," I replied, " some of them extremely able, I understand." " True," he admitted, " but they are not Landauers. Many of them have a *bourgeois* ideology, *kleinbürgerlich* in their interpretation of the revolutionary struggle. Others again are positively counter-revolutionary and a direct danger to Soviet Russia." His tone now was different from his manner at the station or at the luncheon a while ago. It was harsh and intolerant.

Our talk was interrupted by visitors, which I did not regret. I felt much indebted to Radek, but his Communist omnipotence was too much for me. I went back to play with the baby, still free from dogma and creed and refreshing in its innocence of the puerile efforts of all authorities to cast humanity into one mould.

The repeated telephoning of Radek to the commandant of the National about a room for me finally brought results. At ten in the evening he sent me off in his car to the hotel, bundles and all. He was most cordial, assuring me that I could call on him in any emergency.

Moscow at that hour was as deserted as Petrograd and equally dark. Numerous sentries were along the route, halting our automobile with the same stereotyped: "*Propusk, tovarishtch.*" My thoughts were still at the Radeks'. They had given out of the fullness of their hearts to a stranger. But would they have done so if they had found me wanting in their political faith? Poor, loving human heart, so kind and generous when free from class and party strife, so warped and hardened by both.

It was a novel sensation to be with Sasha in the same city and not be able to reach him. Radek had tried all through the day to get hold of him, but he was not in. Seeing my anxiety, Radek had assured me that Berkman would surely be at his lodgings before midnight. He could remain nowhere else, it being strictly prohibited as a protectionary measure against counter-revolution. No one would dare keep him overnight without registering him with the house commandant, and the latter would not permit a person unknown to him to stay after hours. But how could Radek offer to let me pass the night in his apartment, I asked. The Kremlin, he explained, was an exception. It was heavily guarded against unwelcome guests, and as only the most responsible party members lived there, they could be trusted not to harbour undesirable or suspicious strangers. Anyway, I could call Berkman again after midnight, Radek advised; he would surely be in then.

Radek proved right. At one o'clock I reached Sasha. Not having expected me, he had left for the day. He could not come to me then, because his *propusk* was good only till midnight, but he would call in the morning.

Sasha's voice over the telephone was already a great comfort. It helped to take the edge from the loneliness I felt in the great, strange city. My dear old pal arrived bright and early " to drink a cup of coffee with you," he said. He had had nothing like it since he had left Petrograd, he told me, nor much of anything else. A glance at his hollow cheeks convinced me that he had gone hungry. I thought it strange, as I knew he had taken enough provisions from our American supplies to last him several weeks. Lansbury had even teased him about it. As the guest of the Soviet Government he would not go short, Lansbury had said, and of course he would also share with his "comrade Berkman." Sasha had mentioned in his letter to me that he was not feeling well, but not a word about scarcity of food or whether Lansbury had kept his promise. I inquired if he had undergone a cure to reduce for beauty's sake. " No need for that in Russia," Sasha laughed; but his supplies did not go very far, he explained, because he had found so many starving, even if his loaves outdid Christ's in feeding large numbers on a few pieces. As to the comradeship of Mr. Lansbury, it had lasted only until the latter was taken in charge by an official representative of the Foreign Office. The English editor was housed in the palatial home of a former sugar-king, now the residence of Assistant Foreign Commissar Karakhan; but apparently no room could be found there for Sasha, nor had Lansbury shown any interest in whether his travelling companion and interpreter could find lodgings anywhere else. Sasha was informed that he had not been expected. Moreover, he had not a scrap of paper to identify himself. Finally it was decided to send him to a Soviet house on Kharitonenskaya Street. There also the commandant declared that he had no spare room. Sasha was saved from his predicament by a Socialist Revolutionist staying in the house. The man had recently come from Siberia to bring a report to headquarters from the local Communists with whom he was working. He invited Sasha to share his room, even at the risk of rousing the ire of the all-powerful house commandant. This difficulty temporarily solved, Sasha called on Chicherin, who immediately provided him with a credential. That piece of paper proved a veritable magic key, which had already unlocked many doors for him, as well as some hearts. The commandant of the Kharitonensky Soviet house suddenly discovered that there was a vacant room there, after all, and other officials became friendly the moment Sasha produced his talisman!

The food at the Kharitonensky was not bad, but entirely insufficient for adults. The other guests at the house somehow managed to supply themselves with extra morsels, which they would bring to the common dinner-table, but Sasha did not care to do this. His main difficulty, however, was the black bread, which was causing him serious stomach trouble. In fact, he had been compelled to stop eating it altogether. But now he would pick up lost weight quickly, he joked; now that I was in Moscow, he was sure I would manage to prepare good meals out of scraps, as I had always done. My dear Sasha! What amazing capacity for adaptation and what splendid sense for the comic sides of life!

The main attraction of the place where he lived, Sasha related, was the interesting types of humanity domiciled there. Chinese, Koreans, Japanese, and Hindu delegates, come to study the achievements of "October" and to enlist aid for the work of liberation in their native countries.

Our comrades in Moscow, Sasha informed me, seemed to enjoy considerable freedom. The Anarcho-Syndicalists of the group Golos Truda were publishing anarchist literature and selling it openly at their book-shop on the Tverskaya. The Universalist Anarchists had club-rooms with a co-operative restaurant and held open weekly gatherings at which revolutionary problems were freely discussed. A little anarchist sheet was also published by our old Georgian comrade Attabekian, a close friend of Peter Kropotkin, who had his own print-shop. "What an extraordinary situation," I remarked, "to grant anarchists in Moscow so much freedom, and none at all to the Petrograd circle! Most of the dreadful charges I heard there against the Bolsheviki must have been mere fabrication, but one thing was obvious: they were compelled to meet in secret." Sasha explained that he had come upon quite a number of strange contradictions. Thus, many of our comrades were in prison, for no cause apparently, while others were not molested in their activities. But I would have ample opportunity to learn everything at first hand, he added; the Universalist group had invited us to a special conference where the anarchist angle of the Revolution and current events would be presented by three able speakers.

I could hardly wait for the approaching meeting, which held out the hope of better understanding of Russian reality. In the meantime I tramped Moscow many hours a day, sometimes with, but more often without, Sasha. He lived too far away, a full hour's walk from the National, and there were no street-cars and but few *izvostchiky*. But I urged Sasha to have at least one meal a day with me. He needed building up, and I had brought with me part of our groceries from Petrograd. The markets in Moscow were wide open, doing a rushing business. I saw no betrayal of the Revolution in buying necessaries there. Zorin had indeed told me that trading of any kind was the worst counter-revolution and was strictly prohibited. When I had called

his attention to the open markets, he had assured me that only speculators were to be found there. I thought it was sheer nonsense to expect people to starve to death in sight of food. There was no heroism
in that, nor could the Revolution profit by it. Starving people could
not produce, and without production revolution is doomed to failure.
Zorin had insisted that the blockade, the Allied intervention, and the
White generals were responsible for the lack of food. But I had grown
weary of the same rosary about the causes of Russia's ills. I did not
dispute the facts as presented by Zorin and other Communists, but I
did think that if the Soviet Government failed to prevent food reaching the markets, it should at least close them. If food was allowed to
be sold in public places, it was adding insult to injury to forbid the
masses to take advantage of securing provisions, the more so as
money was permitted to circulate, the Government coining it wholesale. To such arguments Zorin replied that only my theoretic conceptions of revolution were obscuring the needs of the practical situation.

The main market in Moscow was the once famous Soukharevka,
which presented the most amazing picture of incongruity I had yet
seen in Russia. People of every kind and station were gathered there,
stripped of the trappings of caste and station. The aristocrat and the
peasant, the cultured and the uncouth, the *bourgeois,* the soldier, and
the worker rubbed elbows with the enemy of yesterday, pitifully crying out their wares or feverishly buying. Former barriers were broken
down, not by the equity of communism, but by the common need for
bread, bread, bread. Here one could find exquisitely carved ikons and
rusty nails, beautiful jewelry and gaudy trinkets, damask shawls and
faded cotton quilts. Amidst the remnants of former luxury and the
last cherished objects of wealth, the crowds jostled, motley gatherings
scrambling to possess themselves of coveted articles. Truly an overpowering spectacle of primitive instincts, asserting themselves without
restraint or fear.

The Soukharevka made more flagrant the discrimination against
smaller places of barter. The little market near the National was being constantly raided. Yet there were but the poorest of the poor
desperately trying to keep alive: old women, children in tatters,
derelict men, their wares as wretched as themselves. Ill-smelling
tshchi (vegetable soup), frozen potatoes, biscuits black and hard, or
a few boxes of matches — they held them out to the passers-by with
trembling hands, in trembling voices pleading: " Buy, *barinya* (lady),

buy, for the love of Christ, buy! " In the raids their measly wares would be seized, their soup and kvass poured out on the square, and the unfortunates dragged off to prison as speculators. Those lucky enough to escape the raiders would soon crawl back, gather up the matches and cigarettes strewn about, and begin their wretched trade again.

The Bolsheviki, in common with other social rebels, had always stressed the potency of hunger as the cause of most of the evils in capitalist society. They never grew tired of condemning the system that punished the effects while leaving their sources intact. How could they now pursue the same stupid and incredible course, I wondered. True, the appalling hunger was not of their making. The blockade and the interventionists *were* chiefly responsible for that. More reason, then, it seemed to me, why the victims should not be hounded and punished. Witnessing such a raid, Sasha had been aroused by its cruelty and inhumanity. He had vigorously protested against the brutal manner in which the soldiers and the Chekists dispersed the crowd, and he had been himself saved from arrest only by the credential Chicherin had given him. Forthwith the Chekist had changed his tone and manner, offering profuse apologies to the " foreign *tovarishtch*." He was only doing his duty, he said, carrying out the orders of his superiors, and he could not be blamed.

It was evident that the new power in the Kremlin was feared no less than the old, and that its official seal had the same awesome effect. " Wherein is the change? " I asked Sasha. " You can't measure a gigantic upheaval by a few specks of dust," he replied. But were they mere specks, I wondered, for they seemed to me gusts that were threatening to pull down the entire revolutionary edifice I had constructed in America around the Bolsheviki. Yet my faith in their integrity was too strong to charge them with responsibility for the evils and wrongs I was witnessing at every step. These kept growing daily, ugly facts utterly at variance with what Soviet Russia had been proclaiming to the world. I tried to avoid facing them, but they lurked in every corner and would not be ignored.

The National, almost exclusively occupied by Communists, was manned by a large kitchen force that was wasting time and precious foodstuffs in preparing uneatable meals. Next to it was another kitchen with private servants cooking all day for their masters, prominent Soviet officials. They and their friends were permitted special privileges, often receiving three and even more rations, while the ordinary mortals were wearing out their depleted strength to attain their meagre due.

The housing arrangements disclosed similar favouritism and injustice. Large and well-furnished apartments were easily obtainable for a monetary consideration, but it required weeks of humiliation before petty officials to secure one room in a dismal flat without water, heat, or light. Lucky indeed the person if, after all his exhausting efforts, he did not find someone else occupying the same room. This seemed entirely too fantastic to believe, but the personal experience of various friends, among them a young girl I knew, as well as of Manya and Vassily Semenoff, old comrades from the States, left no doubt. They had been among the first to hasten back to Russia at the very outbreak of the Revolution. Since then they had faithfully worked in Soviet institutions at the hardest tasks, yet they had been compelled to wait months and canvass numerous departments before they were granted lodgings. Their happiness was, however, short-lived. On reaching the place assigned to her the young woman found a man already in possession of it. " But we can't both live in the same room," she had told him. " Why not? " he replied; " in Soviet Russia one mustn't be so particular. I worked too hard to secure this hole and I can't afford to give it up. But I can sleep on the floor and let you have the bed," he offered. " It was very decent of him," the girl said, " but I could not face such close proximity with an utter stranger. I left the room and resumed my search for another place."

The hideous sores on revolutionary Russia could not for long be ignored. The facts presented at the gathering of the Moscow anarchists, the analysis of the situation by leading Left Socialist Revolutionists, and my talks with simple people who claimed no political affiliations enabled me to look behind the scenes of the revolutionary drama and to behold the dictatorship without its stage make-up. Its rôle was somewhat different from the one proclaimed in public. It was forcible tax-collection at the point of guns, with its devastating effect on villages and towns. It was the elimination from responsible positions of everyone who dared think aloud, and the spiritual death of the most militant elements whose intelligence, faith, and courage had really enabled the Bolsheviki to achieve their power. The anarchists and Left Socialist Revolutionists had been used as pawns by Lenin in the October days and were now doomed to extinction by his creed and policies. It was the system of taking hostages for political refugees, not exempting even old parents and children of tender age. The nightly *oblavas* (street and house raids) by the Cheka, the population frightened out of sleep, their few belongings turned upside down and ripped open for secret documents, the dragnet of soldiers left behind to haul in the crop of unsuspecting callers at the besieged house. The penalties for flimsy charges often amounted to long prison terms, exile to desolate parts of the country, and even execution. Shattering in its cumulative effect, the essence of the story was the same as told me by my Petrograd comrades. I had been too dazzled then by the public glare and glitter of Bolshevism to credit the veracity of the accusations. I had refused to trust their judgment and their viewpoint. But now Bolshevism was shorn of its pretence, its naked soul exposed to my gaze. Still I would not believe. I would not see with my inner eye the truth so evident to my outer sight. I was stunned, baffled, the ground pulled from under me. Yet I hung on, hung on by a thread as a drowning man. In my anguish I cried: " Bolshevism is the *mene, tekel* over every throne, the menace of craven hearts, the hated enemy of organized wealth and power. Its path has been thorny, its obstacles many, its climb steep. How could it help falling behind at times, how could it help making mistakes? But to belie itself, to play Judas to the fervent hope of the disinherited and oppressed, to betray its own ultimate aims? No, never could it be guilty of such an eclipse of the world's most luminous star! "

Even the Moscow Anarchist Conference had not gone so far in its indictment. The Soviet State was different from capitalist and *bourgeois* governments, they had told us when we objected to their absurdly illogical resolution asking for the legalisation of their work and the release of our comrades from prison. " In no country have the anarchists ever begged favours from the government," we argued, " nor do they believe in loyalty to the State. Why do it here, if the Bolsheviki have broken faith? " The Bolshevik government was revolutionary in spite of its offences; it was proletarian in its nature and purposes, the Russian comrades insisted. Whereupon we had signed the petition and agreed to present it to the proper authorities.

Both Sasha and I held on to the firm belief that the Bolsheviki were our brothers in a common fight. Our very lives and all our revolutionary hopes were staked upon it. Lenin, Trotsky, and their co-workers were the soul of the Revolution, we were sure, and its keenest defenders. We would go to them, to Lunacharsky, Kollontay, Bala-banoff. Jack Reed had spoken of them with deepest admiration and affection. They were capable of other criteria than a membership card in estimating people and events, Jack had said. They would help me see things in their proper light. I would seek them out. And our old teacher, Peter Kropotkin — we had drifted apart over our stand on the World War, but our love and esteem for his great personality and acute mind had not changed. I was certain that his feeling for us had also remained the same. We had been eager to see our dear comrade immediately upon our arrival in Russia. He was living in the village of Dmitrov, we had been informed, about sixty versts from Moscow, in his own little house, and he was well supplied with all necessaries by the Soviet Government. Travel was impossible then, but our trip would be arranged in the spring, Zorin had assured us.

Seeing Peter was too imperative for me now to stop at the hard-ships of travel. I would reach him somehow, I decided. He, of all people, would best be able to help me out of the pit of doubt and de-spair. He had returned to Russia after the February Revolution and he had witnessed the " October." He had seen some part of his cher-ished dream realized. His was a penetrating mind. He would strike the right key. I must go to him.

Alexandra Kollontay and Angelica Balabanoff were within easy reach, as they were living in the National. I sought out the former first. Mme Kollontay looked remarkably young and radiant, consider-ing her fifty years and the severe operation she had recently under-gone. A tall and stately woman, every inch the *grande dame* rather than the fiery revolutionist. Her attire and suite of two rooms bespoke good taste, the roses on her desk rather startling in the Russian grey-ness. They were the first I had seen since our deportation. Her hand-shake was limp and aloof, though she did say that she was glad to meet me at last in " great, vital Russia." Had I already found my place, she inquired, and the work I wanted to do? I replied that I still felt too uncertain of my ground to decide where I could be of best use. Perhaps I should know better after I had talked with her about the things that disturbed me, the contradictions I had found. I should tell her everything, she said; she was sure she could help me over my first difficult period. Every new-comer passes through the same state, she assured me, but everyone soon learns to see the greatness of Soviet Russia. The little things do not matter. I tried to tell her that my problems did not concern themselves with little things; they were vital and all-important to me. In fact, my very being depended on their right interpretation. "All right, go ahead," she remarked nonchalantly. She leaned back in her arm-chair and I began speaking of the harrowing things that had come to my knowledge. She listened attentively without interrupting me, but there was not the slightest indication in her cold, handsome face of any perturbation on account of my recital. "We do have some dull grey spots in our vivid revolutionary picture," she said when I had concluded. "They are unavoidable in a country so backward, with a people so dark and a social experiment of such magnitude, opposed by the entire world as it is. They will disappear when we have liquidated our military fronts and when we shall have raised the mental level of our masses." I could help in that, she continued. I could work among the women; they were ignorant of the simplest principles of life, physical and otherwise, ignorant of their own functions as mothers and citizens. I had done such fine work of that kind in America, and she could assure me of a much more fertile field in Russia. "Why not join me and stop your brooding over a few dull grey spots?" she said in conclusion; "they are nothing more, dear comrade, really nothing more."

People raided, imprisoned, and shot for their *ideas*! The old and the young held as hostages, every protest gagged, iniquity and favouritism rampant, the best human values betrayed, the very spirit of revolution daily crucified — were all these nothing but "grey, dull spots," I wondered! I felt chilled to the marrow of my bones.

Two days later I went to see Anatol Lunacharsky. His quarters were in the Kremlin, the impenetrable citadel of authority in the popular mind of Russia. I bore several credentials, and my escort was a "Sovietsky" anarchist held in high esteem by the Communists. Nevertheless we made very slow progress in reaching the seat of the People's Commissar for Education. Repeatedly the sentries scrutinized our *propusks* and asked questions regarding the purpose of our coming. At last we found ourselves in a reception room, a large salon filled with many objects of art and a crowd of people. They were artists, writers, and teachers awaiting an audience, my companion explained. A sorry and undernourished lot they were, their gaze steadily riveted on the door leading to the Commissar's private office. Hope and fear burned in their eyes. I too was anxious, though my rations did not depend on the man who presided over the cultural positions. Lunacharsky's greeting was warmer and more cordial than Kollontay's. He also inquired whether I had already found suitable work. If not, he could suggest a number of occupations in his department. The American system of education was being introduced in Soviet Russia, he said, and I, coming from that country, would undoubtedly be able to make valuable suggestions in regard to its proletarian application. I gasped. I forgot all about the purpose of my visit. The educational system found wanting and rejected by the best pedagogues in the United States now accepted as a model in revolutionary Russia? Lunacharsky looked much astonished. Was the system really being opposed in America, he inquired, and by whom? What changes had they suggested? I should explain the whole matter to him and his teachers, and he would call a special conference for the purpose. I could do much good, he urged, and I could be of great help to him in his struggle with the reactionary elements among the teachers who were clamouring for the old methods in dealing with the child and who even favoured prison for the mental defectives.

His eagerness to learn lessened somewhat my resentment at the attempt to transplant to Russia the American public-school system. It was evident that Lunacharsky knew nothing of the insurgent movement that had for years been trying to modernize that hoary and futile institution. I must point out to the educators of Russia the absurdity of aping those antiquated methods in the land of new life and values. But America was millions of miles away from my mind. Russia was consuming me, Russia with all her wonders and woes.

Lunacharsky continued to talk of his difficulties with the conservative instructors and of the controversy raging in the Soviet press about defective children and their treatment. He and Maxim Gorki were standing out against prison as a reformative influence; he himself was even opposed to milder forms, in fact to any form, of coercion in dealing with the young. "You are more in tune with the modern approach to the child than Maxim Gorki," I said. In part, however, he agreed with Gorki, he replied, for most of Russia's young generation were tainted with bad heredity, which the years of war and civic strife had accentuated. But rejuvenation could not be brought about by punishment or terror, he emphasized. "That is splendid," I remarked; "but are not terror and punishment the methods of dictatorship? And do you not approve of the latter?" He did, but only as a transitory factor, while Russia was being bled by the blockade and attacked on numerous fronts. "Once these have been liquidated, we will begin in earnest to build the real Socialist Republic, and the dictatorship will then go, of course." He considered it stupid to hold Denikin, Yudenich, and their kind responsible for all the shortcomings of Soviet Russia while ignoring the evil of the growing new bureaucracy and the increasing power of the Cheka. It was also very bad policy to proclaim Russia's educational achievements from the house-tops, he thought. Much was being done for the child, but the real herculean task was still ahead. " Rather heretical! " I remarked. He replied laughingly that he was considered even worse than a mere heretic because he had insisted that the intelligentsia, besides being indispensable, was, after all, also human and should not be forced to die by starvation. He had great faith in the proletariat, but he refused to swear by its infallibility. " If you don't look out, you'll be excommunicated," I warned him. " Yes, or put in a corner under the watchful eye of a teacher," he countered, with a knowing smile.

Lunacharsky did not give the impression of a vital personality, but he had broad humanity and I liked him for that. I wanted to broach my own problems, but I had already taken up too much time and I was conscious of the people waiting behind the door and undoubtedly cursing me. Before I left, Lunacharsky once more reiterated that his department was the right place for me, and that I must not leave Moscow until I had addressed the conference he was going to call.

On my way back to the National I learned from my escort that the People's Commissar for Education was considered not only sentimental, but also a scatter-brain and a wastrel. He was doing very little for the *proletcult* (proletarian culture), spending huge sums instead to protect *bourgeois* art. Worst of all, he was devoting most of his time to saving the last remnants of the counter-revolutionary intelligentsia. With the co-operation of Maxim Gorki he had succeeded in reinstating the old professors and teachers in the Dom Utcheniy (Home of the Learned). There they could keep warm while at work and get their rations without standing in line. He had also committed a grave offence in establishing the so-called academic ration for the more noted writers, thinkers, and scientists of Russia, irrespective of party affiliation. The academic ration was far from luxury and by no means too plentiful; many of the responsible Communists received even better provisions, but they were bitter against Lunacharsky for " favouring " the intelligentsia, my informant declared.

The poor bigots, I thought, to whom the Revolution meant only vengeance and a rung on the social ladder! They were the dead weight threatening to sink the revolutionary ship. Lunacharsky was aware of it. And Kollontay? I was certain she too knew better. But she was a diplomat trying to smooth over crude and hard places. Would Balabanoff also turn out to be of the same type, I wondered. Presently I had an opportunity to convince myself that she was quite the reverse.

The two leading Communist women of Russia proved the greatest contrast. Angelica Balabanoff lacked what Kollontay possessed in abundance: the latter's fine figure, good looks, and youthful litheness, as well as her worldly polish and sophistication. But Angelica had something that far outweighed the external attributes of her handsome comrade. In her large sad eyes there shone profundity, compassion, and tenderness. The tribulations of her people, the birth-pangs of her native land, the suffering of the downtrodden she had served her whole life were deeply graven on her pallid face. I found her ill, crumpled up on the couch of her small room, but she immediately became all interest and concern for me. Why had I not let her know that I was her neighbour, she asked. She would have come to me at once. And why had I waited so long before seeking her out? Did I need anything? She would see to it that my wants should be looked after. Coming from the States, I must find it very hard to adjust myself to Russia's poverty. It was different with the native masses, who had never known anything except hunger and want. Ah, the Russian masses, their power of endurance, their capacity for suffering, their heroism in the face of such fearful odds! Children in their weakness, giants in their strength! She had come to know them better since " October " than in all her previous years in Russia. She had grown to believe in them with a more abiding faith and to feel with them an all-embracing love.

It was dusk; the city's noises did not penetrate the cell-like room. Yet it was vibrant with stirring sounds. The face before me, shrunken and ashy, was beauteous now in the glow of its inner light. Without a word from me Angelica Balabanoff had guessed my doubts and travail. I sensed that her tribute to the Russian masses was her unique way of making me feel that nothing mattered so much to the ultimate triumph of the Revolution as the spiritual resources of the people themselves. I inquired whether that was her meaning, and she nodded assent. She knew from her own struggle that mine must be very hard and she wanted me never to lose sight of the peaks of the " October " ascendancy.

I walked to her couch and stroked her thick braided black hair, already streaked with grey. I must call her Angelica, she said, drawing me to her heart. She asked me to ring for a comrade on the same floor to bring the samovar. She had some *varenya* (fruit jelly), and Swedish comrades had given her some biscuits and butter. She felt very guilty to enjoy such luxuries when the people did not have enough bread. But her stomach was bad; she could digest nothing, and so perhaps she was not so inconsistent as it might appear. Such selflessness amidst the callous indifference I had found everywhere moved me deeply. I broke down and wept as I had not since I had held my dear Helena in my arms at our final parting. Angelica became frightened. Had she said anything to cause me pain, or was I ill or in trouble? I opened my heart to her and poured out everything, my shocks, disillusionments, and nightmares, all the dreadful things and thoughts that had been oppressing me since my arrival. What was the answer, what the explanation, and where the responsibility?

Life itself is behind all frustration, Angelica replied, in an individual as well as in a social sense. Life was hard and cruel, and those who would live must also grow cruel and hard. Life is replete with eddies and whirlpools; its currents are violent and destructive. The sensitive, those shrinking from hurt, cannot hold their own against it. As with man, so with his ideas and ideals. The finer they are, the more humane, the sooner their death from the impact of Life. " But this is fatalism with a vengeance," I protested; " how can you harmonize such an attitude with your socialistic views and materialistic conception of history and human development? " Angelica explained that Russian reality had convinced her that life, and not theories, dictates the course of human events. " Life! Life! " I cried impatiently, " what is it but what the genius of man imparts to it? And what is the use of human striving if some mysterious power called Life can turn it to naught? " Angelica replied that there really was no particular sense in our efforts, except that living meant striving, reaching out for something better. But I should not mind her, she hastened to add. She was probably all wrong, and those others right who could pay the full measure life exacts. "You must go to see 'Ilich,'" she advised; only he, Lenin, could help me, for he knew how to meet the demands of Life. She would arrange an interview for me.

I left the dear little woman with mixed feelings. Soothed and comforted by her rich fount of love, I at the same time disapproved of her acquiescence in the evils and abuses about her. I had known of her as a fighter, always firm and unflinching in her stand. What had made her so passive now, I wondered. Communists enjoyed the right of criticism, as I had learned from the Bolshevik press. Why, then, did Angelica not use her pen and voice in and out of the party? It kept worrying me and I sought an opportunity to speak to her woman comrade who had served us tea. From her I learned that Angelica had been secretary of the Third International. In that capacity she had fought determinedly against the growing bureaucracy of the clique led by Zinoviev, Radek, and Bukharin. As a result she was most unceremoniously kicked out and denied all responsible work. It was not that Angelica cared about the personal injustice and insult. But she felt that the methods of intrigue and slander employed against her were also being used against other sincere comrades at variance with the leaders. This poison was eating into the very body of the party, and Angelica knew that it was fraught with disastrous results to the Revolution. "Is there no way of putting a stop to such nefarious methods?" I asked Angelica's friend. There was none, she assured me, none within Russia, and no one would think of a protest abroad as long as the Revolution was in danger. This awareness had undermined Angelica's health and had paralysed her will. Her mental state was due to the methods employed by her party, including the widespread suffering, the terror, and the cheapness of human life. Angelica could not face them.

Dear, sweet Angelica — I began to understand her better and what she meant by the currents of life. But I could not share her attitude. I could not submit. I must probe into the hidden sources of Russia's ills, I felt; I must unearth their causes and proclaim them aloud. No party clique should tie my tongue.

I had not seen Sasha for several days. The long trip from Kharitonenskaya to the National was too exhausting, he said. But the morning after my visit with Angelica I received a hurry call to come to his lodgings. I found Sasha ill in bed, with no help near. I dropped everything and took up my old profession of nursing. His fever was stubborn, but his dogged will to live presently won out. His illness left him weak and spent, however, and in no condition to remain alone. I could not stop at the Kharitonenskaya, nor could Sasha, for that matter, for the house commandant had informed him that his time had expired and that he would have to vacate his room. We were planning to leave for Petrograd within a week and it was therefore useless to argue with the official *tovarishtch*. We went to the National, my room fortunately being larger than the one I had occupied in the Astoria, and provided with an extra couch. When Angelica learned of Sasha's illness and his presence in the National, she immediately constituted herself his guardian angel. Her family of Swedish, Norwegian, and Dutch comrades seemed to increase all the time, and from them she would bring Sasha same delicate morsels. I had learned through various sources that Angelica was looked upon by her comrades as a " sentimental *bourzhooy*." She was wasting her time, they said, on philanthropy, always trying to procure milk for some sick baby, extra things for a pregnant woman, or old clothes for people of useless age.

When Angelica had suggested that I go to see Lenin, I decided to work out a memorandum of the most salient contradictions in Soviet life, but, not having heard anything more about the proposed interview, I had not done anything about the matter. Angelica's telephone message one morning, informing me that " Ilich " was waiting to see Sasha and me, and that his auto had come for us, was therefore most disconcerting. We knew Lenin was so crowded with work that he was almost inaccessible. The exception in our favour was a chance we could not miss. We felt that even without our memorandum we should find the right approach to our discussion; moreover, we should have the opportunity to present to him the resolutions our Moscow comrades had entrusted to us.

Lenin's auto rushed at furious speed along the congested streets and into the Kremlin, past every sentry without being halted for *propusks*. At the entrance of one of the ancient buildings that stood apart from the rest, we were asked to alight. An armed guard was at the elevator, evidently already apprised of our coming. Without a word, he unlocked the door and motioned us within, then locked it and put the key into his pocket. We heard our names shouted to the soldier on the first floor, the call repeated in the same loud voice at the next and the next. A chorus was announcing our coming as the elevator slowly ascended. At the top a guard repeated the process of unlocking and locking the elevator, then ushered us into a vast reception hall with the announcement: " *Tovarishtchy* Goldman and Berkman." We were asked to wait a moment, but almost an hour passed before the ceremony of leading us to the seat of the highest was resumed. A young man motioned us to follow him. We passed through a number of offices teeming with activity, the click of typewriters, and busy couriers. We were halted before a massive door ornamented with beautifully carved work. Excusing himself for just a minute, our attendant disappeared behind it. Presently the heavy door opened from within, and our guide invited us to step in, himself vanishing and closing the door behind us. We stood on the threshold awaiting the next cue in the strange proceedings. Two slanting eyes were fixed upon us with piercing penetration. Their owner sat behind a huge desk, everything on it arranged with the strictest precision, the rest of the room giving the impression of the same exactitude. A board with numerous telephone switches and a map of the world covered the entire wall behind the man; glass cases filled with heavy tomes lined the sides. A large oblong table hung with red; twelve straight-backed chairs, and several arm-chairs at the windows. Nothing else to relieve the orderly monotony, except the bit of flaming red.

The background seemed most fitting for one reputed for his rigid habits of life and matter-of-factness. Lenin, the man most idolized in the world and equally hated and feared, would have been out of place in surroundings of less severe simplicity.

"Ilich wastes no time on preliminaries. He goes straight to his objective," Zorin had once said to me with evident pride. Indeed, every step Lenin had made since 1917 testified to this. But if we had been in doubt, the manner of our reception and the mode of our interview would have quickly convinced us of the emotional economy of Ilich. His quick perception of its supply in others and his skill in making the utmost use of it for his purpose were extraordinary. No less amazing was his glee over anything he considered funny in himself or his visitors. Especially if he could put one at a disadvantage, the great Lenin would shake with laughter so as to compel one to laugh with him.

His sharp scrutiny having bared us to the bone, we were treated to a volley of questions, one following the other like arrows from his flint-like brain. America, her political and economic conditions — what were the chances of revolution there in the near future? The

American Federation of Labor — was it all honeycombed with *bourgeois* ideology or was it only Gompers and his clique, and was the rank and file a fertile soil for boring from within? The I.W.W. — what was its strength, and were the anarchists actually as effective as our recent trial would seem to indicate? He had just finished reading our speeches in court. " Great stuff! Clear-cut analysis of the capitalist system, splendid propaganda! " Too bad we could not have remained in the United States, no matter at what price. We were most welcome in Soviet Russia, of course, but such fighters were badly needed in America to help in the approaching revolution, " as many of your best comrades had been in ours." " And you, *Tovarishtch* Berkman, what an organizer you must be, like Shatoff. True metal, your comrade Shatoff; shrinks from nothing and can work like a dozen men. In Siberia now, commissar of railroads in the Far Eastern Republic. Many other anarchists hold important positions with us. Everything is open to them if they are willing to co-operate with us as true *ideiny* anarchists. You, *Tovarishtch* Berkman, will soon find your place. A pity, though, that you were torn away from America at this portentous time. And you, *Tovarishtch* Goldman? What a field you had! You could have remained. Why didn't you, even if *Tovarishtch* Berkman was shoved out? Well, you're here. Have you thought of the work you want to do? You are *ideiny* anarchists, I can see that by your stand on the war, your defence of ' October,' and your fight for us, your faith in the soviets. Just like your great comrade Malatesta, who is entirely with Soviet Russia. What is it you prefer to do?"

Sasha was the first to get his breath. He began in English, but Lenin at once stopped him with a mirthful laugh. " Do you think I understand English? Not a word. Nor any other foreign languages. I am no good at them, though I have lived abroad for many years. Funny, isn't it?" And off he went in peals of laughter. Sasha continued in Russian. He was proud to hear his comrades praised so highly, he said; but why were anarchists in Soviet prisons? " Anarchists?" Ilich interrupted; " nonsense! Who told you such yarns, and how could you believe them? We do have bandits in prison, and Makhnovtsy, but no *ideiny* anarchists."

" Imagine," I broke in, " capitalist America also divides the anarchists into two categories, philosophic and criminal. The first are accepted in the highest circles; one of them is even high in the councils of the Wilson Administration. The second category, to which we have the honour of belonging, is persecuted and often imprisoned. Yours also seems to be a distinction without a difference. Don't you think so?" Bad reasoning on my part, Lenin replied, sheer muddle-headedness to draw similar conclusions from different premises. Free speech is a *bourgeois* prejudice, a soothing plaster for social ills. In the Workers' Republic economic well-being talks louder than speech, and its freedom is far more secure. The proletarian dictatorship is steering that course. Just now it faces very grave obstacles, the greatest of them the opposition of the peasants. They need nails, salt, textiles, tractors, electrification. When we can give them these, they will be with us, and no counter-revolutionary power will be able to swerve them back. In the present state of Russia all prattle of freedom is merely food for the reaction trying to down Russia. Only bandits are guilty of that, and they must be kept under lock and key.

Sasha handed Lenin the resolutions of the anarchist conference and emphasized the assurance of the Moscow comrades that the imprisoned comrades were *ideiny* and not bandits. "The fact that our people ask to be legalized is proof that they are with the Revolution and the Soviets," we argued. Lenin took the document and promised to submit it to the next session of the Party Executive. We would be notified of its decision, he said, but in any event it was a mere trifle, nothing to disturb any true revolutionist. Was there anything else? We had fought in America for the political rights even of our opponents, we told him; the denial of them to our own comrades was therefore no trifle to us. I, for one, felt, I informed him, that I could not co-operate with a régime that persecuted anarchists or others for the sake of mere opinion. Moreover, there were even more appalling evils. How were we to reconcile them with the high goal he was aiming at? I mentioned some of them. His reply was that my attitude was *bourgeois* sentimentality. The proletarian dictatorship was engaged in a life-and-death struggle, and small considerations could not be permitted to weigh in the scale. Russia was making giant strides at home and abroad. It was igniting the world revolution, and here I was lamenting over a little blood-letting. It was absurd, and I must get over it. "Do something," he advised; "that will be the best way of regaining your revolutionary balance."

Lenin might be right, I thought. I would take his advice. I would start at once, I said. Not with any work within Russia, but with something of propaganda value for the United States. I should like to organize a society of Russian Friends of American Freedom, an active body to give support to America's struggle for liberty, as the American Friends of Russian Freedom had done in aid of Russia against the tsarist régime.

Lenin had not moved in his seat during the entire time, but now he almost leaped out of it. He swung round and stood facing us. "That's a brilliant idea!" he exclaimed, chuckling and rubbing his hands. "A fine practical proposal. You must proceed to carry it out at once. And you, *Tovarishtch* Berkman, will you co-operate in it?" Sasha replied that we had talked the matter over and had already worked out the details of the plan. We could start immediately if we had the necessary equipment. No difficulty in that, Lenin assured us; we would be supplied with everything — an office, a printing outfit, couriers, and whatever funds would be needed. We must send him our prospectus of work and the itemized expenses involved in the project. The Third International would take care of the matter. It was the proper channel for our venture, and it would afford us every help.

In blank astonishment we looked at each other and at Lenin. Simultaneously we began to explain that our efforts could prove effective only if free from any affiliation with known Bolshevik organizations. It must be carried out in our own way; we knew the American psychology and how best to conduct the work. But before we could proceed further, our guide suddenly appeared, as unobtrusively as he had left, and Lenin held out his hand to us in good-bye. "Don't forget to send me the prospectus," he called after us.

The methods of the "clique" in the *politbureau* of the party were also pervading the International and poisoning the entire labour movement, Angelica's friend had told me. Was Lenin aware of it? And was that also a mere trifle in his estimation? I was certain now that he knew everything that was going on in Russia. Nothing escaped his searching eye, nothing could take place without first having been weighed in his scale and approved by his authoritative seal. An indomitable will easily bending everyone to its own curve and just as easily breaking men if they failed to yield. Would he also bend or break us? The danger was imminent if we made the first false step, if we accepted the tutelage of the Communist International. We were eager to help Russia and to continue our work for America's liberation, to which we had given the best years of our lives. But it would mean a betrayal of our entire past and the complete abrogation of our independence to submit to the control of the clique. We wrote Lenin to that effect and enclosed a detailed outline of our plan, carefully prepared by Sasha.

We agreed with Lenin in one thing, the need of getting to work. Not, however, in any political capacity or in a Soviet bureau. We must find something that would bring us in direct touch with the masses and enable us to serve them. Moscow was the seat of the Government with more State functionaries than workers, bureaucratic to the last degree. Sasha had visited a number of factories, all of them in a palpably neglected and deserted condition. In most of them the Soviet officials and members of the Communist *yacheika* (cell) far outnumbered the actual producers. He had talked with the workers and found them embittered by the arrogance and arbitrary methods of the industrial bureaucracy. Sasha's impressions only served to strengthen my conviction that Moscow was no place for us. If at least Lunacharsky had kept his promise! But he was swamped with work, he wrote, and unable just then to call the teachers' conference. It might take weeks before it could be done. He understood how difficult it was for people used to doing things in their own independent manner to fit themselves into a groove. But it was the only effective place in Russia and I would have to reconcile myself to that. Meanwhile I must keep in touch with him, his letter concluded.

It was a subtle hint that the dictatorship was all-pervading and that it would brook no independent effort. Not in Moscow, at any rate. After all, every seat of government inevitably breeds the martinet and the flunkey, the courtier and the spy, a herd of hangers-on fed by the official hand. Moscow was evidently no exception. We could not find our place there, nor come close to the toiling masses. One more thing we would attempt — get to see our comrade Kropotkin and then back to Petrograd, we decided.

We learned that George Lansbury and Mr. Barry were about to go to Dmitrov in a special train. We decided to ask permission to join them, though we were not elated over the prospect of seeing Peter in the presence of two newspaper men. We had not been able to arrange a trip to Dmitrov, and this was an unexpected and exceptional opportunity. Sasha hastened to see Lansbury. The latter consented to have us accompany him and even expressed his willingness that we bring with us anyone else we might want. He assured Sasha that he had long wanted to see me again and that he would be delighted at the chance. Considering that he had all along known of my presence in Moscow and that he had not taken the trouble to look me up, his delight seemed rather questionable. But the main thing was to meet Peter, and we also invited our comrade Alexander Schapiro to come with us.

The train crawled snail-like, stopping at every water-tank. It was late evening when we at last reached the house. We found Peter ill and worn-looking. He appeared a mere shadow of the sturdy man I had known in Paris and London in 1907. Since my coming to Russia I had been repeatedly assured by the most prominent Communists that Kropotkin lived in very comfortable circumstances and that he lacked neither food nor fuel; and here were Peter, his wife, Sophie, and their daughter, Alexandra, actually living in one room by no means sufficiently heated. The temperature in the other rooms was below zero, so that they could not be inhabited. Their rations, sufficient to exist on, had until recently been supplied by the Dmitrov co-operative society. That organization had since been liquidated, like so many other similar institutions, and most of its members arrested and taken to the Butirky prison in Moscow. How did they manage to exist, we inquired. Sophie explained that they had a cow and enough produce from her garden for the winter. The comrades from the Ukraine, particularly Makhno, had contrived to supply them with extra provisions. They would have managed to better advantage had not Peter been ailing of late and in need of more nourishing food.

Could nothing be done to rouse the responsible Communists to the fact that one of the greatest men of Russia was starving to death? Even if they had no interest in him as an anarchist, they must know his worth as a man of science and letters. Lenin, Lunacharsky, and the others in high position were probably not informed about Peter's situation. Could I not call their attention to his condition? Lansbury agreed with me. " It is impossible," he said, " that the big people in the Soviet Government would let so great a personality as Peter Kropotkin want for the necessaries of life. We in England would not stand for such an outrage." He would immediately take the matter up with the Soviet comrades, he declared. Sophie had been repeatedly pulling at his sleeve to make him stop. She did not want Peter to hear our talk. But that dear soul was deeply immersed in conversation with the two Alexanders, quite unaware that we were discussing his welfare.

Peter would accept nothing from the Bolsheviki, Sophie told us. Only a short time previously, when the rouble still stood well, he had refused the offer of 250,000 roubles from the Government Publication Department for the right to issue his literary work. Since the Bolsheviki had expropriated others, they might as well help themselves to his books, he had said. But it would not be done with his consent. He had never willingly dealt with any government and he had no intention of doing so with the one that in the name of socialism had abrogated every revolutionary and ethical value. Sophie had not even been able to induce Peter to accept the academic ration Lunacharsky had ordered for him. His increasing feebleness had compelled her to take it without his knowledge. His health, she apologized, was more important to her than his scruples. Besides, as a scientific botanist she was herself entitled to the academic ration.

Sasha was speaking to Peter of the maze of revolutionary contradictions we had found in Russia, the varied interpretations we had heard of the causes of the crying evils, and our interview with Lenin. We were eager to hear Peter's view-point and get his reactions to the situation. He replied that it was what it had always been to Marxism and its theories. He had foreseen its dangers and he had always warned against them. All anarchists had done so, and he himself had dealt with them in nearly every one of his writings. True, none of us had fully realized to what proportions the Marxian menace would grow. Perhaps it was not so much Marxism as the Jesuitical spirit of its dogmas. The Bolsheviki were poisoned by it, their dictatorship surpassing the autocracy of the Inquisition. Their power was strengthened by the blustering statesmen of Europe. The blockade, the Allied support of the counter-revolutionary elements, the intervention, and all the other attempts to crush the Revolution had resulted in silencing every protest against Bolshevik tyranny within Russia itself. " Is there no one to speak out against it? " I demanded, " no one whose voice would carry weight? Yours, for instance, dear comrade? " Peter smiled sadly. I would know better, he said, after I had been awhile longer in the country. The gag was the most complete in the world. He had protested, of course, and so had others, among them the venerable Vera Figner, as well as Maxim Gorki on several occasions. It had no effect whatever, nor was it possible to do any writing with the Cheka constantly at one's door. One could not keep " incriminating " things in one's house nor expose others to the peril of discovery.

It was not fear; it was the realization of the futility and impossibility of reaching the world from the inner prisons of the Cheka. The main drawback, however, was the enemies surrounding Russia. Anything said or written against the Bolsheviki was bound to be interpreted by the outside world as an attack upon the Revolution and as alignment with the reactionary forces. The anarchists in particular were between two fires. They could not make peace with the formidable power of the Kremlin, nor could they join hands with the enemies of Russia. Their only alternative at present, it seemed to Peter, was to find some work of direct benefit to the masses. He was glad that we had decided on that. " Ridiculous of Lenin to want to bind you to the apron-strings of the party," he declared. " It shows how far mere shrewdness is from wisdom. No one can deny Lenin's shrewdness, but neither in his attitude to the peasants nor in his appraisal of those within or outside the reach of corruption has he shown real judgment or sagacity."

It was growing late and Sophie had been trying to prevail upon Peter to retire. But he persistently declined. He had been so long cut off from his comrades — indeed, from any kind of intellectual contact, he said. Our visit at first seemed to exert a bracing effect upon him. But presently he began to show signs of exhaustion, and we felt it was high time to go. Gentle and gallant was our Peter even in his fatigue. Nothing would do but he must see us to the exit and once more clasp us lovingly to his heart.

Our train was not to start till two a.m., and it was only eleven. The woman porter was fast asleep. She had forgotten to look after the fire, and the car was bitterly cold. The boys set to work over the stove, but it would yield nothing except smoke. Meanwhile Lansbury, wrapped up to his ears in his great fur coat, held forth on what a pity it was that Peter Kropotkin's age disqualified him from taking an active part in Soviet affairs. Living away from the centre, Kropotkin was not in a position to do justice to the grandiose achievements of the Bolsheviki, he reiterated. I was almost frozen and too miserable over Peter's condition to argue. But the boys did it for the three of us. At the Moscow station Sasha had another tilt with the London editor. Starved and half-naked children besieged us for a piece of bread. I had sandwiches on hand and we gave them to the kids, who devoured them ravenously. " A terrible sight," Sasha remarked. " Look here,

Berkman, you are too sentimental," Lansbury retorted; " I could show you any number of poverty-stricken children in the East End of London." " I am sure you could," Sasha replied, " but you forget that the Revolution *has* taken place in Russia, not in England."

Our journey laid me up with a heavy cold and fever for a fortnight. Angelica was again beautifully solicitous, calling every day to look after me and never empty-handed. The comrades of the Universalist Club were also very helpful. Their care and that of gentle Angelica enabled me to leave my sick-bed much quicker than if I had been less fortunate in friends and attention. They urged me to stay at least another week. Travelling was dangerous at best and I was not yet completely recovered. But I could not bear Moscow any longer. It had grown into a veritable monster that I had to escape lest it destroy me. Petrograd held out the hope of relief in useful labour. And there was also my gnawing longing for news from my old home. Five months had passed without a word from anyone. The address we had left with our friends in America was Petrograd. My yearning was mingled with some unaccountable apprehension, both combining into the *idée fixe* that I must hasten back to the northern city.

Mail was actually awaiting us there, received four weeks previously. Why had it not been forwarded, we asked Liza Zorin. " What was the use? " she replied; " I did not think anything from America so important and interesting as what you must have seen and heard in Moscow." The letters were from Fitzi and Stella. Not " so important " — only news of the death of my beloved Helena. What could personal sorrow mean to people who had become cogs in the wheel that was crushing so many at every turn? I myself seemed to have turned into one of the cogs. I could find no tears for the loss of my darling sister, no tears or regrets. Only paralysing numbness and a larger void.

My deportation, Stella wrote, had proved the last blow to Helena's shattered condition. She had grown steadily worse from the moment she had heard about it. Death was more kind to her than life: it came quickly through a stroke. Dear, sweet sister, merciful indeed was your end, your supreme wish fulfilled since David's loss. Your tortured spirit at last found release in eternal rest, my beloved. You are at peace. Not so those whose lives are strewn with the autumn leaves of hope, the withered branches of a dying faith.

Fitzi's letter contained another blow. Our friend Aline Barnsdall had made all arrangements to go to Russia and she had invited Fitzi to come with her. But at the last moment Washington had refused them passports. M. Eleanor Fitzgerald was too well known as " a notorious anarchist, the co-worker of Alexander Berkman and Emma Goldman," the authorities had declared, and she was therefore not allowed to leave the country. Aline Barnsdall's affiliations with radicals had also been traced through the cheque she had given me. Fitzi had no means, even if she could have found some *sub rosa* way of reaching Russia. She was all broken up over her failure to join us, but she knew we would understand.

On our return to Petrograd we found our fellow-passengers of the *Buford* considerably dimininished in numbers. Some of them had succeeded in getting sent to their native places. Others, who in America had been bitter opponents of our defence of the Bolsheviki, became reconciled to the Soviet régime. In Rome now, they argued, they would howl with the Romans. The eleven Communists among the deportees were entirely in clover. They found the flesh-pots prepared for them, and the tables laden. They had but to grab the best place and morsels.

The remaining group was in a deplorable condition. Their attempts to secure useful work, for which years of labour in the United States had qualified them, brought no results. They were being sent from one institution to another, from commissar to commissar, without anyone able to decide whether their efforts were needed and where.

Here was Russia, famished for what these men could and longed to give, yet their productive capacities were compelled to lie fallow, and everything was being done to turn their devotion to hatred. Was this to be the lot of other workers to be deported from the United States and of those who would flock to Soviet Russia to aid the Revolution, we wondered. We could not sit by without at least essaying some effort to prevent the repetition of such criminal stupidity. Sasha proposed a clearing-house for the American deportees, those already in Russia and the others that were being expected. He worked out a plan for their reception, which was to be less ostentatious than on the occasion of our arrival, but which would assure greater security of food and lodging, better economy and practical sense. His project included the classification of the refugees by trade and occupation and assignment to useful and needed work. " Think of the gain to the Revolution if American training and experience were sensibly directed into productive channels," Sasha commented. His plan also provided an immediate opening for our own usefulness and that of other deportees in the city.

I suggested that we get in touch with Mme Ravich about the matter. Herself a prodigious worker and very efficient, she would be quick to see the value of Sasha's idea. Chicherin's representative in the Petrograd Foreign Office was also chief of the city's militia as well as commissar of the factory women's collectives. She lived in the Astoria and we knew the long hours she remained at her desk. I phoned to her at two a.m. and asked for an appointment. She requested me to call at once, adding that she had just received a message from Chicherin for "*Tovarishtchy* Goldman and Berkman."

A large contingent of American deportees were on their way to Russia, Mme Ravich informed us, and Comrade Chicherin had instructed her to put us in charge of their reception. It was a most propitious occasion to broach Sasha's plan. Regardless of the late hour and her fatigue, Mme Ravich would not consent to our leaving until we had fully explained the project. We could count entirely on her co-operation, she assured us, and she would immediately issue directions to her secretary to facilitate our work in every way.

Mme Ravich kept her word, even supplying us with an automobile to save time in getting about. Her assistant, Kaplan, proved an earnest and willing aid, arming us with numerous *propusks* to secure us access to various departments. In his eagerness to help he even proposed to have a *tovarishtch* Chekist accompany us, to enable us to get quicker results. I assured him that I knew of a less drastic and more effective way, ironic and humbling though it was to admit it. Was there really such a method in the Soviet Republic, he inquired. Alas, not home-grown, but imported from the United States, I told him. It was American chocolate, cigarettes, and condensed milk. Their softening and soothing effect had proved irresistible to many Soviet hearts, inducing action and willingness where coaxing, commands, and threats had failed.

Now they achieved in a fortnight what Ravich and Kaplan admitted would have ordinarily taken months to accomplish. Three old germ-eaten buildings were renovated and equipped for the use of the expected deportees; the distribution of their rations organized so as to save their standing in queues, medical attention prepared in case of need, and employment secured for the "swimming" contingent.

Sasha and Ethel had in the meantime taken charge of the welcome to be given the deportees on the Latvian border. They were awaiting them there, with two trains held in readiness to bring the expected thousand refugees to Petrograd. They spent two weeks in vain waiting, only to find out that another blunder had been added to the chaos and confusion of the Soviet situation. The wireless announcing returning war prisoners had been misread by the Foreign Office to mean American deportees. Sasha had repeatedly telegraphed to Chicherin to explain the mistake and offering to use his trains for bringing the war prisoners to Petrograd. He was ordered, however, to remain on the border to await the American deportees; the war prisoners would be taken care of by the War Commissariat. But Sasha had positively ascertained from the war prisoners' convoy that no political refugees were on their way from America. Instead of keeping his trains and provisions for the mythical deportees, as directed by Moscow, and leaving the fifteen hundred war prisoners to their fates on the uninhabited plain, without food or medical aid, Sasha decided to put his trains at their disposal and send them on to Petrograd.

We proposed to use the buildings we had prepared for the benefit of the war prisoners, and Mme Ravich favoured the suggestion. But the men were under the jurisdiction of the War Department, and she felt she must first get permission. Nothing further was heard of the matter. The quarters renovated with so much effort and time were sealed up and three able-bodied militiamen stationed on guard. All our labour was wasted, and Sasha's plan of organizing the deportees or the war prisoners for useful work was allowed to go by the board.

The same disheartening results met our other attempts to do practical work outside of the State machine. We would not be daunted, however.

The palatial residences of the former rich in the part of Petrograd known as Kammenny Ostrov (Island) were to be turned into rest-homes for toilers. "Marvellous idea, isn't it?" Zorin remarked to us; "we must complete it within six weeks." Only American speed and efficiency could accomplish the job on time. Would we help? We took the work in hand and became absorbed in it, until again we struck the impassable wall of Soviet bureaucracy.

From the start we had insisted that at least one warm meal a day should be provided for the workers employed in the preparation of rest-homes for their brothers. I had undertaken to supervise the cooking and the equitable distribution of the rations. For a while all went well; the men were satisfied with the arrangements, and their labours were making unusual progress — unusual for Russians, at any rate. But presently the Bolshevik staffs and their favourites began to increase and the rations of the workers to diminish. The latter were not long in perceiving that they were being robbed of their share for the sake of unnecessary office-holders and hangers-on. Their interest in the work showed signs of waning and presently the effects became apparent. We protested to Zorin against the farce of ill-treating one set of workers to enable another set to enjoy leisure and a rest. Equally we objected to the peremptory eviction from their homes of people whose only offence was a university degree. Old teachers and professors had been occupying some houses on the island ever since October, and no one had troubled them in any way. Now they and their families were to be deprived of home without any possibility of securing another roof over their heads. Zorin had requested Sasha to have the eviction orders carried out. But Sasha emphatically refused to act as the bully of the Communist State.

Zorin felt indignant at our " rank sentimentality." A man with Berkman's revolutionary record, he said, should not shrink from any task; it made no difference whether the *bourgeois* parasites ended in the gutter or threw themselves into the Neva. We replied that translating Communism into the everyday life of Russia was more revolutionary than its denial and betrayal in behalf of an alleged future. But Zorin had become too blinded by his creed to see its disintegrating and devastating effect. He ceased calling for us on his daily ride to the island. We did not want him to think that our interest in the work depended on the comfort of his car and we continued to make the long journey on foot, which required about three hours' walk. Before long, however, we found others in our places, persons more pliable in the hands of the political machine. We understood.

The rest-homes were inaugurated with much éclat. To us the rows of rusty iron bedsteads in the vast salons, with their furniture of faded silk and plush, looked tawdry, cold, and uninviting. No worker with any self-respect could feel at ease or enjoy a rest in such surroundings. Many shared our views, and some even felt convinced that none but those within the party or hanging on to its coat-tails would ever see the inside of the Rest Homes for Workers on the Kammenny Ostrov.

We went our way in painful contemplation of the real tragedy of the Revolution become overgrown with poisonous weeds sapping its precious life. Still we would not despair or give up. Somewhere, somehow it must be possible to undertake the clearing of the path. The smallest beginning, we wanted nothing more. Surely we should find that much, if only we persevered in our search.

The Sovietsky soup-kitchens were an abomination, Zorin had repeatedly told us. Could we suggest some improvement, he asked. Sasha again became all interest, completely immersing himself in his new project of reorganizing the nauseating dining-rooms. In a few days he had outlined a complete project, every item provided for in his usual painstaking manner. A chain of cafeterias was to cover the entire city, planned to eliminate the great waste of food and the superfluous employees in the existing kitchens. Even with the given supplies, scarce though they were, simple but palatable dishes would be served in clean and cheerful surroundings. Sasha would undertake the work, and he was sure I would assist. A few cafeterias to begin with, later to be extended.

An amazing idea, Zinoviev said approvingly. Why had no one thought of it before? Very simple and easily carried out. There was great enthusiasm over it on all sides, and plenty of promises. Petrograd was filled with stores, locked and sealed since the Revolution. Sasha could select the necessary furnishings, get men to remodel the places and have the supplies and everything else needed. My pal was again on deck, his organizing ingenuity on fire in behalf of his plan.

This time there could be no hitch, we were assured. But again the bureaucracy blocked every move initiated without them. Difficulties began to appear in the most unexpected quarters. Officials were too busy to aid Sasha's work, and, after all, wholesome eating-places were not so important in the scale of the world revolution that was expected to break out momentarily. It was absurd to lay stress on immediate amelioration in the face of the general situation. At best it could have no vital effect on the course of the Revolution. And Berkman could do more important work. He should not busy himself as a reformer. It was most disappointing, for everyone had thought him to be a revolutionist of steel and iron. It was naïve of Berkman to claim that feeding the masses was the first concern of the Revolution, the care of the people, their contentment and joy, its main hope and safety, and indeed its only *raison d'être* and moral meaning. Such sentimentality was the purest *bourgeois* ideology. The Red Army and the Cheka were the strength of the Revolution, and its best defence. The capitalist world knew it and was trembling before the might of armed Russia.

One more hope perished, like the preceding ones. Yet to be reborn again in every pulse-beat of a stout heart. Sasha's determination and strength had never been greater. My Yiddish perseverance also refused to surrender. All Soviet streams do not lead to the same muddy pools, we thought. There must be others running into the deep, bracing sea. We must persevere and strike out for other fields.

I talked to the wife of Lashevich, Zinoviev's friend, high in the Bolshevik councils, about the condition of the hospitals. I was a trained nurse and I should be happy to give my services in improving them. She volunteered to call the matter to the attention of Comrade Pervoukhin, the Petrograd Board of Health Commissar. Weeks passed before I received word to call on him. I hastened to the Board of Health.

A trained nurse, months in Russia already and yet not assigned to him for service, Pervoukhin exclaimed. I should have known that he was desperately in need of just such aid. The hospitals were in a wretched condition; there was great scarcity of dispensaries and a lack of trained help, not to speak of the dearth of medical facilities and surgical instruments. He could use several hundred American nurses and here I had been doing nothing all this time. I must start in at once, he urged. As to co-operation, I could count on him to the limit, including an auto to make my rounds. He would take me for the first tour of inspection as soon as I was ready to start. Could I report to him in the morning?

I would come early, I replied, but he should not over-estimate my abilities and importance in the colossal task on hand. I would do my utmost, of course, I could promise him that. He would expect nothing else from a *tovarishtch*, he replied, from an old revolutionist and Communist, as he had been informed. I was indeed a Communist, I assented, but of the anarchist school. Oh yes, he understood that, but there was really no difference. Many anarchists had realized this and they were entirely with the party, working with the Bolsheviki and doing finely. "I also am with you," I said, "in the defence of the Revolution, even to my last breath." Not with the Communism of the dictatorship, however, I explained. I had not been able to reconcile myself to that, for I could not see the remotest relationship between the coerced and forced form of State communism and that of the free and voluntary co-operation of anarchist communism.

I had so often seen Communists on such occasions instantly alter their tone and manner that I was not surprised at the sudden change in Commissar Pervoukhin. The kindly physician so deeply concerned in the people's health, the humanitarian who had a moment previously so lamented his lack of nurses to minister to the ill and afflicted, immediately became the political fanatic fairly oozing antagonism and resentment. Did my differing view-point matter in the care of the sick, or did he think it would affect my usefulness as a nurse, I inquired. He forced a sickly smile, replying that in Soviet Russia everyone who wants to work is welcome. His ideas are not questioned, provided he is a true revolutionist willing to set all political considerations aside. Would I do so? I could make no pledges except one, I replied. I would help him to the best of my ability.

I called the next day and every day for a week. Pervoukhin did not take me on the planned tour of inspection. For hours he kept me in his office arguing the infallibility of the Communist State and the immaculate conception of the Bolshevik dictatorship. One must either accept them without question or be shut out of the fold. Ghastly hospitals, lack of medical supplies, no adequate care of the patients — those were piffling matters as compared with the required faith in the new trinity. I was evidently no longer " desperately needed." I was shut out.

With the help of my Astoria Hotel neighbour, young Kibalchich, I succeeded in visiting a few hospitals. Their condition was appalling. The true cause of it was not so much poor equipment or the lack of nurses. It was the omnipresent machine, the Communist " cell," the commissars, the eternal suspicion and surveillance. Physicians and surgeons with splendid records in their profession, touchingly devoted to their work, were hampered at every turn and paralysed in the atmosphere of dread, hatred, and fear. Even the Communists among them were helpless. Some of them had not yet been entirely divested of human feeling by the régime. Being of the intelligentsia, they were considered doubtful characters and were kept in leash. I understood why Pervoukhin could not have me on his staff.

These rude awakenings in the Soviet Arcadia of dictatorship were followed by repeated and more forcible jolts. They helped still further to uproot my cherished belief in the Bolsheviki as the clarion voice of " October."

The militarization of labour, rushed through the ninth Party Congress with typical Tammany Hall steam-roller methods, definitely turned every worker into a galley-slave. The substitution of one-man power in the shops and mills in place of co-operative management placed the masses again under the thumb of the very elements they had for three years been taught to hate as the worst menace. The "specialists" and professional men of the intelligentsia, formerly denounced as vampires and enemies guilty of sabotaging the Revolution, were now installed in high positions and clothed with almost supreme power over the men in the factories. It was a step that with one stroke destroyed the principal achievements of " October," the right of the workers to industrial control. Insult was added to injury by the introduction of the labour book, which virtually stamped everyone a felon, robbed him of the last vestiges of freedom, deprived him of the choice of place and occupation, and fastened him to a given district without the right of straying too far, on pain of severest penalties. True, these reactionary and anti-revolutionary measures were determinedly fought by a substantial minority within the party, as well as denounced by the people at large. We were among them, Sasha even more vigorously than I, although his faith in the Bolsheviki was still very strong. He was not yet ready to see with his inner vision the things already obvious to his outer eye, nor prepared to admit the tragic fate that the Bolshevik Frankenstein monster was pulling down the " October " edifice.

For hours he would argue against my " impatience " and deficient judgment of far-reaching issues, my kid-glove approach to the Revolution. I had always depreciated the economic factor as the main cause of capitalist evils, he declared. Could I fail to see now that economic necessity was the very reason which was forcing the hand of the men at the Soviet helm? The continued danger from the outside, the natural indolence of the Russian worker and his failure to increase production, the peasants' lack of the most necessary implements, and their resultant refusal to feed the cities had compelled the Bolsheviki to pass those desperate measures. Of course he regarded such methods as counter-revolutionary and bound to defeat their purpose. Still, it was preposterous to suspect men like Lenin or Trotsky of deliberate treachery to the Revolution. Why, they had dedicated their lives to that cause, they had suffered persecution, calumny, prison, and exile for their ideals! They *could* not go back on them to such an extent!

I assured Sasha that nothing was further from my thought than to charge the Bolsheviki with treachery. Indeed, I considered them quite consistent, truer to their aims than those of our own comrades who were working with them. Especially did I feel Lenin as a man hewn out of one piece. To be sure, his policies had undergone extraordinary changes; there was no denying his great agility as a political acrobat. But he had never deviated from his objective. His bitterest enemies would not accuse him of that. But his objective was the very crux of Russia's tragedy, I insisted. It was the Communist State, its absolute supremacy and exclusive power. What if it destroy the Revolution, condemn millions to death, and drench Russia in the blood of its best sons and daughters? That could not dismay the iron man in the Kremlin. They were " trifles, a little blood-letting." It could not affect his ultimate purpose. In point of clarity of vision, concentration of will, and unflagging determination Lenin had my respect. But as to the effect of his purposes and methods upon the Revolution, I considered him the greatest menace, more pernicious than the combined interventionists, because his objective was more elusive, his methods more deceptive.

Sasha did not gainsay this, nor was he less convinced than I of the hopelessness of our further attempts to fit into the garrotte of the political machine. But he thought that I was holding Lenin and his co-workers responsible for methods imposed upon them by dire revolutionary necessity. Shatoff had been the first to emphasize this. All the level-headed comrades, Sasha claimed, shared that attitude. And he himself had come to see that revolution in action is a quite different thing from revolution in the realm of theory mouthed by parlour radicals. It meant blood and iron, and it was unavoidable.

The dear companionship of my old pal and our intellectual harmony had mitigated much of the lacerating process of finding my way through the Soviet labyrinth. Sasha was all that had been left me from the tornado that had swept over my life. He represented everything dear to me, and I felt him a safe anchor in the roaring sea of Russia. Our disagreement, springing up so suddenly, overwhelmed me like a mighty wave, leaving me bruised and battered. I was certain my friend would in time realize the falsity of his position. I knew that his desperate attempt to defend Bolshevik methods was his last stand in a lost battle, the battle we had been the first to wage in the United States in behalf of the October Revolution.

Among our many callers during our Moscow stay had been an interesting young woman, Alexandra Timofeyevna Shakol. She had learned from Schapiro of our presence in the city, and, an anarchist herself, she was eager to meet her famous American comrades. Besides, she wanted to talk to us about a project initiated by the Petrograd Museum of the Revolution. An expedition was being planned, she explained, that was to cover the length and breadth of the country in search of documents bearing on the Revolution and the revolutionary movement of Russia since its inception. The collected material would ultimately serve as archives for the study of the great upheaval. Would we join such a venture?

For a moment we had been carried away by the plan and by the opportunity it offered to see Russia in her Revolutionary everyday life, to learn at first hand what the Revolution had done for the masses and how it affected their existence. We might never have such another chance. But on second thought we felt it bitter irony that would condemn us to collect dead material amidst the raging life of Russia. Thirty years long we had stood in the very thick of the social battle, always on the firing line. Could we now be content with anything less in our reborn native land? We longed for more vital work, something that would enable us to give out of the fullness of our hearts and the best of our abilities to the great task.

Since our return to Petrograd we had been so busy chasing Soviet windmills, so eagerly reaching out for a new hold, that we had hardly thought of our comrade Shakol and her proposal. But with every hope of useful work gone, her offer once more came to our minds. It might afford an escape from our meaningless existence. If the material we should collect would aid future historians in establishing the right relationship between the Revolution and the Bolsheviki, it would be worth the effort, Sasha and I agreed. Perhaps it would also help us to get the right perspective. The various parts of the country we should visit, the people we should come in contact with, their lives, customs, and habits, would prove a useful school, we comforted each other. We finally decided to try it, since nothing else was open to us. " If only the new project will also not turn out a bubble," I said to

Sasha on our way to the Winter Palace, where the Museum of the Revolution was located.

We found Shakol absent and we were distressed to learn that she had barely escaped death from typhus, which she had contracted in Moscow. She was convalescing now, but she would not be back to work for another fortnight. She had informed the museum, however, that we had promised to visit it, and we were received by the secretary, M. B. Kaplan, a man in the middle thirties, of pleasant and intelligent appearance. He offered to take us through the institution and show us what had already been accomplished. A number of rooms were filled with valuable material, among them the secret archives of the tsarist régime, including the records of the Third Political Section, disclosing the workings of its spy system. Much of the vast collection had already been arranged, classified, and prepared for exhibition in the near future. "Our task is only beginning," the secretary explained; " it will require years to achieve our object of establishing in Russia a museum more complete and unique than anything existing at present in any other country, not excepting the British Museum, the more so as no country contains such a wealth of revolutionary treasures scattered about the land and waiting to be rescued from loss and destruction." It was for that reason that the museum was anxious to send the collecting expedition as soon as possible, because much was being lost by delay. Kaplan was heart and soul for the project, and his collaborators were equally enthusiastic about the future of the museum and the work planned by it. All were anxious to secure our help.

Though it was the latter part of May, the vast chambers of the Winter Palace were breathing a penetrating chill. We were warmly clad, yet we quickly felt benumbed with the cold. We marvelled at the men and women working in the fearful dampness all through the severe months of the Petrograd winter. They had been employed there for almost three years now. Their faces were streaked with blue blotches, their hands frost-bitten. Some had contracted severe cases of rheumatism and tubercular affections. His own health had become undermined, the secretary admitted. But it was revolutionary Russia, and he and his co-workers were happy to be privileged to help in building its future. Most of them, like himself, were non-partisan.

He was all eagerness to be able to count on our aid. His enthusiasm was too infectious to resist, and we agreed. " Then you had better report for duty at once," he suggested. There was a great deal to be done yet to get the expedition under way. The necessary equipment for the journey was to be procured and two railroad cars prepared, one for the staff, which was to consist of six persons, the other to hold the material to be collected. Various formalities had also to be looked after, the consent of numerous departments, *propusks,* and supplies to be secured, and the right of way for the expedition. Haste was imperative and we must begin immediately.

We left the genial secretary and his collaborators in a more cheerful frame of mind. We did not yet feel about the work before us as did the other members of the museum. We knew we could not for long be content with merely collecting parchments when more important work was so urgently needed which we might do. But the devotion and fortitude of those people had lifted the weight of despair from our hearts. It was the most encouraging feature of Soviet life. Frequently we had come upon this new spirit of Russia, even in entirely unexpected places. In the darkest hours of our groping we would often discover the most heroic endurance and devotion hidden under the official Soviet surface. Not the kind daily acclaimed in public places and feasted with showy demonstrations and military display. No one outside the party believed in that official brand. Even within its ranks there were large numbers who hated the empty bombast and pretence, though they were powerless against the machine. They made up for the vulgar ostentation by their own singleness of purpose and probity. Silently they plodded at their tasks, giving their all to the Revolution and asking nothing in return for themselves either in rations, praise, or other recognition. These great souls redeemed for us much that was hateful in the Bolshevik régime.

Preparations for the expedition were progressing rather slowly, leaving us time to visit museums, art galleries, and similar places of interest, as well as to attend to other things. A report had reached us of the arrest of two anarchist girls, aged fifteen and seventeen, charged with the circulation of a protest against the degrading aspects of the labour book and also against the unbearable conditions of the politicals in the Shpalerny and Gorokhovaya jails in the city. Several Petrograd comrades called on us in the matter and we immediately addressed ourselves to the leading Bolsheviki. Zorin had long ago given us up as lost for his heaven. Zinoviev did not seem to like me particularly; the sentiment was, indeed, mutual. He was always extremely nice to Sasha, however, and the latter therefore called to see him about the arrested anarchists. On the same errand I visited Mme Ravich, whom I still greatly admired for her simple and un-assuming personality and her readiness to admit and undo official abuses. Unfortunately, political prisoners were outside her jurisdiction. Such matters were under the control of the Cheka, whose Petro-grad chief, the Communist Bakayev, was known as very vindictive towards anarchists. On the very first day of the arrival of the *Buford* deportees Bakayev had impressed upon them that "no anarchist foolishness is tolerated in Soviet Russia." Such luxuries were fit only for capitalist countries, he had told them. Under the proletarian dic-tatorship anarchists had either to submit or to be squelched. Upon our boys' resenting such a greeting, Bakayev had ordered the entire group of two hundred and forty-seven under house arrest. We had learned of it only the third day and we had been much wrought up over it. Zorin had minimized the occurrence as an unfortunate mis-understanding and had also prevailed upon his Chekist comrade to withdraw the armed guard from the dormitories of our people in the Smolny. Alas, since then we had seen too many of such "unfortunate misunderstandings."

On this occasion a wink from Zinoviev and Mme Ravich had im-mediate effect upon Bakayev. He also lived at the Astoria and he phoned me to call on him. He would release the arrested anarchist girls, he informed me, provided we were willing to vouch for it that that would stop their "bandit activities." I expressed amazement at his application of the term to two young girls guilty only of publishing a protest against the methods they considered counter-revolutionary. "Your party cannot be very sure of itself or it would not be constantly haunted by imaginary bandits and counter-revolutionists," I said. I declined to vouch for anyone, knowing that I myself would not keep silent if I saw the need of voicing my senti-ments. Nor could I speak for Comrade Alexander Berkman, I in-formed Bakayev, though I knew that he would refuse to bind anyone by making promises for him. As to the ill treatment of political prisoners, I assured the Cheka chief that it would be grist to the American prison mills to learn that the jails in Soviet Russia were no better than those in the States. This seemed to reach Bakayev in the right spot. He would give the girls another chance, he declared, for, after all, they were proletarians even if they had not yet realized that they must not injure their own class by criticizing the dictatorship. He would also see what improvement the jails required, though conditions had been greatly exaggerated.

Getting people out of jail had been among our various activities in America. But we had never dreamed that we should find the same necessity in revolutionary Russia. Certainly not we who had fought fiercely the least suggestion of such a preposterous eventuality. Yet our only positive work so far had been just that — pleading for our imprisoned comrades with Lenin, with Krestinsky, and now with a lesser light. We were still able to see the pathos and the humour of the situation and we had not yet forgotten how to laugh at our own follies, though more often my laughter only thinly veiled my tears.

Nevertheless we had reason not to regret our efforts, particularly in the case of one of our finest comrades, Vsevolod Volin. He had been educationally active in the ranks of the Ukrainian peasant rebels headed by the anarchist Nestor Makhno, whom the Bolsheviki had formerly acclaimed as an effective leader of the masses, a man of great strategic acumen and exceptional courage. Not without reason, since it had been Makhno and his *povstantsy* army who had routed various counter-revolutionary adventurers and who had materially helped the Red forces to drive back the hordes of General Denikin. For refusing to submit his army to the absolute command of Trotsky, Makhno had been declared an enemy and bandit and his entire forces denounced as counter-revolutionary. Volin was an educator and in no way a participant in the military operations of Makhno. But the Ukrainian Cheka made no such fine distinction. At the first opportunity they had arrested Volin and held him incommunicado in the Kharkov prison, dangerously ill with fever though he was. Our comrades in Moscow realized the perilous position of Volin, for Trotsky had in the meantime sent telegraphic orders to have him executed. They tried to get the prisoner transferred to Moscow, where he was well known to the leading Communists as a man of revolutionary integrity and high intellectual attainments. They had circulated an appeal for his transfer, which was signed by every anarchist then present in the capital, and they had chosen Sasha and the local comrade Askaroff to present the petition to Krestinsky, Secretary of the Communist Party.

Krestinsky proved very fanatical and bitter against the anarchists, claiming at first that Volin was a counter-revolutionist deserving death, and again pretending that he had already been brought to Moscow. Sasha succeeded in convincing him that he was wrong on both points and that Volin be at least given a chance to state his case, which opportunity he would not have in Kharkov. Krestinsky finally yielded to Sasha's arguments. He promised to telegraph to the proper authorities in Kharkov to have Volin removed to the capital. Apparently he kept his word, because before long our comrade was brought to Moscow and placed in the Butirky prison. Shortly after that Vsevolod Volin was entirely released.

Having finally effected the release of the two Petrograd girls, we felt we might turn to other things before the expedition would be ready to start on its long journey. First of all we proceeded to visit the industries.

I had heard various rumours about factory conditions, but as I had not yet been able to gain access to the factories, I was loath to credit the stories. I had long ago realized that in a country deprived of press and speech, public opinion must needs be based on exaggerations and falsehoods. I would have to inspect the mills and shops myself, I always told my informants, before reaching conclusions.

My long-awaited opportunity to visit factories and possibly to talk to the workers at the bench came when Mme Ravich requested me to act as guide to a certain American journalist who had suddenly appeared in Petrograd. It was, I discovered, one of the newspaper men who had interviewed us on our landing in Terryoki, on our way through Finland. It seemed ages and ages ago. The man had repeatedly tried to get into Soviet Russia, as he had informed Sasha on the border, requesting him at the same time to speak a good word for him to Chicherin, in whose hands lay the decision about the admission of journalists. The young man had made a favourable impression by his frank expression and manner, but aside from that we knew about him nothing whatever, not even his name nor the paper he represented. Only at the last moment, as we walked across the border, did he hand us his card. Sasha had promised to transmit his message to the People's Commissar for Foreign Affairs, stating, however, that he could not plead in his behalf. Sasha had indeed kept his promise, having informed Chicherin that the young journalist, John Clayton by name, was anxious to come to Russia, and that he represented the Chicago *Tribune,* one of the reactionary newspapers in the United States.

We had heard no more about the matter, and in the hectic life of Russia we had forgotten all about Clayton's existence. I was therefore not a little surprised when on my return to Petrograd Mme Ravich telephoned me to inquire whether I knew a man by the name of John Clayton. He had been arrested on the border trying to cross over to Russia and he was being held by the Cheka. He had given our names as proof that he knew trustworthy people and that they would intercede for him. I repeated to Ravich what Sasha had previously told Chicherin, adding that, since the man was already on Soviet soil, it would be better policy to set him free. He could not see more than the Soviet government would permit, and he could not send out any news without the Bolshevik censorship passing upon it. Why, then, be afraid? Mme Ravich decided to report to the border Cheka what I had said and leave the matter to them for final action. Again there was nothing more heard about Clayton, and great was my astonishment to meet him one day at the door of my room in the Astoria. "Where do you come from?" I blurted out before even inviting him in. "Oh, don't ask me," he replied piteously; " I have risked my life to get into the country. I come with the best intentions and am treated worse than a dog." "What has happened?" I demanded. "For the love of Mike," Clayton cried, "aren't you mean not even to ask me to step into your room? I need a whole day to tell you all my adventures." The poor man did look forlorn, and I never liked to be rude, even to an American reporter, though few people had as good reason as I to be so. "Come in, old fellow, and make a clean breast of it," I said lightly. His face brightened. "Thanks, E.G.," he replied, "I knew they couldn't turn you into a hardened Bolshevik." "Nonsense," I corrected him, "all Bolsheviki are not hardened, and those that are have been made so largely by the grace of your Government in league with the others to starve the Russian masses."

Clayton related that he had ski'd and bribed his way from Finland, had been caught, thrown into a filthy Cheka prison, and finally

shipped to Moscow, where he had been " free " the past six weeks.
" Free ? " I inquired in surprise. Yes, but he might as well not have
been for all he had got to see or to hear. Not a scrap of anything
even for a first measly story. As for himself, every kind of discrimination and chicanery had been employed against him ever since
he had reached Moscow. " Rotten I call it, and bad judgment to
treat a newspaper man so," he declared bitterly.

The way to a man's heart is proverbially through his stomach, and
something was needed to sooth Clayton's ruffled spirit. " Plenty of
time to discuss all that," I said, " after you have had a cup of coffee."
" Gee, that would be a real treat," he cried in glee. After having
partaken of two cups his chagrin somewhat subsided and he became
more amenable to reason. Before we started on our factory-inspection
tour, Clayton was willing to admit how untenable his position was
and how absurd it was to feel hurt. After all, he was an unknown
quantity, and his credentials from the Chicago *Tribune* anything but
reassuring. Spies and conspiracies had become a mania with the Communists. It was natural in view of the persecution Russia was enduring from the enemies of the Revolution. He would have to see
his unpleasant experiences in a larger light if his intentions were
really as good as he had assured me. Else he would be able to report
only the same stupidity as his colleagues about the alleged nationaliza-
tion of women, *bourgeois* ears and fingers fed to the people, and
similar juicy atrocities that had been published by the American press.
Clayton swore he would never be guilty of such misrepresentation.
" Wait and see," he assured me. I had waited for thirty years, searching all the time with a Diogenes lantern for fairness or accuracy
among American newspaper men. I had found some exceptions, of
course, very few and far between. None of them, however, on the
Chicago *Tribune*. I hoped he would prove to be one of the exceptions.

The function of an official cicerone was not exactly to my liking.
But I did not care to refuse Ravich who had always been responsive
to my intercession for unfortunates. Moreover, I felt that the Russian
situation was too great and vital and that I had not yet grasped it
fully, though I had reached a definite decision not to work within
Bolshevik political confines. Most important to me was it not to be
quoted by any American paper against Soviet Russia, not while the
latter was still forced to fight for life itself on so many fronts. I was
therefore in the predicament of not wanting Clayton to secure

information by my aid and I did not cherish the prospect of having to tell him deliberate lies. I reasoned that Mme Ravich knew what she was about when she had given Clayton permission to visit factories. They were probably not so bad as had been reported to me. Or she may have thought that with me as guide things would be made to appear less harsh. Fortunately Sasha was accompanying us. That would give one of us a chance to lag behind and talk to the workers while the other would interpret to Clayton the official version of conditions.

The Putilov works proved to be in a forlorn state, most of the machines deserted, others out of repair, the place filthy and neglected. While Sasha was explaining to Clayton what the superintendent of the shop was relating, I lingered behind. I found the men very unwilling to talk until I mentioned that I was a *tovarishtch* from America and not a Bolshevik. That made a big difference. They could tell me a great deal, they said, but even the walls had ears. Not a day passed but what some of their fellows failed to return to work. Sick? No, but they had protested a little too loud. I urged that, as the authorities had informed me, the workers in the Putilovsky, being engaged in one of the vital industries, received considerably better rations than other toilers — two pounds of bread a day and special shares of other products. The men stared at me in amazement. I might try their bread, one of them suggested, holding out a black chunk to me. "Bite hard," he said ironically. I tried, but knowing I could ill afford a dentist's bill, I had to return the leathery piece, much to the amusement of the group clustered about me. I suggested that the Communists could not be blamed for the bad bread and the scarcity of it. If the Putilov workers and their brothers in other industries would increase production, the peasants would be able to raise more grain. Yes, they replied, that was the yarn given them every day in explanation of the militarization of labour. It had been hard enough to work on empty stomachs when they were not being driven. Now it was altogether impossible. The new decree had only added to the general misery and bitterness. It was taking the workers too far away from their villages, which formerly had helped them out with provisions. Besides, the number of officials and overseers had been increased and they too had to be fed. "Of the seven thousand employed here, only two thousand are actual producers," an old worker near me remarked. Hadn't I seen the markets, another man demanded in a whisper. Had I noticed much scarcity there for those who had the price to pay? There was no time for a reply. At a warning from their neighbours the men hastened back to their benches and I joined my companions.

Our next objective looked like a military camp, with armed sentinels stationed all around the huge warehouse and about the mill inside. "Why so many guards?" Sasha asked the Commissar in charge. The flour had of late been disappearing by the carload, came the reply, and the soldiers were there to cope with the evil. They had not succeeded in stopping the thefts, but some offenders had been apprehended. They had proved to be workers misled by a gang of speculators. Somehow the official explanation did not sound plausible. I slackened my pace in the hope of getting close to some of the millmen. I knew the right password: " From America, bringing you the solidaric greetings of the militant proletariat and their gift of cigarettes." A young chap with a firm jaw and intelligent eyes attracted my attention as he passed me with a sack of flour on his shoulders. When he returned to pick up another, I tried my magic key. It worked. Would he tell me why armed soldiers were there? Didn't I know of the new decree *militarizing* labour, he demanded. The workers had resented it as an insult to their revolutionary manhood. As a result their brother soldiers, who had helped them during the October days, were now installed over them as watch-dogs. I asked about the theft of flour and whether the guards were not there to prevent it. The man smiled sadly. No one knew better than the commissars, he said, who was stealing the flour, for they themselves passed it through the gates. "And the Revolution? Has it given you workers nothing?" I questioned. "Oh, yes," he replied, " but it has been checked long ago. Now it is a stagnant pool. It will break out again, though, never fear."

In the evening, when Sasha and I compared notes, we agreed that we had seen all we wanted to know of Soviet factory conditions. We could leave the doubtful honour to the official guides, who were less squeamish about turning black into white, and grey into crimson hues. Sasha emphatically refused to act again as cicerone and I completed my unsolicited job by taking Clayton the next morning to the Laferm Tobacco Works. We found them in good condition, because the former owner and manager himself was still in charge.

Before long, Clayton departed, declaring that he would soon return for a longer stay and a more thorough study of conditions. His wife was Russian, he said, and she would serve as his guide, which would make it unnecessary for him to impose on our time and good will. He would guard against making misleading statements concerning Russia, he faithfully promised.

" Misleading," I mused. The poor chap could not know that every day of my Russian existence was misleading, misleading others as well as myself. Would the time ever come when I should once more stand firmly in my own boots, I wondered.

Preparations for the expedition were progressing very slowly, while my nervous tension almost reached breaking-point. Whatever poise I had of late gained had been destroyed by my recent impressions of the appalling conditions under which the masses were living and toiling. The arrival of Angelica Balabanoff somewhat helped to lighten my frame of mind.

She had been sent from Moscow to complete arrangements for the reception of the expected British Labour Mission. Poor Angelica, she too had been relegated to the rôle of guide, and I was certain she would agonize as much as I in having to play hide-and-seek with the shadow of her once glowing faith.

The Narishkin Palace on the Neva, one of the most beautiful in the capital, was assigned to the use of the distinguished English guests. It had been locked up since the October days, and Angelica asked me to help her put it in order. I cheerfully consented, though she really did not need me for the work. An array of servants had been commandeered to do the cleaning that three efficient persons could have accomplished in less time. I guessed that Angelica was lonely, and a glance at her showed me that she was again in bad health. She felt at home with me and I loved to be with her even if I could never get myself to talk frankly to her about the subject we both had most at heart. It would have been like digging into an open wound. Angelica was also very fond of Sasha and she had already secured his help as interpreter and translator of the testimonials of welcome that were being prepared in honour of the visitors.

The mission at last arrived, most of its members of the usual Anglo-Saxon better-than-thou attitude. They were against intervention, of course, and they boasted of having repudiated the attacks on Soviet Russia, but as to revolution or communism, no, thank you, none of that for them. Their reception was calculated to speak to the larger audience of the British labouring masses and to the workers of the entire world. No effort was to be spared to make the occasion propagandistically effective. The grand military display on the square of the Uritsky Palace was but the initial part of the program. Other functions were to prove even more persuasive. The dinners at the Narishkin Palace, its tables laden with the best starving Russia could command, the personally conducted tours through the model schools, selected factories, and rest-homes, theatrical performances, ballets, concerts, and opera, with the members of the mission in the former Tsar's loge, composed some of the festivities. British reserve could not resist such hospitality. Most members of the mission fell for the show and became the more pliable the longer they stayed.

Some of them exerted their best logic to persuade me that the dictatorship and the Cheka were inevitable in a country as backward as Russia, with her people for centuries used to despotic rule. "We Englishmen would not stand for it," one delegate declared, "but it is different with the ignorant Russian masses, strangers to civilized ways." The Soviet Government, he argued, had shown amazing intelligence and skill in having succeeded so well with its raw human material. But the average Englishman, of course, would not put up with such things. "The average Englishman," I retorted, "prefers to run three blocks after a cab so he can act the flunkey for a gentleman and earn the munificent sum of twopence." "If you saw such a sight in London, it was certainly only the dregs of the city," he replied. "Precisely," I said; "there is more than enough of such dregs in England and they would be the worst stumbling-block to any fundamental economic changes in your country. But I forget that you Englishmen will have none of revolution. That could only happen in ignorant and uncivilized Russia."

I walked away to the rear of the box to watch the rest of the ballet undisturbed by British complacent superiority. Presently the door opened and a man in military uniform entered. When the lights went on again, I recognized him as Leon Trotsky. What a change in his appearance and bearing within three years! He was no longer the pale, lean, and narrow-chested exile I had seen in New York in the spring of 1917. The man in the box seemed to have grown in breadth and height, though he showed no superfluous flesh. His pale face was bronze now, his reddish hair and beard considerably streaked with grey. He had tasted power and he looked conscious of his authority. He carried himself with proud mien, and there was disdain in his eyes, even contempt, as he glanced at the British guests. He spoke to no one and soon left. He did not recognize me, nor did I make myself known to him. The gulf between our worlds had widened too far to be reached across.

There were certain members of the British Mission, however, not entirely inclined to look in open-mouthed wonder at the things about them, with their mental eyes shut. These were not of the labouring element. One of them was Mr. Bertrand Russell. Very politely but decisively he had from the very first refused to be officially chaperoned. He preferred to go about himself. He also showed no elation over the honour of being quartered in a palace and fed on special morsels. Suspicious person, that Russell, the Bolsheviki whispered. But then, what can you expect of a *bourgeois*? Angelica almost broke her heart over such talk. She argued that it was stupid and criminal to try to pull the wool over everybody's eyes. People should be allowed to see conditions as they were, she insisted, to realize the harrowing want and misery of blockaded Russia. Perhaps that would help to arouse the conscience of the world against the powers that were starving the country. But the Cheka thought otherwise, though it did not too obviously interfere with the movements of the delegates.

Mr. Russell called on us one day with Henry G. Alsberg, an American correspondent accompanying the mission, who was representing the New York *Nation* and the London *Daily Herald*. John Clayton, whom Alsberg had met in Esthonia, had informed him that we were staying at the Astoria and had also given him some provisions for us. The unexpected replenishment of our larder deserved some kind of celebration, and we invited our callers to stay for lunch, which I proceeded to prepare in my improvised kitchenette. It was by no means an elaborate meal, but our guests assured me that they enjoyed it more than they would have the repast at the palace served in the festal Narishkin salon on damask and fine plate. With us, they said, one could speak freely and get a segment of Russian reality free from fear or favour. It was our first contact with the world outside of Russia, with persons earnestly concerned in the weal of the country. We cherished every moment with our visitors and I liked Henry Alsberg in particular. He brought with him a whiff of the best that was in America — sincerity and easy joviality, directness and *camaraderie*. Mr. Russell was of a more reserved nature, but of gracious and simple personality.

Angelica had invited us to the last social function for the Mission before its departure for Moscow. We went in the capacity of interpreters. The same evening she left with the delegates. Nothing would do but she must have Sasha with her. He had much to attend to for the museum expedition, as no car had yet been secured for our journey. But who could refuse Angelica?

All was ready for our expedition except the principal thing — a railroad car. The Commissar of the Museum of the Revolution, Yatmanov, a prominent Communist, and Secretary Kaplan had for weeks been trying to get one for us, but without success. They were sure Sasha could manage the matter through Zinoviev, with whom he seemed to have a pull. But Sasha was still in Moscow with the British Labour Mission. It was exasperating to remain idle for one whose whole life had been filled with intense activity. I had learned, however, since I came to Russia, to possess my soul in patience. The dictatorship of the proletariat was building for eternity; what could a few weeks, months, or even years matter?

Sasha presently returned and with him a more intense drive for a car. He had not been happy in the capital. The Punch and Judy show for the British Labour Mission had distressed him. Poor Angelica had of course nothing to do with it. She had been thrust aside as soon as she had delivered the guests to Karakhan and his hosts of managers at the Moscow station. They had carried the Britishers off, leaving only Bertrand Russell behind. No one seemed to know him or his place in the world of science and advanced thought. Sasha had saved the situation by hailing Karakhan, who was about to drive off in his luxurious automobile, which he was occupying alone. Karakhan inquired who the man was, remarking that he had never heard of Bertrand Russell. However, he would take Sasha's word for it that the man with him was worth bothering about, upon which he invited Sasha and Russell to his car.

Sasha had absented himself from the public exhibitions and demonstrations in honour of the British Mission. He had had enough of those shows. Nor did he feel that he could serve as interpreter of the bombastic speeches at the public functions and the falsehoods palmed off on the unsuspecting Englishmen. He had translated for Angelica some resolutions and he had accompanied the delegates to shops and factories on tours of inspection. Karl Radek had asked him to translate something Lenin had written and had sent one of the official autos to bring Sasha to the headquarters of the Third International. There Radek had handed him Lenin's manuscript on the " Infantile Diseases of Leftism." " Imagine my surprise," Sasha related, " when a glance at the pages showed me that it was a vitriolic attack on all the revolutionists differing from the Bolshevik attitude. I told Radek I would translate it only on condition of being permitted to write a preface to the brochure." " Radek must have thought you mad to be guilty of such *lèse-majesté,*" I remarked. " Yes, he was so mad he took me for his brother lunatic," my humorous friend replied. Radek did not press the matter any further and Sasha had gone his way. But there were other things that soon engaged his entire attention in Moscow. A number of our people were in prison again, among them our comrade Abe Gordin, of the Universalist Club, who had taken a prominent part in the revolutionary events of 1917. They were being held without any charges made against them. Their repeated demands to know the reason for their arrest having failed to bring results, they had declared a hunger-strike in protest. Sasha had been kept busy trying to induce the authorities to specify our comrades' offence or release them. After much difficulty he had succeeded in getting an audience with Preobrazhensky, Secretary of the Communist Party. Sasha urged that the men in jail had grown dangerously weak from their long hunger-strike, and Preobrazhensky coldly declared that " the quicker they died, the better for us." Sasha had assured him that the Russian anarchists had no intention of obliging him or his party. Moreover, if his régime continued to persecute his comrades, it would have only itself to blame for anything that might happen. " Is this a threat? " the Secretary had demanded. " Only an unavoidable fact, which you as an old revolutionist should know," Sasha had replied.

Our Moscow comrades had enjoyed a modicum of freedom. What could be the purpose of the new policy of deliberate extermination, we wondered. Sasha thought it was due to the stand of the Moscow anarchist conference expressed in the resolutions we had handed to Lenin. The reply of the Communist Party Executive, a copy of which had been expressly sent to us, declared that " *ideiny* anarchists are working with the Soviet Government." The others, who did not, were considered enemies of the Revolution and as such not entitled to more consideration than counter-revolutionists like the Social Revolutionists or the Mensheviki. The Cheka had taken the hint and proceeded accordingly.

It was a terrible situation, but we were powerless. Any protest on our part within Russia would have no greater effect than that of Peter Kropotkin or Vera Figner. With the country endangered on the Polish front, we felt we could not issue any appeal to the workers abroad.

At the first news of war with Poland I had set aside my critical attitude and offered my services as nurse at the front. Mme Ravich was absent from Petrograd at the time and I went to Zorin about it. Since the birth of Liza's child I was again seeing a great deal of the Zorins. Mother and child had been very ill and I had taken care of them. This somewhat softened Zorin's disapproval of us since our disagreement over the rest-homes. My offer to aid Soviet Russia in her hour of need seemed to move him deeply. He had known that Sasha and I would finally come to collaborate with his party, he declared. We only needed time, he thought, to realize that the dictatorship and the Revolution were identical and that to serve one meant to work for the other. He promised to see the proper authorities about my offer and to inform me of results. But he never did. That of course could have no bearing on my determination to help the country, in whatever capacity possible. Nothing seemed so important just then.

Sasha had in the meantime succeeded in securing a car for the Museum Expedition. It was an old dilapidated Pullman containing six compartments, but soon he had it cleaned up, painted, and disinfected for our use. Having proved so successful where others had failed, the museum appointed Sasha general manager of the expedition. Shakol was nominated secretary, while I was entrusted with three jobs, besides the work of collecting historical material, in which we all shared. I was chosen treasurer, housekeeper, and cook. A Russian couple on our staff were supposed to be experts on revolutionary documents. The sixth in our group was a young Jewish Communist, whose special work was to visit local party institutions. As the only Communist in our circle he felt at first quite lost, being among three anarchists and two non-partisans.

Our car needed mattresses, blankets, dishes, and similar utensils, for which I received an order from Yatmanov on the supplies of the Winter Palace. Equipped with this " order," I went down to the basements of the palace, where the Tsar's household goods were stored. The transitoriness of station and power had never before struck me so forcibly as when looking at the wealth that had but recently been used by the reigning family on its State occasions. The toil of every country and clime was gathered there in priceless porcelain, rare silver, copper, glass, and damask. Room after room was stacked to the ceiling with utensils and plate, thickly covered with dust, mute witnesses to the glory that was no more. And there I was, rummaging in all that magnificence for dishes for our expedition! Could any legend be more fantastic, more significant of the ephemeral nature of human destiny?

It took a whole day to select what was suitable for our use, and even at that the things were more fit for a museum. I could not get excited over the fact that we should eat our herring and potatoes, and if lucky also *borscht,* from the plate that had fed the Lord of all the Russias and his family. It amused me to think, however, how the newspapers in America would play up such an incident. Berkman and Goldman, arch-anarchists, using the crested linen and china of the Romanovs! And the free-born Americans, such as the Daughters of the Revolution, dying for the sight of royalty, dead or alive, or even for some souvenir of an old boot that had squeezed a royal foot!

On June 30, 1920, just seven months after we had landed on Soviet soil, our renovated car was hitched to a night train, known as " Maxim Gorki," and headed for Moscow. It being the " centre," we had to stop off there for additional credentials from various departments, including those of education and public health, and from the Foreign Office, not forgetting also the Cheka. From the latter we had to secure a document giving us immunity for the possession of counter-revolutionary documents, the collection of which was part of our task. We expected that a few days in the capital would suffice to complete our arrangements, but it took two weeks instead.

The city was in a ferment over incidents of recent occurrence. The bakers had been on strike; their entire executive committee was now dissolved and its members in prison. The Printers' Union had met a similar fate for a more heinous offence. They had organized a meeting with the members of the British Labour Mission as their guests. The surprise of the occasion was the sudden appearance on the platform of Tchernov, leader of the Social Revolutionists and former President of the Constituent Assembly. The Cheka had for a long time been looking for Tchernov, who was in hiding. He appeared disguised by a long black beard, and he was not at first recognized. His impassioned speech against the Bolsheviki roused the assembly to an ovation, but when the communist chairman of the meeting called for the arrest of the man, he had disappeared in the crowd about him.

There was great excitement in the city, due to the arrival of a number of foreign delegates for the Second Congress of the Red Trade-Union International. Among them we were delighted to find some Anarcho-Syndicalists from Spain, France, Italy, Germany, and Scandinavia. There were also labour men from England, more militant and less comfortable than their countrymen on the British Mission. Learning of our presence in Moscow, they sought us out and we had many conferences together. The clearest minds among them were two anarchists, Pistania from Spain and Augustin Souchy from Germany, representing the Anarcho-Syndicalists labour bodies of their respective countries. These two men were entirely with the Revolution and sympathetic with the Bolsheviki. They were, however, not the kind who could be fêted into seeing everything in roseate colours. They came as earnest students of the situation, desirous of getting the facts at first hand and of observing the Revolution in action. They inquired, among other things, how our comrades were faring under the Communist State. All sorts of rumours had filtered to Europe about the persecution of anarchists and other revolutionists. The comrades abroad, they told us, had refused to credit such reports as long as they had not heard from us about the matter. They had asked that we send back word through Souchy and Pistania about the actual state of affairs. Sasha explained that the rumours were unfortunately not unfounded. Anarchists, Left Socialist Revolutionists, militant workers and peasants were imprisoned in Soviet jails and detention camps, denounced as bandits and counter-revolutionists. They were nothing of the kind, of course, but sincere comrades, most of whom had taken an active part in the October days. Our efforts had been effective for but few of them. Possibly the Anarcho-Syndicalist delegates, as representatives of large Left labour organizations abroad, would be more successful with the Soviet authorities. They should insist on their right to visit the prisons and talk to the prisoners. Sasha also suggested that the delegates demand redress for our people. But he was reluctant to talk to the men of the general situation. His own impressions had not yet sufficiently clarified, he said; he could not speak the final word and he did not want to prejudice the delegates. They would have to learn for themselves.

I felt differently on the matter. Our foreign comrades were accredited representatives of militant labour bodies. They were not likely to use anything I might tell them to the detriment of the Revolution, as newspaper reporters might do. I had no intention of biasing them, but neither did I think that I should keep the facts from them. I wanted at least our own comrades in Europe and America to behold the reverse side of the shiny Soviet medal. Souchy, Pistania, and a British I.W.W. man attentively listened to my narrative, but I could read on their faces that they were as incredulous as I had been of Breshkovskaya, Bob Minor, and the other friends who had told me of the actual conditions in Russia. Nor did I blame them. To the oppressed of the world the Bolsheviki had become the synonym of the Revolution itself. The revolutionists outside of Russia could not easily credit how far that was from the truth. One seldom learns from the experience of others. Nevertheless I did not regret having talked frankly to the delegates. Whatever their own impressions, they would know that I had not denied them my confidence and trust.

Europe and America seemed removed from me by decades. It was gratifying to have them brought closer by our foreign visitors and to learn from them about the anarchist and revolutionary labour activities outside of Russia. To the request of the delegates that I send a message to the workers abroad, I replied: " May they emulate the spirit of their Russian brothers in the coming revolution, but not their naïve faith in political leaders, no matter how fervent their protestations and how red their slogans! That alone can safeguard future revolutions from being harnessed to the State and enslaved again by its bureaucratic whip."

A great and most welcome surprise came to me in Moscow with the opportunity to see the famous Maria Spiridonovna and her friend Kamkov, leaders of the Left Socialist Revolutionists. Maria was living under cover, disguised as a peasant, and great precaution was necessary to keep her whereabouts from the Cheka. She therefore sent a trusted comrade to bring Sasha and me to her place.

Spiridonovna occupies one of the highest places in the galaxy of the heroic women of Russia. Her attack on General Lukhanovsky, Governor of Tambov Province, had been an extraordinary feat for a girl of eighteen. Maria had dogged the man's steps for weeks, patiently waiting for a chance to strike the notorious executioner of the peasants. When the train bearing Lukhanovsky steamed into the station, Maria jumped on to the running-board and shot the Governor dead before his guards realized what the girl was about. No less remarkable had been her behaviour during the tortures she had been subjected to after her arrest. Pulled about by her hair, her clothes torn off, and her naked flesh burned with cigarettes, her face beaten into a pulp, Maria Spiridonovna had remained silent and contemptuous of her tormentors. When this treatment had failed to force her to involve others in her act or to break her spirit, she was tried behind closed doors and condemned to die. She was saved by the tremendous protest in Europe and America, and her sentence was commuted to exile to Siberia for life. Twelve years later the historic tables were turned. Tsar Nikolas was hurled from his throne, and the victims of absolutism, numbering into the thousands, were brought back in triumph from their dungeons and exile. Among them was Maria Spiridonovna, whose Calvary was well known to the radicals everywhere. Her glowing personality had exalted and spurred me on in my work in the United States, and she was among the first I longed to meet when I came to Russia. But no one seemed to know her whereabouts. The Communists I had questioned, including Jack Reed, had told me that she had suffered a nervous break-down and was being nursed back to health in a Soviet sanatorium. It was only when I got to Moscow the first time that I learned from her comrades about the life and struggle of Maria Spiridonovna since her liberation from Siberia. Shattered in health from the agonies she had suffered, and broken down by tuberculosis contracted in prison, she had nevertheless refused to spare herself. Russia needed her, and the peasants to whom she had dedicated her young life were calling her. Now more than ever they needed her, having been betrayed by Kerensky and his party, which had also been hers and by whose order she had killed Lukhanovsky. The Socialist Revolutionist

Provisional Government was forcing the people to continue the world slaughter, and Maria would have nothing to do with it.

Together with the more radical wing of the party, including Kamkov, Dr. Steinberg, Trutovsky, Izmailovich, Kakhovskaya, and others, Maria Spiridonovna organized the Left Socialist Revolutionist Party. Side by side with Lenin and his comrades they worked for the October upheaval and unwittingly helped the Bolsheviki to power. Not unmindful of the ardent support of Spiridonovna and her comrades, Lenin had approved the choice of Maria by the Peasant Congress as its president, his own party's appointment of Dr. Steinberg as People's Commissar for Justice, and Trutovsky as Commissar for Agriculture. But the break with the Bolsheviki came over Brest-Litovsk, the Left Socialist-Revolutionists considering peace with the Kaiser a fatal betrayal of the Revolution. Maria was the first to refuse further co-operation with the Bolsheviki. With her wonted determination she turned from the Communist Government as she had from Kerensky's régime, and her comrades followed her lead. Then her martyrdom began all over again. There followed arrest and incarceration in the Kremlin prison, escape, re-arrest, and more prison. Her influence among the peasantry continued, however, even growing with her persecution. The Communists resorted to the convenient explanation that Maria had gone mad and had to be restrained.

On the sixth floor of a large tenement in Moscow, in a room not much larger than my cell in the Missouri penitentiary, a little old woman embraced me tenderly, without uttering a word. It was Maria Spiridonovna. Though only thirty-three years of age, she was shrivelled in body; a hectic flush was on her emaciated face, her eyes were feverishly brilliant, but her spirit remained unchanged and unfettered, still scaling the heights of her indomitable faith. Anything I could have said at that moment would have sounded banal. Nor did I trust myself to speak. Her hands in mine had a steadying effect and the silence about us was soothing, like her tender touch. Maria spoke and I listened. For three days, with little interruption, I listened tense in every nerve. Her tone was calm, her mind clear, and her presentation keen. Her facts were incontestable and documented by peasant letters from every part of Russia. They cried to her to enlighten them on the great misfortune that had befallen their

beloved *matushka Rossiya*. They had believed in the Revolution as
in the second coming of Christ. They had prepared for its promised
blessings, the freeing of the soil from the masters, the peace and
brotherhood it would bring. She knew best, they wrote, how hard
they had worked and how fervently they had believed in the holy
power of the revolution. Now everything was crushed, their hopes
turned to ashes. They had taken the land from their old masters,
but their produce was now being taken from them by the new bosses,
even to the last seeds for planting. Nothing had changed except the
methods of robbing them. It was the Cossack and the *nagaika* before,
the Chekists and shooting now. The same browbeating and arrests,
the same heartless brutality and drive. Everything the same. They
could not grasp it, could not understand it, and there was no one
to explain, whose word they could believe. They still had her, their
angel Maryussa. She had never played them false and she must
now tell them whether the new Christ also was crucified and whether
he would rise still once more to redeem their suffering land.

Maria was in possession of scores of these pitiful outpourings,
written on slips of coarse paper or dirty cloth and smuggled to her
under the greatest difficulties.

" The Bolsheviki maintain that forcible confiscation has been imposed on them by the peasants' refusing to feed the cities," I remarked. There was no truth in it, Maria assured me. The peasants
had indeed refused to deal with the " centre " through its commissars.
They had their soviets and they insisted that the latter be in direct
touch with the soviets of the workers. They had taken the meaning
and purpose of the soviets literally, as simple folk always do. The
soviets were their medium of keeping in touch with the city toilers
and exchanging with them needed products. When this was denied
them and in addition their General Soviet dissolved and its members
imprisoned, the peasants became aroused against the dictatorship.
Moreover, the forcible collection of produce and the punitive expeditions against the villages had antagonized and embittered the rural
population. These methods could not win with the peasants. The
saying among them was that Ilich could exterminate the peasants,
but he could not conquer the peasantry. " They are right," Maria
commented, " for Russia is eighty per cent agricultural, and that is
the very backbone of the country. It may take some time for Lenin to
find out that the peasant will force his hands, not he the peasant's."

All through her recital Spiridonovna had said not a word about herself, her persecution, illness, or want. Her mainsprings poured into the vast human sea, I felt, each ripple rushing back to her all-embracing heart. I saw no sign of any personal current crossing her universal stream until just shortly before we bade her good-bye on the third day of our visit.

Sasha had been present at our sessions, together with Boris Kamkov. The latter, like his friend Maria, was also calm and collected in his arraignment of the evils wrought among the peasantry by the three years of the dictatorship. At no time during our stay did Maria betray by word or look that the man stirred in her other emotions than those of the solidarity of a common ideal. Now Kamkov was about to leave on a journey to the interior and he very emphatically insisted that he needed nothing for his trip except some bread. He would take nothing from Maria's share. Someone had brought her eggs and cherries, and while Kamkov was talking to Sasha, Maria stealthily stuck her little bundle of provisions, packed in a handkerchief, into the sack of literature her friend was taking with him. She stood near him, diminutive alongside of his great height and breadth. She did not speak, she only looked up into his eyes and lightly brushed her slender white hand over his sleeve, imperceptibly leaning against him. He was going on a dangerous mission and Maria felt that he might never return. No poet ever sang of greater love and longing than her simple gesture expressed. It was beautiful and moving beyond words, laying bare in a flash the rich fount of her soul.

Our red-painted car on a side track at the Moscow railroad station attracted many visitors, among them Henry G. Alsberg and Albert Boni, who had come to Russia. Both were envious of our trip and eager to come with us. Of the two men, Sasha and I liked Alsberg the best. We told him we would prevail on the members of our expedition to allow him to come with us if he would get the necessary credentials from the Soviet authorities.

On the day of our departure he arrived with written permission from Zinoviev, the Foreign Office and the Cheka. The representative of the Cheka in the Foreign Office insisted, however, Alsberg would have to secure an additional visa from the local Moscow Cheka. Karakhan's secretary (Foreign Office), under whose jurisdiction he

was, definitely informed him that he did not need this extra visa and
the Foreign Office "guaranteed" he would not be molested if he
went on the expedition. Alsberg hesitated but we urged him to take
a chance without the *proposk* of the Moscow Cheka. His American
passport and the fact that he represented two pro-Soviet newspapers
should save him from serious difficulties. Our secretary consented that
he should join us, and there was an extra bunk in Sasha's compartment. Thereupon he decided to become the seventh member of our
company.

Our Moscow stay had been rich in surprises. The final one came just
an hour before our departure. A man dashed up, all out of breath, in
search of us. " Why, E.G., don't you recognize me ? " he cried; " I am
Krasnoschokov, formerly Tobinson, of Chicago. Have you forgotten
your chairman at the Workers' Institute meeting, your and Sasha's
co-worker in the Windy City? " The change in him was as complete
as Trotsky's. He seemed taller and broader, of proud carriage, but
without the military severity and disdainful expression of the Commissar of the Red Army. He was, Tobinson-Krasnoschokov related,
President of the Far Eastern Republic, and he had come to Moscow
for an important conference with the Party Executive. He had been
in the city for a week, eager to meet us again, but he had failed to
locate us till the very last moment. He had many things to talk over
and we must remain a few days to celebrate our reunion, he insisted.
He had travelled from Siberia in his own railroad car, bringing plenty
of provisions and his own cook, and he would give us our first real
feast in Soviet Russia. Krasnoschokov had remained the same free
and generous fellow he had been in the States, but we could not alter
our plans and we had only a few hours to spend with him.

Sasha was still in the city, attending to last-hour commissions, but
he would soon be back. Meanwhile Krasnoschokov was regaling me
with his adventures since his arrival in Russia. He had become the
chief executive of the Far Eastern Republic; Bill Shatoff was also
there, as well as other anarchists from America, all working together
with him. Free speech and press prevailed in his part of Russia, he
assured me, and there was every opportunity for our propaganda.
Sasha and I must come, he insisted. He needed our help and we could
count on him. Shatoff was doing great work as Commissar of Railroads and he had warned him not to dare return without us. " Free
speech and free press — how does Moscow stand for that? " I asked.

Conditions were different in that far country, Krasnoschokov explained, and he had been given a free hand there. Anarchists, Left Socialist Revolutionists, and even Mensheviki were co-operating with him and he was proving that free expression and joint effort were giving the best results.

An enchanting picture indeed, I commented, and I should certainly like to see it for myself. Perhaps when we had completed our present tour, we might induce the museum to send our expedition to Siberia. Presently Sasha arrived and there was renewed rejoicing. Alas, only for a short hour. Our visitor was loath to let us depart and we had to promise faithfully to let him know when we would be ready to come to his Far Eastern Republic. He would facilitate our journey and promise us all the liberty we wanted and carloads of material for the museum.

Our first important stop was at Kharkov. It looked prosperous after Petrograd and Moscow. The people, fine physical types of humanity, appeared well fed and carefree in spite of the numerous invasions, changes of government, and the ravages the city had experienced. There was evident a scarcity only of wearing-apparel, particularly of shoes, hats, and hosiery. Men, women, and children were bare-legged, some wearing queer-shaped sandals of wood and straw. The women were especially incongruously attired in dresses of the finest linen and batiste, wearing hand-made lace and multi-coloured kerchiefs. The brightly embroidered native costumes predominated, presenting a pleasant sight after the monotony of the Moscow streets. And the people! I had never seen such a collection of beauty in one place. The men dark-haired and bearded, bronze of skin, with dreamy eyes and shining teeth. The women with crowns of hair, lovely complexions, and flashing black eyes. They seemed a race entirely different from their northern brothers.

The markets were the main gathering-places and centres of attraction. The stalls spread for blocks, piled high with fruit, vegetables, butter, and other provisions. One had no longer believed such profusion existed in Russia. Some of the tables were laden with toys in carved and painted wood, mountains of them of curious shape and design. My heart ached for the children of Petrograd and Moscow, with their broken and mis-shaped dolls and the battered wooden monstrosities they called Cossack steeds. For two dollars in Kerensky paper money I carried off an armful of wonderful toys. I knew that the joy they would give to my Petrograd youngsters would transcend any monetary value.

Bringing anything into another city without special permission was considered speculation and treated as a counter-revolutionary offence, often subject to the " supreme penalty," which meant death. Neither Sasha nor I could see the wisdom or justice, let alone the revolutionary necessity, of such a prohibition. We agreed that speculation in food-stuff was indeed criminal. But it was absurd to decry everyone as a speculator who tried to bring in half a sack of potatoes or a pound of bacon for his family use. Far from deserving punishment, we argued, one should be glad that the Russian masses still possessed such indomitable will to live. Therein alone was the hope of Russia, rather than in mute submission to a slow death by starvation.

Long before we had started on our expedition, we had agreed that if it was right to import dusty documents for future historians, it could not be wrong to bring back some provisions for the relief of present want, particularly for the sick and needy among our friends. The abundance of food on the Kharkov markets made us more determined to lay in a supply on our return trip. We only regretted that we could not take with us enough to feed every man, woman, and child in the stricken cities.

Moscow had been hot, but Kharkov was ablaze, with the railroad station miles from the town. It was physically impossible to spend the day in collecting material and then return to our car for meals. Comrades in the city helped me to secure a room where I could also prepare meals for our secretary, Alexandra Shakol, Henry Alsberg, Sasha and myself. As a pro-Soviet American correspondent Henry had no difficulty in getting a room, which he invited Sasha to share with him. Shakol preferred to sleep in the car. The Russian couple shifted for themselves, having friends in the city, and our Communist member was taken care of by his party comrades. These arrangements completed, we set out on our labours, each member being assigned to cover certain Soviet institutions. Sasha's task was to visit labour, revolutionary, and co-operative organizations; mine included the departments of education and social welfare.

Our reception at those institutions was anything but cordial. Not that the officials were openly disagreeable, but one could sense the frigidity of their manner. I wondered what could be the reason until

Sasha reminded me of the resentment the Ukrainian Communists felt against Moscow for depriving them of self-determination in their local affairs. They saw in our mission a new imposition of the centre. Not daring to ignore orders from Moscow, they could yet sabotage our work. We therefore decided to fall back on our old talisman, emphasizing that we were *tovarishtchy* from America on a tour of study of the revolutionary achievements of the Ukraine, about which we were to write. The change was instantaneous. No matter how busy the officials happened to be, they would drop their work, become wreathed in smiles, supply us with the information we needed, and send us away with stacks of material. In that manner we succeeded in seeing and learning more of the methods and effects of the dictatorship in the Ukraine than would have been possible in any other manner. We were able to collect more than the Russian members of the expedition, including even the Communist in our party.

The poor boy was really treated abominably by his southern comrades. They refused to give him data or documents. Moscow was on their backs heavily enough, they said, directing their every move. They were not going to let the centre rob them of their historical wealth to boot.

The amusing side of the family quarrel was that whenever we came upon some mismanaged institution or ugly state of affairs, the Ukrainians would explain them away by the interference of Moscow. On the other hand, if the Communist in charge was from the centre, he would argue that the Ukrainians were sabotaging the work of Moscow because they were anti-Semites and obsessed by the notion that almost the entire northern Communist Party consisted of Jews. Between the two we had little difficulty in learning the facts of the situation and the real cause of the widespread antagonism towards Moscow.

A Russian engineer who had just returned from the Don basin and whom we met in Kharkov threw considerable light on the Ukrainian situation. It was silly to put the entire blame for conditions on Moscow, he said. The Communists in the south in no way differed from the followers of Lenin in the north in their methods of dictatorship. If anything, their despotism was even more irresponsible in the Ukraine than anywhere else in Russia. His experience in the mines had convinced him of their ruthless persecution of those of the intelligentsia who were unwilling to co-operate with them. As to their inefficiency and inhumanity, a visit to the prisons and concentration camps would convince us as it did him. Only in one thing they differed from their comrades in the north: they took no stock in the imminence of the world revolution and they were not interested in it or in the international proletariat. All they wanted was to have their own independent Communist State and to command in the Ukrainian instead of in the Russian language. That was their main reason for dissatisfaction with Moscow, he thought.

I inquired about the feeling of anti-Semitism in the Ukraine. The engineer admitted that it was widespread, though it was not true that all Ukrainian Communists were against the Jews. He knew many Bolsheviki who were free from that racial prejudice. In any event, it was unjust of the northern Communists to charge their Ukrainian brothers with anti-Semitism, for they knew very well how prevalent the feeling was among themselves. There was a great deal of it in the Red Army. Moscow was trying to keep it down by iron force, though it did not entirely succeed in preventing anti-Jewish outbreaks on a small scale. In the Ukraine the Whites had so far been the only ones responsible for pogroms. Whether the Ukrainian Red forces would be willing and able to cope with the evil was yet to be seen.

We decided to visit the local prison and detention camp. The greatest difficulty, however, we met from the woman superintendent at the head of the Workers' and Peasants' Inspection, a sort of super-watch recently instituted over the other watchers of abuses in Soviet institutions. Concentration camps and prisons being under her jurisdiction, we presented our credentials to her. She frowned. The prison conditions in Kharkov were the concern of the local authorities and of no one else, she declared categorically. Disappointed, we left her office, meeting on the way a man who introduced himself as *tovarishtch* Dibenko, the husband of Alexandra Kollontay. He had heard from her about me, he explained, and he would be glad to be of help. He requested us to wait while he talked matters over with the superintendent. He was evidently in her good graces, because presently she returned with him quite softened. She had not known that we were such well-known American *tovarishtchy*, she said, and of course we could visit the prison and camp. She would immediately take us there in her auto.

Both penal institutions bore out the statement of our engineering acquaintance as regards Ukrainian Communist management and despotism. The camp, called *kantslager,* occupied an old building without any provisions for sanitation and not half large enough for its thousand inmates. The dormitories, overcrowded and smelly, were barren except for wide boards that served as beds and had to be shared by two and sometimes three persons. During the day they had to squat on the floor and even eat their meals in that position. For an hour they were taken out in sections to the yard, the rest of the time being kept indoors without anything to occupy their time and minds. Their offences ranged from sabotage to speculation, and they were all counter-revolutionists, as our stern guide impressed upon us. " Could not some useful occupation be provided for the prisoners? " I inquired. " No time for such *bourgeois* dilly-dallying with the enemies of the Revolution," she replied; " after the fronts are liquidated, we will send them away where they can do no more harm."

The political prison of tsarist times was again in full operation. Those who dared question the right of rulers, divine or self-appointed, were held captive, now as then. The old régime prevailed, with most of the former guards as keepers. During our inspection we halted before two locked doors. The others having been open, we inquired the reason. Our woman escort was evasive at first. We remarked that prison-investigators in America were usually shown only the most obvious things and then wrote knowingly about penology. But we could not be content with such superficiality. Finally the superintendent consented to make an exception in our case. We would understand, she hoped, that behind all measures in Soviet Russia, including the prison régime, was revolutionary necessity. The occupants of locked cells were dangerous criminals, she assured us, one, a woman, was a member of the counter-revolutionary bandit army of Makhno, and the man occupying the adjoining cell had been caught in a counter-revolutionary plot. Both deserved severest treatment and the supreme penalty. Nevertheless she had ordered their cell opened for several hours a day and she had given permission to the other prisoners to talk to them in the presence of a guard.

The Makhnovka, an old peasant woman, was crouching in the corner of her cell like a frightened hare. She blinked stupidly when the door was opened. Suddenly she threw herself headlong before me and shrieked: " *Barinya,* let me out, I know nothing, I know nothing! " I tried to quiet her and get her to tell me about her case. Maybe I could help her, I urged. But she was frantic, whining piteously that she knew nothing about Makhno. In the corridor I told our guide that it seemed absurd to consider that stupefied old creature dangerous to the Revolution. She was half-crazed with the solitary and the fear of execution, and if kept locked up much longer, she would surely go stark mad. " It is mere sentimentality on your part," the guide upbraided me; " we live in a revolutionary period, with enemies on all sides."

The man in the next cell was sitting on a low stool, his head bent. With a sudden jerk he turned his eyes on the door, a terrorized and hunted look in their anticipation. Just as quickly he pulled himself together, his body stiffened, and his look fastened on our guide with concentrated contempt. Two words, no more audible than a sigh, yet petrifying in their effect, broke the silence. " Scoundrels! Murderers! " A horrible feeling overcame me that he believed us to be officials. I took a step towards him to explain, but he turned his back upon us and was standing erect and forbidding beyond my reach. With heavy heart I followed my companions out of the corridor.

Sasha had said nothing, but I felt that he was affected no less than I. With seeming nonchalance he sauntered along the corridors, his object being to find a young anarchist imprisoned in the place, as we had been confidentially informed. I was kept back by the superintendent, enlarging on my *bourgeois* sympathies.

I let her talk to give Sasha an opportunity for his quest. My thoughts were with the two prisoners I had just left. I knew what doom was awaiting them. The man especially had shown pride and independence. Where was mine, I pondered, that I still kept holding on to the shell whose kernel I knew to be worm-eaten through and through.

When alone with Sasha, I learned what our imprisoned comrade had communicated to him. The head of the Workers' and Peasants' Inspection was a former Chekist and she attempted to run the prison in the usual Cheka manner. She had introduced most severe restrictions, including solitary confinement for the politicals. The inmates sought to effect a change without resorting to drastic methods. But when the half-witted peasant woman and the man doomed to die were isolated from the rest and kept under lock, the entire prison protested. A hunger-strike followed. Though it failed of the desired results, it succeeded in opening the cells part of the day for their two fellow inmates. Another hunger-strike was being planned in the near future to compel a change in the despotic régime.

I understood the terrorized expression on the face of the man and the hate in his cry: " Scoundrels! Murderers! " He was being kept in isolation previous to execution, all the time in uncertainty as to when the fatal shot would silence his palpitating heart. Could any " revolutionary necessity " explain such refined cruelty? If only I had come to Russia in the October days, I thought, I might have found the answer or a fitting end to my past. Now I felt caught in a coil that was growing more strangling every day.

The people who least understood my travail were my own comrades in Kharkov. Most of them were from America and had been affiliated with my work there, among them Joseph and Leah Goodman, Aaron and Fanya Baron, Fleshin, and others. Fleshin had been working with us in the *Mother Earth* office and knew me more intimately. The Kharkov comrades, with the heroic personality of Olga Taratuta at their head, had all served the Revolution, fought on its fronts, endured punishment from the Whites, persecution and imprisonment by the Bolsheviki. Nothing had daunted their revolutionary ardour and anarchist faith. They had no painful hesitations, no torturing doubts, no unanswerable questions. They were shocked to find me so undecided. I had always been sure of myself, they said, unswerving in every issue. Yet in Russia, where I was so badly needed, I seemed to have lost my grip. And Sasha, always so clear and determined — why did he at least not join them in organizing and propaganda work instead of wasting his energies on collecting dead parchments?

Our coming to Russia had been a great impetus to them, they told us. They had been sure that we would continue on Soviet soil the work we had so energetically carried on in the United States. They knew, of course, that we would not give up our faith in the Bolsheviki until we became convinced that they had gone back on their revolutionary slogans. For that purpose Joseph and Aaron Baron had been sent to us by their organization, the Nabat, risking their very lives in the attempt to reach us in Petrograd. Had not their story of the Bolshevik emasculation of the Revolution sufficed to convince us? Their persecution of the anarchists, their perfidy and double-dealing in regard to Nestor Makhno? Had not their proofs demonstrated to us that the dictatorship had betrayed the very spirit of the Revolution? Surely we had heard and seen enough to make up our minds as to where we stood in regard to the Communist State.

Aaron Baron and Joseph had indeed visited us in Petrograd. They had come secretly, both having been outlawed by the Bolsheviki. For two weeks they had held our tense interest by their vivid description of conditions and the causes that had gradually turned the Communists into traitors to the Revolution. But those who knew us could not expect us to give up our belief in the revolutionary integrity of men like Lenin, Trotsky and their co-workers because of their mistaken policy towards Makhno or even towards our own comrades. Our Kharkov people were willing to concede that they had been too hasty in their expectations. But now, they argued, after eight months in Soviet Russia, with all the opportunities we had enjoyed of learning conditions at first hand, why did we still hesitate? Our movement needed us. The field was large and promising. We could easily organize the anarchists of the Ukraine into a strong, federated body that would reach the workers and the peasantry by its propaganda. The latter in particular, through the aid of Nestor Makhno. He knew the peasants and they trusted him. He had repeatedly urged the anarchists throughout the country to take advantage of the propaganda possibilities the south offered. He would put everything necessary at our disposal, including funds, a printing-press, paper, and couriers, our comrades urged, pleading for our speedy decision.

If I should make up my mind to become active in Russia, I explained to them, the support of Makhno would lure me no more than Lenin's offer of aid through the Third International. I was not denying Makhno's services to the Revolution in the struggle against the White forces, nor the fact that his *povstantsy* army was a spontaneous mass movement of the toilers. I did not think, however, that anarchism had anything to gain from military activity or that our propaganda should depend on military or political spoils. But that was beside the point. I was not in a position to join their work, nor was it a question of the Bolsheviki any more. I was ready to admit frankly that I had erred grievously when I had defended Lenin and his party as the true champions of the Revolution. But I would not engage in active opposition to them so long as Russia was still being attacked by outside enemies. I was no longer deceived by their mask, but my real problem lay much deeper. It was the Revolution itself. Its manifestations were so completely at variance with what I had conceived and propagated as revolution that I did not know any more which was right. My old values had been shipwrecked and I myself thrown overboard to sink or swim. All I could do was to try to keep my head above water and trust to time to bring me to safe shores.

Fleshin and Mark Mratchny, the most intelligent comrades I had met in Kharkov, grasped my difficulties and supported my stand in refusing to lead others where I myself had lost my way. The rest of the group Nabat was dissatisfied and indignant. They refused to recognize the Emma Goldman of their American conception in her present pale image. They turned to Sasha with greater expectations. They knew that *he* would never doubt the Revolution, no matter what demands it made on him. He had always been a better conspirator than I and he would see the great value of working with Makhno or at least of accepting his co-operation. Joseph and Leah, most genuine and lovable people, were particularly set on winning Sasha for their plans. They were presently joined by Fanya Baron, who had just arrived from Makhno's camp with an invitation to us. Would we come? She would safely guide us to him. " Will you come? " Sasha asked. If he insisted on going, I should be with him, I replied; under no circumstances would I let him face such danger alone. But what about the expedition? We had given our word to remain with it to the end and he had undertaken most of the responsibilities of the venture. Could we go back on that? In the first flush of the chance to get to Makhno and his *povstantsy* army Sasha had given little thought to the museum and our expedition. However, " a pledge is a pledge," he declared; " We must stick; perhaps we shall find another opportunity to meet the peasant leader."

Our stay in Kharkov came to a sudden end. Our secretary learned that our material was in danger of being held up by the Party Executive and not permitted to leave the Ukraine. We needed no further hint. The same night we managed to get our car hitched to a train going to Poltava, and off we lurched.

We speed-spoiled Americans could scoff and make fun of such slow travel, but to the congested humanity at every railroad station in Russia, waiting for days and even weeks to get on a train, the creeping pace was of great advantage. An appalling sight they were — these rag-covered, bundle-loaded, exhausted people, shouting, cursing, and falling over each other in the mad skirmish to swing on. Pushed off, often by the butt of a soldier's gun, not once but many times, doggedly they would try again and again until they succeeded in clinging to the railing or steps. It was an Inferno awaiting the master hand of a Russian Dante.

An entire car occupied by only eight persons, including our porter, with hundreds clamouring for a place on the platform or roof or even on the bumpers was not an unalloyed comfort. Yet we could do nothing to aid. Aside from the imminent danger of typhus infection, the people being vermin-eaten, we could allow no one into our car on account of the valuable material we carried. Thievery, in places high and low, was no new phenomenon in Russia. Years of disintegration and want had increased its scope and perfected its dexterity. We could not hope to safeguard our collection or anything else in the car against such artistry. We could take none of the woeful mob into our car, that was certain. However, we might permit some women or children to ride on the platforms, I suggested. The Jews of our company favoured the plan, the Gentiles were against it. The Russian couple had proved very disagreeable from the start. It seemed their special mission to inject a jarring note. Shakol was Slavic with a vengeance, now bursting with sympathy and compassion for her fellow-men, now talking like a lady of a feudal manor. She could not bear to feel the filthy creatures so near, she said, and she was mortally afraid of catching typhus or some equally dangerous disease. She could not risk another infection. Poor child, she had had a narrow escape and I could not blame her. I promised to scrub and disinfect the platforms every morning, but even that did not prove as persuasive as Sasha's suavity. It was the art of my old chum to lead people gently to where he wanted them and make them think they had been dying to get there all along. With Shakol on our side, we were able to carry our point.

Everything in life is relative, looming in value according to one's necessity. The platforms of our car were coveted more than palaces They offered to a few creatures a night's security against wind and hot soot and preserved them from falling off the roof of the car, a thing that was a common occurrence on the road. Life was cheap and people too preoccupied with their own little share of it to get excited over such matters. No one knew whether he might not come next and no one cared. Once squeezed past the soldiers to the tiniest spot on the train, they looked neither behind nor ahead. The present moment alone was theirs and they snatched at it greedily. Quickly they forgot their tears, their cursing and shrieking. They felt sociable again and capable of fun and frolic. Once more they could give vent to their rich imagery and song. What a people! What kaleidoscopic changes of spirit!

Our credentials from the centre found greater favour in Poltava than in Kharkov. The secretary of the *Revkom* (revolutionary committee acting as the local government) received us pleasantly and gave us *carte blanche* to every Soviet department. With such aid our expedition had no difficulty in gathering a goodly crop of material. It included a large amount of counter-revolutionary documents left behind by the various bands and the armies that had invaded Poltava, finally to be routed by the Red forces. Records, decrees, manifestoes, military emblems, and an assortment of curious weapons were unearthed by our secretary and Sasha and carried in triumph to our car.

Together with Henry Alsberg I made a tour of inspection. Henry wanted to interview the main local Soviet officials, as well as persons outside of the Communist Party. He invited me to act as his interpreter and I gladly accepted.

Curiously enough, Poltava showed but few physical traces of the numerous invaders. Hardly any damage had been done to buildings and parks. Her stately trees were in their appointed places, looking contemptuously down from their great height upon the puny thing called man. Flowers were profuse, vegetable patches at their side, with no armed guards or even a fence to protect them from despoilers. After the distressing scenes of our journey from Kharkov the sight of nature's bounty and a walk along the shady alleys were heaven indeed.

The Soviet institutions presented little interest. They were running true to type, managed in conformity with the established one-track idea and according to the Moscow formula. The official interviews added no new note. It gave us time to look for the tabooed part of the population. Inadvertently we came upon two of that class and by their aid met a larger group held together by their common fate, though widely separated in ideas. Our discovery was two women, one of them the daughter of Vladimir Korolenko, the last of the old school of Russian writers. The other was the head of the " Save the Children " organization, founded in 1914 and continued through all the vicissitudes of the intervening years. They invited us to their home, where we came in contact with others of their circle. They were of the old radical intelligentsia that had always been dedicated to the enlightenment and succour of the Russian masses. They were not able to reconcile themselves to the dictatorship, they frankly admitted; nor were they actively engaged against it. In fact, they were co-operating economically with the Bolsheviki and working in the social welfare departments. Nevertheless they were being persecuted as *sabotazhniky* and the " Save the Children " society had been repeatedly raided by the local authorities as a counter-revolutionary body. This in spite of Lunacharsky's express permission to continue their work.

Henry remarked to our hosts that, no matter what might be said against the Bolsheviki, they could not be charged with neglecting the children. They were doing more in that direction than any other country. Why, then, the need of private welfare associations? Our hostesses smiled sadly. They had no intention whatever, they said, to deprecate the sincerity of the Bolsheviki in relation to the child. They had done much for it and would no doubt do still more. That referred, however, only to a privileged class of children. The destitute ones had alarmingly increased in numbers, and thousands were constantly added. Prostitution, venereal diseases, and every form of crime were rampant among the children of even tender age, and pregnancies frequent among girls of ten and eight. The more thoughtful Communists were aware that the scourge could not be cured by political decrees or the Cheka. It had to be dealt with from other angles and by different means. They welcomed the co-operation of the " Save the Children " society. Lunacharsky, for instance, was most generous in aiding it. The trouble was with the *local* authorities. They cared nothing about Lunacharsky and his enlightened view-point. They saw a traitor, actual or potential, in every intelligent non-partisan and treated him accordingly.

The magnificent spirit I had so often found in the hated and harassed elements was also manifested by Miss Korolenko and her colleagues. They asked nothing for themselves, but they begged me to intercede with Lunacharsky in behalf of their work and the children in their charge. The handicraft of the young folks of the society consisted of toys made from waste paper, rags, straw, and even from discarded shoes. It presented a unique collection of animals, dolls, and fanciful beings, specimens of which the women pressed upon us " for the children in America." I assured my hostesses that they would be much more appreciated by my toy-starved young friends in Petrograd.

Vladimir Korolenko was convalescing after a severe illness and not accessible to visitors. His daughter promised, however, to see her father about us and invited us to come to the home of her parents the next day.

In the evening I called on Mme X, chairman of the Political Red Cross. In the past the organization had been aiding the political victims of the Romanovs. I was interested to learn what they were being permitted to do by the new régime. Mme X was a beautiful woman with snowy white hair and large, tender blue eyes. She was the best type of the old Russian idealist, rarely met with nowadays. Warmth, kindliness, and utmost hospitality had been their characteristics, and my hostess had lost none of these qualities, although she had lived through every phase of misery since 1914. It was a hot evening and we sat out on the little balcony, with the puffing *samovar* between us. The bright moon and the glowing coal in the large tea-urn lent romance to the scene. But our conversation was of Russian reality, of the unfortunates who had filled the Tsar's dungeons and places of exile. The activities of her group were more limited now, the old lady informed me. They were becoming more circumscribed all the time and harassed by many difficulties for reasons that had not existed in the past. The dictatorship and the persecution of everyone even remotely suspected of disagreement with the régime robbed the politicals of their former ethical status and the high regard they had enjoyed in all but the most reactionary circles. Now they were denounced as bandits, counter-revolutionists, and enemies of the people. The public at large, deprived of any means of verifying the terrible accusations, believed the Bolshevik charges. The new régime had thus gone further than the old in branding the flower of Russia with the mark of Cain and alienating from them popular esteem. " I consider it the blackest crime of the Bolsheviki, the most reprehensible even from their own view-point of so-called revolutionary necessity," Mme X said bitterly. The Red Cross was now compelled to operate on two fronts, she continued; to aid the politicals materially and save them from death by starvation, and to dispel the cruel lies spread against them. It was a most difficult task, for it was well-nigh impossible to reach the public mind, because the least attempt to enlighten the people on the subject was considered counter-revolutionary and would result in the entire suppression of the organization and the arrest of everyone connected with it. Another obstacle lay in the general disorganization of the railroads and other means of communication, which made it very hard to visit the imprisoned politicals or to keep in touch with them. The most vital thing, even more important than food, was denied the idealists of Bolshevik Russia — encouragement and the inspiration of their comrades at large. That was the hardest for them to bear, my hostess concluded.

I related to her my great shock on first learning of the Jesuitical methods resorted to by the Bolsheviki to slay their opponents, and my long struggle against crediting such things. I told her of my interview with Lenin and his contention that only bandits and counterrevolutionists were in prison. It seemed unbelievable that a man of his mental stature should stoop to such despicable falsehoods to justify his methods. Mme X shook her head. It was apparent, she said, that I was not conversant with Lenin's habitual ways. In his early writings I would find that he had for years advocated and defended such methods of attack against his political opponents, methods to "cause them to be loathed and hated as the vilest of creatures." He had used such tactics when his victims could defend themselves; why should he now not add insult to injury when he had the whole of Russia as his forum? "Yes, and the rest of the radical world," I added, "for in Lenin it sees the revolutionary Messiah. I had believed him that myself, as did also my comrade Alexander Berkman. We had been among the earliest crusaders in America in his behalf. Even now we find it bitter hard to free ourselves from the Bolshevik myth and its principal spook."

It was growing late and I was anxious to hear from the old lady about Korolenko. I knew that like Tolstoy he had for decades been a great moral force in Russia. I wondered what influence he had been able to exert since 1917. I had been informed that Mme X was Korolenko's sister-in-law and very close to the great writer. I begged her to tell me about him.

The prophet of Yasnaya Polyana, she said, had fortunately been spared the spectacle of the old autocracy surviving the Revolution in a new dress. He was saved the agony of writing letters of protest to the new Tsar. Not so her brother-in-law. Though almost seventy and in poor health, Vladimir Korolenko had to spend most of his time in the Cheka pleading for some innocent life or penning entreating letters to Lenin, Lunacharsky, and Maxim Gorki to put a stop to the wholesale executions. Maxim Gorki, she continued, had proved a great disappointment. No, Maxim found the company of Lenin a safer haven, and the Kremlin a pleasanter abode, than exile in a desolate village. Maxim Gorki had not even the courage, she added, to live up to the honoured tradition among Russian authors of encouraging and helping members of the profession and standing by them in distress.

My own experience with Maxim Gorki came to my mind. I recalled his lame apology for Bolshevik autocracy. Still I was not willing to impute ulterior motives to the man I had once so admired. After all, Gorki had done some good, I pleaded in his behalf. He had helped to organize the Dom Utchonikh for the benefit of old scientists and authors, and he had also protested against the system of taking hostages and had raised his voice against the Government monopoly of everything published in Russia. Mme X readily admitted where credit was due to Gorki. But she thought it insignificant for a man of Gorki's former wide and sympathizing humanity. What little good he had done was merely to salve his conscience; it was not prompted by a sense of justice and decency. Still I stressed the point that Maxim Gorki might really believe in the righteousness of Lenin's policies. He was a poet, not a politician; it was probably the glamour about Lenin's name that made him worship. I preferred to think so rather than to believe Gorki capable of selling his birthright for a mess of pottage.

I expressed my surprise that Korolenko was still permitted to be at large, in view of his repeated offences of *lèse-majesté*. Mme X did not consider it strange. Lenin was a very clever man, she explained. He knew his trump cards: Peter Kropotkin, Vera Figner, Vladimir Korolenko were names to reckon with. Lenin realized that if he could point to them as remaining at liberty, he could effectively disprove the charge that only the gun and the gag were applied under his dictatorship. The world actually swallowed that bait. It remained silent while the Calvary of the real idealists was going on. " The tsarist prisons are reaping a rich harvest, and shooting is being kept up as a matter of course," Mme X concluded.

I felt too stifled to return to the narrow quarters of my compartment. It was past two in the morning, the break of day already near. I suggested to the friend who accompanied me that we take a walk. The air outside was balmy, the streets deserted. Poltava was soothing in her sleeping peace. Silently we walked on, each absorbed in the impressions of the evening. I was trying to see beyond the immediate and reaching upward to a point that might hold out the hope of a renaissance in the life of Russia. Approaching steps, their thud fall-

ing regularly on the granite walk, startled me. A detachment of soldiers marched by, rifles slung over their shoulders, a group of huddled
people in their midst. "And shooting is being kept up as a matter of
course," flitted through my mind.

In the morning, still in the throes of the preceding evening, I went,
together with Henry Alsberg, to the Korolenko home. It was a little
green gem, entirely hidden from view by trees and vines — an enchanting place, with its old native furniture, ornate copper, brass, and
colourful Ukrainian peasant handiwork.

Vladimir Korolenko, white of hair and beard, in girdled peasant
tunic, suggested amid the surroundings of his home a world removed
by centuries. But the illusion was quickly dispelled the moment he
began to speak. He was intensely alive and deeply interested in everything we could tell him of America, of which he seemed very fond.
He knew a great many persons there, he said; they had always responded generously to every appeal of the Russian people and he
admired the country for its broad democracy. We assured him that
he would find very little of it left now except in some small circles that
were too timid and politically confused to exert any influence. We
were much more interested, however, to hear Korolenko on Russia
and we gently led the conversation into that channel. The subject was
apparently an open wound with the old writer and I soon regretted
having dug into it. He relieved my sense of guilt somewhat by remarking that he would give me copies of two letters he had written
to Lunacharsky, treating the very problems on which we had come to
interview him. They were the first of a series of six that Lunacharsky
had asked him to write and which would contain the frank expression
of his attitude towards the dictatorship. "The letters may never see
the light of day," he commented, "but your museum shall have all
of them when they have been written." Alsberg inquired whether
Korolenko could be quoted in America, and our host replied that he
had no objections, because the time for silence had long passed. He
was aware of the danger still facing Russia, he said, but "great as it
may be, it is not anything nearly so grave as the inner menace threatening the Revolution." It was the Bolshevik claim that every form
of terror, including wholesale execution and the taking of hostages,
is justifiable as a revolutionary necessity. To Korolenko it was the
worst travesty on the basic idea of revolution and on all ethical
values.

"It has always been my conception," he added, "that revolution means the highest expression of humanity and justice. The dictatorship has denuded it of both. At home the Communist State daily divests the Revolution of its essence, substituting for it deeds that far exceed in arbitrariness and barbarity those of the Tsar. His *gendarmes,* for instance, had the authority to arrest me. The Communist Cheka has the power to shoot me, as well. At the same time the Bolsheviki have the temerity to proclaim the world revolution. In reality their experiment upon Russia must retard social changes abroad for a long period. What better excuse needs the European *bourgeoisie* for its reactionary methods than the ferocious dictatorship in Russia?"

Mme Korolenko had cautioned us that her husband was yet far from recovered and should avoid much strain. But once the old man had started on Russia, it was difficult for him to stop. He seemed considerably spent and we dared not prolong our stay. I could not leave, however, without telling him that he had given new impetus to my revolutionary faith. His own fine view of the meaning and purpose of the Revolution had strengthened mine, which eight months in Soviet Russia had almost destroyed. I could never be sufficiently grateful to him for it.

I should have loved to remain awhile longer in beautiful Poltava and to spend some more time with the wonderful spirits I met there. But our expedition had finished its labours and we had to proceed. Our next destination was to be Kiev, but the contrariness of Russian engines compelled us to stop at Fastov.

We did not regret the delay. We had heard and read of ghastly anti-Jewish pogroms, but we had never before come face to face with their ravages. On our way to the town we met neither human being nor beast until we reached the market square. A dozen stands displayed a miserable assortment of cabbages, potatoes, herring, and cereals. Their owners were mostly women. Instead of showing some animation at the sudden avalanche of so many customers, they hurriedly pulled their handkerchiefs over their foreheads and shrank back in fright. But their eyes remained riveted in terror on the men with us, consisting of Sasha, Henry, and our young Communist collaborator. We were completely nonplussed. Being the best-versed in Yiddish, I addressed an old Jewess near by. Except for our woman companion, I told her, we were the children of *Yehudim,* and we had come from America. Would she not tell me why the women acted so strangely? She pointed to the men. " Send them away," she begged.

The men withdrew. I remained with our secretary, Shakol, and the women approached nearer. Soon the whole group surrounded us, each competing with the rest in their eagerness to tell us the story of their *tsores* (troubles).

The news of the arrival of Americans spread quickly, and presently the whole village was on its feet. Men came running from the synagogue, women and children hurried towards us to behold the strangers from afar. We must come to the house of prayer, a man declared, to hear the story of the Fastov *goles* (servitude). The march began, and on the way we were met by the rabbi, the *khasin* (singer) and the *magid* (preacher) as honoured guests. Everybody was fearfully excited, gesticulating and talking, most of the women laughing and crying, as if Messiah had indeed come at last.

Our three male companions joined us in the synagogue. The whole assembly tried to tell us the tragic story of their town, all at once. We suggested that they choose a committee of three, each in his turn to relate to us what had happened. In that way we were able to get a coherent account of one of the worst pogroms that had taken place in the Ukraine. Fastov had repeatedly been the scene of Jewish massacres, perpetrated by the hordes of every White general who had invaded the district. They had suffered from Denikin, from Petlura and the other enemy forces. But the pogrom organized in 1919 by Denikin had been the most fiendish one. It had lasted a whole week and had taken the lives of four thousand persons outright and of several thousand more that had perished while escaping to Kiev. But death had not been the worst infliction, the rabbi said in a broken voice. Far more harrowing had been the violation of the women, regardless of age, the young among them repeatedly and in the presence of their male kin, whom the soldiers held pinioned. Old Jews were trapped in the synagogue, tortured, and killed, while their sons were driven to the market square to meet similar fates.

The old rabbi being too shaken to continue, the narrative was taken up by another of the committee. Fastov had been, he said, one of the most prosperous cities in the south. When the Denikin hordes tired of their blood orgy, they pilfered every home, demolished the things they could not carry away, and set the houses on fire. The larger part of the town was destroyed. The survivors, a mere handful, most of them old women and small children, were now doomed to slow extinction unless help quickly came from somewhere. God had heard their prayers and had sent us at the moment when they had almost despaired of the Jewish world's learning of their great calamity. "*Borukh Adonai!*" he cried solemnly, "blessed be Thy name." And everyone repeated after him: "*Borukh Adonai!*"

Their religious fervour was all these people had rescued from their hideous experiences, and, in spite of all certainty that there was no Jehovah to hear them, I was strangely stirred by the tragic scene in the poverty-stricken synagogue in outraged and devastated Fastov. The Jews of America were more likely to answer their prayers, and, alas, neither Sasha nor I had access to them. All we could do was to write about the dreadful pogroms. Excepting the anarchist press, however, we had no assurance that any paper would publish our account. It would have been too cruel to tell these people that in America we were considered *Ahasverus*. We could make known their great tragedy only to the radical labour world and to our own comrades. But there was Henry. He could do a great deal for these unfortunates, and I was sure he would. Our fellow traveller had been with us six weeks and he had witnessed some heart-rending scenes. Yet I had never seen him so affected as in Fastov. Not that he did not feel deeply in a universal sense. Henry was a bundle of emotions, though his male pride would have stoutly denied such an imputation from a mere woman. Nevertheless it was true that his kind heart ached more when Jews were being persecuted, which in view of the fearful Denikin atrocities was not at all surprising. The people gathered in the synagogue no doubt sensed that in him Heaven had sent them the right messenger. They threw themselves upon him with avidity and would not let him go.

We were besieged by the inhabitants with letters and messages for their kin in America. Truly pathetic were the women who brought their little scribbles to us to be forwarded to a son, a daughter, a brother, or an uncle. They were somewhere "in Amerike." We asked the addresses or at least the names of the places where their relatives lived. They had none. Some thought just the name of their loved ones would be enough. They wept bitterly when informed that "Amerike" was somewhat larger than Fastov. We should take their letters anyhow, they implored; maybe they would be delivered somehow. We had not the courage to refuse. We could send them through our people to the Yiddish press in the States, Sasha suggested. No more solemn blessings were ever bestowed on anyone than were showered upon us at our departure.

In the whole gruesome picture of Fastov two redeeming features stood out. The Gentiles of the town had had no share in the massacres. And no pogroms had taken place since the Bolshevik forces had entered the district. Our informants admitted that the Red soldiers were not free from anti-Semitism, but the establishment of Soviet authority in Fastov had lifted the dread of new massacres, and the villagers had been praying for Lenin ever since. " Why only for Lenin? " we asked; " why not also for Trotsky and Zinoviev? " " Well, you see, Trotsky and Zinoviev are *Yehudim*," an old Jew explained with Talmudic intonation; " do they deserve praise for helping their own? But Lenin is a *goi* (Gentile). So you can understand why we bless him." We too felt grateful that the *goi* had at least one saving grace in his régime.

One Gentile was pointed out to us as a physician who had done heroic rescue work during the Denikin pogrom. Repeatedly he had braved grave danger to save Jewish lives. The community fairly worshipped him and gave us numerous instances of his noble valour. We invited the doctor to our car to share with us our evening meal. He had kept a diary of the pogroms in Fastov and he held our attention tense while reading from it till the dawn of morning.

The nightmare of travel we had experienced between Kharkov and Fastov was again repeated during the six days that it required to reach Kiev. It left us bruised and battered and made us realize anew the incredible persistency of the Slav in overcoming the greatest hardships.

The masses of desperate human beings fighting at every station to get on the train were increased by the village poor, the destitute and ragged children presenting the most awful sight. Of various ages and covered with filthy tatters, they besieged us with hungry eyes and pleading voices for a piece of bread. These innocent victims of war, strife, and inhumanity were to me always the most heart-breaking sight in the fearful panorama of our journey.

The crowds at the stations, Sasha and Henry reported, were as nothing compared with the swarms at the village markets. There they were thick as ants and as determined in their attacks. They were the torment of hucksters and of the militiamen ordered to drive them off the streets. No sooner were the markets cleared of them than they would flock back, apparently in even larger numbers. " Drive them away — what solution is that? " I remarked to Henry. " With the blockade starving Russia, there seems no other way," he replied. I wished I could still believe that it was only the blockade and not general inefficiency and the bureaucratic Frankenstein monster which were mainly responsible for the situation. No governmental machinery can cope with great social issues, I said to Henry. Even the United States, with its vast resources and powerful organization, had to enlist the co-operation of the social forces in the war. Trained and efficient men and women outside the Government limits won the World War for Woodrow Wilson rather than his generals. The dictatorship would have none of the social elements to help, and their energy and abilities were compelled to lie fallow. Thousands of Russia's public-spirited men and women were eager to render service to their country, but were refused participation because they could not swallow the twenty-one points of the Third International. How, then, could one hope that the Communist State would ever succeed in solving difficult social problems?

Henry insisted that my impatience with the Bolshevik régime was due to my belief that a revolution *à la Bakunin* would have brought more constructive results, if not immediate anarchism. Yet as a matter of fact the Russian Revolution had been *à la Bakunin,* but it had since been transformed *à la Karl Marx.* That seemed to be the real trouble. I had not been naïve enough to expect anarchism to rise phœnix-like from the ashes of the old. But I did hope that the masses, who had made the Revolution, would also have the chance to direct its course. Henry did not believe that the Russian people would have been capable of accomplishing constructive work even if the dictatorship had not monopolized all power. He was certain, however, that the Bolsheviki would do better, once the blockade had been lifted and the military fronts liquidated. How I wished I could share his hope! But I could not see the slightest sign of the reins being loosened. On the contrary, there was an unmistakable tightening up until all the life was pressed out of the original Revolution.

We never got much further in our discussions. Still it was a great relief to talk these matters over with Henry. One could never discuss them with the Russians in our party, least of all with our secretary, Shakol. She was as aware of conditions as I, but she could not bear the least derogatory remark regarding Russia or the régime. I loved her, though her Slav tendency to mope was very trying at times.

Our need for a thorough scrub and a real night's rest was compelling. Not less so was our eager anticipation of the rich material, particularly counter-revolutionary data, to be found in Kiev. The city on the Dnieper had been the pivot of all the battles in the Ukraine between the Red and the White forces. Only recently the Poles had invaded Kiev.

While still in Petrograd, Sasha and I had shared the indignation of the Soviet press over the vandalism of the Polish occupation. They had demolished all the art treasures of the city, Lunacharsky and Chicherin declared. The ancient cathedrals, the Sophia and the Vladimir, famous for their architectural beauty, had been wrecked. We feared that on our arrival we should find the greater part of the old Russ capital in ruins. But we had failed to take into account the Soviet methods of propaganda, of turning a mole-hill into a mountain. The Poles may have indeed intended much damage to Kiev, but they had evidently not succeeded in accomplishing their purpose. Several small bridges and some railroad tracks were all that had been destroyed. No other ruins were awaiting our arrival. On the other hand, we were assured that the enemy had left behind a wealth of material, but to get possession of it proved a most difficult task. The native Communists fairly oozed antagonism to Moscow, disdainfully ignoring our credentials from " the centre." They evidently had no love for any of their northern comrades, with the exception of Lenin, who seemed everybody's patron saint. They bristled at the very mention of Zinoviev, and apparently they thought us his personal emissaries come to spy on them. " Who is Zinoviev, indeed? " they cried bitterly; " who is he to order us to hand over our valuable historical material? " Safe in the luxurious Kremlin and Smolny, they said, it was easy for Zinoviev to issue commands. But they, the people of the Ukraine, and particularly of Kiev, were living in constant danger. Their *Ispolkom* (Executive Committee) was in hourly dread of a new invasion. Could they bother about Zinoviev's orders? They had more important things to look after. The life of the city had to be organized and they could waste no time on our mission.

Dispirited, our secretary returned from her interview with *Tovarishtch* Vetoshkin, chairman of the all-powerful *Ispolkom*. She was almost in tears. The official was adamant and absolutely refused to aid our efforts. It were better to continue our journey without further loss of time. In spite of her pessimism we decided to try our American sesame. It had worked in seemingly hopeless situations before.

Why not in Kiev? We had a real, honest-to-goodness native American son with us, and a full-fledged correspondent at that. The authorities would not be able to withstand his importance, we said. Henry grinned assent. With a mischievous twinkle in his fine eyes he declared that as his interpreter I had already induced people to say more than he had intended to ask them and that I had succeeded in making them think they would be serving posterity by helping the Museum of the Revolution. Between the two of us he was sure we should succeed in inducing the Ukrainians to co-operate with our mission.

Henry's press card worked like a charm. Not only did Vetoshkin come out in person to greet us, but we were invited into his sanctum and treated to a lengthy and interesting account of Petlura, Denikin, and other adventurers who had been driven out of the Ukraine by Red forces. When we emerged from Vetoshkin's office, we were equipped with an order to the housing-department for two rooms and with instructions to his secretary to give us all the assistance possible. I also received from Vetoshkin an order on the Party Commissary for rations, which I accepted for the Russian members of our group, but declined for Sasha and myself. The markets were well stocked with provisions, and trading was not interfered with, and we preferred to pay our way, I informed the chairman.

The return of the Bolsheviki to the city was but recent and we soon realized that the Soviet departments had almost no material that could serve our purpose. There was too much confusion in the new Government to keep any records. No one knew what anybody else was doing, and orders were given and countermanded with no rhyme or reason.

The Whites had also left very little valuable material. Fourteen different times Kiev had changed hands, and only in one thing the various governments had agreed and co-operated — in pogroms against the Jews.

In the Jewish hospital, now known as the Soviet Clinic, we came upon the victims of the Denikin outrages in Fastov. Though considerable time had elapsed since the last pogrom in that city, many of the women and girls were still very ill, some of them crippled for life as a result of their injuries. The most fearful cases were those of children suffering from the shock of having been forced to witness the torture and violent death of their parents. From Dr. Mandelstamm, the surgeon of the institution, we learned of his gruesome experiences during the pogroms, whose battle-field had been the hospital. He also spoke of the Denikin fury as the worst of all the attacks. Not a patient would have been left alive, he related, nor the building intact, but for the heroic resistance of his staff, most of whom were Gentiles. Bravely they had remained at their posts, rescuing many of their charges. " Fortunately the Bolsheviki came back, bringing with them security from further atrocities," he said.

One of the startling finds I made in Kiev consisted of copies of *Mother Earth*. They were given to me by a man we had called to see in reference to data on pogroms. He had shown little interest in our mission, but the next day he came to our car with a bundle of the magazine I had published in the States. Why had I not explained who Berkman and I were, he chided me; he would not have given us such an indifferent reception. He had received the copies only the previous evening from a friend whom he had told about the visit of " the Americans." Only then he learned whom the Jewish colony of his city had in their midst. How did the magazine get to Kiev, I wondered; I was sure it had never been sent to Russia. Our caller explained that his friend Zaslavsky had received some copies from his brother in America. "Zaslavsky?" I inquired; "not our old comrade of Brooklyn, New York?" "The very same," the man replied. Now that he knew of our identity, he declared, we must come to his house for tea, and he would also invite the local Jewish intelligentsia to meet us. They would never forgive him when they learned that we had been in Kiev and they were not apprised of our presence. Before leaving, the man informed me that he was Latzke, former Minister for Jewish Affairs in the Rada (Ukrainian National Assembly).

In the Russian cataclysm my former life in America had receded into pale memory, becoming a dream bereft of living fibre and I myself a mere shadow without firm hold, all my values turned to vapour. The sudden appearance of the *Mother Earth* copies revived the poignancy of my aimless and useless existence. Yearning, sickening yearning, possessed me, chilling the very marrow of my being. I was pulled back to reality by the arrival of Sonya Avrutskaya, a very sympathetic local comrade. With her was a stranger, a young woman in peasant costume, who was introduced to me as Gallina, the wife of Nestor Makhno. I forgot my distress at the peril that threatened her, Sonya, and all of us. I knew that the Bolsheviki had set a price on Makhno's head, dead or alive. They had already killed his brother and several members of his wife's family in vengeance for their failure to capture Makhno. Anyone even distantly suspected of having any relationship with him was in imminent jeopardy of his life. Discovery would mean certain death for Gallina. How could she risk coming to our place, well known to the authorities as it was and open to every caller, including Bolsheviki? She had faced danger too often to care, Gallina replied. The purpose of her visit was too important to be entrusted to anyone else. She was bringing a message from Nestor to Sasha and me, asking us to consent to a *coup* he was planning. He was not far from Kiev, with a detachment of his forces. His plan was to hold up our train on its journey south, to take us prisoners, as it were. The rest of our expedition could proceed on its way. He wanted to explain to us his position and aims and he would give us safe conduct back to Soviet territory. Such a manœuvre would clear us of suspicion of deliberate dealing with him. It was a desperate scheme, he was aware, but so was also his situation. Bolshevik lies and denunciations had blackened him and the revolutionary integrity of his *povstantsy* army and misrepresented his motives as an anarchist and internationalist. We were his only opportunity to give his side of the situation to the proletarian world outside Russia, to explain that he was neither bandit nor *pogromshtchik,* that he had in fact punished with his own hands individual *povstantsy* guilty of offences against the Jews. He was with the Revolution to the last breath and he hoped and urged that we would render him this vital and solidaric service, to let him talk to us and present his aims. Would we consent to his plan?

It was an ingenious scheme, recklessly daring, its adventurous quality enhanced by the beauty and youth of Makhno's messenger. Presently Sasha and Henry arrived and we were all held spellbound by the passionate pleading of Gallina. Sasha's conspiratory imagination caught fire and he was almost ready to consent. I also felt strongly tempted to accept. But there were others to consider, our companions of the expedition. We could not lead them blindly into something that was undoubtedly fraught with grave consequences. There was also something else that acted as a restraining influence. I had not yet been able to cut the last threads that bound me to the Bolsheviki as a revolutionary body. I felt I could not be guilty of deliberate deception towards those whom I was still trying to exonerate emotionally, though intellectually I could not longer accept them.

In the entire city there was no hiding-place for Makhno's wife. My room offered scant security, but it was her only cover for the night. Tense and moving were the hours spent with Gallina. We sat in darkness, except for the pale moonlight that lit up now and then her lovely face. She seemed completely oblivious of the danger of her presence in my quarters. She was vital, and hungry for information about the life and work of her sisters abroad, particularly in America. What were the women doing there, she questioned, and what have they accomplished in independence and recognition? What was the relationship of the sexes, woman's right to the child and to birth-control? Amazing was the thirst for knowledge and information in a girl born and bred in primitive surroundings. Her passionate eagerness was infectious and revived my own mainsprings for a while. The break of morning compelled us to part. Gallina walked out into the dawning day with brave and sure gait. I stood behind the portières, watching her receding figure.

After Gallina's visit I no longer felt at ease in accepting aid even for our official mission. Not that I was conscious of any breach of confidence so far as the Bolsheviki were concerned. Makhno's wife was in my estimation no counter-revolutionist; and even if I had thought her one, I should not have turned her over to certain death at the hands of the Cheka. Just the same, I realized that I had no business with the *Revkom* and I decided not to visit it any more.

The arrival of Angelica in Kiev brought a new interest. She came as the guide of the Italian and French Mission. Her greeting when I sought her out was so full of tenderness and love that the local Bolsheviki began to consider me as one of their very own. In addition dear Angelica had felt moved to disclose to Vetoshkin our American past and he reproached us for coming to him merely as members of the museum expedition. We had been nearly two weeks in the city and we had not even hinted at our real identity, he complained. He begged us to give up our quarters and become the guests of the Soviet house.

Alexandra Shakol had once told me that she would forgo half her life to wake up a Communist, so as to give herself unreservedly to the party's demands and service. Now I understood what she had meant. I felt that I would also give anything to be able to take Vetoshkin's hand and say: " I am with you. I see your cause with your eyes and I will serve with the same blind faith as you and your sincere comrades." Alas, there was no such short and easy way out of the mental anguish for those who seek for life beyond dogma and creed.

We did not move to the Soviet house and we assured Vetoshkin that we had no need of anything. We accepted, however, Angelica's invitation to the banquet arranged in honour of the Italian and French Mission that she was chaperoning. We had been south for over two months, completely cut off from the Western world as well as from the rest of Russia. Angelica was the first friend from the north we had met since our departure. Unfortunately she could tell us but little, as she herself had been constantly on the road. But she brought us the disturbing news of the arrest of Albert Boni. Suspected as a counter-revolutionary, she told us. " Absurd ! " I laughed. Albert was just a publisher and very far from rebelling against any established institution, whether revolutionary or otherwise. I hastened to call Sasha and Henry. They were much amused to hear that Boni was considered dangerous to the Soviet Government. We knew, however, that landing in the Cheka was no joking matter and we begged Angelica to send a telegram to Lenin, signed by us, to which she readily assented.

On the way to the banquet Sasha fell into a Cheka *oblava* that had encircled the entire street. Every pedestrian was halted and searched for documents. Though Sasha's were in perfect order, the officer held on to him as for dear life, and no explanations would induce the Chekist to permit him to go his way. Fortunately a heated argument was started by a near-by group in the same predicament. No Russian could escape the temptation to join in. The Chekist forgot for a moment his captive, and without much ceremony Sasha left.

The former Commercial Club and its elaborate rooms and gardens were brightly illuminated for the festive occasion and decorated with fresh-cut flowers. The wine and fruit on the tables gave little indication of the storms that had swept the city. It might still have been the good old time when stout ladies tightly laced, their necks and arms bedecked with jewels, sauntered about the place, and no less stodgy gentlemen in swallow-tails feasted in these halls. The gold and plush of the club made an incongruous background for the pale-faced proletarians in shoddy clothes. Of the hundred and fifty or more persons that sat down to the gala affair Angelica was probably the only Communist to suffer from the vulgar display. Even the presence of her beloved Italian comrades could give her little comfort. Serrati to her right and the French Communist Sadoul on her left kept her engaged in conversation. But her pained and roaming eyes expressed better than words how utterly out of place she felt and how out of touch with the entire farce in honour of Lenin, Trotsky, Zinoviev, the Red Army,

the Third International, and the world revolution. Intoxicating words
to those that had no ear for jarring dissonances. They made her wince
as they did me, though our leitmotifs were in vastly different keys.

Two Anarcho-Syndicalists whom we discovered among the French
delegates induced us to remain at the affair till the end. They were to
leave with the mission the same night and they invited us to accompany them to the station so that we could have a talk. They had been
impressed by much that had been shown them, they told us, but they
had also made disturbing observations. They had collected information and data about the political machine that convinced them that
the proletariat had very little share in the actual dictatorship. They
meant to use the material in their report to the syndicates on their
return to France. They looked at us in amazement when we warned
them to be careful about taking out their data. They might not be
permitted to do so, we informed them. " Preposterous! We are not
Russians, nor bound by the discipline of the Communist Party," they
exclaimed. They were Frenchmen, representatives of large syndicalist
organizations. Who would dare molest them? " The Cheka, of
course," we explained. We were unduly anxious, they thought.

The evening arranged for us at Latzke's had none of the affluence
of the mission banquet, though our hosts had spread the best they
could afford. Its interest to us was not the repast, however, but the
unrestrained good will and spirit that prevailed. Everyone felt free
to express himself, and there was no lack in the variegation of opinion
and sentiment. Every profession of the Yiddish intelligentsia was
represented. All came to meet the American visitors, to exchange
with them their views, hopes, and fears. None was a Communist, yet
almost every one of them was an ardent defender of the régime, for
racial reasons. Like Dr. Mandelstamm, who was also present, they
frankly admitted that their main concern was the safety of the Jew.
The Bolsheviki were preventing pogroms and therefore the Jews
should support the Soviet Government, they argued. I inquired
whether they were content with or could believe in permanent protection of their people in an atmosphere of general terror and insecurity. They agreed that the dictatorship was fatal to individual
initiative and effort. But since they had no choice, it was gratifying
to know that at least the Jews as a race had been freed from the
discrimination suffered for centuries. Their feeling was the result
of fear, understandable enough in surroundings surcharged with anti-

Semitism, as the Ukraine was. But as a criterion for releasing social energies it was worse than useless. To me that was the prime consideration. I could not translate the October upheaval into terms of Jew or Gentile, but only into values accruing to all of humanity, or at least to all the people in Russia.

The younger element at our gathering had a different view-point. They did not deny the Bolsheviki full credit for stopping pogroms, but they held that the Soviet régime itself was fertile soil for the poisonous weed of Jew-hatred. Under the tsarist autocracy the pest had been limited to the most reactionary elements. Now all sections of the country were infected by it. The peasant, the worker, and the intelligentsia all saw in Jews Communists and commissars responsible for punitive expeditions, forcible food-collection, militarization, and intimidation. Bolshevism was an impetus to Jew-baiting, they insisted, rather than a safety-valve against it.

Sasha stressed the point that both sides were making the mistake of denouncing the abuses of power, while the evil was in the thing itself. It was the Communist State and dictatorship that had subordinated the aims of the Revolution to those of the ruling party. The purpose of October was to release the creative energies of Russia for the free upbuilding of a new life. The object of the dictatorship was to organize a formidable political machine as the absolute master. That was the source of the disintegrating forces at work in the country. Increased anti-Semitism, return to the churches, anti-revolutionary feeling on the part of the peasantry and the workers, the cynicism of the young generation, and similar manifestations were the direct result of the failure of the Bolsheviki to keep the solemn promises made by them during the October days.

Some of those present favoured our view-point, others fought it determinedly, but without rancour or ill feeling, and therein lay the charm of the gathering at the home of Latzke.

Sasha gathered a wealth of material from the Mensheviki he had met. They had been a potent educational and social force during the first two years of the Revolution in the south, but they had since been liquidated by the Bolsheviki and the Social Democratic unions hitched to the Communist wagon. The Mensheviki had succeeded in rescuing valuable data bearing on the history of Ukrainian labour and of their party and they turned them over to Sasha, together with a lot of personal notes and diaries. He had also somehow ferreted out a counter-revolutionary archive in a desk drawer of the Labour Soviet head-quarters. It consisted of a strange conglomeration of police records, minutes of the Rada sessions, commercial statistics, and similar matter. In that helter-skelter Sasha had also chanced upon the first *Universal* issued by Petlura as dictator of the Ukraine, containing his official declaration of principles of the Southern National Democracy. A most important find was also made by our secretary, consisting of reams of Denikin material stored in the public library of the city and apparently forgotten. The librarian, a rabid nationalist, remained deaf to the pleas of Shakol. But he became all attention when faced with the argument that he could not afford the ridicule and disgrace if it should become known in America that he had preferred to leave the valuable documents to become the prey of rats in his cellar rather than have them preserved for future generations by the Museum of the Revolution.

Our last day in Kiev was a Sunday and we took the opportunity to journey along the beautiful Dnieper. Excursion boats enlivened the view, and in the distance lay the magnificent cathedrals and churches. At a point farther on along the river we came upon an old village with an ancient monastery. The hospitable nuns fed us on bread and honey from their own hives. Between their prayers and labours they had remained untouched by the events in their country and totally ignorant of all that had happened. Steeped in centuries of superstition, they could not realize the meaning of the new life struggling all about them to be born. Their saving grace was the work they were doing, raising vegetables, cultivating bees, teaching the village children to sew and mend, and their kindliness to strangers. Not so their brother monks in the Sophia and the Vladimir cathedrals. They continued to thrive on the credulity of their dupes, still very numerous, as we were assured. The solemn humbugs kept busy showing people through the caves and enlarging on the miracles performed by the saints whose dried bones were exposed to view. A strange sight, indeed, in revolutionary Russia!

On the way to Odessa we lost our good friend Henry Alsberg. Inadvertently he had caused his own arrest. Henry had joined the expedition without having secured the consent of the Moscow Cheka and he could have continued till the end of our journey without the eagle eye of the Soviet being able to discover his whereabouts. But he had added his signature to the telegram we had sent to Lenin in behalf of the arrested Albert Boni. As a result the All-Russian Cheka in the capital had at once sent orders to apprehend the criminal who had dared absent himself without its permission. Things moving at a snail's pace in Russia, the command failed to reach Kiev while we were there. It was wired to every station along our route and overtook us in Zhmerinka.

All our protests failed to save Henry. The Cheka in charge declared that Alsberg's papers were in perfect order and his credentials from Chicherin and Zinoviev valid, but he lacked permission from the Moscow Cheka, and they had strict orders to arrest him. We could not permit Henry to go alone, and we proposed that Sasha or I accompany him to Moscow. But Henry would not hear of it. He knew enough Russian, he joked, to keep his escorts in good humour. Why, he could say *pozhaluysta* (please), *nitchevo* (nothing), and *spassibo* (thank you), and was not that enough for all practical purposes? If need be, he could also muster up a few less polite expressions. Besides, he possessed something policemen everywhere appreciated best — *mezuma*. He had no fear and we need not be anxious about him, he assured us. Brave old Henry! One thing I insisted on, however: that he should not take his notes with him. They would be sure to get him into trouble and they would be safer with us and he without them.

We immediately dispatched telegrams to Lenin, Lunacharsky, and Zinoviev in behalf of Alsberg, but we did not feel very sanguine that they would reach their destination.

Henry had endeared himself to us by his fine spirit, joviality, and ready wit. It was with a heavy heart that we saw him leave, led away by the Chekists. The poor boy had already met with misfortune recently, having been robbed of his wallet. The loss of one's last sou is nowhere very pleasant, but in Russia it was a calamity. I did not have a chance to console my friend, because the boys missed the train and did not rejoin us until many hours later. They were bubbling over with their adventure. "But the thief!" I exclaimed; "was your money recovered?" "Fine chance to find the one among the many," Henry laughed.

Alsberg's arrest proved the beginning of a chain of adversities that pursued us for the rest of our journey. Barely out of Zhmerinka we received the news of the defeat of the Twelfth Army and the advance of the Poles on Kiev. The line was clogged with military trains on their retreat, and at the stations everything was in the wildest confusion. Our car was repeatedly attached to trains ordered south and as many times detached again to be sent in the opposite way. At last we were lucky enough to get into an echelon actually going in the direction of our next destination, the great city on the Black Sea. From there we planned to reach the Caucasus, but the movements of General Wrangel decided otherwise. His forces had just invested Alexandrovsk, a suburb of Rostov, thus shutting off the route we were to take to the Crimea. Our credentials were to expire at the end of October and we knew that months would be required to get them renewed by mail. It would be courting danger to remain south longer than our documents permitted, but, once in Odessa, we hoped to find a way out of the difficulty.

At last we reached the great city on the Black Sea, only to find that a devastating fire had laid the main telegraph office and the electric station in ashes the previous day, leaving the city in utter darkness. The holocaust was declared to be the work of White incendiaries, and the city was placed under martial law. The general nervousness was increased by the report that the Poles had taken Kiev and that Wrangel was advancing north. The public had no means of learning the truth of the situation, which only increased their trepidation.

An atmosphere of suspicion and fear dominated the Soviet institutions. All eyes were turned on us as Shakol, Sasha, and I entered the *Ispolkom*. Our credentials were carefully scrutinized and we were examined as to our identity and purpose before we were permitted to come into the august presence of the *predsedatel*. He proved a rather youngish man, obviously conscious of the importance of his position. He neither responded to our greeting nor asked us to sit down. He kept buried in the papers on his desk, then examined our documents, studying them long and carefully, till at last he seemed satisfied with them. All he could do, he told us finally, was to supply us with a pass to the other Soviet departments and with written permission to be out on the streets " after permitted hours." He could aid us no more and he was not interested in museums, anyhow. It was a sinecure for the intelligentsia, but the workers had more important things to do to defend the Revolution. Everything else was a waste of time, he declared. The man's attitude and curt manner did not augur well for our efforts. Nor did his words sound convincing as to his own integrity. Sasha thanked him, remarking that we appreciated his revolutionary zeal and that we would not impose on his good nature any longer. His sarcasm was lost, however, on the man standing rigid at his desk.

My co-workers shared my impression that it was mostly hatred of the intelligentsia that motivated the chairman of the *Ispolkom.* I had met many proletarian Communists permeated with bitterest resentment against intelligent people, but never anyone so brutally frank about it as the Odessa *predsedatel.* I could not help feeling that such zealots were more harmful to the best interests of the Revolution than armed enemies. We decided that no member of our expedition should call again at the *Ispolkom* and that we would try to accomplish in the city whatever possible by ourselves.

As we were walking down the stairs, several young people approached us. They stared at us a moment and then shouted: " Hello, Sasha! Emma! You here?" The unexpected encounter with our comrades from America was a pleasant surprise after the sight of the Bolshevik martinet. When they learned of our mission, they assured us that we could take the next train out of the city; no help was to be expected from the officials, they were certain. With the *Ispolkom* chairman in the lead, most of them were anti-centre and anti-everything that was not local Communist. They were reputed as the worst *sabotazhniky.* The chairman, a dogmatic zealot, hated anyone whose education transcended the A.B.C.'s; he would have all intellectuals shot, one of the boys declared, if he had his way. Our comrades suggested that we might be aided in our efforts for the museum by our American comrade Orodovsky, who held a responsible position in the city, and there were several others who might also assist us. The Mensheviki, too, could supply us with information and material. They had recently been cleared out of the unions; still, some of them were so influential with the rank and file that the Bolsheviki had not dared to arrest them.

Orodovsky was a first-class printer and a man of a practical turn of mind. He had managed to get into the Government publishing house and he organized it in a manner to astonish the authorities. From the confiscated and neglected materials he formed the best printing shop in the city, and great was his pride in showing us through the place. It was a model of cleanliness, order, and efficient production. His efforts were hampered at every turn; he was not considered one of their " own " and therefore he was under suspicion. He loved the work and he felt he was doing something for the Revolution, but it made him sad to foresee the inevitable approaching. " Ah, the Revolution," he sighed, " what has become of it? "

Through Orodovsky we were enabled to meet several other anarchists active in the economic department. All of them felt themselves, like Orodovsky, only temporarily tolerated and in constant danger of getting into trouble as men who were " not entirely " with the established standards of opinion. The most interesting of them was Shakhvorostov, of proletarian origin, whose whole life had been spent among the workers. He had fought for them under the autocracy and he continued to fight their battles even under the Bolsheviki. He was one of the most militant anarchists and was greatly beloved by the toilers.

On nearer acquaintance Shakhvorostov proved all we had been told of him, besides being most genuine and human. There was about him none of the rigidity and hardness of the chairman of the *Ispolkom*. He was all interest and kindliness, and his manner utterly simple.

" Sheer luck," he said, when asked how he managed to keep at liberty, " and the support of the workers," he added. They knew his sole purpose was to help them in their struggle against the constant encroachments of the Communist State. He realized that it was a losing battle, but all the same it was his duty to keep it up as long as he remained free.

Shakhvorostov substantiated the charges of widespread sabotage made by our young comrades. He added that, while most Soviet officials were simply inefficient, others were downright *sabotazhniky,* purposely hampering every effort for the welfare of the people. He related the particularly gross instance of the recent general raid on the *bourgeoisie* to apply Lenin's slogan: " Rob the robbers." Every house, shop, and shanty had been invaded and the last remnants ransacked and confiscated by the emissaries of the Cheka. It was a big haul, because the raid had taken the owners by surprise. The workers had been assured a supply of clothing and shoes, which they sorely stood in need of. When they learned of the new expropriation, they demanded that the promise be made good. " And it was," Shakhvorostov commented with a wry face; " we in the Public Economy Department received a dozen boxes of goods, but when we opened them, we found nothing but rags, old and torn things that one would not offer a beggar. The raiders had had first pick, and then they stocked the markets and the *bourgeoisie* quickly bought back everything they had lost. The scandal was so great that it could not be hushed up. The decent men in the party demanded an investigation, and the result was that some subordinates were shot. But corruption is rampant, and it is not to be eradicated by shooting."

Shakhvorostov and a comrade from the Metal Workers' Union promised to call a conference of the chairmen of the various labour bodies to acquaint them with the project of the Museum of the Revolution and interest them in our efforts. Sasha was to address the delegates and explain our mission.

A week's canvass of the Soviet institutions convinced us that, far from exaggerating, our comrades had not painted half the picture of Odessa sabotage. The local officials proved the worst shirkers we had ever come across in Russia. From the highest commissar to the last *barishnya* (young woman) typist they made it a habit of coming to work two hours late and quitting an hour earlier than closing time. Often the clerk's window would be shut right in the face of an applicant who had spent hours waiting his turn, only to be told that it was "too late" and to come tomorrow. We received almost no assistance in our work from the Soviet authorities. "Too busy, without a minute to spare," they would assure us. Yet most of them stood about smoking cigarettes and talking by the hour, while the "young ladies" were engaged in polishing their nails and rouging their lips. It was the most open and shameless official parasitism.

The Workers' and Peasants' Inspection, created specially to fight this kind of sabotage, seemed to take little interest in the purpose of their existence. Most of them were notorious speculators, and if anyone wanted tsarist or Kerensky money changed, though the practice was strictly forbidden, he would be advised to go to some well-known official to have the transaction attended to. "Ordinary citizens are shot for such speculation," a well-known Bundist [1] commented to us, "but who can touch these officials? They all work hand in glove." The corruption and autocracy of the highest Soviet circles were an open secret in the city, the man related. The Cheka in particular was nothing more than a gang of cut-throats. Extortion, bribery, and indiscriminate shooting of victims who could not pay

[1] Member of the *Bund*, Jewish Social Democratic organization.

were its common practices. It was a frequent occurrence that big speculators, sentenced to die, were set free by the Cheka for the payment of exorbitant ransom. Another practice was to notify the relatives of some prominent prisoner that he had been executed. While the family would be plunged in grief, a Cheka emissary would arrive to inform them that it had been a mistake. The condemned man was still alive, but only a certain sum, invariably very large, could save his life. Family and friends would divest themselves of everything to secure the necessary amount, and the money was always accepted. There would come no more emissaries to explain that the alleged mistake had been no mistake at all. If anyone dared show signs of protest, he would be arrested and shot for " attempting to corrupt " the Cheka. Almost every morning at dawn a truckload of those that were to die would clatter down " Cheka Street " at a furious pace towards the outskirts of the city. The doomed ones were forced to lie in the wagon face down, their hands and feet tied, armed guards standing over them. Chekists on horseback accompanied the truck, shooting at anyone who showed himself at an open window along their route. A narrow strip of red in the path of the returning truck would be all that was left to tell the story of those taken on their last ride to be *razmenyat* (destroyed).

The Bundist called again a few days later in the company of a friend whom he introduced as Dr. Landesman, a Zionist and member of a circle that included the famous Jewish poet Byalek and other public-spirited men. No doubt we knew, the doctor said, that Rosh Hashona was at hand, and he would be happy to have us celebrate the great day together in the company of his family. We confessed that we had not been aware of the approach of the Jewish New Year, but we were Jews enough to want to spend the holiday with him.

The home of the Landesman family, adjoining his former private clinic, now turned into a Soviet sanatorium, was beautifully situated. Perched on a high elevation, it was buried amidst a profusion of trees and shrubbery on one side, while the other faced the Black Sea, its waters beating against the foot of the hill. We arrived about teatime, as requested, because some of the other guests had no permits to be out after dark, Odessa being under martial law.

Dr. Landesman's clinic had enjoyed the reputation of being the best in Odessa. The Bolsheviki had confiscated it for a workers' resthome, but not a single proletarian had yet been sent there, not even the ordinary party member. Only the highest officials came, with their families. Just now the Chief of the Cheka, Deitsch, was taking the cure for a bad " nervous break-down."

" How can you bear to treat him? " I asked the doctor. " You forget that I have no choice," he replied; " besides, I am a physician and bound by professional ethics to refuse medical aid to no one." " Such *bourgeois* sentimentality! " I laughed. " With the Cheka Chief getting the benefit of it," he retorted in the same spirit.

We were sitting on the terrace, the *samovar* before us, the sky streaked with blue and amethyst, the sun a ball of fire slowly sinking into the Black Sea. The city with all its terror and suffering seemed far off, and the green bowered nook an idyll. If it would last awhile longer, I mused . . . but one lived in seconds only.

New guests arrived, Byalek among them, square-set and broad-shouldered, looking more like a prosperous merchant than a poet. A slender man with vibrantly sensitive features was introduced as a famous authority on Jewish persecution and pogroms. Sasha immediately engaged him in conversation on the subject, but in the midst of it, during the meal, he suddenly grew deathly pale and begged to be excused. Together with Doctor Landesman, I reached Sasha just in time to save him from falling in a faint. He was writhing in pain and gasping for breath, and presently he became unconscious. After a half-hour that seemed an eternity the good doctor had him somewhat restored. Packed in hot water bottles, he felt relieved, but still very weak. I told Landesman that my friend had been very ill when he left the United States, and that he had never been quite well since. The black bread in particular seemed to affect his condition, and he had showed considerable improvement since we had been able to procure white bread in the south. Our hosts insisted that we remain over-night with them in view of the possibility of Sasha's suffering another attack. " What good will it do? " the patient suddenly piped up. " The expedition must proceed to Moscow." The doctor suggested that the expedition proceed, but that Sasha and his nurse remain in Odessa until he could find out the cause of the trouble. Presently Sasha fell quietly asleep and I sat watching his thin, pale face intently. It had lost nothing of its endearment to me since we had met so many, many years ago. What would it mean to lose him, and in Russia? I shuddered at the thought, my mind unable to follow up the cruel possibility. My pal lay peacefully resting, and I went back to the dining-room, my thoughts upon my life and the struggle I had gone through together with my friend and comrade.

The dishes were about to be cleared away when Sasha suddenly entered as if nothing had happened. Did they think he would be so easily done out of his share of the meal, he demanded with a broad grin. His appetite was great, he announced, and he would not think of allowing a little indisposition to stand between him and Mme Landesman's culinary art. The company roared with laughter. The doctor, however, vetoed heavy dishes, but Sasha read him the riot act about attempting to keep an anarchist from eating what he likes. I stared at him in wonder. It was the same boy who had called for extra steak and coffee in Sachs's restaurant in New York just thirty-one years before. The patient of an hour ago not only ate heartily, but became the spirit of the company. He had found the man for whom he had been looking for a long time, he declared, and he held on to the expert investigator of pogroms for the rest of the evening.

The man proved a walking encyclopædia on the subject. He had visited seventy-two cities where pogroms had taken place, and he had collected a wealth of data. Jew-baiting during the various Ukrainian régimes, he stated, had been of more fiendish character than the worst massacres under the tsars. He admitted that no pogroms had taken place since the Bolsheviki had come to power, but he agreed with the younger element of the Kiev writers that Bolshevism had intensified anti-Semitic feeling among the masses. Some day it would break out, he was certain, in the wholesale slaughter of vengeance.

Sasha argued heatedly with him. Speculations about future possibilities aside, he emphasized, it remained a generally recognized fact that the Bolsheviki had put the lid down on pogroms. Did that not point to a sincere and determined purpose to eradicate every violent manifestation of the old disease, if not the disease itself? The investigator denied it, asserting that the Bolsheviki had deprived the Jews of their right of self-defence, forbidding them to organize for the purpose. They were even suspected of plotting against the Soviet Government because they had applied for permission to arm themselves against future attacks. Doctor Landesman added that the local authorities had refused to allow him to form a Yiddish boy-scout unit. He had intended such a group to serve not only as a defence for the Jews, but also for the protection of the citizens generally against the notorious ruffian bands from whom no one was safe in Odessa.

On closer examination the doctor found Sasha suffering from an ulcerated stomach and offered to place him in his sanatorium for treatment. " Give a doctor a chance at your insides and he is sure to find something radically wrong there," Sasha joked, waving aside the good physician's offer. The expedition had to proceed, he insisted, and he with it.

We heartily thanked the Landesmans for their generous hospitality. In social ideas we were far removed from each other, but they were among the most human and friendly beings that it had been our good fortune to meet in Russia. We had exhausted the historical possibilities of Odessa and we had to leave. The Crimea was definitely out of the question, the entire route being in the line of the Wrangel advance. We were promised connexion with a train that was to depart for Kiev within forty-eight hours. We hardly dared to expect such luck, but we clung to the hope. Meanwhile our secretary and Sasha decided to explore Nikolayevsk, where valuable archives were supposed to await rescue. Shakol had been confidentially told that a military auto truck was about to leave for that city and that the soldiers might be persuaded to permit her and Sasha to join them. It was but a slight chance, but nothing could stop those two venturesome spirits.

I remained with the other members of the expedition in Odessa to prepare our car for the journey to Kiev. In the midst of my washing and scrubbing a young woman entered. She addressed me in English and, without stopping to introduce herself, began telling me she had known me in the States. In Detroit she and her husband had attended my lectures. She had learned of our presence in the city and she had come to invite Comrade Berkman and me to her home for a cup of tea. She regretted that her husband would not be present. He was ill, in a hospital, but eager to see us. In fact, it was he who had sent her to request us to visit him, since he could not come to us, his old comrades. Berkman was away, I explained, and I had a great deal of work on hand. I could not come to her home, much as I appreciated her invitation. But I would call on the patient. " One forgets the existence of flowers in Russia," I remarked, " else I should be glad to take some to your husband." Then I asked my caller's name and the address of the hospital. " My husband is in the former Landesman sanatorium," she replied; " his name is Deitsch." I jumped from my chair as if stung by a viper. The woman also sprang to her feet. For some seconds we stood glaring at each other. At last I found my voice. Pointing to the exit, I commanded: " Go, go at once! We want none of you or your husband." " What do you mean talking to me like that? " she cried wrathfully, " you probably don't know that my husband is Chairman of the Cheka! " " I know, I know too much to want to breathe the same atmosphere with you. Go! "

Instead of leaving she brazenly sat down and began upbraiding me for hob-nobbing with Zionists and *bourgeois*. Had I also become a counter-revolutionist, she demanded, that I preferred such bandits to her husband, a comrade who had worked himself ill in the service of revolutionary Russia. Deitsch could compel me to come to him, she said, and he probably would when she told him what his teacher E.G. had become. I let her talk. My social edifice had been crumbling piece by piece. One more edge ruthlessly chopped off could hardly matter. I had not the energy to argue or the faith that I could make that woman grasp the monstrous thing that was being acclaimed as the Revolution, and the monstrosities that were serving it.

Sasha returned with our secretary twenty-four hours later than they had expected. Only when the train pulled out of Odessa did I relate to them my encounter with the wife of the all-powerful Chekist.

My companions told the story of their exciting journey to Nikolay-evsk. They had gone through harrowing experiences, visiting villages devastated by the *razviorstka* (forcible collection of produce) and by the Bolshevik punitive expeditions. The Chekists accompanying the military supply truck on which my two friends had made the trip carried on as irresponsible autocrats in a conquered country, commandeering for their own use everything they could carry, even to the last chicken from the poorest farm-house. All along the route to Nikolayevsk, Sasha said, they had met long lines of peasants, flanked by Chekist troops, carting their confiscated grain to Odessa.

On our journey back to Kiev we did as the Romans. The markets still displayed quantities of foodstuffs, but the prices had risen enormously since our previous visit. We were sure that in Petrograd they were even more prohibitive, if anything could be procured at all. We therefore felt it imperative not to return with empty hands to our friends. Of course, there was the risk of arrest as speculators. What other motive could induce anyone to expose himself to such danger and obloquy? Sympathy, the desire to share with others, the need of alleviating misery and suffering? These terms no longer existed in the dictionary of the dictatorship. We knew too well that we should be pilloried not only in Russia, but also abroad. We should have no means of making ourselves heard, in our own defence, either on the charge of speculation or on our present attitude to the Bolsheviki. Notwithstanding all this, it was impossible to forgo the opportunity of securing food for starving friends in the north. Most decisive, however, was my concern about Sasha and his health. We had not gone very far out of Odessa when he again collapsed. This time his attack lasted longer and was more serious. The black bread and the wormy cereals would have been poison to him in his condition. I knew no law of the Communist State for which I would jeopardize his life, least of all the absurd order that made it a counter-revolutionary offence to bring provisions to a hungry population. I would therefore lay in a supply of food and take the consequences, I decided. No one would accept Soviet roubles as payment. "What can we do with these scraps?" the peasants and shopkeepers would ask. "They are of no use even as wrapping-paper, and for cigarettes we already have sacks of them." Tsarist money or even that of Kerensky they would accept, although they preferred woollens, shoes, or other apparel.

Our return to Znamenka brought Henry back to our minds with vivid sadness. Not that we had forgotten him or had ceased to be concerned in his fate. But our experiences since he had been torn from us had been so sapping that they had centred all our energies. I felt his involuntary departure most because he had been such a splendid companion and a most dependable help in our cuisine. No one else in our group, outside of myself, knew how to cook. Henry was an expert in making flapjacks, in which he took great pride, and he was always ready to give me a vacation from the cooking of two meals a day for seven persons. To do so on a primus in a small compartment on a moving train during the heat of a Ukrainian July and August would have been a torture were it not for my willing assistant. Znamenka revived these memories and made me feel doubly hard the loss of our good old Henry.

Kiev had not been taken by the Poles, as had been reported, but the enemy was almost at its gates, we were informed on our arrival. The population was embittered even more than before, because it was continuously exposed to danger and hardships from whoever possessed itself of the city. They had become somewhat reconciled to the Soviet régime, and now the latter was about to evacuate. At the *Revkom* no one seemed better informed about the actual situation than the man in the street. Vetoshkin was out and his secretary would rather talk of Odessa. " *Tovarishtch* Rakovsky," he said, " recently returned with a glowing account of how well things are going there." We assured him that only in one thing had Odessa reached a high state of proficiency, and that was sabotage. " You really mean it? " he exclaimed in glee; " Rakovsky had given us the dickens that we had not succeeded as well as Odessa."

The Soviets would remain at their post, in spite of all danger, the officials declared, but they urged us to depart for Moscow before the roads became blocked. Sasha brought the good news that a train would be leaving the next day northward, and that he had arranged to have our car attached to it. We felt depressed at not being able to proceed farther on our journey to the Crimea, but that was out of the question under the circumstances. Yet Sasha would not allow us to remain long in bad humour. He was especially jolly that evening, relating anecdotes and cracking jokes and making us laugh in spite of ourselves.

Early in the morning Shakol and I were torn out of sleep by some-one knocking on our door. Still dazed, we heard Sasha's voice demanding to know why we had played such a fool hoax on him. On opening the door of our compartment I saw him standing there wrapped in his blanket. " Where are my clothes? " he asked; " you girls have hidden them from me! " The secretary roared at the sight of him and we assured him that we were quite innocent of the prank. Thereupon he returned to his compartment. Presently he announced that excepting his portfolio of documents and some Sovietsky money, everything was gone. The robbers had made a clean haul, not leaving him a thing to put on. Even the valuable Browning which the secretary of Mme Ravich had lent Sasha for the journey, and a little gold watch, a gift from Fitzi, were missing. They had hung over Sasha's bed directly above his head, and the thief must have been very skilful not to have awakened him or anyone else in the car. Borrowing the most necessary things from the other men, Sasha rigged himself out and prepared to report his loss. In the midst of it he began chuckling to himself. " The fellow that swiped my pants will be fooled, though," he laughed, " for my money is in a secret pocket there that he'll never find." For a moment I did not grasp what he meant; then it struck me that Sasha had also been robbed of our entire fortune of sixteen hundred dollars. Six hundred of it I had turned over to him only the previous evening while my petticoat, in which I had kept it, was drying. " Our independence! " I screamed; " it's gone! "

Through all the bitter disappointments in Russia and our struggle to find ourselves and our work I had been sustained by one thought — our material independence. We did not have to beg or cringe like so many others who were driven by hunger. We had been able to keep our self-respect and to refuse any truck with the dictatorship because we had been made secure by our American friends. Now all was gone! " What now, Sasha? " I cried. " What is going to become of us? " Impatiently he replied: " You seem more concerned about the damned money than about our lives. Don't you realize that if I had stirred, or anyone else in the car, the burglars would have shot us dead? " He had never known me to cling to material things, he added; it was funny I should have thought of the money first of all. " Not so funny when one is compelled to forswear all one holds high in order to exist," I replied. I simply could not face the possibility of eating out of the hand of the Bolshevik State. For myself I should have preferred to be finished by our night callers.

I had been unable to sleep that night because of the stifling heat in our compartment and I had gone out several times into the corridor for a breath of air. Sasha had left the door of his compartment ajar in order to get some air from the corridor window opposite it. I had had a feeling that the window should be closed. Not that I anticipated robbery. Our car was in full view of the station, patrolled by Soviet soldiers. No one could enter or climb into it unobserved. But one could easily help himself to the large chunk of bacon that hung in a bag at the side of the window. It would be too hot for Sasha, I had decided. But the very thing I had thought might be stolen was still in its place. In Petrograd a thief would have certainly taken the meat, but in Kiev clothing was apparently more coveted. In any case it looked as if the robber must have been a railroad worker, since he had been able to enter our car, and undoubtedly he had the co-operation of the soldiers on guard. Our porter, who had been acting queerly for some time, was also not above suspicion. Sasha insisted on recovering his things or at least the money. While he was gone, our car was moved away from the spot where it had stood during the night. Such a proceeding was nothing unusual and we paid no attention to it. We realized its significance, however, when Sasha returned with two militiamen and a police dog. The hound sniffed about, but the traces had been destroyed by the steam of the engine. Undaunted, Sasha in the company of several comrades started a search of the markets in the hope that his clothes might be offered for sale. But apparently the thieves were too careful. They could afford to bide their time. Far from giving up the search, Sasha arranged with some comrades to visit the markets every day for at least a month and to buy back his trousers at any price. "Don't worry," he kept consoling me; "they'll never find that secret pocket with the money." I wished I could share the optimism of my irrepressible pal.

In Bryansk we were greeted with the joyful news of the complete rout of Wrangel. Strange to say, Nester Makhno was being proclaimed a hero who had materially helped to bring about the great victory. But yesterday denounced as a counter-revolutionary, a bandit, the aid of Wrangel, with a large price on his head — what had brought the sudden change of front on the part of the Bolsheviki, we wondered. And how long would the love-feast last? For Trotsky had in turn eulogized the leader of the rebel peasant army and in turn condemned him to death.

Sad news clouded our joy. In a Soviet paper we read of the death of John Reed. Both Sasha and I had been very fond of Jack and we felt his demise as a personal loss. I had last seen him the previous year when he returned from Finland, a very sick man indeed. I had learned that he was put up at the Hotel International in Petrograd, alone and without anyone to take care of him. I had found him in a deplorable condition, his arms and legs swollen, his body covered with ulcers, and his gums badly affected as a result of scurvy acquired in prison. The poor boy suffered even more spiritually, because he had been betrayed to the Finnish authorities by a Russian Communist, a sailor whom Zinoviev had sent with him as a companion. The valuable documents and the large sum of money Jack was taking to his comrades in America all fell into the hands of his captors. It was Jack's second failure of the kind and he took it much to heart. Two weeks' nursing helped put him on his feet again, but he remained fearfully distressed over the methods of Zinoviev and others in jeopardizing the lives of their comrades. " Needlessly and recklessly," he kept saying. He himself had twice been sent on a wild goose chase without any trouble having been taken to find out whether there was any possibility of the venture's succeeding. But at least he could take care of himself and he went into it with open eyes. Moreover, as an American he did not run the same grave risks as the Russian comrades. Communists, mere youngsters, were being sacrificed by the score for the glory of the Third International, he had complained. " Perhaps revolutionary necessity," I had suggested; " at least your comrades always say so." He had believed it also, he had admitted, but his experience and that of others had made him doubt it. His faith in the dictatorship was still fervent, but he was beginning to doubt some of the methods used, particularly by men who themselves always remained in safety.

In Moscow we learned of the presence in the city of Louise Bryant, Reed's wife. Ordinarily I should not have looked her up. I had known Louise for years, even before she was with Jack. An attractive, vivid creature, one had to like her even when not taking her social protestations seriously. On two occasions I had realized her lack of depth. During our trial in New York, when Jack had bravely come to our assistance, Louise had studiously avoided us. They were planning to go to Russia and she was evidently afraid of having her name connected with ours during that dangerous war period, though she had always protested her great friendship in times of peace. I considered it of no great importance, however.

A much graver offence, and one that had angered me considerably, was her misrepresentation of anarchism in her book on Russia. My niece Stella had sent me the volume at the Missouri prison and I was indignant to find repeated in it the stupid story of Russia's nationalizing women that had made its rounds in the American press. Louise charged the anarchists with having been the first to issue the decree. She had taken no trouble to adduce any evidence for her wild assertions, nor had she done so in reply to my letter demanding it. I considered it on a par with the cheap journalistic libelling of the Bolsheviki and I decided to have nothing more to do with Louise.

That seemed ages ago now. Louise had suffered the loss of Jack and she was all broken up over it, I was told by common friends. I went to her without any mental reservations, too deeply moved by her tragedy to remember the past. I found her a wreck, completely shattered. She broke down in convulsive weeping that no words could allay. I took her in my arms, holding her quivering body in a silent embrace. She quieted down after a while and began relating to me the sad story of Jack's death. She had made her way to Russia disguised as a sailor and under great difficulties, only to find on landing in Petrograd that Jack had been ordered to Baku to attend the Congress of Eastern Races. He had begged Zinoviev not to insist on his going, because he had not yet fully recovered from his experience in Finland. But the chief of the Third International was relentless. Reed was to represent the American Communist Party at the Congress, he had declared. In Baku Jack was stricken with typhus and he was brought back to Moscow shortly after Louise had arrived.

I sought to console her by the assurance that all possible care must have been given Jack after his return to Moscow, but she protested that nothing had been done for the boy. A whole week had been lost before the physicians agreed in their diagnosis, and after that Jack had been turned over to an incompetent doctor. No one in the hospital knew anything about nursing, and only after a protracted argument had Louise succeeded in getting permission to take care of Jack. But he had been delirious in his last days and he had probably not even been aware of the presence of his beloved. " Didn't he speak at all? " I inquired. " I could not understand what he meant," Louise replied, " but he kept on repeating all the time: ' Caught in a trap, caught in a trap.' Just that." " Did Jack really use that term? " I cried in amazement. " Why do you ask? " Louise demanded, gripping my hand. " Because that is exactly how I have been feeling since I looked beneath the surface. Caught in a trap. Exactly that."

Had Jack also come to see that all was not well with his idol, I wondered, or had it only been the approach of death that had for a moment illumined his mind? Death strips to the naked truth — it knows no deception.

We were to leave for Petrograd the next day to report to the Museum of the Revolution, but Louise begged us to remain for the funeral. She felt lonely and deserted, and we were the only friends she had, she implored. Now that Jack was gone, she had ceased to interest the Bolsheviki. She had already been made to feel that, she said. Public funerals had always been an abomination to me;

nevertheless I promised to remain to be near her and to help her over the painful ordeal. I told Louise that Sasha might also attend if he could prevail upon the other members of the expedition to postpone their departure for a day.

Louise gave me a message left by our friend Henry Alsberg. It was to the effect that, owing to the friendliness of the guard who had brought him back to Moscow, Alsberg had been saved from the Cheka prison. The *tovaritsch* had permitted him to see his friends in the Foreign Office before delivering him to the Cheka. Nuorteva, whom he was especially anxious to see, detained him there and arranged his release after communicating with the Cheka officials. Had he ever reached the Cheka building, Henry's message continued, it would have taken months for his friends to find him and get him away from their tender care. Henry had since departed for Riga, but he was planning to return in the spring. He had left with Louise the money we had given him at his arrest, which was only two hundred dollars, but a veritable fortune to us now. For a few months at least we should be materially independent, as we had been before Sasha was robbed.

No mail had reached us during our entire journey, but at the Foreign Office our old friend Ethel Bernstein now handed us quite a bundle of it from America. At the same time she gave me a clipping from the Chicago *Tribune*. It was by John Clayton and it told how " E.G. was praying before an American flag on her wall to get back to the States." I had complained to him bitterly, it stated, about the Bolsheviki and their treatment of me. " Of course no one here believes this rotten story," Ethel remarked, " but just the same you ought to see Nuorteva about it." The man she mentioned was in charge of the Publicity Department of the Foreign Office. I saw no reason for offering any apologies. But I was disgusted at having believed that Clayton would prove more honest and decent than the other American reporters who had pestered me in Russia. Yet Clayton had impressed me as trustworthy. Could it be that his story had been doctored by the desk editor? The flag he referred to was a miniature emblem that Jack Reed had once jokingly stuck over Fitzi's picture on my wall and that I had forgotten to take off. The innocent frolic of a friend turned into a fantastic lie! It was sickening. And my complaining about the régime, when I had been particularly reticent with Clayton in regard to such subjects! Well, the Soviet people might believe what they pleased, I decided, but they should get no explanation from me.

Nuorteva received me most kindly and gave me a large package of letters. He did not mention the Clayton story, nor did I. With considerable pride he spoke of having left America on the first Soviet passport submitted to Washington. He was now at the head of the Anglo-Russian Department of the Foreign Office and he would be glad to be of help in the matter of mail. I felt gratified at his tact in not bringing up the wretched matter of Clayton's write-up.

I hastened to our car to read my mail. Letters from Stella, Fitzi, and other friends expressed intense satisfaction at our having at last found a sphere of work. They did not doubt, they wrote, that now we would have the greatest expression for our energies and ideals. Letters of a later date contained clippings of the Clayton story, including one that I read and reread in utter stupefaction. It was a letter for Stella that I had given to Jack Reed to mail and that had been taken from him when he was arrested in Finland. After several readings it dawned on me that the newspaper editor had turned my epistle to Stella into a love missive to John Reed! " Poor Louise, how little she knows of my alleged love-affair with Jack! " I laughed to Sasha.

From our comrades in Moscow we learned of the city-wide raids that had taken place in the early part of October. Among the many victims was also Maria Spiridonovna. She had been ill with typhoid at the time, but the Cheka had arrested her and sent her to a prison hospital. Great, idealistic soul! There was no end to dear Maryusa's martyrdom.

Fanya and Aaron Baron, who were in Moscow, informed us about the developments in regard to Nestor Makhno. The Red forces had proved unable to stand up against Wrangel, and the Bolsheviki had turned to the *povstantsy* leader for aid. He and his army had consented on condition that all the anarchists and Makhnovtsy be released from prison, and that the Soviet Government grant them the right of a general conference. Makhno had named Sasha and me as his representatives in drawing up the agreement. This had never been communicated to us, but the Bolsheviki had accepted Makhno's demands and had actually released a number of the *povstantsy* and some of our comrades. They had also given permission for the gathering, which our comrades from all over Russia had agreed to hold in

Kharkov. Volin and others had already departed for that city, and comrades were expected from every part of the country.

A grey sky overhanging Moscow, rain steadily drizzling its melancholy tune, and artificial wreaths that had served at other funerals were Jack Reed's farewell in the Red Square. No beauty for the man who had loved it so, no colour for his artist-soul. No spark of the red-white flame of the fighter to inspire those who in bombastic speeches claimed him as their comrade. Alexandra Kollontay alone came close to the spirit of John Reed and found the words that would have pleased him most. During her simple and beautiful tribute to Jack, Louise crumpled to the ground in a dead faint just as the coffin was being lowered into the grave. Sasha had almost to carry her to the automobile Nuorteva had put at our disposal. Our old American friend Dr. W. Wovschin, a recent arrival, accompanied us to aid the desolate Louise.

In the Museum of the Revolution, in Petrograd, we were hailed as heroes come back from the front. It was a considerable achievement to return alive after four months of such a journey as we had made, they said, and to have also rescued a whole carload of material of historical value. The future, they assured us, would reward us according to our deserts. All the museum could do now was to give us a month's rest. We were henceforth on the permanent staff of the museum, Yatmanov and Kaplan informed us, and we need not look for other activities. Within a month we should start on a new journey. Our expedition would be granted the privilege of choosing its destination and route. Either the Crimea, which had since been entirely cleared of the Wrangel forces, or Siberia, where Semenoff and Kolchak had been finally routed, would be our objective point. In either place there was much material awaiting us, and we were expected to enrich the museum with it.

"Not to Siberia during the winter," shuddered our Russian members. We also did not particularly welcome the idea, though we remembered Krasnoschokov's invitation to come to the Far Eastern Republic. But there was no need for an immediate decision, the museum chief declared. Alexander Ossipovich and Emma Abramovna (meaning Sasha and me), he insisted, looked as if they indeed needed a vacation.

Sasha and I had definitely decided to apply to the Housing Department for rooms where we might live like the rest of the non-Communist population. The prospect of another trip within a month caused us to defer our plan till some other time, for it would take more than a month to secure lodgings. We should have liked to remain in our car, but there was the problem of heating and of reaching the city. Mme Ravich suggested that we take up our abode at the Hotel International. It was used for foreign visitors, the guests paying for their rooms and meals, and the charges were very reasonable, being fifteen dollars a month for a room and two daily meals. Its main attraction was cleanliness and an opportunity to take a bath. It was the first place of its kind in Russia for other mortals than Communists and we were relieved at the chance to be quartered there.

The museum material, not considered contraband, was easily transferred from our car. Not so the food we had brought with us. Entitled to pass freely through the railroad gates, we aroused no suspicion, though it required a week and four persons to remove the stuff. In the apartment of a friend everything was made up in parcels and sent to sick friends and to those who had children needing fats and sweets. Quite selfishly I had intended to keep enough white flour for the winter to safeguard Sasha from black bread. Now that we were soon to start on another journey, the unpleasant task became unnecessary. It was no small satisfaction to be able to relieve the need of a few more persons, if only for a little while.

In spite of all planning we went neither to the Crimea nor to the Far Eastern Republic. Instead we journeyed to Archangel, " to round out the year," as Yatmanov said. That district having been the centre of the interventionist operations, in which my erstwhile country had played such a disgraceful part, I was glad we were given the opportunity to explore it.

We were only three on that trip. The Russian couple preferred to hug their stove in Petrograd, while our young Communist collaborator had to resume his studies at college.

On the way to Archangel we made two stops, at Yaroslavl and Vologda. Both cities had served as centres for plotters against the Revolution. The former had been the base of the once celebrated revolutionist Savinkov's uprising, drenched in the blood of thousands.

Vologda had been the headquarters of the American Ambassador Francis and other wirepullers in favour of intervention.

Yaroslavl still bore witness to the fratricidal strife; its prison was filled with officers of the Savinkov army that had escaped death. In neither city did we find anything of special value for the museum.

Archangel, at the mouth of the northern Dvina, was separated from the railroad terminus by the frozen river. On arriving we found a temperature of fifty below zero, but the brilliant sun and the dry, crisp air made the cold far less penetrating than in Petrograd. My thoughtful niece, Stella, had pressed her fur coat on me on her last visit to Ellis Island. But I had never worn it because of an idiosyncrasy that made me feel as if the beast were alive and creeping over my neck whenever I put on furs. Everybody had warned us against the Archangel frosts, and as a precaution I had taken the coat with me. Great was my relief when I realized that I could go about in my old velour coat and sweater and even feel too warm in the sun. It was invigorating to walk across the frozen expanse of the river and along the clean streets of Archangel, quite a novelty in a Russian town. In fact, the city presented numerous surprises. Our credentials, scorned in the south, here proved a veritable magic wand, opening wide the doors of every Soviet institution. The chairman of the *Ispolkom* and all other officials went out of their way to aid the efforts of our mission. They exerted themselves to make our stay a memorable experience, as indeed it proved to be. Their fraternal attitude to the population, their equitable efforts to supply them with food and clothing so far as was in their power, made us feel that here principles different from those of " the centre " were operating. The men and women at the helm of affairs in Archangel had grasped the great truth that discrimination, brutality, and hounding were not calculated to convince the people of the beauty or desirability of communism or to cause them to love the Soviet régime. They sought more effective methods. They abolished speculation in food by organizing a more just distribution of rations. They did away with the humiliating and exhausting standing in line by instituting co-operative stores where the inhabitants received due attention and courteous treatment. They introduced a friendly tone and atmosphere in every Soviet institution. While this had not converted the whole community into disciples of Marx or Lenin, it had helped to eliminate the dissatisfaction and antagonism widespread in other parts of the country.

People said that the Communists had acquired organization, efficiency, and order from the example of the Americans quartered in the city. If so, they certainly proved apt pupils. For the usual characteristics of Soviet life, including sabotage, waste, and confusion, were almost entirely missing in Archangel.

Those sturdy sons of the north apparently had something that was very unsovietsky — respect for human life and recognition of its sanctity. Former nuns, monks, White officers, and members of the *bourgeoisie* put to useful work instead of against the wall were an extraordinary revelation. The mere suggestion of such a thing elsewhere in Russia would have marked us as very suspicious characters if not out and out counter-revolutionists. Here the new method had rescued hundreds of lives and had gained for the régime additional workers. Not that the Cheka was absent or capital punishment abolished. A dictatorship could hardly exist without these. But in Archangel the Cheka had not attained the unlimited powers it enjoyed in other places. It did not constitute a State within the State whose sole function was terror and vengeance. If these measures were really dictated by revolutionary necessity, the barbarous methods of the Whites in northern Russia would have certainly justified their use. Not only Communists, but even those remotely sympathetic with them had been subjected to torture and death. Entire families had been ruthlessly exterminated by the Whites. Kulakov, chairman of the *Ispolkom,* for instance, had lost every member of his family. Even his youngest sister, a mere child of twelve, had not escaped the fiendishness of the enemy, and there was hardly a radical or liberal home that had not felt the cruel hand of those that had come to crush the Revolution.

" Naturally we could not meet such fury with gloved hands," the chairman of the educational department said to us. " We fought back desperately, but when the enemy had been driven to flight, we saw no need of retaliation or terror. We felt that vengeance would serve no other purpose than to antagonize the population against us. We set to work to bring order out of the chaos left by the Whites and to reclaim as many lives as we could among our captives."

" Did all your comrades agree with such ' sentimental ' methods? " I asked in astonishment. " Of course not," he replied; " there were many who insisted on drastic measures, and there are those who still insist that we shall yet have to pay dearly for what they call our reformist attitude to those who had conspired against the Revolution."

However, the chairman continued, the more level-headed comrades had prevailed, and experience proved that even former White officers could be utilized in various walks of life. A number of them were employed as teachers and they were doing faithful and useful work. The same held good of several other departments. Moreover, even such dark and bigoted elements as nuns and monks had responded to humane treatment. It was not at all sentimentality, but good common sense that taught him, he added, that the will to life was not dictated by creeds. Nuns and monks were as subject to that law of nature as any average person. After they had been dispossessed from the cloisters and monasteries and faced death if they continued plotting, or starvation if they refused to work, they proved themselves only too eager to make themselves useful in some way. We could convince ourselves of it, he said, by visiting the schools, nurseries, and arts and crafts studios.

We did. We went unannounced and unexpected and we found conditions in those institutions exemplary. I talked to some of the nuns employed there, a number of whom had dwelt apart from the world for a quarter of a century. Mentally they still lived in the cloisters. They understood nothing of the new and changing forces at work about them, but they were doing beautiful work, including pottery, agriculture, illustrations for children's stories, stage scenery for their theatre, and similar things. I also talked to some artisans and woodcarvers of unusual skill. Several of them had been caught red-handed in counter-revolutionary conspiracies. One lamented that his work was not bringing him in as much money as in former days. But his life had been spared and he was allowed to continue the labour he loved. He wanted nothing better, he said.

A few days later I had occasion to meet one of the White officers considered among the best teachers. He could not approve of the dictatorship, he frankly admitted, but he had come to realize the folly and crime of foreign intervention. The Allies had promised much to his country, but all they had done was to divide the Russian house against itself. The Americans had been decent, he thought. They had kept to themselves, their soldiers were off the streets after dark, and they had also been generous with provisions and clothing. At their departure they had distributed their surplus supplies with open hand. The British were different. Their soldiers molested the native women, their officers were arbitrary and haughty, and General Rollins had ordered huge supplies sunk in the open sea before the British ships departed. He was through with intervention. He loved teaching and he was very fond of children and now he had the opportunity of his life.

Similar sentiments we found reflected by persons in various political groupings. Nearly every one agreed that the Soviet régime was sincerely and successfully carrying out the policy of reclamation, and that the social scope was being gradually widened for those even that did not agree with the Communist view-point. In other words, no one was being discriminated against on account of his past.

Among the vast material we gathered in the north were a number of revolutionary and anarchist publications that had appeared underground during the régime of the Tsar and all through the period of occupation. Most appealing was the last message of a sailor condemned to death by the invaders, containing a minute description of his torture by British officers to exact information. There were also photographs of men and women mutilated by the counter-revolutionists. In addition Sasha had also collected interesting material from Bechin, the chairman of the labour soviet, in whom the Provisional Government had tried to crush the revolutionary labour movement of the north. Together with others, but as the responsible factor, Bechin had been tried for treason and condemned to a slow death in the fearsome prison of Yokanan in the arctic zone. He had kept a diary of his arrest, trial, and imprisonment, and after much persuasion he had given it to Sasha for the museum.

Archangel proved so absorbing that we overstayed our time by two weeks. We still had Murmansk to visit, while our credentials were good only till the end of the year. With regret we left the friends we had made and the splendid people we had met in the city.

Within three days' distance from our objective we had to turn back. Heavy snow-storms blocked our route, and our progress resembled that of a snail. It would have required weeks to reach our destination, the road having first to be cleared of mountain-high snow. Fifty miles from Petrograd we were again stalled, this time by a blinding blizzard. Luckily we had fuel and provisions for several days. We settled down for a patient wait, for there was nothing else we could do under the circumstances.

On Christmas Eve, still held up on the road, Shakol and Sasha gave me a surprise. A wee pine-tree, decorated for the occasion and

studded with coloured candles, gaily lit up our compartment. America
contributed the gifts, or rather my women friends who had sent presents before we sailed. A good hot grog, brewed from the rum supplied
us in Archangel, helped to make the festivity complete.

I thought of our Christmas of a year ago — of 1919. Sasha and I,
together with many other undesirable rebels on the *Buford,* torn away
from our work, our comrades, and our loved ones, cruising to an
unknown destination. In enemy hands, under rigid military discipline,
our male companions herded below deck like cattle and fed on
wretched food, all of us exposed to imminent danger from war mines.
Yet we did not care. Soviet Russia was beckoning us, liberated and
reborn, the fulfilment of the heroic struggle of a hundred years. Our
hopes ran high, our faith flamed red-white, all our thoughts centred
on our *Matushka Rossiya.*

Now it was Christmas 1920. We were in Russia, her soil serene
after the raging storms, her attire of white and green under a jewelled
sky. Our house on wheels was warm and cozy. My old pal was at
my side and a new dear friend. They were in a holiday mood and
I longed to join in their merriment. But in vain. My thoughts were
in 1919. Only a year had passed, and nothing was left but the ashes
of my fervent dreams, my burning faith, my joyous song.

We reached Petrograd at the height of the excitement over the
fate of the labour unions. The problem had already been discussed
at the party sessions the previous October and ever since in preparation for the Eighth All-Russian Congress of the Soviets. The trade
unions must serve as a school of communism, Lenin had declared,
and the opposing views of Trotsky, of the old Marxian scholar
Ryazanov, of Kollontay, leading the labour circles, had to capitulate
to the dictum of Ilich. Trotsky insisted that the only thing that could
save the Revolution was the militarization of labour and the entire
subserviency of the unions to the needs of the State. Lenin treated
all his opponents with equal contempt. Trotsky did not know his
Marx, Lenin declared, while the views of Kollontay were half-baked.
As to Ryazanov, he was forbidden all public utterance for a period
of six months on the ground that he did not know what he was talking about.

The great explosion was finally precipitated by Kollontay and
the old Communist Shlyapnikov, representing the labour opposition.

The Revolution had been fought by the workers, they insisted, and the world had been assured that the real dictatorship of Russia was that of the proletariat. Instead the masses were stripped of all rights and denied any say in the economic life of the country. These two daring leaders of labour were indeed articulating the thoughts and feelings of the toiling masses, of the rank and file of the Communists even, who had no way of making themselves heard.

The storm that followed threatened the disruption of the party. Something had to be done, and Lenin was equal to the occasion. He heaped ridicule upon the heretics who dared voice sentiments of " petty *bourgeois* ideology." Quickly the opposition was strangled. Kollontay's pamphlet on labour demands was suppressed and its author severely disciplined, while old Shlyapnikov, of weaker metal, was silenced by being made a member of the Executive Committee of the party and ordered to take a much-needed rest.

Our expedition was being reorganized and arrangements made for our third tour, which was definitely decided upon as a journey to the Crimea. But at the eleventh hour our plans were blocked by an order of the *Ispart,* the newly created Communist body for the purpose of collecting data on the history of the Communist Party. The Museum of the Revolution was curtly notified that henceforth the new organization would take charge of all expeditions, the *Ispart* claiming precedence, by virtue of its Communist character, in all such undertakings. It would also commandeer our car, though the Museum of the Revolution would be granted the privilege of assigning some of its members to the work of the *Ispart.*

The arbitrariness of the new institution was felt by every member of the museum as a deliberate attempt to curtail its independence and limit the scope of its work. Even Commissar Yatmanov, a devoted Communist, expressed himself in no gentle terms about the party zealots who insisted on having everything in their hold. It was unthinkable to submit to such methods without a fight, he declared. He would immediately take the matter up at the Petrograd end, while we must proceed to Moscow. Sasha was to see Zinoviev about it and I should see Lunacharsky, they being the chairmen of the Petrograd Museum. The decision of the *Ispart* was an infringement upon Zinoviev's jurisdiction over Petrograd; he would surely protest against it; while Lunacharsky, as the head of all the cultural efforts of

Russia, would not tolerate such invasion of his domain, Yatmanov asserted.

We had but little hope of success, but we consented to go to Moscow. We declared, however, that should the *Ispart* win in the matter, we would discontinue our affiliation with the museum, distressing as such a step would be to us. We knew too well the meaning of having a political commissar control our work and movements. It signified dictatorship and espionage and it involved clique interests, strife, and disruption. We had declined the offer of many high positions because we would not submit to such tutelage.

Zinoviev was indeed much incensed over the attempt of the *Ispart* to monopolize the work of the Petrograd Museum and to interfere with his program for it. He wrote a letter of protest to his comrades of the new institution and he turned it over to Sasha for presentation and argument. The Museum of the Revolution was not trespassing on the field of the *Ispart;* it had mapped out its own work, in no way in conflict with that of the Moscow body, and he as the head of the Petrograd Museum's executive committee would not tolerate such autocratic interference, Zinoviev wrote. He further assured Sasha that he would take the matter up with Lenin himself if the *Ispart* persisted in its arbitrary decision.

Lunacharsky also was angry with " the fools who would put all cultural endeavour under their own thumb." He promised to protest against such tactics, but soon I had occasion to learn that he was in reality quite without authority. The real power in the All-Russian Commissariat of Education was Pokrovsky, a Communist of old standing, and it was he who had founded the *Ispart*. Lunacharsky was a mere figure-head, exploited by the party because of his presumed European influence, since he had lived many years abroad and was well known in cultural circles there.

Finding lodgings in Moscow was always a difficult problem, but fortunately we were spared the disagreeable task of begging for a roof over our heads. Our good friend Angelica Balabanoff was in charge of a Russo-Italian bureau quartered in a house that had formerly been occupied by a foreign organization. She and her staff were now living there, and, having two vacant rooms, Angelica invited us to stay with her.

Our efforts in behalf of the Petrograd Museum were being blocked on every hand by the concentrated authority of Communist machinery and were proving fruitless. Petrograd urged a personal report and we decided to return there. We had already bought our tickets when word came from Dmitrov that our old comrade Peter Kropotkin had been stricken with pneumonia. The shock was the greater because we had visited Peter in July and had found him in good health and buoyant spirits. He seemed then younger and better than when we had seen him the previous March. The sparkle in his eyes and his vivacity had impressed us with his splendid condition. The Kropotkin place had looked lovely in the summer sunshine, with the flowers and Sophie's vegetable garden in full bloom. With much pride Peter had spoken of his companion and her skill as a gardener. Taking Sasha and me by the hand, he had led us in boyish exuberance to the patch where Sophie had planted a special kind of lettuce. She had succeeded in raising heads as large as cabbages, their leaves crispy and luscious. He himself had also been digging in the soil, but it was Sophie, he had reiterated, who was the real expert. Her potato crop of the previous winter had been so large that there was enough left over to exchange for fodder for their cow and even to share with their Dmitrov neighbours, who had few vegetables. Our dear Peter had been frolicking in his garden and talking about these matters as if they were world events. Infectious had been the youthful spirit of our comrade, carrying us along by its freshness and charm.

In the afternoon, assembled in his study, he had again become the scientist and thinker, clear and penetrating in his judgment of persons and events. We had discussed the dictatorship, the methods forced upon the Revolution by necessity and those inherent in the nature of the party. I wanted Peter to help me to a better understanding of the situation which was threatening to bankrupt my faith in the Revolution and in the masses. Patiently and with the tenderness one uses towards a sick child he had sought to soothe me. There was no reason to despair, he had urged. He understood my inner conflict, he had assured me, but he was certain that in time I should learn to distinguish between the Revolution and the régime. The two were worlds apart, the abyss between them bound to grow wider as time went on. The Russian Revolution was far greater than the French and of more potent world-wide significance. It had struck deep into the lives of the masses everywhere, and no one could foresee the rich harvest humanity would reap from it. The Communists, irrevocably adhering to the idea of a centralized State, were doomed to misdirect the course of the Revolution. Their end being political supremacy, they had inevitably become the Jesuits of socialism, justifying all means to attain their purpose. Their methods, however, paralysed the energies of the masses and terrorized the people. Yet without the people, without the direct participation of the toilers in the reconstruction of the country, nothing creative and essential could be accomplished.

Our own comrades, Kropotkin had continued, had in the past failed to give sufficient consideration to the fundamental elements of the social revolution. The basic factor in such an upheaval is the organization of the economic life of the country. The Russian Revolution proved that we must prepare for that. He had come to the conclusion that syndicalism was likely to furnish what Russia lacked most: the channel through which the industrial and economic upbuilding of the country could flow. He was referring to anarcho-syndicalism, indicating that such a system, by aid of the co-operatives, would save future revolutions the fatal blunders and fearful suffering Russia was passing through.

All this came vividly back to my mind at the sad news of Kropotkin's break-down. I could not think of leaving for Petrograd without seeing Peter again. Skilled nurses were scarce in Russia and I could take care of him and do at least that much for my dear teacher and friend.

I learned that Peter's daughter, Alexandra, was in Moscow and about to go to Dmitrov. She informed me that a very competent nurse, a Russian woman trained in England, was in charge of the case. Their little cottage was too crowded already, she said, and it was not advisable to disturb Peter at the moment. She was leaving for Dmitrov and she would telephone to me about father's condition and the advisability of my seeing him.

The Petrograd Museum was waiting for Sasha's report on his conferences with the *Ispart*, necessitating his immediate departure for the north, while I remained in Moscow ready for a call from Dmitrov. Several days passed without my receiving word from Alexandra, which led me to conclude that Peter was improving and that my services were not needed. I thereupon left for Petrograd.

I had hardly been in the city an hour when Mme Ravich telephoned to inform me that my presence was urgently called for from Dmitrov. She had received a message from Moscow on the long-distance wire urging my immediate coming. Peter had grown worse and the family had begged for me to be notified to come at once.

My train ran into a raging storm and we arrived in Moscow ten hours behind schedule. There was no train for Dmitrov until the following evening, and the roads were blocked by snow-drifts too great for an automobile. All telephone wires were down and there was no way to reach Dmitrov.

The evening train moved with exasperating slowness, repeatedly stopping to refuel. It was four in the morning when we arrived. Together with Alexander Schapiro, an intimate friend of the Kropotkin family, and Pavlov, a comrade from the Bakers' Union, I hastened to the Kropotkin cottage. Alas, too late! Peter had ceased breathing an hour before. He died at four a. m., February 8, 1921.

The distracted widow told me that Peter had repeatedly inquired whether I was already on my way and how soon I would arrive. Sophie was near collapse, and in the need of looking after her I forgot the cruel combination of circumstances that had prevented my rendering even the least service to him who had been such a potent inspiration in my life and work.

We learned from Sophie that Lenin, when informed of Peter's illness, had sent the best Moscow physicians to Dmitrov, together with provisions and delicacies for the patient. He had also ordered that frequent bulletins of Peter's condition should be sent him as well as published in the press. It was a sad commentary that so much attention should have been given on his death-bed to the man who had twice been raided by the Cheka and who had thereby been compelled to go into undesired retirement. Peter Kropotkin had helped to prepare the ground for the Revolution, but had been denied a share in its life and development; his voice had penetrated Russia in spite of tsarist persecution, but it was strangled by the Communist dictatorship.

Peter had never sought or accepted favours from any government nor tolerated pomp and display. We therefore determined there should be no intrusion from the State at his funeral, and that it should not be vulgarized by the participation of officialdom. Peter's last days upon earth should rest in the hands of his comrades only.

Schapiro and Pavlov departed for Moscow to call out Sasha and other Petrograd comrades. Together with the Moscow group they were to take charge of the obsequies. I remained in Dmitrov to help

Sophie prepare her precious dead for the transfer to the capital for burial.

In the silent presence of my comrade I came upon treasures in his being that his utter lack of egotism would not have permitted me to discover. I had known Peter for over a quarter of a century, was familiar with his life, his works and colourful personality. But only his death disclosed his cherished secret that he had also been an artist of unusual quality. I found, hidden away in a box, a number of drawings Peter had made in his all too few leisure moments. Their exquisite line and form proved that he might have achieved as much with his brush as he had with his pen had he cared to devote himself to it. In music also Peter would have excelled. He loved the piano and he could find expression and release in his fine interpretation of the masters. In the drab Dmitrov existence his sole delight consisted in the playing and singing of two young women friends of the family. With them he would feast his love of music on regular weekly evenings.

Richly endowed with creative ability, Peter had been still richer in his vision of a noble social ideal and in his humanity, which embraced all mankind. For that more than for anything else he had laboured during the conscious part of his almost fourscore years. In fact, until the very day when he had to take to his bed, Peter had continued working, under most distressing conditions, on his volume on *Ethics,* which he had hoped to make the supreme effort of his life. His deepest regret in his last hours was that he had not been given a little longer to complete what he had begun years before.

In the past three years of his life Peter had been cut off from close contact with the masses. In his death he found full contact with them. Peasants, workers, soldiers, intellectuals, men and women from a radius of many miles, as well as the entire community of Dmitrov, streamed through the Kropotkin cottage to pay their last tribute to the man that had dwelt among them and had shared their struggle and afflictions.

Sasha arrived in Dmitrov together with a number of Moscow comrades to assist in the removal of Peter's body to Moscow. Never had the little town rendered so great homage to anyone as it did to Peter Kropotkin. The children had known and loved him best because of his childlike playfulness with them. The schools were closed for the day in mourning for their departed friend. In large numbers they marched to the station and waved their farewell to Peter as the train slowly steamed out.

On the way to Moscow I learned from Sasha that the Peter Kropotkin Funeral Commission, which he had helped to organize and of which he was the chairman, had already been subjected to chicanery by the Soviet authorities. Permission had been granted the commission to publish two of Peter's pamphlets and to issue a special *Peter Kropotkin Memorial Bulletin*. Later the Moscow Soviet, under the presidency of Kamenev, demanded that the manuscripts of the *Bulletin* be submitted for censorship. Sasha, Schapiro, and other comrades protested that the proceedings would delay the publication. To gain time they had pledged that nothing but appreciations of Kropotkin's life and work should appear in the memorial issue. Then the censor suddenly remembered that he had too much work on hand and that the matter would have to await its regular turn. It meant that the *Bulletin* could not appear in time for the funeral, and it was evident that the Bolsheviki were resorting to their usual tactics of holding up things until too late for their effectiveness. Our comrades decided to resort to direct action. Lenin had repeatedly appropriated that anarchist idea, and why should the anarchists not recapture it from him? Time was pressing and the object was important enough even to risk arrest. They broke the seal the Cheka had placed on the printing establishment of our old comrade Atabekian, and our friends worked like beavers to prepare the *Bulletin* in time for the funeral.

In Moscow the expressions of esteem and affection for Peter Kropotkin became a tremendous demonstration. From the moment the body arrived in the capital and was placed in the Trade Union House, and all during the two days that the dead lay in state in the Marble Hall, there began an outpouring of the people such as had not been manifested since the days of " October."

The Funeral Commission had sent a request to Lenin to release temporarily the anarchists imprisoned in Moscow to enable them to take part in the last honours paid their dead teacher and friend. Lenin had promised and the Executive Committee of the Communist Party had directed the Veh-Cheka (the All-Russian Cheka) to free " according to its judgment " the imprisoned anarchists for participation in the obsequies. But the Veh-Cheka apparently was not disposed to obey even Lenin or the supreme authority of its own party. Would the Funeral Commission guarantee the return of the prisoners to jail, it demanded. The commission pledged itself collectively. Whereupon the Veh-Cheka declared that there were "no anarchists in the Moscow prisons." The truth, however, was that the Butirky and the inner jail of the Cheka were filled with our comrades arrested in the raid of the Kharkov Conference, though the latter had been officially permitted according to the Soviet agreement with Nestor Makhno. Moreover, Sasha had gained admission to the Butirky and there talked with more than a score of our imprisoned comrades. Accompanied by the Russian anarchist Yarchook, he had also visited the inner prison of the Moscow Cheka and there conversed with Aaron Baron, who represented on the occasion a number of other imprisoned anarchists. Still the Cheka insisted that there were "no anarchists imprisoned in Moscow."

Once again the Funeral Commission was compelled to resort to direct action. On the morning of the funeral it instructed Alexandra Kropotkin to telephone to the Moscow Soviet that a public announcement of its breach of faith would be made and that the wreaths laid on the bier of Kropotkin by Soviet and Communist organizations would be removed forthwith if the promise given by Lenin was not kept.

The large Hall of Columns was filled to the doors, among those present being also several representatives of the European and American press. Our old friend Henry Alsberg was there, recently returned to Russia. Another correspondent was Arthur Ransome, of the Manchester *Guardian*. They would be sure to make the Soviet breach of faith widely known. After the world had been daily apprised for weeks of the care and attention bestowed by the Soviet Government upon Peter Kropotkin in his last illness, the publication of such a scandal had to be avoided at all costs. Kamenev therefore pleaded for more time and solemnly promised to have the imprisoned anarchists released within twenty minutes.

The funeral was held up for an hour. The great masses of bereaved outside kept shivering in the bitter Moscow frost, all waiting for the arrival of the imprisoned pupils of the great dead. At last they came, but only seven of them, from the Cheka jail. There were none of the Butirky comrades, but at the last moment the Cheka assured the commission that they had been released and were on their way to the hall.

The prisoners on leave acted as the honorary pall-bearers. In proud sadness they carried the last remains of their beloved teacher and comrade out of the hall. In the street they were received in impressive silence by the vast assembly. Soldiers without arms, sailors, students, and children, labour organizations of every trade, and groups of men and women representing the learned professions, peasants, and numerous anarchist bodies, all with their banners of red or black, a multitudinous mass united without coercion, orderly without force, stretched along the long march of two hours to the Devichy Cemetery, on the outskirts of the city.

At the Tolstoy Museum the strains of Chopin's *Funeral March* greeted the *cortège,* and a chorus by the followers of the seer of Yasnaya Polyana. In appreciation our comrades lowered their flags, as a fitting tribute of one great son of Russia to another.

Passing the Butirky prison, the procession came to a second halt, and our flags were lowered in token of Peter Kropotkin's last greeting to his courageous comrades who were waving their adieu to him from their barred windows.

Spontaneous expressions of deep-felt sorrow characterized the speeches made by representative men of various political tendencies at the grave of our departed comrade. The dominant note was that the death of Peter Kropotkin was a loss of a great moral force, the equal of which was well-nigh extinct in their native land.

For the first time since my coming to Petrograd my own voice rang out in public. It sounded to me strangely hard and inadequate to express all that Peter had meant to me. My grief over his passing away was bound up with my despair over the defeat of the Revolution, which none of us had been able to avert.

The sun, slowly disappearing below the horizon, and the sky, bathed in dark red, made a fitting canopy over the fresh soil that was now Peter Kropotkin's eternal resting-place.

The seven paroled boys spent the evening with us, and it was late at night when they reached their prison-house. Not expecting them, the guards had locked the gates and retired. The men had fairly to break into the place, so astounded were the keepers to see anarchists foolish enough to live up to the pledge given for them by their comrades.

The anarchists in the Butirky prison had not appeared at the funeral, after all. The Veh-Cheka had assured our commission that they had declined to do so, though offered the opportunity. We knew that it was a lie; nevertheless I decided upon a personal visit to our prisoners to secure their side of the story. This unfortunately involved the hateful necessity of applying to the Cheka for a permit. I was taken into the private office of the presiding Chekist, who proved a mere youth with a gun in his belt and another on his desk. He met me with outstretched hands, profusely addressing me as his " dear comrade." His name was Brenner, he informed me, and he used to live in America. He had been an anarchist and of course he knew " Sasha " and me well and all about our activities in the States. He was proud to call us his comrades. Naturally he was now with the Communists, he explained, for he considered the present régime a stepping stone to anarchism. The Revolution was the main thing, and since the Bolsheviki were working in its behalf, he was co-operating with them. But had I ceased to be a revolutionist that I refused to grasp the proffered comradely hand from one of its defenders?

I had never in my life shaken hands with detectives, I replied, and much less would I do so with one who had been an anarchist. I came for a pass to the prison and I wanted to know whether I could secure one.

The Chekist turned white, but he kept his composure. " All right about the pass," he said, " but there is a little matter that needs explanation." He drew out a clipping from a desk drawer and handed it to me. It was the silly Clayton article that I had already seen months before. It was imperative that I retract its contents in the Soviet press, Brenner declared. I replied that I had long ago cabled my version of it to friends in America, and that I had no intention of doing anything more in the matter. My refusal was sure to go against me, the Chekist remarked. As a *tovarishtch* he felt it his duty to warn me. " Is it a threat?" I asked. " Not yet," he muttered.

He rose and walked out of the room. I waited for half an hour, wondering whether I was a prisoner. Everyone's turn comes in Russia; why not also mine, I mused. Presently steps approached and the door was thrown open. An old man, evidently a Chekist, gave me a slip of paper permitting me to enter the Butirky.

Among a large group of imprisoned comrades I met several I had known in the States: Fanya and Aaron Baron, Volin, and others who had been active in America, as well as the Russians of the *Nabat* organization whom I had met in Kharkov. They had been visited by a representative of the Veh-Cheka, they related, who had offered to release several of them individually, but not as a collective group, as had been arranged with the Funeral Commission. Our comrades had repudiated the breach of faith and insisted that they would attend the Kropotkin funeral in a body or not at all. The man informed them that he would have to report their demand to his superior officers and that he would soon return with the final decision. But he never came back. The comrades said it did not matter at all, because they had held their own Kropotkin memorial meeting in the corridor of their prison wing, and the occasion had been honoured by appropriate speeches and revolutionary songs. In fact, with the help of the other politicals they had turned the prison into a popular university, Volin remarked. They were conducting classes in social science, political economy, sociology, and literature, and they were teaching the common prisoners to read and write. They were enjoying more freedom than we on the outside and we should envy them, they joked. But their haven, they feared, would probably not last much longer.

Sophie Kropotkin, whose whole life had been wrapped up in Peter and his work, was completely shattered by her loss. She could not bear to go on without him, she told me, unless she could devote the rest of her days to the perpetuation of his memory and efforts. A Peter Kropotkin museum was her idea as a fitting testimonial, and she pleaded with me to remain in Moscow to help her realize the project. I agreed that her plan would be a most appropriate monument to Peter, though I did not consider Russia at present the best place for it. The work would involve continual begging from the Government, and that would certainly not be in conformity with Peter's views and wishes. But Sophie insisted that Russia was, everything considered, the most logical place for such a museum. Peter had loved his native land and had had the greatest faith in its people, notwithstanding the Bolshevik dictatorship. Heart-breaking as conditions were, he had often told her, he was determined to spend the rest of his life there. She also had always been devoted to Russia, and, with Peter now resting in Russian soil, it had become doubly sacred to her.

She felt that, with Sasha and me on the museum committee, the main support would come from America and very little would therefore have to be asked from the soviets. The members of the Kropotkin Funeral Commission favoured Sophie's plan. Whatever the nature of the dictatorship, they held, the fact remained that the great Revolution had taken place in Russia, and that country was therefore the proper home for a Kropotkin museum.

The Peter Kropotkin Funeral Commission reorganized itself into a Memorial Committee, with Sophie Kropotkin as its chairman, Sasha as general secretary, and me as manager. In addition I was also to substitute for Sophie during her absence in Dmitrov. The organization, which consisted of representatives of the various anarchist groups, decided to apply to the Moscow Soviet for the old Kropotkin family house as a home for the museum, as well as to request that the Kropotkin cottage in Dmitrov be secured for the widow of Peter.

Together with Sasha I returned to Petrograd to sever our connexions with the Museum of the Revolution. We both regretted having to give up our active association with its staff, who had been so splendid in their relationship with us. But the *Ispart* had irrevocably decided to set up a political commissar over the museum expeditions, and neither Sasha nor I would continue work under such conditions. Moreover, we considered the work of a Peter Kropotkin museum more vital than our labours for the Petrograd Museum and we were already in active charge of the preliminary work. Our presence in Moscow was urgent and we should have to live there. Alexandra Kropotkin was leaving for Europe, and Sophie had promised that we could have the two small rooms they had occupied in an apartment on the Leontevsky Pereulok. At last we should be able to live like the rest of the non-official population.

In my early Russian period the question of strikes had puzzled me a great deal. People had told me that the least attempt of that kind was crushed and the participants sent to prison. I had not believed it, and, as in all similar things, I had turned to Zorin for information. " Strikes under the dictatorship of the proletariat! " he had exclaimed; " there's no such thing." He had even upbraided me for crediting such wild and impossible tales. Against whom, indeed, should the workers strike in Soviet Russia, he had argued. Against themselves? They were the masters of the country, politically as well as industrially. To be sure, there were some among the toilers who were not yet fully class-conscious and aware of their own true interests. These were sometimes disgruntled, but they were elements incited by the *shkurniky,* by self-seekers and enemies of the Revolution. Skinners, parasites, they were, who were purposely misleading the dark people. They were the worst kind of *sabotazhniky,* no better than out and out counter-revolutionists, and of course the Soviet authorities had to protect the country against their kind. Most of them were in prison.

Since then I had learned by personal observation and experience that the real *sabotazhniky,* counter-revolutionists, and bandits in Soviet penal institutions were a negligible minority. The bulk of the prison population consisted of social heretics who were guilty of the cardinal sin against the Communist Church. For no offence was considered more heinous than to entertain political views in opposition to the party, and to voice any protest against the evils and crimes of Bolshevism. I found that by far the greatest number were political prisoners, as well as peasants and workers guilty of demanding better treatment and conditions. These facts, though rigidly kept from the public, were nevertheless common knowledge, as were indeed most things that were secretly going on beneath the Soviet surface. How forbidden information leaked out was a mystery, but it did leak out and would spread with the rapidity and intensity of a forest fire.

Within less than twenty-four hours of our return to Petrograd we learned that the city was seething with discontent and strike talk. The cause of it was the increased suffering due to the unusually severe winter as well as partly to the habitual Soviet near-sightedness. Heavy snow-storms had delayed the meagre supplies of food and fuel for the city. In addition the Petro-Soviet had committed the stupidity of closing down several factories and cutting the rations of their employees almost in half. At the same time it had become known that the party members in the shops had received a fresh supply of shoes and clothing, while the rest of the toilers were wretchedly clad and shod. To cap the climax the authorities vetoed the meeting called by the workers to discuss ways of ameliorating the situation.

It was the common feeling in Petrograd among non-Communist elements that the situation was very grave. The atmosphere was charged to the point of explosion. We decided of course to remain in the city. Not that we hoped to avert impending trouble, but we wanted to be on hand in case we could be of help to the people.

The storm broke out even before anyone expected it. It began with the strike of the millmen at the Troubetskoy works. Their demands were modest enough: an increase in their food rations, as had long ago been promised them, and also the distribution of the foot-gear on hand. The Petro-Soviet refused to parley with the strikers until they returned to work. Companies of armed *kursanty,* consisting of young

Communists in military training, were sent to disperse the workers gathered about the mills. The cadets sought to incite the crowd by firing into the air, but fortunately the workers had come unarmed and there was no bloodshed. The strikers resorted to a more powerful weapon, the solidarity of their fellow-toilers, with the result that the employees of five more factories laid down their tools and joined the strike movement. To a man, they streamed from the Galernaya docks, the Admiralty shops, the Patronny mills, the Baltiysky and Laferm factories. Their street demonstration was promptly broken up by soldiers. From all accounts, I gathered that the handling of the strikers was by no means very comradely. Even such an ardent Communist as Liza Zorin had been aroused to protest against the methods used. Liza and I had drifted apart a long time ago and I was therefore much surprised that she should feel the need of unburdening her heart to me. Never would she have believed that Red Army men would rough-ride over workingmen, she protested. Some women had fainted at the sight of it, and others had become hysterical. A woman standing near her had evidently recognized her as an active party member and had no doubt held her responsible for the brutal scene. She turned on Liza like a fury and hit her full in the face, causing her to bleed profusely. Though staggered by the blow, dear old Liza, who had always teased me about my sentimentality, told her assailant that it did not matter at all. " To reassure the distracted woman I begged her to let me take her to her home," Liza related. " Her home — it was a dreadful hole such as I thought no longer existed in our country. One dark room, cold and barren, occupied by the woman, her husband, and their six children. To think that I have lived in the Astoria all this time ! " she moaned. She knew it was not the fault of her party that such appalling conditions still prevailed in Soviet Russia, she continued. Nor was it Communist wilfulness that was responsible for the strike. The blockade and the world imperialist conspiracy against the Workers' Republic were to blame for the poverty and suffering. Just the same, she could not remain in her comfortable quarters any longer. That desperate woman's room and her frostbitten children would haunt her days. Poor Liza ! Loyal and staunch she was and of sterling character. But oh, so blind politically !

The plea of the workers for more bread and some fuel soon flared into decided political demands, thanks to the arbitrariness and ruthlessness of the authorities. A manifesto, pasted on the walls no one knew by whom, called for " a complete change in the policies of the Government." It declared that, " first of all, the workers and peasants need freedom. They don't want to live by the decrees of the Bolsheviki; they want to control their own destinies." Every day the situation grew more tense and new demands were being voiced by means of proclamations on the walls and buildings. At last appeared a call for the *Uchredilka,* the Constituent Assembly so hated and denounced by the ruling party.

Martial law was declared and the workers were ordered to return to the shops on pain of being deprived of their rations. This entirely failed of any effect, whereupon a number of unions were liquidated, their officials and the more recalcitrant strikers placed in prison.

In helpless misery we saw groups of men, surrounded by armed Chekists and soldiers, led past our windows. In the hope of making the Soviet leaders realize the folly and danger of their tactics Sasha tried to get hold of Zinoviev, while I sought Mme Ravich, Zorin and Zipperovich, head of the Petrograd Trade Union Soviet. But they all denied themselves to us on the excuse that they were too busy defending the city from counter-revolutionary plots hatched by the Mensheviki and Socialist-Revolutionists. This formula had grown stale by three years' repetition, but it still helped to throw sand into the eyes of the Communist rank and file.

The strike kept spreading, all extreme measures notwithstanding. Arrests followed upon arrests, but the very stupidity with which the authorities dealt with the situation served to encourage the dark elements. Anti-revolutionary and Jew-baiting proclamations began to appear, and the wild rumours of military suppression and Cheka brutality against the strikers filled the city.

The workers were determined, but it was apparent that they would soon be starved into submission. There was no means by which the public could aid the strikers even if they had anything to give. All avenues of approach to the industrial districts of the city were cut off by massed troops. Moreover, the population itself was in dreadful want. The little we could gather in foodstuffs and clothing was a mere drop in the ocean. We all realized that the odds between the dictatorship and the workers were too uneven to permit the strikers to hold out much longer.

Into this tense and desperate situation there was presently introduced a new factor that held out the hope of some settlement. It was the sailors of Kronstadt. True to their revolutionary traditions and solidarity with the workers, so loyally demonstrated in the revolution of 1905, and later in the March and October upheavals of 1917, they now again took up the cudgels in behalf of the harassed proletarians in Petrograd. By no means blindly so. Quietly and without outsiders knowing about it, they had sent a committee to investigate the claims of the strikers. Its report roused the sailors of the warships *Petropavlovsk* and *Sevastopol* to adopt a resolution in favour of the demands of their brother workers on strike. They declared themselves devoted to the Revolution and the soviets, as well as loyal to the Communist Party. They protested, however, against the arbitrary attitude of certain commissars and stressed the need of greater self-determination for the organized bodies of workers. They further demanded freedom of assembly for labour unions and peasant organizations and the release of all labour and political prisoners from Soviet prisons and concentration camps.

The example of these brigades was taken up by the First and Second Squadrons of the Baltic Fleet stationed at Kronstadt. At an open-air meeting on March 1, attended by sixteen thousand sailors, Red Army men, and workers of Kronstadt, similar resolutions were adopted unanimously with the exception of only three votes. The dissenters included Vassiliev, president of the Kronstadt Soviet, who was chairman of the mass meeting; Kuzmin, the Commissar of the Baltic Fleet; and Kalinin, President of the Federated Socialist Soviet Republics.

Two anarchists who had attended the gathering returned to tell us of the order, enthusiasm, and fine spirit that had prevailed there. Not since the early days of October had they seen such spontaneous demonstration of solidarity and fervent comradeship. If only we had been there, they lamented. The presence of Sasha, for whom the Kronstadt sailors had made such a valiant stand when he was in danger of extradition to California, in 1917, and of me, whom the sailors knew by reputation, would have added weight to the resolution, they declared. We agreed that it would have been a wonderful experience to participate in the first great mass meeting on Soviet soil that was not machine-made. Gorki had assured me long ago that the men of the Baltic Fleet were born anarchists and that my place was with them. I had often longed to go to Kronstadt to meet the crews and talk to them, but I had felt that in my disturbed and confused state of mind I could give them nothing constructive. But now I would go to take

my place with them, though I knew that the Bolsheviki would raise
the cry that I was inciting the sailors against the régime. Sasha said
he did not care what the Communists would say. He would join the
sailors in their protest in behalf of the striking Petrograd workers.

Our comrades emphasized that the expressions of sympathy on the
part of Kronstadt with the strikers could in no way be construed as
anti-Soviet action. In fact, the entire spirit of the sailors and the
resolutions passed at their mass meeting were thoroughly Sovietist.
They were strongly opposed to the autocratic attitude of the Petrograd authorities towards the starving strikers, but at no time had
the gathering shown the least opposition to the Communists. In fact,
the great meeting had been held under the auspices of the Kronstadt
Soviet. To show their loyalty the sailors had met Kalinin on his arrival
in their city with music and song, and his talk was listened to with
respect and attention. Even after he and his comrades had attacked
the sailors and condemned their resolution, Kalinin had been escorted
back to the station in the greatest friendliness, our informants stated.

We had heard the rumour that at a gathering of three hundred
delegates from the fleet, the garrison, and the trade-union soviet
Kuzmin and Vassilev had been arrested by the sailors. We asked our
two comrades what they knew of the matter. They admitted that the
two men had been detained. The reason for it was that at the meeting
Kuzmin had denounced the sailors as traitors, and the Petrograd
strikers as *shkurniky,* and had declared that henceforth the Communist Party " would fight them to a finish as counter-revolutionists."
The delegates had also learned that Kuzmin had given orders for the
removal of all food and munitions from Kronstadt, thereby virtually
dooming the city to starvation. Therefore it was decided by the sailors
and the garrison of Kronstadt to detain Kuzmin and Vassilev and to
take precautions that no supplies be removed from the town. But that
was no indication whatever of any rebellious intentions or that they
had ceased to believe in the revolutionary integrity of the Communists.
On the contrary, the Communist delegates at the gathering were permitted an equal voice with the rest. Further proof of their confidence
in the régime was given by the delegates in sending a committee of
thirty men to confer with the Petro-Soviet with a view to an amicable
settlement of the strike.

We felt elated over the splendid solidarity of the Kronstadt sailors
and soldiers with their striking brothers in Petrograd and we hoped

that a speedy termination of the trouble would soon result, thanks to the mediation of the sailors.

Alas, our hopes proved vain within an hour after we had received news of the Kronstadt proceedings. An order signed by Lenin and Trotsky spread like wildfire through Petrograd. It declared that Kronstadt had mutinied against the Soviet Government, and denounced the sailors as " tools of former tsarist generals who together with Socialist-Revolutionist traitors staged a counter-revolutionary conspiracy against the proletarian Republic."

" Preposterous! It's nothing short of madness!" Sasha cried as he read the copy of the order. " Lenin and Trotsky must be misinformed by someone. They could not possibly believe the sailors guilty of counter-revolution. Why, the crews of the *Petropavlovsk* and *Sevastopol* in particular had been the staunchest supporters of the Bolsheviki in October and ever since. And did not Trotsky himself greet them as ' the pride and flower of the Revolution '! "

We must go to Moscow at once, Sasha declared. It was imperative to see Lenin and Trotsky and to explain to them that it was all a horrible misunderstanding, a blunder that might prove fatal to the Revolution itself. It was very hard for Sasha to give up his faith in the revolutionary integrity of the men that had appeared as the proletarian apostles to millions throughout the world. I agreed with him that Lenin and Trotsky might have been misled by Zinoviev, who was nightly telephoning to the Kremlin detailed reports about Kronstadt. Zinoviev had never been famed even among his own comrades for personal courage. He had become panicky at the first symptoms of discontent shown by the Petrograd workers. When he learned that the local garrison had expressed sympathy with the strikers, he completely lost his head and had ordered a machine-gun placed at the Astoria for his protection. The stand of Kronstadt had put terror into his heart and had caused him to bombard Moscow with wild stories. I knew all that, as did also Sasha, but I could not believe that Lenin and Trotsky actually thought the Kronstadt men guilty of counter-revolution or capable of co-operating with White generals, as charged in Lenin's order.

Extraordinary martial law was declared over the entire Petrograd Province, and none but specially authorized officials could leave the city. The Bolshevik press opened a campaign of calumny and vituperation against Kronstadt, proclaiming that the sailors and soldiers had made common cause with the " tsarist general Kozlovsky," and declaring the Kronstadt people outlawed. Sasha began to realize that the situation involved a good deal more than mere misinformation on the part of Lenin and Trotsky. The latter was to attend the special session of the Petro-Soviet where the fate of Kronstadt was to be decided. We resolved to be present.

It was my first opportunity in Russia to hear Trotsky. We might remind him of his parting words in New York, I thought: the hope he had expressed that we should come to Russia soon to assist in the great work made possible by the overthrow of tsarism. We would plead with him to let us help settle the Kronstadt difficulty in a comradely spirit, to dispose of our time and energies, even of our lives, in the supreme test to which the Revolution was putting the Communist Party.

Unfortunately Trotsky's train was delayed and he failed to appear at the session. The men who addressed the gathering were beyond reason or appeal. Fanaticism run mad was in their words, and blind fear in their hearts.

The platform was heavily guarded by *kursanty,* and Chekist soldiers with fixed bayonets stood between it and the audience. Zinoviev, who presided, seemed on the point of a nervous collapse. Several times he rose to speak and then sat down again. When he finally began talking, he kept his head jerking to the left and right as if fearing a sudden attack, and his voice, always adolescently thin, rose to a high-pitched shrillness, extremely jarring and in no way convincing.

He denounced " General Kozlovsky " as the evil spirit of the Kronstadt men, though most of the audience knew that that military officer had been placed in Kronstadt by Trotsky himself as an artillery specialist. Kozlovsky was old and decrepit and of no influence whatever with the sailors or the garrison. That did not prevent Zinoviev, as chairman of the specially created Committee of Defence, from proclaiming that Kronstadt had risen against the Revolution and was seeking to carry out the plans of Kozlovsky and his tsarist aids. Kalinin shed his usually grandmotherly manner and attacked the sailors in vicious terms, forgetful of the honours paid him in Kronstadt but a few days previously. " No measure can be too severe for the counter-revolutionists who dare to raise their hand against our glorious Revolution," he declared. The lesser lights among the speakers followed in the same strain, rousing their Communist zealots,

ignorant of the real facts, to revengeful frenzy against the men yesterday acclaimed heroes and brothers.

Above the din of the howling and stamping mob a single voice
strove to be heard — the tense, earnest voice of a man in the front
rows. He was a delegate of the striking employees at the arsenal
works. He was moved to protest, he declared, against the misrepresentations uttered from the platform against the brave and loyal men
of Kronstadt. Facing Zinoviev and pointing his finger directly at him,
the man thundered: " It's the cruel indifference of yourself and of
your party that drove us to strike and that roused the sympathy of
our brother sailors, who had fought side by side with us in the Revolution. They are guilty of no other crime, and you know it. Consciously you malign them and call for their destruction." Cries of
" Counter-revolutionist! Traitor! *Shkurnik!* Menshevik bandit! "
turned the assembly into a bedlam.

The old worker remained standing, his voice rising above the
tumult. " Barely three years ago Lenin, Trotsky, Zinoviev, and all of
you," he shouted, " were denounced as traitors and German spies. We,
the workers and sailors, had come to your rescue and saved you from
the Kerensky Government. It was we who placed you in power. Have
you forgotten that? Now you threaten us with the sword. Remember
you are playing with fire. You are repeating the blunders and crimes
of the Kerensky Government. Beware that a similar fate does not
overtake you! "

The challenge made Zinoviev wince. The others on the platform
moved uneasily in their seats. The Communist audience seemed awed
for an instant by the portentous warning, and in that moment there
rang out another voice. A tall man in a sailor's uniform stood up in
the back. Nothing had changed in the revolutionary spirit of his
brothers of the sea, he declared. To the last man they were ready to
defend the Revolution with their every drop of blood. Then he proceeded to read the Kronstadt resolution adopted at the mass meeting
on March 1. The uproar his daring evoked made it impossible for any
but those nearest to hear him. But he stood his ground and kept on
reading to the end.

The only reply to these two sturdy sons of the Revolution was Zinoviev's resolution demanding the complete and immediate surrender of
Kronstadt on pain of extermination. It was rushed through the ses-

sion amidst a pandemonium of confusion, with every opposing voice gagged.

The atmosphere, surcharged with the hysteria of passion and hate, crept into my being and held me by the throat. All evening I wanted to cry out against the mockery of men stooping to the lowest political trickery in the name of a great ideal. My voice seemed to have left me, for I could not utter a sound. My thoughts reverted to another occasion where the spirit of vengeance and hate had run amuck — the eve of registration, June 4, 1917, at Hunts Point Palace, New York. I had been able to speak out then, entirely oblivious of danger from the war-drunk patriots. Why could I not now? Why did I not brand the impending fratricide by the Bolsheviki, as I had Woodrow Wilson's crime that had dedicated the young manhood of America to the Moloch of war? Had I lost the grit that had sustained me all through the years of fighting against every injustice and every wrong? Or was it helplessness which paralysed my will, the despair that had settled on my heart with the growing realization that I had mistaken a phantom for a life-giving force? Nothing could alter that crushing consciousness or make any protest worth while.

Yet silence in the face of the threatened slaughter was also intolerable. I had to make myself heard. But not by the obsessed, who would choke back my voice as they had done with the others. I would make known my stand in a statement to the supreme power of the Soviet Defence, that very night.

When we were alone and I spoke to Sasha about the matter, I was glad to learn that my old pal had conceived the same plan. He suggested that our letter should be a joint protest and deal exclusively with the murderous resolution passed by the Petro-Soviet. Two comrades who had been with us at the session shared his view and offered to sign their names to our joint appeal to the authorities.

I had no hope that our message would exert any sobering or restraining influence on the events decreed against the sailors. But I was determined to have my attitude registered in a manner to bear future witness that I had not remained a silent party to the blackest betrayal of the Revolution by the Communist Party.

At two o'clock in the morning Sasha got in touch by telephone with Zinoviev, to inform him that he had something important to communicate to him regarding Kronstadt. Perhaps Zinoviev assumed that it was something that might aid the conspiracy against Kronstadt. Otherwise he would have hardly troubled to rush Mme Ravich over at that hour of the night, ten minutes after Sasha had talked to him. She could be trusted absolutely, Zinoviev's note said, and she was to be given the message. We handed her our communication, which read:

To the Petrograd Soviet of Labour and Defence,
Chairman Zinoviev:

To remain silent now is impossible, even criminal. Recent events impel us anarchists to speak out and to declare our attitude in the present situation.

The spirit of ferment and dissatisfaction manifest among the workers and sailors is the result of causes that demand our serious attention. Cold and hunger have produced dissatisfaction, and the absence of any opportunity for discussion and criticism is forcing the workers and sailors to air their grievances in the open.

White-guardist bands wish and may try to exploit this dissatisfaction in their own class interests. Hiding behind the workers and the sailors, they throw out slogans of the Constituent Assembly, of free trade, and similar demands.

We anarchists have long since exposed the fiction of these slogans, and we declare to the whole world that we will fight with arms against any counter-revolutionary attempt, in co-operation with all friends of the Social Revolution and hand in hand with the Bolsheviki.

Concerning the conflict between the Soviet Government and the workers and sailors, we hold that it must be settled, not by force of arms, but by means of comradely, fraternal revolutionary agreement. Resort to bloodshed on the part of the Soviet Government will not—in the given situation—intimidate or quiet the workers. On the contrary, it will serve only to aggravate matters, and will strengthen the hands of the Entente and of internal counter-revolution.

More important still, the use of force by the Workers' and Peasants' Government against the workers and sailors will have a reactionary effect upon the international revolutionary movement and will everywhere result in incalculable harm to the Social Revolution.

Comrades Bolsheviki, bethink yourselves before it is too late. Do not play with fire; you are about to make a most serious and decisive step.

We hereby submit to you the following proposition: Let a commission be selected, to consist of five persons, inclusive of two anarchists. The commission is to go to Kronstadt to settle the dispute by peaceful means. In the given situation it is the most radical method. It will be of international revolutionary significance.

Petrograd
March 5, 1921

ALEXANDER BERKMAN
EMMA GOLDMAN
PERKUS
PETROVSKY

Proof that our appeal had fallen on deaf ears came to us the very same day on the arrival of Trotsky and his ultimatum to Kronstadt. By order of the Workers' and Peasants' Government, he declared to the Kronstadt sailors and soldiers, he would " shoot like pheasants " all those who had dared to " raise their hand against the Socialist fatherland." The rebellious ships and crews were commanded to submit immediately to the orders of the Soviet Government or be subdued by force of arms. Only those surrendering unconditionally might count on the mercy of the Soviet Republic.

The final warning was signed by Trotsky, as Chairman of the Revolutionary Military Soviet, and by Kamenev, the Commander-in-Chief of the Red Army. Daring to question the divine right of rulers was again to be punished by death.

Trotsky kept his word. Having been helped to authority by the men of Kronstadt, he was now in a position to pay his debt in full to the " pride and glory of the Russian Revolution." The best military experts and strategists of the Romanov régime were at his service, among them the notorious Tukhachevsky, whom Trotsky appointed commander-in-chief of the Kronstadt attack. In addition there were hordes of Chekists, with three years' training in the art of murder; *kursanty* and Communists specially picked for their blind obedience to orders; and the most trusted troops from various fronts. With such a force massed against the doomed city the " mutiny " was expected to be easily quelled. Especially after the soldiers and sailors of the Petrograd garrison had been disarmed and those that had expressed solidarity with their besieged comrades removed from the danger zone.

From my room window in the Hotel International I saw them led by in small groups, surrounded by strong detachments of Cheka troops. Their step had lost its spring, their hands hung at their sides, and their heads were bowed in grief.

The Petrograd strikers were no longer feared by the authorities. They were weakened by slow starvation and their energy sapped. They were demoralized by the lies spread against them and their Kronstadt brothers, their spirit broken by the poison of doubt instilled by Bolshevik propaganda. They had no more fight nor faith left to come to the aid of their Kronstadt comrades who had so selflessly taken up their cause and who were about to give up their lives for them.

Kronstadt was forsaken by Petrograd and cut off from the rest of Russia. It stood alone. It could offer almost no resistance. " It will go down at the first shot," the Soviet press proclaimed. They were mistaken. Kronstadt had thought of nothing less than of mutiny or resistance to the Soviet Government. To the very last moment it was determined to shed no blood. It appealed all the time for understanding and amicable settlement. But, forced to defend itself against unprovoked military attack, it fought like a lion. During ten harrowing days and nights the sailors and workers of the besieged city held out against a continuous artillery fire from three sides and bombs hurled from aeroplanes upon the non-combatant community. Heroically they repulsed the repeated attempts of the Bolsheviki to storm the fortresses by special troops from Moscow. Trotsky and Tukhachevsky had every advantage over the men of Kronstadt. The entire machinery of the Communist State backed them, and the centralized press continued to spread venom against the alleged " mutineers and counter-revolutionists." They had unlimited supplies and men whom they had masked in white shrouds to blend with the snow of the frozen Finnish Gulf in order to camouflage the night attack against the unsuspecting men of Kronstadt. The latter had nothing but their unflinching courage and abiding faith in the justice of their cause and in the free soviets they championed as the saviour of Russia from the dictatorship. They lacked even an ice-breaker to halt the onrush of the Communist enemy. They were exhausted by hunger and cold and sleepless nights of vigil. Yet they held their own, desperately fighting against overwhelming odds.

During the fearful suspense, the days and nights filled with the rumbling of heavy artillery, there sounded not a single voice amid the roar of guns to cry out against or call a halt to the terrible blood bath. Gorki, Maxim Gorki, where was he? His voice would be heard. "Let us go to him," I pleaded with some of the intelligentsia. He had never made the slightest protest in grave individual cases, neither in those concerning members of his own profession nor even when he knew of the innocence of doomed men. He would not protest now. It was hopeless.

The intelligentsia, the men and women that had once been revolutionary torch-bearers, leaders of thought, writers and poets, were as helpless as we and paralysed by the futility of individual effort. Most of their comrades and friends were already in prison or exile; some had been executed. They felt too broken by the collapse of all human values.

I turned to the Communists of our acquaintance, imploring them to do something. Some of them realized the monstrous crime their party was committing against Kronstadt. They admitted that the charge of counter-revolution was a downright fabrication. The supposed leader, Kozlovsky, was a nonentity too frightened about his own fate to have anything to do with any protest of the sailors. The latter were of sterling quality, their sole aim the welfare of Russia. Far from making common cause with the tsarist generals, they had even declined the help offered them by Chernov, the leader of the Socialist-Revolutionists. They wanted no outside aid. They demanded the right to choose their own deputies in the forthcoming elections to the Kronstadt Soviet and justice for the strikers in Petrograd.

These Communist friends spent nights with us — talking, talking — but none of them dared raise his voice in open protest. We did not realize, they said, the consequences it would involve. They would be excluded from the party, they and their families deprived of work and rations and literally condemned to death by starvation. Or they would simply vanish and no one would ever know what had become of them. Yet it was not fear that numbed their will, they assured us. It was the utter uselessness of protest or appeal. Nothing, nothing could stop the chariot-wheel of the Communist State. It had rolled them flat and they had no vitality left, even to cry out against it.

I was beset by the terrible apprehension that we also — Sasha and I — might reach the same state and become as spinelessly acquiescent as these people. Anything else would be preferable to that. Prison, exile, even death. Or escape! Escape from the horrible revolutionary sham and pretence.

The idea that I might want to leave Russia had never before entered my mind. I was startled and shocked by the mere thought of it. I to leave Russia to her Calvary! Yet I felt that I would take even that step rather than become a cog in the machinery, an inanimate thing to be manipulated at will.

The cannonade of Kronstadt continued without let-up for ten days and nights and then came to a sudden stop on the morning of March 17. The stillness that fell over Petrograd was more fearful than the ceaseless firing of the night before. It held everyone in agonized suspense, and it was impossible to learn what had happened and why the bombardment had ceased. In the late afternoon the tension gave way to mute horror. Kronstadt had been subdued — tens of thousands slain — the city drenched in blood. The Neva a grave for masses of men, *kursanty* and young Communists whose heavy artillery had broken through the ice. The heroic sailors and soldiers had defended their position to the last breath. Those not fortunate enough to die fighting had fallen into the hands of the enemy to be executed or sent to slow torture in the frozen regions of northernmost Russia.

We were stunned. Sasha, the last thread of his faith in the Bolsheviki broken, desperately roamed the streets. Lead was in my limbs, unutterable weariness in every nerve. I sat limp, peering into the night. Petrograd was hung in a black pall, a ghastly corpse. The street-lamps flickered yellow, like candles at its head and feet.

The following morning, March 18, still heavy with sleep after the lack of it during seventeen anxious days, I was roused by the tramp of many feet. Communists were marching by, bands playing military tunes and singing the *International*. Its strains, once jubilant to my ear, now sounded like a funeral dirge for humanity's flaming hope.

March 18 — the anniversary of the Paris Commune of 1871, crushed two months later by Thiers and Gallifet, the butchers of thirty thousand Communards. Emulated in Kronstadt on March 18, 1921.

The full significance of the "liquidation" of Kronstadt was disclosed by Lenin himself three days after the frightfulness. At the Tenth Congress of the Communist Party, staged in Moscow while the siege of Kronstadt was in progress, Lenin unexpectedly changed his inspired Communist song to an equally inspired pæan to the New

Economic Policy. Free trade, concessions to the capitalists, private employment of farm and factory labour, all damned for over three years as rank counter-revolution and punished by prison and even death, were now written by Lenin on the glorious banner of the dictatorship. Brazenly as ever he admitted what sincere and thoughtful persons in and out of the party had known for seventeen days: that " the Kronstadt men did not really want the counter-revolutionists. But neither did they want us." The naïve sailors had taken seriously the slogan of the Revolution: " All power to the Soviets," by which Lenin and his party had solemnly promised to abide. That had been their unforgivable offence. For that they had to die. They had to be martyred to fertilize the soil for Lenin's new crop of slogans, which completely reversed the old. Their *chef d'œuvre* the New Economic Policy, the NEP.

Lenin's public confession in regard to Kronstadt did not stop the hunt for the sailors, soldiers, and workers of the defeated city. They were arrested by the hundreds, and the Cheka was again busy " target-shooting."

Strangely enough, the anarchists had not been mentioned in connexion with the Kronstadt " mutiny." But at the Tenth Congress Lenin had declared that the most merciless war must be waged against the " petty *bourgeoisie*," including the anarchist elements. The anarcho-syndicalist leanings of the labour opposition proved that these tendencies had developed in the Communist Party itself, he had said. Lenin's call to arms against the anarchists met with immediate response. The Petrograd groups were raided and scores of their members arrested. In addition the Cheka closed the printing and publishing offices of the *Golos Truda,* belonging to the anarcho-syndicalist branch of our ranks. We had purchased our ticket to Moscow before this happened. When we learned about the wholesale arrests, we decided to stay a little longer in case we too should be wanted. We were not molested, however, perhaps because it was necessary to have a few anarchist celebrities at large to show that only " bandits " were in Soviet prisons.

In Moscow we found all except half a dozen anarchists arrested and the *Golos Truda* book-store closed. In neither city had any charges been made against our comrades, nor had they been given a hearing or brought to trial. Nevertheless, a number of them had already been sent away to the penitentiary of Samara. Those still in the Butirky and the Taganka prisons were being subjected to the worst persecution and even physical violence. Thus one of our boys, young Kashirin, had been beaten by a Chekist in the presence of the prison warden. Maximov and other anarchists who had fought on the revolutionary fronts, and who were known and respected by many Communists, had been forced to declare a hunger-strike against the terrible conditions.

The first thing we were asked to do on our return to Moscow was to sign a manifesto to the Soviet authorities denouncing the concerted tactics to exterminate our people.

We did so of course, Sasha now as emphatic as I that protests from within Russia by the handful of politicals still out of prison were entirely futile. On the other hand, no effective action could be expected from the Russian masses, even if we could reach them. Years of war, civil strife, and suffering had sapped their vitality, and terror had silenced them into submission. Our recourse, Sasha declared, was Europe and the United States. The time had come when the workers abroad must learn about the shameful betrayal of " October." The awakened conscience of the proletariat and of other liberal and radical elements in every country must be crystallized into a mighty outcry against the ruthless persecution for opinion's sake. Only that might stay the hand of the dictatorship. Nothing else could.

This much the martyrdom of Kronstadt had already done for my pal. It had demolished the last vestiges of his belief in the Bolshevik myth. Not only Sasha, but also the other comrades who had formerly defended the Communist methods as inevitable in a revolutionary period, had at last been forced to see the abyss between " October " and the dictatorship.

If only the cost for the profound lesson taught them had not been so terrific, I should have taken comfort in the knowledge that Sasha and I were again united in our stand, and that my Russian comrades hitherto antagonistic to my attitude to the Bolsheviki had now come closer to me. It would be a relief not to have to grope further in distressing isolation and not to feel so alien in the midst of people whom I had known in the past as the ablest among the anarchists, not to have to choke back my thoughts and emotions before the one human being who had shared my life, my ideals, and my labours through our common lot of thirty-two years. But there was the black cross erected in Kronstadt and the blood of the modern Christs trickling from their hearts. How could one cherish personal comfort and relief?

On our way to the Leontevsky we ran into a parade more demonstrative and showy than the usual variety. What was the special occasion, we inquired. Had we just come to Moscow that we were ignorant of the grand event? Why, it was the return of General Slaschov-Krimsky that was being celebrated. "What!" cried Sasha and I in the same breath, "the White General, the Jew-baiter, the man who had with his own hand snuffed out the lives of Red soldiers and Jews, the sworn and relentless enemy of the Revolution?" The very one, we were assured. He had recanted and had begged to be readmitted to the fatherland he loved so well, swearing to serve the Bolsheviki faithfully henceforth. He was now being received with military honours and fêted at the order of the Soviet Government by workers, soldiers, and sailors singing revolutionary songs for the edification of one of the most implacable foes of the Revolution. We walked over to the Red Square to see the spectacle of Leon Trotsky, the Commissar of the Revolutionary Army of the Socialist Republic, reviewing his forces before the tsarist general Slaschov-Krimsky. The grand stand was not far from John Reed's grave. Within its shadow Leon Trotsky, the butcher of Kronstadt, was clasping the blood-stained hand of his comrade Krimsky. A spectacle indeed to make the gods weep with laughter!

Shortly after this, General Slaschov-Krimsky was ordered to Karelia, a desolate district in the north, to "liquidate the counter-revolutionary uprising there." The simple Karelians, assured of their right to self-determination, had found the Communist yoke too irksome and had naïvely protested against the abuses they had been made to suffer. Who more competent to bring the "mutineers" to reason than General Slaschov-Krimsky?

One solace was left us. We did not have to eat out of the slayer's hand. My dear old mother and our friend Henry Alsberg had saved us from that degradation. Through a friend my mother had sent me three hundred dollars, and Henry had left Sasha some clothing to exchange for food. In our new mode of living these would go a long way to keep us above water.

We had not yet adapted ourselves to the process of existence that the bulk of the non-privileged were forced to undergo. Waylaying peasants at dawn for a supply of wood, pulling it home on a sleigh, chopping it with frozen hands, carrying it up three flights of stairs; then fetching water several times a day from a long distance and up to our quarters; cooking, washing, and sleeping in a little hall bedroom, Sasha's smaller even than mine and never quite warm — this was bitter hard, at first, and terribly exhausting. My hands were chapped and swollen, and my spine, never very strong, was full of aches. My dear friend also suffered a great deal, especially from the return of his old trouble with his legs, the ligaments of which he had stretched by his fall in New York and which had crippled him for a year.

However, physical pain and weariness were as nothing to our inner liberation — the spiritual release we felt that we no longer had to ask or accept anything from the powers that had dealt the final blow to " October " by the slaughter of Kronstadt.

Considering the complete collapse of all the revolutionary pretence of the dictatorship, a Peter Kropotkin museum under its protection struck me as a direct desecration of his name. Sasha had also come to see the incongruity of a memorial to Peter within the citadel of Lenin, Trotsky, and Slaschov-Krimsky. Our Russian comrades agreed with us. Still they clung to the idea of the museum as the only centre of anarchist thought that the Bolsheviki would not dare lay hands on. Sophie, however, did not want the Kropotkin museum turned into anarchist headquarters. Her ambition as the lifelong companion and co-worker of Peter was a testimonial to *all* of Peter's versatile activities — in the fields of science, philosophy, letters, humanism, and anarchism. While I understood Sophie and felt with her, I nevertheless had to sustain my comrades in their desire to emphasize the anarchist in Kropotkin. He himself had willed it so. He had chosen anarchism as his goal, and its exposition as his supreme interest in life. It was therefore Kropotkin the anarchist who should be given first place in a museum dedicated to him. Yet I could not ignore the importance of Sophie's part in the project. She alone had the devotion, the loving patience, the time and freedom necessary to bring the memorial to life and to watch over its development and growth. I pointed out to our comrades that, though they were still at liberty, they were in danger of arrest by the Cheka at any moment. How could they undertake to build and keep up the museum? Even when free, they could not do it. Their daily toil, added to the consuming task of securing their rations, would leave them neither time nor strength to accomplish anything for Peter's memorial. My part in the project would be limited to an appeal to our people in the United States, and even that I would make only because I wanted to help Sophie. I thought it very inconsistent to have a Kropotkin museum in present-day Russia, nor did I believe in asking or accepting help for it from the Soviet autocrats.

Sasha agreed to join me in the appeal, but under no circumstances would he have any further dealings with the men responsible for the Kronstadt blood bath, for the wholesale persecution of our comrades and the night assault on the politicals in the Butirky prison. The Romanov dynasty, he emphasized, had rarely been guilty of such a wanton attack on politicals. In the Socialist Republic Chekists and soldiers had fallen upon men and women asleep in their cells, beat them, dragged the women by the hair down the stairs, and thrown them into waiting trucks to be sent off no one knew where. No person with any humanity or revolutionary integrity could have anything to do with such criminals, Sasha declared passionately.

It was not often that my comrade was aroused to such a pitch or showed his indignation, no matter how deeply he felt it. But the letter we had received from one of the victims of the frightful night raid had been the last straw to Sasha's wrath, which had been accumulating for the past two months.

The letter bore out the rumours that had come to us during the day following the assault. It read:

Concentration Camp, Ryazan

On the night of April 25 we were attacked by Red soldiers and armed Chekists and ordered to dress and get ready to leave the Butirky. Some of the politicals, fearing that they were to be taken to execution, refused to go and were terribly beaten. The women especially were maltreated, some of them being dragged down the stairs by their hair. Many have suffered serious injury. I myself was so badly beaten that my whole body feels like one big sore. We were taken out by force in our night-clothes and thrown into wagons. The comrades in our group know nothing of the whereabouts of the rest of the politicals, including Mensheviki, Socialist-Revolutionists, Anarchists, and Anarcho-Syndicalists.

Ten of us, among them Fanya Baron, have been brought here. Conditions in this prison are unbearable. No exercise, no fresh air food is scarce and filthy; everywhere awful dirt, bed-bugs, and lice. We mean to declare a hunger-strike for better treatment. We have just been told to get ready with our things. They are going to send us away again. We don't know where to.

The reason for the outrage was that the Cheka could not tolerate the comparative freedom our men had established in the Butirky, and their organization of classes, lectures, and discussions. Also the politicals had pleaded for reforms in the treatment of the ordinary prisoners. Constantly locked in their cells, given abominable food, their excrement-buckets often not emptied for two days, fifteen hundred inmates had gone on strike. It had been entirely due to the politicals that the demands of the unfortunates had been satisfied and the trouble terminated. The Cheka had not forgiven the set-back it had received through the intervention of the politicals. Hence the night assault of April 25.

Repeated inquiries by the Moscow Soviet about the fate of the three hundred Mensheviki, Socialist-Revolutionists, and Anarchists forcibly removed from the Butirky elicited the information that they had been distributed among the Orlov, Yaroslavl, and Vladimir prisons.

Shortly after the raid students of the Moscow University protested in an open meeting against the horrors of April 25. The initiators were promptly arrested, the university closed, and the students, who had come from different parts of Russia, given three days to return to their native places. The official explanation given for these drastic measures was lack of rations. The young people declared that they would do without them if permitted to continue their studies. But they were ordered to leave just the same. A short time later the university was opened again. " Henceforth no political activities of any kind will be tolerated," declared Preobrazhensky, Dean of the university. Dropping professors from the faculty and suspending students if they dared to protest had been a daily occurrence. Only the public did not know about it. After Kronstadt and the New Economic Policy the academic gag became more severe and quite unashamed; it ceased to be a star-chamber proceeding. Alexey Borovoy, a well-known anarchist and professor of philosophy, who had been free to teach in the Moscow University during the régime of the Tsar, was forced to resign under the Bolshevik dictatorship. His offence consisted in that the students attended his classes *en masse* and heard him gladly.

The arrested students were exiled, among them even girls of the age of seventeen and eighteen, charged with belonging to a circle that was studying the works of Kropotkin. In view of the situation it was almost childish to think that the Bolsheviki would hesitate to lay hands on the Peter Kropotkin Museum. But most of the committee members refused to be convinced. Sasha and I needed no further justification for our stand. Besides, we had definitely decided to leave Russia.

In the first weeks of Sasha's anguish that followed the massacre of Kronstadt I had not dared to mention the idea of definitely leaving Russia that had come to me during the siege. I feared it might add to his agony. Later, when he had bravely pulled himself together, I broached the subject to him, not at all sure that he would want to go, but certain that I could not leave him behind under the murderous régime. I was therefore immensely relieved to find that Sasha had spent many sleepless nights brooding over the same idea. After we had discussed every possibility for making our lives count for more than mere existences in Russia, we had come to the conclusion that no word nor act of ours would be of value to the Revolution or to our movement or of the least help to our persecuted comrades. We might proclaim from the market-place the anti-revolutionary nature of Bolshevism, or we might hurl our lives against Lenin, Trotsky, and Zinoviev and go down with them. Far from serving our cause or the interest of the masses by such an act, we should be merely aiding the dictatorship. Its skilful propaganda would drag our names through the mire and brand us before the world as traitors, counter-revolutionists, and bandits. Nor could we continue gagged and chained. Therefore we decided to go. Once Sasha was clear that there was nothing vital for us to do in Russia, with the Revolution crushed by the iron hand of dictatorship, he insisted on our leaving soon and illegally. We should not be given passports, he said. Why, then, keep up the torture? Leave Russia like thieves in the night, I protested, Russia that had promised the fulfilment of our hopes? I could not do that, not until we had tried other means. I pleaded that we should get in touch with our comrades abroad to find out what country would admit us. Syndicalist delegates were sure to attend the Congress of the Red Trade Union International to be held in July in Moscow. We might entrust a message to them, or still better to Henry Alsberg, who was about to leave Russia. He would not be like the others who had promised to deliver our message to our people in America and to tell them frankly of the situation. Most of them either had not done so or had misquoted us. No wonder Stella and Fitzi still kept writing enthusiastically about our wonderful opportunity for activity in Russia. Henry was absolutely dependable;

we must wait until he saw our comrades in Germany. Sasha agreed, though reluctantly. He would find no more peace with Kronstadt on his mind, he said.

I shared his grief, as indeed did all our people and nearly everyone else who still had revolutionary fibre left. Our place in Moscow became the oasis for our comrades, as well as for others outside of our ranks. They came at all hours of the day and even late at night, hungry, spiritless, in black despair. The meals intended for ourselves and perhaps for one or two invited guests had to perform the miracle of Christ's loaves for the many who would drift in by the time we sat down to eat. To assure them that there was enough to go round I had to invent all kinds of reasons for my poor appetite: headaches, stomach trouble, and the vice of cooks who always have their pick of the best before the meal is served. I minded the faintness that would sometimes overcome me much less than the lack of privacy. But these people had no other place to go, nowhere where they might feel at home or free to communicate their troubled spirit. It was the only service we could render and we did so out of the fullness of our hearts.

We had other guests not quite so wearing, though no less distressed by the travail of their native land. Alexandra Shakol, our secretary of the expedition, arrived for a short stay in Moscow. It was good to see her again, to exchange thoughts with her, and to help dispel her gloom by treating her to the most cherished delicacy, gogglemoggle, as she called it (egg-nog), which she considered the acme of bliss.

Through Shakol we were able to renew our acquaintance with Vera Nikolayevna Figner, one of the loftiest figures in the pioneer revolutionary movement known as the *Narodnaya Volya* (the People's Will). I had met her the previous year and had been shocked to find her in poor health and underfed. I had inquired whether she was receiving the academic ration which, though not plentiful, was enough to live on. Vera Nikolayevna was too proud to ask for it and she had been overlooked, Shakol informed me. Lunacharsky, whom I had gone to see about the matter, was as indignant as I. He had known nothing about it and he immediately ordered the ration for Vera Figner. Now she looked better and younger. Despite her almost fourscore years, she was still a figure to feast one's eye upon, much of her former beauty being left, the beauty that had inspired poets. Equally

marvellous was her spirit after twenty-two years spent in the Schlüs-
selburg Fortress and the years of struggle since the Russian drama
unfolded itself before her. Gracious of manner, witty, and with
infinite humanity, Vera Nikolayevna held us rapt by her reminiscences
of the heroic revolutionary epoch, the comrades of the *Narodnaya
Volva* period and their extraordinary fortitude and daring. They
were the real precursors of anarchism, Vera thought, wholly dedicated
to its realization by the masses, and without least thought of self.
She had known almost all of them and her tribute reflected her own
pure vision and grandeur, especially when she spoke of Sophie
Perovskaya, the high priestess of the most significant revolutionary
epoch in the world. Vera's narrative always renewed my hope that
what had been might come again to life in our *Matushka Rossiya*.

An unexpected arrival from America was our old friend Bob
Robbins, of the quaint auto-house and the anti-Semitic dog. He also
had " got religion " — Russia was in his blood. He had cut loose
from his affiliations, comrades, and friends in the United States, and,
taking his savings of years, he had come to the home of the soviets to
help in its labours and to glory in its gains. His wife, Lucy, had
chosen the smoother and safer way of the American Federation of
Labor. Bobby was a strong link with our past. Poignantly real for a
while, it was soon again overshadowed by the black clouds in the
Russian sky. Louise Bryant suddenly appeared, no longer grief-
stricken and in despair. Seven months had passed since Jack's death,
and Louise was young and greedy for life. No wonder she aroused the
misgivings and censure of her husband's comrades. She powdered her
nose and rouged her lips and she was careful of her figure. Such
heresies in Soviet Russia! Perhaps Louise had never been a Communist, but only the wife of one. Why might she not go her own way,
I pleaded in her defence. That was grist to the Communist ascetics.
I was a *bourzhouy* like Louise and others of her kind, they charged,
always championing individual rights when there was only one purpose — the dictatorship and its aims.

Louise asked me to go with her to Stanislavsky for an interview. I
was glad of the chance to meet the man whose great art and that of
his group had often lifted me out of the drab reality. Lunacharsky
had given me a letter of introduction to him as well as to Nemirovich-
Danchenko on my first visit to Moscow. They had both been ill at the

time, and since then Russia's wave had swept over me.

We found Stanislavsky among mountains of trunks, boxes, and bags. His studio had again been requisitioned. It had happened so many times before that he no longer minded it any more than his periodic house arrests, he told us. He felt much more discouraged about the poverty of the Russian drama. Nothing of any merit during the past four years, he said. The growth of a dramatic artist depends on the living source of creative art; when that is dried up, the greatest must needs become sterile. He was not despairing, he hastily added; no one could despair who knew the treasures of the Russian soil and soul. From Gogol to Chekhov, Gorki, and Andreyev the line has apparently broken, but is not entirely lost. The future will prove that, Stanislavsky prophesied.

The visitor closest to us was Henry Alsberg. He came often, somehow divining the moments when we were alone. He was always laden with gifts to replenish our larder, and his ready wit and fine human qualities helped dispel our gloom. Henry no longer talked about the great political changes that would follow when the fronts should be liquidated. Since he had returned to Russia, every front had indeed been terminated, even the Kronstadt front. The only one left was Karelia and General Slaschov-Krimsky was attending to that. Civil strife was at an end. The time had come for the hopes of Alsberg to be fulfilled: free speech, free press, and amnesty for the thousands of politicals in Soviet prisons. " Where are they, Henry? " I once asked him; " where are the liberties you had expected from Lenin and his party? " He was intellectually too honest to deny that he was haunted by Kronstadt, as all of us were, and oppressed by the wholesale arrests of the politicals and their inhuman treatment. His lack of clarity about the nature, meaning, and purpose of the Social Revolution was his trouble. He remained the knight-errant, blaming the Revolution, the backwardness of the country and its people, the interventionists, and the blockade for every crime that was inherent in the dictatorship, in the mania for power to subjugate everybody and everything for the greater glory of that cold monster the Communist State. His attitude sometimes taxed my patience, but never my affection for our easy-going, good-natured friend. Nor did it affect the bonds of our fellowship. In Bolshevik Russia perhaps more than anywhere else one had to laugh sometimes to keep back one's tears.

On one of his last calls at our place Henry again brought a large bundle of clothing. "Well," he drawled to Sasha, "if Lenin can become a shopkeeper, why not also Alexander Berkman?" "Sure," Sasha replied, "it is kosher now, only I beat Lenin to it. I traded things while we were in the Ukraine before the pope in the Kremlin gave it his benediction." "You forget," I interjected, "that you engaged in trade as a 'speculator and bandit.' Lenin does it in the holy name of Karl Marx. That's the difference."

Yes, therein was the difference. The unfortunates in the market in front of the National Hotel had given way to a large pastry shop. It was stacked with fresh loaves of white bread, cake, and *pyroshky*. The owner, perhaps not a Communist, was a business man according to Lenin's own heart. He knew how to attract customers. The place was crowded and business brisk. Outside stood the rabble, pale-faced and faint with hunger, their eyes bulging with craving for the miracle displayed in the show-window, luxuries they had not seen in years. "Where do these things come from?" a woman protested as I was passing there. "A little while ago it was dangerous to have a bit of white bread in one's possession. And look at this. Look at those loaves of fine cake! Is it for this that we have made the Revolution?" she moaned. "I thought we were through with the *bourgeoisie*," a man cried; "look at them going in and out of the place! What are they and who are they?" The crowd took up the refrain, and some clenched their fists. "Go on now, disperse!" came the order of a militiaman on guard at the store. The sacred rights of property had to be protected.

A store on the Tverskaya that had been closed for three years now opened its doors with a large stock of choice fruit, caviar, fowl, and other things one would not have believed existed in Russia. The crowd that gathered outside seemed too overwhelmed to realize what it was all about. It was a brazen challenge to their hunger. Their amazement soon turned to indignation and loud resentment. Those nearest rushed into the store, the rest following. But Lenin's good business man was prepared. Guards had been stationed inside to meet such an emergency. They did their duty. They were the only force in Soviet Russia that worked efficiently.

The Nep spread. The hour of the new *bourgeoisie* had arrived. No further need to worry about Sovietsky soup or rations with such an assortment of delicacies on hand. No further anxiety to hide the loot taken from the predecessors of the new privileged class. I could hardly trust my eyes when at the Stanislavsky First Studio I met a number of women dressed in velvet and silks, wearing costly shawls, and bedecked with jewelry. Why not? The Sovietsky ladies knew how to appreciate fine clothes, even if they were somewhat crumpled from their hiding-places and not exactly in keeping with the latest Parisian fashions!

The grey and drab continued, however, among the masses, wearing out their already depleted strength in the long wait for an order for a hole to live in, a bit of calico or medicine for their sick family or even a coffin for their dead. This was no hallucination of my exhausted brain. It was one of the many ghastly realities. One such case was related to me by Angelica Balabanoff. She had been sent back to a little room in the National and completely divested of her Soviet functions. Ill, disillusioned, and broken, she suffered more than most of her comrades from the latest somersault of her idol Ilich. To see constantly the hungry crowds around the bakeries and pastry-shops was torture to one who, like Angelica, felt guilty to accept the gift of even a few biscuits from her Swedish friends. It was a purgatory which only we, who knew her well, could appreciate.

In a feverish state she told me of the suicide of a friend, a Communist woman, who had been in the revolutionary ranks for a quarter of a century. Having heard of quite a number of Communists who had ended their lives after the new economic policy had been introduced, I thought it was a case of similar nature. But it was not that, Angelica explained. Her comrade had shot herself in the hope that her violent death would call attention to the plight of her son, who was ill in a hospital. She had lost one son at the revolutionary front. The second, a mere lad, was tubercular and the commissar had notified the mother that her boy had overstayed his time in the hospital and that she would have to take him home. She had tried to get an order for a room in the National, where the boy would be assured some comfort. Failing in that, she had decided to die so that her shot might induce the Party Executive Committee to secure a room for her child. " The poor creature must have been insane," I protested. Angelica assured me that the woman had been quite in her mind, but she had been unable to see her son die like a dog. The horror of it had completely overtaken Angelica on the day of the burial. She had gone with a comrade to the cemetery by the last request of their dead friend. No one else was there, nor the body of the deceased. Angelica was near a collapse and her escort insisted on turning back. On the way they met two Communist women with a pushcart for a hearse. The delay had been due to the difficulty of getting an order for the coffin and a burial certificate.

The Nep flourished, and the inspired, flocking to the holy grail, were assured that the proletariat was in full control and that money was no more needed in Soviet Russia because the workers had free access to the best the land produced. A large contingent of the devout believers from America had confidingly turned over to the reception committee on the border all their possessions. In Moscow they were packed like sardines in common quarters, given a small ration of bread and soup, and left to their fate. Within a month two children of the group died of undernourishment and infection. The men became despondent, the women ill, one of them going insane from anxiety about her children and the shock of the conditions she had found in Russia. Our friend, little Bobby, his hopes already shattered, came to tell us of the case on the very day when another woman and her two children had walked two miles from the Moscow station to lay their tragedy at our door. Mrs. Konossevich, her husband, their fourteen-year-old daughter and little boy had been deported from America after they had experienced a dose of Mitchell Palmer's régime. They came to Russia with high enthusiasm in their hearts, though not quite so credulous as the others who had been deported with them. They had heard that Russia was naked and starved and they decided to distribute their possessions among the needy. Two weeks later Konossevich, together with his family, were taken off the train on their way to their native village in the Ukraine. He was accused of being a Makhnovets. He had just arrived from the States, where he had been maltreated and deported for his pro-Soviet stand, he explained to the Cheka, and he had never even heard of Makhno. His protests did not help. He was arrested, his baggage confiscated, and his wife and two children left at the station without enough money to exist a week.

It was at any rate work for us to try to save the wife of one comrade from going mad, to find work for Mrs. Konossevich, and to rescue her husband from probable execution. Over and above this crazy pattern of Soviet life, the famine suddenly loomed across the land; want and death spread through the Volga region and threatened the rest of the country. The Soviet Government had known for two

months that millions were likely to perish unless immediate steps for
relief were taken. Agricultural specialists and economists had warned
the authorities of the impending calamity. They had frankly declared
that the main cause of the situation was inefficiency, mismanagement,
and bureaucratic corruption. Instead of setting the Soviet machinery
to work to relieve the calamity, to acquaint the public with the situation and rouse it to the danger, the report of the specialists had been
suppressed.

The few non-Communists who knew of it were powerless to do
anything. We were among the latter. In the heyday of our faith in
the Bolsheviki we should have knocked at the door of every leader
and given our help in relief work. We had learned better since Kronstadt. Nevertheless we informed the Left elements accessible to us of
the threatened calamity and begged to be permitted to join in a campaign to succour the famine-stricken. They hastened to offer suggestions and aid to the Government, but it was declined. The Right wing
was given a more favourable reception. Apart from Vera Figner,
who had joined that group out of human interest, most of the others
were Constitutional Democrats who had bitterly fought the October
Revolution. They had repeatedly been arrested as counter-revolutionists, but now they were accepted with open arms as the " Citizens'
Committee." Every facility was given them in their work : a building,
telephones, typists, and the right to publish a paper. Two numbers
appeared, the first containing an appeal by Patriarch Tikhon, who
called upon his flock to contribute their donations to him since he
would be responsible for their distribution. The irony of this love-
feast between the *avant-garde* of the proletariat and its enemies was
demonstrated by the *Bulletin* the latter issued. It was nothing else
than the resurrected old *Vyedomosty,* the blackest reactionary sheet
of the tsarist régime, which it resembled in every detail save in name.
It was now called *Pomoshch (Aid).*

Once more the geniuses of the Soviet circus had scored over Barnum
and Bailey. Indeed, western Europe would no more dare say that
political liberties were extinct in the Communist State, or that the
Soviet Government did not welcome the co-operation of all parties in
the crucial hour of famine.

After the glad tidings had been heralded abroad and generous aid
found in the American Relief Administration, the love-feast came to
a sudden end. The alliance was declared off, the bride not merely

jilted, but even thrown into the Cheka jail. The members of the
" Citizens' Committee " were again denounced as counter-revolutionary, and its leaders exiled to distant parts of the country. Vera
Figner was spared, but she refused the honour. She went to the Cheka
and demanded to share the fate of her co-workers, but the Government did not think it wise to touch her for fear of the storm of indignation that would have been raised abroad.

President Kalinin, of Kronstadt infamy, travelled in a train *de luxe*,
with carloads of Lenin's wisdom, and royally entertained a host of
foreign correspondents. The world was to learn how solicitous the
Soviet State was of its afflicted people.

The actual workers of the relief, however, were the foreign bodies
that had meantime organized their aid. The workers of Russia and
the majority of the non-Communist population were performing
superhuman labour to succour the famine-stricken districts. The intelligentsia accomplished miracles. In their capacity as physicians, nurses,
and distributors of supplies scores of them sacrificed themselves.
Many died of exposure and infection, and a number were even killed
by the dark and crazed people whom they had come to help. With
millions of lives devoured by the famine, the loss of a few hundred
bourgeois was hardly worth noticing by the Government. It was more
important for the world revolution that the Soviet régime suddenly
discovered the wealth contained in the churches. It could have been
confiscated before without much protest from the peasantry. But now
the expropriation of the Church treasures added fuel to the fires of
hate which the dictatorship had engendered in all classes of the people.
Another demonstration of the continued revolutionary zeal of the
Communist State was to order its own members to deliver forthwith
all the valuables they had in their possession, even to the last trinket.
It was a shock to learn that Communists should be suspected by their
own party of hoarding jewelry or other valuables. But apparently
there actually were such members. The editor of the *Izvestia,* the
well-known Communist Steklov, whose specialty was to hound non-
Communist revolutionists as bandits, was discovered to have a large
collection of silver and gold, things a Communist was not supposed to
own. They could not shoot a prominent party editor as they had shot
a Fanya Baron. Neither could he be allowed to remain in the sanctum.
The rank and file might muster up courage to demand why such
discrimination was practised. Steklov was therefore suspended from

the paper, and other Communists were sent to the Crimea.

The famine continued its devastating march. But Moscow was far from the stricken region, and great events were being prepared for within its gates. Three international congresses were to take place: those of the Communist International, of the Women's Organizations, and of the Red Trade Unions. A number of buildings adjoining the Hotel de Luxe were being renovated and the city cleaned up and decorated for the occasion. The blue and gold of the cupolas on the forty times forty churches intermingled with the scarlet hues of the bunting and flags. All was ready for the reception of the foreign delegates and visitors from every part of the world.

Among the early arrivals were two I.W.W. delegates from America, Williams and Cascaden. Others also soon came, among them Ella Reeve Bloor, William Z. Foster, and William D. Haywood. How could " Big Bill " come, we wondered, for we knew that he was out on twenty-thousand-dollar bail and under sentence of twenty years' imprisonment. Was it possible that he had jumped his bond? Sasha was inclined to believe it; he had lost faith in Bill since 1914, when the latter had shown himself weak-kneed during the free-speech fights that Sasha had conducted in New York. I defended Bill hotly, pointing out that our actions are not always to be judged so easily. " Not even your own, old man," I said. But Sasha refused to come with me to the hotel where Haywood was lodged. " He will come to us if he is really anxious to see us," he declared. I laughed at such ceremony with Bill.

Bill Haywood had often been under our roof, by day and by night, always our welcome guest, our comrade in many battles, though not sharing the same ideas. I hastened to the Hotel de Luxe, where the most favoured delegates were quartered, to find the old war-horse, of whom I had always been very fond. Bill received me in the same warm and genial manner that had captured all his friends. In fact, he immediately embraced me, before the whole crowd. A roar went up from the boys, who began teasing Bill for keeping it secret that E.G. was among his many lady-loves. He laughed good-naturedly and drew me down to a seat at his side. I had come only for a moment, I told him, just to welcome him and to tell him where and when he could find us. I still could give him a cup of coffee " as black as night, as sweet as love, as strong as revolutionary zeal." Bill smiled in remembrance. " I'll come tomorrow," he said.

In the crowd surrounding Haywood I noticed several interpreters, whom I knew as Chekists. They were Russian-American Communists who had risen in station and importance for their services to the party. They felt ill at ease in my presence and eyed me suspiciously. I was glad to see Bill again and also several others from the States, including Ella Reeve Bloor, who had visited me in the Missouri penitentiary and who had always showed affection for me and interest in my work. I paid no further attention to the "interpreters" and soon I left.

Sasha was out when Bill arrived in the late afternoon the following day. My visitor transferred me back to America, my old arena of so many years' effort. I plied him with questions about my friends, about Stella and Fitzi, Elizabeth Gurley Flynn, and many others whom I still had in my heart. I wanted to hear about the general situation, the labour movement, and the I.W.W., which had since been all but demolished by the war phobia, as well as about my own comrades. Bill stopped my volley of questions. Before we proceeded, he said, he would first have to make his own position clear to me. I noticed that he was under the nervous tension that used to come over him when he stood before a large audience, his big frame shaking with suppressed feeling. He had jumped his bail, he said suddenly; he had run away. Not because of the twenty years of prison that faced him, though that was no small matter at his age. "Ridiculous, Bill," I interrupted; "you would never have to serve the whole sentence. Gene Debs was pardoned and Kate Richard O'Hare also." "Listen first," he interrupted; "the prison was not the deciding factor. It was Russia, Russia, which fulfilled what we had dreamed about and propagated all our lives, I as well as you. Russia, the home of the liberated proletariat, was calling me." He had also been urged by Moscow to come, he added. He was told he was needed in Russia. From here he would be able to revolutionize the American masses and to prepare them for the dictatorship of the proletariat. It had not been easy to decide to leave his comrades to face their long terms in prison alone. But the Revolution was more important and its ends justified all means. Of course, the twenty-thousand-dollar bail would be paid by the Communist Party. He had been given a solemn pledge for that. He hoped, he said, that I would understand his motives and not think him a shirker.

I did not ask any more about America, nor did I satisfy his request

to tell him my impressions of Russia. With a shock I realized that
Bill was as blindfolded as we had been on our arrival in the country.
Would he also undergo the excruciating operation that would remove
the scales from his eyes? And what would become of Bill when his
house of cards had tumbled over him, and all his hopes were buried
like ours? He had burned his bridges in America, and never again
could he fire the imagination of the proletarian youth of his country
and justify to them his escape at a time when they needed him so
desperately. Who would again entrust his life to a captain who had
been the first to abandon his sinking ship? And later on, when he
would come to see Soviet Russia with open eyes, what would he do?
He would be cast on the refuse-pile, like so many before him, after
he had served the propaganda purposes of Moscow. Bill, so rooted in
his native soil and its traditions, so alien to Russia, ignorant of her
language and her people —

I had almost forgotten the presence of my guest in the contemplation of the tragic future that was awaiting him. "Why so silent?" he
asked. "Because silence is more golden than speech," I joked. Later,
after he had got his bearings in the new country, we might talk again,
I added. Could he come often, he asked, "just as in the days of
210 East Thirteenth Street?" "Yes, dear Bill," I replied, "any
time, if you still want to after you have been taken in hand." He
did not understand, nor did I explain.

Sasha ridiculed the motives Bill had given for running away. Russia
and all the other reasons were not convincing to him. They were no
doubt contributory factors, but the main reason was that Bill quaked
before the twenty years in Leavenworth. In late years he had repeatedly shown the white feather. I need have no anxiety about Bill's
future, Sasha assured me. He would fit in, even when he came to see
the stupendous delusion foisted on the world by Moscow. There was
no reason why he shouldn't. Bill had always stood for a strong State
and centralization. What was his One Big Union but a dictatorship?
"Bill will be in clover here," Sasha concluded; "just wait and see."

Two days later William Z. Foster telephoned to ask whether he
could come up. It was my wash-day and I was too busy, but Sasha
offered to receive Foster in his room until I should be through with
my work. It occurred to me that Foster might like to meet Schapiro
and other comrades still free. But when I asked him about it, he said
he was not interested in Russian syndicalists. He only wanted to talk

to Sasha and me. Foster had been among the first in America to advocate revolutionary labour tactics in the economic struggle, which the Russian Anarcho-Syndicalists had applied. It seemed strange that he should decline to meet these rebels and to hear from them what place, if any, syndicalism had in the Communist régime.

He arrived in the company of Jim Browder, a Kansas boy, whom we used to know as an active I.W.W. Sasha took them in charge. At noon, when my work was finished and lunch prepared, I invited our guests to share it with us. Vegetables and fruit were plentiful on the market and much cheaper than meat and fish. We lived almost entirely on this diet. The boys had evidently not lost their American appetite. They ate with relish and expressed appreciation of E.G.'s skill in preparing such dishes. Foster said nothing during the meal except to inform us that he was in Russia in the capacity of a reporter for the Federated Labor Press. Browder talked a great deal about the marvels of the Communist State and the wonderful things the party had achieved. I inquired how long he had been in the country. "About a week," he replied. "And you have already discovered that all is wonderful?" "Indeed," he said, "it can be seen at a glance." I congratulated him on his extraordinary vision and turned our conversation into less turbulent waters. Our callers soon left, which I did not regret.

Two other Americans came to see us, Agnes Smedley and her Hindu friend Chato. I had heard a good deal about Agnes in the States in connexion with her Hindu activities, but I had never met her personally. She was a striking girl, an earnest and true rebel, who seemed to have no other interest in life except the cause of the oppressed people in India. Chato was intellectual and witty, but he impressed me as a somewhat crafty individual. He called himself an anarchist, though it was evident that it was Hindu nationalism to which he had devoted himself entirely.

Cascaden, the Canadian I.W.W. delegate, visited us often, daily looking more distressed over the political intrigues going on in the preliminary sessions. The other American delegates had already been roped in by the Communists, he told us, and made to dance to the tune played by Losovsky, the prospective president of the Red Union International. Cascaden was holding out against their wiles, but he foresaw that he would have no chance at the Congress. We consoled him by telling him that no one with independence and character would have any chance. The Congress would be packed by marionettes of the Russian Bolsheviki, who would vote on every subject as directed by "the centre." Cass, as we familiarly called him, was brave; he would fight to the last for the instructions given him by his organization, he assured us.

The other delegates kept aloof from us, including my erstwhile devoted Ella Reeve Bloor. Bill Haywood also did not return. They had all been warded off by their "interpreters," as were also Robert Minor, Mary Heaton Vorse, and Tom Mann. They were in Moscow and they could not help knowing that we were living in the city. Bob Minor had "changed his mind a little ": he had become a Communist. We had read his confession in the *Liberator,* which had, in effect, been an open letter to the man he had idolized, his closest friend and teacher, Alexander Berkman. Mary Heaton Vorse, an intimate of my New York circle, was a kind soul and a charming companion. Her political views came to her by proxy. She had been an I.W.W. when vivid Joe O'Brien was her husband, and no doubt she must be a Communist now that she was with Minor. Reason enough why Mary should not have allowed her superficial political leanings to obscure the friendship that she had formerly so often proclaimed.

There was also Tom Mann, the old champion of syndicalism and bitter foe of every political machine, the man who had shown the greatest concern for my welfare in London during the exciting days of the Boer War. He had been our guest in New York during his American tour, which the efforts of the *Mother Earth* group had saved from disaster. All these delegates lived in the Hotel de Luxe, a stone's throw from us. "How can human beings go back so easily on their old affiliations?" I remarked to Sasha. I should not take it so much to heart, he replied. They had been told that we were in ill repute with the Bolsheviki and therefore they were afraid to come near us. For himself, he didn't give a damn, and he did not see why I should. I wished I possessed his simple and direct attitude.

The Latin delegates had also been given a gentle hint in regard to us, we learned. But they were of different mettle from the Anglo-Saxons. They informed their "guides" that they did not propose to deny their comrades or to be dictated to about whom they should associate with. The French, Italian, Spanish, German, and Scandinavian Anarcho-Syndicalists lost no time in seeking us out. In fact, they made our place their headquarters. They spent with us every free hour they had, eager to know our impressions and views. They had heard of the alleged persecution of the Left-wing elements by the Communists, but they had taken it as a capitalist fabrication. Their French Communist friends, who had made the journey with them, were also sincerely desirous to learn the facts. Among them Boris Souvarine was the most intelligent and alert inquirer.

The Cheka was of course well aware that these men were coming in and out of our place. Our attitude since Kronstadt had also not remained a secret from them. In fact, Sasha had gone to the head of the Soviet printing house in Petrograd and had demanded back the copy of his *Prison Memoirs,* which they were to publish in Russian. He had openly declared on that occasion, as well as to Zinoviev personally, that he was through with the Bolsheviki because of Kronstadt and all that it involved. We were prepared to take the consequences and we spoke freely to our visitors. Souvarine was quite shaken by our account. It could not be that Lenin and Trotsky knew about the real state of affairs, he thought. Had we tried to talk to them? We had, but we had not been received. Yet Sasha had written a letter to Lenin explaining the situation and our stand in regard to it. But all such efforts were as futile as our protests and proposal to the Petrograd Soviet of Defence during the Kronstadt siege. Nothing was being done in Russia, we informed our visitors, without the knowledge and approval of the supreme authority, the Central Committee of the Communist Party, and Lenin was the head of it.

The Communists in France were co-operating on many occasions with their anarchist comrades, Souvarine argued. Why could not the same conditions be brought about in Russia? The reason was not far to see, we explained. The French Communists had not yet attained political power in their country. They had not yet achieved a dictatorship there, but when that hour arrived, their comradeship with the French anarchists would be at an end, we assured Souvarine. He thought it impossible and he insisted that he should discuss the subject with the leading Bolsheviki. He wanted to bring about an amicable relationship between his Russian comrades and ours.

Just at that moment Olya Maximova called. Pale and trembling, she told us that Maximov and twelve other comrades in the Taganka prison had declared a hunger-strike to the death. They had repeatedly demanded the reason for their imprisonment since March. Information was refused them, nor had any charges been brought against them. Having failed to receive a reply to their protests, they had decided to call the attention of the foreign delegates to their intolerable situation by means of a desperate hunger-strike.

The syndicalists present jumped to their feet in great excitement. They would have never believed such a state of affairs possible in Soviet Russia, they declared, and they would immediately demand an accounting. They would raise the question at the opening of the Red Trade Union Congress the following morning. Souvarine implored them to wait and first to see the trade-union leaders, among them Tomsky, the labour head, Losovsky, and others. An open discussion at the public sessions would be working into the enemy's hand, he argued; the capitalist press and the *bourgeoisie* in France and other countries would make the most of it. The matter must be settled quietly and in a friendly way, Souvarine pleaded. The delegates left, assuring us that they would not rest until justice was done to our suffering comrades. They returned late at night to inform us that the trade-union leaders had begged them not to make the scandal public and had promised to do their utmost to get redress for the imprisoned anarchists. They had suggested a committee of one delegate from each country, including Russia, to confer with Lenin and Trotsky. Our comrades from Europe were only too glad to avoid a breach and they had willingly accepted the proposal.

I went with Sasha to the opening session of the Congress to see whom we might get to act on the committee. We were sure that Tom Mann would be anxious to serve on it, for had he not fought against political persecution all his life? And Bill Haywood would certainly not refuse. When on trial for his life in Idaho, he had faced death, from which the anarchists had helped to save him; they had always given him and his I.W.W. organization solidaric assistance at every arrest and during every trouble, as well as during the war. " Tom Mann may help," Sasha said, " but Haywood won't. I may try to get Bob; he would hardly refuse me," he added.

The Marble Hall in the Trade Union House was the theatre where the grand review had been carefully prepared and rehearsed. We found the principal performers all grouped on the stage. The orchestra seats were packed by delegates from every part of the world, the Russians predominating. Not the least important among them were the delegates of such large industrial centres as Palestina, Bokhara, Azerbaijan and similar countries.

Outside of the railing, separating the official representatives from the general audience, were benches for the public. We took our seats in the first row, which the delegates had to pass on their way to the platform. Bill Haywood was in the place of honour. He saw us come in and he turned his head away. Having gone back on his comrades in distress, it was not surprising that he should also deny his former friends. Sasha had been right: there was no need to worry about Bill's future. He could see no more with his good eye than with his blind one and he would " fit in." I felt no anger; I was only unspeakably sad.

Tom Mann stopped short when he recognized us. Like Bill's, his greeting had been profuse only a short time ago. He drew back, however, as soon as I mentioned the proposed committee. He knew nothing about the matter, he said, and he would first have to investigate. Sasha violently upbraided Tom for his lack of stamina and for his fear to displease the Bolshevik bosses. Tom winced at the rebuke from one who had paid with an agony of years for his loyalty and devotion, while Tom had merely been spouting. " All right, all right," he said, shamefacedly, " I'll serve on the committee."

As we walked out of the hall during the noon intermission, we collided with Bob Minor and Mary Heaton Vorse. They were startled at the unexpected meeting and looked very much embarrassed. They pretended a friendly grin, Bob hastening to say that he had meant to look us up, but had been too busy; he would call on us soon, however. " Why these apologies? " Sasha retorted; " they are unnecessary, and please don't come out of duty." He did not mention the committee to Bob.

On our way my dear chum kept silent. I knew how sad he felt. He cared a great deal about Bob and he had trusted in his sense of fair play.

The committee was at last organized and ready to call on Lenin. None of them was a match for the shrewd Grand Mogul. He knew better how to divert their attention than they to compel his. Tom Mann, always anathema to the ruling class of his country, now accepted and made much of by the head of the new dynasty, proved clay in Bolshevik hands. He was too weak to resist Lenin and he was overcome like a débutante first receiving male homage. No less overawed were most of the other members of the committee, but the Labour Syndicalists refused to be side-tracked by the solicitous inquiries of Ilich about the conditions of labour abroad, the strength of the Syndicalists and their prospects. They insisted on knowing what he had to say about the revolutionary hunger-strikers in Russia. Lenin stopped short. He did not care if all the politicals perished in prison, he declared. He and his party would brook no opposition from any side, Left or Right. He would consent, however, to have the imprisoned anarchists deported from the country, on pain of being shot if they should return to Soviet soil. Lenin's ears had become attuned for nearly four years to shooting and he had grown infatuated with the sound of it.

His proposal, submitted to the Central Committee of the Communist Party as a matter of form, was of course approved by it. A joint committee was formed, representing the Government and the foreign delegates, to arrange for the immediate release and deportation of the Taganka hunger-strikers and the imprisoned anarchists.

On the eighth day of the strike there was still no definite action taken, because the high authority of the All-Russian Cheka, with Dzherzhinsky and Unschlicht at its head, insisted that " there were no anarchists in Soviet prisons." There were only bandits and Makhnovtsy, they declared. They demanded that the foreign delegates first submit a list of those they wanted liberated for deportation. The ruse was an obvious attempt to sabotage the entire plan and to gain time till the Congress adjourned and the foreign delegates departed. Some of the latter began to realize that nothing would be done and that our comrades might starve to death. They again threatened to take the matter up at the Congress and have it discussed in open session. But this was just what the Soviet authorities were anxious to prevent. They pleaded for a private conference with the delegates and faithfully promised to bring about a satisfactory arrangement without further loss of time.

Our people in the Taganka were beginning to break down under the torture of the protracted hunger-strike. One of them, a young student of the Moscow University, a consumptive, had already collapsed. His co-strikers urged him to terminate his fast, but he loyally refused to desert them, even in the face of death. We were powerless to aid in any way. With heavy hearts Sasha and I kept after the syndicalist members of the joint committee, urging and pleading for speedy action. One day, while on our way to the Congress, we were met by Robert Minor, who handed Sasha a large bundle. " Some provisions," he said sheepishly; "we at the Luxe get too much. Maybe you'll give it to the hunger-strikers. Some light things — caviar, white bread, and chocolate. I thought — " " Never mind what you thought," Sasha interrupted; " you are a rotter to add insult to the injury the Taganka men have already endured. Instead of protesting against the hounding of men for their political views, you try to bribe our comrades into breaking their strike by offering the leavings of your overfed fellow delegates." " By the way," I added, " you had better stop Mary Heaton Vorse from her irresponsible talk about our friend Bob Robbins. Does she want to land him in the Cheka ? "

Bob mumbled that Lucy Robbins had allied herself with Gompers, who was fighting the Russian Revolution. Sasha replied that the fact that Lucy was working with the American Federation of Labor, while showing poor judgment, did not stamp her husband as a counter-revolutionist. He had better curb Mary's tongue. It meant a man's life.

Bob grew pale, his eyes shifted uneasily from Sasha to me and back, and then he started to say something. I stopped him. " Give your parcel to the women and children shivering outside your Hotel de Luxe and greedily picking up the crumbs that fall from the wagon-loads of white bread brought to feed the delegates." " You people make me sick," Bob cried, trying to control his rage; " you make a big fuss over the thirteen anarchists in the Taganka and forget that it is a revolutionary period. What do those thirteen matter, or thirteen hundred even, in view of the greatest revolution the world has ever seen ? " " Yes, we've heard that before," Sasha retorted; " but I should really not be angry with you, considering that I myself believed the same stuff for fifteen months. But I know better now. I know that this ' greatest revolution ' is the greatest fraud, masking every crime to keep the Communists in power. Some day, Bob, you may also come to realize it. We'll talk then. Now we have nothing more to say to each other."

On the tenth day of the hunger-strike the joint committee finally met in the Kremlin. Sasha and Schapiro had been asked by the Taganka prisoners to represent their demands. Trotsky was to be the spokesman of the Central Committee of the Communist Party, but he failed to appear and Lunacharsky took his place. Unschlicht, acting head of the All-Russian Cheka, treated the delegates with open scorn and finally left the room without even a greeting to them. The " comradely " session might have ended in the arrest of the foreign delegates had not the coolness of Sasha and Schapiro smoothed matters. It required all his self-restraint, Sasha later told me, not to hit Unschlicht for his arrogant behaviour, but the fate of our sufferers was at stake. The air was surcharged with antagonism, and it was only after long bickering that an agreement was reached. A letter signed by the joint committee, but not concurred in by Alexander Berkman, was forwarded through Unschlicht to the Taganka men, containing the following statement:

Comrades, in view of the fact that we have come to the conclusion that your hunger-strike cannot accomplish your liberation, we hereby advise you to terminate it.

At the same time we inform you that definite proposals have been made to us by Comrade Lunacharsky in the name of the Central Committee of the Communist Party. To wit:

1. All anarchists held in the prisons of Russia who are now on a hunger-strike will be permitted to leave for any country they may choose. They will be supplied with passports and funds.

2. Concerning other imprisoned anarchists or those out of prison, final action will be taken by the party tomorrow. It is the opinion of Comrade Lunacharsky that the decision in their case will be similar to the present one.

3. We have received the promise, endorsed by Unschlicht, that the families of the comrades to go abroad will be permitted to follow them if they so wish. For conspirative reasons some time will have to elapse before this is done.

4. The comrades before going abroad will be permitted two or three days at liberty before their departure, to enable them to arrange their affairs.

5. They will not be allowed to return to Russia without the consent of the Soviet Government.

6. Most of these conditions are contained in the letter received by this delegation from the Central Committee of the Communist Party, signed by Trotsky.

7. The foreign comrades have been authorized to see to it that these conditions are properly carried out.

[Signatures]

ORLANDI
LEVAL } Spain

SIROLLE
MICHEL } France

A. SCHAPIRO—Russia
[signed] LUNACHARSKY

The above is correct.

Alexander Berkman declines to sign because:

   a. he is opposed to deportation on principle;

   b. he considers the letter an arbitrary and unjustified curtail-
ment of the original offer of the Central Committee according to which all the anarchists were to be permitted to
leave Russia;

   c. he demands more time at liberty for those to be released,
to enable them to recuperate before deportation.

Kremlin, Moscow
  13/VII/1921

I was glad Sasha had refused to concur in the outrageous decision
that established the precedent of deportation of revolutionists from
Soviet Russia, of men who had valiantly defended the Revolution,
had fought on its fronts, and had suffered untold danger and hardships. What a commentary on the Communist State outdoing Uncle
Sam! He, poor boob, went only as far as deporting his foreign-born
opponents. Lenin and Company, themselves political refugees from
their native land only a short time ago, were now ordering the deportation of Russia's native sons, the best flower of her revolutionary
past.

Despair is often more compelling than hunger. The Taganka comrades were motivated by that, rather than by their eleven torturous
days, in terminating their hunger-strike. They accepted the conditions
that were to set them adrift. They were completely exhausted by their
long fast, some of them laid up with a high temperature. The coarse
prison food would have been fatal to them, but Lenin had declared
that he did not care if they perished in jail. It would be absurd to look
for more humanity from the prison authorities or to expect them to
supply suitable light diet. Fortunately the Swedish delegates had
given us a suitcaseful of provisions, and these served to feed our
prisoners during the critical days of recuperation.

The sequel of the " amicable settlement " Souvarine and his fellow
French delegates had hoped for was supplied by Bukharin at the
eleventh hour of the Red Trade Union Congress. In the name of
the Central Committee of the Communist Party he made a ferocious
attack on the men in the Taganka and the Russian anarchists in
general. They were all counter-revolutionists, he declared, who were
plotting against the Socialist Republic. The whole Russian anarchist

movement was nothing but banditry, he charged, the ally of Makhno and of his highwaymen who had fought the Revolution and had murdered Communists and Red Army men. The flagrant breach of the agreement to avoid publicity in the Taganka trouble, which the Bolsheviki themselves had insisted upon, came like unexpected thunder in the final session of the Congress. The Latin delegates, outraged by such underhand tactics, were immediately on their feet. They demanded to be heard in protest, in rebuttal of the denunciation of their Russian comrades. Chairman Lozovsky had obligingly given the floor to Bukharin, though the latter was not a delegate and had no right to address the Congress. But now Lozovsky resorted to every possible trick to deprive the foreign delegates of a chance to answer the libellous charges of Bukharin. Even some of the Russian Communist delegates were dismayed by the proceedings and supported the demand of the Latin delegates to be heard. Of the Anglo-Saxon delegates only Cascaden rose in protest. Tom Mann, Bill Haywood, Bob Minor, William Foster, and Ella Reeve Bloor were silent in the face of the crying injustice and suppression. The lifelong champions of free speech could find no word of protest against its denial in Soviet Russia. In the tumult and uproar that followed Bukharin's attack on the anarchists few persons in the hall noticed Rykov, chairman of the All-Russian Soviet of Economy, signalling to the attending Chekists. A detachment of soldiers clattered into the hall, adding fuel to the blaze ignited by Bukharin's speech.

Sasha and I elbowed our way to the platform. This time I should speak, I told him, even if I had to resort to force, unless Schapiro or some Syndicalist delegate got the floor. He would rush the platform, if necessary, Sasha said. In passing he caught sight of Bob Minor. He gripped his cane, about to strike him. " You're a yellow cur, you son of a b—," Sasha roared at him. Minor recoiled in fright. Sasha took up his stand on one side of the platform steps, while I stood on the other. The majority of the delegates were on their feet, clamouring to be heard and protesting against Lozovsky's autocratic conduct. Beset on all sides, he was finally forced to give the floor to Sirolle, the French Anarcho-Syndicalist. Roused by the Jesuitical machinations of the Communist Party, Sirolle in thunderous voice denounced the double-dealing tactics of the Soviet Government and brilliantly refuted the cowardly charges against the Taganka men and the Russian anarchists.

When the news of the approaching deportation became known, the Left Socialist-Revolutionists, comrades of Maria Spiridonovna, decided to benefit by the presence of the foreign delegates and labour men. In a statement distributed among them they set forth that Maria, taken from her sick-bed the previous year, was still being kept in prison. She had undergone several hunger-strikes in protest and had demanded her release and that of her life-long friend and companion Izmailovich. She had twice been at death's door and was now in a most precarious state. Her comrades would supply the means of sending Maria abroad for medical treatment, the statement read, if the Soviet authorities would permit her to go.

Dr. I. Steinberg requested me to interest the delegates of the International Women's Congress, then taking place in Moscow. I went to see Clara Zetkin, the famous old Social Democrat, who was now high in the councils of the Government. She was working to rally the support of the women of every country for the world revolution, she informed me. Well, Maria Spiridonovna had already served that cause, I told her, served it the greater part of her life. She was indeed the very symbol of that revolution. It would do irreparable harm to the prestige of the Communist Party if Maria was to be extinguished in a Cheka prison, I urged, and it was Clara Zetkin's duty to prevail upon the Government to permit Maria Spiridonovna to leave Russia.

Zetkin promised to intercede in behalf of Maria. But at the close of the Congress she sent me word that Lenin was too ill to be seen. She had spoken to Trotsky in the matter, and the War Commissar had told her that Maria Spiridonovna was still too dangerous to be at liberty or to be permitted abroad.

The Red Trade Union Congress was over. Its most pathetic harlequin proved to be Bill Haywood. The founder of the I.W.W. in America and its dominant figure for twenty years, he allowed himself to be persuaded to vote at the Congress for the Communist plan to "liquidate" the militant minority labour organizations, including the I.W.W., and force their members to join the American Federation of Labor, which Haywood had for years denounced as "capitalistic and reactionary."

The smaller fry among his comrades, the Ella Reeve Bloors, the Browders, and Andreychins. took the cue from their chief. Andreychin had never been blessed with much backbone. During the Mesaba Range strike he had been willing to make any compromise to save himself from deportation. Sasha had interested Amos Pinchot and other influential liberals in his behalf and through them had stayed the hand of the Immigration Bureau. While Andreychin was in Leavenworth, he again showed the white feather. I ascribed his weakness to the fear of tuberculosis, which had begun to undermine his health. I was at the time in the Missouri prison, but in compliance with Andreychin's repeated requests I urged Stella and Fitzi to raise the ten thousand dollars needed to release him on bail. The faithful girls had worked like galley-slaves to secure bonds for many other victims of the war mania, but they would not refuse me. They procured part of the bail, while a friend gave the balance. Andreychin, spineless creature that he was, emulated his teacher Bill Haywood and jumped his bond. On the very first day of his arrival in Moscow he delivered a public speech in which he denounced his I.W.W. fellows in the United States and pledged the Bolsheviki his help in destroying the organization. Yet I felt that this treachery was not so much the fault of Andreychin, Bill Haywood, and the many others who were on their knees before the holy shrine of the Kremlin. It was rather the appalling superstition, the Bolshevik myth, that duped and ensnared them, as it had also formerly done to us.

Soviet Russia had become the modern socialist Lourdes, to which the blind and the lame, the deaf and the dumb were flocking for miraculous cures. I was filled with pity for these deluded ones, but I felt only contempt for those others who had come, had seen with open eyes and understood, and had yet been conquered. Of these was William Z. Foster, once the champion of revolutionary syndicalism in America. He was keen-eyed and he had come as a press correspondent. He went back to do Moscow's bidding.

No word had arrived from our comrades in Germany in reply to the letter sent them about securing visas. Sasha was chafing under the delay of getting out of Russia. He could stand the fearful tragicomedy no longer, he said. A German Syndicalist delegate, member of the Seamen's and Transport Workers' Union, had also taken a letter from us and had promised to see our people in Berlin. There was no news yet. As in his early days after his coming out of the Western Penitentiary, Sasha became very restless. He could not endure being indoors or seeing people. He would roam the streets of

Moscow most of the day and late into the night, and my anxiety about him grew.

In his absence one day Bob Minor called. Not finding Sasha, he edged out. I did not try to detain him, for our old ties had snapped. Shortly after, there arrived a letter from him, addressed to Sasha. He read it and handed it to me without comment. Bob's letter dilated on the "momentous and world-revolutionizing resolutions" passed by the Congress of the Third International. He had always known Sasha as the clearest mind in the anarchist movement in America and as an indomitable and fearless rebel. Could he not see now that his place was in the Communist Party? He belonged there, and it offered him a large field for his abilities and devotion. He could not give up the hope that Sasha would yet come to realize the supreme mission of the Communist dictatorship in Russia and its approaching conquest of capitalism throughout the world.

Bob was sincere, Sasha commented, but the veriest blockhead politically and blind as a bat socially. He should have stuck to his real field, that of art. I urged Sasha to reply to Bob's letter, but he refused. It was useless, he said, and he was weary of talk and arguments. How well I understood his weariness! I also felt completely fagged out. The physical drudgery of our existence and the excessive summer heat had sapped my strength. The stream of visitors, the long hours without sleep, and the great strain of the Trade Union Congress made me feel tired to death.

Sasha returned from one of his long tramps in the city looking unusually pale and distressed. When he made sure that I was alone, he said in a whisper: "Fanya Baron is in Moscow. She has just escaped from the Ryazan prison and she is in great danger; without money or papers and no place to go."

I was struck dumb with horror of the fate awaiting Fanya if discovered. Fanya in the very fortress of the Cheka! "Oh, Sasha, why did she come here, of all places?" I cried. "That isn't the question now," he returned; "better let us think quickly how we can help her."

Our own place would be a trap for her. She would be discovered within twenty-four hours. The other comrades were also being watched. To give her shelter would mean death for them as for her. Of course, we would supply her with money, clothing, and food. But how about a roof over her head? She was safe for the night, Sasha said, but on the morrow something would have to be devised. There was no more sleep for me that night — Fanya weighed heavily on my mind.

Early next morning Sasha left the house with money and things for Fanya, and I remained in sickening suspense until the late afternoon, beset by fears for both. My friend had a less anxious look when he returned. Fanya had found shelter with a brother of Aaron Baron. He was a Communist and his place therefore safe for Fanya. I stared in amazement. " It's all right," Sasha said, trying to soothe my fears, " the man has always been fond of Aaron and Fanya. He will not betray her." I was dubious of a Communist allowing family ties or personal feelings to interfere with his party's commands. But I could suggest no safer place and I knew that Fanya could not remain out on the streets. Sasha felt so relieved that Fanya was under cover that I did not want to arouse his fears again. I plied him with questions about the daring girl — why she had come to Moscow and when I could see her.

That was entirely out of the question, Sasha declared. It was enough for one of us to take the risk. I had already courted enough danger, he argued, by my visits to the Arshinov family. The Bolsheviki had set a price on Pyotr Arshinov's head, dead or alive, as the closest friend and associate of Nestor Makhno. He was in hiding and he could only venture out after dark to call on his wife and infant in the city. I had indeed been repeatedly to see them and to take things for their baby, and once Sasha had accompanied me. Now he insisted that I promise not to attempt to see Fanya. My dear, faithful pal was so concerned about my safety that I would have promised anything to reassure him. But at heart I determined to visit my haunted comrade.

Fanya's mission in Moscow, Sasha confided to me, was to prepare the escape of Aaron Baron. She had learned of the persecution he was undergoing in prison and she had determined to rescue her lover from his living death. Her own escape was made for that very purpose. Brave, wonderful Fanya, dedicated to Aaron as few wives are, yet not tied by law! My heart went out to our splendid comrade in trembling fear for her mission, her sweetheart, and herself.

Sasha's account of his meetings with Fanya served to allay my anxiety about her and him. It even made me laugh. The city was crowded and the parks filled with spooning couples. Ladies of pleasure were about everywhere, entertaining some of the foreign delegates in return for real valuta or delicacies from the Hotel de Luxe. Sasha and Fanya were no doubt considered by the passers-by as engaged in similar propaganda activities. Fanya looked much improved physically and was in fine spirits. She was less worried about Aaron now, because his brother, to whom she had confided her mission, had promised to aid her scheme. Again I felt my heart flutter at the risk Fanya was taking, but I kept my own counsel.

Then the blow came and left us stunned. Two of our comrades fell into the Cheka net — Lev Tchorny, gifted poet and writer, and Fanya Baron! She had been arrested in the home of her Communist brother-in-law. At the same time eight other men had been shot at on the street by Chekists and taken prisoners. They were *existy* (expropriators), the Cheka declared.

Sasha had seen Fanya the preceding evening. She had been in a hopeful mood: the preparations for Aaron's escape were progressing satisfactorily, she had told him, and she felt almost gay, all unconscious of the sword that was to fall upon her head the following morning. "And now she is in their clutches and we are powerless to help," Sasha groaned.

He could not go on any longer in the dreadful country, he declared. Why would I persist in my objection to illegal channels? We were not running away from the Revolution. It was dead long ago; yes, to be resurrected, but not for a good while to come. That we, two such well-known anarchists, who had given our entire lives to revolutionary effort, should leave Russia illegally would be the worst slap in the face of the Bolsheviki, he emphasized. Why, then, should I hesitate? He had learned of a way of going from Petrograd to Reval. He would go there to make the preliminary arrangements. He was suffocating in the atmosphere of the bloody dictatorship. He could not stand it any more.

In Petrograd the " party " that traded in false passports and aided people to leave the country secretly turned out to be a priest with several assistants. Sasha would have nothing to do with them, and the plan was off. I sighed with relief. My reason told me that Sasha was right in ridiculing my objection to being smuggled out of Russia. But my feelings rebelled against it and were not to be argued away. Moreover, somehow I felt certain that we should hear from our German comrades.

We planned to remain in Petrograd for awhile, since I hated Moscow, so overrun by Chekists and soldiers. The city on the Neva had not changed since our last visit; it was as dreary in appearance and as famished as before. But the warm welcome from our former co-workers in the Museum of the Revolution, the affectionate friendship of Alexandra Shakol and of our nearest comrades, would make our stay more pleasant than in the capital, I thought. Plans in Russia, however, almost always go awry. Word reached us from Moscow that the apartment on the Leontevsky where we had stayed had been raided and Sasha's room in particular had been ransacked from top to bottom. A number of our friends, among them Vassily Semenoff, our old American comrade, had been caught in the dragnet laid by the Cheka. A *zassada* of soldiers remained in the apartment. It was apparent that our callers, who did not know we were away, were being made to suffer for our sins. We decided to return to Moscow forthwith. To save the expenses of our trip I went to see Mme Ravich, to inform her that we were at the call of the Cheka whenever wanted. I had not seen the Petrograd Commissar of the Interior since the memorable night of March 5 when she had come for the information Zinoviev had expected from Sasha regarding Kronstadt. Her manner, while no longer so warm as before, was still cordial. She knew nothing about the raid of our rooms in Moscow, she said, but would inquire by long-distance telephone. The next morning she informed me that it all had been a misunderstanding, that we were not wanted by the authorities, and that the *zassada* had been removed.

We knew that such " misunderstandings " were a daily occurrence, not infrequently involving even execution, and we gave little credence to Mme Ravich's explanation. The particularly suspicious circumstance was the special attention given to Sasha's room. I had been in opposition to the Bolsheviki longer than he and more outspoken. Why was it that his room was searched and not mine? It was the second attempt to find something incriminating against us. We agreed to leave immediately for Moscow.

On reaching the capital we learned that Vassily, arrested when he had called on us during our absence, had already been liberated. So were also ten of the thirteen Taganka hunger-strikers. They had been kept in prison two months longer, despite the pledge of the Government to free them immediately upon the termination of their hunger-strike. Their release, however, was the sheerest farce, because they were placed under the strictest surveillance, forbidden to associate with their comrades, and denied the right to work, although informed that their deportation would be delayed. At the same time the Cheka announced that none of the other imprisoned anarchists would be liberated. Trotsky had written a letter to the French delegates to that effect, notwithstanding the original promise of the Central Committee to the contrary.

Our Taganka comrades found themselves " free," weak and ill as a result of their long hunger-strike. They were in tatters, without money or means of existence. We did what we could to alleviate their need and to cheer them, although we ourselves felt anything but cheerful. Meanwhile Sasha had somehow succeeded in communicating with Fanya in the inner Cheka prison. She informed him that she had been transferred the previous evening to another wing. The note did not indicate whether she realized the significance of it. She asked that a few toilet things be sent her. But neither she nor Lev Tchorny needed them any more. They were beyond human kindness, beyond man's savagery. Fanya was shot in the cellar of the Cheka prison, together with eight other victims, on the following day, September 30, 1921. The life of the Communist brother of Aaron Baron was spared. Lev Tchorny had cheated the executioner. His old mother, calling daily at the prison, was receiving the assurance that her son would not be executed and that within a few days she would see him at liberty. Tchorny indeed was not executed. His mother kept bringing parcels of food for her beloved boy, but Tchorny had for days been under the ground, having died as the result of the tortures inflicted on him to force a confession of guilt.

There was no Lev Tchorny on the list of the executed published in the official *Izvestia* the next day. There was " Turchaninov " — Tchorny's family name, which he almost never used and which was quite unknown to most of his friends. The Bolsheviki were aware that Tchorny was a household word in thousands of labour and revolutionary homes. They knew he was held in the greatest esteem as a beautiful soul of deep human kindliness and sympathy, a man known for poetic and literary gifts and as the author of the original and very thoughtful work on *Associational Anarchism*. They knew he was respected by numerous Communists and they did not dare publish that they had murdered the man. It was only Turchaninov who had been " executed."

And our dear, splendid Fanya, radiant with life and love, unswerving in her consecration to her ideals, touchingly feminine, yet resolute as a lioness in defence of her young, of indomitable will, she had fought to the last breath. She would not go submissively to her doom. She resisted and had to be carried bodily to the place of execution by the knights of the Communist State. Rebel to the last, Fanya had pitted her enfeebled strength against the monster for a moment and then was dragged into eternity as the hideous silence in the Cheka cellar was rent once more by her shrieks above the sudden pistol-shots.

I had reached the end. I could bear it no longer. In the dark I groped my way to Sasha to beg him to leave Russia, by whatever means. "I am ready, my dear, to go with you, in any way," I whispered, "only far away from the woe, the blood, the tears, the stalking death."

Sasha was planning to go to the Polish frontier, to arrange for our leaving by that route. I was afraid to let him go alone in his present condition, his nerves shattered by the fearful shock of recent events. On the other hand, it would arouse suspicion if both of us should disappear from our quarters at the same time. Sasha realized the danger and consented to wait another week or two. The idea was for him to proceed to Minsk; I was to follow when he should have made the necessary arrangements. As we should have to travel like the rest of the damned portion of the population, Sasha insisted that I take no baggage. He would carry with him what we absolutely needed; the rest of our things were to be distributed among our friends. We had come to starved and naked Russia overflowing with the need of giving of ourselves as well as of the trunkfuls of gifts we had brought with us. Our hearts were empty now and so must be our hands.

Our preparations had to be made in the strictest privacy, at night, when the rest of the tenants in the apartment were asleep. Manya Semenoff, her lovable Vassily, and a few other trusted ones knew of our plan. It was tragic indeed, this scheming to steal out of the country that had held our highest longings and hopes.

In the midst of the packing the long-expected letter from Germany arrived. It contained an invitation for Sasha, Schapiro, and me to attend the Anarchist Congress that was to take place in Berlin at Christmas. It sent me spinning round the room, weeping and laughing at the same time. "We shan't have to hide and cheat and resort to false papers, Sasha," I cried in glee; "we shan't have to sneak out like thieves in the night!" But Sasha did not seem elated over it. "Ridiculous," he retorted, "you don't mean that our Berlin comrades can exert any influence over Chicherin, the Communist Party, or the Cheka! Moreover, I have no intention of applying to them for anything. I've already told you that." I knew from experience that it was useless to argue with my stubborn pal when he was angry. I would wait for a more propitious time. The new hope held out by the letter had reawakened my objections to leaving secretly the land that had known the glory and the defeat of the great " October."

I sought out Angelica. She had told me that she would help us secure the consent of the Soviet authorities to leave the country. She herself was planning to go abroad to regain her health in some quiet spot. She, too, had reached the spiritual breaking-point, though she would not admit it even to herself. Dear Angelica immediately offered to get the necessary application blanks, and she would go to Chicherin and even to Lenin, if need be, to vouch for Sasha and me. " No, dear Angelica," I protested, " you shall do nothing of the kind." I knew what it meant to leave such security. We would not have anyone endangered for us, nor did we care to have the benediction of Lenin. I informed Angelica that all I wanted of her was to help quicken action if passports were to be granted at all.

In the space in the application reserved for the promise of loyalty and the signature of two party members vouching for the applicant I wrote: " As an anarchist I have never pledged loyalty to any government, much less can I do it to the R.S.F.S.R., which claims to be Socialist and revolutionary. I consider it an insult to my past to ask anyone to stand the consequences of anything I may say or do. I therefore refuse to have anyone vouch for me."

Angelica was considerably perturbed by my declaration. She feared it might spoil our chances of securing permission to leave the country. " Either we go out without any strings attached to us, or we will find another way," I declared. We would leave no hostages behind. Angelica understood.

I went to the Foreign Office to find out whether a request from our German comrades that we be permitted to attend the Anarchist Congress had been received. I was called before Litvinov, who was acting in behalf of Commissar Chicherin. I had never met him before. He looked like a *commis voyageur,* short and fat and disgustingly content with himself. Reclining in an easy chair in his luxurious office he began to ply me with questions as to why we wanted to leave Russia, what our intentions were abroad, and where we meant to live. Had the Foreign Office not received any communication from the Berlin anarchists, I inquired. It had, he admitted, and he knew we had been invited to attend the Anarchist Congress in Berlin. That was explanation enough, I told him; I could add nothing further. " But if you are refused? " he demanded suddenly. If his Government wanted it known abroad that we were being kept prisoners in Russia, it could certainly do so, for it had the power, I replied. Litvinov peered at me steadily out of little eyes bulging from his puffy face. He made no comment, but asked whether our Berlin comrades had made sure that the German Government would admit us. Certainly the latter would not be anxious to increase the number of anarchists in its territory. It was a capitalist country and we could not expect the reception there that Soviet Russia had given us. " Yet, strange to say," I replied, " the anarchists continue their work in most European countries, which cannot be said to be the case in Russia." " Are you singing the praises of the *bourgeois* countries? " he demanded. " No, only reminding you of facts. I have been strengthened in my anarchist attitude that all governments are fundamentally alike, whatever their protestations. However, what about our passports? "

He would let us know, he replied. At any rate, the Soviet Government would not undertake to supply us with visas. That was our own look-out, and, saying so, Litvinov closed the interview.

Sasha had left for Minsk, and ten days passed before I received a sign from him. Then a short note arrived in a roundabout way, informing me that the trip had been hideous, but that he had finally reached his destination and was busy " collecting historical material for the Museum of the Revolution." He had given this as a reason for his journey when he had purchased his ticket.

I was somewhat distracted from my anxiety and worry by the glad news that Maria Spiridonovna had been released. She was almost at death's door from another hunger-strike. Fearing she was about to die in prison, the Cheka had permitted her friends to take her out for a rest and recuperation. Should she get well and show the least sign of renewed activity, the authorities had warned, she would be immediately arrested and imprisoned again. Her friends had indeed to take Maria away bodily, as she was too weak and ill to walk. Her companion Izmailovich was permitted to accompany her, and both women were installed by their friends in Malakhovka, near Moscow. The Government stationed Chekists about the place to guard against any attempt to spirit Maria away.

There was to be no end to Maria's martyrdom, but I felt that she would at least be with her own friends and comrades, and those who loved her would be privileged to look after her needs. It was a comforting thought.

On the twelfth day, when I had about given up hope of hearing from the Foreign Office again, Angelica telephoned to me that passports had been issued to us. I should call for them at the Foreign Office, she said, and take with me dollars or English pounds to pay for them. Cabs were a luxury when so many of our people were in dire want, but I did not have the patience to walk. I wanted to see the passports with my own eyes before I would believe that they had actually been granted. It proved true, however, really true. Sasha and I would not have to hide and cheat to leave the country. We should be able to go as we had come — in the open, even if desolate and denuded of dreams.

Our comrade A. Schapiro had applied independently and I was happy to learn that his passport was also ready and awaiting his call.

I telegraphed Sasha: " This time I win, old scout. Come back quickly." It was probably cattish, but revenge was sweet. In my joyous exuberance I had not stopped to consider the anomaly of the Foreign Office demanding *valuta* when the possession of such currency was strictly prohibited. Well, I mused, laws were made to be broken, and none so skilful as the lawmakers themselves.

Passports on hand, I was now beset by other misgivings. Visas — how were they to be obtained? Our Berlin comrades notified us that they were trying their utmost to secure our admission to Germany. If we could somehow reach Latvia or Esthonia, it would be easier to get visas, they wrote.

Sasha burst into the house unannounced. He looked a fright, unshaven and apparently unwashed for days, tired and exhausted, and without the suit-case he had taken with him. " What's this? " he demanded; " just a hoax to get me back here? " He had made all preparations, he said, to cross the border and had come to fetch me. The papers would be awaiting us in Minsk and he had given fifty dollars' deposit on them. " Is the money to be lost? " he demanded. " And the suit-case," I returned, " is that to be lost too? " He grinned. " That's already lost," he replied; " you know, they are clever, these

Russians. I was told the safest way on trains is to tie your bags to your legs. I did so, and the rope was strong. But the car was pitch-dark — no lights whatever — and so crowded I had to stand all the way. The train stopped at innumerable stations and I must have dozed off. When I looked at my suit-case — well, the rope was there, but no suit-case. Couldn't find it anywhere in the car. Clever of them, wasn't it?"

"Clever of you, too — the third time, isn't it?" "You're a hard loser, old girl," he teased, "you ought to be glad it wasn't sixteen hundred dollars again." What could one do with such an irrepressible one? I had to laugh with him.

Triumphantly I held out the passports. He scrutinized them from every side. "Well," he drawled, "I was sure they'd refuse. A fellow may be wrong, sometimes."

But I could see he felt relieved that it would not have to be the Minsk route. His trip must have been ghastly. It took him a week to recuperate from it.

The Lithuanian visa was granted for two weeks. A transit through Latvia was obtained without much trouble. We could leave any day. The certainty made us feel doubly the plight of the comrades and friends whom we were leaving behind — in want, distress, fettered and utterly helpless in the Soviet void. The Taganka men awaiting deportation were still kept in uncertainty. Exhausted by their daily chase after the authorities to secure some definite statement or action, they were spending most of their time in the corridor of our apartment trying to reach the Cheka by telephone. There was no lack of promises, but not a single one of them had been kept during the four months that had passed since the agreement to deport the men. Every gamut of human suffering had been experienced by them, every physical and spiritual torture for opinion's sake. Yet they were undaunted. Nothing could affect their ideal or weaken their faith in its final triumph. Mark Mrachny, recently robbed by death of his young wife, with a poor little sickly infant on his hands, remained brave and unbent. Volin, with his four small children doomed to starvation before his very eyes, and with his wife ailing in their cold and barren quarters, still continued to write poetry. Maximov, his health broken by several previous hunger-strikes, had lost nothing of his studious interests. Olya Maximova, delicate and sensitive, who had for seven months twice weekly carried heavy loads of provisions to the Taganka prison in continuous stress and anguish about the fate of her beloved Maximov, could still crave beauty and social fellowship. Yarchook, a dauntless fighter, with trials and tribulations to break the strongest, had also withstood all the Taganka horrors. The rest of the men awaiting deportation were of the same fibre and grit. Amazing were they, and those other wonderful friends and comrades we had met in the Ukraine and all through Russia, men of courage, ability, and heroic endurance for the sake of their ideals. I owed much to them, and in my heart I felt grateful for having known them. Their staunch comradeship, understanding, and faith had helped to sustain me spiritually and had kept me from being swept away by the avalanche that had passed over all of us. Their lives had become one with mine; the approaching parting would, I knew, be a wrench and bitter hard. My special favourites were Alexey Borovoy and Mark Mrachny, the first because of his brilliant mind and gracious personality, the other for his sparkling vitality, ready wit, and understanding of human frailty. It was hardest for me to leave them behind; and of course also our dear Manya and Vassily. To ease the pangs of parting, our dear friends kept assuring us that by leaving our tragic Russia we should be aiding them, for we could do much more for the country abroad than in Russia, work for a better understanding of the chasm between the Revolution and the régime and for the political victims in Soviet prisons and concentration camps. They were certain our voices would be heard in western Europe and America to good advantage, and they were glad we were leaving. They pretended a gay mood to cheer us at our farewell party.

Belo-Ostrov, January 19, 1920. O radiant dream, O burning faith! O *Matushka Rossiya,* reborn in the travail of the Revolution, purged by it from hate and strife, liberated for true humanity and embracing all. I will dedicate myself to you, O Russia!

In the train, December 1, 1921! My dreams crushed, my faith broken, my heart like a stone. *Matushka Rossiya* bleeding from a thousand wounds, her soil strewn with the dead.

I clutch the bar at the frozen window-pane and grit my teeth to suppress my sobs.

CHAPTER LIII

RIGA! JOSTLING CROWDS AT THE STATION, STRANGE SPEECH, laughter, and glaring lights. It was bewildering and it aggravated my feverish condition from the bad cold I had contracted on the way. We planned to go to our comrade Tsvetkov, who was employed in the Soviet transport department. He and his lovely wife Maryussa had been our close friends in the early Petrograd days. Little Maryussa, delicate as a lily, together with Tsvetkov and others, had guarded Petrograd against General Yudenich. Rifle over shoulder, brave Maryussa had been prepared to lay down her life for the Revolution. Later they had endured untold privation and hardships, which undermined Maryussa's health, and finally she succumbed to typhus. Both she and Tsvetkov were of sterling quality. He remained unchanged in his ideas, notwithstanding that he was compelled to earn his living in the employ of the Bolshevik régime. I knew he would bid us a hearty welcome. Still, I shrank from renewed contact with what I had left behind. Nor was I in a condition to meet people and argue the questions I had definitely settled for myself. I needed a rest and I wanted to forget — to shut out the nightmare behind me and not to have to think of the void before me. We considered it inadvisable to go to a hotel: we would arouse too much attention and we were particularly anxious to avoid newspaper men. At Tsvetkov's we could live quietly.

Our first thought was to prepare a manifesto setting forth the appalling conditions of the politicals in the Communist State and urging the anarchist press in Europe and America to help save them from a slow death. It was our desperate cry after twenty-one months of forced silence, the initial step of fulfilling the pledge given our people to make known to the world the colossal fraud wrapped in the Red mantle of " October."

News from Germany was reassuring. Our comrades were working to secure our admission and they were confident of success. But they needed a little more time and therefore we must get our Latvian visa extended for a few days. The few days dragged into three weeks. Owing to our persistency, the visas were renewed, but only in driblets. We would have to get out of their country, the local authorities informed us, go anywhere or back to Russia, where we belonged " as Bolsheviks." The officials were almost without exception mere youths. Their new statehood had evidently gone to their heads like suddenly acquired riches. They were " climbers," coarse and arrogant, overbearing to the point of disgust.

A ray of hope broke at last through our dark sky. " All is settled," our Berlin comrades notified us. The German Consul in Riga had been given instructions to issue the necessary visa. We hastened to the Consulate. It was all right about our visa, we were told there, but our application must first be sent on to Berlin. Within three days we would receive them.

In high spirits our boys again went to the Consulate, confident of securing the visas this time. When they returned, I knew the result without a word being spoken. Our application was refused.

Again it was necessary to procure a prolongation of our stay in Latvia. The sullen youngsters in office demurred, but finally permitted us another forty-eight hours. At the expiration of that time we must leave, they insisted, whether we procured any visa by then or not. " You'll go back to your own country," they declared peremptorily. Our country? Where was it? The war had destroyed the ancient right of asylum, and Bolshevism had turned Russia into a prison. We could not return even there. Nor would we if we could. We'll go to Lithuania, we thought, and we should have really gone there if we had not missed the train on our arrival in Riga.

Our friend Tsvetkov would not hear of it. Lithuania was a trap, he declared. It would be impossible for us to get to Germany from there, nor could we return to Riga again. He would arrange a *sub rosa* route. He knew some freighters whose crews were syndicalists, and he would manage the matter. But could Emma stand being stowed away? I bristled at the implication that I could stand less than the boys. " But your cough — it will give you all away! " he retorted. I protested vigorously. To escape my feminine indignation our friend left to establish the necessary connexions. But his scheme proved a bubble — luckily for us all. For on the following day, the last we could remain in Latvia, came Swedish visas that our syndicalist comrades in Stockholm had obtained. Mr. Branting, the Socialist Prime Minister, had proved more decent than his German comrades.

Accompanied by Tsvetkov and Mrs. C., Secretary Shakol's sister, who had befriended us and supplied us with a large lunch-basket for the journey, we went to the railroad station to board the train which was to take us to Reval. As it pulled out, we heaved a deep sigh of relief. For a while, at least, our visa troubles were over! But the train was barely out of the sight of our friends when we discovered that we had an escort with us. It proved to be three Latvian secret-service men. They demanded our passports, which they immediately confiscated, declaring that we were all under arrest. In vain were our protests against the sudden interruption of our journey, when they could have arrested us during our stay in Riga. The train was stopped and we were taken off, bag and baggage, bundled into an already waiting automobile, and driven by a roundabout route to the city. The car came to a halt before a large brick building, and great was our astonishment when, some feet distant, we recognized the house where we had occupied rooms in the apartment of Tsvetkov. It was the Political Police Department and we could not help laughing at the manœuvres of the authorities to " catch " us when all the time we had been so close at hand.

One by one we were taken into an inner office and examined about our " Bolshevism." I informed the official that, though I was not a Bolshevik, I refused to discuss the subject with him. He evidently realized that it was useless to threaten or coax me, and he ordered me taken to another room, for later disposition.

The room was filled with officials, sitting about, talking, apparently with nothing to do. I had a book with me, and as in the olden days in my adopted country — how far away and long ago it seemed now! — I was soon lost in reading. I did not even notice that the men had left and I was alone. Another hour passed and there was still no sign of my two companions. I grew somewhat uneasy, though I was not alarmed. I knew that Sasha was seasoned in handling difficult situations, and Schapiro was also no novice in such matters. He had had previous experience with the police. During the war, as editor of the London Yiddish weekly, the *Arbeiter Freund,* he had taken over the editorial duties of Rudolf Rocker, who had been interned. Before

long he was arrested and had to serve six months for an article someone else had written. He was a man of discretion and cool-headed. I
felt confident that whatever might happen to my two friends or to
me, we should at least have a chance for a fight. It would reach the
outside world and would thus serve our ideas.

Someone broke in on my reflections. A large policewoman stood
before me. She came to search me, she announced. " Really? " I remarked; " the three hours I was waiting here were more than enough
time to destroy any evidence of the conspiracy the police suspect us
of." Her stolidity was not affected by my raillery. She proceeded to
search me to the skin. But when she attempted to go further, I slapped
her face. She dashed out of the room vowing she would bring men to
finish the job. I dressed in order to receive the gentlemen without
shocking their modesty. Only one came, who invited me to follow him
to my cell, which he locked upon me. He was an obliging chap. Silently
he pointed to the adjoining cells, indicating that my two friends were
there. That was a pleasant surprise and gave me great relief. I was
in solitary confinement, yet I had not felt so free and at peace for the
past twenty-one months. I had ceased to be an automaton. I had regained my will. I was back where I had been in the past — in the
fight. And my comrades were near me, separated only by a wall.
Great peace came over me, contentment and sleep.

On the second day I was taken downstairs for examination. A youth
in his twenties was my inquisitor. He demanded to know about our
secret Bolshevik mission in Europe, why we had stayed in Riga so
long, with whom we had associated, and what had become of the
important documents he knew we had smuggled into the country. I
assured him he still had much to learn to achieve fame and fortune as
an interrogator of such an experienced criminal as he had before him.
I would not take him into my confidence, I told him, even if I had
any information that he might want. I would divulge, however, that
I was an anarchist not a Bolshevik. As he did not seem to know the
difference, I promised him some anarchist literature, which I would
forward to him after leaving the country. He might exchange information and tell me why we had been arrested and on what charge.

He would within a few days, he promised. Strange to say, he kept
his word. The day before Christmas he came to my cell to inform me
that " it was an unfortunate mistake." I started at the familiar phrase.
" Yes, an unfortunate mistake," he repeated, " and the fault is with

your friends the Bolsheviki, not my Government's." I scorned his insinuation. "The Soviet Government gave us passports and permitted us to depart. What interest could it have to land us all in your jail?" I demanded. "I cannot reveal State secrets," he replied, "but it is true, just the same." We would find out later that this was no idle talk. By right we should be immediately released, he added, but there were some formalities to attend to, and all the superior officials had already left for their holidays. I assured him it did not matter. I had spent more than the birthday of Jesus in prison, and that was, after all, the place where the Nazarene would now find himself if he happened to visit our Christian world. The man was duly scandalized, as behooved a prospective State prosecutor.

The guard did my Christmas shopping for me, bringing me fruit, nuts, cake, coffee, and a can of evaporated milk. Luxuries they were, but I was anxious to prepare a Christmas feast for my friends in the adjoining cells. In return for a tip the old guard's heart softened and he permitted me the use of the kitchen situated on the same floor. I took my time and found excuses for going back and forth to my cell, humming all the time: "Christ has risen, rejoice, ye heathen!" and finding a chance to whisper a few words to my invisible companions. Two neatly wrapped packages and a large thermos bottle of steaming coffee were carried by the guard to the two desperadoes next door in return for a little Christmas gift to his family.

We were finally released with profuse apologies. My friends related their experiences to me. They had also been searched to the skin, the lining of their coats ripped open, and the bottoms of their suit-cases torn out for the secret documents we were supposed to have brought out with us. It had been a real burlesque to watch the eager faces of the guards gradually turn to baffled disappointment. Sasha, old jail-bird that he was, had managed to signal at night with lighted matches to a young fellow who sat reading in a house opposite. He threw out notes to the man, one of which the latter picked up, and Sasha hoped it might reach our friends in the city. Schapiro had repeatedly tried to get in touch with me by tapping. I had answered, but he could not make me out. "Nor I you, old man," I confessed. "Next time we'll agree on the key." Even if I could not understand his good old Russian prison signals, he added, I somehow always managed to start a cuisine. "She loves to cook, and even prison can't stop her," Sasha interposed.

At last, on January 2, 1922, we departed from Reval, Esthonia. To avoid a repetition of our Riga adventure we went directly to the steamer, though the boat was not to leave until the following morning. We made good use of the free day to see the quaint town, much older and more picturesque than Riga.

Our reception in Stockholm was fortunately unofficial. Neither soldiers nor workers were ordered out to meet us with music and speeches, as on our arrival in Belo-Ostrov. Just a few comrades genuinely glad to see us. Our good chaperons were Albert and Elise Jensen, who steered us safely past the shoals of American newspaper men. Not that I was averse to greeting my enemies who had been so eager to lie about my doings in Russia. But I preferred not to be misquoted on the Soviet experiment until I had a chance to express my thoughts over my own signature. With the Stockholm *Arbetaren,* our daily syndicalist publication, and the *Brand,* an anarchist weekly, open to us to have our say, there was no need to be interviewed by reporters, and we were all grateful to our friends for saving us from falling into their hands.

Letters from Berlin explained the sudden change of heart on the part of the German Consul in Riga after he had led us to believe that the visa would be issued to us. He had been warned by a Chekist that we were dangerous conspirators on a secret mission to the Anarchist Congress in Berlin. This also shed a light on the insistence of the Lettish officials that " our friends the Bolsheviks " had been behind our trouble in Riga. The Latvian Government had known of our presence in Riga, and the repeated extensions of our stay had been registered with the local police. They would have hardly waited with our arrest till we were leaving the country, except that they were at the last moment supplied by the Soviet emissary with the same information he had given the German Consul in Riga. Our examiners everywhere stressed our alleged possession of secret documents. Their exceptionally thorough search also tended to indicate that our good friends in the Kremlin had denounced us.

I realized with a shock what strong hold the Bolshevik superstition still had on me. Well knowing the nature of the beast, I had yet protested vehemently against the insinuations of the Lettish officials in regard to the Soviet people in Moscow. Notwithstanding my two years' daily experience of Bolshevik political depravity, I was yet unable to credit such Jesuitism on their part — to give us passports and at the same time make it impossible for us to enter any other country. I fully understood now the significance of Litvinov's assurance that "the capitalistic countries will not be anxious to have you." But why, then, did they let us go out of Russia, I wondered. My companions said that the reason was obvious. To refuse us permission to leave would have caused too much protest abroad, as in the case of Peter Kropotkin. He had in fact never attempted to leave Russia, but the mere rumour that he had not been permitted to do so had aroused the entire revolutionary and liberal world abroad and rained endless inquiries on the Kremlin. Moscow evidently did not want to invite a similar uproar again. Our arrest in Russia would have caused undesirable publicity. On the other hand, the Cheka, aware of our stand on the dictatorship and of our part in the protest of the foreign delegates in regard to the Taganka hunger-strike, could not leave us at large much longer. The best solution of the situation was therefore to permit us to depart. It was better policy to appear magnanimous and do the dirty work against us outside the territory of the R.S.F.S.R. This was also the view expressed by our Berlin correspondents. The German Consul in Riga had communicated to his uncle Paul Kampfmeier, the well-known Social Democrat, the rôle played by the Bolshevik Chekist in the matter.

Our Swedish anarchists and anarcho-syndicalists were certain we could remain in their country as long as we pleased. We might as well live there as anywhere else and carry out our plan of writing about our Russian experiences. The *Arbetaren* was anxious for articles from us, as was also the *Brand*. But Sasha as well as I felt that America, our old home, had first claim on us. It had been our field of activity for over thirty years. For good or evil we were known there and we could reach a wider audience than in Sweden or in any other country. We agreed, however, to be interviewed for the *Arbetaren* and the *Brand* and to write appeals in them for the politicals imprisoned and exiled in Russia.

No sooner had our first article appeared in the *Arbetaren* than Mr. Branting had his secretary notify the Syndicalist Committee that had obtained our visa to Sweden that "it was inadvisable for the Russians to appear in print." Branting was a Social Democrat and was opposed to the Bolsheviki. But he was also Prime Minister, and Sweden was at the time discussing the recognition of the Russian Government. An additional reason was the bid the Bolsheviki were making for a united front with the Social Democrats, whom but yesterday they had been denouncing as social traitors and counter-revolutionists. Moreover, the reactionary press started a campaign of denunciation against Branting for having given asylum to anarchists and Bolsheviks. The latter charge referred to Angelica Balabanoff, who was then in Sweden. We were informed that another extension of one month had been given us, but at the expiration of that time we would be expected to shake the dust of Sweden off our revolutionary feet. Poor Branting seemed anxious to quiet the storm against him by securing our departure as soon as possible. He would not drive us out, of course, his secretary assured our people, but we should try at once to find some other country for our abode.

Comrades in half a dozen lands were working hard to secure asylum for us. Our Berlin friends kept up their strenuous efforts. In Austria our old comrade Dr. Max Nettlau was exerting himself in our behalf. In Czechoslovakia others were working to obtain visas. Also in France. The smaller countries were hopeless, Denmark and Norway having already signified to our comrades that there was "nothing doing."

The situation was rather desperate, made more so by several other circumstances. The cost of living in a Stockholm hotel had bankrupted us within a month. The hospitable Jensens invited me to share their two-room apartment, which I accepted in the belief that it would be only for a short time. Sasha had found a room with a Swedish family whose place was too small even for themselves. He regretted that we had not followed his original plan of going by the Minsk route. It had been stupid to ask Moscow for passports. At any rate, he would not apply for a visa any more and he was determined to leave without giving notice and to enter without permission. I could do as I pleased, he declared.

There was something else that had come between us — the question whether I should or should not permit the New York *World* to publish my series of articles on Soviet Russia. Stella had cabled me that the *World* was eager for the story of my Russian experience. I had already been informed to the same effect in Riga by a *World* representative. In fact, he told me his paper had tried to reach me several times while I was still in Moscow. If I had been informed about it there and even if I could have safely sent out an article from R.S.F.S.R., I should have declined to write for a capitalist paper on so vital an issue as Russia. I was just as loath to consider the offer that came through Stella. I wrote her that I preferred to have my say in the liberal and labour press in the United States, and that I should be willing to have them publish my articles without any pay rather than have them appear in the New York *World* or similar publications.

Stella tried the *Freeman* with an article on the martyrdom of Maria Spiridonovna. It was declined. The other American liberal papers showed equal illiberality. I realized that in addition to being stamped an Ishmaelite I should also be gagged on the question of the Bolsheviki. I had kept silent long enough. I had witnessed the slaughter of the Revolution and had heard its death-rattle. I had weighed the evidence that was daily being added to the mountain of Bolshevik crimes. I had seen the collapse of the last vestige of revolutionary pretence of the dictatorship. And all I had done during the two years was to beat my chest and cry: " I have sinned, sinned." In America I had presumed to write *The Truth about the Bolsheviki* and to uphold and defend them in the sincere and ignorant belief that they were the protagonists of the Revolution. Now that I knew the truth, was I to be forced to slay it and keep silent? No, I must protest. I must cry out against the gigantic deception posing as truth and justice.

This I told Sasha and Schapiro. They also were determined to speak out, and, indeed, Sasha had already written a series of articles dealing with various phases of the Bolshevik régime, and they were being published in the anarchist press. But both he and Schapiro emphasized that the workers would not credit my story if published in a capitalist paper like the New York *World*. I did not mind Schapiro's objection because he was of the old sectarian school that had always frowned on the idea of anarchists' writing for *bourgeois* publications, though nearly all of our leading comrades had done so. But Sasha knew that the bulk of workers, particularly in the United States, read nothing but the capitalist papers. It was they whom he wanted to enlighten on the difference between the Revolution and Bolshevism. His attitude hurt me very much and we argued for days. I had repeatedly written for the New York *World* in the past, as well as for other similar publications. Was it not more important how and what one said than where? Sasha insisted that it did not apply in this case. Anything I might write in the capitalist press would inevitably be used by the reactionaries against Russia and I would justly be censured for it by our own comrades. I was well aware of it. Had I not myself condemned the old revolutionist Breshkovskaya for speaking under the auspices of *bourgeois* sponsors? Nothing my comrades would say against me could be so lacerating as the compunction I suffered for having sat in judgment over *Babushka*. Fifty years of her life had gone into the preparation of the Revolution, only to see it exploited by the Communist Party for its political aims. She had witnessed the great *débâcle* while I had been thousands of miles away. And I had added my stone to the pile hurled against her when she had been in America. For that very reason I must speak out now. But Sasha urged that we could do so by means of pamphlets that our people would circulate. He had several of them in preparation; a number of his articles had already appeared in our press; three of them had also been published in the New York *Call*, the Socialist daily. Why could I not do the same? The comrades of the International Aid Federation in the United States were also urging similar means for my presentation of the Russian situation. They had cabled and written, stressing that I refrain from writing for the capitalist press. Their main point was that it would hurt the cause. Their condemnation left me cold. But it was different with Sasha. He was my lifelong comrade in arms, my friend and fellow fighter in a hundred battles that had scorched our beings and tested our souls. We had gone our separate ways while in Russia regarding the question of "revolutionary necessity." There had been no break between us, however, because I also had been uncertain for a long time in my stand. Kronstadt had cleared our minds and had brought us closer again. It was harrowing now to have to take a position so divergent from my friend's attitude. Days and weeks went into the conflict, the hardest life had allotted me. All through the spiritual torture it beat against my brain: I must, I would be heard, even if it should be for the last time. Finally I cabled to Stella to turn over the articles, seven in all, to the New York *World*.

In my decision I was spared the bitterness of complete isolation. Our Grand Old Man Enrico Malatesta, Max Nettlau, Rudolf Rocker, the London *Freedom* group, Albert and Elise Jensen, Harry Kelly, and several other friends and comrades whose opinion I valued expressed their approval of my stand. I should have walked the way of Golgotha in any event. But it was balm to have their support.

I was too far away to witness the fury my articles aroused in the

Communist ranks or to be affected by their poisonous venom. But from the descriptions sent me about Communist meetings against me and from their press I could see the similarity between their blood-lust and that of Southern whites at Negro lynchings. One such occasion must have been most edifying: the gathering presided over by Rose Pastor Stokes. Once she had sat at E.G.'s feet — now she was calling for volunteers to burn E.G., at least in effigy. What a picture! The chairlady intoning the *International,* and the audience holding hands in an orgiastic dance round the flames licking Emma Goldman's body to the tune of the liberating song.

The stereotyped accusation that I had forsworn my revolutionary past, by people who had no past to forswear, was also nothing to worry about. What did trouble me was that the New York *World* had not rated my literary value as highly as did my Communist admirers. It had paid me a paltry three hundred dollars for each article, or twenty-one hundred dollars for the series of seven. And it was being heralded by the Communist chorus that thirty thousand dollars had been paid to the traitor E.G. I was wishing it were true! I might have saved at least some portion of it for the Russian political victims who were suffering cold, hunger, and despair in the prisons and exile of the Bolshevik paradise.

Under pressure from the Swedish syndicalists Branting had extended permission for us to stay for another month. It was to be the last. Visas to other countries were not in sight, and Sasha and Schapiro decided to take matters into their own hands. The latter soon left and Sasha was to go next. A comrade in Prague had secured a visa for me to Czechoslovakia and I implored Sasha to allow our friend to do the same for him. But the mere suggestion of it aroused his wrath.

Sasha stowed away on a tramp steamer, but before the boat pulled out of Stockholm word reached me from the Austrian Consulate that a visa had been granted us. Sick with fear that the boat might leave before I should have the visa in my hands, I did not care if the chauffeur broke all speed limits. I found the visa ready for all three of us, but with it a demand of the Austrian Minister for Foreign Affairs that we give a written pledge not to engage in any political activities in his country. I had no intention of doing so, and I was confident that neither of the boys would consent to it. However, I could not disclose the clandestine departure of the one and the impending going of the

other. I would consult my comrades, I told the Consul, and return
with the answer the next day. It was not altogether a lie, as I still
had time to reach Sasha. A blizzard had descended on the city, and
the boat was held up for forty-eight hours. It afforded me the chance
to send word to Sasha about the Austrian visa and the string attached
to it. I did not expect him to accept it, but I felt he should be informed
about it. A young Swedish friend, the one comforting association of
my dismal sojourn in Stockholm, brought back word that Sasha had
decided on his course and would not be swerved from it. I hovered
about the neighbourhood of the wharf in the deep snow to be near
our stowaway, whom fate had woven into the very texture of my life.

A week after Sasha's departure I also decided on a *sub rosa* route.
Accompanied by my young companion, I travelled to the southern part
of Sweden in the hope of finding there means to be smuggled over to
Denmark. Some sailors my friend knew had agreed to aid me for
three hundred kronen, equal to about a hundred dollars. At the last
moment they demanded double the amount. I was not impressed with
their reliability and we dropped the scheme. We found a man with a
motor boat. We were instructed to get aboard before midnight, the
" lady to lie flat and covered with a blanket until the inspector had
made his rounds." I did. It was not the inspector, however. It was a
policeman. We explained that we were lovers and destitute, and we
had taken refuge on the boat. He was a kindly man, but he wanted
to arrest us just the same, until a generous tip changed his mind. I
could not help laughing at our impromptu story, for it really expressed
the situation.

My friend was crestfallen at the way things were bungled. I consoled him by saying that I had always been a bum conspirator and
that I was glad the scheme had failed. It had certain advantages,
however — did it not give me a chance to see a warmer part of Sweden and more attractive women than the capital, and — not the least
— forty new varieties of hors-d'œuvre that would inspire the most
fastidious gourmet.

Upon my return to Stockholm the next day, I found a letter from
the German Consul. A visa for ten days had been granted me.

CHAPTER LIV

A T THE GERMAN BORDER I FELL RIGHT INTO THE LOVING ARMS
of two stalwart Prussian officials whose Kaiser Wilhelm mous-
taches had lost nothing of pride by the ignominious retreat of their
namesake. Quickly they led me into a private office. I was confronted with a dossier comprising all the events of my life, almost
from my cradle days, whereupon they began grilling me for an hour.
I congratulated them on their German thoroughness in having kept
such a complete record that there was nothing I could add. What were
my intentions in Germany? Honourable, of course: to find a millionaire old bachelor in search of a handsome young wife. At the expiration of my visa I would proceed to Czechoslovakia on the same quest.
"*Ein verflixtes Frauenzimmer*" they roared, and after a further exchange of compliments I was escorted back to the train.

Five months after our comrades had begun the campaign to enable
me to enter Germany, I landed in Berlin, with no more hope that I
should be more successful than they in securing a longer stay. I accepted Czechoslovakia as a last resort — a place of exile. I had no
connexions or friends there; the comrade who had helped to secure
my visa was about to leave the country. I knew I should be cut off
from everybody I cared about. Moreover, the cost of living was high.
But in Germany I was on familiar ground: its language was my mother
tongue. Whatever schooling I had received was in that country, and
my early influences were German. Most important, there was a strong
anarchist and anarcho-syndicalist movement in which I might take
root. My friends Milly and Rudolf Rocker and many other dear comrades were also in Berlin. I would try my luck there, and, should I
have to leave, it would not be without a fight!

Much to everybody's surprise, the Foreign Office made no difficulties about granting me a month's stay. At its expiration I was in-

formed that two more months had been secured for me, and that I
was to call at the Foreign Office. I found the Secretary engaged with
a man who looked like a Russian. The latter was evidently leaving
for his native land; the Secretary was seeing him to the door and impressing upon his visitor not to forget to bring back caviar and *ein
Pelz*. Then the official turned on me with good old Prussian politeness. What did I mean by coming back, he shouted, after he had told
me I should have to leave at the end of the month? My time would be
up tomorrow, he said, and I'd have to go or I should be forcibly put
across the border. His changed manner made me think that Moscow
and its Berlin satraps were again at my heels. The man who had just
left was probably a Chekist.

However, I could not afford to lose my temper. I explained in as
ladylike a tone as I could under the circumstances that another two
months had been granted me and that I came to have my passport
stamped for that. He knew nothing about it and he would not give
me the extension if he did know, he declared. I had better leave
the country quietly or be kicked out. In that case, I replied, he would
have to send several men to carry me out. I left him confounded by
my *Frechheit* and went to the Reichstag in search of my sponsors.
They kept me waiting three hours, too busy with affairs of State
to see me. I was in a disturbed state of mind, but soon I forgot my
troubles in watching the antics of what Johann Most used to call
" the House of Marionettes."

Judging by the continuous stream of deputies to the refreshment
rooms, the latter seemed to be the real seat of the august body. There,
amid quantities of *Stullen, Seidels* of beer, and gusts of cigar-smoke,
the weal and woe of the German masses was being decided. In the
legislative hall someone was talking against time, no doubt to hold the
fort till his political group should have recouped themselves sufficiently to knock the other on the head. It was an entertainment I
should have been sorry to miss.

The day's hard work over, my sponsors turned to me. After listening to my account of the interview at the Foreign Office, they took up
the telephone. A rather warm argument followed, in the course of
which the party at the other end was told that he would be reported
to his chief for " suppressing the extension issued to Frau E. G. Kerschner." The threat seemed to be effective as indicated by " Well,
then — we knew you'd be sensible." The following morning my

passport was stamped for another two months' stay.

With this respite, I decided on a little apartment. I had been driven about so much that I felt bruised in every bone and I was in need of a rest under my own roof. I wanted some peace to collect my thoughts before beginning my book on Russia. I longed for my flaxen-haired, blue-eyed Swedish boy, whose tender devotion had been my mainstay in the three and a half months of my existence in Stockholm. I'd send for him and have two months of personal life in a lifetime that had never been my own. Vain hope! I realized it the moment I met my friend at the station. His fine eyes had not lost their friendliness, but the glow that had rekindled my soul was no longer there. They had come to see what I had known from the start, yet did not wish to realize — that he was twenty-nine and I fifty-three.

Would that the adventure had ended at its height, a golden memory on my thorny road! But his eagerness to rejoin me, and my own heart-hunger had been hard to resist. " Berlin soon! " had been our parting word. Only four weeks had passed since, and his flame had burned out. I was too staggered by the unexpected blow to think clearly and I clung to the straw that I might reawaken the love that had been mine.

There were various reasons why I could not tell him to go. He had avoided conscription and he had aroused the suspicion of the Stockholm police because of his attempt to help Sasha with some papers. He had no means and he would not be permitted to work in Germany. I felt I could not send him away. What if his love had died? Our friendship would still be sweet — my affection for him strong enough to be content with that, I reasoned. The rest and joy I had hoped for were turned into eight months of purgatory.

My misery was increased by Sasha's lack of sympathy with my struggle, the more surprising because he had been kind and solicitous when I fought against the growing infatuation for my friend. He had ridiculed the silly conventions regarding difference in age, and advised me to follow my desire for the youth who had come into my life. Sasha was fond of the boy, and as for the latter, he worshipped my old chum. But my young Swede's arrival in Berlin and his presence in the same apartment somehow changed their former fine comradeship into silent antagonism. I knew they did not mean to hurt me, and yet in their male short-sightedness they did nothing else.

I was in no state of mind for writing a book on Russia. The thought of that unfortunate country and of its political martyrs was ever present with me and I felt I was betraying their trust. I was doing nothing to make their condition and the even more poignant drama of " October " known. I tried to salve my conscience by a contribution I made from the sums earned by my articles and from the brochure the London group had published at my expense. Sasha was doing splendid work, writing articles and issuing pamphlets on *The Russian Tragedy, The Communist Party, Kronstadt,* and related subjects. Our Taganka deportees were now also in Germany and they were making themselves heard in the anarchist press and on the platform regarding the Soviet reality. And even before our voices were raised, our able comrades Rudolf Rocker and Augustin Souchy had been enlightening the German workers on the true conditions in Russia.

Through Herbert Swope, of the New York *World,* and Albert Boni, Clinton P. Brainard, then president of Harper's, became interested in my planned work on Russia. He proved a jovial old man, a breezy Westerner, expansive in manner and conversation; but he did not seem to have the slightest idea of books and their relation to their authors. " Six months for a book on the Soviets! " he exclaimed. " Nonsense! You ought to be able to dictate it right off the bat in a month." "Your name and the subject will make the book, not its literary quality," he asserted. He would bet anything that a volume by Emma Goldman on the Bolsheviki, with an introduction by Herbert Hoover, would prove the greatest thriller of the day. " Why, it means a fortune for you! Did you ever expect that, E.G.? " " No, never in all my life," I admitted, wondering whether he was joking or so incredibly ignorant of my life, my ideas, the importance of Russia to me, or why I wanted to write about it. I felt that Mr. Brainard was so naïve, so like the average American mind, that I could not take offence at his suggestion of Mr. Hoover, another perfect average American, to introduce my poor book to the world.

I expressed surprise to Albert Boni that anyone so limited as the president of Harper's should be at the head of a publishing house of quality and reputation. He explained that Mr. Brainard's domain was business and not the literary department, which was some relief.

I had had no experience with publishers, our books in America having always been issued by ourselves through the *Mother Earth* Publishing Association. Albert Boni, representing Brainard and the McClure Newspaper Syndicate, did not find it necessary to enlighten

me on their commercial methods. The result was that I sold to Mr.
Brainard the world rights to my book on Russia for $1,750 advance
against the usual royalties and fifty per cent for the serial rights. It
seemed a very satisfactory arrangement to me, the most gratifying
provision in the agreement being that nothing could be changed in
my manuscript without my knowledge and consent.

My visa was renewed for another two months and the hope held
out that I could have further extensions. My living-expenses were now
also secured. I could proceed with my book. I had lived with it since
Kronstadt and had worked it out in all its aspects. But when I came
to write it, I was overwhelmed by the magnitude of my subject. The
Russian Revolution, greater and more profound than the French, as
Peter had rightly said — could I do it justice in one volume and in
the limited time set? Years were needed for such a work, and a far
abler pen than mine to make the story as vivid and moving as its
reality. Had I gained the necessary perspective and detachment to
write without personal grievance or rancour against the men at the
helm of the dictatorship? These doubts assailed me at my desk, gaining momentum the more I tried to concentrate on my task.

My immediate surroundings were anything but helpful. My young
friend had got into the same slough as I. He had not the strength to
leave, nor I to send him away. Loneliness, the yearning to be cared
for in an intimate sense, made me cling to the boy. He admired me as
a rebel and as a fighter; as a friend and companion I had awakened
his spirit and had opened to him a new world of ideas, books, music,
art. He did not want to live away from me and he needed the fellowship and understanding that he found in our relationship, he said.
But the difference, the ever present difference of twenty-four years,
he could not forget.

My friends Rudolf and Milly Rocker sensed the physical and mental stress I was going through. I had not seen them since 1907, when
we had known each other only as comrades. During my stay in Berlin
I came to appreciate and love their beautiful spirit. Rudolf was very
much like my old companion Max, as understanding, tender, and generous, and not given so much to paralysing introspection. Intellectually brilliant and with a prodigious capacity for work, he was a force
in the German anarchist movement and an inspiration to everyone
who came in contact with him. Milly was also sensitively attuned to
human suffering and unstinted in her sympathy and affection. They

were a soothing help in the battle I was fighting to get control of myself. I desperately needed to begin my book.

The arrival of my beloved Stella and Ian, my baby almost as much as hers, somewhat dulled my gnawing pain. I had not seen them for three years and I had longed for their coming. One week went by in sweet harmony with my own, in reminiscences of the past, with all its joy and travail, of what is admirable and what is hateful in my adopted land.

A dissonant note soon disturbed our idyll. Stella had always kept me on a pedestal. She could not bear to see my feet of clay. She had suffered through my relation to Ben, and now again my dear one resented that her adored *Tante* should " throw herself away." My young Swede was quick to sense the disdain of my niece. He became more contrary and went out of his way to be particularly disagreeable to her.

Ian, a beautiful youngster of six, wild and unbridled as a young colt, found our apartment too small for his energies. He knew no German and he could not understand why everybody should walk as on glass because " granny's " nerves were on edge. There was wisdom from the mouth of a child. Even our baby had learned to go by years, and, fool that I was, I still felt young, reaching out hungrily for the fire of youth. Fortunately my sense of the ridiculous had not entirely forsaken me. I could still laugh at my own folly. But I could not write, or do as my Swede — run away!

He would go to the seashore for a few days, so that Stella and I could be with each other undisturbed, he said. I did not protest; I felt rather relieved. The two days lengthened into a week without a word to reassure me that all was well with him. My anxiety grew into an obsession that he had taken or lost his life. To escape the torturing thought I tried once more to start my book. As if by magic the load I had carried for months was lifted; the harrowing shadows disappeared together with the boy and my frustrations. I myself became dissolved into the picture that was taking form on the paper before me.

A storm began in the late afternoon and continued throughout the night. Thunder and lightning, followed by wind and rain, beat against the windows of my room. I wrote on, oblivious of everything except the storm in my own soul. I found release at last.

The storm outside had stopped. The air was still, the sun slowly rising and spreading its red and gold over the sky in greeting of the new day. I wept, conscious of the eternal rebirth in nature, in the dreams of man, in his quest for freedom and beauty, in the struggle of humanity to greater heights. I felt the rebirth of my own life, to blend once more with the universal, of which I was but an infinitesimal part.

The Swede returned hale and sound. He had not written because he was trying to muster up courage to go his own way. He failed. He was drawn back by his need of me. Would I accept him again? I did, certain that he could not consume me as before. I was back in Russia now, in her triumph and defeat, my every fibre intent on re-creating the tremendous panorama I had witnessed for twenty-one months.

My dear old pal Sasha, though rarely sympathetic with my affairs of the heart, never failed me in our common activities or in his co-operation with my literary efforts. Just as soon as he saw me working in earnest, he came back with his old eagerness to help. I should have made considerable progress now but for a new disturbance.

Young people are rarely generous to each other, nor have they patience with each other's shortcomings. My secretary, an intelligent and efficient Jewish-American girl, and my young Swede could apparently not get on. They argued violently and quarrelled over every trivial matter. The strain was aggravated when the girl moved into our apartment. It was large enough, and each of us had his own room. But the two young things glared and fumed at each other every moment they were together.

Soon I discovered the truth of the German saying: *Was liebt sich, das neckt sich*. The two young people had fallen in love with each other and were fighting to distract my attention from their real feelings. They were too unsophisticated to be guilty of deliberate deception. They simply lacked the courage to speak and were perhaps afraid to hurt me. As if their frankness could have been more lacerating than my realization that their show of indifference was only a shield! At heart I had not ceased to believe that my love would rekindle his affection, so rich and abundant during our months in Stockholm.

I could not endure the silly hide-and-seek going on before my eyes. I assured them that nothing would change my affection for them, and that I wanted the girl to continue with me until the manuscript was typed, but I would ask them to find quarters of their own. It would be less wearing for the three of us.

They moved out. The girl continued to do my secretarial work, but her attitude towards me had changed. The young Swede kept coming to see me, generally in the evening, when his sweetheart was not present. She could not bear to see him with me, he said, or to be made to feel that I was his inspiration. I would always remain that, he reiterated. It was something of a consolation; still, it would be best if he stayed away altogether, I told him. I was past minding. Their love was young, and it was unkind to cause it pain. He took my advice and he did not come again until shortly before he left with the girl for America, and then only to say good-bye.

I still had the hardest part of my book to do — an Afterword that was to set forth the lessons of the Russian Revolution which our comrades and the militant masses will have to learn if future revolutions are not to be failures. I had come to realize that with all the Bolshevik mania for power they could never have so completely terrorized the Russian people if it were not inherent in mass psychology to be easily swayed. I was also convinced that the conception of revolution in our own ranks was too romantic, and that miracles cannot be expected even after capitalism shall have been abolished and the *bourgeoisie* eliminated. I knew better now and I wanted to help my comrades to a clearer understanding.

I felt that for an adequate treatment of the constructive side of revolution I myself had to get away from the phantom of the Communist State far enough for objective writing. I did not want my book to go out into the world without some definite conclusions. Yet in my state of mind I found it impossible to go into the complex problems of the subject. After weeks of conflict I decided to jot down a few thoughts, some fragments that might serve as a sketch for a larger work on the vital subject. Sasha agreed that in the light of the Russian events a thorough revision of the old conception of revolution had become imperative. He or I or both of us might undertake it later. There was no need to fret about the matter now. A book of impressions, such as mine, was no place for an analysis of theories and ideas. Rudolf also held this view. As a result of the advice of my two friends, whose judgment in such questions rarely erred, and because of my own feeling about it, I wrote a closing chapter suggesting in general outline the practical, constructive efforts during revolution.

I had reasons for a double celebration. I had regained my emotional sanity and I had completed the manuscript of " My Two Years in Russia." Sasha also had cause to be exceedingly glad. The precious diary he had kept in Russia, which had escaped the Chekists who ransacked his room because I had it hidden in mine, had been lost after it was smuggled out of Russia. While Sasha was in Minsk, a friend had taken his note-books to Germany, promising to deliver them to the Rockers. Great was our shock on learning that our Berlin friends had failed to receive the precious package. Nothing could replace the day-by-day record Sasha had kept of every incident and event during our stay in Russia. Luckily the priceless diary was discovered after many an anxious week.

Months passed after my manuscript had been mailed to the McClure Newspaper Syndicate, but no word came about its receipt. I wrote with every sailing and spent a little fortune on cables, but there was no reply. Stella and Fitzi, whom I had asked to see Brainard about it, reported that they had been told that the man had not appeared in his office since his return from Germany, and no one at the Syndicate knew anything about my manuscript. I then cabled Mr. Swope, of the New York *World,* begging him to go after the president of Harper's. I saw Garet Garrett, of the *Tribune,* while he was in Berlin and asked him to help me locate the manuscript. I gave Albert Boni no peace. All these frantic efforts brought no results. Unable to endure the worry about my book any longer, I turned the matter over to my old friend and counsellor Harry Weinberger. I was confident he would succeed in making the McClure people or Brainard give me an account.

In addition to this anxiety came the news of the frightful calamity that had happened to my Stella. She had lost the sight of her right eye. Specialists who had treated her nearly brought her to the grave by their experiments. One of them dismissed her case as a detached retina that could not be cured, and hinted at complete blindness. Germany is famous for its eye specialists and I was entirely free now to devote myself to my niece. I urged her to come to me at once. She came, a shadow of the radiant girl that had visited me the previous year. A specialist diagnosed her case as tuberculosis of the eyes and held out no hope for recovery.

Dr. Magnus Hirschfeld, whom I knew for his pioneer work in sex psychology, came to our rescue. He suggested Dr. Count Wiser, of

Bad Liebenstein, in Thüringen. He was a remarkable man, Dr. Hirschfeld said, a great diagnostician and an innovator in the treatment of eye affections. The doctor added that I should be particularly interested in Wiser because he had been proscribed and persecuted by the profession, as I had been in the political field and he himself in his humanitarian and social prophylactic work. I smiled at the idea that an aristocrat should meet with the same opposition as a social rebel or even as Dr. Hirschfeld, a Jew working to clear away the sexual prejudices of the German *Michel*. However, we were willing to try Count Wiser.

Though we had been informed about the attitude of the medical profession towards Dr. Wiser, we were rather dismayed by the circular handed us in his office when we arrived for a consultation. It was an appeal to the Medical Department of the War Ministry to have Dr. Graf Wiser suppressed on grounds of professional incompetence, quackery, and dishonesty, and it was signed by twenty-two of the foremost eye specialists of Germany. For a moment the thought came to me that there must be something wrong with Dr. Wiser to have called forth the enmity of his illustrious colleagues. Our unpleasant impression was somewhat mitigated by the fact that Wiser did not hesitate to let his patients know the professional attitude against him. He could not undertake to treat any person, he stated in a foot-note, unless assured of confidence in his method. This raised him considerably in my estimation and respect.

My first personal meeting with the proscribed doctor freed me entirely from the last doubt raised by the circular. His entire demeanour belied the accusation against him. His simplicity and sincerity were evident in every word. Though he had a line of people waiting, he took an hour and a half to examine Stella and then declined to form a definite opinion about her condition. He was certain, however, that she had neither a detached retina nor tuberculosis. He expressed the view that probable overstrain had resulted in excessive blood-pressure, causing a hæmorrhage that formed a blood clot over the optic nerve. He hoped he could treat it in such a manner that it would be absorbed in her system. Time and care would tell. Much would depend on the patient herself. His treatment was rather rigorous, and " The patience of an angel is required to keep it up," the doctor remarked, with a smile that lit up his fine features. Six hours or more of daily exercises with various lenses was a strenuous process that called for complete rest and relaxation after the ordeal. His charm and human interest convinced me that there was a beautiful personality beneath the physician who loved his profession. Every day strengthened my first impression of Dr. Wiser.

Our presence in Liebenstein brought to us many of our friends from America. Fitzi and Paula, whom we had not seen since our deportation, came for a stay. Ellen Kennan, our old Denver friend, Michael Cohn and his new wife, Henry Alsberg, Rudolf and Milly Rocker, Agnes Smedley, Chatto and comrades from England. My life had not been so replete with friendship and affection in many years. Joy over Stella's improvement filled my cup of happiness to the brim. " Queen E.G. and her court," teased Henry at the lovely surprise party my family arranged for my fifty-fourth birthday. This much life had given me: friends whose love neither faltered nor changed with the years, a treasure few possess.

Among the many birthday gifts and messages I received was also one from my faithful friend and counsellor, Harry Weinberger. It brought the good news that my manuscript had been sold by Brainard to Doubleday, Page and Company and that the book would be out in October of that year (1923). I cabled that page proofs be sent to me. The publishers replied that it would delay the issue of my book and assured me that they would keep strictly to the manuscript.

After three months' treatment by Dr. Wiser, Stella regained partial sight of her blind eye. Nor was that the only achievement of " our *Graf,*" as we began to call him. Every day in his private clinic I had occasion to study various cases, afflictions similar to Stella's, that had been given up as hopeless and that Dr. Wiser succeeded in curing, partially or completely. I thought it incredible that anyone so skilled and eager to give relief should have been put in the pillory.

From my talks with Dr. Wiser's patients, some of whom had known him for years, I learned of the most amazing conspiracy I had ever heard of in the professional world. The statement sent to the War Ministry by the group of eye specialists was only a minor part of the dossier manufactured against the *Graf.* They had even gone to the extent of sending one of their worthies to spy on him. Among the accusations against him was that he was mercenary. I never knew anyone less concerned with money than Wiser. When the value of the mark was going down five times a day, he never asked a pfennig from his patients until they had finished their treatment. This involved losses that caused him to close his public clinic, where the poorest were given the same treatment and attention as those who could afford to pay. Sixty-three years of age, in delicate health, Dr. Wiser worked twelve hours a day, seven days a week, and though he had scores of patients, he and his wife lived in the utmost frugality. At the same time he freely helped everybody who came to him, not only professionally, but from his limited means as well.

Dr. Wiser's greatest offence in the eyes of his detractors, apart from the fact that he achieved results where they had failed, was his reluctance to return soldiers to the front who had had their sight impaired. In one of the many interviews I had with him, he remarked: " I know nothing about politics and I care little about it. I only know suffering humanity, the flower of the land shot to pieces by senseless hate. My aim, my sole interest, is to help them and instil in them new faith in life."

Stella, having begun to show signs of strain from the three months of daily application, Dr. Wiser ordered her to take a complete rest. It was part of his general system to have his patients recuperate from time to time before continuing the treatment. She was planning to visit Munich for the approaching Wagner-Strauss festival, with the latter conducting his own operas. Sasha, Fitzi, Paula, and Ellen were also going and they all urged me to join them.

Bavaria being the stronghold of German jingoism, I was dubious about the suggestion, but the girls insisted and I accompanied them. Forty-eight hours after reaching Munich came again the familiar knock on my door. Three men invited me to accompany them to the *Polizei Presidium*. They were not nearly so polite as my early callers in Berlin, but they consented to wait long enough to enable me to apprise my friends of my arrest.

The dossier in the Munich rogues' gallery was as complete as the one on the German border. It contained material dating back to 1892 — nearly everything I had ever written or said — all about Sasha's activities and mine, and a complete collection of photographs. The most surprising exhibit was a picture taken in New York by my uncle, a photographer, in 1889. My vanity flattered at seeing myself so young and attractive, I offered to buy a copy. The police grew quite angry at such " flightiness " in the face of my arrest and certain deportation. After several hours inquisition I was permitted to return to my hotel for lunch on condition that I come back again. I was grateful for the hour with my family. My one regret was that I had heard only *Tristan and Isolde* and *Electra,* and that my subscription to the rest of the cycle would be lost.

Among the charges against me was that I had been in Bavaria in the Fall of 1893 on a secret mission. I denied the allegation because I had then been " otherwise engaged." " What was it ? " they demanded. " I was taking a rest-cure at Blackwell's Island Penitentiary in New York." And I had the effrontery to admit it ? Why not ? I had not been there for stealing silver spoons or silk handkerchiefs. I was there for my social ideas, for the very ones for which they were about to expel me. " We know those ideas," they roared, " plotting conspiracies, bombs, killing of rulers." Were they still afraid of such trifles after the world slaughter they and their Government had helped to launch ? Oh, that was for the protection of the Fatherland, but I could not be expected to understand such holy motives. I cheerfully admitted my limitations.

In the late afternoon I was sent back to the hotel with a body-guard and ordered to leave on the evening train. How to get Sasha away was my main problem. My young police escort unwittingly suggested a way. He complained that he had been on duty since early morning and now he would be unable to get back to his wife and child until he saw me leave Munich. I remarked that he could just as well turn me over to the hotel porter, who would take me to the station. He hesitated only long enough to see me pull out a five-dollar bill. The matter could be arranged, he said, if I would promise not to jump out of the train after it left the station. Reassured that I had no intention of committing suicide, he went his way.

In the hotel I held a hurried conference with the members of our party. We agreed that Sasha must get out of Munich at once, for it was certain that the police would find him if he remained another day. Fitzi, looking very ladylike in spite of her many " plots " while she had been with us in America, saw Sasha to the station. We met on the train when it was well out of Bavaria.

The police returned to the hotel the next morning in search of Alexander Berkman, and the same day Stella was expelled from the country because she was the niece of Emma Goldman. They did not bother the other girls, but the latter decided that they had had enough of Bavarian hospitality.

Stella went back to Wiser and I remained in Berlin till Fitzi's sailing. I planned to join my niece as soon as dear Fitzi should have departed. It became unnecessary, because Stella could not longer stand the separation from her son and his father. Moreover, Dr. Wiser felt anxious about her because of the threatening political situation in Germany. He knew the temper of the reactionaries in his country and he would not expose his foreign patients to it. He advised Stella to return to America, impressing upon her the necessity of the utmost precaution against exposing her sick eye. He also mapped out a system of treatment that she could continue herself until the spring, when he expected her to come back. I fought against her leaving. I dreaded some mishap — a cold, something unforeseen, that might throw her back. But there was no holding Stella any longer, and the reassurance of our *Graf* quieted my fears.

Stella had hardly left when I received a blow that staggered me. A copy of my book arrived with the last twelve chapters missing and with an entirely wrong title. As printed, the volume was an unfinished work, because the last chapters and particularly my Afterword, which represented the culminating essence of the whole, were left out. The unauthorized name was fearfully misleading: *My Disillusionment in Russia* was sure to convey to the reader that it was the Revolution that had disillusioned me rather than the pseudo-revolutionary methods of the Communist State. The title I had given my work was simply " My Two Years in Russia." The spurious title was a veritable misfit. I wrote a statement for the press, which I sent to Stella, explaining that my manuscript had been amputated, and I cabled Harry Weinberger to demand of the publishers an explanation. I wanted the sales stopped till the matter should be straightened out.

In reply, Doubleday, Page and Company cabled that they had bought from the McClure Syndicate the world rights to the twenty-four chapters in the belief that they comprised my complete story. They had also been authorized to use their own title. They had known nothing about the existence of the other chapters.

Energetic Harry Weinberger would not give up. He succeeded in inducing Doubleday, Page and Company to publish the missing chapters in a separate volume, the cost of printing to be guaranteed by us. I appealed to our comrade Michael A. Cohn to extend the loan, which he did without delay.

Meanwhile Stella had suffered a relapse. In crossing the Atlantic she had done the very thing the *Graf* had warned her against. She remained on deck during a storm without the prescribed bandage to protect her eye. On landing she was caught in the vortex of family worries, which helped to aggravate her condition. She regretted bitterly not having remained in Wiser's care, and I reproached myself for permitting her to leave when she was making such progress.

I had written a story on Wiser's work and planned to send it to the New York *World*. But it was out of the question now. My readers could not be expected to take my word that Dr. Wiser was not responsible for Stella's relapse. I decided to withhold my article until she could again come under his care. However, the story appeared after all, in the *New Review,* a magazine published in Calcutta in the English language. Agnes Smedley and Chatto, the latter having also been treated by the *Graf,* believed in the success of his new method and they wanted to make him known in India. Its publication resulted in a number of Hindus' coming to Dr. Wiser as patients. It was the only comfort in my grief over Stella's condition.

The reviews of *My Disillusionment in Russia* showed as much discernment as the representative of Doubleday, Page and Company who had bought three-quarters of a manuscript as a complete work. Among the scores of reviewers only one guessed that the book was an abortion. It was a Buffalo librarian, who pointed out in the *Journal* that Emma Goldman's narrative ended with Kiev, 1920, while in her Preface she stated that she had left Russia in December 1921. Had nothing happened in all the intervening time to impress the author? The man's perspicacity strikingly reflected on the dullness of the " critics " who presume to pass literary judgment in the United States.

The Communist response to my volume on Russia could have been foreseen, of course. William Z. Foster's " review " was to the effect that everybody in Moscow was aware that Emma Goldman was receiving support from the American Secret Service Department. Mr. Foster knew that I should not have lasted a day in Russia if the Cheka had believed such a thing. Other Communists, who wrote as kindly as Mr. Foster, also knew that I had not been bought. There was only one who had the courage to say so: René Marchand, of the French group in Moscow, who stated in his review that, though he regretted my misguided judgment, he could not believe that my stand against Soviet Russia was motivated by material reasons. I appreciated his giving me credit for my revolutionary integrity, and I wished he were brave enough to admit that he was unable to reconcile

himself to some of the methods the Bolsheviki practised in the name
of the Revolution. Commandeered to work in the Cheka, René Marchand had seen enough to plead for his removal, as otherwise he would
be compelled to leave the Communist Party. Like many other sincere
Communists he did not understand the Revolution in terms of the
Cheka.

Not so Bill Haywood. As Sasha had foreseen, he easily took the
Bolshevik bait. Three weeks after his arrival in Russia he wrote to
America that the workers were in full control and that prostitution
and drunkenness had been abolished. Lending himself to such obvious
falsehoods, why should Bill not also credit me with motives he knew
were absurd? "Emma Goldman did not get the soft jobs she was
looking for; that was why she wrote against the Dictatorship of the
Proletariat." Poor Bill! He began rolling down the precipice when
he ran away to save himself from the burning house of the I.W.W.
He could not stop himself in his fall.

My Communist accusers were not the only ones to cry "Crucify!"
There were also some anarchist voices in the chorus. They were the
very people who had fought me on Ellis Island, on the *Buford,* and
the first year in Russia because I had refused to condemn the Bolsheviki before I had a chance to test their scheme.

Daily the news from Russia about the continued political persecution strengthened every fact I had described in my articles and in my
book. It was understandable that Communists should close their eyes
to the reality, but it was reprehensible on the part of people who
called themselves anarchists to do so, especially after the treatment
Mollie Steimer had received in Russia after having valiantly fought
in America for the Soviet régime.

For her activities in behalf of Soviet Russia and against intervention Mollie Steimer had been railroaded by an American court to
fifteen years in prison. Before she had begun her sentence in the Missouri State Prison, she had endured incredible cruelty for six months
in the New York workhouse. After eighteen months in the Jefferson
City Penitentiary Mollie, together with three other members of her
group, had been released to be deported to Russia. Surely these
young people deserved well of the Communist State. The boys, more
adaptable to the new wrongs, managed to move safely among the
cliffs of the dictatorship. Not so Mollie, who was of different fibre.
She found the Soviet jails filled with her comrades, and, while she

could not make her protest heard as she had against the crimes in the United States, she undertook to raise funds to supply food to the incarcerated anarchists in the Petrograd jails. Such counter-revolutionary work could not be tolerated on Soviet soil.

Eleven months after Mollie had come to Russia, she was arrested, charged with the heinous offence of feeding her imprisoned comrades and corresponding with Alexander Berkman and Emma Goldman. A protracted hunger-strike and the vigorous protest of the Anarcho-Syndicalist delegates to the Congress of the Red Trade Union International brought about Mollie's release, but not freedom of movement. She was forbidden to leave Petrograd, placed under Cheka surveillance, and ordered to report every forty-eight hours. Six months later Mollie's room was raided and she was again arrested. In the Cheka Mollie was grilled, kept in a filthy cell, and once more compelled to hunger-strike.

Finally Mollie was deported by the Russian Socialist Federated Soviet Republic which she had so staunchly championed in America and for which she had willingly taken fifteen years' imprisonment. Could anything express more forcibly the degeneration of the Kremlin rulers, once revolutionists themselves? Yet some anarchists censured me because I had refused to handle the Bolshevik fetish with kid gloves. The case of Mollie and of her friend Fleshin, both of whom had gone through the same persecution and suffering, would have been enough for me to brand the Moscow outfit. They came straight to us in Berlin — starved, ill, penniless, without a possibility of finding work in Germany or of being admitted to any other country. Yet their spirit was undaunted none the less. They had escaped the Bolshevik inferno. Not so thousands of other true rebels who remained in the Communist paradise. What mattered to me the condemnation and attacks of the zealots in comparison with my inability to help the Mollies and the thousands of others in prison and exile? I had done nothing for them since my arrival in Germany.

The German Revolution was only skin-deep, but it succeeded in establishing certain political liberties. Our comrades could publish their papers, issue books, and hold meetings. The Communists carried on their propaganda with little molestation, condemning in Germany the abuses they defended in Russia. The reactionary nationalist elements were also not interfered with. Their arrogance knew no bounds, equalling that of the militarists of the old Prussian régime. With two such I had an encounter in a subway train. They were railing against the *verdammte Juden* as idle vampires and the cause of the ruin of the Fatherland. I listened for a while and then remarked that they were talking nonsense. I had lived in a land where there were millions of Jewish workingmen, I told them, and many of them brave fighters for the betterment of humanity. " Where is that? " they demanded. " In America," I replied. It drew a volley of abuse from them. America had tricked Germany out of victory, they cried. As the train reached my station and I alighted, they shouted after me: " Wait till things change and we'll fix such as you just as we did Rosa Luxemburg."

Though in a desperate economic situation, Germany enjoyed considerable political freedom. That is to say, the natives. But I was not a German and consequently I had no right to express opinions. It was not a matter of mere arrest: it meant expulsion. There was apparently no other country willing to let me in, but I thought I might try Austria again. Like his tribe in other lands, the Austrian Minister for Foreign Affairs signified his readiness to admit me, but on condition that I abstain from all political activity. Naturally I refused.

My friends Rudolf and Milly Rocker favoured one of the two ways out of my dilemma: the legalization in Germany by marriage, or England. The first method had been a frequent practice among the Russian intelligentsia and revolutionists in the days when women had no political status apart from their husbands or fathers. In Germany Rosa Luxemburg had contracted such a nominal marriage to enable her to remain in the country and follow her work. Why couldn't I do the same? I, they said, should go through with the ridiculous ceremony and end my troubles. Such a step had long before been suggested in America. Several comrades had been willing to sacrifice themselves for the cause, among them my old friend Harry Kelly. It would have prevented the United States from deporting me, Milly reiterated. But I had been unable to do the ludicrous and inconsistent thing, having opposed the institution of marriage all my life. Moreover, there had been the lure of Russia, the glowing dream. That too was dead now, together with the notion that one could remain on earth without making compromises.

My difficulties in Sweden and other countries made me amenable to the suggestion of marriage in order to gain a foothold now in some corner of the world. Harry Kelly was still ready to keep his promise.

On his visit to Sweden he had again offered to take me back to America as his bride. Good old scout! He had been unaware of the new law by which an American husband was no longer a protection for his foreign-born wife.

No such law existed in Germany, Rudolf informed me, and I might as well give some man a chance to make a " respectable woman " of me! If not that, then I should go to Great Britain. It was still politically the freest country. He himself would go back there if he could. He had deeper roots in England than in his native land, having lived and worked in that country nearly as long as Sasha and I had in America. He could understand why I felt alien everywhere and why I did not want to be bound to Germany. I would probably never be content anywhere, cut off from my old moorings. The next best was England.

I was dubious. It did not seem possible that Great Britain had escaped the reaction following upon the war any more than had other countries; still, it might be worth trying. My present position was insupportable. The only public meeting I had addressed in behalf of the Russian politicals brought me an official warning against expressing any further criticism of the Soviet Republic.

Another difficulty was how to earn my living by my pen. The German press was out of the question; too many native writers were starving. At the same time America's hatred of Germany was still strong. Two articles I had sent the New York *World* were refused. One treated of Gerhart Hauptmann in connexion with his sixtieth anniversary, celebrated on a national scale. The *World* had cabled its consent to my going to Breslau, where the main festivities were taking place, but declined my article on the ground that it was " too high-brow." My second essay was on the Ruhr occupation, with its resulting bitterness and suffering. A third article, on the experimental new schools in Germany, and a fourth on the foremost women in German art, letters, and labour, were returned by a dozen magazines. I had not the least chance of earning my salt by writing on German topics. From Brainard, who had broken our agreement and botched my book, there was no hope of any income.

England did not appear very enticing. Still, it might afford me asylum with comparative political freedom, and perhaps also an opportunity to earn my livelihood through lectures and articles. Frank Harris was in Berlin, keeping open house. His interest and kindness, as when I was in the Missouri prison, had not changed. It would be quite easy to get me to England, he said. He knew almost everyone in the Labour Government and he would try for a visa for me. Soon after, Frank left for France, and several months passed before I heard from him again. He informed me that the Home Office had asked no questions about my political views or intentions. It had merely inquired whether I had means of support. Frank had replied that I was an able writer who earned my living by my pen. Moreover, he could name a dozen persons who would consider it a privilege to support his friend and he was one of them. Shortly afterwards I was notified by the British Consulate in Berlin that a visa had been granted me.

Except for the parting from Sasha and from the other friends who had endeared themselves to me, I had no regrets on leaving Germany. Vicissitudes of many kinds, not the least the death of my mother in America, had not brought me cheer and joy. Enforced inactivity embittered even the occasional hours of tranquillity during my stay of twenty-seven months. Sasha had finished his *The Bolshevik Myth;* he was in good health, had acquired a circle of friends, and was devoting himself to the work of aid for the revolutionary politicals in prison and exile in Russia. For the rest, I was glad to get away. England might let me take root, offer an outlet for my energies, respond to an appeal for the doomed and damned in the Soviet land. That was worth going to England for; it was a new hope to cling to.

With this thought to give me courage, I left Germany on July 24, 1924, via Holland and France, for England.

My Dutch visa permitted a stay of only three days, yet long enough to address the twentieth anniversary celebration of the Anti-Militarist Society, organized by our grand champion of peace, our old comrade, Domela Nieuwenhuis. Dutch secret-service men watched the house of my host, de Ligt. They followed us to the station and waited until my train pulled out. At the same time the Dutch Government was entertaining another visitor, a Soviet representative. No limit was put on his stay, nor were his movements shadowed. When I expressed surprise that a reactionary government like that of Holland should offer hospitality to an emissary of the Communist State, my friends smiled. " Russia is a wheat-producing country and Rotterdam a good centre for the distribution of her exports," they explained.

My French transit visa was for two weeks. The inspector at the border insisted that it did not permit me to stop and ordered me to connect immediately with the boat train for England. I refused to budge. After a long parley, greased by American cash, I was allowed to proceed.

The two weeks in Paris, the city I love best in Europe, were enjoyable in the company of friends from America. There were Paula, who had come from Berlin, Harry Weinberger, little Dorothy Miller, Frank and Nellie Harris, and many others, some of whom I had not seen in five years.

"Two weeks!" objected Weinberger; "I'll get you an extension for a month at least."

"How can you — an unknown person here?" I retorted.

"Unknown — me? And coming straight from the Lawyers' Congress, received by the King of England, and presented to the President of the French Republic?" Harry protested indignantly. "You wait and see."

Dressed in morning clothes, wearing a top hat, with ribbons on his coat, Harry presented himself with me at Quai d'Orsay. His client, Madame Kerschner, had come from Germany, he announced, to confer with him on important business matters that would take at least a month. One look at Harry's regalia, and the extension was granted.

"Unknown?" said Harry triumphantly. "Say it again if you dare." I was as meek as a lamb.

In appreciation I offered to chaperon him through Paris. In the same group with my friend were several of his colleagues. The one I liked best was Arthur Leonard Ross. He was of the rare type that one gets to consider in a short time as a good friend.

My dear old friends were thinning out. I had been more fortunate in my friendships than most people, and I gained new ones, among them Nellie Harris, Frank's wife. I had never met her before; it was love at first sight on my part, and Nellie seemed to like me also. Frank continued to be eternally young; at sixty-eight he could still run twelve blocks for exercise after an elaborate meal and enough drink to make most men unsteady. Wine only made him more witty and sparkling. What if he loomed largest in his own estimation? So do most people whose gifts are not nearly so brilliant as his. He was extremely entertaining with the stories of the people he had known in every clime and station in life, from bricklayers, cowboys, and statesmen to the geniuses of art and letters. Frank was an extremist in his loves and hates. If he cared for you, no praise was too generous; if he disliked you, he saw you all black. His enemies, real or imaginary, had no redeeming qualities. Often he was unfair and unjust and we gave and took many verbal blows from each other.

My stay in Paris served to increase my aversion to going to London. I dreaded its fogs, bleakness and chill. Frank urged me to delay no longer. He expected the Labour Government to be defeated in the coming elections; the Tories would probably ignore my visa. To encourage me he enlarged on the many interesting people I should meet there who would welcome me and help in my contemplated campaign in behalf of the Russian politicals, as well as in my lectures on the drama and literature.

Helpful as ever was Frank, but he could not make London's autumn and winter attractive to me. Perhaps if I could secure a return visa to France, I might find England less irksome. Harry Weinberger had sailed and most of the people I knew in Paris lacked the necessary connexions to help me to a return visa.

My meeting with Ernest Hemingway held out some hope. It was at a party given by Ford Madox Ford. The affair might have been duller had not Hemingway been there. He reminded me of both Jack London and John Reed because of his simplicity and exuberance of spirit. He invited me to dinner together with a newspaper friend of his who, Hemingway believed, could secure a French visa for me. Ernest, in his rôle as proud father of a buxom baby, looked younger and was gayer in his home setting. His journalist friend did not impress me, nor could he do anything about a visa, though he had promised much. Instead he wrote a silly story about me, purporting to be an interview on Russia, not one word of which was true.

CHAPTER LV

ONE IS CERTAIN TO BE DISAPPOINTED IN AMERICAN REPORTERS, YET never in the London weather during autumn or winter. It was foggy and drizzling when I arrived in September, and it did not let up until May. Unlike my visit in 1900, when I lived in a basement, my quarters this time were on the heights: a bedroom on the third floor in the house of my old friend Doris Zhook. I even had the luxury of a gas-stove, which I kept going all day. The monster fog mocked my futile attempts to keep the chill out of my old bones, even when I tried to snatch a little cheer from an occasional ray of sunlight. Doris and the other comrades insisted that it was " not really cold." American steam-heated apartments had spoiled me for the " mild British climate," they said. They would not have their homes centrally heated if they could. Fire-places were "more sensible, more healthful, and pleasanter." I told my friends that I had been away from America five years and had forgotten its material blessings. I had been in Archangel when the temperature was fifty below zero and I had not felt so chilly. Poetic fancy, they teased. If the damp makes one miserable, it produces good complexions, rich foliage, and the strength of the British Empire. Delicate skins, the luscious green lawns and meadows, are due to the weather, and the need to escape from his own climate has made the Englishman foremost among globe-trotters and colonizers.

I soon realized that physical handicaps would be the least of my difficulties. The anarchists of London were my friends of many years, solicitous and willing to assist in anything I wanted to do. They were the remnant of the old guard of the pre-war groups, including John Turner, Doris Zhook, her brother William Wess, Tom Keell, and William C. Owen, a former co-worker of mine in America. But they were divided among themselves. Tom Keell, the publisher of *Free-*

dom, and Owen, its editor, had kept the paper alive in spite of all vicissitudes. But there was no real movement in London or in the provinces, I soon learned. Coming as I did from the seething anarchist activities in Berlin, the situation in England was depressing. The general political conditions were worse than I had anticipated. The war had created greater havoc with traditional British liberalism and the right of asylum than it had in other lands. Getting into the country was extremely difficult for anyone of advanced social ideas. More difficult to remain if one engaged in socio-political propaganda. The Labour Government was expelling people on as slight pretexts as had the Tories before. My comrades thought it extraordinary that I should have been granted a visa, and expressed doubt that I would be allowed to remain long if I became politically active. The anti-alien laws had almost destroyed the Yiddish anarchist movement, as everyone active in the East End feared expulsion at any time. The disruption in radical ranks brought about by the nefarious methods of Moscow served to strengthen the hands of reaction. In former days the liberal and radical groups used to take a common stand against every encroachment on political freedom and in opposition to economic injustice. Now they were all at each other's throats over the question of Russia.

The older rebels were disillusioned by the collapse of the Revolution. The younger generation, as far as it was at all interested in ideas (which was little enough), was carried away by the Bolshevik glamour. Communist intrigue and denunciation were doing the rest to widen the chasm.

It was a disheartening picture. But I was in England and I did not propose to run away, notwithstanding the odds against me. My comrades agreed that my name and knowledge of Russian conditions might rally the radical and Labour factions to the support of the political victims of the dictatorship. They were certain that my presence in England would be a stimulus to our own comrades. I did not feel sanguine about the situation. I did not know how to reach the British people, and the only suggestion I could make was a dinner at some restaurant as my début before the London liberal public. My comrades were elated over the idea, and set to work.

My note to Rebecca West brought a kind of reply and an invitation to lunch. I was pleasantly surprised to find her anything but English in her manner. But for her speech I should have thought her an Oriental, she was so vivacious, eager, charming, direct. Her friendliness, the cosiness of her room, the hot tea, were grateful after a long, cold ride in the drab autumn afternoon. She had not read my writings, she frankly admitted, but she knew enough about me to add her welcome to that of the others and she would be happy to speak at the dinner. She would also arrange an evening to have her friends meet me. I was not to hesitate to call on her for anything I might need. I left my hostess with the comforting feeling that I had found a friend, an oasis in the desert London seemed to me.

The day of the dinner began in darkness and ended in a downpour. I went to the restaurant with a sinking heart. Doris tried to reassure me that no one in England minded the weather; I was known and would draw a crowd. "Scotland Yard, the newspapers, and perhaps a few persons acquainted with American liberal thought," I retorted. There was no use to deceive ourselves; I should not set England afire. "An incurable pessimist," my friend laughed; she could not understand how I had kept up the struggle for so many years. Poor Doris nearly collapsed when we reached the hotel. There wasn't a baker's dozen present at seven o'clock. But at eight she walked on air; two hundred and fifty people had crowded into the dining-room, and additional tables had to be laid for guests who continued to come, even after the speeches had begun. I was profoundly moved that so many should venture out on such a night to welcome me.

The spirit of the evening, the messages of greeting from Havelock Ellis, Edward Carpenter, H. G. Wells, Lady Warwick, Israel Zangwill, and Henry Salt, and the beautiful tributes paid to my past efforts by Colonel Josiah C. Wedgwood, our chairman, by Rebecca West, and by Bertrand Russell completely swept me off my feet. Surely the hospitality and generosity shown political refugees in England, often described to me by Peter Kropotkin, were not dead. I should at last find my sphere of action. With a feeling of gratitude I began my address on the purpose of my coming to England and the things I wanted to do. I have rarely had a more attentive audience until I mentioned Russia. Shifting of chairs, turning of necks, and disapproval on the faces before me were the first indications that all was not going to be so harmonious as it seemed at first. I went on with my speech. It was important that the main reason for my presence in England should be clear to everyone. I reminded my hearers of the Russian Revolution of 1905 and the horrors that followed it. It was my illustrious comrade Peter Kropotkin, then living in England, who had aroused the conscience of the radical and liberal world to protest against the frightful persecution of politicals. His "*J'accuse!*" was taken up in the House of Commons, and it succeeded in checking the autocracy. "You will be shocked to learn that a similar situation exists in Russia today," I said. "The new rulers are continuing the old terror. Alas! There is no Kropotkin to indict them at the bar of humanity." I did not feel, I continued, the equal of my great teacher in brain or personality, but I was determined to do all I could to make known the fearful state of affairs in Russia. With whatever ability and voice I possessed I would cry out my "*J'accuse!*" against the Soviet autocracy responsible for political persecution, executions, and savage brutality.

The applause was interrupted by loud protests. Some diners jumped to their feet and demanded the floor. They never would have believed, they said, that the arch-rebel Emma Goldman would ally herself with the Tories against the Workers' Republic. They would not have broken bread with me had they known that I had gone back on my revolutionary past. It was growing late. The evening meant too much to me to have it end in a row. We were planning a meeting in Queen's Hall, I informed the audience, and there we all should have opportunity to discuss the matter in detail.

The reports of the dinner in the London daily press were copious and fair. Only the *Herald* was evasive about my talk, though it printed a short paragraph about the other speeches. I was informed that its editors, George Lansbury and Hamilton Fife, were indignant at my "breach of faith." They had added their names to that of George Slocombe, who had assured the Home Office that my sole purpose in coming to England was to do research work in the British Museum. I explained to my friends that Mr. Slocombe was the man through whom Frank Harris had got permission for me to enter England. Neither Harris nor I had authorized him to make any pledges on my behalf. As to the gentlemen of the *Herald,* their share in helping secure a visa for me was news to me. I did not know Mr. Fife. Mr. Lansbury I had met in Russia, and from what I knew of his attitude to the Communist State it would have never occurred to me to ask favours of him. But I could understand Mr. Lansbury's chagrin over my intended campaign to shed light on the Russian situation. The author of the statement that the teachings of Jesus had been realized in Russia could not afford to be made ridiculous.

My conviction that governmental scene-shifting does not alter the economic situation of the masses had not changed. The Socialists in power, including those of Great Britain, had strengthened my attitude on the question of the State. Nowhere had they helped to improve the life of the worker. I was certain that Mr. MacDonald would do no more during his second term than he had in his first. But there was one matter of utmost importance that the Labour Government could accomplish: recognition of the Soviet Government. I was vitally interested in that, because I knew it would remove the halo of martyrdom from the brow of the Communist State. The international proletariat would then realize that the Soviet Government was of the same clay as the others. I therefore decided not to talk about Russia during the campaign.

Now it was over and my speeches could not affect the fate of the Independent Labour Party. It was its own incompetence in dealing with the poverty and distress of the country while still in office that defeated it. I felt free to write for *The Times* and the London *Daily News* the articles they had requested. It was not only that I had financially reached bottom, but mainly because we needed funds for our mass meeting in Queen's Hall. The British anarchists were too poor to contribute more than a few shillings, and so far no one of means had volunteered to aid. I was glad to earn forty pounds and at the same time speak to a wider public.

Owing to the elections and the approaching holidays, our meeting had to be postponed till January. My friends insisted that the backing of a numerous committee was indispensable to the moral success of our undertaking. I chafed at the delay and resented the idea of a committee. I told my friends of the large birth-control meetings my co-worker Ben Reitman had managed with just a few comrades to assist him; the big demonstrations Sasha had organized and our antiwar protests. We had had no prominent support. Why was it necessary in London? In America Sasha and I were well known, but it was different in England, my friends replied. Here people moved in a herd, at the direction of their shepherd, and this applied alike to party organizations, societies, and clubs. We must have backing to reach the public ear. They agreed with what Rebecca West had told me about free-lance lecture work. "It is not done in England," she had said. London audiences paid admission to lectures only for charitable purposes.

In my public career I had been affiliated with groups only temporarily. I worked for them, not with them. Whatever value my activities had in America was due to my free-lancing and independent position. My London friends urged that my first large public appearance must have the proper support. The dinner had already called attention to my presence in London and to my purpose. The meeting would pave my way for further efforts. After all, they knew best how to reach the British public, and I was willing to follow their advice.

For two weeks I bombarded with letters every name on the list of the prospective committee, but the response was negligible. Most of them did not even reply. Others gave evasive reasons why they could not serve. Mr. Zangwill wrote that, owing to poor health, he had given up all public participation; besides, he did not believe that a committee of known Labour people would do me the slightest good. I might approach the Society for Democratic Control, of which both he and Bertrand Russell were members. He could suggest nothing more. He was sorry I had had to go to Russia to find out what he had known all along: that the Moscow dictatorship was tyranny.

Havelock Ellis sent a kindly note. While he was certain of the sincerity of my motives, he feared my criticism of Russia would give comfort to the reactionaries. They had never protested against the tsarist autocracy and he had no patience with their opposition to Bolshevism, which was only " inverted tsarism." At any rate he did not like committee functions.

The venerable Mrs. Cobden-Sanderson, an old friend of the Kropotkins, who had co-operated with them against the political persecutions of the tsarist régime, Lady Warwick, Bertrand Russell, and Professor Harold Laski invited me to come to them for a talk.

Two persons consented to be on our committee without any reservations: Rebecca West and Colonel Josiah Wedgwood. Edward Carpenter wrote that because of age he could not venture out in the evening, but he was ready to back my efforts, which, he was confident, stood for freedom and justice.

Rebecca West had already given me considerable help. At her home I had met her colleagues on the feminist publication *Time and Tide* — Lady Rhonnda, Mrs. Archdale, and Rebecca's sister, Dr. Letitia Fairfield, as well as a number of others interested in the women politicals in Russia. My circle of acquaintance kept enlarging, and invitations to luncheons, teas, and dinners began to pour in. Everyone was most hospitable, attentive, and cordial — all very pleasant if I had come to England for social entertainment only. But I had come for a purpose. I wanted to arouse the sensibilities of fair-minded Englishmen to the purgatory of Russia, to stir them to a concerted protest against the horrors parading as Socialism and Revolution. It was not that my hosts and their friends were not interested or that they questioned the facts I presented. It was their remoteness from the Russian reality, their lukewarmness to conditions they could not visualize and hence did not feel.

The Labour leaders were callous. In the words of a British Socialist, " It would spell political disaster to my party to declare to its constituents that the Bolsheviks had slain the Revolution." Mr. Clifford Allen, secretary of the Independent Labour Party, declared that " Emma Goldman is an old-time Christian, still believing in the Truth and speaking it out." The most important issue was trade with Russia, he asserted. I had met Mr. Allen in Petrograd, in 1920, when he had come with the British Labour Mission, for which Sasha had acted as interpreter in Moscow. Both of us had been impressed by Allen's independent and idealistic personality. It was somewhat of a shock to discover that in his official capacity he would allow considerations of business to loom higher than human values. I admitted that I was not a shopkeeper, but I believed enough in liberty to let his party be one. Yet I failed to see the connexion between " trade with Russia " and acquiescence in the criminal doings of the Cheka. England had traded with the Romanovs, but liberty-loving Englishmen had often protested against the horrors of the tsars, not merely by words, but by deeds. Why should it be different now? Had the British sense of justice and humanity been shell-shocked that they could remain deaf to the desperate cry of thousands in Soviet dungeons? Did I mean to compare the rule of the Tsar with that of the Bolsheviki? Politically their régime was worse, I told my hearers, its tyranny more irresponsible and Draconic. The Soviet Government was proletarian, after all, and its ultimate aim socialism, Mr. Allen expostulated. He did not approve of all the methods of the dictatorship, but neither he nor his party could afford to join a campaign against it. Most of the others shared his view.

Among the scores of people I met, very few showed such kindly concern as Lady Warwick. I had experienced so many setbacks and disappointments that I clung to the hope that her interest in Russia was vital and that she could be depended on to induce her comrades to join our committee, or at least do so herself. But presently Lady Warwick informed me that it would be necessary to postpone the conference arranged to meet at her house because she had been requested by the Labour men to await the return from Russia of the British Trade Union Delegation. She seemed to be very much afraid that any move on her part might bring back the Tsar. Apparently she continued in that fear, for I never heard from her again.

When I first called on Professor Harold Laski, he expressed the opinion that I ought to take some comfort in the vindication anarchism had received by the Bolsheviki. I agreed, adding that not only their régime, but their stepbrothers as well, the Socialists in power in other countries, had demonstrated the failure of the Marxian State better than any anarchist argument. Living proof was always more convincing than theory. Naturally I did not regret the Socialist failure, but I could not rejoice in it in the face of the Russian tragedy. If I could at least arouse the labour and radical elements! So far I had made no progress. Outside of Rebecca West and Colonel Wedgwood I had found no one who really cared about the woe of Russia. In America I had never met such lack of response to any appeal. Laski thought I would find even the most radical elements reluctant to oppose the Bolsheviki. They were too enthusiastic about the Revolution to draw lines of demarcation. In time I might interest the labour ranks. He would do his best to aid me; he would invite his friends for the next Sunday afternoon to hear my story. Once more hope sprang from what seemed a hopeless and futile quest.

It was impossible for me to speak dispassionately about Russia, but on this occasion I sought to suppress all personal feeling. I spoke in a conversational tone and as objectively as I could. At the conclusion of my talk most of my questioners demanded whether I could point out " any political group more liberal than the Bolsheviki, more efficient for establishing a democratic government should the Soviet régime be overthrown." I replied that I did not want the Communist State overthrown, nor would I aid any group that attempted such a *coup*. Fundamental changes were not made by parties, but by the awakened consciousness of the masses. That had happened in March and October 1917 and would happen again, though probably not in the near future. The dictatorship had discredited all social ideals, and the people were exhausted by years of civil strife. It would require a long time to rekindle their revolutionary fire. I was not interested in a change of rulers in Russia, but I was vitally concerned in the plight of the political victims of the Kremlin autocrats. I believed that strong radical opinion in the United States and Europe would affect the Soviet government as it had that of the Romanovs. It might help to curb their despotism, stop persecution for mere opinion, convictions without trial, and wholesale executions in the cellars of the Cheka. Were not these simple human demands worth trying for? " Yes, but it might lead to the return of autocracy."

The same evasions and objections, the same faint-heartedness, I came across in every group I addressed. It was appalling. At last realizing the futility of my efforts, I resolved not to waste more time on the élite, the Labour politicians, or the ladies dabbling in socialism. Anarchists had always carried on their work without so-called respectable backing and they would have to do so now. Better small meetings under our own auspices and without obligation to anyone than the support of the *bourgeois* world. The dozen members of our little group agreed to go ahead in any way I should suggest, and they procured South Place Institute for our meeting. They reminded me that many a brave voice had pleaded from that platform for freedom and justice. I recollected that I had spoken there in 1900, during the Boer War, under the chairmanship of Tom Mann. Many scenes had been shifted since. Mann was in the bosom of the new church and I was still proscribed by both sides, the capitalist and the Communist.

Professor Laski notified me that his friends were of the opinion that the I.L.P. should abstain from attacking Soviet Russia. He added that Bertrand Russell, though he disliked the Soviet methods, doubted the advisability of my propaganda. Others were convinced that I was more anxious to attack the Bolsheviki than to obtain redress for the politicals; they would not support such an outspoken opponent of Russia. Some held that action must come from the Trade Union Delegation and not from non-English sources. Professor Laski concluded by stating that the Labour leaders would do nothing that might involve them in a controversy with the Soviets. On the whole he agreed with Bertrand Russell that a campaign in behalf of the politicals must not be under anti-Bolshevik auspices "such as yours."

Bertrand Russell's stand was a disappointment to me. I had seen him and talked with him at length. While he had not promised to act on the proposed committee, saying he would have to think the matter over, he had shown no indication that he did not care to affiliate himself with an avowed anarchist. It was rather discouraging to find the brilliant critic of the State, the man whose spiritual attitude was anarchistic, fight shy of co-operation with an anarchist. And Laski, too, the bold exponent of individualism!

The Trade Union Delegation returned from Russia on fire with the wonders they had seen — rather, had been shown! They waxed enthusiastic in the *Daily Herald* and at meetings about the splendid Soviet achievements. They had spent all of six weeks in Russia; could one speak with greater knowledge and authority?

If I failed to arouse the Britishers, I succeeded in impressing a few Americans in England, most of them Rhodes scholars, who invited me to address them. My visit to Oxford was quite an event, not only on account of the splendid meeting the boys had arranged in spite of opposition from the " Coolidge gang," but also because of the hospitality and generous aid given me by Professor S. E. Morison, of the American History Department, and by the dozen young chaps, the most thoughtful and wide-awake of the group, who became my ardent friends. This at least I had gained after four months of effort. The genuine interest and the sincere desire to help of such new friends as David Soskice, the well-known Russian revolutionist and one-time editor of *Free Russia,* of Mrs. Soskice, the writer and sister of Ford Madox Ford, as well as their two vivid boys, was a most satisfying recompense.

Thanks to the faithful and energetic work of my comrades, among them Doris Zhook, William Wess, A. Sugg, Tom Keell, and William C. Owen, our South Place Institute meeting was crowded, notwithstanding the downpour and the admission charged. The tact of our chairman, Colonel Josiah Wedgwood, my American student friends, some " real " proletarians to keep order, and my usual sang-froid on the platform saved the situation.

We had reason to rejoice over our success. Without backing, either moral or financial, we covered the expenses of our meeting and had some surplus left to send to the Berlin Fund for political prisoners. With Tom Sweetlove as treasurer, and A. Sugg, as secretary, the committee was launched as a permanent body for systematic activity. Though numerically small, it had ambitious aims: a series of lectures on Russia, the circulation of the *Bulletin* of the Joint Committee for the Defense of the Imprisoned Revolutionists in Russia, published in the English language in Berlin under Sasha's editorship, and the raising of funds. The *Bulletin* contained accurate information and data on political persecution, as well as letters from the incarcerated and exiled which Sasha and other members of the Joint Committee were receiving *sub rosa* from Russia.

Our main trouble was that I found myself between two fires. I had no hope of a hearing by the Independent Labour Party or in the trade unions; neither would I speak under the auspices of the Tories. From the latter I received a number of invitations to lecture on Russia, but I had to decline because I learned that they were exclusive Conservative clubs. Another came from the Woman's Guild of the Empire in Paisley. I inquired about its political character and was informed that it stood for " God, King, and Country." I wrote to the Guild that as an anarchist I repudiated social arrangements which raised some to the throne and condemned others to pauperism. I did not discriminate against any audience, whatever its social, political, or religious beliefs; in the United States I had lectured before the most diversified crowds — longshoremen and millionaires, poor working and professional women; in halls behind saloons and in drawing-rooms, in mines hundreds of feet below the ground, from pulpits and soap-boxes. From our own platform I should be willing to treat the subject of Russia, no matter who came to hear me. On any other topic I should be willing to talk in the House of Lords, in Windsor Castle, or before the Conservative Party. But not on Russia.

I doubted that our committee could succeed with independent meetings in reaching the general public. The members were not dismayed. They would experiment with English lectures, and the *Arbeiter Freund* group volunteered to organize Yiddish meetings in the East End. Thus encouraged, I started my weekly rounds from one end of London to the other, in rain, sleet, fog, and chill, for three months. Not even in my pioneer days in the United States had I found it quite so bitter to break new ground as I did in this venture. The result was hardly worth the effort, though the committee insisted that it was. Expenses were covered, some money was added to the Political Prisoners' Fund, and conditions under the Communist State were made known to hundreds of people.

My tour through the north of England and south Wales was

little to boast of. The Welsh people were impressionable and easily aroused, but not always dependable, John Turner had once told me. After the English icicles I had tried to melt, I welcomed the Welsh crowds and their enthusiasm. The difficulty was not the indifference of the workers, but their dreadful poverty. Many had been unemployed for a long time, and those who were fortunate enough to have jobs earned the barest pittance. The amazing thing was that people living in such bleakness should come to meetings at all; it seemed extraordinary that they could muster up enough sympathy in their suffering brothers in far-away Russia. The pale, pinched faces of these toilers made me painfully aware of my own position. Like all missionaries I was appealing for " charity for China " when help was so desperately needed at home. If I could at least enter their lives, share in their struggles, show them that anarchism alone has the key that can transform society and secure their well-being, my begging would have some justification.

Already in London after my first lectures I had begun to chafe under my compulsory silence on the frightful economic conditions in England. The social wrongs in Great Britain could of course in no way justify similar evils in Russia. Nor did I feel it just to talk about the dictatorship and ignore the situation close at hand. This feeling was constantly increasing and adding to my inner struggle. I could not go on much longer with my anti-Soviet activities without voicing my stand on the general social question. That opportunity denied me in England, as indeed everywhere else, I should have to stop discussing the Bolshevik State. I could not close my eyes to the fact that I owed my asylum to my attitude on Russia — a doubtful and uncomfortable hospitality, which I could not accept indefinitely. My comrades urged me to remain for my work. I had no reason to feel that I must not appeal for the imprisoned revolutionists in Russia because I could not take part in the social struggle in England, they argued. I was the first anarchist returned from the Soviet country to explain in Great Britain the relation of the Bolsheviki to the Revolution; such knowledge was vital everywhere, but nowhere more so than in England, where many of the labour leaders were emissaries of Moscow. This applied particularly to south Wales, where certain officials of the Miners' Federation were espousing the miracle of the Communist State. The simple trust and faith of my comrades was deeply touching. Proletarian from infancy, their lives barren of beauty and joy, they clung to their ideal as the sole hope of a new and free world. Typical of them was James Colton, who at the age of sixty-five was still compelled to slave in the mines for his daily bread. He had given the greater part of his life to active service in our ranks, and with much pride he told me that, like myself, he had become an anarchist as a result of the judicial murder of our Chicago martyrs. With no chance for an education, he had picked up much knowledge and a clear understanding of social problems. He devoted his native ability as a speaker to the cause and he contributed to the propagation of anarchism from his meagre earnings. The comrades in his group, younger men with families to support, were carried along by " Jimmy's " energy and inspired by his love and consecration to the ideal.

The Trade Union Report on Russia, signed by all the delegates, including John Turner, proved a complete whitewash of the Soviet régime. The ground it covered would have required several years' study, extensive travel, and a long stay in the country. The Labour delegates had been in Russia six weeks, more than a week of which was spent in trains, as John told me. Obviously their report could not represent the personal knowledge and observation of its authors. As a matter of fact, it was a compilation of the documents specially prepared for them by the authorities. Inasmuch as most of the delegates had been pro-Soviet before coming to Russia, it was quite natural that they should swallow the whole Bolshevik bait. Their interpreters, one of them a naval attaché of the British Embassy in the tsarist days, another in the diplomatic service for a long time, were past masters in mustering official data to good effect. They had winked at the old autocracy in the interests of their Government, and now, as adherents of the I.L.P., they had also to do considerable winking. That was their profession and I had no quarrel with them. But I was shocked to see John Turner sign the report. The more so because his article in *Foreign Affairs,* the interview he gave to a representative of the New York *Forward,* as well as his talk at our meeting, flatly contradicted the pæans of the report. I wrote him frankly how he had disappointed me and the other comrades. He replied in almost the identical phrase Lansbury had used to Sasha in 1920: he could show me " any number of poor, destitute and starved in London." I failed to see the connexion between the misery in England and the statement in the report that the Russian toilers, though politically bound, were economically free and contented. Turner and his co-delegates knew that this was no more true regarding the masses in Russia than in reference to the British workers.

It was imperative to unmask the deception. I suggested to our committee a reply and I was instructed to prepare it, with the help of Doris Zhook. The brochure we issued compared the statements in the report with quotations from the Soviet press during the visit of the British delegates. It contained no comments whatever, as we were willing to let the Bolsheviki themselves disprove the extravagant claims of the report. The Communists immediately charged us with using material from the forged *Izvestia* and *Pravda,* allegedly published by counter-revolutionists abroad. It was absurdly silly, but it was sad to see even so good an insurgent as Colonel Josiah Wedgwood change front. He wrote me that he would take no responsibility for the pamphlet and requested that his name be taken off the committee. Wedgwood, like most of the others, including even my comrade John Turner, moved in a groove and lacked the independence to stand out against the Communist rooters.

The one exception in these ranks was Rebecca West, who did not permit her affiliations to influence her attitude or curtail her freedom of action. Though extremely occupied with her own work, she nevertheless found time to interest her friends in my efforts, to put me in touch with a literary agent who might place *My Disillusionment in Russia* with a British publisher, to write a preface for it, and to preside at one of my lectures. But, then, Rebecca West is an artist, not a politician.

Mr. C. W. Daniel was another unfettered spirit; a publisher, he did not consider trade the all-embracing issue of life. He cared more for the ideas and literary quality of works he was issuing than for the money they might bring him. Was he, too, an old-fashioned Christian to prefer truth to business, I inquired, adding that I was charged with that offence. I admitted that it was naïve of me to expect more from the I.L.P. than from any other political party. I had always known that, like the beasts, they never change their natures, however much they may shed their skins. Alas, one grows older but not wiser or I should not have been so shocked to find radicals argue the life and death of thousands in terms of commerce. On closer acquaintance Mr. Daniel did not prove wiser than I, even if younger. He undertook to publish a British edition of *My Disillusionment in Russia,* fully aware that though it might secure glory from posterity it could not bring him much trade. My book had already appeared in complete form in a Swedish edition, but it did not mean so much to me as to see my work, so atrociously bungled in America, in one volume in England, with a preface by Rebecca West.

My Disillusionment, the articles in the New York *World,* reprinted and circulated by the London *Freedom,* my contributions to the *Westminster Gazette* and the *Weekly News,* besides those that had appeared in the London *Times* and been syndicated in the provinces, the article in the *Daily News,* and, finally, our brochure refuting the fiction of the trade-union delegates contained a wealth of information accessible to all but the wilfully blind.

Sasha had also not been idle; his *The Bolshevik Myth* now appeared, published in New York by Boni and Liveright. But the latter had eliminated the concluding and most vital chapter as being an " anticlimax." Thereupon Sasha issued it as a brochure under that very title and circulated it at his own expense. Sheets of the book had been imported to England and the volume sold at a prohibitive price without the author's knowledge or consent, and without his receiving a cent of royalties. The reviews were splendid, the critics agreeing that *The Bolshevik Myth* was a convincing and moving work of first-rate literary merit. In addition Sasha had gathered a wealth of data and documents about political persecution under the Soviet dictatorship. He secured the stories and affidavits of numerous politicals who had escaped or been deported from Russia. Added to similar matter collected by Henry G. Alsberg and Isaac Don Levine, the whole constituted a collective indictment of Bolshevik terror overpowering in its effect. On the strength of it Alsberg and Levine procured letters of protest against the Moscow despotism by men and women of international fame, and the entire material was published in New York by the International Committee for Political Prisoners in a volume entitled *Letters from Russian Prisons.*

We kept our pledge to our suffering comrades in Russia. We made known their cause as well as that of all other persecuted revolutionists. We demonstrated the abyss between the Bolsheviki and " October." We would continue to do so, Sasha through the *Bulletin* of the Joint Committee for the Defense of Political Prisoners, and I whenever and wherever the opportunity presented itself. Now was the time for me to turn to other matters. After eight months' absorption in the Russian situation I felt justified in seeking different subjects for expression. This was especially imperative because I could not go on indefinitely accepting support from my family and American friends. I should not have been able to keep going but for such dear and devoted friends as Stewart Kerr, for instance, who never allowed a month to pass without a gift. Now that I might become self-supporting by means of lectures on the drama, I decided to discontinue my Russian work, at least for a while.

Shortly after my arrival in England Fitzi had appointed me her representative for the Provincetown Playhouse, to which she had already given years of labour and love. My credentials afforded me free access to some of the theatres, yet what I saw did not whet my appetite for further exploration of the London stage. English friends spoke highly of the Birmingham Repertory Theatre, the only outstanding group of artistic merit. It had grown out of amateur beginnings, they informed me, and it owed its first start and splendid development to the skill and generosity of its founder, Barry V. Jackson. My experience with British intellectual hospitality had made me somewhat sceptical. Opportunity to judge for myself came when the Birmingham Repertory Company opened in London with Shaw's *Cæsar and Cleopatra,* and I made haste to present my credentials as Fitzi's European ambassador. At no theatre in the British metropolis had I been received with greater courtesy. The performance proved to be a revelation. Such settings, atmosphere, and ensemble acting I had not seen since the Stanislavsky Studio days, and even there the scenery did not compare with this feast for the eyes. Cedric Hardwicke's Cæsar surpassed that of Forbes-Robertson, whom I had seen in New York. He succeeded in making the old Roman intensely human, with enough wit to laugh at himself. Miss Gwen Ffrangçon-Davies as Cleopatra was an exquisite creature. For the first time in England I was able to banish the gloom the travail of eight months had settled on my spirit.

Nearer acquaintance with Barry Jackson, Walter Peacock, Bache Matthews (Mr. Jackson's director), and several other members of the company saved me from judging the nature of a whole people by the bitter experiences I had with some groups. They knew I was a stranger struggling to gain a foothold in their country, and that was reason enough for them to offer their help. The possibility of losing votes or support and disagreement with my views on social subjects did not affect them. They were interested in the human, in a fellow-creature adrift in an alien land. They made me welcome at their theatres and put me in touch with circles that could enable me to establish myself by means of lectures on the drama.

Mr. Peacock introduced me to a number of people, among them Geoffrey Whitworth, the Honourable Secretary of the British Drama League. Mr. Matthews interested the secretary of the Birmingham Playgoers in my work, which soon brought me an engagement from that society; and Barry Jackson, one of the busiest men in London, always found time for me when I needed his kindly aid. Mr. Whitworth generously turned his entire office over to my work; the assistant secretary of the league, the library, and the list of affiliated societies were put at my disposal. Mr. Whitworth also invited me to speak at the conference of the Drama League, which was to take place in Birmingham.

In the lovely Repertory Theatre I lectured on the Russian theatre, discussing the studios, the Kamerny, and Meyerhold. The atmosphere was free from strife or rancour, the audiences were receptive, the questions keen and intelligent. Intermission brought everyone together in easy sociability that was most encouraging to me.

Too late I learned that in England it is customary for clubs and societies to arrange their lecture courses six months in advance. Still, I succeeded in securing seven engagements for the early autumn from the Playgoers in Manchester, Liverpool, Birkenhead, Bath, and Bristol. In the last city a series was also being planned by our own people. The Drama Study Circle I had organized in London was planning several lectures on the origin and development of the Russian drama, and the anarchists in the East End of London asked for the same course in Yiddish. I could look forward to a busy time doing work I had always loved.

During my early days in England, when everything seemed bleakest, Stella had written me that London was a cold beauty that required much wooing before revealing her charms. "Who cares to woo a cold beauty?" I replied. Now I had been paying court to her for nine months. Could it be that I was beginning to touch her heart?

London was really beautiful now in its profusion of green and abundance of flowers and sun, as if it would never wear mourning or weep torrents again. One begrudged every moment indoors, knowing how short-lived the glory was. But six hours every day was the very least I needed to cope with the historic treasures I discovered in the British Museum on the Russian theatre and drama. This institution had been one of my objectives in coming to England, but it was only now that I had the time, the interest, and the need for availing myself of all it offered. The longer I worked in the museum, the more information I unearthed on stage arrangement, old plays, scenery, and costumes. This led to wider fields, embracing the political and social backgrounds of the dramatists of different periods, and their correspondence that reflected their feelings and reaction to Russian life. It was a fascinating study and so absorbing as to make me forget the closing-hour. One thing became plain from the start. I could not hope to cover even a fraction of the material in six lectures, or in a dozen. An entire volume would be required. Professor Wiener, Peter Kropotkin, and others had written such works on Russian literature. It occurred to me that my drama series might serve as an introduction to a larger book to be written at some later date.

My meetings with Havelock Ellis and Edward Carpenter stood out as the fulfillment of a wish cherished for a quarter of a century. Not that I learned to know them better through our fleeting personal contact than I had through their works. I saw Ellis for a bare half-hour in his London apartment and we were both rather tongue-tied. But if I had lived near him for years, I should not have realized better the oneness of the man with his life's labours, so expressive of his unique personality and lofty vision was every line that had spoken to me out of the pages of his liberating work.

My visit with Edward Carpenter lasted the greater part of an afternoon in his modest cottage at Guildford. He was nearly eighty, frail and feeble. Alongside of his dapper companion, whom everybody addressed as George, his clothes looked shabby. But there was distinction in his carriage, and grace in every gesture. Dear Edward had little chance to be heard, for it was George who did most of the talking about the work " Edward and I " had written while they were in Spain, and the book "we're planning this summer." Patient and forbearing was Edward towards the conceit of small people, viewing it with the wisdom of the sage.

I attempted to tell him how much his books had meant to me — *Towards Democracy, Angel Wings, Walt Whitman*. He stopped me, gently putting his hand over mine. Instead I should rather tell him about Alexander Berkman, he said. He had read his *Prison Memoirs,* a profound study of man's inhumanity and prison psychology, and of his own martyrdom, portrayed with extraordinary simplicity." He had always wanted to know "Sasha" and "the Girl" in the book.

Havelock Ellis and Edward Carpenter! My summer was indeed enriched by these two grand seigneurs of intellect and heart.

It brought also other interesting events outside of my research work. Fitzi arrived for a brief visit, and through her I came to know Paul and Essie Robeson, as well as several of Fitzi's associates in the Provincetown Playhouse. They had come to London to put on *The Emperor Jones* with Paul Robeson. Essie was a delightful person, and Paul fascinated everyone. I first heard Robeson sing a group of spirituals at a party given by my American friend Estelle Healy. Nothing I had been told about his singing adequately expressed the moving quality of his voice. Paul was also a lovable personality, entirely free from the self-importance of the star and as natural as a child. He never refused to sing, no matter how small the circle, if the company was congenial. The Robesons liked my cooking, especially my coffee, and so we exchanged compliments. I would prepare dinner for a chosen few or arrange a party of my English friends to meet the Robesons, and Paul would hold everyone spellbound by his glorious voice.

The summer was rich, the richest in years. Now that the sunny days were drawing to an end, my friends were departing. Work I loved lay before me and I still had a stout heart. But by December there was little left of it or anything else to help face the London winter. My venture into the Playgoers' societies was quite satisfactory. Gratifying also were the Liverpool and Birkenhead organizations, because of their mixed membership. The others were purely middle-class, with no vital interest in the drama and no feeling for its social and educational value. Nevertheless the experience proved that I could establish myself with the Playgoers if I could hold out long enough to become better known in England, for a year or two. I had no means for it, nor the inclination to become an adjunct.

The independent lectures in London and Bristol again demonstrated the truth of the British saying that "it isn't done in England." The London failure was particularly disappointing because the work had started with every promise of success. Keats' House, quaintly beautiful and permeated by the genius and spirit of England's great poet, was our meeting-place; Claire Fowler Shone, our secretary, a skilful organizer and prodigious worker, widely known in labour and trade-union ranks, with a dozen friends to assist her. A review of my drama work by Rebecca West and Frank Harris circulated in thousands of copies; Barry Jackson, Geoffrey Whitworth, A. E. Filmer, and others, no strangers in the world of the drama, were announced as chairmen. Yet the attendance was small and the receipts barely covered the expenses. True, the audiences were of a high intellectual order. That and the joy of collecting my material were the only satisfaction I gained from nearly six months' effort.

I spent three weeks in Bristol with similar results. My second attempt to take root in the United Kingdom had thus also gone by the board. The fogs and wet remained faithful and wandered through my system at their own sweet will. I was laid up with chills and fever when an invitation came from my dear friends Frank and Nellie Harris to visit them in Nice.

In June I had married the old rebel James Colton. British now, I did as most natives do who can scrape up enough to escape their country's climate. The *American Mercury* had sent me a cheque for my sketch on Johann Most, so I was able to pay my fare to the south of France. The Harrises were marvellous hosts, sparing no pains to surround me with care and help restore my health and cheer. I had spent many interesting hours with Frank before, but never enough to see more than the artist, the man of the world, the interesting *causeur*. In the intimacy of his home I was able to penetrate beneath what everyone considered Frank's egotism and conceit. I found that my host knew himself much better than anyone else did. He knew the human, all too human in his make-up. He had his gnawing doubts whether he was indeed the supreme artist he proclaimed himself, whether his works would live and he be given an immortal niche. Frank was not deceived about his own foibles, however blind he might be to those of his friends or mistaken in those he looked upon as enemies. Frank Harris, when he turned himself inside out, far from lessening my affection, brought himself nearer to me. We had few ideas in common, especially on social problems. We fought often, but always in the best of feeling, for we knew that no matter how far apart we might drift, our friendship would not weaken.

My meeting with Nellie Harris in Paris the year before had shown me little of her personality, except for her obvious loveliness and charm. During my visit all her rare and exquisite qualities unfolded like a flower before me. I had met wives of creative men on previous occasions. I had seen their bitterness to their husbands' friends, their jealousy of female admirers, and well I knew how overbearing and cattish my sex can be to the wives of their idols. My sympathies were often with the wives, for it seemed martyrdom enough to be the spouse of an artist. I should have thought no less of Nellie had I found her ungenerous to the admirers of Frank. But Nellie was an angel, a large and loving spirit, incapable of harshness, and no mere reflection of her famous husband, but an individual in her own right, a keen observer of people and affairs, a better judge of human nature than dear old Frank, and more patient and understanding.

I was loath to leave my good friends, but necessary research in the Bibliothèque Nationale called me back to Paris before returning to England. I still had some engagements to fill with the Playgoers' societies in Liverpool on the little-theatre movement in America. I had addressed them before on the works of Eugene O'Neill, and a woman reporter had reviewed my " sensitive hands and gold coloured lining of the opera cloak, rather startling in an anarchist," but the Play-goers must have liked my talks, because they invited me again. I had also consented to deliver another course of lectures on Continental and American plays in a popular hall, with one-shilling admission. My comrades were sure it would bring a crowd, but on the appointed day there were no crowds. Strindberg, the German expressionists, Eugene O'Neill, and Susan Glaspell did not interest the British public when presented without the seal of an organization or party. " It isn't done in England." I was compelled to realize that a much longer period than I had thought would be necessary to break through the wall of what " isn't done." Five years, perhaps, if not more. But I did not have many more years to throw about. Meanwhile I was faced with the problem of making ends meet. Not till my deportation had I ever given a thought to this question; I had felt that as long as I could use my voice and pen, I could easily earn my living. Since then I had been haunted by the spectre of dependence, and it grew after my tour of south Wales and the provinces. I would rather take a job as a cook or housekeeper than get my living from my activities among the underpaid miners and cotton-mill workers. I could not allow them to defray my railroad fares, let alone the expenses of my lectures. The drama meetings not paying for themselves, I saw no way of continuing my work in England.

A friend had once said jokingly that I was like a cat; " drop her out of a sixth-story window and she'll land on her paws." After the last failure I felt as if I had indeed been thrown from the top of the Woolworth Building. Two things brought me on my paws again. One was my plan of a volume on "The Origin and Development of the Russian Drama"; the other, a tour through Canada. The anarchists there had invited me to come, and a New York comrade promised to raise my expenses. I would go to some little place in France and devote the summer to writing and would leave for Canada in the fall. The two ventures, I hoped, might secure me for a year or two to live and be active in England. I made sure of my going to Canada by immediately reserving my passage.

The incentive to devote the next four months to writing had come from C. W. Daniel, my patron publisher. He had taken the keenest interest in my lectures on the Russian dramatists, had sent a stenographer to take them verbatim, and held out the hope of issuing my book in the not too distant future. Besides *My Disillusionment* he had also published an English edition of Alexander Berkman's *Prison Memoirs of an Anarchist,* for which Edward Carpenter had written a preface, and he had imported sheets of *Letters from Russian Prisons,* neither of which undertakings added much to his coffers. But it in no way discouraged him from wanting to try his luck again.

I was about to leave London when the general strike was declared. I could not think of running away from an event of such overwhelming importance. Workers and helpers would be needed and I must remain and offer my services. John Turner was the most likely man to get me in touch with the people in charge of the strike. I explained to him that I was willing to do any kind of work to aid the great struggle: look after the relief of the strikers' families, organize the care of their children, or take charge of feeding-stations. I wanted to help the rank and file. John was delighted. It would dispel the prejudice my anti-Soviet stand had created in trade-union circles and would demonstrate that anarchists not merely theorized, but were capable of practical work and were ready for any emergency. He would take my message to the strike committee and put them in direct touch with me. I waited for two days, but no word came either from trade-union headquarters or from John. On the third day I again made the long trip on foot to see John and to inquire about the matter. He had been told that all help in the strike situation was drawn from trade-union ranks, and that no outside aid was needed. The excuse was flimsy; clearly the leaders feared it would leak out that the anarchist Emma Goldman had some connexion with the general strike. John was loath to admit my interpretation, nor could he deny that I might be right. It was the old story: the centralized machinery in every walk of British life left no room for individual initiative. It was torture to remain neutral where the line between masters and men was so sharply drawn, or to stand by idly while the leaders were making one blunder after another; nor would I leave by rail or ship manned by strike-breakers. I found some relief in being out on the streets mingling with the men and getting their reactions. Their spirit of solidarity was wonderful, their fortitude great, their disregard of the hardships the strike had already imposed admirable. No less extraordinary was their good humour and self-control in the face of provocation from the enemy: armoured cars rattling along the streets, taunts and ridicule from the young bullies in charge, and the affronts of the wealthy in their luxurious automobiles. A few encounters had taken place, but on the whole the strikers carried themselves with pride and dignity, confident of the justice of their cause. It was inspiring, but it also increased my misery at my own helplessness. On the tenth day of the strike, there still being no sign of a settlement, I decided to leave England by airplane.

CHAPTER LVI

FRIENDS HAD UNEARTHED A LOVELY SPOT IN SAINT-TROPEZ, AN ancient, picturesque fishing-village in the south of France. An enchanted place it was: a little villa of three rooms from which one caught a view of the snow-covered Maritime Alps, with a garden of magnificent roses, pink and red geraniums, fruit-trees, and a large vineyard, all for fifteen dollars a month. Here I regained something of my old zest for life, and faith in my ability to overcome the hardships the future might hold. I divided my time between my writing-desk and my *ménage*. I even found time to learn to swim. I prepared the meals on a quaint, red-bricked Provençal stove in which only char-coal could be used. Many friends from America and other parts of the world found their way to my new home in Saint-Tropez.

Georgette Leblanc, Margaret Anderson, Peggy Guggenheim, Law-rence Vail, and many others came for an hour or a day to discuss serious matters or in jolly company. Peggy and Lawrence lived not far from us in a village called Pramousquier and there I first met Kathleen Millay and Howard Young. The latter reproached me for not writing my autobiography. "A woman of your past!" he ex-claimed; "just think what you could make of it!" I would, I told him, if I could secure an income for two years, a secretary, and some-one to scour my pots and kettles. He would undertake to raise five thousand dollars on his return to America, Young promised. In honour of my prospective benefactor, Peggy added a few more bottles of wine to those already emptied at dinner.

The four months in Saint-Tropez passed all too quickly in labour and play. A golden dream, not without its rude awakening, however. Mr. Daniels informed me that conditions in England since the general strike had grown from bad to worse; there being no sign of coming improvement I should not feel bound to his firm with my manuscript on the Russian drama. That was the first ripple in my azure sky, yet not so disconcerting as the cable from the New York comrade who had promised to raise the initial fund for my Canadian tour. "It is off," he announced.

The Canadian Government had probably declared I would not be admitted, or our own people had reconsidered their invitation, I thought. But my conjectures proved false. Canada remained blissfully ignorant of the danger threatening it, and our comrades assured me they were expecting me without fail.

My sponsor was apparently afraid of the bodily harm I might meet at the hands of the Communists. His fears were not entirely groundless; Communists in New York had broken up radical meetings and had even physically attacked their opponents. The hard times would also affect the success of my lecture tour, the comrade wrote. I appreciated his good intentions to protect me and my interests, but I could not be very gracious about the right he had assumed to cancel my tour. Had this new blow come while I was yet in England, I should have thought my world at an end. But life in Saint-Tropez had restored my strength and with it my fighting spirit. I cabled three friends in the States for loans. They responded simultaneously, though they lived in different parts.

While in Paris, I lunched with Theodore Dreiser. "You must write the story of your life, E.G.," he urged; "it is the richest of any woman's of our century. Why in the name of Mike don't you do it?" I told him that Howard Young had put the question first. I had not taken it very seriously and I was not surprised that I had received no word from him, though he had been back in America several months. Dreiser protested that he was greatly interested in seeing my story given to the world. He would secure a five-thousand-dollar advance from some publisher and I would hear from him very soon. "All right, old dear, see what you can do! If you also forget or if you fail, I will not sue you for breach of promise," I laughed.

I entered Canada as unheralded as I had England two years previously. In Montreal I learned that no English anarchist had been heard in Canada for a great many years. The only active people were the Yiddish-language group, but they had no experience in organizing English lectures. My friend Isaac Don Levine had promised to help with the publicity work, but even before he reached Montreal, the newspapers announced that the dangerous anarchist Emma Goldman, masquerading under the name of Colton, had managed to get by the immigration authorities and had come to Montreal. To save the Montrealers further trepidation and to satisfy the curiosity of the press Don issued a statement setting forth how and why I had come to Canada and inviting press interviews. The telephone and door-bell of my hosts, the Zahlers, worked overtime, and the papers were lurid with the news that romance still lived in this crassly materialistic age: Emma Goldman and James Colton, a southern Welsh miner, had rediscovered their mutual affection after twenty-five years and had joined their lives in matrimony. The immigration authorities were reported to have stated that there was no intention of interfering with my presence in Canada as long as I " did not advocate bombs."

The Moscow fanatics sought to boycott my lectures by a house-to-house canvass of the radical Yiddish population. A few of the more decent and sensible Communists deprecated these tactics. They suggested a debate between Scott Nearing and myself. I should have preferred some Communist who had lived in Russia longer and knew the situation better than Mr. Nearing. Still, I was quite willing to discuss with him the question of Life under the Dictatorship. Not so Mr. Nearing. His reply was that if E.G. were dying and he could save her life, he would not go round the corner to do so.

Besides my lecture in the theatre and an address at the Eugene Debs Memorial gathering I delivered six Yiddish lectures and spoke at a banquet where several hundred dollars were subscribed for the Russian politicals. The most satisfying result of my visit in Montreal was the group of women I gathered into a permanent body to raise funds for the imprisoned revolutionists in the Communist State.

The Toronto anarchists were more numerous and better organized. They were carrying on intensive propaganda in Yiddish and exerting an influence in their community, but they sadly neglected the natives. They were eager, however, to assist me to any extent with my program of English lectures. They had done a great deal of preparatory work that promised success for my first appearance. Support came also from an unexpected quarter. I had notified the Toronto newspapers of my visit to their city, but only the *Star* showed sufficient interest to send a representative, Mr. C. R. Reade. I was amazed to find him thoroughly informed about the anarchist philosophy and familiar with its exponents and their works. He might as well be one of us, I joked. Life was difficult enough without being an adherent of such an unpopular cause or sharing its ideas with a dull world, he laughed. His understanding and friendly attitude exerted a proselyting effect on his editors. In the words of the Communists, the *Star* became an " Emma Goldman propaganda sheet." The explanation given for my " pull " with the paper was that its owner had in the past been a " philosophic " anarchist and remained hospitable to advanced ideas. But I felt that it was due mostly to Reade's good offices. Both he and Mrs. Reade became my enthusiastic sponsors. Mrs. Reade even volunteered to organize a course of my drama lectures. They were among the few kindred intellectual spirits I enjoyed during my stay in Toronto.

Dear members of my family came to visit me from the States, and it was a great joy to be within their reach, even if they had to come to me instead of my going to them. Not that the opportunity was not offered me. Various friends were eager to smuggle me across the border. With my picture in every rogues' gallery in the United States, I could not have remained there long without being recognized, and there was no object in hiding. Those of my friends and comrades who could afford it would come to see me. For the rest, I never liked sensation for its own sake. There still was a large place in my heart for my erstwhile country, regardless of her shabby treatment. My love for all that is ideal, creative, and humane in her would not die. But I should rather never see America again if I could do so only by compromising my ideas.

The expense of travel in Canada and the great distances between the larger cities decided me to go no farther than Edmonton, Alberta. Winnipeg nearly became my Waterloo. The city was extremely cold and in the throes of a grippe epidemic, to which I succumbed in the first twenty-four hours. Lack of cohesion in our ranks, badly organized meetings, and Communist obstruction at every gathering made the situation anything but a cheerful prospect. Hugging my bed by day, in a half stupor from drugs to break my cold, I managed to pull through the Sunday evening mass meeting in spite of the rough-house created by the Moscow bigots. Later I added a course of drama lectures to my schedule. The six weeks in Winnipeg, though strenuous to exhaustion, were not entirely without compensation. The alert and active young people in the *Arbeiter Ring* organization, and the girl students of the University who invited me to speak, were the saving grace of my ordeal. I also succeeded in welding together the radical women into a relief society for the imprisoned revolutionists in Russia and added some money to the fund.

Edmonton, Alberta, proved a record-breaker. I came there for two lectures. I stayed to deliver fifteen in one week, some days speaking three times. All the Jewish organizations in town and most of the Canadian labour, social, and educational groups invited me to speak. The two extremes of the variegated audiences I addressed that week were factory girls during their lunch hour in the shop and the faculties of Edmonton College and the University of Alberta at a tea arranged in one of the hotels by Mrs. H. A. Freedman, the president of the Council of Jewish Women. The extraordinary interest my presence in Edmonton aroused was entirely due to the kindly efforts of three people, none of whom was an anarchist. Mrs. Freedman was a staunch and sincere adherent of the present political order, E. Hanson was a Socialist-Nationalist, and Carl Berg was an I.W.W.

A note from Peggy Guggenheim on my return to Toronto expressed surprise that I had not answered Howard Young's letter regarding my autobiography. Had I changed my mind about permitting him to raise a fund to enable me to write the book? He was planning to proceed with it and she would open the subscription with five hundred dollars. I replied that I had never received Howard's letter, but it was all right for him to go ahead. Yet I should prefer to have my old friend W. S. Van Valkenburgh in charge of the hard work the appeal would entail. I knew that if energy and indefatigability could avail, Van was sure of success. With Peggy Guggenheim and Howard Young as my first sponsors, Kathleen Millay as the official secretary, and Van to do the heavy correspondence, the project was finally launched to secure funds for my writing the " masterpiece that would set the world afire."

Meanwhile my Toronto comrades kept on insisting that I was wanted in their midst. They had never believed that their city could respond so warmly to anarchist propaganda. They urged that I make Toronto my permanent home or that I remain there several years at least. They offered to foot all bills and I should consider myself engaged, they declared. Most of these Yiddish anarchists were working-men, barely earning their living: expansive Maurice Langbord and his wife, Becky, toiling to support their six adorable children, with large appetites; A. Judkin, weighing no more than ninety pounds, with

a sick wife, running a newspaper delivery truck; genial and kindly
Joe Desser, ill for months; Gurian, Simkin, Goldstein, and other comrades — every one of them with heavy burdens to carry. I would not
consent to accept support even from Julius Seltzer, the only " millionaire " in our ranks, let alone from them. Nor could I think of spending the rest of my life in Canada. But I would risk it for a year.

The special drama course, arranged by my two artist friends Florence Loring and Frances Wylie, had left a surplus. My family sent
cash as their birthday gifts. The two Bens, Big and Little, and other
friends had also remembered me on the occasion. I would have enough
to keep going for part of the summer. I thought I would rest up for
a while and then buckle down to prepare a new lecture course. But
I lost all desire for a rest with the impending murder of Sacco and
Vanzetti.

The first knowledge of their arrest had reached me in Russia; then
nothing more till I was in Germany. So overpowering were the proofs
of their innocence, it seemed impossible that the State of Massachusetts would repeat in 1923 the crime Illinois had committed in 1887.
Surely some progress had been made in America in the past quarter
of a century, some change in the minds and hearts of the masses to
prevent the new human sacrifice, I reasoned. Strange that I, of all
people, should have thought so. I who had lived and struggled in the
United States for more than half my life and had witnessed the inertia
of the workers and the unscrupulousness and the inhumanity of the
American courts! With our Chicago men innocently slain, with Sasha
doomed to twenty-two years for an offence that legally called only
for seven, with Mooney and Billings buried alive on perjured testimony, the victims of Wheatland and Centralia still in prison, and all
the others I had seen railroaded! How could I have believed that
Sacco and Vanzetti, however innocent, would escape American " justice "? The power of suggestion had taken me off my guard. The
whole world had repudiated the monstrous possibility that Sacco and
Vanzetti would be denied a new trial or that the sentence of death
would be carried out. I had been influenced by it and had done little
to help stay the hangman's hand reaching out for these two beautiful
lives. Only after I had come to Canada did I fully realize my mistake.
Talking seemed inconsequential and futile. Yet it was all I could do
to call attention to the black deed about to be committed across the
border, after the seven years' purgatory suffered by the two persecuted

men. Alas, my feeble voice, like that of millions, cried in vain. America remained deaf.

My comrades organized a memorial meeting. I consented to speak, though I knew that no pæan of their valour and nobility could raise them to greater glory in the eyes of posterity than Vanzetti's own beautiful song or Sacco's last simple and heroic words.

Absorption in some vital interest had often helped me over the savagery man inflicts on his brother. Concentrated study of the material for my winter's work might dull the pain over our great and poignant loss.

The Public and University libraries in Toronto were lacking in modern works on the social, educational, and psychologic problems occupying the best minds. " We do not buy books we consider immoral," a local librarian was reported as saying. I acquired a librarian of my own in Arthur Leonard Ross, best of friends, who sent me two boxes of the latest reference books on the subjects I was preparing. I also came upon a rich Walt Whitman collection, owned by Mr. H. F. Saunders, secretary of the Toronto Walt Whitman Fellowship, who invited me to speak at the annual gathering in memory of the Good Grey Poet.

My luck in Toronto far exceeded my deserts. Kind hearts supplied my every wish. " A secretary? " " Why, there's Molly Kirzner — she'll do your work." Within the year Molly changed her name to Ackerman, but not her loyalty to me. " A centrally located place for our publicity? " " Why, there's C. M. Herlick, the lawyer. Don't you fear, he is also a Socialist and eager to put his office at your service." A physician, a dentist, and tailors at my call, and a kidnapper whose cozy home soon became mine. The dear woman, Esther Laddon, was about my own age, but she mothered me as if I were her child. She fretted about my health, worried about my meals, and buttonholed everybody to warn them not to dare miss hearing the great orator E.G. Indeed, my luck exceeded my deserts.

In January 1928 I delivered my final talk in a series of twenty, embracing various problems of our time. The last evening, on which I discussed Ben Lindsey's *Companionate Marriage,* brought out an audience equalling the total attendance of four other meetings. I was assured that I had performed a feat no public speaker had ever attempted in Toronto before. I had come as a stranger without funds or a manager. Within a year I had created enough interest to secure audiences twice a week for eight months. Most important, my friends thought, was the effect of my lecture on corporal punishment in the schools. The campaign organized to abolish the savage practice was the direct result of it, they said. I could not have achieved what I did had it not been for the effective support of such friends as the Reades, Robert Low, Mary Ramsey, Jane Cohen, the Hugheses, Florence Loring and Frances Wylie, and my comrades in Toronto. Their share was no less than mine, nor should their credit be.

The week in Montreal before sailing was free from the gloom and disappointments of my previous visit. I came as the guest of the Women's Aid Society, the group I had organized for the relief of the persecuted revolutionists in Russia. My year's absence had not dampened their ardour nor lessened their efforts. Mrs. Zahler, Lena Slackman, Minna Baron, Rose Bernstein, and the other hard workers had surpassed my expectations in the amount of financial aid they had succeeded in sending to Berlin for the Russian Political Prisoners' Fund. They proved equally efficient with the two meetings they arranged for me, the largest and most interesting I had had in Montreal. I greatly enjoyed the fine fellowship at the farewell dinner they gave me. Other friends added to the interest and pleasure of my stay, among them Mr. and Mrs. H. M. Caiserman, enthusiastic Judaists, who gathered the Yiddish intelligentsia to attend my lecture on Walt Whitman at their home. They were proud that I was one of their race, they reiterated. It was worth coming back to Montreal to reach their Yiddish hearts by the grace of the *goi* Walt Whitman.

Evelyn Scott was in the city and I spent some lovely hours with her. I had read and admired her *Escapade* years before we met. Our friendship began in London and was cemented by Evelyn's letters, no less masterly than her literary work. We laughed to tears over the recollection of our recent meeting in Cassis, France. She had invited Sasha and me to dinner and we had arrived in the company of Peggy and Lawrence at four in the morning, hungry as wolves. Dazed with sleep, Evelyn had announced that she could offer us only coffee; not a scrap had been left from the sumptuous dinner.

The call to arms for "E.G.'s Life" had not brought battalions to the fore, Van ruefully reported; no more than a thousand dollars had come in, though he had bombarded everyone within reach. His face lit up when he learned that the comrades of the *Freie Arbeiter Stimme* had, through the efforts of its editor, Joseph Cohen, B. Axler, and Sarah Gruber, raised nearly as much, and that Toronto and Montreal had not lagged behind. But we were still only half-way towards the needed five thousand dollars. Van was not discouraged: he would continue to pester those who had once proclaimed their friendship for E.G. What were my plans? Would I wait before beginning my work? Did he dare suggest that a good anarchist would stop half-way, I teased my impresario. In fifteen months I had raised over thirteen hundred dollars for the political fund, some money for the fight to rescue Sacco and Vanzetti and for similar causes. I had paid my debts, amounting to twelve hundred dollars, and I had enough left to cover my return passage, aside from the new fund for my autobiography.

I was returning to France, to lovely Saint-Tropez and my enchanting little cottage to write my life. My life — I had lived in its heights and its depths, in bitter sorrow and ecstatic joy, in black despair and fervent hope. I had drunk the cup to the last drop. I had lived my life. Would I had the gift to paint the life I had lived!

INDEX